COMMITTIES AND COMMISSIONS IN INDIA 1947-73

Details of Published Volumes

COMMITTEES AND COMMISSIONS IN INDIA 1947-80

(In 18 Vols.)

Vol. 1	1947-54	Rs. 1500
Vol. 2	1955-57	Rs. 1500
Vol. 3	1958-59	Rs. 1500
Vol. 4	1960-61	Rs. 1500
Vol. 5	1962-63	Rs. 1500
Vol. 6	1964-65	Rs. 1500
Vol. 7	1966	Rs. 1500
Vol. 8	1967	Rs. 1500
Vol. 9	1968-69	Rs. 1500
Vol. 10	1970	Rs. 1500
Vol. 11	1971-73	Rs. 1500
Vol. 12	1974	Rs. 450
Vol. 13	1975	Rs. 450
Vol. 14	1976	Rs. 450
Vol. 15A	1977	Rs. 450
Vol. 15B	1977	Rs. 450
Vol. 15C	1977	Rs. 450
Vol. 15D	1977	Rs. 450
Vol. 16A	1978	Rs. 450
Vol. 16B	1978	Rs. 450
Vol. 17A	1979	Rs. 450
Vol. 17B	1979	Rs. 450
Vol. 18A	1980	Rs. 450
Vol. 18B	1980	Rs. 450

COMMITTIES AND COMMISSIONS IN INDIA 1947-73

Volume III
1958-59

Virendra Kumar

CONCEPT PUBLISHING COMPANY, NEW DELHI-110059

ISBN 81-7022-212-5 (Vol III)

First Published 1977
Reprinted 2004

Published and Printed by
Ashok Kumar Mittal
Concept Publishing Company
A/15-16, Commercial Block, Mohan Garden
NEW DELHI-110059 (India)

Phones : 25351460, 25351794
Fax : 091-11-25357103
Email : publishing@conceptpub.com

Dedicated to
revered Sh. D. R. Kalia
who continues to inspire me
to see through this project

INTRODUCTION

The Third Volume attempts to understand and analyse the activities of the various "Committees and Commissions" during the period 1958-1959 which have received as far as the previous volume is concerned scant attention from even bibliophiles and documentation experts. It is known that the governments all over the world largely rely on the Committees and Commissions for their decisions on particular subjects. Governments make an extensive use of the Instrument of the Public Inquiries which ultimately help in lessening managerial tensions as well as quietening the allegations of misrule. According to John Stuart Mill, "A man seldom judges right, even in his own concerns, still less in those of the public, when he makes habitual use of knowledge but his own or that of some single adviser." Thus the "Committee System" greatly helps the proper functioning of a democratic set-up.

A Commission is a "Governmental agency created to perform a particular function such as special investigations or on governmental regulations of business." It is appointed mainly when it is thought that a matter involves some financial questions. There are other reasons for which a commission is appointed, e.g., in matters pertaining to the welfare of the state and its citizens and for improving the efficiency in an administration. The status of a Committee is also the same as that of a Commission, but it does not possess as wide powers as are enjoyed by a Commission and has to limit itself in relation to specific work assigned to it under its terms of reference. While arriving at decisions in the form of recommendations, a Committee or a Commission ensures that such decisions are representative of interests of various types of people and also a safeguard against abuse of power.

The Committees and Commissions always advise a Government, offering valuable suggestions and recommendations for smooth operation and efficiency in administration for the welfare of the people.

A Committee or a Commission comprises a Chairman, the Members and Member-Secretary (sometimes there is also a Vice-Chairman and an Assistant Secretary). In some cases there are even one-man Commissions and the enquiries conducted by such Commissions are entrusted to an Official-on-Special Duty or a Judge of the High Court.

The Chairman of a Commission is a person well versed in legal affairs and is often a retired Judge of a High Court or the Supreme Court of India. Occasionally, a member of Parliament is also appointed to the post of Chairman of a Commission. Regarding Committees, the Chairman is usually a specialist in the subject of the Committee. He can be a Leader or a Convenor also if he heads a Panel, Study Group, Working Group or a Delegation etc.

The members of a Commission, Committee, Panel, Study Group, Working Group etc., are specialists in their respective fields and provide valuable guidance to the Commission in making recommendations.

The Member-Secretary or Secretary is nominated from among the experienced officials who have the requisite competent knowledge of the subject on which the Commission or the

Committee is appointed.

The study of the "Committees and Commissions" is divided into two main parts :—

(I) *Pre-Independence :* From 1772 to August 1947; and

(II) *Post-Independence :* From August 1947 to 1973.

The first volume covers the period from August 1947 to 1954. The second volume covers the period from 1955 to 1957. The present book, Volume III, in the series covers the period from 1958 to 1959.

The work provides information on subjects like Bibliographical Data of the Committees and Commissions; Chairman, Leader, Convenor etc. of the Committees and Commissions; Appointments; Terms of Reference; Contents; and Recommendations.

Arrangements : The arrangements in the "Committees and Commissions" are chronological and items have been arranged according to their dates of appointment and not according to their dates of publication.

I am sure that this reference work will continue into a number of volumes for it is unique in nature. I have spared no efforts to make it a comprehensive reference work and it will be of great use to the research scholars, sociologists, historians, economists, students of political science as well as to all those connectedwith the study of administration and legal affairs. I have tried my level best to rectify all omissions or errors that I noticed in the previous volumes. It will be my effort to go on improving these volumes. The introductory part in Volume I deals in detail with the *why*, *what* and *how* of the "Committees and Commissions".

In the end I must express my gratitude to the Press that reviewed and appreciated the first volume. I am also indebted to my friends who have helped me a lot in the process of compilation of this volume.

I am also grateful to my wife and children who have sacrificed their personal comforts by providing me every facility to make this volume ready for publication within a reasonably short time.

New Delhi
Akshayatritiya
April 21,1977

Virendra Kumar

CONTENTS

1959

1958

PANEL ON NATIONAL WATER SUPPLY AND SANITATION SCHEME, 1958—REPORT

New Delhi, Committee on Plan Projects (Buildings Projects Team), 1961. 74p.+iip.

Chairman : Shri N.V. Modak.

Members : Shri P.C. Bose; Shri R.D. Varma; Shri S. Rajagopalan.

Secretary : Shri T. S. Vedagiri.

APPOINTMENT

The Panel was constituted in 1958 under the Committee on Plan Pro jects in consultation with the Ministry of Health to study the problem in detail and make suitable recommendations.

TERMS OF REFERENCE

To study the problem in detail and make suitable recommendations.

CONTENTS

Introduction; The Panel and its Work; A Survey of the Situation; An Analysis of the Problem; The Magnitude of the Problem Ahead; Measures for Immediate Implementation: Long Range Reforms; Rural Water Supply and Sanitation; Summary of Important Recommendations; Appendices I to V.

RECOMMENDATIONS

The existing procedure of allocating funds on a year-to-year basis and the belated information to the State Governments regarding availability of funds for any year leave very little time for the authorities in the States to plan for the projects, to procure materials and incur expenditure. The only practical solution to speed the pace of work would be to place the financing of this programme on a three or at least two-year basis as a special case.

The preparatory work required to be done before a

scheme is taken up for planning is prolonged and cumbersome. It should be possible for the State Governments to reduce procedural delays, fix up priorities for various schemes and take preparatory work on them well in advance. It is equally essential for the State Governments to detail special staff for the advance investigation and preparation of projects.

State Governments should take advance action in regard to land acquisition proceedings relating to water supply and sanitation schemes so that there is no avoidable delay in the execution of component works of the scheme.

Inter-State sales tax at the rate of seven per cent is charged from the Corporations and other Local Bodies while the State Governments have to pay only one per cent on their inter-State purchases. Government should consider this and remove the disparity in the levy of sales tax.

The concerned agency in the State should furnish details of the schemes in the specific form laid down for the purpose, in order to avoid unnecessary duplication of work and delay.

The Health Ministry may explore ways and means of cutting short existing procedural delays in according sanctions to schemes.

An analytical study should be made of the actual expenditure incurred by Government Departments on various schemes planned and executed by them on behalf of local bodies with a view to fixing centage charges on a rational basis.

State Governments should set up a separate Public Health Engineering Department where they have not done so.

The cadre of municipal engineers should be provincialised and integrated with Public Health Engineering Department to ensure inter-changeability and continuity of experience of personnel in all aspects of water supply and santitation works.

It is desirable to arrange for refresher courses to the different grades of in-service-personnel at suitable centres in the States.

A National Water and Sewage Works Association should be formed to act as common forum for free exchange of ideas on the problems met with in the operation and maintenance of water treatment and sewage disposal works.

The Conference of Public Health Engineers should be held at least once a year.

It is necessary to standardise the qualifications and training of plant operators of different grades in order to bring them under National Certificate Scheme. The Ministry of Health should take the necessary measures in this behalf in consultation with the State Governments.

A common code of practice laying down standards and specifications in design and execution of Public Health Engineering Works is an imperative need.

The Central Public Health Engineering Research Institute may intensify research work in regard to preconditioning and filtration of drinking water and the preliminary and secondary treatment of sewage and industrial wastes in order to evolve rational design criteria for future adoption.

There is a need for putting up a pilot plant wherever big schemes are envisaged. The pilot plant can be constructed in collaboration with the CPHERI as part of the comprehensive scheme.

To foster research work on all problems relating to public health engineering, sufficient money must be earmarked for operational research.

In view of the responsibilities that the Central Public Health Engineering Organisation has to shoulder, it is essential that its status should be elevated and the head of the Organisation should enjoy at least the same status as that of the Chief Engineer in the Central Government.

The personnel of the Central Public Health Engineering Organisation should be periodically inter-changed with State Public Health Engineering officers in order to promote better understanding of each other's viewpoints.

There is an imperative need for stepping up the production of C.I. Pipes of the smaller sides. Side by side, attention should also be paid to step up the manufacture of C.I. specials.

Water meter industry has a great future in the country. It is essential, therefore, that it is built up and promoted on efficient lines in order to get meters of good quality at reasonable cost.

A cheap and durable fool-proof device for chlorinating rural water supply should be evolved.

Special emphasis is laid on the need for cheap, simple and robust pump suited for rural water supplies as the success of a rural water supply scheme depends upon the quality of the pump itself.

The hydraulic pressures in the rural distribution system are not normally high and should, therefore, permit the use of pipes of cheaper material.

A class of pipe lower than the present 'B' class should be manufactured in order to avoid the use of 'B' class pipes everywhere. A judicious use of spun concrete pipes wherever possible will release cast iron pipes for use elsewhere.

Every encouragement must be given for the manufacture of pre-stressed concrete pipes in the country after laying down suitable standards and specifications in this behalf.

Careful collection of data regarding the daily performance of all existing plants should be enforced as that would be very valuable in designing future expansions and in building new ones elsewhere. The authorities may make proper use of the facilities afforded by the Central Public Health Engineering Research Institute for this purpose.

Local Bodies should take steps to impose water and drainage tax where they have not done so and strictly collect the same. This would act as an incentive for the house owners to take connections quickly.

The engineers in charge of public health engineering works should use their discretion in designing civil structures with a view to effect maximum economy.

The installation of water supply scheme in any urban area makes a sewerage scheme for that area inescapable. It is, therefore, necessary to treat water supply and sanitation schemes as combined utility projects financed on a common basis.

For making the schemes self-supporting the cost must have a practical relation to the paying capacity of the local population. A practical way to keep down the cost would be to design schemes with minimum standards to start with, with provisions for expansion at later stages.

The method of financing and the agency for executing water supply and sanitation schemes as combined projects will have to be patterned to suit local conditions. Local Bodies in the present status cannot undertake this job. It therefore becomes necessary that a number of municipalities in a region are given the benefit of the services of a Regional Statutory Water and Sewage Board which would act on behalf of these municipalities in the region, taking over such functions and duties from them as are necessary to work the Plan to success.

To foster and develop the growth of public health engineering profession, it is necessary to frame now rules for registration, licensing and conduct of business. The Union Health Ministry should take action in this behalf.

Mapping of water resources in the different parts of the country and laying down policies for its economic and efficient utilisation is a matter of great importance. Equally important is the need for effecting adequate control over pollution of water resources. A broad based Board should be set up for this purpose in each State.

The National Water Supply and Sanitation Programme should not only include selective types of supply for groups of villages from a single source but also rural water supply schemes which involve engineering skill and experience either in the development of the source or in the distribution of the supply and its maintenance.

The Public Health Engineering Department of the State should be effectively associated with the implementation of rural schemes under different programmes in order to achieve efficiency and economy.

The preparation of basic inventory by each State Government of the rural water supply needs, resources and forecasts is essential. It will be desirable to include in the coming national census operations, collection of comprehensive data on the present status of the rural national water supply and sanitation facilities.

Self-closing taps of robust and approved make should be provided for all stand posts as part and parcel of schemes approved by State and Central Governments in order to avoid wastage of water.

It is desirable that the scope of the National Water Supply and Sanitation Programme is modified in order to give more equitable opportunities to urban communities under the loan disbursement. The programme may include a 25 per cent of grant-in-aid for villages or towns with a population between five to 20 thousand. This will give an element of rationale in the aid contemplated under the programme and would approximate to a slab system of help to the rural, semi-rural and urban population in the country.

SELECTED BUILDINGS PROJECTS TEAM ON INDUSTRIAL ESTATES, 1958— REPORT

New Delhi, Committee on Plan Projects, 1959. 33p.+Plates.

Leader : Shri S.K. Patil.

Members : Shri Sarup Singh; Dr. Eng. A. Carbone; Shri C.P. Malik.

Secretary : Shri T.S. Vedagiri.

APPOINTMENT

In view of the large and growing outlay on the plan projects undertaken in the First and Second Five Year Plans, and the necessity to explore all possible avenues of economy in cost and consumption of materials in their execution, the National Development Council constituted the Committee on Plan Projects in September 1956. As buildings form a substantial portion of the total capital outlay, the Committee on Plan Projects set up the Buildings Projects Team in 1958, to carry out an evaluation of selected buildings projects particularly with regard to planning and execution with a view to making suggestions for economy in design and execution.

TERMS OF REFERENCE

(a) Technical service and research schemes, e.g., training-cum-production or training-cum-demonstration centres and polytechnics;

(b) Production schemes of a pilot character initiated departmentally with a view to being turned over to industrial cooperatives or private enterprises;

(c) Production schemes of a commercial character and loans to private concerns under State Aid to Industries Acts; and

(d) Schemes for supply of power.

These provisions are according to the Second Five-Year Plan.

CONTENTS

Introduction; Objective of Industrial Estates; Approach to the Problem; Main Observations; Planning and Layout; Design Details, Services and other Amenities; Organisations for Execution and Maintenance; Recommendations for reducing Cost of Construction; General Observations; Summary of Important Recommendations; Remarks by the Selected Buildings Projects Team; Appendices I to V; Plates I to VII.

RECOMMENDATIONS

A detailed survey must be carried out in and around the town near which an industrial estate is proposed to be set up.

It must be the endeavour of engineers and architects to plan the Estate in such a way that area under factory plot is about 60-65 per cent of total area.

Standard plans of 30 ft. and 40 ft. can be adopted for work sheds.

The internal division of the covered area of the worksheds into workshops, office, stores, etc. should be left to the allottee.

Large sheds may be detached, medium ones can be semi-detached and the smaller ones can be of row construction.

Area under roads should not exceed 20 per cent of the total area of the estate.

Expenditure on unproductive works such as administrative buildings, etc., should be avoided in the initial stages.

Where possible, timber trusses should be adopted for the sheds.

Pre-cast RCC trusses and purilus should be adopted for roofing of worksheds.

It is essential to foster the technique of pre-stressing and train, if necessary, more people who can guide the work at site.

Financial allocations for various industrial estates should be made in advance in order to help advance planning.

Utmost care must be exercised in selecting the site for industrial estates.

The hire-purchase and outright sale of work sheds deserve greater attention.

Where an Industrial Estate is located near a city, the project should be coordinated with city improvement and slum clearance schemes.

It is desirable to locate industrial estates near towns with a population of about 50,000.

In the first instance, location of industrial estates in rural areas should be on an experimental basis and extended enly if it proves a success.

Entrepreneurs should make more possitive use of the service institutes.

COMMISSION OF INQUIRY INTO THE AFFAIRS OF THE LIFE INSURANCE CORPORATION OF INDIA, 1958—REPORT

Delhi, 1958. 25p. (Memeograph)

Chairman : Shri M.C. Chagla.

APPOINTMENT

The Commission of Inquiry into the Affairs of the Life Insurance Corporation of India was constituted under the Government of India vide their notification dated January 17, 1958.

TERMS OF REFERENCE

To inquire into and report on the transactions of the Life Insurance Corporation of India relating to the purchase of shares in the companies mentioned in the Schedule and, in particular—

(i) Whether the purchases were in accordance with normal business principles or practice;

(ii) The propriety of the purchases;

(iii) The person or persons responsible for the purchases; and

(iv) Any other circumstance which to the Commission may appear to be relevant.

The companies mentioned in the Schedule are:—

1. Angelo Brothers Limited, Calcutta.
2. The British India Corporation Limited, Kanpur.
3. Smith Stanistreet & Co. Ltd.. Calcutta.
4. Jessop & Company Ltd., Calcutta.
5. Richardson & Cruddas Ltd., Calcutta.
6. The Osler Electric Lamp Manufacturing Co. Ltd., Calcutta.

CONTENTS

Report; Annexure 'A'.

RECOMMENDATIONS

Life insurance was nationalised and the Life Insurance Corporation was set up on September 1, 1956 and in nationalising life insurance Government placed very high ideals before itself. Although there was criticism of the policy of nationalisation in certain sections of the public, on the whole the people responded favourably as they shared the same ideals as Government and the public expectantly watched to see these ideals translated into practice. On January 19, 1956, the then Finance Minister Mr. C.D. Deshmukh broadcast to the public on the eve of the promulgation of the Ordinance which brought about nationalisation and which ultimately brought into existence the Life Insurance Corporation. In this broadcast he stated that the nationalisation of life insurance was a further step in the direction of more effective mobilisation of the people's savings, and he emphasised the fact that a nation's savings were the prime mover of its economic development, and he drew attention to the fact that with the Second Five-Year Plan in the offing involving an accelerated rate of investment and development, the widening and deepening of all possible channels of public savings had become more than even necessary, and he wound up his broadcast by saying that the nationalisation of life insurance would be another milestone on the road the country had chosen in order to reach its goal of a socialistic pattern of society and in the implementation of the Second Five Year Plan it was bound to give material assistance. In the Lok Sabha speaking on the Life Insurance (Emergency Provisions) Bill on February 29, 1956, he gave as one of the reasons for nationalization that life insurance today was not being managed either efficiently or with an adequate sense of responsibility and it was not functioning in India in the most efficient manner possible so as to attract the savings of the average man to the maximum extent. He laid great emphasis on the concept of trusteeship which should be the corner-stone of life insurance. I may add that although it is true in the general sense that all revenues collected by the State are held in trust for people of the State, life insurance funds are held in trust in a more special sense. The funds represent the savings of millions of hard-working people of the country and there is a special obligation cast upon those who administer those funds to administer them for the benefit of the policy holders. Dealing with the policy of investment, Mr. Deshmukh rightly pointed out that the funds must be invested so as to secure the maximum yield for the policy holders that it may be possible to secure consistent with the safety of capital, and he sounded the right note when he said that insurance was an essential social service which a welfare State must make available to its people and the State must assume the responsibility for rendering this service once it is clear beyond reasonable doubt that it cannot be provided in any other manner. On March 20, 1956, Mr. Deshmukh again made clear what the investment policy of the Corporation would be:

"There have been suggestions made in regard to the investment policy of the Corporation. All I can say at present is that the Corporation will be guided by the advice given to it by the Investment Committee which will be constituted for this purpose, and on which there may be, besides the members of the Corporation, others who have expert knowledge of the subject. It is our intention to indicate in a broad manner what type of investment the Corporation should avoid, and which particular types of investment it should view with favour. The investment in ventures established in pursuance of the Plan would be given preference over others, and the investment policy would be governed in the main by major considerations such as the interests of the policy holders, and the interest of the development envisaged in the Second Five Year Plan and subsequent Plans."

This is the historical background in relation to which the transactions of the Life Insurance Corporation, which I have to investigate, must be considered.

Before I deal with the transactions themselves, I would like to consider the legal background. Section 3 of the Life Insurance Corporation Act, 1956, provides for the establishment of the Life Insurance Corporation with a perpetual succession and a common seal. Section 4 deals with the constitution of the Corporation, which shall consist of such number of persons not exceeding 15 as the Central Government may think fit to appoint and one of them shall be appointed by the Central Government to be the Chairman thereof. Section 5 provides that the original capital of the Corporation shall be five crores of rupees provided by the Central Government. Section 6 lays down what the functions of the Corporation are and this Section provides that it shall be the general duty of the Corporation to carry on life insurance business and so to exercise its powers as to secure that life insurance business is developed to the best advantage of the community. Sub-section (2) of that Section confers certain powers upon the Corporation, and one of the powers with which we are concerned is contained in sub-clause (b) and which is to invest the funds of the Corporation subject to the rules, if any, made by the Central Government, in such manner as the Corporation may think fit and to take all such steps as may be necessary or expedient for the protection or realisation of any investment. Sub-section (3) provides that in the discharge of any of its functions the Corporation shall act so far as may be on business principles. Section 19 deals with the committees of the Corporation. One of them is the Executive Committee and the other the Investment Committee. Section 20 provides for the appointment of one or more persons to be the Managing Directors of the Corporation. Then we come to the important Section, Section 21, which provides that in the discharge of its functions under this Act, the Corporation shall be guided by such directions in matters of policy involving public interest as the Central Government may give to it in writing. Sub-section (1) of Section 43 provides for the application immediately of certain Sections of the Insurance Act of 1938 to the Corporation, and sub-section (2) provides for the application of some other Sections of the Insurance Act to the Corporation subject to such conditions and modifications as may be specified in the notification which was to be issued by the Central Government as soon as may be after the commencement of this Act, and among these sections what is necessary to note for our purpose is Section 27-A. Section 48 confers upon the Central Government the power to make rules to carry out the purpose of the Act, and Section 49 confers power upon the Corporation, with the previous approval of the Central Government, to make regulations not inconsistent with the Act and the rules made thereunder to provide for all matters for which provision is expedient for the purpose of giving effect to the provisions of the Act.

Turning to the Regulations which have been framed under Section 49, Regulation 12 provides for an Executive Committee and it is to consist of the Chairman, two Managing Directors and two other Members of the Corporation to be nominated by the Corporation, and under Regulation 17, without prejudice to the generality of powers conferred by Regulation 16, certain powers are conferred upon the Executive Committee which are subject to such limitations and directives as may from time to time be imposed or given by the Corporation, and under sub-clause (ix) of this Regulation one of the powers is: "subject to the provisions of the Insurance Act and taking into consideration the advice of the Investment Committee, to invest and deal with any moneys of the Corporation not immediately required including its Insurance Funds." Then Regulation 18 provides for the Chairman being the Chief Executive and that in an emergency he shall be competent to exercise all the powers of the Executive Committee enumerated in Regulation 17. Regulation 19 provides for the appointment of Functional Directors, and Regulation 20 lays down that any matter pertaining to the business of the Corporation may be decided upon by any such Functional Director, subject to such general or special directions as the Executive Committee or the Chairman may give from time to time. Regulation 22 provides for the constitution of an Investment Committee consisting of the Chairman, a Functional Director and five other persons, one of whom at least shall be a member of the Corporation, and Regulation 24 provides that the Investment Committee will advise the Corporation in matters referred to it relating to the investment of its funds. Regulation 25 provides that the Investment Committee shall meet as often as may be necessary and such meetings shall be governed by the procedure that may be decided upon from time to time by the said Committee.

It will be apparent from these provisions that the Life Insurance Corporation is an autonomous corporation. It is independent of Government and it cannot be looked upon as merely one of the many departments of Government. In the investments it may make, and in the investment policy it may pursue, it must be guided by its own officers and by the Statutory Committees set up under the Act. The only control that Government can exercise is under Section 21 and that control is restricted to matters of policy involving public interest, and what is equally important is that the control can only be exercised by directions given in writing. Now, there is very good reason why Parliament provided that Government should not interfere with the working of the Corporation or try to control its actions except by means of the statutory direction to be given under Section 21. If Government were to interfere with the working of the Corporation otherwise than in the manner laid down in Section 21, the Corporation would have lost its autonomy. Further, it was clearly intended that Government must take the responsibility of dictating to the Corporation what policy it should pursue in a particular matter and that policy could only become clear if it was embodied in a direction given in writing. Such a direction could then become a matter of discussion and debate both in Parliament and in the public. In my opinion, Section 21 embodies the ideal compromise between the autonomy of a statutory corporation and the control which must be exercised by a welfare State over such a corporation. While leaving the Corporation complete independent to manage its own day-to-day administration, while leaving it free to invest its funds in the interest of the policy holders, Government could only control its discretion when a question of policy involving public interest arose. Government could not tell the Corporation that it should or should not invest in any particular shares, it could not tell the Corporation that it should help a particular industry, much less a particular individual; but it could tell the Corporation that it should invest its funds in certain industries which were essential for the successful working of the Second Five-Year Plan or to give effect to a particular economic or financial policy laid down by the Government. In my opinion, it is most unfortunate that the wise and sound principle laid down in Section 21 has not been adhered to in the working of the Life Insurance Corporation. The evidence before me, which I will discuss later, clearly shows that there was a tendency on the part of the Finance Ministry to look upon the Corporation as a wing or branch of that Ministry and to issue orders to it in the belief that the Corporation was bound to carry out those orders. If one thing is more important than any other, it is that the Chairman of the Corporation should be an independent official who is conscious both of his own position and the status of the Corporation under the Act. But this salutary principle has been completely overlooked. The very first Chairman of the Corporation was Mr. Patel who, while he held the office of the Chairman, continued to hold the office of the Principal Secretary to the Finance Ministry. It is not surprising that the clear dividing line between the functions of the Corporation and the power and authority of Government tended to be completely blurred. Mr. Patel cannot be blamed if he felt that in administering the Corporation he was doing nothing more than administering a department of Government. Mr. Patel was the Chairman from September 1, 1956 to June 5, 1957, and on that date Mr. Kamat, who had been Deputy Chairman, was appointed as Chairman in place of Mr. Patel. Mr. Kamat is also a member of the Indian Civil Service as Mr. Patel is. Mr. Kamat is junior ins ervice to Mr. Patel. Mr Kamat held an important post in the United States of America before he was brought to the Corporation, and therefore as far as Mr. Kamat was concerned the position he occupied in the Corporation was merely one rung in the ladder of promotion. Mr. Patel continued to hold the office of Principal Secretary after he ceased to be the Chairman of the Corporation and, as the evidence will disclose, the contact between Mr. Patel and Kamat continued; and it is not to be wondered at that Mr. Kamat should be guided by any suggestion or advice given by Mr. Patel who was not only a senior civilian but also the Principal Secretary of the Finance Ministry. But if the matter stopped at Mr. Kamat being guided by Mr. Patel there would be nothing seriously wrong with the situation. But the record shows, what technically took the shape of advice, was in reality an order issued by Government and that is how it was looked upon by the officials of the Corporation. In my opinion, it is very necessary that appointments to important offices in the Corporation should not be looked upon as merely the transfer of an officer from one department to another. There should be some security of tenure and a fairly long duration of office and it should be impressed upon these who are appointed to these posts that they have to discharge their duty to the Corporation irrespective of whether their actions find favour with Government or not.

Another serious criticism which I have to offer with regard to the working of the Corporation is the fact that Section 27-A of the Insurance Act was never brought to force. Section 27-A lays down what approved investments are in which the funds of the Corporation may be invested and it is the general opinion that very salutary safeguards with regard to investments have been laid down in this Section. The intention of Government, in the first instance, was not to make this Section applicable to the new Corporation. Mr. Deshmukh, speaking in the Lok Sabha on May 18, 1956, said:

"Another strongly pressed suggestion is that the provisions of the Insurance Act relating to investment, namely Section 27-A, Section 29 and Section 30, should also be applied. Here also, the reason for not applying them is the same, namely, that they appear to be needless. These provisions which incorporate some of the well-known canons of investment were enacted to prevent the management from misusing the policy-holders' money to benefit themselves. In terms of the Bill, the investments are to be made under the guidance of a high powered Investment Committee. This is the further safeguard that the Central Government have the right to give directions to the Corporation in the matter of investment. It is, therefore, inconceivable that any wrong policy could be followed by the Corporation. I trust Hon. Member will agree that whenever we have made any portion of the Insurance Act inapplicable to the new Corporation, it has been for good and compelling reasons."

On May 23, 1956, Mr. Deshmukh stated :

"...... I am saying that in case the Hon. Member wants to make a point about investment, as he did yesterday or the day before yesterday in his speech, the Corporation should be obliged to adhere to the creteria which at present govern investments by a life insurance company in the private sector. I am prepared, therefore, to accept 27-A being added on in subclause (2) of section 43."

Therefore, there is not only the assurance given by the then Finance Minister that section 27-A would be made applicable to the Corporation and the criteria laid down in that Section would be followed in making investments, but that assurance took a statutory form inasmuch as, as already pointed out. Sub-section (2) of Section 43 cast a duty upon the Central Government, as soon as may be after the commencement of the Act, to make Section 27-A applicable to the Corporation subject to such conditions and modifications as may be specified; but that Section has not yet been made applicable. I may also point out that no rules have been framed by Government as contemplated by Section 6(2)(b) and in respect of which express power has been conferred under Section 48(2)(g) which provides for rules to be made with regard to the manner in which and the conditions subject to which investments may be made by the Corporation.

We might now turn to the machinery which has to be employed by the Corporation in order to make investments. It may be pointed out that the amount to be invested by the Corporation is extremely large, as much as about Rs. 10 lakhs a day. It is therefore obvious that the investments of the Corporation should be made with the best knowledge available with regard to the investment market so as to secure to the policy holders the best return from these investments. Now, as pointed out, under the Regulations, the power to invest is conferred upon the Executive Committee. What is important to note is that this power can only be exercised after taking into consideration the advice of the Investment Committee. Under Regulation 24, the Investment Committee has to advise the Corporation in matters referred to it relating to the investment of its funds, but inasmuch as the Executive Committee cannot act without taking into consideration the advice of the Investment Committee, all questions of investment must necessarily be referred to the Investment Committee. The Investment Committee is so constituted as to make available to the Corporation proper advice as to investment. In March 1957, the Investment Committee consisted of Mr. Patel as Chairman, Mr. Jha, Secretary for Heavy Industries Department, Mr. K.R.P. Aiyangar, Joint Secretary of the Company Law Administration, and Mr. Vaidyanathan, the Managing Director. These are the officials. The non-official members were Mr. Chaturvedi, the President of the Calcutta Stock Exchange, Mr. K.R.P. Shroff, President of the Bombay Stock Exchange and Mr. Parekh, Deputy General Manager of the Industrial Credit and Investment Corporation. The same Committee continued throughout 1957 with only the change that Mr. Kamat as Chairman took the place of Mr. Patel. It appears that in practice the Executive Committee did not consider the question of investments at all and in justification of this practice my attention was drawn by Mr. Kamat to a resolution passed by the Executive Committee on February 19, 1957, by which it resolved :

"It shall be the responsibility of the Chairman to direct the purchase and rule of investments. In this he will be guided by the Investment Committee and he will make the investments bearing in mind the recommendations of the Investment Committee."

It is extremely doubtful whether the Executive Committee could delegate its power to the Chairman. But without going into legal technicalities, I am prepared to assume for the purpose of this inquiry that the practice followed by the Corporation with regard to investments was one authorised by law and the practice was that investments were considered by the Investment Committee, and advice was given by the Investment Committee. It is true that the Chairman or the Managing Director did make investments without previous consultation with the Investment Committee and then reported these investments to the Investment Committee. This had to be done because the Investment Committee was not continually in session, and if investments had to be made from day-today and if the market had to be watched and good bargain secured, authority had to be given to some officials of the Corporation. But as I shall point out later, the Investment Committee had laid down rules of guidance and had also advised that Section 27-A as modified should constitute a criterion for making investments and in making day-to-day investments the Managing Director or the Chairman had to keep the modified Section 27-A and the rules of guidance in mind. Therefore, so long as there was no departure from the principles laid down by the Investment Committee there was no danger that any investment might be made by the officials of the Corporation which would not be sound and prudent investments.

Having dealt with this historical and legal background, I will now come to the transactions in question and I propose, in the first instance, to give a brief narrative of the undisputed facts. It appears that on June 18, 1957, the Finance Minister, Mr. T.T. Krishnamachari, was in Calcutta and he addressed a meeting of businessmen and financiers to explain to them the Government's economic and financial policy. At that date were also present Mr. Patel, the Principal Secretary of the Finance Ministry, Mr. Iyengar, the Governor of the Reserve Bank, and Mr. Bhattacharyya, the Chairman of the State Bank, and all the three were present at this meeting which was addressed by the Finance Minister. Mr. Patel left Calcutta on June 18, and arrived in Bombay on June 20, and the Finance Minister arrived in Bombay on June 21. On June 21, Mundhra, about whom I will have to say a great deal later, requested Mr. Patel to see him and Mr. Patel complied with that request. Mundhra told Mr. Patel that he had various suggestions or proposals to sell or mortgage some of his assets without having to make large sales through the Stock Exchange. Mr. Patel told him that he should submit, in writing, a full Statement of his proposals and whatever he had to say. This Mundhra did on the same day and we have a letter of June 21, 1957, addressed by Mundhra to Mr. Patel. In this letter he states that he had a discussion with Mr. Patel that morning in connection with his financial position and that he had tried to explain to him the problems that he was faced with at present. With this letter he attached a list of his total liabilities which amounted to five crores and 24 lakhs of rupees. This consisted, among others, of liability to various banks in the sum of Rs. three crores 93 lakhs, and liabilities to different brokers in the sum of Rs. one crore 31 lakhs, and he gave the value of his assets which were free from all encumbrances at Rs. one crore 55 lakhs. He points out that it was essential to avoid any selling pressure from the brokers, that their accounts be cleared, and that the shares be taken delivery of after settling their dues, as this would relieve undue pressure on the markets and also upon him. With this object in view he makes these proposals that the Corporation should buy shares worth Rs. 80 lakhs and further shares of the value of Rs. 30 to 40 lakhs direct from the market to create confidence and to make the situation healthier. The sccond proposal was that the Corporation should give him a loan of Rs. one crore and he undertook to give the Life Insurance Corporation business to the extent of Rs. one crore. He also proposed that the Corporation should buy fresh issues of Preference Shares in B.I.C. and Jessop and Co. to the extent of Rs. one crore 25 lakhs, and he agreed to offer to the Corporation fire insurance business to the extent of Rs. 15 lakhs a year. He further stated that he was prepared to consider any alternative proposals which would help to stabilise and improve the atmosphere and also to free him from financial worries. On June 22, Mr. Patel discussed the proposals of Mundhra contained in the letter of June 21, with Mr. Kamat, the Chairman of the Corporation, and Mr. Kamat was not prepared to consider any other proposal except the proposal of buying shares of the various companies. On June 23, the next day which was a Sunday, Mr. Patel, Mr. Kamat and Mr. Bhattacharyya, the Chairman of the State Bank, met Mundhra and at this meeting it was agreed in principle to consider the purchase of shares worth about Rs. one crore, and the proposals made by Mundhra in the letter of June 21, were considered in detail and Mundhra was asked to make definite proposals with regard to the sale of his own shares to the Life Insurance Corporation and bring them the next day, viz., June 24 when the details would be considered. On June 24 again in the presence of Mr. Patel, Mr. Kamat and Mr. Bhattacharyya, Mundhra placed his proposals as embodied in his letter of June 23, 1957. At this meeting Mr. Vaidyanathan, the Managing Director of the Corporation, was also present. In this letter Mundhra states that he is placing before Mr. Patel and also before Mr. Bhattacharyya and Mr. Kamat, whom he thanks for the opportunity given to him to explain the proposals as stated by him in his letter of June 21, the following proposals to relieve him of his present situation, and then we have the number of shares in different companies, the price and the value, and the total comes to Rs. 94,74,000. He also states that the prices of the shares in his group are very much depressed at present due to several factors and that in order to create confidence in the market it was essential that they should be brought to such levels as they should ordinarily be, and this the Corporation should do by buying shares worth Rs. 50 lakhs direct from the market through their brokers. He also thanks Mr. Patel for the assurance given for considering favourably the proposal for purchasing the proposed new issue of Preference Shares of B.I.C. and Jessop and Co., and he wants Mr. Patel to reconsider the proposal for a loan of Rs. one crore. At this meeting Mr. Patel made various alterations in the number of shares to be purchased by the Corporation. The price to be paid for these shares is a matter of dispute with which I shall deal later. The alterations made in the letter of June 23, were embodied by Mundhra in his letter of June 24, also addressed to Mr. Patel, and he starts the letter by saying that he thanks Mr. Bhattacharyya, Mr. Kamat and Mr. Patel for the assistance given to him in his present difficult situation by agreeing to buy the following shares held by his brokers, and then follow the shares, the value of which at the prices mentioned comes to Rs. 1,19,49,500. He mentions that he is arranging to take delivery of the above shares from his brokers and deliver them to the Life Insurance Corporation at the above rates. He also agrees to issue the Preference Shares in B.I.C. and Jessop and Co. already referred to. He also confirms having agreed to place with the Life Insurance Corporation general insurance business to yield a minimum premium of Rs. 15 lakhs per year. He also thanks Mr. Patel for agreeing to purchase shares through the brokers from the market which would help to bring them to the ordinary level. Mr. Bhattacharyya pointed out to Mr. Patel and Mr. Kamat at the meeting of June 24, that he had heard rumours of some defective scrips floating about, and in order to safeguard against such scrips a letter was taken from Mundhra dated June 24, 1957, and addressed to the Life Insurance Corporation by which Mundhra made himself personally responsible for any defects which might be found in the shares from the time of delivery to the bankers of the Corporation until the same were registered in the Corporation's name. If any defect was found, Mundhra agreed to replace the defective scrips or get them registered in the name of the Corporation by the different companies. In the afternoon of June 24, Mr. Kamat and Mr. Vaidyanathan met Mundhra and they refused to consider the purchase of shares of Duncan Stratton and Co. which had also been mentioned at the discussion in the meeting which took place on the morning of June 24, and which were also referred to in Mundhra's letter of June 24. In place of the shares of Duncan Stratton and Co., the Corporation agreed to accept, 4,000 additional Preference Shares of Richardson and Cruddas and also 2,000 additional Preferenee Shares of Osler Electric Lamp Mfg. Co. and 50,000 additional Ordinary Shares of Osler Electric Lamp Mfg. Co. Mr. Vaidyanathan obtained the prices prevailing on that date in the Calcutta Stock Exchange of Ordinary Shares of British India Corporation, Ordinary and Preference Shares of Jessop and Co. and Preference Shares of Smith Stanistreet and Co. from brokers on the telephone and a letter was written by the Corporation to Mundhra on June 24, 1957, agreeing to purchase 7,00,000 Ordinary Shares of B.I.C. at Rs. 6 per share, 6,000 Preference Shares of Jessop and Co. at Rs. 90 per Share, 78,000 Ordinary Shares of Jessop and Co. at Rs. 24 per share, and 7,500 Preference Shares of Smith Stanistreet at Rs. 78 per share. The prices mentioned were the prices obtained by Mr. Vaidyanathan as already stated. Mr. Vaidyanathan could not get the prices of other shares which the Corporation had agreed to purchase from Mundhra. On June 25, he obtained the closing price on June 24, of Ordinary Shares of Angelo Bros. from the Times of India of June 25. It appears that Mundhra and Mr. Sodhani went to the office of the Times of India and asked Mr. Shah, the Secretary to the General Manager of the Times of India, to obtain through the P.T.I. the closing prices on June 24, of Smith Stanistreet Ordinary Shares, Richardson and Cruddas Ordinary and Preference Shares, and Osler Electric Lamp Mfg. Co., Ordinary and Preference Shares. These prices were obtained and the letter of June 25, 1957, was sent by the Corporation to Mundhra agreeing to purchase 19,000 Preference Shares of Richardson and Cruddas at Rs. 80 per share, 1,50,000 Ordinary Shares of Richardson and Cruddas at Rs. 15.25 per share, 25,000 Ordinary Shares of Smith Stanistreet at Rs. 13 per share, 25,000 Ordinary Shares of Angelo Bros. at Rs. 20.25 per share, 6,000 4½ per cent Preference Shares of Osler Electric Lamp Mfg. Co. at Rs. 75 per share, and 1,00,000 Ordinary Shares of Osler Electric Lamp Mfg. Co. at Rs. 4 per share. The prices mentioned in this letter were obtained as just stated. Therefore, the transaction of June 24, 1957, is embodied in the two letters of June 24 and 25, 1957. The Corporation agreed to purchase the shares mentioned in these two letters at the prices also stated in these two letters, and the total amount which the Corporation had to pay as a result of this transaction was Rs. 1,26,65,750. Out of the shares so purchased by the Corporation, delivery could not be given by Mundhra of 9,675 Ordinary Shares of Angelo Bros. and 505 Preference Shares of Jessop and Co. In place of these the Corporation agreed by its letter of August 9, 1957, to purchase 8,700 Ordinary Shares of Richardson & Cruddas at Rs. 13.62 per share, and 5,300 Ordinary Shares of Jessop & Co. at Rs. 23.25 per share. The price of all these shares was paid by the Central Bank, which are the bankers of the Corporation, to Mundhra against delivery of the share certificates.

Although the Inquiry has been mainly directed to considering the nature of the transaction of June 24, it would perhaps be mentioned here that apart from this there were certain other transactions entered into by the Corporation with regard to Mundhra shares. The first of these transactions was on March 9, 1957, when the Corporation purchased 10,000 Ordinary Shares of Jessop and Co. through a firm of brokers. This was the very first time that the Corporation was purchasing any shares of a company with which Mundhra was concerned. Then there is a transaction of April 5, 1957, when 50,000 Ordinary Shares of Jessop & Co. were purchased, and the third transaction is of April 25, 1957, when a further lot of 50,000 ordinary shares of Jessop & Co. were purchased. These two transactions were entered into directly with Mundhra. There are some transactions with Mundhra concerns after June 24, 1957. There is a transaction of September 3, 1957, for the purchase of 3,900 preference shares of Richardson & Cruddas, a transaction on September 14, 1957, for the purchase of 1,000 ordinary shares of Richardson & Cruddas, and a transaction of September 20, 1957 and September 23, 1957, for the purchase of 9,000 and 1,500 ordinary shares of Richardson and Cruddas respectively. All these four transactions were entered into through a firm of brokers.

The first thing that I have to consider is the propriety of the transaction entered into by the Corporation on June 24, 1957, and also whether it was entered into in accordance with business principles. In considering the propriety, I should first like to consider the ethics of this transaction. We are not dealing here with a business man out to make profits without considering how and by what means those profits are made. We are dealing with a statutory Corporation set up by the Government of India which in its business transactions must maintain certain standards. It would be clearly wrong for the Corporation to utilise its funds to help an individual or the concerns of an individual. It would be even more wrong for the Corporation to deal with an individual who was suspected to be a law-breaker and possessed a doubtful financial reputation and whose antecedents were of a most questionable character. Mundhra is a man who has a flamboyant personality and is a financial adventurer whose only ambition is to build up an industrial empire by dubious methods. He is not very particular about the means he employs so long as the end is achieved. Starting from scratch with no education and no means, he succeeded in acquiring control in several large concerns. He is not an industrialist in the real sense of the term. His interest does not lie in developing or enlarging the industrial output of the country, but his interest lies in being a financial wizard who can swallow up concern after concern. It may be said that this is the picture of Mundhra that emerges after many facts have come to light after June 1957, and what we are concerned with is the state of knowledge of the Finance Ministry in June, 1957. The record makes it perfectly clear that all that I have just said about Mundhra and more was known to the Finance Ministry. As far back as August 23, 1955, Mr. T.T. Krishnamachari, who was then the Commerce Minister, wrote to Mr. Deshmukh, the then Finance Minister, pointing out that during the last one year Mundhra had been operating in a big way in the matter of acquiring control over British owned concerns in India, and he expresses his surprise that despite so many stringent measures in the Companies Act, right under their very nose, Mundhra could do what he liked, and he suggests an inquiry into possible amendments to the Companies Act to prevent similar activities of Mundhra in future. On February 17, 1956, Mr. Rama Rau, the then Governor of the Reserve Bank, had drawn the attention of Mr. Patel, who was the Secretary to the Finance Department, saying that he had been rather disturbed by the activities of Haridas Mundhra. He points out that Mundhra had seen him in the last month with various documents with a view to showing how he secured funds to acquire a controlling interest in so many big firms, and Mundhra also informed Mr. Rama Rau that he, Mundhra, had explained the position personally to the Finance and Commerce Ministers. To this letter Mr. Rama Rau annexed a note prepared by Mr. Ram Nath, Deputy Governor of the Reserve Bank, explaining the operations of Mundhra, and in the note Mr. Ram Nath states that the picture presented as a whole is correct and is sufficiently disturbing to warrant consideration whether action should not be taken to impose some restraint on his operations. Mr. Ram Nath says that Mundhra is building up an industrial empire of considerable magnitude. He does not, however, appear to possess either the experience or the background necessary for successfully working the large enterprises whose control has now passed into his hand. He also quotes a remark of Mr. Justice Tendolkar in a petition filed by Mundhra where the learned Judge observed that a thoroughly dishonest attitude had been adopted by Mundhra. Mr. Ram Nath also draws attention to the fact that apart from the question of the efficient working of these institutions (in which Mundhra has obtained controlling interest), there is the problem of the stability of these concerns and the interests of the shareholders, as also the position of the banks which are involved in financing them. The funds of the different concerns instead of being used for legitimate purposes of the undertaking have been utilised for purchasing a controlling interest in other concerns, with the result that there is a considerable inter-locking of assets. Mr. Ram Nath sounds a note of warning that the entire edifice built up by Mundhra was liable to collapse, and according to him it was necessary that action should be taken calculated to put some restraint on the activities of Mundhra not only in the interests of the shareholders and the banks which are involved, but also in the interest of promoting the soundness of the industrial structure of the country. To Mr. Ram Nath's note is annexed a letter of December 8, 1955, from Mr. Lahiri of the Ministry of Finance to Mr. Jeejeebhoy of the Reserve Bank of India, in which Mr. Lahiri says that there is grave suspicion that the shareholders of F. & C. Osler Ltd. have been defrauded to the extent of about

Rs. 6 lakhs. On March 9, 1956, Mr. Ram Nath wrote to Mr. Patel, enclosing a copy of a preliminary report sent by the Inspecting Officer of the Reserve Bank considering the manipulations in the accounts of the associated concerns of Mundhra. Mr. D.L. Mazumdar, Secretary of the Ministry of Finance, Company Law Administration, gave evidence before me and he stated that the activities and operations of Mundhra had been before the Company Law Administration and the Government of India, Ministry of Finance, from 1954 onwards. He also stated that the Prime Minister came to know about this from some source at about that time and he wrote letters to the Commerce Minister and to the Finance Minister that he was hearing a great deal of a new star which had made its appearance and he wanted them to look into the matter. When Mr. Mazumdar was asked what was the state of knowledge of the Ministry of Finance with regard to Mundhra in the beginning of June 1957, he answered that the state of the knowledge was that he was using dubious methods, that he was a dashing young industrialist keen on building up an industrial empire, whose methods were not above board, and that his antecedents were not very reputable and his reputation was not such as could be trusted. The Prime Minister in his characteristic way summed up the character of Mundhra, when he was acting as Finance Minister in the absence of Mr. Krishnamachari, and when papers relating to Mundhra were submitted to him, in his note that he made on that occasion, viz., on September 19, 1957, by saying "So far as I know, the reputation of this gentleman is not good." Certain prosecutions had also been launched against Mundhra for breaches of the provisions of the Companies Act. Mundhra had also dealings with the State Bank and two of his concerns, the B.I.C. and Richardson & Cruddas, had an overdraft account with the State Bank which had been overdrawn to the utmost limit, and both Mr. Iyengar, who had been the Chairman of the State Bank before he became the Governor of the Reserve Bank and Mr. Bhattacharya, the present Chairman of the State Bank, told me that the state of both these accounts caused the bank considerable anxiety. Mr. Patel himself frankly confessed that Mundhra was not a man in whom complete confidence could be placed.

It is not disputed that Mundhra had a controlling interest in all the companies, the shares of which were purchased by the Corporation on June 24. It is also an admitted fact that the transaction of June 24 was the largest single transaction ever entered into by the Corporation and also the first transaction, apart from the two earlier transactions to which reference has been made, in which the Corporation had dealt direct with the owner of the shares and had not purchased the shares through brokers. The letters, to which reference has been made, between Mundhra and Mr. Patel also make it amply clear that Mundhra was appealing to the Corporation to relieve him of his financial difficulties. Therefore, prima facie, the transaction entered into by the Corporation was a transaction with an individual of doubtful reputation about whom the Finance Ministry entertained most serious suspicions, and effected for the purpose of relieving him of his financial difficulties or, to put a more charitable construction on the transaction, to relieve the financial difficulties of the various concerns which he had succeeded in acquiring by dubious methods and in which he had a controlling interest. It is necessary at this stage clearly to understand what were the real difficulties of Mundhra which the Corporation was trying to overcome. A large number of shares of these concerns had been purchased by Mundhra of which he could not take delivery and which were held for him by his brokers. The prices of these shares were going down and many of the brokers were demanding additional margin from Mundhra. The brokers were themselves in difficulties because they had obtained moneys from the banks on the strength of these shares in order to hold on to these shares. To put it in the language of the Stock Exchange, these shares were weakly held by the brokers and there was a possibility of the brokers not being able to hold on to these shares and to throw them on the market. If that had happened, the prices of these shares obviously would have been further depressed. It is therefore the case of Mr. Patel that he came to know of the situation while he was in Calcutta on June 18, that serious representations were made, among others, by Mr. Chaturvedi, the President of the Calcutta Stock Exchange, that some brokers also made these representations to Mr. Iyengar, the Governor of the Reserve Bank, that Mundhra shares constituted a drag on the market and it was necessary that this drag should be removed, and the main justification for the purchase of these shares is that it was done for the purpose of stabilising the Calcutta Stock Exchange. I find it very difficult to accept this explanation as providing an answer to the criticism which I have already made that the Corporation was dealing with a person with whom it should never have dealt and was trying to help concerns which had been acquired by Mundhra by objectionable methods.

In the first place, there is evidence before me which I accept that the ordinary investor had practically lost all interest in the Mundhra concerns. The reputation of Mundhra was not only known to the Finance Ministry. The public have an uncanny instinct of scenting trouble and of knowing that all is not well with some concerns which are controlled by an individual in whom they have no confidence. Therefore, in removing this so-called drag and raising the price of the Mundhra shares, the Corporation was not in any way helping the general investing public. It was not seeking to cure any general malaise that affected the market. The only possible result of this transaction could have been to give a breathing time to Mundhra, to get his brokers out of their difficulties and to raise the prices of some of the shares which were dealt with on the Calcutta Stock Exchange. Whether it is the legitimate purpose of the Corporation to invest its funds for the purpose of stabilising the market or not—and I shall deal with this aspect of the matter later—what the Corporation did on this occasion did not and could not had that effect. The proper policy for that purpose was the policy enunciated by the Finance Minister himself on the floor of the Lok Sabha and which has now come to be known as the Blue Chip Policy. The Finance Minister stated that he took full responsibility for that policy which could only be of support being given to the Stock Exchange by the Corporation by buying good equity shares in order to raise the price level of shares on the Stock Exchange and keep the Stock Exchange in a healthy condition. When I deal with the nature of these investments I hope to make it clear that by no stretch of imagination could it be said that a large number of shares purchased by the Corporation in this transaction were good equity shares or could be looked upon by any person with any knowledge of shares as Blue Chips. It is true that the Stock Exchange both in Calcutta and Bombay was in a depressed state and that state had continued from August 1956 when various Government policies were announced, and it would be understandable if in June 1957, the Corporation had continued its policy of buying good shares in order to prevent further depression in the market or even to raise the level of the prices in the market. It is not suggested that good shares were not available or that there was any difficulty in the Corporation investing in these shares. On the contrary, the whole case as presented to me, both by the Corporation and Mr. Patel, is that the Corporation deliberately and advisedly after due consideration decided to purchase these Mundhra shares.

It has been forcefully put to me both by Mr. Krishnamachari and Mr. Patel that I should divorce the reputation of Mundhra from the shares that the Corporation was purchasing. It was said that if an investor buys shares from a person, he does not consider whether the owner of the shares is a good or a wicked man, but what he considers is what would be the effect of the buying of those shares upon his own fortune. This argument would be sound if Mundhra was an ordinary owner of these shares who had no concern with the companies, the shares of which he was selling. But the inescapable fact in this Inquiry is that Mundhra had a controlling interest in these concerns. It is an equally inescapable fact that the Corporation did nothing whatever with regard to Mundhra's controlling interest while buying this arge block of shares. Therefore the Corporation was quite prepared to have its money sunk in these concerns while Mundhra continued to control them and to carry on with his financial manipulations. It was open to the Corporation to provide that one of its representatives should be on the Board of Directors of these concerns. But no such obvious safeguard was taken.

It may be mentioned in this connection that these investments were reported to the meeting of the Board of Directors held on July 8, 1957, and at that meeting one of the members raised a question that various important particulars with regard to Mundhra concerns had not been obtained by the Corporation. Thereupon a letter was addressed by the Corporation to Mundhra on July 10, 1957, calling upon him to furnish particulars with regard to various matters mentioned in that letter, such as the present Directors of the company, nominees of Mundhra on the Board, the present holding of Mundhra or his nominees in these companies, etc. One should have thought that these particulars should have been obtained before the transaction was effected. Even if the particulars turned out to be unsatisfactory, the purchases had already been made and the most that the Corporation could do would have been to sell these shares possibly at a loss.

It has also been said that Mundhra's controlling interest in these companies did not result in his interfering with the day-to-day administration of these concerns. But his controlling interest did make it possible for him to juggle with the finances of these concerns, and that such a thing could happen is now borne out by the fact that one of the allegations made with regard to one of the best of these concerns, Jessop & Co., is that Mundhra is alleged to have purchased, out of the reserves of Jessop & Company, shares of Richardson & Cruddas of the value of about Rs. 61 lakhs, and although it is alleged that the money has disappeared the share certificates are not forthcoming. Equally so, it has been in the case of Richardson & Cruddas, because the Life Insurance Corporation itself moved the Calcutta High Court for the appointment of an administrator of the company on behalf of the Corporation.

It is also significant that although the aim of this transaction was the removal of this so-called drag on the Calcutta Stock Exchange, no precaution was taken to see that the shares which were purchased were obtained from the brokers. There is nothing whatever on the record to show from whom Mundhra obtained the share certificates which were handed over to the Central Bank against payment. I have also not been able frankly to understand why it was necessary to buy this large quantity of shares from Mundhra direct in order to raise the prices of his shares. The same purpose could have been achieved and more effectively achieved if the Corporation had given instructions to its brokers to buy these shares in the open market. A curious answer has been given to this suggestion that if the brokers had been instructed and if the people in the market had known that the Corporation was a buyer, the prices would have shot up. But that is exactly what the Corporation wanted to bring about. Therefore, the real reason for buying these shares does not seem to be to stabilise the market or to remove the drag or to raise the prices of the shares, but somehow or other to acquire this large block of shares at prices that were agreed upon. In other words, the object was to finance Mundhra to the extent of a crore and a quarter by the purchase of his shares. It is also interesting to note that although the Corporation was aware that there was danger of spurious share certificates being given to them against the payment of price, the only safeguard that the Corporation took was the extraordinary one of a personal guarantee from Mundhra himself. It is clear that such a guarantee was entirely worthless. Situated as Mundhra was, he could never have made good any loss caused to the Corporation by defective share certificates being given to them. This action shows the almost pathetic confidence that the Corporation had in Mun dhra personally.

In this connection attention may be drawn to the fact that when Mundhra was not in a position to deliver some of the shares as pointed out, it was open to the Corporation to pay Mundhra less to that extent, but instead of doing that they bought other shares of Mundhra concerns in order to make up roughly the amount of one crore and a quarter. This action reinforces what I have already said that the object of this deal seemed to be to help Mundhra financially by paying him a definite amount as the price for the shares of his concerns purchased by the Corporation. Mention may also be made to the agreement arrived at between the Corporation and Mundhra by which the Corporation agreed to take up the preference shares to be issued by B.I.C. and Jessop & Co. This agreement had clearly nothing to do with stabilising the market or removing the drag on the market. This agreement on the face of it bears the imprint of the desire on the part of the Corporation to help Mundhra or Mundhra concerns out of their difficulties.

The other aspect of this transaction which raises serious doubts as to its propriety is the haste with which it was effected. I could not help feeling as I was listening to the evidence that there was a sense of urgency about this transaction. The transaction was negotiated and effected by hurried meetings held in the Reserve Bank while Mr. Patel was busy with more important questions of public importance. It did not seem to have dawned upon anyone of those concerned with this transaction that there was a statutory Investment Committee which might be consulted when so large an amount was being invested in concerns of doubtful financial stability. It is true that all the members of the Investment Committee are not in Bombay, but an urgent meeting could easily have been convened within two or three days. Mr. Kamat, the Chairman of the Corporation, was new to the ways of the Stock Exchange. He was not familiar with all the concerns. He had not studied their balance-sheets. He did not know whether some concerns had been giving any dividend at all and some very little dividend. The obvious thing for Mr. Kamat to have taken a little time to consider whether the large investment he was making was a sound and prudent one. Even Mr. Vaidyanathan, who was the Managing Director, studied the analysis reports of these concerns after the transaction had been effected. Even the price had to be fixed in a hurry because, as already pointed out, the services of the P.T.I. had to be requisitioned in order to obtain the rates from the Calcutta Stock Exchange. Therefore, it is clear that there was some compelling reason, some motivating force, which was driving all these actors into this precipitate action. The explanation of Mr. Patel is that there was a danger of the price shooting up in the market and also that in as-much as the Minister of Finance was in Bombay the decision should be taken immediately. I have already dealt with the first explanation. With regard to the second, it was not necessary that the decision should be taken while the Minister was in Bombay. If he was consulted and his general approval taken, that would have been quite sufficient, and the Corporation could have made the investment after following the normal procedure. The third reason suggested by Mr. Patel which requires more serious consideration is that the atmosphere in the Calcutta Stock Exchange was such that if the difficulties were not removed it would lead to serious consquences. In other words, what is suggested by Mr. Patel is that there was a danger of a crisis and the hasty decision was taken to avert such a crisis.

Let us, therefore, consider what the situation of the Calcutta Stock Exchange was in the middle of June. I have here a graph prepared by the Reserve Bank showing the trend of share prices on the Calcutta Stock Exchange, and this graph shows a steady and continuous decline in the price of shares from August 1956 till about the 10th of June, 1957. As a matter of fact, after June 10, there is a little spurt in the market and the prices went up till the month of August when there was again a further decline. Therefore, as far as this graph is concerned, it does not warrant any suggestion that the market was so steeply going down that something had to be done immediately to restore its confidence. Even with regard to Mundhra shares the official price report of the Stock Exchange shows that the prices of some of these shares were going up after June 10. Therefore, even if the object was to come to the rescue of these shares, there did not seem to be an immediate urgency. I have also the reports of Messrs. Place Siddons & Gough, leading share broker of Calcutta, dealing with the market about this time, and it is curious that in these reports there is no reference whatever either to a threatened crisis in the Stock Exchange or to a drag constituted by the Mundhra shares. Mr. Esplen, a partner in the firm of Place Siddons & Gough, also gave evidence and his opinion was that between June 15 and 20, the market was slightly depressed, but really was recovering from the shock, the shock being the policy of Government, and he denied the suggestion that there was any crisis at that time. Mr. Esplen's explanation for the improvement in the Market in the middle of June was the visit of the Finance Minister to Calcutta and the investment by the Life Insurance Corporation in first class shares. He further said that the so-called drag of Mundhra shares had been in the Calcutta market for two years or more. He further expressed his opinion that the Mundhra group of shares was not in a position to create a crisis because in his opinion a large percentage of these shares was helped by European banks and as they had very little margin they would not throw these shares on the market and suffer a loss. Therefore, to sum up what required the transaction to be put through with such haste was neither a crisis in the Stock Exchange, nor the danger of the prices going up, nor the short stay of the Minister in Bombay, but the threatening financial difficulties of Mundhra himself, and as I have already pointed out, he had made no secret of his own extremely difficult financial situation.

In considering the propriety of the transaction and as to whether it was effected according to business principles, I must now consider the amazing manner—that is the only expression I can use—in which the price which the Corporation had to pay for the shares was fixed. One should have thought that when one is entering into a transaction of this magnitude, the most important term in the contract would be the price, and yet everyone concerned with this transaction seemed to have attached the least importance to this aspect of the matter. In one of the letters exchanged between Mundhra and Mr. Patel on the one hand and the Corporation and Mundhra on the other it is clearly stated as to what was the basis on which the price had to be fixed. Mundhra in his letter of June 24, quotes certain prices and the Corporation in its two letters of June 24, and June 25, quotes its own prices at which it had agreed to purchase these shares. It may be said that if the basis of the price to be paid had been settled in the discussion between Mr. Patel, Mr. Kamat and Mundhra, then perhaps it was not necessary to set out that basis in correspondence if the figures were arrived at in conformity with that basis. But the difficulty in this case is that there is no agreement between the principal participants in this discussion as to what was the basis on which the price was fixed. Turning first to Mr. Patel, he said that in negotiating the deal he was not prepared to accept the price quoted by Mundhra. He was only prepared to pay the prevailing market rate. He was not clear in his mind as to what the prevailing market rate was. Now, this transaction was effected on the 24th and Mr. Patel is clear that the price was not to be fixed on the basis of the rate prevailing on the 24th. Therefore, it may be that it would be the prevailing market rate on the day before the 24th when the market was open, which happens to be the 21st. But even there, there is a difficulty. Was it to be the closing rate of the 21st? Was it to be the average, if there were several transactions on that date? Faced with this difficulty Mr. Patel admitted that what he understood by the prevailing market rate was the trend of the market. This is understandable, because in order to avoid manipulations in the market it is always safer to take a rate which is consistent with the trend of the market over a given period. Mr. Vaidyanathan's understanding also is that the prevailing market rate should be taken as the basis, but according to him the prevailing rate was to be on the 24th and not on any previous day. Mr. Kamat's understanding is again different and his understanding is that the rate was to be the closing market rate on the 24th or the rate mentioned by Mundhra in his letter of the 24th, whichever was lower. It is clear from the evidence that none of these officials made it clear what price was to be paid before the meeting of June 24, came to an end, nor did they take the elementary precaution of reducing the agreed basis to writing. The result of Mr. Vaidyanathan's and Mr. Kamat's understanding of what the price fixed was led to most serious consequences, highly detrimental to the interests of the Corporation.

The negotiations for this deal had been going on in Bombay since June 21, and there is evidence that this fact was known in Calcutta a week before the 24th. If Mundhra was to get the price which was quoted on the Stock Exchange on the 24th, nothing was easier for him than to manipulate the market by raising the price of his scrips on the 24th. This manipulation neither requires much finance nor much ingenuity. A small transaction could be put through on the 24th at a higher rate which would become the closing market rate for that day. We are not in the realm of speculation because there is actual evidence that with regard to two quotations, one of Osler ordinary shares and the other of Jessop & Co. ordinary shares, the Calcutta Stock

Exchange discovered that these were not quotations of genuine transactions in the market, and with regard to the quotation of Osler shares the closing quotation was actually struck off and the quotation of the previous transaction substituted as being the correct closing quotation.

Now let us see how much more the Corporation paid by fixing the price on the basis of the closing quotations on the 24th rather than the closing quotations on the 21st. The price of Richardson & Cruddas ordinary shares on June 21, was Rs. 13.50 and on June 24, it was Rs. 15.25. The price of Richardson & Cruddas preference shares on the 21st was Rs. 61 and on the 24th, it was Rs. 82. With regard to Jessop & Co., the price of ordinary shares on the 21st was Rs. 23.37 and on the 24th, it was Rs. 24.50, and the price of preference shares on the 21st was Rs. 89 and 24th it was Rs. 91. The price of Angelo Bros. shares on the 21st was Rs. 16.87 and on the 24th, it was Rs. 20.25. The price of Osler ordinary shares on the 21st was Rs. 2.84 and on the 24th it was Rs. 4. (This is the quotation which, as I have already pointed out, was ultimately deleted.) The price of Osler preference shares on the 21st was Rs. 60 and on the 24th, it was Rs. 75/. The price of Smith Stanistreet ordinary shares on the 21st was Rs. 11.69 and on the 24th it was Rs. 13. The price of Smith Stanistreet preference shares on the 21st was Rs. 87 and and on the 24th it was Rs. 77. This is the only instance where the price is less on the 24th than on the 21st. The price of B.I.C. ordinary shares on the 21st was Rs. 5.85 and on the 24th it was Rs. 5.90 and that of preference shares on the 21st was Rs. 106 and on the 24th it was Rs. 105. There is a slight fall in this also. The prices accepted by the Corporation in its letter of the 24th June were based upon the quotations received from brokers by Mr. Vaidyanathan, but it will be noticed that in some cases the price paid was even more than the closing rate on the 24th, and in the case of preference shares of Smith Stanistreet & Co., the price was Rs. 3 more than the price quoted by Mundhra himself in his letter of June 24. Turning to the letter of June 25, it will be noticed that although the quotation on the 21st of Richardson & Cruddas preference shares was Rs. 61, the price paid was Rs. 80 based on the quotation of the 24th, which was Rs. 82. The price paid for Richardson & Cruddas ordinary shares was Rs. 15.25 as against the quotation of Rs. 13.50 on the 21st and as against the offer by Mundhra of Rs. 15. The price paid for Smith Stanistreet ordinary shares was Rs. 13, as against the quotation of Rs. 11.69 on the 21st. The price paid for Angelo Bros. shares was Rs. 20.25 as against the quotation of Rs. 16.87 on the 21st and as against the offer of Mundhra of Rs. 20. The price paid for Osler preference shares was Rs. 75 as against the quotation of Rs. 60 on the 21st. The price paid for Osler ordinary shares was Rs. 4 as against the correct price on that date of Rs. 2.88 and as against Rs. 2.84 on the 21st. But the surprising feature with regard to the fixing of the price does not stop here. Mr. Kamat has told us that when the letter of June 25 was brought to him, be found that the market price of Richardson & Cruddas preference shares was Rs. 82, but the offer made by Mundhra was Rs. 80 and therefore he persuaded Mundhra to accept the price of Rs. 80 and not Rs. 82, because according to him the price fixed was the closing market rate on the 24th or the price offered by Mundhra, whichever was lower. When his attention was drawn to the fact that in some cases the Corporation had in fact paid more than the price offered by Mundhra in the letter of June 24, his answer was that his attention was not directed to these discrepancies. Therefore, we have this extraordinary position here that not only a large bulk of shares is purchased at a price fixed on a basis which is unwarranted by any business principle, but even that basis is not adhered to and in some cases even more than that price has been paid.

It may be pointed out that Mr. Kamat's understanding about the basis on which the price was fixed is borne out by the letter which he wrote on July 16, 1957, to Mr. Kaul, Joint Secretary, Ministry of Finance, in order to apprise him of all the details of the transaction of June 24, and it will be found that the Finance Minister also in the Lok Sabha stated that the price was the closing market rate on the day of the transaction or the price quoted by the Mundhra, whichever was less.

It has been urged that this was a package deal and the considerations that may apply to purchase of small block of shares cannot apply to this large deal. Package deals are not unknown in business circles and if we apply the business principles to such package deals, we will find that those principles have been departed from in this case. If a party wishes to buy certain good shares and the dealer is only prepared to sell them provided the buyer also buys other shares which are not as good or which are bad, the buyer may agree to take all the shares in the package deal provided he gets substantial concession in the price which he is paying for the good shares. But in this case, as I will point out later, good, bad and indifferent shares have been bought without any concession being made to the Corporation at all with regard to the price it was paying for what might be considered reasonably good shares.

The transaction is also open to challenge on the ground that it was not really a transaction effected by the Corporation in the exercise of its statutory duty and discretion. The evidence is clear beyond doubt that the transaction was brought about as a result of interference by Government and the transaction may be characterised as a dictated transaction. I have already referred earlier in this Report to the danger of an order from Government masquerading as a mere advice, and the transaction I am considering brings out in full force how Government can dictate to the Corporation although in form it may appear as a mere advice.

There can be no doubt that the leading part in bringing about this transaction was taken by Mr. Patel. Even the letters written by Mundhra offering to sell the shares and containing other offers are addressed to him and he asked Mundhra to communicate these offers to him rather than to Mr. Kamat of the Life Insurance Corporation. It is also clear on the evidence that at the meetings held with Mundhra in the Reserve Bank, his was the dominating personality. Even the alterations made in the offer of Mundhra contained in the letter of June 23, are in his handwriting. Let us consider now in what light the so-called advice given by Mr. Patel was considered by those to whom it was given. The evidence of Mr. Vaidyanathan is clear and categoric. He says that when the Finance Secretary asked them to do something they looked upon it as a directive from Government. He even went to the extent of saying that he looked upon Mr. Patel as Government and Government had got the right to supersede the Investment Committee. He made no secret of the fact that the decision to buy the shares was solely that of Mr. Patel and the Corporation had nothing to do with it. We have, therefore, here the spectacle of the will of the Chief Executive Officer of the Corporation completely paralysed in the presence of the Secretary to Government, so paralysed that he completely abdicated his own duties and functions and merely carried out the direction of Mr. Patel as an order of Government. With regard to Mr. Kamat, it is true that the evidence discloses that he discussed various details with Mr. Patel and Mundhra. But even he, wittingly or unwittingly, was influenced by the fact that the suggestion to buy these shares was being made by a Senior I.C.S. official and Secretary to Government. If he had been so influenced, he would never have agreed to enter into this transaction without satisfying himself as to the soundness of the investment. He frankly admitted that if he had the knowledge about Mundhra, which he now has, he would never have entered into this transaction. Mr. Parekh, a member of the Investment Committee, who wrote a minute with regard to these transactions, with which I will deal later, also says that the decision to purchase Mundhra shares without consulting the Investment Committee represented Government instructions.

The transaction also suffers from this serious blemish that it was effected without consulting the Investment Committee. I have already pointed out the legal aspect of this matter and also apart from the legal aspect the practice followed by the Corporation in the past with regard to its investments. I find no justification whatsoever in the Corporation investing this large amount without seeking the advice of a statutory body which has been set up for the very purpose of advising the Corporation with regard to the investments it wishes to make. In making this investment, the Corporation has also contravened the clear directions given by the Investment Committee with regard to the investments to be made. It appears that at the meeting of the Investment Committee held on September 15, 1956, it suggested modification of Section 27-A and considered Section 27-A as so modified as affording a broad basis for the investment policy of the Corporation, and it also laid down general rules of guidance regarding investments. Now, in two important respects this investment which we are considering has deviated from both the provisions of modified Section 27-A and the general rules of guidance. The modified Section 27-A provides that preference shares of a company should be bought, which company has paid dividends for five years immediately preceding or for at least five out of the six or seven years immediately preceding, and with regard to ordinary shares the Corporation can only invest in shares of a company on which dividends of not less than four per cent have been paid for the five years immediately preceding or for at least five out of seven years immediately preceding. In the rules of guidance the Investment Committee advised that investment in preference shares should yield at least four-and-a-half per cent net and in ordinary shares at least five per cent net. Now with regard to three types of shares purchased by the Corporation, there was a clear departure from these provisions and these shares are the ordinary and preference shares of Osler Electric Co. and the ordinary shares of B.I.C. The modified Section 27-A also provides that the Corporation shall not, out of the controlled fund, invest or keep invested in the shares or debentures of any one company more than 30 per cent of the capital of the company except with the prior permission of the Central Government, and when we look at the result after the investment had been made in June 1957, the result is that in the case of Osler Electric Co. and Smith Stainstreet & Co., the limit of 30 per cent was exceeded. It is sought to be argued that it is open to the Corporation under Sub-section (3) of the modified Section 27-A to invest funds in unauthorised investment so long as the investment does not exceed 15 per cent of the amount of its controlled fund. But such an investment in unauthorised shares can only be made on the advice of the Investment Committee, and inasmuch as no advice was taken, the Corporation cannot rely on this provision in modified Section 27-A. My attention was also drawn to the provision in the rules for guidance that the Managing Director should be authorised to make investments in consultation with the Chairman in the case of fairly big transactions and on his own initiative in the case of smaller transactions, where there was a possibility of good investment opportunity being missed by waiting for calling a meeting of the Investment Committee. Now, surely, it cannot be said of the purchase of Mundhra shares that if the meeting of the Investment Committee had been called, a good opportunity would have been missed. This was a case of needy seller and not a case where the Corporation was looking for a good bargain to invest its funds. Mr. Kamat does not seriously maintain that there was no contravention of these rules of guidance. What he has urged is that these are mere rules of guidance and there was no obligation upon him, legal or otherwise, not to deviate from them under any circumstance. A statutory Investment Committee can serve no purpose if its advice is not taken into consideration and if it is treated as purely superfluous to be consulted or not according to the sweet will of the Chairman or the Managing Director. I could have understood a case of emergency, a case of something having to be done in a hurry in the interest of the Corporation, which might necessitate the by-passing of the Investment Committee. But as I have already pointed out, in this case there was no emergency and the transaction was by no means a good bargain from the point of view of the Corporation.

Assuming that the transaction was entered into not to relieve Mundhra of his financial difficulties but to stabilise the market and remove the drag on itas suggested by Mr. Patel, even so the investment has been made for an extraneous purpose and not solely in the interest of the policy holders. It is obligatory upon the Corporation to consider every investment on its own merits and to decide whether it is sound and prudent investment. It is only when Government has issued a directive in writing under section 21 that it would be incumbent upon the Corporation to carry out that directive, even though in its opinion the investment may not be a sound one from the point of view of the yield which it might give or the security of the capital. But as no such directive was given in this case by Government, the Corporation's function should have been confined to considering the investment on its own merits. It must be further borne in mind that this is not a case where Government could possibly have given a directive, even if that was its intention, under Section 21. Government cannot under that Section direct the Corporation to buy shares of a particular concern or belonging to a particular individual and therefore Government could not ask the Corporation to buy these specific shares of Mundhra concerns. I now come to consider the most important aspect of this transaction, and that is whether the investment was sound and prudent from a business point of view. The Bombay Shareholders Association submitted a memorandum to me and it laid down the following criteria for making investments in large blocks of shares of limited companies :—

(a) A close scrutiny of audited accounts, and Directors' reports for the preceding few years, say, about five years, which would give a reasonably fair idea about the working and financial position of the Company.

(b) Good and steady return on capital for the previous five to seven years.

(c) Sound financial position and policy as can be seen from the audited accounts and Directors' reports.

(d) Future prospects.

(e) Integrity, reputation and credit of the controlling management.

(f) Marketability of the scrip.

If these be sound criteria, and I think they are, then it will be immediately noticed that all these investments suffer from having failed to conform to one important criterion, viz., integrity, reputation and credit of the controlling management. There is impressive evidence of Mr. A.D. Shroff, who has a wide and varied experience of investments for over 30 years, that knowing what he did about Mundhra and his activities, he would have hesitated to buy any shares in which Mundhra had a controlling interest. There is general agreement with regard to three concerns, viz., Jessop & Co., Angelo Bros. and Smith Stanistreet, that they are sound concerns apart from the question of Mundhra's association with them, that they have been paying regular dividends, and the yield also is satisfactory, with regard to Richardson & Cruddas, although its dividend record is good and it has been paying regular dividends, Mr. Esplen, partner in Messrs Place Siddon & Gough, told me that he would hesitate to buy these shares. Mr. A.D. shroff was of the same opinion. In his opinion, profits shown by Richardson & Cruddas were either false or that the company was not well run. The further reason he gave for not buying these shares was that there were a large number of spurious share certificates of this concern on the market. According to him, the danger of the spurious shares was well known to the brokers on the market. Mr. Mody, an experienced Chartered Accountant, valued the ordinary shares of Richardson of Cruddas at Rs. 14, and it will be remembered that the Corporation brought these shares at Rs. 15.25. With regard to B.I.C. and Osler shares, the evidence is emphatic that they were bad and unsound shares. With regard to dividends, B.I.C. paid only one and a quarter per cent in 1954, no dividend at all in 1955, and two per cent in 1956, and Osler has at no time paid any dividend on its ordinary shares and even with regard to preference shares the dividend has only been paid up to the end of July 1949. Mr. Esplen's opinion was that investments in Osler and B.I.C. shares were neither sound nor prudent, and Mr. A.D. Shroff emphatically said that he would never have touched either B.I.C. or Osler shares. Mr. Mody has valued B.I.C. ordinary shares at only Rs. 3 per share, and Osler shares at Rs. 2/8/-per share. With regard to B.I.C., I may also mention that an application for a loan was made by the B.I.C. to the N.I.D.C. The N.I.D.C obtained a report from the Textile Commissioner and on the report of the Textile Commissioner the loan was refused. I heard a great deal about the potentialities of these concerns and I was told that although, in the case of B.I.C. and Osler, the yield was very little or none, both the companies gave promise of giving a good return in the future. The past record of a company constitutes a certain data, the future must largely rest on speculation, and the speculation becomes even more risky when the potentialities depend upon the management of a person like Mundhra. As I have pointed out before, I could have understood the argument if the Corporation had assumed control of these concerns and could have moulded their policy and made sure of their being run on sound lines. But leaving the concerns in Mundhra's hands and hoping for the best was neither a wise nor a prudent act. In this connection reference may be made to a note made by Mr. Parekh, a member of the Investment (Committee, after these investments) were reported to that Committee. He points out in his note that Rs. 50 lakhs were invested which would practically yield no return. He also says that the action had the effect of indirectly supporting wanton acts of persons who might have taken over control of companies without having the resources, by means of financial manipulation without intent to run industrial concerns in a serious fashion. In so far as this operation has the outcome of condoning questionable practices in the field of industrial management, it lays down a precedent not capable of serving the best interests of the policy holder, unless suitable safeguards are taken. Mr. Chaturvedi, another member of the Investment Committee, was in favour of purchasing the shares of Richardson & Cruddas, Angelo Bros., Smith Stainstreet and Jessop & Co. With regard to Osler, he pointed out that there were no reports of the company for a number of years and there were rumours on the Stock Exchange that moneys had been taken out from the company. He was also against the purchase of B.I.C. shares because the progress record of that company was not encouraging. Mr. Govardhandas, who is a leading stock-exchange broker in Bombay, said that he would not ask any of his investors to touch any of the Mundhra scrips with a pair of tongs. He also mentioned that reports were current that B.I.C. shares were forged and a notice was actually issued by the B.I.C. on August 29, 1956, that great care should be exercised by all those who were dealing with or handling in certificates purporting to cover ordinary shares of the Corporation, as the Corporation had recently received for verification a certificate which was clearly a clever forgery and there was reason to believe that more forged certificates might be on the market. He also mentioned that an application was made to the Bombay Stock Exchange for putting Richardson and Cruddas on the forward list, but because the Exchange were aware of the antecedents of Mundhra, the Stock Exchange considered that it was not in public interest to put the company on the forward list and the application was rejected. This was in early part of 1955. Mr. Vaidyanathan confessed that if he had the knowledge which he had today, he would not have invested the Corporation's money in these shares. He said that he had not been trained in the tradition to go in for shares so large in number of one particular individual unless of course he was exceptionally sound. As he put it, his must be a very high sounding name, not otherwise. He also thought that it was wrong for the Corporation to put all the eggs in one basket unless the basket was an exceptionally good one. As a matter of curiosity it may be pointed out that when Mr. Kamat wrote to the Finance Minister on July 12, 1957, giving him information which he wanted relating to the holdings of the Life Insurance Corporation in Blue Chips, he only mentioned the holdings of the Corporation in B.I.C. and Jessop & Co. and did not include the other shares. Therefore, clearly, according to Mr. Kamat, the other shares which the Corporation had purchased were not Blue Chips, or in other words, good equity shares. It may be said that it is not a fair criterion to apply to the purchase of shares to consider subsequent depreciation in their value. A purchase may be sound when it is made and yet circumstances and factors which were not present at the time of the investment may bring about a depreciation in the value of the shares. If the stock market as a whole becomes depressed, then all shares, good or bad, would suffer depreciation. But in my opinion, it would not be wrong to consider what depreciation in value the shares of the Corporation would have suffered if they have brought good equity shares in comparison with the depreciation suffered by them in the shares which they purchased in the Mundhra concerns. Taking the three scrips which have been described as the aristocracy of the share market, the depreciation in the value of Tata Iron & Steel shares between June 24, 1957 and January 16, 1958, was 1.5, in that of Indian Iron & steel 2.9 and in that of A.C.C. 5.1. As against this the depreciation in the value of B.I.C. is 34.33, Osler Electric 49.33, Richardson & Cruddas ordinary 51.50 and in preference 32.50, and even with regard to shares that are considered good, the depreciation in Jessop preference is 7.78 and in ordinary 11.46 and 8.60 and the depreciation in Smith Stainstreet preference shares is 28.21 and in Angelo Bros. 12.35. There is only appreciation in Smith Stainstreet ordinary shares which is

0.92. Taking an overall view of the investment of June 24, the amount invested in the three scrips which may be considered good comes to Rs. 37,10,000. The investment in Richardson & Cruddas, which is a doubtful investment, comes to Rs. 39,23,000, and taking the investment in shares which on the overwhelming evidence must be held to be bad was Rs. 50,49,000. From a view of this evidence it seems clear to me that whatever might be said about Jessop, Angelo Bros. and Smith Stainstreet, the purchase by the Corporation of Richardson & Cruddas, B.I.C. and Osler shares did not constitute a sound and prudent investment. It would therefore be seen that this particular transaction was not entered into in accordance with business principles and was also opposed to propriety on several grounds.

Before I pass on to another aspect of the matter, I should like briefly to consider the transactions entered into in Mundhra shares prior to June 24, and subsequent thereto. With regard to the transaction on March 9, 1957, which was for 10,000 ordinary shares of Jessop & Co., the Investment Committee was consulted and the transaction was put through a firm of brokers. With regard to the transaction of April 5, 1957, of 50,000 ordinary shares of Jessop & Co., although it was a transaction direct with Mundhra, the investment Committee was consulted. With regard to the transaction of April 25, 1957, which was also for 50,000 ordinary shares of Jessop & Co., the Investment Committee was not consulted and the evidence is that Mr. Patel put through a trunk call from Delhi to Mr. Vaidyanathan and asked him to make this investment. At this time Mr. Patel was both the Chairman of the Corporation and the principal Finance Secretary, and it is not quite clear in what capacity Mr. Patel was giving this direction to Mr. Vaidyanathan. Nor is it clear why the Investment Committee was not consulted. It may be that Government was beginning to take interest in investing shares in Mundhra concerns. A letter from Mr. Vaidyanathan to Mr. Patel on April 25, 1957, shows that there was some hesitation in paying the cheque in respect of the sale proceeds of these 50,000 shares Mr. Vaidyanathan wanted to consult the State Bank with regard to Mundhra's indebtedness to that Bank.

With regard to the four transactions subsequent to June 24, except with regard to the transaction of September 14, 1957, the Investment Committee was not consulted. All these transactions were entered into through brokers and with regard to the transaction of September 20, 1957, there is some further evidence. On September 10, 1957, Mr. Patel wrote to Mr. Kamat enclosing an extract from the weekly report received from the Reserve Bank, Calcutta. It gave in brief the market gossip regarding Mundhra and his concerns. Mr. Patel says that it might be necessary to seek a representation on the Board on behalf of the Corporation and he advised picking up such shares as Mr. Kamat can of Jessop & Co. and possibly also of Richardson & Cruddas and pursuant to this 9,000 shares were purchased of Richardson and Cruddas ordinary on September 20, and 1,500 on September 23. It may be that Mr. Patel advised this purchase in order to increase the holding of the Corporation in these two concerns so that it would be easier to get representation on the Board of Directors of these concerns. It may be mentioned that the total investment by the Corporation from March 9, 1957, to September 23, 1957, in Mundhra concerns aggregate to Rs. 1,56,42,645.

Turning to another and equally important aspect of the matter, I have to determine who should be held responsible for entering into the transaction of June 24, which is the main transaction with which I am concerned. Legally and technically the responsibility was that of the Corporation and of the Executive Officers, Mr. Kamat and Mr. Vaidyanathan, who formally put through this transaction. In law, in the absence of any direction in writing, it was the duty of the Corporation to make investments of its funds. If the funds have been utilised unsoundly and imprudently, the Corporation and its Executive Officers must be held responsible. In fact both Mr. Vaidyanathan and Mr. Kamat failed to exercise the responsibility. Mr. Vaidyanathan completely surrendered his judgment to Mr. Patel. Mr. Kamat was overawed by his senior collegue in the service and failed to satisfy himself about the real nature of the transaction. He failed to consult the Investment Committee. He said he was not even aware of the regulation which made it incumbent that the Investment Committee should be consulted. Formally the action was that of Mr. Kamat, therefore it many be said that although the hands were the hands of Mr. Kamat, the voice was Mr. Patel's voice. It was a grave error of judgment on the part of both Mr. Kamat and Mr, Vaidyanathan to have been overborne by Mr. Patel, but in extenuation of their conduct I must point out that they trusted the higher authority and better knowledge of Mr. Patel. Mr. Kamat, it may be added, did not know anything about Mundhra till June 22. He also did not have much experience of the Stock Exchange as he was in the United States from January 1954 to November 1956. As far as Mr. Vaidyanathan is concerned, his responsibility is greater. He had been dealing with day-to-day investments of the Corporation. He was familiar with the Stock Exchange. He had experience of the Oriental Insurance Company, one of the largest life insurance companies in India, with an extremely conservative investment policy and he allowed his judgment to be paralysed by Mr. Patel.

I now come to consider the more difficult and more serious question with regard to the responsibility of Mr. Patel and the Finance Minister. There can be no doubt on the evidence that Mr. Patel was primarily concerned with this transaction. Negotiations with regard to this transaction were carried on by Mr. Patel with Mundhra as is clear from the fact that letters were addressed by Mundhra to Mr. Patel and not to Mr. Kamat or Mr. Vaidyanathan. It is also clear from the evidence that he took a leading part in the discussion which took place between Mr. Patel, Mr. Kamat, Mr. Vaidyanathan and Mundhra. Mr. Patel's case is that he was advising the Corporation to adopt a particular course of action and that advice was based on the policy of Government and was tendered with the knowledge and approval of the Minister of Finance. I have already come to the conclusion that what Mr. Patel gave was not advice but was an order or direction from Government. But the question still remains to be considered whether Mr. Patel was acting on his own responsibility or whether he was giving effect to ministerial policy or ministerial directions.

In the first place, I should like to consider the evidence on the record before I consider the constitutional aspect of the matter. It seems rather strange that Mundhra should have approached Mr. Patel in Bombay on June 21, and should have put in the form of a letter his detailed proposals as to how the Corporation should help him without there having been any prior discussion of the matter in Calcutta where both the Minister and Mr. Patel were on June 18. The only evidence with regard to what happened on June 18, is that there was a meeting of business men at which the Governor of the Reserve Bank, the Chairman of the State Bank, Mr. Patel and the Finance Minister were present, and at this meeting it was mentioned, especially by Mr. Chaturvedi, the Chairman of the Calcutta Stock Exchange, that there was a drag of Mundhra shares on the market. Mr. Patel has denied that there was any discussion with Mundhra in Calcutta or that the question of buying Mundhra shares was discussed. With regard to what happened in Bombay, Mr. Patel's evidence is that on June 22, there was a meeting with the Governor of the Reserve Bank of India, the Minister, the Chairman of the State Bank and himself, and at this meeting a number of financial matters were discussed. At this meeting Mr. Patel brought up the proposals which he had received from Mundhra. They were discussed briefly and it was ageeed that he (Mr. Patel) should take up the question with the L.I.C. whether they could appropriately accept any of these proposals. It is further the evidence of Mr. Patel that after it was agreed in principle with Mundhra to buy his shares worth about a crore of rupees, he mentioned the fact to the Minister and his general approval was obtained. According to Mr. Krishnamachari, all that happened in Bombay between him and his Principal Secretary was that the latter mentioned to him that some kind of offer had been made by Mundhra and some of the Mundhra concerns were mentioned and all that Mr. Krishnamachar told Mr. Patel was that there were some rumours about some of the concerns and he should look into the matter. He also says that he did not go very much behind the matter. He was quite clear that he had not given any instructions to Mr. Patel nor did it occur to him that he was called upon to give any directions. According to the Minister the whole thing appeared to him as a matter which was casually mentioned by Mr. Patel and took no interest in the matter, and when he was asked that the manner in which the transaction was put through showed that there was some driving force behind it, he said that he did not supply that force. He was quite clear that Government did not give any direction to the Corporation. The Corporation acted on its responsibility and the Government was not interested in the matter at all. He also said that as far as his advice to the Corporation was concerned, it was restricted to the Corporation buying Blue Chips and this advice was given by him after the introduction of the Budget in 1957. With regard to Calcutta, the Minister's evidence was that he was told that the policy of the Corporation of entering the market had created steady conditions to a large extent and the people whom the Minister met were reasonably satisfied with the condition as it existed. He also said that he had no interview with Mundhra and no discussion with regard to the Corporation investing in the Mundhra concerns. There is, therefore, a conflict between the testimony of the Finance Minister and Mr. Patel whereas according to Mr. Patel the question of investing in Mundhra concerns was discussed with the Minister and his general approval obtained before the transaction was put through, the Minister has not stated that he gave his approval to this transaction. But whereas Mr. Patel is explicit in his evidence and has a clear recollection of what happened at the two interviews between him and the Minister, the Minister was reproducing before me what he recollected at that date of what had transpired some months ago. There are two more witnesses to resolve this conflict. One is Mr Bhattacharya, the Chairman of the State Bank. Mr. Bhattacharya has a clear recollection of both these interviews. Mr. Bhattacharya stated that on June 22, after the business of the meeting was over at which Mr. Patel, Mr. Bhattacharya, the Minister and the Governor of the Reserve Bank were present, Mr. Patel mentioned to the Minister that a letter had been received by him from Mundhra in which he proposed the sale of certain shares of his concerns to the Life Insurance Corporation and the Minister, as far as he remembered, said "you might look into it". With regard to the second meeting between Mr. Patel and the Minister, Mr. Bhattacharya said: "After the State Finance Ministers conference was over on the 23rd, Mr. Patel and the Minister had a conversation and Mr. Patel told the Minister that a principal was willing to sell shares and that L.I.C. was willing to buy and the Minister said that if the L.I.C. was buying there was no harm in it and he added that Mr. Patel should be careful because there were some rumours about certain scrips being spurious and asked him to take precautions". He also said that Mr. Patel told the Minister that the amount involved was a crore of rupees and that he also mentioned at least some of the concerns in which the amount was to be invested and the Minister said that if the L.I.C. decided to invest in those concerns there was no harm. As far as Mr. Iyengar, the Governor of the Reserve Bank, is concerned, his evidence is purely negative. He said that no conversation took place between Mr. Patel and the Minister within his hearing. I would prefer to accept the positive evidence of Mr. Patel and Mr. Bhattacharya, especially as Mr. Patel's version is strongly supported by the probabilities of the case and also by certain subsequent events to which I would draw attention. I think Mr. Patel rightly said that the decision arrived at to buy Mundhra shares was a decision of some importance and that it was impossible that he should proceed to finalise it on his own. He further said that he was acting in his official capacity as the Finance Secretary and if he felt that his view of the matter was not acceptable to the Minister, then obviously he would not have advised the Corporation to go into the matter. It is difficult to believe that when the Minister was in Bombay and easily available and when Mr. Patel was "advising" the Corporation to enter into the largest transaction it had so far entered into in its history and that too with a man whose antecedents Mr. Patel knew, he would act on his own responsibility without obtaining the approval of the Minister. I quite understand that there are occasions when Secretaries have to act on their own responsibility. Administration would become impossible if a Secretary has to told his hands until he has received the formal consent or approval of his Minister. In day-to-day administration, in cases of emergency, the Secretary must take the responsibility and must act in a manner which according to him would ultimately meet with the approval of his Minister. But this was neither a case of day-to-day administration nor a case of emergency. Government were going out of their way to ask the Corporation to invest a large amount which was done without consulting the Investment Committee, and that too for the specific purpose of removing the drag on the Calcutta Stock Exchange created by the Mundhra shares. Why should Mr. Patel act on his own responsibility with regard to so unusual and doubtful a transaction? And if there was some conversation with regard to this transaction, as the Finance Minister admits that there was, why should Mr. Patel have stopped at merely discussing the generalities and not getting the specific approval of the Minister? As a matter of fact, one of the reasons given by Mr. Patel for the haste with which the transaction was put through was the necessity of availing himself of the presence of the Minister in Bombay.

It appears that Mr. Patel left India on June 29 and returned on July 18. There is a letter of July 6, 1957, from Mr. Raman, Research Officer in the Research Section of the Reserve Bank of India, Calcutta, to Mr. Madan, Principal Adviser to the Reserve Bank of India, Bombay, which letter specifically mentions that the recent Life Insurance Corporation's support to buy Mundhra shares has relieved the market of the floating stocks to the extent of over a crore of rupees. "The opinion of the Life Insuranee Corporation buying of such shares is itself divided. While some say that to the extent that it has avoided a crisis and imparted some stability, the Life Insurance Corporation has done a good job. There are others who say that it has only temporarily plugged the loop hole and has therefore only postponed D-day. In any case, the truth is that Mundhra is now on a slightly firmer ground although he is far from being out of the woods." A copy of this letter was forwarded to the Ministry of Finance and Mr. Kaul, the Joint Secretary in the Ministry of Finance, has told me that these papers received from the Reserve Bank of India are submitted to the Minister. The Parliamentary Session Commenced about the middle of July, and one of Mr. Kaul's duties is to supply briefs to the Minister in connection with Parliamentary questions and short notice questions, Mr. Kaul had come to know that there was a possibility of some questions being asked in Parliament with regard to the Mundhra investments. Mr. Kaul himself was a Director of the Life Insurance Corporation, but at the relevant time he was on leave and therefore he wanted to be in possession of all the facts with regard to this particular transaction. He therefore wrote to Mr. Kamat and asked him to supply a full statement of facts and Mr. Kamat wrote to Mr. Kaul on July 16. This letter is of considerable importance. The letter gives a detailed history of how this transaction came about. He points out that wlth the announcement of the Budget proposals in May, equity values began to drop sharply and the Life Insurance Corporation then entered the market as a substantial purchaser of some prominent shares at their low values. These transactions assisted in bringing about a measure of stability in the market. The bear spectaculars then diverted their activity to several other scrips and the shares of the group of important companies in which Haridas Mundhra held a controlling interest received their particular attention. Mundhra who had in the past borrowed heavily from several banks on the security of these shares tried to support the values of these shares by taking up offers of sale made by several brokers. Gradually, his commitments to brokers reached a sizable proportion and he then approached the Life Insurance Corporation for assistance. He then sets out the course of negotiations as appears from the various letters exchanged between Mr. Patel and Mundhra and the Corporation and he then says that putting through this transaction "we have averted what might have been a serious position in the market arising from Mundhra's large liabilities to the brokers". He also points out that there is adverse criticism of this transaction and in answering these criticisms he says that by timely intervention in a falling market an institution like the L.I.C. can, therefore, moderate these trends and may even help to stimulate real investor interest. He also says that the purchase of Mundhra shares was made not with a view to rescue him from his financial difficulties (this is his version of the transaction), but with a view to avert possible financial difficulties in the market and to acquire at bargain prices share holdings in sound and potentially sound concerns. He also says that the apprehension that Mundhra with his controlling interest in these companies may feel tempted to interfere in the internal financial management of these campanies may well be a legitimate criticism of the purchase.

The first question with regard to the Mundhra transations was asked in the Lok Sabha on September 4, 1957, by Dr. Ram Subhag Singh and the question was:—

"Will the Minister of Finance be pleased to refer to a report in The Statesman (Delhi edition) of August 3, 1957, to the effect that a sum of Rs. one crore from the funds of the Life Insurance Corporation had been invested in a private enterprise with its headquarters in Kanpur and state:

(a) the name of the private enterprise in which the funds have been invested;

(b) the tolal amount invested so far; and

(c) the reasons for investing the funds in a private enterprise?

Now it is in evidence that before answer to a question is finanlised, the file with regard to the relevant papers goes to the Minister who has to give the reply and there can be not doubt that this letter of July 16, must have gone to the Minister with the file. Therefore, some time before September 4, the Minister must have been in possession of all the facts with regard to this transaction. It is most unfortunate that in answering the question the Minister did not think it proper to place all the facts fully and frankly before the Lok Sabha. Without disrespect, the answer given seems to be equivocal because the information that Dr. Ram Subhag Singh was obviously seeking was with regard to the transaction of June 24, and because he made the mistake of suggesting that one crore of rupees had been invested in a private enterprise with its headquarters in Kanpur, the only answer given by the Minister was that the Life Insurance Corporation had not invested a crore of rupees in any single private enterprise with headquarters in Kanpur. It is quite true that technically the answer was correct and that one crore of rupees had not been invested in the British India Corporation. There was a further question in the Lok Sabha on November 29 by the same Dr. Ram Subhag Singh. Obviously, Dr. Singh had then obtained more detailed information about this transaction and Mr. Bhagat, the Deputy Minister, informed Dr. Singh that the Life Insurance Corporation had, about the end of June 1957, purchased shares of the value of Rs. 1,26,86,100 in concerns in which Mundhra is said to have an interest. What is important to note are the answers given to the supplementary questions put to him, and the Minister said that the investment policy of the Corporation was dictated by the Investment Committee of the Life Insurance Corporation and that the Government had no hand in the purchases from time to time. He further said that the investment by the Life Insurance Corporation was being done solely with a view to getting a return and making a safe investment and that was the policy which was behind whatever investment they made. The question was not one of favouring any particular individual or any particular group but seeing that the Corporation benefited by the investment. He also said that the Corporation already owned shares in the Mundhra concerns and then wanted to augment the shares because they were able to purchase them at that time at an advantageous price. He also made it clear that so far as he was concerned the Life Insurance Corporation was not interested either in the Stock Exchange or in the brokers. They were essentially interested in their own investments. It is again unfortunate that with the letter of July 16, before the Finance Ministry he should have said that the investment policy was dictated by the Investment Committee of the L.I.C. when there was no suggestion in the letter of Mr. Kamat of July 16, that the Committee had been consulted. Again, this letter of July 16 clearly showed that the L.I.C. was interested in the Stock Exchange and also that the shares were not purchased at advantageous prices but they were purchased at prices fixed on the basis of the closing rate on June 24 or the rates quoted by Mundhra whichever were lower. Advantageous price would suggest that the Corporation had obtained these shares at a lower rate than the one prevailing in the market.

In the Lok Sabha debate which took place on December 16, 1957, the Minister pleaded guilty to having asked the L.I.C. to carry out the policy of Blue Chips. But he made it equally clear that apart from that policy that he had not imposed any other policy on the Corporation. Therefore, according to him, if the Corporation were buying these shares in pursuance of some other policy, then it would be on their own responsibility and not pursuant to any directions given by Government. Now Mr. Patel was clearly stated in his evidence that his understanding of the Government policy was not that of the Minister.

There was another letter from the Reserve Bank on September 5, 1957, again from Mr. Raman to Dr. Madan in which Mr. Raman points out that the opinion of many in the market is that Mundhra had not yet set his house in order and that he had practically reverted to the position as it was prior to the commencement of the L.I.C. support. He also says that the market is distressed over the fact that the actual disbursement of B.I.C. dividends which used to take place normally around April every year has still not been made. He further says that the fact that the accounts of Jessop & Co. have not been released so far is also interpreted to mean that all is not well with them. He also points out that the feeling is that the very least that the Government could do is to conduct an inquiry into the affairs of his concerns so that they may be in possession of information necessary to formulate any policy in regard to his concerns. A copy of this letter in the ordinary course came before the Finance Minister and he made a note addressed to the Principal Secretary on September 9 to the following effect: "The attached report from Raman does not make good reading. Can we do anything about it?" On September 15, Mr. Patel made a note that he had sent the relevant extracts from this report regarding Mundhra to Mr. Bhattacharya and Mr. Kamat and he also suggested that L.I.C. might try and buy further shares of Jessops and Richardson & Cruddas. This explains the letter of September 10, by Mr. Patel to Mr. Kamat to which reference has already been made. The importance of these documents lies in the fact that whether the Minister was aware of what Mr. Patel had done on June 24 or not, when he did come to know of these transactions he never repudiated the action of Mr. Patel. Therefore, clearly there is accquiescence on the part of the Minister in the part played by Mr. Patel in bringing about the transaction of June 24. The lack of repudiation on the part of the Minister would go to support Mr. Patel's story that the Minister had approved of the transaction in Bombay of June 24.

In my opinion, in any case, it is clear that constitutionally the Minister is responsible for the action taken by his Secretary with regard to this transaction. It is clear that a Minister must take the responsibility for actions done by his subordinates. He cannot take shelter behind them, nor can he disown their actions. The doctrine of ministerial responsibility has two facets. The Minister has complete autonomy within his own sphere of authority. As a necessary corollary he must take full responsibility for the actions of his servants. It is true that this may throw a very great burden on the Minister because it is impossible to expect that in a highly complicated system of administration which we have evolved the Minister could possibly know, leave alone give his consent to, every action taken by his subordinates. But it is assumed that once the policy is laid down by the Minister, his subordinates must reflect that policy and must loyally carry out that policy. If any subordinate fails to do so, he may be punished or dismissed, but, however vicariously, the responsibility of his action must be assumed by the Minister. It may be said that a Minister is merely part of the Government and his policy is the policy of the Government as a whole, and if the Minister should take the responsibility for his subordinate's actions, equally so must the Cabinet. But it is well established that the Cabinet only takes the responsibility for the Minister's action if the Minister reports the matter to the Cabinet and obtains Cabinet's sanction before he puts into effect this policy. Then the policy becomes the Cabinet policy and not only the Minister but the whole Cabinet must take the responsibility for whatever might have been done by a subordinate. In this case, therefore, Mr. Patel, who admittedly was acting as the Principal Secretary of the Minister, cannot be fastened with the responsibility of having effected this transaction in his own secretarial capacity. The Minister must fully and squarely accept the responsibility for what Mr. Patel did and if the transaction is improper and unjustified, although Mr. Patel may be actually responsible for the transaction, constitutionally the responsibility is that of the Minister.

This inquiry would have served no purpose whatever if no lessons could be derived from it. I think, if I may say so without presumption, that the following principles seem to be established as a result of a careful consideration of all the materials that have been placed before me :

(1) That Government should not interfere with the working of autonomous statutory corporations; that if they wish to interfere, they should not shirk the responsibility of giving directions in writing.

(2) That Chairman of corporations like the L.I.C., which has to deal with investments in a large way, should be appointed from persons who have business and financial experience and who are familiar with the ways of the Stock Exchange.

(3) That if the Executive Officers of the Corporation are to be appointed from the Civil Services, it should be impressed upon them that they owe a duty and loyalty to the Corporation and that they should not permit themselves to be influenced by senior officials of Government or surrender their judgment to them. If they feel that they are bound to obey the orders of these officials, they must insist on these orders being in writing.

(4) The funds of the Life Insurance Corporation

should only be used for the benefit of the policy-holders and not for any extraneous purpose. If they are to be used for any extraneous purpose that purpose must be the larger interest of the country. The public is entitled to an assurance from Government to this effect.

(5) In a Parliamentary form of Government, Parliament must be taken into confidence by the Ministers at the earliest stage and all relevant facts und materials must be placed before it. This would avoid difficulties and embarrassment being caused at a later stage when Parliament gets the necessary information from other sources.

(6) That the Minister must take full responsibility for the acts of his subordinates. He cannot be permitted to say that his subordinates did not reflect his policy or acted contrary to his wishes or directions.

(7) That Government should immediately apply to the Corporation Section 27-A of the Life Insurance Act of 1938, modified as circumstances require to carry out the solemn statutory assurance given in the Life Insurance Corporation Act.

SHIP REPAIRS COMMITTEE, 1958—REPORT

New Delhi, Ministry of Transport and Communications, 1959. 160p.

Chairman : Shri O. V. Alagesan.

Members : Shri Amarnath Aggarwal; Shri Narendra P. Nathwani; Rear Admiral T.B. Bose; Captain T.N. Kochhar; Shri H.C. Raut; Shri P.N. Rabady; Shri T.M. Sanghavi; Shri F.V. Badami.

Secretaries : Shri H.M. Trivedi; Shri P.R. Subramaniam.

APPOINTMENT

The proposal to appoint a Committee to enquire into the question of improvement of ship repair facilities in Indian ports appears to have been mooted originally in 1957, and a reference was made to this proposal in Parliament by the then Minister for Transport and Communications during the discussions in the budget session of that year. The appointment of this committee was, however, actually announced in a Resolution of the Government of India which was published in the Ministry of Transport and Communications Notification, No. 54-1 (2)/57 dated January 22, 1958.

TERMS OF REFERENCE

(i) To enquire into and report on the extsting ship repair facilities in Caleutta, Bombay, Madras, Visakhapatnam, Cochin, Kandla and at such other places where, in the opinion of the Committee, the problem needs looking into;

(ii) To recommend what improvement and expansion is required in such facilities in order to meet adequately the requirements of the developing merchant shipping of India as well as of non-Indian shipping which may require repairing facilities at Indian ports;

(iii) To report particularly whether facilities for dry docking available at present are adequate and, if not, what improvements/additional facilities are required and at which places;

(iv) To report whether materials, stores, etc., required for ship repairing are available adequately within the country or whether the country is deficient in this respect. If the latter is the case, to recommend what steps should be taken for reaching self-sufficiency in this field as far as possible:

(v) To consider and recommend the steps which are to be taken;

(a) by Government, and

(b) by the private sector,

for securing such improvement and/or expansion in the ship repairing facilities as the Committee may recommend.

CONTENTS

Introductory; Terms of Reference; Ships Repair Industry—General Considerations; Nature of Ship Repairs—Facilities Required and their Importance; Ship Repair Facilities in Foreign Ports; Ship Repairs Expenditure—Present Position and Future Potential; Ship Repair Workshops—Capacity and Turnover; Dry Docks and Repair Berths at Major Ports; Time and Cost of Repairs—Clarification of Policy Regarding Port Facilities; Recommendations regarding Ship Repair Workshops; Recommendations regarding Dry Docks; Recommendations regarding Repair Berths; Minor Ports; Ship Repair Materials and Ship Stores; Customs Procedure; Governmental Control and Advisory Machinery; Miscellaneous Matters; Summary of Recommendations, Annexures I to IX.

RECOMMENDATIONS

General

Government and the port authorities should accept the principle that it is part of their responsibility to provide for the requirements of the ship repair industry and Government should clarify their policy in this matter accordingly.

Subject to the implementation of the recommendation made by us regarding port dry docks in Calcutta and Bombay, there is no need to consider the provision of additional dry docks for merchant ships in these ports at present.

In order to make the industry more broad based, the new dry docks should preferably be constructed in Visakhapatnam and Cochin rather than in Calcutta and Bombay.

The provision of 12 fully equipped repair berth for both Calcutta and Bombay should be accepted as the ultimate target.

In the ports of Visakhapatnam, Madras and Cochin, one of the new berths should be equipped as a repair berth and allotted for repairs whenever required.

The port authorities should provide all essential facilities like cranes, electric power, compressed air, water supply, etc., as the dry docks controlled by them and also at the berths earmarked for ship repairs.

Government should encourage the privately owned workshops to undertake modernisation of their workshops, if necessary, with a scheme of financial assistance on favourable terms.

The private workshops should be encouraged to develop facilities for various items of repair work which cannot at present be carried out in India with such assistance as may be required from Government.

The Indian Naval Dockyard should make available its dry docks for merchant ships whenever they require them for routine dry docking etc. to the extent their own work permits.

To the extent the I.N. Dockyard Workshop has facilities for special types of work, they should be made available to ship repair firms or shipping companies whenever they need them.

The facilities of the port workshops at Visakhapatnam, Madras, Cochin and Kandla should as a matter of policy be made available to merchant ships requiring repairs.

The Hindustan Shipyard should, as a matter of policy, extend its activities to ship repair work and take early steps to fully equip itself for this purpose.

The formation of an all-India organisation of ship repairers and shipbuilders is necessary and desirable and the Government should encourage the formation of such an organisation and accord recognition to it, when formed.

It is desirable to set up an all-India advisory body with representatives of ship repairers, shipbuilders, shipowners, major ports and the departments of Government concerned. This body should advise Government on all matters pertaining to the industry as a whole. This body may be attached to the Ministry of Transport and Communications and be presided over by the Minister.

Until repair facilities are improved at other major ports, there is scope for local advisory committees only at Calcutta and Bombay. These may be presided over by the Chairman of the Port Commissioners or Port Trust and should include the representatives of the Government departments and the commercial interests concerned. These committees should deal with matters concerning improvements in repair facilities, repair berth and dry dock programmes, shortage of materials etc.

Major Ports

Calcutta

The six large port craft may continue to use the larger dry docks (i.e., K.G. dry docks and K.P. dry docks Nos. 1 and 2 for their requiremenrs. When these craft require the use of the dry dock for long periods, they may preferably be docked in K.G. dry dock No. 1.

All other craft should, as far as possible, be docked on the post shipways, the Island Workshop dry docks and Kidderpore dry dock No. 3 and they may use the larger dry docks only when it is unavoidable.

When the port vessels are docked in the longer dry docks, the port authorities should arrange for work to be done round the clock so that it is completed in the shortest possible time.

A heavy lift crane in the K.G. dry docks and additional compressors and flood lighting in both the K.G. and K.P. dry docks should be provided within the remaining period of the Second Plan.

Improved compressed air supply, A.C. and D.C. power, drinking water facilities, sanitary arrangements and telephone facilities, as recommended by us at both the K.G. and K.P. dry docks should also be provided within the remaining period of the Second Plan.

The Kidderpore dry docks should be renovated and a 15-ton travelling crane provided during the Third Plan period.

The three lay up berths in K.P. Dock (off 28 and 29) and K.G. Dock (G. berth) should be earmarked for ship repairs, dredged to a minimum depth of 18' and equipped with certain essential facilities as recommended by us during the remaining period of the Second Plan.

Provision for certain additional facilities like travelling cranes, compressed air, etc., at these berths should be made in the Third Plan.

During the Third Plan period, the 'H' berths in the K.G. Dock should be adapted and equipped as a repair berth. In addition, two berths in the new basin proposed to be built in the K.G. Dock should be constructed as repair berths as a part of that plan.

Bombay

As some 30 port craft will in future be of such draft and dimensions that they cannot be docked on the port slipways, the Port Trust should construct a small dry dock near the port workshop large enough to take all such craft.

Thereafter, all port craft should, as far as possible, be docked in this dry dock or the port slipways and they may use the larger dry docks only when it is unavoidable.

Pending the constructions of the new dry dock, whenever the port craft use the larger dry docks, the port authorities should arrange for the work to be done round the clock, so that it is completed in the shortest possible time.

The proposal to lengthen the Hughes dry dock by 125′ so as to make two T. 2 tankers should be considered and taken up for execution as early as possible and completed early in the Third Plan period.

Improved compressed air supply, A.C., and D.C. power, drinking and salt water supplies, sanitary arrangements and telephone facilities, as recommended by us, at both the Hughes and Mereweather dry docks should be provided within the remaining period of the Second Plan.

A reservior of suitable size for storage of fresh water should be constructed near the Hughes dry dock.

A 15-ton travelling crane should be provided solely for the use of the Mereweather dry dock.

The Port Trust and the Mazagon Dock should co-operate to achieve increased utilisation of the Ritchie and Mogul dry docks which are controlled by the Mazagon Dock. The Port Trust should be prepared to accept responsibility for dredging and maintenance of the channel and the approaches to these dry docks and the Mazagon Dock, on their part, should be agreeable to incur capital expenditure on lengthening and deepening the Ritchie dry dock, which would make it suitable for docking large merchant ships. They should also not be averse to hiring out the Mogul dry dock to shipping companies who wish to utilise the services of the ship repair firms other than the Mazagon Dock.

The inner northern half of K.L.M. berths and the northern half of N and O berths in the Prince's Dock should be reserved for the ships needing repairs.

No. 9 berth in the Victoria Dock should also be earmarked for ship repairs.

All the above berths should be equipped with the various facilities, as mentioned in the case of Calcutta, during the remaining period of the Second Plan and in the Third Plan period.

In addition to the above, one berth in the outer dock wall should be made available as a repair berth during fair weather. It should be dredged to maintain a minimum depth of 18′ and equipped with necessary facilities.

The Kassara Basin should be put into use as a repair basin for medium sized vessels. This will necessitate dredging of the basin and the approach channel fitting of a lock gate, strengthening of the piers and providing various repair facilities. This should be included in the Third Plan.

In any scheme for construction of new basins or docks in Bombay, two fully equipped berths for repair purposes should be planned as part of the scheme.

Visakhapatnam

The scheme under consideration by the Hindustan Shipyard for the construction of a dry dock should be taken up at an early date. The dry dock should be capable of accommodating T.2 type tankers. The proposal of the port authorities for lengthening and deepening their dry dock should be considered in the light of the above.

Kandla

There is no need to consider the provision of a dry dock at this port at present.

Madras

It is not necessary to consider the provision of a dry dock at this port at present.

The use of the port slipway for docking small sea-going vessels based on this port should be permitted.

Cochin

The construction of a fully equipped dry dock, either as a port of the second shipyard scheme or otherwise, should be planned and completed by the end of the Third Plan period.

Minor Ports

There is scope for improving the existing facilities at the ports mentioned below to serve the needs of small coastal vessels for dry docking and repairs and also of deep sea ships for repairs afloat.

Mandapam

The dry dock should be lengthened and deepened so as to dock vessels of 350′ length and 15′ draft and the approach channel dredged during the Third Plan period.

The slipway should be brought into use for docking and repairs to small vessels and craft plying in the area.

The workshop should, as a matter of policy, undertake repairs to privately owned vessels.

Tuticorin

The provision of a ship repair workshop and a fully equipped repair berth at this port should be considered as part of the general plan for development of Tuticorin as a major port.

Bhavnagar

The existing dry dock should be extended and deepened so as to dock vessels of 350′ length, 45′ breadth and 15′ draft.

The port workshop should, as a matter of policy, undertake repairs to privately owned vessels and the workshop should be expanded for this purpose.

In the new port one of the new berths proposed to be built should be earmarked for ship repair work and fully equipped with all repair facilities

Okha

The workshop at this port should be equipped for carrying out maintenance and running repairs to merchant ships.

Bedibunder

The dry dock at this port should be renovated and the lock gates repaired.

Veraval

The dry dock may be used in future for docking small vessels and sailing vessels which are being mechanised.

Ship Repair Materials and Ship Stores

While a policy of progressive manufacture of these items indigenously should be pursued, it is necessary to take a liberal view of applications for import of materials if the industry is to be in a state of competitive efficiency.

High priority should continue to be given to the steel requirements of the ship repair industry and steps taken to eliminate avoidable procedural delays. Quota certificates should be issued before the end of the quarter to which they relate.

The Iron and Steel Controller should make every possible effort to fulfill the quotas allotted to ship repair firms both in terms of total tonnage and also of the specified categories applied for. To the extent the quotas cannot be fulfilled from indigenous producers or stockists the repair firms concerned should be enabled to obtain the balance from abroad by issue of necessary import licences.

To meet emergency requirements of shipping companies and small ship repair firms not registered with the Development Wing, the Iron and Steel Controller should on the recommendation of the Director General of Shipping, make ad hoc supply available to them without delay from the producers or stockists.

The entire position regarding supply of steel should be reviewed after the three Government steel plants have been in production for some time in consultation with the all India Advisory Body recommended by us.

Imports of required quantities of Oregon pine and Lignum Vitae should be allowed until regular supplies of indigenous substitutes are available.

In the case of certain materials essential for ship repairs, workshop spares and equipment should have the same preferential treatment as raw materials have for other industries.

In view of the special position of the industry its imports requirements should be dealt with separately from those of other industries importers and provision made to meet them directly.

A separate foreign exchange quota should be established for the ship repair industry for import of materials required for ship repairs and workshop spares and equipment. It may be administered by the Development Wing and a liberal licensing policy should be followed in respect of their imports subject to proved non-availability from indigenous sources. All policy questions regarding this quota should be dealt within consultation with the All India Advisory Body recommended by us.

A special foreign exchange quota should be established for import of spares, ship stores etc., required by shipping companies. This quota may be administered by the Directorate General of Shipping. All policy questions regarding this quota should be dealt with in consultation with the Indian National Steamship Owners Association.

The decisions of the Development Wing and the Directorate General of Shipping as to the necessity for imports should be accepted by the Import Control Authority for issue of licences.

A more liberal policy in regard to imports of essential ship stores by ship chandlers should be followed.

Customs Procedure

The present Customs procedure does not take account of the special requirements of the ship repair industry, and affects it adversely. The entire policy should be reviewed and necessary changes made in the procedure.

The present machinery pass system results in increasing the time of ship repairs in Calcutta and Bombay owing to delays in complying with the procedure. A new procedure should be evolved, which should be simple in operation and remove the factors which result in delays.

As regards the changes to be made, the Master or Chief Engineer of a ship and the supervisor of the repair firm should be authorised to sign the machinery pass. It should be endorsed by the Customs officer at the gate after necessary check. To protect Government's interests an overriding guarantee should be furnished by the sbipowners or the agent and the ship repairer accepting responsibility for the actions of their officers.

One or two gates in each dock in Calcutta and Bombay may be specified through which all lorries carrying repair materials should pass both outward and inward.

Pending revision of the procedure, as suggested above, urgent steps should be taken to make available in these two ports an adequate pool of Customs officers, both during and outside working hours. The Customs staff handling this work should be strengthened and all Customs inspectors available in the dock concerned should be authorised to deal with all matters connected with machinery passes. Special officers with telephone facilities should be earmarked to deal with machinery passes outside working hours.

Although difficulties are experienced in other ports also as a result of the machinery pass system, they will be overcome by the general procedural changes recommended by us.

The shipment of spares, materials, etc., for repairs should be treated differently from ship stores and they should be allowed to be shipped freely subject to such formal documentation as may be prescribed for record purposes. A responsible officer of the shipowner, agent or ship repairer may be required to certify the items which are proposed to be shipped.

No restrictions should be imposed on the fitting of new parts on ships undergoing repairs by transfer of parts from another ship of the same owner or from bond or by import from abroad.

Shipowners and ship repairers should be allowed to avail themselves of bonding facilities on a liberal scale and at a reasonable cost.

Miscellaneous

Two sludge larges of approximately 100 tons should be provided in Calcutta and Bombay for discharge of sludge. Shore sludge tanks should also be provided for discharge of sludge from the barges.

Space should be made available to the principal repair firms at the major ports in the dock area for maintaining a small workshop-cum-office. Facilities should be given to use a part of the premises for a small bonded store.

Garbage bins should be provided near the dry docks and the repair berths to collect waste materials from ships.

Every effort should be made to return the existing quantum of chipping and painting work in Indian ports by suitable measures.

The procedure for disposal of scrap should be simplified and the Iron and Steel Controller should be given authority to issue final disposal instructions without the ship repair firms having to enter into prolonged correspondence with furnace owners and/or re-rolling mills.

The procedure should be so modified that the existing formality of levying Customs duty on ship stores etc., when repairs exceed three months, does not arise,

State Governments should consider sympathetically applications from ship repair firms for exemption from Section 58 of the Factories Act relating to overlapping shifts and Section 64 relating to overtime work.

The port authorities should take steps to improve fresh water supplies for ships' requirements when necessary. The port authorities should also permit private parties to own and operate water barges within the ports for supplies to ships in stream.

Applications from ship repairers for operating two-way V.H.F. sets between ships and workshops should be sympathetically considered by the P. and T. Department.

The terms on which port craft or equipment are hired to ship repairers should be reviewed so as to eliminate any onerous conditions which would restrict their use or availability.

In cases of prolonged occupation of berths for repairs the Bombay Port Trust should discontinue levying extra charges under clause (d) of Section IV of the B.P.T. dock scale of rates, except in extreme cases.

It would be of assistance in future if the port authorities and shipping companies keep certain essential information regarding dry docks, berths, time and expenditure on ship repairs, etc.

AD-HOC COMMITTEE ON FRUIT AND VEGETABLE PRESERVATION INDUSTRY, 1958—REPORT

Delhi, Manager of Publications, 1960. 100p.+iip.

Chairman : Shri T. R. Sathe.
Member : Shri V. A. Mehta.
Secretary : Shri P. H. Bhatt.

APPOINTMENT

Ministry of Commerce and Industry, Government of India vide letter No. 23 (1) 57-MC, dated January 24, 1958, constituted an Ad-Hoc Committee to review the development of the preserved fruit and vegetable industry in India.

TERMS OF REFERENCE

(i) To review the steps so far taken to develop preserved fruit and vegetable industry in India on the basis of recommendations made by various bodies like Planning Commission, Tariff Commission etc.

(ii) To examine the present position of the industry in regard to installed capacity, production, consumption, availability of raw materials and export of finished products.

(iii) To assess the scope for further development of the industry in different regions of the country keeping in view the available facilities.

(iv) To examine the extent and future scope for the indigenous production of different types of chemicals, raw materials and machinery required for the fruit and vegetable preservation industry.

(v) To make such recommendations as the Committee may consider necessary having regard to the objective of developing fruit and vegetable preservation industry.

CONTENTS

Preface; Introduction; Production (Fruit Products Order); Raw Materials; Equipment and Machinery; Tariff Enquiries; Exports; Research and Investigational Work; Second Five-Year Plan; Suggestions for Future Development of the Industry; Summary and Recommendations; Appendices A to H.

RECOMMENDATIONS

Ministry of Commerce and Industry, Government of India, constituted an Ad-Hoc Committee in January, 1958, to review the development of preserved fruit and vegetable industry.

The need for horticultural development in India is essential for the healthy growth of our population Fruit and Vegetable Preservation Industry is linked up with the development of horticulture.

India does not lack in adequate resources for developing this industry as only 0.12 per cent of the production of fresh fruits and vegetables is estimated to be utilised by the industry as against nearly 15 to 20 percent of fresh fruits and vegetables which go waste due to transport and other bottlenecks.

There is immense scope for the development of industry in fruit growing regions which are at present suffering from transport and marketing difficulties.

The total estimated production of fruit and vegetable products during the year 1956 was 30,000 tons valued at Rs. 334 lakhs and for 1957, 32,000 tons valued at Rs. 388 lakhs.

Production of different varieties of fruit and vegetable products is carried out throughout the year.

Bombay, Delhi, Punjab, West Bengal and Uttar Pradesh are important States for the industry. Beverages, pickles, canned fruits and vegetables and preserves are important items of production.

The fruit product industry is controlled under the Fruit Products Order, 1955, issued under the Essential Commodities Act, 1955.

The number of licence holders who manufacture fruit and vegetable products has been on the increase and was 990 in 1958. Although the number of factories is quite large, units which have a production of over Rs. one lakh per year in value are only 51. The larger units contribute considerably to the total production and deal mainly in products like fruit beverages, chutney, canned fruits and vegetables.

Most of the larger units in the country fulfill all the requirements of hygiene, sanitation and standardisation of quality laid down under the Fruit Products Order, 1955.

The major raw materials required by the industry are fruits, vegetables, cans, bottles, (fuel, barrels, chemicals like pectin), citric acid, acetic acid, preservatives, food colours, essences, flavours, salt, spices, edible oils, water softening agents, detergents, packing and labelling materials.

Due to lack of data regarding the suitability for processing of different varieties of fruits and vegetables, the industry has been mainly using known varieties which are more suitable for table purposes.

The requirements of sugar for the industry is hardly

0.3 per cent of the total production of s ugar in the country.

The total requirement of tinplate containers is estimated at 2,000 tons per year out of which 1,000 tons is of special type which is imported at present. It would be necessary to continue the use of imported tin-plate till the country starts the production at Rourkela of cold reduced hot dipped tin-plate manufactured from suitable quality of steel.

The murrabba and pickle industry are using canisters made from ordinary type of tin-plate. The advisability of using such a material requires to be investigated by the Central Food Technological Research Institute, Mysore.

It is estimated that 50 per cent of the production of fruit and vegetable products is packed in bottles.

The trend for glass packing is likely to improve but the major obstacles are (a) the price of glass, (b) the quality of bottles particularly for packing products hermetically and processing in pressurised system, (c) development of better closures and (d) higher cost of transport due to heavier gross weight.

The industry has been facing difficulties in obtaining good quality bottles at reasonable prices particularly in the southern region of the country.

The manufacture of barrels from special woods needs to be investigated by the Forest Research Institute, Dehra Dun. There is scope for increase in the use of barrels for packing varieties of food products.

The existing technological institutes have not been paying adequate attention to imparting training in the cooperating techniques and packing in barrels.

Scope for the manufacture of pectin from apple and citrus waste should he explored.

Production of citric and acetic acids in substantial qualities within the country would enable the industry to obtain the requirements indigenously at reasonable prices.

The use of peservatives and food colours is regulated under the Fruit Products Order and the Prevention of Food Adulteration Rules.

Excessive use of food colours is not desirable.

The requirement of equipment and machinery by the unorganised sector of the industry is insignificant. In the organised sector considerable amount of manual labour is employed in India and mechanisation is avoided as far as possible.

Fabrication of cartain types of food machinery has been recently undertaken within the country. Some of the specialised equipment and machinery are still required to be imported.

Fruit and Vegetable Presevation Industry enjoyed tariff protection for a period of about 10 years. In the last tariff enquiry held in the year 1957, Tariff Commission recommended de-protection of the industry and made certain recommendations for its future development.

The export of fruit and vegetable products was to the extent of Rs. 31.13 lakhs in the year 1957. The main items exported were chutney, pickles, canned fruits, pulps and juices.

There is possibility of promoting export trade of canned fruits, pulps and canned vegetables.

In exploring the export markets, it is recommended that an official delegation having representatives of the industry may be sent to a few selected countries. The target for export of fruit products has been fixed at 11,000 tons by 1960-61 and the Committee feels that this could be fulfilled by a more vigorous drive in giving publicity to our products in foreign countries and by participation in exhibitions and international fairs.

State Trading Corporation may usefully contribute to the promotion of export of fruit and vegetable products.

The industry should voluntarily subject itself to compulsory quality check on exported fruit products.

For evolving a development programme for fruit preservation industry during the Second Five-Year Plan, a Panel was set up which submitted its report to Government in 1955.

The target for increased production by the industry during the Second Five-Year Plan has been fixed at 50,000 tons by 1960-61.

On the recommendation of the Tariff Commission and the Panel, Government of India has agreed to the scheme for subsidy on tin-plate used in the manufacture of open top sanitary cans. The subsidy has reduced the cost of cans to industry by 22 per cent on an average.

With a view to develop the industry in various parts of India, a scheme for loans to the industry has been sanctioned and in the year 1957-58, loans to the extent of Rs. nine lakhs were sanctioned. Loan facilities would accelerate the development of the industry considerably.

Decentralisation of research on fruit and vegetable preservation industry has been recognised and it is proposed to establish 10 regional research stations in various regions of India by 1960-61.

Some of the important recommendations of the Panel have been put into effect recently, amongst which are :

(a) Rebate of excise duty on sugar used in exported fruit products.

(b) Inclusion of Fruit Preservation Industry in the Industries Development and Regulation Act.

(c) Formation of Development Council for food processing industry.

Industry has been given facilities for replenishment of quota for tin-plate used in exported fruit-products as well as for drawback of import duty on tin-plate and glass bottles used in packing the products which are exported.

The State Bank of India has recently extended liberalised terms of finance for fruit and vegetable preservation industry.

A total ban has been imposed at present on the import of fruit and vegetable products.

Research and investigational work carried out at the Central Food Technological Researeh Institute, Mysore and other institutions has, besides solving certain technical problems of the industry, helped the development of new products and improvement of existing processing technique.

The estimated target of production in the Third Plan is visualised as 100,000 tons by 1965-66. It is estimated that the level of production may go up to 400,000 tons per year on the basis of long-term development.

The export target for fruit and vegetable production by 1965-66 is estimated as 20,000 tons.

Implementation of several schemes which were included in the Second Five-Year Plan for the benefit of the industry have been delayed. These schemes should be carried over and projected in the Third Five-Year Plan.

The Committee recommends that a coordinated programme of horticulture and fruit and vegetable preservation should be chalked out.

Steps should be taken to help the industry in exploring and developing new markets for fruit and vegetable products.

The Committee emphasises the need for quality control and recommends that compulsory standardisation should be adopted for exports.

The need for technical training programmes at various levels as well as for foreign training of technicians has been recognised and adequate provision should be made for such training during the Third Five-Year Plan.

The Committee recognises the need for development of refrigeration expeditiously in the Third Five-Year Plan.

The development of fruit processing industries would necessitate the development of allied group of industries like tin containers, closures, fabrication of equipment and machinery, manufacture of food colours, flavours and chemicals, etc,

ADVISORY COMMITTEE ON SLUM CLEARANCE, 1958—REPORT

New Delhi, Ministry of Works, Housing and Supply, 1958. 48p.

Chairman : Shri Asoke K. Sen.

Members : Shri M.R. Sachdev; Shri N.N. Wanchoo; Shri K. Ram; Shri Hari Sharma; Shri P.P. Agarwal; Dr. P.C. Alexander; Shri A.V. Venkatasubban; Shri S.L. Khurana; Shri G. Mukherji.

Secretary : Shri N.P. Dube.

APPOINTMENT

In his minute dated January 25, 1958, the Prime Minister made the following observations on the subject of slum clearance:

(a) The question of removing the slums is intimately connected with housing and of future urban planning;

(b) Providing employment to the slum dwellers must form an important part of any slum clearance programme. Calcutta is the worst affected city in India from the point of view of insanitary living conditions, over-crowding and unemployment and Bombay, Kanpur and other big cities are not very much better;

(c) It might be possible to start small industries in the slum areas with the help of small machines and tools;

(d) In Delhi there are a number of authorities, with overlapping jurisdiction, which deal with the problem of slum clearance in some way or the other. There has been some coordination of late under the Delhi Development Authority which works under the Health Ministry. Other authorities concerned in Delhi are the Ministry of Works, Housing and Supply and the Ministry of Home Affairs. The Ministry of Finance naturally come into the picture, and so does the Ministry of Commerce and Industry, if small industries are to be considered.

The Prime Minister, therefore, constituted an Advisory Committee to collect material on what has been done in the major cities of India and to present its report or suggestions on the various approaches to the problem of slum clearance. The committee was to take special interest in the principal cities and particular attention was to be given to the slum situation in Calcutta.

TERMS OF REFERENCE

(i) To collect material on what has been done in the major cities of India and to present its report or suggestions on the various approaches to the problem of slum clearance.

(ii) The Committee was to take special interest in the principal cities and particular attention was to be given to the slum situation in Calcutta.

CONTENTS

Terms of Reference; Introduction; Nature and Extent of the Problem; Improvement of Slums; Short-term Objective; Clearance of Slums; Long-term Objective; Financial Implications of the Slum Clearance Programme; Raising Additional Revenue; The Foreign Exchange Component; Compensation and Acquisition of Land; Slums and Urban Development; Summary of the Main Recommendations; Appendices I and II.

RECOMMENDATIONS

Slum clearance should be viewed as a part of the problem of urban development and all activities relating to social welfare, including the provision of fruitful employment, should be integrated to bring about the development of the depressed and slum areas.

It will be desirable to entrust this urban community development to one Ministry at the Centre which could integrate the activities of the other Ministries in respect of town-planning, slum clearance, housing, health, education and industries in order to develop completely the particular slum areas chosen for treatment.

To start off with, the worst slum area in the six cities of Calcutta, Bombay, Madras, Delhi, Kanpur and Ahmedabad may be taken up for treatment.

In the States, in which the first six experiments are to be conducted, the urban community development organisations may be headed by Administrators. These Administrators will draw up and implement, in consultation with the Ministry in charge of urban community development and with the State and local bodies concerned, the composite urban development scheme for the selected areas.

The short-term objective of providing the basic amenities in the existing slums should be carried out with expedition and vigour.

In order to make more effective the Ministry of Works, Housing and Supply's Slum-Clearance Scheme, which has for its objective, the eradication of the slums, it will be necessary to:

(i) Provide an increased financial allocation for slum clearance, especially for the cities of Bombay, Calcutta, Madras, Delhi, Kanpur and Ahmedabad;

(ii) Find the entire subsidy envisaged under the Scheme from the Centre's own financial resources;

(iii) Set up medium, small scale and cottage industries in order to provide the slum-dwellers who have to be moved away, to distant sites, means of employment in the new neighbourhoods; and

(iv) Acquire land in bulk on the payment of reasonable compensation and to develop it for use in the housing and slum-clearance programme.

It is suggested that there should be a levy of terminal tax on goods and passengers carried by rail, in order to initiate the programme of urban community development, to implement more effectively the present Slum Clearance Scheme and to acquire and develop land in advance.

COMMITTEE ON THE INTRODUCTION OF STANDARDS OF WEIGHTS AND MEASURES BASED ON THE METRIC SYSTEM, 1958—REPORT

Ernakulam, The Coir Board, 1960. 23p.

Chairman & Convener : Shri T.M.B. Nedungadi.
Vice-Chairman : Shri C.T. Jacob.
Members : Shri N. Kunjuraman; Shri J. Murukandi; Shri B.S. Krishnan; Shri Revi Karunakaran; Shri P.K. Nayar; Shri T.K. Divakaran; Shri T.D. Venkataraman.

APPOINTMENT

The Committee on the Introduction of Standards of Weights and Measures Based on the Metric System was constituted under the Coir Board at its 15th meeting held on February 26, 1958.

TERMS OF REFERENCE

(i) To study the problems connected with the transition to metric system of weights and measures and to assess the difficulties that may crop up consequent on the introduction of this system; and

(ii) To suggest ways and means for overcoming them, paying special attention to the recalibration of weighing devices in use in factories, specifications for the size and quality of coir products and the difficulties of exporters of coir products.

CONTENTS

Introduction; Terms of Reference of the Committee; Meetings of the Committee; General; Metric System and Coir Industry; Recommendations of the Committee; Appendices I to V.

RECOMMENDATIONS

The metric system of weights and measures be introduced in the organised sector of the coir industry, viz.:

(i) Factories engaged in the processing of coir yarn or manufacture of coir products, in so far as they undertake the purchase of coir or coir yarn or the sale of coir, coir yarn or coir products;

(ii) In Central Coir Cooperative Societies in so far as they undertake the purchase of coir yarn or the sale of coir, coir yarn or coir products.

As far as the coir industry and coir trade are concerned, introduction of the metric system of weights and measures in the place of the present foot-pound system should be taken up by the Coir Board.

The metric system of weights and measures will be enforced in the coir industry only in October 1959, in view of the various difficulties facing the industry.

The continuance of the use for a period of two years from the date of introduction of the metric system of any weights and measures which was in use immediately be fore that date in respect of that sector of coir industry to which the system is made applicable.

In order to popularise the new system to the public concerned with the industry, the Coir Board should launch upon a programme of intensive publicity.

The list of various types of weights and measures now in vogue in the industry (Appendix III) may be forwarded to the Central Government and the Central Government may be requested to notifiy the equivalents for all these types of weights and measures required by the industry as required under the Act.

The Central Government may be requested to take urgent steps in the matter of unrestricted production and distribution of the commercial weights and measures in the new system to the trade so far as the coir industry is concerned.

The Board should get printed in large scale, charts giving the comparative terms of the weights and measures in current use and their equivalents in metric system. Similarly, a conversion table of the prices on the basis of the present terms and their metric equivalents should also be prepared and copies printed. Printed copies of these comparative charts and conversion table should be widely distributed free of cost amongst all concerned in the trade and the industry as early as possible.

The Board should in all its future publications, wherever necessary, publish quotations of prices/rates of coir and coir goods on the basis of the current weights and the measures along with their metric equivalents. The local papers who publish rates/quotations daily, weekly, fortnightly or monthly should also be requested to do so on the basis of the conversion table to be supplied to them by the Board.

AGRICULTURAL ADMINISTRATION COMMITTEE, 1958—REPORT

New Delhi, Ministry of Food and Agriculture, 1958. 85p.+vip.+xlvip.

Chairman : Raja Surendra Singh of Nalagarh.

Members : Dr. J.S. Patel; Shri J.V.A. Nehemiah; Shri M.L. Wilson; Shri K. Sachidanandam.

Co-opted Members : Secretary to Government in-charge Agriculture; Director of Agriculture; Registrar, Cooperative Societies of the States visited.

Secretary : Dr. R.N. Mathur.

APPOINTMENT

At the Conference of State Ministers of Agriculture, held in Srinagar in October, 1957, it was observed that serious delays in the execution of several agricultural production schemes in the States were due to administrative complexities and over-centralisation of powers both administrative and financial. The Conference suggested that the Central Government should set up a Committee, consisting of experts and administrators, both from the Central and State Governments, which should visit four or five States and recommend for the consideration of the State Governments a model agricultural organisation in the States, as well as measures for the delegation of powers to agricultural officers at all administrative levels. The Government of India, in accordance with the recommendation of the Conference of State Ministers of Agriculture appointed this Committee vide their letter No. 3-35/57-GMF (Co), dated February 28, 1958, to make recommendations on the lines of the resolution passed at the Srinagar Conference.

TERMS OF REFERENCE

(i) To suggest simplification of administrative and financial procedures in order to expedite the implementation of agricultural production schemes; and

(ii) To suggest a model agricultural organisation in the States, along with suggestions for delegation of suitable powers at various levels in the States, so that agricultural production schemes may be carried out speedily.

CONTENTS

Introductory; Growth of Agricultural Departments and the Prevailing Service Conditions; Training and Assessment; Coordination; Evaluation and Assessment of Development Work; Programme Planning; Budgeting, Sanctions, Procedures and Delegation of Powers; Supply Procedures; Model Agricultural Organisation to Suit Present Needs; Organisation for Agricultural Research and Education; Summary of Recommendations; Appendices I to IX.

RECOMMENDATIONS

Growth Of Agricultural Departments And The Prevailing Service Conditions

The growing tendency of depending upon stimulus from the Centre for taking action on subjects which are the responsibility of the States, needs to be discouraged. States should examine periodically, the structure, objectives and policies of the State Department of Agriculture with a view to providing balanced growth and enunciating programmes and policies. This review should be undertaken once in five years by a special Committee of agricultural scientists, administrators and progressive farmers.

A similar Committee is recommended at the Centre for examining programmes and policies of the Central Commodity Committees and other Central Institutions dealing with agriculture.

The Royal Commission on Agriculture made important recommendations in 1928 with regard to improving service conditions, but unfortunately most of these recommendations have not been implemented. Present day problems of low morale and inefficiency are attributable to non-implementation of these vital recommendations made 30 years ago.

A very large number of temporary posts—30 per cent to 80 per cent still exist in State Departments of Agriculture. All temporary posts continuing for more than three years and having reasonable chances of continuing should be added to the State cadre and made permanent. Pensionary and other rights such as annual increments etc. of agricultural workers who have served for many years should be protected.

Willingness to recognise the Agriculture Department as a major and important department is still lacking and there is strong need for planning and distribution of national intellect.

Low scales of pay do not attract talent. To attract the best talent available in the country to the field of agriculture they should be paid at par with the administrative services. The existing disparity has lowered the stature of agricultural services in this country.

The scales of pay of gazetted, as well as, subordinate agricultural services should not be lower than those for other services, requiring comparable training and subsequent prospects of promotion and prosperity in the service.

The District Agricultural Officers and the Regional Deputy Directors who play the role of an adviser, should be upgraded in status. Avenues for promotion should be increased by introducing more senior and selection grade posts.

If technical qualities and competence are to be promoted, there should be adequate recognition of merit at all stages and advancement should not depend merely on seniority.

Creation of supernumerary posts in superior cadres is necessary for retaining technical personnel of requisite aptitude and competence in their fields of specialisation, without allowing their prospects of promotion to suffer.

For raising the morale and prestige of agricultural services and for attracting equally suitable human material and for bringing about uniformity of standard, an All-India Agricultural Service should be created. The scales of pay and prospects should be at par with the I.A.S.

Till such time that an All-India Service can be created, an 'Agricultural' or 'Technical' Cadre or Pool may be created in the I.A.S. cadre to which 38 per cent of the technical officers of State Class II Services and above, should be recruited by the Union Public Service Commission strictly on the basis of merit and competence.

State Departments of Agriculture should frame or

revise rules for recruitment, confirmation and promotion. An experienced Administrative Officer from the Appointments Department should be deputed with the Secretary, Agriculture, for drafting or revising the rules of Agricultural Services.

Only those persons who have an aptitude for agriculture should be recruited in agricultural departments. Suitable tests for aptitude should be devised, especially for research.

Qualifications for various posts in the agricultural departments have been suggested.

In Extension and Farm Management Branches, 40 per cent of the posts should be filled up by direct recruitment; similarly, 50 per cent of the posts of the Deputy Directors should be filled up by direct recruitment so as to attract bright youngmen in the services, before they have lost their initiative and drive by serving long periods in subordinate positions. The introduction of fresh blood will tend to tone up the services.

Suggestions have been made for grouping of posts, promotion quotas and qualifications required for various branches of the Agriculture Departments.

The posts of Principal of Agricultural College and Joint Directors of Agriculture, Research, Education and Extension, etc., should be treated as selection grade posts and should not be filled merely on the basis of seniority. In filling these posts, as well as those of Deputy Directors and Heads of Sections the need for recruiting officers with merit, initiative and drive is paramount.

Training And Assessment

The fast disappearing concept of taking training of subordinates as an important duty needs to be restored.

Fresh agricultural graduates recruited by the Agricultural Departments should be given orientation as well as 'on the job' training. Old staff, whether engaged in research teaching or extension or when transferred from one agro-climatic zone to another should also receive this training.

It is important that training courses are conducted by senior, experienced and competent officers.

Job training should impart a practical working knowledge of different types of jobs to be entrusted to the trainees. It is necessary that a systematic and regular programme of training is drawn up and the officers expected to fill higher posts given such training.

In order to keep agricultural officers abreast of latest developments and researches, arrangements should be made permanently for imparting refresher courses in a systematic and automatic manner. These refresher courses should be followed by examinations and those who fail to pass in these examinations should stand to lose; those who pass should stand to gain in matter of promotions.

Short-term intensive courses should also be organised during summer vacations at postgraduate colleges for the benefit of the research, teaching and extension staff. Due weightage should be given to the examinations passed at the time of promotion.

Special training facilities need to be organised for imparting training in Farm Management and Farm Planning on a few selected farms ,as it is only through well managed farms, running at a profit, that modern practices can be demonstrated to the cultivator in a convincing manner.

The need for foreign training should be assessed on a long term basis and panels of selected candidates should be kept by the State Departments of Agriculture. Ad-hoc selections should the avoided. After receiving training, officers should be posted back to the subject of their specialisation.

In all the cadres of the agricultural departments where there are more than eight to 10 posts in a subject, a training and deputation reserve should be created. This should be in addition to the normal leave reserve. The need for training is felt more keenly in the case of the extension or the field personnel.

Periodical examinations should be prescribed for officers. Those who fail to pass should not be confirmed, promoted or permitted to cross the efficiency bar.

The existing system of evaluating officers leaves much to be desired. For proper assessment of subordinates, competent Boards should be set up; gazetted officers should be assessed by Boards of Agricultural Scientists and technical men of repute from different parts of India. These reports will enable the Director of Agriculture to assess the work of his departmental officers.

Coordination

Coordination of work is a knotty problem and what is urgently required is coordination of mind and action. There is tendency for coordinating bodies to function in a routine manner. These bodies do not meet often enough and follow up action is lacking. For coordination to operate successfully adequate authority and power should be vested in the coordinating bodies at all levels. For this purpose it is suggested that the Development Commissioner should have a status higher than the Secretary to Departments.

Field Officers are burdened with too many reports, and returns. Multiplicity of returns does not ensure coordination; what is more important is that coordinating bodies should meet frequently on predetermined dates.

Research programmes should be examined by working parties, consisting of specialists in concerned subjects and then by a Research Committee consisting of Heads of Research Sections, Professors, Principals and Deputy Directors of Agriculture. For suggesting research problems there should be Regional Advisory Committees, as in some States, consisting of District Agricultural Officers, leading farmers and selected Extension Officers and Farm Managers.

There should be a similar Committee at the State level for formulating and coordinating extension programmes and also Regional Advisory Committees to discuss the district programmes.

Similarly, educational programmes should be prepared by the Educational Programme Committee at the State level, with representatives from Research, Education, Extension and the Community Development Departments. Training programmes for Farm Leaders V.L.W.'s, and farmers drawn up at the divisional level should be considered by this Committee.

There is a gross lack of coordination between Irrigation and Agriculture departments, both in planning and execution. This has resulted in the irrigation resources of the country not being fully utilised. It is suggested that Irrigation Department should have special Agricultural Officers to serve as a liaison between the agriculturists and the State Departments of Agriculture, ensuring maximum utilisation of water.

Evaluation And Assessment Of Department Work

For evaluating and assessing progress of works and schemes, a small unit has been suggested at the headquarters of the Director of Agriculture. This unit should conduct every year detailed studies of a few schemes. These studies will help in revising procedures and avoid pitfalls.

The progress made in extending the recommendations of the Research Sections to field practices, should be evaluated by Heads of Research Sections.

The feeling that officers have discharged their duties once they have completed the specified work or distributed aids such as seeds, fertilisers, implements, etc., should be discouraged. An intensive drive to promote follow-up work should be built up through intensified supervision.

Inspections and supervision seem to have been relegated to the background and deal more with procedures, accounts and irregularities, rather than with technological standards adopted in Demonstrations, Extension, etc. Inspections should be purposeful and pre-planned to provide technical guidance and solutions on the spot. It should also be checked up whether earlier advice and instructions given have been acted upon on correct lines.

A regular system of oral reports from subordinates is recommended, by which senior officers should remain in continuous touch with the progress of work. Such opportunities should also be utilised by subordinate officers to discuss with their seniors local problems and thus help to keep the work under continuous review.

Programme Planning

It has been noticed that gradually and imperceptibly, the propaganda or the extension branch of State Departments of Agriculture was converted into a machinery for executing land development works and for distributing supplies; the principal task of educating the farmers for adopting new methods of cultivation receded into the background.

The important role which the Agriculture Departments should play in framing policies which contribute to production has been indicated. The knowledge gained through experiments has not been translated into practical field application. It is essential that a "technological balance" is maintained in planning programmes for different areas.

Adoption of self-help programmes, which benefit the small non-creditworthy farmer is recommended. This constitutes supply of small quantities of nucleus seed to villages and organising the farmers for multiplying the seed and exchanging it locally. This process has the advantage of decentralising the work completely.

For building up soil fertility, a programme of green manuring in irrigated areas and the production of compost in non-irrigated areas should be adopted. Planting of fuel trees and shrubs, for eliminating the conversion of cow dung into fuel for cooking purposes, has been neglected. These three basic items are capable of universal adoption, leaving the department of agriculture free for carrying out their educational programmes.

Cultivators should be persuaded and helped to own their equipment, individually or cooperatively, for spraying and dusting their crops against insect pests and diseases.

The Agricultural Department should evolve plans for increasing agricultural production in every village, rather than for executing the targets for distribution of seeds, fertilisers, etc. If integrated plans for increasing the production in a village are prepared and executed, the targets prescribed for the Second Five-Year Plan will be taken care of automatically.

The present system of fixing targets State-wise and then breaking them district, tehsil and village-wise is defective, as resources are locked up in the slow moving areas. The locking up of resources in the slow moving areas should be avoided and initially only 50 per cent to 60 per cent of the resources should be earmarked for an area for utilisation in four to six months; additional amounts being given according to actual performance.

Budgeting, Sanctions, Procedures And Delegation Of Powers

Means must be devised urgently to avoid concentration of expenditure during the last quarter of the financial year.

The various stages of action from the formulation of

schemes to their implementation should be completed more expeditiously and unnecessary references to the Centre and State Finance Departments should be eliminated. Personal discussions among officers should be encouraged.

Plan schemes should be taken immediately on the advent of the financial year and no administrative or financial delays should be allowed to stand in the way of execution.

The technical and financial scrutiny of schemes should be completed before the financial provision is made in the budget. The schemes should be prepared initially in greater detail and the financial authorities should issue standing instructions indicating the minimum data to be furnished in respect of each scheme.

A lump sum provision may be made in respect of schemes for which complete and detailed examination cannot be made due to lack of technical data, expenditure sanctions being issued after detailed scrutiny. In respect of schemes spread over a number of years, the issue of administrative and expenditure sanctions during the second and the succeeding years should be regarded as a formality only.

Once schemes have been included in the budget after proper scrutiny, a second reference to the Finance Department for expenditure sanction before their implementation should not be necessary.

In the case of Union Territories, after the budgets are voted, sanction for the implementation of schemes has to be given by the administration concerned through the Home Ministry who again refer to the Administrative Ministries and Finance. This second reference to the Government of India should be dispensed with.

Organisational improvements such as the posting of an Internal Financial Adviser with powers to take decisions in the State Departments of Agriculture should be undertaken. The officers of the Finance Department responsible for scrutiny and sanction of the schemes should preferably, have actual experience of formulation and implementation of plan schemes.

In case a scheme has been sanctioned as a whole, there should be no need to obtain separate sanction of the various component parts of the scheme such as staff, equipment, etc.

There should be the greatest delegation of powers at all levels from the Director of Agriculture downwards. The powers that could be exercised only by the senior officers should be specified clearly and in respect of matters not so specified the officer implementing a scheme should be free to operate on his own. The financial powers of officers at all levels should be examined urgently and wherever necessary, revised, keeping in view the general rise in cost of services and commodities and the changing needs of the expanded development programme. Suggestions have been made by the Committee for financial and administrative powers which may be delegated to officers at various levels in the State Agriculture Departments. Steps should be taken to codify all financial and administrative powers delegated.

Officers taking initiative and responsibility should feel that Government trusts them in the exercise of their powers and the delegation of powers should be both in letter and in spirit. Executive instructions which circumscribe normal financial and administrative powers of officers should be issued only after due consideration and for very weighty reasons. A review of all such instructions should be made every six months preferably, by a Committee appointed by the State Governments, with a view to removing them or making them part of the permanent rules where considered absolutely necessary. Temporary restrictions should not be allowed to remain in force for more than six months.

Each officer should be given as an ad-hoc measure, powers to execute specified schemes for which budget provision has been made even though the expenditure on a particular item may exceed his normal financial powers.

Indenting departments should be authorised to purchase direct, instead of through the State Purchasing Organisations, technical stores and stores of petty value, after observing codal formalities.

Discretionary powers should be given to officers-in-charge of State Transport vehicles engaged on essential food production work to get emergency repair done outside the Departmental workshops, where the interest of the public service justifies it.

Supply Procedures

It is generally felt in the States that not only sufficient fertilisers are not being allotted by the Government of India, but the fertilisers allocated from Sindri and other factories are not received by them regularly and in time for application to the crops.

To overcome difficulties and delays in procurement and supply of chemical fertilisers, it is suggested that proper advance planning should be taken up by the Ministry of Food and Agriculture in consultation with the State Governments.

Centrally administered godowns, conveniently situated in several parts of the country should be started to receive and store fertilisers for supply to the consuming centres.

The payment of interest charges to Government of India on short term loans advanced to the States for fertilisers may be deferred till such time as the fertiliser is actually required for use on the land.

Adequate storage facilities for stocking fertilisers are also not available in the States and the number of distributing centres is not sufficient to meet the requirements.

Agricultural Departments should confine their attention only to propagation of improved pedigree seeds.

The quota of iron and steel for agricultural purposes should be increased substantially according to demand made by the States and placed at the disposal of the State Agricultural Departments, who should organise the manufacture of improved agricultural implements for supply ultimately to the cultivators through the Cooperative Organisations.

The entire organisation for the supply of fertilisers, improved seeds, insecticides, agricultural implements etc. should be separated from the extension and technical functions of the Agricultural Departments and transferred to the Cooperative Organisations. These agencies may be helped financially in the initial stages, if necessary.

The present system of providing credit does not fulfil the needs of the non-creditworthy cultivators. Government policies should be moulded to the needs of the small cultivators and credit facilities extended to them despite the greater risk involved.

Model Agricultural Organisation To Suit Present Needs

In order to fulfil the expectations of the people in the field of agriculture, State Departments should be organised to handle the growing demands of the farmers in an efficient manner. Among other things the Department should provide facilities for educating and training the farmers, demonstrate better methods of cultivation and disseminate knowledge through audio-visual channels, organise farmers for adopting improved techniques of production and for working together, pick up problems of the farmers and pass them for solution to the research sections and transmit their solutions back to the farmers.

Agricultural extension agency should concentrate entirely on educating and organising the farmers to produce more. The Departments of Agriculture should deal with technical knowledge rather than trade in supplies.

It is suggested that in States, the feasibility of the portfolio of Agriculture and Irrigation being held by one Minister should be considered. This will ensure rapid progress. There may be two Secretaries under the Minister for Agriculture; one for Agriculture dealing with Agriculture, Land Reclamation, Soil Conservation (in agricultural lands), Animal Husbandry and Veterinary Science and the other for Irrigation, Forests (including soil conservation in forest areas), Cooperation and Agricultural Marketing.

Frequent changes in Ministers and Secretaries should be avoided, as these dislocate the execution of work.

It is suggested that Minor Irrigation Works, costing not more than Rs. 10,000 should be handled by the Community Development agency; works costing above Rs. 10,000 but not more than Rs. 80,000 may be handled by the Agricultural Department and those costing even more may be handled by the Irrigation Department.

It is recommended that a Works Division be set up within the Directorate of Agriculture under a Joint Director of Land Development with full powers of a Superintending Engineer. This will ensure speedy implementation of minor irrigation and building programmes within the Agriculture sector. A Research Division for agricultural implements and machinery should also be added to this circle.

Soil conservation of agricultural lands should be the function of the Agriculture Department and in forest areas of the Forest Department and no independent Soil Conservation Department should be allowed to spring up.

A separate Land Development Wing is also required in the Department of Agriculture to look after land reclamation, minor irrigation, flood control, soil conservation and drainage. As already mentioned, this Wing should be under the charge of the Joint Director for Land Development, and should also deal with agricultural machinery and implements.

The Director of Agriculture should be further assisted by Joint Directors in charge of Extension, and Research and Education. A Deputy Director may be necessary to help the Joint Director of Research and Education depending upon the volume of work.

There should be a Deputy Director (Farm Management) under the Joint Director for Extension who should be fully responsible for running all the Agricultural Farms, including a large number of Seed Farms established recently.

The Joint Director of Extension should be assisted by, at least, four Extension Subject Matter Specialists in Agronomy, Plant Protection, Soils and Soil Fertility, and Horticulture and any other subject depending upon local conditions.

At the headquarters of the Director of Agriculture and subordinate to him, there should be an Administrative Officer and a Budget and Accounts Officer to relieve the executive officers from routine administrative and accounts matters. Smaller States may combine the two posts and have one administrative and accounts officer.

There should be a Progress and Evaluation Officer, assisted by a small unit of staff for the continuous evaluation of programmes and collection of development statistics. This unit is intended to function as the eyes and ears of the State Department of Agriculture with respect to all schemes.

The Extension Specialists at the headquarters of the Director of Agriculture should be assisted by similar Specialists at the District level and ultimately at the

Block level also. These Extension Specialists should belong to the research sections.

The workload in districts where there would be more than 12-15 blocks justifies the appointment of the Sub-Divisional Agricultural officers. An experienced Deputy Director can guide work in 100-125 Blocks, while a District Agricultural Officer of 3-4 Sub-Divisional Officers look after 10-12 Blocks each. In this case the District Agricultural Officer should be in Class I cadre and the Deputy Directors should be included in selection grade corresponding to Superintending Engineers.

Until the supply functions are transferred from the Department of Agriculture to other appropriate agencies such as, Cooperative, District Agricultural Officers and the Deputy Directors should be provided with gazetted Personal Assistants to relieve them of routine accounts, bills and supply work.

The Farm Advisory Service to be fully effective should be supported by an Agricultural Information Service consisting of trained staff specialising in mass communication methods. It is important that agricultural information work should be distinguished from publicity and propaganda work which is the normal function of the Information and Publicity Department of a State.

Organisation For Agricultural Research And Education

The total research programme under way at present is not considered adequate to meet the needs and the demand for improved agricultural materials and practices in the country.

There is a clear necessity for establishing major Research Stations for serving the needs of each agro-climatic region. These research stations should have a suitable complement of plant breeders, soil scientists, entomologists, mycologists, agronomists and horticulturists. Ultimately, agricultural colleges and training centres should be built up around these major research stations. Subject matter specialists working at district stations should frequently visit the regional stations. The expenditure incurred should bear some relation to the area and importance of the crop in the region.

At least one of the Regional Stations should be developed into a first rate post-graduate training institution, with tripartite organisation for research, education and extension. There should be one Principal or Dean for education and research and two Deputies, one for education and one for research where the regional research station and the agricultural college are both located at one place.

Agricultural Colleges and Research Institutes should organise two separate sections for research and teaching in the fields of Agricultural Extension and Agricultural Economics.

Each district should have one Vocational School of Agriculture, imparting practical training in agriculture, extending over a period of two years for those who have passed the secondary examination.

Short duration courses and hostel facilities should be provided for the farmers who come for training in the district schools. These schools should be under the charge of Regional Deputy Directors of Extension but, under the over-all control of the Dean or Principal of the Agricultural College of the region.

College coordination between research, education and extension branches should be maintained through a system of annual conferences held at the major research stations which should be attended by all officers working in the region. Similar meetings should be held at District level once in three or four months.

To relieve the research staff from administrative and accounts work, there should be properly trained administrative and accounts staff, who should take full responsibility in these matters.

The talents of retired specialists who have settled down in different parts of the country should be utilised by associating them with research institutions or with local supervision of schemes.

PIECE-RATE REVIEW COMMITTEE, PORT OF CALCUTTA, 1958—REPORT

New Delhi, Ministry of Labour, 1958.

Chairman : Shri F. Jeejeebhoy.
(One-Man Committee)

APPOINTMENT

The Piece-Rate Review Committee was constituted under the Ministry of Labour, vide their Notification No. Fac. 175(16)/58, dated March 7, 1958, to examine the report of the Calcutta Piece-Rate Committee appointed by the Notification of the Government of India in the Ministry of Labour No. S.R.O. 742, dated March 1,

1957, and after hearing such organisations and persons as the Committee may deem fit to make such recommendations to the Central Government as it may consider suitable.

TERMS OF REFERENCE

(i) To examine the report of the Calcutta Piece-Rate Committee appointed by the Notification of the Government of India in the Ministry of Labour No. S.R.O. 742, dated March 1, 1957, and after hearing such organisations and persons as the Committee may deem fit to make such recommendations to the Central Government as it may consider suitable;

The Government of India, Ministry of Transport and Communications by its letter No. 23-PLA (40)/56, of March 13, 1958, also authorised this Committee to:

(ii) Examine the said Report for the shore workers and crane drivers of the Port of Calcutta.

CONTENTS

Report; Schedule A; Appendices A to E; List of Appearances at Calcutta at the hearings between July 22, and July 31, 1958.

RECOMMENDATIONS

The shore workers were represented by Shri Anthony Pillai and Shri Makhan Chatterjee who expressed their whole-hearted readiness to have a piece-rate scheme. Dr. Mrs. Maitreyee Bose represented the shore workers as well as the coal workers and the stevedore workers. She has no objection to a piece-rate scheme being applied to the coal workers, but she is allergic to the entire scheme so far as the stevedore workers are concerned. It is however manifest that the Committee had been required to frame a scheme on the lines of the Bombay award, and it is a basic assumption that the scheme would apply as in Bombay to stevedore workers as well. The question as to whether the stevedore workers should be excluded from the scheme does not arise, for a piece-rate scheme on the lines of the Bombay scheme necessarily includes the stevedore worker. Dr. Mrs. Bose however has made her submissions as regards revising the scheme as given, not only as to the shore and coal workers, but also as to the stevedore workers.

Stevedore labour was further represented before me by Shri Sisir Roy who though opposed to a piece-rate scheme for stevedore labour nevertheless asked for amendments of the scheme on the basis of the expected application of the scheme to the stevedore workers also. It was urged that a piece-rate scheme would not be suitable for stevedore labour and that they were unwilling to accept it; that the lightermen had been excluded which made overside work difficult for the stevedore worker, that the wages of the new entrants had been reduced and that the pay scales of pre-June 1955 was recognised whereas the later emoluments should have formed the basis of the piece-rate scheme; that the pay differential given by the scheme would cause resentment among the stevedore workers who should have a higher processing wage based on present wages; that the piece-rate scheme took away the special facilities for employment of extra gangs given by the Expert Committee as also relief gangs as were being supplied for hazardous, dirty and obnoxious cargo like sulphate of ammonia, sulphur, cement, caustic soda. It was pointed out to Shri Sisir Roy that the lightermen were not likely to hold up the work of the stevedore workers, and that the experience of Bombay supported this view; it was not correct that the wages of new entrants had been reduced under the scheme, for the scheme would benefit all the stevedore workers to a very great extent; the willing worker, working with reasonable efficiency, could comfortably reach the datum figures; the wage structure of the stevedore workers was so constructed that there would be no reduction in the emoluments of existing workers, but it had to be recognised that a piece-rate scheme was to be so phased that the wage rates had to start low and advance progressively; although the processing wage was held in check; the differentials gave to the present workers the advantage of their present higher earning; it was true that the Expert Committee's Report (framed at a time when conditions were not normal) would now vanish with the application of the piece-rate scheme, but that was inevitable, because under the piece-rate scheme everybody in a gang working to datums in a shift will get the same benefits; the Expert Committee's Report did not apply to shore labour, and in a piece-rate scheme, the labour of the stevedores and of the shore workers had to be coordinated; as regards hazardous and injurious cargo, safeguards as already specified in the Indian Dock Labourers Act and Regulations would be provided as has been done here and is done in Bombay, but if extra hands were required it would follow that the datums would have to be raised and that was undesirable; no additional men are provided either in Bombay or in Madras for such work, and mouth pads are given to workers handling cement and sulphur on board in Bombay, and also gloves and gum boots when handling drums of caustic soda; and so far as the Madras workers are concerned they have not asked for any extra men as it would reduce the quantum of handling. Calcutta already supplies gloves and gum boots and will now give mouth pads. The pre-June 1955 wage was taken for the purpose of processing because of the reasons which have been stated in the Report under review and to which reference has also been made in the Bombay Award; it was not possible to process on the high wages which were given to the stevedore workmen in Calcutta at a time when they were getting bookings for only five to 12 days; these matters have already been carefully considered previously; the fact remains that no existing worker will get less than what he had been getting because his differential by way of personal pay would cover the difference; as regards future entrants the wage graph is already higher than that of the shore worker in Calcutta and also higher than that of the stevedore workers in Bombay and Madras, and otherwise more than adequate, and in actual fact the question of the potential workers does not assume any importance at this stage. I am therefore unable to accept the view of Shri Sisir Roy that the wage graph for stevedore labour should be altered.

The recommendation contained in paragraph 27 of the original Report that a reserve pool worker who is available for work but for whom no work can be found should be paid attendance allowance at Rs. 1.50 per day for the day on which he attended for work but could not get it, shall be applicable when the stevedore workers work under this piece-rate scheme.

I shall now deal with the points raised as regards the shore workers.

It has become necessary to fix the hours of work of the piece-rate workers in the light of the observations of the Central Government in its Resolution of July 20, 1958, wherein it is provided that there should be adequate breaks within a shift for rest and recuperation. There were considerable differences of opinion on the subject, and it was ultimately agreed that the shore and stevedore shifts should function as follows:

Shore And Stevedore Shifts

First shift nine hours (6.30 a.m. to 3.30 p.m.) with one hour recess (between 10.30 a.m. and 11.30 a.m.).

Second shift seven hours (3.30 p.m. to 10.30 p.m.) with half hour recess (between 7 p.m. and 7.30 p.m.).

Third shift seven hours (10.30 p.m. to 5.30 a.m.) with half hour recess (between 2.00 a.m. and 2.30 a.m.).

For cargo dock it was agreed that whenever it was necessary to work longer hours, labour would be under obligation to work overtime on payment of prescribed rates between the hours of 5.30 a.m. to 6.30 a.m. They would also work overtime during recess, if they had no objection. It was further agreed that the recess would be subject to adjustment to suit requirements during the Ramzan month so as to synchronize with the time for breaking fasts and starting fasts.

It was agreed that similar provisions mutatis mutandis would apply to the coal docks, the shift hours of which are by consent fixed as follows.

Mechanical Berths And Trimmers

First shift nine hours (6.30 a.m. to 3.30 p.m.) with one hour recess (between 10.30 a.m. and 11.30 a.m.).

Second shift seven hours (3.30 p.m. to 10.30 p.m.) with half hour recess (between 7 p.m. and 7.30 p.m.).

Third shift seven hours (10.30 p.m. to 5.30 a.m.) with half hour recess (between 2.00 a.m. and 2.30 a.m.)

Labour Berths

First shift nine hours (6.30 a.m. to 3.30 p.m.) with one hour recess (between 10.30 a.m. and 11.30 a.m.).

Second shift seven hours (7.30 p.m. to 2.30 a.m.) with half hour recess (between 11.30 p.m. to midnight).

Special shift nine hours (8 a.m. to 5 p.m.) with one hour recess (between 10.30 a.m. and 11.30 a.m.).

The next important claim made on behalf of the shore workers was to the effect that the daily wage should be raised from Rs. 3-13-0 as at present to Rs. 4-8-0. It was urged inter alia in support of this claim that Madras had been given Rs. 3-15-0 and that there was an existing difference between Madras and Calcutta of 0-4-0 annas per day on account of house rent allowance and compensatory allowance. It was therefore suggested that the daily wage here should be not less than Rs. 4-3-0. It was also claimed that as the Bombay shore worker had the advantage of baroots for the purpose of sorting and stacking general cargo weighing above 140 lbs. and piling men for stacking bag cargo weighing over 140 lbs., some allowance should be made in favour of Calcutta workers. It was on the other hand established that a considerable portion of the cargo in Calcutta is delivered direct from the wharves and is not taken into the sheds, with the result that the shore workers in Calcutta have an easier time than in Bombay. There was considerable discussion on this subject and all aspects were fully explored, and ultimately I suggested that the daily wage be raised to Rs. 4, to which the parties were not averse, and the deliberations thereafter proceeded on that basis. The wage graph is accordingly framed with a daily wage of Rs. 4. This will necessitate an alteration of the wage graph and of the components of the processing. The components of the daily wage will now be as follows:

Basic	Re.	1-0-0
Dearness allowance	,,	1-5-4
House Rent allowance	,,	0-5-4
Compensatory allowance	,,	0-4-0
Processing allowance	,,	0-5-0
Interim adjustment allowance	,,	0-9-0
Special adjustment allowance	,,	0-3-0
Total	Rs.	3-15-8-Rs. 4

During the course of the arguments the parties were reliying upon the Bombay scheme and at the same time on the Madras scheme, which while founded on the Bombay scheme was based largely on agreed solutions, as if the two schemes could be utilised interchangeably for any argument which a party chose to advance. It was, however, pointed out that the Bombay Award laid down the principles which governed that decision, and that the piece-rate scheme of Calcutta was to be designed to incorporate those same principles. The Madras scheme also followed the same principles, but there were agreed solutions on many points, and those agreed solutions could not be invoked in the present case as if they were the decisions of an award; agreed solutions represent the results of bargaining and are entitled to respectful consideration, and within the principles of the Bombay Award are based upon the particular circumstances prevailing in the locality.

Concurrently, with the question of raising the daily wage was the claim of labour to an allowance for stacking. In the course of the discussions it was suggested by the parties that there might be a fixed consolidated daily allowance to be given to the shore worker to cover (a) this claim on account of certain alleged difference in work in the sheds in Bombay and in Calcutta and (b) the double hook and multiple hook allowance which appears as item 14 of Appendix 'B' of the Report under review. It was ultimately agreed between the parties that a consolidated sum of 0-11-0 annas should be paid to each cargo dock worker working piece-rate per shift under this scheme to cover payment under item 14 of Appendix 'B' as well as to make an allowance for certain features in the stacking of cargo. I have had some misgivings as to the wisdom of this agreement, but as the parties have agreed and are satisfied about it I accept this settlement as a compromise. Perhaps it is a desirable agreement having regard to the topography of the Port. The stevedore workers have no parallel problem, nor has any been raised.

In the result, for the shore worker doing piece-rate work under this scheme:

(a) The daily wage is raised to Rs. 4, and the consequential adjustments will be made. The weekly off will also be paid at the rate of Rs. 4.

(b) A consolidated sum of annas 0-11-0 will be paid to each cargo dock worker doing piece-rate under this scheme every day in lieu of payment under clause 14 of Appendix 'B' of the Report under review regarding the double/multiple hook allowance and also to allow for certain features in the stacking of cargo.

(c) The shore workers shall do stacking up to the following limits:

Bags up to 140 lbs. each.	...	6 ft. high
Bags exceeding 150 lbs. each	...	6 ft. high or 6 high whichever is less
Cartons, ingots and general packages upto 140 lbs. each	...	6 ft. high
General packages between 140 lbs. and 400 lbs. per package	...	3 high
General Packages above 400 lbs. per package	...	2 high
Drums above 400 lbs. each	...	2 high
Yard Cargo	...	As is being done now.

It was also agreed that for stacking cargo beyond the above limits additional labour will be provided by the Port Commissioners and such labour will be paid according to the existing rates, and not under this progressive piece-rate scheme.

Dr. Mrs. Bose and Shri Sisir Roy contended that no scheme of piece-rate could be introduced until the lightermen had been brought within its ambit. It was their case that unless the lightermen collaborated, the piece-rate would not succeed. It is true that quite a considerable portion of cargo in Calcutta is handled overside from and into lighters; but the number of the men in the lighters is fixed according to licence, which answers Shri Anthony Pillai's apprehension that the lighters might be undermanned. In Madras the lighters were incorporated into the piece-rate scheme, but the conditions there are different. In Madras the lighters are owned by the Port Trust and are regarded as a projection of the docks. Here the lighters belong to any number of lighter contractors. But that does not mean that the workmen on the lighters are likely to be slack in their work; they may not have the incentive of the piece-rate scheme, but they have the stimulant to work applied by the contractors who are mostly paid by the ton. I am quite unable to accept the view that the piece-rate scheme will fail unless the lightermen are brought into it; lightermen do not fall within the Calcutta Dock Workers (Regulation of Employment) Scheme, and admittedly they cannot be brought into the piece-rate scheme so long as they are as at present working under the contractors; and this position is recognised by all parties. And the contention that the lightermen are an essential part of the piece-rate scheme is not acceptable; they are no more a link in the chain than the mobile crane drivers or tractor drivers who are on time rate. In Bombay, the lightermen are time-rated, and there has been no complaint that they have retarded the tempo of work. As to the difficulty of placing the lighter alongside during high tide, this is common to most ports; any delay will be compensated by idle time and lowered datums. In my view the absence of the lightermen from the piece-rate scheme will not adversely affect its success.

It was vigorously urged that the coal trimmers should be given the same wage as stevedore labour. At present they have been given the average piece-rate earnings of the coal shore worker, with whom they work, plus Rs. five per month as trimming pay and also an extra 12½ per cent of the daily wage. It was pointed out by the Port Commissioners that the coal trimmer's work is lighter than that of a stevedore worker and is of an intermittent character. The coal as it descends tends to settle down by its own weight. It is true that trimming of coal is a dirtier type of work, but nevertheless the actual work involved in trimming is of short durations and does not require the same amount of sustained skill or effort as in the case of stevedore labour. Furthermore, the wage of the trimmer with the allowance given compares favourably with the expected earnings of a stevedore worker. In my opinion no change is necessary.

Shri Makhan Chatterjee raised the question of long lead at coal docks. Anything above 300 ft. is at present regarded as a long lead presumably as a result of the opinion of a senior officer of the Port Commissioners who is conversant with the conditions of the Port. It appears however that a Sub-Committee of the port Commissioners had been constituted for the purpose of deciding what would amount to a long lead and it recommended anything over 250 ft., and Dr. Mrs. Bose protested against non-acceptance of this Sub-Committee's decision. I am of the view that the interests of justice would be served by fixing a long lead at anything over 275 ft. beyond which two extra men will be allowed. It is understood that the lead will be calculated according to the normal and reasonable route from wagon to ship or chute, as the case may be.

A claim was next made that the chute khalasis should be put on piece-rate. Their duties are primarily to flip a lever so as to release the door through which the coal runs down the chute into the tub. It was urged on behalf of these khalasis that they also directed the crane to lower the tubs into the pit. But the work done by these khalasis is comparatively simple and light. It is of a limited character, and has nothing to do with the physical loading of the tub which is done automatically from the chûte. They flip a lever to open the door from the chute to the five ton tub by a simple movement, and do a little signalling, and sometimes also see that the automatic lever is again fully in the closed position, but this does not entitle them to participate in the piece-rate scheme. This conclusion is as much the result of my observations on the spot as of the arguments advanced before me. Alternatively, it was claimed that they should be given a premium for the work that they do. In my opinion the nature of their work does not call for any special emoluments. The tub descends on the average once in say seven to ten minutes inclusive of the time taken for filling the tub; thus the work of the chute khalasi is very intermittent and he has a lot of idle time.

Subject to the general objection to the application of the piece-rate scheme to stevedore workers the representatives of the stevedore workers wanted a 10 per cent reduction in datums on the ground that the work in Calcutta dock is more difficult than in Bombay. There is no dispute that a larger amount of cargo is handled overside from and into lighters in Calcutta than in Bombay. But that does not make the work of the stevedore workers any more difficult. The datums were fixed originally by consent of all parties present in Committee, and nothing that has now been said was not said before. Here the subject has again been scrutinised but no grounds exist for the general reduction of stevedore datums as now sought. Taken all in all, the conditions of work in Bombay and Calcutta are comparable. No doubt there are some differences but they tend to cancel each other. There are also some differences for which provision is made in the scheme. But there are no grounds for reducing the datums as urged on behalf of the stevedore workers. Dr. Mrs. Bose relied upon a resolution of her union claiming a general reduction of 10 per cent of the datums for stevedore and shore workers but no arguments were addressed in support of it. Judging by actual output figures of hooks the datums are altogether favourable to labour.

It have dealt with the major points of dispute so far and the agreed decisions reached during the hearing. There were other agreed solutions and agreed clarifications which I am incorporating in Schedule A to this Report. I accept those agreements.

I shall now deal with the disputed points, as to which agreements were not reached, other than those to which reference has already been made.

As regard datums, it was first urged that there should be a clarification of what "bulk grain" meant for which a datum of 98 has been given. It means grain discharged in bulk, for bag cargo including grain is already provided for with a datum of 103. In this connection it was urged by the shore workers that the datums should be reduced from 98 to 65; but as I have said before, datums had been fixed originally after very careful consideration and having regard to the datums which Bombay has been operating with considerable advantage to labour, there was no reason why there should be any reduction in bulk grain. In fact bulk grain is hardly ever landed in Calcutta so that the discussion as to reducing the datum is academic. Contrary to Bombay the procedure here as in Madras is for the bulk grain to be bagged in the hold before being landed. Shri Anthony Pillai complained that in Madras they were unable to achieve the datum; but it was shown that the bottleneck in the case of Madras was due to an insufficiency of baggers and stitchers; in Madras the baggers and stitchers were five and four respectively, whereas in Calcutta they are 16 and six per hook per shift, and Calcutta has never suffered from shortage in ready bags. There is thus no ground for reducing the datum as given.

Similarly, the union asked for reduction of 15 per cent in the datum for bags fertilisers, but it was difficult to understand on what basis this claim could be sustained.

There is no essential difference between bags of grain and bags of fertilisers for the purpose of handling, and it has been shown that the difficulty Madras has experienced in the quick landing of bag cargo like grain has been due to the insufficiency of baggers and stitchers. This insufficiency does not prevail in Calcutta.

A third objection was raised as regards coastal cargo and it was said that the words "Karachi" and "Chittagong" should be excluded. It is not in dispute that in shipping circles the word 'coastal cargo' has reference to the Ports of Karachi on the West and Chittagong on the East, and coastal licences have to be taken to take cargo to Karachi. There is nothing improper that Karachi and Chittagong should be included as the limits of coastal cargo, because they are the two extremities within which the coastal trade has its natural limits. A claim was next made that item five with a datum of 72 for East Coast coastal cargo should have a reduced datum of 64, which would make it the same as the West Coast coastal cargo. There is, however, the difference in the pattern of trade between eastern coastal cargo and the western coastal cargo and in order to provide for that difference the datum of 72 was given to eastern coastal cargo, and that too as a result of a compromise after very considerable discussion, as there are no grounds for changing it. Connected with this question is the claim of the shipping companies that the 50 per cent rule should apply to coastal cargo. The rule was deliberately made inapplicable because of the nature of the coastal cargo, and there is no reason why a change should now be made.

As regards ores in bulk, it was the claim of the union that the datum of 80 in the exports list should be reduced. In respect of the handling of ore, there are some differences between Bombay and Calcutta but in the balance there is nothing much. For instance, in Bombay the ore is brought in wagons and lorries and is directly transported in tubs to the ship. In Culcutta too this is sometimes done, but more often the ore is brought and stacked and then loaded into tubs to be lifted into the ship. As against the easier method of handling in Bombay there are certain disadvantages in Bombay arising out of the limited number of wagons which can be brought to the site. In Calcutta there is the advantage of ore being readily available for loading. There is no doubt that the datum for ores in bulk in Bombay has been considerably exceeded, and there is no reason to expect otherwise in Calcutta. I am, therefore, unable to accept the position that the datum for ores in bulk should be reduced below 80. It was further contended in this connection that the 50 per cent rule should not apply to iron ore, even though it might apply to manganese. There is, however, no material difference in the handling of manganese and iron ore, and there are no grounds for making a distinction between the two.

The last point regarding the question of ores in bulk was the shipping company's contention that the datum should be raised to 200 tons for two gangs ashore and two aboard working ore at 5 King George's Dock. It is true that this being a mechanical berth has considerable advantages in the case of loading of ore; but it has been pointed out by the unions that there is a difference in the manner of stacking and handling of the iron ore at 5 King George's Dock and at the other berths; at 5 K. G. Dock, the ore is stacked within small islands whence they are put into tubs, and the tubs are taken alongside the ship by a locomotive and are lifted by the crane and discharged into the steamer; it is also the procedure to fill the tubs direct from the wagons whenever it is possible to do so. At the other docks the ore is stacked at the wharves and is put into tubs by baskets which are carried from the pile to the tubs. On a totality of considerations there is probably not a very great difference between the two in the matter of ease of loading but there is no doubt that at the mechanical berths the speed is accelerated. At 5 K. G. Dock, the cranes are of five ton capacity and the tubs are of three ton capacity whereas at the other berths the cranes are of 35 cwt. capacity or two tons and the tubs have a capacity of little more than one ton. Thus in this way time is saved in 5 K. G. Dock. On a consideration of these factors, I would fix the two gangs ashore and two gangs aboard datum for 5 K. G. Dock at 170 tons. If one gang is employed ashore and one aboard then the datum will be 85 for eight hours' work.

In connection with the datums, the shipping companies raised certain specific points. They wanted pig iron to be excluded from iron and steel. There was strong opposition from Shri Anthony Pillai about loading the datums against him by divorcing specific cargo from the general line datums, and this is an aspect of the matter which must receive consideration. In this case, item 17 deals with "iron and steel not packed in cases, crates, boxes or other covering" which would include pig iron. It must also be remembered that the shipping interests were parties to the original fixation of datums and they had no objection to the datums as fixed, and indeed they raised no objection as far as I am aware until this Committee was constituted. The shipping interests also asked that chemicals which come in bags exceeding 112 lbs., as also sulphur, should be grouped with item 12 which is "salt in bags exceeding 112 lbs." and has been given a datum of 103. The datums as given to Calcutta follow Bombay, and are otherwise sound, and I see no reason for altering the position.

The last point on datums to be raised by the shipping companies was to the effect that the 50 per cent rule should apply on a quantitative basis instead of the percentage basis. Apart from the question whether this suggestion should be accepted, to introduce this innovation would entail a general revision of the datums, and it would be unwise to do so. I am therefore unable to accede to this claim.

On behalf of the union it was urged that for a team of four men in chute lines at 19 and 20 berths the datum of 38 which has been given should be reduced to 29. I have already indicated the facilities at the chute lines and see no reason to reduce the datum below 38, which was fixed by agreement of the union now represented by Dr. Mrs. Bose. I have no doubt that this datum of 38 will be largely exceeded. A similar claim was made that for a team of four men in Basket Lines at 19 and 20 coal berths, the datum should be reduced below 19. This is not possible. I was present at the docks one morning when I found that a first shift unit had nearly cleared a wagon of approximately 22 tons before 9-30 A.M.

As regards the wage structure of the cranemen, the union claimed that for the purposes of the wage structure the basic wage should be Rs. 60 and not Rs. 50, in anticipation of certain revision which is expected. I must fix the wage in accordance with the existing wage structure, which includes not only the basic wage but also other emoluments. I cannot here say what would be the effect of any change in the scale. Similarly, the claim that some extra allowance should be given to the cranemen for working against more than one unit on the shore at 19 and 20 berths cannot be allowed because under this scheme the cranemen are to receive the average benefit of the piece-rate work done by coal labour as part of their emoluments, and that is quite sufficient.

It was claimed that the trimming pay of the trimmers should form part of the processing of their wages instead of being a differential. The trimming pay of Rs. five is given as an allowance and therefore it is right that it should be considered as a differential. As I have said before the wage of the trimmer compares favourably with that of the stevedore worker almost at all stages.

It was next urged that the interim adjustment allowance of 0-9-0 annas given to the shore workers and to the trimmers should be treated as part of their basic pay. This interim adjustment allowance was given for a specified purpose and was subject "to the provision that the amounts of any increase in the minima of basic wage scales or scales of allowances of the basic porter shall be first set off and adjusted against this allowance". The processing wage of the shore worker has already been stepped up very considerably, and if this interim adjustment allowance is now added to the basic it will unduly increase the wage at that stage, apart from being contrary to principle. Furthermore, labour has already received a considerable advantage in the Rs. five extra dearness allowance which has been given subsequent to the first report to all employees; this amount has been added by the Port Commissioners ex-gratia as a differential, whereas it might well have been deducted from this interim adjustment allowance. To that extent the workmen have already benefited.

The shipping interests represented before me that rule 14 of Appendix 'D' regarding the allowance for double and multiple hooks working in the same batch should be removed. It was their contention that the modern ship comes with much longer hatches and that the work of double and multiple hooks in such hatches does not cause any obstruction so as to justify the allowance. There is no doubt that this rule will require reconsideration in the near future if the present tendency of longer hatches continues. But at the present moment there is no satisfactory indication that the existence of the larger hatches has become so general as to call for a change in these proceedings. That being so I do not think that this rule needs any modification here.

On the subject of allowances it was claimed on behalf of the coal dock workers that they should receive 0-3-0 annas per day extra because the shore cargo dock worker had received something extra by way of an allowance for certain features of stacking. There is of course no analogy at all. The shore workers get it for the features of stacking on shore, whereas there is no such stacking done by the coal workers.

A point which was urged before me on behalf of the unions was to the effect that leave salary and provident fund contribution should be calculated on the piece–rate earnings of the last six months. This has been declined in our original report and has not been granted by the Government of India in its Resolution. If the provident fund and leave salary are to be allied to piece-rate earnings the total emoluments might become so high as to necessitate a modification of the datums and/or for the wage graph. It is not possible for me to accede to this request.

The question of pit cleaning came up for consideration. This is the pit into which the tubs at 19 and 20 berths land and pick up the coal from the chutes. During the process of transporting the coal from the wagons into the tubs through the chute a certain amount of coal drops into the pit, and it is material to remember that this coal which drops into the pit is paid for at the existing piece-rate and labour has had the advantage of it. The same gangs do not retrieve this coal from the pit, which is a large rectangular well below the surface about 10 ft. deep. The Port Commissioners have to utilise other labour everyday for the purpose of retrieving the coal from the pit and stacking it on the side, and for this purpose they pay at the rate of 0-10-0 annas per ton, roughly by visual assessment. On behalf of such labour as is employed for the purpose it was said that the handling of this coal was very arduous and therefore a higher rate should be given, but no higher rate was specified. I do not think that the work is more difficult than the normal carrying of coal; but of course it has to be done in or about the pit; and there is a certain amount of water in the pit, which is continuously being pumped out. Alternatively, labour says that if piece-rate gangs from idle time are required to do this work they should receive an allowance of 0-3-0 annas per hour, over and above the idle time, which proposal of course would be contrary to one of the agreements already reached. The existing piece-rated worker gets daily his dearness allowance etc. of Re. 1-9-0 plus a minimum of 0-12-0 annas as his basic wage, and also a monthly minimum of Rs. 92-50, and his rate for non-shipment miscellaneous work is 0-10-0 annas per ton. The normal capacity for this pit work would be one-and a-half tons per day in which case he would at present be earning 0-15-0 annas as his basic for the day. I direct that the pit cleaner should be paid at the rate of 0-15-0 annas per ton which would be more suitable for the type of work he is required to do.

As regards relieving men a claim was made that a specific set of men should be kept as reliefs for cranemen and winchmen. The Port Commissioners undoubtedly must provide sufficient relief for the cranemen, and in fact they have agreed to do so in order that the work may not be impeded; but it would be wrong for me to specify any particular number of relief cranemen to be appointed for the purpose. The suggestion that it should be one craneman for every four would not be acceptable, because it may happen at times that a craneman is free on idle time and could be utilised as a relief, and to have a separate craneman at the same time would be surplusage. As regards the winchmen, I am told that in Bombay there is one relief winchman for every eight and the relieving winchman also relieves the signaller. I think it is undesirable to specify the exact proportion of relief men to cranemen or winchmen, and we must leave it to the good sense of the Port Commissioners and of the stevedore employers to provide prompt relief. In fact in their own interests they will do so.

The shipping interests suggested that clause 25 of Appendix 'B' and 29 of Appendix 'D' which provide for adjustment of errors by supplementary payment or deduction should cover a period of a few months; in Bombay they have actually reached an agreement that the period should be six months. Apparently the adjustments are very minor, and payments against each shipment is really unnecessary and leads to needless haste in accounting for the sake of very minor differences. I see no objection to these adjustments being made once in three months, and the clause will be altered accordingly.

The union has asked for the abolition of the following clause:

"Any material long-term change in conditions which go to determine the expected standard output (i.e., the datum) may necessitate fixing a new datum, like a material change in the composition of cargo or pattern of trade or a like change in the process of loading or unloading or introduction of different gear may require a new datum."

Labour is apprehensive that this clause may be frequently utilised in order to reduce their earnings. In my opinion this clause should remain, and it has within itself all the safeguards which labour can expect. This clause will not apply unless there is "any material long-term change in conditions which go to determine the expected standard output"; and it must be remembered that labour itself might utilise this provision on an appropriate occasion. I cannot agree to the deletion of this clause which in fact gives effect to an implied condition of all piece-rate schemes.

As regards payment for weekly-off, it was urged on behalf of casual labour that they should be paid for weekly off after six consecutive days of work or whenever a worker qualified for weekly off with pay. This subject has been covered by paragraph 11(e) of the Government of India's Resolution of July 20, 1958, and I can do nothing further about it.

Dr. Mrs. Bose claimed that the minimum monthly guarantee under this scheme should be Rs. 125 for the cargo and coal dock workers. The present minimum guarantee is Rs. 92.50 and it is a principle of a piece-rate scheme that the minimum wage should not be so high as to act as a disincentive, and that principle could not be challenged. If the sum of Rs. 92.50 is raised to Rs. 125, there is always the danger of a workman taking the minimum and doing less than what he should do, and thus the piece-rate scheme would become infructuous. So far as the Federation is concerned, there was an agreement between the Federation and the Port Commissioners that Rs. 92.50 should remain the monthly minimum. I am unable to increase the sum of Rs. 92.50 as the minimum.

There was a claim that payment rate for non-shipment work should be increased but that is a matter with which this Committee is not concerned.

Apart from the other specific points a few general points were raised. It was urged that something should be said in the body of the Report that the daily wage is processed upon the present incremental wages and without prejudice to any revision that may be effected in the future. This Report shows how the piece-rate wage has been processed. It has taken into account the present emoluments and liberally fortified it with a dose of processing allowance, so as to provide an adequate piece-rate wage. The implication that a revision of scales will automatically invalidate the wage graph is therefore not an acceptable proposition.

Certain clarification was sought as to the wage of the stevedore worker working sub-normally for 21 days in a month on piece-rate. The stevedore workmen are assured under the Dock Labour Board Scheme of 21 days' employment and therefore that is the minimum that they will get. If he had 21 chances during the month, he would get his minimum; and if he works sub-normally he would have a minimum of Rs. 82 under this scheme. If, however, he worked for some days above normal he would earn much more. On the days he works piece-rate, he gets his piece-rate earnings.

I am happy to say that there was a large measure of agreement as to the details of the scheme not withstanding the stevedore union's apprehension that the scheme would be detrimental to the interests of the stevedore workers. The several points raised by the parties were thoroughly discussed before me and every effort was made to give the fullest consideration to them. It was urged on behalf of stevedore labour that they were not used to a progressive piece-rate scheme as presented here and that in the past they have been working well, and therefore some simple incentive scheme nor the elements thereof were presented to the Committee for consideration. I do not think that the apprehensions of labour have any foundation. Dr. Mrs. Bose took the view that the application of the piece-rate scheme would result in hazards to health through overwork and that it would lead to a higher incidence of tuberculosis; but it was pointed out to her that a proper appreciation of the dignity of labour and the higher emoluments achieved commensurate to the effort of the workmen would necessarily lead to a higher standard of living which should mean better health and better existence for the worker and his family. Dr. Mrs. Bose, however, took the view that the extra money would be used in drinking and gambling and immoral indulgences. I offered to put a ceiling on the emoluments of the workmen, but she was not agreeable to that course. Paradoxically, Dr. Mrs. Bose wants the piece-rate scheme to be applied at once to the coal workers, thereafter gradually to be extended to the shore workers, and lastly to the stevedore workers. But having regard to the experience gained and to the trend of the discussions in this Committee, I think it would be a serious mistake to introduce the piece-rate scheme in parts; it should be introduced at once as a whole applicable to coal workers, stevedore workers and shore workers at the same time. In any event it is not possible to have the scheme applicable to shore labour if stevedore labour is not brought into it.

With the emergence of the piece-rate scheme, there will have to be a re-adjustment of existing practice as envisaged in para 11(ii) of the Central Government's Resolution of July 20, 1958. It becomes necessary that 'A' and 'B' category workers must now accept bookings for any shift on any day in a proper scheme of rotation, and that will have to be done as a necessary part of an equitable piece-rate scheme ; there is already rotation of this character in the coal docks.

It is a pleasure to record that at the conclusion of the hearing both Shri Anthony Pillai and Shri Makhan Chatterjee wanted the scheme to be put into operation as soon as possible; that is a very healthy augury and indicates the confidence which they have in the character of the scheme. Shri Anthony Pillai had taken note of the reluctance of stevedore labour to accept the piece-rate scheme; as far as I can make out from the correspondence, this Review Committee was appointed with the specific understanding that all labour interests would accept my decision as final, and therefore it was rather surprising that stevedore labour should voice its objection to the scheme.

Shri Anthony Pillai has suggested that until the stevedore labour participates in the scheme the shore labour should be given a minimum guarantee as if production of 100 per cent had been achieved. I do not visualise the possibility of stevedore labour staying out of the scheme, and, therefore, this question does not arise. In any event the Port Commissioners have been approaching these labour problems in a spirit of liberality and with a broad outlook and they will surely be able to meet any particular contingency which might arise. With the coal workers and the shore workers so eager to get on to the piece-rate scheme, it is difficult to imagine that stevedore labour will lag behind; and if they do lag behind it would be contrary to their own interests. I cannot entertain the further claim of shore labour that they should be guaranteed 100 per cent during the first three months of the introduction of the scheme. No such assurances have been given either in Bombay or in Madras and no grounds exist for giving the assurance here. In Bombay too labour had been averse to piece-rate, but when the advantages of piece-rate became a reality nothing could stop them from making a success of it.

Shri Anthony Pillai and Shri Makhan Chatterjee wanted the scheme to be brought into operation by October 1. I agree that it should be put into operation as soon as possible but a certain degree of administrative flexibility should be allowed. The success of the scheme depends to quite an extent on its proper implementation, and therefore, proper arrangements have to be made for the purpose. During the course of the hearing, all parties present agreed that the training of the staff for the piece-rate scheme should proceed apace and I have no doubt that it has been done.

IRRIGATION AND POWER TEAM ON MINOR IRRIGATION WORKS (KERALA STATE), 1958—REPORT

New Delhi, Committee on Plan Projects, 1960. 41p.+iip.+Maps and Charts

Leader : Shri N.V. Gadgil (replaced by Dr. A.N. Khosla).
Members : Shri M. Narasimhaiya; Shri Lal Singh; Shri Mahavir Prasad.
Secretary : Shri D.S. Borker.

APPOINTMENT

The Irrigation and Power Team on Minor Irrigation Works (Kerala State) was constituted under the Committee on Plan Projects vide their Memorandum No. COPP/(4)/9/58, dated March 26, 1958.

TERMS OF REFERENCE

1. The minor irrigation projects may be divided for study into two parts:

(a) Works already in existence.

(b) Works which are now being constructed.

2. Case studies should be made of a number of projects of each type under the above headings with a view to judging their efficiency having regard to the objectives with which such works were carried out.

3. The following points should be especially borne in mind:

Existing Projects

(i) The present state of repair and maintenance.

(ii) The system of keeping works in proper maintenance with particular reference to the customary obligations of villagers for keeping such works in a sound condition from year to year, the team should also examine the extent to which these obligations are enforced, the reasons for the failure to do so and the steps that should be taken to carry out such obligations efficiently.

(iii) Reasons, if any for non-utilisation of water by cultivators.

(iv) Improvements necessary to make the projects more efficient either in the matter of better agricultural planning and practices or in respect of engineering works.

(v) Cost of restoration if the project is in a state of disrepair and whether it has been included in the Plan.

New Projects

(i) Method of selection—procedure and principles on which priorities are based.

(ii) Flow Chart of the Construction Project should be prepared to examine whether any avoidable delay has occurred in its completion.

(iii) Whether fullest use is made of catchment capacity in preparing designs.

(iv) Economics of design.

(v) State of agricultural planning with a view to optimum utilisation of benefits.

(vi) Institutional arrangements provided for the proper maintenance of new works with special reference to the customary obligation of villagers in this regard.

(vii) Cost of actual construction compared to estimated costs—the reasons for increase if and the care with which the initial estimates were framed.

4. Any other matter which the Team considers necessary to report upon having a bearing on economy and efficiency of such projects.

5. The following information should be gathered by the Team for each State, taken as a whole in regard to existing minor irrigation works:

(i) The total area irrigated from them according to settlement registers.

(ii) The area actually irrigated from year to year beginning from 1947.

(iii) The reason for the reduction, if any, in the area irrigated.

6. In addition, the Team will carry out a study of the tubewell schemes of the Punjab and the U.P. with reference to the fact whether optimum use has been made of the facilities available by ensuring scientific crop planning and by improving agricultural practices. The study should be based on an examination of individual tubewells, which may be divided into most successful, successful and least successful varieties for the purpose of study. The Team should also select a few tubewells for which alternative crop planning and practices may be recommended that are being carried out at present in order to make them more successful. The consideration mentioned regarding minor irrigation works in paragraph three mutatis mutandis be taken into consideration for the study of tubewells also.

CONTENTS

Preface; General; Agricultural Aspects; Irrigation Planning; Types and Design of Minor Irrigation Works;

Selection, Execution and Maintenance of Minor Irrigation Works; Irrigation Administration and Cess; Summary of Recommendations; Appendices I to V; Isohyetal Map of Kerala.

RECOMMENDATIONS

Experiments should be conducted on underground filter-taps as an alternative to spring tanks in the case of future works, as also to supplement supplies to existing tanks, so as to:

(i) avoid wastage of land;

(ii) reduce evaporation losses; and

(iii) avoid contamination of drinking water, etc.

Some storages should be provided to stabilise water supplies on diversion schemes. This will increase their scopes considerably.

Steel gates and structures required for irrigation projects may be fabricated in local workshops as far as possible, in preference to ordering the same on Tungabhadra Workshops etc. in order to avoid delay.

In view of their established utility, schemes such as Lift Irrigation, Salt Water Barriers and Punja De-Watering, may be taken up in increasing numbers.

Design practices of earthen bunds and waste-weirs may be reviewed so that adequate spillway capacity is provided and the bund slopes are not too steep on the water side. Also, necessity of providing adequate silting capacity in the reservoirs is emphasised.

Use of hume-pipe conduits or overhead flumes supported on trestless is recommended on lift irrigation schemes wherever economical in place of surface channels in cuttings or embankment so as to:

(a) avoid acquisition of land from unwilling people; and

(b) reduce percolation losses.

The proposal to entrust the maintenance of tanks irrigating less than 200 acres to the Panchayats is commendable. These Panchayats may also be authorised to levy suitable cess to finance the maintenance and repairs costs. Further, each Panchayat may employ necessary technical staff in addition to routine maintenance staff.

The water rates for all the crops are very low both in Travancore-Cochin and Malabar regions and need upward revision in accordance with the recommendations contained in the Taxation Enquiry Committee's Report.

As the liabilities on lift schemes cannot be met fully by paddy crops, lift waters may be utilised for growing cash and perennial crops like sugarcane. Also, so as to minimise the operational costs of lift and encourage economic use of water, cooperative management of the lift schemes may be introduced. Government may offer financial and technical assistance to such cooperatives.

Speedy legislation of a new Irrigation Act providing for proper Water Rates for different crops and Betterment Levy and speedy implementation of the same, may be considered by the State Authorities.

JOINT COMMITTEE IN REGARD TO CONTROL AND ERADICATION OF CHOLERA, 1958—REPORT

New Delhi, Indian Council of Medical Research, 1959. (Bound with Joint Committee on Smallpox). pp. 66—181.+viiip.

Chairman : Dr. C.G. Pandit.

Members : Dr. M.S. Chadha; Lt.-Col. Barkat Narain; Dr. B.S. Yajnik; Dr. R.V. Sathe; Dr. K. Venkatraman; Dr. S.C. Seal.

Secretary : Dr. C.V. Ramchandani.

Representatives of the States Expert Committees : Dr. C.R. Naidu (Andhra Pradesh); Dr. D.N Phukan (Assam); Dr. S.R. Chatterjee (Bihar); Dr. M.S. Boparai (Delhi); Lt.-Col. P. Chandra (Himachal Pradesh); Dr. R. Sankararaman (Kerala); Dr. A.M. Francis (Madras); Dr. G.L. Sharma (Madhya Pradesh); Dr. Babu Lal Verma (Madhya Pradesh); Dr. S.D. Narayana Gowda (Mysore); Dr. N. Pattanayak (Orissa); Dr. D.D. Sharma (Punjab); Dr. Satya Deo Arya (Rajasthan); Dr. R.S. Bhatnagar (Rajasthan); Dr. P.K. Topa (Uttar Pradesh); Dr. Saroj Kumar Chatterjee (West Bengal).

APPOINTMENT

The Joint Committee in regard to Control and Eradication of Cholera was constituted under the Indian Council of Medical Research in May, 1958.

TERMS OF REFERENCE

(i) To examine in detail all the aspects of cholera;

(ii) Recommended measures for combating them and

also indicate ways and means for the ultimate eradication from the country.

CONTENTS

Preamble: Incidence; Epidemiology: (a) Factors influencing Endemicity and Epidemicity of Cholera; (b) Special Features of the Epidemiology of Cholera in the States; (c) General Pattern of Spread of Cholera based on the Study of Epidemics during 1956, 1957 and 1958; Present Methods of Control of Cholera [(a) Use of Cholera Vaccine; (b) Isolation of Cases; (c) Chlorination of Water Supplies in Urban and Rural Areas; (d) Control Measures at Fairs and Festivals]; Recommendations (Need for Concerted Efforts for Cholera Control in certain Key Areas of Endemicity; Need for Interdepartmental Coordination; Establishment of Epidemiological Units; Control Measures in Epidemic Areas [(a) Legal Provisions for ensuring Prompt Action in Fighting Epidemic of Cholera: (b) Early Detection and Notification of Cases of Cholera: (c) Isolation and Treatment of Cases; (d) Use of Sulphaguanidine in preventing the Spread of Infection: (e) Technical Aspects of Cholera Vaccine Prophylaxis—(i) Efficacy of Vaccine; (ii) Strains of Cholera Vibros for the Production of Vaccine; (iii) Potency of the Vaccine; (iv) Supply, Storage and Distribution of Vaccine; (v) Meeting Cost of Vaccine; (iv) Dosage of Vaccine; (f) Chlorination of Water Supplies; (g) Disinfection of Cholera Discharges and formaties; Formation of Anti-Epidemic Committees at the District Level; Health Education; Pilot Projects; Need for Further Research; Central Smallpox and Cholera Control Commission]; Estimate of Costs involved in Implementing the Recommendations; Abstract of Recommendations; Appendices, Charts and Maps.

RECOMMENDATIONS

Need For Concerted Efforts For Cholera Control In Certain Key Areas Of Endemicity

The Committee recommends that the eradication programme should be implemented in West Bengal and Orissa in the first instance.

In West Bengal, the area to be chosen for the eradication programme would be about 500 sq. miles, extending some 10 miles south and 40 miles north of the city of Calcutta. The city forms the major focus of infection, and its problem is specific and requires to be tackled on a high priority basis.

In Orissa, the eradication programme should be carried out in the area around Puri and Cuttack.

There is reason to believe that the total picture of Cholera in the rest of the country would be materially altered for the better, if measures recommended above are taken in those two key areas.

Need For Interdepartmental Co-ordination

The Committee recommends the strengthening of the Public Health Engineering Organisation in each State and establishment of a machinery to bring about close cooperation between that organisation and the State Health Directorate. The Committee further recommends that the resolutions passed by the Central Council of Health at its seventh meeting in Shillong in January, 1959, should be implemented.

Establishment Of Epidemiological Units

The Committee recommends that epidemiological studies should be carried out in the States by these Units to elucidate the factor or factors responsible for the spread of the epidemic within the State and to other States and to perform the other functions recommended earlier in the report.

Control Measures In Epidemic Areas

Legal Provisions for Ensuring Prompt Action in Fighting Epidemic of Cholera: The Committee recommends that a Central Infectious Diseases Control Act should be promulgated, more or less on the lines of the Central Food Adulteration Act, to ensure adoption of uniform procedures all over the country in respect of control of cholera.

Early Detection and Notification of Cases of Cholera The Committee recommends that:

(i) Whenever an epidemic of gastro-enteritis assumes the clinical picture of cholera it should be reported as cholera for administrative purposes, and the use of the word 'gastro-enteritis', which has been adopted in one State, should, as far as possible, be avoided, unless there is ample evidence from a recognised laboratory to the effect that it is undeniably gastro-enteritis and not cholera.

(ii) Responsibility of notification should be placed on the Panchayats, because the Chowkidar or the Gram Sewak or the Village Headman will all be presumably under the control of the Panchayat;

(iii) The Panchayat Secretary should transmit the information to health authorities by telegram if a telegraph office is within easy reach, otherwise by a special messenger, and the doctor in charge of the Primary Health Centre or the Sanitary Inspectors and the District Medical Officer of Health should be informed by him simultaneously;

(iv) Special instructions should be prepared for the guidance of (chowkidars and others to help them) recognise cases and which should also highlight the necessity of reporting cases without delay.

Isolation and Treatment of Cases: The Committee recommends that:

(i) Mobile hospitals with adequate personnel and

equipment should be established in each State for the rural areas; and

(ii) Special isolation wards should be created in district and taluk hospitals to serve the needs of the urban areas.

Use of Sulphaguanidine in Preventing the Spread of Infection: The Committee recommends that medicine chests with adequate supplies of sulphaguanidine should be provided in villages prone to epidemics of cholera and in other areas threatened with outbreaks of the diseases in order to facilitate immediate treatment pending the arrival of mobile hospitals.

Technical Aspects Of Cholera Vaccine Prophylaxis

(i) **Efficacy of Vaccine:** The Committee recommends that regulations for the proper utilisation of vaccine, which could be enforced without delay whenever and whenever required, should be drawn up.

(ii) **Strains of Cholera Vibrio for the Production of Vaccine:** The Committee recommends that the vaccine for use during epidemics should be manufactured from both the Inaba and Ogawa strains of Cholera vibrio in equal proportion.

(iii) **Potency of the Vaccine:** The Committee recommends that, in order to facilitate manufacture of a standard vaccine, one centre should be established in the country with the following functions:

(a) Distribution of suitable strains of cholera vibrio to manufacturing centres;

(b) Determination of potency of the vaccine produced by different centres;

(c) Distribution of diagnostic sera for use by the public health authorities;

The Committee further recommends that, pending the establishment of such a centre on a permanent basis, one of the existing laboratories, which is suitably equipped, should be entrusted with the tasks suggested.

(iv) **Supply, Storage and Distribution of Vaccine:** The Committee recommends that:

(a) States, which do not have facilities for manufacturing vaccine in large quantities, should take immediate steps to increase production;

(b) Adequate stocks of the vaccine should be maintained at district headquarters and there should be subsidiary depots at *thana* headquarters;

(c) The Administrative Medical Officer or the Director of Health Services of each State should bear the responsibility of coordinating procurement and distribution of vaccine within the State.

(v) **Cost of Vaccine:** The Committee recommends that the State Governments should accept the responsibility of meeting the cost of vaccine for use within the State (and that they should ensure that) routine administrative and financial procedures do not hamper the effective and timely utilisation of the vaccine.

(iv) **Dosage of Vaccine:** The Committee recommends, as a standard procedure, that one dose of vaccine (1c.c.) should be given to adults in all mass inoculation programmes. The Committee further recommends that contacts of cholera cases should also be inoculated and children should receive dosage of vaccine according to age.

(vii) **Inoculation of Special Groups:** The Committee recommends that a special programme should be instituted for the inoculation of labour employed in the industrial establishments, both in the public and private sectors, as well as of immigrant labour employed in agricultural and other operations. Inoculation of labour should be repeated once every six months.

Disinfection Procedures: The Committee recommends that, in the disinfection of water supplies, cholera discharges and fomites, standard procedures, as laid down in the report and in Appendices II and III, should be followed.

Formation Of Anti-Epidemic Committees At The District Level

The Committee recommends the formation of District Anti-Epidemic Committees as an essential step in the over-all drive against cholera.

Health Education

The Committee recommends that preparations for health education, as indicated in the report, should be taken in hand as soon as the principle of the eradication programme is accepted and education of the population carried out with increasing tempo so that people are fully ready to receive the programme when it is launched.

Pilot Projects

The Committee recommends that, in order to arrive at a fairly comprehensive estimate of the requirements in respect of funds and manpower, each State, in which cholera is at present a major public health problem, should institute a pilot project in selected area prone to frequent epidemics of cholera.

Need For Further Research

The Committee recommends the establishment of a permanent unit, with full-time staff, for the purpose of continuing research on the various problems of cholera on the lines indicated in the report.

Central Smallpox And Cholera Control Commission

The Committee recommends that the Government of India should constitute a Central Small-pox and Cholera

Control Commission, consisting of members appointed on a full-time basis, on the lines indicated in the report, for the execution of the programme for the control and eradication of smallpox and cholera.

JOINT COMMITTEE IN REGARD TO CONTROL AND ERADICATION OF SMALLPOX, 1958—REPORT

New Delhi, Indian Council of Medical Research, 1959. (Bound with Joint Committee on Cholera) pp. 1—65.+viiip.

Chairman : Dr. C.G. Pandit.
Members : Dr. M.S. Chadha; Lt.-Col. Barkat Narain; Dr. B.S. Yajnik; Dr. R.V. Sathe; Dr. K. Venkatraman; Dr. S.C. Seal.
Secretary : Dr. C.V. Ramchandani.
Representatives of the States Expert Committees : Dr. C.R. Naidu (Andhra Pradesh); Dr. D.N. Phukan (Assam); Dr. S.R. Chatterjee (Bihar); Dr. M.S. Boparai (Delhi); Lt.-Col. P. Chandra (Himachal Pradesh); Dr. R. Sankararaman (Kerala); Dr. A.M. Francis (Madras); Dr. G.L. Sharma (Madhya Pradesh); Dr. Babulal Verma (Madhya Pradesh); Dr. S.D. Narayana Gowda (Mysore); Dr. N. Pattanayak (Orissa); Dr. D.D. Sharma (Punjab); Dr. Satya Deo Arya (Rajasthan); Dr. R.S. Bhatnagar (Uttar Pradesh); Dr. Saroj Kumar Chatterjee (West Bengal).

APPOINTMENT

The Joint Committee in regard to Control and Eradication of Smallpox was constituted under the Indian Council of Medical Research in May, 1958.

TERMS OF REFERENCE

(i) To examine in detail all the aspects of smallpox;

(ii) Recommended measures for combating them and also indicate ways and means for the ultimate eradication from the country.

CONTENTS

Preamble; Incidence of Smallpox in India; Registration of Births and Deaths; Existing Legal Provisions regarding Primary Vaccination and Revaccination; Present Methods of Control of Smallpox [Manufacture and Supply of Vaccine Lymph; Administration of Vaccination Programmes: (a) Control of Vaccination Programmes; (b) Training of Vaccinators; (c) Supervision of Vaccinator's Work]; Steps taken by States to Intensify Vaccination Programmes; Recommendations [General Recommendations—Registration of Births and Deaths; Legal Provisions for Ensuring Prompt Action in Fighting Epidemics of Smallpox; Early Detection and Notification of Cases of Smallpox; Technical Aspects of Vaccine Lymph Manufacture: (a) Purity of Lymph; (b) Potency of Lymph; Utilisation of Lymph in the Field: (a) Age of Child when Primary Vaccination can be given; (b) Interval between Primary Vaccination and Revaccination; (c) Techniques of Vaccination; (d) Number of Insertions; Specific Recommendations for instituting Smallpox Eradication Programme—Augmentation of Vaccine Lymph Supplies; Use of Freeze-dried Vaccine Lymph; Storage and Distribution of Vaccine Lymph; Programme Schedule and Recruitment and Training of Vaccinators; Equipment; Some Essential Aspects of the Mass Vaccination Campaign: (a) Preparation of Registers of Births and Deaths; (b) Vaccination Programme; (c) Record of Vaccinations; Health Education; Formation of Anti-epidemic Committees at District Level; Pilot Projects; Epidemiological Units; Organisation of the Vaccination Campaign: (a) Organisation at the District Level; (b) Organisation at the State Level; (c) Organisation at the Central Ministry of Health Central Smallpox and Cholera Control Commission; Estimate of Cost of Smallpox Eradication Programme; Time-table of the Eradication Programme; Abstract of Recommendations; Appendices and Charts.

RECOMMENDATIONS

Registration Of Births And Deaths

In view of the multiplicity of practices in regard to registration of births and deaths leading to unsatisfactory results and with the object of improving the situation, the Committee recommends:

That there should be an Act making registration of vital events compulsory and that that Act should legislate for the provision of proper facilities for registration, setting up of registering offices easily accessible to those reporting vital events, and awarding of punishment for lapses in the duties of reporting or recording of vital events.

That the Secretary of Gram Panchayat should be appointed Registrar of births and deaths for his area.

That the Secretary of Gram Panchayat should send figures of vital statistics to the Block office from where such information could be forwarded to the Sub-Division or District office.

That arrangements should be made for the peripheral reporting officials to send information about births and deaths by post on unstamped cards, the postage charges being recoverable by the postal authorities later on in consolidated amount in a manner similar to the one adopted in respect of commercial concerns; or perhaps, the Committee felt, the Centre could give exemption from affixing of postage stamps on communications notifying births and deaths.

That the registers containing records of vital events should be preserved.

That the officers of the health administration should have the right to inspect these registers.

That before a child is admitted to a primary school, even in the villages, the parents should be required to produce a certificate of his/her birth. Such a practice, the Committee felt, would compel the parents to have the births of their children registered.

That the power to prosecute for lapses in reporting or registration of vital events should be vested in the District Health Officers instead of the Tehsildars.

Legal Provisions

A Central Infectious Diseases Control Act should be promulgated, more or less on the lines of the Central Food Adulteration Act, to ensure uniform procedures all over the country in respect of control of smallpox.

One authority in each State should be entrusted with the task of enforcement of legal provisions in respect of vaccination.

Both primary vaccination and revaccination should be made compulsory.

Early Detection And Notification Of Cases

In view of the importance of early recognition of cases, and taking into account the several views expressed in this regard, the Committee recommends that:

It would be better to place the responsibility of notification on the Panchayats because the Chowkidar or the Gram Sevak or the Village Headman will presumably be under the control of the Panchayat.

The Panchayat Secretary should transmit the information to health authorities by telegram, where a telegraph office exists, otherwise by a special messenger, and the doctor in charge of the Primary Health Centre or the Sanitary Inspectors and the District Medical Officer of Health should be informed by him simultaneously.

For the guidance of Chowkidars and others, special instructions should be prepared to help them to recognise cases and impress on them the necessity of reporting them without delay.

Purity And Potency Of Vaccine Lymph

Purity: The Committee recommends that, while vaccine lymph has to conform to the specifications laid down in the Drugs Act of 1940, suitable laboratory procedures should be adopted for the elimination of pathogenic staphylococci from lymph.

Potency: To secure uniformity in the potency of lymph and to know whether issued lymph, during the period between its despatch and use, has not lost its potency, the Committee recommends that:

(i) Batches of lymph manufactured by different laboratories should be tested at a central place designated for the purpose as a reference laboratory, and

(ii) Arrangements should be made to return random samples of the lymph issued for use in the field to the issuing laboratory for re-testing.

By adopting the procedures mentioned at (i) and (ii) above, it would become possible to take appropriate measures to remedy defects when noticed.

Utilisation Of Lymph In The Field

Age when Primary Vaccination can be Given: The Committee, while recommending that the practice of giving primary vaccination within the age period of four to six months should be continued, saw no scientific reason why vaccination should not be performed even at an earlier age, should that become necessary because of the presence of smallpox in the area.

Interval between Primary Vaccination and Revaccination: In view of the fact that immunity conferred by primary vaccination gradually diminishes, it is necessary to boost it up by periodic revaccinations. The first revaccination should be done at the age of five and subsequent ones should be given every five years till the age of 15 is reached. To facilitate fulfilment of this recommendation, arrangements should be made to vaccinate all children at the time of entry to school again at age of 10 and then at the time of leaving school. The question of giving revaccination after the age of 15 will require to be considered in the light of the results obtained from the proposed programme.

Technique of Vaccination: As regards the technique of vaccination, the Committee recommends that, while the multiple pressure method would normally be the method of choice, the rotary lancet technique should continue to be employed in the mass vaccination campaign because of its simplicity and the familiarity of the vaccinators with its use.

Number of Insertions: The Committee recommends that the number of insertions in primary vaccination should be four, two on each arm, or, if so desired, three on one arm. In case of primary vaccination in persons who have passed the age of 12, only one insertion should be given.

Smallpox Eradication Programme

The Committee recommends that steps should be taken to launch with the least possible delay a national smallpox eradication programme, with the avowed object of successfully vaccinating the entire population as far as practicable, and completing the programme within a period of three years. This would necessitate a concerted and simultaneous action in all the States of India.

The Committee further recommends that, in order to attain the aforesaid object, immediate action should be taken on the lines indicated in the subsequent part of this section, to:

(a) Ensure availability of adequate supplies of vaccine lymph;

(b) Recruit and train adequate number of vaccinators and other personnel required for the campaign,

(c) Obtain necessary equipment for vaccination work and storage of vaccine lymph at all levels,

(d) Bring into being a suitable organisation, both at the Centre and in the States, to ensure smooth functioning of the campaign; and, above all,

(e) Prepare the population well in advance to receive the programme as outlined.

Augmentation Of Vaccine Lymph Supplies

The Committee recommends that:

Immediate steps should be taken by each of the manufacturing centres to augment its lymph production.

The States which do not have lymph producing facilities, should take necessary action to set up lymph producing centres.

Estimates of lymph requirements should be worked out by each State for itself, taking into account the need to maintain adequate reserves so as to ensure continued availability of supplies in the event of breakdowns in lymph production.

Use Of Freeze-Dried-Vaccine

The Committee realised that freeze-dried vaccine, if made available would facilitate the implementation of mass vaccination programme. However, the Committee wished to point out that the control and ultimate eradication of smallpox need not depend on the availability of freeze-dried vaccine and that liquid vaccine, which is more easily prepared, can serve the purpose equally well when kept and transported under suitable conditions.

Storage And Distribution of Vaccine Lymph

The Committee recommends that subsidiary storage depots should be established at district headquarters and at some selected thana headquarters, taking into consideration the size of the districts and the availability or otherwise of suitable communications.

Recruitment And Training Of Vaccinators

The Committee recommends that:

About 20,000 vaccinators should be recruited to complete the programme within the stipulated period.

The vaccinators should be recruited from within the district and given the necessary training at district headquarters.

It should be accepted as sufficient if those who have studied upto middle vernacular or seventh standard are chosen for such training.

The period of training should be one month during which some essential knowledge of health education techniques should also be imparted.

The Committee further recommends that the required number of Vaccinators should be recruited one month prior to the inauguration of the campaign, so that, after training, their services can be immediately utilised for the mass vaccination work. The period of service of the Vaccinator should be deemed to have begun from the date they were recruited for training.

Equipment

The Committee recommends that steps should be taken well in advance for securing the necessary vehicles for the use of the field staff as well as refrigerators, projectors, generators, etc.

Some Important Points To Be Attended To For The Success Of The Mass Vaccination Campaign

The Committee recommends the preparation, well in advance, of family-wise birth and death registers to be maintained for each village, drawing up of a vaccination programme to ensure ready supplies of lymph so as to facilitate uninterrupted work of the vaccinators, and making of arrangements for recording the results of vaccinations.

The Committee further recommends that, while the newly recruited vaccinators should do vaccination work, the existing trained vaccinating staff of each State should be entrusted with the task of supervising the vaccinators' work and recording results of vaccination.

Health Education

The Committee recommends that preparations for health education of the people should be taken in hand as soon as the principle of the eradication programme is accepted, and education of the population should be carried out with increasing tempo so that the people are fully ready to receive the programme when it is launched.

Formation Of Anti-Epidemic Committees At The District Level

The Committee whole-heartedly supports the idea of formation of District Anti-epidemic Committees.

Pilot Projects

The Committee recommends that, in order to estimate the requirements of the eradication programme in respect of manpower and finances, each State should institute a pilot project for this purpose in an area with a total population of not less than 60,000.

Epidemiological Units

The Committee recommends the formation of Epidemiological Units in each State for the continuous study of the smallpox problem.

Organisation Of The Vaccination Campaign

In order to ensure the success of the campaign as envisaged, the Committee recommends that a suitable administrative machinery should be created at the District and State level, as well as in the Central Ministry of Health, with adequate powers to deal effectively with the day-to-day administrative problems and take decisions on any matter concerning the campaign.

Central Organisation

The Committee recommends that the Central Organisation should be named the Central Smallpox and Cholera Control Commission.

Estimates Of Cost Of Smallpox Eradication Programme

The Committee recommends a total provision of Rs. 7.5 crores for the smallpox eradication campaign. In arriving at this estimate the Committee has not taken into account the expenditure incurred by each State on its routine vaccination programmes.

Time-Table Of The Eradication Programme

The Committee recommends that the entire programme should be completed in three years and should be carried out in two phases, the first phase relating to the period of planning and the second phase to the actual execution of the campaign. Priorities of procedures are indicated.

THE STUDY TEAM ON SOCIAL WELFARE AND WELFARE OF BACKWARD CLASSES, 1958—REPORT

Delhi, Manager of Publications 1959, 2 vols.

Leader : Smt. Renuka Ray.
Members : Shri M. S. Gore ; Shri H. C. Heda; Shri Viyogi Hari (resigned; replaced by Smt. Sarojini Varadappan) ; Shri Thakur Phool Singh; Shri R. L. Jangde; Shri J. S. Lall.

APPOINTMENT:

The Study Team on Social Welfare and Welfare of Backward Classes was constituted under the Committee on Plan Projects on May 1, 1958.

TERMS OF REFERENCE

(1) The Team will study the programme of work relating to Social Welfare, included in the Plan in the Central and State Sectors, with a view to economy and particular reference to the work of the Central Social Welfare Board. In making this study, it will keep the following points in view:

(a) The modifications necessary in the context of the programme and in the scheme of priorities relating to the various fields of activities comprising it having regard to the efficient utilisation of resources and the objectives set for the programme.

(b) The changes required in the methods of work adopted for the implementation of the programme. In particular, the Team should review the arrangements for coordination as among the Central Social Welfare Board, the Centre and the States and as between different agencies including local bodies, within the Central and State Governments.

(c) The quality of the personnel engaged upon the implementation of the programme and the training schemes formulated for improving upon it with special reference to the need and feasibility for establishing a cadre of workers for the adminisration of the programme.

(d) Assessment to the extent to which the existing programmes have succeeded in utilising local initiative and in creating institutions to ensure management of the programme in future by the local community itself.

(e) Examination of the working of the grants-in-aid programme of the Central Social Welfare Board with special reference to :

(i) The development of voluntary institutions in areas inadequately served at present so as to secure a more even distribution of grants-in-aid;

(ii) The evolution of certain minimum standards in the welfare services provided by aided institutions;

(iii) An examination of the criteria employed by inspecting officers; and

(iv) An assessment of the effect of the aid programme on the resources of voluntary agencies.

(f) To consider the suggestion made for setting up of coordinating councils for voluntary welfare agencies at various levels particularly in important district towns.

(g) To make such other suggestions on any aspect of the programme as would lead to economy and efficiency in the utilisation of resources and/or expediting the working of the programme.

(2) The terms of reference at (a), (b), (c), (d) and (g) above will also govern *mutatis mutandis* the work of the Team relating to welfare projects for Scheduled Castes/Tribes and other backward classes.

(3) In addition, the Team shall make recommendations on the necessity and feasibility of evaluation machinery of a continuous nature for both the types of projects and on methods adopted for reporting upon the results of the programme.

CONTENTS

RECOMMENDATIONS

Introductory

Role Of Voluntary Organisations

No separate allocation for enlisting public cooperation in officially sponsored programmes should be made in the Plans. Instead, grants-in-aid for specific schemes should be given to voluntary organisations of standing and repute for mobilising public cooperation.

In the organisation of welfare services, emphasis should now shift from residential institutions to setting up of non residential community welfare services with family as the basic unit.

The voluntary organisations should reorient their fund raising programmes, so that they depend on the willing support of the large majority of citizens, rather than on the generosity of a few philanthropists.

Steps should be taken to ensure the formal representation of voluntary organisations in addition to the present practice of associating non-official workers in their individual capacity.

Coordinating Councils should be set up at the district, State and national levels. Initially the proposed Councils may be convened at the State level, by the State Governments, in consultation with the State Social Welfare Boards. The Councils once established should organise themselves and function under rules of procedure evolved by them.

Social Welfare

Central Social Welfare Board

Functions of the CSWB may be restated as follows:

(i) To cause a comprehensive survey to be made of the needs and requirements of social welfare organisations;

(ii) To lay down broad policy and priorities for the grants-in-aid programme and to allot funds to the State Boards for the administration of this programme;

(iii) To organise a field counselling service as an effective supplement to the working of the grants-in-aid programme and to assess the programmes and projects of aided agencies;

(iv) To coordinate the various grants-in-aid programmes for voluntary social welfare agencies available at the Centre;

(v) To promote the setting up of voluntary organisations in areas uncovered at present;

(vi) To promote the setting up of the rural welfare projects to be administered through the agency of the State Social Welfare Boards;

(vii) To initiate the organisation of pioneering welfare services; and

(viii) To stimulate effective coordination among voluntary welfare agencies, especially at the national level and among agencies covered by the grants-in-aid programmes.

The composition of the CSWB should be revised as follows:

(i) The number of the members of the Board should be raised to 15 non-officials in addition to ex-officio members;

(ii) The Chairman and five members (non-officials) should be nominated by Government from among eminent social workers;

(iii) Three representatives should be elected by Parliament (two by the Lok Sabha and one by the Rajya Sabha either from within Parliament or from outside);

(iv) Three members be nominated, one each by three institutions selected in rotation, by Government from a list of approved voluntary organisations;

(v) Three members be nominated by Government from among Chairmen, State Social Welfare Boards, in rotation; and

(vi) The existing basis of representation of Central Ministries should continue.

The Central Social Welfare Board should be constituted as a statutory autonomous body.

The tenure of office of the Chairman and Members of the CSWB should be for a period of three years.

State Social Welfare Advisory Boards

The functions of the State Social Welfare Boards may be revised as follows:

(i) To promote the growth of voluntary social welfare agencies, with special reference to development of welfare services in areas uncovered at present;

(ii) To administer the grants-in-aid programme:

I. On behalf of the CSWB for development and capital grants; and

II. On behalf of the State Government for maintenance grants;

(iii) To assist the CSWB in the provision of a field counselling service for aided agencies;

(iv) To administer the programme of rural welfare projects (WEP's);

(v) To stimulate effective coordination among voluntary welfare agencies at the State and local levels; and

(vi) To assist the CSWB and the State Government in the further development of welfare services.

The State Social Welfare Advisory Boards should be redesignated as State Social Welfare Boards and should serve as independent executive bodies to assist the CSWB as well as the State Welfare Departments in their programmes. The status, form and organisation may be redefined in a statute in which the relationships of the State Boards with the State Governments and the Central Social Welfare Board should also be brought out.

The composition of the State Social Welfare Boards should be revised on the following lines, viz.:

(i) That the Chairman and five non-official members should be nominated by the CSWB and the State Government by joint consultation from among eminent social workers and experts;

(ii) That three representatives should be elected by the State Legislature (one from Legislative Council where such a Council exists);

(iii) That three representatives should be selected by the State Government from a list of approved State level welfare organisations in rotation;

(vi) That three representatives should be nominated from among Chairmen, PIC's;

(v) That the representation of State Government departments dealing with welfare programmes should be continued on the existing basis; and

(vi) That in the selection of members to serve on the State Board, the criteria of district-wise representation, especially of districts relatively uncovered by welfare services, should be taken into account.

The tenure of office of the Chairmen and Members of the State Boards should be for a period of three years.

Welfare Extension Projects

Steps should be taken to remove the existing difficulties in the setting up and efficient functioning of coordinated pattern WEP's,—the accepted pattern for all WEP's to be set up in the future.

Original pattern WEP's located outside a C.D. block area should continue to function on the present basis until such time as the area is covered by a C.D. block, when the WEP should be recognised on the coordinated pattern.

Original pattern WEPs located at present within a C.D. block area should be reorganised on the coordinated pattern without delay.

Welfare programmes for women and children in the C.D. block area conducted by the block staff should be so organised as to provide the basis for the subsequent setting up of a full-fledged WEP. The block staff (a woman SEO and two gram sevikas) should initiate a limited programme with say two project centres under the supervision of a Sub-Committee consisting of women voluntary social workers appointed by the Block Development Committees.

The provision in the budget of both the Stage-I and Stage-II blocks should be set at a minimum of Rs. 40,000.

Similar welfare programmes for rural women and children conducted by other welfare departments should be integrated into one standard pattern for the organisation of these welfare services.

A separate PIC should continue to function at the Block level for the administration of welfare programmes for rural women and children.

The number of representatives of the Block Panchayat/Block Development Committee on the PIC should be increased so that their association in running the programme will prepare the way for the ultimate transfer of welfare responsibilities to the block level authorities.

The composition of the PIC in the coordinated pattern WEP's, should be revised as follows:

	Number
(i) Chairman selected from among women voluntary social workers in joint consultation between Chairman, State Board and the block level authority.	1
(ii) Members nominated by the State Board from among local women social workers.	3
(iii) Members elected by the block panchayat either from among its non-official members or from outside.	3
(iv) Ex-officio members including Block Development Officer, Extension Officer (Industries), etc.	3
Grand Total	10

Non-official members of the PIC should, as far as possible, be selected from among persons residing within the block area or, at least, from among persons who can devote sufficient time to this work.

The Chairman and non-official members of the PIC should pay special attention to the following functions:

(i) Preparing the village community in the project area to receive the WEP programme and to participate in the activities on an effective basis; and

(ii) Organising and conducting the programmes of raising popular contributions.

Popular initiative, preferably expressed through representative local organisations, should be an essential criterion in deciding on the area in which the project is started and the village centres are located; and

In applying this criterion, care should be taken to ensure that the centres are located in a compact area capable of effective coverage and supervision.

The educational content of the balwadi programme should be standardised in consultation with the appropriate educational authorities and the training programmes for gram sevikas should be suitably reoriented to meet the needs of this programme.

Regularity of attendance at the balwadi should be emphasised.

Steps should be taken to effectively strengthen the balwadi programme through the provision of supplementary nutrition on regular basis and the conduct of a periodic medical check-up of the children.

The maternity and infant health service to be provided through an auxiliary nurse-cum-midwife should be extended to cover:

(i) Advice and guidance in family planning;

(ii) Training in mother-craft; and

(iii) Assistance in improving the standards of local dais.

The State Board should ensure a regular and adequate supply of medicines to the centres; the PIC's being authorised to make local purchases, subject to certain specified limits.

The infant health service should receive adequate emphasis and there should be a comprehensive programme for the regular medical check-up of children and prevention of common children's diseases.

Craft programmes undertaken at the project centre should concentrate on purposeful domestic crafts directly related to the needs of the family.

The responsibility for the organisation of a craft programme with a substantial economic content on a production basis should be undertaken by expert bodies under the aegis of the State Governments. The PIC should, however, take the initiative in the location of these centres and in the selection of women workers.

In the conduct of the craft programmes referred to at (b) above, priority in employment should be given to unattached destitute or indigent women and those exposed to moral danger who are in need of special assistance.

The budget of the WEP should include provision only for the programme of domestic crafts. The budget provision for running the production centres having economic crafts should be made from outside the WEP budget.

The adult literacy classes in the social education programme should give an increased emphasis to the education of younger girls instead of the adult women.

The cultural and recreational programmes should be oriented to provide for participation of all sections of the village community.

As the various items of the WEP programmes are gradually absorbed into the general pattern of normalised services, arrangements should be made for their progressive transfer to the appropriate authorities.

The post of the craft instructor should be abolished and the gram sevika should be entrusted with the responsibility of providing training in domestic crafts.

The post of the dai should be upgraded to that of a nurse-cum-midwife capable of undertaking family planning, mothercraft classes and improving the standards of the local dais.

Immediate steps should be taken to expand existing training facilities for the auxiliary nurse-cum-midwife and as an interim measure, a trained dai should be posted at each centre.

Arrangements should be made to strengthen the staffing pattern in the centres by the appointment of gram sahayikas on payment of suitable honoraria.

All staff under coordinated projects should be recruited by a joint committee at the State level consisting of the representatives of the State Social Welfare Board and the concerned departments of the State Government.

All project staff, who are now under the CSWB, should be taken into Government service and should be given the same terms and conditions of service as applicable to the corresponding employees in Government service.

Having integrated all staff, the services of field workers and supervisors in projects should be placed under the administrative and technical control of the PIC.

In integrating the C.D. and WEP staff the minimum qualifications for selection and employment should be equated for each category of staff who should undergo a standardised programme training.

The training programme of the supervisory workers should be related to and based on the training courses given to the field workers.

Instead of providing as at present, two supervisors, i.e., the mukhya sevika and the woman SEO to function in the same coordinated project, only one supervisor should be appointed with the designation of mukhya sevika.

The project budgets should be formulated by the Project Implementing Committees on a more realistic basis by taking into account the varying local needs and conditions and spending potentials of the projects in the light of past performances.

There should be an approved plan for the activities to be undertaken in a project during a period of years, which may be co-terminus with the Plan period. The project budgets should, however, be prepared from year to year in the manner obtaining in the Government organisations.

As in the case of the State Plan Schemes, the ceilings of expenditure on activities undertaken by the State Board in each State may be fixed after consultations with the Central Board and the representatives of the State Government in the beginning of each year. But the project budgets should be finally approved by the State Boards, in terms of programmes of work and the allocations among different sub-heads.

The present pattern of assistance to the projects may be continued.

Funds from the Ministry of Community Development, the State Governments and the CSWB may be made available to the State Boards for working of the projects.

Grants from the Central Social Welfare Board should be made available to the State Boards en-bloc in the beginning of a year.

Grants from the State Government including the funds payable from the Community Development budget should be made available to the State Boards in two instalments, the first to the extent of 50 per cent of the estimated share of expenditure for the year on receipt of a statement of accounts of the previous year's grants and the second representing balance of the grant on receipt of the audited statement of accounts of the previous year.

The State Boards may release an advance for two months, in the beginning of the year, to the Project Implementing Committees. Subsequent instalments may be paid monthly in the light of actual requirements and on the basis of monthly statements of account.

The State Boards should take steps to review the progress of expenditure in the Welfare Extension Projects every month. The Project Implementing Committees should be asked to explain promptly the reasons for substantial excesses/shortfalls, if any, before the subsequent instalment of the grant is released

An increasing emphasis should be laid on contributions received in terms of services and the Project Implementing Committees should make efforts to mobilise such services.

A scientific method of computing the cost of services towards local contributions may be devised in consultation with the State Governments.

Services such as voluntary labour, assistance towards conducting the programmes in centres and other such services should be taken into account in assessing the local contributions.

Suitable staff having an experience of finance and accounting may be made available by the State Governments to the Projects Implementing Committees.

The State Governments should guide the State Boards generally in the application of the financial rules and procedure.

The frequency of inspection of the projects by members of the State Boards should be increased with a view to keeping a close watch over the financial administration of the projects.

There should be unified financial responsibility in the drawal and spending of funds with the Chairman of the Project Implementing Committees.

The Central Board should take steps to ensure that the rules regarding the maintenance of jeeps are properly enforced.

Grants-in-Aid Programmes

The initiative for defining minimum institutional standards should be taken by the CSWB; and in defining and revising these standards and introducing suitable regional variations, the CSWB should work in close coöperation with State Governments, State Boards and experienced social workers and experts.

The State Governments should organise a system of recognition for all welfare institutions on the basis of certain prescribed institutional standards. The field counselling service should provide the necessary inspectorial assistance for making this programme of recognition more effective.

The administration of the grants-in-aid programme covering the consideration of applications and sanctioning of grants should be the responsibility of the State Boards.

The programme of development grants should be organised on the following basis:

(i) The funds for the payment of development grants should be made available by the CSWB;

(ii) The agency for the administration of the programme of development grants at the State level should be the State Social Welfare Board;

(iii) The CSWB should allot these funds each year to the State Boards. In establishing the quota for each State, special weightage should be given to the building up of new institutions and services in relatively backward areas;

(iv) The CSWB should work out, in consultation with each State Board and in line with its special needs and problems, a pattern of priorities and allocate amounts for different purposes to different fields of welfare activities, e.g., the welfare of women, children, handicapped, etc.

(v) The State Boards should be left free to re-appropriate the funds between the respective fields of welfare upto a prescribed percentage;

(vi) The grants should be made available to a certain number of institutions selected from among the list of recognised institutions that have displayed the potential for undertaking development projects; and

(vii) The grants should not exceed 25 per cent of the normal level of expenditure of the institutions.

With regard to capital grants:

(i) The funds for the payment of capital grants should be made available by the CSWB;

(ii) The agency for administration of the programme of capital grants should be the State Social Welfare Board;

(iii) The principles laid down for the administration of development grants should also be applied to capital grants;

(iv) The ceiling of capital grants should also be raised so as not to let a development programme suffer on account of marginal inadequacy of the grant.

With regard to maintenance grants:

(i) The State Governments should provide funds for assisting recognised institutions with maintenance grants;

(ii) The agency for the administration of the programme of maintenance grants should be the State Social Welfare Board; and

(iii) The position of resources for financing this aid programme may be examined by the Planning Commission and additional funds made available to the State Governments, if necessary, for this purpose.

The CSWB should organise an effective field counselling service with the assistance of adequately trained and experienced officers.

The field counselling officers should be posted by the CSWB to work with the State Social Welfare Boards.

The field counselling service should be made available to aided agencies receiving—

(i) Development and capital grants from the CSWB; and

(ii) Maintenance grants from the State Governments.

Suitable arrangements may be made to extend the field counselling service to other institutions that may ask for this help.

The CSWB should organise a programme for assessing the work of aided agencies on the basis of data made available by the field counselling service and from such other sources as are available to the CSWB.

The visits by State Board members to institutions applying for grants should be more frequent and more intensive. These visits should be supplemented by the reports of the field counselling staff.

The decisions of the State Board, whether in terms of acceptance or rejection of an application, should invariably be conveyed to the concerned institutions.

Provision should be made for reviewing the cases of those institutions which are not satisfied with the decision of the State Board.

Special measures should be taken to encourage the development of new services in relatively uncovered areas either through existing welfare organisations or new institutions on the following basis, viz.:

(i) In the case of new institutions of recent standing, the condition of recognition and eligibility for grant may be suitably relaxed and institutions assisted in making a good start through frequent visits and guidance given by the members of the State Board and the field counselling staff; and

(ii) In the case of existing organisations of long standing, the proportion of matching contributions may be reduced. The amount of grants may be fixed in a higher proportion to the total expenditure and administrative charges and salaries of paid staff may be included in estimating expenditure on the project.

Grants to voluntary institutions should be provided for in the Central Board's budget under different subheads indicating the broad purposes of grants such as child welfare, welfare of women, etc.

An index of basic data on individual institutions should be maintained in the office of the State Board so that while dealing with subsequent applications, only such additional data, as is necessary, may be called for from the institutions.

The application form should be printed in the regional languages by the State Boards and each State Board should be responsible for the submission of a consolidated return to the CSWB.

The form of application also requires to be considerably simplified. It should only call for the data having a direct and immediate relation to the conditions of the grants and should exclude such information as can be found in published reports.

A simpler form of application, on the lines suggested by the Team should be adopted for purposes of development and maintenance grants.

The conditioning of maintaining a separate account of grants received from the Board may be relaxed in favour of the institutions receiving funds also from local bodies, public donations, etc. Audited statements of accounts for the entire expenditure incurred by the institutions may be accepted in such cases.

State Governments should evolve a common system of audit applicable to the audit of grants paid by the CSWB and by the State Governments through the State Boards. A suitable panel of auditors drawn from the Government organisations or commercial firms should be nominated by the State Governments for this purpose. In some States, audit could also be entrusted with advantage to the Examiners; Local Funds.

Second and subsequent instalments of grants-in-aid may be released on receipt of mere statements of accounts provided that the last instalment of each year may not be released till audited statement of accounts of the previous year is received.

Social Defence Programmes

Juvenile Delinquency

It is necessary to bring the various Acts into one uniform pattern, especially with regard to vital clauses relating to age limits and the categories of juvenile offenders covered under the Act.

The State Governments should provide the necessary machinery for implementing these Acts and, wherever necessary, additional funds should be earmarked for this purpose.

Juvenile courts should be organised without delay in places where no such courts exist at present and arrangements should be made to provide special magistrates to handle these cases.

Special police officers should be appointed to deal with the cases of juvenile offenders. It is important that they bring to their task a certain measure of sympathy and understanding so important in dealing with such a sensitive problem.

If the role of the probation officer is to be understood by the concerned magistrates and police officers, it is necessary to appoint the probation officer from among persons with adequate background and training and wherever possible orientation courses should be organised for concerned officers to enable them to appreciate the process in probation work.

In organising an effective machinery for the implementation of the various Acts, it is necessary to provide for setting up an adequate number of Remand Homes, Certified Schools and Fit Persons Institutions.

Special attention should be paid to juveniles living in urban slum areas as under-privileged children from the low income groups. Effective steps should be taken to enable these children to derive the maximum benefit from existing welfare programmes.

Social And Moral Hygiene

Voluntary agencies should be associated more directly with the execution of the programmes.

The advisory character of the managing committee should be modified so as to give the committee greater executive responsibility, with certain financial safeguards to be retained by the State Government.

Adequate advisory and supervisory staff should be provided both at the Centre and in the States for the administration of the programme. Efforts should be made to transfer the responsibility for the administration of individual units from the nominated managing committee to a committee composed of representatives of voluntary agencies.

The overall responsibility at the Centre for the Social and Moral Hygiene programme should be transferred to the Central Social Welfare Board.

The responsibility at the State level for the Social and Moral Hygiene programme should be transferred to the State Social Welfare Board.

Every step should be taken to establish independent Protection Homes as visualised in the Act.

The location of the Homes/Shelters should be preceded by an assessment of the need for such a facility and should be located in places where the problem is acute, e.g., where prostitution is rampant and where large scale recruitment for prostitution takes place.

The case of every woman who is admitted in a Home should be carefully assessed on admission and it should be the object of each Home to so tackle each case that the inmate is able to become a useful member of the society within a reasonable period.

Production units allocated to the State Homes should be organised simultaneously with the establishment of the Homes as otherwise economic rehabilitation of the inmates is not possible.

Work in the field of Social and Moral Hygiene is difficult and complicated and social workers employed in these programmes should be well qualified in the methods and techniques of handling the work.

The workers employed for the management of the Homes should necessarily be women and even in the appointment of members of the Managing Committees preference should be given to women.

It is necessary to provide for compulsory licensing of voluntary institutions working in the field of Social and Moral Hygiene.

The recommendations of the Advisory Committee on Social and Moral Hygiene relating to sex education in educational institutions, child guidance clinics, marriage guidance and counselling, encouragement of parent-teacher associations, treatment of venereal diseases and strengthening the family planning programme should be effectively implemented. Voluntary agencies should also be helped to undertake countrywide programme to advocate suitable changes in social life and in community practices and customs.

The After-Care Programme

The responsibility at the State level for the after-care programme should be transferred to the State Social Welfare Boards.

The need for an after-care service unit should be established prior to the setting up of any such institution through the conduct of the necessary surveys and experiments.

Where no justification can be found for an existing after-care unit, it should be either closed or converted into a care institution. (The revised 'care' basis should be clearly emphasised.)

The present pace of development of the after-care programme should be immediately reviewed. The tempo of extension may be reduced and attempts made to consolidate existing after-care service units on sound lines.

The facilities of such a specialised service should not be made available on a general basis but only to such individual discharges whose potential for rehabilitation has been established and who are in need of such a specialised service. Each individual application should be examined by trained staff at the pre-discharged stage.

Production units should be organised as an integral part of the services provided by an after-care unit. Arrangements should be made to set up production units at the same time as the after-care homes are opened. These production units should preferably be organised on a cooperative basis. Apart from organising such production units, simultaneous efforts should be made to explore other avenues of resettlement and employment.

The training programmes of care institutions should be so dovetailed with the production programmes of after-care institutions that trainees proficient in selected vocations and crafts can be utilised in the after-care units for the organising of a production programme on an economic basis.

Voluntary agencies should be associated more directly with the detailed execution of the after-care programmes.

The advisory character of the Managing Committee should be modified so as to give the Committee greater executive responsibility with certain financial safeguards to be retained by the State Government.

Adequate advisory and supervisory staff should be provided both at the Centre and in the States for the administration of the programme and efforts should be made to transfer the responsibility for administration of individual units from the nominated Managing Committees to voluntary after-care agencies.

Socio-Economic And Other Programmes of the CSWB

Socio-Economic Programmes

The programme should more appropriately be designated as the "Urban Socio-Economic Project".

The selection of items of production for these industrial units should be related to the availability of raw material, marketing facilities and the ease with which skill and proficiency can be acquired so that the programme can provide gainful employment on competitive terms.

Steps should be taken to establish the units on a sound economic basis and to encourage the cooperatives to assume full responsibility for the running of the units.

The CSWB should coordinate their work with the production programme of the All India Industrial Boards on the following lines, viz.:

(i) By starting welfare extension projects (rural and urban) in areas with a concentration of professional artisans ; and

(ii) By using the WEP's as the organisational base for starting separate production units, where there are sufficient numbers of professional artisans in the area.

While the CSWB should continue to give grants for such programmes, it should attempt to interest the All-India Industrial Boards in providing the technical assistance for starting and running the production units and financing these programmes.

The scheme for the supply of sewing machines to women has a special significance in view of the relevant training programmes conducted in the WEP centres and, therefore, the CSWB should examine the possibilities of taking up this scheme once again. The responsibility for organisation and supervision should not be undertaken by the CSWB, as in the earlier arrangement. Instead, applications for sewing machines should be sponsored by the State Social Welfare Board and Cooperatives should be organised with arrangements for the services of a master tailor and suitable marketing facilities.

Pilot Urban Welfare Extension Projects

The activities of the urban pilot welfare extension projects should not be restricted to women and children and the programme should take the family as the basic unit as stated in the objectives of the scheme.

The welfare programmes in the urban welfare projects should be coordinated from the very outset with similar programme in the urban areas so as to avoid duplication and overlapping which have been noticed with regard to welfare programmes in the rural areas.

The programme of urban WEP's should be extended to towns/cities with a population of more than 50,000 persons. The programme should be undertaken in consultation with the concerned municipalities.

Night Shelters

Night shelters should be developed in close cooperation with the concerned municipality or the corporation and the programme should be fitted into the overall pattern of development conceived of by the civic authority.

Condensed Course Of Training For Adult Women

(i) The condensed course should prepare candidates for the Matriculation or equivalent examination;

(ii) The course may suitably be extended to two or three years; and

(iii) The candidates eligible for this course should have a minimum qualification of Primary School pass.

Institutions taking up the condensed course, should be located in smaller towns and preferably in rural areas.

Hostels For Working Women

Instead of sanctioning grants on an ad-hoc basis, the CSWB should undertake, at an early date, a preliminary survey in a few major towns and cities, to assess the need for establishing such hostels. Once the acquirements are assessed, the CSWB should induce, by suitably relaxing the conditions prescribed for the building and other grants, leading women's welfare institutions of standing and repute to take up construction of such hostels.

Rs. 15,000, which is set as the maximum ceiling at present, is too low to cover costs of construction in a crowded city where the problem of providing accommodation to working girls primarily exists. The ceiling, therefore, should be suitably raised.

Assistance under the present scheme should be restricted to the construction of buildings and provision of minimum furniture and fixtures.

Welfare Schemes Of State Governments And Local Bodies

Welfare Schemes Of Local Bodies

Municipal Corporations and Municipal Committees should be recognised as the principal welfare agencies in the urban areas.

The resources of a Municipal Corporation or a Municipal Committee, to meet the costs involved in undertaking the welfare programme, should consist of:

(i) Grants-in-aid by the Central Government to be made available from out of the special funds provided at the Centre for welfare programmes including those provided for the welfare of backward classes; and

(ii) State assistance in the form of grants which may be provided from out of the special provision made in the Plans of the States both for social welfare programmes and for programmes for the welfare of backward classes.

The Municipal Corporations and the Municipal Committees should undertake, in particular, the following types of programmes:

(i) The Welfare Schemes should be designed in a manner that they cover sweepers, scavengers and Harijan employees of the Municipal Corporations and the Municipal Committees and also persons engaged in the so-called unclean occupations such as flaying, canning and leather work by providing for them cleaner surroundings and housing sites with flaying yards and tanning pits outside their localities.

(ii) Setting up of Balwadis in slum areas.

(iii) Provision of milk supply.

(iv) Maintenance of playgrounds.

(v) Provision of recreational facilities.

(vi) Construction and maintenance of night shelters (Rein Baseras).

(vii) Programmes which would cover beggars, juvenile delinquents and other underprivileged sections of the population.

The Municipal Corporations and Municipal Committees should undertake an overall programme of Community Development by establishing a suitable machinery to prepare plans and initiate pilot projects. The projects should aim at initiating and achieving the desired changes through the maximum citizen-group participation and minimum professional leadership.

The Corporations/Committees should encourage welfare institutions working within their jurisdiction by giving them grants-in-aid for sponsoring welfare services which the Corporation or Municipality would not, otherwise, be in a position, for want of suitable machinery to execute by themselves.

The pilot schemes for urban community development under the Central Social Welfare Board or State Boards, which are being carried out through voluntary organisations, should be drafted and implemented in consultation with the concerned Municipal Corporations or Municipal Committees.

Due representation should be given to Municipal Corporations/Committees both at the Central level as well as at the State levels, in drawing up welfare programmes intended to cover the areas falling within their jurisdiction.

Youth Welfare Services

The scheme of Labour and Social Service Camps should be discontinued.

As a part of this programme physical standards should be prescribed for different age-groups separately for boys and girls, and special programmes should be designed so as to achieve these standards. Popular interest may be created through the organisation of national and regional competitions for developing physical standards.

Special concessions and financial assistance should be given to enable youths from low income groups and from among Scheduled Castes, Scheduled Tribes, etc., to avail themselves of the facility of educational tours.

The Team wishes to endorse the recommendation of the Estimates Committee on Special Education with regard to shifting the venue of the inter-university youth festival from Delhi to other cities through a system of rotation.

Students' organisations and educational institutions should be provided with the necessary technical assistance and guidance so as to enable them to redraft their programmes on a readily acceptable basis.

Arrangements should be made to provide students with information on employment opportunities and training facilities at the stage of bifurcation in the educational system or at the end of the secondary stage of education.

Employment bureaus should be established in the universities on the lines of the employment bureau in the Delhi University.

Career masters should be appointed in major schools at the district headquarters level so that they can act as a channel of vocational information for students.

Organisations at the district and taluka level should be encouraged to promote cultural and recreational activities for non-student youth. Social education programme should also be specially directed towards meeting the educational needs of this category of the general population.

Child Welfare Services

In the drafting of a comprehensive welfare programme, the first priority should be given to schemes for the welfare of children.

Within the field of child welfare priority should be given to schemes for the welfare of the normal child with special attention to the needs of the children of the under-privileged groups including those living in urban areas. In working out schemes for child welfare, greater attention has to be paid to the preventive side so that the underlying causes of all the social problems and the disabilities of the children are effectively controlled.

Child welfare legislation should be enacted in all States with some measure of uniformity.

The Model Children's Bill should be recirculated among the State Governments in order to arrive at a certain measure of agreement.

Steps should be taken by the State Governments to enforce these Acts immediately and, where necessary, funds should be provided for the purpose.

The trained staff should be given the necessary incentives, by way of allowances and better living conditions, to restore the balance between their demand and supply in the rural areas. The mobility of such trained staff could be increased if training programmes are planned on a regional basis, using a common language to reach the people and to overcome local barriers and prejudices.

Additional efforts should be made to secure improvements in the school health service. In so doing the scope of the scheme should also be extended from mere medical inspection, as at present, to providing the requisite follow-up treatment as well.

In the immediate future attention should be focused on extending the scheme of mid-day meals at least to the following categories of children, viz.:

(i) Children attending primary schools in the urban and rural areas, preferably from among low income groups; and

(ii) Children residing in areas more prone to famine, floods and scarcity conditions.

In this respect, it may also be necessary to pay attention to the full and proper utilisation of milk and other supplies made available by the U.N. and other agencies.

Balwadis should be organised in the urban areas, preferably in slum areas, so as to benefit the children from low income groups.

The Municipal authorities in cities with a population of between fifty thousand and one lakh persons should provide adequate parks and playgrounds and should organise supervised recreation in cooperation with local voluntary organisations, if necessary, with financial assistance from the Government.

Children's literature, produced in India, should be sold at prices within easy reach of the people and should be widely distributed. To ensure effective distribution of this literature, it should be made available to children's sections, especially set up in public libraries, wherever necessary, and to school libraries at concessional subsidised rates.

The possibility of using the Census Organisation for the collection of data on the problem of the handicapped children should be considered.

There should, at least, be a minimum set of services for the welfare and education of each of the categories of the handicapped in every State and such a minimum programme should be worked out on a model basis.

A National Commission for Child Welfare, for improving the pattern of child welfare services and for drawing up an integrated national programme, to be adopted as part of the Third Five-Year Plan should be set-up.

Welfare Of Backward Classes

General Principles

While still retaining the Schedules of Castes and Tribes for special assistance, an economic criterion should be applied within the groups of Scheduled Tribes and Scheduled Castes so as to ensure that more benefits go to those who are economically less advanced.

An economic rationale should be introduced in the schemes of assistance concentrating on aid to those individuals who are economically less advanced among the other backward classes.

Standard norms based either on revenue or income tax or some other local tax which are easily assessable should be adopted.

These norms should be objectively determined and should be applied in no ungenerous or rigid manner. They may be periodically reviewed in the light of the changing position.

The extension methods should be properly adopted so as to suit the tribal psychology and should be so applied as to enable the tribals to develop according to their own genius.

The traditional tribal institutions should be actively associated with planning and execution of welfare and development programmes. In doing so, however, the process of democratisation should be progressively introduced. One possible method would be to make these authorities elective and leave tribal bodies to work out methods of functioning in keeping with their traditions.

Plan for tribal welfare need to be very simple. It is important, at least in the initial stages, to concentrate on a few selected programmes, that have a vital bearing on the felt needs of the people so as to secure ready understanding and willing participation on the part of the tribals.

Constant vigilance should be exercised to ensure that action under various schemes, which are inter-dependent is properly synchronised so as not to cause delay or failure in their implementation and consequent frustration among the people.

Welfare And Development Programme For Scheduled Tribes

The overall order of priority should be as follows:

(a) Economic Development and Communications;
(b) Education; and
(c) Public Health.

While the above three major programmes should receive a higher priority than the rest, *inter se* they should receive simultaneous attention because success in each of them is dependent upon the progress in other spheres.

A carefully integrated programme of development of tribal economy based on agriculture, forestry, handicrafts and village industries should be organised. The exact degree of emphasis upon each of them would be determined by a systematic survey of the needs and possibilities in each area.

One of the first few steps that should receive higher priority in the programme of agricultural development in tribal areas is that of surveying the areas of cultivable land. Wherever it is not possible to carry out detailed survey, it would suffice to ascertain the extent and location of land available for allotment and reclamation.

This should be immediately followed by a plan of allotment in which due emphasis should be given to allotting land to shifting cultivators and landless tribals.

Settlement of tribals on land should be encouraged on a cooperative basis wherever circumstances permit and people are in favour.

Also where the land is insufficient but is available in a compact and contiguous stretch, cooperative cultivation be promoted subject to above.

The assistance given to the settlers should be adequate so as to enable the tribesmen to derive maximum benefit out of the allotted land.

Subsidiary occupations should also be provided in order to supplement the earnings from land.

The utility of existing provisions for protecting the land rights of tribals should be re-examined by the States and measures taken to bring them in line with the needs of the situation prevailing today. This could perhaps be done by the same committee suggested to examine measures to end exploitation.

Subsidies should be given for soil conservation measures on individual and community holdings, the tribal's contribution being accepted in the form of labour.

In respect of new land, schemes of settlement should be worked out first and conservation measures adopted on the principles stated above.

Prohibition or regulation of cultivation on higher slopes should be linked with schemes for cultivation of cash crops which have proved successful in experiments.

The tribals should be attracted to come and settle around places where gainful occupation is assured.

It would be better to provide suitable home-steads around the allotted land making sure that there is a perennial source of clean drinking water available at hand.

Research and experimental farms should be set up on a regional basis.

Demonstration farms should be established locally within each block or in any other convenient regional unit so that improved methods of cultivation can be demonstrated under typical conditions prevailing therein.

Some practices may have to be demonstrated actually on people's own holdings by moving parties or teams of extension workers.

Individual cultivators should be selected, who aided with equipment, seeds and technical guidance in improved agricultural practices, would undertake the application of research findings. Selection of these individuals can be entrusted to the tribal communities or their representative bodies subject to fulfilment of certain requirements from the technical point of view.

Promotion of animal husbandry among tribal agriculturists should proceed cautiously.

Those tribals who have a traditional love of cattle should be chosen to develop animal husbandry among them.

A close supervision and guidance should be provided to enable them to take better care of cattle and to realise the importance of the use of animal power in agriculture.

Forest Department should, as far as possible, employ only tribals in the forests in tribal areas; suitable training may be given to employ them in higher grades.

Steps should also be taken to introduce a system of guided management, whereby the tribals or their representative bodies, will be progressively associated in the management and exploitation of the forests in tribal areas.

Village forests for domestic use should be carved out and placed under the management of tribal village councils.

In addition, the entire revenue from these village forests should be given to these councils to be used for the development of their village.

Vigorous measures should be taken up for afforestation in the appropriate seasons during the year. Some of the operations should be carried out in the lean months so as to provide gainful employment to tribal cultivators who may then be idle.

Their wages should be paid partly in food and the balance in cash.

Commercial exploitation of forests should be entrusted to forest labour cooperatives rather than to contractors, the Bombay scheme being adopted with such modification as may be necessary and operation profits to be utilised for tribal welfare.

Societies may either be sponsored by the official or non-official organisations and coordinated by the State Government themselves.

Cooperatives on the same lines should be set up to exploit minor forest products.

No deposits should be demanded from these cooperative societies; pledging of timber or whatever be the forest produce should be considered as an adequate surety.

In most cases substantial loans will have to be advanced for the cooperatives to launch the initial exploitation of forest coupes on a profitable scale.

Transport and marketing facilities should also be provided for these cooperative societies.

The extension of communications in tribal areas should be directly linked up with the implementation of development plans in the area so as to minimise the dangers of exploitation.

All the main tribal and scheduled areas not yet opened up should be served atleast by one motorable road useable throughout the year so that the produce of the area can find ready market without the help of intermediaries. An area equivalent to that of a special multi-purpose block, namely, 200 sq. miles, should constitute the unit in regard to the construction of such main roads.

The cost of inter-district roads and State highways should be debited not to the provision for development of communications in tribal areas but to the general budget for development of roads.

The main roads should be connected with the feeder roads which bring the outlying areas effectively into contact with the outside world. It will be enough if these cart tracks serve the normal purpose of commerce. In some cases, e.g., in hilly areas, even bridle tracks will suffice.

Labour cooperatives may be sponsored in the tribal areas and may be given preference over the contractors.

Necessary technical assistance should be made available to them.

The concept of the development of region along with the welfare of the community should be further extended to all areas which are inhabited by tribal people. This may be done without reference to the formality of placing the area on the schedule.

The State Governments should exercise more freely the authority or varying the schematic budgets in keeping with the general priorities recommended by the Team in an earlier section and more particularly in conformity with the felt needs of the local community.

There should be an initial period of pre-planning, say

of six months, which should not be deducted from the block period though the cost may have to be debited to the block budget.

This period should be utilised for selection and posting of staff, mobilisation of resources, procurement of equipment and construction of buildings so that the work can start on the opening day itself.

This planning should be carried out by a skeleton staff headed by the Block Officer designate.

For speedy construction of buildings, local styles and designs may be suitably adopted keeping in view the requirements of public health and utility.

To stimulate initiative in this direction a prize may be awarded to the block which may construct the best buildings on the basis of adopted local patterns.

In the selection of staff, services of suitable tribal candidates should be utilised to the maximum possible extent. The authority to relax educational qualifications should be exercised in the case of tribal candidates at least for the next few years. It is needless to add that wherever choice is available preference should be given to the tribal candidates.

In either case, special training must be given to the staff to be posted in the special multi-purpose blocks. To the non-tribal candidates at least one local dialect should also be taught during the period of training.

In view of the living conditions in tribal areas, there should be extra allowances, e.g., 25 per cent of the salary in respect of the Block Development Officer and other extension officers and higher allowances upto 50 per cent of the salary in respect of village level workers and other lower staff.

A representative of the department dealings with tribal welfare should serve as a member on the block committee. Since the Tribal Welfare Department is responsible for the welfare of tribal communities in the block areas before and after the intensive stage, it is necessary that the Tribal Welfare Department should be actively associated with the preparation of block plans and with the subsequent implementation.

It would be desirable to extend these blocks to all areas predominantly inhabited by the tribal communities. An overall survey of the future requirements in terms of personnel, equipments and other resources should be undertaken in advance so as to use the pre-planning period for mobilisation of public cooperation.

The programme of opening new special multi-purpose blocks should be suitably incorporated in the phased schedule covering the entire country by 1963.

The general pattern of education prevalent in the country should be extended to tribals so as to evolve one common pattern of education in the country. Assuming that at the primary and upper primary stages a genuine basic system would prevail, there would be enough scope for choice of agriculture and other related tribal crafts in the schools in tribal areas.

The principle of bifurcation which has been recognised for all students is equally necessary in tribal education. This would ensure that tribal students who discontinue at a lower stage are not alienated from their own cultural millieu.

The accepted principle of imparting instruction at primary level in the mother-tongue of the child should be extended to tribal children as well.

Wherever there are minor variations in local dialects of different tribal communities residing in contiguous tribal areas, the main tribal language should be chosen as the medium of instruction at the primary level.

In areas where the regional language has been adopted by the tribals, the same may be adopted as the medium of instruction. Regional and national languages should be introduced at the Secondary stage.

As for the script, the Devanagari should, as far as possible, be introduced except in areas where the prevailing script of the regional language is more easily adaptable and acceptable stage.

Regional and national languages should be introduced at the Secondary stage.

The text books in primary schools in tribal areas may have to be based largely on reading material related to tribal life without substantially deviating from the general outline of the common syllabus for all primary schools.

From the Secondary stage onwards, however, there should be common text books based on the integrated pattern of education. They should include material derived from both tribal as well as non-tribal sources. Lessons on national heroes, festivals, places of historical interest and the like should also include selections from tribal life and conditions.

It is necessary that early surveys should be carried out to assess the number and standards of the teachers required in tribal areas. This assessment should take into consideration the probable requirements in the Third Five-Year Plan.

Based on the results of such surveys, a regular scheme of education and training of tribal teachers should be undertaken.

If sufficient number of suitably educated tribals are not available, the required number may be made good by recruiting non-tribals who may show evidence of an aptitude for working among the tribal communities. Their training should include proficiency in at least one of the tribal languages and a sympathetic understanding of their customs and traditions.

Similarly, an adequate number of women should be recruited and trained to serve as school teachers in tribal areas so that there is at least one woman teacher in every tribal school by the end of the Third Five-Year Plan.

It is obvious that the terms and conditions of the teachers serving in tribal areas should be made more attractive so as to draw most suitable candidates.

The school hours, as also the holidays and vacations, in the tribal areas should be so adjusted as to synchronise with their occupational seasons and social festivities.

There should be at least one reliable drinking water well or any other source in each village.

In hills special provision should be made for tapping perennial sources with pipe connections or even with bamboos or carved out hollowed trunks of palm trees.

All-out efforts should be made to eradicate major diseases in cooperation with appropriate international and United Nations agencies.

An extensive network of indoor hospitals and sanatoria, with a much wider network of outdoor centres, should be organised. The latter should organise campaigns for prevention of and early detection of the major diseases while the former may offer timely and effective indoor treatment.

A far-reaching follow-up service, with carefully kept case records, is necessary to supplement a programme of medical and public health in tribal areas.

As for normal medical aid, dispensaries, mobile health vans and in areas where motor vans cannot reach, peripatetic health squads should be provided.

Considering that the tribal preference is for herbal medicines because they are cheap and dependable, an effort should be made to carry out systematic researches into the ingredients of medical herbs instead of rejecting them outright. Their efficiency should be tested and a measure of standardisation should be introduced and the acquired knowledge may be embodied in a kind of indigenous pharmacopoeia.

Knowing the resistance of tribal women to outsiders, the local dais should be provided with training and the necessary kit to continue to practise in their own areas.

A certain measure of resistance is known to have come forth from the local dais for any regular training, it is hoped, however, that with a programme of health education they will be persuaded to do so in course of time.

It cannot be over-emphasised that terms and conditions of working and living in tribal areas should be made attractive enough to draw suitably qualified health personnel to settle and serve in tribal areas.

The schemes for tribal housing should be governed by the conditions as stipulated in para 62 of the Report.

Once it is decided to offer housing facilities to a particular group, they or their representatives should be closely associated in the planning and construction of the houses.

The design and pattern of housing should, as far as possible, closely approximate to their natural habitats with only certain minimum standards consistent with the requirements of public health and hygiene.

While introducing diversions from the natural tribal pattern, the essential features of the original habitat which give them adequate protection against the climate and the geographical factors should be ensured.

Construction should be undertaken through tribals themselves either individually or through labour cooperatives with the necessary technical assistance provided by the concerned department.

Some standing arrangement should be made to see that the colony develops into a regular neighbourhood and the tribals should be educated to maintain the colony in a condition fit for their habitation.

The tribal research institutes in the States should be reorganised so as to cover the following functions:

(i) To prepare monographs on the major tribes with as comprehensive a documentation of facts as possible. This should be accompanied by a study of the tribal linguistics and authoritative glossary of the tribals in the State;

(ii) To study, test and adopt for application in the tribal areas, ideas and methods which may be considered useful, in the local setting;

(iii) To disseminate the results of observation, experimentation and evaluation through publication of reports, brochures and other literature;

(iv) To conduct short term training courses for welfare workers and administrators in tribal areas. In doing so it must be ensured that the institutes are appropriately staffed to undertake this additional function; and

(v) To carry out such other functions as would help in the review of policies and programmes for tribal welfare so as to be increasingly effective in the context of regional conditions.

A Central Institute of Tribal Welfare, on the lines discussed in the Report, should be established.

The Central Institute will have the following functions:

(i) To coordinate research on an all-India basis;

(ii) To make studies of special problems which extend beyond the jurisdiction of any one State;

(iii) To pool ideas and to disseminate them among the State Governments and other authorities charged with the implementation of tribal development and welfare; and

(iv) To provide expert advice and guidance.

The Director should be assisted by suitably qualified research staff to cover each major branch of tribal welfare, e.g., education, social organisation, economic development, etc.

This Institute should function under the same Union Ministry which deals with tribal affairs.

Programmes Of Development For Backward Classes

For those, who practise craft as a subsidiary occupation, it must be related to their agricultural or forest operations and should enable them to supplement their earnings appreciably.

For others who take craft as the main occupation, it must continue to be a profitable venture in the face of severe competition that is offered by purely commercial ventures.

Systematic surveys should, therefore, be carried out with the assistance of the technical staff of the development and industries departments to explore the possibilities of development of handicrafts and village industries on sound business lines.

On the basis of the findings of the surveys, broadly two types of schemes should be planned. The first category should include crafts and industries which may produce articles of domestic utility for local consumption. The second category of schemes should cover such crafts and industries as may promise profitable production for outside markets. Here, the stress should be laid on employing those who have the necessary aptitude and environment in terms of traditional family occupation.

The crafts of domestic utility should offer subsidiary occupations to men and women in their spare time and during the lean periods when agricultural operations are not on.

The commercial crafts and village industries, on the other hand, should offer scope for full-time substantial gainful employment to those who depend on them as major occupations.

The existing emphasis on training in the training-cum-production centres should be reversed and greater emphasis be placed on the production aspect. Training programmes should be linked up with the production activity so that apart from acquiring the manual skill in a particular craft, the trainees would also acquire knowledge of the methods of business organisation in the respective trades.

Hostel facilities should be provided by the training centres so that trainees can be drawn from a wider area and they can return to their respective places to practise the trade. Wherever it is not possible, the training centres should be mobile. After training a batch or two it should be shifted to another uncovered area.

Every successful trainee should be enabled to settle down in his trade in one of the following ways:

(i) Working as an artisan doing job work;

(ii) Employment as a wage earner in a production unit; and

(iii) As a member-worker of a producers' cooperative society.

The particular method of rehabilitation for each trainee should be determined keeping in view, on the one hand, the economic possibilities of the particular trade and the aptitude and interest of the individual trainee on the other.

The multiplier principle should be adopted so that more qualified and talented trainees are further coached to take positions as instructors in the other training centres.

Financial assistance should be made available to the successful trainees or to their cooperatives in two parts, viz., non-recurring and recurring.

The cost of non-recurring equipment should be given as an outright grant and the provision for recurring expenses should be advanced as a loan on easy terms.

The terms of financial assistance should be so regulated that net profits go to the cooperative societies and not to the Government as in the case with regard to certain types of forest cooperatives in some parts of the country.

No scheme of commercial nature should be started unless arrangements for raw material and marketing are secured in advance. A survey of the demand for the particular commodity or service should be made to ascertain the marketing possibilities.

The Committee suggested under 'Land Tenure' in para 12 of Chapter II (Part III) may also be asked to review and examine the working of various Acts that have a bearing on the protection of backward classes particularly Scheduled Tribes and Scheduled Castes and to suggest measures for amendment wherever necessary.

In particular, these Committees, might examine the extent to which Prevention of Land Alienation Acts and other legislative measures for the liquidation of indebtedness have succeeded. The same Committees should also suggest ways and means whereby the enforcement of these Acts and measures is made more effective.

States which have not yet enacted such measures might try to emulate these measures.

The law governing organisation and conduct of cooperatives should be simplified so as to make the organisation of cooperatives easy and their maintenance smooth.

Suitable training programmes should be instituted to train tribals and other backward classes in the methods of cooperative organisation. If such programmes are started for the rural masses in general, backward class individuals should be given due place in them.

In order to ensure that some of these exploiters do not get into cooperative organisations disguising their intentions and methods of exploitation, adequate safeguards must be provided.

It is necessary that the rules of procedure should be so revised as to make it possible that credit is given promptly and in adequate measure.

Sufficient discretion should be allowed to managing committees of cooperative societies who sanction loans for production purposes with little or no security. It should be considered adequate to advance a loan against an undertaking, duly supported by recognised local individual or authority, to repay the amount on receipt of cash after the sale of the produce.

In order to enable the backward class individuals to become members of the cooperative societies, loans should be advanced to them for purchase of minimum necessary shares.

In extending the scheme to other States, however, care should be taken to avoid pitfalls experienced by the States which have done the pioneering work, that is issuing of grain to fictitious borrowers, collection of grain without issue of receipts, and the like.

In order to implement these recommendations with greater measure of success, it is proposed that either the panchayats or cooperative societies should be entrusted with this work.

Government may open fair price shops for sale of food and other articles of daily necessities and also for purchase at reasonable prices, of the produce such as grain and craft goods from the farmers and artisans.

Government should take active steps to discourage contractors foregoing the administrative convenience of assigning departmental contracts to single individuals. If necessary, specifications of job requirements may have to be suitably revised and technical assistance may have to be provided.

Hostels should be common for students of all communities; reservation of an adequate proportion of seats being made for backward class students.

The existing hostels should be converted into general hostels as per above, and the names be changed so as to give them a more cosmopolitan outlook.

The manner of working out this conversion should be such as not to jeopardise the position of Scheduled Castes, Scheduled Tribes or other backward classes in regard to the number of seats available for them in hostels both existing and new.

Students belonging to sweepers' and scavnegers' communities should be admitted into local hostels.

The usual condition that no student residing within five miles radius of the concerned town or city would be allowed admission in the local hostels should be waived in the case of students belonging to *Bhangi* community.

Minimum standards should be prescribed and enforced in regard to accommodation, food, sanitary arrangements, medical care and recreational facilities. These should apply equally to hostels run by Government and non-Government organisations.

Recognition and assistance may be granted only to hostels managed by bona fide voluntary welfare organisations. Hostels run by individuals should neither be recognised nor assisted.

Daily programmes should be so organised as to leave enough time for rest and recreation.

Recreational and cultural programmes should also include locally popular games and activities.

Stress should be laid on developing national outlook among backward class students, particularly, among the Scheduled Tribes students living in isolated areas, through the organisation of national days like the Republic Day, the Independence Day, daily singing of national songs and the like.

At least one common girls' hostel should be set up at each divisional headquarters with adequate number of seats being kept for girls belonging to backward classes.

At other levels, additional girls' hostels should be provided wherever sufficient number of backward class girls is forthcoming.

Post-matric scholarship should be administered at the State level so as to decentralise the procedure and to cut down the delays. The system of associating popular representatives with the consideration of applications could still be retained with advantage by constituting similar scholarships boards at the State level consisting both of the backward class representatives as well as concerned officials.

The centralised grant of scholarships at the Union level can still be justifiably retained in respect of scholarships to students seeking admissions to all-India institutions of higher education in scientific and technical subjects.

The power of sanction of under-matric scholarships should be delegated to the District level where a suitable committee consisting of officers and popular representatives should be set up.

The forms of application and the conditions of award need to be drastically simplified. Verification should be deemed as valid on the basis of a certificate from the Sub-Divisional Officer or from the Sarpanch, countersigned by the Sub-Divisional Officer.

In regard to continuing scholarships, the practice of automatic renewals which has already been started in some States, should be extended to all States and adequate amounts should be placed at the disposal of the local officers or institutional heads for timely payments.

Recommendations in regard to the simplification of procedure and other aspects of their adequacy or otherwise are as much applicable to the post-matric scholarships as to those up to the Matriculation standard.

The rate of payment of scholarships and stipends should be rationalised for each State and there should be uniformity for each equivalent category of scholars.

In view of the backwardness of the girls' education at all stages of education, they should be given stipends adequate enough to cover hostel expenses, wherever necessary and they might be exempted from paying admission fee in advance.

All scientific and technical institutions which have

not prescribed minimum qualifications for admission should do so.

These minimum qualifications should be common to all students.

A certain number of seats should be reserved for backward class students who should be considered for admission on the basis of the prescribed minimum qualifications.

Office Of The Commissioner For Scheduled Castes And Scheduled Tribes

As regards the qualifications and the background of the incumbent who can ably and independently discharge the functions of the Commissioner he should preferably be a non-service person, as at present.

The Commissioner should concentrate on evaluation of the working of the welfare schemes for the backward classes.

Assistant Commissioners for Scheduled Castes and Scheduled Tribes should preferably be drawn from among the I.A.S. or equivalent services from the cadre of a State other than that to which they are required to be posted.

The Reports of the Commissioner may present a State-wise analysis and that the Governments should issue explanatory Memoranda on the shortcomings and inadequacies pointed out in the Commissioner's Report. The Reports and the Memoranda should be discussed in the Parliament and the State Legislatures every year.

Special Problems Of Scheduled Castes

The Village Panchayats, Welfare Extension Project Centres, Community Development Blocks and non-official institutions should celebrate national festivals such as Independence Day, Republic Day, Children's Day and Martyr's Day in such a manner as to persuade Harijans to actively participate in greater numbers.

In regard to the observance of socio-religious functions such as Vijaya Dashmi, Dewali, Pongal, Holi, Ram Naumi, Durga Puja, and Shivaratri, venues should be selected near Harijans' Bastis. The village leadership may give a start by visiting the houses of Harijans on these occasions.

Festivals which are observed exclusively by Harijans should be accepted and celebrated as common functions in which all communities should participate on equal terms.

Steps may be taken which may lead to marriages between Harijans and non-Harijans. This should more be an indirect result of a congenial atmosphere that voluntary workers and organisations would have created rather than be the outcome of any direct campaign for this purpose.

Social workers and voluntary organisations working in the field of Harijan welfare and social reform should persuade carefully selected caste-Hindu families to adopt Harijan children.

A change should be introduced in the scope and method of awarding prizes for the removal of untouchability. The award need not be restricted to the official campaign in the villages and should be given to any individual institution, panchayat or a village rendering meritorious services which may lead to the removal of untouchability.

The conditioning of enrolling a certain proportion of members from among Harijans should be strictly adhered to. If the Harijans in the neighbourhood are not in a position to join the society for reasons of economic backwardness, a special grant may be given to such Harijans to enable them to become members of the society.

With regard to legal remedies the following measures would adequately strengthen the law so as to make it sufficiently deterrent :

(i) The first offence should be tried summarily so that justice is not inordinately delayed.

(ii) The minimum fine in the first offence should not be less than Rs. 50/-.

(iii) For the second offence the fine should not be less than Rs. 200/- together with compulsory imprisonment for not less than one month.

(iv) Second offence should not be compoundable.

(v) Panchayats can play an effective role in the removal of untouchability. The question of investing them with adequate statutory powers in this regard should be examined.

The Central and the State Governments should increase their share of grants to municipalities to enable them to abolish, within a specified period, the practice of carrying night-soil in open baskets on the head.

Wherever possible scavenger-free latrines should be installed. This could form an important activity of the programmes of slum clearance, town improvement and new habitation.

The condition of assistance which insists that municipalities should introduce the reforms in the entire areas under their jurisdiction, should be relaxed or waived. Also, wherever wheel-barrows or hand carts cannot be introduced, tightly covered portable buckets may replace the baskets.

Leather and tanning industry should be reorganised in such a manner that others may also be attracted to take up various occupations in the industry without dislodging those already engaged in them.

Government should extend all possible facilities to the cooperatives to establish flaying and tanning centres outside village boundaries.

Scientific methods should be progressively introduced so as to eliminate or minimise the 'unclean' part of the various processes in the leather and tanning industry.

Sufficient safeguards should be provided so as to reduce the incidence of occupational hazards or diseases prevalent among the workers in the industry.

Cooperatives should be organised with substantial Government support for the purpose of raw material and sale of the finished products of the tanning and leather industry.

In the construction of new colonies or in the development of new suburbs and townships, mixed habitation of Harijans and non-Harijans should be encouraged by reserving a certain proportion of house sites or houses for Harijans.

Wherever free house-sites are provided, care should be taken to see that their location is such as would promote integration rather than segregation of Harijans from the rest of the community. This should apply in all cases of assistance whether by grants or loans.

In the first instance, the basis of assistance for housing should be rationalised. Those below a particular income level should be given outright grants and those above, subject to a maximum, should be given incentives by way of loans on easy terms.

A maximum and a minimum should be fixed in accordance with regional considerations.

The amount of assistance must be fixed in accordance with the local conditions such as in the case of building material and transport. But there should be no variations in the size of the amount within the same area.

Labour should be provided as far as possible, by the grantees themselves.

It must be ensured that the Harijans are not evicted from the land or from the house constructed thereon. It should be the duty of the local and district authorities to ensure this and they should be given the necessary powers to deal with this problem effectively.

A special provision should be made in the appropriate law that the transfer of ownership of a house from a Scheduled Caste individual to any other should be deemed as valid only when certified as a bona fide deal by the appropriate authority.

In regard to the provision of quarters for the sweepers and scavengers who are municipal employees it must be made an obligatory duty of local bodies and the Central and State Governments should provide substantial contributions towards the schemes.

Once this assistance is provided, a time limit must be set within which all municipalities and corporations should provide housing of a suitable standard to all members of their conservancy staff.

The municipal colonies must provide for various income groups in all departments and should not be restricted to sweepers and scavengers or to employees belonging to the lowest income bracket. Each colony should, however, reserve an adequate number of housing units for the conservancy staff.

Standing arrangements should be provided to ensure the proper maintenance of these colonies so that they do not deteriorate into slums.

In all housing schemes cooperative effort should be encouraged as compared to assistance to isolated individuals. This would facilitate civic amenities and community services.

The problem of providing perennial supply of protected drinking water should be tackled as such without reference to the removal of untouchability.

In places where Harijan bastis are separate, convenience of Harijans must be given first priority in deciding upon the location of wells.

In areas where mixed habitation exits or is encouraged, the location would depend upon common convenience.

Financial assistance for construction of wells should be regulated according to the cost of construction in varying local conditions.

Denotified Communities

A correctional and welfare approach as against a penal one should be adopted in practice towards the rehabilitation of the denotified communities.

The habitual criminals among them should be isolated and treated under the ordinary law of the land.

The economic programme should go hand in hand with a dynamic and suitably oriented programme of social education so as to wean them away from socially undesirable tendencies.

The substantive economic content should be provided in the welfare programmes for denotified communities, keeping in view the adventurous spirit and traditional skills that prevail among them.

Where production-cum-training centres meant for backward classes in general are not easily accessible to them, separate production-cum-training centres should be started in the denotified community settlements opening out to every individual three avenues of gainful employment:

(i) Work as an individual aritsan;

(ii) Seeking employment in any vocation or trade in private or public sectors; and

(iii) Organisation of producers' cooperatives or industrial cooperatives.

With a view to removing the stigma attached to these tribes in the past, the Government should give a lead in offering them employment in Government.

Community Welfare Centres should be opened in all these settlements with particular emphasis on programmes for children's and women's welfare so that they can be moulded into a new way of life.

Opportunities may be provided to children, above seven years of age, to study in hostels away from settlements. The measures should be so adopted as to provide new education to the children of these communities without alienating them from these families.

Administration Training And Evaluation

Administrative Set-up

Social welfare subjects (excluding the welfare of backward classes) should be brought under one administrative agency at the Centre. A separate Department may be set up immediately for the purpose under the Ministry of Education which may be appropriately redesignated as "Ministry of Education and Social Welfare".

The Department for the welfare of Scheduled Castes, Scheduled Tribes and other backward classes may be set up under the Ministry of Home Affairs.

The functions of the proposed Social Welfare Department at the Centre, may be stated as under:

(i) Administration of national social welfare policy;

(ii) Initiating, reviewing, and watching implementation of social welfare legislation by the State Governments;

(iii) Coordination of social welfare schemes of the State Governments on a broadly uniform pattern;

(iv) Promotion of social research; and

(v) Constitution and administration of a Central cadre of welfare administrators.

A unified Welfare Department in each State dealing with social welfare as also the welfare of backward classes should be set up. The executive machinery for social welfare and the welfare of backward classes should, however, be kept separate.

Where the allocation of funds, the quantum of work or the proportion of population makes it necessary, the States may consider the desirability of setting up a separate Department of Harijan or Tribal Welfare without prejudice to the provision of Article 164(1) of the Constitution.

The State Governments may bring about the required flexibility in administration by reorganising the methods and procedure in their Directorates dealing with welfare services or by setting up Boards with a certain measure of autonomy and executive responsibilities.

The functions of the proposed Department at the State level may be stated as follows:

(i) Initiation and execution of welfare schemes other than those undertaken by the State Social Welfare Advisory Boards;

(ii) Social welfare legislation;

(iii) Introduction of the system of recognition and registration of institutions based on minimum institutional standards;

(iv) Administration of maintenance grants to voluntary social welfare institutions through the State Boards;

(v) Promotion of Coordinating Councils of voluntary organisations on the advice of the State Boards; and

(vi) Constitution and administration of a cadre of social welfare administrators at the State level.

The Director for the Welfare of Backward Classes and Tribal Welfare, as the case may be, should be vested with the powers of a Joint or a Deputy Development Commissioner and may be designated as such. We believe that Director will then be in a position to exercise an overall authority over execution of the development schemes for the backward classes and to ensure that the money disbursed to other departments for this purpose is fully and properly spent.

The Central Advisory Boards for Harijan Welfare and Tribal Welfare should exercise the following functions:

(i) Association with planning;

(ii) Periodical assessment of the work of various welfare schemes; and

(iii) Consideration of the difficulties encountered by beneficiaries in the actual operation of the various welfare schemes.

The composition of the Central Advisory Boards for Harijan and Tribal Welfare may be revised as follows:

(i) One-third from among the M.P.'s (Tribal representatives in the case of the Board for Tribal Welfare and Harijan representatives for the Board for Harijan Welfare).

(ii) One-third from among social workers.

(iii) One-third from among the social scientists.

With the revised composition and extended functions it is necessary that these Boards should meet more frequently than at present. Further, in order that a certain measure of continuity is assured to the Boards, their tenure of membership should be extended to at least two years with a provision for re-nomination of a certain proportion of members.

Advisory Boards for Harijan and Tribal Welfare Board should be constituted by all the States as soon as possible so that they function as effective counterparts to the Central bodies in the execution of the welfare schemes. In line with the functions envisaged for the Central bodies, the functions of these bodies should also be expanded similarly, so that they function with greater responsibility and the welfare plans are brought on a footing of a measurable and recognised popular association. So far as the composition goes, the pattern of representation should also be on the lines suggested for the Central Board with the only difference that there should be Members of Legislative Assemblies and/or Legislative Councils in place of Members of

Parliament.

(a) The Collector should be in overall charge of supervision and coordination of all welfare schemes in the District. Funds should be transferred from the Welfare Department to the Collector in respect of all schemes with the exception of those mentioned in (c) below, for the implementation of the schemes.

(b) Apart from such schemes as the Welfare Department may frame, the District Level Committee may be encouraged to originate schemes based on local needs.

(c) In respect of supra-district schemes, moneys may be transferred direct to implementing departments.

(d) (i) In respect of schemes in (b) above, execution will proceed directly under the supervision of the Collector.

(ii) In respect of schemes under (c) above, the execution will be through the implementing departments. These arrangements will have to be incorporated in standing orders in accordance with which the local officers of implementing departments will automatically act under the Collector's instructions.

To assist the Collector in all welfare schemes which need to be executed in the district, there should be a full-time District Welfare Officer for each district. He should have a status and adequate powers to be able to discharge effectively the functions mentioned below:

(i) In addition to the other duties which would normally, devolve on a District Welfare Officer, he may be empowered to acquire land and allot it for purposes of house sites and for agriculture.

(ii) He should also arrange for free legal aid in respect of offences arising out of the Untouchability (Offences) Act, 1955, unauthorised ejectment, harassment or fraud by money lenders, etc.

Staff under the District Welfare Officer should be adequate both in numbers as well as qualifications in relation to the volume and nature of work in the district.

The District Planning Committees may themselves constitute special Sub-Committees for Harijan Welfare, Tribal Welfare, etc., according to the local requirements. The composition and functions of these Sub-Committees should be regulated more or less on the lines of the functional Sub-Committees of the Block Panchayat Samitis as proposed in our recommendations later. There are certain aspects of backward classes welfare which should receive close attention at the hands of the District Committees. These would ensure among others, the proper observance of forest rights and the retail and wholesale rates in the local weekly markets, for which they may have local committees consisting of non-official leaders and local officials. These committees should also have sufficient powers to intervene effectively in case of suspected exploitation of tribals.

The pattern existing in Madras, viz., the Assistant Women Welfare Officers at the district level being Members of Project Implementing Committee, may be adopted in other States also.

Nomination of members to the functional sub-committees for Harijan and Tribal Welfare, of the Block Panchayat Samitis need not be restricted to the members of the Samitis but should include other leading Harijans or Tribals in the area as also trusted and tried social workers devoted to the cause of the welfare of Harijans or Tribals.

In all cases, the statute should lay a definite responsibility for the welfare of Scheduled Castes and Scheduled Tribes on the Samitis and a portion of the budget should be earmarked for certain welfare activities for their benefit.

A certain minimum number of Harijans or Tribal members, as the case may be, should be prescribed in the composition of functional sub-committees of the Block Panchayat Samitis.

As an additional safeguard, the list of members of the functional sub-committees should be approved by the District Magistrate and he should be authorised to ensure that the amount specially set apart for the welfare of these groups is spent fully and properly for the purpose for which it is meant.

It would be desirable to reconstitute the existing Coordination Committee by the addition of the Secretary and the required number of officials of the Social Welfare Department. The Minister for Education and Social Welfare may appropriately be the Chairman of this Committee. Similar coordinating Committees may also be appointed at the State level.

The Central Family Planning Board should take on its body, representatives of the proposed Social Welfare Department apart from the Chairman, Central Social Welfare Board, who is already a member of the Board.

The planning of rehabilitation schemes following emergencies may be made by an ad hoc Committee consisting of representatives of the Central Social Welfare Board, the Department of Social Welfare and the Ministry of Home Affairs as also the State Welfare Departments and the State Welfare Boards of the concerned States.

Joint meetings of the Women's Advisory Committee, the Central Social Welfare Board and the Social Welfare Department may be held from time to time under the aegis of the Ministry of Community Development, to plan the social welfare schemes in the block area as also the programmes in coordinated projects.

A study group, consisting of the representatives of the Health and the proposed Department of Social Welfare, may be set up to work out the demarcation of responsibility and to devise the appropriate manner in which the process of treatment and rehabilitation could be coordinated at the Central level, and to demarcate responsibility between the different departments.

The Social Welfare Department should set up a Standing Coordinating Committee presided over by the Minister of Education and Social Welfare and consisting of the Secretaries and Advisers of the concerned Ministries and Departments to coordinate and take decisions on schemes of the Social Welfare Department to be dealt in some aspects by other Ministries and Departments and vice versa. For an effective coordination it is also desirable for these committees to meet at least quarterly every year.

Coordination Committee consisting of the representatives of all Central Ministries concerned with the development schemes should be constituted by the Department of Welfare of Backward Classes under the Ministry of Home Affairs, which would review the working of the development programmes in relation to the welfare of backward classes and suggest such changes as would be necessary from time to time.

The State Welfare Departments may set up Coordination Committees consisting of Secretaries and Advisers of other concerned departments, presided over by the Minister Incharge of the Welfare Department.

It will be desirable to reconstitute the Standing Committees of the Ministry of Commerce & Industry by taking in representatives of the CSWB, Social Welfare Department and the All-India Boards. Such Committees consisting of the representative of the State Boards, the State Welfare Departments and the State branches of All-India Boards may also be set up at the State level.

There should be periodic conferences of the Secretaries of the Welfare Departments, the concerned Directorates, and the Secretary and other officers of the Social Welfare Department in the Ministry of Education and Social Welfare. Representatives of the Central Social Welfare Board and the State Social Welfare Boards may also be invited to these conferences.

Coordination may be achieved through the representation of State Boards in the proposed Inter-Departmental Coordination Committees to be set up by the Welfare Department.

Financial Administration

It may be considered whether the date for the formulation of schemes could be somewhat advanced without ignoring the need for having a realistic assessment of resources.

On the analogy of certain schemes in the Centrally-sponsored programme it may be prescribed that, in respect of the schemes not exceeding a total outlay of Rs. 25 lakhs over the plan period or of Rs. 10 lakhs during the year, the Central Ministry should accord their approval on the basis of a statement from the State Governments to the effect that the schemes have obtained the approval of the respective technical departments or bodies in the State.

A suitable re-allocation of subjects in each group of schemes may be attempted in consultation with the State Governments.

The requirement of prior Central approval may be done away with in respect of the Centrally-sponsored schemes, as in the case of the schemes in the State Plans. However, the Central Government may specify the areas or the categories of schemes in which more intensive effort is required and may earmark specific sums for the purpose which cannot be appropriated to other schemes.

The Central Government may consider the sharing of expenditure on additional establishment in the field in respect of schemes for backward classes in the State Plans.

The present procedure regarding release of grants may be reviewed at the end of the Second Plan with reference to the progress noticed in the performance on the schemes.

The State Governments should take steps to see that the prescribed progress reports reach the Home Ministry on the stipulated dates. It will be useful to have a Central Cell in the State Department to collect the information on a continuous basis.

The State Governments should make efforts towards formulation of schemes in relevant details in time for the annual Plan discussions, and that no scheme should be provided for in the Plan or in each year of the Plan till its chances of being taken up during the said period are fairly certain.

The scrutiny legitimately exercisable by the Finance Department, should, with advantage, be carried out in all its details at only the budgetary stage, i.e., before the schemes are included in the budget with the safeguard that for schemes involving a substantial outlay (ceilings to be specified) a reference has to be made to them again before they are sanctioned.

The State Government may, on the analogy of the Central Government, discontinue the practice of making lump-sum provision in their budgets.

The situation regarding the scrutiny and approval of the Technical Departments may be remedied in one or more of the following ways:

(a) The representatives of all the Technical Departments concerned may be associated at the time of the formulation of the schemes at the budgetary stage and their approval obtained. In case it is not possible to finalise certain aspects or details of the schemes at that stage or certain doubts or differences are not settled then, it should be possible for the sponsoring Department to obtain the approval of the Technical Departments on these specified matters later during the course of the year.

An attempt may be made to segregate small scale

schemes which are not very significant from the technical point of view from other schemes and some delegation in respect of the former may be made in favour of the sponsoring department or executing department, as the case may be. The State Governments may consider in this connection, the raising of the limit of expenditure beyond which it is necessary to obtain approval of the Works Deptt., provided the works are brought to a standard approved design. In some cases it may not really be necessary to prepare detailed plans and estimates and the work may be left to be carried out by the beneficiaries themselves.

On the analogy of the experiment made in Bihar, a unit of the Works Department may be earmarked for speedy sanction and approval of works programmes in the scheme for welfare of backward classes.

For schemes which must necessarily have the approval of the Technical Departments and are such as cannot be finalised at the budgetary stage, it will be desirable to entrust execution also to the Technical Departments, as this will cut short the delay in the process of obtaining approval by the sponsoring Department.

The Department dealing with the welfare of backward classes should have a separate budget grant of its own for which it would be answerable to the Legislature.

The area of execution by other Departments may cover only :

(i) Such schemes which are not different in content and form from other schemes of development ; and

(ii) The schemes which require technical expertise available only to those Departments.

The officers of other Departments executing the schemes should be directly responsible and accountable to the sponsoring Department irrespective of the fact that the expenditure has to be sanctioned by the executing Department.

For schemes to be executed by the Department dealing with backward classes the District Welfare Officers of the Department may be given wider power of execution than at present. For example, minor adjustment between items of a scheme need not be referred by them to the Directorate for prior approval and they may have more funds at their disposal for contingencies, etc.

The Government of India, in consultation with the Comptroller and Auditor General, may devise a suitable method to ensure the accuracy and authenticity of the expenditure on schemes for the welfare of backward classes in the State Plans as also in the Centrally-sponsored programmes financed from the Central grants.

An attempt should be made to ascertain the expenditure incurred by the State Governments on the welfare of backward classes in relation to schemes other than those that are assisted by the Home Ministry. The Ministries in the Central and the State Governments, should periodically furnish the Home Ministry with accounts of grants by the Central Government on the welfare of backward classes so that the Home Ministry are in a position to co-relate them with the special assistance given by them to the State Governments.

The Central Government may consider a change in financial year from April 1, as at present, to July 1.

Recruitment And Training Of Welfare Personnel

(a) Category (a)—positions—'administrative and senior supervisory'—should be filled by persons with minimum graduate qualifications plus two years of training in social work.

(b) Category (b) positions—'intermediate supervisory'—should be filled by persons recruited at the intermediate level with two years of training in social work, or in the alternative, from among graduates with one year of training in social work.

(c) Category (c) positions—'field level workers'—should be drawn from among matriculates with two years of training in social work.

The Advisory Board on Social Welfare should be suitably reorganised and provided with the necessary executive machinery to undertake the following functions:

(i) Organisation of a system of recognition for training institutions in the different fields of welfare;

(ii) Approval of the syllabii of these institutions and definition of minimum standards for educational practice;

(iii) Development of text books and teaching materials based on Indian conditions; and

(iv) Development of field work programmes under the supervision of trained staff as an integral part of the various training programmes.

Steps should be taken to relate the admission policy of training institutions with the requirements of welfare personnel to man development programmes ; personnel requirements should be estimated on a five-year basis and the admission policy should cover not only the total numbers involved but should also take into account the special welfare fields for which personnel are required.

As most of the existing training institutions are located in the urban areas, new training institutions should, as far as possible, be located in or within easy reach of the rural areas so that the training programmes are conducted in a more appropriate setting.

While all new recruits will be drawn from among trained personnel, orientation courses should be organised for untrained personnel, already in position.

Undergraduate training programmes should be organised on a two-year basis to prepare students for specific careers as mukhya sevikas, superintendents of welfare institutions, etc.

The undergraduate and graduate training programmes should be linked together so that experienced welfare workers could qualify themselves for higher responsibilities on the completion of suitable training courses.

The duration of the training course for gram sevikas should be extended to a minimum period of two years.

The various courses taught at the training centres should be directly related to the actual duties and problems that the staff will be called upon to deal with in the field, and more time should be set apart for courses on child-psychology, pre-school education and an understanding of the social forces that govern rural life.

A distinction should be drawn between domestic crafts and economic crafts and the gram sevikas should be made proficient to teach domestic crafts, as an alternative to providing a separate craft instructor.

Training programmes should integrate class-room instruction with a field-work programme supervised by trained staff, this field-work programme should be phased over the two-year training period on the following basis:

(i) A period of field-work in a project centre with limited responsibility given to the trainee for running specific items of the programme over a period of a year as a supplement to class-room instruction ; and

(ii) An extended period of field work, say three months, during which time the trainee will be posted to work with a gram sevika and will shoulder responsibilities that are almost equivalent to the actual work situation.

In order to further enrich the field-work experience, Government should entrust the training institutions with projects and programmes on an experimental basis. The successful methods evolved in these projects could also be adopted in other projects.

New training centres should appropriately be located near other training centres at block headquarters.

The two district training programmes for gram sevikas, conducted at present by Kasturba Gandhi National Memorial Trust and the Home Economics Wing, should be integrated at an early date on the following lines :

(i) The content of the two training programmes should be identical ;

(ii) Minimum training standards should be observed by both programmes in respect of the number of trained teachers, the teacher-pupil ratio, the organisation of field work, the maintenance of libraries and the scientific orientation given to trainees;

(iii) Text books should be prepared in the context of field conditions; and

(iv) Each training centre should have at least one trained teacher drawn from the field of education, another from home economics and a third from social welfare. The cooperation of visiting lecturers can be secured from the rural extension training centres for the conduct of courses on agriculture and animal husbandry.

Periodic refresher courses should be organised for trained field staff, who have completed a period of service on the lines followed by the Home Economics Wing.

For those already serving in the field or in supervisory positions, short-term in-service training should be provided so as to bring them on par with others who may receive the proposed training.

Orientation courses should be provided for all the technical personnel, namely, teachers, engineers, overseers, doctors and other health personnel who are required to work among Scheduled Tribes or in Scheduled Areas.

With regard to the extent of the training programmes for the auxiliary nurse-cum-midwives undertaken by the Ministry of Health, a standard syllabus should be followed which should include a course in family planning.

Minimum standards should be maintained in the recruitment of teachers for the training centres in terms of training and experience in their particular fields of specialisation, e.g., education, home economics and social welfare work.

Incentives should be given to attract teachers of the necessary calibre to these training centres in terms of improved salary scales, special allowances and arrangements for deputation from existing departments.

Orientation programmes should be provided for these teachers in terms of special requirements of a welfare programme.

Refresher courses should be organised at intervals to keep these teachers in touch with changing problems in the welfare field.

The minimum educational qualification of the trainees should be the matriculation standard.

The trainees may perferably be drawn from within the age-group 25-35 years.

The trainees should be selected from among persons with a rural background.

The trainees, especially those recruited for work in tribal areas, should be assisted during the training period in acquiring proficiency in the local language.

The field staff at present employed by the CSWB, for the purposes of the WEP programme, e.g., gram sevikas, mukhya sevikas should be absorbed into permanent Government service and should then be deputed to work in the WEP's.

The salary scales of the field staff should be equated with the scales paid to other field staff under other departments.

Opportunities should be provided for promotion of gram sevikas on the basis of merit to the next higher post of mukhya sevika.

Adequate and cheap accommodation should be provided for the gram sevikas in the village centres.

Welfare programmes at the planning, administrative, supervisory and field levels must be executed with the aid of trained personnel.

Union and State cadres for welfare personnel should be constituted.

Recruitment to these cadres should be done through Public Service Commissions from among candidates with qualifications prescribed by the Advisory Board on Social Welfare.

As an interim measure, the senior posts may be filled by officers from the administrative services to the extent trained and experienced welfare workers are not available to take over these responsibilities.

Opportunities should be provided for workers to move to the higher levels on the basis of merit and experience.

In addition to direct recruitment to these cadres, opportunities should be given for the absorption of persons already on the job on the completion of prescribed training programmes.

Evaluation Of Welfare Programmes

The Office of the Commissioner for Scheduled Castes and Scheduled Tribes should continue to undertake an evaluation of the work of the Central and the State Governments for the welfare of backward classes and the office of the Commissioner should be strengthened with appropriately qualified research personnel.

A new unit should be set up in the Programme Evaluation Organisation and staffed with appropriately qualified persons to undertake the work of evaluation of social welfare programmes.

Evaluation machinery both of the Programme Evaluation Organisation and the Commissioner's office will have to be duly strengthened particularly at the State level.

Non-official experts should be associated with the evaluation undertaken by the proposed agencies.

ROAD TRANSPORT REORGANISATION COMMITTEE 1958, REPORT

New Delhi, Ministry of Transport and Communications, 1959, 154p.

Chairman : Shri M.R. Masani.

Members : Shri Harish Chandra Mathur; Shri C.R. Pattabhi Raman; Shri Mahabir Prasad Bhargava; Shri Chandan Mal Baid; Shri Govind Sahai; Shri D.S. Rathor; Shri J.B. Bowman; Shri T.S. Santhanam; Shri Kundan Lal; Shri S.R. Kalyanaraman.

Secretaries : Shri C.S. Nair; Shri P.S. Rajagopala Raju.

APPOINTMENT

In order to secure the fuller development of road motor transport and its expansion to meet the demand created the Second Five Year Plan, it is essential that there should be suitable machinery in the States to look after the various problems facing the industry and to plan and foster its development. It is felt that the existing administrative set-up in most States is concerned more with the regulation of motor transport rather than its planned development. To assist the States in reorganising their transport administration, the Government of India have decided to appoint an Ad Hoc Committee to conduct a comprehensive enquiry and make recommendations for the re-organisation of the transport administrative set-up in the States. Accordingly this Committee was constituted under the Ministry of Transport and Communications (Department of Transport) vide their Resolution No. 31-T(39)/55, dated May 5, 1958.

TERMS OF REFERENCE

(1) To survey the existing machinery for the administration of motor transport in the States, with particular reference to the working of the Regional Transport Authorities and State Transport Authorities and their suitability of look after the development, coordination and regulation of road transport consistently with the economic development of the country *vis-a-vis* our successive Five-Year Plans and the need to expand motor transport to rural areas in order to develop village economy.

(2) To suggest a model administrative set-up which will ensure:

(a) The fair and speedy disposal of applications for permits;

(b) The healthy growth of motor transport, providing efficient services and adequate amenities to the public;

(c) The elimination of inhibitory factors which stand in the way of the development of motor transport;

(d) Adequate development of truck-trailer combinations;

(e) The fullest use of available road facilities and transport vehicles and

(f) Proper coordination with the activities and functions of the Inter-State Transport Commission.

(3) To make any other recommendations germane to the subject matter of the inquiry.

CONTENTS

Introduction; A Bird's Eye View; Retrospect; Inhibitory Factors; Licensing Policy; Administrative Set-up; Summary of the main Conclusions and Recommendations; Note of Dissent; Annexures; List of Appendices to Report; Appendices I to VIII.

RECOMMENDATIONS

A Bird's Eye View

The mileage of roads in relation to territory and population compares unfavourably with that in other countries and even the existing roads are not being fully and properly utilised.

The transport business is generally lucrative but unfortunately this is not always reflected in the prosperity and well-being of those engaged in it.

Conditions in passenger transport leave a great deal to be desired. In regard to goods transport the public suffers from the limitations of transport arising from the policy of restrictive licensing.

There is no uniformity in the various States in the structure of administration that deals with road transport.

The staffing of the transport administration at various levels, including the Transport Department at the Centre in far from satisfactory and the expansion of facilities under the momentum of economic forces has far outrun the administrative machinery provided to deal with it.

Retrospect

The Motor Vehicles Act, 1939, created for the first time comprehensive machinery for the administration of road transport.

The pattern that might have emerged for the healthy development of motor transport was, however, distorted because of the non-availability of vehicles and the paucity of spare-parts due to World War II.

In 1945 even though transport shortage was still continuing, the Government of India issued a Code of Principles and Practice which resulted in throttling the development of road transport.

The burden of taxation which was one of the causes of retarded development, was aggravated as certain States made use of specific recommendations of the Motor Vehicle Taxation Enquiry Committee, 1950, to enhance their revenues instead of accepting its general recommendation of a ceiling on taxes.

In spite of the amendments to the Motor Vehicle Act in 1956, designed to meet the growing needs of road transport there has been little improvement in the general condition of transport. Most States have failed even to frame rules under the new Act.

Out of 18 States and centrally administered areas, 17 administrations have partially nationalised passenger services within their territories, some fairly extensively as in Bombay and Uttar Pradesh and others to a smaller extent. Only three of these administrations have established corporations under the Road Transport Corporations Act, namely, Andhra Pradesh, Bombay and the former Pepsu, while some States are contemplating doing so. In the majority of the States the nationalised services are run departmentally as State Undertakings. Quantitatively, nationalised services are run departmentally as state undertakings. Quantitatively, nationalised services operate only a small proportion of the total volume of road transport.

Inhibitory Factors

Inadequate surfaced roads and bridges, rigid load restrictions, lack of encouragement to truck-trailer combinations, inadequate supply of vehicles, multiplicity of taxes, absence of reeiprocal agreements between States, absence of viable units, lack of proper credit facilities and the fear of nationalisation or some of the inhibitory factors that stand in the way of the development of transport.

Roads and Bridges

A larger provision for road construction with improved surface and width is necessary to cope with modern vehicles including trailers.

Particularly high priority should be given to the allocation of foreign exchange for buying high tensile steel required to construct about 116 major bridges which are holding up through traffic on our National Highways.

Interim arrangements like providing suitable diversions, allowing the use of railway bridges, ferrying motor vehicles in rail cars and providing ferries should be made pending the construction or strengthening of bridges and culverts.

A fresh examination is necessary to permit a fuller utilisation of national investment both in roads and motor vehicles as the present limits of laden weights are low and unduly conservative in character. The Roads Wing of the Ministry of Transport and Communications and the Indian Roads Congress may consider placing the services and advice of experts at the disposal of the States in ascertaining whether the existing limits cannot safely be revised.

So far as Nātional Highways are concerned, a uniform limit of 12 tons on two axles may be prescribed. The unscientific method of fixing maximum vehicle weights irrespective of the number of axles should be replaced by a scientific way of ascertaining safe axle load.

The use of trailers and semi-trailers is an effective means of maximising transport facilities within the available truck manufacturing capacity of the country and of protecting the roads and bridges through the distribution of loads. They will also help in reducing the cost of operations and affording economies in foreign exchange.

To encourage the extensive use of the multiple unit vehicles, tax concessions and preference for Government contracts should be provided.

Supply Of Vehicles

The present gap in the supply of transport vehicles should be looked into by the Ministries of Transport and Communications and Commerce and Industry and the Planning Commission who may devise ways and means to accelerate the production of commercial vehicles.

There is need for larger allocations of foreign exchange to ensure an adequate supply of vehicles, parts and tyres for the development of transport.

Taxation

Octrois, wheel taxes and other imposts charged by municipalities as well as the tax on passengers and goods carried should be discontinued, octroi being merged in the general sales tax and the other imposts in the vehicle tax.

Sales tax on trucks and buses should not be at luxury rates but at rates applicable to essential goods.

In certain States the fees charged are so high as to contain a substantial element of taxation. Fees should be so lowered to correspond to the services rendered and amounts realised should be spent on providing adequate services in the Department.

Impediments To Diesel

With reference to the increased duty proposed to be levied on diesel oil, the Committee is of the opinion that having regard to the efficiency of diesel fuel, no impediments should be placed in the path of dieselisation. Necessary supplies of diesel oil should be obtained as it is worthwhile paying the price in foreign exchange.

Reciprocal Agreements

Multiple taxation is a great hindrance to through traffic between States. Legislation paying down the principles of taxation and providing for a single point tax should be introduced in Parliament.

Viable Units

The formation of efficient enterprises should be encouraged in all reasonable and legitimate ways, but no ban should be placed on the owner of a single truck in the case of goods transport.

For intra-regional operation of goods services, there should be on ban no the owner of a single truck but, for a State-wide operation, the unit should consist of a minimum of five vehicles and for inter-State operations of 10 vehicles.

For the operation of passenger transport services, a minimum of at least five buses should be required as an operator with a single bus cannot guarantee efficient or regular service.

The form of ownership should not be of any relevance since what is of importance is the efficiency of management. Ownership may vest in a joint stock company, a partnership firm, an individual, a cooperative society or members of a Union.

Rules should be framed for licensing the booking and forwarding agents.

Credit Facilities

The Reserve Bank may issue directives to the State Bank and Scheduled Banks to advance money to hire purchase concerns and Cooperative Banks and operators for helping the industry.

The State Finance Corporations also should lend money to operators and proper machinery should be set up to regulate the interest to be charged by the intermediaries.

The development rebate granted to the shipping and scheduled industries should be granted to the road transport industry also.

Nationalisation

The expansion of road transport has been grossly inadequate and there is ample room for both the State and private sectors to expand.

Nationalisation should be resorted to only if such a step is necessary in the opinion of the State Government for providing efficient, adequate, economic and properly coordinated services. For the efficient working of the private sector a sense of security should be instilled in them by nationalising only according to a phased programme.

The existing moratorium on nationalisation of goods transport should be extended for a period of at least 10 years from the end of the Third Five-Year Plan.

Licensing Policy

The Motor Vehicles Act, 1939, contains many provisions which create an impression that its objective was to restrict rather than develop road transport.

Restrictions on road transport have meant loss of revenue to the Centre and the States.

Road transport will inevitably play a far greater role in India than at any time in the past and will have to be developed on a large scale.

The principle of road-rail coordination has been working in a one-sided way. This is evident in the persistent attempts to impose distance limits on goods transport.

Technological developments in the field of transport in other countries clearly show a definite trend towards roads and any attempt to cling to Railways would be to do grave injury to the interests of the country.

The task of the planner in a democratic society is to balance the free choice of the consumer with the needs of the maximum utilisation of resources invested in the various forms of transport.

The fact that Railways are allegedly losing revenue because of road competition is a clear indication of the preference of road transport by public. It is desirable that railway freight rates should have some relation to the cost of operation. They cannot ask for restrictions on other forms of transport on the ground that they follow a rate structure of a particular pattern.

The claim of the Railways that it is not in the national interest to encourage road transport because their average cost of carriage is less than the road cost is not borne out by facts.

Private carriers' permits for bona fide use should be issued without any restrictions and the permits may be valid in the State or as many States as desired.

Within the estimated overall capacity of the State, the issue of intra-State public carriers' permits should be free and unrestricted subject to the allocation of a certain number of permits to each region in order to ensure all-sided development.

All intra-State permits issued for goods vehicles should be valid for the whole of the State subject to the proviso that any operator can confine himself to a region and pay a lower rate of tax. The present permit holders should be given the option to secure State-wide validity subject to eligibility.

Stage carriage permits should continue to be issued for specific routes but the number of stage carriages that should ply on each route should be fixed and reviewed annually.

A more liberal policy should be followed in the grant of stage carriage permits until travel facilities catch up with the demand, and permit holders with good records should have a guarantee of renewal.

All applicants for new stage carriage permits should own at least five vehicles, but in order to allow suitable new operators to enter the field, permits for intra-regional operation may be granted to them subject to the condition that the permit holder should join a viable unit within a period of four months.

The qualifications for inter-State permits should be operation of a minimum of 10 vehicles in the case of goods vehicles and five vehicles in the case of stage carriages.

States may be left free to initiate and negotiate proposals but the Inter-State Transport Commission should be invested with powers to issue permits in case of need. The Commission should also be armed with necessary executive staff for proper functioning instead of being wholly dependent on the States.

The Inter-State Transport Commission may function on the lines of U.S. Inter-State Commerce Commission.

On the basis of the present powers vested in the Inter-State Transport Commission the Committee recommends that the Commission should receive proposals from the States relating to inter-State traffic by the end of December every year and take necessary action.

Permits for inter-State transport of goods should be issued following a liberal policy somewhat on the system prevailing in the U.S.A., where the governing factor is public convenience and necessity, to meet all felt needs.

The possibilities of developing tourism are almost unlimited. Lack of comfortable vehicles, difficulty in obtaining permits and double taxation on vehicles are handicaps to the development of tourism.

Permits for tourists vehicles should be issued freely to operators with viable units having suitable facilities.

Steps should be taken to expand transport facilities in rural areas.

Those who are willing to operate stage carriages exclusively on unmetalled roads should be given every encouragement including tax concession.

Private goods vehicles of upto 8,000 lbs. laden should require no permits.

There is avoidable delay and litigation in the matter of grant of permits and other matters and there is great need to simplify the procedure to avoid these things. The following suggestions are *inter-alia* made for the simplification of procedure:—

(i) The number of stage carriage and public carrier's vehicles should be fixed by the State Transport Authority on the recommendations of the Planning and Development Wing.

(ii) The time taken for publishing the applications should be reduced and they should be disposed of within three months.

(iii) Permit holders with good record should have guarantee of renewal and permits should be deemed to have been renewed if orders are not passed within a specified time.

(iv) Rules should be framed for selecting applicants for grant of stage carriage permits.

(v) Applications for variation of permits should be treated as applications for new permits.

(vi) All appeals and revisions should end at the level of the State Transport Appellate Tribunal.

(vii) All amendments made by the States prior to the Central amendments of 1956 should be repealed.

Administrative Set-Up

The present administrative set-up in the States is altogether inadequate for the task of developing road transport and should be overhauled.

There should be a Transport Ministry in each State to deal exclusively with Roads and Road Transport and such a Ministry should be under the Transport Minister exclusively devoted to these subjects. In the Ministry there should be a Roads Wing under a Chief Engineer and a Transport Wing under a Transport Commissioner. There should be a Secıetary to coordinate both the Wings.

Under the Transport Commissioner there should be three Deputy Transport Commissioners each one separately dealing with (i) enforcement, (ii) licensing and registration of vehicles and (iii) planning and development.

A Planning and Development Wing should be created and the Deputy Transport Commissioner-in-charge should be an expert in economics of transport and traffic engineering. He should be provided with suitable and adequate staff for collecting reliable data and assessing traffic.

State Transport Authorities should be constituted with an official Chairman with judicial experience, two other official members and two non-official members. The Transport Commissioner should normally be the Chairman of the State Transport Authority. Non-officials should be representatives of bodies like Chambers of Commeree and Trade Associations.

Neither the Railways nor road transport Operators should be represented on the State Transport Authorities.

The size of a region of a Regional Transport Authority may remain flexible depending on the administrative convenience. But the criteria in determining the size should be the convenience of the public and in case of large-sized regions there should be a Branch Office of Regional Transport Authorities at each district headquarters.

A single member Regional Transport Authority constituted with an official with requisite experience is best suited in view of the scheme of administration that the Committee has suggested.

The Secretaries of Regional Transport Authorities should be full-time officers.

All appeals and revision petitions should be heard by a State Transport Appellate Tribunal constituted with a full-time judicial officer and no provision for a second appeal need be made.

In Centrally administered areas roads and road transport should be dealt with one and the same officer at the Administrative level. The Secretary of the State Transport Authority should be a full-time officer and Head of the Department in the place of Transport Commissioner suggested for States. The State Transport Authorities should be constituted with Judicial Secretary as Chairman and two-official members and two other non-official members. The Chief Commissioner or a member of the judiciary should be the Appellate Tribunal to hear all appeals and revisions.

The rationing of permits and the consequent shortage of essential services is the root cause of corruption.

The main responsibility for ensuring purity in administration should be placed on the executives of the State Transport Authorities and Regional Transport Authorities.

The present dual control of the Police and Transport departments regarding enforcement is not satisfactory and complaints of harassment are numerous. For better enforcement the functions of the two departments should be specified. The Transport Department should be in full charge of enforcement excepting traffic with which the police should be concerned.

Operators should not be punished unless their connivance in offences committed by drivers is proved and minor offences should be compounded.

Registration, licensing and taxation should be attended to by Regional Transport Officers or Assistant Regional Transport Officers.

The registering authorities should maintain and supply relevant statistics not only to State Transport Authorities but also to those applying for them.

Claims Tribunals should be set up in all States to ensure the payment of compensation to those involved in accidents.

The anomalous position of one and the same officer being in charge of the administration of the Motor Vehicles Act and running the State Transport services is not favoured. It is imperative that wherever transport is nationalised the operation and administration should be kept independent of each other.

There should be a Transport Advisory Committee in each State composed of heads of departments concerned with various aspects of transport, members of the Legislative Assembly, representatives of road transport, operators of other forms of transport, nominees of Chambers of Commerce and Commercial interests and organisations interested in the development of road transport, with the Transport Minister as President to advice on the development of road transport.

The organisation of the transport department at the Centre is sketchy. It already has a large volume of work to handle and its duties will increase considerably under the new set-up.

The strength of the Transport Wing in the Union Ministry of Transport and Communications should be considerably enlarged and the head of the Department should be a Joint Secretary dealing exclusively with road transport.

IRRIGATION AND POWER TEAM ON KOYNA PROJECT (BOMBAY STATE), 1958—REPORT

New Delhi, Committee on Plan Projects, 1959, 130p.+iiip+Maps & Charts.

Leader : Shri N.V. Gadgil.
Members : Shri Balwant Singh Nag; Shri M.P. Mathrani.
Secretary : Shri D.S. Borker.

APPOINTMENT

The Irrigation and Power Team on Koyna Project (Bombay State) was constituted under the Committee on Plan Projects vide their Memorandum No. COPP/4/(14)/58, dated May 13, 1958.

TERMS OF REFERENCE

To make a study of various aspects of the Projects, in particular :

(1) The aspects of the Project having a bearing on economy and efficiency with special reference to :

(a) Utilisation of trained personnel and materials;

(b) Utilisation of machinery and equipment;

(c) Construction Plant lay-out;

(d) Adequacy of original estimates and designs as evidenced from actual construction of the project;

(e) Phasing of construction with a view to studying whether:

(i) Timely utilisation of benefits accruing from the project has been ensured;

(ii) It is possible to accelerate accrual of benefits; and

(iii) Benefits could be increased by rephasing the project at this stage;

(f) Sufficiency of investigations conducted at the planning stage with a view to the formulation of project estimates;

(g) The effect of the above study on the financial results of the Project, if any.

(2) Generally to assess the progress made in construction, the reasons for shortfall, if any, and to suggest measures for improvements in the future;

(3) To examine the possibility of decreasing dependence upon imported materials and equipment required for the project.

(4) To examine whether adequate steps have been taken by the authorities concerned for fixing and realising the contemplated water rates, betterment fees and/or any other rates, cesses or taxes; and

(5) To report on any other aspect that the Team may like, in order to ensure economy and efficiency in the construction of the project.

CONTENTS

Preface; History and Scope of Project; Administration; Power Generation and Utilisation; Industrial and Irrigation Development; Phasing of Construction Programme; Features of Design and Construction; Costs of Project; Agencies of Construction; Summary; Appendices i to xi; Maps and Charts.

RECOMMENDATIONS

The present Koyna scheme envisages utilising 67,500 million cu.ft. of water for an installed generating capacity of 4,80,000 KW of electricity and providing 41,000 million cu.ft. of water for irrigation purposes. The first stage of the scheme, in its present form to develop 240,000 KW of power, was finalised in December 1952 when it was estimated to cost Rs. 33.22 crores. This estimate was revised to Rs. 38.28 crores in October 1956 so as to accommodate the technical changes recommended by Swiss Consultants and the higher tendered costs. The delivery of power was scheduled for October 1960 and it has now been revised to July 1961.

Establishment for the project is sanctioned from year to year. The Team, however, recommends that an overall sanction should be given for the period of the project and the Chief Engineers authorised to operate thereon. This will save time and labour both of the Chief Engineers and the Control Board.

The Team further recommends the following with a view to providing necessary incentive to the temporary personnel on the project :

(i) Immediate implementation of the Control Board's recommendation to give temporary subordinate staff a lien in permanent Circles of Public Works Department; and

(ii) Immediate creation of permanent posts, both gazetted and non-gazetted, required on completion of the project and absorbing deserving personnel against them.

All the 240,000 KW of electricity generated on completion of the first stage of the project is expected to be consumed by October 1964 and therefore it would not be possible to postpone the second stage by 10 years as originally contemplated. It is therefore necessary to merge the second stage with the first and to rephase the project so that the fifth unit of the Project is commissioned soon after October 1964. It would therefore seem necessary that the dam should be raised in continuation of the first stage to a height sufficient to store 57,000 M.C. Ft. of water required for second stage power generation.

The cost and selling rate of power are stated in October 1956 Project Report as 0.38 and 0.45 anna per unit respectively. These rates are neither related to what the industries can pay without detriment to their progress nor to costs of thermal power as an alternative. It is hoped that the Tariff Committee will duly weigh these factors and decide upon tariffs which, after meeting the working expenses, interest and depreciation charges, will yield sufficient surplus for reserves and contingencies.

It is the view of the Team that the main concern in utilisation of power should be to avoid concentration of industries in Bombay area, if the problems arising from such concentration are to be avoided. It would therefore be desirable to give priority to the establishment of as many industries in the Koyna area as possible thereby enabling exploitation of the natural resources locally available such as bauxites as well as other raw materials which can be economically brought by sea for electro-chemical and other industries.

The ample tail waters should help in developing the Dabhol Creek into a port. The potentiality of this Creek in this regard needs to be speedily assessed and exploited.

It should be possible to irrigate about 5,000 acres of land on the banks of the tail race channel by diverting a fraction of the tail waters. This as well as other possible uses of tail waters such as water supply to towns and villages, etc. should be investigated.

The Koyna Dam was originally planned to store 98,000 M.C. Ft. of water (57,000 for power, 31,000 for irrigation in Satara and Bijapur Districts and 10,000 for carryover). Since November 1956, Bijapur District has been transferred to the reorganised Mysore State. In May 1958 the Bombay Government decided to utilise 16,000 M.C. Ft. of water for flow irrigation of about 1 lakh acres in North and South Satara Districts in Bombay State. The project estimate for this irrigation scheme is not yet ready. The feasibility of this irrigation scheme therefore cannot be judged at present. The Government of Bombay addressed the Government of Mysore in may 1958 regarding sharing the cost of storage required by Mysore State. The Mysore Government has not yet taken a decision. The two States should come to an early agreement so that the programme of construction for the full development can be finalised.

The Team wishes to stress the importance of undertaking the immediate re-allocation of Krishna waters, consequent to reorganisation of States.

The tempo of some of the works like concreting of the dam and excavation of pressure shafts is not at present adequate to achieve the revised target of power generation in July 1961. The capacity of the concreting rig is only about 60% of that required for completing the job in time and needs to be supplemented immediately. Similarly, steps need to be taken to improve the technique of excavation of the pressure shafts so as to achieve the required progress. The steel lining of pressure shafts may also prove a bottleneck and may require foreign expert supervision. The project authorities have standing arrangements with their Swiss Consultants for obtaining advice and assistance of experts in the line when necessary. This may be availed of if any difficulty is experienced.

The Thana Creek Crossing which is a complicated work may prove yet another bottleneck unless immediate steps are taken to start construction there.

According to October 1956 estimate, the spillway portion of the dam was to he constructed to full width required for the final storage of 98,000 M.C. Ft. both in foundation and superstructure. In the non-spillway portion the foundations were to be of full width required for the final storage, but the superstructure was to be of a width required for the first stage storage of 36,000 M.C. Ft. On account of the expected rapid load development, as it would not have permitted of a time lag of 10 years between construction of first and second stages which was considered necessary for attaining equilibrium of the first stage concrete before the second stage concrete could be started, the Bombay Government have modified this programme. In this modified programme it it proposed to construct foundations of the spillway portion to full width required for final storage, but the superstructure has been reduced to suit a storage of 73,000 M.C. Ft. required for power and irrigation in Bombay state. The non-spillway portion is proposed to be constructed both in foundation and super-structure of width required for a storage of 73,000 M.C. Ft. This modification in the programme is likely to make the construction work for the final storage of 98,000 M.C. Ft. both difficult and costly. The cost of the extra work on dam for storing 98,000 M.C. Ft. instead of 73,000 M.C. Ft. will be only Rs. 2.2 crores.

This extra cost is amply justified both on account of the additional benefits of power and irrigation.

The modification in the construction programme to finish both the foundation and the superstructure of the dam to full width required for 98 T.M.C. Ft. storage would involve an additional quantity of 3.7 M.C. Ft. to be finished by May 1961. It is understood that this increase in quantity of concrete to be finished by May 1961 will lead to complications with the contractors in respect of rates and completion programme. It is considered that any further postponement in generation of power will have serious dislocating consequences in the industrial activity in Bombay region. In view of these difficulties it would not be advisable to alter the programme of construction materially. It is, however, considered that there will be great difficulty in thickening the superstructure of the spillway portion later on. Apart from constructional difficulties, there will be very limited time during the working season to do this work. The total extra quantity of concrete involved in this work is 0.88 M.C. Ft. of which only 0.55 M.C. Ft. will need to be done before May 1961. This will mean an increase of about two per cent in the quantity of concrete or about a fortnight's work for the concrete laying equipment. The Team, therefore, recommends that the present programme of construction may be adhered to except for the small modification suggested in the spillway superstructure in constructing it to a thickness required for ultimate storage of 98,000 M.C. Ft.

After completion of the first stage work, the work of the second stage should be carried out in continuation upto the level for storage of 57,000 M.C. Ft. required for power.

Subsequent work should be coordinated with irrigation schemes of the Koyna both in Bombay and Mysore.

In view of the necessity to develop the second stage power by 1965, the third and fourth pressure shafts and second cable tunnel will also have to be completed before that time. This work may be carried out departmentally as rock excavation work at present being executed by the department is much cheaper than similar work done through contractors. It would be desirable to take up this work immediately the tail race tunnel, which is being executed departmentally, is finished. This should be suitable as it would combine organisational interests with the requirements of the project.

The Dam is being built in rubble concrete which weighs more but costs less than ordinary concrete. Therefore, successful development of the technique of laying such concrete would go a long way in providing a cheaper alternative to pure concrete.

It is suggested that senior officer may be deputed for liaison work to arrange for the import licences, etc. At present there are considerable delays in obtaining them. This matter deserves immediate attention of Commerce and Industry Ministry, as there is the risk of targets not being attained, if such delays are not avoided.

The project authorities anticipate an excess of Rs. 2.31 crores on certain items and a saving of Rs. 2.16 crores on other items. No major excesses are anticipated.

The total project expenditure forecast for the period ending March 1958 was about Rs. 18.9 crores and the actual expenditure was only Rs. 9 crores. This has necessitated rephasing of expenditure.

A comparison of provision of residential area and expenditure thereon for different categories of personnel on various projects reveals a great deal of diversity. The Team recommends that the Ministry of Irrigation and Power should lay down standards both for type of construction and size of accommodation in consultation with the Buildings Projects Team of COPP.

The tenders for the works of Dam and Appurtenances, Approach and Ventilation Tunnels and Intake to Emergency Valve Tunnel, have all exceeded the estimated cost by 19 to 30 per cent. On some of the important items like concreting of the head race tunnel and pressure shafts the excess is of the order of 50 to 100 per cent. Under the terms of contracts 90 per cent of funds are advanced and foreign exchange provided to the contractors for purchase of machinery. In spite of these high rates and the facilities provided to the contractors, the works are not likely to be completed within the target date of October 1960 for generation of power. Therefore, the Team is of the opinion that such large works involving use of heavy machinery and extending over a number of years may be carried out departmentally using Government machinery and employing small contractors or piece-workers.

There has been a growing tendency towards curtailment of the powers of the Chief Engineers specially after the separation of the Chief Engineer's post from that of the Secretary to Government. For efficient departmental execution of such large projects, the Chief Engineer should be vested with full powers to give technical sanctions within project provisions, to place orders for plant and machinery required for the project after inviting public tenders, to order spare parts as and when required and to employ work-charged staff on suitable salaries after making detailed provision in the working estimates.

The work of tail race tunnel is the only big work being executed departmentally. The rate of underground excavation of the tunnel as reported by the Chief Engineer is about 66 per cent of the contractor's rate for similar work. Valuable data will be available when the concrete lining of this tunnel is oompleted departmentally.

The Team is glad to place on record that this large and complicated project was investigated thoroughly and has been prepared carefully, and that its execution is vested in an authority of the proper type.

IRRIGATION AND POWER TEAM ON NAGARJUNASAGAR PROJECT (ANDHRA PRADESH), 1958 REPORT

New Delhi, Committee on Plan Projects, 1960. 197p.+iiip.+Charts.

Leader : Shri N.V. Gadgil (replaced by Dr. A.N. Khosla).

Members : Shri Balwant Singh Nag; Shri M.P. Mathrani; Shri Lal Singh.

Secretary : Shri D.S. Borker.

APPOINTMENT

The Irrigation and Power Team on Nagarjunasagar Project (Andhra Pradesh) was constituted under the Committee on Plan Projects vide their Memorandum No. COPP/4(14)/58 dated May 13, 1958.

TERMS OF REFERENCE

To make a study of the various aspects of the two projects and of the following ones in particular :

1. The aspects of the project having a bearing on economy and efficiency with special reference to :

(a) Utilisation of trained personnel and materials;

(d) Utilisation of machinery and equipment;

(c) Construction Plan Lay-out;

(d) Adequacy of original estimates and designs as evidenced from actual construction of the Project;

(e) Phasing of construction with a view to studying whether.

(i) Timely utilisation of benefits accruing from the Project has been ensured;

(ii) It is possible to accelerate accrual of benefits; and

(iii) Benefits could be increased by rephasing the Project at this stage;

(f) Sufficiency of investigations conducted at the Planning stage with a view to the formulation of project estimates; and

(g) The effect of the above study on the financial results of the Project, if any.

(2) Generally to assess the progress made in construction, the reasons for shortfall, if any, and to suggest measures for improvements in the future;

(3) To examine the possibility of decreasing dependence upon imported materials and equipment required for the Project;

(4) To examine whether adequate steps have been taken by the authorities concerned for fixing and realising the contemplated water rates, betterment fees and/or any other rates, cesses or taxes; and

(5) To report on any other aspect that the Team may like, in order to ensure economy and efficiency in the construction of the Project.

CONTENTS

Preface; Scope of the Project; Availabitity of Water; Feasibility of First Phase Project; Integration of Srisailam and Nagarjunasagar Projects; Design Features; Construction Features; Phasing of Construction Programme; Power Development; Construction Costs; Irrigation Development and Agricultural Aspects; Summary; Appendices.

RECOMMENDATIONS

Scope And Estimated Cost Of The Project

The Joint Report prepared by Andhra and Hyderabad States in 1954 forms the basis of the present Project. The First Phase of the same, as estimated in October 1956, was to cost Rs. 85.5 crores to irrigate 20.6 lakh acres. This phase envisaged construction of a dam to a partial height up to F.R.L. 525, but to a full thickness required for the ultimate height up to F.R.L. 590. Irrigation was to be done as under :

	Lakh Acres
Delta	
First Crop	1.5
Second Crop	1.5
Right Bank Canal (140 miles)	
First crop	9.7
Left Bank Canal (108 miles)	
First Crop	6.7
Second Crop	1.2
	20.6

The estimate has since been revised due to increased cost of cement, steel, etc., and now amounts to Rs. 91.12 crores. The Control Board has given its approval to this estimate, but sanction of the Government of India is yet to be accorded.

Availability Of Water

The question of adjustment of allocations of Krishna waters, on the basis of 1951 Award, due to the reorganisation of the States is under consideration in the Ministry of Irrigation and Power. The Team recommends that this question should be finalised at an early date as already suggested in the Team's Report on Koyna Project.

The 1954 Nagarjunasagar Project is based on the yields of the Krishna river for the year 1929-30, which are 12 per cent in excess of the dependable yield assumed in the 1951 Award of the Planning Commission and give a dependability of 76 per cent against 86 per cent in the Award. On the basis of dependable yield of 1745 T.M.C. Feet assumed in the Award, there is just sufficient water for irrigation at Nagarjunasagar of the area provided in the final phase of 1954 Project. No water is available for (i) irrigation and evaporation losses at Srisailam and (ii) the extension of three-and-a-half lakh acres of irrigation on Nagarjunasagar left Bank Canal as now contemplated. The Central Water and Power Commission and the Project Authorities have suggested that in the interest of increasing production of food crops the dependability for assured irrigation projects in the Krishna Basin may be fixed at about 75 per cent. The Team recommends that 75 per cent dependability may be accepted for the purpose of sanctioning projects in the Krishna Basin. On this basis the above extra irrigation uses at Nagarjunasagar and Srisailam can almost be met.

The Project provides for 1.5 lakh acres of additional first crop irrigation in the Krishna Delta area. The area has already been provided with Krishna water under minor irrigation programme. The Project Authorities have now proposed taking up an equivalent additional area on Nagarjunasagar Canals. It is pointed out that water is not available, even on the basis of 75 per cent dependability, for this additional area. This point should be kept in mind in considering the availability of water for Krishna-Pennar Canal in case this additional area is retained on Nagarjunasagar Canals.

Feasibility Of First Phase Project

The Working Tables for the First Phase of 1954 Project are based on an assumption that no new projects out of the allocations of 1,000 T.M.C. Feet of Krishna waters to the various States will be undertaken by the Upper States, whereas a number of new projects are already under construction above Nagarjunasagar. The F.R.L. of 525 of Nagarjunasagar Reservoir provided in the First Phase of 1954 Project is hardly adequate for the irrigation of 20 lakh acres of first crop as the lowest reservoir level is shown as R.L. 486, in Table No. III of 1954 Project Report, whereas the sill level of the head sluices of the two Canals is at R.L. 490.

In spite of the above difficulty, the scope of the First Phase has been further increased in the 1956 First Phase estimate. The irrigation provided consists of 17.9 lakh acres of first crop, 2.7 lakh acres of second crop and 7.65 lakh acres of catch crops on the Left Bank Canal. No working tables seem to have been prepared to see, if it would be possible to do the second crop irrigation with F.R.L. 525 proposed for the revised First Phase. The Team has prepared Working Table No. 1.A for the first Phase irrigation as provided in 1956 Project for the year 1937-38, which is a year of 75 per cent dependability, on the assumption that the upper States will be utilising half of their allocations for the new projects which roughly tallies with the actual constructions undertaken. On this basis it is seen that only about two-thirds of the first crop irrigation and no second crop provided in the First Phase can be done. In view of these limitations it would be necessary (i) either to curtail the length of the Canals to do about two-thirds of the first crop irrigation or (ii) to complete the masonry of the Dam to the final height, leaving the installation of the gates to be done in the Second Phase and to do as much irrigation as possible with the raised F.R.L. 546 which is recommended to be kept as the sill level of the spillway gates.

The Team has prepared Working Table No. 1-B with F.R.L. 546 from which it will be observed that full first crop irrigation provided in 1956 Project and 1.25 lakh acres of the second crop in the Krishna Delta can be done. In addition, about 40 MW of continuous firm power can be generated. The extra masonry involved would be only aboul 20 M.C. Feet which is one extra season's work. This will cost about Rs. 2.5 crores if done in continuation of the present programme. It will cost much more, if postponed to the final phase. In view of the several advantages, the Team recommends the second alternative. The extra funds of Rs. 2.5 crores will be required in the first year of Fourth Five-Year Plan.

Integration Of Srisailam And Nagarjunasagar Projects

The storage provided in the final phase at Nagarjunasagar up to F.R.L. 590 is just adequate for the irrigation provided in the 1954 Project without support from any upper dams. By proper integrated working of Nagarjunasagar Dam with the Srisailam Dam to be constructed 64 miles upstream, the F.R.L. of Nagarjunasagar could have been lowered to F.R.L. 544 for all the assured irrigation benefits provided in 1954 Project and additional 3.5 lakh acres proposed to be provided on Left Bank Extension. This would have resulted in a reduction of Rs. 7.5 crores in the cost of the Dam.

The Srisailam Hydro-electric Project as contemplated by the State Government provides for a storage of 308 T.M.C. Feet upto F.R.L 885 of which 150 T.M.C. Feet from R.L. 885 to 854 is proposed to be let down in regulated flows for developing firm power of 260 MW at 60 per cent load factor. The minimum draw down level of 854 at Srisailam has been determined by the requirements of the Krishna-Pennar Canal.

The Team is of the view that there is scope for development of more firm hydro-power to the extent of 377 MW at 60 per cent load factor at Srisailam by lowering the draw-down level from R.L. 854 to R.L. 830, thus utilising 210 T.M.C. Feet of stored water for gene-

ration of power. The draw-down level will go below R.L. 854 for three fortnights only. It is feasible to install suitable reversible hydro-generating sets at Krishna-Pennar Canal intake. These units will be generating power normally; when reversed, they can pump water into the Krishna-Pennar Canal, when the lake levels are lower than the Canal supply levels. The power required for pumping in the three fortnights is small as compared with extra generation of 117 MW of firm power which is possible by lowering the Srisailam lake level to R.L. 830. However, it should be recognised that construction of any of the other proposed power reservoirs upstream of Srisailam will enable maintaining of minimum reservoir level at Srisailam above R.L. 854. As such upper power potentials will doubtless be exploited in due course, whether any installation of pumping scheme for Krishna-Pennar Canal at Srisailam is at all necessary, may be determined with reference to the phasing of the projects upstream of Nagarjunasagar. The Team's method of operation will also give an extra saving of not less than Rs. 62 lakhs annually in the integrated power system due to the greater generation of hydro-energy.

It has been suggested by the Central Water and Power Commission that surplus storage in Nagarjunasagar Reservoir above the level of 544 required for the full contemplated assured irrigation will be most useful for irrigating additional second crop in surplus years. The team has worked out the scope for such additional irrigation with F.R.L. 590 and found that an area of 3.3 lakh acres of additional second crop can be done annually on an average. This will give a return of 3.3 per cent on the capital of Rs. 7.5 crores required for raising the F.R.L. from 544 to 590. From general considerations and the revenue return on the capital involved which compares favourably with the return of 2.2 per cent in the First Phase, it would not be desirable to lower the height of the Dam at this stage particularly as the actual saving will now be much less as the masonry of the Dam is being built for the full section required for F.R.L. 590.

First crop irrigation is partly done from storage, and partly from the river flows in the monsoon season, but the second crop irrigation has to be done entirely from costly storage water in the winter season. The Team, therefore, recommends that the water-cess for the second crop paddy may be raised from Rs. 7.50 to Rs. 12 per acre, that for the first crop paddy being Rs. 15 per acre as proposed in the Project Report.

Design Features

It is seen that many important design features of the Dam have been changed and these changes will materially affect the estimate of the Project. It is, therefore, essential that a revised project estimate should be prepared at the earliest possible date on the basis of the changes made to get a realistic picture of the likely cost.

The spillway was originally designed for a high flood discharge of 10.27 lakh cusecs with an additional capacity of 20,000 cusecs through the Dam sluices. For this purpose twenty-seven spillway bays of 60′×30′ and twelve river sluices of 6′×9′ were provided. When the construction work was started, the flood capacity was increased to 11.87 lakh cusecs for 100 years frequency and for this purpose twenty-four bays of 50′×40′ and twelve river sluices of 5′×9′ were provided. The high flood discharge for 1,000 years' frequency was worked out by Central Water and Power Commission as 13.85 lakh cusecs, which the Team considered to be low. This discharge was calculated to pass over the spillway with a rise of four feet above F.R.L. of 590 by encroaching on the free board. The safety of the Dam was checked for M.W.L. of 594 and it was found to be structurally safe.

As a result of discussions with the Team, the Central Water and Power Commission have since stated that high flood discharge for 1,000 years' frequency at the Dam site will be 15.31 lakh cusecs and that the same will still pass over the designed spillway with a rise of four feet above F.R.L. 590 as a result of routing of the flood through the Reservoir which was not taken into account previously.

Previous model experiments had indicated that the co-efficient of discharge adopted in working out the flood discharge at Vijayawada Anicut, on the basis of which the flood discharges at the Dam site were estimated, was on the low side. Fresh model experiments are proposed to be made by the Project Authorities. If these experiments indicate a higher co-efficient of discharge than hitherto used, the high flood discharge of 15.31 lakh cusecs estimated for a 1,000 years, frequency will need to be further increased.

In the adjoining Godavari Valley, in connection with the Rampadsagar Project, the high flood discharge for 1,000 years' frequency was worked out as 30.6 lakh cusecs was recorded on August 15, 1953. Another high flood of similar magnitude occurred on September 17, 1959. Thus within a short period, a high flood approaching that of 1,000 years' frequency has already been experienced on this river twice. On the basis of the further data, the 100 years' and 1,000 years' frequency floods would far exceed those assumed in the Project. It would not be unreasonable to expect a similar situation arising in the adjoining Krishna Valley.

It would be most unwise to take any chances with the safety of a large dam, like the Nagarjunasagar Dam, considering the nature and the magnitude of the risks involved. The Team is of the view that the spillway capacity of this Dam should be designed for a flood of

the magnitude of a 1,000 years' frequency, at present estimated at 15.31 lakh cusecs, but to be further increased, should the proposed model experiments indicate a higher co-efficient of discharge for the Vijayawada Anicut. This capacity should be without encroachment on the free board.

To cater for a flood discharge of 15.31 lakh cusecs, the present spillway capacity can be increased by providing three extra bays, which is possible under present stage of construction and by providing 44 feet high gates instead of 40 feet gates. The extra cost involved is about Rs. 35 lakhs. Any additional capacity later found necessary can be provided on the left bank, as it is understood that there is a suitable site for a saddle spillway in the Tiger Valley on that bank.

There have been some major changes in the designed sections of the Right Bank and the Left Bank Canals which will affect the Project estimates. The Team has suggested to the Project Authorities that the revised project estimates should be prepared as early as possible.

The Left Bank Canal, which was originally designed for a full supply discharge of 11,000 cusecs is now being constructed on the basis of a full supply discharge of 15,000 cusecs. The increase in discharge is intended to irrigate an extra area of 3.5 lakh acres beyond the tail reach. The earthwork is being done for a discharge of 11,000 cusecs, but the masonry structures are being constructed for a discharge of 15,000 cusecs. The extra cost of the masonry structures in the First Phase will be Rs. 40 lakhs. Water will be available for the extra area on the basis of 75 per cent dependability. There is no alternative source for irrigating most of this additional area. The remodelling of the masonry structures later on will not only be difficult but would involve greater cost. The State Authorities should obtain the concurrence of the Government of India to this change which is desirable due to the above considerations and which the Team supports.

Many changes have been made in the design features of the Left Bank Canal in the head reach, presumably from economic considerations, but without fully considering their effect on the working operations of the Reservoir. The full supply level of the Canal at the head has been raised from about R.L. 508 to R.L. 524.5. Originally twin tunnels with a waterway of 1,100 square feet for a discharge of 11,000 cusecs and giving a velocity of 10 feet per second were provided in the head reach. The flume section in rock cutting was 20′×50′. In the revised design one tunnel with a waterway of 850 square feet has been provided for a discharge of 15,000 cusecs and the flume section has been changed to 40′×32′. The velocity in the tunnel is over 18 feet per second. These changes have resulted in considerable loss of head and in the minimum reservoir level being kept at R.L. 520 against R.L. 510 provided in the original Project. Thus the storage between R.L. 520 and 510 cannot be used to the same advantage as it can be done if the full supply level of the Left Bank Canal was lowered by ten feet.

There are two alternatives for lowering the full supply level of the Left Bank Canal by 10 feet. One alternative would be to increase the size of the tunnel under construction from 32 feet diameter to 38 feet diameter and to lower the bed of the flume upstream of the tunnel. The second alternative would be to provide a second tunnel of appropriate size later when the extension of Left Bank Canal is undertaken but to construct suitable approaches upstream and downstream of the tunnel now. As it will be several years before the Left Bank Canal Extension is constructed, the second alternative appears advisable. The Project Authorities have accepted this. The resulting advantages of lowering the full supply level of the Left Bank Canal will be:

(i) The full supply level of the Left Bank and Right Bank Canals will be close to each other, resulting in both the Canals making use of the storage under similar conditions;

(ii) The velocity in the tunnel will decrease from over eighteen feet per second to under thirteen feet per second. This will increase the life of the concrete lining of the tunnel considerably; and

(iii) The minimum operation level will be reduced from R.L. 520 to R.L. 510 originally envisaged in 1954 Project. This will result in more water becoming available in surplus years for additional second crop irrigation which on an average will be about 42,000 acres per annum. This will give an extra revenue of Rs. 3.15 lakhs on the basis of Rs. 7.50 per acre assumed in the project report and Rs. 5 lakhs on the basis of Rs. 12 per acre recommended by the Team.

Construction Features

It is noticed that a railway line has been constructed from Macherla to the Right Bank side of the Dam at an approximate cost of Rs. 50 lakhs for a distance of about 14 miles, for bringing about 6 lakh tons of cement and about one lakh tons of other material. A black topped road has also been constructed from Macherla to the Dam site at a cost of about Rs. 14 lakhs. The haulage charges for cement by railway would be Rs. 2.75 per ton exclusive of the depreciation charges on the capital cost of Rs. 50 lakhs. The cement will have to be transported by road in bulk cement carriers for a distance of three miles by double-handling from the railway terminus to the batching plant on the left bank, which will involve extra cost. The Project Authorities were transporting cement in bags by road upto the batching plant at a cost of about Rs. 3 per ton, before the railway line was completed. The Team observes that the cement could have been conveniently and

economically brought in bulk cement carriers by road and construction of the railway line costing Rs. 50 lakhs could have been avoided.

A road bridge has been constructed on the downstream side of the Dam with a road width of 38 feet at a cost of about Rs. 36 lakhs against a normal width of 22 feet for a highway road bridge. The extra width of 16 feet was provided for two narrow gauge lines which are likely to be used. The normal width of 22 feet would have been adequate for all the traffic that is required between the two banks.

Five separate colonies have been constructed which are rather scattered far apart. The Team considers that the lay-out of the colonies for large projects should be compact as far as possible so that the expenditure on services like lighting, water-supply, roads and sanitation etc., can be kept down to the minimum.

The savings of Rs. 70 lakhs in the special tools and plant assumed in the revised project on account of use of some old machinery received from the project is not likely to materialise.

The total cost of machinery purchased to end of 1958-59 amounts to Rs. 5.45 crores of which the earth moving machinery amounts to Rs. 3.56 crores. The average daily utilisation of machinery for the years 1957-58 and 1958-59 for which data are obtained from the reports prepared by the Project Authorities and submitted to the Control Board is as under:

Name of work	1957-58 Hour	Minutes per working day	1958-59 Hours	Minutes per working day
Dam	2	13	3	04
Right Bank Canal	2	11	1	34
Left Bank Canal	2	33	1	07

The Project Authorities have since suggested that an allowance should be made for rainy days and for days the machines were not in commission. On the basis of the revised statements supplied by the Project Authorities, the average daily utilisation of machinery is as under:

Name of work	1957-58 Hours	Minntes per working day	1958-59 Hours	Minutes per working day
Right Bank Canal	4	23	5	33
Left Bank Canal	3	11	3	30

There is scope for improving the overall working efficiency specially by working two shifts. At present the machinery is worked for one shift only.

It may be mentioned that the earth moving machinery involves considerable capital cost and on account of shortage of foreign exchange, it is very scarce. It should, therefore, be utilised to the best advantage. Such machinery should be worked at least in two shifts. The Team recommends that the greatest caution should be exercised in purchasing further machinery for this Project particularly earth moving machinery.

There are considerable delays in procurement of spare parts due to difficulty of foreign exchange, which prevent full use being made of the machinery. This has been noticed by the Team in their study of other projects also. It is suggested that the necessary steps should be taken at the highest level to avoid costly and scarce machinery remaining idle for lack of spares.

At present the hire charges are based on the norms recommended in the Cost and Rates Committee's Report for the purpose of debit to works, but the poor working efficiency will result in the actual costs being higher per unit rate of output of earthwork.

Phasing Of Construction Programme

The First phase of Nagarjunasagar Project estimated in 1956 to cost Rs. 86.57 crores was to be completed by 1963-64 and the phased expenditure was Rs. 1.11 crores, 57.4 crores and 28.06 crores in the First, Second and Third Five-Year Plans. The allocation of funds to the project in the Second Five Year-Plan is, however, expected to be only Rs. 37.98 crores. On account of the reduced allotment for the Second Five-Year Plan the construction programme has had to be modified and the project is now expected to be completed not before 1965-66.

The total quantity of masonry in the Dam to be done in the approved First Phase is 160 M.C. Feet of which 36 M.C. Feet has been done by the end of 1959-60. In order to complete the remaining quantity of masonry within the Third Plan, the average annual output will have to be 24 M.C. Feet. As there will be restricted space available for laying masonry specially in the last two years, the peak annual out-turn for next three years will have to be 30 M.C. Feet, which should be aimed at.

The construction of the masonry of the Dam will be the controlling factor in the completion of the project. Because of the high level of the take-off Canals, irrigation benefits will start accruing on them only when the Dam is nearing completion. Therefore, in allocating funds for the various units of work on this Project, the Dam should receive preference.

Power Development

No hydro-electric power is envisaged in the First phase. The 1954 project envisaged an ultimate development of 75 MW of firm power at 60 per cent load factor. For this purpose five penstocks of 10 feet diameter were provided. The firm power potential is determined by the discharge required for the second crop irrigation in the Delta in the non-monsoon months. This is approximately 2,250 cusecs. When no water is required for irrigation in the Delta in some fortnights it is proposed to let down about 20 T.M.C. Feet of water annually for firming up power. It is now proposed by the Central Water and Power Commission to provide eight penstocks of 16 feet diameter "taking into account all possible eventualities and the possibility that Nagarjunasagar Station may have to operate at a very low load factor of the order of even 25 per cent in conjunction with future base load nuclear and thermal stations". To utilise eventually the potential of power at Nagarjunasagar for peaking, the present provision for embedding in the masonry of the Dam, eight penstocks of 16 feet diameter is in order. A provision of Rs. 50 lakhs has been made for the same in the 1956 estimate.

In the First Phase the masonry of the Dam will need to be constructed to F.R.L. 546 against F.R.L. 525 provided in the First Phase Project as already explained earlier. Apart from providing irrigation for the full area of first crop of First Phase and for 1.25 lakh acres of second crop in the Delta, it will result in a power potential varying from 40 MW to 230 MW at 100 per cent load factor. There is shortage of power in the region which is inhibiting both medium and large scale industrial development. The power potential at Nagarjunasagar can be developed conveniently and very economically as the incremental cost for the Hydro Plant will be about Rs. 400 per KW only. The Team, therefore, recommends the exploitation of this power potential in the First Phase itself by providing a power house with two units of 50 MW each at an approximate cost of Rs. four crores. 132 KV transmission lines from the power house to the two main load centres at Hyderabad and Vijayawada and necessary sub-stations and sub-transmission lines will be required in the first instance to utilise the power; the additional cost for these will be about Rs. four crores.

Additional expenditure to develop 100 MW power at Nagarjunasagar and to distribute it, may, therefore, amount to Rs. eight crores or Rs. 800 per KW. This will cost approximately Rs. 80 per KW year at the main receiving sub-stations. If bulk power is priced at the receiving station at 3.25 np per KW hour, at which it can be readily marketed at present, the gross revenue that can be realised will be Rs. 171 per KW year at a load factor of 60 per cent. This will give an extra net revenue of Rs. 70 lakhs per annum, which will help materially to augment the total earnings from the First Phase Nagarjunasagar Project. At the same time it will permit phasing to later stages, building of relatively costlier thermal power capacity or exploiting other hydro power potentials; in the latter case funds will be necessary for civil works (Dams) as well as for the Hydro-Power Station.

Construction Costs And Financial Forecast

According to the 1954 joint Project Report, the First Phase was estimated to cost Rs. 85.5 crores. However in September 1954, the two Chief Engineers for Irrigation of Andhra and Hyderabad States indicated the possibility of reducing the outlay on the First Phase to Rs. 75 crores. The irrigated area was shown as 23.6 lakh acres and the revenue return as 5.05 per cent on the net capital. The Planning Commission approved this scheme in February 1955. Soon after the Project was started, it was realised that the estimated cost, irrigation benefits and percentage return could not be adhered to. A fresh estimate amounting to Rs. 86.6 crores was prepared in 1956 and irrigated area was shown as 0.60 lakh acres and percentage return as 2.64 per cent at the end of the 10th year after completion on the basis of 4.5 per cent simple interest. This estimate was also not prepared in detail, but was more or less based on 1954 Project estimate. On account of increase in cost of cement, steel and oil, this estimate has been further revised to Rs. 91.12 crores. This estimate also does not take into account the important changes made in the design, etc.

The working rates for masonry and concrete do not allow for sufficient depreciation on special tools and plant purchased and do not take into account actual working expenses for machinery and services like water-supply, lighting, sanitation, huttings, etc. The earthwork rates for earthen flanks of the Dam are also likely to be exceeded. It is. therefore, necessary that a revised estimate for the Dam incorporating all the changes made in the designs may be prepared at the earliest possible date on the basis of the actual working rates.

On the basis of the estimates of earthwork for the portion of the Right Bank Canal from head to mile 45 which have been prepared by the Project Authorities, the Team anticipates that there is likely to be some excess on the earthwork for the length of the Right Bank Canal to be done in the First Phase. The Project Authorities anticipate that there will be an excess of 10 per cent in earthwork and rock excavation quantities.

In the revised estimate amounting to Rs. 91.12 crores the provision for cross drainage works on the two canals has been increased by Rs. 72 lakhs. Even this increased provision is likely to prove inadequate, as there is already an excess of over Rs. 32 lakhs on the four masonry works for which estimates have been sanctioned so far. For the Delta area there is a provision of Rs. 100 per acre for distribution system in the revised estimate. The provision for this item on the Right Bank Canal is Rs. 82 per acre of ayacut and that in the case of the Left Bank Canal is only Rs. 50 per acre, which is likely to be exceeded. The Project estimate should again be reviewed and revised early in order to give a clear picture of the overall excess anticipated on this Project.

The 1956 Project showed a return of 2.64 per cent at the end of the 10th year after completion with the project cost of Rs. 86.56 crores. It was based on assumptions which were too optimistic. These have been somewhat modified in the new financial forecast for the revised project cost of Rs. 91.12 crores. The return now expected is 2.3 per cent at the end of 10th year after completion decreasing progressively thereafter. The actual position may be somewhat worse if, as is feared, the working expenses come to more than Rs. two per acre and the full irrigation development takes more than four years allowed for in the financial return.

The Team makes the following suggestions for improving the financial return :

(i) Increase from Rs. 7.50 per acre to Rs. 12 per acre in water-cess for second crop paddy for which the entire water is to be provided from expensive storage;

(ii) Reduction in percentages of wet crops and increase in percentage of dry crop which will bring more revenue for the same quantity of water;

(iii) A uniform rate of Rs. 10 per acre as water-cess for dry crops on both the Canals instead of Rs. 7.50 per acre on the Left Bank Canal and Rs. 10 per acre on the Right Bank Canal;

(iv) Exploitation of power potential in the First Phase which will give an extra revenue of Rs. 70 lakhs;

(v) As the second crop requires water entirely from expensive storage and as very much more revenue can be realised from non-paddy rabi crops than from second paddy for the same quantity of water, it would be desirable to develop non-paddy rabi crops as far as possible; and

(vi) Revision of the existing low water-cess rates in the Delta, on account of making assured supplies available from Nagarjunasagar Reservoir.

The Team is of the view that the the Project Authorities are in a position to spend much more than what is being allotted annually. The Team, therefore, suggests that the available funds in the Third Five-Year Plan should in the first instance be concentrated on this Project in perference to new projects in the state so that this Project will start giving irrigation benefits at an early date.

Irrigation Development And Agricultural Aspects

The irrigation demands, duties and rates of water-cess provided by Hyderabad and Andhra were on different basis. Now that the whole area lies in the reorganised Andhra Pradesh, it would be desirable to have uniformity as far as possible.

Some cotton is grown in the ayacut area on natural rainfall but it gives very poor yield. If its sowing is done a month or two earlier before rains come—say April-May —with the help of canal water, the yield would increase considerably as has been the experience in Punjab and elsewhere and this should be tried by the State Agriculture Department. In about 75 per cent of the years there will be some extra water available from the storage over and above the requirements of assured irrigation. Some of this can be used for early cotton sowing and green manure crops for improving the poor fertility of the soil. Even in the remaining 25 per cent of the years it should be possible to provide some water for early cotton with slight adjustment in the pattern of wet and dry crops on the two Canals.

The present plan of the Project Authorities in localising the ayacut is to omit the areas at the ridges i.e., areas adjoining the distributaries and to provide irrigation to the low lying areas adjoining the nalla banks. The main consideration by the Project Authorities appears to be that salts from upper lands under irrigation will be leached and carried down to lower lands and thereby ruin lands lower down would be easily drained by the natural drainage system, when irrigation is applied there. However, this approach of the Project Authorities appears to overlook the following important considerations:

(i) The areas near the ridges being relatively flat are easily adaptable to flow irrigation without much need for levelling;

(ii) The salt contents of soil at ridges do not appear to be high, probably because of continuous drainage by rainfall over a long period;

(iii) Cultivation of deep rooted plants like fruit trees, etc., would not only utilise the sub-soil water but also help in preventing rise of salts to the surface,

(iv) Application of canal water to low lands would result in a heavy loss of water due to seepage into nallas whereas water applied to upper lands would get stored in the subsoil of the lower lands and would be available for lift irrigation, and

(v) Precluding ridge lands from irrigation would involve long lengths of water course for irrigating more distant low lands, thus increasing water losses. Apart from these considerations, the unpleasant task of acquiring land from the land-owners on the ridges and at the same time depriving them of irrigation facilities will be avoided.

Therefore, the Team suggests that these factors should be given full consideration before the lands adjoining the distributaries on the ridges are deprived of irrigation benefits.

The Team suggests that the lands lower down the distributaries adjoining the natural drainages should be reserved for lift irrigation by making use of the sub-soil water, which is already high enough and which will rise still further due to irrigation in the upper lands. This would prevent water logging of the lower lands in addition to maximising irrigation, benefits, to encourage lift irrigation the Team recommends liberal loans for digging of wells and installing pumps etc., and lower water rates on such irrigation.

As an Anti-malarial measure, the Project Authorities intend precluding from irrigation areas within two miles of each town and half a mile of each village. Lands around towns and villages are not only very expensive but are also generally fertile and can readily bear betterment levy. Such lands are ideally suited for growing vegetables, fodder crops and fruit trees—the latter are also known to minimise the rigours of extreme heat. The team, therefore, suggests that such areas should be given light irrigation, and only heavily irrigated crops like sugar-cane and paddy should be debarred.

The present plan for localisation of irrigated area envisages permanently ear-marking different areas for (a) wet cultivation or heavy irrigation such as rice, (b) semi-wet or dry cultivation (crops requiring light irrigation) and (c) areas left out of irrigation. Such a step might give rise to resentment among the cultivators denied irrigation or permitted only light irrigation for all times to come. Secondly, no crop rotation would be possible under this system. The Team suggests that the irrigation area of each village may be divided into three parts, two parts for dry and one for wet in a particular season but crops being rotated in every season.

Change over from dry cultivation to wet cultivation brings about revolutionary changes, not only in agricultural economy and pattern, but even in the methods of cultivation and agricultural practices, etc. Necessary experimental work has to be undertaken to find solutions to the numerous problems that will face the cultivators with the advent of canal irrigation. While it is gratifying to note that the Agricultural Department is fully alive to this problem and the Project Authorities are also very keen in the matter and there also exists a Development Committee, much headway has not yet been made in starting the experimental work. As it takes years of experimentation, before authentic results become available, the Team recommends establishment of at least two experimental stations forthwith—one on the Right Bank and the other on the Left Bank Canal, to carry out experiments regarding varietal trials on important crops like paddy, sugarcane, cotton, etc., manurial experiments to find out the nutritional requirements of different crops, cultural practices, water requirements of different crops and varietal trials of fruit trees etc. Apart from this, demonstration farms would also be necessary which may be at the rate of one for every twenty-five square miles.

The existing roads in the ayacut are in an unsatisfactory state and are totally inadequate even now. After the development of irrigation, there will be greater need for better roads for transport of the extra agricultural produce. Therefore, the Team recommends that provision of suitable and adequate roads and marketing facilities in the ayacut should be given full and early consideration.

The Team suggests that the survey of sub-soil water table should be taken up at an early date so that timely remedial measures can be taken in the 'danger zones' against water-logging.

The Team is glad to record that the Project staff is working with a fine team spirit.

NATIONAL COMMITTEE ON WOMEN'S EDUCATION, 1958—REPORT

Delhi, Manager of Publications, 1959. 335p.+ixp.

Chairman : Smt. Durgabai Deshmukh.

Members : Miss S. Panandikar; Shri P.N. Mathur; Smt. Kulsum Sayani; Shri J.P. Naik; Smt. Zahra Ahmed; Smt. O.C. Srinivasan.

Secretary : Km. Sarojini Rajan (At the special request of the Committee, Dr. Phulrenu Guha, Vice-Chairman, West Bengal State Social Welfare Board, agreed to associate herself with its work and function as a member.)

APPOINTMENT

The problems of the education of girls and women in our country have acquired a new significance since the attainment of Independence and there is an ever increasing realisation, both in the minds of the people and the Government, that unless every effort is made to find solutions for them, the rapid progress of the country which is the aspiration of every one will be seriously impeded. Planners and administrators, both at the Centre and in the States, have been discussing these problems with this end in view.

The Education Panel of the Planning Commission, at its meeting held in Poona in July, 1957, recommended that "a suitable Committee should be appointed to go into the various aspects of the question relating to the nature of education for girls at the elementary, secondary and adult stages and to examine whether the present system was helping them to lead a happier and more useful life." This recommendation was placed before the Conference of the State Education Ministers (held in September, 1957) who also agreed that a special Committee should be appointed to examine the whole question of women's education.

The National Committee on Women's Education was accordingly set up by the Government of India in the Ministry of Education under Government Resolution No. F. 34-12/57-B.5 of May 19, 1958

TERMS OF REFERENCE

(i) To suggest special measures to make up the leeway in women's education at the Primary and Secondary levels;

(ii) To examine the problems of wastage in girls education at these levels;

(iii) To examine the problem of adult women who have relapsed into illiteracy or have received inadequate education and who need continuation education so as to enable them to earn a living and participate in projects of national reconstruction;

(iv) To survey the nature and extent of material and other facilities offered by voluntary welfare organisations for the education of such women and to recommend steps necessary to enable them to offer larger educational facilities to them, and

(v) To examine the possibility and methods of encouraging a larger number of women to go into vocational trades by providing suitable vocational training as a part of formal education or through special courses designed for adult women.

CONTENTS

Introduction; Basic Approaches and Fundamental Considerations; Education of Women in India : a Historical Survey 1800-1947; Statement of the Problem; Education of Girls in the Age-group of 6 to 11 (Primary Stage); Education of girls in the Age-group of 11 to 17 (Middle and Secondary Stages); Wastage and Stagnation in the Education of Girls at the Primary and Secondary Stages; Curricula and Syllabii; Training and employment of Women Teachers; Professional and Vocational Education; Special Educational Facilities for Adult Women; Role of Voluntary Organisations; Some Special Problems; Organisation, Administration and Finance; General Conclusions; Recommendations; Documents and Data relating to the Work of the National Committee on Women's Education

RECOMMENDATIONS

The recommendations made in this Report are grouped here under three main categories, viz.,

(1) Special recommendations which require Top Priority and immediate consideration.

(2) Other special recommendations.

(3) General recommendations.

By 'special' recommendations, we mean those recommendations which concern themselves exclusively with educational programmes for girls and women; and by 'general' recommendations, we mean those recommendations which may concern themselves with educational programmes for both girls and boys and women and men.

I. Special Recommendations

The following recommendations made in this Report need top priority and immediate attention at the hands of Government.

(1) The education of women should be regarded as a major and a special problem in Education for a good many years to come and a bold and determined effort should be made to face its difficulties and magnitude and to close the existing gap between the education of men and women in as short a time as possible.

(2) The highest priority should be given to schemes prepared from this point of view and the funds required for the purpose should be considered to be the first charge on the sums set aside for the development of education.

(3) Necessary steps should be taken, without delay, to create a special machinery to deal with the problem of the education of girls and women and to assign adequate funds for the purpose.

(4) Steps should be taken to constitute as early as possible, a National Council for the Education of Girls and Women.

(5) The problem of the education of women is so vital and of such great national significance that it is absolutely necessary for the Centre to assume more responsibility for its rapid development. This responsibility will be threefold :

(i) It should be a responsibility of the Centre to see that parity between the education of boys and girls is reached as early as possible, and also to see that the education of girls and women is developed evenly in all parts of the country;

(ii) The Centre should prescribe targets to be attained and also guide the States in preparing comprehensive development plans for the education of girls and women in their areas;

(iii) The Centre should assist the States financially in implementing the approved plans.

(6) There should be a senior officer of the rank of Joint Educational Adviser at the Centre to look after the education of girls and women.

(7) It would be necessary to create a separate unit in the Ministry of Education to deal with the problems of the education of girls and women. This unit would naturally be under the control of the Joint Educational Adviser, who should also be the *ex-officio* Member-Secre-

tary of the proposed National Council for the Education of Girls and Women.

(8) The State Governments should establish State Councils for the education of girls and women.

(9) In each State, a woman should be appointed as Joint Director and placed in charge of the education of girls and women. She should be responsible for the planning, organising and execution of all the programmes pertaining to their education.

(10) The magnitude of the problem of the education of girls and women is so great that it can be solved only if all the resources of Government and of non-official organisations are combined and fully geared to the task.

(11) It is also necessary to enlist the cooperation of all semi-official organisations, local bodies, voluntary organisations, teachers' organisations and members of the public to assist in the promotion of the education of girls and women.

(12) To the extent that private affort is not forthcoming, direct action should be taken by the State to develop the education of girls and women and to establish special institutions for the purpose under its immediate control.

(13) A sum of not less than Rs. 10 crores in addition to provisions that already exist should be earmarked for the education of girls and women during the remaining period of the Second Five-Year Plan, and an adequate special provision made for their education in the Third Plan.

(14) The amount will thus be set aside for the development of the education of girls and women during the remaining period of the Second Five-Year Plan should be utilised for the following purposes :

(1) Development of middle schools for girls;
(2) Development of secondary schools for girls;
(3) Development of training institutions for women;
(4) Construction of hostels for girls and staff quarters for girls' institutions at all levels; and
(5) Organising special educational facilities for adult women.

(15) Every State should be required to prepare comprehensive development plans for the education of girls and women in its area. For this purpose, two plans—one for the remaining period of the Second Five-Year Plan and another for the period of the Third Plan—are necessary.

(16) The system of matching grants should be done away with in so far as the development of the education of girls and women is concerned and the entire financial responsibility for this programme should be that of the Government of India.

(17) During the Third Plan, there should be a special programme for the development of the education of girls and women, which is not covered by any of the general programmes and a sum of not less than Rs. 100 crores should be allocated for it.

(18) The University Grants Commission which is a statutory body empowered to deal with colleges and universities, should set apart a special fund of not less than Rs. one crore for the remaining period of the Second Five-Year Plan for giving necessary grants to colleges, including training colleges, for the construction of hostels for girls. While sanctioning these grants, preference should be given to colleges in rural areas and to semi-urban institutions. The funds should be utilised either for purpose of grant-in-aid or for loans. When grants are given, they should cover 75 per cent of the total expenditure and, in case of rural colleges, grants on 100 per cent basis may be given. The loans should cover the entire cost of the projects and should preferably be interest-free. Their repayment should be spread over a fairly long term.

(19) The Planning Commission should set up a permanent machinery to estimate, as accurately as possible, the woman-power requirements of the Plans from time to time and make the results of its studies available to Government and the public.

(20) Governments should set up, as early as possible, a high-power Committee to examine the so-called wastage in the medical and professional educations of women.

II. Other Special Recommendations

The following are the other special recommendations made in this Report. They all relate exclusively to the special problems of the education of women.

Primary Education (Age Group 6-11)

(21) School mothers should be appointed in al. schools where there are no women teachers, on the staff.

(22) In every co-educational school separate lavatory arrangements with necessary privacy should be made for girls.

(23) Concessions in kind (not in cash) should be given to all girls, whether from rural or urban areas, of parents below a certain income level. Such concessions should cover the cost of books and stationery, school uniform or clothing and other such necessary educational equipment.

(24) Government should encourage the opening of more creches for the care of the younger children. These creches can be located at Community Centres, *Mahila Samities*, in buildings attached to schools or in other suitable places. They may be run as part of Welfare Extension Projects or by Voluntary workers.

(25) The Government should formulate a scheme for awarding prizes to the village which shows the largest proportional enrolment and average attendance of girls in each small group of villages, a block, a *taluka* or a *tehsil*. Rotating shields may also be instituted for

the purpose, the village showing the best progress being allowed to win and keep the shield for one year.

(26) Graded attendance allowances to teachers on the basis of average attendance of girls, in their classes, may be introduced in rural areas.

(27) (a) Two or three prizes in the form of useful articles may be awarded to girls in every primary school for regular attendance.

(b) Attendance Scholarships in the form of useful articles may also be given to poor girls.

(28) The mere passing of compulsory legislation would be of no avail unless suitable conditions for encouraging parents to send their daughters to schools are created. Greater emphasis, therefore, should be laid on the creation of such conditions rather than on giving the authorities concerned more penal powers.

(29) The Government should recognise the great importance of creating a strong public opinion in the country in favour of the education of girls and women and take all possible measures for the purpose.

These measures may include:

(i) Organising of a women's education week every year,

(ii) Carrying on social education work among adult women,

(iii) Associating village women and *Mahila Mandals* through school Committees etc. with the work of increasing the enrolment of girls in primary schools.

Middle And Secondary Education (Age-Group 11 To 17)

(30) In so far as middle-school education is concerned the existing disparity between the enrolment of boys and girls may be brought down to a point where the percentage of girls in schools is at least half of that of boys in schools the estimated disparity at the end of the Second Plan being 3.2:1 by the end of the Third Plan; parity between the two being aimed at by the end of the Fourth Plan. So far as secondary education is concerned it is difficult at present to lay down any precise target.

(31) (a) At the middle school stage more and more co-educational institutions should be started, subject to the conditions that adequate attention is paid to meet the special needs and requirements of the girls;

(b) But for the secondary stage, separate schools for girls should be established specially in rural areas, at the same time giving parents full freedom to admit their girls to boys' schools if they so desire. Although co-education at the secondary stage has not been recommended, all the same every effort should be made to remove the genuine difficulties and valid apprehensions that exist today in regard to co-education, at this stage. One way to do this is to take special care in recruiting the right type of staff including Heads for co-educational schools. Parents should also be given the opportunity of paying periodical visits to schools and of coming to know directly about the work and the atmosphere there. The appointment of women teachers and, if possible, of women Heads in co-educational institutions would instil great confidence in the parents and thus be a real help in increasing the enrolment of girls.

(c) Where co-education is not acceptable, an alternative is to start separate shifts for boys and girls in the same school building, so as to avoid duplication of buildings and equipment.

(32) (a) All girls (and all boys also) of parents below a prescribed income level should be given free education upto the middle stage. The income level to be prescribed for the purpose may have to vary from place to place and as such its determination may be left to the judgment of the State Governments and local authorities.

(b) In the secondary stage free education has not been recommended but in so far as girls are concerned, liberal exemptions—full and partial—from tuition and other fees should be granted to them.

(33) (a) Suitable hostel facilities should be provided in as many schools as possible and non-matching building grants given for construction of the hostel buildings.

(b) The board and lodging arrangements in these hostels should be cheap, and payment in kind should be permitted wherever required.

(c) Free and half-free board and lodging should be made available to poor and deserving students.

(34) As far as possible, free or subsidised transport should be made available to girls in order to bring middle and secondary schools, within easy reach.

(35) Certain necessary special facilities should be provided to girls in co-educational schools to as full an extent as possible.

(36) (a) Up to the middle stage all girls from rural and urban areas, of parents below a certain level of income should be given help in cash or kind to cover the following items (i) books, stationery and other necessary educational equipment (ii) school uniform or clothing.

(b) In the secondary stage this help should be extended only to such deserving and poor girls about whom there exists some certainty that after completion of their secondary education they may take up some vocation.

(37) There should also be adequate provision for awarding scholarships on merit to girls in the middle and secondary stages.

(38) In order to make the education of girls more purposive and practical, effective guidance services should be provided in all schools as far as possible.

(39) The recommendations regarding (i) Part-time education, (ii) Night schools, (iii) Creches, made in

regard to primary education are applicable, *mutatis mutandis* to middle and secondary education also.

(40) The importance of educating public opinion in regard to middle and secondary education of girls is in no way less than what it is in respect of primary education. For the education of public opinion, among other measures (i) teacher-parent cooperation and (ii) education of adult women are particularly recommended.

Curriculum And Syllabi

(41) A good curriculum should have the following objectives:

(i) Creating right attitude in life—individual and social;

(ii) Imparting useful knowledge;

(iii) Giving practical training for life;

(iv) Developing good personal habits;

(v) Inculcating a sense of social awareness and a spirit of service to society.

(42) As needs and circumstances change, there should be a periodical review of all courses.

(43) There should be identical curriculum for boys and girls at the primary stage with the proviso that, even at this stage subjects like music, painting, sewing, needle work, simple handwork, and cooking (in the last two years of the primary stage) should be introduced to make the courses more suitable for girls.

(44) At the middle school stage, and more especially at the secondary stage, there is need for differenciation visualised, however, does not imply a totally different course of study but indicates merely an improvement of the existing courses, either by suitable changes within them or by inclusion of subjects more useful for girls, or by both.

(45) At the middle school stage, steps should be taken to provide a number of electives, so that girls may choose subjects according to their individual tastes and aptitudes, and in keeping with the career which they wish to take up later on in life. The diversification at this stage should also include some pre-vocational education which would help girls to choose such careers as that of a *Gram-Sevika*, a social worker, a mid-wife a health visitor, a nurse, a craft teacher, etc.

(46) At the secondary stage, diversified courses so far introduced for girls have been framed chiefly with a view to preparing them for home-making. This approach is too narrow and taking into consideration the various vocational opportunities open to women, some additional diversified courses of pre-vocational educational, suitable for girls, should be introduced. These may include:

(i) Secretarial courses to include pre-vocational training in correspondence filing, typing, etc.;

(ii) Courses useful for Secretaries of Organisations and office assistants which should include training in taking notes, writing minutes of meetings, giving press reports, maintaining accounts, correspondence, etc.

(iii) Courses leading to social work of various types;

(iv) Crafts like leather work, tailoring at an advanced stage and other home-crafts which could be taken up as part-time occupations.

(v) Courses in education; leading to training as pre-primary and primary teacher or Social Education worker.

(47) There is a great need for the simplification of the existing courses at the primary and middle stages.

(48) Educational activities in schools should include programmes that would help in developing the moral sense of the students.

(49) The knowledge of systemic history and geography should be imparted in suitable form and content at the primary, middle and secondary stages.

(50) The existing courses in general education up to the secondary stage should be thoroughly examined and modified with a view to making them less academic and more suitable to giving an insight into the problems of society.

(51) An examination of the text books and other reading material used at present as well as the content of the existing curricula shows a neglect of the needs and problems of the life of girls and women. This imbalance in our education has to be corrected.

Training And Employment Of Women Teachers

(52) The State Governments should be requested to take vigorous measures to increase the output of women teachers and to employ them in increasing numbers so that the existing low proportion of women teachers is substantially raised in the near future.

(53) Immediately steps should be taken to set up additional training institutions for women teachers in all such areas of the country where a shortage exists at present.

(54) The average training institution for women should be of a fairly small size and an attempt should be made to start at least one such training institution for women primary school teachers in every district.

(55) Training schools for primary school teachers and girls' secondary schools should be developed together as a combined institution wherever possible and especially in rural areas.

(56) A determined effort should be made to locate the training institutions for women primary teachers in rural areas.

(57) With a view to inducing women from urban areas to accept posts of teachers in rural schools, the following steps should be taken:

(a) Adequate provision should be made in the

Third Plan for providing women teachers serving in rural areas with quarters which should be, as far as possible near the school.

(b) A village allowance may be given to such teachers.

(c) Where both husband and wife are qualified to work as teachers, both of them should be employed and posted together in one and the same place.

(d) Liberal inducements should be offered to teachers to train their wives as teachers or as school mothers.

(58) In order to increase the supply of women teachers from the rural areas, the following measures should be taken:

(a) In employing women teachers, preference should always be given to persons from rural areas, whenever available.

(b) Girls from rural areas who have passed the Middle School or an equivalent examination should be recruited as primary teachers.

(c) In selecting candidates for admission to training institutions, girls from rural areas should be given preference.

(d) A large number of scholarships should also be instituted in training institutions to be awarded to girls from rural areas only. The amount of the scholarship should be such that the trainee should not be required to seek any other assistance to maintain herself at the institution.

(59) The maximum age limit for entry into service may be relaxed as much as possible in the case of women teachers. The relaxation should be made at least up to 40 or 45 years of age.

(60) The age of retirement may be extended to 60 in all States provided the teacher is physically and otherwise fit.

(61) Women teachers who take up employment at a late age in life do not get adequate protection for old age under the existing rules. Government should, therefore, have this problem examined and amend the existing rules suitably, with a view to making a reasonable provision for old age for these adult women.

(62) (a) It is desirable to exempt all women trainees in the training institutions, for primary school teachers from the payment of tuition fees.

(b) In respect of secondary school teachers, however, all women trainees whose guardians have an income below a specific level should be exempted from the payment of tuition fees.

(63) A sufficient number of scholarships should be instituted in all training institutions so that all women trainees in need may receive adequate financial assistance to cover their expenses, other than tuition fees while under training.

(64) Suitable pupils, particularly from rural areas, who wish to become teachers may be picked out during the last two years of their middle or secondary school course and given free secondary education and even special scholarships, if they are prepared to work in rural areas.

(65) In selecting women candidates for training, special consideration may be given to:

(a) The background of the candidates;

(b) Adult women, particularly widows and others who may have to maintain themselves; and

(c) *Gram-Sevikas* who might be released from Social Welfare Projects.

(66) Government should take immediate steps for provision of hostels in all training establishments. Rented accommodation may be provided as a transitional measure.

(67) Voluntary organisations conducting training institutions for women should be assisted for construction of hostels either by a grant-in-aid, or a loan which would cover the total cost and be interest-free, if possible.

(68) Steps on the lines indicated above for hostels should also be adopted in so far as the provision of staff quarters for training institutions is concerned.

(69) Although residence in hostels should ordinarily be compulsory for trainees, women, who have unavoidable responsibilities at home, may be exempted under such circumstances.

(70) In training institutions for women teachers, arrangements should be made for creches for the care of the children of the trainees, whenever necessary.

(71) Adequate provision for instruction in fine arts and home crafts should be made in training institutions for women teachers.

(72) Preparatory classes, for the the training of adult women with inadequate educational qualifications through condensed courses to prescribed standards of admission, should be attached to all training institutions for women teachers.

(73) Coaching classes should be organised for women who have obtained less than the required percentage of marks in some subjects. Their progress should be examined after coaching and if found satisfactory, they should be admitted to regular training institutions.

(74) Part-time courses for the preparation of women teachers should be organised, wherever possible.

(75) Every training institution for women teachers should set up a placement centre which would assist its trainees in securing employment. Arrangements should also be made under which a placement centre would give a grant or a loan to a trainee to enable her to attend an interview.

(76) Demand and supply lists of women teachers should be maintained by all Education Departments and

Coordinated by the Ministry of Education.

(77) Part-time employment of women teachers should be encouraged as largely as possible in order to enable women to manage their responsibilities at home as well as to do some teaching work.

(78) The practice, followed in some areas, of discharging untrained teachers at vacation time should be abandoned generally in the case of all the teachers. If that is not possible, it should be abandoned in respect of women teachers at least.

Professional And Vocational Education

(79) In order that women may be enabled to attend to their homes properly as well as to take up some suitable vocation, the employment of women on a part-time basis, wherever feasible, should be accepted as a policy and more and more opportunities should be thrown open to women in the form of part-time work, which can be undertaken in and outside the home.

(80) A thorough study of the vocational training needs and of the employment opportunities for women should be undertaken immediately by the Government with a group of experts and representatives of concerned Ministries with adequate time and ample resources at their disposal. Such a survey will discover the occupations available for women in different parts of the country.

(81) Wherever women come forward to organise a cottage or a small scale industry as individuals, the Government should provide necessary assistance and guidance. Assistance may be in the form of loan, subsidy, supply of raw material and adequate marketing arrangements for sale of the products. Cooperatives or other organisations may also be helped in a like manner.

(82) Government should formulate a number of "Small Scale Industries Schemes" calculated to meet the needs of women, in consultation with the departments concerned.

(83) (a) Vocational training courses with "Primary" as basic qualification may be conducted in schools during the day, alongside general education. This training may also be given in training-*cum*-production centres.

(b) Courses with "Middle" and "Secondary" as basic qualifications may be organised in vocational sections of middle and secondary schools, in multipurpose schools, in separate vocational schools, in apprenticeship classes, in Training Centres, in workshops and/or in continuation schools.

(84) Government should take immediate action by providing additional seats for women in existing training institutions and/or starting new Training Centres in vocations suitable to women.

(85) The number of seats available for women in commercial courses should be increased.

(86) Difficulties are being experienced by girls in getting admission to polytechnics in some States. These should be removed.

(87) Polytechnics, which provide courses suitable for both boys and girls should be made co-educational.

(88) A thorough grounding should be given to women in courses of secretarial and administrative work to enable them to do such work efficiently.

(89) Training in home economics should be so organised that in addition to preparing women for home making, it would also prepare them for earning a living.

(90) The system of part-time training is most suited to the needs of Indian women and should be expanded as largely as possible.

(91) In order that a larger proportion of girls and women from rural areas may be enabled to join vocational training courses, such training should be provided in boarding schools, where they may be given room and board free.

(92) Girls should be encouraged to take up courses in Commerce, Engineering, Agriculture, Medicine, etc., at the University stage by offering them scholarships and other concessions.

(93) In the case of women, vocational institutions should restrict courses of training to occupations for which there is a local need sufficient to absorb them after training in the same locality, as far as possible.

(94) Vocational guidance services should be organised on a wider scale and services of qualified "career masters" be made available to assist pupils in choosing a field of training and select the appropriate vocational courses.

(95) Leaders of Industry should be given all facilities for formulating their needs in respect of qualifications or recruits and their advice is always essential to give proper guidance to trainees as to the occupations for which training may be sought.

(96) Employment Exchanges should give women financial assistance, if needed, to attend an interview. This assistance may be a grant or a loan reçoverable on employment.

(97) Career information centres should be set up in girls' High Schools and higher secondary schools and even primary schools and other educational institutions for girls and women.

(98) Educational and trainining institutions for women should have trained counsellors to help women choose appropriate careers.

(99) Educational institutions for women should organise regular career conferences to acquaint the students leaving the institutions and their guardians about the occupational opportunities open to them and the qualifications required for them.

(100) Government should prepare besides pamphlets, a number of career films and film strips on occupations available for women.

(101) Each Employment Exchange area should have a coordination Committee consisting of the nominees of the proposed National Council for Women's Education, Employment Exchange, Social Welfare Boards and representatives of prominent women's organisations.

(102) It is important to organise campaigns to mobilise public opinion for creating proper conditions in offices and establishments in which women can work freely.

(103) Government should take adequate steps to ensure that girls and women who complete their training courses are, as far as possible gainfully employed, immediately after training.

(104) The employment officers should visit training institutions and other Centres in their area to render necessary information regarding employment opportunities and also to register those who pass out of the training institutions.

(105) The Government should take necessary steps to encourage the entry of an increasing number of women into all suitable occupations.

(106) In the case of women taking up an employment other than teaching under Government or Semi-Government organisations the maximum age requirement may be relaxed to 35 years of age. Such women who enter service at a later age, should be allowed to work beyond the usual retirement age, which may be extended upto 60 years in the case of women.

(107) Wherever feasible, hostels for working women should be started.

(108) Facilities like creches and free care of children may be extended to all women in employment. Creches may be started in suitable places and their need properly coordinated.

Special Education Facilities For Adult Women

(109) Special educational facilities for adult women should be provided for three valid reasons partly (1) on humanitarian grounds, partly (2) as an act of pure social justice; and partly (3) because women workers are needed for a number of Plan projects.

(110) The fear that condensed courses for adult women will lead to a fall in standards and the argument that these facilities are costly are not quite sound and they should not stand in the way of providing such facilities.

(111) Educational facilities in the form of condensed courses (1) that prepare women for the Middle School Examination and (2) those that prepare them for the High School or Higher Secondary Examination should be provided more extensively in all States.

(112) Provision should also be made of condensed courses, which train women for suitable vocation after completion of necessary continuation education.

(113) The duration of the condensed courses should be made variable, depending upon the previous education of the women concerned, their individual capacities, the conditions for study, etc. But it should usually be possible to complete the general education of the middle standard in 2 or 3 years and further training for a vocation in one or two years.

(114) In order to make the duration of the condensed courses as short as possible, residential arrangement should be made for the trainees and the classes kept small.

(115) Women undertaking such condensed courses should appear for the same final examination as the pupils of primary or secondary schools, but the question of exempting them from appearing for certain subjects or parts thereof needs thorough examination.

(116) The course in each school subject should be divided into small suitable units so that, after the completion of a unit in the period of a month or two months, new units can be commenced in that subject.

(117) The general principles as given in paragraph 12 of Chapter XI should be followed in condensing courses.

(118) For certain jobs—such as that of the *Gram-Sevika*—an orientation course of one year would be sufficient for these adult women. But in the case of primary school teaching full two years training is needed; in the alternative, those adult women who have completed their general education up to the required minimum level can be given a short orientation course of about eight weeks duration as is being done under the scheme of relief to educated unemployed. In due course, they should take their regular training of two years.

(119) As many institutions providing special educational facilities for adult women as possible should be located in rural areas.

(120) Every preference should be given to voluntary organisations of standing and repute to organise these special educational facilities for adult women.

(121) A separate section for institutions which provide such special educational facilities for adult women should be included in the Grant-in-aid Codes of all State Governments and Administrations.

(122) (a) This section should be based on the following broad principles :

(i) The rules regarding the grant of recognition to such institutions should be as simple as possible.

(ii) No fees should be charged in such institutions.

(iii) There should be no conditions of minimum enrolment and attendance.

(iv) The grant-in-aid should ordinarily be liberal enough to cover the entire expenditure of the institution, subject however to such general ceilings of grant-in-aid per capita as may be prescribed by the State Governments in view of their local conditions.

(v) Non-recurring grants (or loans at a very low rate of interest, repayment of which may be spread over a fairly long period) for hostels should be liberally given in addition to recurring grants.

(vi) As attendance at such institutions should ordinarily be lower than in urban areas the ceilings for the per capita grant-in-aid should be higher in rural areas.

(b) The Central Government should accept responsibility for provision of grants-in-aid to selected organisations doing some significant work in the field of the education of women and for this purpose adequate provision should be made in the Central budget from year to year.

(123) Concessions to adult women taking up these condensed courses should be given in the form of scholarships and/or loans. Wherever necessary, the maintenance of dependent children should also be provided for.

(124) The State Governments and the Administrations should be requested to take without delay a decision regarding :

(i) The provision of such special educational facilities for adult women.

(ii) The nature and amount of non-recurring and recurring financial assistance that would be available to institutions which would undertake to organise the activity as well as to the trainees who would join the courses.

(iii) It would also be desirable to assure the women that they would be employed as soon as they have completed their training satisfactorily.

(iv) This scheme should be given wide publicity so as to evoke the interest of and response from as many adult women as possible.

(125) Such of the managements as are doing this work in rural areas at present should be contacted by the officers of the Education Department and be persuaded and encouraged to organise and expand this activity as early and on as large a scale as possible.

(126) If the required number of women teachers and other women personnel are to be made available by 1961-62, the commencement of the Third Plan, it is necessary that a very large beginning in the provision of special educational facilities for adult women should be made immediately. A lump sum provision of one crore of rupees should, therefore, be earmarked for this from the 10 crores proposed in Recommendation number 13.

(127) This programme should receive great emphasis and high priority at the hands of the Government of India and of the State Governments and the Administrations an adequate funds required for the purpose should be provided in the Third Plan.

Role Of Voluntary Organisations

(128) The services of the voluntary organisations should be extensively used in the field of middle, secondary, higher, social and vocational education of women. Their services should also be utilised in teacher-training and in providing special educational facilities for adult women.

(129) Some of the main difficulties experienced by voluntary organisations are as follows :

(i) Private institutions are not treated on a par with Government institutions, though their functions are identical.

(ii) Grant-in-aid rules are not sufficiently liberal.

(iii) There is irksome Departmental control.

(iv) The procedure for the release of funds is unduly complicated.

Steps should, therefore, be taken to remove these difficulties and private effort enabled to play the part which is expected of it.

(130) The existing grant-in-aid codes of the States need a thorough revision. on the following broad principles in so far as the institutions for the education of women are concerned :

(i) There should be a substantial and significant difference in the rates of grants-in-aid as between girls institutions and boys' institutions at all levels.

(ii) The conditions of aid for girls' institutions should be made easier.

(iii) The conditions generally imposed by Boards of Secondary Education and Universities in respect of buildings and reserve funds should be relaxed in the case of all educational institutions for girls.

(iv) Institutions for the education of girls in rural areas should receive more liberal grants-in-aid, both recurring and non-recurring. The purposes of the non-recurring grants-in-aid should include building and equipment. In rural areas, hostels and staff quarters must be included where necessary.

(v) In the case of middle and secondary schools for girls, training institutions for teachers and institutions which provide special educational facilities for adult women, there should not be any condition requiring a matching contribution. In other cases, a matching contribution up to 25 per cent could be insisted upon.

(vi) The grants-in-aid given to voluntary organisations of established standing and repute for non-recurring purposes should be given on a hundred per cent basis (at least in so far as primary, middle and the secondary schools and training institutions including the special institutions for adult women are concerned).

(vii) On the recurring side, the grant-in-aid should ordinarily cover the entire deficit, subject to the ceiling that the aid per capita will not be more than the cost per pupil in a State institution of a similar type.

(viii) In the case of other voluntary organisations matching contributions may be expected, but not more than half of what is expected in the case of boys' schools.

(131) (a) A scheme similar to the Central Government scheme to assist voluntary organisations doing some experimental or valuable work in education should be prepared for girls' institutions only and special funds allocated for it.

(b) A detailed scheme for giving loans for non-recurring purposes—particularly for hostels and staff quarters—should be drawn up for immediate implementation.

Institutions applying for aid under these schemes should be permitted to apply direct with a copy of the application to the State Government concerned.

(132) Wherever possible, the establishment of new institutions working in rural areas only should be encouraged. Where this is not possible, the existing voluntary organisations, whose activities are confined to urban areas only should be persuaded to extend their activities to rural areas also.

(133) Steps should be taken to organise in all States associations of devoted women workers and necessary assistance extended to them for educational activities.

(134) Women's Welfare Organisations should be encouraged to take up educational schemes for which aid should be given from the special fund proposed to be created for the development of the education of girls and women.

(135) The liberalisation of grants-in-aid rules, which is meant primarily to ensure operational convenience should not be at the cost of quality and standards.

Some Special Problems

(A) Education Of Women At University Stage

(136) A fairly large number of scholarships should be instituted for poor and deserving girls in all colleges, both Government and private. The amount of these scholarships should be such as would enable the girls to continue their education without being a burden on their families.

(137) A large number of girls continue their studies at college under great social and economic handicaps. It is necessary that the State should recognise these handicaps and provide a sufficiently large number of scholarships to be awarded to girls on merit.

(138) Government should draw up a scheme under which assistance could be made available to poor girls for purchase of educational equipment and books.

(139) It is necessary to establish a few good institutions in different parts of the country which would be able to devote themselves exclusively to the study of the special problems of the education of women.

(140) There should be a special budget provision for such schemes in the Plans of the Government of India and an attempt should be made to develop them on proper lines through grants-in-aid on a hundred per cent basis. The immediate object of this programme should be to develop these institutions to the university level and to make them centres of experimental and pioneer work as well as of fundamental thinking with regard to the education of women.

(B) Pre-primary Education

(141) Government of India should appoint, as early as possible, a suitable Committee to examine all aspects of the problem of pre-primary education.

(142) Government should accept the responsibility for the training of women teachers for pre-primary schools and private effort working in the field should be liberally encouraged. The grants-in-aid to training institutions for primary teachers as well as the assistance to be given to the trainees should be on the some lines as those recommended for the training of primary teachers.

(143) Women who have received pre-primary training should be considered eligible for appointment in primary schools also (especially for Classes I and II) and regarded as trained primary teachers for purposes of pay and allowances.

(C) Education Of Women Belonging To Backward Classes

(144) In the funds sanctioned for the welfare of the backward classes, a special provision should be made for the education of women from the backward communities.

(D) Education Of Handicapped Children

(145) The Central Government should see that adequate facilities are provided for the training of teachers for handicapped children.

(E) Social Education

(146) A determined effort should be made to increase the number of classes for making women literate, particularly in rural areas.

(147) Mass literacy campaigns to spread literacy among women should be organised both in rural and urban areas

(148) (a) Social Education classes for imparting simple useful skills and for creating certain new attitudes necessary for present day conditions should be widely expanded through the agency of *Mahila Mandals* in rural areas.

(b) The method of a well-equipped mobile mission should be tried to implement the programme of imparting such skills and attitudes.

(F) **Professional Education**

(149) The study group of the Planning Commission have indicated that there would be great shortages of women personnel for various projects of the Third Plan. Steps which will reduce these shortages should be taken from now.

Organisation, Administration and Finance

(150) The existing proportion of women officers in the Education Departments should be substantially increased.

(151) At the primary and middle stages, an increasing number of women inspecting officers should be employed and all new vacancies should be filled by women as far as possible.

(152) At the secondary stage, girls' schools should be ordinarily inspected by women officers.

(153) Government should undertake a special programme for the development of the education of girls and women during the Third Plan which should include the following items:

Primary Stage (Age-Group Six-11)

(i) Attendance prizes and scholarships to girls in the age-group six-11;

(ii) All items and programmes connected with the drive to enrol more girls into schools;

(iii) The appointment of school mothers;

(iv) Supply of free educational equipment and clothes to girls;

(v) Attendance allowance to teachers;

(vi) All expenditure required to provide special amenities needed by girls in co-educational schools;

(vii) Construction of quarters for women teachers in rural areas.

Middle Stage (Age-Group 11-14)

(i) Scholarships to girls to enable them to continue their education further;

(ii) Establishment of separate middle schools for girls as well as the development of existing ones;

(iii) Supply of free educational equipment and clothes to girls.

Secondary Stage (Age-Group 14-17)

(i) Scholarships to girls on merit;

(ii) Scholarships to girls to enable them to continue their education;

(iii) Grant-in-aid to private institutions in lieu of concessions in fees given to girls at this stage;

(iv) Supply of educational equipment and clothes to girls; and

(v) Establishment of more secondary schools for girls and further development of existing ones, especially in rural areas, with provision for staff quarters, hostels and even free or subsidised transport, where necessary.

University Stage

(i) Scholarships to girls on merit;

(ii) Scholarships to girls for continuation of their studies at this stage

(iii) Grant of educational equipment to girls attending colleges;

(iv) Grants to be given to a few selected institutions to develop themselves into institutions specially devoted to the education of women.

Training of Teachers

(i) Non-recurring grants required for the development of existing institutions and for the establishment of new training institutions for women primary teachers, especially in rural areas. These grants should include grants for building, equipment, staff quarters and hostels ;

(ii) Award for scholarships to girls, especially from rural areas while under training.

Vocational And Special Education

(i) Grants-in-aid to institutions providing special education facilities for adult women;

(ii) Social education programmes for adult women;

(iii) Vocational training to Women;

(iv) Grants to private institutions providing vocational training to women; and

(v) Increasing the existing facilities available to women for vocational education.

Administration And Supervision

(i) All expenditure connected with the National Council for the education of Girls and women;

(ii) All expenditure connected with the State Councils for the Education of Girls and Women; and

(iii) All expenditure required for organising educative propaganda for developing the education of women.

(154) The old practice including a special Chapter on the education of girls and women in the Annual Reports of the Directors of Education of the States, which was discontinued at the suggestion of the Sargent Report should be revived.

(155) A special Chapter on the education of girls and women should also be included in the Annual Reviews of Education which are being published by the Ministry of Education.

III. General Recommendations

The following is the list of general recommendations

which concern not only the education of girls, but of boys as well.

Primary Education (Age Group Six to 11)

(156) Wherever primary education is not free, immediate steps should be taken to make it free and the Government should compensate the private schools for the loss in revenue resulting from the introduction of Free Education in case they are the only schools available in a particular area.

(157) Whenever new schools are started; the rural region should be given priority consideration. In fact a definite plan based on a survey should be followed by the Government so that there would be no unnecessary duplication and the distribution of schools would not be lopsided but would be even.

(158) Small and scattered habitations in hill, forest or desert areas and nomadic populations lack the necessary schooling facilities. In such cases some other solutions will have to be found. They may take the form of peripatetic teachers, central schools with hostels arrangements and/or .transport facilities or some other arrangements feasible in the local situation.

(159) Co-education should be adopted at the primary stage as a general policy. But as a transitional measure, separate schools for girls may be permitted as an exception in places where there is a strong public demand for them and the enrolment of girls is large enough to justifiy their establishment. Propaganda should be made in all such areas to remove the existing prejudice against co-education and create a positive opinion in its favour.

(160) The shift system should be adopted only as a temporary device and under special conditions of emergency. It should be introduced only wherever enrolment warrants it. It should be organised on a daily basis and not on alternate days. Wherever the shift system is in force one shift may be for boys and the other for girls, if it is likely to lead to greater enrolment of girls.

(161) The condition of primary schools needs much improvement in respect of staff, buildings, equipment educational activities and content and subjects actually taught as well as methods of teaching employed. Therefore, an order of priority should be fixed by each state among the various items mentioned above in accordance with the situation prevailing in each area.

(162) New patterns of cheap but healthy and convenient school buildings should be devised.

(163) The largest possible provision of part-time instruction, suited to the needs of each locality should be made in all parts of the country for children of poor parents, especially girls.

(164) Night schools should be started for those children who cannot attend day schools.

(165) Inducement through the provision of mid-day meals should also be offered to influence parents to send their children to schools. This provision should be a permanent feature of the primary school programme. The meals should be supplied free of charge only to such of the pupils as are ascertained to be poor and for them free supply is necessary and justified. They may not be free of charge for children of well-to-do families.

(166) There is a good deal of waste involved in the existing system in which a number of agencies operate in the field independently of each other. Instead of having a number of agencies, providing some form of refreshment or other to school children, each in a limited way, it is better if the Ministry of Education in collaboration with other Ministries works out a well-coordinated and clear cut Scheme by pooling all resources including public donations, and associating and encouraging voluntary efforts.

(167) Heads of schools should convene periodical meetings of the guardians/parents and give them opportunities of directly coming into contact with the life of school as a whole.

(168) Particular attention should also be paid to the following two measures :

(i) Improvement of schooling facilities ;

(ii) Encouragement of voluntary effort in expanding middle and secondary education.

Wastage And Stagnation

(169) Although the extent of wastage and stagnation in the case of girls is slightly higher than that in the case of boys, remedial measures to be adopted to reduce them should generally be the same for boys and girls, for these problems are common problems of the educational system as a whole.

(170) As a scientific study of the problem of wastage on an all-India basis is needed, the Ministry of Education should carry out special studies of this problem in all parts of the country to throw light on both the causes and extent of wastage at the different stages of the educational ladder.

(171) The Government of India should also carry out sample investigations into the problems of stagnation in select areas in different parts of the country.

(172) The necessary statistics to show the extent of stagnation should be collected from each State by the Government of India and included as a part of the statistical tables annually published.

(173) The following steps should be taken to reduce the extent of stagnation in Class I :

(i) All fresh admissions to Class I should be made in the beginning of the school year and not later than 60 days after the beginning of the first session.

(ii) It should be a specific responsibility of teachers particularly in rural areas, to see that proper attendance is maintained in the school and due consideration should be given to this aspect while assessing their work.

(iii) The age of admission should be raised to six plus.

(iv) Standards of teaching should be improved.

(174) The stagnation in Classes II to V can be reduced if :

(i) Attendance of children is increased.

(ii) Standards of teaching improved.

(iii) Internal examinations are introduced wherever necessary and possible and the teachers trained properly in evaluating the work of the students.

(iv) Books and educational equipment needed by poor children are supplied in good time.

(175) About 65 per cent of the cases of wastage at the primary level are due to economic causes. This wastage can be eliminated only if provision for part-time instruction is made for those children who cannot attend on a whole-time basis.

(176) School hours should be adjusted to the needs of the situation and steps should also be taken to adjust the vacations to suit local needs.

(177) About 25 to 30 per cent of the cases of wastage at the primary level are due to the indifference of parents. This cause can be eliminated partly by educative propaganda and partly by a rigorous enforcement of the compulsory education law.

(178) The other causes of wastage at the primary level are educational and can be eliminated if (i) the extent of stagnation is reduced, (ii) the quality of education is improved, (iii) provision of free supply of books and educational equipment (and even clothing in the case of girls) is made, (iv) incomplete primary schools, that is schools which do not teach all the five classes, are eliminated, and (v) the law for prevention of child marriages is rigorously enforced.

(179) Experimental pilot projects should be conducted by the Ministry of Education during the period of the Second Five-Year Plan itself to determine the causes of wastage and the methods of removing them. At least one such project should be undertaken in every State.

(180) Wastage at the middle and secondary stages is mainly due to economic reasons and in the case of girls, to early marriages. The average age of marriage will, therefore, have to rise still higher if this wastage is to be reduced; and the economic factors can only be met by provision of part-time instruction in the age-group of 11 to 14 and the provision of adequate financial assistance to poor and deserving girls of the age-group of 11 to 17 to continue their studies further.

(181) Stagnation and wastage are not independent evils by themselves. They are really symptoms of a number of other evils among which the most important are four :

(i) Lack of adjustment between the school sysetm and the social and economic environment of the community for whom they are intended.

(ii) Poor standards of the average schools which lack buildings, equipment and above all good teachers.

(iii) Absence of adequate economic assistance to children of poor parents to enable them to continue their studies further; and

(iv) Absence of facilities for part-time instruction.

If suitable action on the lines recommended is taken to remedy these fundamental evils of the educational system, the symptomatic evils of wastage and stagnation would disappear automatically.

Training And Employment Of Women Teachers

(182) Taking into consideration the increase in the cost of living as it obtains today the present scales of pay of teachers should be suitably revised.

(183) There should be no distinction between the scales of pay and allowances paid to teachers in Government and Local Board or Municipal institutions and those that are paid to teachers working under private managements.

(184) The triple-benefit scheme called the Pension-cum-Provident Fund-cum-Insurance Scheme should be made applicable to every teacher who is employed permanently in an institution.

(185) When teachers are required to work in areas where children speak dialects peculiar to the region, steps should be taken to give adequate instruction to the teachers in the local dialects.

KERALA AND MADRAS FOOD POISONING CASES ENQUIRY COMMISSION, 1958—REPORT

New Delhi, Ministry of Health, 1958. 117p.

Chairman : Shri Justice J.C. Shah.
Members : Major Ceneral Sarup Narain; Captain T.B. Bose.
Secretary : Shri V.R. Gadkari.

APPOINTMENT

The Kerala and Madras Food Poisoning Cases Enquiry Commission was constituted under the Ministry of Health vide their Notification No. F. 24-83/58-PH dated May 23, 1958, by Govt. of India in exercise of the powers conferred by Sec. 3 of the Commission of Inquiry Act, 1952 (60 of 1952).

TERMS OF REFERENCE

To inquire and report :

(a) The circumstances in which the causes whereby the food or food stuffs used in preparing the food came to be contaminated;

(b) Whether the contamination could have been avoided or detected in time;

(c) The action, if any, taken by the person or persons concerned after detection of such contamination to prevent further distribution of the contaminated food or food stuffs;

(d) Whether there has been any failure in taking adequate measure for the avoidance or timely detection of such contamination and the person or persons responsible for such failure; and

(e) The measure to be taken to safeguard against similar occurrences in future.

CONTENTS

Introductory; Voyage No. 166 of S.S. Jai Hind from Bombay to Cochin; Food-poisoning Cases in Kerala; Folidol; Conclusions and Recommendations; Monograph on Folidol by Major General Sarup Narain; Appendices I to V.

RECOMMENDATIONS

Special Recommendation About Disposal Of Food Stuffs Attached By The Kerala State

We are of the view that before any part of the foodstuffs which have been attached under orders of the State Government of Kerala can safely be released for consumption, representative samples from each bag or container should be obtained after a thorough mixing up of the contents of the bag or container in the presence of some health authority and subject to proper precautions in drawing the samples, and those samples must be subjected to independent tests in more than one laboratory and unless the findings are negative for parathion by the Averell and Norris tests as well as the spectrophotometric test and such other tests as the authorities may deem necessary to apply, the foodstuffs should not be permitted to be released for consumption.

General Recommendations

Control should be imposed by a comprehensive statute or statutes on the manufacture, storage, transport, distribution and use of insecticides which are regarded as highly toxic, especially dinitro-phenols and their salts, dinitro-substituted phenols and their salts, organo-phosphorous compounds and preparations or mixtures containing any one or more of the aforesaid insecticides; and substances to which the statute may, by notification to be made, apply.

Provision for regulations may be made under the statute for precautions to be taken in the matter of manufacture, formulation or processing of the insecticides in the matter of providing protective clothing, facility for ventilation, in the factories supplying masks, eye-shields, rubber gloves and rubber aprons and washing facilities for all workmen employed in the manufacture, formulation or processing of the scheduled insecticides and for decontamination and care of equipment used in the application of the insecticides.

Regulations should be made for frequent medical examination of workmen engaged in the manufacture, formulation, processing or application of the insecticides.

Regulation should be made for supervision over the workmen during the process of manufacture, formulation, processing and application of insecticides, and for preventing the workmen from eating, drinking or smoking in the course of their work and in the area of application.

Other regulations for ensuring the safety of workmen against special hazard to the workmen incidental to their employment in the manufacture and application should also be made.

Regulation imposing an obligation upon the manufacturer, processor or formulator to store insecticides in special containers, and to use specified containers if the authority constituted in that behalf so directs.

Regulation for certification of suitable containers for insecticides by one of the national laboratories or other approved institutions should be made.

Regulations for provision of separate storage of insecticide in warehouses should be made.

In the matter of transport, we recommend that the Indian Merchant Shipping Act and the Indian Merchant Shipping (carriage of Dangerous Goods) Rules, 1954, be amended by making it obligatory upon the shipper to make a declaration under Rule 4, and by providing a penalty of imprisonment for a substantial period for infringement of the rules. Similar provision should also be made requiring the consignor to make a declaration in writing as regards the identity of the goods, the nature of the danger to which the goods give rise, and indicating at the same time the category of poison even when the transport is by rail, road or air, and imposing penalty for breach of the same, and for separate storage when the insecticides are transported by rail, air, road or even boats.

The manufacturers and distributors should be licensed and be obliged to give necessary instructions to the purchaser of insecticides about the toxic quality of the insecticide sold by them, and to maintain record of the sales of the insecticides.

Regulation for providing labels for containers and packages in which they are stored and the forms thereof which give precise and adequate information to the persons dealing with the containers and packages of insecticides in conformity with the international recommendations in that behalf should be made.

Regulation for giving information to the health, agricultural and municipal authorities regarding the use of insecticides within their jurisdiction should be made.

Setting up of Pest Control Laboratories with special facility for study of insecticides, their properties, behaviour and effect, and for development of insecticides which are less toxic to human beings.

Provision of facility for training and education of all concerned in the matter of handling and use of insecticides, decontamination of equipment, and contaminated articles and disposal of containers.

Research in the matter of evolving protective devices in an effort to discover which equipment will give complete protection against contamination by insecticides without interfering with the comfort and safety of the workmen.

TEXTILE ENQUIRY COMMITTEE, 1958—REPORT

Delhi, Manager of Publications, 1958. 84p.

Chairman : Shri D.S. Joshi.

Members : Prof. D.G. Karve; Shri N. Majumdar; Shri Kanhaiyalal Mehta; Shri Padampat Singhania; Shri Krishnaraj M.D. Thackersey; Shri S.R. Vasavada; Shri R. Venkataswamy Naidu.

Secretary : Shri K.R. Aravamuthan.

APPOINTMENT

The Cotton Textile Industry has been for sometime past, experiencing difficulties by way of accumulation of yarn and cloth and also by a fall in exports generally. Apart from the relief recently given by reductions and rationalisation of excise duty, Government consider it necessary that an examination of the structure of the industry, with special reference to production, management, finance, modernisation and allied problems, should now be undertaken and have accordingly set up this Committee under the Ministry of Commerce and Industry vide their Resolution No. 1(9)-TEX(A)/58 dated May 29, 1958.

TERMS OF REFERENCE

(i) To enquire into the present condition of the Cotton Textile Industry;

(ii) To suggest necessary remedial measures to overcome the difficulties of the industry.

CONTENTS

Introductory; Difficulties of the Industry; Demand for Cloth and Rated Capacity; Marketing and Finance; Excise Duty and Handloom Rebate; Coal, Fuel, Electricity and other Charges; Production Controls and Costing; Export Promotion; Textile Mill Closures; Rationalisation and Modernisation; Management; Concluding Remarks; Summary of Conclusions and Recommendations; Annexures; Statistical Data.

RECOMMENDATIONS

Several factors were adduced to have contributed to the malady faced by some sections of the industry.

The deep rooted causes refer to the need for the replacement of outdated machinery, rationalisation, modernisation, major repairs and overhauls, rectification of inefficient management purchases and sales as also improvement of productivity of labour.

Other causes are—decline in purchasing power, increases in cost structure of the industry, high taxation and over production of certain varieties of coarse cloth. Steep increase in excise duties in September 1956 was also stated as an additional factor.

There has been a significant increase in the production of coarse varieties particularly coarse dhoties and sarees.

The consumers' preference is for better and finer varieties of cotton textiles.

The Committee considers that:

(i) Specialisation of products in each unit should help to maintain and improve the quality and at the same time result in economy in production.

(ii) In view of consumer preferences for better quality goods processing facilities to the necessary extent should be allowed.

The extent to which the anticipated increase in the handloom production falls short, the per capita availability of cloth will be affected.

The spinning sector caters to the demand of handloom industry and is therefore interlinked with the vicissitudes of the handloom cloth production and sale.

The Government of India have already set up a Wage Board consisting of members from the Industry and Labour as well as experts. The Committee feels that questions relating to wage and DFA should be left to the judgment of the Wage Board.

Since the economic development is not at the rate envisaged in the Plan, the Committee does not anticipate that the per capita consumption will exceed 17.5 yards.

It does not appear that mill production will be running at too high a figure. If due to unforeseen circumstances the position deteriorates in future, it is necessary to adjust the production in the different sectors revising the allocations for cach Sector.

The rated capacity of the Industry can be fixed at 5,100 to 5,200 million yards.

The spinning capacity is bound to increase when all the outstanding licensed spindles of 1.5 million are installed.

There is at present a sizable surplus of yarn available for export without injury to the handloom industry.

The Committee has noted that Government have recently announced a policy for the next three years as regards the export of yarn to the extent of performance during 1958 by exporting mills plus additional 1.2 lakh bales.

The Committee recommends that further installation of spindles even already licensed should be stopped after examining each case. The Textile Commissioner should be armed with powers to regulate production of free yarn both by spinning and composite mills.

The question of marketing of cloth forms an important field which guides producers on changing tastes and preferences of consumers. Marketing intelligence or research is an indispensable adjunct. There is a need for more continuous and sustained study in this field which may be undertaken by the Industry and the Textile Commissioner's organisation.

The co-related statistical information about stocks from the production to the consumer's end may also advisedly be undertaken on a sampling basis.

Subject to the normal precautions being taken by banks in lending to the Industry and Trade the Committee would recommend liberal financing by the banks.

The Committee strongly feels that introduction of changes in excise duty in the middle of financial years should normally be avoided.

The overwhelming evidence before the Committee was in favour of change over of duties to *ad valorem* basis.

The low duties coupled with rebate on extra production led to a phenomenal increase in the production of coarse dhoties and sarees.

The Committee considers that the present structure of duties is weighted more heavily on plain cloth and unprocessed cloth compared to processed cloth of various descriptions. Both on the grounds of equity and on the grounds of fairness to the mills without processing equipment, it is essential that the pattern of excise duty is changed to provide for a closer approximation to *ad valorem* duties.

For the handloom industry the question of assistance available by way of rebate be based on a fairly stable basis. The Government should announce the measures of assistance by way of rebate on an annual basis as far as possible.

The Committee would urge that positive assistance designed to ensure the efficiency and impoving the quality of the products of the handloom sector should be pursued with even greater vigour.

The Committee considers that any measure of additional taxation by the State Governments consequent on replacement of sales tax by excise duty would run counter to an expectation of bona fide replacement.

The Committee considers that some of the provisions of Production Control Order have become obsolete and may be modified and others while they may continue in existence their operations would be suspended.

In the context of the unmistakable shift in the pattern of consumer demand for cloth of improved quality and in processed condition rather than grey goods of cheaper quality, the Committee is of the opinion that the Industry will have to go in increasingly for the production of bleached, dyed, printed and finished cloth to suit the consumers' taste.

It is recommended that Government should examine the granting of printing quotas question in the light of the requirement of the needy mills.

The Committee also would recommend costing analysis by spot investigation for a few selected units of the industry at least half-yearly.

A uniform or standard costing system should be introduced in the textile industry.

The Committee urges that larger funds should be made available to the Cotton Textiles Export Promotion Council to open offices in other countries so that the demand in those countries could be properly assessed and stimulated and recommends certain other measures.

The Committee recommends that as an experimental measure, up to 3,000 additional automatic looms should be allowed to be installed, on condition that the entire production of such looms is exported.

The main reasons for closure seem to be bad condition of machinery in many cases neglected continuously without proper attendance and repairs and replacements. In efficient management has also been one of the main reasons.

It is difficult to have a common remedy for enabling the closed mills to reopen. While each case will have to be investigated on its merit, the Committee recommends adoption of certain measures.

Problem of rationalisation in the textile industry has to be solved adequately if the industry was to progress and make full use of the results of technological advancement.

Industry cannot be expected to modernise unless it is allowed to rationalise simultaneously.

The Committee has used the term "Rationalisation" to mean a reorganisation in an unit of the industry which ensures elimination of all waste and the most scientific utilisation of men, material and machinery.

Rationalisation without the cooperation of labour results in strained relations between the labour and the management leading to breach of industrial peace.

The Committee feels that having regard to the need for ensuring industrial peace and obtaining the fullest cooperation from the workers, rationalisation with or without modernisation subject to the conditions of the 15th Labour Conference may not be quick enough for some centres where margin of excess labour is large.

The Committee suggests setting up a Rationalisation Sub-Committee for the Industry as a whole for considering and laying down policies and principles governing rationalisation from time to time.

The Committee also suggests formation of sub-Committees on a regional level working within the framework of such principles and dealing individual schemes of rationalisation within their areas before implementation.

In view of the large majority of machines in existence today having outlived their usefulness the need for rehabilitation is urgent. Non-replacement of such machinery would result in low production, bad quality of products, engagement of a large number of workers and high cost of production.

The rate at which rehabilitation could be effectively undertaken is limited by availability of foreign exchange, paucity of funds with the mills, non-availability of certain essential items of machinery from indigenous sources etc.

There is at present no adequate machinery which goes into individual requirements of mills for rehabilitation.

The Committee feels that a small consultative Sub-Committee to advise Government on the principles and procedures to be followed in deciding these applications should be set up.

Management is the single most important factor that makes the difference between success and failure of a textile undertaking.

We still find that a number of marginal and sub-marginal units which are not making the best use of their resources and thereby are causing avoidable losses to the community in general are creating a situation which leads to closures or threatened closures.

Mills with inadequate and dilapidated machinery which have been reported by experts as beyond redemption should definitely not be allowed to restart in the same condition. It would be better to allow them to be scrapped and to be replaced, if necessary, by better equipped units.

There is no machinery in existence today which would ensure a timely survey of the operations of individual mills particularly of those found to be operating on unsound or inefficient lines.

The Committee feels that an Advisory Committee consisting of all interests and Government representatives from all the important centres should be set up. This Committee should be available for advising the Textile Commissioner on all important matters affecting the working of the units of the textile industry.

In order that this Advisory Committee can be adequately furnished with up-to-date information about the working of mills, the Special Survey Wing of the Textile Commissioner's organisation should be strengthened with adequate staff.

Where the management is unresponsive, or the weaknesses have taken deeper roots, it would be necessary to invoke the relevant provisions of the Industries (Development and Regulation) Act, to not only institute formal enquiries but also ultimately to take over the management of such mills.

The Committee does not feel that it would be advisable for Government either to manage or own and manage mills taken over under the Act as a Department of Government. The Committee recommends that an autonomus Corporation functioning independently of the Government should be constituted for this purpose with adequate capital. The Board of Management of the Corporation should be so constituted as to attract experienced and public spirited millowners, responsible leaders of labour, technicians and expert managers.

The Committee is firmly of the opinion that Government should give the greatest weight to the advice rendered by the Advisory Committee not only in regard to proposals of taking over the management of mills but also to all items which have been placed before it for advice.

The Committee is of the opinion that the Corporation should not enjoy any discriminatory advantages compared with well run mills under private management.

DIRECT TAXES ADMINISTRATION ENQUIRY COMMITTEE 1958—REPORT

Delhi, Manager of Publications, 1960. 578p.+ivp.+vp.

Chairman : Shri Mahavir Tyagi.
Members : Shri Rajendra Pratap Sinha; Shri B.M. Gupte; Shri G.P. Kapadia; Shri K.S. Sundara Rajan.
Secretary : Shri F.H. Vallibhoy.

APPOINTMENT

This Committee was appointed by the Government of India in pursuance of Resolution No. 4 (59)/ 58-TPL dated June 3, 1958, the main part of which reads as under:

"The Government of India have had under consideration for some time the question of having an efficient system of direct taxation which will be sufficiently broad based and will also be determined according to the capacity to pay. With a view to achieving this end, necessary legislation has been undertaken recently to impose taxes on wealth, expenditure and gifts and the exemption limit for payment of income-tax has also been reduced. The integration of the tax structure has thus been completed so far as legislation is concerned.

2. The entire work in connection with the assessment and collection of these taxes has fallen on the Income-Tax Department. This Department was organised for the assessment and collection of income-tax only. In recent years, it has been expanded to take on the new burdens but it is necessary to ensure that the administrative organisation and procedure are such as would secure the basic objectives of the present taxation policy. It is equally important that the administrative machinery should be effective in checking evasion of taxes and function without giving any scope for public complaint."

TERMS OF REFERENCE

To advise Government on the administrative organisation and procedures necessary for implementing the integrated scheme of direct taxation with due regard to the need for eliminating tax evasion and avoiding inconvenience to the assessees.

CONTENTS

Introduction; General; Assessments I—Procedures; Assessments II—Special Problems; Appeals and Revisions; Collection and Recovery; Refunds; Evasion and Avoidance; Administration; Public Relations; Summary of Conclusions and Recommendations; Appendices I to XV; Memorandum of Dissent, Comments and Recommendations by Shri G.P. Kapadia; Index.

RECOMMENDATIONS

General

Until such time as the Department and the taxpaying public gain sufficient experience of the working of the existing statutes, the present position of administering the various taxes under the different Acts should continue.

It is not worthwhile to introduce a system of asssessment on the basis of one comprehensive return of the income, wealth, expenditure and gift.

The designation of the assessing officers under all the direct taxes Acts should be changed to 'Direct Taxes Officers' and the designation of the other authorities to Appellate Assistant Commissioner, Direct Taxes, Inspecting Assistant Commissioner, Direct Taxes, Commissioner of Direct Taxes and Direct Taxes Appellate Tribunal. It is also necessary to change the designation of the Income-Tax Department into the 'Direct Taxes Department.

Frequent changes in the statutes adversely affect the efficiency of the Department and should, therefore, be avoided.

All substantial changes in the law should, as far as possible, be effected through specific amending Acts which would provide opportunities for detailed consideration by the Parliament, instead of through the Finance Bills as at present.

Simplification of taxing statutes is not an easy task. However, if changes in the statutes are reduced to the barest minimum and the provisions are arranged more logically and expressed in clearer language much of the existing ambiguity would disappear.

It is essential that appropriate measures are taken to enable the State to secure its due amounts of taxes. For this purpose, the administration has to be so geared that the state is able to collect the taxes in full without causing any undue inconvenience to the assessees.

Assessments I (Procedures)

Total Quantum And Arrears Of Assessments

The department should endeavour to complete all assessments, as far as possible, in the assessment year itself and save in exceptional cases, no assessment should remain pending for more than two years.

Measures For Expediting Disposal

Assessees having income from business, profession or vocation should be statutorily required to file the returns of income within four months after the close of the accounting year or by June 30, following that year, whichever is later. For all other assessees, the last date for filing of returns should be June 30, regardless of their accounting year. In suitable cases, where the accounting period for business, profession or vocation ends after December, 31, the assessing officer should be empowered to grant on his own appropriate extensions of time for filing the return, up to a date not exceeding beyond a period of six months from the end of the accounting year. In any other case, extension should be granted by him only after obtaining the previous permission of the Commissioner and on conditions which might include the furnishing of adequate security for the tax that might become due. In all cases of extension, the levy of interest at six per cent per annum on the tax that would become payable on assessment, should be compulsory and statutorily laid down. Assessees who do not file the returns by the prescribed or the extended date should be subjected to deterrent penalties which should vary according to the period of default.

The statutory provision, under Section 22 (i) of the Income-Tax Act, for the issue of a general public notice should be deleted. Instead, a simple advertisement should be issued in the beginning of each assessment year, reminding the public about their liability to file their returns within the perscribed dates.

As a matter of convenience, the Department should send return forms to the existing assessees by ordinary post under a general certificate of posting so as a reach them before April 30. However, if a person does not file the return within the time-limit or within the extended time, he should be considered to be in default unless he can show that he had applied for return from the assessing officer in time and the same had not been supplied to him.

The responsibility for a preliminary scrutiny of returns should be specifically assigned to the Inspector or Head Clerk. Such a scrutiny should be restricted to pointing out technical defects which have a material bearing on the assessment.

Though assessment proceedings may have to be adjourned on account of genuine difficulties of assessees, adjournments should not be given as a matter of course, but only where they are justified.

The assessing officers should have full discretion to fix their programmes of assessment work. They should however, have no objection to adjusting these programmes to suit the convenience of assessees' representatives, should the latter so request.

Assessing officers should give a minimum of eight days' time from the date of service of a notice for its compliance.

The need for planning of work and prior study of a case before fixing it for hearing is nowhere greater than in the Income-Tax Department.

The use of standardised questionnaire in respect of important industries, trades and professions should be restricted to big cases only and be relevant to the facts of the case.

Each assessing officer should chalk out, in the beginning of the year, a plan of his work for the year. In doing so, be should take due care that revenue-yielding and-arrear cases are taken up sufficiently early in the year, that all pending assessments in a case are taken up together and that the assessments under the various direct taxes Acts in a case are disposed of simultaneously.

Wherever sufficient numbers of cases of similar trades, businesses, etc., are available, functional circles should be organised to deal separately with the cases of each trade, business, etc.

Small Income group Scheme

The amount of time and labour devoted to cases of different categories should bear relation to their revenue potential. The time and energy being spent on small cases appears to be totally disproportionate to the revenue yields therefrom. The Department must get out of the present groove and make a bold departure in respect of the assessment of small income cases. In such cases the income returned should be generally accepted after preliminary scrutiny and the assessment made under Section 23(1) of the Income Tax Act without calling the assessee to the tax office. Detailed examination of accounts and other scrutiny would be made only once in four years. This new approach will have a psychological effect and improve the relations between the Department and nearly five lakhs of assessees.

The proposal for having on-the-spot assessments is not favoured. However, in big cities like Bombay, Calcutta, Madras and Delhi, the assessing officers dealing with small income cases should have their offices in the various localities, if the number of cases justifies such local offices. In the mofussil areas, an assessee should be called to the nearest place which the assessing officer visits during the year, unless the assessee requests for a hearing at the headquarters of the officer.

Middle And Large Income Group Assessees

Cases of large income group assessees should be segregated, wherever possible, and entrusted to experienced and competent officers.

Where returns or accounts have been accepted in the past, they should not be subjected to detailed enquiry every year, unless the assessing officer comes in possession of definite information regarding concealment of income etc., in such cases.

The proposal for deleting the proviso to Section 13 of the Income-tax Act relating to estimated assessments is not favoured. However, to remove various difficulties experienced in the application of this proviso, the following steps should be taken:

(a) The Department should, after due study of the local conditions and practices, and in consultation with the various chambers and trade associations, consider the feasibility of prescribing the minimum accounts and the type of accounts which should be maintained in respect of each trade, business or vocation. If accounts are kept in the prescribed form or maintained in proper manner with sales and purchases supported by vouchers or otherwise proved, they should be accepted unless there are grave omissions or there is evidence of suppressed sales or undisclosed purchases.

(b) In any case where it is proposed to reject the results shown by the account books, the assessee must be given an opportunity to explain his viewpoint. Before finalising the assessment, the assessing officer should also give to the assessee an indication of the rate of gross profits that is proposed to be adopted and the relevant particulars of comparable cases, ensuring that such information does not enable the assessee to identify the person to whom the particulars relate.

(c) In cases where accounts are reliable in part, estimates should be restricted only to such other part as is not acceptable.

(d) Gross profit rates registers in the prescribed form should be maintained, tradewise, in each tax Circle or Ward.

(e) A list of the cases where the proviso to Section 13 of the Income-tax Act had been applied should be sent, every fortnight, by each assessing officer to the Inspecting Assistant Commissioner.

(f) In their orders on appeals against the invoking of the proviso and the gross profit rates applied, the appellate authorities should fully and properly reason out the relief which they give.

A provision should be made in the Income-tax Act requiring all assessees to furnish statements of total wealth every fourth year along with their returns of income.

Before finalising an assessment, the assessing officer should make a tentative computation of the total income, wealth, etc. Where the additions or disallowances proposed to be made are of small amounts only, he may discuss them orally with the assessee and/or his representative and record the result of the discussion on the order sheet. However, where substantial additions are proposed, he should allow an opportunity to the assessee, in writing, to give his point of view within a fortnight.

Audit of accounts in all non-company cases of business, profession or vocation, where the assessed total income in any of the last three years exceeds Rs. 50,000 should be made compulsory by law and the auditors should be required to give audit certificate in a prescribed form. Such an audit should also be compulsory in those cases of business, profession or vocation where the returned income, for the first time, exceeds Rs. 50,000.

Improvements In Methods Of Work

In cases where production of books of accounts is necessary and the assessments could be completed in one hearing, notices under Sections 23(21) and 22(4) of the Income-tax Act should be issued simultaneously and preferably in a combined form.

It is not desirable to revive the cadre of Examiner of Accounts in the form in which it existed till 1945. However, the assessing officers should be permitted to utilise the assistance of the Inspectors in the matter of routine examination of accounts or detailed examination on specific issues. In addition, there should be a set of experienced Examiners, preferably Chartered Accountants, at important centres of various Commissioners' charges to assist the officers in examination of complicated cases.

Suitable administrative instructions should be issued to the effect that in bona fide cases, expenses should be allowed after scrutiny on broad lines without going into meticulous details, and that interest, rebates and other trade discounts should be allowed in the years in which such adjustments are recorded in the books.

It should be ensured, by executive action, that assessment order is passed by the assessing officer as early as possible, after the final hearing, but in no case later than thirty days. There should be a statutory provision in all the direct taxes Acts requiring the assessing officer to send a certified copy of the assessment order along with the notice of demand.

In order to reduce complications in the calculations of tax, the following steps should be taken :

(a) The basic rates of income-tax should be incorporated in the statute itself.

(b) To meet the budgetary requirements from time to time, variations should be made in the rates of surcharges through the annual Finance Acts. Whenever necessary, however, the basic rates may also be increased or decreased.

(c) Without affecting any of the reliefs at present admissible, such of the sur-charges on income-tax as go to the divisible pool should be merged with the basic income-tax rates.

(d) In the case of company taxation, instead of prescribing the rate of super tax at 50 per cent and then providing several rebates therefrom for various types of companies, the effective rate of super tax for each of these types should be specified in the Act itself.

(e) In the case of registered firms having total income exceeding Rs. 40,000, the procedure for allowing rebates to the partners should be suitably amended so as to simplify the calculations of tax, without affecting the incidence or quantum of taxation.

(f) Ready-reckoners for calculations of taxes should be made available to the departmental officials immediately after the passing of the Finance Bill.

(g) All tax offices should be equipped with one or more calculating machines.

Internal audit parties for conducting post-audit of tax calculations, etc., should be established on a permanent footing in all commissioners' charges and they should be adequately staffed. They should be as zealous in pointing out mistakes which have resulted in excess recoveries of tax from assessees as they are in detecting cases of under payment. There should also be a more comprehensive and systematic pre-audit of tax calculations than is being done at present.

The assessing officers should maintain two separate order sheets—one for recording brief details of all the proceedings relating to an assessment and the other for noting matters of confidential nature like inter-departmental correspondence, etc. The former order sheet alone should be open to inspection by assessees and copies thereof should be made available to them, subject to the usual rules.

Assessment proceedings should not be delayed in any case merely because there would be no further recovery of tax or a refund might result.

Assessing officers should be administratively required to report to their higher authorities cases where assessments have not been completed within 12 months from the date of the filing of the returns, giving reasons therefor.

Precautionary assessments should be made only in exceptional cases where there is a likelihood of irretrievable loss to revenue.

The present return forms require simplification in certain respects. They should be so revised and rationalised that the columns which are mostly superfluous are deleted, that each assessee is required to give details only in respect of those matters which are relevant to his assessment and that such enquiries of a general nature which are almost invariably made at present, in the course of assessment proceedings, are incorporated in these forms.

The power of the Central Government to grant relief under Section 60(2) of the Income-tax Act in accordance with the rules already laid down should statutorily vest in the Commissioners of Income-Tax.

Assessments II
(Special Problems)

Foreign Branches

The Department should take special steps to ensure that the statutory provisions and instructions of the Central Board of Revenue for keeping the tax demands relating to foreign income and assets in abeyance, until monies can be repatriated to India, are strictly followed by the assessing officers and no harassment is caused to the assessees.

While the income from or value of shares in Indian companies having assets in foreign countries, which have imposed restrictions on the repatriation of profits or capital to India, should continue to be included in the hands of the shareholders for assessment purposes the amount of tax to be covered should be limited to the sum that would have been payable, had the income or assets in these countries not been included in the assessee's total world income or wealth. The balance of the demand should not be recovered until restrictions on their repatriation are removed.

The certificates of assessment issued by the foreign taxation authorities in regard to transactions in foreign countries should be invariably accepted as a sufficient proof, unless there are reasons to suspect the bona fides of such certificates. In such cases there should be no need for insisting on the production of account books or even audited balance sheets or statements of accounts.

Depreciation Allowances

The existing method of allowing depreciation on the basis of 'written down value' for assets other than ocean-going ships, should continue.

The present method of allowing depreciation on the basis of the number of months of use of an asset in a year should be changed. Depreciation at full rates should be allowed in respect of an asset which has been used for the business for six months or more during the 'previous year'. For an asset which has been used for more than a month but less than six months, depreciation should be allowed at half of the prescribed rates. No depreciation should be admissible as regards an asset which has not been used for a total period of more than a month during the 'previous year'.

The present procedure for making changes in the categorisation of assets and rates of depreciation prescribed in Rule 8 of the Income Tax Rules is satisfactory and should continue. However, in future, before making any changes or amendments in this regard, the views of the Direct Taxes Central Advisory Committee which is being proposed, should be obtained and duly considered by the Central Board of Revenue.

Provisions of Section 10 (2) (vii) of the Income-tax Act should be applicable to 'furniture' also.

Where an asset is purchased and sold in the same year, no depreciation should be allowable, and the difference between its purchase value and the sales price should be treated as capital gain or loss, as the case may be.

Expenses of repairs to leased properties used for the purposes of business, profession or vocation, and normal depreciation on alterations or additions made by the lessee to such properties should, by executive instructions, be allowed in his assessment to the extent to which he would have been entitled to them; had he been the owner of the premises. This concession should be available only for the period of the lease. Any residual depreciation which cannot be given or remains unabsorbed, owing to the termination of the lease, should not be carried forward, either in the hands of the lessee or the lessor.

In order to avoid difficulties arising out of different methods of calculating depreciation in the cases of electricity undertakings for income-tax purposes and for the purposes of Electricity (Supply) Act, 1948, the latter Act should be suitably amended so as to provide for appropriate reserves of depreciation in earlier years.

Development Rebate

The condition that for the allowance of development rebate, the asset should not be sold or otherwise transferred to any person other than the Government for a period of 10 years needs to be relaxed. This period should be reduced to eight years. The restrictions should not apply to transfer or sale of assets to Government Companies, Statutory Corporations and public utility companies, and those resulting from the absorption of one company, by amalgamation or otherwise, by another company.

If a firm which had been allowed development rebate in respect of certain assets converts itself into a private limited company within the period prescribed for allowance of such rebate, and the share capital of the partners of the erstwhile firm in the company remains either the same or is more and the amount of development rebate kept in reserve by the firm is transferred *en bloc* to the company which also keeps it under the same conditions as would have applied to the firm, had it continued, the rebate should not be forfeited.

There should be a general provision in the statute conferring on the Central Board of Revenue, residuary power of relaxation of the various conditions for entitlement of development rebate in exceptional cases.

In cases of companies which acquire new machinery entitled to development rebate but which incur overall losses within the statutory period of 10 years, the rebate should not be withdrawn, if such a withdrawal results in the levy of tax.

The intention of the legislature with regard to the word 'installed' for the purposes of allowing development rebate should be clarified beyond all doubts by suitable amendment of the Income-tax Act. Development rebate should also be admissible in respect of mobile plant and machinery, such as earth removers, cranes, bulldozers, aero-engines, coal mining machinery, etc., as well as on trucks and tractors and other machinery which are used exclusively in connection with mining operations.

Bad Debts And Irrecoverable Loans

Assessing officers should not disallow the claim of a bad debt on purely technical grounds. If the officer is satisfied about the genuineness of a bad debt, he must allow it either for the 'previous year' in respect of which it is claimed or for any of the earlier 'previous years' in which, according to the officer, the debt had actually become bad, provided that such earlier 'previous year' is not more than four years anterior to the 'previous year' in which the debt is claimed to have become bad and actually written off. The assessing officer's findings in this respect should be appealable. The appellate authorities should, in such appeals, give a definite finding as to the year within the four years' period to which the bad debt relates. The effect of the appellate order should be given by the assessing officer by rectification of the relevant assessment order under section 35 of the Income-tax Act. These considerations should equally apply to claims of irrecoverable loans.

If the assessing officer finds that the write off of a bad debt is premature, he must make a specific note to this effect in the assessment records and allow the bad debt in the relevant year irrespective of the fact that the debt has been written off in the earlier year.

In the case of public banking companies, although statements giving all relevant particulars in regard to claims of bad debts and irrecoverable loans in respect of their assessments should continue to be supplied by them, the assessing officer should not exercise any meticulous check over them, nor call for additional information except in cases where he has reasons to doubt the genuineness or the correctness of their write off.

Mutual Associations

Government should enter into suitable long-term administrative arrangements with chambers of commerce, trade and professional associations, etc., so as to tax them on the entire surplus of receipts over outgoings without allocation between mutual and non-mutual activities. Annual subscriptions paid by members of these bodies should be deducted from their income and so also the surplus distributed to the members, such surplus being taxed in the hands of the recipients. The proposal for total exemption of chambers of commerce from tax is not approved.

Section 23-A Companies

The existing provision of Section 23-A of the Income-tax Act relating to statutory percentages of the net distributable profits which should be distributed as dividends by Section 23-A companies should continue. The administrative discretion for relaxing these percentages which was available upto 1957 in the form of Sub-sections 3 and 4 of Section 23-A should not be revived.

The provisions of Section 23-A (2) should be so amended as to provide that the company would get an opportunity to make further distribution of its profits and gains to make up the statutory percentage, if:

(a) The distribution made by the company falls short of the statutory percentage by not more than 15 per cent of its total income, as reduced by the amounts referred to in clauses (a), (b) and (c) of Section 23-A(i); or

(b) The company had distributed not less than the statutory percentage of the total income as reduced by the amounts, according to the return made by it under Section 22 (2), but in the assessment made by the assessing officer, a higher total income is arrived at and this difference is due to any reason other than deliberate concealment.

The provisions of the old Sub-Section (6) of Section 23-A of the Income Tax Act were equitable and easily administerable, and they should, therefore, be restored.

Such of the foreign profits which could not be remitted and also the taxes thereon should both be excluded in the calculation of the distributable income for the purposes of Section 23-A of the Income-tax Act. Simultaneously, it should be made clear in the statute that if and when such profits are repatriated they would be included in the distributable income.

The time-limit for passing on order under Section 23-A of the Income-tax Act in cases of normal assessment should be limited to four years in the same way as for making assessments. Such a time-limit should not apply to cases of companies whose assessments are reopened or made under Section 34 of the Act.

It should be made clear in the statute itself that the mere fact that the articles of association of a company give general discretion to its Directors to allow or disallow the transfer of its shares would not mean that the shares are not freely transferable so as to invite the application of Sections 23-A of the Income-tax Act.

The Department should, under administrative instruction, give, on request, a clearance to the companies as to whether on the facts stated to them, the provisions of Section 23-A would be applicable or not.

Speculation Losses

No change is considered necessary in the fundamentals of the provisions of Section 24 (1) of the Income-tax Act relating to set off of loss sustained in speculative transactions. However, the following steps should be taken for removing some of the difficulties experienced in the application of the existing provisions :

(i) Explanation 2 to Section 24 (1) of the Income Tax Act should be expanded so as to clearly specify the various types of hedging transactions which would not be regarded as speculative for the purposes of this Section. Hedging transactions in connected commodities should not be treated as speculative transactions, provided the total of such hedging sales does not exceed the actual stocks and purchase transactions.

(ii) Bona fide hedging transactions entered into by a dealer or investor in shares different from those held by him, up to the amount of his holdings in stocks and shares should not be treated as speculative.

(iii) Suitable administrative instructions should be issued giving illustrations in order to make the intention of the Government clear as to what constitute speculative transactions and what are hedging transactions.

(iv) Genuine hedging transactions with parties outside the country should be treated at par with the hedging transactions inside the country.

(v) Suitable administrative instructions should be issued so as to make it clear that speculative loss, if any, carried forward from the earlier years or the speculation loss, if any, in a year should first be adjusted against speculation profits of the particular year before allowing any other loss to be adjusted against these profits.

Registration Of Firms

Once a firm is registered, there should be no obligation on it to apply for renewal of registration every year, provided the firm files a declaration along with the return of income to the effect that there had been no change in its constitution. Unless a partner who has left a firm intimates the act of his having done so to the assessing officer, he should continue to remain liable for the tax on his share of the profits.

Assessing officers should point out technical errors, if any, in a partnership deed, or application for registration and offer the partners of the firm an opportunity to rectify such technical defects within a month.

It should be provided in the Income Tax Act or the rules thereunder, that the firm or firms as constituted during the accounting year should be registered and the demand should be raised against the partners constituting the firms during that year. It should further be provided that the successor firm and/or its partners would also be liable for the tax liability of the succeeded firm or its partners.

Reopening Of Assessments

No change in the time-limits for taking action under Section 34 of the Income-tax Act is called for. However, before reopening an assessment under this section, the assessing officer should intimate to the assessee the grounds on which the action is proposed to be taken, and give him 10 days' time to send his reply. It is after proper consideration of the reply of the assessee that the decision to reopen the case should be taken.

Section 34 (3) of the Income Tax Act should be so amended as to give the Department at least one year's time from the date of filing of a return under Section 22 (3) of the Income Tax Act for completing that assessment.

The proposal for incorporating in the direct taxes Acts provisions similar to those of Section 66 of the U.K. Income Tax Act, 1952 is not favoured.

Neither the assessee nor the Department should be entitled to have assessments reopened on points of law already concluded merely because there is a later decision of the High Court or the Supreme Court to the contrary.

Taxation Of Non-Residents

The proposal for adopting in the Indian Income Tax Act the provisions of U.K. Income Tax Act in regard to taxation of non--residents is not favoured. Executive instructions issued by the Central Board of Revenue regarding the interpretation of the term 'business connection' and in respect of the provisions for the taxability of non-resident should be widely publicised both within and outside the country.

Applications for the issue of certificates under the second proviso to Section 42 (1) of the Income Tax Act regarding the extent of the tax liability of the agent of a non-resident should be promptly attended to by the assessing officers and disposed of within one month of their receipt.

The Department should avoid proceeding simultaneously against the non-resident and his resident agent.

Place Of Assessment

Where an assessee has more than one place of business, profession or vocation, the assessment should be done at the place which is the most important from the point of view of his business activities.

It should be made clear that the place of assessment should be taken in relation to the assessment year and not the 'previous year'.

Suitable administrative steps should be taken to put a stop to the illegal and incorrect practice of some of the officers to proceed with the assessments without referring the assessees' objections about jurisdiction to the Commissioner, although the objections had been raised by the assessees in time.

The provisions of the Explanation to Section 5 (7A) of the Income Tax Act should be made applicable to all cases where jurisdiction is transferred from one officer to another.

The Central Board of Revenue should take suitable administrative measures to see that the assessing officer assessing at the head office, businesses having various branches obtains necessary information regarding the latter from the respective officers.

Definition Of Income

There is no need for giving an all-embracing definition of the term 'income' in the statute.

Definition Of Expenses

The following categories of expenditure should be considered as allowable deductions in computation of total income under the Income Tax Act :—

(a) Interest paid or payable on monies borrowed by a partner for investing in the firm as his share of capital;

(b) Expenses incurred prior to the commencement of a business but in connection with the activities leading to such commencement;

(c) Expenses incurred for tax representation during assessment proceedings for settlement of liabilities under the Income Tax, Wealth-Tax, Expenditure-Tax and Gift-Tax Acts.

Right Shares

While computing the profits made on the sa.e of right or bonus shares, a reduction should be allowed for the fall in the value of the original shares.

Problems Relating To Other Direct Taxes Acts

A Central Valuation Department for the purposes of valuing different types of assets would be advantageous to both the Department and the assessees. However, to begin with, a Valuation Cell may be created in the Central Board of Revenue for valuing shares of limited Companies. With gain in experience, the Cell may extend its valuation activities to other categories of assets and may ultimately mature into a full-fledged Central Valuation Department.

Arbitration by valuers should continue to be available only at the appellate stage before the Tribunal. However, in cases where the valuation of more than one type or category of assets is in dispute, it should be permissible for the assessee as also the Department to name a valuer for all types of assets instead of having separate valuer for each of the type or category of assets.

The valuers appointed for arbitration should give their award within six months, as under the Arbitration Act, unless further time up to three months is allowed.

Value of an immovable property adopted for one assessment under the Wealth-Tax Act and accepted by the assessee should not normally be disturbed for five years.

The only qualification for approving Chartered Accountants for appointment as valuers should be ten years practice in the profession. No change is suggested in regard to the qualifications prescribed at present for appointment of valuers in jewellery.

The following procedure should be adopted for valuation of shares:

Where quotations are available in the stock exchange the latest quotation anterior to the valuation date should be adopted. In other cases of public limited companies where shares are not quoted in the stock exchanges, the value of their shares may be taken at the price at which transfers of a bona fide character have been made before the valuation date. In the case of shares of private limited companies, the break-up value should not be the only criterion for determining the value of the shares, but all other relevant conditions and factors should also be taken into consideration.

For the purposes of Wealth Tax assessments, the formula of taking the value of a building at 20 times the municipal annual rental valuation less permissible expenses should not be applied too rigidly and due regard should be had for other relevant factors, including the age and condition of the building.

In no case should a life interest in trust property be computed at a figure exceeding the value of the entire trust property itself. Nor should there be double assessment of the same assets, once in the hands of the trust and again in the hands of a beneficiary having a life interest therein.

The Central Board of Revenue should formulate rules for valuation of annuities.

The basis for valuation of assets left in Pakistan should not be the face value for which the claims have been admitted by the Rehabilitation Authorities of the Government of India, but the realisable value of such claims.

It should be provided in Section 2 (m) (iii) of the Wealth Tax Act that in cases, where the tax is disputed in appeal and is, therefore, not paid, the disputed liability would be adjusted by rectification as and when the appeal is decided.

The Central Board of Revenue should issue instructions prescribing a broad basis for a rational allocation of liabilities in relation to assets chargeable to Wealth Tax and those exempted from this tax.

When a certain amount of expenditure is admitted by an assessee, the Expenditure Tax officer should not make any roving enquiries about that. The instructions already issued by the Central Board of Revenue on this point should be further emphasised.

There should be a statutory time-limit of four years from the date of filing of the return for the completion of an Estate Duty assessment. Where assessments are made ex pare, the time-limit should be four years from the date the return was due.

In mofussil circles the same officer who assesses the assessees for the other direct taxes should also deal with the estate duty cases. In cities, the present circles for dealing exclusively with estate duty cases should continue.

Where an accountable person discharges the debts or other liabilities of the deceased and the Department is satisfied that such discharge is bona-fide, such debts should be allowed to be deducted from the value of the life interest in the trust or other property.

The present requirement of the verification in the Estate Duty Return to be made before a magistrate should be removed. Verification for estate duty purposes should have to be made in the same way as for income-tax purposes.

Appeals And Revisions

Appellate Assistant Commissioners

The Appellate Assistant Commissioners should be transferred from the control of the Central Board of Revenue to that of the Ministry of Law.

Appeals from Central Circles, Special Circles, Company Circles as well as other cases involving large sums in dispute should be grouped together in 10 or 12 special Appellate Ranges in important centres and these should be manned by experienced Appellate Assistant Commissioners.

There is scope for improvement in the methods and procedures of work of the Appellate Assistant Commissioners which can he helpful in expediting disposals and in redressing the grievances of the appellants.

Appellate Commissioners

Two Appellate Commissioners who would be of the same status and rank as Commissioners but functioning under the administrative control of the Ministry of Law should be appointed for exercising administrative control over the Appellate Assistant Commissioners, and carrying out annual administrative inspections, with a view to ensuring quicker disposal of work and the maintenance of uniform standards in their approach to problems. In addition, they will also hear appeals on assessments made by Inspecting Assistant Commissioners as well as function as Appellate Controllers of Estate Duty when the Estate Duty (Amendment) Act comes into force.

Appellate Tribunal

The Appellate Tribunal is a necessary and suitable appellate organisation and should continue.

The President of the Appellate Tribunal should be a serving High Court Judge, deputed to act as such by the President of India for a fixed tenure.

As far as possible, officers of the Department of the status of Commissioners of income-tax or Assistant Commissioners senior enough to become Commissioners, should be selected for appointment as accountant members. Serving District and session Judges should, as far as possible, be selected for the posts of judicial members.

As far as possible, the Appellate Tribunal should give reasoned and detailed orders giving full facts and findings so that a clear picture of the issues involved, the arguments advanced and the conclusions arrived at, would emerge.

The Appellate Tribunal being the final fact finding authority, it should not be granted enhancement powers under the Income-Tax Act. Enhancement powers now vested in it under the other direct taxes Acts should be withdrawn.

The Department or the assessee may be permitted to file a memorandum of cross objections against so much of the order of the Appellate Assistant Commissioner as was against the Department or the assessee in instances where one of them might have gone in appeal.

Panel Of Advisers

Introduction of non-official element, at the appellate stage by constituting a panel of advisers is not favoured.

Rights Of Appeal

Rights of appeal should be provided against the order passed under the following sections of the Income-Tax Act and the corresponding sections of the other direct taxes Acts wherever applicable.

(i) Section 18(7) under which the person responsible for deducting tax at source and paying it to the credit of the Central Government could be treated as an assessee in default;

(ii) Sections 18 A (6), 18A (7) and 18A (8) authorising levy of interest and Sections 18A (9) and 18A (10) authorising levy of penalty in instances of late payment or non-payment of the correct amount of advance tax;

(iii) Section 23 (6) governing the determination of the income of a firm and its division amongst the partners;

(iv) Section 23A (1) authorising inclusion of deemed dividends in the total income of a shareholder.

(v) Sections 25 (3) and 25 (4) governing grant of exemption from tax in cases of succession and discontinuance of business;

(vi) Rule 6-B under which registration, granted to a firm under Section 26-A, could be cancelled;

(vii) Section 35 authorising rectification of mistakes in the orders passed;

(viii) Section 43 under which a person can be treated as agent of a non-resident; and

(ix) Section 144 under which liability could be fixed on partners of firms and members of associations in instances of dissolution or discontinuance of business.

In addition, appeal should also be statutorily provided against orders of the Appellate Assistant Commissioner under the different direct taxes Acts where he refuses to extend time for filing an appeal or dismisses an appeal as not filed in time.

Modification in the existing stages of appeal is not favoured.

No restrictions should be placed on the existing rights of appeal under the Income-Tax Act on the basis of the monetary limit of the income or tax involved. Introduction of such a system under the other direct taxes Acts is also not favoured.

There should be no restriction on the rights of appeal in instances where an assessee fails to submit returns or comply with notices.

The difficulties caused to the Department on account of assessees' filing writ petitions do not call for a change in the Constitution. However, it should be ensured through appropriate Rules of the High Courts that the Courts give precedence in the matter of hearing of all applications concerning assessment and collection of the direct taxes, issue of notices of hearing to the Department at the stage of admission of writ petitions, and insist, in suitable cases, on the petitioners furnishing adequate securities to cover taxes in dispute before granting stay orders.

Disposal Of Appeals

The placing of statutory time limit within which the appeals should be disposed of is not favoured.

The measures adopted by the Central Board of Revenue with regard to disposal by Appellate Assistant Commissioners have proved effective but the matter must be kept under constant review. If found necessary, the number of Appellate Assistant Commissioners should be increased.

The present strength of the Appellate Tribunal is inadequate and the number of benches should be increased immediately.

The Chief Justices of the various High Courts should be requested to examine the position and take suitable measures such as the constituting of special benches for dealing with reference applications under direct taxes and giving priority to them so that the disposal of such cases is expedited.

The Chief Justice of the Supreme Court should be approached with a request for constituting a special direct taxes benches to deal with appeals under the direct taxes Acts.

Uniformity In Interpretations

The present procedure of issuing copies of the instructions of the Central Board of Revenue to the Appellate Assistant Commissioners should continue. However, these will not be binding on them. On a question of law involved in an appeal before the Appellate Tribunal; if varying judgments had been given by different High Courts, the President of the Tribunal may, on a request made to him, refer the question directly to the Supreme Court for a decision.

Adducing Of Evidence

The present system under which admission of fresh evidence before the Appellate Assistant Commissioner is left to his discretion should continue. No modifications are necessary at present with regard to adducing of evidence before the Appellate Tribunal.

Collection Of Taxes In Dispute

The present provision for the stay of disputed demands at the discretion of the assessing officer should continue but the assessees should be provided with a right to approach the Inspecting Assistant Commissioner, the Commissioner and the Central Board of Revenue in instances where his request is not acceded to.

Provisions analogous to what is contained in section 66 (7) of the Income-Tax Act and the corresponding sections of the other direct taxes Acts should not be introduced to cover instances of appeals before other authorities.

Costs In Tax Appeals

The practice of awarding costs prevalent in Civil Courts cannot be easily adopted for appeal proceedings under the direct taxes Acts as far as appeals before the Appellate Assistant Commissioners and Appellate Tribunal are concerned.

The existing procedure of granting expenses incurred in connection with proceedings before the assessing authorities itself constitutes an extra statutory concession and, there is no justification for a further extension of the concession to cover costs incurred in appeal.

Representation Of The Department Before Appellate Authorities

There is a need for improvement in the matter of representing the Department before the various appellate authorities. The Senior Departmental Representative before the Tribunal should invariably be a person of the status of an Assistant Commissioner.

Revisionary Powers Of Commissioners

In view of the discretionary power of the Commissioner to condone delays, no change is called for with regard to the time limit under Section 33-A of the Income-Tax Act and the corresponding sections of the other direct taxes Acts. The commissioners should condone delays freely, especially in cases of over-assessments.

While in instances where the assessee does not require a hearing the revision free may continue to be Rs. 25 as at present, in instances where the assessee desires a hearing by the Commissioner, he should pay a fee of Rs. 75. The Commissioner should not, however, be precluded from granting a hearing to the assessee in cases of the former category if, for any reason, he considers it necessary.

It is necessary not only to ensure that the pending petitions are disposed of immediately but also that the tendency towards an increase in their number is arrested.

Collection And Recovery Problem Of Arrears

The total amount of taxes in arrears, appears to be substantial. However, when the sums held in abeyance for settlement of relief claims and others which should be written off are taken into consideration, the effective arrears are much less.

Causes Of Arrears

Broadly, it can be stated that both belated assessments as well as over assessments are responsible for a major portion of the existing arrears.

Writing Off And Scaling Down Of Demands

By a suitable modification of the Delegation of Financial Power Rules, the powers of write off of Commissioners should be limited to irrecoverable demands not exceeding two lakhs in a case should be effected by a Committee consisting of the Chairman and two members of the Central Board of Revenue.

A system of scaling down of demands should be adopted subject to the monetary limit and other conditions mentioned with regard to write off of irrecoverable demands. The details of write off and scaling down of demands above a certain limit and the attendant circumstances should be presented to the Parliament through the annual administration reports of the Department.

Procedural Measures For Improving Collection

An improvement in collection is possible within the existing legal frame work by proper planning of assessment work, securing agreement on payment of taxes in cases involving substantial demands at the stage of assessment itself, issuing and serving notices of demand without delay, disposing of appeals involving large sums expeditiously, disposing of applications under Section 27 of the Income-Tax Act and passing of orders of rectification etc. expeditiously, improving the manner of issue of recovery certificates to the Collectors, relieving assessing officers of their routine administrative duties, issuing distress warrants on a larger scale and establishing better relationship between Central and State officials.

Deduction Of Tax At Source

In instances where contracts are granted by the Central or State Governments, local authorities or statutory corporations, the paying authorities should insist on tax clearance certificates for granting the contracts and should, in addition retain $2\frac{1}{2}$ per cent of the total value of the contract from the final or earlier instalments of payment, till the assessee produced a tax clearance certificate. There is no scope for extending the principle of deduction to tax at source either to cover further items under the Income-Tax Act or to cover items under the other direct taxes Acts.

Rule 11-A of the Income-Tax Rules should be modified in such a way that in deserving cases, while the payment of tax deducted should be made every month, the employers may be allowed to submit even quarterly or half-yearly statements.

Advance Payment Of Tax

The system of payment of tax in advance has been found useful and should be continued.

An assessee should be liable for interest and penalty only if his estimate of advance tax turns out to be less than 75 per cent of the tax eventually assessed, after making adjustments for items of income on which tax is deductible at source and also the variations in the rates of tax made by the subsequent Finance Acts.

The power vested with the Income-Tax officer to revise demands under Section 18-A of the Income-Tax Act on the basis of the latest assessed income should be utilised even in cases where such a procedure might be beneficial to the assessees. The position should be made clear in the statute itself and the term appearing as 'may' in the third proviso to Section 18-A(1) should be changed to 'shall'.

The liability arising under Section 42 of the Income-Tax Act is on the non-resident and there is no case for exempting income under this Section assessed through an agent from the provisions of Section 18-A.

The present basis of calculation of tax at the rates of the current financial year for issue of a notice under Section 11-A should be modified and the Income-Tax Officer should merely repeat the demand relating to the assessed income of the latest year.

The Department should continue to issue the notice under Section 18-A in the case of assessees who are already on its records.

The date for the payment of the last instalment of advance tax should be advanced by 15 days. Correspondingly, the dates for the payment of the other instalments should also be similarly advanced.

Extension of the system of payment of tax in advance to the Wealth-Tax and Expenditure-Tax Acts is not necessary for the present.

Provisional And Self Assessments

The introduction of a system of self-assessment either as an addition or as an alternative to the existing procedure of provisional assessments under the Income Tax Act is not favoured.

Assessments under Section 23-B of the Income Tax Act should generally be confined to cases where the income returned is above Rs. 20,000. Income shown in Section D of Part I of the Income-Tax Return and claimed to be not taxable should not be included in the provisional assessments.

The Wealth Tax and Expenditure-Tax Acts should be amended to provide both for a system of provisional assessment on the lines of Section 23-B of the Income-Tax Act, and a system of self-assessment under which assessees would pay tax along with the returns as per their wealth or expenditure declared in them.

Facilities For Payment Of Taxes

In all cases a month's time from the date of service

of notice should be given for payment of taxes.

Arrangements should be made in the tax offices for making payments of tax and cash counters should be opened for this purpose in all the important places. The possibility of opening Government accounts or accounts of the Reserve Bank with scheduled banks into which taxes could be paid should be explored. Cheques drawn on all scheduled banks should be accepted towards payment of tax. The Reserve Bank and the State Bank should be approached for opening branches in Income-Tax Offices. The assessees in the small income group should be given facility of remitting the due amount of tax by money orders and for this, a special type of money order form as now exists in certain States for payment of land revenue should be introduced.

Rebates And Discounts

Introduction of a system of rebates and discounts as obtaining under the Gift-Tax Act, in the other direct taxes Acts is not favoured.

Section 18(3) of the Gift-Tax Act should be so modified as to provide that the amount of tax to be paid under Sub-Section (1) of Section 18 of the Gift-Tax Act should be the tax that would have been payable under the Schedule had all gifts made during the previous year, including the gifts under consideration, been assessed to gift-tax at the rates given in the Schedule.

Interest And Penalty In Case Of Default

Without prejudice to Section 46(1) of the Income-Tax Act and to corresponding sections of the other direct taxes Acts, the Acts should be amended to allow for automatic accrual of interest at six per cent where taxes are not paid on the due dates.

Lieu In Favour Of Revenue

Revenue should not be granted an unrestricted lieu, without any time limit, over the assets of an assessee.

The law should be amended to secure that where the Commissioner is satisfied at any time that an assessee is trying to alienate his assets to defraud the State of its revenue, he may direct the Income-Tax Officer to immediately assess the total income of the assessee from the expiry of the last previous year to any such date as well as for the years not assessed, on the lines of Section 24-A(1) of the Income-Tax Act.

Recovery From Companies And Shareholders

Section 530 of the Companies Act should be modified to the extent of allowing preferential payments of one year's assessment if assessed for a period prior to the winding up notwithstanding that the assessment was made subsequent to the winding up.

The statute should be amended to secure that the priority for the recovery of tax in the case of companies in which the public are not substantially interested within the meaning of Section 23-A of the Income-Tax Act obtains without any time-limit.

The Companies Act should be amended to cast obligations on the liquidator of the company to give intimation regarding liquidation proceedings on the lines of Section 148 of the Internal Revenue Code, 1952 of U.S.A. If necessary, the taxing statutes should also be suitably amended.

Statutory provisions should be made requiring the Registrar of Companies not to strike off a company from the register of companies without obtaining the tax clearance certificate from the Income-Tax Officer.

In the case of companies in which the public are not substantially interested within the meaning of Section 23-A of the Income-Tax Act, the liability for the direct taxes should first fall on the assets of the company, then on the directors of the company and lastly on the shareholders in proportion to their holdings.

It should be statutorily provided that if the existing shareholders or directors do not come forward to purchase the shares of private limited companies belonging to defaulting directors or shareholders on the basis of the fair value determined according to the provisions of the Wealth-Tax Act, the Department shall have the right to sell the shares by auction and the purchasers shall be registered as shareholders of the company, notwithstanding any provisions to the contrary contained in the Memorandum and Articles of Association of the Company.

Recovery From Firms And Partners

Suitable amendments in the Income-Tax Act should be made to secure that all the assets of the firm are liable to be proceeded against for releasing tax due from the defaulting partner of a registered firm in so far as the demand relates to his share of income from the firm.

Recovery From Transferred Assets

Where it is not possible to recover taxes from the assessee in respect of the income aggregated under Sections 16(1)(c) and 16(3) of the Income-Tax Act, the Department should have the right to proceed against the legal owner of the assets in respect of the share of tax payable on account of the inclusion of the proportionate income from such assets. However, in a case where the assessment has resulted from a finding of fact that the transfer was a mere *benami* transaction effected with an intent to evade tax; no such restrictions are necessary.

Section 46(5A) Of The Income-Tax Act

Section 46 (5A) of the Income-Tax Act should be amended to allow the Department powers to attach joint accounts also.

Granting powers to Income-Tax Officers under Section 46 (5A) of the Income-Tax Act to enquire into and decide questions of title etc. is not favoured. However, the law should be modified to provide that even where a garnishee on whom the notice is served disputes or denies the liability the account is frozen. The Income-Tax Officer should be empowered to file a suit in the civil court to establish the liability of the garnishee.

Publicising Names Of Defaulters

Publicising names of defaulters as a means for effecting speedy collections is not favoured.

Functional Division Between Assessment And Collection

No functional division resulting in the assessing officers being divested entirely of the responsibility for collection, is called for. However, they should be relieved of the unnecessary routine work so as to enable them to devote more time to recovery work.

Central Revenue Recovery Code

A self-contained Central Revenue Recovery Code, complete in all respects, should be enacted for the purposes of effecting recoveries of direct taxes levied by the Central Government.

The recovery of direct taxes levied by the Central Government under the Central Revenue Recovery Code should be effected by the Department of the Central Government itself.

Refunds

Direct Refund Claims

The special procedure for the disposal of the refund applications on the very day of their receipt, as obtaining at present at some places like Ahmedabad and Calcutta, should be extended to all the refund circles.

The Department should give sufficiently wide publicity to the system of exemption certificates. The refund circles, in particular, should advise the refundees to obtain exemption certificates in fit cases. The exemption certificates should be issued freely and they should be valid for a period of three years.

The Department should pay to the assessees interest at six per cent per annum for the amount of refunds due in respect of direct refund claims payment of which is delayed beyond six months from the date of the refund application, unless the applicant is himself mainly responsible for the delay. Interest at a similar rate should be payable in cases where the payment of the refund resulting from appellate or revisionary orders etc. is delayed beyond one month from the date of the receipt of the order concerned by the assessing officer. In cases where settlement of the refund claim is being held up due to non-cooperation from the claimant, a written intimation should be sent to him warning that the settlement of his claim for refund is being held up on account of his non-compliance with the Department's requirements (which may be specified therein) and that no interest will be payable to him for the consequent delay in the issue of refund.

As quick disposal of refund claims is an important means for establishing good relations with the taxpayers, greater importance than at present should be given for disposal of refund applications.

Refund And Dividend Taxation

The new scheme of taxation of companies and their shareholders as laid down in the Finance Act 1959, is sufficiently simple and easily workable. In order to avoid any difficulty to the shareholders, the Deparment should issue the exemption certificates freely and should give as many attested copies of the certificates as required by them.

In cases where grossing up of the dividends not covered by the new scheme of company taxation is necessary, settlement of the refund claims involving dividend income should not be kept pending for want of the relevant correct 'grossing factor' and that the claims should be disposed of provisionally on the basis of either the latest 'grossing factor' previously adopted for the company concerned, or the 'grossing factor' that may be ascertained from the company's certificate, whichever is more appropriate in the circumstances of each case.

Other Refunds

In cases where assessees have paid advance tax under Section 18-A of the Income-Tax Act in excess of the amount due on the returns filed by them, if the assessment is not finalised within three months of the filing of the return of income, provisional refund of the excess payment should be given to the assessee concerned in the same way as provisional assessment is made under Section 23-B of the Income-Tax Act for collecting the tax payable, or alternatively, the Department should pay interest at six per cent on the amount refundable from the date of the filing of the return to the date of the issue of the refund order.

There should be no objection in allowing the assessees to seek adjustment of the refunds due to them on account of excess advance payments against other tax demands in cases where the Income-tax Officers have failed either to finalise the assessments within three months or give provisional refunds.

Double Taxation Relief

In cases where the claim for double taxation relief

cannot be filed within four years from the expiry of the relevant assessment year on account of non-completion of the assessment whether in India or in the foreign country within such time, the claim may be allowed to be made within one year from the date of assessment either in India or in the foreign country, whichever is later. In cases where the claims are filed beyond the permissible time-limits and are thus technically time-barred, the Commissioners of Income-Tax should, in deserving cases, condone the delay or extend the time for filing the claims where circumstances warrant such condonation or extension.

In order to avoid the necessity for claiming refunds of double taxation relief and the hardships attendant thereto, the Government should conclude bilateral agreements for avoidance of double txation with as many countries as possible.

The government should take special steps to ensure that the "Two-man" committee consituted to arbitrate in cases of disagreement between India and Pakistan regarding the allocation of the income chargeable to tax in either country, meets regularly and decides cases of disagreement.

A provision should by made to statutorily extend the time-limit of one year for production of the certificate of foreign assessment in order that the abate ment in tax admissible to the assessees under the agreements for avoidance of double taxation is not forfeited. Alternatively, the Government should make some other suitable provision to safeguard the interest and rights of the assessees.

Payment Of Refunds

Strict instructions should be given to the officers to issue Refund Orders immediately after the refund claim has been settled and to write them out correctly so that there is no difficulty in their encashment.

The currency of the Refund Orders should be the same as for treasury cheques, i.e. three months instead of one months, which obtains at present.

When a refundee makes a request for the payment of the refund to him in cash, it should be paid to him either in cash at the cash counter or remitted to him by postal money order, provided that the amount of refund does not exceed Rs. 250.

When there is no dispute amongst the legal heirs, the refund due to the estate of a deceased should be paid to his son/widow or other legal heirs on their furnishing an indemnity bond and without requiring the production of succession certificates or letters of administration etc.

Evasion And Avoidance

Introductory

Tax Evasion and Tax Avoidance are neither new nor peculiar to India. They constitute a problem which is prevalent in almost all countries.

Whatever be the method an assessee adopts—whether it be avoidance or evasion—the consequence of his action is the same, viz., loss of revenue to the state and increase *pro tanto* in the burden of tax on the other tax-payers who do not resort to such practices.

The quantum of tax-evasion, though undoubtedly high, is not of the magnitude indicated by Prof. Kaldar in his report.

Causes Of Evasion

While it cannot be denied that the higher the rate of tax, the greater will be the temptation for evasion and avoidance, the tax rates by themselves are not to blame for the large extent of evasion in the country.

The complicated provisions of the direct taxes Acts, not all of which are easily intelligible, are responsible, to some extent, for tax avoidance and evasion.

The inadequacy of the powers vested in the personnel of the Department is yet another cause for tax evasion.

It is necessary to have in the Department sufficient numbers of trained and experienced personnel to cope with the current as well as arrear load of assessment and investigation work. Simultaneously, the organisation and procedures of the Department should be so improved as to bring it to the highest pitch of efficiency.

Unless it is brought home to the potential tax-evader that all attempts at concealment will not only pay but also actually land him in jail, there could be no effective check against tax evasion. Non-resort to prosecutions and non-levy of deterrent penalties have undoubtedly encouraged the growth of evassion.

The pressure of public opinion is a major deterrent against any offence and, if the secrecy provisions of the direct taxes Acts are relaxed even to a limited extent, they will go a long way towards checking tax evasion.

Suppression of the sales in the case of retail trades in an attempt to evade sales tax also results in evasion of income-tax.

A reformed moral outlook of the citizens and development of a better civic conscience would go a long way in eliminating tax evasion.

Mutual distrust between the assessing officers and the taxpayers also encourages, to some extent, tax evasion. The Administration has to take the initiative and trust the assessees and conduct itself with a high sense of justice and fair play.

Not only should the depertmental officials be honest but they must also be above suspicion and they should so conduct themselves in their private as well as official life that no wrong motives could be attributed to any of their actions.

Methods Of Enquiry And Investigation

More importance should be given to external survey

work, by re-organising the Survey Circles and augmenting the staff in them. In larger cities like Bombay, Calcutta, Madras and Delhi, an Inspecting Assistant Commissioner should be placed exclusively in charge of survey work

It should be the responsibility of the Inspecting Assistant Commissioners of the various ranges to see, during the course of inspection, that the information collected during survey is properly utilised by the assessing officers. Particular attention should be paid in survey to the collection of information regarding construction of house properties and the rental incomes therefrom.

Inspecting Officers as well as the Commissioners should see, by periodical test-checks, that the work of internal survey is not neglected and does not fall in arrears.

The special Investigation Branches should be reorganised and placed under the charge of Assistant Commissioners in Bombay and Calcutta and under senior Income-Tax Officers in other charges.

Rules may be framed casting an obligation on the Government departments and quasi- Government bodies for communicating information about the payments made to contractors etc., to the Collation Branch of the Income-Tax Department.

The Collation Branch should be placed under the control of the Director of Investigation and Intelligence, with a Deputy Director of Inspection in-charge.

It should be the responsibility of the Inspecting Assistant Commissioners to see that the information received by the assessing officers from the Collation Branch is utilised properly.

More special Circles may be created, as and when necessary.

In order to make for better guidance on the spot, greater utilisation of local knowledge and more expeditious disposal of work, control over the Special Circles even in regard to the technical work of making investigations and assessment should be transferred to the territorial Commissioners of Income-Tax.

The Central charges have proved quite effective in handling cases of tax evasion and they should continue. The arrear cases in these charges are, however, very large, and as large amounts of revenue are involved, greater emphasis should be laid on bringing the assessments up to date. As soon as the investigations for the relevant period are completed and the assessments brought up to date, such cases should be re-transferred to the territorial charges and fresh cases requiring investigation taken over by the Central charges.

The Directorate of Inspection (Investigation) should be reorganised into a Directorate of Investigation and Intelligence. It should function in a more positive way by itself gathering all useful information and directing the investigational activities of the Department.

The Directorate should organise, and be responsible for the collection, collation and dissemination of all such information as will be useful in determining the correct tax liability of the assessees.

The Directorate should not only coordinate the investigations carried on in the different Commissioners' charges, but it should also render expert technical assistance in the investigations of specially complicated cases.

The Directorate as well as certain Commissioner's offices should be equipped with modern mechanical aids like the photostat machines, infra-red photographic equipment and the ultra-violet equipment.

Establishment of a Board of specialists consisting of non-officials would not be of much help in checking tax evasion. However, officers with proved efficiency and experience in assessments of particular trades and industry should be appointed as specialists in the Directorate of Investigation and Intelligence. For the present, six specialists may be appointed, one each for the following industries and connected trades :

(i) Cotton textiles.
(ii) Other textiles including rayon, and paper.
(iii) Sugar and connected industries.
(iv) Iron and Steel and Engineering Industries.
(v) Cement manufacture and building contractors.
(vi) Mining and Quarrying, Petroleum and allied products.

Once the Income-Tax Investigation cases are disposed of, there will be no need for a special body like the Directorate of Inspection (Special Investigation).

The constitution of a separate body lke the Income-Tax Investigation Commission for dealing with cases of large scale evasion is neither feasible nor necessary in the present circumstances.

The system of group Assistant Commissioner's charges, apart from having other advantages, helps in checking evasion.

Total wealth statements as recommended earlier would be one of the most effective methods of checking tax evasion.

Compulsory audit of accounts in cases of income above Rs. 50,000 from business, profession or vocation (suggested earlier under the heading "Assessments-Procedure") will help the assessing officers in the detection of concealments and manipulation of accounts.

Powers

The suggestion that all traders should be statutorily required to keep closed and adjusted accounts on mercantile basis is not capable of implementation at this stage.

Any scheme requiring the assessees to write their accounts in books previously signed and stamped by the officials of the Department will not work satisfactorily and is likely to do more harm than good.

In order to avoid any inconvenience to the assessees, the checking of the current accounts should be done in the business premises of the assessees, after obtaining the permission of the Commissioner.

The statutory provisions regarding search and seizure are, on the whole, adequate and no major charge is called for. Timely action is, however, of utmost importance.

The feasibility of requiring the banks and other credit institutions to give names and addresses of their constituents, the sum total of whose deposits or withdrawals exceeds rupees one lakh a year, should be examined by Government, in consultation with the Reserive Bank of India.

The Life Insurance Corporation should be statutorily required to furnish the name and address of every person taking life insurance policies for sums aggregating to Rs. 50,000 or more, whether in his own name or jointly with another. The general insurance companies should also be statutorily required to furnish brief particulars of general insurance policies of the value of Rupees five lakhs and above, whether taken under one cover or more than one cover by the same person.

The suggestion that it should be statutorily provided that payments of money above a specified limit should invariably be made by crossed cheques is not practicable and is therefore, not favoured.

It is necessary that the activities of the various revenue Departments in checking evasion of taxes should be properly coordinated, and that, for this purpose, there should be a regular and systematic exchange of the useful information available with the various Departments. The existing liaison arrangements between the various Departments should be improved and placed on a more systematic footing.

The suggestion that the production of a tax clearance certificate from the assessing officers should be insisted upon by the registration authorities before registering the transfer of properties whose value exceeds a certain limit, is not favoured as such a restriction does not appear to be necessary.

The system of automatic reporting as suggested by Prof. Kaldor in his report would throw an undue volume of work and is unworkable under the conditions existing in India today.

In order to discourage tax evaders from entering into *benami* transactions for the purpose of achieving their object, statements made by any party to such a transaction before the direct taxes authorities with regard to the ownership of an asset should be made available, to the other party concerned in the case, if he applies for a copy of it. The secrecy provisions of the direct taxes acts should be modified to secure this.

By means of blank transfers dishonest assessees are able to conceal their income from the Department and even if the concealments are detected and assessed, they can avoid the payment of the taxes as the shares are not registered in their names, and they cannot, therefore, be attached and sold. The only effective remedy against blank transfers is to provide that all transfer deeds executed by the transferor should be registered by the Stock Exchange and simultaneously date stamped. It should be secured by statute that the transfer deeds should have a currency of only six months from the date of stamping and that multiple transfers will be permitted only within that period of six months.

The restrictions in the preceding recommendation should not be applied in cases :

(a) Where the shares are handed over to a banking company either as a security or for safe custody; or

(b) Where the shares are held on blank transfers by the directors of a company or partners of a registered firm or trustees in a fiduciary capacity.

The banks, however, should be required to communicate to the tax authorities, through an annual statement, brief particulars of the shares held by them under blank transfers.

While the present practice of rewarding the informers should continue, a statutory provision should be made for the punishment of informers who give wrong information. The Department should also be provided with the power to grant immunity from penal proceedings or prosecutions to those who having abetted an offence in this respect, come forward to give evidence against an assessee. No action should be taken on anonymous or pseudonymous petitions unless they contain some specific information.

The present system of requiring contractors, applicants for import and export licences. etc., submitting a tax clearance certificate from the assessing officers, and the conditions attached to their issue, are effective in checking tax evasion and defaults in the payment of taxes. Tax clearance certificate should not be refused to those who have evaded or defaulted once but have thereafter kept a clean record with the tax authorities for atleast three years continuously.

Penalties and Prosecutions

A detailed schedule of penalties should be drawn up and incorporated in the statute book in place of Section 28 of the Income-Tax Act and corresponding Sections of the other taxes Acts. The schedule should make a distinction between cases of deliberate concealment or gross or wilful neglect, the levels of penalty for the latter category being much lower than those for the former. The maximum penalty leviable for concealment or deliberate furnishing of inaccurate particulars should continue to be 150 per cent of the tax sought to be evaded as at present.

The penalty provisions of the direct taxes Acts should be brought in line with Section 49 (1) of the Income-Tax Act, 1952 of the United Kingdom so that the onus of proving that the omission to disclose income, wealth, etc., did not proceed from any fraud or wilful neglect, is placed on the assessee himself.

The prior approval of the Inspecting Assistant Commissioners for the levy of penalty should be obligatory only in cases of more serious offences, where the quantum of penalties leviable are heavier. Further the Inspecting Assistant Commissioners should be statutorily required to give a hearing to the assessees before according his approval to the levy of penalty in such cases. The law should be amended requiring the completion of the penalty proceedings within one year of the passing of the relevant assessment order or of the appellate order of the Appellate Assistant Commissioner or the Appellate Tribunal or of the revision order of the Commissioner, as the case may be.

Failure to institute prosecutions even in clear cases of tax evasion cannot be justified. In all cases of deliberate concealment, where there is sufficient evidence, the Department should, as a rule, resort to criminal prosecution.

Government should consider whether Sections 177, 191, 192, 199 and perhaps 181 of the Indian Penal Code, should also be specifically referred to in the direct taxes Acts. Resort should be had more frequently to the provisions of the Indian Penal Code than to those of the taxing statutes and there should be a specific provision in the direct taxes Acts permitting the Department to take action also under the Indian Penal Code, Deliberate concealment of income, wealth, etc., should be made a specific offence punishable under Section 52 of the Income-Tax Act and corresponding provisions of the other direct taxes Acts. There should be a footnote in the return form itself to the effect that false or incorrect declaration would attract the penalty provided under sections 28 and 52 of the Income-Tax Act or the corresponding provisions of the other direct taxes Acts, as the case may be, and Sections 177 and 199 of the Indian Penal Code. The relevant sections should also be reproduced *in toto* in the return form.

Enhancing the maximum period of imprisonment will not in itself serve any useful purpose at the present moment when, pratically, no prosecutions have been launched for the past several years. It is also not necessary at the present stage to provide for a minimum period of imprisonment, but if in actual practice hereafter the Department finds that the courts are averse to awarding imprisonment, the question of amending the existing law so as to provide for a minimum period of imprisonment in cases of conviction may be examined.

There should be an Enforcement Branch in each Commissioner's charge with the specific responsibility for examining cases suitable for prosecution and for initiating and pursuing prosecution proceedings. Prosecutions in cases of offences referred to in Section 51 of the Income-tax Act and the corresponding provisions of the other direct taxes Acts should be launched with the prior approval of the Commissioner. Prosecutions for offences mentioned in Section 52 of the Income-tax Act and the corresponding provisions of the other direct taxes Acts or any of the provisions of the Indian Penal Code should be launched with the prior approval of the Central Board of Revenue, in order that there may be an uniform policy in this matter.

While the existing powers to compound offences for which prosecutions are launched may continue, such powers should be exercised only in exceptional cases and not as a matter of course. In particular, there should be no attempt at compounding an offence merely because the composition fee offered is substantial. Compounding in any case should be done only with the approval of the authority sanctioning the prosecution.

Provisions of Section 28 (4) of the Income-Tax Act and the corresponding provision of the other direct taxes Acts which bar prosecutions in respect of the same facts on which a penalty has been imposed, should be deleted.

Abetment of evasion of tax should be made punishable under the tax laws. A provision similar to the one contained in the Income-Tax (Amendment) Bill. 1951 should be introduced in all the direct taxes Acts.

The income-tax return form, in cases of income above Rs. 20,000 and the return forms prescribed under the other direct taxes Acts should provide for a declaration and certificate in a prescribed form to be given by the representative who prepares or assists the assessees in the preparation of the return.

Voluntary Disclosures

The introduction of a voluntary disclosure scheme on the lines of the 195 Scheme is not justifiable under the circumstances prevailing at present.

Powers of settlement available, at present to a limited extent, under the Income-Tax Act, for specific types of cases, should be enlarged and the Central Board of Revenue authorised to arrive at settlements with the assessees at any stage of the proceedings under the direct taxes Acts. Administratively, it may be ensured that the disclosure cases are settled by the Commissioner of Income-Tax, where the tax involved is Rupees two lakhs or less, and where the tax is over Rupees two lakhs, the case should be settled by a committee consisting of the Chairman and two Members of the Central Board of Revenue.

Suggestions To Amend The Law

The existing law should be amended on the following lines in order to plug the various loopholes :

(1) Remittances of foreign profits which are at present exempt under section 4 (i) (b) (iii) of the Income-Tax Act, should be made taxable.

(2) The existing provisions relating to exemption of the income of charitable trusts under section 4 (3) (1) should be amended as follows :

(a) The accounts of all charitable institutions, with the exception of those audited under the requirement of any other law or regulation, having an income of Rs. 5,000 or over, must be compulsorily audited and a certificate from the auditor in a form to be prescribed should be furnished to the assessing officer in support of its claim for exemption from tax.

(b) A charitable trust carrying on a business which is not in the course of carrying out the primary object of the trust itself should not be entitled to the exemption under section 4 (3) (i) of the Income-Tax Act and this should be made clear in the substantive part of the section itself.

(c) Where a trust deed contains a clause that the funds of the trust should also be utilised for the relations and family members of the donor or that in carrying out the charitable objects of the trust priority should be given to such relations or members, exemption should not be available under section 5 (1) (i) of the Wealth-Tax Act.

(d) If any charitable trust had invested, at any time during the previous year, in the shares or capital of an industrial or commercial undertaking, in which the donor was himself substantially interested, an amount more than five per cent of the paid up capital of that undertaking, then the dividends or share income from such investments should not be eligible for exemption and should the taxed in the hands of the trustees.

(e) As regards the other incomes of the trust, they will be exempt if the conditions under section 4 (1) (i) of the Income-Tax Act are fulfilled, but if more than 25 per cent of such income of a trust is set apart for being spent subsequently for charitable purposes, the amount set apart in excess of 25 per cent should be taxed in the year in which it is so set apart. The Central Board of Revenue should, however, be empowered to increase this percentage in fit cases

(f) If on enquiries into the use to which the properties belonging to a charitable trust were being put to, the assessing officer found that they were being utilised (i) by the donor or his nominees or any of his family members, or (ii) by a trustee or his nominee or his family, the properties should not be allowed exemption admissible under Section 5 (1) (i) of the Wealth Tax Act, unless in the case of (ii) above the occupation of the property by the trustee was necessary for carrying out the objects of the trust. The assessing officer should also ensure that gift-tax is recovered in respect of the properties enjoyed by such persons.

(3) Section 10 (1) of the Income-Tax Act should be amended so as to be consistent with the second proviso to section 10 (2) (vii), providing that even where the assessee had discontinued his business, profession or vocation, profits resulting from the sale of machinery or other assets would be treated as income and subjected to tax. The business expenses incurred ofter the closing of the business should also be allowed.

(4) There is no justification for continuing the tax exemption to cooperative societies which are running transport services or controlling large commercial and industrial undertakings, since their dealings are mostly with non-members. It should be specifically laid down in Section 14 (3) of the Income-Tax Act that the exemption would not be available to the cooperative societies if their total income execeeds Rs. 20,000. In view of the tax holiday given to new industrial undertakings under Section 15-C of the Income-tax Act and also the limitation on the distribution of the profits of the co-operative societies under the various State laws, the changes proposed would not interfere with the growth of genuine cooperative societies.

(5) A provision similar to Section 16 (3) of the Income Tax Act should be made so as to cover cases of assets transferred by wife to the husband. A further amendment may also be made to Section 16 (3) of the Income Tax Act so as to cover transfers of assets to minor children by the mother.

(6) The law should be modified so as to provide that in cases where a father creates a trust for the benefit of his minor daughter with a stipulation that the income of the trust should be accumulated and added to the corpus and that the daughter should be entitled to receive the income only after attaining majority, such income of the minors would be taxed.

Section 9 (2) of the Income Tax Act should be suitably amended so as to provide that in cases where, after transferring the ownership of a residential property to his wife or minor child, without adequate consideration, the transferor continues to reside in it along with the transferee, there is no escapement of proper tax liability.

Section 46 A of the Income Tax Act should be amended so as to include the liabilities under the Wealth Tax Act, Expenditure-tax Act and Gift Tax Act also within the scope of that Section.

There is no justification for giving the marriage and children's allowance both to the husband and the wife where they are separately taxable. The law should be suitably amended.

Any industrial or public utility undertaking run as a department of the State Government should also be subjected to tax and, for this purpose, provision should be made in law as envisaged in Article 289 (2) of the Constitution.

The law should be so amended that even on the assessee's cessation of his business, etc., or retirement from profession or death, income received after such cessation, retirement or death would be taxed.

In the case of companies in which the public are not substantially interested, set off of the earlier years' losses against subsequent profits should be allowed only if the shareholders in the year in which the income is earned are substantially the same as those in the years in which the losses were incurred.

Publicity

Evasion could be effectively checked by making public the information relating to the income, wealth etc., declared by the assessees in their returns. The Government may adopt either of the following two methods and prescribe the necessary procedure therefor :

(i) Communication to any member of the public, on the payment of a specified fee, the amount of income, wealth, etc., declared by a person in his return;

(ii) Publication annually in a printed booklet form the names, addresses and declared income, wealth, expenditure, etc., of either all assessees or those above a certain limit.

In view of the deterrent effect it would have on attempts at evasion, the names of all persons in whose cases penalties have been imposed for Rs. 5,000 or more for the concealment of income, wealth, expenditure, etc., should be published by the Commissioners, in the gazette as well as in the press, giving details of their names, addresses and amounts of penalities. If the assessee concerned is a company or firm, the names of all the directors of the company or partners of the firm, as the case may be, should be published unless it has been established that only a particular director or partner was responsible for the evasion. The publication should be made only after the penalty has become final in appeal and reference. Central Board of Revenue should have discretion to withhold the publication of names in suitable cases, but the number of cases in which such information was withheld and the reasons therefor, should be given in the annual administration report but without mentioning the names of such persons.

Arousing Public Conscience

The following measures may be useful in arousing public conscience against tax evasion:

(i) People should be educated with regard to the real object of the collection of direct taxes, through press, radio and films.

(ii) Steps should be taken to convince the tax-payers that the money collected through taxes is not spent wastefully but put to proper use.

(iii) No official patronage or recognition or awards should be given to persons who have been penalised for concealment or in whose case prosecution proceedings have been taken. Such a person should not be allowed to become a member of any Committee or Commission appointed by Government.

(iv) Tax evaders should be strictly dealt with and brought to book by the Department in future so that the widely-held feeling in the minds of the public that evasion pays and that evaders are treated lightly is removed. Prosecution proceedings should be launched wherever necessary.

(v) The cooperation of the chambers of commerce and other professional bodies such as bar associations, medical associations, etc., should be enlisted in the matter of wiping out evasion.

(vi) A special drive should be undertaken to rouse public conscience by enlisting the cooperation of leaders in the various walks of life.

Administration

Central Board Of Revenue

It is neither practicable nor desirable to divorce administration entirely from policy making. The Central Board of Revenue should continue to function as the Deparment of Revenue.

It will facilitate the joint functioning of the Central Board of Revenue, to a large extent, and result in a more efficient administration of the different tax laws, if the administration of the direct taxes and that of indirect taxes are entrusted to two separate Boards. However, as the new direct taxes have been introduced recently, and the bifurcation of the present combined Board might involve additional expenditure, the formation of two separate Boards for direct and indirect taxes is not immediately necessary. For the present, there should be two distinct Wings of direct and indirect taxes in the Central Board of Revenue with a common Chairman. After examining the working of the two separate Wings Government may consider the feasibility of constituting separate Boards for direct and indirect taxes.

A list of functions of the Central Board of Revenue where the Members should function jointly and individually should be drawn up and strictly adhered to. There should not be frequent changes in the status of the post of the Chairman or in the composition of the Board.

There should be a separate Secretary for the Department of Revenue and this post and that of the Chairman of the Central Board of Revenue should be combined.

The Central Board of Revenue should have one more

Member to look after the general administrative and organisational matters relating to direct taxes.

It should be laid down that each member of the Central Board of Revenue can function independently on behalf of the Board in respect of the specific work allotted to him and that all orders passed by him should be treated as orders of the Board. In respect of appeals, however, it should be provided that at least two Members of the Board should hear them jointly. Applications for settlement, write off, etc., should be dealt with by the Chairman and two Members acting jointly. On matters of administrative policy as well as those relating to promotions and postings of officers, all the three Members along with the Chairman should take a joint decision.

At least half the Members of the Central Board of Revenue dealing with direct taxes should be selected from amongst the officers of the Department. The tenure of appointment as a Member should normally be five years.

The recruitment of the officers of the Income-Tax Department to the Central Administrative cadre (Pool) of Officers should be increased considerably and greater facilities made available to them to acquire experience of other work.

The officers and other staff in the administrative and technical sections of the Central Board of Revenue should be appointed, as far as possible, from amongst the departmental personnel, who have field experience. There should also be a periodical exchange of officers and staff between the Board and the field officers.

In order to provide the Central Board of Revenue with expert legal advice in day-to-day work, a senior solicitor or advocate with adequate experience in direct taxes matters should be appointed as Legal Adviser in the office of the Board and given appropriate status and pay.

There should be no false economy in engaging experienced and leading members of the Bar and paying the requisite fees of representation on tax matters for the Department.

Directorates

The existing three Directorates of Inspection should be reorganised into the following four Directorates:

(a) Directorate of Inspection.

(b) Directorate of Investigation and Intelligence.

(c) Directorate of Vigilance.

(d) Directorate of Training, Statistics, Research and Publications.

The Directorate of Inspection should carry out administrative inspections of the offices of the Commissioners and Inspecting Assistant Commissioners of Income-Tax. It should also review and test-check the inspection of the work of the assessing officers carried out by the Inspecting Assistant Commissioners and suggest improvements for the organisation and methods of the working of the Department.

The functions of the Directorate of Investigation and Intelligence are noted earlier. It should have six experienced Assistant Commissioners working as Specialists to deal with tax problems in respect of specified important industries and trades like textiles, iron and steel, sugar, paper, cement, mining, etc.

It is of the utmost importance that the revenue administration should maintain the highest standards of morality and integrity. Besides keeping a constant vigil over the number of personnel at different levels, the Directorate of Vigilance should see that cases of complaints and disciplinary proceedings are expeditiously dealt with and that dishonest officials are properly brought to book.

The Directorate of Training, Statistics, Research, and Publications should look after the work of the Training College for the gazetted officers, coordinate the training programmes of the non-gazetted staff, see to recruitment of personnel and departmental examinations, compile all the statistical information, carry out research studies in tax matters and be in charge of the publication of tax literature, books and manuals, bulletins and journals, etc. The present office of the Statistician (Income-Tax) should be merged with this Directorate.

An Annual Administration Report should be published by the Department and laid on the table of the Parliament.

Commissioners Of Income-Tax

One more Commissioner of Income-Tax should be appointed in each of the West Bengal, Bombay City and Bombay North charges.

The cadre of Commissioners of Income-Tax, Grade II should be abolished, and all the Commissioners should be in one unified grade and get the same scale of pay as given to other heads of departments like the Accountants General, Postmasters General, Divisional Commissioners, etc., as well as to the members of the Income-Tax Appellate Tribunal.

There should be further decentralisation and delegation of enlarged powers to the Commissioners of Income-Tax in respect of incurring of expenditure on printing and purchase of stationery, legal charges, etc., as well as with regard to appointments, promotions and transfers.

Deputy Commissioners

Creation of posts of Deputy Commissioners is not favoured.

Assistant Commissioners

The Inspecting Assistant Commissioners should

continue to advise and guide the assessing officers in assessment matters. Pre-assessment guidance and control by them is necessary for improving the quality of assessments and checking tax evasion.

Inspecting Assistant Commissioners should give to the assessees, whenever asked for, an opportunity of being heard before issuing instructions to the assessing officers.

As a general rule, Inspecting Assistant Commissioners should not do assessment work. However, about 10 Assistant Commissioners should be entrusted with actual assessment work in important cases involving large revenues, detailed investigations and complicated questions of facts and law.

The system of group charges should be extended and 25 more such charges created in important cities.

The number of assessing officers under an Inspecting Assistant Commissioner in a non-group charge should be reduced to about 20 so that both administrative and regular inspection of assessment and collection work of each assessing officer is carried out every year.

The Inspecting Assistant Commissioners in the group charges should also inspect the work of the assessing officers in the group.

Assessing Officers

The Class II cadre of the Income-Tax Officers should continue. There should be only one grade for Class I service with an integrated pay scale.

The number of Class I posts of Income-Tax Officers should be increased by about 100 and a corresponding decrease made in the number of Class II Officers.

Income-Tax Officers promoted from Class II to Class I should not be given any weightage *vis-a-vis* direct recruits to Class I.

The present sanctioned strength of the Income-Tax Officers should be increased by about 50.

For purposes of evaluation of work and control of output of the assessing officers, categorisation of cases and fixation of disposal in standard units are necessary.

The assessing officers should be relieved of the routine administrative work which should be attended to by the office Supervisor.

Inspectors

The assessing officers and the Inspecting Assistant Commissioners should exercise stricter control and supervision over the work done by the Inspectors.

Inspector should be given statutory status under the other direct taxes Acts as under the Income-Tax Act. He should carry a written authority under the signature and seal of the assessing officer specifying the points on which he has to make survey and other enquiries.

Merger of the existing two grades of Inspectors, i.e., Ordinary and Selection Grade is not favoured.

The present sanctioned strength of Inspectors should be increased by 250.

Ministerial And Other Staff

Each tax office except that of the Appellate Assistant Commissioner should have a whole time supervisory officer. There should be one supervisory officer for every 10 clerks and out of the total supervisory posts at least one-third should be in the cadre of Supervisor.

Merging the cadre of Head Clerks with that of Supervisors is not favoured. Grade II cadre of Supervisors should be abolished and there should be only one grade of Supervisor. The present pay scales of the two grades should be integrated for this purpose. There should be Administrative Officers of Gazetted rank in the offices of the Commissioners and Directorates.

The direct taxes offices should be equipped with adequate ministerial staff.

The number of Notice Servers and Class IV servants should be suitably reduced, the strength of the latter being too large. The anomaly in the classification of the Notice Servers and Daftries with similar scales of pay should be removed. Class IV staff should not be required to do private and domestic work of the officers, and the nature of their official duties should be clearly defined.

Recruitment, Training And Promotion

Both direct recruitment and promotion in specific proportions are necessary to secure a correct and balanced blending of fresh talent and mature experience. The normal quota for promotion to the cadres of Inspectors and Upper Division Clerks should remain at 50 per cent as obtaining at present, and no direct recruitment need be made to the cadre of Class II Income-Tax Officers. Merit and efficiency should be the sole criteria for filling of selection posts in any cadre and quality should not be sacrificed merely for reaching the quotas fixed.

While allotting the candidates who are successful in the combined competitive examination held by the Union Public Service Commission, to the various Class I services, a due proportion of the higher ranking candidates should be posted to the direct taxes Department.

The ministerial staff should also be recruited on the basis of open competitive examinations. Preference should be given to persons possessing commercial and accountancy qualifications. The final selection should be made by Committees consisting of at least three persons.

There should be a whole time Principal in charge of the Training College for Income-Tax Officers. He should be assisted by a complement of full time instructors in the various subjects.

The Training College should provide specialised

training for sixteen months, after the four months foundational training course for all services. Greater attention should be paid to the practical training of the Probationary Income-Tax Officers. Emphasis should be laid on developing the qualities of leadership, initiative and self-confidence amongst them. Adequate instruction should also be given in the techniques and problems of public relations and administration.

Officers appointed as Income-Tax Officers on promotion from the lower ranks should be given a restricted course of training for at least six months in the Training College.

The Training College should organise regular refresher courses of four months' duration for senior assessing officers with five to eight years of service.

Selected Assistant Commissioners should be sent periodically to the Administrative Staff College at Hyderabad for an all-round advance course in administration and management.

There should be four regional centres for training of Inspectors each under the charge of a senior Income-Tax Officer.

Arrangements for the training of ministerial staff under the charge of a selected senior Supervisor should be made in each Commissioner's charge preferably at the respective headquarters.

Instructors should themselves be qualified and given a short course of training.

No change in the existing classification of the various posts, for purposes of promotion into 'Selection' and 'non-Selection' posts is considered necessary except with regard to Inspectors (Selection Grade).

The present forms of annual confidential reports should be rationalised. The counter-signing officer should, in particular, give his own views about the suitability of the person reported upon for promotion to the next higher grade.

Seniority for purposes of promotion to the next higher grade should be regulated with reference to the date or the year of passing the departmental examination prescribed for the grade concerned.

The existing restriction not permitting a person to appear in the departmental examination for a higher grade until he is actually working in the immediate lower grade should be relaxed. A period of five years should be fixed for taking the next higher examination after the person concerned has passed the lower examination.

The benefit of granting two advance increments on passing the departmental examination for the next higher grade should be made available to all categories of staff including the steno-typists and stenographers. The benefit should also not be limited to the minimum of the pay scale of the next higher grade.

Conditions Of Service

The officers of the Income-Tax Department in particular require special consideration in respect of pay scales and conditions of service having regard to their nature of work and the difficult duties they have to perform. The pay structure of all ranks, specially in respect of the gazetted officers of this important Department should be commensurate with their powers and responsibilities.

Every effort should be made to depute a sufficiently large number of the officers of the Income-Tax Department to other departments and organisations, but they should come back to the Department after a specified tenure.

The delay in confirming temporary officiating officials should be avoided, and such of the temporary posts as have been in existence for more than three years and which are not likely to be discontinued should be made permanent.

Periodical transfers of staff from one station to another and from one post to another are necessary, but they should not be too frequent.

One month's notice of transfers should generally be given to the officers. During this period they must pass final orders in all cases where hearings and investigations have been completed and endeavour to complete as many of the partly heard matters as possible. Before handing over charge on transfer, officers of all ranks should be required to send to their immediate superior officers, a certificate to the effect that all fully heard cases have been disposed of. A list of the partly completed work with full details and reasons for the pendency should also be furnished by such officers.

The Government should, in consultation with the Comptroller and Auditor General, devise suitable means for avoiding delays in the issue of pay slips, payment of leave salaries and settlement of pension, gratuity and provident fund claims, etc.

All staff employed in survey and outdoor enquiry work as also assessing officers in special survey circles should be given reasonable conveyance allowance.

Suitable arrangements should be made with the State Governments to ensure that there is no discrimination against Central Government officers in the matter of providing accommodation in Circuit Houses, Rest Houses, Inspection Bungalows, etc., belonging to the different States, and in regard to the charges for such accommodation as compared to the facilities given to the State Government officers.

Adequate funds should be specifically allotted for the construction of residential houses for the officers and staff of the Department. So long as this is not done, arrangements should be made to hire suitable accommodation for them.

The Central Government should organise schools in

the various important cities and towns for the education of the children of all the Government servants. In the meantime, arrangements should be made with the State Governments and important educational Institutions for securing admission on a priority basis to the schools for the children of a transferred official.

Adequate medical facilities should be afforded to the staff of the Department.

The Department should provide cheap holiday houses at hill stations and other health resorts for its employees.

The various staff welfare activities should be further enlarged.

Staff Committees should be constituted in all Commissioner's charges at their respective headquarters.

A sense of discipline and responsibility should be inculcated in the staff. Cases of indisciplined conduct should be promptly looked into and due steps taken to punish the wrong doers, wherever necessary.

Office Equipment And Accommodation

Better accommodation and necessary supply of office equipment and appliances will not only improve the working conditions of the staff but will result in increased efficiency and greater convenience to the assessees.

Timely and adequate supply of stationery and the forms to the tax offices should be ensured. For this purpose, the requirements of the Department should be given a sufficiently high priority. The responsibility for arranging supply of stationery and printing of forms, etc., for the Department should be entrusted to a separate section of Printing and Stationery. The Commissioners should have full financial powers for the local purchase of stationery or printing of forms if their requirements are not met by the Controller of Printing and Stationery in time. The subordinate authorities should also be given suitable financial powers for such local arrangements.

Typewriters should be supplied to the offices in sufficient numbers and other modern appliances also made available looking to the needs and exigencies of work.

Sufficient funds should be specifically allotted for the construction of office buildings for the Department and the rules regarding hiring of private accommodation be also suitably liberalised.

Cost Of Collection

The increase in the cost of administration during the past years was justified and necessary. The cost of administration should, no doubt be kept as low as practicable but it should not be at the cost of the Department's efforts in checking tax evasion and improving its overall efficiency.

Prevention Of Malpractices

Highest standards of integrity, honesty and fair play are essential in the Department. The stakes involved in a Revenue Department are very high and, therefore, a very strict vigilance is called for. The Department should have a strong and effective machinery but at the same time the procedures and the methods of work should be so designed as not to cause any fear of harassment or inconvenience to the assessees.

Apart from the Directorate of Vigilance, there should be vigilance sections in each Commissioner's charge for organising and coordinating the vigilance work in the charge and for making expeditious enquiries into complaints received and early finalisation of the disciplinary proceedings.

All officials of the Income-Tax Department should be required to send every fourth year a complete statement of their total wealth, both immovable and movable, including those in the names of wife and children and other family members. The income-tax assessments of the gazetted officers of the Departments should be centralised in a circle at headquarters.

Accepting of gifts on weddings and other occasions from other than relations of close friends and the acceptance of private hospitality, free entertainments, and other obligations from the public should be strictly discounted.

Undue importance, particularly in a taxing department, should not be attached to anonymous and pseudonymous complaints and nothing should be done to disturb the morale of the officers in the discharge of their duties.

The Government should take a policy decision so as to prevent the officers of the Department leaving Government service prematurely and joining private employment.

Provisions similar to Section 13(3) as well as Sections 7(7) and 50(1) of the U.K. Income-Tax Act, 1952 should be incorporated in the direct taxes statutes, but to safeguard against the misuse of these powers, the complaints should first be made to the Central Board of Revenue who would initiate proceedings after making necessary enquiries.

Representation Of Assessees By Tax Experts

Restriction of the right to represent assessees to the Chartered Accountants and the Lawyers would cause undue hardship to the small income assessees and the Income-tax practitioners should, therefore, be allowed to continue.

To improve the quality of representation by Income-tax practitioners, the minimum educational qualification for them should be a degree in commerce of any of the recognised Universities. In addition they should be required to pass a written examination to accountancy and tax laws to be held by the Department. The existing Income-tax practitioners should, however, be allowed to continue to represent assessees irrespective of their qualifications and they should be exempted from taking this test. The income-tax practitioners should also be permitted to represent tax payers under all the direct taxes laws.

It would be neither practicable nor desirable to completely prohibit Departmental persons from tax practice after retirement or resignation. However, they should not be allowed to represent assessees for a period of two years after retirement or resignation without the previous permission of the Central Board of Revenue except in cases of persons who desire to engage in tax practice on resigning within a period of three years after joining the Department. The Board should give the permission subject to the condition that the person concerned will not be entitled to tax practice in the state or the Commissioner's charges where he had served at any time during the three years immediately preceding his retirement or resignation. As regards the officers having all-India jurisdiction like the Directors, permission for tax practice should be given to them on the further condition that they should not represent assessees whose cases have been dealt with by them during the three years preceding their retirement or resignation.

Admission of the various classes of professional experts to tax practice should be regulated by a system of registration with the Department.

Disciplinary jurisdiction over the Income-tax practitioners should continue to remain with the Commissioners, who should use their authority with greater vigilance.

In the case of lawyers and chartered accountants the present procedure with regard to disciplinary action and the ultimate jurisdiction of the High Court as provided for under Section 10(1) of the Bar Council Act, 1926 and Section 21 of the Chartered Accountants Act, 1949 should continue. However a slight departure from the general procedure would be justified. The report of the enquiry of the Bar Council or the District Judge in the case of misconduct by a lawyer and of the Disciplinary Committee of the Institute of Chartered Accountants in case of one of its members should be submitted to the President of the Income-tax Appellate Tribunal, who will pass orders after hearing the complainant, the respondent and the Council of the Institute of Chartered Accountants or the Bar Council as the case may be. This procedure is suggested subject to our recommendation about the appointment of a High Court Judge as the President of the Income-tax Appellate Tribunal being accepted. Any appeal from the decision of the President of the Income-tax Appellate Tribunal will go to the respective High Courts.

The Government nominee on the Disciplinary Committee of the Council of the Institute of Chartered Accountants should be a representative of the Central Board of Revenue. Similarly, whenever such a case regarding the conduct of a lawyer before the direct taxes authorities is inquired into by the Bar Council, the Standing Counsel of the Department should be coopted as a member of that Council for this purpose, if he is not already a member of the Bar Council concerned.

If a tax expert is finally convicted for evasion of tax as a result of prosecution under the provisions of the direct taxes Acts, he should be straightaway disqualified from tax practice and his name removed from the register. Similarly, the conviction of a tax expert under the direct taxes Acts on charges of abetting or aiding his clients in tax evasion, should result in automatic disqualification from tax practice. Any tax expert, who is penalised under the direct taxes Acts for concealment of income, wealth, estate, gift or expenditure should be disqualified from representation after the penalty proceedings have become final. However, the usual disciplinary procedure should be followed in such cases of penalty and disqualification should not be automatic.

The standards about the code of conduct and responsibilities that apply to Chartered Accountants and Lawyers in the United Kingdom should apply to Chartered Accountants and Lawyers in India.

Public Relations

Factors Influencing Public Relations

While the officers of the Department have necessarily to be firm in the discharge of their duties, and function without fear or favour, they must be sympathetic to the taxpayers, and show due consideration for their doubts and difficulties.

It must be the duty of every officer of the Department to bring to the assesses' notice any allowance, rebate or relief that may be legitimately due to them. The higher authorities should view any omission in this regard very seriously and take such punitive and remedial action as may be necessary in the circumstances of the case.

The criterion for judging the worth of the assessment work, should be not the highly-pitched assessments which are ultimateiy reduced in appeals, but the making of realistic assessments which stand the test of appeal. The existing administrative instructions to this effect, need to be re-emphasised.

Effective steps should be taken to see that the records are kept properly and that there is a fool-proof system for getting and filing of necessary receipts for the various documents, papers, payments, etc.

The targets for disposal of assessments and collection of taxes must be so fixed as do not, in any way, lead to over-assessments and harassment of the assessees.

The Central Board of Revenue should see that its

instructions prohibiting the officers from fixing up all the cases at the same hour of the day, and requiring them to call the assessees at suitable intervals distributed throughout the day are scrupulously followed and the daily cause list placed on the notice board.

The officers should observe the office hours punctually and should see that the assessees are not made to spend more than the minimum necessary time in the tax offices.

The officers should spare at least half an hour of their working own to make various enquiries and seek clarifications. The period for interviews should be prominently notified. Besides, all tax offices should have Enquiry Counters where the assessees can make various routine enquiries without having to wait to see the officers.

The staff dealing with the issue of tax clearance certificates should be strengthened, and in particular, the number of Income-Tax Officers, Foreign Section, entrusted with the issue of the certificates under Section 46-A of the Income-Tax Act should be enlarged so that there is at least one such officer at the headquarters of each state or the Commissioner of Income-tax.

An applicant for tax clearance/Exemption Certificates under Section 46-A of the Income-Tax Act should be required to furnish, in duplicate, an application in the prescribed form to his assessing officer who should deliver one copy of the Authorisation to the applicant and send another copy of it along-with a copy of the application, duly endorsed, to the Income-Tax Officer, Foreign Section, concerned. The applicant or his representative should then present the Authorisation to the Income-tax officer, Foreign Section for exchanging it with the tax clearance/Exemption Certificate.

All the forms necessary for obtaining the various certificates should be standardised and printed, and made freely available to the assessees on request.

All complaints of inconvenience in the tax offices should be quickly remedied. Adequate and proper amenities, such as waiting rooms, furniture, reading material, cool drinking water, canteens, public telephones, sanitary arrangements, parking space, etc. for the assessees and their representatives should be provided in all tax offices.

Information And Guidance To The Assessees

Greater attention should be paid to organised departmental publicity, and more tax literature in the form of pamphlets, booklets, etc. dealing with the various branches of taxation should be issued. Detailed explanatory notes about the various forms of returns should also be made freely available to the public. The Department should also publish a Tax Journal.

The various notifications and circulars issued by the Central Board of Revenue having a bearing on the application of the taxation laws and affecting the assessees' interests, directly or indirectly, should be made known to the public.

The modern media of Communication with the public such as radio, motion pictures and other visual aids, should be regarded as eesential in the programme of developing public relations.

In places other than those where Public Relations officers function, Enquiry Counters, should be responsible for assisting the assessees in filling up various return forms, explaining their difficulties and doubts, answering their various queries and guiding them in all possible ways.

Facilities provided by the chambers of commerce etc. to educate their members about the tax matters should be further enlarge and the Department should usefully establish some liaison arrangements with them for this purpose.

It will facilitate the administration of the tax laws and avoid under inconvenience to the assessees if the Central Board of Revenue or the Commissioner gives opinion on the points referred to by the assessees provided that all the facts relevant to the points at issue are made available and the relevant points are not pending for decision before any appellate authority.

Redress Of Grievances

All the gazetted officers of the Department, in particular, the Inspecting Assistant Commissioners and the Commissioners, should keep their doors open for any member of the public to walk in and voice his grievances. These officers should, for the sake of convenience, keep certain fixed hours everyday for the public to meet them. Complaint and suggestion boxes should be provided in all tax offices including those of the Assistant Commissioners, Commissioners and Appellate Tribunal Benches.

Public Relations Officers

The Public Relations Officers can prove very useful and helpful in promoting better relations between the Department and the Public. There should be a whole-time Public Relations Officer in the charge of each Commissioner of Income-tax. The Public Relations Officers in important places like Bombay and Calcutta should be of the rank of Assistant Commissioners, and those in other places should be at least senior Class I Grade I officers.

One of the Members of the Central Board of Revenue should be in specific charge of 'public relations.'

Direct Taxes Advisory Committees

A Direct Taxes Central Advisory Committee should be set up for the Headquarters organisation under the Chairmanship of the Union Minister for Revenue and Civil Expenditure. In addition, similar Committees should be constituted separately for the various regional organisations under the Chairmanship of the Union Minister for Revenue and Civil Expenditure. In addition, similar Committees should be constituted separately for the various regional organisations under the Chairmanship of the Commissioner concerned. These Committees should fully represent the important interests and view points, and consist of Members of Parliament, representatives of Central and/or State Governments, commerce, industry and other organisation and professional tax experts. They should advise the Administration on measures for developing and encouraging mutual understanding and cooperation between the tax-payers and the Department.

COMMITTEE ON FISHERIES EDUCATION 1958—REPORT

New Delhi, Ministry of Food and Agriculture, Department of Agriculture, 1959. 144p.+iiip.

Chairman : Dr. N.K. Panikkar.

Members : Dr. G.L. Kesteven, Prof. G.M. Gerhardsen, Dr. B.N. Chopra.

APPOINTMENT

The facilities established by the Government of India in the First Five-Year Plan and in the initial stages of the Second Plan, for training of fishery workers were essentially *ad hoc* intended to provide specialised personnel rather than to constitute an integrated system of education in this field. However, as the development schemes progressed, the manpower problems became so pressing that the entire question came up for review early in 1957; with the result the Government decided to appoint a Committee to examine the needs of the fishery programmes for trained persons and the facilities required for training them. In the Government of India Resolution No. F.7-15/57-FY(D), dated June 4, 1958, this Committee was appointed.

TERMS OF REFERENCE

(1) To review and assess the training requirements for fisheries personnel to man the administrative and executive and research projects in India and for the growing needs of the Industry.

(2) To examine the need for higher or ancillary training facilities in the field of fisheries in the light of the present and future requirements of the Second and Third Plans and of the training courses now available.

(3) To recommend the location, courses of study, the staff required and other practical details for the establishment of such training institute (institutes).

CONTENTS

Introduction; Indian Fisheries and Their Development; Fisheries Administration in India; Manpower Requirements; Existing Arrangements for Training in Fisheries; Proposals for a Central Institute of Fisheries Education (CIFE); Ancillary Training; Summary of Conclusions and Recommendations; Acknowledgements; Appendices I to X.

RECOMMENDATIONS

Manpower Deficiency

The Committee is convinced that progress in development of Indian fisheries has been hampered by acute shortage of suitably trained personnel. Shortages of operatives and lower level administrative staff have been partially overcome by training provided by Government but no training exists for high level developmental and managerial staff. Accelerated development during the Third and successive Plans will not be achieved without such trained staff. The Committee recommends that immediate steps be taken to establish facilities for this training.

Such training along with certain other ancillary training courses in fisheries should be organised by the Central Government (Ministry of Food and Agriculture) in an Institute which should be established for this purpose and not as an adjunct to any of the existing establishments or Universities.

Interim Arrangements

The Committee reiterates and recommends for adoption its proposal made in an Interim Report that pending the establishment of this Institute, immediate arrangements be made at Bombay for a provisional training course for District Fisheries Development Officers. The Committee recommends that this course should start in July, 1959.

Status Of The Course

The provisional course of study prescribed for the

District Fisheries Development Officers should develop into a regular professional training in Fisheries, which should be on a par with the Bachelor Degree Course in Agriculture, Forestry and other applied Sciences. Although starting as a diploma course, this should eventually become a Degree course in Fisheries at Bachelor level.

Scope For Specialisation

Having fully examined whether separate training should be provided for marine and inland fisheries, the Committee recommends that the proposed course at the Fisheries Training Institute should be common for both marine and inland fisheries. The course should, however, provide for specialisation in one of the following subjects or any other subject within the curriculum approved by the Institute:

(i) Inland Fisheries.
(ii) Fish Handling and Processing Technology.
(iii) Fishing Gear Technology.
(iv) Fishery Economics and Business Management.
(v) Fish Marketing and Trade.

Qualification For Admission

Minimum educational qualification for admission to the training course for District Fishery Development Officers should be a Degree in Science with Zoology as one of the subjects. Preference should be given to those who have taken Chemistry, Botany, Statistics or Economics as an additional subject.

Duration Of Training

The duration of the training course should be two years, of which nearly half should be spent in prescribed field work.

Number Of Trainees

To meet the requirements of trained personnel in the Third Plan, the Committee's opinion is that at least 30 candidates should be trained at the Institute each year. If the Institute becomes a regional or an international training centre, steps should be taken to ensure that adequate number of seats are reserved for Indian trainees.

Selection Of Trainees

The trainees should include nominees of Central and State Governments as well as private candidates. For the first two or three batches of trainees, it is expected that all seats will be taken up by Governmental nominees.

Nominations

The trainees nominated by the State Governments should include persons either already in service or selected against existing or anticipated posts.

Stipends

The trainees should be given stipends during the period of training and also provided with adequate travel grants. The Committee recommends a stipend of Rs. 200 per month. Employees of Central/State Governments should be paid full salary and allowances and if the total emolument is less than the stipend, they should be given additional allowance upto the prescribed stipend.

Location Of The Institute

Having studied the various criteria necessary for the successful functioning of the Training Institute, the Committee feels that the Institute should be located at a centre where the fishery industry is well developed and where adequate port facilities are available for the ships of the Institute. Since the main centre of training must thus be a coastal city, the Committee recognises the need for a sub-centre at which to give field training in inland fish cultural practices

On strictly technical grounds the Committee considers that Cochin is the most suitable place for the location of the Training Institute.

For the location of the Inland Fisheries Training Sub-Centre, the Kausalyaganga area near Bhubaneswar in Orissa offers the best facilities.

Physical Facilities

The Institute should have its own library, workshop, training ships, pilot processing plants, laboratories, lecture rooms and other essential facilities for a self-contained training establishment.

It is most essential to provide hostel facilities for the trainees, regardless of the location of the institute.

If the Institute is situated at some distance from the city, residential accommodation for all members of the staff should be provided in the vicinity of the Institute. In any case, it would be necessary to provide accommodation for the Director and a part of the staff in the premises of the Institute.

Training Vessels

The Training Institute should have two vessels—one capable of being used for different types of fishing, about 85 to 90 feet and the other, a smaller vessel of about 35 feet. These ships should have berthing and servicing facilities within a reasonable distance from the Institute. Both the vessels should be staffed by competent personnel and fully equipped for fishing with different kinds of gear, exploratory work and training. It is likely that the services of a skipper and a senior Engineer for the larger vessel will have to be obtained from abroad for a period of three years.

Staff

The Committee places great emphasis on the high professional standing of staff to be appointed for the Institute. It should have a Director, who will be in-charge of the whole organisation, assisted by a Registrar to help him in purely administrative matters. There should be one professor for each of the following Divisions :

1. Fishery Biology.
2. Fishery Economics and Co-operation.
3. Fishery Technology.

There should be six Assistant Professors for the subjects indicated below:

A. Division Of Fishery Biology

1. Oceanography, Meteorology and Limnology.
2. Inland Fisheries.

B. Division Of Fishery Economics

1. Statistics, Commerce and Business Administration.
2. Marketing and Co-operation.

C. Division Of Fishery Technology

1. Fishing Technology and Naval Architecture.
2. Fish Processing and related subjects.

In addition to the Assistant Professors, there should be demonstrators, field instructors, administrative personnel, secretarial staff, etc.

The Committee considers that it will be necessary to engage experts from abroad to occupy the senior posts at the Institute during its formative years. Suitable Indian counterparts should be appointed to work with the foreign experts and be trained by them to take over the responsibilities within a period of about five years.

In addition to the permanent staff of the Institute, the Committee envisages the need for visiting lecturers from India and abroad for giving special courses.

Placement Of Qualified Trainees

The trainees after successful completion of the course should normally be eligible for appointment as District Fisheries Development Officers. In some cases, it may be necessary for administrative reasons to appoint them initially to lower posts such as Inspectors, but there should be a reasonable prospect of their promotion as District Officers in three to five years.

To attract good trainees, fisheries positions in Government service should have adequate remuneration. The status and salaries of District Fisheries Development Officers should, by no means, be lower than those prescribed for corresponding position in Agriculture or Forestry. The Committee wishes to emphasise that in its view much of the purpose of the Institute would be nullified if candidates of the right kind do not come forward for training.

Training Of Junior Fisheries Officers

To meet the requirements of staff at levels lower than that of the District Fisheries Development Officer in inland States and for inland areas in maritime States, the existing training course at Barrackpore should be suitably overhauled. For this purpose, additional staff will have to be provided and the syllabus revised to give more practical training in inland fisheries. When facilities become available at the proposed Sub-Centre of the Institute at Kausalyaganga, this course should be transferred to that place.

Operative Training

The Committee is convinced that there is great need for training operatives at various levels of skill in fishing, navigation, boat-building, marine engineering, fish handling and processing, marketing, etc. Training in these skills should be separate from the training for Development Officers. For such vocational training, preference should be given to fishermen wherever possible.

The Committee recommends that in addition to the training for fisheries Development Officers the Institute should conduct or arrange for certain courses in subjects ancillary to fisheries.

AD-HOC ENQUIRY COMMITTEE ON GAMES AND SPORTS, 1958—REPORT

Delhi, Manager of Publications, 1959. 56p.

Chairman : H.H. The Maharajadhiraj of Patiala.

Members : Shri Naval H. Tata; Rajkumari Amrit Kaur; Shri S.M. Moinul Haq; Dr. P. Subbarayan; Shri Jaipal Singh; Gen. K.S. Thimayya; Shri M.S. Duleepsinhji; Shri N.N. Wanchoo; Shri P.N. Kripal.

Secretary : Shri M.N. Masud.

APPOINTMENT

The Government of India appointed this Committee on July 1958, to investigate the persistence of low standards in sports in India and the performance of Indian teams in international contests such as the Olympic and Asian Games and to recommend measures for improvement.

TERMS OF REFERENCE

(i) To enquire into the reasons for the poor performance of Indian competitors in International contests;

(ii) To suggest measures to arrest the gradual decline in the level of performance; and

(iii) To recommend steps for the improvement of standards.

CONTENTS

Introduction; National Federations/Associations; Services Sport Control Board; Other Sports and Games; All-India Council of Sports and State Sports Councils; Coaching in Sports and Games; Selection of Teams; Management of Teams; Promotion of Sports in Rural Areas; Playgrounds and Equipment; Procedure for Grant of Assistance by the Government of India; Judging, Refereeing and Umpiring; Amateurism; Summary of Recommendations; Minutes of Dissent.

RECOMMENDATIONS

Introduction

As other countries have improved their performances very much more, we have to accelerate our rate of improvement. It is, therefore, necessary that more facilities and better opportunities for training and competition are provided and greater administrative efficiency achieved.

The contribution of our educational institutions to the development of sports and games in the country has not been as great as that of educational institutions in some other countries who are far ahead in the field of sports. Unless more opportunities and greater facilities are provided in educational institutions in the form of equipment, playgrounds, funds, etc., sports and games will not be popular in schools and colleges and the contribution of educational institutions to the development of sports and games will remain as poor as it has been all these years.

Incentives in the form of credit for achievements in sports and games are also desirable.

It has been proved that there is a definite correlation between athletic proficiency and achievements in competitions like the Olympic Games, on the one hand, and, on the other, factors such as sports traditions and social and nutritional habits which have a bearing on the general health of the people. Health, power of endurance, physical well-being are all dependent to a large extent on proper nutrition. Natural abilities in our young people must be helped by environmental forces in addition to improvement in nutrition.

National Federations/Associations

It is necessary that conditions detrimental to the development and popularising of sports should be eliminated. People with integrity, love and knowledge of sports should feel that they are welcome in organisations governing sports. The following measures have been recommended:

(i) The term of the office bearers in a National Federation/Association should be limited to three years with option for re-eleetion for another term of three years.

(ii) No office bearer in one National Federation/Association should simultaneously hold office in any other National Federation/Association.

(iii) All National Federations/Associations should get themselves registered under the Registration of Societies Act, 1860.

(iv) Every National Federation/Association should have a stipendiary Assistant Secretary.

All India Council Of Sports And State Sports Councils

The All-India Council of Sports should be reconstituted and it should consist of 11 to 15 members, including a Chairman, [nominated by the Government of India, who have knowledge standing and experience of sports and their administration. No extraneous considerations should influence the selection of members. The Council of Sports in the States should also be reconstituted on the pattern of the All-India Council of Sports. They should consist of seven to nine members nominated by the Government of the State. The powers and functions of the All-India Council of Sports and the State Sports Councils should be redefined so that they should not interfere with, encroach upon or usurp the functions or authority of the Sports Associations at the National or State level.

Coaching In Sports And Games

Planned coaching at all stages is essential. Coaching as it is at present has not even touched the fringe of the problem. There is a vast talent potential in the country which can and must be exploited by intensive and planned coaching. There should be a Central Plan to ensure a reservoir for a regular supply of trainees for the coaches. An expert from a foreign country may be appointed to assist in the formulation of the Central Plan.

A beginning should be made immediately with the establishment of a Central Training Institute to provide first class coaches in different sports and games. Admission to the Institute should be regulated according to the requirements of a planned coaching scheme so that coaches graduating from there are distributed according to the plan. Physical Education teachers, by virtue of their numbers and the fact that they are spread all over the country, should play a very important role as primary coaches of the youth of the country.

A cadre of coaches should be built up as soon as possible and security of service assured to coaches on a contract basis for a minimum period of five years subject to a probationary period of six months. Coaches will have to be paid different rates according to their stature in the profession, their qualifications, experience, etc., and the specific purpose for which they are appointed. Until such time as the recommendations of the Committee are implemented, the existing Coaching Schemes should continue.

Selection Of Teams

National Federations/Associations should appoint their Selection Committees, as far as possible, on a permanent basis and every Selection Committee may be constituted for a period of two years. These Selection Committees should be small consisting of not more than five members. Of these, two should wherever possible be persons who have played that particular game in an international competition. The Captain should be appointed by the Executive Body of the Federation/Association on the recommendation of its Selection Committee and he should assist the Committee in the selection of the team.

Management Of Teams

National Federations/Associations should choose as Managers the right type of persons for the performance of their difficult and onerous task.

The duty of the Manager is primarily with his team and it is only incidental if he serves on boards, committees and in other places.

Discipline is essential for the success of a team. The Manager should be able to maintain descipline. He has to see that there is a spontaneous response from the team to its officials.

In a contingent where several teams are included it should be the duty of the chief official to see that the various units are welded into a homogeneous whole which feels and acts like one team, and that all members of the contingent with his assistance and under his guidance prove themselves good ambassadors of their country.

Promotion Of Sports In Rural Areas

There has been little or no activity in the field of sports and games in rural areas. Sports and games should be organised in such areas through *Vyayamshalas*, *Vyayam Mandals*, *Akharas*, etc., and in cooperation with the Community Projects, Sports Festivals should be organised and sports events encouraged on the occasion of Fairs etc. Indigenous sports like *Kabaddi* and indigenous style of wrestling should be encouraged.

Playgrounds And Equipment

There is inadequacy of playgrounds and equipment in the country. In educational institutions the position in respect of these is still worse. If schools and colleges and universities have to play their part in the development of sports and games in the country, they must have the minimum requirements in respect of play grounds and equipment. The following standards have been recommended:

A College with a student population of 1000 to 1500	... 10 acres for playgrounds.
A High School with a student population of 500 to 1000	... 5-6 acres.
A Middle School with a student population of 200 to 500	... 3-5 acres.
A Primary School	... 1 acre.

Where separate playgrounds cannot be made available for each educational institution, a common pool for a group of institutions should be created.

Stadiums are necessary for sports, but in consideration of the fact that our financial resources are limited, the possibility of harnessing voluntary effort, including *shramdan* wherever possible, is strongly recommended. Only utility type stadiums instead of expensive ones should be built. Even with the help of voluntary effort building of stadiums may prove expensive and, therefore, it is preferable to provide a larger number of enclosed playgrounds to serve a wider purpose in the development of sports and games.

No indoor sports arenas exist at present, although it is necessary to have indoor sports arenas for the improvement of standards in games like, Badminton and Table Tennis, both of which are popular in the country.

Standard equipment should be manufactured in the country so as to be available at cheap rates to all and facilities for its manufacture should be provided.

Procedure For Grant Of Assistance By The Government Of India

The available funds with the Government of India for the development of sports and games during the remaining portion of the Second Five-Year Plan should be distributed as follows:

1. Improvement of standards in sports. ... 30 per cent
2. Popularisation of sports and games in educational institutions and in rural areas ... 65 per cent
3. On organisational expenses for the National Federations Associations, etc. ... 5 per cent

Funds should be distributed, through the State Governments concerned, on the recommendation of the All-India Council of Sports and State Sports Councils.

Judging, Refereeing And Umpiring

The existing standards in umpiring and refereeing are generally low. For the development of sports and games in the country it is essential that umpiring and refereeing should be of a high order. Apart from other efforts that are being made to increase the number of these officials and improve the standards of officiating, all qualified coaches should also be trained to be qualified officials. This should be a part of their training.

Amateurism

The rules on amateurism laid down by the International Federations and the International Olympic Committee should be strictly followed in the country.

COMMITTEE FOR PLANNING MEASURES AGAINST FLOODS AND SIMILAR CALAMITIES IN DELHI, 1958—REPORT

New Delhi, Ministry of Works, Housing and Supply, 1959, 106p.+Charts.

Chairman : Shri K.C. Reddy.
Members : Shri Dharma Vira; Shri V.K.B. Pillai; Shri A.D. Pandit; Shri P.R. Nayak; Shri J.M. Rijhwani; Shri S. Vohra; Shri G. Mukharji; Shri Kanwar Sain; Shri M.A. Lokhande; Maj. Gen. R.E. Aserappa.
Convener : Shri M.R. Sachdev.
Assisted by : Shri Walter George; Shri Karnail Singh.

Appointment

Flooding of large parts of the Capital during the monsoon has been quite a common occurrence for a number of years. The all-time record of rainfall of more than 10.5″ in 24 hours, with a maximum intensity of 2.8″ in one hour, on July 20 and 21, 1958 flooded large areas in the Capital, causing damage to some roads and buildings and paralysing Communications.

The Prime Minister called a meeting on July 23, 1958 of the Ministers concerned, the Mayor of Delhi and other civil and Military officers concerned to consider the situation that had arisen and, after discussions, appointed a Committee for Planning Measures Against Floods and Similar Calamities in Delhi.

Terms Of Reference

(i) To consider protective measures from consequences of floods, heavy rains, etc.;

(ii) To examine the adequacy of existing drainage and sewerage systems and to suggest improvements,

(iii) To go into the problem of water-logging, low-lying land and sub-soil water;

(iv) To examine the bridges, bunds, etc., from the structural point of view; and

(v) To look into the matter relating to equipment, such as pumps, etc., necessary to deal with emergencies.

CONTENTS

RECOMMENDATIONS

Stormwater Drainage

The stormwater drainage system of the urban and rural areas has been considered separately. In respect of urban areas, the drainage system has been recommended to be remodelled for a storm likely to occur once in two years. This represents a rainfall intensity of 1.65 inches per hour. The run-off is to be worked out taking into consideration the intensity of rainfall corresponding to the time of concentration of the drain and also the proportion of built-up to unbuilt areas. In the case of rural areas, the consideration will be to limit the period of flooding of crops to three days for a storm of frequency of once in five years. The run-off corresponding to this is 10 cusecs per sq. mile.

For the purpose of investigation of the stormwater drainage, the Delhi State has been divided into four blocks on the basis of natural topography of land.

Block No. 1 comprises the New Delhi area and areas on the south and is mainly drained by the Barapulla Nalla and its tributaries.

Block No. II comprises the rural areas of West and North Delhi, drained by the Najafgarh Drain and its tributaries.

Block No. III comprises the Old Delhi city area.

Block No. IV comprises the Shahdara area.

Block No. I

The improvements suggested to Block I will take the following forms :—

(a) Improving the intercepting arrangements in the pre-1939 colonies.

(b) Increasing the capacity of the existing drainage system in the pre-1939 colonies to take a run-off of ½ inch against the original design of ¼ inch.

(c) Improving the outfall conditions in case of the post-1939 colonies where flooding occurred.

(d) Providing pumps in areas which cannot be drained by gravity.

(e) Increasing the restricted waterways under railway and road bridges wherever necessary.

(f) Desilting and re-sectioning of the open outfall nallas.

Action on (b) above should be taken on the basis of observations on the performance of the drainage system after removal of all the existing obstructions. The cost of all these improvements has been estimated at Rs. 2.37 crores.

Block No. II

This comprises the catchment of the Najafgarh Drain and its tributaries, 508 sq. miles in extent. The flooding of the urban areas in this catchment was partly due to the inadequacy, under the present conditions, of the waterway under the bridge across the Deryala Nalla, a tributary of this drain. It is now proposed to remodel this bridge to provide an adequate waterway.

Regarding the rural areas of Alipur and Najafgarh Blocks, the proposal is to regrade the bed of the Najafgarh Drain in a reach of 10 miles as an immediate measure. For providing substantial interim relief, it is proposed to compeletely re-section this drain in a reach of 13 miles, increasing its bed width where the drain has a restricted waterway. For complete relief, it is proposed to provide a catchwater drain around the Jheel, improve the Najafgarh Drain throughout its length and regrade and divert the Manageshpur and Nangloi Drains. Before execution of this work, the desirability of draining the Jheel completely should be examined bythe C.W. & P.C. in consultation with the Ministry of Food and Agriculture. In addition, pumping of arrangements will be required for certain low pockets as also improvements to a few other drains. The total cost of all these improvements is estimated at Rs. 1.7 crores.

Block No. III

Block No. III covers the Old Delhi city area. The problem here is the separation of sewerage from stormwater drains. The estimated cost of separation is Rs. 30 lakhs.

Block No. IV

This comprises the Shahdara area. It is proposed to drain this area by gravity through suitable open channels running north-south, taking the rainwater to a point below the Okhla Weir where adequate fall in the river is reported to be available. As this scheme is based on a general study of conditions at site, detailed investigations are necessary before the necessity for pumping can be ruled out. The cost of this scheme has been estimated at Rs. 42 lakhs.

Summing up, the total cost of the improvements to the existing drainage system is Rs. 4.79 crores, i.e. Block No. I Rs. 2.37 crores, Block No. II Rs. 1.70 crores, Block No. III Rs. 30 lakhs and Block No. IV Rs. 42 lakhs.

As the outlay involved is large and the implementation of all the works is likely to take considerable time, these works have been divided into three phases :—

(1) Works that should be completed before the next monsoon.

These are estimated to cost Rs. 19 lakhs.

(2) Works of an urgent nature which should be taken up for execution as soon as the investigation work is completed, and should be completed before the monsoon of 1960.

These are estimated to cost Rs. 129 lakhs.

(3) Remaining works which are estimated to cost Rs 331 lakhs.

The Committee accepts the necessity for all these works and recommends their speedy execution. Before any further steps to augment the capacity of the drainage system of the pre-1939 New Delhi area are taken, the Committee would recommend that the performance of the system should be watched after the removal of all obstructions.

Sewerage

The urban areas of the Delhi State have been divided into four zones for the purpose of investigation of the sewerage system. These are the South-East Zone, the North Zone, the West Zone and the Shahdara Area. Reference may be made to Plan No. 3 for these zones.

South-East Zone

This zone comprises the Old Delhi and New Delhi areas. Of the three trunk sewers serving this area, two are overloaded. Some of the branch sewers in the New Delhi are also overloaded. The Old Delhi area is, at present, served by a combined system whereby stormwater also enters the sewers. The Okhla sewage treatment plant is no longer adequate to deal with the entire sewage flow and parts of the plant are also due for renewal. As a result, crude sewage overflows into the Jamuna at several places. Many of the outlying colonies are still unsewered. There are a number of subsidiary pumping stations involving a heavy recurring expenditure.

The Delhi Corporation is laying a relief trunk sewer from the Delhi Gate to the Ring Road. Certain additions are also being made to the Okhla treatment plant. Action is also being taken for providing sewerage to some of the unsewered colonies. The further improvements, which are necessary and which we recommend for execution, are :

(a) Laying relief branch sewers in the New Delhi area.

(b) Extension of the new trunk sewer from the Delhi Gate to the Red Fort, duplicate rising main from the Ring Road Pumping Station to the high-level gravity duct and cross-connection between old and new sewers.

(c) Providing internal sewers in Civil Lines and Kotla Mubarakpur, outfall sewers for the Friends' Colony and Malvia Nagar.

(d) Additional secondary treatment plant at Okhla for 30 m.g.d. Extension of irrigation channels and renewal of machinery of the activated sludge plant.

(e) Gas utilisation works at Okhla.

(f) Elimination of subsidiary pumping stations.

(g) Separation of stormwater and sewage in the Delhi city area.

Excluding the last item, provision for which has been made in the stormwater drainage estimate, the cost of the schemes is estimated at Rs. 166 lakhs.

North Zone

This zone covers the urban areas in North Delhi, such as Karol Bagh, Subzi Mandi, Model Town, etc. Some of the colonies are sewered, some have septic tank arrangements and the rest are at present unsewered. Part of the sewage from the sewered colonies is pumped into the trunk sewers in the South-East Zone, further aggravating the overloading of the latter.

A new treatment plant, capable of dealing with the entire sewage of this zone, has been set up near the Coronation Pillar. The main trunk sewer to feed this treatment plant is also being laid. The further works, which are necessary and which we recommend for execution, are:

(a) Additional secondary treatment units for 10 m.g.d. and gas utilisation works at the treatment plant.

(b) Extension of the trunk sewer from the Delhi-Ambala railway line up to the Old Rohtak Road.

(c) Branch sewers.

These are estimates to cost Rs. 81 lakhs.

West Zone

This zone covers the urban areas of West Delhi. Excepting the Cantonment area, none of the colonies is sewered. A new treatment plant has been setup by the Corporation at Tilak Nagar to deal with the entire sewage and industrial wastes of this zone. One trunk sewer is being laid along Road No. 34 and the Najafgarh Road. The further works, which are necessary and which we recommend for execution, are :—

(a) Providing irrigation channels at the Tilak Nagar Plant.

(b) Laying a trunk sewer along the Najafgarh Drain.

(c) Laying a trunk sewer south of the Najafgarh Road parallel to the railway line.

(d) Branch sewers.

These are estimated to cost Rs. 88 lakhs.

Shahdara Area

The entire Shahdara Area is at present unsewered. Due to development difficulties, it will not be easy to provide underground sewerage in this zone immediately. As an immediate measure, we recommend the setting up of two night-soil digestion tanks at an estimated cost of Rs. 7.6 lakhs. The pace of development is, however, likely to quicken in the near future and it will not be long before we shall have to think of providing sewerage arrangements. The probable cost of providing sewerage facilities, complete with purification works, has been estimated by the Corporation at Rs. 1.39 crores.

Summing up, the total cost of improvements to severage is Rs. 4.82 crores as shown below :

(a) South-East Zone	...	Rs. 166 lakhs
(b) North Zone	...	Rs. 81 lakhs
(c) West Zone	...	Rs. 88 lakhs
(d) Shahdara Area	...	Rs. 147 lakhs
		Rs. 482 lakhs

The Committee recommends the phasing out of the works on the basis of priority.

The Problem of Sub-Soil Water

The Ad Hoc Committee on Sub-soil water has finalised its study of the causes of the rise of sub-soil water and suitable measures to lower it.

It has divided the New Delhi area into three zones :

Zone I : The areas where the sub-soil water table in October is within six feet from the ground surface. These are termed as 'Badly Affected'. These are the areas where the maximum damage to buildings, roads and vegetation can take place as a result of water-logging.

Zone II : This zone, termed as "Moderately Affected" areas, covers the areas where the water table is six feet to 10 feet from the ground surface.

Zone III : Areas where the water table in the month of October is at a depth greater than 10 feet from the ground surface.

From the Iso-hydrographs drawn every year, it is observed that more and more areas under zone III are passing into zone II and, similarly, areas from zone II are passing into zone I. The statement given below indicates the alarming rate at which large areas of land, which were "safe", have passed on to what are termed as "moderately" and "badly" affected areas:

Sr. No.	Depth of Water Table from Ground in October	Area in Acres in Oct. 1954	Area in Acres in Oct. 1955	Area in Acres in Oct. 1956	Area in Acres in Oct. 1957	Area in Acres in Oct. 1958
1.	Within 6 feet	256	545	920	1,040	3,200
2.	From 6 feet to 10 feet	3,114	3,415	3,470	3,930	6,000
3.	More than 10 feet	6,430	5,840	5,410	4,830	600

Apart from this, the other conclusions that have been reached are as follows :

(1) The sub-soil water table rises from June to October.

(2) It falls from October to June but there is generally a net rise from June to June.

(3) Heavy rainfall is responsible for the abnormal rise during the monsoon period.

(4) Since 1912, there has been a general rise in the sub-soil water table, varying from 1.67 feet to 15.87 feet.

(5) The net annual rise of sub-soil water is the least in the case of badly affected areas, and is the maximum in the case of "safe" areas.

(6) Whether a state of equlibrium has been reached in the badly affected areas is difficult to say. A final conclusion on this point will be possible only when the results of observations for a long period are available.

According to the Ad Hoc Committee, the rise in sub-soil water is due to additions to the underground water table by way of percolation or seepage.

The sources of percolation or seepage are :

(i) Holding up of stormwater due to urbanisation; and

(ii) Irrigation.

According to the Ad Hoc Committee, a high water table is harmful to buildings and vegetation. It has, therefore, recommended that the sub-soil water table should be lowered to a depth of 10 feet below the ground level in October and to 14 feet in the pre-monsoon period. It has also confirmed that such lowering is not likely to have any harmful effect on the existing buildings. The remedial measures suggested are :

(a) Improvement of the drainage system.

(b) Economy in the use of unfiltered water.

(c) Physical removal of water from the sub-soil reservoir by tubewells.

(d) Supplementing the underground drainage by laying porous drains in areas to be taken up for development.

The Ad Hoc Committee has ruled out the possibility of utilising tubewell water for irrigation purposes due to its high salinity. It has also recommended the reclamation of areas, which have become saline due to the presence of salts caused by fluctuation in the water table, by using D.D.T. or gypsum.

The Ad Hoc Committee has also recommended further continuance of studies on the behaviour of the sub-soil water table.

Without taking into consideration the cost of improvement to drainage, the cost of various remedial measures suggested for lowering and stabilising the water table has been estimated at Rs. 30 lakhs.

This Committee accepts the various recommendations of the Ad-Hoc Committee on Sub-soil Water and recommends their speedy implementation.

Flood Protection Works

Flood protection works in the Delhi State consist of a series of bunds on both sides of the Jamuna. Improvements to these bunds have been carried out from time to time. During the floods of 1956 to 1958, it has been observed that the right side bund from the Coronation

Pillar to the Shah-Alam Bridge and the left Marginal Bund need strengthening. A new weir is under construction at Wazirabad, as a result of which the high flood level upstream of the weir will rise further, necessitating raising of the bunds upstream of the weir. Schemes for raising and strengthening of the bunds have been finalised, estimates sanctioned and the works taken in hand. The Committee would, however recommend that the top width of the Shahdara Bund, after raising, should be 24 against the proposed width of 15 feet.

The villages between the river and the bunds are unprotected from floods. A proposal has already been finalised to shift these villages to the land side of the bunds. We recommend early implementation of this proposal.

Low-lying areas on either side of the Barapulla Nalla between the railway track aud the Ring Road are also subject to flooding. To remedy this, it is proposed to provide bunds on either side of the Barapulla Nalla in this reach and the cost of this scheme is included in the seuggested improvements to storm water drainage. We recommend early completion of investigation and implementation of this proposal.

Equipment

The equipment required has been subdivided into :

(a) Equipment for execution of the various schemes.

(b) Equipment to deal with emergencies.

The equipment required for execution are well point equipment for the Delhi Municipal Corporation and two drag line excavators for the C.P. W.D, These are estimated to cost Rs. nine lakhs.

The Delhi Municipal Corporation has already made arrangements for procuring the necessary equipment to deal with emergencies in its areas. The N.D.M.C. has, however, yet to procure such equipment for the areas under its jurisdiction and the cost of these is estimated at Rs. 80,000/-.

We recommend immediate procurement of this equipment.

Administrative and Financial Matters

The Improvements suggested would involve a total financial outlay of Rs. 10.05 crores. The allocation of costs, according to the fields of reponsibility, would be as follows :

(i)	Delhi Municipal Corporation	...	Rs. 613 lakhs
(ii)	N.D. M.C.	...	Rs. 202 lakhs
(iii)	Delhi Administration	...	Rs. 154 lakhs
(iv)	Ministry of W.H. & S.	...	Rs. 36 lakhs
			Rs. 1,005 lakhs

The local bodies may find it difficult in the immediate future to raise such large amounts from their own resources. We, therefore, recommeud that, if they approach Government for assistance, such assistance should be rendered by way of loans and grants, as may be necessary.

For carrying out investigations, we recommend that the Corporation should strengthen its field engineering organisation. As regards the N.D.M.C., we recommend that the C.P.W.D. should render such assistance to it as it may require and as Government may approve. As an interim measure, we recommend the continuance of the existing set-up under the C.P.W.D., the Corporation and the C.W. & P.C.

Apart from the technical problems of the Delhi State, dealt with by this Committee, there are also other technical problems of Delhi, as for example, the problems of water supply. We recommend that the responsibility for the formulation of policies and ensuring coordination in regard to all such problems should rest with the Ministry of Home Affairs.

In order to assist the Ministry of Home Affairs in these technical matters and for purposes of securing necessary coordination, we recommend the setting up of a Committee of Secretaries of the Ministries concerned dealing with these technical matters. This Committee should be further assisted by a whole time technical officer of Chief Engineer's rank, functioning as Secretary of this Coordinating Committee.

COMMITTEE TO ASSESS AND EVALUATE THE PRESENT STATUS OF AYURVEDIC SYSTEM OF MEDICINE, 1958—REPORT

New Delhi, Ministry of Health, 246p.+viiip.

Chairman : Dr. K.N. Udupa.
Member : Shri Kaladi Parameswaran Pillai.
Secretary : Shri R. Narasimhan.

APPOINTMENT

The Committee to Assess and Evaluate the present Status of Ayurvedic System of Medicine was constituted under the Ministry of Health *vide* their letter No. F.2-50/58-ISM, dated July 29, 1958.

TERMS OF REFERENCE

(i) To evaluate and assess the work already done in the field of Ayervedic Research and upgrading of Ayurvedic Institutions as a result of grants already given by the Central and State Governments;

(ii) To assess the existing facilities for training and research in Ayurveda;

(iii) To assess the nature, volume and standard of the Ayurvedic Pharmaceutical Products; and

(iv) To find out the factual position in regard to the practice and recognition of the Ayurvedic system of medicine.

CONTENTS

Introduction; Terms of Reference and Methods of Study; General Observations; Training; Research: Pharmaceutical Products; Status of Practice; Final Recommendations; Concluding Remarks; Appendices I to X; Tables I to XIII; Maps 1 to 4; Figures 1 to 13.

RECOMMENDATIONS

Training

In the interests of the resuscitation of the science of Ayurveda, an integration of the old and new will be necessary and as much of modern medical subjects as will be necessary to explain the gaps left in Ayurveda should be taught in Ayurvedic institutions, prominence being given to the principles of Ayurveda.

The Shudh Ayurvedic type of training should also continue, at least for some time to come, subject to the condition that ample provision is made in the institutions concerned for practical training.

The Integrated and Shudh Ayurvedic Physicians and the traditional Vaidyas have a definite place in providing the much-needed medical relief to the country, particularly in rural areas. By properly canalising the training of the Shudh Ayurvedic Physicians and by encouraging all the existing Vaidyas of known reputation, medical relief can be improved considerably.

The Central and State Governments should make an unequivocal declaration of policy recognising the training and practice of Ayurveda.

A Central Council of Indian Medicine should be set up as the very first measure of reform. The suggestions made in the Chapter on Training regarding the constitution and functions of this Central Council may be implemented at an early date. There should be an Executive Committee of the Central Council.

Governments have the main responsibility for providing adequate finances to improve the present unsatisfactory position in Ayurvedic training. Apart from proper provision and maintenance of institutions, Governments should see to it that a sufficient number of freeships, scholarships and other financial concessions are given in order to attract the proper type of students.

Attempts should be made immediately to affiliate all Ayurvedic training institutions to Universities with separate Faculties for Ayurvedic Medicine. This will tone up the standard of teaching, and examinations and improve the buildings, laboratories, equipment, practical facilities, etc. Besides this, the status of teaching staff will improve.

For providing adequate number of efficient teachers at an early date, the Central Government should, in addition to the Post-Graduate Training Centre at Jamnagar, establish three more model Post-Graduate Training Centres to cover the Northern and Eastern, Central and Southern Zones respectively at Banaras, Poona and Trivandrum. In these four Post-Graduate Training Centres, a three-year training course should be instituted for Integrated Degree Holders, Shudh Ayurvedic Title holders and modern medical graduates. In addition there should be special training courses of one year's duration for all existing teachers of Ayurveda. Modern medical colleges should give facilities to suitable integrated graduates to undergo post-graduate courses in modern subjects so that such graduates may teach modern subjects in Ayurvedic teaching institutions. Pending such a step, only top men in the modern medical field holding M.D., M.S., etc., should be appointed as Professors in integrated teaching institutions. The Central Council of Indian Medicine should work out the details of these teachers' training programmes on a uniform basis.

Teaching methods require a greate deal of improvement. Two-fifths of the time should be devoted to lectures and three-fifths to practicals by students themselves. The philosophical aspects of Ayurveda should be emphasised throughout the under-graduate training. Greater attention than at present should be paid to the teaching of Ayurvedic subjects. Each group of subjects should be constituted into a separate department and one subject should be taught by one professor, who should invariably have a lecturer and a demonstrator attached to him. The suggestions made in the Training Chapter regarding teaching of individual subjects may be considered by the Central Council, Universities, Boards and teaching institutions when working out the details of the curriculum of studies. The following further suggestions for improving the teaching methods may also be considered, as they have been adopted with success in foreign institutions, like the tutorial system, a journal club and weekly or fornightly staff rounds in every teaching hospital.

In regard to the curriculum of studies, the present Integrated system should continue. A broad-based curriculum for a five-year course excluding an appropriate period of internship has been suggested in the Chapter on "Training". The Shudh Ayurvedic system should also continue for some time to come, but with the addition of a eertain amount of modern subjects and increased facilities for practical training. In due course it is anticipated that one uniform course of training in Ayurveda can be prescribed. Persons successfully completing the Integrated training should be given a Bachelor's Degree and those successfully completing the Shudh Ayurvedic training should be awarded the Title of Ayurvedacharya or Pravina. The degree and title should, however, be uniform in the whole country. The Central Council of Indian Medicine should work out the details of the two curricula on the basis of the suggestions made by this Committee. The curricula should be somewhat elastic and should be adopted by the authorities concerned to suit local conditions in consultation with the Central Council.

As regards the status of Principals, Professors, Lecturers, etc., in Ayurvedic Training institutions, the Central Council of Indian Medicinc should take appropriate steps at a very early date to bring them on a par with corresponding posts in modern medical colleges.

The basic qualifications for admission of students into Ayurvedic institutions should be so fixed that they will be well-equipped to understand the Ayurvedic subjects taught and that they will know from the very beginning that they will be future practioners of Ayurveda. It should be ensured that the students admitted have interest in the ancient science and aptitude for research and that they are not joining the course merely as a last resort. The basic qualifications for admission to the Integrated course should be Intermediate with Physics, Chemistry and Biology and Sanskrit. The qualifications of admission to the Shudh Ayurvedic course should be Matriculation with Sanskrit or equivalent qualification. Some of the other conditions that will encourage students to take up Ayurveda are that they are assured of equal prospects in the profession as their compatriots in modern medicine and that their privileges are the same as the modern medical practitioners. Finally Governments should encourage girl students to take up Ayurveda particularly because Gynaecology and Obstetrics, Paediatrics, etc., have still to be re-introduced scientifically in the Ayurvedic system. Scholarships and other financial help are necessary for this purpose.

Immediate attention may be given to the writing up of subjeet-wise text books in Ayurveda on a uniform basis and annotations of original texts, as part of the Literary Research Programme. Existing text-books may be reviewed and whatever is suitable may be accepted. A few concise textbooks on modern medical subjects may also be prepared for use in Ayurvedic institutions. Government should encourage the publication of text-books by giving financial assistance, prizes, etc. All text-books should be revised from time to time as science progresses. Every Ayurvedic institution should maintain a proper library under the charge of a trained medical librarian. Professors should induce students to make full use of libraries.

In order to create a suitable atmosphere in Ayurvedic studies, it is necessary to have proper buildings with adequate practical facilities like a medicinal plants garden, museum, pharmacy and hospital (with atleast 150 beds for a student strength of 50). The student of Ayurveda should also be given public health training in order to enable him to render public health services to the villager. Students' hostel and recreational facilities should be provided in ample measure in all teaching centres.

Every Ayurvedic teaching institution or at least one institution in each State should provide for post-graduate courses in Ayurvedic as well as in modern subjects, as part of the development programmes of the State concerned. The Shudh Ayurved may take up post-graduate training in Ayurvedic subjects only, whereas the Integrated Ayurved may take up both Ayurvedic and modern subjects. The modern medical graduate can take up post-graduate courses in Ayurvedic subjects, provided he has an aptitude for it and has undergone some training under established Ayurvedic preceptors and passes a preliminary test.

State Governments should pursue the question of establishing chairs of Indian Medicine in modern medical colleges, both for the under-graduate and post-graduate. In addition there may be an Ayurvedic ward in each of the medical college hospitals, so that the principles of Ayurvedic treatment are better comprehended by the modern men. This will help to remove the bias in their minds, if any.

Research Departments should become part and parcel of Ayurvedic teaching institutions. The two problems of post-graduate and research facilities should be examined by a central body and steps should be taken to combine in the same teaching institution a wing for post-graduate training and another for research work.

Preparation of medicine and practice should be separated if the Ayurvedic Practitioner's status is to be improved. Special courses like B. Pharm (Ayurveda) should be instituted.

Research

At the Central Institute of Research in Indigenous Systems of Medicine, Jamnagar there seems to be a certain amount of lack of close collaboration between the Ayurvedic and modern teams, which has resulted in an accumulation of a large amount of uncompared and uncoordinated data on either side. There should, therefore, be more cooperation between the two teams and the modern team instead of working behind the curtain should closely follow the Ayurvedic treatment at every stage. Productive clinical research can be done only by intensive study of carefully selected cases, rather than the study of a large number of cases. Moreover such research should be undertaken on chronic cases endemic in that area.

The Jamnagar Research Centre should start other types of research, e.g., literary, pharmacological, etc., on a planned basis.

Research work at Jamnagar will be placed on an ideal footing if the Post-Graduate Training Centre and the under-Graduate training institution of the Gulab-Kunwarba Society in the same premises are amalgamated with it in order to form one single unit.

As a first step for the improvement of research in Ayurveda, it is recommended that a Central Council of Ayurvedic Research be established on the lines mentioned in the chapter on "Research".

The Central Government should also establish three more Research Centres on the analogy of the Jamnagar Institute, and these should be amalgamated with the three-Post-Graduate Training Centres referred to in the chapter on "Training".

State Governments should establish Boards of Research, which may follow closely the various lines of research chalked out by the Bombay Board of Research.

It is recommended that in the first instance research work in Ayurveda should be done under the following seven heads:

(1) Clinical;
(2) Literary;
(3) Chemical;
(4) Botanical;
(5) Pharmacognosical;
(6) Pharmacological, and
(7) Basic Principles of Ayurveda.

Clinical Research should precede every other type of research. The other items of work can be done simultaneously after the effectiveness of an Ayurvedic drug has been clinically proved.

In addition to being carried out at various research centres, clinical research may be advantageously done in a separate wing of a modern hospital by Vaidyas in complete collaboration with the modern physicians there. The modern team should closely observe and keep a record of the Ayurvedic treatment and condition of the patient at every stage.

The Central Council of Ayurvedic Research should set up a Joint Committee of Vaidyas and modern scientists for the purpose of planning schemes of chemical research on a uniform basis.

Clinical Research can be done in four directions *viz.*,

(1) Both diagnosis and treatment strictly according to Ayurvedic principles;

(2) Diagnosis under Ayurvedic principles and treatment in accordance with modern medicine;

(3) Diagnosis under modern medical principles and treatment in accordance with the doctrines of Ayurveda; and

(4) Both diagnosis and treatment in modern medical methods as a control measure.

The Central Council of Ayurvedic Research may consider this new approach to clinical research and put it into practice at suitable centres of research.

Literary Research may be taken up under the following heads:

(a) Collection and review of old manuscripts and publication of the more important ones;

(b) Translation of old texts;

(c) Preparation of suitable text-books; and

(d) Establishment of reference libraries.

State Boards of Research should give Literary Research an important place in their programmes and establish well-equipped libraries and start Research journals.

The Central Council of Ayurvedic Research should plan and coordinate literary research in various States. establish a Central Library and also start an Indian Journal of Ayurvedic Research.

Modern scientists should take up Chemical Research on indigenous drugs whose efficacy has been proved clinically. Team work is essential in such investigations. So the active help of Vaidyas of repute should be taken by them. The Central Council of Ayurvedic Research should plan and allot this work to selected modern scientists etc. and help them financially.

In the field of Botanical Research, steps should be taken by the Central Council of Ayurvedic Research to get surveys of medicinal plants in different regions in India carried out by State Governments in collaboration with Forest Departments. Detailed maps of each area showing quantities available should be prepared and circulated to all State Governments and institutions. The Central Council should then plan an extensive cultivation programme on a scientific basis with the advice of the Botanical experts in the country. In this connection the treatises on Vrikshayurveda may be studied with advantage.

Pharmacognosical Research on plants and herbs used in Ayurveda is going on in many centres, but the work is of a time-consuming nature and also requires careful coordination. The Central Council of Ayurvedic Research should prepare a plan for carrying out these studies by 12 to 15 separate units, each consisting of a Botanist, a Vaidya and a Photo-Artist, and should aim at completing the work on the known herbs and plants in about ten years' time.

Pharmacological Research on indigenous drugs should be planned and financed by the Central Council of Ayurvedic Research in cousultation with expert Vaidyas. This work should be allocated to a limited number of places where there are Pharmacologists with real interest in Ayurveda and where special facilities for the work are available. To these pharmacologists should be attached Ayurvedic scholars, chemists, botanists, pharmacists, statisticians and research fellows to the extent necesssary. It is very essential that in all this work the basic principles and recognised practice of Ayurveda should be adhered to.

As far as Research in Basic Principles of Ayurveda is concerned, it is recommended that the theories about Panchabhuta, Tridosha, Mind, Wisdom, Atma, etc., should be investigated by learned Ayurvedic scholars. Similarly research on the various methods of diagnosis and treatment mentioned in Ayurveda should be studied and adopted. For this purpose a suitable standard proforma may be evolved by the Central Council. The results of these scientific studies should be compiled and statistically evaluated, so that a standard and easy method of examination of persons in health and in disease may be adopted.

It is also recommended that the Central Council may plan research in the following branches of Ayurveda, which are now in vogue among traditional Vaidyas:

(a) Dietetics;
(b) Panchkarma;
(c) Bala Chikitsa (Paediatrics);
(d) Treatment of Mental Diseases;
(e) Treatment of eye diseases;
(f) Marmachikitsa (Orthopaedics);
(g) Visha Chikitsa (Toxicology);
(h) Dentistry;
(i) Preventive medicine including Yoga; and
(j) Oil and massage treatment.

Ths present methods of reseasch followed in teaching institutions and by individuals under the Central or State Schemes are not very systematic Adequate facilities do not exist in many places. There is a duplication in the diseases chosen for investigation. The time has come when the Central Council of Ayurvedic Research should systematise the work of these institutions and individuals on a planned basis.

Pharmaceutical Products

A survey will have to be carried out in all the forest regions of the country, in collaboration with the Forest Department and the Botanical Survey of India, to assess both quantitatively and qualitatively the availability of raw herbs and drugs used in Ayurvedic medicine.

Forest authorities should keep certain areas in hills reserved for improving the cultivation and preservation of medicinal plants etc.

The Central Council of Ayurvedic Research should coordinate the work of various persons and institutions in regard to the identification of plants and drugs and to the preparation of a uniform Pharmacognosy and publication of reliable monographs.

A team of expert Vaidyas, modern botanists who have done work on medicinal plants, and research workers should be established for this purpose.

Correct identification of plants and drugs will be helped if State Governments and other agencies including teaching institutions and research centres start as many drug farms as possible. These drug farms will meet the needs of pharmacies, practitioners, etc. apart from helping in the training of Ayurvedic students.

In additlon to drug farms, teaching institutions and research centres should develop museums of plants, drugs, etc., where both the genuine and adulterated specimens should be kept for helping in correct identification.

Central Government should give financial assistance for the setting up of such drug farms and museums.

Standardisation of raw materials, mineral drugs and other organic materials for preparation of Ayurvedic medicine should be undertaken by the Central Council of Ayurvedic Research. Modern techniques like Chromatography may be used if necessary. The part or parts of raw herbs to be used in medicine and the time of collection should be taken into consideration in such standardisation.

Standardisation of the process of manufacture is urgently needed. For this purpose the compilation of a standard Ayurvedic Pharmacopoeia should be taken up immediately. A uniform formulary for each standard medicine should be laid down.

Efforts should be made to lay down uniform weights and measures for preparation of Ayurvedic medicines in accordance with Ayurvedic texts.

Standards for prepared medicines should be laid down in order to avoid variations in individual techniques and to ensure that all the ingredients in a medicinal preparation, particularly the costly ones like gold, saffron, musk, etc., are added in correct proportions.

Storage depots on the model of the Forest Department Depot at Baramula (Jammu and Kashmir State) should be opened on a regional basis in collaboration with Forest authorities, so that Government Pharmacies, Pharmaceutical concerns and individual Ayurvedic practitioners may place their demands on them and get genuine material.

There should be a Central Laboratory on the analogy of the Central Drugs Laboratory, Calcutta, for testing Ayurvedic drugs and medicines, for deciding the standard chemical composition of prepared medicines, where possible and for giving their opinion in disputed cases. This Central Laboratory should preferably be located at Bombay where facilities appear to exist.

Apart from this Central Laboratory, every pharmaceutical concern and every recognised pharmacy should have a well-equipped laboratory where the raw herbs, mineral drugs and other ingredients used in the preparation of Ayurvedic medicines can be tested according to standards prescribed.

In order to make Ayurvedic medicines more popular and more standardised, manual labour in pharmacies and pharmaceutical concerns should be replaced by modern machinery adapted to the needs of Ayurvedic science.

It will be advantageous to have in every State Cooprative Pharmacies of the Adyar (Madras) type so that medicines of recognised standards are readily available to practitioners and the public.

Every recognised pharmacy or pharmaceutical concern should have a specified minimum essential technical staff. This should include Ayurvedic experts, Ayurvedic Pharmacists, mechanical staff, modern botanists and chemists.

Governments should start training courses for Ayurvedic Pharmacists immediately.

A Drugs Act for Ayurvedic Medicine on the analogy of the Drugs Act, 1940 should be passed at an early date in order to enforce the various suggestions for standardisation mentioned in the above paragraphs.

The Central Government should immediately appoint an Ayurvedic Drugs Adviser and also set up a Drugs Advisory Body (Ayurveda) and a Pharmacy Council (Ayurveda).

Status Of Practice

The Central Government should in addition to the Adviser in Indigenous Systems of Medicines, have a team of experts to advise them in all aspects of the development of Indian systems of medicine in the country.

A uniform policy should be adopted so that the provision of medical relief under the modern medical and Ayurvedic systems, especially in the rural areas of the country, may be considerably augmented.

The utility of Ayurveda having been established, it is the duty of Government to approach the problem with sympathy and to unequivocally recognise and encourage the system,

The Ayurvedic Degree Holders should be put in charge of primary health centres under the Community Development Programme. In fact, they are better fitted than the modern medical men to give medical relief in rural areas because they know the life and customs of the villagers far better.

The first and foremost thing to be done is for State Governments to establish an independent department of Indian Medicine, where this has not already been done, with a full-fledged Director of Indian Medicine.

The Central and State Governments should recognise Ayurvedic treatment for purposes of remibursement of medical charges incurred by their employees.

The pay scales of Ayurvedic Practitioners in Government or semi-Government service should be the same as those applicable to modern medical practitioners, the Degree Holders being paid the same grade as the medical graduate, viz., Rs. 200—500 p.m. and the Diploma and Title Holders being paid the same grade as Licentiates of Modern Medicine, *viz.*, 150—300 p.m. Ayurvedic Graduates should be paid the same extra allowance as their compatriots in modern medicine when they hold special posts like Principals, Professors, Lecturers, etc., in Ayurvedic teaching institutions.

Governments should open as many more Ayurvedic hospitals and dispensaries as possible at the State, District and Tehsil levels. Where this is not possible, wards with Ayurvedic out-patient departments should be set up in modern hospitals and the modern medical authorities in such hospitals should give full and willing cooperation to the Vaidyas incharge of these wards.

For popularising Ayurvedic treatment and giving medical relief to a larger section of people than at present, philanthropists should be encouraged to donate hospital or dispensary buildings (as is done in Rajasthan), Governments bearing the other non-recurring and recurring expenditure of such institutions.

Governments should arrange Refresher Courses of short duration to Ayurvedic physicians under their control so that their knowledge is brought up-to-date.

There should be no restriction on Ayurvedic practitioners under-taking surgical, obstetrical or medico-legal cases provided they have had adequate training in their collegiate courses.

Ayurvedic practitioners should be given the same privileges as the modern medical practitioners in the matter of issuing medical certificates of all types.

The imposition of heavy import duties on some of the essential requirements of Ayurvedic practitioners like mercury, Vanshlochan and the taxing of Asavas and Aristas, which are basically needed for the preparation of Ayurvedic medicines, under the Medicinal and Toilet Preparations (Excise Duties) Act of 1955, are putting serious impediments in the practice of Ayurveda. These impediments should be removed by Government at an early date.

Boards of Indian Medicine should be established in the remaining three States *viz.*, Mysore, Orissa and Jammu and Kashmir.

Boards of Indian Medicine should be primarily in-charge of the control of practice only, the educational aspect of Ayurveda being dealt with by Universities, who may, if necessary, take the advice of these Boards.

A comprehensive list of recognised Ayurvedic institutions and practitioners in the whole country, should be prepared and published by the Central Council of Indian Medicine in consultation with the various Boards of Indian Medicine so that a person passing out of the institutions in one State is automatically registered in the other States.

Registration of Ayurvedic Practitioners should be enforced and completed in all States. The registration should be done category-wise, *viz.*, institutionally qualified, traditional and others. Among the institutionally qualified a distinction should be made between the Integrated and Shudh type of practitioners.

Boards of Indian Medicine should publish the names of Registered Ayurvedic Practitioners regularly every year and use the powers vested in them to remove from the lists those who are guilty of professional misconduct, after giving them due warning.

For improving status of Ayurvedic practice, steps should be taken to encourage the practice of all the eight branches of Ayurveda and to make them subjects of post-graduate study.

The so-called "secret remedies" prevalent among some of the traditional Vaidyas should be scientifically investigated in the interest of Ayurvedic practice and in the interest of the public.

Ayurvedic practitioners should strive to keep up the dignity of the profession by strict observation of the ethical codes prescribed by the ancient authorities in Ayurveda.

An all-India Ayurvedic Organisation, representing all types of Ayurvedic practitioners should be formed with the object of safeguarding the rights and obligations of the professionals and thus enhancing the status of practice. This organisation should have a first class library of Ayurvedic books and should initiate the publication of a technical journal for the propagation of scientific ideas.

IRRIGATION AND POWER TEAM ON MINOR IRRIGATION WORKS (ANDHRA PRADESH), 1958—REPORT

New Delhi, Committee on Plan Projects, 1960. 85p.+iip+Map.

Leader : Shri N. V. Gadgil (replaced by Dr. A. N. Khosla).

Members : Shri M. Narasimhaiya; Shri Lal Singh; Shri Mahavir Prasad.

Secretary : Shri D.S. Borker.

APPOINTMENT :

The Irrigation and Power Team on Minor Irrigation Works (Andhra Pradesh) was constituted under the Committee on Plan Projects *vide* Memo No. COPP/(4)/17/58, dated August 4, 1958.

TERMS OF REFERENCE

1. The Minor Irrigation Projects may be divided or studied into two parts :

(a) Works already in existence.

(b) Works which are now being constructed.

2. Case studies should be made of a number of projects of each type under the above headings with a view to judging their efficiency having regard to the objectives with which such works were carried out.

3. The following points should be specially borne in mind.

Existing Projects

(i) The present state of repair and maintenance.

(ii) The system of keeping works in proper maintenance with particular reference to the customary obligations of villagers for keeping such works in a sound condition from year to year, the Team should also examine the extent to which these obligations are enforced, the reasons for the failure to do so and the steps that should be taken to carry out such obligations efficiently.

(iii) Reasons, if any for non-utilisation of water by cultivators.

(iv) Improvements necessary to make the projects more efficient either in the matter of better agricultural planning and practices or in respect of engineering works.

(v) Cost of restoration if the project is in a state of disrepair and whether it has been included in the Plan.

New Projects

(i) Methods of selection—procedure and principles on which priorities are based.

(ii) Flow chart of the construction Project should be prepared to examine whether any avoidable delay has occurred in its completion.

(iii) Whether fullest use is made of catchment capacity in preparing designs.

(iv) Economics of design.

(v) State of agricultural planning with a view to optimum utilisation of benefits.

(vi) Institutional arragements provided for the proper maintenance of new works with special reference to the customary obligation of villagers in this regard.

(vii) Costs of actual construction compared to estimated cost—the reason for increase, if any, and the care with which the initial estimates were framed.

4. Any other matter which the Team considers necessary to report upon having a bearing on economy and efficiency of such projects.

5. The following information should be gathered by the Team for each State, taken as a whole, in regard to existing minor irrigation works :

(i) The total area irrigated from them according to Settlement Registers.

(ii) The area actually irrigated from year to year beginning from 1947.

(iii) The reason for the reduction, if any, in the area irrigated.

6. In addition, the Team will carry out a study of the tube-well schemes of the Punjab and U.P. with reference to the fact whether optimum use has been made of the facilities available by ensuring scientific crop planning and by improving agricultural practices. The study should be based on an examination of individual tube-wells, which may be divided into most successful, successful and least successful varieties for the purposes of study. The Team should also select a few tube-wells for which alternative crop planning and practices may be recommended that are being carried out at present in order to make them more successful. The consideration mentioned regarding minor irrigation works in third paragraph *mutatis mutandis* be taken into consideration for the study of tube-wells also.

CONTENTS

Preface ; Water and Resources and their Land Utilisation ; Maintenance of Minor Irrigation Works ; Design and Construction of Minor Irrigation Works ; Irrigation Development ; Agricultural Aspects ; Water Rates and Betterment Levy ; Summary ; Appendices I to XVI ; Map of Andhra Pradesh.

RECOMMENDATIONS

The Team recommends that the Master Plan for restoring old tanks in Andhra Pradesh be implemented and completed during the Third Five-Year Plan. The Team suggests that the following steps to taken to expedite and systematise restoration works :—

(i) The desirability of having a Special Survey Circle for Andhra Region may be considered so as to expedite the work of restoration of tanks ;

(ii) Standards for the 13,000 tanks taken over from the ex-Zamindars should be drawn out on modern principles ;

(iii) The capacity lost due to silting should be recovered by raising the bunds and waste-weirs. The Desilting-cum-Reclamation Scheme as evolved by the Madras State may be adopted wherever feasible, to reduce submergence ; and

(iv) Cultivation in the fore-shores should be regulated to minimise silting up.

The Team also recommends speedy research in measures to be taken to minimise evaporation losses, and checking weed-growths in the tank bed.

In order to achieve uniformity and efficiency in maintenance of tanks in Andhra Pradesh, taking into account the new Panchayat System, the Team recommends that :

(a) The Revenue Department may maintain tanks with ayacut from 50 to 200 acres ;

(b) All tanks below 50 acres may be maintained by the Panchayats ;

(c) Maintenance of other tanks may be progressively transferred to the Panchayats when they build up sufficient efficiency and experience ; and

(d) Regular maintenance levy may be imposd on the lands irrigated by each tank.

In order to ensure proper routine maintenance, the Team recommends a certain minimum annual grant for each tank in addition to Special grants for repairs when necessary.

The Team suggests grouping up of a number of small

and scattereu ıepair works in the vicinity totalling to about Rs. 50,000 and giving them to bigger contractors, who would then be in a better position to execute the works at reasonable rates, when other agencies are not forthcoming to execute the repair works.

With regard to design practices, the Team points out that :

(a) With a view to minimise the incidence in silting up of channels from diversion weirs, adequate provision of scour sluices near the canal take-off is necessary. Also, wherever feasibls, piers and gates may be preferred to solid weirs.

(b) Adequate surplusing capacities need to be provided so as to avoid frequent breaching of tanks. Tank slopes on the water-side, also need to be not less then 2 : 1 whereas they could be 1½ : 1 on the rearside.

(c) The Madras Specification No. 20-A, providing for consolidation and tamping, be applied to all bank-work of tank bunds.

The Team recommends the following measures to accelerate lift irrigation by pump-sets :

(a) Encouraging diesel-pump-sets until rural electrification is developed by suitably relaxing the criterion that the applicant should possess land worth at least double the loan amount, which is rather too harsh and deters the cultivators from the venture. Loan advances may also be based on the potential of the land rather than on the land assessment, which is normally conservative; and

(b) Encouraging cooperative lift schemes which would enable small farmers to get the benefit of such schemes as a result and publicising the details of successful cooperative lift irrigation schemes so as to popularise the same.

The Team suggests that drainage water from upper irrigatian ayacut may be picked up by means of diversion weirs and channels to further irrigation, preferably on a cooperative basis, with adequate Government help in the form of loans.

Economic returns as also yield per acre from non-paddy crops are in no way less than those from paddy. Therefore, the Team recommends raising of non-paddy crops. Such a reorientation in the cropping pattern will result in (a) higher incomes to the cultivators and greater revenue to the State; (b) bringing additional areas under cultivation thereby augmenting food production; (c) lessening the chances of water-logging; and (d) more balanced diet. A present non-availability of water for Rabi crops is mainly due to increased emphasis on cultivation of paddy which consumes majority of the water stored in the tanks. Rice cultivation should, therefore, be confined to those areas only where its production potential is high. The remaining areas should be put under other crops needing less water. Also, water required for Rabi crops should be obtained by resorting to intensive lift-irrigation.

The Team recommends (i) preservation of soil-fertility by increased use of green and artificial manure and rotation of crops, and (ii) application of super-phosphates for counteracting harmful effects of salinity and alkalinity in the soil, particularly in the low rainfall areas of Nalgonda and Hyderabad Districts.

It is recommended that necessary steps may be taken by the State Authorities to have water channels constructed even by acquiring the necessary lands from the individual owners, so as to reduce loss of water due to extra evaporation and percolation while passing through the fields.

With a view to enhancing the returns to the Government from irrigation works, steps may be taken to earry out a detailed study regarding the current water rates. The Team points out the large scope for upward revision of water rates and recommends introduction of uniform and increased rates on a rational basis, in accordance with the recommendations of the "Taxation Enquiry Commission". The Team also recommends implementation of the Betterment Act.

IRRIGATION TEAM ON MINOR IRRIGATION WORKS (GUJARAT STATE), 1958—REPORT

New Delhi, Committee on Plan Projects, 1963. 123p.+vp.

Leader : Shri M. Thirumala Rao.
Members : Shri Baleshwar Nath; Dr. Arjan Singh; Shri Mahavir Prasad.

APPOINTMENT

The Irrigation Team on Minor Irrigation works (Gujarat State) was constituted under the Committee on Plan Projects *vide* their Memorandum No. COPP (4)/17/58, dated August 4, 1958.

TERMS OF REFERENCE

1. The minor irrigation projects may be divided for

study into two parts :

(a) Works already in existence.

(b) Works which are now being constructed.

2. Case studies should be made of a number of projects of each type under the above headings with a view to judging their efficiency having regard to the objectives with which such works were carried out.

3. The following points should be especially borne in mind :

Existing Projects

(i) The present state of repair and maintenance.

(ii) The system of keeping works in proper maintenance with particular reference to the customary obligations of villagers for keeping such works in a sound condition from year to year, the Team should also examine the extent to which these obligations are enforced, the reasons for the failure to do so and the steps that should be taken to carry out such obligations efficiently.

(iii) Reasons, if any for non-utilisation of water by cultivators.

(iv) Improvements necessary to make the projects more efficient either in the matter of better agricultural planning and practices or in respect of engineering works.

(v) Cost of restoration if the project is in a state of disrepair and whether it has been included in the Plan.

New Projects :

(i) Method of selection—procedure and principles on which priorities are based.

(ii) Flow Chart of the Construction Project should be prepared to examine whether any avoidable delay has occurred in its completion.

(iii) Whether fullest use is made of catchment capacity in preparing designs.

(iv) Economics of design.

(v) State of agricultural planning with a view to optimum utilisation of benefits.

(vi) Institutional arrangements provided for the proper maintenance of new works with special reference to the customary obligation of villagers in this regard.

(vii) Cost of actual construction compared to estimated costs—the reasons for increase if any and the care with which the initial estimates were framed.

4. Any other matter which the Team considers necessary to report upon having a bearing on economy and efficiency of such projects.

5. The following information should be gathered by the Team for each State, taken as a whole in regard to existing minor irrigation works :

(i) The total area irrigated from them according to Settlement registers.

(ii) The area actually irrigated from year to year beginning from 1947.

(iii) The reason for the reduction, if any, in the area irrigated.

6. In addition, the Team will carry out a study of the tubewells schemes of the Punjab and the U.P. with reference to the fact whether optimum use has been made of the facilities available by ensuring scientific crop planning and by improving agricultural practices. The study should be based on an examination of individual tubewells, which may be divided into most successful, successful and least successful varieties for the purpose of study. The Team should also select a few tubewells for which alternative crop planning and practices may be recommended that are being carried out at present in order to make them more successful. The consideration mentioned regarding minor irrigation works in third paragraph *mutatis mutandis* be taken into consideration for the study of tubewells also.

CONTENTS

General Aspects; State Tubewells; Wells and Lift Irrigation; Tanks and Diversion Canals; Performance and Financial Picture; Irrigation in Coastal Areas; Planning and Prospecting of Minor Irrigation Works; Summary of Recommendations; Appendices I to VII.

RECOMMENDATIONS

Gujarat is mostly a water deficient State. A techno-economic appraisal of its minor irrigation schemes, as presented in this study, may thus invoke interest towards bettement of their performance. The study conducted by the Team is, in its very nature, an applied technical research with an economic bias. The recommendations emerging out therefrom have, therefore, generalised implications though they have been inferred from direct field observations made on sample works. Again, the recommendations are orientated to impinge primarily on policy matters leaving out details pertaining to individual works to be attended to by the State authorities. They are enumerated below :

Regular and systematic sub-soil water studies, both quantitative and qualitative, should be carried out in the State, more particularly in the areas, where State tubewells are located.

Responsibility of management and preparation of assessment papers (demand statement) of irrigation works may rest with the Irrigation Department and realisation of water rates be the responsibility of the Revenue Department.

Stoppage of water supply from tubewells to the defaulter cultivators is not conducive to optimum utilisation of water. Effective resources to Section 57 of the Bombay Irrigation Act, 1879 be had, to recover arrears of water rates tili a regular Tubewells act governing the operation and management of State Tubewells is enacted and enforced.

Supply of water to the cultivators in the order in which applications are received involves loss of both water and time. *Osrabandi*—Warabandi System (as in U.P. and Punjab) may be adopted, as necessary.

Where commanded areas are on different contours it would be advisable to provide separate outlets in the delivery tank at corresponding levels, thus obtaining any unnecessary lift.

To keep a watch on the behaviour of tubewells, a regular proforma should be introduced for periodic inspection and check up of discharges and depressions by the supervisory staff.

In the interest of the economy and efficiency the pace of energising the State tubewells working on diesel oil should be accelerated.

Land acquisition procedure for water courses should be suitably amended to accelerate the process of acquisition.

Supply of water on concessional rates for hot weather and green manure crops should be offered in order to encourage cultivation and to secure a balanced irrigation performance throughout the year.

Two-part Tariff consisting of a fixed yearly standing charge on the area in the command and a recurring charge on the area actually irrigated may be introduced to help utilisation of the potential created.

Extensive commands of tubewells be restricted to render service more effective and efficient as well as leading to economy in the water distribution system.

Isolated patches of land at higher elevation be left out of command beeause of unduly heavy cost of reaching water upto them on high embanked water channels.

State agencies be organised to help needy agriculturists to deepen open wells which may otherwise become derelict and costs of deepening be recovered in convenient instalments.

Lifting of water through '*Motes*' could be replaced wherever feasible with modern lifting appliances, *Rahats*, etc.

A bold programme of well sinking and repairing should be undertaken to achieve targets of food production and also to serve as insurance against failure of monsoon.

Closure of irrigation channels during night hours needs to be avoided. Instead irrigation at night should be encouraged.

To effect economy in the use of water, land levelling and grading in the irrigation commands should be done even if State help in the shape of loan or sybsidy is required by the cultivators. This process should be expedited.

Channel sections and outlets need to be checked up and remodelled to standard designs in the interest of efficient, economic and equitable distribution of irrigation supplies.

Practice of field to field irrigation should be discouraged. Instead properly aligned water courses should be laid out.

Irrigation tanks which would come in the command of perennial major or medium irrigation schemes would not be required to be retained. Necessary planning about reclamation and utilisation of tank bed areas should be done well in time.

Correct record of actual irrigation should be maintained to gauge the capacities and capabilities of projects and schemes, whether under fixed or recurring water rate system.

To have a proper assessment of the capacities, it is desirable to conduct regular silt observations on reservoirs likely to get silted.

Basic record of irrigation on which devolves assessment of water rates, should be maintained on prescribed, printed and machine numbered registers and brought under required physical check by the supervisory staff.

Potentialities of schemes located on perennial streams may be exploited with advantage both for kharif and rabi with adoption of suitable cropping patterns, evolved with the coordination of the Irrigation and the Agriculture Departments.

Where serviceability of the diversion weirs located on perennial streams could be extended, possibilities of creating storages in upper reaches may be examined.

Abnormal variations from the original estimate need to be guarded against, with a view to avoid heavy unforeseen financial commitments, through a thorough initial check up of scheme.

Kharif bandharas do not seem to fulfil irrigational requirments effectively. Their further construction may not seem justified.

Gauges need to be fixed at head, tail and other control points of the canals where they do not exist.

The concerning situation in respect of minus financial returns as obtained on some irrigation works should be particularly looked into with a view to secure optimum utilisation of water and to make such works remunerative to the State.

In coastal areas water conservation measures need to be taken along with drainage schemes.

Where the climatic and environmental conditions are favourable, suitable measures should be taken to encourage cultivation of coconut and date-palm, particularly in coastal areas.

Suitable sluice arrangements should be made at river mouths which will prevent the ingress of brackish sea water and at the same time allow the river into the sea so that the river water in the lower reaches does not become saline.

Experiments to produce sweet water from saline sources may be undertaken in areas with precarious water resources through solar radiation process.

Where the cost of mechanical and other allied methods of land reclamation from salinity is prohibitive, salinity resistant species of plants and trees may be grown with advantage.

Early steps need to be taken to enact and enforce a unified Irrigation Code with a rationalised water rate structure, applicable to the whole State.

To achieve wholesome utilisation of irrigation supplies a sense of awareness and pre-preparedness is required to be created amongst the cultivators before any scheme is undertaken and during its execution.

The research programme on the Trial-cum-Demonstration Farms should be re-orientated to suit regional needs.

Stress on soil studies relating to its texture, structure, depth and layers is required to be given so that effective and economic use can be made of available irrigation water.

Determined drive is necessary to increase the area under multiple cropping and substitution of low yielding crops by high yielding varieties.

IRRIGATION TEAM ON MINOR IRRIGATION WORKS (MAHARASHTRA STATE), 1958—REPORT

New Delhi, Committee on Plan Projects, 1963. 87p.+vp.+Maps and Charts

Leaders : Dr. A.N. Khosla (replaced by Shri M. Thirmula Rao).

Members : Shri Lal Singh (replaced by Dr. Arjan Singh); Shri Baleshwar Nath; Shri Mahavir Prasad.

APPOINTMENT

The Irrigation Team on Minor Irrigation Works (Maharashtra State) was constituted under the Committee on Plan Projects *vide* their Memorandum No. COPP/(4)/17/58, dated August 4, 1958.

TERMS OF REFERENCE

The minor irrigation projects may be divided for study into two parts:

(a) Works already in existence.

(b) Works which are now being constructed.

2. Case studies should be made of a number of projects of each type under the above headings with a view to judging their efficiency having regard to the objectives with which such works were carried out.

3. The following points should be especially borne in mind.

Existing Projects

(i) The present state of repair and maintenance.

(ii) The system of keeping works in proper maintenance with particular reference to the customary obligations of villagers for keeping such works in a sound condition from year to year, the team should also examine the extent to which these obligations are enforced, the reasons for the failure to do so and the steps that should be taken to carry out such obligations efficiently.

(iii) Reasons, if any for non-utilisation of water by cultivators.

(iv) Improvements necessary to make the projects more efficient either in the matter of better agricultural planning and practices or in respect of engineering works.

(v) Cost of restoration if the project is in a state of disrepair and whether it has been included in the Plan.

New Projects

(i) Method of selection—procedure and principles on which priorities are based.

(ii) Flow Chart of the Construction Project should be prepared to examine whether any avoidable delay has occurred in its completion.

(iii) Whether fullest use is made of catchment capacity in preparing design.

(iv) Economics of design.

(v) State of agricultural planning with a view to optimum utilisation of benefits.

(vi) Institutional arrangements provided for the proper maintenance of new works with special reference to the customary obligation of villagers in this regard.

(vii) Cost of actual construction compared to estimated costs—the reasons for increase if any and the care with which the initial estimates were framed.

4. Any other matter which the Team considers necessary to report upon having a bearing on economy and efficiency of such projects.

5. The following information should be gathered by the Team for each State, taken as a whole in regard to existing minor irrigation works.

(i) The total area irrigated from them according to Settlement registers.

(ii) The area actually irrigated from year to year beginning from 1947.

(iii) The reason for the reduction, if any, in the area irrigated.

6. In addition, the Team will carry out a study of the tubewell schemes of the Punjab and the U.P. with reference to the fact whether optimum use has been made of the facilities available by ensuring scientific crop planning and by improving agricultural practices. The study should be based on an examination of individual tubewells, which may be divided into most successfull, successful and least successful varieties for the purpose of study. The Team should also select a few tubewells for which alternative crop planning and practices may be recommended that are being carrid out at present in order to make them more successful. The consideration mentioned regarding minor irrigation works in third paragraph *mutatis mutandis* be taken into consideration for the study of tubewells also,

CONTENTS

General; Diversion Canals and Bandharas; Storage Reservoirs and Irrigation Tanks; Ex-Malguzari Tanks; Wells and Lift Irrigation; Agricultural Aspects; Planning and Prospecting of Minor Irrigation; Recommendations; Terms of Reference; Appendices I to IX.

RECOMENDATIONS

Among the States of India, Maharashtra has the lowest percentage of its cultivated area under irrigation. Its rainfall pattern also varies considerably from West to East. While the rainfall in the Ghats area is heavy, there is scarcity of water on the plateau to the West. The water and soil conservation schemes supplemented by minor irrigation works wherever possible are a great necessity for the State. Many points of routine nature as occurred to the Team during their visits were discussed with the local officers. The State authorities will, undoubtedly, give attention to the suggestions which emerge out of such mutual discussions. The Team's recommendations on matters of special significance as a result of the studies are summarised as below:—

For construction of earthern embankments the practice of building *Namunas* (Profiles) ahead of work, should be followed to ensure good quality of work and proper alignment.

Some organisation, either State-managed or cooperative, should be devised to help the cultivators in levelling up their fields, contour bunding and anti-erosion measures wherever irrigation water is made available.

Outlet system on channels should be remodelled, wherever necessary, to enable maximum areas to be commanded through flow irrigation.

Lift irrigation should be allowed, wherever it involves light lifts.

Direct pumping from canals should be forbidden. Sumps for such pumping, if allowed, should be built outside the canal land.

Kharif bandharas do not seem to fulfil any irrigational requirement effectively, Their further construction should be discouraged.

In certain locations, where seepage losses from field channels are high owing to high permeability of soils, application of bentonite map help sealing the soils to some extent. Experiments thereabout may be tried.

Where series of bandharas exist on a river or a stream, they should be integrated into one compact system resulting in a more efficient distribution and economic utilisation of supplies available.

Construction of various schemes should be taken up only after ascertaining adequate supply of water from established hydrological studies and not on ad-hoc basis.

Land acquisition proceedings need to be expedited to enable channel construction to be done speedily.

Phad system needs to be re-examined. It should be amended so as to enable more extensive use being made of the available supplies.

Rabi bandharas should be improved with regard to their supplies, through small storages being created in the upper reaches, wherever possible.

To enable the estimates to be framed on a realistic basis, the yardstick of capital investment per acre should be revised as necessary, as effective capital-cost rates actually attained on a number of projects are much higher than project provided rates.

State Government may take up experimental work on artificial rain-making in areas, where possibility of its success is indicated by meteorological conditions.

Closure of irrigation channels during night hours, which is a wasteful process, should be avoided. Irrigation at night should be encouraged.

Proper gauges should be fixed at the head, tail and other control points of minor irrigation channels as is done on major canal systems.

For economic use of water, existing practice of field to field irrigation, which proves wasteful, should be replaced by a properly aligned water courses on minor irrigation work also, as is the practice on major canals in the State.

An expenditious procedure may be evolved for action being taken in case of reservoirs (particularly those under Revenue Department) showing signs of leakage and needing engineering attention.

Where irrigation is not progressing well, split-rate system of irrigation charges may be introduced.

To enable suitable legislative steps being taken to set matters right on ex-Malguzari tanks, the settlement operations in those areas may be expedited.

To check further deterioration in the condition of ex-Malguzari tanks resulting in a significant drop in their irrigational performance a renovation programme should be taken up on an emergency basis.

Recording of actual irrigation needs to be done on all State-managed works to enable their performance to be judged, irrespective of admissibility for levy of water rates on areas irrigated therefrom.

With irrigation water being available during winter-months, steps should be taken to promote double cropping in Chanda and Bhandra districts.

On suitable tanks, desilting-cum-reclamation plans should be evolved with the dual purpose of increasing capacity of the tanks and reclaiming the fore-shore areas.

Water pumped out from collieries and other types of mining operations, wherever found suitable for agricultural use, should be made use of on the neighbouring lands, if they are fit for cultivation.

The programme of sinking new wells and repairing old ones should be progressed vigorously side by side with soil conservation schemes, to improve irrigated agriculture in the State.

Sinking of new wells should be done after thorough examination of the sub-soil water resources.

Sanction of electric connections for pumping water from wells need to be accorded with due consideration to sub-soil supplies and not merely on the basis of availability of electricity.

The system of irrigation through *mothe* needs to be improved. The practice of pulling up bullocks while retracing steps upslope to the well (as if in a reverse-gear) should be discourged. Also, use of improved lifting appliances should be popularised.

Sitting of lift irrigation schemes be done after investigations about the availability of water in the streams, keeping also in view any previous irrigational or riparian commitments.

To have equitable distribution of water, roastering amongst the share-holders of lift irrigation societies be done and enforced through "warabandi" or "osrabandi" system according to their irrigable areas in the command. This system could also be adopted on other irrigation works in the State wherever necessary.

Maintenance of lifting equipment needs preferably to be entrusted to a competent agency instead of being done by individual cooperative societies with limited technical knowledge and resources.

The State technical agencies may handle lift irrigation cooperative schemes for a couple of years before making them over to the cooperative societies.

For coastal areas, where only one crop is taken in three years, a suitable crop pattern may be evolved to ensure a wholesome use of the land.

Production of wheat needs to be stepped up by evolving high yielding, rust resisting, varieties as also oilseeds and cotton in irrigated areas.

Sowing season of cotton in some areas like Nagpur Division could with advantage be advanced from June-July to April-May leading to greater production per acre.

To restore fertility and counteract the depressing effect of Jowar on land, the existing main crop of the State, adequate manuring, fertilisation and inclusion of legumes and green manuring in the rotation seems necessary.

Stress on green manuring requires to be given also, either before or after rice.

In irrigated areas, production of potato needs to be enhanced and also cultivation of sweet potato and tapioca introduced.

A concerted research programme to deal with all the problems of irrigated farming should be organised to evolve suitable methods of field water use.

Demonstration-cum-trial centres should be opened in increasing number, to ensure adoption of suitable crop patterns by the cultivators, wherever irrigation supplies are available.

A comprehensive survey of the potentialities of minor irrigation works, both State-owned and private, should be done on district or even block-wise basis.

In the wider interest of decentralisation, works in charge of Revenue Department, need to be gradually shifted to the charge of Village Panchayats or Gram Samitis, who may be provided with necessary technical competence to look after them,

Early steps need be taken to evolve and enact a unified Canal Code for the State as a whole,

Study of ground-water-table behaviour may be conducted in areas where sub-soil water is exploited through mechanical pumping from wells and also in areas where new irrigation is introduced.

Some selected areas in the coastal strip may be taken for exploratory tubewell borings.

Pilot project may be started on terracing of selected areas in western slopes for the purpose of improving post-monsoon flow and enabling rabi cultivation to be done on emergent lands in upper contours.

IRRIGATION TEAM ON MINOR IRRIGATION WORKS (ORISSA STATE), 1958—REPORT

New Delhi, Committee on Plan Projects, 1964. 91p.+vp.+Charts.

Leader : Shri Thirumala Rao.
Members : Shri Baleshwar Nath; Dr. Arjan Singh; Shri Mahavir Prasad.

APPOINTMENT

The Irrigation Team on Minor Irrigation Works (Orissa State) was constituted under the Committee on Plan Projects *vide* their Memorandum No. COPP/ (4)/ 17/58, dated August 4, 1958.

TERMS OF REFERENCE

1. The Minor Irrigation Projects may be divided for study into two parts:

(a) Works already in existence.

(b) Works which are now being constructed,

2. Case studies should be made of a number of projects of each type under the above headings with a view to judging their efficiency having regard to the objectives with which such works were carried out.

3. The following points should be especially borne in mind:

Existing Projects

(i) The present state of repair and maintenance.

(ii) The system of keeping works in proper maintenance with particular reference to the customary obligations of villagers for keeping such works in a sound condition from year to year, the Team should also examine the extent to which these obligations are enforced, the reasons for the failure to do so and the steps that should be taken to carry out such obligations efficiently.

(iii) Reasons, if any, for non-utilisation of water by cultivators.

(iv) Improvements necessary to make the projects more efficient either in the matter of better agricultural planning and practices or in respect of engineering works.

(v) Cost of restoration if the project is in a state of disrepair and whether it has been included in the Plan.

New Projects

(i) Method of selection—procedure and principles on which priorities are based.

(ii) Flow chart of the construction Project should be prepared to examine whether any avoidable delay has occurred in its completion.

(iii) Whether fullest use is made of catachment capacity in preparing designs.

(iv) Eeonomics of design.

(v) State of agricultural planning with a view to optimum utilisation of benefits.

(vi) Institutional arrangements provided for the proper maintenance of new works with special reference to the customary obligation of villagers in this regard.

(vii) Cost of actual construction compared to estimated costs—the reasons for increase if any and the care with which the initial estimates were framed.

4. Any other matter which the Team considers necessary to report upon having a bearing on economy and efficiency of such projects.

5. The following information should be gathered by the Team for each State, taken as a whole in regard to existing minor irrigation works:

(i) The total area irrigated from them according to Settlement Registers.

(ii) The area actually irrigated from year to year beginning from 1947.

(iii) The reason for the reduction, if any, in the area irrigated.

6. In addition, the Team will carry out a study of the tubewell schemes of the Punjab and U.P with reference to the fact whether optimum use has been made of the facilities available by ensuring scientific crop planning and by improving agricultural practices. The Study should be based on an examination of individual tubewells, whlch may be divided into most successful, successful and least successful varieties for the purpose of study. The Team should also select a few tubewells for which alternative crop planning and practices may be recommended that are being carried out at present in order to make them more successful. The consideration mentioned regarding minor irrigation works in third paragraph *mutatis mutandis* be taken into consideration for the study of tubewells also.

CONTENTS

General; Small Diversion Schemes; Tanks and Reservoirs: State Tubewells; Lift Irrigation; Planning and Prospecting of Minor Irrigation Works: Recommendations; Terms of Reference; Appendices I to V1.

RECOMMENDATIONS

Apart from mineral resources, the State of Orissa has vast natural resources of land and water, which have not so far been amply exploited. A concerted multi-faced programme—both in industrial and agricultural fields—to utilise the available resources can turn Orissa into a prosperous State. This study pertains primarily to the development of small irrigation schemes and main recommendations as emerge out of the study, are listed below:

Irrigation schemes need be taken up only after adequate agro-technical investigation and scrutiny. That will help excluding unpromising schemes and will ensure a better standard of works.

Possibilities of creation of storages in the upper reaches of the streams may be looked into to augment supplies in the diversion weirs.

On irrigation works piece-meal sanctions need be avoided so as to enable estimates being framed on a comprehensive basis.

On streams where irrigation works are located action need be taken to extinguish less fruitful riparian rights in upper reaches, which otherwise tend to cause obstruction and reduction in flow of water, particularly during critical periods of demand.

Direct lifting of water from canals needs to be prohibited to ensure regulated irrigation supplies to the areas catered for.

On non-perennial streams retention of tanks for conservation of water for use in the ayacut of irrigation works, may be encouraged.

Construction of wells to supplement canal irrigation may be promoted and subsidised in the ayacut, where there are possibilities to tap subsoil resources of water.

Otherwise too, efforts need be made to utilise, where-ever feasible, the subsoil resources of water through open wells, which constitute the common man's commonest resources for irrigation.

Specific rules and regulations for the operations of State Tubewells need to be introduced.

Pre-preparedness is necessary to be carried among the beneficiaries to make use of irrigation supplies as they become available.

Scrutiny of actual ayacut of minor irrigation works need be completed speedily, so that areas outside the authorised command and receiving irrigation, do not escape assessment any longer.

Maximum periods of development need to be fixed for tubewells, lift irrigation schemes, and other irrigation works, so that there does not occur an undue lag of time between creation of potential and its utilisation and efforts are mobilised by all concerned to achieve targeted development within scheduled time limit.

Water rate structure under examination in the State needs to be fixed on rational basis.

Effective recourse to the provision of section 4(7) and 11 of Orissa Irrigation Act XIV of 1959 with respect to construction and maintenance of water courses, is called for to have well laid-out field channels on minor irrigation works to replace the wasteful practice of field to field irrigation.

Re-modelling of canals, wherever necessary, needs to be done to bring them in proper section, slopes and depths.

Where silted areas of tank beds are under unauthorised occupation, suitable action is called for to get the encroachments vacated.

Such areas after recovery, if not required for submergence again, could be profitably disposed of to cover at least some portion of the expenditure incurred on renovation of such old storages.

A judicious combination of desilting-cum-reclamation of silted tanks needs to be undertaken with a view to regain the lost capacities of the reservoirs.

Recording of actual irrigation on minor irrigation works is necessary to have a correct appraisal of their yearly serviceability.

Suitable procedure for physical check of booked up irrigation also needs to be introduced.

Where irrigation by gravity flow is possible even at some extra cost, lift irrigation need not be provided.

Time-lag in completion of works and energisation of tubewells need to be cut to the barest minimum, to ensure early utilisation of the resources created.

Irrigation works—big or small—need to be brought under a unified control of one department having competent technical personnel at all levels, preferably Irrigation Department, as is practised in the States of Northern India, Bihar and Gujarat. Coordination of Irrigation and Agriculture Departments at all levels is called for, to achieve implementation of effective development of irrigated agriculture in the State.

On lift irrigation schemes if the area is such as can be commanded from two different elevations, water need not be pumped to higher elevation.

Effective steps need to be taken to protect winter cropping areas against cattle grazing.

Wherever winter cropping is to be encouraged a start need be made with adequate percentage of fodder crops.

Some of the results of research work carried out at the Central Rice Research Institute, Cuttack, in regard to cultural practices particularly about the placement of fertilizers in the sub-surface zone, are of far reaching importance and need to be widely publicised and adopted.

The practice of taking two crops of paddy with green manure crop in-between, or of growing cotton or groundnut after paddy in winter, requires to be encouraged in the irrigated areas.

IRRIGATION TEAM ON MINOR IRRIGATION WORKS (RAJASTHAN STATE), 1958—REPORT

New Delhi, Committee on Plan Projects, 1965. 77p.+vip.+Charts.

Leader : Shri M. Thirumala Rao.
Members : Shri Baleshwar Nath; Dr. Arjan Singh; Shri Mahavir Prasad.

APPOINTMENT

The Irrigation Team on Minor Irrigation Works in Rajasthan State was constituted under the Committee on Plan Projects *vide* their Memorandum No. COPP/(4)/17/58, dated August 4, 1958.

TERMS OF REFERENCE

1. The Minor irrigation projects may be divided for study into two parts:

(a) Works already in existence.

(b) Works which are now being constructed.

2. Case studies should be made of a number of projects of each type under the above headings with a view to judging their efficiency having regard to the objects with which such works were carried out.

(3) The following points should be especially borne in mind:

Existing Projects

(i) The present state of repair and maintenance.

(ii) The system of keeping works in proper maintenance with particular reference to the customary obligations of villagers for keeping such works in a sound condition from year to year, the Team should also examine the extent to which these obligations are enforced, the reasons for the failure to do so and the steps that should be taken to carrry out such obligations efficiently.

(iii) Reasons, if any, for non-utilisation of water by cultivators.

(iv) Improvements necessary to make the projects more efficient either in the matter of better agricultural planning and practices or in respect of engineering works.

(v) Cost of restoration if the project is in a state of of disrepair and whether it has been included in the Plan.

New Projects

(i) Method of selection—procedure and principles on which priorities are based.

(ii) Flow Chart of the construction Project should be prepared to examine whether any avoidable delay has occurred in its completion.

(iii) Whether fullest use is made of catchment capacity in preparing designs.

(iv) Economics of design.

(v) State of agricultural planning with a view to optimum utilisation of benefits.

(vi) Institutional arrangements provided for the proper maintenance of new works with special reference to the customary obligation of villagers in this regard.

(vii) Costs of actual construction compared to estimated costs—the reasons for increase if any and the care with which the initial estimates were framed.

4. Any other matter which the Team considers necessary to report upon having a bearing on economy and efficiency of such projects.

5. The following information should be gathered by the Team for each State, taken as a whole in regard to existing minor irrigation works:

(i) The total area irrigated from them according to Settlement registers.

(ii) The area actually irrigated from year to year beginning from 1947.

(iii) The reason for the reduction, if any, in the area irrigated.

6. In addition, the Team will carry out a study of the tubewell schemes of the Punjab and the U.P. with reference to the fact whether optimum use has been made of the facilities available by ensuring scientific crop planning and by improving agricultural practices. The Study should be based on an examination of individual tubewells, which may be divided into most successful, successful and least successful varieties for the purpose of study. The Team should also select a few tubewells for which alternative crop planning and practices may be recommended that are being carried out at present in order to make them more successful. The consideration mentioned regarding minor irrigation works in third paragraph *mutatis mutandis* be taken into consideration for the study of tubewells also.

CONTENTS

General; Irrigation Tanks and Storage Reservoirs; Submergence Tanks and Bundies; Rapats and Wells; Planning and Prospecting; Recommendations; Appendces I to VI.

RECOMMENDATIONS

Aridity is a prominent aspect of the climatic complex of Rajasthan. Conservation of water is, therefore, the mainstay of its agrarian economy. Some areas, in the western half of the State face extremely acute shortage of water almost every year. Irrigation accordingly occupies a significant place in agricultural development of the State. Techno-economic appraisal of its minor irrigation works, may thus invoke interest in their performance and consequent improvement. The Team's observations as contained in this Report are based on actual field studies conducted on a number of sample works. But only such recommendations are listed below, as have generalised implications and impinge directly on policy matters.

A schedule of periodic inspection and upkeep of masonry weirs, tanks, reservoirs and appurtenant works needs to be laid down, so that timely repairs are carried out.

With a view to improve agro-economic return per acre inch of water, it seems necessary to examine the possibilities of extending commands on a number of irrigation works, which are using their scarce supplies lavishly. That will, in its turn, lead to a change in the cropping pattern designed to give optimum agricultural production per unit of water, as well as land.

Outletting on irrigation channels should be done on a rationalised and scientific basis, in the interest of equitable distribution of supplies.

Continuous running of channels should be changed over to intermittent running, subject to systematic regulation of supplies and rostering of channels and outlets, so that scarce resources of water are subjected to optimum use and chances of wastage are minimised.

Construction of off-taking channels and water courses should proceed side by side with the construction of reservoirs and their allied works. Delays in completion of irrigation channels cause valuable storage water to remain unutilised, besides unnecessary locking up of the capital.

Duel control exercised on tanks and reservoirs irrigating from 51 to 2,500 acres does not seem to lead to optimum utilisation of irrigation supplies. A reconsideration of the issue seems necessary in the light of experience gained during the past two years.

Annual water budgets for pucca compact irrigation schemes, like the tank at Siliserh in Alwar, need to be drawn up so that the supplies are subjected to maximum possible use for agricultural production.

Unauthorised acts of people leading to wastage of water need to be controlled through punitive action. Wherever possible equitable distribution and economic use of water need to be encouraged through introduction of warabandi and osrabandi.

Agricultural demonstration farms preferably in the cultivators' fields, need to be established in the commands of selected irrigation schemes with a view to evolve new cropping patterns depending on irrigation facility available.

Where 'Chahi' areas interpolate the commands of irrigation works, such commands need to be extended, with a view to ensure improvement in their irrigation efficiency.

Soil suitability needs to be ascertained before schemes of submergence bunds are taken up so that they do not fail to retain water.

The system of assessment for submergence irrigation appears to be different on different works. It needs to be rationalised and brought on a uniform basis.

Drilling of shallow tubewells in the beds of submergence tanks, wherever feasible and practicable, may be encouraged. They could be helpful for subsequent rabi waterings.

Water courses generally do not exist for irrigation from tanks and channels, thus causing lot of wastage. Action needs to be caused for their construction either on self-help basis or through organisational set-ups like Panchayats or through suitable legislative action.

Possibility of imposing some annual cess on the wells benefited by Rapats built by the State need to be looked into.

Feasibility of constructing Rapats without the use of mortar needs also to be considered.

Indisecreet expansion of Rapats needs to be guarded against and resisted in the interest of areas in lower reaches of the Nadis concerned.

In areas where suitable subsoil resources exist people may be encouraged to have more open wells by grant of *taccavi* loans and subsidies.

Replacement of Charsa by iron persian wheels needs to be encouraged. Possibility of lifting water by wind-mills may also be explored.

Further exploration of underground water resource may be carried out in Luni river basin to locate any other rich water yielding site like that at Bourunda.

The deep tubewell exploratory borings like those in Rajakhera area should be put into commission without delay, so that the results of their working could be examined and more tubewells could be planned.

To reduce heavy evaporation losses from tanks in the arid and semi-arid regions of the State, field use of mono-monocular compound like cetyl-alcohol needs to be tried.

It may be worthwhile making rain making experiments in suitable locations *e.g.* Mount Abu, so as to examine possibilities of augmenting natural precipitation wherever possible.

Land capabilities surveys need to be carried out in all such areas as have the benefit of irrigation of one kind or the other, so that cropping patterns leading to potimum agricultural production could be worked out.

To evolve uniform pattern of irrigation rates in the State, the existing rate structure needs to be examined by an expert body or a specific irrigation rates Commission.

In areas subjected to erosion of soils either by rain or wind, steps need to be taken for conservation of soils—more particularly in irrigated areas.

MINOR IRRIGATION TEAM ON STATE TUBE-WELLS IN UTTAR PRADESH, 1958—REPORT

New Delhi, Committee on Plan Projects, 1961. 98p.

Leader : Shri N.V. Gadgil (replaced by Dr. A.N. Khosla).

Members : Shri M. Narasimhaiya (replaced by Shri Baleshwar Nath); Shri Lal Singh.

Ex-Officio Member : Shri Mahavir Prasad.

APPOINTMENT

The Minor Irrigation Team was constituted under the Committee on Plan Projects *vide* their Memorandum No. COPP/ (4)/ 17/ 58, dated August 4, 1958.

TERMS OF REFERENCE

The minor irrigation projects may be divided for study into two parts:—

(a) Works already in existence.

(b) Works which are now being constructed.

2. Case studies should be made of a number of projects of each type under the above headings with a view to judging their efficiency having regard to the objectives with which such works were carried out.

3. The following points should be especially borne in mind:

Existing Projects

(i) The present state of repair and maintenance.

(ii) The system of keeping works in proper maintenance with particular reference to the customary obligations of villagers for keeping such works in a sound condition from year to year, the Team should also examine the extent to which these obligations are enforced, the reasons for the failure to do so and the steps that should be taken to carry out such obligations efficiently.

(iii) Reasons, if any for non-utilisation of water by cultivators.

(iv) Improvements necessary to make the projects more efficient either in the matter of better agricultural planning and practices or in respect of engineering works.

(v) Cost of restoration if the project is in a state of disrepair and whether it has been included in the Plan.

New Projects

(i) Method of selection—procedure and principles on which priorities are based.

(ii) Flow Chart of the construction Project should be prepared to examine whether any avoidable delay has occurred in its completion.

(iii) Whether fullest use is made of catchment capacity in preparing designs.

(vi) Economics of design.

(v) State of agricultural planning with a view to optimum utilisation of benefits.

(vi) Institutional arrangements provided for the proper maintenance of new works with special reference to the customary obligation of villagers in this regard.

(vii) Costs of actual construction compared to estimated costs—the reasons for increase if any and the care with which the initial estimates were framed.

4. Any other matter which the Team considers necessary to report upon having a bearing on economy and efficiency of such projects.

5. The following information should be gathered by the Team for each State, taken as a whole in regard to existing minor irrigation works:

(i) The total area irrigated from them according to Settlement Registers.

(ii) The area actually irrigated from year to year beginning from 1947.

(iii) The reason for the reduction, if any, in the area irrigated.

6. In addition, the Team will carry out a study of the tubewell schemes of the Punjab and the U.P with reference to the fact whether optimum use has been made of the facilities available by ensuring scientific crop planning and by improving agricultural practices. The

study should be based on an examination of individual tubewells, which may be divided into most successful, successful and least successful varieties for the purpose of study. The team should also select a few tubewells for which alternative crop planning and practices may be recommended that are being carried out at present in order to make them more successful. The consideration mentioned regarding minor irrigation works in third paragraph *mutatis mutandis* be taken into consideration for the study of tubewells also.

CONTENTS

Letter of Transmittal; Preface; Need for Tubewell Irrigation in U.P. and its Growth; Organisational Set-up; Financial Picture; Planning, Construction and Operation of Tubewells; Performance of State Tubewells; Agricultural Aspects of Tubewell Irrigation with annexure; Summing-up and Recommendations; Appendices I to XIV

RECOMMENDATIONS

The question of construction, maintenance and operation of State tubewells in Uttar Pradesh and their financial remunerativeness, is of great complexity. In it are implicated many disciplines of science and many aspects of humanity, namely, geology, sub-soil water resources, natural precipitation and its variations, hydrology, engineering, sources of energy, mechnical equipment and their indigenous production, utilisation of water supplies, agronomic practices and their traditional background, agricultural statistics, revenue returns, financial analysis of overall and indirect benefits, State and private interests, frame-work of communal and social life, state taxation policies, betterment levies, cooperative trends, general economic development and above all, the urge of a welfare State to raise its production level and standard of living of its people. The team has, therefore, looked into the question from a broad-based view and minor points indicating shortfalls and short-comings, which came under observation during individual case studies, have not been included in this report. They were, however, discussed with the officers concerned and State authorities will undoubtedly take action to remedy those. Matters involving policy decisions and of wide interest have mostly been taken up and recommendations of the Team are given below:

I. A coordinated approach for development of tubewell areas as envisaged at state level should be extended to Community Development Block and village levels.

II. An expert scientific and detailed evaluation of direct and indirect benefits accruing from tubewell schemes should be made in order to examine whether it is necessary to have modified financial criteria to judge tubewell performance.

III. Minus returns faced by the State should be made up through improvement of operational efficiency, increase in production by better agricultural management than heretofore and consequently in revenue returns.

IV. The siting of tubewells in ribbon like fashion along main roads should be avoided as it involves costly energisation due to long lengths of transmission lines.

V. Unnecessarily large commands of tubewells should be reduced so that areas not adequately served by such tubewells could be developed through alternative means or additional tubewells.

VI. A periodical stock-taking of sub-soil water resources should be made in respect of areas served by tubewells, say every ten years.

VII. Where rebuilding of tubewells involves closure of irrigation service, advance action should be taken so that damage to crops and inconvenience to cultivators are obviated.

VIII. Standard types of equipment, that can be manufactured within the country, should be evolved to replace the present diverse makes when they wear out.

IX. Community Development Block Committees and Panchayats should encourage cultivators to form cooperatives or Committees for the purpose of maintaining water channels on tubewell commands.

X. Earth work formation on water channels should be scientifically compacted on optimum moisture content basis. It should not be left for natural consolidation by rainfall alone.

XI. With a view to minimising percolation losses, lining of channels should be done, as far as possible.

XII. (i) A policy of taking prior undertaking from intending irrigators from State tubewell's should be adopted.

(ii) A Two-Part Tariff consisting of a fixed starting charge and available recurring charge may be introduced.

(iii) Different water rates during slack and active periods should be introduced so as to encourage cultivators to use tubewell supplies.

(iv) Where tubewells are not running to their capacity, waterings at reduced rates should be allowed for special types of crops.

XIII. Osrabandi warabandi *i.e.* water distribution rules should be made more flexible and adjustable. Clause giving option to change turns could, with advantage, be introduced.

XIV. As application of irrigation water in shallow depths at suitable intervals is beneficial to crops, inducive measures should be devised to encourage cultivators to do so.

XV. (i) Areas under high water requirement crops should be limited on each tubewell so as to ensure adequate supply of water to all holdings.

(ii) Levelling of fields being a pre-requisite of wet landfarming it may be undertaken by the State Government on a cost basis, the cost being recoverable from cultivators in easy instalments. The State Government may alternatively advance loans to the affected cultivators and offer technical assistance, if needed for the purpose.

(iii) The State Government should set up a Research Wing to draw upon the experiences and results achieved on demonstration or model farms and on well bores and equipment performance, including the Ground Water Studies conducted at the Irrigation Research Institute, Roorkee. The benefits of research should be made available to all concerned including cultivators.

XVI. (i) In recruitment to the post of operators preference should be given to agriculturally trained persons.

(ii) The staff engaged on tubewells should be given orientation course of training in agricultural practices so that they may be better equipped to devote their spare time to the needs of irrigated agriculture.

XVII. Strains of crops suited to local soil conditions and to the quality of water should be developed and popularised by the Agriculture Department in co-operation with the Irrigation Department.

XVIII. In the context of shortage of manure and high cost of fertilizers, concessional water rates may be offered to cultivators for growing green manure crops.

XIX. (i) Demonstration farms should be organised in areas having a group of ten or more tube-wells.

(ii) Suitable crop pattern should be evolved for areas served by tube-wells and demonstrations with regard to better methods of husbandry, including proper and economic utilisation of tubewell flow should be organised.

COMMITTEE OF THE CLASSIFICATION AND CATEGORISATION OF CLASS III AND CLASS IV EMPLOYEES OF MAJOR PORTS, 1958—REPORT

New Delhi, Ministry of Transport and Communications, 1961. 167p.+iiip.

Chairman : Shri F. Jeejeebhoy.

Members : Shri S. Nanjundiah (resigned); Shri K.M. Palekar; Shri G.H. Kale; Shri Makhan Chatterjee; Shri Kali Mukherjee; Shri T.S. Parasuraman; Shri T.A. Eastment; Shri K.N. Shrinivasan (resigned); Shri C.V. Venkateswaran; Shri Shivakumar Dhindaw; Shri A.W. De Lima; Shri T.K. Parameswaran Nambiar; Shri K. Mitter (replaced by Shri C.R. Reddy).

Secretary : Shri Batuk H. Mehta.

APPOINTMENT

By its Resolution No. 23-PLA(91)/58, dated August 23, 1958, published in the Gazette of India Extra-Ordinary, Part I—Section 1, No. 84A, dated August 25, 1958, the Government of India in the Ministry of Transport and Communications (Department of Transport) constituted this Committee to undertake the work of classification and categorisation of class III and IV posts in the major posts of Bombay, Calcutta, Madras, Cochin, Kandla and Vizagapatnam, and to fit them into one or other of the scales of pay given in the Schedule attached to the Resolution.

TERMS OF REFERENCE

(i) The Committee will examine the duties and responsibillties of the various posts and fit them into one or other of the scales of pay given in the attached Schedule, in the light of the scales of pay of posts with comparable duties and responsibilities in other departments of Government. Should the Committee feel that, owing to the existence of gradations of skill and responsibility or both, the scales given in the Schedule cannot be adopted fully in the case of a particular post or group of posts, they are free to suggest breaking up of longer scales (i.e. a scale extending over a number of years such as Rs. 60-3-81-EB-4-125-5-130) into two or three shorter scales for adoption in those cases;

(ii) Shorter scales may also be suggested in cases where the method of recruitment is not direct but by departmental promotion or a higher start is justified owing to higher qualifications prescribed for the post;

(iii) The Committee is not precluded from recommending scales going beyond the indicated maximum if on a comparison of the duties and responsibilities of the categories of the posts in the Ports with the duties and responsibilities of similar categories in other establishments, the weight of evidence is in favour of such recommendation, provided that the scale recommended does not go beyond the scale adopted in the Government Departments for comparable categories;

(iv) The Committee will also recommend changes, where necessary, in the designation of posts so that standardised nomenclature may be evolved.

CONTENTS

Ports' Scheme; Labour's Replies; Hearings; Meetings for Taking Decisions; The Committee's Approach; Scales of Pay as Fixed by the Committee; Particular Categories; Implementation; Appendices A to H; Schedules I to VI.

RECOMMENDATIONS

Lower Clerical Staff

The Committee considered in detail the various representations made before it by the indoor and the outdoor clerks in the lowest scale, and taking into consideration the nature of their duties and responsibilities in the Ports the Committee has decided that all the clerks in all the Ports, both indoor and outdoor, in the lower division scale or its equivalent should be in the scale of Rs. 60-4-120-EB-5-150. The Committee is not too happy with the present proportion between the strength of the cadres of the Upper and Lower Division Clerks (designated as Clerks, 'B' Scale, or Clerks, Grade II, in Bombay; as Junior Clerks in Kandla; as Clerks, Class II, or Clerk 'E' in Vizagapatnam; and as lower clerical staff of outdoor establishment of Engineering Department in Cochin). Instances have been brought to the notice of the Committee where the number of Upper Division Clerks in a Section is unduly low. The Committee therefore urges upon the Port Authorities the necessity of taking early steps to examine the position so as to rectify any existing anomalies in that regard. In this connection the Committee desires to draw the attention of the Port Administrations to the following recommendation made by Shri P.C. Chaudhuri, I.C.S., Officer on Special Duty, in his report dated September 1, 1957, a recommendation which was accepted in principle by the Government of India, but being administrative in character was left to be pursued at the Ports' level *vide* Appendix I, Part I, sub-paragraph (v) of the Government Resolution dated July 20, 1958.

"(v) In many Administrative Departments, the proportion of Upper Divisional clerical cadre to the Lower Division and the proportion of the Supervisory staff to the clerical strength is quite low in most of the Ports; higher proportions will be more in consonance with work requirements also".

Typists

There is a combined cadre of Clerks and Typists at Bombay, Cochin, Kandla, and Madras Ports, and a separate cadre of Typists at Calcutta and Vizagapatnam; at the latter two Ports there are a few posts of Senior Typist in the Upper Division clerical scale. The Committee is of the view that the promotion opportunities for the Typists at Calcutta and Vizagapatnam ought to be examined by the Port Administrations with a view to improvement.

Stenographers

The Committee has decided that the entry scale into the category of Stenographers should be the higher clerical scale of Rs. 80-5-120-EB-8-200-10/2-220. There should be two promotional scales for the Stenographers, the first being the higher ministerial scale of Rs. 160-10-300 with a higher start of Rs. 260. At Cochin Port there are no posts of Stenographer as such, and an Upper Division Clerk is employed as a Stenographer on his own pay, and a Lower Division Clerk is so employed with a special allowance of Rs. 15. The Committee has decided that all these clerks at Cochin doing Stenographer's work should be designated as Stenographers and paid accordingly.

Railway Staff

The Committee had before it the question whether the extraneous benefits given by the Indian Railways, which are not all given by the Port Railways, would justify a higher scale of pay for the Port Railway employees. The Committee, however, has taken the view that the terms of reference contained in the Government Resolution constituting the Committee are precise, and that extraneous benefits are not to be calculated for the purpose of fixing particular categories into particular scales.

The category designated as "Yard Porter" in the Traffic Department (Railway Transportation) of Calcutta is a composite one, and the incumbents thereof perform different functions in turn, such as Gateman, Chalk-washer, Bellman, Lampman, Weigh-bridge Khalasi, Pointsman, Points-setter and Signalman. The Committee has decided that those Yard Porters who perform the duties of Pointsman, Points-setter, and Signalman should be categorised and classified in the higher scale of Rs. 35-1-50. In this connection the Committee draws the attention of the Calcutta Port authorities to the Das Gupta Award dated December 30, 1957, published in the Gazette of India Extraordinary dated January 30, 1958.

Skilled Artisans

The Committee has given very careful thought to the question whether the skilled artisans of the different Ports should be given the skilled long grade of Rs. 60-3-81-EB-4-125-5-130 or the three short skilled scales, as given in the Schedule to the Government Resolution dated August 23, 1958. It is said that the one long scale as prevailing in the Railways is not satisfactory on the main ground that a long scale inhibits the growth of skills and incentive to improvement. There is on the other hand a legitimate anxiety that if the three short scales are given there might be a hiatus at the end of each scale, as promotion will normally have to await a vacancy. This Committee has decided that the skilled artisans of the Ports should be given the three scales, *viz.* (1) Rs. 60-5/2-75, (2) Rs. 75-3-105, and (3) Rs. 100-5-130. Concommitently with the granting of such scales, it is provided that towards the end of the Rs. 60-5/2-75 scale, and also towards the end of the Rs. 75-3-105 scale, there shall be trade tests before the skilled workmen concerned, with approved service, are allowed to proceed to the next higher scale; but it is also provided that nobody with approved service who has passed the trade test shall be held up in either of the two grades for want of a vacancy, and that the Ports Administrations concerned shall take appropriate steps to ensure such end within the totality of the skilled posts.

For the purposes of categorisation of the artisans of Calcutta Port, the Committee has decided as follows:

(i) Those employees in the Rs. 40-60 scale now prevailing in Calcutta who are holding posts in the semi-skilled grade will remain in that scale; but those who are now in the Rs. 40-60 scale and are holding posts in the existing lowest skilled category shall be fixed in the scale of Rs. 60-5/2-75.

(ii) Those Grade I artisans of Calcutta, who are now in the scale of Rs. 60-75, shall be fixed in the scale of Rs. 75-3-105.

(iii) Grade 'A' workers' shall be regarded as highly skilled and placed in the scale of Rs. 80-5-120-EB-8-160.

As regards the skilled artisans of Cochin Port, it is provided that those now in the scale of Rs. 40-1-50 will be fixed in the scale of Rs. 60-5/2-75, that those now in the scale of Rs. 50-2-60 will be fixed in the scale of Rs. 75-3-105 and those now in the scale of Rs. 60-5/2-75 will be fixed in the scale of Rs. 100-5-130. This classification will apply to the existing personnel in the respective three categories as the Cochin Port Authority is satisfied that the employees concerned have the requisite capacity to be fixed in the three scales without trade tests. As regards future promotions, the employees concerned will have to pass appropriate trade tests in accordance with the Committee's general decision in that behalf.

In the Schedules of the different Ports the skilled scales fixed by the Committee as stated in the foregoing paragraphs have been indicated, and a remark has been entered against the category to the effect that the scale is "in the scheme of skilled scales". It is the intention of the Committee that normally the entry scale for a skilled artisan shall be Rs. 60-5/2-75 and that every skilled artisan, for whom one or the other of the shorter skilled scales has been fixed, should be able, with approved service ultimately to reach the maximum of Rs. 130 by passing the appropriate trade tests wherever applicable, irrespective of the fact that there is no vacancy in the higher grade.

Semi-Skilled Artisans

The Committee has decided that there shall be three scales of pay for the semi-skilled categories, namely, (1) Rs. 35-1-50, (2) 40-1-50-2-60, and (3) Rs. 40-2-60. In this connection the Committee desires to draw the attention of the Port Authorities to the following observations made in paragraph 26 at page 228 in the Report of the Second Pay Commission :

"We, therefore, recommend that the system of basic tradesmen should be worked so as to provide a channel through which, in trades where there is no semi-skilled grade, unskilled workers may advance to the skilled grade, and that posts of basic tradesmen created with this object are not set off against posts in the skilled grade".

Highly-Skilled Categories

The Committee has decided that the "highly skilled" categories shall be fixed in the scales of Rs. 80-5-120-EB-8-160 and Rs. 100-5-125-6-155-EB-6-185, and the Committee has also decided upon certain posts which ought to be in these scales. The Committee however feels that there are possibly other posts entitled to the highly skilled grade, and it recommends that the Port Administrations do examine the requirements of the highly skilled work and create highly skilled posts wherever warranted.

Railway Engineering Staff

The Committee has fixed appropriate scales for the different categories of the Engineering Permanent Way Staff at the different Ports. As regards the category of "Trolleyman" at Bombay and Calcutta Ports, the Committee desires to draw the attention of the Port Administrations to the fact that the post of "Head Trolleyman" existing on the Indian Railways is absent at present from the Bombay and Calcutta Ports Railway Engineering set-up. The Committee also desires to draw the attention of the Bombay Port Administration to the fact that there is no post of "Maistry" over the "Mate" or "Muccadum" as obtaining on the Indian Railways Permanent Way Sections and at other Ports. These matters do call for consideration.

Operational Staff Of Cranes And Other Shore Plants

The Committee considered the classification into different groups of the operational staff of cranes and other shore plants and has decided to classify them into the following five groups and to fit them in the scales shown against each :

Group I—Scale : Rs. 40-2-60

1. Battery Trucks
2. Platform Trucks.
3. Electric Cars
4. Fixed Hydraulic Hoists, or Lifts.
5. Fixed Hydraulic Cranes at Madras Port.

Group II—Scale : Rs. 60-3-81-EB-4-105

1. Motor Cars
2. Ambulances
3. Lorries.
4. Fire Service Lorries.
5. Road Rollers (Steam & Diesel).
6. Diesel Loco. Tow Car.
7. Fork Lifts, 3½ tons and below.
8. Tractors.
9. Wharf Cranes below 10 tons.
10. Travelling or Gantry or Transporter Crane below 10 tons.
11. Mobile Cranes, 3½ tons and below.
12. Steam Rail Cranes upto and including five tons.

Group III—Scale : Rs. 75-3-81-EB-4-125-5-130

1. Mobile Cranes, above 3½ tons and upto and including 15 tons.
2. Wharf cranes, 10 tons and above and below 100 tons.
3. Travelling or Gantry or transporter Crane, 10 tons and above.
4. Break down Cranes.
5. Steam Rail Cranes, above 5 tons.
6. Diesel Rail Crane, 12 tons, at Vizagapatam Port.
7. Fork Lifts above 3½ tons.
8. Scotch Derrick Cranes.
9. Coal loader of Mechanical Coal Loading Plant of Calcutta.

Group IV—Scale : Rs. 100-5-125-6-155

1. All cranes of 100 tons and below 200 tons.
2. Mobile Cranes above 15 tons.
3. Floating Cranes.

Group V—Scale : Rs. 155-6-185

All Cranes of 200 tons and above.

The relevant categories at each Port have accordingly been fixed in the appropriate scales in the respective Schedules.

Divers

The Committee has carefully considered the several categories of "Diver" at the different Ports, the differences between skin divers and dress divers, and between those diving in still waters and those required to dive in a river or in the open sea. The Committee is of the view that the linesman attached to the Diver does a particular kind of job, and higher scale of pay has been fixed for this category for the different Ports. This might involve a departure from the existing scheme of promotion, and the Committee takes the view that the Port Administrations do review the linesman's category for his proper line of promotion,

Lascars (Shore And Flotilla Crews)

As regards Lascars (Shore and Flotilla Crews), the Committee decided that the first group should consist of the lascars on :

(1) Suction Dredgers and floating pipeline
(2) Bucket Dredgers
(3) Propelled Grab Dredgers
(4) Tugs
(5) Pilot Launches of Cochin and Vizagapatam
(6) Propelled Floating Crane
(7) Rock Breaker and Dipper Dredger of Vizagapatam.
(8) Propelled Craft, 40 N.H.P. and over or 226 B.H.P. and over
(9) Hawser Boats of Calcutta
(10) Mooring Launches of Cochin
(11) Light Vessels of Calcutta and that they should be in the scale of Rs. 40-1-50.

The remaining Lascars are Categorised as Lascar, Grade II, and will receive the scale of Rs. 30-1-40-EB-1-50 (to start on Rs. 34/- at Calcutta and at Rs. 32/- at other Ports). The Lascars in this group, Grade II, include Lascars on:

(1) Non-propelled Grab Dredgers.
(2) Launches other than Pilot launches of Cochin and Vizagapatam and Mooring launch of Cochin.
(3) Non-propelled Hopper Barges.
(4) Water Barges.
(5) Mooring Boats.
(6) Diving Boats.
(7) Mooring work at Vizagapatam.
(8) Shore pipeline (Dredging).
(9) Marine Khalasis and Shore Lascars (Marine) in all Ports including Water Supply Khalasis of Vizagapatam.

(10) Propelled Craft of less than 40 N. H. P. or 226 B.H.P.

(11) Jolly Boat Lascars and Khalasis or Lascars of other boats at all Ports and Boatmen of Vizagapatam.

(12) Non-propelled Floating Cranes.

(13) Lighters of all capacities.

As regards Madras, the above principles shall be applied to Lascars in the Engineering Department. Lascars in the grade of Rs. 35-1-50 in Marine Survey in Engineering Department shall be fixed in the scale of Rs. 40-1-50. For the Lascars in the Marine Department in Madras, there will be a single scale of Rs. 30-1-50. Lascars in the Dy. Conservator's yard, who are now on Rs. 35-1-50, shall be fixed in the scale of Rs. 40-1-50-2-60 and those on Rs. 30-½-35 shall be fixed in the scale of Rs. 30-1-40, starting at Rs. 32/-. The Lighterman in the Traffic Department shall be in the scale of Rs. 30-1-40. The Madras Port Administration might examine the question of applying the principles now made applicable to the Engineering Department lascars above to the Marine Department lascars also.

The designation of this category shall be "Lascar" at all the Ports.

Sanitary Staff

The Committee has fixed for the Class IV Sanitary staff at all Ports, generally designated as sweepers/scavengers, rat catchers, the scale of Rs. 30-1-35. In their case the Committee would urge upon the Administrations of the Ports the desirability of giving to these categories such "unclean allowances" as they might consider just.

In the Sanitary Section of the Medical Department at Calcutta there are two categories of 'Jamadar' and 'Literate Jamadar' for whom the Committee has prescribed appropriate scales. In their case it has been urged that some of them are doing work as full-fledged clerks. The Committee, therefore recommends that the Calcutta Port Administration do investigate these two categories and if any of the Jamadars and the Literate Jamadars are found to be doing work as full-fledged clerks they should be classified accordingly and fixed in appropriate clerical scales.

Watch And Ward Staff

The Committee has fixed the scale of Rs. 30-1-35 for the category of watchman, designated as Chowkidar. Sainik, Watchman, etc. at the different Ports. It has been urged before the Committee that promotion opportunities for such staff have been very inadequate, and the Committee would therefore urge upon the Ports the desirability of examining the position with a view to providing adequate promotional opportunities for the Watchman.

Messengers

As regards Messengers in Bombay who have been fixed by the Committee in the scales of Rs. 30-35 and Rs. 35-50, it has been urged that some of them are doing higher class of work; and in this connection particular mention has been made of the Messengers employed in the sub-offices under the control of the Junior Assistant Engineer (Railway) and of the Assistant Manager, Bunders, at Bombay. The Committee would urge upon the Bombay Port Administration to investigate the matter, and if it is found that some Messengers are doing a higher class of work they could be fixed in an appropriate scale.

Cycle Peons

The Cycle Peons at Calcutta, including the category of Cycle Orderly, have been fixed in the scale of Rs. 30-1-35. In this connection the Committee recommends that the Calcutta Port Administration do consider the question of making available to Cycle Peons and Cycle Orderlies some promotional opportunities if they did not exist at present, and of granting them an adequate "Cycle Allowance."

Shore Workers

Members of the Committee representing labour desired that the Porter (Piece-rate) serial No. 1009 of Calcutta now shown as being on Rs. 30-35 should be fitted in the same scale of pay as the Porter (Departmental) serial No. 1007 now given Rs. 30-40 on the ground that their duties and responsibilities are comparable and both are now on the same scale of pay. It was urged that although the category—Porter (Piece-Rate)—is paid under the piece rate scheme his provident fund, gratuity and leave salary are based on a scale of Rs. 30-35. For removing any misapprehension they said that they had no objection to a rider to the effect that the fixation of the scale as suggested by them shall not by itself affect the piece rate scheme.

The details of Piece Rate Schemes vary from Port to Port. It is evident that a piece rate wage cannot be fixed into a monthly time scale. But we find that there has been a practice to utilise a monthly time scale for the ascertainment of Provident Fund benefits, leave pay and gratuity of the piece rater. In view of what has been said above by the Representatives of Labour, this Committee recommends that a monthly time scale of Rs. 30-1-40 may be adopted for the ascertainment of such benefits wherever present quantums are lower.

This would also apply to the Sirdar, Piece-rate, (Serial No. 1012) of Calcutta who will continue to have his differential.

romotion Opportunities

The Committee recommends that a survey similar to the one indicated earlier might be extended with advantage to other categories in the Ports.

INTERMEDIATE PORTS DEVELOPMENT COMMITTEE, 1958—REPORT

Delhi, Manager of Publications, 1960. 285p.+ivp.

Chairman : Shri H. P. Matharani.

Members : Shri D. Sandilya; Capt. W. B. Piggot; Shri M. S. Venkataraman; Shri K. Ranganathan; Shri K. L. Luthra; Shri V. P. Sawhney; Dr. C. R. Krishnamoorthy; Dr. H. B. Mohanti; Shri K. N. Srinivasan; Capt. C. Sankunni; Capt. L. T. Yettie; Shri H. P. Oza; Capt. M. L. Advani; Shri T. M. Goculdas; Shri S. N. Haji; Shri N. L. Kanoria; Shri Ghanshyamlal Gopalji Thakkar.

Asst. Sercetary : Shri D. P. Ohri.

Secretary: Shri I. G. Chacko.

Appointment :

The Government of India *vide* their Resolution No. 1-PDII (24)/57, dated October 27, 1958, appointed a Committee known as the Intermediate Ports Development Committee to select suitable intermediate ports in India for intensive development in order of priority and to determine the extent of development required at these parts,

Terms of Reference

(i) Selection of suitable intermediate ports in India for intensive development in order of priority, taking into account—

(a) Broad national considerations as well as regional requirements;

(b) Engineering aspects with emphasis on economy of construction and maintenance; and

(c) Traffic potential of the hinterland and transport costs.

(ii) Determination of the extent of development required at these ports as well as allied transport development, having regard to the needs of the entire area to be served, and the financial implications thereof.

Contents :

Introductory; Iron Ore Export; Orissa State; Andhra Pradesh; Madras State; Kerala State; Mysore State; Bombay State (Maharashtra Region); Bombay State (Gujarat Region); Allocation of Priorities Amongst Different Ports; General; Summary of Recommendations; Appendices I to XXVII; List of Drawings.

RECOMMENDATIONS

Paradip Port

1. *See* Recommendation after 55 which will become Recommendation No. 1.

2. The present lines of communications and modes of transport of iron ore from the mines to the port, are not satisfactory. If these are improved Paradip will become the natural outlet of the mines in the Tomka-Sukinda region. With this improvement there will be no difficulty in moving 5,00,000 tons of iron ore to Paradip Port even without a railway line from Cuttack to Paradip.

3. Paradip Port should be developed as a fair weather lighterage port for handling 5.5 lakh tons of traffic per annum.

4. When the traffic at Paradip reaches a figure of 5.5 lakh tons per annum, it may be necessary to provide an all-weather port at Paradip together with a railway link from Cuttack to Paradip. Rourkela-Talcher line when it comes will help the development of Orissa State and the port, but this need not be an essential pre-requisite for making Paradip into an all weather port.

5. At Paradip when the traffic exceeds 5.5 lakh tons per annum the Committee recommends the all-weather port to be located in Attarbanki creek lying to the South of the Mahanadi creek with entrance works on the Vizagapatnam model.

6. For handling a traffic of 2.5 lakh tons, the Committee recommends works costing Rs. 99 lakhs to be given first priority as per details given in Appendix X.

7. As the traffic increases upto 2.5 lakh tons and there is indication that the anticipated traffic of 5.5 lakh tons will actually be achieved, the Committee recommends certain additional works costing Rs. 55.3 lakhs as per details given in Appendix X. This may be given second priority.

Kakinada Port

8. Considering the importance of Kakinada, this port should be modernised and improved to handle efficiently an annual traffic of four lakh tons of cargo expected in the next few years. The works which are immediately required at Kakinada are estimated to cost Rs. 25 lakhs as per details in Appendix X. These should be given first priority. Certain additional works estimated to cost Rs. nine lakhs as per details given in Appendix X are also necessary though this may be given a second priority.

Masulipatnam Port

9. A traffic of 4 lakh tons per annum is expected in the next few years. One of the most important development required at Masulipatnam for this purpose is the stabilisation and improvement of the bar at Masulipatnam. This work estimated to cost Rs. 17 lakhs should be given first priority. Initially a sea going cutter section dredger from the proposed dredger pool in the Ministry of Transport and Communications should be utilised for dredging the bar and thus gain experience of the quantum of maintenance dredging is involved. After actual experience of dredging with the help of dredger pool the question of a full time dredger for the port may be examined. Certain additional works estimated to cost Rs. 14.8 lakhs as per details given in Appendix X are also necessary for the development of Masulipatnam Port, though this may be given second priority.

Cuddalore Port

10. The Committee visualises a traffic of roughly 6.5 lakh tons at Cuddalore in the course of the next 10 years. For this, Cuddalore Port should be further developed into a nine ft. harbour. One of the most essentials for this is the stabilisation of the mouth of the rivers and the improvement of the depths over the bar. This can be achieved by the training of the two rivers and the construction of two inclined break waters at the mouth estimated to cost Rs. 50 lakhs as per details given in Appendix X. This proposal should be given first priority. Certain additional works which may be given second priority as per details given in Appendix X are also necessary to complete the development. This will cost Rs. 28.4 lakhs.

Nagapattinam Port

11. The importance of Nagapattinam Port is from the point of view of an established passenger traffic with Malayan ports which is expected to continue in the future. The present bar at Nagapattinam is shallow, narrow and dangerous for the passage of lighters carrying passengers. Accidents to these lighters have been reported in the past resulting in the loss of human life. Works designed to improve the bar at Nagapattinam by the provision of a reinforced concrete pier with needle piles and mobile sand pump mounted thereon, estimated to cost Rs. 10 lakhs as per details given in Appendix X, are therefore considered necessary for for Nagapattinam. This should be given first priority. In addition to this scheme certain other works will also be required to modernise the port and to enable it to handle the estimated traffic of 50,000 passengers and 50,000 tons of cargo per annum. These works are estimated to cost Rs. 12.15 lakhs as per details given in Appendix X. These should be given second priority.

Tuticorin Port

12. The Committee estimates a traffic of one million tons per annum at Tuticorin by the end of 1964-65. For this traffic, the Committee considers a deep-sea harbour with alongside facilities at Tuticorin necessary.

The project recommended by the Committee for the development of Tuticorin into a 30 ft. harbour with four alongside berths, two for coal, one for salt and one for general cargo, works out to Rs. 10.27 crores as per estimate given in Appendix XIV. In essence the scheme consists of having an island harbour in the sea connected to the shore harbour by two embankments of one mile in length to carry road and railway lines. The space between the two embankments will be available for future development of the port. An island will be reclaimed in the sea on which the dock and other port facilities will be located. A turning basin will be sited on the eastern side of the island and will be protected by two inclined breakwaters.

14. Pending the decision of the Government of India regarding Tuticorin's future as an all-weather port with alongside facilities, certain normal development works are immediately necessary if Tuticorin is to continue as a lighterage port even for a few years. These works are estimated to cost Rs. 27 lakhs as per details given in Appendix X and should be given first priority. Certain other works which are also considered necessary but may be given second priority are estimated to cost Rs. 9.5 lakhs as per details given in Appendix X.

A New Intermediate Port At Neendakara

15. Taking into consideration the needs of the entire region near Quilon and the traffic that originates from this region, the Committee recommends that Neendakara should be developed as an Intermediate port to cater for roughly four lakh tons of estimated traffic per annum.

16. The Port of Neendakara should be developed with wharves at Koilthotam to cater for ilmenite trade, a wharf with transit shed on the Quilon side with road and rail approaches for the trade in cashew nuts and

other rail borne traffic and by widening and deepening the existing waterways from the wharves to the Neendakara bar and the stabilisation and improvement of the bar by the construction of two break-waters. The proposal costing Rs. 92.5 lakhs may be given first priority as per details given in Appendix X.

Kozhikode And Beypore

17. The traffic forecast for the ports is 4.75 lakh tons per annum by 1967-68. On this basis it will be necessary to develop Kozhikode and Beypore Ports to deal with this traffic. For this purpose a sailing vessel wharf estimated to cost Rs. 14.56 lakhs as per details given in Appendix X, should be given first priority at Beypore. Certain other items of work estimated to cost Rs. 10.78 lakhs as per details given in Appendix X are also necessary for the development of Beypore Port but these may be given second priority. As far as Kozhikode is concerned the Committee is of the opinion that the present method of handling cargo on the pier by the existing slow and mannually operated crane is inefficient. It will, therefore, be necessary to provide electric cranes on both the north and south piers, estimated to cost Rs. 10 lakhs as work of first priority for Kozhikode, as per details given in Appendix X. Certain other essential works which though necessary, may be given second priority, are estimated to cost Rs. 4.5 lakhs as per details given in Appendix X. Detailed observations should also be undertaken at Beypore in respect of waves, winds, tides, rivers discharge in floods and its silt content and model studies undertaken with a view to ascertain the feasibility of development of an all-weather port at Beypore in the future.

Mangalore Port

18. The Committee estimates a general cargo traffic of five to six lakhs tons per annum excluding iron ore of an all-weather deep draft port is constructed at Mangalore and a railway link is made connecting Mangalore with Hassan for a distance of 123 miles. In view of this and the need for exporting two million tons of iron ore and the advantageous position of Mangalore for exporting both high grade and low grade ores, the Committee considers that Mangalore should be developed as an all-weather port provided it can be made suitable for at least 34 ft. ships in the next five to ten years and if possible for 38 ft. draft ships as a long term measure.

19. The project recommended by the Committee for the development of Mangalore into a 34 ft. harbour with three alongside berths, two for general cargo, and one for ore the last fully mechanised capable of handling six lakh tons of general cargo and two million tons of iron ore in the first stage is estimated to cost Rs. 12.7 crores as per details given in Appendix XXIV. In essence the scheme consists of having a lagoon harbour in the estuary of the Gurpur River after diverting the Gurpur and the Netravati Rivers with the approach channel dredged through the sand spit to the sea and protected by two curved breakwaters. The berths will be developed on the sand spit with the railway and road lines taken across the Gurpur estuary over the Netravati Bund. The scheme should be taken in hand only after investigations are carried out for a 34 ft. harbour.

20. Pending the decision of the Government of India regarding Mangalore's future as an all-weather port with alongside facilities, certain normal development works are necessary even if Mangalore has to continue as a lighterage port for a few years. These works the details of which are given in Appendix X are estimated to cost Rs. 28.00 lakhs and should be given first priority.

21. The economics of developing an all-weather port at Mangalore for 34 ft. draft steamers capable of handling 2.6 million tons of cargo indicate that the project will yield an annual return of about Rs, 43.00 lakhs after making full allowance for depreciation and interest on capital at 4½ per cent.

Karwar Port

22. The present lines of communications from the mines to the port are not satisfactory. This should be improved to handle a traffic of five lakh tons of iron ore through Karwar port.

23. On the basis of the future traffic of six to seven lakh tons per annum at Karwar which can reasonably be expected, Karwar should be developed as an efficient fair weather lighterage port for this purpose. The estimated cost of this is Rs. 25 lakhs as per details given in Appendix X, which can be given first priority. Certain other works which are also necessary are estimated to cost Rs. 9.5 lakhs as per items (i) to (vii) under Second Priority for Karwar given in Appendix X should be given Second Priority. In addition if experimental dredging is successful an alongside berth for 30 to 32 ft. steamers may be provided at Karwar. This is estimated to cost Rs. 152 lakhs as per item (viii) to (xviii) under Karwar in Appendix X.

24. A study of the water supply resources for port purposes near Karwar should be immediately undertaken.

Redi

25. In view of the importance of Redi Port for the export of iron ore, Redi Port should be developed as an intermediate port for handling five lakh tons of iron ore per annum. This development is estimated to cost Rs. 10 lakhs as per details given in Appendix X, and should be given first priority.

26. The Government of Bombay should take over

Redi Port from the mining companies and run the port themselves.

Ratnagiri

27. The passenger traffic at Ratnagiri of the order of 1,00,000 persons per annum as at present, will continue for the next 10 years. For this purpose Ratnagiri should be provided with better fair weather lighterage facilities to enable passengers to be landed at all stages of the tide. A 150 H. P. towing tug to help passenger lighters during unfavourable wind conditions when rowing as is being done at present becomes slow and inefficient should be provided at Ratnagiri. The cost of these is estimated to be Rs. 15.4 lakhs as per details given in Appendix X and should be given first priority. The provision of staff quarters estimated to cost Rs. two lakhs as per details in Appendix X is also necessary but may be given second priority.

28. An all weather port for coastal passenger ships can be located in Mirya Bay. This is estimated to cost about Rs. two crores. This port may be constructed when the traffic justifies and financial resources permit. The harbour is so designed that it can later be made suitable for ocean going ships by extension of its breakwaters.

Surat

29. It is estimated that with the development of lighterage port near Surat the traffic at the place will be 1,00,000 tons. It is, therefore, recommended that a lighterage port be developed at Magdala about eight miles down stream of Surat. This will also avoid the more difficult bars which the sailing craft have to negotiate at present between Surat and Magdala. The cost of this new port is estimated to be Rs. 12.10 lakhs as per details given in Appendix X and are considered of first priority for Surat Port.

Broach

30. The State Government suggested to the Committee for its examination a proposal for an all-weather Port for ocean going steamers at Dahej near the mouth of the Narmada. The Committee found the proposal for an all-weather port unsuitable because of the shallow sea bed and continuous silting at the site. Nor could the Committee find any other suitable site for a deep drafted or lighterage port in the vicinity of the Narmada estuary. The best way to improve the working of the port at Broach is to provide one or more tugs for towing the sailing craft at high water from Broach to the Gulf or *vice versa*, thereby reducing the time taken by sailing craft for the distance of 32 miles from the sea to Broach from about three days to about one day. It will also be necessary to extend the existing reinforced concrete jetty at Broach to reduce the congestion created by the bunching of the craft all of which come at high water. The estimated cost of these proposals together with ancillary facilities estimated to cost Rs. 12.6 lakhs as per details given in Appendix X, should be given first priority.

31. Systematic hydrographic surveys should be carried out of the Narmada river and the channel suitably marked. Introduction of portable type of flashing beacons will further help navigation in the river during the night. Dredging may be undertaken at key shoals with the help of the State Government's dredgers earmarked for internal dredging. The provision for navigational aids for night navigation and the construction of quarters estimated to cost Rs 1.75 lakhs as per details given in Appendix X, may be given second priority for Broach.

Bhavnagar

32. The traffic for purposes of present development at Bhavnagar is estimated to rise to four lakh tons in the next five years.

33. The main problem of Bhavnagar is the silting in Bhavnagar Channel leading to the port from the Gulf. Due to the lack of adequate technical data the Committee is unable to predict the future of Bhavnagar Channel except to say that it would be possible to maintain the approach channel to the port for a number of years by gradually increasing dredging of the Bhavnagar Channel.

34. The Water Impounding Scheme now under construction at Bhavnagar requires certain additional works to make it work more efficiently. These include the provision of wharping jetties on both sides of the entrance, the provision of electric capsterns to facilitate the handling of ships through the entrance and a 750 H.P. tug for handling the ships. The approach channel to Bhavnagar port should also be suitably marked. The estimated cost of these works is Rs. 34.4 lakhs as per details in Appendix X. These works should be given first priority.

35. In view of the fact that the transit sheds at Bhavnagar are located some distance away from the jetty, fork lift trucks should be used to improve the efficiency of handling. In the first instance four Nos. fork lift trucks estimated to cost Rs. 2.4 lakhs should be introduced. This should also be given first priority for Bhavnagar.

36. No provision should be made for any oil berth inside the impounded dock at Bhavnagar, as it is highly undesirable to discharge dangerous oils inside an impounded dock, the gates of which can only be opened at high tide. Oil requirements for this port will have to be met from other sources. For oil bunkering purposes, if trade justifies, barge with tanks and pumps may be maintained.

37. The State Government proposed the construction of three additional berths in the impounded dock. Looking to the traffic expected in a reasonable time, the Committee did not consider the provision of these berths an urgent necessity. To take care of possible bunching of ships that can enter the basin, it will suffice if the turning basin inside the impounded dock is increased to 1000 ft. dia, and one mooring together with an adequate lighterage wharf is provided. It is also necessary to provide suitable office accommodation in the Concrete Jetty areas as the existing office is far away in the town. This will enable better control of dock operation— Repair facilities in terms of portable tools, air compressors, etc. may also be provided in the Concrete Jetty area. The water supply to the port should be augmented. It will also be necessary to construct quarters for essential port staff. The Committee recommends the above works estimated to cost Rs. 40.25 lakhs as per details given in Appendix X to be given second priority.

38. The Ship Repairs Committee had recommended that at Bhavnagar the existing dry dock should be extended and deepened so as to take larger vessels. The Committee was of the opinion that the present dry dock located in the Steel Jetty site should not be extended as the site of this dry dock is a dying site. A new dry dock may be provided in the new port area, when funds permit.

39. In regard to the proposal for earmarking a berth for ship repair work inside the dock, the Committee has not reeommended the construction of any new berth.

Veraval

40. The Committee estimates a future traffic of three lakh tons per annum by the end of the Third Five-Year Plan period. For this purpose, it will be necessary to obtain four electric cranes of half ton to three ton capacity and the 350 H.P. tug for towing the lighters to and from the anchorage. The warehousing accommodation at Veraval should also be increased by another 50,000 sq. ft. The total estimated cost of these works is Rs. 15.5 lakhs as per details given in Appendix X and should be given first priority for Veraval. Certain additional works estimated to cost Rs. 26.5 lakhs as per details given in Appendix X are also necessary for the efficient handling of the traffic at Veraval. These may be given second priority.

Porbandar

41. The Committee expects a traffic of 3.5 lakhs tons at Porbandar by the end of the Third Five-Year Plan. For handling this traffic, it is necessary to construct a lighterage wharf 685 ft. in length, provide a mobile crane and have an additional lighterage capacity of 400 tons. These together with certain ancillary works are estimated to cost Rs. 19 lakhs as per Appendix X and may be given first priority for Porbandar. Certain additional works estimated to cost Rs. 11 lakhs as per details given in Appendix X are also necessary, but these may be given second priority.

42. In regard to the proposal for the construction of an all-weather port, the Committee found that the provision of an all-weather port at Porbandar with two moorings will cost Rs. 5.25 crores. For a trade of 3·5 lakh tons, there would not be economic justification for the development of Porbandar into an all-weather port. As bulk of the expected increase in traffic is in valuable commodities like cement and soda ash, it may be economical to convert this port into an all weather port when there are indications of its rising to about five lakhs tons per year.

Port Okha

43. The Committee expects a traffic of six lakh tons per annum at Port Okha in the next 10 years subject to the conditions that oil traffic will continue as at present. There may be a change in the pattern of oil traffic when the Cambay oil is exploited for commercial use. It is important that oil traffic should be segregated from the general cargo traffic at Port Okha as early as possible. For this purpose an oil tanker berth should be provided at port Okha. In the event of oil traffic disappearing from Port Okha, this berth may be converted into general cargo berth. The provision of this oil tanker berth along with an additional transit accommodation of 40,000 Sq. qt., and the extension of passenger jetty to enable passenger launches to come alongside during all stages of the tide, estimated to cost Rs. 24.5 lakhs as per details given in Appendix X should be given first priority. Certain additional works required at Port Okha as per details given in Appendix X may be given second priority. These are estimated to cost Rs. 18.2 lakhs.

44. The railway authorities should be requested to shift their port station some distance away and to provide sorting lines between the new station and the port railway lines.

45. The need for radio communications between Port Okha and ships at sea coming to Port Okha is essential. The Posts and Telegraphs Department should be requested to provide this facility.

46. The proposal to construct a coastal berth on the eastern side of the pier should be abandoned as this scheme is unnecessary and even harmful.

Sikka Port

47. On the basis of the present traffic of over 1.5 lakh tons and the future traffic of 3.5 lakh tons per annum in the next 10 years forecast by the Committee,

Sikka should be treated as an intermediate port.

48. The immediate necessity at Sikka is the provision of a shallow draft twin screw tug and a lighterage capacity of 600 tons. This is estimated to cost Rs. eight lakhs as per details given in Appendix X and should be given first priority.

Bedi Port

49. The Committee estimated a traffic of 5.6 lakh tons per annum at Bedi Port in the next 10 years. To take care of this traffic, it would be necessary to dredge Bedi Creek in the first stage aiming at a level of +4 at the dock-end of the creek and 0.00 at the sea-end. It will also be necessary to provide a 350 H.P. towing tug. These works would enable a better turn round for the lighters thus increasing the capacity of the port. The estimated cost of these works is Rs. 12 lakhs as per details given in Appendix X. These should be given first priority. Certain additional works estimated to cost Rs. 15.8 lakhs as per details given in Appendix X are also necessary at Bedi Port but these may be given a second priority.

Priorities On An All India Basis

50. The development works given under first priority at each port as details given in Appendix X should be given first priority on an All India basis. These are estimated to cost Rs. 6.12 crores.

51. All works given second priority at each port as per details given in Appendix X should be given second priority. The total cost of these works is Rs. 4.22 crores.

52. All works under third priority as per details given in Appendix X may be given third priority. These are estimated to cost Rs. 42.50 lakhs.

53. The Committee recommends the following priorities for development of all-weather deep draft ports.

Projects	Estimated Amount Rs. in Lakhs	Remarks
First Priority		
Development of a 30 ft. harbour at Tuticorin with four alongside berths, two for coal, one for salt, and one for general cargo.	1,027	
Development of a 34 ft. harbour at Mangalore with three alongside berths, two for general cargo and one for iron ore with a fully mechanised ore loading plant.	1,270	This depends on further studies showing that the port would be suitable for not less than 34 ft. draft and urgency of requirement in respect of export of iron ore.
Second Priority		
Development of Paradip into an all-weather port with one mechanical ore loading berth and four all weather moorings.	954	This depends on traffic exceeding five lakh tons and the construction of Cuttack—Paradip railway line.
Development of Porbandar into an all-weather port with two moorings.	525	This depends on traffic reaching five lakh tons.

General

54. Considering the magnitude of the dredging needs of the various intermediate ports and minor ports, the Dredger Pool recommended as a nucleous by the Dredging Committee be enlarged as early as possible.

55. The provision of dredgers for carrying out internal dredging at the various ports as per details given in Appendix X should be given first priority on an all-India basis along with the other development works at each port which have been recommended to be given first priority.

Iron Ore Exports

In view of the important role iron ore traffic will play in future in deciding the ports to be developed, the Committee went into the question of the future possibilities of iron ore exports from India and the ports through which these ores should be economically routed. The Committee came to the conclusion that there was reasonable prospect of iron ore exports reaching a figure of 13 million tons per year by 1966-67 with a possible increase to 15 million tons a few years later if not by 1966-67. As it is advantageous to develop port capacity ahead of needs, the Committee considered that it would be desirable to accept the figure of 15 million tons for the purpose of planning port development. This traffic will be handled both by the major and intermediate ports. The Committee recommends that the following intermediate ports should be developed for handling the quantities of iron ore shown against them in the next five to 10 years.

Paradip	...	2.5 to 5.0 lakh tons
Kakinada	...	2.0 lakh tons
Masulipatnam	...	3.0 lakh tons
Cuddalore	...	5.0 lakh tons
Mangalore	...	20.0 lakh tons provided this is found suitable for not less than 34 ft. draft.
Karwar	...	5.0 lakh tons
Redi	...	5.0 lakh tons.

Appendix X

Recommended Development Works Of The Various Ports And Priorities At Each Port

Sl.	Port	Name of Work	Estimated amount	Probable Expenditure During third Plan	Remarks
1	2	3	4	5	6
			Rs.	Rs.	
		Orissa			
1.	Paradip	**First Priority**			
		(i) Investigations	1,00,000	1,00,000	
		(ii) Model Study	1,00,000	1,00,000	
		(iii) Lighterage wharf 1600 ft. @ Rs. 1000/- per ft.	16,00,000	16,00,000	
		(iv) 2 Nos. two ton mobile cranes @ Rs. 90,000/- each.	1,80,000	1,80,000	
		(v) 18 Nos. 100-ton lighters @ Rs. one lakh each	18,00,000	18,00,000	
		(vi) Ore tubs and nets	2,88,000	2,88,000	
		(vii) Platform cars and trolly track	2,60,000	2,60,000	
		(viii) 3 Nos. 300 H.P. towing tugs at Rs. four lakhs each	12,00,000	12,00,000	
		(ix) Staff Quarters	5,50,000	5,50,000	
		(a) 5 Nos. officers Qrs. at Rs. 30,000/- each Rs. 1.5 lakhs			
		(b) 15 Nos. class III Qrs. @ Rs. 10,000/- each Rs. 1.5 lakhs.			

1	2	3	4	5	6
			Rs.	Rs.	
		(c) 50 Nos. class IV Qrs. @ Rs. 5,000/- each Rs. 2.5 lakhs			
		Total Rs. 5.5 lakhs			
		(x) Port and customs office	1,00,000	1,00,000	
		(xi) Water supply including one 6″ tubewell, overhead tank and pump house	1,25,000	1,25,000	
		(xii) Electrification	1,00,000	1,00,000	
		(xiii) Navigational Aids:	2,40,000	2,40,000	
		(a) 4 lighted buoys @ Rs. 20,000 each Rs. 80,000			
		(b) 8 unlighted buoys ... Rs. 15,000/- each Rs. 1,20,000			
		(c) 4 beacons @ Rs. 10,000 each Rs. 40,000			
		Rs. 2,40,000			
		(xiv) Roads in port estate four miles	3,00,000	3,00,000	
		(xv) Acquisition of land	1,00,000	1,00,000	
		(xvi) Reclamation including levelling and filling	4,00,000	4,00,000	
		(xvii) Workshop and slipway	5,00,000	5,00,000	
		(xviii) 12″ cutter suction dredger for internal dredging	10,00,000	10,00,000	
		(xix) Water cum-fuel barge	2,00,000	2,00,000	
		(xx) Transit shed 120′×30′	50,000	50,000	
		(xxi) Construction of watering jetty	38,000	38,000	
		(xxii) Construction of road bridge across Attarbanki creek 500×22′	5,00,000	5,00,000	
		(xxiii) Stacking yard for iron ore	1,50,000	1,50,000	
		Total say	99,00,000	99,00,000	
		Second Priority			
		(i) 2 Nos. two ton mobile cranes @ Rs. 90,000/- each	1,80,000	1,80,000	
		(ii) 18 Nos. 100-ton lighters @ Rs. one lakh each	18,00,000	18,00,000	
		(iii) 3 Nos. 300 H.P. towing tugs @ Rs. four lakhs each	12,00,000	12,00,000	
		(iv) Staff Quarters:	15,50,000	15,50,000	
		(a) 5 Nos. officers Qrs. @ Rs. 30,000 each 1,50,000			

1	2	3	4	5	6
			Rs.	Rs.	
		(b) 15 Nos. class III Qrs. @ Rs. 10,000/- each 1,50,000			
		(c) 250 Nos. class IV Qrs. @ Rs. 5,000/- each 12,50,000			
		Total 15,50,000			
		(v) Small field Hospital	2,00,000	2,00,000	
		(vi) Electrification	1,00,000	1,00,000	
		(vii) Improvements to roads in port estate	2,00,000	2,00,000	
		(viii) Expansion of workshop facilities	3,00,000	3,00,000	
		Total	55,30,000	55,30,000	
		Andhra Pradesh			
2.	Kakinada	**First Priority**			
		(i) Development of loading hard area for handling grains and fertilisers	3,00,000	3,00,000	
		(ii) Extension of groynes	8,00,000	8,00,000	
		(iii) Acquisition of a new 12 feet cutter suction dredger	10,00,000	10,00,000	
		(iv) Navigational aids	1,75,000	1,75,000	
		(a) Three Nos. flashing buoys @ Rs. 50,000/-each 1,50,000			
		(b) Radar reflector at Godavari Point 25,000			
		1,75,000			
		(v) Construction of three R.C.C 'T' headed jetties for iron ore	1,25,000	1,25,000	
		(vi) Acquisition of floating dock area for use as fish-cum-ore dock	1,00,000	1,00,000	
		Total	25,00,000	25,00,000	
		Second Priority			
		(i) One grab dredger with two hopper barges of 100-ton capacity	5,00,000	5,00,000	
		(ii) Staff Quarters	2,00,000	2,00,000	
		(a) Nine Qrs. for class III Rs. 72,000			

1	2	3	4	5	6
			Rs.	Rs.	
		(b) 20 Qrs. for class IV Rs. 1,00,000			
		(c) Amenities for labour Rs. 25,000			
		Total say Rs. 2,00,000			
		(iii) Reconditioning of tug 'Godavari' and the conversion of M.F.V. as a despatch vessel.	2,00,000	2,00,000	
		Total Rs.	9,00,000	9,00,000	
3.	Masulipatnam	**First Priority**			
		Stabilising the channel at Masulipatnam including earthern bunds and strengthening of sand spit	17,00,000	15,00,000	Rs. 2 lakhs will be spent during second Plan for provisions exists.
		Total Rs.	17,00,000	15,00,000	
		Second Priority			
		(i) Revetment of channel	2,00,000	2,00,000	
		(ii) Ore Stacking area near bar	1,00,000	1,00,000	
		(iii) Providing approach road and bridge to the new Stacking area	5,60,000	5,60,000	
		(iv) Conversion of S.D. 'Akhanda Godavari' to oil firing	2,00,000	2.00,000	
		(v) Construction of a slipway and provision of essential workshop equipment	3,00,000	3,00.000	
		(vi) Quarters for staff	1,20,000	1,20,000	
		(a) Two Nos. class III Qrs. @ Rs. 8,000. Rs. 16,000			
		(b) 17 No. class II· Qrs. Rs. 5,000 Rs. 85,000			
		(c) Land acquisition Rs. 1,21,000 or Say 1,20,000			
		Total	14,80,000	14,80,000	

MADRAS

1	2	3	4	5	6
4.	Cuddalore	**First Priority**			
		(i) Training works	10,00,000	10,00,000	

1	2	3	4	5	6
			Rs.	Rs.	
		(ii) Construction of break water about 2000' @ Rs. 2,000 per feet	40,00,000	40,00,000	
		Total Rs.	50,00,000	50,00,000	
		Second Priority			
		(i) Capital dredging L. S.	4,00,000	4,00,000	
		(ii) Construction of R. C. C. wharf wall on two sides of spoil Island	7,00,000	7,00,000	
		(iii) Concreting the stacking area on north, central and south wharves	50,000	50,000	
		(iv) Electrification of spoil Island	10,000	10,000	
		(v) Inspection-cum-survey launch	1,00,000	1,00,000	
		(vi) 50 ton steel water barge with equipment	80,000	80,000	
		(vii) Provision of a two ton mobile crane	1,00,000	1,00,000	
		(viii) Reconstruction of 1000 ft. of wharf	4,00,000	4,00,000	
		(ix) Purchase of a grab dredger with necessary pints	3,10,000	3,10,000	
		(x) Provision of a 300 H.P. tug for towing lighters	4,50,000	4,50,000	
		(xi) Providing navigational aids such as lighted beacon and lighted buoys for night work	1,10,000	1,10,000	
		(xii) Provision of quarters for port staff	1,30,000	1,30,000	
		(a) One No. Class II Qr. Rs. 15,000			
		(b) Six Nos. Class III Qrs. @ Rs. 7,000 each Rs. 42,000			
		(c) 12 Nos. Class IV Qrs. @ Rs. 5,000 each Rs. 60,000			
		(d) Land acquisition Rs. 10,000			
		Total say Rs. 1,30,000			
		Total	28,40,000	28,40,000	
		Third Priority			
		(i) Purchase of 12 inch Seagoing cutter suction dredger with pipeline	20,00,000	20,00,00	Provisional requirements at Cuddalore if a full time

1	2	3	4	5	6
			Rs.	Rs.	
					dredger is found necessary from experience.
		(ii) Extension of dry dock	3,00,000	3,00,000	—do—
		Total	23,00,000	23,00,000	
5.	Nagapattinam	**First Priority**			
		Construction of a reinforced concrete jetty with needle piles and mobile sand pump	10,00,000	10,00,000	
		Total	10,00,000	10,00,000	
		Second Priority			
		(i) Reconstruction of wharf wall (southern end)	1,80,000	1,80,000	
		(ii) Improvement to the timber wharf including revetment etc.	2,00,000	2,00,000	
		(iii) Construction of transit sheds in timber wharf area	50,000	50,000	
		(iv) Reconstruction of Passenger Sheds	2,50,000	2,50,000	
		(v) Joining up the 2 ramps in Central and South wharf (120 ft.)	70,000	70,000	
		(vi) Slipway for dredger and tug	1,50,000	1,50,000	
		(vii) Provision of 100 H. P. tug for towing passenger lighters	1,50,000	1,50,000	
		(viii) Provision of quarters for Port Staff (a) Seven Nos. class III Qrs. @ 13,000 Rs. 91,000 (b) 12 Nos. class IV Qrs. @ 4,000 Rs. 48,000 (c) Land acquisition, water supply & electricity Rs. 26,000 1,65,000			
		Total	12,15,000	12,15,000	
		Third Priority			
		(i) Provision of a small suction dredger	6,00,000	6,00,000	

1	2	3	4	5	6
			Rs.	Rs.	
		(ii) Improving the intensity of the light house	1,00,000	1,00,000	
		Total	7,00,000	7,00,000	
6.	Tuticorin	**First Priority**			
		(i) Purchase of one 300 H. P. diesel tug	5,00,000	5,00,000	
		(ii) Two two-ton mobile cranes (20 feet radius) diesel	1,50,000	1,50,000	
		(iii) 2½ cubic yard dumb grab dredger	5,00,000	5,00,000	
		(iv) Three Mudpints with wooden hull (100 tons capacity)	2,50,000	2,50,000	
		(v) Three Nos. 300 ton dumb barges	5,00,000	5,00,000	
		(vi) One dumb barge with reclamation and diluting pumps and pipeline	3,00,000	3,00,000	
		(vii) Construction of shipway for port-craft	2,00,000	2,00,000	
		(viii) Workshop, Equipment etc.	2,00,000	2,00,000	
		(ix) Removal of 'Galatia' wreck	1,00,000	1,00,000	
		Total	27,00,000	27,00,000	
		Second Priority			
		(i) Reconditioning of dredger 'Tuticorin' and extension of ladder	5,00,000	5,00,000	
		(ii) Construction of staff quarters :	4,50,000	4,50,000	
		(a) Class I—Nil			
		(b) Class II—3 Nos. 45,000			
		(c) Class IIIA—3 Nos. 39,000			
		(d) Class IIIB—26 Nos. 1,82,000			
		(e) Class IV—45 Nos. 1,80,000			
		Total say Rs. 4,50,000			
		Total	9.50,000	9,50,000	
		KERALA			
7.	Neendakara	**First Priority**			
		(i) Construction of break-waters at Neendakara	44,00,000	44,00,000	
		(ii) Dredging	2,00,000	2,00,000	
		(iii) Extension of railway siding	1,00,000	1,00,000	
		(iv) Construction of a wharf at			

1	2	3	4	5	6
			Rs.	Rs.	
		Quilon near the additional rest house	3,00,000	3,00,000	
		(v) Construction of transit sheds at Quilon near proposed wharf	2,50,000	2,50,000	
		(vi) Dredging of Ashtamudi lake from Quilon jetty to Neendakara	2,00,000	2,00,000	
		(vii) Widening and deepening of Chavara canal connecting Koilthotam to Ashtamudi lake and dredging in lake to the channel L.S.	5,00,000	5,00,000	
		(viii) Installation of buoys for making ships anchorage	1,00,000	1,00,000	
		(ix) Administration building, signal station and quarters	1,00,000	1,00,000	
		(x) 30 Nos. 50 to 60 ton wooden lighter for Koilthotam at Rs. 30,000 each	9,00,000	9,00;000	
		(xi) Electricity and water supply	1,00,000	1,00,000	
		(xii) Three Nos. 150 H. P. tugs at Rs. 1.75 lakhs each	5,25,000	5,25,000	
		(xiii) Six wooden lighters of 50 to 60 ton capacity for Quilon traffic at Rs. 30,000 each	1,80,000	1,80,000	
		(xiv) One No. 150 H.P. tug for Quilon	1,75,000	1,75,000	
		(xv) One No. 12 ft. cutter suction dredger for capital and maintenance dredging	8,00.000	8,00,000	
		(xvi) Shipway and Workshop	3,85,000	3,85,000	
		(xvii) Additional field offices at Koilthotam and Quilon	30,000	30,000	
		Total	92,50,000	92,50,000	
8.	Beypore	**First Priority**			
		(i) Construction of jetty for sailing craft 500 ft. × 60 ft. including acquisition of land and electrification of wharf	13,56,000	9,00,000	The balance is expected to be spent in second Plan.
		(ii) Investigations and model study for an all-weather port	1,00,000	1,00,000	
		Total	14,56,000	10,00,000	
		Second Priority			
		(i) Three Nos. fixed electric wharf cranes (one five ton and two two-ton)	3,00,000	3,00,000	
		(ii) Water supply	50,000	50,000	

1	2	3	4	5	6
			Rs.	Rs.	
		(iii) Transit sheds 150′×30′	54,000	54,000	
		(iv) 150 H. P. diesel tug for towing tugs and country craft	2,00,000	2,00,000	
		(v) Workshop equipment	1,60,000	1,60,000	
		(vi) Staff quarters	3,14,000	3,14,000	
		(a) Class I—1 No. 4,00,000			
		(b) Class III—17 Nos. 1,70,000			
		(c) Class IV—9 Nos. 54,000			
		(d) Land acquisition (½ acres) 50,000			
		3,14,000			
		Total	10,78,000	10,78,000	
9.	Kozhikode	**First Priority**			
		(i) Provision of fixed electric wharf cranes on north and south piers.	10,00,000	10,00,000	
		(a) North Pier—Two Nos. five ton cranes at 10′ rādius; one No. two ton crane at 20 feet radius.			
		(b) South Pier Six Nos. two ton cranes at 20 feet radius, one No. five ton crane at 10 feet radius at approximately each 1,00,000			
		Total	10,00,000	10,00,000	
		Second Priority			
		(i) Construction of transit shed at south pier 150′×30′	54,000	54,000	
		(ii) Two Nos. one ton electric Capstans for hauling rollies at south and North piers.	15,000	15,000	
		(iii) Additional stacking area at North pier 400×100 (including 600′ of shallow sea wall at Rs, 500/- per ft.)	3,50.000	3,50.000	
		(iv) Construction of signal station.	30,000	30,000	
		Total say	4,50,000	4,50,000	
10.	General	**First Priority**			
		(i) Dredger for internal dredging at intermediate and minor ports.	20,00,000	20,00,000	
		(a) 2 ton grab dredger Rs. 6 lakhs.			

1	2	3	4	5	6
			Rs.	Rs.	
		(b) 3 Nos. 100-ton hopper barges 3 lakhs.			
		(c) 1 No. 200 H.P. tug 3 lakhs.			
		(d) 1 No. 12' cutter suction dredger 8 lakhs.			
		Total 20 lakhs	20,00,000	20,00,000	
		MYSORE			
11.	Mangalore	**First Priority**			
		(i) Provision of a new light house	1,50,000	1,50,000	Rs. 30,000 will be spent during second Plan.
		(ii) Extension of workshop facilities	1,60,000	1,30,000	
		(iii) Beach protection and wind screen with casurina plantation on sand spit on 100 ft. wide belt, length about 1 mile	25,000	25,000	
		(iv) Timber, firewood and hay wharf at Khadathapalli and reclamation 400 ft. in length	4,00,000	4,00,000	
		(v) Investigations for development of Mangalore into an all weather port	1,00,000	1,00,000	
		(vi) Extension of north wharf for iron ore	11,00,000	8,50,000	This is an item included in 2nd Plan on which Rs. 2.5 lakhs are expected to be spent during current plan.
		(vii) Provision of a 300 H.P. tug	5,00,000	5,00,000	
		(viii) Provision of a 100 H.P. launch	1,50,000	1,50,000	
		(ix) One No. two-ton mobile crane	1,00,000	1,00,000	
		(x) Replacing channel marking buoys with lighted buoys	1,25,000	1,25,000	
		Total say	28,00,000	25,30,000	
12.	Karwar	**First Priority**			
		(i) Provision of lighterage wharf 1000 ft. in length including dredging along-side and in the approach channel to a depth of eight feet below L.W.O.S.T. @ Rs. 1960/- per p.f t.	19,60,000	19,60,000	
		(ii) Provision of repair facilities including slipway and workshop.	3,90,000	3,90,000	

1	2	3	4	5	6
			Rs.	Rs.	
		(iii) Provision of Pilot launch	1,50,000	1,50,000	
		Total Rs.	25,00,000	25,00,000	
		Second Priority			
		(i) Provision of a transit shed 200 feet ×50 feet	1,00,000	1,00,000	
		(ii) Provision of water barge with pump and shore installations for supplying water to ships	1,00,000	1,00,000	
		(iii) Provision of 150 H.P. diesel tug for harbour service, towage of passenger boats and sailing craft and for inspection purposes	2,50,000	2,50,000	
		(iv) Navigational aids	30,000	30,000	
		(a) Improvement to Koney light 10,000			
		(b) Two leading lights at Shimshigudh and Kurmagad Isles 20,000			
		Rs. 30,000			
		(v) Provision of quarters for staff	2,95,000	2,95,000	
		(a) One No. class I officers Qr. 37,000			
		(b) One No. class II officers Qr. 21,000			
		(c) 10 Nos. class III Qrs. 96,000			
		(d) 30 Nos. class IV Qrs. 1,20,000			
		(e) Land acquisition 21,000			
		Rs. 2,95,000			
		(vi) Extension of office building	25,000	25,000	
		(vii) Provision of two mooring buoys	1,50,000	1,50,000	
		(viii) Experimental dredging	2,00,000	2,00,000	
		(ix) Land acquisition for future major expansion at Karwar	20,00,000	20,00,000	
		(x) Dredging approach channel, turning basin and mooring area opposite the existing wharf for 30 ft. steamers	49,03,860	49,03,080	This work to be taken up only after traffic exceeds five lakh tons per annum there is economic justification for further development.
		(xi) Provision of channel marks	6,00,000	6,00,000	—do—
		(a) fairway buoy I No.	1,00,000		

1	2	3	4	5	6
			Rs.	Rs.	
		(b) channel marking buoys 10 Nos. @ 50,000 each 5,00,000			
		Rs. 6,00,000			
		(xii) Provision of two tugs 1000 B.H.P. and 700 B.H.P. for manoeuvring of vessels	34,00,000	34,00,000	—do—
		(xiii) Provision of one mooring berth for ocean going steamers including heave up boat for anchors	2,50,000	2,50,000	—do—
		(xiv) Navigational aids	2,00,000	2,00,000	—do—
		(a) Lighted buoy for Parker rock I No. 50,000			
		(b) Lighted buoy for Marriot rock 1 No. 50,000			
		(c) Lighted buoy to mark Gudsav Sanv No. 1 50,000			
		(d) Lighted beacon on rock awash bearing 098 distance 4900 from ft. dyster Rock Light House 50,000			
		Rs. 2,00,000			
		(xv) Diversion of the present main road alongside port wharf and improvement of Binge-Karwar road as an alternative L.S	4,00,000	4,00,000	—do—
		(xvi) Electrification and water supply L.S.	2,00,000	2,00,000	
		(xvii) Provision of one ocean going steamer berth 600 feet at Rs. 5000/- per ft.	30,00,000	30,00,000	
		(xviii) Additional dredging alongside ocean going steamer berth	38,400	38,400	
		Total say	1,61,40,000	1,61,41,860 or say 1,61,40,000	
13.	General	**First Priority**			
		(i) Dredger for internal dredging of various minor intermediate ports including auxiliary craft	10,00,000	7,50,000	This is an item included in the 2nd Plan. An expenditure of Rs. 2.5 lakhs is expected in 2nd Plan.

1	2	3	4	5	6
			Rs.	Rs.	
		(ii) Preliminary investigations	1,00,000	1,00,000	
		(iii) Tools and Plant	1,50,000	1,50,000	
		Total	13,50,000	10,00,000	
		BOMBAY (MAHARASHTRA)			
14.	Redi	**First Prioirty**			
		(i) Construction of wharf 400 feet ×50 feet @ Rs. 1500/- per R. ft.	6,00,000	6,00,000	
		(ii) Construction of puckka approach road	20,000	20,000	
		(iii) Dredging the channel	1,00,000	1,00,000	
		(iv) Providing aids to navigation, buoys, etc.	1,80,000	1,80,000	
		(v) Ancillary buildings	60,000	60,000	
		(a) Office-cum-store building 30 feet×30 feet @ Rs. 20/- per sq. ft. Rs. 18,000			
		(b) Staff quarters			
		Class III two Nos. Rs. 24,000			
		Class IV two Nos. Rs. 16,000			
		Land acquisition 2,000			
		Rs. 60,000			
		(vi) Water supply arrangement for port	40,000	40,000	
		Total	10,00,000	10,00,000	
15.	Ratnagiri	**First Priority**			
		(i) Raising by about 12 feet and widening low level jetty from 5 feet to 15 feet with landing facilities (Caisson construction for pier) 600 feet × 15 feet @ Rs. 80/- per sq. ft.	7,20,000	7,20,000	
		(ii) Extending jetty by 300 feet × 15 feet on R.C.C. piles, 300 feet @ Rs. 80/- per sq. ft.	3,60,000	3,60,000	
		(iii) Parking space with reclamation at shore (150 feet × 60 feet) at Rs. 12/- per sq. ft.	1,08,000	1,08,000	
		(iv) Electrification	20,000	20,000	
		(v) Extending road by about 500 feet with pitching on sea side and surfacing	40,000	40,000	

1	2	3	4	5	6
			Rs.	Rs.	
		(vi) Water supply	40,000	40,000	
		(vii) 150 H.P. towing tug	2,50,000	2,50,000	
		Total say	15,40,000	15,40,000	
		Second Priority			
		Staff quarters including land acquisition	2,00,000	2,00,000	
		(a) Class II one No. Rs. 30,000			
		(b) Class III eight Nos. Rs. 1,20,000			
		(c) Class IV two Nos. Rs. 12,000			
		(d) Land acquisition ,, 38,000			
		Total 2,00,000			
		Total	2,00,000	2,00,000	
16.	General	**First Priority**			
		Dredgers for internal dredging	12,00,000	12,00,000	
		(a) Two-ton grab dredger 6 lakhs			
		(b) Three Nos. 100-ton hopper barges 3 lakhs			
		(c) No. 200 H.P. tug 3 lakhs			
		12 lakhs			
		Total	12,00,000	12,00,000	
		BOMBAY (GUJARAT)			
17.	Surat	**First Priority**			
		(i) RCC piled jetty extension 8000 Sft. @ Rs. 80/- per Sft.	6,40,000	6,40,000	
		(ii) Water supply arrangement	20,000	20,000	
		(iii) Electric lighting	20,000	20,000	
		(iv) Three-ton fixed hand crane	30,000	30,000	
		(v) Transit shed 100 feet × 50 feet @ Rs. 16/- per Sft.	80,000	80,000	
		(vi) Office and residence	1,00,000	1,00,000	
		(vii) Three-ton fixed hand crane	30,000	30,000	
		(viii) One 150 H.P. tug for towing sailing craft	2,50,000	2,50,000	
		Total	12,60,000	12,60,000	

1	2	3	4	5	6
			Rs.	Rs.	
		Second Priority			
		(i) Staff quarters Class III-Four Nos. 60,000 Class IV-Two ,, 15,000 Rs. 75,000	75,000	75,000	
		(ii) Navigational aids	1,00,000	1,00,000	
		Total	1,75,000	1,75,000	
19.	Bhavnagar	**First Priority**			
		(i) Improving lock gate working	34,40,000	34,40,000	
		(a) Three additional wharping dolphins at the entrance on the south and two wharping dolphins on the north with cat-walk 15,00,000			
		(b) Channel marking buoys on each side of the channel for a distance of about two miles south from the entrance to the concrete jetty at Rs. 30,000/- for each buoy 2,40,000			
		(c) Two electric capstans at the entrance having a pull of 10-12 tons. 1,00,000			
		(d) 750 HP twin screw Kort nozzle tug of about 10-12 tons Bollard pull 16,00,000			
		Rs. 34,40,000			
		(ii) Four Nos. fork lift trucks	2,40,000	2,40,000	
		Total	36,80,000	36,80,000	
		Second Priority			
		(i) Lighterage arrangements in the new dock at concrete jetty	23,45,000	23,45,000	
		(a) Two mooring dolphins 2,00,000			
		(b) Arrangements for lighterage work to accommodate four barges along with certain work of retention of earth 6,45,000			
		(c) Two portal cranes for jetty and two $1\frac{1}{2}$ ton cranes for lighterage wharf 5,00,000			

1	2	3	4	5	6
			Rs.	Rs.	
		(d) Dredging for turning basin and mooring 10,00,000			
		Rs. 23,45,000			
		(ii) Residential accommodation for staff	6,00,000	6,00,000	
		(a) Class II- 1 No. 29,800			
		(b) Class III A Thiee Nos. of two units-accommodation for six-63,200			
		(c) Class III B-eight Nos. of two unit-accommodation for 16—1,48,000			
		(d) Class IV—38 of two units accommodation for 76— 3,57,000			
		Total say Rs. 6,00,000			
		(iii) Repair facilities at concrete jetty	80,000	80,000	
		(iv) Augmenting water supply from the city mains	7,00,000	7,00,000	
		(v) Post office building at concrete jetty	3,00,000	3,00,000	
		Total	40,25,000	40,25,000	
		Third Priority			
		Shifting sailing craft and lighterage facilities from "steel jetty" to Akwada Creek when the "steel jetty" creck silts.	12,50,000	12,50,000	
20.	Veraval	**First Priority**			
		(i) Four Nos. electric wharf cranes (1½ tones to three tones)	5,00,000	5,00,000	
		(ii) 350 H.P. tug	4,50,000	4,50,000	
		(iii) Warehouses—50,000 Sft Rs. 12/- @ per Sft	6,00,000	6,00,000	
		Total	15,50,000	15,50,000	
		Second Priority			
		(i) 4 Nos. Electric wharf cranes (1½ tons to three tons)	5,00,000	5,00,000	
		(ii) Workshop equipment	75,000	75,000	
		(iii) 600 tons of lighterage capacity	4,80,000	4,80,000	
		(iv) Staff quarters	6,00,000	6,00,000	

1	2	3	4	5	6
			Rs.	Rs.	
		(a) Class II-one No. Rs. 29,820 (b) Class III A-three Nos. of two units 63,200 (c) Class III B-eight Nos. of two units 1,48,900 (d) Class IV—38 Nos. of two units Rs. 3,57,000 Total Say Rs. 6,00,000			
		(v) Road and rail siding two miles in length	4,00,000	4,00,000	
		(vi) Warehouses—50,000 Sft @ Rs. 12/-per Sft.	6,00,000	6,00,000	
		Total say	26,50,000	26,50,000	
21.		**PORBANDAR**			
		First Priority			
		(i) A lighter wharf 685 ft in length	8,60,000	8,60,000	
		(ii) Provision of mobile wharf crane	2,00,000	2,00,000	
		(iii) Road to new wharf	1,20,000	1,20,000	
		(iv) Provision of heavy lift arrangement	1,50,000	1,50,000	
		(v) Additional lighterage capacity of 400 tons	3,20,000	3,20,000	
		(iv) Extension of the port yard lighting and water supply to the new site			
		Total	19,00,000	19,00,000	
		Second Priority			
		(i) Providing railway siding in newly developed sites on the opposite shore	3,00,000	3,00,000	
		(ii) Staff quarters	6,00,000	6,00,000	
		(a) Class II-one No. Rs. 29,820 (b) Class III A three Nos. of two units-accommodation for 6, 63,200 (c) Class III B-eight Nos. two units-accommodation for 16 1,48,000 (d) Class IV 38 Nos. of two units-accommodation for 76 3,57,100 Total say Rs. 6,00,000			

1	2	3	4	5	6
			Rs.	Rs.	
		(iii) Additional lighterage capacity	2,00,000	2,00,000	
		Total	11,00,000	11,00,000	
22.	Okha	**First Priority**			
		(i) Oil tanker berth	16,00,000	16,00,000	
		(ii) Transit shed	5,00,000	5,00,000	
		(iii) Passenger jetty on Okha side	3.50,000	3,50,000	
		Total	24,50,000	24,50,000	
		Second Priority			
		(i) Shunting locomotive	40,000	40,000	
		(ii) 72,000 sft. of storage shed	8,00,000	8,00,000	
		(iii) Reclamation for increase working space for bauxite	1,50,000	1,50,000	
		(iv) Replacing the existing dockyard railway siding with new standard 51 lbs. rails as per railway code.	3,50,000	53.0,000	
		(v) Two fixed fore and a ft. moorings	2,00,000	2,00,000	
		(vi) Workshop equipment (2-air-compressors, a welding set and tools)	1,30,000	1,30,000	
		(vii) Lighting arrangements in the dockyard	1,50,000	1,50,000	
		Total say	18,20,000	18,20,000	
23.	Sika	**First Priority**			
		(i) Lighterage capacity of 600 tons	4,80,000	4,80,000	
		(ii) A shallow draft twin screw tug of 350 BHP	3,00,000	3,00,000	
		Total say	8,00,000	8,00,000	
24.	Bedi	**First Priority**			
		(i) Improving the approach creek by dredging	7,50,000	7,50,000	
		(ii) Replacement of one towing tug of 350 B.H.P.	4,50,000	4,50,000	
		Total	12,00,000	12,00,000	

1	2	3	4	5	6
		Second Priority			
			Rs.	Rs.	
		(i) Railway siding to new wharf constructed during the second plan.	1,80,000	1,80,000	
		(ii) Providing road surfacing of the dockyard road including new roads to the newly development site	2,50,000	2,50,000	
		(iii) Addition to the existing strength of lighters by 800 ton capacity	6,40,000	6,40,000	
		(iv) Replacement of one towing tug of 350 B. H. P.	4,50,000	4,50,000	
		(v) Lighting arrangements in the new area and in the labour colony	60,000	60,000	
		Total	15,80,000	15,80,000	
25. General					
		First Priority			
		(i) Dredger for internal dredging with ancillary craft.	15,00,000	15,00,000	
		Total	15,00,000	15,00,000	

Statewise Abstract Indicating Priorities For Each State

Sl. No.	State	For Priorities	
		First Priority Amount in Rs. Lakhs	Second Priority Amount in Rs. Lakhs
1.	Orissa	99.00	55.30
2.	Andhra Pradesh	42.00	23.80
3.	Madras	87.00	50.05
4.	Kerala	137.06	15.28
5.	Mysore	63.00	161.40
6.	Bombay (Maharashtra)	37.40	2.00
7.	Bombay (Gujarat)	155.50	113.50
	Total	621.00	422.00

N. B.—Figures rounded to the nearest lakh.

Appendix XIV

Estimate For The Development Of Tuticorin Into A 30 ft. Harbour, With Four Alongside Berths Two For Coal, One For Salt And One For General Cargo.

Sl. No.	Items	Quantity or No.	Rate Rs.	Unit	Amount Rs. lakhs	Total
1	2	3	4	5	6	7
1.	Preliminary expenses including road to quarry	L.S	—	—	10.00	
2.	Acquisition of land for rail and road approaches	L.S.	—	—	3.00	
3.	Dredging in turning basin and berth—					
	(a) in ordinary soil	67,770 c. yds.	3.00	c. yds.	2.03	
	(b) in rock	25,96,800 c. ft.	1.50	c. ft.	38.95	
*4.	Construction of reclamation wall including filling with dredged material	—	—	—	352.31	
5.	Construction of breakwaters Noses	2,350 ft.	5,850	1 ft.	137.43	
6.	Construction of Quay	2 Nos.	27.73	lakh each	55.46	
		2, 200 rft.	5,000	1. ft.	110.00	
7.	Navigational aids	L.S.	—	—	1.60	
8.	Transit sheds	60,000 sq. ft.	18/-	sq. ft.	10.80	
9.	Workshop building	27,500 sq. ft.	12/-	sq. ft.	3.30	
10.	Construction of Dry Dock 200′×50′ — sill — 14.00	—	—	—	8.50	
11.	Approach road	9 miles	2 lakhs	mile	18.00	
12.	Internal roads	L.S.	—	—	5.00	
13.	Railway access	10 miles	2 lakhs	Do	20.00	
14.	Construction of warehouse	48,000 sq. ft.	18/-	sq. ft.	8.64	
15.	Railway Sidings and Marshalling yards	L.S.	—	—	20.00	
16.	Cranes					
	(a) Wharf cranes—3 tons capacity	7 Nos.	3 lakhs	each	21.00	
	(b) Wharf cranes—5 ton capacity	1 No.	5 lakhs	each	5.00	
	(c) do-Mobile crane 10 ton capacity	1 No.	3 lakhs	each	3.00	
	(d) For handling Tetrapods and Boulders 5 cranes—2 tons capacity	2 Nos.	5 lakhs	each	10.00	
17.	Purchase of Tugs					
	(a) 1000 HP Twin Screw Diesel tug filled with fire fighting and					

*For details see at the end of Appendix.

1	2	3	4	5	6	7
	salvage arrangements	1 Nos.	20 lakhs	each	20.00	
	(b) 800 HP Twin Screw Diesel tug	1 No.	15 lakhs	each	15.00	
18.	Survey launch	1 No,	1.3 lakhs	each	1.30	
19.	Rock breaker and dipper dredger	1 No.	—	—	20.00	
20.	Grab dredger	1 No.	—	—	15.00	
21.	Dumb hopper barges 100 ton capacity	6. Nos.	1.5 lakh	each	9.00	
22.	Tug for hopper barges 150—H.P.—2 Nos.	2. Nos.	3 lakh	each	6.00	
23.	Narrow gauge Railway truck	3 miles	80,000	mile	2.40	
24.	Diesel locomotives	2 Nos.	36,000	each	0.72	
25.	(a) Tipping wagons	50 Nos.	3,000	each	1.50	
	(b) Flat wagons for tetrapods	20 Nos.	3,000	each	0.60	
26.	Diving boat and diving equipment	L.S.	—	—	2.00	
27.	Mooring Boat	3 Nos.	10,000	each	0.30	
28.	Workshop machinery	L.S.	—	—	7.00	
29.	Office Building	L.S.	—	—	5.00	
30.	Water supply	L.S.	—	—	10.00	
31.	Electricity	L.S.	—	—	10.00	
32.	Stacking area	7,20,000 sq. ft.	130/-	100 sq.ft.	9.36	
33.	Drainage	L.S.	—	—	1.50	
34.	Maintenance during construction	L.S.	—	—	5.00	
35.	Pilot Launch	1 No.	—	—	1.50	
					987.25	
	3 per cent contingencies				29.62	
		Total			1016.87	
	1 per cent Workcharged Establishment				10.17	
		Grand Total say			1027.00	

Location	Distance	Rate	Amount
From—30 to—27	1640 ft.	Rs. 5,400/- 1. ft.	88,56,000
From—27 to—26	560 ft.	@ Rs. 5,160/- 1. ft.	28,9,8600
From—26 to—25	600 ft.	@ Rs. 4,250/- 1. ft.	25,50,000
From—25 to—24	540 ft.	@ Rs. 2,960/- 1. ft.	15,98,400
From—24 to—18	3000 ft.	@ Rs. 2,625/- 1. ft.	78,75,000
Prom—18 to—12	3600 ft.	@ Rs. 2,150/- 1. ft.	77,40,000
From—12 to— 6	800 ft.	@ Rs, 1,645/- 1. ft.	13,16,000
From— 6 to shore	1800 ft.	@ Rs. 760/- 1. ft.	13,78,000
Front wall	1200 ft.	@ Rs. 825/-	10,38,000
		Total	352,81,000
			or
			352.31 lakhs

Appendix XXIV

A. The economics of developing an all-weather port at Mangalore for 34 ft. draft steamers with three alongside berths.

The basis adopted for the following estimates are:-

(a) Receipts on Wet Docks and wharves based on the prevailing rates (handing and shipping fees and wharfage) for Cochin Port.

(b) Receipts from Railway Department, Lands and Buildings and Port Department are derived from the receipts at Cochin Port for the year 1956-57 in the proportion of cargo proposed to be handled at Mangalore to that of Cochin for the year 1956-57.

(c) Expenditure under the heads Administration, Port Department, Traffic Operations, Other Maintenance, Pensions, Provident Funds, Other items, Rent, Rates, etc., Police, and Audit fees, derived on the expenditure at Cochin Port during 1956-57 in the proportion of cargo proposed to be handled at Mangalore to that of Cochin for the year 1956-57.

1. Wet docks and wharves: Rs. 35.67 lakhs

	Quantity Tons	Rate	Amount Rs. in Lakhs
Receipts			
Steamer Traffic*,			
(a) Existing traffic (excluding ore, cashew nuts, coffee, and general cargo).	40,000	4.50 (average)	1.8
(b) Increase due to all-weather working	20,000	4.50 (average)	.9
(c) Traffic from Bhadravati and Bangalore area.	1,00,000	4.5 (average)	4.5
(d) Diverted traffic from other ports.	50,000	4.5 (average)	2.25
(e) Foodgrain and fertilisers.	75,000	4.13	3.10
(f) Misc. general cargo.	15,000	4.5	.68
(g) Iron ore including loading by mechanical ore loading plant.	20,00,000	7.0	140.00
B. Sailing vessel traffic. General Cargo	3,00,000	1.0	3.00
2. Lands and buildings.			16.54
3. Railway Department.			19.06
4. Port Department			11.22
5. Miscellaneous.			5.42
			208.47
Expenditure			
1. Administration.			4.23
2. Port Department.			8.80
3. Traffic Operations.			18.19
4. Dredging.			†15.00
5. Other maintenance.			12.31
6. Pensions.			0.28
7. Provident Fund contributions.			2.51
8. Other items.			6.17

*As estimated by the Committee.

†This assumes maintenance dredging of one million tons at the rate of Rs. 1.50 per ton. This will vary in the light of actual experience.

1	2	3	4	5	6
9.	Rents, Rates, etc.			0.12	
10.	Police.			1.63	
11.	Audit fee.			0.50	
12.	Interest on capital at 45 percent (on Rs. 12.8 crores).			57.15	
13.	Add for depreciation (50 years) 11.3 crores at 2 percent, 1.5 crores at 4 percent.			28.40	
14.	Operation cost of mechanical ore loading plant.			10.00	
		Total expenditure:		165.29	
		Net annual revenue:		43.18	

MANGANESE POISONING ENQUIRY COMMITTEE, 1958—REPORT

Delhi, Manager of Publications, 1961. 143p.+ivp.

Chairman : Dr. M.L. Rawal.

Members : Dr. M.N. Rao, Dr. N.H. Wadia; Dr. T.P. Niyogi; Dr. M.N. Gupta; Dr. M.K. Chakraborty; Dr. B.K. Sengupta;

APPOINTMENT

The Manganese Poisoning Enquiry Committee was constituted under the Ministry of Labour and Emloyment vide their letter No.MI-41 (74)/56, dated November 3, 1958.

TERMS OF REFERENCE

(i) A complete investigation of causation, extent, diagnosis and treatment of the different varieties of manganese poisoning found in the workers of the manganese mines in India; and

(ii) To advise on the preventive measures that may be enforced.

CONTENTS

Formation of the Committee; Scope of Enquiry; Manganese Mining Industry; Manganese Miner and His Environment; Manganese Intoxication—Clinical Manifestations; Manganese Intoxication—Special Investigation; Discussion; Recommendations; Acknowledgement; References; Appendices I to III; List of figures; List of Tables.

RECOMMENDATIONS

Dry drilling must be stopped at all costs and wet drilling introduced compulsorily both underground and at surface.

In general, dust control methods are strongly recommended wherever a hazard exists.

In underground mining practices, the following ventilation standards are tentatively recommended:

(a) Maximum permissible concentration of six mgm. manganese dust per cubic metre of air.

(b) A minimnm air velocity of 50 ft. per minute at the work faces and dead ends at points not more than five feet away from the worker.

(c) As a check, periodic dust and ventilation surveys of the underground environment should be done.

All manganese mines should have suitably qualified medical officers whole time or part time.

All management personnel in the manganese mining should be conversant with the occupational risks in the industry.

Periodical medical examination of all miners should be done and adequate records maintained.

As soon as early diagnostic symptoms and signs are recognised, the worker should be withdrawn from his dusty environment to a suitable surface job and the proper authority notified.

Treatment

The Committee feels that there is no specific remedy for the disease and the affected patients should be rehabilitated in new occupations suitable to their physical condition.

Treatment with Calcium EDTA was given to patients both orally and intravenously without any remarkable success. Parpanit given orally gave considerable symptomatic relief and made walking and movements easier. The beneficial effects of the treatment lasted only as long as the drug was given. Physiotherapy and occupational therapy were useful adjutants in the rehabilitation of these patients. Details of treatment attempted are given in case records.

Manganese poisoning in the mining industry should be made a compensable disease under Schedule III of the Workmen's Compensation Act, relating the extent of compensation to the neurological damage.

COMMITTEE ON GENERAL EDUCATION, 1958—REPORT

New Delhi, University Grants Commission, 1961. 89p.+vp.

Chairman : Shri S. Govindarajulu.
Members : Shri G. C. Bannerjee; Shri S.V. Kogekar; Shri R. Enoch; Prof. Hans Simons.
Secretary : Dr. P.J. Philip.

APPOINTMENT

In December, 1958, while considering requests from Aligarh and Baroda Universities for financial assistance to their programmes of general education, the University Grants Commission suggested that some principles should be evolved in order to assess their needs for additional staff and other facilities. Since several other universities had also decided to introduce general education courses, the Commission desired that a Committee consisting mainly of persons who had first-hand knowledge of the principles and practice of general education be appointed for considering requirements in this behalf in the universities. Accordingly the Commission appointed a Committee.

TERMS OF REFERENCE

To go into the whole question of general education in Indian Universities.

CONTENTS

Preface; Introduction: Background of General Education in India; Present Position of General Education in India; Place of General Education in Indian Higher Education; Observations and Recommendations; Summary and Resulting Recommendations; Appendices I to VII; Bibliography.

RECOMMENDATIONS

Observations And Recommendations General Objectives

One of our assumptions is that general education, as an ally of good education, should be thought of in terms of appropriate educational experiences and development of rational skills and outlook rather than in terms of courses, prescriptions and examinations. Two extreme positions can be taken with regard to this assumption. One view is that general education ought to concentrate on contemporary and the personal problems of students. Another view is that the programme of general education will drift to inconsequential chatter about trivialities without some basic requirements and prescribed courses. The Committee believes that it should be possible to achieve the objectives of general education without subscribing to either of the two extremes. Prescribing basic requirements and courses does not necessarily vitiate the aims of general education; what matters ultimately is how the prescribed courses are taught and by whom.

Most discussions on the philosophy and principles of general education are based on the assumption that integration of the personality of student is possible by integrating the three broad areas of knowledge, viz., the Humanities, the Physical and Natural Sciences and the Social Sciences. This assumption has been challenged on the ground that integration imposed from above or outside may not be meaningful to a student because it may be irrelevant to his present problems and not tuned with his mental equipment. The Committee, while in agreement with the substance of this argument, nevertheless believes that a certain measure of integration of thought, emotions and loyalties is possible if the learner is helped to organise and reorganise his experiences not only around his need to be a socially effective individual but also around his individual and personal needs. All educational effort is based on the postulate that modification of behaviour is possible through education. The snag here is not that integration of personality is impossible through integration of knowledge but that the teacher who is imparting integrated knowledge may not always be an integrated personality.

Again it does not seen necessary to wait till "integration" of knowledge takes place in an individual. All the three broad areas of knowledge have a distinctive contribution to make to the growth of human personnality. Study of sciences should help the students to understand and use the scientific method, to cultivate an active interest in the whole of the physical and biological world and to understand the impact of science on human thoughts and activities. Study of the Humanities should transmit the achievements of the human spirit and enable a student to discover their relevance to contemporary life. Study of the social sciences should promote an understanding of society and of the forces which have brought about its present complexity; it should also produce an awareness of the social "facts" which are too often loaded with prejudice and emotional overtones. As the Radhakrishnan Commission Report suggests, in each field the student should get his bearings, learn the basic vocabulary, become acquainted with the central concepts and with illustrations of cases and should be on the way to life-long interest and self-education in each field. Integration or synthesis of knowledge may be the ultimate ideal; a more practical aim, however, seems to be an honest and intelligent pursuit of the disciplines that underlie each area of knowledge.

Sometimes fears are expressed that imposition of general education on the three-year degree course may result in superficiality, dissipation of interests, lack of standards and insufficient illumination. The Committee realise that it is obviously impossible for a student who has spent three years on a study of, say, Physics and General Education courses to have covered as much ground as intensively in Physics as a student who has spent three years on a study of Physics alone. But it is also to be realised that mere length of time spent on the study of a subject is not a guarantee of intellectual attainment, and judgement has to be made on the quality of work of the student and the teacher. Actually in the hands of competent teachers, general education may prove an ally to specialisation. The kind of discipline inherent in a given area of knowledge may act as a catalyst in the study of another area of knowledge. For instance, it has been observed that science cannot be at its best without a critical understanding of language. We think largely with the use of words and unless the scientist learns to use and organise words effectively, thinking of the scientists may lack precision and accuracy. Again, an engineer may be a better engineer if besides building a bridge of technical perfection, he also understands the social change likely to be brought about by the bridge between two communities on either side of a river. As the American Society for Engineering Education observed in its Report on Evaluation of Engineering Education (1952-55): "Engineering education must contribute to the development of men who can face new and difficult engineering situations with imagination and competence. Meeting such situations invariably involves both professional and social responsibilities."

General education would not be worth having if it undermined in any way specialisation of a high order. We envisage general education to create a milieu in which the speciality can develop its fullest possibilities, and to create that balance and background which can improve the specialists pursuit of creative activity. As the 'Journal of General Education' (Oct. 1947) put it, "Even the success of the most competent specialist depends upon general capacities. The man of deep understanding, of rich culture, of flexible mind will not long be at a disadvantage in competition with those who have merely acquired a vast amount of technical information. The dramatically swift success of the narrowly trained practitioner is ultimately over-shadowed by the achievement of the person of philosophic grounding." If the programme of general education is properly conceived and imaginatively executed by skilful and experienced teachers, it may generate an intellectual climate in which the creative genius of Indian specialists of all kinds will have a chance to grow and flourish.

Methods Of Implementing Specific Objectives

Both the lecture and discussion methods can be used with advantage for imparting general education. Discussion may, as it too often does, degenerate into a series of brief uninformed lectures and the lecture may turn into an uninterrupted monologue. It is well to remember here that even the best method will not avail much in the hands of a bad teacher. The real aim of education, it will be admitted, is to enliven the imagination of the student, to help him discriminate between valid and invalid conclusions and to put him on the path of discovering and integrating knowledge for himself. A skilful teacher can do so either by the lecture method, or by the discussion method or by both in combination. In fact and indeed a really inspired teacher could use all the tools that modern developments in science and education have placed at his disposal.

The Committee therefore feel that the pivotal problem of general education, as indeed of all education, is the teacher on whom will depend the success or the failure of the scheme. Relegating the programme of general education exclusively to junior members of the staff or to new recruits is to work a process whose failure can easily be foreseen. It is just not enough to have an Expert Committee at the top and entrust the execution of the programme to junior or new teachers. To the question who should teach courses in general education we have no ready answer. But, it should not be difficult to visualise a happy situation in which the really top-men in a university find time to make the programme a success. The Committee would cite the instance of Dr. S. Radhakrishnan who when he was the Vice-Chancellor of Banaras Hindu University, used to give weekly discourses on the Gita.

Development Of Language Skills

Curricular requirements in our universities have

undergone marked changes during the last fifty years or so. Till about the appearance of the Sadler Commission Report, the general pattern of course in the school and the first two years of the colleges in India was one of compulsory core subjects almost without any provision for electives. Even in the last two years of the college course, two languages, viz. English and an Indian classical or modern language which together accounted for half of the lecturing time, were obligatory for most of the students, the other half being available for the subjects chosen by the student. The two obligatory languages for the B.A. degree were largely intended to serve the purpose of liberal or general education. But as the reports of numerous expert committees and commissions point out, the teaching of languages has ceased to cultivate the mental attitude needed for great literature and thought. In some universities not only are languages taught merely for the purpose of passing the examination but an increasing number of science students do not have any familiarity with any language except perhaps the rudiments of English. We endorse the view of Govindarajulu Report that here is the one place where general education can repair a neglect and also revive some of the attitudes usually associated with liberal education.

The Committee is aware of the fact that even the best general education programmes will be useless, if the students have not developed adequate language skills by the time they enter the university. Enough attention is probably not given to this in schools. We recommended therefore that the pre-university class should be used for improving language skill in English and in the regional language. While importance of English is on the whole recognised, it is doubtful, whether it is taught well at the present time. In view of the increasing importance of the regional language as a medium of communication at the local and regional levels, the student should also have a greater experience of the regional language. We think that it is appropriate to combine at the pre-university level a programme of general education with the development of language skills. For example, the prescribed books in languages could include books dealing with ethical, aesthetic and spiritual values. In view of the poor standard of English of the average pre-university student, it may be desirable to have a majority of these books in the regional language while attempts are made to improve their knowledge of English through special courses.

Another reason why we recommend combined programme of languages and general education is that the workload of the pre-university class in many universities is already quite heavy. For example, besides the usual subjects, the pre-university student at Aligarh has to study Muslim Theology or Islamic Civilisation. Again, apart from English, Aligarh has also to do both Hindi and Urdu. In fact, faced by such a situation, the university has decided to give up general education courses for pre-university students from the next year. While we appreciate the special difficulty of this university, and other universities similarly placed, we still think that the experiment of imparting general education through the compulsory languages is possible and feasible.

General Education In The Three-Year Degree Course

We recommend that science students may be given the regular science course and a general education course in the Social Sciences and the Humanities. Similarly, non-science students may be given the regular course of their departments with a general education course in Science. *Inter-alia*, such a course for arts students should bring out the relation between man and his physical environment and the role that experimental and scientific methods have played in advancing the boundaries of human knowledge and man's conquest of nature. Among other things, the Social Science course for science students should attempt to emphasise the relationship between man and his social environment and cultural heritage. As another alternative, if requirements for further education do not stand in the way science students may be given instead of the normal science course a specially devised general education course in science of equal weight. Similarly, in the place of the normal course in Arts, a specially devised general education course in the Social Sciences of equal weight may be provided. Welding general education with normal arts and science courses should, however, not result in bringing down the standards of the first degree examination.

As a third alternative, some universities may find it possible to devise a common general education programme for all students. In view of the fact that General Science and the Social Studies form an integral part of the scheme of higher secondary examination courses all over the country, an experiment in this direction seems attractive. However, this possibility seems to be circumscribed by the poor standard of students at the higher secondary level.

Reading Material

The problem of selection of reading material is not easy. The present range of human knowledge is so vast that any attempt to give even a bird's eye view of it would seem to be impracticable. Selection has, therefore, to be made judiciously. Here, we would like to recommend the criterion suggested by Whitehead, "A student should not be taught more than he can think about. Selection is the essence of teaching. Even the most compendious survey is only the rudest outline from reality. Since the problem of choice can under no circumstances be avoided, the problem becomes what, rather than how much, to teach : or better, what principles and methods to illustrate by the use of information''. It should however, be remembered that general education is not about a subject but of a subject based on definite knowledge.

Production of reading materials for general education courses will reflect in many ways the philosophy and the intellectual climate of a university. For this reason, if for none other, the Committee recommends that the utmost core and thought should be given to this matter.

Further, appropriate and adequate reading material for general education courses is important for two reasons. First, if colleges can ensure that this material is actually read by the students, we shall have achieved some revival of the reading habit and more than justified the introduction of these courses. Secondly, if the reading material is chosen suitably to provide for more than one point of view on the same question, it will help students to form judgements of their own.

The Committee had an opportunity of noting the effort made by the M.S. University of Baroda to produce some reading material. This was intended by them for use in their own university. Aligarh Muslim University has, however, a much bigger scheme and has been engaged for sometime in producing material which, it was hoped, would be useful to many universities in India. It would, undoubtedly, be advantageous if the reading material produced by one university could be used by other universities wholly or in part. But, the probability is that each university or the universities in a particular region will want to produce reading material to suit their own syllabi and requirements. More important, this reading material, once produced, should not become sacrosanct and unalterable.

In Baroda and Aligarh Universities, we found two matters for comment. The small treatises which are produced for the purpose of covering a part or the whole of the syllabus in a given area do not always encourage an original and independent approach to the problems and issues in those treatises. Books of this type may also generate the feeling that the views expressed through them are the views of the university. Further, there is always the possibility of using those 'text-books' as vehicles for propagating particular views and attitudes rather than the thoughts of great men on great issues. Secondly, as experience in Baroda has shown, such treatises are open to the danger of being memorised for the purpose of the examination. And, it may not be too long before cheap bazar notes are written on these books.

These observations do not however, constitute a disapproval of lectures being written out by persons, delivering them for the benefit of their colleagues.

Assistance will have to be given to universities for producing suitable reading material for general education courses. Persons entrusted with the responsibility of selecting the reading material may be given suitable remuneration. In some cases universities might find it desirable to get the reading material transplanted into the regional languages; translators may have to be paid while ordinary printing and publishing cost may be recovered from the students.

Library And Equipment

We feel that for proper implementation of the scheme of general education it will be necessary to strengthen the libraries of the colleges as well as to provide equipment for the teaching courses in science and fine arts. We envisage a sum of Rs. 10,000 (NR) and Rs. 2,000 (R) per annum for the addition of books concerned with general education and an equal amount for equipment and audio-visual aids. These items of expenditure may be met by outright grants by the University Grants Commission and suited to the content of general education. A number of sets of the books may be provided. They should be of the kind and in the language that could be easily understood by the students. The position with regard to the Science equipment already available may have to be reviewed and additional grant given, if necessary.

Accommodation

In most colleges rooms are not available at present for holding discussion groups. We think it may be necessary to provide for four to six discussion rooms, one lecture hall, one office room and a store room for the purposes of general education. The following areas are suggested :

Discussion Rooms (four to six rooms)	1,600 sq. ft.
Large Hall (to accommodate 200 students)	2,000 ,, ,,
Store Room	400 ,, ,,
Office Room	400 ,, ,,
Total	4,400 ,, ,,

Assistance to colleges for providing accommodation as specified above may be made available by the University Grants Commission on the usual basis. The committee is of the view that the above mentioned facilities will be necessary for the proper implementation of the scheme of general education. We have noted that in many of the colleges additional space has already been provided under the three-year degree course scheme. This has, no doubt, improved conditions in various colleges but may not be quite adequate for meeting the additional needs of the courses of general education. We noted that buildings are being put up in the universities of Aligarh and Baroda with generous assistance from the Ford Foundation for the accommodation of general education courses. These buildings will, no doubt, facilitate the working of general education programmes in these two universities. We do not, however, envisage the construction of such large buildings in other universities for the purpose.

Seminars, Workshops

The Committee feel that for implementing the programme of general education it will be necessary to hold seminars in general education which would function as workshops for providing orientation and training in the technique of these courses. Responsibility for this will have to be taken by the university to which colleges are affiliated. It is understood that some universities are getting assistance for this purpose from the Ministry of Education.

Additional Teachers

To the extent to which the introduction of general education courses contributes a net increase in the teaching load of the university or college departments, it will be necessary to provide for additional staff. For determining the requirements in this regard we may take into account the size of the class, the size of the discussion group and the number of periods devoted to this work.

We envisage the following methods of teaching and discussion at the pre-university stage :

In the area in which a student has offered a general education course, he will have two lectures and one discussion class and he will have also one lecture and one discussion class in the area which is or is to be his speciality. The size of the discussion class will be 25 : each class of 100 students will be divided into four sections for the purposes of discussion. Thus an arts student will have three periods of general education in science and two periods of general education in arts. The maximum addition for a class of 100 students under this arrangement will be 11 "additional periods per week (three periods for three lectures plus two periods of discussion class for each of the four discussion groups of a class of 100 students). The net addition may actually be less as a result of any reduction in the number of subjects consequent on the introduction of general education course. For a college with 300 students in the pre-university class the net additional requirement of staff would be two or three teachers. In view of the large number of optional subjects and the consequent difficulty in getting together all students at the same time in degree colleges, the addition to the staff may be worked out on the basis of one teacher for every hundred students of the first and second year of the degree class. Thus the total additional staff requirement of a degree college of 1,000 students would be two teachers for the pre-university class with 300 students, two teachers each for first year and second year classes with 250 students in each, i.e. seven teachers in all of whom four may be senior and three junior teachers. One of the three senior teachers may coordinate the programme of general education. In addition, one lecturer who will be arranging demonstration classes, etc., may be provided, if required by the college.

We agree that for the purpose of coordination, it may be necessary to appoint a special staff of atleast three persons of whom one should be given the responsibility for coordination. In addition, it may be necessary to have a technical assistant to take care of the audio-visual and other material aids. We believe that the bulk of teachers should be drawn from the various teaching departments. As already stressed earlier, courses in general education should be given as far as possible by the senior teachers. We are not in favour of the establishment of an independent department of general education but though for purposes of coordination and guidance a general education centre may be created. We envisage general education as a bridge between departments, if it is so, an independent faculty or a separate department of general education, cannot serve the purpose.

Evaluation

Serious thought has been given in recent times to improve our system of examination but the difficulties involved are very great for any radical change to be brought about quickly. On the case of general education however, a change in the system of evaluation is intimately connected with the achievement of the objectives of general education. If the subject matter of general education courses is tested annually by a comprehensive examination, based on papers set by external examiner we shall have to contend with an additional but unnecessary load on the students and such evils as cramming and bazar notes during the final examinations. It is therefore necessary that without waiting for a change in the examination system for all the courses, we should immediately put into operation the many practical improvements that have been suggested. The first of these is that the teacher in-charge of the discussion group should carefully ascertain the reading done by the students from week to week. This may be done by making each student participate in the discussion on the weekly assignment. Secondly, a short quiz of five or seven minutes could be arranged any day without advance notice. The objective of both the discussion and the quiz will be to gauge the depth of understanding a student has reached in a given course.

It is not suggested that the final test in general

education courses should invariably be given by the internal examiners. What is suggested is that due weight, say 50 per cent of the credit in a given course, should be given to the assessment by the teacher in the class-room. This scheme may first be tried in the university colleges which are situated within the university campus or are very near to the university headquarters so that, if necessary, the university can supervise the methods of evaluation with ease and at short intervals.

We believe that it is neither feasible nor practicable to give 50 per cent weightage to the evaluation of class-room teachers in far-flung affiliated colleges. A beginning might be made with 25 per cent in the first instance on the stipulation that an officer of the university, not below the rank of a Reader, will go round the affiliated colleges to check the reliability and validity of their methods of assessment. Madras and Rajasthan Universities have similar procedures for checking the internal awards of their affiliated teachers' training colleges.

General Education in Affiliating Universities

The special problems which confront the affiliating type of universities in introducing general education or, for that matter, any reform, were brought to the notice of the Committee at Madras and Bangalore. Because of the varying quality and quantity of personnel and physical resources available in affiliated colleges, the pace of reform is usually set by those affiliated colleges which are not advantageously placed in relation to the better ones. In order to ensure that at least a minimum of standard is reached by most colleges, the affiliating university is forced to prescribe courses and standards which in the interest of unformity, have to be followed. This leaves, naturally, little room for experimentation with new methods and courses. It is not always possible to see, for example, that the library facilities are adequate in all the colleges. The success of general education, as indeed of any system of education, will be determined by the teachers of competence who are not always plentiful in the affiliated colleges. It is, therefore, necessary to be cautious in regard to developing courses of general education and in devising appropriate techniques of assessment.

While the Committee agreed that the problems peculiar to the affiliating type of universities do not lend themselves to easy and quick solution, nevertheless it is felt that these universities could improve their supervisory role in relation to prescribed requirements. At least some of the better colleges could be entrusted with making experiments both in the development of courses and appropriate test materials for general education. Alternatively a few affiliated colleges in a limited neighbourhood could pool their physical and personnel resources and introduce whatever reforms were possible. The university could also encourage the experiment by providing (a) visiting teachers, (b) books and reference materials and (c) guidance from experts appointed for the purpose. With such supervision from the headquarters colleges or groups of colleges could be helped to create the necessary conditions for a successful implementation of the general education programme.

Affiliating universities with a university college need not feel obliged in our opinion to have the same pattern of general education as in the affiliated colleges. In fact, we think that the university college may adopt a different system which may include experimentation in the same way in which a unitary university can do it. The experience gained by the university college and the persons who have that experience will be helpful to the affiliated colleges to improve their own methods. The trained personnel from the university college can also help in holding periodical tests to minimise the disadvantages of a cumulative external examination. We also suggest that the university may first organise periodical seminars for the mutual exchange of ideas and experiences etc., between teachers of the university college and teachers of the affiliated colleges.

Summary And Resulting Recommendations

Objectives Of General Education

General education concerns itself with a concept of education rather than with the content of courses; it is a different method of teaching and to some extent of learning; it is an approach to knowledge rather than the imparting of knowledge itself; it emphasises the generic rather than the particular. It is a complimentary, not a self-sufficient part of university education, meant to prepare the modern citizen, It emphasises the active more than the contemplative part which the student has to play in it.

Intellectually, general education should evoke curiosity and develop it into a searching interest; it should arouse questions that lead to knowledge, and only eventually to the forming of opinion; it should sharpen reason for controlling emotions and where possible develop controlled emotion into creativity.

General education should lead the student to an awareness of himself and of the place which through his profession he will occupy in relation to his society. It should help him to acquire what may be called an "outlook on life" or a "philosophy of life".

General education should make students understand that learning is a continuous process which does not stop with the earning of a degree. It should also prepare students to develop a spirit of enquiry and intelligent formulation of their doubts and quests and to acquire sufficient information about where to look for answers.

It should instil in students a respect for facts, data and available sources as well as an awareness of problems of human existence which may not be solved through the ordinary process of reasoning.

General Education As An Integral Part Of The Required Curriculum

It is essential that the so-called general education courses are made a regular part of the curriculum. This implies that they take the place of either compulsory or selective courses and that at least a passing mark earned through appropriate tests will be a pre-requisite for admission to the final B.A. or B.Sc. examination.

It is preferable to develop general education courses out of courses that are at present part of the prescribed curriculum for the B.A. or B.Sc. programme. This necessitates some reorganisation of the curriculum, so that general education is imparted through regular course-work in each particular area and also through additional course-work in those areas which are not read at principal level. There is ample opportunity for such changes in the programme for the pre-university year as well as the first and second year of the courses for the first degree examination.

Pilot Projects In General Education

After general education courses have been introduced as a required and regular part of the curriculum for the first degree examination, an attempt should be made to select a few well-established colleges which would be given the freedom to develop courses of general education and to devise a system of reliable and valid internal assessment. Such projects could be initiated in unitary universities where senior members of all faculties are easily available for consultation and guidance. The affiliating universities could start such pilot projects in some selected colleges in a limited neighbourhood where all their resources could be pooled and help could also be secured from the university headquarters in the form of (i) reference materials, (ii) audio-visual aids, (iii) visiting teachers from various faculties; and (iv) advice from experts in the field. Courses and methods of assessment of general education would be open to review in the light of experience gained from these pilot projects.

Organisation Of A General Education Centre

General education will not amount to much unless somebody is fully responsible for its development. Therefore it is essential that universities and colleges which introduce general education establish a general education 'centre' (or whatever it is named) with a limited number of members who give their major attention to this work and who undertake the coordination of the total programme in consultation with the representatives of the different departments of study who, in turn, should be willing to form a reservoir of participants for it.

Nobody in this 'centre' should be concerned exclusively with general education. On the contrary all teachers in general education should remain members of their respective departments, participate in their departmental work, offer courses within the regular curriculum and use departmental research facilities. But in the case of those teachers who devote a major part of their time to general education, the head of the general education centre has to judge their performance and propose their advancement within the university.

The head of the general education set-up does not have to devote himself exclusively to this task. However, unless there is a responsible co-ordinator authorized to call on all faculty members for co-operation, general education cannot make much headway. Unless the senior faculty members are encouraged or if need be persuaded to participate, general education will not have its proper academic status and those participating in it will not have the prestige and security without which they cannot make a success of it.

Even a small college can designate a representative for each of the three major areas (Science, Social Sciences, Humanities) who will form a general education centre and design a programme that the college can carry out. In the universities (unitary universities or headquarters of affiliating universities) this "department" may have a larger number of teachers depending on actual needs.

Reading Material For General Education Courses

Judging from experience in India and elsewhere it is unlikely that general education can be taught with the help of text-books. Even if they can be written and made available they would very soon be out of date, because for a number of years general education in the Indian setting will have to be experimental, flexible and open to revision. Some of the expected results are attainable only by the method of trial and error. This does not mean that there is no need for reading, listening and viewing material (audio-visual aids) all of which is not readily available, but has to be assembled or freshly prepared for the purpose.

Unless it is possible to whet the intellectual appetite of the students for inquiries into the different fields of human knowledge and their interdependence, they will not start reading original sources. Furthermore, unless tests and quizzes cover a broader field than is dealt with in lectures and cyclostyled material, students will not realise the difference between the traditional course circumscribed by the traditional examinations, and the type of knowledge and understanding which tests in general education are meant to foster.

The Teacher Of General Education

Even more than in any other area of the academic enterprise, in general education the teacher is all important. Therefore, it is essential that all ranks participate in this new effort and that it be regarded as a valuable and deserving activity for an academic teacher. The relative isolation of the several departments has to be pierced for this purpose, Flexibility in planning and tolerance in evaluation, mutual visits of teachers to each others classrooms, regular consultation on teaching methods and results, and discussion of student problems in general education have to be part of the duties which the participants must be willing to assume.

Since the general education programme will involve re-examination of the syllabi as well as a completely new working out of lectures and seminars all teachers in general education should for at least the first year be relieved of two hours, for each hour they are engaged in general education, so that they can devote more time to the careful preparation of their new task.

Equally important is the recognition the teacher gets for his efforts in general education. Even though he remains with his department he cannot give it as much time and attention as those who do not participate in general education work. Therefore, he has to be assured that good teaching will be rated equally with publication and research as qualifying him for academic promotion.

Seminars And Workshops

The faculty members who will participate in the general education programme should meet for a seminar during the long vocation. Experienced general education teachers from institutions already engaged in this activity may be invited as advisers. The purpose of such seminars and workshops will be *inter-alia* (a) to discuss the aims and objectives of general education in the changing social order of India, (b) to spell out these objectives in terms of behavioural changes in respect of social, intellectual and academic issues, (c) to discuss the problems arising out of the actual execution of current programmes, (d) to review the materials prescribed or recommended for general education courses, (e) to discuss new experiments in the field, (f) to devise methods of evaluating reaction of students, and (g) to evaluate the success of the programme in relation to accepted aims and objectives.

Assistance By The University Grants Commission Towards General Education Programmes

The Commission may assist colleges and universities in a suitable manner or as indicated in this report in some or all of the following areas :

(a) Cost of conferences and seminars;

(b) Cost of additional teachers,

(c) Cost of translation of reading material needed for general education courses;

(d) Cost of printing or cyclostyling such material which may be later recovered if students pay for such material;

(e) Mechanical equipment like projector, tape-recorder, phonographs, etc., and material like slides, records etc., needed for it;

(f) Additions to the library, selected strictly for general education purposes and kept separate and easily accessible for students working in general education;

(g) Minimum office equipment and small secretarial staff for general education centres at universities and colleges;

(h) Cost of additional rooms and a hall for discussion and general sessions.

Standing Advisory Committee On General Education

The Committee venture to suggest the establishment by the University Grants Commission of a permanent advisory Committee on general education which among other functions might:

(a) Review applications for support in general education with regard to basic principles of educational policy;

(b) Encourage experimentation by universities and even individual colleges, whether constituent or affiliated, within the broad limits proposed in this report;

(c) Review regularly the progress of significant general education experiments and suggest changes in academic and educational policy.

(d) Participate in regional or central conferences.

1959

AGRICULTURAL PRODUCTION TEAM, 1959—REPORT

(Report on India's Food Crisis and Steps to Meet it) New Delhi, Ministry of Food and Agriculture and Ministry of Community Development and Cooperation, 1959. 259p. (Sponsored by the Ford Foundation)

Chairman : Dr. Sherman E. Johnson.

Members : Dr. Marvin A. Anderson; Dr. George M. Beal; Dr. E.M. Cralley; Mr. Gerald Huffman; Dr. A.A. Johnson; Dr. Omer J. Kelley; Dr. Charles E. Kellogg; Dr. Harold Miles; Miss Ellen L. Moline; Mr. Frank K. Naegely; Dean Arthur D. Weber; Dr. Norman Wengert.

APPOINTMENT

The Agriculture Production Team sponsored by the Ford Foundation was constituted under the Ministry of Food and Agriculture and Ministry of Community Development and Cooperation in 1959.

TERMS OF REFERENCE

To study India's food production problems and targets.

CONTENTS

Preface; The Crucial Decisions; **Part I**—The Need for Emergency Measures; **Part II**—Action Highlights; Enabling Village Farmers to Increase Production (Better Economic and Administrative Arrangements; Better Use of Physical and Biological Resources); **Part III**—The Role of Cooperatives in Increasing Food Production—Credit, Supplies and Marketing; Economic Intelligence and Outlook; Some Problems of Foodgrains Marketing; Research in Agricultural Economics; General Comments on Research and Education; Improving Extension Work Through Community Development; Soil and Water Conservation, including Water Use; Chemical Fertilizers; Improvements in Cereal Production, including Plant Protection; Multiplication and Distribution of Improved Seeds; The Promise of Hybrid Maize; Livestock Development and Food Production; Agricultural implements and Mechanisation; Changing Food Habits; Programme

Research and Evaluation; Experimental Projects; Appendix.

RECOMMENDATIONS

The Crucial Decisions

The Third Plan Target

A Third Plan target of 110 million tons of food grains by 1965-66 is reasonable, in view of India's rapidly rising population.

The Impending Gap

If India's food production increases no faster than present rates, the gap between supplies and target will be 28 million tons by 1965-66. This will be about 25 per cent shortfall in terms of need. No conceivable programme of imports or rationing can meet a crisis of this magnitude.

The Need For Emergency Action

A 110-million-ton target, however, can be realised only if an all-out emergency food production programme is undertaken. Food production must be given the highest priorty. It must have the sponsorship of topmost leaders who can and will mobilise the nation for action to meet the impending crisis.

The Need For Stabilisaticn Of Farm Prices

Recommended incentives for increased production are :

(a) A guaranted minimum price announced in advance of the planting season.

(b) A market within bullock-cart distance that will pay the guaranteed price when the cultivator has to sell.

(c) **Suitable Local Storage**—Immediate consideration should be given to using funds available from grain imports under PL-480 and other special programmes to construct needed godowns in village areas.

A Public Works Programme For Increasing Food Production And Village Employment

The Team recommends a public works programme for projects requiring primarily hand labour, such as contour bunding, land levelling, surface drainage, irrigation wells and tanks.

Priorities For Chemical Fertilisers

Procurement of fertilisers and means of producing high-analysis fertilisers be given a top priority, including foreign exchange as necessary.

Intensified Irrigation And Drainage Programmes

India can make greater and more immediate gains in food production by intensifying expenditure of time and effort on water management than by constructing large-scale irrigation projects which take years to develop. The Team recommends that the Third Plan allocate substantial funds for technical assistance to aid cultivators in making better use of available water. Provision must also be made for a more comprehensive approach with coordination of all relevant departments. More emphasis be placed on irrigation projects which will yield rapid returns in food production, such as tube wells and shallow masonry wells.

Millions of acres could be reclaimed and made more productive by drainage improvement. The Team recommends that drainage improvement be given a high priority, and believes that a unified agency is necessary in each state for coordination and improvement of drainage.

Selection Of Certain Crops And Certain Areas For More Intensive Efforts

That those selected crops and those selected areas in each State should be chosen which have the greatest increase potentialities.

Efforts to stimulate food production should be directed more heavily to *rice* and *wheat*, which now make up more than half of total foodgrains. With hybrid maize, India can in five to seven years make more progress in increasing yields than the U.S.A. made in 20 years.

More effort should be concentrated on the most promising areas for wheat and rice production, i.e., those which have had the most rapid rate of increase in the recent past, and which have also the highest potential for rapid large increases in the years immediately ahead. For rice, there are 25 important growing districts; for wheat, there are selected districts in the Punjab, U.P., M.P. and Bihar.

These areas will, the Team believes, increase India's food production more rapidly than others, if given allocation of fertilisers in combination with other improved practices, such as plant protection measures, improved seeds, and water for irrigation. Attention to other areas should not be reduced. But, in the national interest, the Team believes that increased effort should be immediately directed to the most responsive areas.

Security Of Land Tenure And Land Consolidation

Land ceilings and other land reforms should be setled as quickly as possible, and stay settled for the Third Plan. Firm plans should be developed immediately to schedule the completion of consolidation of fragmented holdings, village by village as soon as possible. Improved coordination must be provided.

Immediate Large Scale Credit Through Cooperatives

The present marketing, supply and credit services are major deterrents to increasing food production. Eighty-five per cent of credit is now supplied by money lenders and other individuals. Most marketed grains are sold to local traders at harvest time at depressed prices. Strong cooperatives can break these bonds.

To help cooperatives do so effectively, the Team's major recommendations are that (i) Government must be prepared to provide loans and to assist in developing capable management; and (2) standards of creditworthiness must be redefined to encourage production loans on the basis of expected crop yields and repayment ability, instead of land security.

Progressive Reduction Of Cattle Numbers

The Team recommends that legislation be considered providing for: (1) at tax policy which makes maintenance of useless cattle a burden on their owners (tax receipts could go to villages for improvements); (2) confinement of all bulls and mandatory castration of all bulls not kept for breading; (3) measures to control open grazing; (4) establishment of dessicating plants to process fallen animals, with incentive payments to owners who bring in fallen cattle.

The Urgency Of A High Level Coordinating Food Production Authority

Far-reaching centralised authority with a clear line of command and execution alone can meet the challenge of growing more food. The Team believes that such authority is essential to allocate resources on a priority basis—such as personnel, fertilisers, steel (for sprayers, godowns, fertilisers plants, etc.), to coordinate irrigation, drainage and soil management programmes; and to enforce policy decisions giving priority to food production. The administrative structure, moreover, must be simplified and clear lines of authority and responsibility established at all levels of Government, so that policy decisions are carried out to the village level.

The Role of Community Development And The Technical Ministries

All Ministries concerned with any aspect or programme relevant to food production must give top priority to food production now and for the period of the Third Plan.

India's Capacity To Do The Job

It is within the capacity of India's people to mobilise to meet the great crisis before them.

The Need For Emergency Measures

The Gap In Food Production

Food will have to be provided for 80 million more people by the end of the Third Plan.

The Impending Shortage

The entire nation must be made aware of the impending food crisis and steps must be taken to meet it. Adequate supplies of food may indeed be essential to survival of democracy, because freedom from hunger is a prerequisite to enjoyment of other freedoms. If elementary wants such as food and clothing, are not satisfied, other freedoms may be sacrificed for the promise of food enough.

If foodgrain production increases no faster than indicated by the present trend, the gap between supply and needs in 1965-66 will be about 28 million tons.

In any case, no conceivable programme of imports or rationing could meet a crisis of this magnitude.

A Third Plan target of 110 million tons must be reached if the country is to go forward on its development programme. In fact greatly accelerated expansion of food production is necessary to prevent hunger and possible civil disturbance.

This target can be achieved if. an all out emergency food production programme is undertaken. The best in Indian agriculture is comparable to the best in other countries, but the average level is unduly low. The task before the country is to develop ways of raising the low average to the higher levels that many Indian cultivators have achieved.

Top Priority For Food Production

It is clear to us that food production increases at the rate required to reach a 110-million ton target cannot be realised unless an all out emergency programme is undertaken, and adequate resources are made available. This means that agricultural development must be given the highest priority among all the categories of development for the remainder of the Second Five Year Plan and for the entire Third Plan period.

Resources For Increasing Production

It is clear that India has the soil, climatic and other physical resources to achieve a Third Plan target of 110 million tons of foodgrains. Although land is relatively scarce, the labour supply is abundant, and there are great potentialities for increasing production per acre. The problem is one of organising and combining resources to achieve the food production targets.

To India's physical resources must be added her human ingenuity and effort. There are many ways in which labour can be combined with relatively small capital outlays for fertilisers, pesticides, minor irrigation works, drainage, and improved equipment. From the effective combination of all these resources will come the increased food supply which India needs.

The Labour Resources

One of the major problems of Indian agriculture is,

to find productive employment for the many unemployed and underemployed villagers. If India's present over-abundant supply of agricultural labour can be used to increase output per acre, a wasted human resource will be utilised more effectively, and food production will be increased. There will also be important social gains.

A part of the underutilised labour force can be used directly to apply the combination of improved practices that will increase output per acre. But not all of the surplus labour can be employed productively this way and India cannot afford the waste of resources involved in village unemployment. Consequently, we are proposing, in a later section of this report, a public works programme to provide employment and to produce more food.

Many land and village improvements can be undertaken in a public works programme which requires much labour and little capital equipment, and which will result in immediate increases in food production. Among these improvements are building of contour bunds and other soil and water conservation structures, land levelling, some drainage work, masonry wells and tanks for irrigation, village godowns, and even village-to-market roads.

Capital Resources Required

But labour alone will not accomplish the task. Sufficient capital must also be provided to permit the most effective use of the abundant labour resources. Chemical fertilisers, pesticides, improved seeds, and other materials will have to be made available in adequate quantities. Investments will have to be made in fertiliser plants, in tube wells and other minor irrigation works, and in some other facilities related to food production. In this connection it is important to note that the ratio of capital expenditure to added output will be much less in food production than in most other enterprises, and that the increase in output will generally come more quickly from investments in food production than from investments in heavy industry or very large irrigation projects. Such increases in output consequently will counteract inflationary tendencies from the increased expenditures.

Lack Of Knowledge A Limiting Factor

Most of the improvements needed to double yields are already known to some people. Many improved practices have been adopted by some cultivators, in some areas. But until this knowledge is more widespread and acted upon, food production targets cannot be achieved.

If the known improvements that are adopted to each area were generally adopted in their most effective combinations, food production targets could be attained. But physical potentialities and the steps necessary to their attainment must be distinguished. And it is in this connection that lack of knowledge is crucial. Lack of knowledge exists not only among the cultivators, but also among those who work with them. Thus, training and the dissemination of knowledge are of tremendous importance for better use of India's food production resources.

Combined Practices Required

The evidence is clear that startling increases in food production are possible if the known improvements are adopted in effective combinations.

A few improved practices can be effective if adopted singly, but the full benefit from most improvements can be obtained only if they are adopted in combinations suitable for specific soil and climatic conditions. Sufficient fertilisers, improved seed, pesticides, proper soil and water management practices—all of these, while important in themselves can be fully effective only if adopted in combination with each other. For this reason, improvement programmes should be designed to concentrate on the adoption of those combinations of practices that are most likely to increase food production quickly.

Basic Premises

Programmes to increase foodgrains production will receive funds that are required for such items as credit, fertiliser, seed, soil and water conservation including irrigation and drainage, other land development, plant protection, food storage and processing facilities.

Adequate personnel will be trained and assigned to the job of increasing food production.

At all levels top leadership will be provided and coordination will be achieved among planners, administrators, educators, natural scientists, social scientists, local community leaders and cultivators. Without such leadership and coordination, no production programme can be successful.

Efforts will be concentrated where results will be greatest.

Since most of the risks associated with programmes to increase food production fall on the cultivators, they will be protected from price declines that would discourage expanding of production, and steps will be taken to stabilise food supplies and prices over time and space.

Organising To Meet The Crisis

We are convinced that extraordinary organisational and administrative measures and actions are required to mobilise the nation to meet the challenge of producing food enough to meet minimum requirements of a rapidly growing population.

We believe that the crisis in food requires action at the highest levels of Government. But there must be follow-through at all levels. Legislative as well as administrative branches of Government must be aware of the urgency of the situation. Decisions which are binding on all Ministries of Government and on all levels of Government, and which are supported by political leaders, must be made. The crucial role of agriculture must be recognised and the best technical knowledge on food production must be brought to bear on the problems without equivocation or delay.

Power must be granted to set priorities among activities, including the reallocation of budgeted funds and foreign exchange in the interest of greater food production. Power must also be granted to reallocate and reassign personnel, to redefine programme content and emphasis, including the power to stop on-going programmes and activities which conflict with or detract from immediate food production activities. Finally, power must be granted to require coordination and collaboration among Government agencies to simplify administrative, fiscal and other procedures as necessary to win the battle of food production.

Far-reaching, centralised authority with a clear line of command and execution, alone can meet the challenge of growing more food.

That the urgency of the problem and the need for clear-cut organisational adjustments to meet it must be understood at the State level. Unless State officials recognise the crisis and the need for forceful and direct action, the problem cannot be solved. We emphasise that existing policy conflicts between departments, the present lack of coordinated efforts on food production and the frequent failure to provide adequate funds for agricultural work must be eliminated.

As competent personnel become available for such staffing, they should first be assigned to those areas and blocks where the combination of water, soil, and other resources indicate that food production increases will be greatest.

We would like to emphasise that at each level, agencies and officers should be given well-defined, manageable and inescapable responsibility with full authority to discharge that responsibility. They should be judged by their initiative, their ability to push through the programme, and by their concrete accomplishments in increasing food production.

India faces a crisis of overwhelming gravity, and the administrative structure must positively be simplified and tightened to meet this crisis.

Better Economics And Administrative Arrangements

Price Stabilisation

To encourage increases in foodgrain production, the cultivator should be assured of a price which will enable him to invest in fertiliser, seed and new equipment knowing that, with average crop conditions, he can repay any debts with the added income that results from adoption of improved practices. Such assurance would constitute an important incentive to increase production.

Suggested Approaches To Rice Stabilisation Of Foodgrains

A conscious and consistent price policy is necessary to guide production to planned targets. This policy should aim not merely at reducing price variations but should maintain relative positions among agricultural commodities to attain desired patterns of output. Special price inducements or deterrents should encourage or discourage the use of agricultural resources for particular purposes. It is recognised that the erratic nature of production prevents exact response in the short run; flexibility, therefore, is required to meet changing supply situations.

The major need for price stabilisation is a systematic and continuous effort to maintain foodgrain prices at the desired level. This can be accomplished only by a permanent agency which can formulate price policy and implement this policy with the required action.

We suggest that such an agency be given the responsibility for :

(1) Determining base prices and the permissible range in variation from these prices;

(2) Announcing the prices well in advance of the sowing season ;

(3) Initiating purchase or sales operations as required by citcumstances ;

(4) Establishing the locations for stocks of each foodgrain and the recommended supplies to keep in reserve ;

(5) Determining export and import duties and quotas and such other devices for controlling prices as may be necessary ;

(6) Encouraging the development of an effective grading system.

Determining The Guaranteed Price

The level of minimum prices must be set with great care after consideration of all pertinent factors. Ideally the price guarantee for a specific product should protect the cultivator against unduly low prices and risk of loss. It should also even out seasonal fluctuations by holding prices up during the harvest season and should clear the market over the entire season, except for the quantity retained by the Government for buffer stock operations.

If the price is set too high, it may cause hardship for consumers. It might also bring restrictions on imports to protect the domestic market. On the other hand, if the price for any foodgrains is set too low, the required production and marketing may not take place, and expensive procurement and rationing programmes would have to be established, especially following a poor crop season. The floor price to producers must be set with due regard for the best interests of the economy as a whole.

The price must also not be set so high that price supports will become a drain on the national treasury. No large or sustained transfer payments between the agricultural and other sectors of the economy are feasible.

It is apparent that the level of price guarantees will need to be established on the basis of the best possible estimates of domestic and world supply of foodgrains, and on the basis of import prices as well as estimated domestic demand. It seems doubtful that a rigid formula can be developed which can be followed from year to year. Estimates will need to be made concerning prices for different foodgrains that are likely to clear the market. Then the price guarantees to farmers will have to be established with due regard for competition with other crops, for necessary handling margins and for fluctuations in productions.

The data required for decisions making should be supplied by the economic intelligence and outlook organisation described in a later section. This organisation should have full responsibility for the collection and analysis of agricultural and related economic data. It should review the supply, demand and price situation on a continuing basis and present the results of its appraisal to the policy group as a basis for their decisions.

Flexibility In Developing The Programme

Prudence requires a conservative approach to establishment of price guarantees in the early phase of a price stabilisation programme. It is especially desirable that adequate staff be available to carry out the programme effectively and with despatch. As a beginning we suggest that minimum prices be established only for rice and wheat on an all-India basis, and other important grains on a regional basis. Unless domestic considerations indicate the need for establishing floor prices on the basis of other criteria, considerations should be given to setting the first floor prices 10 to 15 per cent below prevailing import prices for each commodity, depending upon the proportion of imports to production. So long as the floor price is below import price, there need be no fear of financial loss in a country where imports are likely to continue for some years.

The floor price should be announced to cultivators before sowing time and remain in effect for one full year. A further announcement should be made that floor prices will be established for an additional two years at at levels 10 to 15 per cent below the import price, at a stated time each year. The actual prices are likely to rise above the minimum levels, at least in some years.

A floor price established in this way would permit annual adjustments to existing and prospective conditions. After experience has been gained with the first three years of operation, the programme could be renewed. Floor prices for other crops could be added as experience indicates the need for a broader programme.

Storage And Marketing Structure

The price stabilisation programme should leave the major responsibility for the movement of foodgrains to marketing cooperatives or private traders, with the Government intervening only to the extent required to guarantee minimum prices and to even out supplies.

At points of surplus, the Government should stand ready to buy at the minimum price any quantity offered for sale. At deficit points, the Government should stand ready to supply foodgrains through fair price shops. This requires that the Government be in possession at all times of stocks to use as a price lever.

Import of foodgrains can be of maternal assistance in operation of a buffer-stock programme. The foodgrain imports that have been available under special programmes have relieved the pressure on foreign exchange. No exact recommendations can be given an amounts to import in any year because this involves considerations of domestic production, substitution among foodgrains, availability of foreign exchange and willingness of foreign countries to make supplies available under special programmes.

Land Reform And Food Production
Stability Of Tenure

Assurance of stability of land tenure and equitable rental arrangements can contribute substantially to food production, but insecurity of tenure has a retarding effect. Many tenants do not have sufficient security to participate in land improvement, and some of the share-cropping arrangements definitely discourage adoption of improved practices.

In some areas uncertainties with respect to the application of land ceilings are at present retarding private investments in agriculture that could result in additional food production. Such retardation emphasises the urgent need for passage of land reform legislation at the earliest possible dates, and then for immediate execution of the provisions of such legislation. Only in this way can uncertainties be eliminated, and assurance be given to cultivators so that they can safely make desirable land improvements.

We recognise the need for considering programmes for the relief of those who have no land, and of those who cultivate too little land. But it is imperative to achieve this objective in ways that will not retard the increases in food production which are vital to national welfare. Some progress can be made by arranging for reallocation, improvement and operation of potentially productive lands that are now idle, or are being used very ineffectively. Care should be exercised, however, so as not to break up farms that are efficiently and productively operated.

The longer term objectives of a land tenure programme also must be kept in mind. These would include development of a labour intensive, but nevertheless efficient agriculture. To achieve this end requires intelligent and capable leadership on the part of cultivators. This leadership must come from a strong group of progressive cultivators, who will move forward in adopting new technology, and other measures for improvement of the farms and the villages. Land reforms must not discourage development of a progressive group of cultivators who have middle-sized holdings.

Size Of Holdings

Income improvement for the landless and for those with too little land must be sought in ways that will permit subsequent adjustments in land holdings and in farm sizes when non-farm employment opportunities can be arranged for those not needed in agriculture.

Care should be taken to avoid freezing a pattern of land tenure that cannot later be modified to meet changing conditions.

It is just as necessary to establish a minimum standard of land resources per family as it is to set a ceiling on land holdings. The minimum standard necessarily will vary in acreage, depending upon the physical productivity of the land, whether it is irrigated or unirrigated, and its location with respect to markets. Consequently the minimum standard will need to be adopted to local conditions, but the general principle of a minimum unit for adequate living for a farm family must be kept in mind.

The concept of a minimum unit of land per family is equally applicable to private or to cooperative operation of land. If land resources per family are insufficient, neither cooperative nor private operation can provide an adequate living.

Cooperative Farming And Land Use

Present policy discussions include suggestions that joint cooperative farming societies be organised for operation of land now poorly utilised, or for areas acquired by application of land ceilings. It is understood that joint farming cooperatives will be organised on a voluntary basis. Undoubtedly, some time will be required for organisation and efficient operation of many cooperatives of this type.

While experience is being gained by careful analysis of the first cooperative farming ventures that are established, attention can also be centred on alternative ways of accomplishing cooperation in farm operations. Present owners or tenants operating small units could be encouraged to arrange for joint ownership and operation of bullock or mechanical power, and for use of the necessary equipment. Such operation permits individual attention by the cultivator to his unit of land.

Management assistance to cultivators, combined with supervised credit, and perhaps with joint ownership of equipment, offers a way to obtain the advantage of better management while still retaining the incentives gained by individual operations.

Other Means Of Helping The Landless

Other ways of improving the condition of the landless labourers must also be found. Many landless labourers would no doubt consider more secure employment, at some-what higher wages than they now get, just as much of an improvement in their conditions as membership in a joint farming cooperative. The public works programme suggested in the following section would provide temporary work, but the long term solution depends upon economic development that will provide more non-farm employment. In this connection more attention should be given to establishing cooperatives for processing farm products in the villages.

Consolidation Of Fragmented Holdings

By carrying on land consolidation with soil and water conservation planning, land areas can be laid out so that field irrigation, canals, drainage ditches, contour bunds, and stone terraces are on the boundaries between holdings, or parts of holdings. Such locations of field boundaries are very important. It is not always necessary or even desirable to bring all the land of one holder into a single block, especially where two or more contrasting soils of unlike management requirements are involved. It is more desirable to bring together those fragments of holdings that have similar soil.

Since land consolidation requires satisfactory settlement of tenure problems, prompt action on all phases of tenure and land ceilings is urgently needed.

In any area where consolidation is begun, it should be completed within a definite time period in order to avoid uncertainties and a lowering of production.

Immediate steps should be taken : (1) to initiate soil surveys and topographic surveys, where needed, ahead of planning for consolidation and with highest priority to areas of contrasting soils; and (2) to ensure that planning for consolidation takes full account of needed field structures for irrigation, drainage, and contour bunds. In fact, a poor job of planning may result in few benefits and great confusion later when a proper scheme is attempted.

We recommend that firm plans be developed immediately to schedule the completion of the consolidation of fragmented holdings, village-by-village, as soon as possible. The work should be based upon adequate soil surveys and on a coordinated plan through which the boundaries of holdings could fall on the same lines as drainage ditches, irrigation canals, contour bunds, stone terraces, and similar structures. We also recommend that high-level coordinating agencies be established at the Centre and in each State to develop schedules, and to ensure effective coordination with the requirements for soil and water conservation, giving special emphasis to needed structures for water control distribution, and disposal.

Many States now have laws for undertaking land consolidation. Not all have laws to prevent further uneconomic fragmentation. Such laws should be enacted in States and necessary enforcement should be provided for. We therefore, suggest that draft legislation be prepared and submitted for consideration of the States not now having such laws, to prevent fragmentation of small holdings into tiny uneconomic units.

A Public Works Programme To Increase Rural Employment And To Provide More Food

That a public works programme be instituted in the interest of increasing rural employment and at the same time increasing food production.

Projects undertaken under this programme should be limited to those :

(1) Which will have a direct effect on food production;

(2) Which require little or no capital expenditure and can be carried out primarily with hand labour;

(3) Which require little or no scarce material and little or no foreign exchange;

(4) For which people with the necessary skills to supervise the work are available or can readily be trained.

Priority should be given to projects in those areas where serious rural unemployment prevails and, within those areas, to activities which will make the greatest and most immediate contribution to food production.

Bunding And Terracing

An outstanding example of a type of project that can be undertaken in appropriate areas in contour bunding and terracing (including masonry terracing) accurately laid out in relation to contour and slope. Large and immediate increases in food production can result from such work, where it is well done, and where the cultivators are prepared to use such other good farming practices necessary for full effectiveness. Since bunding and terracing work must cover an area completely, it will be necessary for the affected villageıs to agree to the project.

Other Projects

As people can be trained and the work organised, other soil conservation and water utilisation measures can also provide employment and food production increases. Land levelling, surface drainage, minor irrigation works, construction of wells and tanks —all these would provide suitable projects under this programme. Where villages lack adequate approach roads for bringing in supplies and taking produce to market, these could be included as useful projects. Where village godowns are needed for better storage and preservation of food, these too might be constructed.

Although the returns measured in food production would come later, consideration might in some areas be given to the planting of fruit and fuel trees on village common lands. Protection of productive lands from livestock depredations might also provide employment, and in many areas would increase food production significantly.

It should be noted that while wages paid to these workers would increase their purchasing power, more food would be produced not only for those who do the work but for other consumers as well. Hence a works programme of this type need not be inflationary.

A public works programme to serve these purposes will need careful organisation. Arrangements should be made to utilise existing agencies. To the extent practicable, village panchayats should assume responsibility for designating the unemployed and underemployed labourers and for other aspects of particular projects. But to be effective approval of projects and supervision of the work undertaken must be the responsibility of a State or Central Government agency.

The Role Of Cooperatives In Expanded Food Production —Credit, Marketing And Supply

Present credit, marketing and supply services in the villages are a major deterrent to increasing India's food production. Over 85 per cent of the credit which cultivators use is provided by money lenders and other individuals. Most of their small marketable surplus is sold to traders at depressed prices at harvest time. Many cultivators are not getting full value for their produce, are paying exorbitant rates of interest for inadequate credit, and do not have a reliable source of production supplies. Thus, they are unable to adopt many improved practices for increased production.

Yet the cultivators, acting alone, are incapable of breaking loose from their poverty-stricken status. Only by cooperative effort, with Government assistance, can the stranglehold of money lenders and traders be broken.

But there is no magic in the cooperative form of organisation which assures its success. Cooperatives will succeed only if they perform economic functions better than they are now being performed. They will be able to do this only if they are built upon sound business principles. They must have sufficient capital to provide adequate working funds and sufficient income to pay necessary operating expenses, including the cost of competent management. To develop strong cooperatives, therefore, Government help must not be niggardly in respect to both financial and technical assistance.

Extending Credit Through The Primary Society

Present plans make no provision for the States to advance loan funds to the smaller primary societies. We believe that the primary societies must become important in the extension of credit in rural India. To achieve this goal, the State Governments must advance loan funds to supplement the capital investment of the members, to provide a capital base large enough to support the complete borrowing needs of cultivators. If this is done, the Reserve Bank can then provide the necessary loan funds through the cooperative bank system, so that no society will be forced to deny a loan or give an inadequate loan because it does not have sufficient resources.

We believe further that there should be no specific due date by which time the Government advances would be repaid. The advances should be retained by the society until it has adequate resources of its own to serve its members and potential members. The terms for repayment should be established by agreement, and should be based upon the relationship of the society's net worth to risk assets. During this period of capital formation at the local level, the banks and societies should forgo the payment of dividends so that all earnings may be applied to increasing net worth.

We believe that the structure of a primary cooperative society is not as important as the results it achieves. Fundamental principles of cooperation must be adhered to but the type of functions a society performs, the nature of its membership, and the number of villages served will have to be determined by the circumstances found in each situation.

Very little of this type of educational work is being done at the village level. It is the opinion of this Team that the extension staff, especially at the block level, must be strengthened in this respect by adding sufficient personnel to do intensive educational and promotional work on cooperatives. These people would need to work with the central cooperative bank, with the cooperative unions (where they exist) and with the VLW's, but they should take initiative for carrying out the educational and promotional assignment.

Credit Worthiness

There are a variety of standards which can be used to determine who is entitled to credit. In India today creditworthiness is most often based on the value of pledged assets. Although the Reserve Bank and a few States are encouraging production loans upon the basis of expected crop yields and repayment ability, we find that in a large part of India this procedure is taking hold only slowly. Yet we are convinced that if this approach to lending could be adopted immediately by primary societies and cooperative banks, it would make an important contribution towards increasing agricultural production.

Timely Credit Service

It is essential that operating procedures of primary societies and cooperative banks be simplified so that cultivators can obtain loan funds from their society in a reasonable period of time. New applications for short-term production credit should not require over a fortnight for decision. A cultivator with a good record of performance with a society should be able to receive approval of a normal credit request within a few days. For small amounts he should be able to obtain the funds "over the counter". Only by this kind of service can the society meet the entire credit requirements of its members. And until this can be done, the cultivators will have to resort to the money lenders for emergency credit.

Credit And Agriculture Technicians

There should be close working relationship between the agricultural technicians and the officials of both the primary credit societies and the cooperative banks, in order that technical agricultural knowledge be used to strengthen repayment capacity, and enhance loan recovery probabilities.

That agricultural college graduates should be used to a greater extent than presently in the primary societies and cooperative banks. It would seem logical, considering the importance of cooperatives to India, that the agricultural colleges develop a curriculum especially designed for future managers of cooperatives.

Marketing And Supply

We feel that the cooperative departments of the States and their staff in the field should, as rapidly as they are able to do so, assume responsibility for organising and servicing the agriculture supply lines. While there will always be a place for the enterprising honest private entrepreneur who wants to make a business of stocking and selling agricultural supplies, cooperatives must play an important role in supplying the cultivator with the tools, fertilisers, seeds, etc., for an intensive food production campaign.

We believe that strength could be given to marketing and supply cooperatives by using them as agency for price stabilisation.

To be effective, marketing and supply cooperatives must have godowns to provide safe and adequate storage. There should also be a godown available to each village, under control of the primary society in which the small quantities of the marketable crops of the villagers can be stored until delivered to the marketing cooperatives. These village godowns would also provide storage space for supplies, for seeds and foodgrains for village use.

We believe that the possibility of using funds from grain imports for godown construction should be investigated fully. It is possible, for example, that (PL-480) funds resulting from sale within India of grain from the United States might be available for this purpose.

Food Processing

It appears to us that the greatest need today is for more cooperatively owned paddy hulling and rice mills in major rice-producing areas. Efforts to market rice cooperatively have not been too successful and the lack of processing facilities has been frequently reported as a major contributing cause. The present ban on new paddy hulling plants is keeping cooperatives out of this activity. Some means should be found to let cooperatives enter this field.

The future of the cooperative movement in India depends upon the people who lead, direct and manage it. In addition to many qualified people in the Government, India has capable, well-informed and educated people in the cooperative movement itself. This "non-official" group can provide informed and practical information essential to the development of sound and practical policies and plans. Their counsel and advice should be sought. Unless "non-official" leadership is recognised and developed, cooperatives will be led and dominated by Government. This is not India's objective as we interpret her plans.

Improving Extension Work Through Community Development

Extension Programmes

Extension programmes can be improved by focusing them more directly upon local conditions, upon village production problems and production potentials, and by having village farmers participate more actively in programme determinations, including setting the priority order of programme action.

Block extension workers should set up village food production committees through which the local farm people, assisted by block extension personnel and VLW's, first, can assess the present production and optimum productive capacities of village farms, and, second, determine the combinations of improved farming methods necessary to achieve expanded production. Where the village has a panchayat, the food committee could act as a sub-committee of the panchayat.

Targets composed of improved practice quotas handed down to the blocks and villages from national and State levels should be abandoned. The use of targets should be confined to national and State requirements for key food crops and be used by the village cultivators as guides in setting their own food production goals, in consultation with local extension workers.

Special extension programme emphasis should be given to the important contribution that farm women and youth can make in village community efforts to step up food production.

Caution should be exercised in making recommendations for any improved practice uniformly over large areas without adequate regard for their appropriateness for local farming conditions.

Extension Organisations And Administration

To achieve greater farming efficiency and expanded output, we recommend :

The community development organisation from the Centre to the blocks should focus its extension programme more fully on increased food production. The emergency nature of the present food situation requires much more than issuing directives that the VLW's should spend 75 to 80 per cent of their time on agricultural production.

The top priority programme objective of community development in the foreseeable future must be to marshal the educational force and drive that will stimulate village cultivators to produce more food. The application of many more technological improvements, and the vigorous impact of science, are greatly needed at the field level in order to obtain the magnitude of production required. This demands the use of technical agricultural specialists in the blocks and also other adjustments in current block staff assignments.

Additional block agricultural personnel with specialised technical competence to handle local farming problems, such as irrigation, soil conservation, farm management and home science, are needed; and more intensive technical and extension methods training must be given to all present block staffs as rapidly as possible. Adjustments in block budgets are also called for.

Immediate steps must be taken at the Centre, State and District levels to strengthen extension work. Unless the block staffs are adequately supported by a core of agricultural subject matter specialists up the line—specialists who are continuously in touch with current research developments—the local staffs cannot be expected to carry on successful extension programmes to increase crop yields by modern farming methods.

At the Centre, some of the nation's most competent agricultural technicians and scientists – in such fields as rice and other cereal crop production, irrigation, plant protection, soil fertility, animal husbandry, farm management and agricultural economics—must be recruited to give broad, general leadership of State extention specialists. The men selected must be capable of commanding the complete respect of their opposite numbers in research. At State and District levels men of similar qualifications are needed to give leadership and direction to the men in blocks and villages.

The shortage of technical personnel requires that care be exercised in building up this technical staff to avoid undue disruption to on-going research work important to food production. In some cases, research workers at colleges and experiment stations might be used for this purpose on a part-time basis,

The kinds of State-wide and District farming problems impeding greater food production should determine the special technical qualifications of these extension workers.

In the interest of securing more rapid farming improvements throughout the country, the approximately 2,000 "shadow" blocks (that is, the blocks not yet under the community development programme) should receive at least a minimum of extension educational assistance. These areas should be manned with a full complement of agricultural assistants and field demonstrators, and these extension workers should also receive periodic subject-matter and extension methods training.

The following charges in assignments of officers at the block level should be made :

(a) **Village Level Workers** : Relieve the Gram Sewak of service tasks, such as handling farm supplies, loan collections, etc., as rapidly as these jobs can be assigned to other persons. Direct more of the activities of the Gram Sevikas to teaching improved agricultural practices to farm women.

(b) **Agricultural Officer** : Relieve him of service responsibilities such as seed, fertiliser, and insecticide handling, assigning this to cooperatives and to the Co-operative Officer.

(c) **Animal Husbandry Officer** : Reorient his work toward food production, for example, giving greater emphasis to poultry production, where applicable and, greater emphasis to forage utilisation and controlled grazing.

(d) **SEO (Man)** : Assign him as a staff officer to assist the BDO and other block officers in organising facilities and in preparing visual materials and other teaching aids with particular reference to agricultural production, and to assist the VLW in organisation, method demonstrations, etc.

(e) **Cooperative Officer** : Encourage him to take greater responsibility for developing an understanding of the purpose, objectives and opportunities of co-operatives and aiding in their organisation. Make him responsible for the supply functions such as seed and fertiliser currently usually handled by the agricultural officer.

(f) **Other Officers** : The work of the engineer, panchayat officer, woman social education organiser should be redirected, to the extent possible, to educational activities and development programmes contributing directly to greater production.

State Departments of Agriculture should provide adequate agricultural information services to help extend information on improved practices through mass communication media, such as radio, newspapers and pamphlets and by visual teaching devices—movies, filmstrips, posters, and so on. Information services can support the work of local extension personnel by making farmers more aware of better farming methods, and by providing the local workers visual and other teaching aids.

Conditions contributing to rapid personnel turnover, such as low salaries, job insecurity and limited opportunities for advancement, should be remedied. This is particularly a matter of concern with respect to VLW's but would also improve the quality of work done by extension personnel by the line. A part of these personnel problems can be solved by staff supervision oriented to worker counsel and guidance and to general personnel development rather than to inspection, order-giving and control. Administrative steps must also be taken to correct the more crucial problems of job insecurity and low morale resulting from insufficient opportunities for advancement.

With respect to block budgets and accounting and auditing procedures, greater budget flexibility from block to block is needed. Budgets should reflect priorities set by the local people and the block staff. Accounting and credit inspectors need a better understanding of extension programme objectives. Rigidities and complex paper controls place the local extension workers in "strait jackets" and consume time that should be devoted to the business of aiding farmers to produce more food.

The reports required of extension workers should be simplified, and consist of periodic descriptive statements of extension programme achievements, with expanding food production as the central theme. The present detailed reports of VLW's and block extension officers appear to give more emphasis to mechanical paper control than to assessing programme results.

To mobilise the manpower of State-level personnel concerned with food production programmes fully, each State should convene a working conference of community development and appropriate technical department officers and specialists for the purpose of : (a) assessing and outlining the jobs to be done to aid local extension workers and village cultivators to produce more food, and (b) fixing the specific responsibilities of each department for carrying out the plans. Each such State conference should be followed by a series of District conferences in which all appropriate District personnel, official and non-official would meet to appraise the food production potential of their respective Districts and determine and assign responsibilities for jobs to be done to support block staff extension programmes with technicians, teaching equipment, materials and demonstration supplies.

Extension Methods

Competent instructors in extension education should be secured or trained for the extension training centres, and a more comprehensive and practical work-training syllabus, including content and methods of teaching, should be developed.

A critical analysis should be made, in the field, of extension methods now being used and of any others that may be valuable, to determine how extension programmes in action may most effectively persuade the village farmers to adopt farming implements.

Village leader training camps are an excellent method of extending and maximising the limited resources of local extension staffs available to encourage greater food production. These camps should be continued and expanded in number, so that full advantage can be taken of local progressive farmer leadership, capable of influencing neighbouring farmers to adopt efficient practices. Extreme care should be taken in planning the programmes of these camps to make certain that the subject matter taught relates clearly to increased food production.

Better Use Of Physical And Biological Resources

Soil And Water Conservation (Including Water Use)

India has the basic natural resources of soil, water, climate and labour, for abundant food production. High production results only when combinations of soil, water and crop management are adopted to local conditions and are skilfully applied by individual cultivators. Costs for irrigation works and for contour bunding, for example, are rarely returned unless the water is well controlled and unless fertilisers, good seeds, and other appropriate cultural practices are also used.

This principle of combined practices—of fitting the various practices together as adapted to each kind of soil—is the very cornerstone of any successful programme for soil and water conservation that gives efficient, sustained production at a high level.

80 per cent of the annual rainfall, over the greater part of India, is received in less than four months. Since India has a tropical or sub-tropical climate, it has a potential to grow crops on a year-round basis. An adequate water supply in the soil can provide opportunity for increasing crop production several-fold. Often too much or too little water and its inefficient use are primary limiting factors to increased crop production. India is blessed with one of the largest water supplies of any country in the world, but only a small portion of its potential has been developed. Continued emphasis, therefore, should be given to the development of irrigation water supply through storage reservoirs and direct diversion from rivers and streams which will permit water delivery on a continuous yearly basis.

Wells and Tanks

Wells must be considered as a source of water supply, where stream flow is only seasonal (during monsoons) and where storage from reservoirs is not feasible. In these areas consideration must be given to providing crop requirements either directly from wells or by supplementing stream flow with well water. In determining the feasibility of such projects and the cost of irrigation it is essential to relate the cost of irrigation to the benefits to be derived in terms of physical crop yields and related social benefits.

The tube-well programme should be greatly expanded in those areas where there is now a relatively sure supply of good ground water. This would include large areas in Uttar Pradesh, Punjab, West Bengal, Bihar, Madras, Andhra Pradesh, and parts of Bombay and other States. Those areas which have potential for two and three crops per year should have highest priority.

The programme for shallow masonry wells should be expanded to meet the maximum demand consistent with good irrigation planning.

The development of tanks should be encouraged, and public assistance, through loans or subsidies, should be given for their construction and repair.

Improving Water Conveyance

Improved water conveyance, within the village and on the farm, land preparation for uniform water distribution, and proper practices as to time and amount of water applied for various crops, soils and climates, offer some of the greatest opportunities for increasing food production. To get such practices used correctly on irrigated lands, and for contour bunding, terracing, and land levelling on non-irrigated areas, requires technical assistance to the farmer.

Seepage studies should be made in the canal systems losing more than 15 per cent of their water; where excessive seepage is occurring, action should be taken to reduce it.

Each State should provide for a staff of technicians in soil and water conservation, not only for project work but also for direct technical assistance to cultivators and groups of cultivators as the need is identified by agricultural extension officers.

Good Water Management

An increased effort should be made through technical assistance, extension and demonstration to get improved water management practices, combined with proper fertilisers, recommended seeds and cropping systems on farm fields as rapidly as possible.

Research experiments and demonstrations should be greatly expanded to deal with the proper combination of (a) water management, (b) fertilisers, (c) good seeds, (d) other cultural practices necessary for high production.

An adequate percentage of the total cost of each new major irrigation project should be earmarked and made available through appropriate agencies of the Agricultural Department, so that funds necessary to start demonstrations of irrigation farming and other phases of their programmes will be available; at the same time the engineering construction phases of a new project are begun.

Drainage And Salinity

One agency should be given the responsibility for coordination and improvement of natural and artificial drainage ways, and that the improvement of natural drainage ways be given a high priority.

Research and demonstration should be expanded on the reclamation of water-logged, saline and alkali soils, and that increased efforts should be made to reclaim present areas so affected, but that no tilling or internal drainage should be started until after surface drainage has been effected.

Bunding And Terracing On Dry Lands

Contour bunding and terracing, especially stone terracing, should be given a top priority on soils (a) that can be shifted from rough pasture to good cropland, (b) that can be shifted from one fair crop to two good crops, and (c) that can give increases in production of two-fold or better.

Since contour bunds to be effective must be laid out accurately, and since they must be continuous without breaks, except to well-prepared outlets, legislation should be adopted that permits a majority in a village (or wider area) to vote for contour-bunding or terracing schemes that obligate all landholders in the village (or wider area).

Mechanised Tillage

Heavy tractors (and other mechanised equipment) should be secured, using foreign exchange, if necessary, for use where (1) soil areas will give greatly increased production, and (2) cultivators are prepared to use them without significant subsidy beyond loans.

Erosion Control

Allotments for conservation work should be made in all financial plans for public water-storage structures, and such work should be timed for early completion, and subsidies and loans for constructing tanks should be given only where the plans include measures for ensuring erosion control.

Shifting Cultivation

The Centre develop a research programme for testing improvments and supplements to the existing systems of shifting cultivation.

Control Of Grazing

Enough further demonstrations should be established to permit each rural resident to see the results of controlled grazing.

A vigorous educational programme should be developed.

Appropriate legislation should be formulated for only licensed grazing on public land.

Forestry officers should give added attention to village forest plantings, particularly of fuel trees which can release much needed manure for food production and also control erosion.

Putting More Land Into Full Production

Adequate regulations should be formulated and enforced to provide that unused or poorly used land suited to crop production be leased or otherwise made available to cultivators.

All plans for bringing new land into use and for land consolidation should be made jointly with experts on soil and water conservation on the basis of soil surveys.

Helping Farmers To Adopt Improved Soil And Water Practices

The Soil Conservation Board, in cooperation with State agencies, should work out ways to guarantee cultivators against loss from the adoption of radically different but well-proved systems of soil and water management that promise substantial increases in both yields and income.

Demonstrations of combinations of fertiliser use, bunding, terracing, controlled grazing, and similar practices should be accompanied by explanations of costs and returns.

The Centre should (a) give assistance to States for the coordination of departments dealing with agriculture, irrigation, public works, consolidation of fragmented holdings, land development and allotment, forestry, and related functions; and (b) give the effectiveness of such coordination major emphasis in determining grants to the individual States for projects in soil and water conservation or projects related to it.

Research

We recommend that two central research stations be established to conduct basic research on national and regional soil and water conservation problems, one in an irrigated and one in a non-irrigated area, and that funds be made available for close cooperation with the State Agricultural Departments, agricultural colleges, and other appropriate institutions.

Training

We, therefore, recommend that existing facilities for such training be improved and expanded, including especially the use of combined training and work camps for diploma holders, who can be trained on the job to fill the many positions of local supervision that will be urgently needed.

Chemical Fertiliser—A Top Priority

We commend efforts toward fuller use of manures, composts, and green manures. But at the very best they can substitute for only a small fraction of the chemical fertilisers needed during the next seven years. Only with more abundant chemical fertilisers will the benefits from irrigation, bunding, improved seeds, and other facilities be realised. Hence, the procurement of fertilisers, and of the means of producing high-analysis fertilisers, must be given a top priority, including necessary foreign exchange.

The targets for fertiliser to be made available at the end of the Third Plan, developed in the Ministry of Food and Agriculture, are soundly based but conservative in relation to need. These amount to 1,500,000 tons of nitrogen, 750,000 tons of phosphoric acid, and 200,000 tons of potash. These will mean a nine-fold increase in use of nitrogen and considerably larger increases in the others, the use of which has just started. Even then we feel these are the very minima for meeting food production targets.

Allocation Policy

So long as fertilisers are in short-supply, they should be allocated primarily to growers of food crops, according to (1) the opportunities for increased food production and (2) the extent to which cultivators are using the other practices necessary for fertiliser to be most effective.

High-Analysis Fertilisers

Unhappily, traditions in India favour fertilisers of low analysis, especially ammonium sulphate and superphosphate. These materials are very costly per pound of plant nutrient because of bagging, freight, and handling charges. Emphasis should be given to high-analysis fertilisers for (a) research-testing of high-analysis materials already proved in other countries, (b) importation of such materials for test-demonstration, (c) large-scale importation for general use as soon as possible, and (d) industrial research for the manufacture of such materials within India.

Research

Commendable progress on fertiliser research and soil testing has been made in recent years in India. To reach projected food goals, continued strong research effort is needed within the specific area of fertiliser use and the interactions of fertiliser use with cropping systems and other practices.

Specifically, added emphasis should be given to :

(1) The standardisation of laboratory soil tests with field experiments on the important kinds of soil;

(2) Coordination of the soil-testing scheme with the soil survey;

(3) Follow-through by field officers of test results;

(4) Full recognition of other factors besides test results of surface soil that influence recommendations;

(5) A wider network of village demonstrations;

(6) Estimates of economic returns along with physical demonstrations of the results of fertiliser use; and

(7) Developing definite cooperative relationships in the soil-testing scheme with the Soil Conservation Research Stations and all other experimental stations doing research on or conducting demonstrations with soils or crops.

Fertiliser Technology

A strong central group of chemists and engineers should be selected to give attention to the many problems of fertiliser manufacture and supply. We, therefore, recommend an all-India centre of fertiliser technology for research and advice within the Ministry of Food and Agriculture.

Improvements In Cereal Production

Technological information is available in India to make possible immediate and significant increases in cereal production. But much more research is needed to bring both long-run and short-run production nearer to the maximum.

Potential For Immediate Production Increases

Special consideration should be given to about 25 rice districts in various States and to special wheat districts in Punjab, parts of Uttar Pradesh, Madhya Pradesh and Bihar. In many of these specified districts yields of rice and wheat can be doubled, if the scientific approach is utilised, and all factors of production are made available in optimum quantities.

Plant Breeding

Rice : A number of rice-breeding projects are in progress in India and work of the following type should be intensified :

(1) **Breeding for Strong Straw :** Most of the varieties now grown have weak straw and efficient response to high soil fertility levels is not always obtained. Promising hybrids have been developed from Indica-Japonica crosses which have stiffer straw and better response to high fertility levels than local varieties. These improved varieties seould be made speedily available to the cultivator.

(2) **Breeding for Early Maturation Period :** There is a need for high-yielding varieties with a maturation period of about 100 to 120 days. They can be grown in areas where the water supply is limited, because they require less water than the 166-170 day maturity types. Varieties of the short as well as long maturity types are also needed which are non-sensitive to photo period.

(3) **Breeding for Disease and Insect resistance :** Only slight gains have been made in these areas and the research work should be strengthened since diseases and insects are often a major limiting factor in rice production.

(4) **Breeding for Drought Conditions :** About 65 per cent of the rice acreage is non-irrigated, and ample water is often not available for these areas. Plant breeders and plant physiologists should cooperate on this project because basic research is needed for a scientific basis for the breeding work.

Wheat : New high-yielding, rust-resistant varieties have been developed, yet older rust-susceptible varieties are grown over large areas in certain States. Consequently, rust epidemics are a serious threat.

Wheat-breeding work should be intensified in the important wheat-growing States and the Centre, giving special emphasis to high-yielding varieties which have resistance to rust as well as other serious wheat diseases. Laboratories for testing rust samples should be enlarged so that larger samples may be tested and new races more quickly identified. Special effort should be made to ensure rapid adoption of the improved varieties by the cultivator.

Hybrid Maize : Significant increase in yield over local varieties can be obtained with hybrid maize. Hence a real potential for increased food production lies in the substitution of hybrid maize for local verieties, and in increasing acreage sown to hybrid maize since diseases and insects pose a serious threat to hybrid maize, breeding work must be done in cooperation with the plant pathologists and entomologists.

Millets : Millets, including sorghum, represent an important group of food plant crops in India. But they have not received enough attention from the plant breeder. Recently a coordinated sorghum-breeding project has been inaugurated and this project should receive a high priority because of a recently discovered mechanism for utilising hybrid vigour in sorghum production.

Plant Protection

Unnecessary yield losses are registered annually because plant diseases and insects are not adequately controlled. More equipment, such as dusters and sprayers, must be made available to the cultivator, and additional plant protection specialists must be added to the field staff to make timely pest surveys and advise on technological phases of pesticide applications. In case of widespread out break of insects, control by aerial application should be emphasised.

The need for close cooperation between plant protection personnel and research centres is necessary. Timely refresher courses for plant protection personnel are important, since new plant protection materials are continually being developed, and up-to-date information is necessary on selectivity, timing, rate and number of applications, and toxicity hazards.

Mechanisation

A strong engineering department is nedeed where present equipment can be improved in design, where new equipment can be developed, and where imported equipment can be checked for adaptability;

Special emphasis should be given to the improvement and design of mechanical equipment which can be used for weed control. For example, the rotary weeder, used extensively in rice cultivation, and similar equipment, should be improved in design.

Culture Practices

Japanese "Method" of Paddy Cultivation : Experments show that 67 to 70 per cent (seven maunds per acre) of the increase in production from the "Japanese system" of paddy cultivation is due to the use of organic and inorganic fertilisers. The yield increases associated with cultural practices alone are about two maunds per acre. It should be understood that the Japanese method can and should be adopted in areas under irrigation but that a high priority must be given to the use of commercial fertilisers in order for the system to result in high yield increases.

Fertilisers

As indicated in the preceding section, organic manures and mechanical fertilisers are complementary, and since organic manures alone cannot be relied upon to achieve production goals, a high priority must be given to commercial fertilisers if proposed cereal production goals are to be met.

Improved Varieties

The acreage of grain crops planted to improved varieties is estimated at only 15 to 20 per cent of the total. This acreage must be substantially increased through (1) an efficient seed multiplication programme and (2) a vigorous educational programme to convince cultivators of the need and economic advantage of planting improved seed. Full benefits from other improved practices (such as irrigation, application of fertilisers and plant protection) cannot be realised unless improved varieties are grown. There is a critical need for wider testing of new varieties to determine the areas for which they are suitable. Regional State tests should be more widely employed and should include varieties from all States, Centre, as well as promising importations. Testing of foreign varieties should be encouraged for all crops.

Crop Production Research

Despite the fact that research scientists in India have made notable contributions, it must be stated that there are not enough trained scientists in any field of crop production to satisfy the requirements for a true scientific approach to increasing crop production. Much more emphasis must be placed on applied research in order that the cultivator's production problems can be solved. Strangely enough, because of low salaries and unrealistic promotion and retirement policies, the full potential of the available scientists is not being realised. In certain State research centres library facilities are not sufficient to allow research workers to keep abreast of the world scientific literature.

In view of the shortage of research personnel and equipment, we believe that more progress could often be made if research talent and facilities were concentrated at certain centres to permit a cooperative approach among technicians with varied training. For example, in the development of improved varieties, much more rapid progress can be made if there is close cooperation between the plant breeders, plant pathologists, entomologists, agronomists, geneticists, and plant physiologists. Closer cooperation between the States and between the States and the Centre would also result in greater and more efficient research output.

The Multiplication And Distribution Of Improved Seeds

A vigorous effective seeds multiplication and distribution programme is an absolute necessity to increase food production in India.

The Need For Seed Specialists

The needed progress in improved seed multiplication and distribution can only occur under the leadership of competent seed specialists.

Education, Supply And Quality Control

We recommend that (1) village, block and district extension workers should be responsible primarily for improved seed education, (2) the State departments of agriculture should be responsible for seed certification, and (3) cooperative and private growers should be encouraged to assume the role of supplying improved seed. In the interim, as recommended in the section of the report on extension, the block cooperatives officer should assume primary responsibility for improved seed supply. In this transitional period, it is important that improved seed programmes do not suffer.

Seed Certification Standards

If seed improvement schemes are to be successful, the Centre and State Governments should develop and enforce uniform seed certification standards of all crops.

Maintenance Of Varietal Purity

The plant breeder must maintain recurring supplies of pure Breeder seed of improved varieties, and seed multiplication methods must be employed which will maintain varietal purity in seed increases.

Importance Of High Quality Seed

Effective steps should be taken to upgrade the quality of seed included in improved seed programmes. As an aid in accomplishing this, the States should establish and operate modern seed-testing laboratories and enact suitable seed laws.

Stock Seed Farms

We recommend that Government stock seed farms should be established only at the rate at which competent management can be trained and recruited. Fewer of larger size will more fully utilise competent managers and equipment.

Improved Seed For The Villager

Increased production of improved seed should be concentrated in each block in one or at the most two, selected "seed multiplication villages". These villages should receive special technical assistance, fertiliser allocations, plant protection measures, etc., to facilitate maximum production of high-quality seed. Wherever feasible, improved seed multiplication should also utilise the well-managed middle or larger sized farms.

An excessive number of improved varieties clutters listings in many States. This dilutes multiplication and distribution effort. Some varieties are superior, far too many are mediocre. All too frequently States fail to utilise the best varieties evolved in other States or the Centre. An all-India scheme for variety testing for all important crops, adopted to regions and crops, should, therefore, be inaugurated immediately under the leadership and financial assistance of the Centre. To get maximum value from coordinated variety testing, "Variety Release Committees" should be established in Centre and States to pass on all varieties, new and old, which are to be included in seed multiplication schemes. It is vital that only the best varieties be included in State seed schemes regardless of origin. Data on disease resistance and other desirable characteristics, determined in well-equipped laboratories. should also serve as criteria in accepting varieties. Centre scientists should be represented in State seed committees in an advisory capacity.

Merchandising Of Seed

Seed merchandising, including attention to seed quality, has not received enough attention in seed schemes. This deficiency is fast becoming the major deterrent to successful improved seed programmes. India does not now have a seed industry to take leadership in seed merchandising, or to engage in either seed multiplication or distribution. As a result, local extension personnel are increasingly devoting their time to inadequately organised seed distribution schemes, often at the expense of the educational programme.

All possible speed should, therefore, be used in developing supply cooperatives, and where feasible private enterprise, to assume major responsibility for certified seed distribution along with other agricultural supplies,

Special Crops

An all-India coordinated research and development programme should be inaugurated to discover and put to use the most suitable areas for the multiplication of pure high quality seed of improved varieties of certain crops, including vegetables.

Maize

We strongly recommend that India embark immediately on a vigorous hybrid maize seed multiplication and distribution programme. It is essential that this scheme be developed on an all India coordinated basis, with Centre financing and with policy to be established by a State-Centre Board. We believe that an autonomous corporate structure free to organise and carry through a successful hybrid maize programme can best do this job.

Such a coordinated scheme will also fit the development of hybrid sorghum seed.

Storage

Storage to maintain high planting value of improved seeds, particularly in the hot humid season, is a major problem. Heavy losses may occur in large central seed godowns as well as in the villages. It is imperative that the accumulated knowledge of seed storage for tropical climates be fully applied in India, both as a type of storage and protection from insects, rodents and fungi.

Progress Evaluation

Progress in improved seed schemes can be ascertained by determining the proportion of the acreage planted to recommend varieties. Such data has in the past often been improperly determined and reported. Grossly misleading data is less useful than no data. Hence only statistically sound methods of reporting acreage planted to improved seeds should be employed. Such determinations should also include consideration of seed quality.

Livestock Development And Food Production

The objective clearly should be to improve the efficiency of draft power and to increase the quantity of animal products without using more land, or, better still, to produce more power and more animal products from less land than is now being used for these purposes.

Too Many Cattle

There is widespread recognition, not only among animal husbandry officials and technicians, but among citizens generally, that India's cattle population is far in excess of the available supplies of fodder and feed. The bovine population of India is estimated to be 203 millions, of which 155 millions are cattle and 48 millions buffaloes. This is one-fourth of the world's total, and more than the bovine population of any other country. Only Denmark has more cattle per square mile than India. At least one-third, and perhaps as many as one-half, of the Indian cattle population may be regarded as surplus in relation to the feed supply. The problem is being accentuated greatly by a substantial annual increase in cattle numbers.

Authentic figures are not available upon which to base a reliable estimate of the total loss to the nation because of cattle which neither work nor produce milk. But it is known, for example, that more dung is produced when a given quantity of feed is consumed by one animal than when is shared by two animals. The magnitude of the loss to the nation from feeding useless cattle and buffaloes may best be illustrated, however, by calculating the quantity of milk that would be produced if the feed now being consumed by such useless animals were added to the rations of milch animals whose maintenance requirements are already being provided for. If this transfer of feed were possible, it is reasonable to assume that at least one additional pound of milk per day could be produced as a result of eliminating one useless animal. Thus, for each animal eliminated, 365 pounds of milk would be gained annually. This quantity of milk, if valued at 13 annas per seer (the price now being paid at many points in India), would be worth Rs. 148. On this basis, the total amount gained annually by the nation from eliminating useless cattle and buffaloes would exceed Rs. 70 crores. Of perhaps even greater significance than the monetary gain is the fact that each pound of additional milk thus made available would provide the suggested daily nutritional allowance for one Indian child.

Programme For Reducing The Number Of Cattle

Modifications of the ban on cattle slaughter by the States so as to permit the economic utilisation of stray and useless cattle would contribute significantly to the attainment of the objective for animal husbandry programmes set forth in the Second Five-year Plan.

Unless problems associated with excessive cattle numbers and the attendant shortage of feed supplies are dealt with realistically, contribution of animal husbandry to increased food production will be extremely difficult, perhaps impossible.

This report and the recommendations contained herein have been prepared in the belief that progress can be made within the limitations imposed by the doctrine of *ahimsa* along with a deep sense of obligation to point out how the ban on cattle slaughter complicates the problem of increasing food production. Furthermore, a study of food production of India manifestly, would be incomplete without some consideration of the cattle slaughter question.. This should not be taken to mean that it is necessary for outsiders making such a study to take a position for or against cattle slaughter in India. The question is one which can be dealt with by India alone under her own political and socio-religious systems.

Recommendation For Reducing Cattle Numbers

A graduated tax on cattle which would make the maintenance of useless cattle a burden on their owners.

Compulsory confinement of all bulls kept for natural service.

Mandatory castration of all young bulls not required for breeding.

Compulsory sterilisation of surplus cows and heifers.

Measures to control open grazing,

Dessicating Plants

It is recommended that dessicating plants, fully equipped to process animal carcasses, be established on a sub-district, district or regional basis and that incentive payments be made to owners who bring fallen animals to these plants.

Poultry Production

It is strongly recommended that steps be taken immediately to encourage a marked expansion of the poultry industry.

Integration Of Livestock Production And Crop Production

There must be one programme for animal husbandry, including the all-India key village scheme, mixed farming projects and dairy development, irrespective of where the work is done or who does it.

It is recommended that the Indian Council of Agricultural Research evolve a plan for shaping and carrying out animal husbandry projects. This plan should stress : (1) the interdependence of livestock production and crop production ; and (2) coordination and teamwork among agencies and technical personnel concerned with (a) production and use of fodder and feed, (b) the improvement of livestock, and (c) the marketing of milk, eggs and poultry.

Over the long term, there are certain other activities which need to be started to ensure sustained future increases in food production. These include : (1) a constructive programme of grassland improvement and management ; (2) applied research on practical animal husbandry problems ; (3) basic and applied research in animal nutrition ; and (4) a country-wide marketing organisation linked to mixed farming.

The Role Of Cooperatives In Expanded Food Production

The individual cultivator is incapable, by himself alone, of breaking loose from his poverty-stricken status. Cooperative effort is required to break the strangling grip of the money lender and traders on the marketing supply and credit functions in the villages. Central and State participation is necessary in the form of loan advances to supplement the share capital of the primary societies, loans and subsidies for the construction of required godowns and other physical structures, and staff services for education and managerial assistance during the stages.

The Situation Today

Thus India has had considerable experience with various approaches to cooperative development at village level but she has not, as yet, found a basis for a programme on which all can agree. Until this is done, India can accomplish little in this phase of cooperative development.

We find that there is considerable inertia in all sectors of the cooperative movement today. Our inquiries into the reason for this has brought many different responses but most frequently mentioned are : administrative "red tape", the multitudinous requirements imposed by Governments before societies can be registered and State and Centre funds used ; fragmented responsibility for educational and promotional work on cooperatives ; and shifting policy at the national level.

Government Help

Government assistance to cooperatives must be given in a timely and helpful manner and with confidence if it is to contribute the maximum to the development of cooperatives. This is not to say that Government audit or inspection is not necessary. It must be maintained and strengthened in many States. Cases of bad faith must be dealt with firmly, impartially and without delay. Direct participation of Government employees in operations, on the other hand, contributes to delay and frustration and, if continued, may cause the whole system to fail.

Requirements Of Successful Cooperative

A cooperative organised to perform economic functions is a business organisation. If it is to make a significant contribution toward increasing India's food production, it must be built upon sound business principles.

The structure of a cooperative society is not so important as the results it achieves. Fundamental principles of cooperation must be adhered to, but the type of functions a society performs, the nature of its membership and the number of villages served will have to be determined by the circumstances found in each situation.

The flexibility is of great importance in a developing nation, because as the rural areas develop economically and socially the people will begin to look beyond their village walls and the boundaries of their lands. New problems as well as opportunities will be revealed and new social and economic groupings will develop.

This will be brought about by improved communication and transportation, by the cultivators purchasing more of their production requirements and selling more of their produce in the markets, by their joining with the people of other villages to develop their lands cooperatively and perform mutually beneficial services, and by their being better educated and informed. The people's cooperatives must not be rigid in structure but must be able to adapt to the future as well as the present.

Cooperative Leaders

That the counsel and advice of qualified and dedicated non-official cooperators should be sought when considering either State or national policy or plans to implement policy.

Unless non-official leadership is recognised and developed, cooperatives will be led and dominated by Government. This is not India's objective as we interpret her plans. Obviously, if there are any non-official leaders who have selfish designs they must be weeded out, or they will cause the whole movement to fail and the whole economic development programme will suffer a severe blow.

Auditors And Inspectors

The attitude of auditors and inspectors is important. They must approach audit and inspection with a helpful attitude rather than a strictly critical one which places emphasis upon minor details. In any new development, honest errors in judgment are bound to occur. If these are magnified and responsible employees severely criticised for such errors, initiative is stifled and the programme suffers. The State registrars can be of material assistance to the cooperative movement by developing in their employees this philosophy of assistance and encouragement, and by stressing the necessity for them to distinguish important from non-important infractions of rules and errors of judgement. There must, however, be no compromise with dishonesty, selfish designs, or general incompetence.

Personnel Training Of Officers And Employees

The flexible approach to cooperative development requires a concentration of training in the requirements of successful operation.

It is our view that it is especially important for the senior officers of all cooperative societies, cooperative departments and cooperative banks to have at least enough training in agriculture to develop a full appreciation of the many agricultural problems in India and a greater knowledge of their possible solution.

Training At The Village Level

We have found very little of this essential educational work being done in India. Therefore, we strongly recommend that the registrars for cooperatives in the various States provide sufficient personnel in the extension blocks to do concentrated educational and promotional work on cooperatives.

Government-Appointed Directors

It is especially important that the cooperative banks have their board members elected as soon as possible, by the primary societies and other cooperatives served. We were informed on numerous occasions that cooperative banks were more urban than rural minded. Where this situation exists, it should be changed as soon as possible.

Managerial Assistance

Management is so important that, despite the urgency of the situation, no cooperative should begin operations until the board is confident that they have a qualified man who will command the confidence of the people and be able to build the organisation.

Cooperative Institutes And Cooperative Unions

The cooperative institutes and unions can make their greatest contribution. The unions should work hand-in-hand with the men in the extension blocks who have responsibility for educational and developmental activities. They should help plan and execute educational and developmental programmes. This work may, in fact, be delegated to them by the State, in certain areas where they are capable of doing the job. Delegation of the work to cooperative institutes and unions would not, however, relieve the State of its own responsibility for educational and developmental activities.

The institutes and unions are now performing many valuable services to cooperatives. They are articulate in regard to proposed policies and programmes affecting cooperatives and they are doing important educational and developmental work.

Their work should be continued and expanded. However, we believe they could make an even greater contribution if they were entirely supported by cooperatives and could be relieved of having to ask the Government for support. Only when they reach this position can they be the completely unfettered representatives of cooperatives. During this developmental period, their work is so important that Government assistance is, in our opinion, justified. But they should try to become free of Government support as soon as possible. This is in conformity with the policy we recommend for cooperatives.

The Primary Society

If cultivators are going to produce more food, they will need more credit, more production supplies such as fertilisers, improved seeds, agricultural chemicals, etc. They need also an improved marketing system to give them more assurance that they will benefit from greater production.

These are all requirements of cultivators, whether they are landlords, tenants or owner-operators. The requirements are closely related and are complementary one to the other. Thus they can all logically be handled by a single primary society operating at the village level. Usually a primary society in India can perform all these functions together better than it can perform a single function. On this point there is general agreement. Our discussion of primary societies is, therefore, based upon the assumption that their original functions will be to extend credit, distribute supplies and assist members in the marketing of their products.

Extending Credit Through The Primary Society

An adequate, dependable and timely credit service at reasonable cost is a prime requisite of rural development and increased agricultural production.

Government Financial Assistance To Primary Societies And Cooperative Banks

We believe that if primary societies are to become important in the extension of credit in India, the State Governments must advance loan funds to supplement the capital investments of the members to the extent necessary to provide a capital base adequate to support the complete borrowing needs of cultivators.

But we are unable to see how a primary society will be able to provide the services (especially the credit services) needed in a village without Government advances to supplement the capital of members.

We are of the opinion that all net earnings should be kept in the business until the Government loan advances are paid or nearly paid.

We believe that there should be no specific date established when the Government's advances would be repaid.

Relation Of Primary Societies To Central And Apex Banks

There must be a direct and close working relationship between the Central Banks and the primary societies.

If Central Banks become or continue to be rural-minded, they must have a responsibility for the successful operation of the primary societies. It is for these reasons that we have recommended that the officials of Central and also the Apex Banks have some training in agricultural and why we have recommended that the Directors of Central Banks be elected by the primary societies and other cooperatives, and as soon as possible.

Creditworthiness

But if the lender's objective is to provide maximum economic assistance to the borrower by the extension of credit, he will concern himself with the purpose for which the loan is being sought and the likely effect of loan upon the borrower's well-being as well as his repayment capacity and the value of his pledgable assets. Agricultural credit societies must approach credit with this objective before them, if they are to perform the function for which they were created. It is our observation, however, that many of the societies and cooperative banks are still approaching credit with maximum safety as the major objective.

An immediate change in philosophy regarding creditworthiness could make an important contribution toward increasing agricultural production in India.

In brief a cultivator is considered to be creditworthy and entitled to credit, if he is honest and can repay his loan from production.

Nothing would cause greater havoc to a credit system than to intermingle credit with subsidy or relief payments to cultivators.

Credit And Agricultural Technicians

If credit for production purposes is extended upon the basis of repayment capacity, there needs to be a functioning inter-relationship between the agricultural technicians of the departments of agriculture and the officials of both the primary credit societies and the co-operative banks in order to maximise repayment capacity and enhance recovery probabilities.

We are of the firm opinion that only by a coordinated combined effort of the various agencies of Government can a rapid and significant increase in food production be obtained in India. We, therefore, believe that projects of the nature of the Paddy Project in Bombay, with some strengthening of the marketing phase, should be inaugurated in other States, in areas where the potential for increased food production is greatest.

Timely Credit Service

It is essential that operating procedures of credit societies and cooperative banks be simplified so that cultivators can obtain funds from their societies in a reasonable period of time. Requests of new applicants for short-term production credit should not require over a fortnight for a decision and a cultivator with a good record of performance with the society should be able to receive approval of a normal credit request within a few days. For small amounts he should be able to obtain the funds "over the counter". Only by this kind of service can the society meet all the production credit requirements of its members. This is, therefore, the only way the societies can compete effectively with the money lenders and become dominant in the production credit field.

There is no India-wide system for bounding employees as a protection against loss because of bad faith, defalcations, unfaithful performance of duty, etc. It appears that this might be an activity in which the States could engage on a self-supporting basis, by the collection of premiums from organisations wishing the protection of bonded employees. With this added protection there should be less need for double checking for the safety of the banks and societies.

Consumer Credit

Consumer credit, coupled with a programme to make a greater variety of consumer goods available to cultivators might be a stimulant to production and could induce cultivators to sell more of their produce. To the extent that an increased marketable surplus was induced, credit extended for consumer goods would not be inflationary. More information is needed before a final judgement can be made on how much encouragement should be given to promoting consumer credit in rural areas. A study of the effect of consumer credit extended by primary societies should be of value in determining policy and developing an appropriate educational programme.

There is no question, however, that primary societies are going to have to extend some consumer credit if they are to maintain the interest and loyalty of their members.

Special Problems Of Land Mortage Banks

The land mortgage banks have an excellent opportunity to make a real contribution and to develop business and prestige if they can develop a sound scheme of financing which will assist the cultivators to properly develop their land.

Although we believe that the term of the debentures sold by the banks should generally be related to the term of loans made, we do not believe that this policy need be so rigid as to prevent the issuing of some shorter-term debentures (perhaps five years should be as short a term as the banks should issue at this time), when money is more available in that sector of the market.

The Role Of The Primary Society

The Rural Credit Survey recommended that "agricultural credit societies may also supply members' requirements for crop production and also basic, but standardised, consumer goods on the basis of indents or established demand". Further the Plan provides for the establishment of 1800 marketing societies. "They are set up at important marketing centres, and agricultural credit societies as well as agriculturists belonging to villages from which there is a natural flow of harvested crops to these centres, are enrolled as their members. When production loans are given by credit societies, the borrower signs an agreement to deliver the crops raised with the loan at the marketing society to which the credit society is affiliated, and that the marketing society may recover his productions loan for the credit society either out of the sale proceeds of the crops or out of any loan it may advance on the produce left in its godown".

It will be seen from these quotations that it is intended that the primary society will extend credit, distribute supplies, and assist members to market their crops. Obviously, each primary society should have a godown nearby in order to carry out these functions. The primary society does not actually market the crop, nor does it have responsibility for arranging the purchase of supplies. But it is a stockholder in, and has representation on, the board of directors of (its affiliated) marketing cooperative, which has these responsibilities. The primary society functions more in the nature of an agent for the marketing cooperative. This coordination makes it possible for the primary society to extend a part of its credit in kind and also to be in a position to effect recoveries better.

"Marketing" cooperatives are intended to perform both the supply and marketing functions in India.

The Supply Functions

We have been impressed with the ever-recurring problem of how to get the needed supplies to the cultivator at the time they were required, and in the variety and the quality recommended by the block staff and within a bullock-cart haul distance of the cultivator.

Distribution of Fertilisers: Of the projected increase in foodgrain production under the Second Plan about 25 per cent is expected from fertilisers and manures and 10 per cent from improved seeds.

Marketing fertiliser through cooperatives should help strengthen the cooperative movement by providing additional responsibilities, increasing contacts with cultivators and increasing volume of business.

The Marketing Functions

Although cooperative marketing is accepted as a desirable goal, it has not attained wide adoption in India.

It is suggested that strength be given to the cooperatives by using them as an agency for price stabilisation.

Processing of Crops for Market: Since costs of hand pounding are reported to exceed machine milling costs, we believe that the cooperatives in areas having substantial marketable surpluses of rice should be encouraged to establish, either individually or jointly with other cooperatives, cooperative paddy hullers or rice mills. This can facilitate the improving of rice quality and result in higher prices for the milled product.

Storage

The possibility of using funds from grain imports for godown construction should be investigated fully. It is possible, for example, that funds available from grain imports under PL 480 and other special programmes might be used to construct needed godowns in village areas. This could be especially desirable as domestic supplies of steel and cement become more available.

Legislation

It is evident that there is need for legislation in the various States to modernise their laws relating to cooperatives. A review of these laws is now in progress. We have not had time to study present or proposed laws but we would state as a general policy that the legislation finally enacted should permit the States to assist primary cooperatives financially and otherwise during their developmental period. The States should have continuing authority to protect the interests of members and the public interest through audit and inspection. But the responsibility for day-to-day operations must rest with the board of directors and managers of the cooperatives. Only by having local responsibility for operation can the cooperatives be responsive to local needs and develop local leadership and initiative.

There is need also for the States to clarify and perhaps modify their laws relating to property rights in land following land reform legislation, in order that the land mortage banks might safely extend long-term credit upon the security of land. Specific legislative measures to accomplish these objectives could be properly drawn only after a careful study of the present laws in each State by an appropriate committee or agent representing the cooperative banks and societies.

It appears also that there needs to be review of present State laws as they apply to crop production loans. Since the policy of making production loans on the basis of expected crop yields is relatively new, it is likely that there need to be some changes in law to give adequate protection to the lender.

Economic Intelligence And Outlook

We suggest the development of an Agricultural Economic Intelligence Organisation at the Centre with the responsibility for making short-term and long-term forecasts and summaries for foodgrains and other agricultural commodities. This involves the collection and organisation of the necessary data, and rapid processing of the data to permit timely analysis for use in decision and reporting. An excellent beginning has been made within the Ministry of Food and Agriculture. The major need is to broaden the data-collecting process, speed up the processing and improve the dissemination of the results. The information provided by an economic intelligence organisation is not only essential for administrators; it will provide a basis for obtaining an understanding of the food situation by cultivators and the general public. As cultivators learn the need for expanded food production, and the production potentials of their own village, they can participate intelligently in establishing production targets that represent realistic achievements village by village and area by area.

It is believed that by assessing the forces that are likely to operate in the future and by working out the uantitative relationships involved, the improvements in decision-making will repay all the costs of the enlarged Agricultural Economic Intelligence Organisation.

Market Information For Cultivators

We suggest that in view of the need for market information to cultivators, a programme be initiated to install and maintain a radio in every village in India for dissemination of market reviews by the All-India Radio. It is suggested that an immediate test be made in one district in each State. The daily press should also be encouraged to carry commodity prices, market reports and similar information.

Some Problems Of Foodgrain Marketing

Our limited observations indicate that the present marketing system in India fails to perform in an efficient manner the individual marketing functions. Yet substantial progress is being made in improving transportation, storage, processing and other functions.

Grades And Standards

We suggest that the Ministry of Food and Agriculture experiment with tentative grades for grains. A number one or premium grade could include the superior or very best commercial delivery; the number two could have quality requirements to include the bulk of the produce; the number three grade would be basically wholesome but include a larger proportion of admixtures and damaged or broken kernels; and the number four grade would be of low quality, suitable only for livestock feed or requiring expensive cleaning for human consumption.

Popularising and securing general adoption of grading will require a concerted effort on the part of all Government-sponsored institutions involved in marketing. Regulated markets and cooperative marketing societies, for example, should adopt statutory grades for their trade transactions as soon as possible. Similarly, the official reporting agencies should quote prices in terms of official grades wherever possible. It might be advisable to give higher priorities to graded foodgrains in booking railway cars. This would encourage proper cleaning of grains early in the marketing process. Only by a concerted effort can the economies and other benefits of graded produce be realised.

Regulated Markets

It is suggested that the development of regulated markets be stressed especially in areas with large marketable surpluses of foodgrains. The cooperative marketing societies may continue to meet with opposition and competition from established traders. But if a representative of the marketing cooperative is a member of the market committee in the regulated market, he can protect the interests of the cooperative. The cooperative will operate to the best advantage if the programme for price stabilisation is conducted through the marketing cooperatives and at the regulated markets.

MARKETABLE SURPLUS OF CEREALS

(Calculated from production adjusted on 1955-57 final estimate)

Year	Rice (31.5 per cent of Production)	Wheat (35 per cent of Production)	Jowar (23.8 per cent of Production)	Bajra (26.5 per cent of Production)	Maize (24.5 per cent of Production)	Ragi (18.9 per cent of Production)	Barley (26 per cent of Production)	Small Millets (16.14 per cent of Production)	Total Cereals
				(Million Tons)					
1949-50	7.5	2.3	1.6	0.8	0.6	0.3	0.6	0.3	14.0
1950-51	6.6	2.3	1.5	0.7	0.5	0.3	0.6	0.3	12.5
1951-52	6.7	2,2	1.6	0.6	0.6	0.2	0.6	0.3	12.8
1952-53	7.2	2.6	1.7	0.8	0.7	0.2	0.7	0.3	14.2
1953-54	8.9	2.8	1.9	1.1	0.7	0.3	0.7	0.4	16.8
1954-55	7.9	3.1	2.2	0.9	0.7	0.3	0.8	0.4	16.3
1955-56	8.5	3.0	1.6	0.9	0.6	0.3	0.7	0.3	15.9
1956-57	8.9	3.3	1.7	0.8	0.7	0.3	0.7	0.3	16.7
1957-58	7.8	2.7	1.9	0.9	0.8	0.3	0.6	0.3	15.3

Research In Agriculture Economics

We believe that an immediate start should be made to initiate research that will arrive at solutions to each of the major economic problems facing agriculture. We find the same needs for research answers in India as in other countries, and a great deal of experience and methodology can be adapted to India. The International Conference of Agricultural Economists held in Mysore in August 1958 demonstrated very clearly that India has competent leaders in agricultural economics. But many more are needed, and funds must be available for productive research on pressing problems.

A programme has gone forward between five Indian educational institutions and The Ford Foundation to train graduate students in social science research methodology. Similar programmes on an expanded scale should be initiated by the Centre.

There is urgent need for one outsanding centre for graduate training in agricultural economics. Emphasis should be placed on training in economics of farming in view of the crisis in food production. Research programmes should be expanded as more trained workers become available. We believe that the resulting improvements in the planning and execution of food programmes will more than pay for all of the costs involved.

Special attention should be devoted to types of farm management research that can provide guidance to the food production programme.

We suggest that farm management research be developed along the following lines:

Every State Department of Agriculture should establish a section on agricultural economics which would be responsible for development of both farm management research and extension within the State and for cooperation with the Centre on research of nationwide importance.

In so far as possible, the actual research in farm management should be centred at the agricultural colleges. Those who are teaching agricultural economics would then have an opportunity to study actual farm and village problems, and to use the results in their teaching as well as making them available for programme guidance. A close working relationship should be maintained with the extension farm management specialists stationed at block headquarters.

The research should concentrate on case studies of farms that would be representative of sizes and types most important in the area under study. Available census or sample survey data should be used to determine the representative character of the farms selected for study. Care also should be taken to select, for case study, farms with soil and water conditions broadly representative of the area to be covered.

An inventory should be made of the resources of case-study farms. The present crops and livestock should be analysed to determine the inputs and practices used, and the physical outputs. An estimate would then be made of income, expenses and net returns from the present system of farming.

Estimate should be made from all available information of the results that might be obtained from introducing new crops, new practices and better feeding and care of livestock. The income results should be compared with the present system and attempts made to persuade cultivators to adopt the improved system.

Similar analyses should be made of the case-study farms in succeeding years. The results of the improvements made would be evaluated in this way. If farmers could be persuaded to keep simple records, the analysis would be facilitated, but on farms of the usual size adequate estimates can be made by the cultivator and checked by the researcher.

If year-to-year case farm studies of the type outlined could be made in a large number of areas, the results could be used to indicate the potentialities of programmes for increasing food production and the well-being of cultivators. The returns on the farms where major changes have been made would serve as one indicator of progress. The gaps in other research information would be revealed by such studies and steps could be taken to fill them.

Other types of farm management research should be undertaken as problems come to the forefront, but we believe that case farm studies in areas with broadly similar production opportunities will contribute most directly to food production efforts.

General Comments On Agriculture Research And Education

Clearly research must pave the way for the far-reaching changes in Indian Agriculture. Clearly too, if India expects to have food enough for its rapidly growing population, it must have an increasing number of increasingly better trained agricultural scientists, educators, extension workers, and agricultural administrators.

Agricultural Research

To assure that research is making its proper contribution to food production, an inventory of agricultural research should be made to determine what information may be lacking, what research gaps need to be filled, and what new projects should be undertaken.

We would urge that India give greater consideration to team approaches in both planning and implementing research. Most agricultural problems are complex and can often be solved most effectively by the combined efforts of scientists from two or more disciplines. Indeed there are few problems which cannot be solved more effectively by a team approach, in less time and with less expenditure of effort and money.

All research activities, research findings and technical knowledge must be related to the cultivators, who in the final analysis must apply the results of research to their own farming operations. The bridge between the researchers and the cultivators is the agricultural extension worker.

It is especially desirable for research workers at the agricultural colleges to be closely tied into field problems so that their work might similarly make a direct contribution to food production. We endorse the policy of relating the agricultural colleges to specific blocks in their vicinity and urge its full implementation.

Agricultural Education

We would encourage each institution to develop its own programmes based on the geograhphical area it serves and the problems of agriculture in the community. More graduate work should be provided in India, but only at fully competent institutions. The Team has been impressed with the pioneering efforts of the Indian Agricultural Research Institute at New Delhi, and believes that this Institute may well set the pattern for sound developments in the field of graduate education.

The Team expresses a word of caution. Instead of increasing the number of agricultural colleges and training institutions, it would seem desirable to expand and consolidate those already in existence. Where possible, agricultural and animal husbandry institutions should be located on the same campus to permit economies in teaching of basic courses and to encourage joint teaching of such courses as forage and feed production, animal breeding and genetics, and livestock production and marketing.

We are convinced that colleges with enrolments of a few hundred students suffer in effectiveness and quality. They often cannot afford the facilities, such as laboratories and libraries, nor the calibre of faculty, that a larger institution can support. In this connection the Team endorses the concept of the "Rural University" as set forth in the plans of the University Education Commission headed by Dr. S. Radhakrishnan.

Improving Extension Work Through Community Development

Extension Programmes And Their Development

A study of agricultural extension work demands that attention be given to the adaptation of an extension programme to local needs; the degree to which the programme is directed to the particular interests of all people capable of making a contribution to increased food production; the extent of village cultivator participation in its development; the scientific validity of the practices recommended. Each of these points will be considered as they apply to India's present agricultural extension observations.

Determining The Block Programme

In the opinion of the Team present agricultural extension programmes in India would be capable of making a much greater contribution to increased food production if they were focused more directly upon local conditions, village production problems, and village potentials.

Production Targets And Local Programme Adaptation

The Team believes that national and State production targets are necessary but that their use should be confined to the role of indicating national and State food and other crop requirements for the guidance of local programming, rather than serve as specific quotas handed down from above.

The Programme And The People

To be effective, a programme to increase agricultural production must take into account the people whose behaviour is to be changed and the factors that affect their behaviour or limit the possibilities of change. It would appear that extension programmes in India have not given sufficient concern to the factors of human motivation.

Food production objectives and programmes to achieve them must be related to the group that ultimately increases food production, the cultivators themselves. Unless the behaviour of this group can be changed unless they can effectively be motivated to take steps which will increase production on their fields, no extension educational programme can succeed. From observations in the field, the Team believes that this fact is often lost sight of in the multiplicity of directives, campaign leaflets and procedures used in current extension work.

While the cultivator should be the primary focus of efforts to increase food production, farm women and youth can also make substantial contribution to greater farming efficiency and increased production. It appeared to the Team that these groups were not being given the attention that they merit in present extension programmes.

Women play an important role in the selection and storage of seed and in such field work as planting, weeding and harvesting. New varieties may not be accepted because women do not like the grinding or cooking qualities of the grain. Women often share in the decision-making process when major expenditures are considered for such items as fertiliser. It is clear that village women are an important clientele to be reached, and that a great deal of teaching of agriculture can be done through village women's groups and training camps.

Even more important in the long run are the young people. They characteristically respond to group organisation and action. They accept new and different ideas. Properly structured and organised, with provision for satisfactions and rewards, an organised youth movement can materially contribute to stated objectives in the short run and more specifically in the long run. Not only is there opportunity for the acquisition of skills directly by youth members but they in turn are influential in achieving change among their parents and others who come in contact with them and their projects.

Involving People In Planning

The Team observed that village leaders have been used in some instances to gain acceptance of goals assigned to the blocks. The procedure followed began with village circle camps. The team noted that village leaders were trained in these camps to assist the VLW's and block officers by conducting subsequent meetings in their own villages. In a series of three such meetings in each village, problems are analysed with the cultivators, production potentials are assessed, resources needed are determined, and finally cultivators pledge their intentions with respect to food production increases. It is noteworthy that where this procedure has been followed, targets have often been surpassed. We believe that if participation had occurred earlier in the planning process (instead of starting from goals passed down from higher levels), production achievement might have been even higher.

Involvement of local people in planning processes is difficult and time-consuming. However, to meet higher production goals, and to achieve the objectives of human development and leadership, more emphasis must be placed on local participation in programme planning. It is clear that plans, not accepted by those people who alone can carry them out, are only paper plans. To project more fertiliser use where farmers refuse to use more fertiliser is futile. To plan for the activities which cultivators would do in any case is obviously wasted effort in India's critical food situation. Hence, there is really no alternative to increasingly effective local planning in which the cultivators themselves are involved.

As has been indicated earlier, the cultivators and other people of the village, as well as the professional staff, have roles to play in this planning process. Because of their training and background, the VLW's and block officers herein perform their roles as educators and guides in the process of planning for greater food production. In this connection, they can use statistically expressed targets from higher sources as guides to what is needed, to measure resources and to challenge interest.

Once production goals are set locally and methods for accomplishing them are agreed upon, the professional staff members can proceed to outline their own work plans for aiding the villagers to attain the stated goals. Ultimate performance, of course, is by the cultivators and they must be involved in the day-to-day actions and later in the evaluation of achievements.

Village Agricultural Production Committees

We realise the kind of planning process here proposed cannot be adopted overnight. Its development will require time and patience. More importantly, it will require a change in thinking about the role of the people in extension programme planning. But a beginning must be made. It is recommended, therefore, that initially one village food production committee be set up in each VLW circle so that the VLW's and the block staff can develop the skills needed to expand this approach to the greater involvement of local people in food programme planning.

Staff Work Planning

There is also need for effective work planning by members of the block staff, as a group on a long-range basis, annually or semi-annually.

Summary And Recommendations on Programmes

Agricultural extension programmes in India are not now having the impact upon food production that is necessary for the nation's survival. They can be improved. We therefore recommend :

The programmes should be focused more directly upon local conditions, village production problems and production potential, and the village farmers should participate more actively in programme determinations, including setting the priority order of programme action. This process in itself leads to mental growth and development of leadership in village people.

Block extension workers should set up village food production committees through which the local farm people, assisted by block extension personnel and VLW's can, first, assess the present production, and optimum production capacities of village farms; and, second, determine the combinations of improved farming methods necessary to achieve the production potentials.

Targets composed of improved practice quotas handed down to the blocks and villages from above should be discontinued. The use of targets should be con ined to national and State requirements for key food and other crops and be used as guides by the local people and extension workers for programme planning for increased production.

Special extension programme emphasis should be given to the important contribution that farm women and youth can make in village community efforts to step up food production.

Caution should be exercised in making recommendations for any improved practice uniformly over large areas without adequate regard for their appropriateness for local farming conditions.

The Block Level As A Focus Of The Programme

It is important that an organisational and team relationship be developed in the block that will complement and not compete with agricultural programmes.

There is need for a more careful analysis of the specific tasks which need to be undertaken in each block. This need arises out of the present uniform staffing and budget allocation for all organised blocks over India. Admittedly, the problems and opportunities vary from block to block and from State to State. Block staffing should reflect block resources, needs, problems and opportunities.

The Village Level Worker

In the opinion of the Team, corroborated by Indian officials, many VLW's now possess greater aptitude and skill than other officers in working with people at the village level. Given the training in this task, he can become even more effective. To fulfil this role adequately necessitates a broad understanding of village problems, particularly in agriculture. Over-time he will need more and higher and constant upgrading. But the VLW will still need the support and guidance of adequate and competent specialists at the block level.

It is a temptation to say that the extension worker should slough off these chores, but often alternate ways of handling them are not available. Institutions for service may not exist. Moreover, performance of services may prepare the way for educational contacts. Often the services are of such a crucial character that withdrawal may cause a failure of the programme. We can only conclude under the circumstances that such vital service activities be continued only for as short a time period as necessary, and that immediate steps be taken to develop other provisions for rendering these necessary service functions.

Extension Officers On the Block Staff

We recommend the following changes in assignments for officers at the block level :

(a) **Agriculture Officer** : Relieve him of service responsibilities such as seed, fertiliser and insecticides. assigning these duties to cooperatives and the Cooperative Officer.

(b) **Animal Husbandry Officer :** Reorient his role to place greater emphasis on poultry and milk production where applicable, greater emphasis on forage utilisation and controlled grazing which have more immediate impact on food production.

(c) **S.E.O. (Man) :** Assign him to the B.D.O. as a staff officer to assist the entire staff in organising facilities, preparing material, visual aids and other teaching techniques with particular bearing on agricultural production. To the extent of his time and abilities he would train and assist the VLW in organisation, method demonstrations, etc. In this role, he would perform a staff function and would give service to selected programmes rather than carrying certain programmes alone. This idea is consistent with the objective that these skills eventually become common to all Extension Officers. It is, therefore, a step toward developing the organisational and methods competence of each staff officer.

(d) **SEO (Woman) :** Assign responsibility for kitchen gardens and for education and training of village women in pertinent aspects of food production.

(e) **Cooperative Officer :** Assign him responsibility for teaching and connselling in regard to the purposes, objectives, and opportunities through cooperatives and aid in their organisation. Make him responsible for the supply functions such as seed and fertiliser currenty handled by the agriculturul officer.

(f) **Other Officers :** Assign them responsibilities which would contribute more directly to food production, *i.e.*, the panchayat officer should give leadership and assistance to organising and servicing village food production committees ; the engineering officer should aid in the construction of godown and farm-to-market roads. Training programmes may be necessary if such officers are to make their maximum contribution.

With the above real location of resources of the officers of the block staff, the agricultural officer will be free to spend greater effort in the educational tasks of food production. In addition, each officer will have an opportunity to make a more direct contribution to the immediate needs of food production.

We fully concur in the recommendation of the report of the Agricultural Personnel Committee. of the Planning Commission that "the block staff be strengthened by the addition of four agricultural graduates with some special training in selected subjects". Due to the lack of trained personnel to implement this realistically, this recommendation may be a long-range objective, at least for application uniformly across the country. However, priorities can be established so that as agricultural officers become available, they may be placed where they can make maximum contribution to India's food production.

"Shadow" Block Areas

It is recommended that steps be taken to ensure shadow blocks with full staffing of agricultural inspectors, assistant inspectors, *kamdars*, particularly in those blocks located in good farming areas. Attention should be given to the farming of these men in improved agricultural practices and in extension teaching methods.

District Organisation And Staff

The Report of the Agricultural Administration Committee recommended additional district extension specialists, their subject matter to depend upon the types of farming carried on in the various districts. The Team fully supports this recommendation and hopes that this can be implemented at an early date. As a shorter run recommendation, the Team suggests that the present duties of the district agricultural officers and animal husbandary officers should be re-arranged so that some of the routine administrative duties of these officers can be reduced and the servicing functions be transferred to the district cooperative officers.

Organisation And Staffing At The State Level

With respect to State-level direction, leadership and technical guidance for agricultural extension workers in the field, the Team supports reccommendation made in the Agricultural Administration Committee Report. It is important that each State promptly establish and fill with best qualified candidate the position of extension joint director. It is neceesary also that several extension subject matter specialists be posted with the extension joint director to guide field staff in a programme of extension education soundly based upon research.

These State extension specialists should work in continuous liaison with counterparts in research in order that research information be made available to the village cultivators through the field service, and that local problems retarding production be transferred to the attention of the research staffs. State extension units in agricultural departments should be confined strictly to agricultural extension functions. Responsibilities for supplies and regulatory activities should be transferred as rapidly as feasible to the cooperative and other appropriate departments.

Central Government Responsibility For Agricultural Extension

The Team recommends that some of the topflight agriculturists be recruited to build up the strength of this Central Office for the duration of the current food emergency. The men selected should be nationally renowned for their competence in the production of the nation's key crops and also in livestock husbandary. They should be persons commanding the respect of their corresponding colleagues in research and also have the capacity to work with the State Directors of Agriculture in staffing and training competent State subject-matter specialists for the State services. A limited staff of this calibre could provide broad subject-matter guidance and overall programme leadership to the state Departments of Agriculture in their own efforts to strength block and district agricultural extension programmes.

Finally, since agricultural extension programmes in the NES blocks are carried on by personnel under the administrative direction of the State Development Department and under the general guidance of the Central Ministry of Community Development, the staff of the other Directorate of Extension in the Central Ministry of the Food and Agriculture needs to continue and further strengthen the close liaison maintained with appropriate personnel in the Ministry of Community Development for purposes of administrative and operational coordination. The current effort to step up food production makes imperative the closest possible coordination.

Information Service : State And Centre

Mass media communications are among the most effective methods for creating "awareness" about an idea or practice. These methods also support the process of accepting and adopting new ideas. The potential of reaching large numbers of people through the use of such mass communication devices as radio, newspapers, pamphlets and other similar materials, movies, slides, film strips and other visual aids has not yet been fully exploited.

Since mass communications are among the means of conducting educational programmes, it follows that these means should be at the disposal of the agency responsible for the programme. Agricultural production is of importance enough and agricultural educational information is of such a unique character that we are impressed with a need to set up agricultural information services in both the States and the Centre. We agree with the principle partially accepted in some States that there should be a separate agricultural information bureau or unit in the Ministry of Agriculture and agriculture departments so placed that it can serve as an aid to extension education. The unit should thus be an integral part of extension with guaranteed liaison to the research workers. It is important also that because of its special skills, the information staff help in the planning of action programmes and in using the most effective communication devices for success in action.

Three general areas of opportunity exist for an information unit:

(1) Preparation of material which is intended for the direct consumption of the cultivator and his family. Included in this are circulars, posters, radio programmes, press releases, etc.

(2) Preparation of materials to equip the cores of workers who do direct teaching (BDO, ADO, VLW). Examples of this are hand books, procedural outlines, campaign guides, supporting and additional technical information, film strips, movies and other teaching aids.

(3) Preparation of materials which will permit engaging the support from other Governmental and non-Governmental mass media sources. Groups involved include radio networks and newspaper and magazine editors.

On the production side of mass communication, we find that the State information offices are inadequately equipped, staffed and budgeted to take advantage of their present and expanding opportunities. Steps need to be taken which will:

(1) Provide additional information staff of editors, artists, radio and visual aid specialists ;

(2) Provide additional facilities for posters, bulletins circulars, radio tapes, transcriptions;

(3) Establish budgets for personnel and facilities on a continuing basis;

(4) Expand and improve the training workshops for State information staff; for State workers such as specialists, district level workers, BDO's, block officers and VLW's; for newspaper editors who can become more aware of their expanding opportunities to provide agricultural information to cultivators.

Specialised Administrative Functions

There are several special areas of extension administration, including budgeting, accounting and auditing and reporting, along with the management, supervision and training of the staff, that are also essential to the conduct of extension work. These elements of administration, with primary attention to block operation, are considered below.

Budgeting

The following recommendations are offered:

Block budgets for all aspects of food production programmes should be more flexible, and should, in total amount and in detailed breakdown, reflect priority programme needs and potentialities as identified at the block level.

Budget procedures should be drastically simplified to permit more final decisions to be made at the block level without the delays now part of the complex sanctioning system. Similar reforms are also necessary at other levels, as has been pointed out in the recent Report of the Agricultural Administration Committee.

Greater emphasis should be placed upon programme budgeting and on appraising expenditures in terms of programme accomplishments, than on elaborate and refined controls before expenditure. This emphasis on programme is necessary if the goal of rapid, flexible and effective food production programme administration is to be achieved.

Accounting And Auditing

The Team suggests that steps be taken to develop a fuller understanding of programme objectives in accountants and auditors dealing with emergency food production programmes. More particularly they must be made to realise:

(a) That programmes moving into new substantive areas move on untrodden paths; hence more numerous errors of judgment may be expected, and greater margins of error must be permitted;

(b) That where many new employees are being brought into a new and expanding programme, the chances for errors of judgment are increased, and hence a greater margin of error must be permitted;

(c) That the criteria for evaluating administrative financial decisions should include the standard of reasonableness of the action under the circumstances of the time and place;

(d) That the food production programme requires a high level of initiative and experimentation;

(e) That the overall basis of appraisal should be programme results that are a contribution to increased agricultural production.

Records And Reports

The Team would suggest that appropriate representatives of the Community Development Organisation and others concerned should make an appraisal of the current reports and records required of the block staffs in order to determine the extent to which they make a specific contribution to the block and village programmes for achieving increased food production, rather than serve largely for administrative control.

A limited number of administrative reports relating to financial expenditure are, of course, necessary in connection with block development projects and service activities. However, it would appear that reports directed toward supervision and administrative understanding of extension results should be reduced to short, periodic and descriptive statements of programme achievement. With respect to the food production programme, the focus of records and reports should be programme accomplishments toward the ultimate goals of more food. Beyond that, reports for administrative intelligence and overall programme appraisal need not go. For purposes of supervision, however, worker reports also need of include a periodic review of teaching methods used, along with self-appraisals of the effectiveness of extension methods in obtaining programme results,

Management Procedure Experimentation

The Team has been critical of a number of current budgetary, accounting, auditing, and reporting procedures, expressing the view that these often hamper the realisation of programme objectives. A number of general recommendations have been made to alter these procedures. It is suggested that an experimental approach be adopted with respect to these changes. A district area might be selected in each State in which greater control over budget allocation, without the need for superior approval, be given to the BDO's. Accounting and auditing criteria might also be experimented with, and in sample blocks or village circles, the reporting requirements might be reduced to a bare minimum in order to determine the best ways to simplify and decentralise certain administrative operations that reflect upon food production programme effectiveness.

Personnel Policies

The Team believes that more attention should be given to the preparation of job descriptions related to specific jobs to be done, and to the particular needs, problems and opportunities of individual blocks and village level worker circles. It is believed that job descriptions of this kind, prepared by the individual workers and their immediate supervisors, would provide greater understanding of the task assigned and of the performance expected.

The Team observed that there is considerable job turnover of block personnel. To a degree this problem is inevitable in the dynamic expending activity of community development. But insofar as it is affected by controllable conditions, steps should be taken quickly to deal with these conditions lest they continue to retard the quality of extension operations.

Among the conditions which the Team believes are contributing to job turnover are :

Low salaries, especially when compared to roughly similar jobs in India generally.

Lack of respect and status for agricultural employment.

Insecurity in the job.

Limited promotional and salary increase opportunities except by moving to other positions.

Political influence in appointment in some areas.

There is need for a more realistic recognition of the limits of coordination and of the need for and importance of individual choices and decisions which are then translated into action through supervision and guidance. This is an especially acute problem where persons with differing technical training are involved.

The Team has observed considerable variation in the attitude of the different bloc personnel regarding their role of supervising the village level workers. In several blocks visited the block staff viewed their supervisory job as that of issuing directives and orders to the village level workers and then making inspections of what work the local staffs had accomplished. In other blocks the BDO and extension officers considered their supervisory function to be that of giving counsel and guidance to the local workers, of helping them analyse problems impeding effective work, and also showing concern and giving advice on local living conditions and other personal matters.

The Team believes that a higher state of village level worker performance, and of extension programme effectiveness in achieving greater food production, will occur where supervision is viewed in the latter light. Block officers and also district officers should be encouraged to develop this positive and staff developmental side of supervision.

This Team has been impressed by the way in which a large number of Government departments have been involved in building new institutions, setting up syllabi, staffing the institutions and training various types of extension workers. From the standpoint of achieving greater food production, competent agricultural extension workers, trained in technical substance and in extension teaching methods, are a prime need.

The Team believes that India needs to look to the future training of village level workers, block officers, appropriate district officers and others most directly involved in the drive for increased food production, with several criteria in mind. With special consideration to the need for greater food production, staff training of extension workers, including women workers, needs to consider (a) integration of the training programme now widely dispersed, (b) more specific attention to who is trained, (c) the specific purpose of the training. (d) the content of the training in terms of getting more food produced through extension work, (e) the methods used in training, (f) adequacy of training for specific job assignments.

Block Development Officers : For those BDO's who do not have an agricultural background, additional training must be given in the field of agriculture and extension methods. There is also need for training all new BDO's in the field of democratic administration and supervision.

Agricultural Officers : The attempt is made to secure agricultural college graduates for these positions. Unless the status of the professional agricultural workers is raised, the best students will not be attracted to the agriculrural colleges. There is a need for more agricultural specialists for teaching, research and extension. The suggested pattern of agricultural specialists at the block, district, and State levels makes this need even more imperative. The present system of using a common general syllabus does not allow for subject-matter specialisation. There should be fiexibility to allow for specialisation in the various agricultural sciences and in the problems singular to the areas served by the colleges. For those college students who intend to enter extension work, provision needs to be made in the college curricula for courses that will be of special use to them, for instance, extension methods.

Animal Husbandry Officers: They must have additional, training in animal breeding, feeding, management and in the proper care of farm animals. The same general type of orientation training and induction training should be given to animal husbandry officers as to the agricultural officers.

Cooperative Officers : If the cooperative officers are to perform more of the agricultural supply "servicing" recommended earlier, they must have additional training in basic agriculture, the role of credit in agricultural production and in organising and administering farm supply and farm product marketing functions.

They also need the training that will enable them to conduct successful cooperative member education programmes.

Women Social Education Officers : The women social education officers carry on certain activities directly related to food preservation, food production and preparation. Since women SEO's are the immediate supervisors of the Gram Sevikas in a technical sense, it is imperative that their pre-service and in-service training include subjects relating to the work of the Gram Sevikas in the fields of agricultural production, home food storage, family nutrition and so on.

It is recommended that training syllabi of these officers be re-evaluated in terms of the present food production emergency with a view to strengthening the food production and family food preservation subject matter presented in training courses (both pre-service and in-service).

Gram Sevak : The Gram Sevaks have a primary responsibility for the motivation and stimulation of farmer interests in extension education directed toward increased food production. They must also have a reasonable degree of knowledge in the skills of farming and in farm management and the methods of informing farmers about improved practices, as well as in methods of involving village farm leaders in developing a programme to step up food production.

The team had only limited opportunities to study village level worker training programmes. However, it appears that some of the training given is highly theoretical and abstract. A way must be found to bring some of the more successful block agricultural extension officers into the instructorships for Gram Sevak training. As to the practical training of Gram Sevaks in village circles near the training centres, these training circles should be staffed with experienced successful Gram Sevaks in order for the trainees to secure practical teaching skills that will help them when placed in their own village circles.

Gram Sevikas : The Team strongly recommends that steps be taken to improve the training programmes of the Gram Sevikas, both in terms of content that will better prepare them to aid farm women in their food production tasks, and in terms of actually performing the improved farm and home practices that they will later be expected to demonstrate to the village people.

In addition to what has been said above about block staff training, it is to be noted that continnous in-service training is essential through short seminars, training conferences and tours as well as through adequate and positive supervision. Such meetings and tours can best be conducted by extension subject-matter specialists at the district and State levels. This provides an additional reason for the placing of more specialists at these levels in order to give the continuous block staff training needed during the critical food emergency.

Extension Methods

The Team observed a number of areas where there is great potential for increasing educational effectiveness. The following areas, with examples, are given to illustrate the point.

Understanding Social-psychology : The extension worker needs to have the understandings that will enable him to determine the mental make-up of the cultivator with whom he must communicate. In approaching and working with people (and choosing methods), much more attention needs to be given to such things as their values, attitudes, aspirations and perceived needs.

The extension worker should be able to do a more effective educational job if he secures the following kinds of information about the cultivator. What is the cultivator's perception of the extension worker ? Is he seen as a friend, an outside exploiter, a person who must prove himself, or a person with sound practical information ? What are the cultivator's attitudes toward changing his ways of farming and what is the basis of these attitudes? What does the cultivator see as his problems and why are these things problems? Does the cultivator have aspirations to farm better? Does he think he can improve his farming methods? In many cases one of the first steps in the educational process may be to convince the farmer he can, with his limited resources, do a better job of farming.

The Learning-Acting Process

There needs to be greater understanding of the learning-acting process. For instance, even an over simplified conceptualisation of this process should be of great aid to the professional worker in bringing about desired change in a cultivator. The process can be thought of in terms of :

Awareness—Attention. Knowing about the practice but not understanding its intrinsic qualities.

Interest—The desire for and the receipt of more detailed information on the practice.

Evaluation—The mental process of weighing the advantages and disadvantages of the new practice over the traditional practice.

Trial—The physical trial of the new practice on the land.

Adoption—The process of interpreting and evaluating the trial results which lead to rational satisfaction with the trial and commitment to use.

The Villager In His Social Setting

There needs to be greater depth of understanding of the social setting in which the villager lives, communicates and acts. Many programmes, and workers, assume that the village is an integrated community when in reality it may be made up of many factional groupings. There is a tendency to over simplify the complex leadership, power, influence and communication networks that exist in the village.

The Communication Process And Extension Methods

We recommend :

Instructors with competence in extension education must be secured or trained for the extension wings of colleges and the various training centres.

A syllabus covering the psychology of learning and character of group action should be developed as soon as possible for in-service training programmes. It should also include methods of teaching. Instructors must be trained in the content and use of the syllabus for training the various levels of workers.

A planned programme of in-service training should be developed and initiated as soon as feasible with the objective of increasing the understanding and skills of all levels of workers in using this type of knowledge on the job. The first priority of training is probably with people at the block level—BDOs, other block level officers and VLW's.

Individual Contacts

We recommend:

Personal contact should continue to be used as an important extension educational method. However, because of its time-consuming quality, it is important to use intensive personal contacts with those cultivators who have the greatest potential in helping increase food production, directly or indireetly through influencing other cultivators.

Block and district agriculture officers must make enough personal cultivator contacts to keep them in touch with the practical farming problems of cultivators.

Result Demonstrations

The use of demonstrations as a teaching device should be encouraged. However, steps should be taken to make sure that they are set up properly. Additional training and supervision is needed in the case of demonstrations set up by VLW's.

Whenever possible emphasis should be placed on the demonstration of the proper combination of practices.

The Group Approach and Group Techniques

Additional use should be made of the small interest group approach in educating and motivating farmers.

A study should be made by the syllabi committees to determine the efficacy of increasing the training on group formation and group techniques for the various levels of extension workers.

The possibility of in-service training in this area should be investigated.

The recommended group techniques could be utilised by skilled people who have charge of the various refresher courses and workshops that are now being held and thus demonstrate their use to the participants.

Leader Training Camps

The adoption of the Leader Camp idea at this stage of the educational process seems to have great potential. Camps should be encouraged. In terms of their importance and the amount of resources that are used, great care should be used in planning and executing them to assure maximum educational impact.

The Campaign Approach

Immediate steps should be taken to provide additional agricultural visual aids, and visual aid equipment and materials for use in the block.

Agricultural educational films, film strips and slides should have top priority in village educational programmes.

Soil And Water Conservation, Including Water Use
The Cultivator Makes His Arable Soil

The point is especially important in India, since most tropical soils are not highly productive under simple management. But many of them can be made so by the cultivator's art as improved by science and aided by the products of industry. It is thus that a strong and efficient agriculture develops with a strong and efficient industry.

Stream Flow And Surface Storage Water

In determining the feasibility of projects and the cost of irrigation, it is essential to relate the cost of irrigation to the benefits to be derived in terms of physical crop yields and related social benefits. The current system of determining the merits of a scheme in terms of irrigation charges alone may not be conducive to good irrigation development.

Continued emphasis should be given to the development of irrigation water supply through storage reservoirs and direct diversion from rivers and streams where water delivered is based on a continuous yearly supply.

Well Water

The tube-well programme should be greatly expanded in those areas where there is now a relatively sure supply of good ground water. This would include large areas in Uttar Pradesh, Punjab, West Bengal, Bihar, Madras, Andhra Pradesh, and parts of Bombay and other States. Those areas which have potential for two and three crops per year should have highest priority.

The programme for shallow masonry wells should be expanded to meet the maximum demand consistent with good irrigation planning.

Water Conveyance

Seepage studies should be made in the canal systems losing more than 15 per cent of their water. Where excessive seepage is occurring, action should be taken to reduce it.

Water Application

A number of villages should be selected in irrigated areas for an experimental programme using all the best known water-management practices, necessary fertilisers, recommended seeds and cropping systems, and good cultural practices combined into a farming system.

An adequate percentage of the total cost of each new major irrigation project should usually be earmarked and made available through appropriate agencies of the Agricultural Department, to start their educational and the necessary technical work on irrigated lands at the same time that the engineering construction phase of the project is begun. This would include research and demonstrations (using water from wells or tanks) as long in advance as possible.

Research experiments and demonstrations should he greatly expanded to deal with the proper combinations of (a) water management, (b) fertilisers and green manures, (c) good seeds, and (d) other cultural practices necessary for high production.

Surface Drainage

A single agency should be given the responsibility for coordination and improvement of natural and artificial drainage ways, and improvement of natural drainage ways should be given a high priority.

Salinity And Internal Drainage

Research and demonstration should be expanded on the reclamation of saline and alkali soils and increased efforts should be made to reclaim present areas affected by salinity and alkali.

Bunding And Terracing On Dryland

Increased effort should he made on accurate contour bunding with first priority on better soils (1) that can be shifted from rough pasture to cropland, (2) that can be shifted from Kharif crops alone to both Kharif and Rabi crops, or (3) that can produce much higher yields.

Legislation should be adopted to provide that a bunding or terracing scheme be undertaken in a village, or larger unit, only where a clear majority have voted for it with full understanding of the works to be done. The work should be done on all land required to make the scheme successful and charged as part of the taxes against the land if necessary. The Government should maintain the bunds for two years, after which the responsibility for maintenance should be given to the village. In order to protect the welfare of the majority, the Government should inspect the bunds thereafter and make necessary repairs if any bunds are not maintained, charging the cost as part of the taxes against the land.

Tillage Practices

Special studies should be made of the need for tractor-drawn ploughs or other tillage implements, with a view to their procurement and use (1) where the soil areas will yield far greater increases in food production than is possible with other tillage implements, and where the cultivators have the ability, willingness, and organisation to make effective use of the implements without significant subsidy beyond loans; (2) where neglected and compacted soils of derelict village commons can be brought into use; and (3) where new land development requires heavy initial ploughing or earth moving. Even scarce foreign exchange should be allocated for such machines where the benefits are very substantial,

Erosion Control

Joint conferences among agriculturists and highway engineers should be held, in order to find ways to develop mutually satisfactory methods for joint planning for handling water in ways most helpful to soil stability and agricultural production.

Suitable allotments for soil and water consevation works, including forest planting and protection from over grazing, should be made within all plans for works of public improvement, such as water storage reservoirs; and these improvements in the catchment area should be timed to begin as soon as firm decisions on the project are finalised and soil surveys can be made.

Public assistance, through loans or subsidies, should be given for constructing or repairing tanks, only where the designs provide (1) for as deep tanks as are practicable (considering the problem of sealing them against leakage by the use of special earth materials or chemicals sealers) in order to conserve soil area and reduce evaporation, (2) grass silt traps at the margins, and (3) proper bunds, diversions, spill ways, and chutes to control erosion in the catchment area so that they may continue for a reasonable life span.

Controlled Grazing'

Demonstrations of the great value of guarding vegetation, including grasses, shrubs, and trees, and of the other associated practices should be increased as rapidly as facilities permit, along with plant selections, seed multiplication, and reseeding of the desirable species of grasses, shrubs, and trees so that as many cultivators and herdsmen as possible can see the results.

In the light of the growing body of evidence, the Board of Agriculture of the ICAR should give this problem of grazing control a top priority for appropriate study and recommendations, working in full cooperation with leading experts in soil and water conservation, range management, farm management, and legal matters relating to rural lands. This kind of coordinated study should result in preparing and promulgating a widespread and intensive educational programme along cultivators and herdsmen and drafting of model legislation for controlled grazing, including the licensing of grazing, on all public lands under management systems that permit adequate protection of plants, soils, and water supplies.

Farm And Village Forestry

Forestry officers should give increased emphasis to farm and village forestry, to continued selection of species and varieties most adopted to such conditions, and to the breeding and propagation of superior strains of trees for local plantings.

Shifting Cultivation

The Centre should develop an adequate research programme for testing likely possibilities for improving and supplementing the existing systems of shifting cultivation, and for developing new techniques, with full attention to the existing experience of local cultivators and to the results already achieved in Africa, especially by INEAC, Yangambi, Belgian Cango, in rationalization of such systems. Such researches should be closely associated with the soil survey programme and with programmes for demonstrations of the new crops and practices as rapidly as their soundness has been established.

Reclamation And Use of Unused Land

Adequate laws should be developed to provide that unused or very poorly used land well suited to crop production be leased on fair terms to qualified cultivators for food production.

The development of new land areas should be planned jointly with experts in soil and water conservation on the basis of adequate soil surveys, so that adequate layouts of holdings are ensured for efficient soil and water management and so that holdings have comparable potential for food production.

Risk Insurance For Soil And Water Conservation

The Soil Conservation Board should work out reasonable ways to guarantee cultivators against loss from the adoption of radically changed systems of soil and water management that promise substantial increases in food production and income.

College Teaching

Appropriate steps should be taken by the Centre to work with agricultural and engineering colleges in order to help them develop statisfactory curricula for the potential soil scientists and conservation engineers so urgently needed in India.

Two Additional Primary Research Stations

Two central research stations should be established to conduct basic research on national and regional soil and water conservation problems; one to be concerned with the irrigated areas and the other to deal with the non-irrigated areas. Funds should be available for close cooperation with the State agricultural departments and colleges.

Soil Surveys

Every effort should be made to secure air photos for high-priority soil survey areas in advance of mapping.

Economic Evaluation Of Soil And Water Conservation Demonstrations

Efforts should be made to have economic evaluations of demonstrations of fertiliser use, terracing, bunding, controlled grazing, and other soil and water conservation practices in combination.

In-service Training

Every opportunity should be taken to strengthen and to expand training facilities at Soil Conservation Research Stations and other centres for professional in service training in soil and water conservation and consideration should be given to the establishment of six month training camps for diploma holders who can become local supervisors, under professional guidance, for expanded public works in soil and water conservation.

Library Facilities

The Librarian of the I.C.A.R. should be asked to form a special study group to develop more nearly adequate lists of books and periodicals for the libraries used by students and field operating staff in soil and water conservation, with special reference to literature in both French and English from African and other tropical areas.

Staff For Technical Assistance

Each State should provide for a staff of technicians in soil and water conservation, not only for project work but also for direct technical assistance to cultivators and groups of cultivators as the need is identified by agricultural extension officers. Beginnings might be made at the State level but the Team suggests that such cadres should be available in district offices.

Coordination For Soil And Water Conservation

As the Centre implements its plan for inspection of all soil and water conservation work for which grants and loans are furnished, the extent and effectiveness of coordination among State departments of agriculture, forestry, irrigation, public works, revenue, and the like, should be a major consideration in the approval of schemes for soil and water conservation put forward for sanction

Chemical Fertilisers

The Urgent Need For Fertilisers

If food goals are to be reached, fertilisers must have greater emphasis and a top priority in both agricultural planning and allocations of foreign exchange, both for fertiliser materials and for any machines needed for constructing new plants to produce high-analysis fertilisers within India.

Priority For Distribution Of Scarce Fertilisers

For as long as fertilisers are in short supply they should be allocated primarily to growers of food crops, mainly according to (1) the opportunities for increased food production and (2) the extent to which cultivators are using the other practices necessary for fertiliser to be most effective.

Wider Cooperation In Soil-Testing Scheme

Added emphasis should be given to (1) the standardisation of laboratory soil tests with field experiments on the important kinds of soil; (2) coordination of the soil-testing scheme with the Soil Survey; (3) follow-through by field officers of test results; (4) full recognition of other factors besides test results of surface soil that influence recommendations; (5) a wider network of village demonstrations; (6) free three-year demonstrations, in areas where fertilisers would produce large increases, for cultivators who will also use other practices to make fertiliser effective; (7) estimates of economic returns along with physical demonstrations of the results of fertiliser use; and (8) developing definite cooperative relationships in the soil testing scheme with the Soil Conservation Research Stations and all other experimental stations doing research on or conducting demonstrations with soils or crops.

Research And Promotion Of High-Analysis Fertiliser Materials

Emphasis should be given to fertilisers of high analysis because of the excessive costs for freight and handling now being paid by cultivators. Immediate plans should be developed for (a) research-testing of high-analysis materials, (b) importation of such materials for test-demonstration on important soils and crops, (c) large-scale importation for general field use as soon as possible, and (d) industrial research for manufacture of such materials within India.

Early consideration should be given to the organization of an all-India Centre of fertilizer technology within the Ministry of Food and Agriculture to deal with the pressing problems of fertilizer development, manufacture, import, supply, transport, and related problems.

Other Opportunities Should Be Looked For

Each State should have a well-trained, experienced senior officer, with a small staff, to coordinate the fertiliser programme of the State under the Director of Agriculture. This officer should be a soil scientist well trained in chemistry and agronomy, or an agricultural chemist with field experience in soil science and agronomy.

Improvements In Cereal Production, Including Plant Protection

Plant Breeding

The rice and wheat breeding research work should

be intensified in the States as well as the Centre to supply the needed high yielding, plant-disease and insect-resistant, stiffer strawed varieties that will respond to higher levels of soil fertility. The production of hybrid maize and sorghum should be intensified because of their immediate potential for increasing production.

Interaction Of Improved Crop Varieties With Other Improved Practices

Testing Of Improved Varieties

There is a critical need for wider testing of new varieties to check the area of adaptation. Regional tests should be more widely employed and should include varieties from all States and Centre as well as promising exotic varieties.

Rice: Soil Fertility

Experiments both at the Central Rice Research Institute, at other experiment stations, and in the cultivators' fields have shown that application of nitrogen in the form of ammonium sulphate in sub-surface (plough sole) is much more efficient than surface application. This practice should be advocated for adoption in all rice growing areas.

Organic manures and chemical fertilisers are complementary in function and since organic manures cannot be relied upon to achieve immediate production goals, a high priority must be given to the use of chemical fertilisers. To obtain efficient fertiliser utilisation more attention should be given to certain factors such as: N.P.K. ratios, timing of applications, split applications and placement.

It is necessary that in attempts to increase acre yields, the Japanese method of intensive cultivation of rice should be extended to practically all irrigated areas. It should be mentioned that the essential elements of the "Japanese method" are related and the lack of any one of these elements is likely to reduce the efficiency of the others. The lack of commercial fertiliser will reduce the production potential of the system.

Mechanisation

A strong engineering department is needed at some centre where imported equipment can be checked for adaptability, present equipment can be improved in design, and new equipment can be designed for rice production. In the breeding work, emphasis should be placed on development of varieties suitable for mechanisation. More applied research is needed to determine how mechanisation can fit in with overall cultural practices. Educational work should be expanded on the maintenance and proper use of mechanical equipment.

The Multiplication And Distribution Of Improved Seeds

The use of highest yielding adapted crop varieties by the cultivators is one of the most economical means of increasing agricultural production. Seed is a basic crop production cost, and is a cost present whether cultivators use good or poor seed. It is thus vital that only the best seed be used.

Organising And Training A Seed Specialist Cadre

It must, however, be recognised that India's improved seed programme is today fulfilling only a small fraction of the increasing demands which will be made on it in the years ahead. There are increasing needs and demands for improved seed of better quality and in greater quantities.

The Team recommends that a cadre of trained seed specialists be recruited, trained and organised at the earliest possible moment. The need is so great, and so essential to the whole improved seed programme that the setting up of such a cadre is given as our first recommendation. The recommendation is based on the knowledge that in no country is high-quality seed of improved varieties successfully produced except under the direction and leadership of competent specialists. India is no exception. The Team's inquiries revealed that in situations where competent specialists supervised the work, the seed multiplication was well conducted. In other situations (and these are the majority), seed which was badly mixed as to varietal purity and unsatisfactory in other quality factors was being produced. Seed of unsatisfactory quality was therefore being produced, even though in some instances officials—from the VLW up to state officers—expressed satisfaction with the progress being made.

To provide continuity in improved seed multiplication schemes it is necessary to keep seed specialists at seed posts. Seed multiplication is not an administrative type of post where a generalist can be effective. It is necessary to provide advancement and inducement for deserving seed specialists in this field of specialisation.

Levels Of Specialists Needed In Centre And States

It is recommended that a cadre of seed specialists at the following levels be trained and recruited as early as possible:

At the Centre: A botanist with post-graduate training or suitable experience and competence in improved seed programmes is needed at the Centre. This specialist will require intimate knowledge of improved seed production techniques and procedures for the wide variety of crops found in India. His primary role would be to work towards expediting recommendations made by the Centre Expert Seed Committee and by other Centre Committees or officials concerned with improved seed schemes. Leadership qualities are thus of paramount importance.

The specialist should be the leader in developing special training for seed specialists at the State, district and block levels, He would work towards the development of uniform seed certification standards and seed legislation among the States for the several crops, and maintain liaison with improved seed development in other countries. In seed supply, such a specialist could act as a clearing house for information regarding available supplies of improved seeds. This will help expedite seed movement between States.

The Centre specialist's primary role should be one of teaching and leadership in organising improved seed schemes.

In the States: Here a counterpart post to the one recommended for the Centre should be set up, under a specialist with comparable training and ability, such as a botanist with improved seed programme competence. This post should correspond in level to the Deputy Director of agriculture. The specialist should preferably be responsible to the top administrative officer in State agricultural extension. The specialist's primary responsibility should be seed training of district, block and village workers. The specialist could also advantageously assume overall technical responsibility for operation of the Government seed farms.

His other functions would be development of State seed certification standards; maintenance of contact with the Centre, other States and districts on supplies of the various classes of certified seed; preparation of teaching information on recommended crop varieties. In general, he should work towards the maximum use of improved crop varieties in association with other improved crop production practices. It is especially important that the State seed specialist maintain close contact with plant breeding research stations.

At the District Level: It is recommended that seed specialists also be established at the district level and made responsible to the State seed specialist. Depending on the local situation, one specialist may occasionally serve more than one district. Seed specialists in district should be agricultural college graduates with plant breeding and agronomy training and the needed "in-service" training in seed technology and improved seed programmes.

District specialists would adapt improved seed recommendations for use at the block and village levels. They should provide training for personnel making village field and seed inspections. They would coordinate certified seed supply needs from within the district and from outside of the district. While their work as district seed specialists would be primarily directed to training block and village level workers, it must be borne in mind that until cooperative and private dealers are developed, the agriculture departments will continue to supply seed to the cultivators. Upgrading of certified seed quality through training of seed inspectors and supply coordination will therefore be an important function of district seed specialists.

At the Block Level: The Government has set a goal of a Government seed farm to serve each block. The Team recommends that direct supervision of Government seed farms for Foundation seed production, whenever feasible, be placed under the direction and supervision of a trained seed specialist at the block level. A resident seed farm manager would in most cases also be necessary to conduct day-to-day operations. In most blocks, as the occasion demands, it is recommended that one of the four additional block specialists recommended in the section on extension be primarily responsible for improved seeds. In technical matters, such as inspections for certification, this block specialist should be administratively responsible to the district seed specialist or appropriate District Agricultural Officer.

A block seed specialist would be valuable in assuring high quality of Foundation, Registered, and Certified seed. He could personally train department of agriculture personnel making field and seed inspections at the village level. He should, until an agriculture department certification staff is developed, personally make a large share of the necessary field and seed inspections. This is particularly true if certified seed multiplication is concentrated on larger land holdings or in special seed multiplication villages. The block seed specialist should also aid in popularising improved seeds through working side by side with the village level worker in establishing demonstrations and related teaching devices.

At the Village Level: A high degree of seed specialisation is not feasible at the village level. The VLW should receive training on improved seed through the State, district and block seed specialists. Such training should be properly inter-related to training in other crop production practices. The VLW should primarily be a demonstrator and village teacher of improved seed practices. As soon as possible, he should be relieved of improved seed supply and seed inspection functions. Except by intense and adequate training, the VLW cannot become a satisfactory improved seed production specialist.

Seed Training Programmes

Adequate training of the proposed Centre, State, district and block seed specialists is a formidable task. It is nevertheless a need which cannot be postponed if India is to capitalise on improved seed, one of the most economical means of increasing food production.

Three Aspects Of Solving The Improved Seed Problem

For some time to come the State departments of

agriculture will necessarily continue to conduct at least a portion of the three aspects of improved seed programmes. The three aspects should, however, be separated into three distinct functions as soon as possible. Under such separation, cooperatives and private growers should assume the supply role, community development and agriculture departments should assume the educational functions, and agriculture departments should assume the inspection function.

The block cooperative officer should be assigned the duty of organising and arranging for cooperatives to assume responsibility for distribution of Certified seed to village cultivators, along with other agricultural supplies. Plans for needed improved seed production should be developed by the block seed specialist in cooperation with district seed specialist and the block cooperative officer.

The Need For Uniform Nomenclature And Quality Standards

The increased yield potential of an improved variety is entirely or partially lost when the cultivator plants seed which is mixed, is of less than 90 per cent or better germination, or is contaminated with weeds and other crops or infected with seed-borne diseases. The widespread use of improved crop varieties associated with seed of high quality must go hand in hand if the improved varieties are to make their full contribution to increase food production.

There is good evidence that administrative, research and extension officers of the States, and the cultivators, are relying on the mere spread or saturation of improved varieties to bring about increased production.

A general improvement in the quality of seed used by the cultivator would result if all Breeder, Foundation, Registered and Certified seed handled or distributed under State Government auspices were tested in properly equipped official seed laboratories. If large quantities of high quality pure certified seed were distributed, varietal contamination and quality deterioration would be minimised in the last one or two stages of village seed increase. Under such a scheme, it would be imperative that seed failing to meet the minimum seed certification quality standards should be rejected.

Nomenclature And Definition

To facilitate the development of uniform seed-certification standards among all States, it is important that there be a uniform nomenclature and definition for each succeeding generation of improved seed. Seed uniformity would facilitate the movement of the various classes of seed from one State to another.

The following nomenclature and definition for succeeding generations of certified seed approved by F.A.O. are recommended for use in India.

(a) **Breeder Seed :** Breeder seed is seed directly controlled by the originating or in certain cases, the sponsoring plant breeder or institution, and which provides the source for the initial and recurring increase of Foundation seed.

(b) **Foundation Seed:** Foundation seed shall be seed stocks that are so handled as to most nearly maintain specific genetic identity and purity and that may be designated or distributed by an agricultural experiment station.

Production must be carefully supervised or approved by suitable representatives of the appropriate Government agency. Foundation seed shall be the source of all other certified seed classes, either directly or through Registered seed.

(c) **Registered Seed:** Registered seed shall be the progeny of foundation or registered seed that is so handled as to maintain satisfactory genetic identity and purity, and that has been approved and certified by the certifying agency. This class of seed should be of a quality suitable for the production of certified seed.

(d) **Certified Seed:** Certified seed shall be the progeny of foundation, registered, or certified seed that is so handled as to maintain satisfactory genetic identity and purity and that has been approved and certified by the certifying agency.

The breeder, foundation and registered seed classes are primarily intended as stock seed (for further multiplication), while the certified class is the large volume of seed to be planted by the cultivators. In actual village use, registered and certified seed may overlap, though certified seed should never be used to produce registered seed. In hybrid maize and hybrid sorghum, the generation sequence is breeder, foundation and certified.

Seed Quality Standards

There is evidence that there is now much variability in seed quality between States. This could be remedied by the development and enforcement of uniform certification standards.

Maintenance Of Breeder Seed

The plant breeder has, however, a continuing responsibility to maintain recurring supplies of genetically pure breeder seed as long as the variety is included in a seed multiplication scheme.

Government Stock Seed Farms

The larger efficiently managed seed farms will serve India's improved seed needs better than rigid adherence to proposals for one small farm for each block. This is because trained seed specialists are not available to manage competently the very large number of smaller farms on a one-per-block basis. Further, some mechanisation is necessary. This is better suited to the larger farms serving several blocks. To speed up the spread of new improved varieties, effective effort must be made to produce maximum yields of foundation seed (the early generation). It is also important that Government seed farms be self-supporting.

Wherever feasible it is recommended that the block seed specialist be assigned technical supervision of the Government Seed Farms.

Certified Seed Multiplication Villages

In view of the slowness with which certified seed is multiplied and spread when seed farms are in every village, and of the questionable seed quality produced under a village system, it is recommended that an effort be made to organise certified seed multiplication at the block level on the basis of one or at the most two seed multiplication villages per block.

It is recommended that the certified seed multiplication village scheme be given high priority in the seed multiplication effort. As a start, it is urged that such a plan be concentrated in those areas of India that have the greatest opportunity for response in increased food production. i.e. surplus production or alleviating severe food shortages. Since superior organisational ability is needed to make such a plan succeed, the most competent seed specialists should be assigned to this effort. An adequate staff must be provided. As experience is gained the programme can be extended to the other areas.

To assure success, it may be necessary to enact legislation sanctioning one-variety areas in villages.

Multiplicity Of Varieties—"Variety Release Committees"

It is apparent that an inadequate variety-testing programme has thus far failed to identify the very best varieties for each State. It is, therefore, urged that a coordinated variety-testing programme for the important crops be inaugurated under the technical leadership and financial assistance of the Centre.

Uniform variety tests should be made up for each of the major crops on a regional basis. These tests should then be conducted throughout each region by the States and Centre. Reports on each test should be submitted to the Centre where all tests are to be compiled into a regional or all-India report. Varieties found to be superior over a wide region should be given top priority in seed multiplication schemes.

It is recommended that the Centre and each State establish committees or boards officially to sanction the release and recommendation of new improved varieties. The Centre Committee should be made up of scientists and appropriate administrators of the Centre with adequate representation from the States. These committees might be called, "Variety Release Committees".

Basic criteria for accepting new varieties are high yield, disease resistance, wide adaptation, responsiveness to fertiliser and water management, etc. The same criteria should apply to all varieties irrespective of origin only the very best varieties should be included in improved seed programmes.

Improved Seed Storage

Larger central seed storage will be needed at Government seed farms and where registered seed is multiplied. It should also be normal procedure to carry a reasonable inventory of seed from year to year. A perpetual inventory of from 10 to 15 per cent of the quantity of certified seed handled annually would be a minimum reserve. In the case of breeder and foundation seed, reserves must be larger.

The Need For a Seed Industry

If cooperatives and private dealers are to make a substantial contribution to the multiplication of improved seeds, every effort must be made to create a favourable economic climate for such operations.

It is recognised that the national welfare demands that improved seed programmes be carried forward even though Government subsidy may be required to keep the programme from bogging down.

Vegetable Seed Production

Examine vegetable varieties from other countries and as soon as possible initiate a comprehensive vegetable breeding programme.

Seek out and use the best vegetable seed-growing areas in India for the various kinds of vegetables.

Increase vegetable seed production research and development.

In seed multiplication schemes involving cross-fertilised vegetable varieties,

(a) Obtain from foreign sources recurring supplies of 100 per cent pure breeder seed from the originator of the variety or other thoroughly reliable sources. Only small quantities are needed in relation to the total used in India.

(b) Multiply the breeder seed in the most favoured areas for high seed yield and under conditions of enforced isolation and roguing so as to minimise varietal contamination.

(c) Use a minimum number of generations from breeder seed in seed multiplication, i.e. breeder, foundation, registered, certifide.

Establish and enforce seed certification standards among the various vegetable seed-producing States. These standards should designate minimum requirements for varietal purity and other seed quality factors.

Work toward development of an all-India coordinated scheme of vegetable seed multiplication and distribution.

The Promise Of Hybrid Maize

Potentials Of Hybrid Maize In India

There is clear evidence that this great pool of genetic diversity when properly combined will result in unprecedented yield increase. Available here also is the accumulated knowledge and experience of maize improvement, culture and seed multiplication. These resources represent a tremendous opportunity in maize improvement. In view of india's food crisis, failure to make the most of this opportunity is a grave responsibility.

Hybrids with flint or flint-dent characteristics demanded by Indian consumers are also being developed.

An intensive and integrated research programme will be necessary to solve insect, disease, cultural and breeding problems. However, rarely has the opportunity in any country been as great for a major breakthrough in increased acre-yield for an important crop as is now available to India in hybrid maize.

The yield of maize in India can easily be increased by 100 per cent by the use of hybrids with increasing supplies of fertilisers, water for irrigation, drainage, and plant protection measures. With better farming practices and the willingness of the cultivators to change, both yield and acreages, planted to maize should increase sharply.

The Need For A Coordinated Maize Seed Programme

Seed Stocks: It is recommended that this vital activity be coordinated on an all-India basis, to enable the Seed Stocks Organisation to produce and utilise seed most effectively.

Producing The Double Cross Seed

As to land requirements, it is recommended that priority be given in seed multiplication to the larger land tracts either owned by the State and Central Governments or by individuals. High priority should also be given to expansion of hybrid maize seed acreage on "garden colonies" where an entire village produces seed of one hybrid. The use of the proper male single cross for limited acreages would be an end in obtaining needed isolation.

Hybrid maize seed multiplication must be conceived in terms of large quantities, considerable capital and a high degree of specialisation.

Achieving A Coordinated Hybrid Maize Seed Programme.

In view of the magnitude and nature of the hybrid maize seed problem, it is recommended that an all-India fully coordinated hybrid maize seed multiplication scheme be developed and put into immediate operation.

This should be an organisation operating from the Centre under Centre charter with branches operating in the respective States under State charter. Double cross maize seed multiplication should remain the primary responsibility of the several States; the States thus need freedom of action to develop adequate State programmes.

Livestock Development And Food Production

It is not enough to conduct systematic work in animal husbandry on Government livestock farms. The real test is what happens in the villages and on the land.

Reducing Cattle Numbers

A study of food production in India manifestly would be incomplete without some consideration of the cattle slaughter question. This should not be taken to mean that it is necessary for outsiders making such a study to take a position for or against cattle slaughter in India. The question is one which can be dealt with by India alone under her own political and socio-religious systems.

Other Means Of Reducing Cattle Numbers

While an outsider may properly conclude that he should leave the question of cattle slaughter for India's political and professional leaders to deal with, he also may just as appropriately feel that it is within his province, when his advice on animal husbandry is requested, to recommend other means of reducing the number of cattle and of controlling the rate of reproduction. With this in mind, the following practices and procedures are recommended :

(1) A Tax On Cattle: Tax exemptions bullocks required for farm work and on the number of breeding cows justified by the size of holding could he authorised. A graduated tax schedule for animals, with such suitable exemptions, would help to bring cattle numbers in balance with feed supplies by making the maintenance of such animals a financial burden on their owners. Cattle for which people take responsibility should be identified by appropriate means; and all animals not identified by the village should be declared outlaws. All taxes collected on cattle should go to the panchayat for agricultural development.

(2) Compulsory confinement of all bulls kept for natural service.

(3) Mandatory castration of all young bulls not required for breeding. The operation should be performed before the bulls become of serviceable age.

(4) Compulsory sterilisation of surplus cows and heifers.

(5) The advisability of enacting a law prohibiting open grazing should be investigated. In any event, on educational campaign to eliminate open grazing should be undertaken so that regeneration of grasslands may be accomplished. Compulsion to keep animals within the farm premises would help to control cattle numbers.

Dessicating Plants

It is recommended that dessicating plants be established on a sub-district, district or regional basis. These plants should be equipped to salvage hides and fats and to produce meat meal, bone, and animal by product fertiliser.

Production And Use Of Fodder And Feed

It is recommended that forage research be increased particularly to identify and develop varieties suitable (a) for intensive production in small areas and (b) for use in rotations. Initially, such programmes should stress the testing of existing varieties.

A clear cut statement of animal husbandry objectives is urgently needed. This statement should be concerned with the production and use of fodder and feed as well as livestock improvement and marketing. Thus far, Five-Year Plans contain only isolated items dealing with animal husbandry development.

Cattle Breeding And Dairy Development

Without improvement in the feeding of village cattle, little progress will be made in upgrading either draft or milk producing ability. That is, why a coordinated programme of mixed farming is so important.

Merely because a bull is raised on a Government farm does not ensure that his offspring will be better than the ordinary run of cattle. There is an urgent need to identify the really outstanding breeding sires among those available on Government farms and then to make as extensive use as possible of the semen of these superior individuals. To do this, most testing procedures will have to be revised to emphasise the performance of a bull's daughters, instead of his own appearance or even his dam's record.

There is need to develop new and higher producing strains or breeds of dairy cattle. This will require more extensive and more systematic cross-breeding programmes than are now being undertaken.

Poultry Production

Poultry production has a tremendous, potential in India. It is strongly recommended, therefore, that steps be taken immediately to encourage expansion of the poultry industry. The following lines for expansion should be exploited : (a) as a village enterprise, (b) as a backyard project for residents of urban areas, and (c) as a commercial business. Here again, the effort in each State should be concentrated on key villages and a limited number of commercial enterprises so that production and market development can be integrated effectively. The immediate objective should be to produce results which will serve to demonstrate the practicability of achieving much higher production.

Poultry excel all other animals in the efficiency with which feed is converted into human food. Other advantages of poultry make them especially useful in India. Among these advantages are : (a) small investment required to get started; (b) their suitability as a family enterprise; (c) small area required, even for large units; and (d) quick financial returns.

Extensive use of food by-products and waste materials would make expansion of the poultry industry possible without competing with humans for scarce and costly cereal grains. The use of considerable quantities of grains for poultry production may be justified, however, when more grains are produced, especially those not commonly used as food by humans.

It is recommended that encouragement, including Government aid if necessary, be given for the production of balanced poultry feeds.

Sheep and Goat Breeding

Continued emphasis should be given to the development of improved strains of both wool and mutton types of sheep. Goat breeding projects should be confined to the milch type.

Changing Food Habits

We suggest that the increases in total food demand be channelled toward the food which will contribute most to health. People should be strong and capable of doing a full day's work able to resist disease and to enjoy living. This requires a well-balanced diet.

The following results of a diet survey made during 1945-48 is reported by The Indian Council of Medical Research, New Delhi, 1951. This survey has the disadvantage of a limited sample, but it is the best information available comparing the customary Indian diet with recommended standards.

Recommended And Actual Food Consumption

Classes of food stuffs	Recommended Intake in Ounces	Actual Average Intake in Ounces
Cereals	14.0	16.6
Pulses	3.0	2.3
Leafy vegetables	4.0	0.9
Other vegetables	6.0	4.1
Ghee and vegetable oil	2.0	0.9

Milk and Milk products	10.0	3.3
Meat, fish and eggs	4.0	0.9
Fruits and nuts	3.0	0.6
Sugar and jaggery	2.0	0.7
Condiments	—	0.4

Programme Research And Evaluation

There is need for greater concern at all levels for programme research and evaluation especially related to food production. Specifically, it is recommended that each State explore the possibility of setting up a small programme research unit to work on problems and programmes of special importance to the individual States.

There is need for more precise statements of goals and procedures for the various programmes and subphases of programmes.

The programme research and evaluation people should be brought into the planning process of action programmes at an early stage.

There should be greater emphasis placed on the study of the attitudinal factors involved in programme planning and execution.

There should be increased efforts placed on "process" studies. There have been some "before" and "after" studies made to measure the change brought about by specific programmes.

There should be more effective use made of the case study method.

Additional attention should be given to input-output relations.

Research and action people should be aware of the problem of "feedback" in experimental research.

There should be a clear understanding of the role of "ideal" experiments.

There is need for more research on administrative structure.

Programme research and evaluation groups have the opportunity to make a contribution to the basic theory of human motivation, social action and programme, planning and execution.

Experimental Projects On Increasing Food Production

The team recommends that the following three projects be given a high priority:

(1) Experimental projects to determine realistic food production potentials of Indian villages under optimum field conditions.

(2) Experimental projects to determine the value of trained farm management assistance in helping cultivators increase food production and income.

(3) Experimental projects to measure the effectiveness of the intensified use of mass media and visual aids as a part of an increased food production educational effort.

An Intensified Programme To Determine Realistic Food Production Potentials

We suggest that each State undertake such an experiment with a core staff of three people serving approximately five contiguous villages. The productive potential of the villages selected should be moderately high. The staff should be made up of college graduates with extension field experience. One staff member should be a farm management specialist. The other two staff members should be chosen on the basis of the most important needs of the experimental area. For example, a specialist in water utilisation might be assigned full time if production could be increased significantly by improving water management.

COMMITTEE ON PLAN PROJECTS, BUILDINGS PROJECTS TEAM, PANEL ON STORAGE STRUCTURES, 1959—REPORT

New Delhi, Committee on Plan Projects, 1961. 39p.+iiip.+Plates.

Chairman : Shri U.J. Bhatt.

Members : Shri V.D. Bhandari; Shri O. Muthachan; Dr. S.V. Pingle; Shri K.V. Thadaney; Shri K. G. Rajagopalan; Shri R. P. Mhatre (replaced by Shri S.D. Pathak).

Secretary Shri T. S. Vedagiri.

APPOINTMENT

The Committee on Plan Projects took up the study of grain godown in 1957 when difficulty was experienced in getting structural steel sections. The Panel set up for this purpose analysed a number of alternative designs, namely, (a) timber trusses and purlins with sheeted roofing, (b) pre-stressed concrete girders and rafters with sheeted roofing, (c) modified steel trusses and purlins, with sheeted roofing and (d) shell construction.

Considering the acute shortage of timber for structural purposes and the necessity of putting up large number of godowns for storage, the Panel did not recommend the adoption of timber roofing for godowns at that time. Similarly, the pre-stressed concrete alternative was ruled out due to want of high tensile steel wire and equipment. The Panel could not recommend steel trusses as the very purpose of setting up of the Panel was to explore ways and means of curtailing the use of structural steel. After processing a number of other alternatives in concrete, the Panel came to the conclusion that shell construction with a chord width of 90 feet and a double span of 35 feet would meet the requirements. The width of 90 feet was chosen to eliminate the central row of columns and the valley gutters which are always a source of trouble and recurring expense.

The report of the Panel was accepted by all concerned and the C.P.W.D. has already constructed a few godowns with shell roof in Calcutta and has programmed to extend it to Delhi and Bombay. The solution then proposed was an *ad hoc* one to meet the immediate needs of the situation, especially for large sized storage.

In the planned development of the country, emphasis is being laid on increasing the production of foodgrains. Noticeable progress has already been made. At the beginning of the First Plan, in 1950-51, the foodgrains production amounted to 52.2 million tons. At the end of the First Five-Year Plan, in 1955-56, it amounted to 65.5 million tons and in 1958-59, to 73.5 million tons. At the end of the Second Five-Year Plan, the production is expected to go up to 75 million tons and by the end of the Third Five-Year Plan, to 100-105 million tons. Along with the efforts to increase production, it is proposed to maintain sufficiently large quantities of foodgrain in reserve to stabilise prices and meet emergencies.

It is estimated that about 30 to 35 per cent of foodgrains produced in the country move through trade channels. These would need storage facilities right from the centre of production to the centre of consumption. Construction of storage structures with varying capacities, therefore, becomes essential. Further, large scale imports of foodgrains are expected in the next few years, which would require additional storage facilities. Considering the magnitude of the problem and the changing situation in the availability of steel, the Committee on Plan Projects considered it worthwhile to re-examine the question in a broader perspective and evolve several alternative designs which could be adopted at different places in the country, to suit the needs of different regions and the demands of varying situations.

This Panel to consider this question, was set up in consultation with the Ministry of Food and Agriculture, in 1959.

TERMS OF REFERENCE

It is estimated that about 30 to 35 per cent of foodgrains produced in the country move through trade channels. These would need storage facilities right from the centre of production to the centre of consumption. Construction of storage structures with varying capacities, therefore, becomes essential. Further, large scale imports of foodgrains are expected in the next few years, which would require additional storage facilities. Considering the magnitude of the problem and the changing situation in the availability of steel, the Committee on Plan Projects considered it worthwhile to re-examine the question in a broader perspective and evolve several alternative designs which could be adopted at different places in the country, to suit the needs of different regions and the demands of varying situations.

CONTENTS

Introduction; Sizes and Spans of Warehouses; Structural Pattern; Specifications and Costs; Suggestions for Further Economy; Appendices I to VI; Plates.

RECOMMENDATIONS

Sizes And Spans Of Warehouses

The capacity of storage at different places has to vary with the purpose of storage and the demands of different locations. Keeping in view the programme before the Ministry of Food as also that of the Warehousing Corporations, the Panel would recommend that storage buildings should be of three categories: small, medium and large. The small storage buildings will have a capacity of 100 to 500 tons, the medium will have a capacity of 500 to 1,000 tons and the large ones above 1,000 tons.

The size of warehouses for these different capacities depends upon the size and shape of plot available, the mode of transport, rail or road or both, the stacking arrangements for optimum utilisation of godown space and the lead involved in handling within the godown.

Godowns of small capacities will be required in interior locations where transport will be invariably by road. There is no necessity to provide elaborate platforms in these cases. A covered doorway would suffice. The spans adopted should be such as to facilitate the use of materials like timber where good quality is available at comparatively low cost. The fixing of spans also depends on the special storage requirements of commodities like spices and copra which require relatively narrow godown space. Considering these factors as well as the size of stacks for optimum space utilisation, the Panel would recommend the adoption of single or double spans of 20 feet. The length can be adjusted to suit the requirements.

For medium storage, single or double spans of 30 feet would be suitable. Platforms can be provided on one side or both the sides according to requirements. There is, however, no need to roof the platforms fully. Suitable covers over doorways should suffice.

For large godowns, double spans of 45 feet or a single span of 90 feet would be advantageous. Platforms on both the sides one to serve the rail and the other to serve the road would be necessary. Roofing should normally be provided over these platforms except in places where rainfall is very low. Where there is no roofing, suitable covers may be provided at entrance doors.

Structural Patterns

Having decided upon the size and spans of godowns of different capacities, the Panel analysed various structural arrangements that are possible. It is obvious that no single pattern can be prescribed for these godowns as the availability of material, labour and fabricating capacity vary widely from place to place. Further, the time element involved in construction also plays a prominent part. Considering this, the Panel would recommend the adoption of the following patterns for different spans, as given below:

20 Feet Span

(a) Timber trusses and rafters with sheet roof.

(b) RCC gable frame and RCC purlins with sheet roof.

(c) Precast RCC rafters and sheet roof.

30 Feet Span

(a) Timber trusses and purlins with sheet roof.

(b) RCC gable frame and RCC purlins with sheet roof.

(c) Space purlins of structural steel with sheet roof.

(d) Precast prestressed truss and purlins with sheet roof.

45 Feet Span

(a) RCC gable frame and RCC purlins with sheet roof.

(b) Space trusses of steel and steel purlins with sheet roof.

(c) Tubular trusses with sheet roof.

(d) RCC semi-elliptical shell.

(e) RCC segmental shell with 90 feet chord width without central row of columns.

(f) Precast prestressed truss and purlins with sheet roof.

(g) Timber truss with sheet roof.

The Panel would emphasise that while choosing the particular type of structure to be adopted the economic aspects of several alternatives should be studied in a realistic manner taking into account not only the initial cost of outlay but also the recurring cost of operation and maintenance including insurance and the effect of economic lives of different structures.

In such an analysis it is possible to exhibit and account for the tangibles such as the cost of operation and of maintenance. There will be certain intangibles which will not be susceptible for evaluation in monetary terms. All these have been listed out so that a comprehensive consideration is possible while deciding upon the type of structure at a particular location at a poin[t] of time, *vide* Appendix II.

In order to justify the expenditure of time and money an economy study on the basis of the following is quite necessary:—

(1) It should be based upon consideration of al[l] available factors.

(2) The cost of construction, etc., should be intelligently estimated in the light of experience and sound judgment.

(3) The study should show a measure of financia[l] efficiency based on any of suitable methods listed below.

(4) The study should contain a recommended course of action together with the reasons for the recommendations.

There are several procedures for making such studies. Each procedure has certain advantages and limitations. Some of them are applicable only to industrial processes. The patterns suitable for application to public work[s] where alternative structures of different lives are to be considered are (a) the Present-Worth-Cost Method and (b) the Capitalised-Cost Method. Of the two the Present-Worth-Cost procedure provides a more satisfactory and realistic basis.

The Present-Worth-Cost may be computed in two ways. The first determines the present worth of th[e] annual costs. In this case depreciation, taxes, operation and maintenance costs, and amortisation of non-recurring expenses are included. The procedure is mos[t] advantageous when the annual cost will be uniform throughout the life. For these conditions the basi[c] pattern is Present-Worth-Cost, (D+O+M+I)aL where

$$D = \text{Depreciation (Annual)} = \frac{\text{Original Cost-Scrap Value at the end of Life.}}{\text{Amount of Annuity of 'One' for Life in Years}}$$

O = Operation Charges (annual)

M = Maintenance Charges (annual)

I = Interest on borrowed Capital (annual)

aL = Present Worth conversion factor for 'L' Number of years of life.

L = Life in Years (period).

More generally, the expenditure is not uniform every year. For this condition the present worth of all lump-sum expenditure plus the present worth of any recurring annual expenditure is determined.

It is customary to include the first cost of all assets thus eliminating the consideration of amortisation costs. The inclusion of first cost provides for recovery of capital plus a return on the investment. Using this very general concept the basic pattern for a Present-Worth-Cost is

$$C+(O+M+I)_1v^1+(O+M+I)_2v^2+\ldots\ldots\ldots\ldots\ldots\ldots$$
$$+(O+M+i)_nv^n+\ldots\ldots\ldots\ldots+(O+M+I)_lv^l$$

Where

C equals First Cost of Assets;

O, Operation Charges;

M, Maintenance Charges;

I, Interest on Borrowed Capital; and

V^n the Present-Worth Conversion Factor.

The importance of such an analysis lies in the fact that it takes into account not only the capital cost of construction but also the cost of operation and maintenance throughout the life of the structure. Where lives of two structures are different, the effect of this also is reflected in the analysis.

Applying this principle of Present-Worth-Cost, six alternative structures for twin spans of 45 feet have been analysed and the results are given in Appendix III. The method of arriving at the Present-Worth-Cost is given for three cases in Appendix VI for reference.

The alternatives suggested for storage structures above may be broadly grouped into two categories namely (a) structures with sheeted roof, (b) structures with non-sheeted roof. The sheeted roof structure can again be subdivided into those having Tubular Truss, Welded Frame, RCC, or Prestressed Concrete supporting structures etc. The relative merits of these structures are given in Appendix II.

Specifications and Costs

The godown must satisfy the basic requirements of storage. They should be leak proof, damp proof and rodent proof. The specifications for different components of the structure must satisfy its requirements commensurate with its economy. Certain suggestions of the Panel in this behalf are listed below:

(i) **Foundation :** The present practice is to take the foundation of the columns to a depth of four feet below ground level under normal conditions, the longitudinal panel walls to a depth of two feet six inches and the globe end walls and platform retaining walls to a depth of three feet below ground level. This is quite satisfactory.

(ii) **Plinth Height :** The plinth height adopted at present is three feet six inches above ground level to facilitate loading and unloading from railway wagons. Where there is no provision for railway siding, plinth height can be reduced to two feet six inches and in particularly high location even to two feet. To keep off the storm water the top of the coping over the edge of platform may be kept three inches lower than the floor level of the main godown, the difference being effected by providing a fall of one and a half inches across the doorway and one and a half inches across the platforms.

(iii) **Height of Walls :** The height of wall depends upon the type of roofing and the height of stacks. It has been possible to increase the height of stacks to 15 feet. Further increase may not be possible as the grain in the lower layers will get crushed. It would be sufficient if one-and a half feet clearance is given above the edge of stacks near the wall provided further clearance is available towards the ridge. This is possible in roofs without tie beams. In these cases the height of wall can be so kept that a clearance of 16½ feet is available at a distance of two feet six inches from the wall. In cases where ties and bracings are to be adopted the wall height must be 17 feet six inches. In particular cases where the height of stacks can be further increased the wall height may go upto 20 feet.

(iv) **Thickness of Walls :** The present practice of constructing brick masonry walls 13½ inches thick may be continued. This may be increased suitably in case of 20 feet high walls in heavy wind pressure zone. Where stone masonry is adopted, the walls may be 15 inches or 18 inches thick according to the quality and size of stone available.

In gable ends, pillar and panel construction can be adopted with either masonry or reinforced concrete pillars and 13½ inches thick panel walls in between pillars.

(v) **Flooring :** The flooring in a grain godown should be damp-proof, rigid and durable. It is considered that nine inches thick layer of pure sand, free from all deleterious materials, especially clay, or cinder, whichever is cheaper should be provided under the rigid part of the floors. Prior to sand or cinder filling, the earth filling under the floor must be properly stabilised as otherwise, there would be danger of settlement and cracks.

The top layer of the floor may consist of four inches lime or lean cement concrete 1 : 4 : 8 with two inches thick wearing surface of rich concrete 1 : 2 : 3.

The provision of Ironite, Hardonate or Rockite is prohibitive and may be avoided.

Where the subsoil water level is within five feet of the prevailing ground level or conditions otherwise demand, a membrane of tar-felt (three ply) or alkathere sheets film of not less than 400 G., may be introduced between the base course and the wearing surface.

If it is difficult or expensive to obtain clean sand, two-coat treatment of Bitumen at 50 lbs. per 100 sft. should be given above the lean concrete course. In such cases, the thickness of the sand layer can be reduced to six inches.

(vi) Finish of Walls: For cleanliness it was considered necessary that the inside of the walls may be plastered and white washed. The outside may be pointed or plastered.

(vii) Ventilation : Adequate ventilation within the godown is essential for preservation of grain. Ventilators, therefore, must be provided in all walls both at top and bottom. The top ventilators should have wire gauze protection on the external side and provided with central or bottom hung scutters to keep off moisture. The lower ventilators should have expanded metal or grill protection outside and sliding or hinged shutters and wire gauze on the inside.

(viii) Lighting : The light desired from the ventilators on all sides appears to be quite sufficient, more so if the length of the godown is limited to 100 feet to 200 feet. Hence it is considered that the provision of skylight in the roof is not essential.

(ix) Platform Protection: The Platforms should have a minimum width of eight feet. Where they are utilised weighing, batching, drying and temporary storing of grains, they require adequate covering also. The present practice is to have eight feet wide platform on roadside and 10 feet wide platform on railside.

To prevent damage to the platform by the backing of transport vehicles, it should be provided with wooden fenders throughout, backed by hard rubber backing at intervals.

(x) Drainage : It is considered desirable to avoid location of down water pipes and drains inside the godown. This could be made possible if the length of the godown is limited to about 150 feet where water can be drained off along the valley right outside the godown. This would require a fall of nine inches on either side which can be achieved by raising the central columns by nine inches and arranging the height of other columns suitably.

Costs

Details of estimates of cost and requirement of materials have been worked out for the several types of structures cited above. The estimates are based on the current schedule of rates applicable for Delhi. The designs have been made to suit the wind pressure of Zone III and for bearing capacity of soil of one ton per sq. ft.

The Panel hopes that the information regarding cost and consumption of materials will be useful to the authorities in making comparative economy studies, for fixing up the type of structure to be adopted.

Suggestions For Further Economy

The recommendations in the earlier section of the report deal with the structural pattern and specifications to be adopted for grain godowns with a view to achieving economy and efficiency. It is possible to effect further economy through standardisation, institution of work study on the entire pattern of handling and storing of grains and other commodities and organised research on the type of structure and materials to be adopted for such construction.

Standardisation

The need for finalising designs and specifications before the award of work needs no special emphasis. Experience shows that frequent and major changes during execution are not uncommon leading to contractual obligation and delay in execution. With the material available in this report it is hoped that it would not be difficult for the departments concerned to standardise the designs for grain storage structures in order to minimise, if not totally avoid, the changes during execution.

Where shell or folded plate construction is adopted, it will be an added advantage to standardise the shuttering and supply the same departmentally to contractors or else tenders may be called for group of godown in an area in order to facilitate repititive use of shuttering which will certainly lead to reduction in cost.

Application Of Works Study

Works study represents a philosophy of management and all that it implies and connotes is "techniques and analysis with a view to better fact-finding, more orderly thinking of work practices and scheduling and ensuring better quality of work within the specified time commensurate with targets fixed." The technique of work study which includes in its purview methods, works measurement etc. has been successfully adopted in U. S. A. and U. K. for critical evalution of all types of industrial processes. The utility of this technique in assessing and modifying various work procedures with a view to economy and efficiency has been increasingly recognised and its sphere of application is widening day by day. The handling and the storage of grains are such operations where systematic works study may yield rich dividends.

The lay out of stacks within the godowns, the operation of receipt and despatch of grain bags are some of the items where detailed works study would be able to pinpoint sources for economy. In a limited works study sponsored by the Panel, it was found that the utilisation of space within the godowns could be improved by about 10 per cent by changing the length of stacks to 29 feet and 34 feet alternately with a constant width of 25 feet. The aisles in between the stacks could be so manipulated to be brought beneath the roof trusses thus obviating the inconvenience in fumigation. It is gratifying to note that already this factor has been considered and put into practice in less humid regions.

Similarly, the study of handling and operation may be useful in deciding the width of platforms and the necessity of providing platforms on either side. It may also be considered whether it will be possible to eliminate altogether one of the platforms by making a study of the movement of trains and trucks to and fro.

Research

The Panel during its study has examined a number of structural patterns for adoption, though only a few of them have been recommended in the report. There are other structural patterns such as hyperbolic paraboloid and folded plate construction which have found increased application in foreign countries, especially U.S.A. The Central Building Research Institute in India has recently put up a laboratory with folded plate roof. They have also prepared a type design for grain godowns with roof of folded plate construction.

The advantages of folded plate construction are that the shuttering required is quite simple and with repetitive use, the cost of shuttering would decrease considerably. This type of construction also leads to considerable economy in the consumption of materials in additions to giving an architecturally pleasing appearance. The Panel feels that this type of construction has a great future in this country. The Central Building Research Institute should study in detail the performance and cost aspects of such structure and produce illustrative brochure with a view to promoting this form of construction.

Appendix II

Relative Merits Of Different Structures

SL. No.	Description of Structure.	Tubular Truss	Welded Frame	R.C.C. Gable	R.C.C. Shell (Elliptical)	R.C.C. Shell (Segmental)	Prestressed Prefabricated Truss
1.	2	3	4	5	6	7	8
1.	Capital cost per sft. of godown area (C)	9.95	8.05	8.25	9.89	10.32	8.54
2.	Maintenance cost (comparative) in terms of present-worth per sft. of godown area (M)	2.14	2.12	1.93	1.92	2.05	1.96
	Total : C+M(i.e., Items 1+2)	12.09	10.17	10.18	11.81	12.37	10.50
Intangibles							
I. Execution							
	(a) Skilled labour or ordinary labour	Ordy.	Skilled	Ordy.	Ordy.	Ordy.	Skilled
	(b) Competent firms (A) or ordinary firms (B)	B	A	B	A	A	A
	(c) Special trained supervision or ordinary supervision	Ordy.	Special	Ordy.	Special	Special	Special
	(d) Special equipment or ordinary equipment	Ordy.	Special	Ordy.	Ordy.	Ordy.	Special
	(e) Time of execution more or less	Less (6 months)	Less (7 months)	Less (7 months)	More (9 months)	More (9 months)	Less (7) months)
	(f) Foreign exchange involved, if any	Nil	Nil	Nil	Nil	Nil	Yes
	(g) Many godowns in a place for economic repetitive use of centering and mould or not	No	No	Yes	Yes	Yes	Yes
II. Efficiency :							
	(a) Economic Life or structure	Equal	Equal	Equal	Equal	Equal	Equal
	(b) Relative maintenance cost	More	More	Less	Less	Less	Less
	(c) Flexibility of layout inside Godown	Less	Less	Less	Less	More	Less
	(d) Leakage through roof and Valley Gutters	More	More	More	Nil	Nil	More
	(e) Effective volume inside Godown	Less	More	More	Less	More	Less
	(f) Dispersion of natural light	Less	Less	Less	More	More	Less
	(g) Insulation against heat and cold	Less	Less	Less	More	More	Less

(h) Consumption of materials :—						
(i) Structural Steel	Nil	More	Nil	Nil	Nil	Nil
(ii) Mild Steel	Less	Less	More	More	More	Less
(iii) M. S. Tubes	More	Nil	Nil	Nil	Nil	Nil
(iv) High Tensile Steel	Nil	Nil	Nil	Nil	Nil	Yes
(v) Accessories	More	More	More	Less	Less	More
(vi) Cement	Less	Less	More	More	More	More
(i) Resistance to fire	Less	Less	More	More	More	More
(j) Insurance rates	More	More	More	Less	Less	More

N.B. As long as there is shortage of structural steel in the country, the adoption of these alternatives will involve foreign exchange directly or indirectly.

Appendix III
Cost Study Of Alternative Structures

Sl. N.	Description	Unit	Tubular Truss with A.C. Sheet	Welded frame with A.C. Sheet	R.C.C. Gable Frame (with A C. Sheet)	Shell Roof (with Ellip-tical)	Shell Roof (Segmen-tal)	Prefabri-cated Precast and Pre-tensioned (with A.C. Sheet)
1	2	3	4	5	6	7	8	9
I.	Size of godown (clear dimension)		148′-9″ × 87′-6″	142′-0″ × 88′-10½″	150′-0″ × 87′-9″	130′-0″ × 89′-0″	140′-10″ × 88′-9″	148′-6″ × 88′-3″
	(a) Plinth area	sft.	16,335	15,850	16,524	15,322	15,880	16,602
	(b) Godown area	sft.	13,016	12,620	13,163	12,282	12,500	13,105
	(a) Cost of frame work	Rs.	75,800	48,100	52,500	73,000	75,000	57,000
	(b) Cost of filler work	Rs.	53,700	53,500	56,100	48,500	54,000	55,000
	(c) Total cost	Rs.	1,29,500	1,01,600	1,08,600	1,21,500	1,29,000	1,12,000
4.	(a) Cost of frame work per sft. of godown area	Rs.	5.82	3.81	3.99	5.94	6.00	4.35
	(b) Cost of filler work per sft. of godown area	Rs.	4.13	4.24	4.26	3.95	4.32	4.19
	(c) Total cost per sft. of godown area	Rs.	9.95	8.05	8.25	9.89	10.32	8.54
5.	(a) Equated cost of maintenance per year	Rs.	1,300	1,250	1,200	1,100	1,200	1,200
	(b) Equated cost of maintenance over capital cost percentage	%	1.00	1.23	1.12	0.91	0.93	1.04
	(c) Present worth cost of maintenance per sft. of godown area	Rs.	2.14	2.12	1.93	1.92	2.05	1.96

6.	Present worth cost of capital and maintenance 4 (c)+5(c)	Rs.	12.09	10.17	10.18	11.81	12.37	10.50
7.	Quantity of Steel per 100 sft. of godown area							
	(a) Structural Steel	Cwts.	Nil	2.31	Nil	Nil	Nil	0.07
	(b) M. S. reinforcement	Cwts.	1.57	1.29	4.03	4.36	4.26	1.14
	(c) M. S. tubes	Cwts.	2.40	Nil	Nil	Nil	Nil	Nil
	(d) Accessories	Cwts.	0.19	0.19	0.19	0.05	0.09	0.35 (H.T. Steel) 0.19
	(e) Total Quantity of steel (a+b+c+d)	Cwts.	4.16	3.79	4.22	4.41	4.35	1.75
8.	Quantity of cement per 100 sft. of godown area	Cwts.	18.89	17.91	21.12	27.52	29.60	18.01
9.	Economic life of structure	Years	75	75	75	75	75	75
10.	Time of construction	Months	6	7	7	9	9	7
11.	Materials for frame and filler works							
	(a) Cement	Cwts.	2,525	2,300	2,750	3,420	3,580	2,650
	(b) Steel							
	(i) Mild steel	Cwts.	204	163	530	535	532	150
	(ii) Structural steel	Cwts.	Nil	292	Nil	Nil	Nil	10
	(iii) High tensile steel	Cwts.	Nil	Nil	Nil	Nil	Nil	45
	(iv) M.S. tubes	Cwts.	316	Nil	Nil	Nil	Nil	Nil
	(v) Accessories	Cwts.	25	25	25	8	12	25
	(c) Sand	Cft.	10,000	9,000	10,400	12,000	12,800	10,000
	(d) Ballast							
	(i) 1½″ size	Cft.	6,200	6,000	6,500	6,000	6,000	6,500
	(ii) ¾″ and ½″ size	Cft.	4,700	3,600	4,500	10,200	9,500	4,500
	(e) Bricks	Nos.	1,85,000	1,80,000	1,80,000	1,50,000	2,00,000	2,05,000

Note : (1) The costs apply to Delhi and will vary at other places according to basic rates of material and labour.
(2) All structures are suitable for Zones, I, II and III of wind pressure. The estimate of welded frame structure relates to Zone III, and quantity of steel and cement will be higher for Zone I.
(3) Quantity of sand in II (c) does not include sand used in basement filling.

Appendix VI

Table 1

Present-Worth-Cost Study Of Tubular Roof Truss Structure

Data :

(1) Godown Area : 13016 sft.
(2) Capital Cost Rs. 1,29,500/-
(3) Rate per sft. of Godown Area: Rs. 9.95
(4) Rate of Compound Interest (i) =4.5 per cent per annum

Maintenance

Sl. No.	Description	Quantity	Rate	Per	Amount	Sinking fund factor (divided by)	Sinking fund value
1	2	3	4	5	6	7	8
			Rs.		Rs.	No.	Rs.
I.	1. White washing—every year	18,500 sft.	0.62	100 sft.	115	1.000	115.00
	2. Painting iron work—once in three years	600 sft.	7.50	100 sft.	45	3.133	14.40
	3. Painting iron work—once in four years	4,800 sft.	7.50	100 sft.	360	4.267	84.37
	4. Replacing valley gutter once in four years	156 rft.	4.30	rft.	671	...	...
	Deduct salvage value 10 per cent				67		
					604	4.267	141.60
	(5) (a) Replacing A.C. sheet—once in 15 years	18,700 sft.	80.00	100 sft.	14,960		
	(b) Replacing eave gutter—once in 15 years	312 rft.	3.80	rft.	1,186		
	(c) Replacing ridge—once in 15 years	312 rft.	2.24	rft.	699		
					16,885		
	(d) Deduct salvage value				842		
					16,043	20.156	795.94

Sheet 5 per cent
Gutter 5 per cent
Ridge 5 per cent } $\frac{16,885}{20}$

						148.69
	6. Miscellaneous	...	...	...	Total	1,300
	7. Annuity of maintenance	...	...	...	...	...
	8. (a) Present worth cost of maintenance Present value of an annuity of one for a period of 75 years at 4.5 per cent compound interest $=\frac{1-v^n}{i}$ where $v^n=\frac{1}{(1+i)^n}$			21.401		—
	(b) Present-worth cost of maintenance per sft. of godown area	...	...	$\frac{1300\times 21.401}{13,016}$	...	2.14
	9. Equated cost of maintenance per year per sft. of godown area	$\frac{1300}{13016}$	...	... 0.10	...	...
	10. Percentage cost of maintenance over capital cost	$\frac{1300\times 100}{1,29,500}$		1.00%		
II.	Capital cost Cost per sft. of godown area	1,29,500				9.95
III.	Present worth cost of trusses replaced at 50th year. Cost=39000 Present-worth-factor$=\frac{1}{(1\times i)}=0.1109$ Present worth-cost-per sft. of godown area	$\frac{39000\times 0.1109}{13016}$				0.31
IV.	Total outlay :					12.40
V.	*Deduct* Salvage value of the truss replaced at 50th year=39000×25 per cent=9750. Present worth cost per sft.	$\frac{9750\times 0.1109}{13016}$				0.08
VI.	Salvage value at 75th year					
	(a) A.C. sheet (b) Eave gutter (c) Ridge (d) Valley gutter	5 per cent of cost 876				
	(e) Doors, ventilators etc.	2000				
	(f) Salvage value of tubular truss at 25th year	31692				
		34568 or	34600			
	(g) Present worth cost per sft. of godown area for a period of 75 years	$=\frac{34600\times 0.0369}{13016}$	0.10			

$$\left[\frac{I}{(I \times i)75} \text{ i.e. } \frac{I}{\left(I \times \frac{4.50}{100}\right)75} = 0.369\right]$$

VII.	Total	0.18
VIII.	Net present worth cost per sft. of godown area	12.22

Table 2

Present-Worth-Cost Of R.C.C. Gable Roof Structure

Data :
1. Godown area : 13163 sft.
2. Capital cost : Rs. 1,08,600
3. Rate per sft. of godown area : Rs. 8.25
4. Rate of compound interest (i)=4.5 per cent per annum

Maintenance

Sl. No.	Description	Quantity	Rate	Per	Amount	Sinking fund factor (divided by)	Sinking fund value
1	2	3	4	5	6	7	8
			Rs.		Rs.	No.	Rs.
	1. White washing—every year	17600	0.62	100 sft.	109	1.000	109.00
	2. Painting wood work—once in 3 years	700	7.50	100 sft,	53	3.133	16.92
	3. Painting Iron work—once in 4 years	1750	7.50	100 sft.	131	4.267	30.70
	4. Replacing Valley Gutter—once in 4 years	154	4.30	rft.	622		
	Deduct 10% salvage				66	...	...
		...	...	...	596	4.267	139.60

5. Replacing Asbestos Sheet—once in 15 years	18600	80.00	100 sft.	14,800	—	—
Ridge—once in 15 years	308	3.80	rft.	1,170	—	—
Eave Gutter—once in 15 years	308	2.24	rft.	690	—	—
				16,740		
Deduct Salvage Value Sheet 5 per cent, Gutters 5 per cent, Ridge 5 per cent } 16740 / 20				837	20.156	788.90
				15,903		1085.12
6. Miscellaneous	...	...	...	...	...	114.88
7. Present cost of maintenance per sft.	1200×21.401 / 13163					1200.00
8. Equated cost of maintenance	1200 / 13163			0.09	—	1.95 —
9. Percentage cost of maintenance	1200×100 / 1,07,000			1.12%		
10. Deduct salvage value						
Roof 5 per cent	837	—	—	—	—	—
Doors 1/5×5120=1024	1024	—	—	—	—	—
Ventilators 1/20×4000=200	00	—	—	—	—	—
Frame 30000 / 10	3000	—	—	—	—	—
Miscellaneous	939	...	...	...	...	0.02
	6000×·0369 / 13163					1.93
11. Capital cost :		—	—	—	—	8.25
12. Present worth cost of capital and maintenance per sft. of godown area	—	—	...	—	—	10.18

Table 3

Present-Worth-Cost Study Of R.C.C. Semi-Elliptical Shell Roof Structure

Data :
1. Godown Area : 12,282 sft.
2. Capital Cost : Rs. 1,21,500
3. Rate per sft. of Godown Area : Rs. 9.89
4. Rate of Compound Interest (i) = 4.5 per cent per annum

Maintenance

Sl. No.	Description	Quantity	Rate	Per	Amount	Sinking fund factor (divided by)	Sinking fund value
1	2	3	4	5	6	7	8
			Rs.		Rs.	No.	Rs.
	1. White washing—every year	35500	0.62	100 sft.	220	1.000	220.00
	2. Painting wood work—once in three years	600	7.50	100 sft.	45	3.133	14.40
	3. Painting iron work—once in four years	1700	7.50	100 sft.	128	4.267	30.00
	4. Replacing tarfelt—once in eight years	1700	45.00	100 sft.	7650	9.378	815.80
							1080.20
	5. Miscellaneous	L.S.		...	...	...	19.80
	6. Present worth of maintenance	1,100×21.401 / 12,282					1.92
	7. Equated cost of maintenance per year per sft. of godown area	1100 / 12,282		...	0.09	—	—
	8. Equated percentage cost of maintenance per year over capital cost	1100×100 / 21,500		...	9.91%	—	—
	9. Capital cost per sft. of godown area	121500 / 12,282					9.89
	10. Total Capital cost and maintenance		...	...	...	...	11.81
	Deduct Doors : 5120×1/5=1024 Ventilators : 3700×1/20=185 Miscellaneous L.S. =291 Present worth per sft.	1500 1500×0.0369 / 12,282	...	...	...	...	0.01
	11. Net Present worth cost per sft. of Godown Area		...	...	...	...	11.80

REVIEWING COMMITTEE ON THE INDIAN INSTITUTE OF TECHNOLOGY, KHARAGPUR, 1959—REPORT

New Delhi, Ministry of Scientific and Cultural Affairs, 1961. 98p.+ip.

Chairman : Sir Willis Jackson.
Members : Prof. M. Mujeeb; Shri D. L. Deshpande; Dr. Atma Ram; Shri S. Ratnam.
Secretary Shri G. N. Vaswani.

APPOINTMENT

The Reviewing Committee on the Indian Institute of Technology, Kharagpur was appointed by the President of India in his capacity as Visitor of the Indian Institute of Technology, Kharagpur, in exercise of the powers vested in him under sub-section (2) of Section 9 of the Indian Institute of Technology (Kharagpur) Act, 1956 (51 of 1956) in 1959.

TERMS OF REFERENCE

(i) To review the work and progress of the Institute since its inception in 1951; and

(ii) To make recommendations in regard to the further development of the Institute.

CONTENTS

Chairman's Letter to the President of India; **Section I** : Constitution of the Reviewing Committee and Terms of Reference; An outline of the Procedure of Work and Programme of the Committee; Summary of the Committee's Recommendations; **Section II** : Brief History and Present State of Development of the Institute ; **Section III** : The Trends and Needs of the Technological Development ; **Section IV:** The Place of the Institution in the Educational Structure of India; **Section V:** The Number of Students and Related Questions; **Section VI** : Campus Amenities; **Section VII** : Staff and Staff-Student Relations ; **Section VIII** : Departments; **Section IX** : Appendices I to V.

RECOMMENDATIONS

Progress in technology now-a-days involves the collaborative team efforts of groups of scientists and technologists. It is imperative, therefore, that the education of technologists should embrace an advanced and broad-based study of the fundamental sciences in appropriate relationship to the particular technology which the individual specialises. In developing this point, the committee draw a clear distinction between the 'techologist' and the 'engineering technician' as these terms are understood in the United Kingdom.

The purpose of the Indian Institute of Technology, Kharagpur, is to produce technologists of high calibre in the foregoing sense. The attainment of this objective will call for radical changes in the character of the under-graduate courses at the Institute. With this and other considerations in mind, the Committee recommend a reduced intake of under-graduate students.

The Committee are disappointed with the smallness of the post-graduate population in the technological departments and also in the fact that too few of the present post-graduate students have had prior industrial or similar experience. They consider 12 months' internal experience of this kind a minimum pre-requisite for post-graduate entry.

The Committee suggest what in their view should be the maximum intake to the several under-graduate technologies and on the extent of the financial assistance that should be made available to the entrants.

The Committee indicate the directions in which improvements should be effected in the Campus amenities.

The Committee suggest certain measures which in their opinion would improve staff and staff-student relations.

The Committee review and make certain recommendations about the work of the departments, and in the introduction to this section they comment on the system of examinations obtaining at the Institute.

The Committee recommend that the Institute be allowed a revolving advance of about Rs. 10 lakhs to enable payments to be made during the opening months of the financial year before Government grants are received.

TEAM ON LOCAL GOVERNMENT IN YUGOSLAVIA, 1959—REPORT

New Delhi, Ministry of Community Development and Cooperation, Department of Community Development, 1960. 91p., Diagrams

Leader : Shri B. Mehta.
Member : Shri G. F. Mankodi.

APPOINTMENT

The Team on Local Government in Yugoslavia was constituted under the Ministry of Community Development and Cooperation (Department of Community Development) in 1959.

TERMS OF REFERENCE

To study Local Government in Yugoslavia for a period of about eight weeks from November 1959 to January 1960.

CONTENTS

Introduction; Historical Background; State Organisation—Levels of Government—Federal and Republican; Local Government—Its Growth; Local Government—People's Committee; Local Government—Organisation—Executive, Administrative and Judicial; Local Government—Functions; Local Government—Resources and Budget; Local Government—Services; Local Government—Relationship and Control; Local Government and Planning; Local Government and Social Management; Local Government and Social Welfare; Local Government and Other Organisations; Local Government in India; General Observations and Recommendations; Summary of Recommendations; Appendices A to D.

RECOMMENDATIONS

Three tier system recommended by Balwant Ray Mehta Team be adopted, but functions of Panchayat may need revision.

Pattern of Local Government should find a place in the country's Constitution.

Distinction berween rural and urban development should disappear. A beginning may be made by integrating rural and urban programmes in a District by the Zila Parishad.

Creation of a House of Producers is not feasible in India.

Nomination of candidates for election is not recommended.

25 to 33 per cent of the strength of Panchayat Samiti should be by direct election with a limited electorate.

Yugoslavian pattern of various councils discharging executive-*cum*-administrative functions is recommended for de-concentrating power and larger involvement of people.

President should not himself punish the employees but refer disciplinary action to a district level body predominantly non-official.

Secretary, *i.e.*, Chief Executive Officer of Panchayat Samiti should be recognised as a vital functionary and treated as a Head of the paid administration of the Samiti and allowed full disciplinary control over other employees.

Early consideration should be given to Urban Community Development and necessary additions to the functions recommended by the Balwant Ray Mehta Team should be considered to achieve this.

Making Block (Panchayat Samiti area) a basic administrative unit instead of Tehsil or Taluk should be studied by a high powered committee consisting of representatives of a few States, of concerned Central Ministries and the Planning Commission.

Reducing the multiplicity of agencies representing Central, State and Local Governments, operating in the area of Local Bodies is urgent. It should be coordinated and rationalised.

Budget Reserve Fund : The idea of budget reserve fund is worth considering.

Transfer of revenues from certain taxes wholly and others partly to the local bodies will provide incentive to tax collection and help development.

Ultimate aim should be to transfer the entire income from land revenue to local bodies.

Use of a percentage of small savings in area of its collection should be considered.

A Local Government Service Commission should be constituted for recruiting servants for rural and urban areas in the jurisdiction of Local Governments. For promotions, services in the State Government should be open to local government servants and be considered continuous.

Block Development Officer, as Secretary of the Panchayat Samiti, should be a highly qualified person with high calibre, if possible from the State Service.

The idea of issuing instructions should be replaced by idea of advice and guidance from higher bodies. Collector may also have to play a vital role in supervision on these lines.

Intensive and continuous training programme for the people as a whole, for people's representatives and frequent meetings of voters are essential for growth of local bodies. There is extreme shortage of useful literature for this purpose.

Zila Parishad should act as eldermen to guide lower bodies rather than control them.

State Government will have to retain the necessary powers of correction and control over local bodies and Collector will have to be vested with them, though he may rarely use them.

Role of Commissioner is very important. He should be relieved of most of routine administrative work so that he could act as Programme Adviser. He is the vital link between people and Government.

Role of Development Commissioner should be replaced by Commissioner and he should become Special Secretary to Government and coordinate activities of different departments.

Panchayat Samitis and Municipalities should be the base for drawing up plans which should be integrated at the district level.

The system of self-management in enterprises industrial or agricultural, cannot be adopted in India.

Principle of beneficiaries managing education and other institutions should be given trial by stages starting with schools upto middle standard in urban areas.

An institution on the lines of Standing Conference of Towns in Yugoslavia may be set up in each State.

A mechanism for improving administrative organisations and methods of work of local bodies should also be set up either as wings of the Institute of public administration or by State Governments.

Expert organisations, State Governments, and institutes like Mussoorie Institute should provide general guidance to the State organisations referred to above.

Ministry of Community Development should take steps to get subjects like cooperation, community development and local Government included in the curriculum for Graduate and Post-graduate classes in the University.

REVIEW COMMITTEE ON BIOCHEMISTRY IN INDIAN UNIVERSITIES, 1959—REPORT

New Delhi, University Grants Commission, 1963. 70p.+ixp.

Chairman : Dr. B. C. Guha.
Members : Dr. B. Mukherjee ; Dr. P. S. Sarma; Dr. P. S. Krishnan ; Dr. Hussain Zaheer ; Dr. V. Jagannathan.
Secretary : Dr. B. D. Laroia.

APPOINTMENT

Early in 1959, the University Grants Commission felt it necessary to have a systematic assessment made of the present status and standards of teaching and research in various science subjects and the facilities available in the country for training in each subject and to critically estimate the impact of the grants made by the University Grants Commission to the Indian Universities during the first and the Second Plan periods for rehabilitation, renewal of equipment, procurement of fresh equipment of modern design, strengthening of central and sectional libraries, improvement of salaries of teachers, etc. Such a stock-taking of the results of the work done during the first two Plan periods should prove helpful guide in the formulation of Commission's programmes of assistance in future, *i.e.*, during the Third Plan period and onwards. Accordingly, the Chairman, University Grants Commission appointed Review Committee in various science subjects, including one in Biochemistry.

The Review Committee on Biochemistry was appointed by the University Grants Commission in January, 1959.

TERMS OF REFERENCE

The Review Committee enjoyed wide terms of reference and was free to make out its own programme of work. Amongst other things, the Committee was, especially, to examine the following main items :

(a) The stage of development attained up till now in training and research in Biochemistry ;

(b) Qualitative and quantitative appraisal of the researches in progress ;

(c) Trends of research, its potentialities and steps to be taken for expansion of training and research facilities ;

(d) The syllabi and examination system at different levels and suggest improvement and modernisation of syllabi ;

(e) Ways of coordination between Universities and non-university institutions of teaching and research ;

(f) Improvement of facilities and amenities for students and teaching staff.

CONTENTS

RECOMMENDATIONS

The practice in some of the universities of teaching biochemistry in a section of the chemistry department is unsatisfactory as it tends to keep the standard of teaching low, denies biochemistry its importance as an independent discipline ond thus inhibits its development. Departments of biochemistry should, therefore, have the status of independent departments.

Teaching of biochemistry should start at the post-graduate level and should be for a period of two years leading to the M. Sc. degree. The Committee is not in favour of teaching biochemistry at the under-graduate level since the teaching of biochemistry needs a good grounding in subjects like chemistry and biology. A student who has just come out of the higher secondary school will not ordinarily be a suitable person to take to the study of biochemistry. Teaching of biochemistry at a lower level than M. Sc. would tend to divert the attention of the student from the fundamental subjects of chemistry and biology, which form the basis for studies in biochemistry.

The first year of the two-year course for M. Sc. should be devoted to advanced training in branches of chemistry, particularly physical and organic, with a bias towards biochemistry. The courses in the first year should also cover the basic principles of biology and physiology along with some biochemical subjects. Thus, before going to the final year of the M. Sc. course, a student should prepare himself in all allied subjects on which teaching in biochemistry is based so that he will be ready in the final year to take specialised training in biochemistry.

Admission to the post-graduate classes in biochemistry should be open to those who have taken chemistry as a major or a minor subject at the B. Sc. level, preference being given to those who have studied chemistry as a major subject along with any two of the following : (a) physics, (b) mathematics, (c) botany, (d) zoology, and (e) physiology. Those who have taken a medical degree and wish to specialise in biochemistry may also be admitted, wherever suitable.

Each centre selected for training in biochemistry should normally admit 10 to 12 students every year. Only in special cases these units may be doubled, provided adequate facilities, laboratory space and staff are available.

The new centres of biochemistry should be allowed to develop at such places only where chemistry departments are fully developed and are functioning efficiently. Similarly, for expansion of the present facilities preference for developing biochemistry should be given to those universities which have well established chemistry departments.

In addition to the existing independent departments of biochemistry in the universities, 10 more centres should be developed to provide facilities for training in biochemistry. Preference should be given to those universities which already have sections of biochemistry functioning as parts of the departments of chemistry.

Any department of biochemistry selected as a centre for purposes of post-graduate training should possess minimum equipment needed for reasonable coverage of the syllabus given in the text and provide practical training in all the important branches of biochemistry. The syllabus given indicates the coverage of the subject and is to be regarded as only illustrative.

Expensive equipment should be provided where they are needed for researches already in progress or for initiating new lines of research and where trained personnel are available to handle such specialised equipment so as to ensure proper utilisation of equipment.

For purposes of research it is desirable to develop on regional basis three or four centres to provide facilities in almost all the major branches of biochemistry in the initial stages. When more funds are available, these facilities should be extended to all centres.

In those universities where the situation does not warrant establishment of independent departments of biochemistry but where the departments of other biological sciences namely, botany, and zoology are strongly developed so as to require the services of a biochemist, a biochemist of the rank of a reader should be made available, either individually or jointly for such departments.

The subject of biochemistry has not been developed in any centre in the north-western region including the central universities teaching science subjects and the committee desires that necessary steps may be taken to develop at least one centre in this region.

The biochemistry departments should make the best use of the cooperation from other related departments such as, chemistry, zoology and botany.

The system of introducing teaching assistantships on a fixed remuneration and encouraging Ph. D. students who have considerably progressed in their work to take up such assistantships is highly commendable.

There is a growing need for providing short-term courses in certain specialised areas of knowledge. Certain university centres may be selected to provide such short-term courses.

Scholarships both merit as well as post-graduate research scholarships which were being awarded by the Commission up till now should be continued to be awarded. The basis of selection should be the merit of the candidate. If, however, a university-wise allotment were to be made, the number of scholarships to be given for the study of biochemistry should be at least two per year for each of the departments recommended by the Committee. The value of research scholarships should be increased from Rs. 200 to Rs. 250. Similarly, the Commission should continue to award post-doctoral Junior and Senior Research Fellowships. The value of Junior post-doctoral fellowship should be increased from Rs. 300 to Rs. 400, as in the case of the fellowships awarded by the Council of Scientific and Industrial Research, the National Institute of Sciences of India and the National Research Fellowships of the Government of India. The number of such fellowships may be increased to 100. The number of Senior Research Fellowships of the value of Rs. 500 may be increased to 40 per year

A short term course in instrumentation and analytical techniques in biochemistry should be arranged in two suitable centres, perhaps, Calcutta and Bangalore to begin with, where facilities for imparting this training are available. Adequate financial aid with regard to personnel, equipment and recurring expenses should be provided and this may be determined in consultation with the centres of training chosen.

The minimum requirements of staff, equipment and space required for training 10-12 students for the M.Sc. course in Biochemistry are indicated. For doctorate and particularly post-doctorate students more space and facilities would be needed.

The training of 150-200 M.Sc.'s in Biochemistry per year is aimed at during the Third Plan period. They should be absorbed in universities, medical, agricultural and veterinary Institutions, government scientific and technical services and in State and private industry. The fact that most medical and agricultural institutions in the country do not have full-fledged independent departments of biochemistry is pointed out. These departments should be rapidly built up so that these institutions concerned with national welfare can run on modern lines as in other advanced countries. Biochemists for appointment in medical colleges need not necessarily have a medical qualification but should be well-trained biochemists. Insistence on a medical degree will be inhibitory to progress.

Professors-in-charge of departments should not be bogged in administrative duties. They should have administrative secretaries to look after routine duties. Some "Research Professorships" on the same scale of pay as the other professorships should be created to allow some professors to give their wholetime to research and occasional teaching and they should be relieved entirely of administrative duties.

Annual block research grants should be provided for all teachers so that they can proceed with researches on a long term basis. These grants may be supplemented by grants from other bodies like the Council of Scientific and Industrial Research, Indian Council of Medical Research, etc.

Facilities for the improvement of research abilities of teachers are indicated including the arrangement of seminars and summer schools and the provision of travel grants and subbatical leave.

WORKING GROUP ON SMALL SCALE INDUSTRIES, 1959—EVALUATION REPORT

New Delhi, Ministry of Commerce & Industry, 1959. 153p.

Chairman : Shri P. B, Advani.
Members: Shri H. C. Mathur ; Dr. P. S. Lokanathan; Shri G. L. Bansal; Shri P. C. Basu ; Shri M. Bhatnagar; Shri L. N. Renu.

Secretary : Dr. S. L. Sharma.

APPOINTMENT

The working Group on Small Scale Industries was constituted under the Ministry of Commerce and Industry. Government of India *vide* their Memorandum No. SSI(A)-28 (83) /58, dated January 30, 1959, as modified on March, 20, 1959, for evaluation of Small Scale Industries programme.

TERMS OF REFERENCE

To undertake evaluation studies on the following:

(i) Provision made and the actual expenditure in the first three years and the main items on which the expenditure has been incurred ;

(ii) Increase in production levels of development and employment achieved as a result of the outlay ;

(iii) Improvements achieved in technicues of production and quality of products;

(iv) Increase in the earnings of artisans;

(v) Number of persons trained and the number of trained persons absorbed in the industry;

(vi) Increase in exports of products or diminution in imports of corresponding products;

(vii) Improvements in administrative and organisational set up for the efficient implementation of the programme, with special reference to the programme of industrial cooperatives;

(viii) Shortfalls in expenditure, if any, below the provisions made and the reasons therefor ;

(ix) Shortfalls in production/development, if any, below the targets or levels of development envisaged and the factors accounting for the same ;

(x) A general appraisal of the extent to which the results achieved have been commensurate with the outlay, with particular reference to the cases in which the results have been poor or disappointing (the appraisal should include an examination of the extent to which the industry has been stabilised and thus enabled to reduce its dependence on subsidies, Government-assisted marketing, Government finance and other forms of Government assistance);

(xi) An assessment of the extent to which the shortfalls in (viii) and (ix) above were due to temporary causes or special difficulties of an unavoidable character and how far they are due to the basic weaknesses of the programmes or limiting conditions of a durable character;

(xii) Whether the difficulties of small-scale industries in obtaining their fair share of raw materials are being overcome;

(xiii) Whether under the new arrangements credit can be obtained without undue harassment ;

(xiv) Whether the provision of technical know-how and assistance is adequate ; and

(xv) Lessons of experience for the Third Five Year Plan.

CONTENTS

Introductory ; Small Industries Programme; Plan Provisions and Actual Expenditure in the first Three Years of the Second Five Year Plan; Increase in Production Levels of Development and Employment and Increase in Earnings as a Result of Outlay ; Shortfalls in Production/Development, if any, Below the Targets or levels of Development Envisaged and the Factors Accounting for the Same ; An Assessment of the Extent to which the Shortfalls in (iii) and (v) Above were due to Temporary Causes of Special Difficulties of an Unavoidable Character and how Far they are due to the Basic Weaknesses of the Programme or Limiting Conditions of a Durable Character ; Improvements, Achieved in Techniques of Production and Quality of Products ; Number of Persons Trained and the Number of Trained Persons Absorbed in the Industry ; Improvements in Administrative and Organisational Set-up for the Efficient Implementation of the Programme with Special Reference to the Progress of Industrial Cooperatives ; Whether the Difficulties of the Small Scale Industries in Obtaining their Fair Share of Raw Material are being Overcome ; Whether under the New Arrangements Credit can be Obtained without undue Harassment ; Increase in Exports of Products or Diminution in Imports of Corresponding Products ; General Appraisal of the Extent to which the Results Achieved have been Commensurate with the Outlay Including an Examination of the Extent to which Industries have been Stabilised ; Lessons of Experience for the Third Five-Year Plan; Summary and Conclusions ; Appendices I to XVI.

RECOMMENDATIONS

Plan Provision

The total amount provided in the Second Plan for village and small industries has been revised from Rs. 200 to Rs. 176 crores. The Sum earmarked for small industries alone has been revised from Rs. 61 crores to Rs. 56.57 crores.

State And General Schemes

A provision of Rs. 35 crores was made for State Schemes and a provision of Rs. six ¾ crores for general schemes, now merged with the State schemes. The Planning Commission has now revised the total provision for State and general schemes to Rs. 33.18 crores, but has not revised the five years allocations, the necessary adjustment being made through the annual plans.

Plan Provision And Expenditure

Up to the end of 1958, total expenditure of various States amounted to only 63 per cent of the amount provided for three years and 30.8 per cent of the total Plan provision. The shortfall in the first year of the Plan was the heaviest *i.e.*, about 48 per cent of the provision made for that year. Ever since the rate of expenditure has been gradually increasing every year. Cumbersome machinery for sanctioning the scheme, suspension of construction work, States' reorgnisation and shortage of technical and administrative staff are the main reasons for the shortfall in expenditure.

Streamlining Of Sanction Procedure

The sanction procedures have recently been streamlined. Shortfalls in State expenditure have now been reduced to the minimum. The expenditure for 1958-59 has been as high as 92 per cent of the sanctioned amount. The highest percentage expenditure upto March was by Madras (84.5 per cent) and the lowest by Bombay and Madhya Pradesh. Although some States have not been able to gear up their machinery to the full, the performance as a whole has shown appreciable improvement as a result of the streamlining of the procedure.

Category-wise Analysis Of Expenditure

Expenditure on schemes of loans under the State Aid to Industries Act and Industrial Cooperatives has been as high as 80 per cent and 60 per cent respectively and on other schemes it ranges between 32 per cent to 47 per cent. The amount provided for strengthening the staff has been fully utilised.

Capital Assets And Current Outlay

The group feels that a break-up of expenditure into capital and current development expenditure is very important for planning purposes and therefore should hence forward be attempted.

Industrial Estates

Not much progress was made as regards the construction of Industrial Estates in the First Plan. During the Second Plan, the Planning Commission has accepted the proposal to put up 97 Estates for which revised plan allocation of Rs. 11.12 crores has been made. The progress of expenditure incurred on the construction of Industrial Estates has been satisfactory. Slow acquisition proceedings and delays caused by PWD's have been the main reasons for some of the States to lag behind in construction of Industrial Estates.

In view of the popularity and importance of the Industrial Estates programme, it is considered necessary not only to restore the original number of 110 Estates but also, if possible add a few more to the Estate programme during the current plan.

Central Schemes

A sum of Rs. 11.38 crores has been provided for in the plan for programme of development of small scale industries directly by the Centre.

Industrial Extention Service

A net-work of Small Industries Service Institutes, Branch Institutes and Extension Centres has been planned all over the country. The percentage of expenditure for the years 1956-57 to 1958-59, over the amount provided is 60.

Year-wise expenditure reveals that only 40 per cent was spent on land and buildings. The reasons for this shortfall are to be located mainly in procedural delays of an administrative character.

It is necessary that so far as the execution of the work is concerned, the C.P.W.D. and W.H.S. Ministry should only be concerned with laying down the broad principles, and the rest of the work should be decentralised and given over to the Ministry.

It should also not be necessary to refer cases again and again to a multitude of authorities for getting the sanctions.

Machinery

The expenditure on machinery in the first three years works out to only 39 per cent of the amount provided. The main cause for this shortfall has been want of suitable accommodation for installing the machinery,

Staff

Expenditure on "Staff" and 'other charges' has amounted to as much as 88 per cent and 100 per cent respectively. (A view was taken in the Group that this was rather strange in view of the fact that on buildings only 41.6 per cent and on machinery only 25.4 per cent of the budgeted amounts were spent.) This does not give a satisfactory picture of the staff position because provisions for staff are made on a conservative basis. It is necessary to strengthen staff in all Institutes and Extension Centres especially, the newly created ones which are poorly staffed. Technical advice to a substantial extent has been given which would have been more satisfactory if workshops had been in position.

National Small Industries Corporation

NSIC has been undertaking such activities as (a) marketing service, (b) Supply of machinery on hire-purchase basis, (c) construction and maintenance of Industrial Estates at Naini and Okhla and (d) establishment of the Proto-type production-*cum*-training centres. During the three years of its working, *i.e.*, 1956-57 to 1958-59, the Central Government has financed this Corporation to the extent of Rs. 382.75 lakhs.

Increase in Production

Industry outlook reports issued by the Small Industries Organisation, NSIC's date about factories working in the Okhla Industrial Estate and the impact of Hire-Purchase Scheme on production/employment ; its Government Purchase Programme, results of loan assistance to small units by the State Directors of Industries under the State Aid to Industries Act and a rapid survey of 300 units conducted by the D.C.'s Organisation—all show that production in the small-scale sector has generally been on an increase ever since the programme of development of small scale industries was launched by the Government.

Increase/Decrease In Employment

Increase in employment has not been recorded to the same extent.

In the case of majority of units that received assistance, production increases were more significant than employment increases. It is not possible to precisely determine the gain due to various types of assistance rendered, but it is evident that without such help such gains would be much less.

Ancillary Production

Ancillary development forms an integral part of any small industries programme. Efforts made by the NSIC to promote a few ancillary units around large scale factories as perpetual feeders of components and parts at pre-determined prices have resulted in setting up ancillary units.

Incentive To Promote Ancillaries

Despite the steps taken both by the Government and NSIC, the group feels that development of ancillaries has made no satisfactory headway.

New large-scale industries wherever feasible should be licensed and regulated so as to develop a broad base of small-scale units. Factories in the Public sector should give the lead and set this pattern before the country. Some special steps will need to be taken to accelerate the development of ancillary industry.

Increase In The Earning Of Artisans

It has been brought out by the rapid survey of 300 units that in most cases the wage-increase have been more than the increase recorded by the Consumer Price Index (Working Class) during 1954 to 58.

Although no conclusive evidence is available regarding the extent of increase in wages for various categories of workers, it is found that in great majority of cases skilled labour benefited more than semi-skilled and semi-skilled more than unskilled from the programme.

Targets Of Production

The Planning Commission in consultation with the Ministry of Commerce and Industry, fixed targets of production for three small scale industries—bicycles, sewing machines and storage batteries. The SSI Board has recommended in May 1959, that targets for a few selected small scale industries should be fixed.

Sewing Machines

There has been an expansion of production of Sewing machines in the small scale sector to the extent of 85 per cent. Contribution of the small-scale sector in 1958, has been 13 per cent of the total production of sewing machines in the country, or 38 per cent of its approved capacity target.

Storage Batteries

No production programme for manufacturing storage batteries in the small-scale sector has been formulated.

Restriction On Large Scale Industries

Restrictions have also been placed on the expansion of the capacity in the large-scale sector in industries like furniture making, pencil, small hand tools, sports goods footwear, etc.

No further expansion of capacity during the Second Plan was envisaged for the large scale tanning leather and radio receivers industries.

There has also been a demarcation of the spheres of production in respect of large and small scale producers of agricultural implements and a restrictive policy is being followed in regard to expansion thereof in the large scale sector.

Shortfalls In Targets Of Production

The momentum gathered by certain small scale units as a result of various types of assistance—technical, financial, marketing—given by the Small Scale Industries Organisation, should be sustained and increased. Further, the strides already made by the various branches of the Small Scale Industries Organisation may be supplemented by strengthening them through more and better equipment, additional staff, more advanced trainning etc.

Institutes' Buildings

The need for composite buildings for each Institute

and Extension Centre cannot be over-emphasised if technical assistance has to be made effective.

Staff

While staffing the Institutes and Extension Centres, special needs of the under-developed areas should be fully kept in view. In order to ensure maximum utilisation of the available resources, there should be fullest coordination between installation, supply of machines, staff recruitment and posting.

Supply Of Raw Materials

To render more effective demonstration/trainning and other service, Institutes should be assisted with supplies of the required type and variety of raw materials on a continuous basis.

Workshops And Laboratories

To make extension service and technical assistance more efficient, it is necessary for the Institutes to have their own workshops and laboratories. It is understood that remedial measures are being taken to ensure that the machinery and equipment are installed espeditiously in the buildings which are now being constructed.

Quality And Production

The quality marking schemes which have been in the States of U.P. and Punjab should be introduced in other States.

NSIC And DGS & D Encouragement To Quality Production

Small-Scale units are now taking increasing interest in producing quality goods as a result of the sales promotion activities of the NSIC and Stores Purchase Programme of D.G.S. & D.

Type Of Assistance Given

Small scale units have taken a great interest in improving their production techniques, quality marking services, utilisation of proper raw materials and new and improved type of machines, knowledge of management practices, business management training, library Service, help in cost acccountancy, etc.

Designs And Drawings

The Group notes with satisfaction the recent decision to make available the services of Industrial Designers to all the Institutes and Centres.

Designing Equipment

Improved designs cannot be adopted satisfactorily in the small scale units in the absence of suitable machinery.

Model Schemes And Technical Bulletins

So far, 339 model schemes and 198 bulletins have been prepared and arrangements have also been made to translate them into Hindi and other regional languages.

Mobile Workshop Demonstrations

Demonstrations through mobile workshops have aroused interest of the artisans in the use of improved hand tools and hand operated machines. They have also been supplied technical information at the door.

Result Of Demonstration

In order to assist the artisan towards effecting improvements in the techinques or quality of products a more intensive training for longer duration will have to be undertaken.

Supply Of Machinery On Hire Purchase And Quality

Some improvement in the quality of the products and production of new items has resulted from the supply of machinery by the NSIC on hire-purchase basis.

Future Requirements

It is necessary not only to extend the existing activities of the Institutes but also to start new branch Institutes and Extension Centres equipped with a large field staff in order to cater to the growing needs.

Need And Scope For Expanding Technical Services

In view of the expanding requirements it would be further necessary to expand the technical services, There is considerable scope for developmental activities of the Institutes and Extension Centres. The ground is now more than prepared for a more intensive and extensive development of the services rendered by the Technical Institutes and Extension Centres.

Indian And Foreign Technicians

In order to utilise the services of foreign consultants more effectively it is recommended that (i) job specifications and descriptions should be worked out in detail writting for each post before the arrival of each consultant, (ii) the maximum number of Indian counterparts should be attached full-time to each foreign consultant, (iii) the work of the foreign consultants and their Indian counterparts should be carefully followed-up, (iv) the foreign consultants should be given all assistance possible—like modern drafting machines, tools, reference, library, books, etc.

Intensive Training Programme

In view of the development under contemplation, a more intensive programme for sending staff of the Small Scale Industries Organisation abroad as well as for training and refresher courses in suitable Indian concerns and refresher courses must be developed. More of Ford Foundation funds should be used for training our young men abroad from the S.S.I. Organisation of the Centre and States.

On The Job Or In-Plant Training

A training programme should be developed by the SSI Organisation under which persons with basic qualifications should be recruited for the various posts in the SSI Organisation and given on the job or in-plant training for one to two years within the country.

Technical And Apprentice Training

Early action should be taken on the recommendations of the Technical Training Committee and Apprentices Training Committee which submitted their reports in 1957 and 1958 respectively.

Training At The H.M.T. Factory

The suggestion made by the Committee set up by the Ministry of Commerce and Industry that the Government should assist small scale industries by deputing suitable personnel for specialised training at Hindustan Machine Tools Factory, Bangalore is a step in the right direction and will go a long way in improving the quality of products of small scale industries.

Training By The State Directors Of Industries

Most State Governments organise training under their vocational training programme.

Employment Of Trained Persons

In Andhra Pradesh, it is reported that about 99 per cent of the trainees have been absorbed in industries and 45 persons have set up their own industies. In Madras, U.P., and Punjab also most of the trainees have either been self-employed or got employment in factories. The progress in other States is slow.

Training Courses And Syllabi

There is no uniformity in the duration of course and the syllabi followed by States. The progress of absorption of trainees has not been followed up properly. Due to unattractive remunerations, the training-*cum*-production centres have not been manned by proper and efficient teachers. Inadequate stipends offered by the State Governments often deter artisans from joining these centres.

It is imperative that there should be uniformity in the syllabi of training in all the States.

As far as possible emoluments should be raised in order to attract properly qualified teachers.

Utilisation of Existing Facilities

For training skilled craftsman with a view to atsisting them in improving their techniques, existing facilities in the Small Scale Industries Organisation should be fully utilised. The value of stipends should be adequately raised in order to attract the real artisans for such training.

Steps should be taken to ensure that all the trainees after completing their course are gainfully employed either by self-employment or through employment in factories.

Training of B.L.E.O.'s

There is considerable under-utilisation of existing training facilities provided by the Central Government for the training of block level extension officers (Industries) of the State Governments.

Business Manogement Training

There is wide interest among the small businessmen to avail of the business management training. In view of the increasing demand for such courses and the necessity for them, it should be possible to expand these facilities further at other Institutes/Centres also.

Existing Staff Shortage in DC's Organisation

There is acute shortage of technical and other administrative staff, gazetted and non-gazetted, required for working an extensive programme of small scale industries development both at the Centre and the States. The general reasons assigned for this are shortage of technical and qualified administrative personnel, delays in obtaining sanctions and procedural delays in recruitment of staff.

Special efforts should be made to select qualified persons as expeditiously as possible and give them in-plant training both in India and abroad.

A Special Officer in the Office of the Development Commissioner should be exclusively occupied with the whole process of recruitment, training and placement.

Decentralisation Of Authority

Delegation of authority with a view to expediting the small scale industries programmes is necessary. Some States have already taken suitable steps in this direction. The Group is in favour of the principle of decentralisation of power and authority to the fullest extent consistent with safeguarding the Government's interests and carrying out policies and programmes laid down from time to time.

Rectifying the Procedure

Decentralisation is not an end in itself. It is a question of fixing responsibility upon each level of officer and giving him the right and authority for taking decisions. Officers' efficiency should be judged not by the few mistakes they make but by the nature and quality of decisions they take and the speedy action which follow their decisions.

Review Of Personnel Requirements

While assessing the personnel requirements connected with the small industries the amount of work involved and the number of officers required to execute it must always be borne in mind. Both the number and the quality of personnel and their outlook need to be greatly improved in the Centre as well as the States. There is great need for consolidating activities at different levels. Expansion of activities without consolidation will result in waste which sometimes can lead to demoralisation.

The progress with a few exceptions recorded by industrial cooperatives has not been very significant. The financial assistance given by the Directors of Industries to such cooperatives is not very significant which suggests that the whole programme needs to be reviewed for its fuller development.

Raw Material Shortage

The survey reports show that the majority of the units are experiencing raw material shortages, both controlled and imported; the degree of their shortage differs from unit to unit and industry to industry.

Overall Shortage Of Steel

Allocation of steel to the small scale units during the past three years has been limited. However, with the expected improvement in the supply position during first quarter of 1959-60, allocation has much improved.

Director Of Industries To Be Overall In-charge

It is recommended that the Director of Industries in the State should be the only officer in-charge of small scale industries for the assessment and distribution of controlled raw materials and duplication of these duties by the Iron and Steel Controller in the State, if any, be avoided. In appropriate cases small industrialist should be given import quotas for their requirements of imported iron and steel.

Role Of Association And Raw Materials

Excess quantities of controlled materials, for free sale with registered stockists be made available to small units, preferably, through Associations and Corporations of small industrialists.

SSI Board's Recommendation For Raw Material Depots

The Group feels that the recommendation of the SSI Board that each State should set up atleast two raw material depots before March 31, 1960, should be implemented.

NSIS's Efforts To Supply Non-ferrous Metals

The supply position of copper, zinc, tin, etc., continues to be unsatisfactory. Efforts are being made by the NSIC to obtain brass scrap from Ordnance factories for distribution to small units under a scheme. The Group recommends that the scheme be accepted and pursued vigorously.

When a commodity or component is needed by a small scale industry, it is to be considered on an *ad hoc* basis and import licence issued.

Sanctioning Of Loan Applications

The time taken in sanctioning loans under the State Aid to Industries Act to small-scale units varies from State to state. In Orissa and Rajasthan it takes one to three months while in other States it is between three to 12 months depending upon the amount of loan and securities offered.

Results of Industry Surveys

According to the Industry surveys conducted by the Small-Scale Industries Organisation, loans from private sources are still very common which involves minimum delay and formalities at the hands of the lending agencies as compared with Government agencies.

Departmental Loans

Loans sanctioned through the State Department of Industries to the small scale units amounted to Rs. 520 lakhs or 66 per cent of the total loans sanctioned by various agencies.

Security And Disbursement Rules

Considerable time is taken by the lending authorities in knowing the credit-worthiness of the applicants and evaluating the securities offered, completion of legal formalities etc.

Working Group On State Aid

The working group appointed by the Small Scale Industries Board in January 1958 had recommended certain measures for eliminating differences of procedures and rules at the State levels and for evolving more simplified ways so as to avoid all possible delays in disposing of the loan applications. These recommendations are under consideration of the State Governments.

Inadequancy Of Funds

Except in Punjab all other State Governments feel that the funds placed at their disposal under

State Aid to Industries Act often fall short of their requirements.

State Financial Corporations

Routing of Government funds through the State Financial Corporation has been possible only in six States.

Limiting Loan Operations to Medium Scale Units

State Financial Corporations, in addition to the agency work, also advance loans to small-scale units out of their own funds. But most of these loans so far have been granted to more credit-worthy and medium scale units.

State Bank of India : Loan Facilities

The State Bank of India's Pilot Scheme of granting credit to small-scale units has now been extended to all its branches. A test check conducted by the Development Commissioner's Organisation has shown that Bank has been favouring 'Lock and Key' loans instead of 'clean' or 'factory' type loans. Since the former caused inconveinence to the borrower, the State Bank has further liberalised its terms and conditions and is now prepared to advance the 'factory' type loan.

Routing Of Government Funds

State Bank of India and the Government should give serious consideration to the suggestion of the SSI Board that Government funds should also be routed through the State Bank. This would enable larger number of people to avail of the facility. Other banks can also take up this work on behalf of the State Governments.

Commercial Banks

It is to be regretted that, thus far, commercial banks in the country have been rather averse to the idea of financing Small-Scale Industries. Standing Committee of the SSI Board is already seized of this matter and it has taken up the issue with some of the commercial banks in the country.

Urban Cooperative Banks

Only Bombay and Mysore States have so far accepted the SSI Board's suggestion of routing at least 10 per cent of the funds, available under State Aid of Industries Act, through six urban cooperative Banks in each State.

Financing of Industrial Cooperatives has largely been the function of Cooperative Banks. But progress in this field, except in Bombay State, has been very insignificant. State Bank of India was approached by the SSI Board to take up this function also, to which it has agreed. Also, the Working Group on Industrial Cooperatives appointed by the Government of India in 1957 has made certain valuable recommendations for accelerating the development of Industrial Cooperatives.

Other Schemes

The State Bank of India has agreed to open cash credit accounts for small-scale units reommended by the National Small Industries Corporation. The Bank also advances loans to such units against security of raw materials without maintaining the usual margin between the value of the security and the amount advanced.

The State Governments have been advised by the SSI Board to assist the small-scale units participating in the State Governments Purchase Programme by getting them credit from the State Bank of India, as NSIC has done.

Re-Financing By Reserve Bank

The Reserve Bank of India is considering to include leather industry under its approval list of selected industries for financing by the Bank.

Expansion Of Production And Reduction Of Imports

An overall expansion in the production of certain items like electric fans, Sewing machines, paints and varnishes and bicycles, which are quite prominent in the Small Scale Sector, has been accompained by reduction in imports from abroad. The percentage fall in imports (during 1955-56) and 1958, of electric fans, soap, bicycles, and sewing machines was 82, 68 50 and 65 respectively.

Difficulty Of Assessing Replacement Of Imports

There has been, correspondingly, an appreciable increase in the production of Small Scale Sector, though no definite correlation could be worked out to assess the replacement of imports by such increased production.

Exports

Although shoes have been sold to some East European countries, no significant advance has been made by the Small Scale Industry in pushing up its share in country's exports.

Export Promotion By The NSIC

In Punjab, Delhi and U.P. the NSIC has been able to procure orders for export of shoes to Russia and Poland. In Bombay too one unit, with NSIC's assistance, has been exporting paints and varnishes to Afghanistan under 'Jansevak' Brand.

Export Of Shoes

According to an *ad hoc* survey by the NSIC, the export order of shoes has resulted in doubling the production of quality shoes in the main producing centres. It has meant increase in aggregate employment and enhanced total wage bill.

Trade Inquiries

The mounting figure of trade enquiries received from Far East, America, Europe, Africa and Australia bears testimony to the export potentialities for Indian goods which exist there.

Exhibition And Sample Display

NSIC has been participating in international exhibitions for promoting small scale industries, products, specially guava slices, jelly, sports goods and wollen hosiery products.

Quality Control

There is great necessity to adhere to specifications and quality in products required by the foreign buyers. Small scale units would gain more if they kept the quality of their products consistent. Special consideration for small scale products is desirable at the hands of the export promotion directorate.

Scope Of Expansion

There are as many as 29 small scale industries for which good scope for expansion of exports is noticed. Wood screws, bolts and nuts, wire netting, panel pins, microphones, electric fans, gramophone needles being some of important ones.

Contribution Of Small Scale Industries In Exports

By and large, Industries where indigenous production is short of domestic requirement or where rising trends of exports promise further expansion or where imports are rapidly decreasing indicate that small scale units can play an increasingly important part in adding to the production of such items.

Export Possibilities

In so far as small scale industries are expected to replace foreign products it is necessary to relax import restrictions on some of the finished products used as samples which would enable the small scale producers in improving the quality on their basis.

Impact Of The Programme

The assistance rendered by the erstwhile Regional Institute, although commendable, has not been followed by a very appreciable growth of the small-scale industries. The main bottleneck has been in respect of raw materials, equipment, trained personnel, factory building etc. State Governments need to intensify their efforts, if the small scale sector in their respective economies is to make rapid progress.

Progress Of The Industrial Estate Programme

Though the small scale units have taken full advantage of the facilities available in the Industrial Estates, the programme itself has generally been slow, because of the difficulties in obtaining suitable land, long time taken in their construction etc. The revised programme of Industrial Estates is likely to be completed by May 1961.

Dependence Of Industries On Government Assistance

The small-scale units, with the execption of a few, are still dependent on the State for their development. However, in Punjab, a few industries are reported to be less dependent now on Government assistance. Concerted efforts are needed at the State level to activise the programme for bringing about the desired development of the small-scale industries.

Small Industries Programme—Initial Difficulties Tided Over

The Small Scale Industries Programme has got over its teething troubles and has gathered considerable momentum. Nevertheless, progress has been slow in various spheres to various limitations mentioned in the previous Chapters.

Progress Towards Decentralisation

Progress has been restricted with regard to Industries Estates programme. The extent and degree of decentralisation than can be fostered here finally to depend on the availability of electricp ower and other services. A time has now come when greater attention should be given to the establishment of industrial estates in smaller towns and rural areas.

Objectives Of Employment

The recent revision of definition of small industries in respect of the employment limit is also likely to increase employment by the working of additional shifts.

Balance Between Capital Intensive And Labour Intensive

In order to create larger employment and increased production, a balance between capital intensive and labour intensive small scale industries has to be struck.

Necessity For Electrification

Concerted efforts to carry electricity to the rural areas must be backed by a drive to educate the village artisan in the use of power operated machines, and equipment, supplied possibly on hire-purchase. It is recommended that local grids be established on the basis of medium thermal stations for taking electricity to rural areas.

Reservation Of Spheres Of Production

No action has so far been taken on the first item of the Common Production Programme envisaged under the First Plan, *viz.*, reservation of the spheres of production.

Norms Of Production

It is of importance to fix fresh production targets for cycles, sewing machines and storage batteries industries as well as certain scheduled and non-scheduled industries for the small scale sector.

Development Of Ancillaries

To accelerate the growth of ancillaries for which there is great scope, suitable positive measures will have to be taken.

Summary

Practical steps should be taken to ensure the establishment of adequate number of new small industrial units capable of producing goods of the approximate value of Rs. 250 to Rs. 300 crores per year from the end of the Third Plan period. If a provision of about Rs. 212 crores excluding private investment and working capital is made available for the small Industries Programme during the Third Plan and other recommended steps are taken it would be possible to achieve this production and also create about 3,50,000 new jobs.

New Jobs To Be Created

It is proposed that something like half of production and employment suggested in para above should be planned in small towns and rural areas. This can probably best be done by setting up adequate number of industrial estates in suitable localities which may provide workshop sheds for units with total employment potential of about 1,75,000 persons. Certain number of workers in existing industries will also have to be provided for in these estates. For this purpose a sum of Rs. 50 crores will be necessary.

Machinery

Steps should be taken to arrange for machinery required by the small scale sector to be made in the country in adequate quantity. These steps should be taken immediately so that machinery starts to be available immediately the Third Plan period starts. Possibilities of starting more proto-type centres be also examined.

Cost Of Machinery

The estimated total cost of machinery required for 350,000 new jobs is 140 crores ; 20 per cent of this sum or 28 crores will be found by entrepreneurs and the balance provided to them as loans.

Technical Know-How

It is essential also to implement expeditiously the recommendations of the Technical Training and Apprentice Training Committee appointed by the SSI Board, with a view to ensuring that sufficient technical know-how for starting and manning industries is available. Facilities for advanced managerial-*cum*-organisational training of such technically qualified persons or science graduates as are potential entrepreneurs should also be developed in collaboration with State or private undertakings on a large-scale.

National Small Industries Corporation

The NSIC should be developed substantially for much large-scale operations than it has undertaken so far.

Removal Of Bottlenecks

The important objective of the Third Five Year Plan should be to remove shortages of raw materials, power, technical know-how and cheap finance, on account of which the progress of small scale industries has suffered.

The State Dept. to of Industries should be considerably strengthened. The existing State administrative machinery should also be suitably modified to ensure better results.

A System of regular meetings between the representatives of various Central Government and StateG overnment authorities should be evolved with a view to achieving more effective utilisation of Central funds.

Development Commissioner may also examine the possibility of recruiting men with basic qualifications and sending them for training to factories for one to two years after binding them to serve his Organisation for atleast two to three years after their return.

Statistics

Necessary steps should also be taken and machinery created for the systematic collection and analysis of the requisite statistical data.

Development Commisioner's Organisation And State Deptt. Of Industries And Subsidising Losses

A fairly large sum should be necessary (about Rs, 40 crores) in the Third Plan period for strengthening the various branches of the D. C's Organisation and State Dept. of Industries.

A sum of Rs. 10 crores may be required for making provision for subsidising (a) price preference given for Government purchases publicity and participations in exhibition etc. and (b) losses or covering interest in so far as commercial and other financing agencies will be required to route Government loans or grant financial assistance on their own.

Total Financial Provision

The total sum envisaged for the development of small scale industries (other than the money to be found by entrepreneurs) for the Third Plan period will be Rs. 197 crores, which will create about 3,50,000 new jobs. This does not include the estimates of working capital.

WORKING GROUP ON FLOW-OF-FUNDS, 1959—REPORT

New Delhi, Cabinet Secretariat, Department of Statistics, Central Stastical Organisation, 1963. 89p.

Chairman : Shri P. C. Mathew.

Members : Dr. N. S. R. Sastry ; Shri S. L. N. Simha; Dr. D. N. Saxena ; Shri M. Mukherjee ; Dr. S. G. Tiwari, Shri B. K. Barpujari (died. replaced by Shri K. C. Sharma).

APPOINTMENT

For India the suggestion to construct a model of flow-of-funds system of accounts was first made in December 1955 by Shri C. D. Deshmukh, the then Finance Minister. As a result, in May 1956 some tentative arrangements were made between the Central Statistical Organisation (CSO) and the Reserve Bank of India (RBI) and it was proposed that the CSO should do the preliminary work on Government sector and the RBI on banking and corporate sectors. Some exploratory studies were made in the Reserve Bank to examine the feasibility of casting the available data relating to banking and corporate business sectors into money flows accounts and in 1957, an attempt was made to construct the accounts for these two sectors for the First Plan period. This tentative effort revealed that, though the available data were inadequate in many respects, it was possible to cast them in the form of money flows accounts. Early in 1959, prof. H. W. Arndt of the Australian National University visited India at the invitation of the Indian Statistical Institute (ISI) and held discussions on the subject with the officials of CSO, Ministry of Finance and RBI. He prepared a Memorandum on flow-of-funds entitled "Financial Flows of Indian Economy, 1951-52—1957-58". In his memorandum, the economy was divided into four broad sectors, *viz.*, Government, banks, rest of the world and residual. However, his analysis was confined to lending and borrowing only, since the main object of the accounts was to show as to how and in what forms domestic savings had become available to Governent for financing its expenditure.

The CSO arranged for a preliminary meeting of the representatives of the RBI, Ministry of Finance and ISI, in February 1959 to consider the Memorandum of Prof. Arndt and for formulating proposals for further study of the subject. In this meeting, this Working Group was constituted to arrange for the collection and compilation of data necessary for the preparation of accounts for the year 1957-58 which was the latest year for which the data were available and to study the methods to be followed for the purpose.

TERMS OF REFERENCE

(i) To arrange for the collection and compilation of data necessary for the preparation of accounts for the year 1957-58, which was the latest year for which the data were available; and

(ii) To study the methods to be followed for the purpose.

CONTENTS

Section I : Introduction; Flow-of-Funds System of Accounts—General Concepts; The Frame-work of Accounts for India; **Section II :** Non-Financial Flows—Households; Banking Sector; Other Financial Institutions; Private Corporate Business; Government Sector; Rest of the World; Consolidated Accounts; **Section III :** Financial Flows—Households; Banking Sector; Other Financial Institutions; Private Corporate Business; Government Sector; Rest of the World; Consolidated Accounts; **Section IV :** Limitations of the Accounts and Recommendations; Appendix.

RECOMMENDATIONS

Household Sector

A system of national income and product accounts is the starting point for construction of flow-of-funds system of accounts for this sector. The National Income Committee in their first report suggested a framework for social accounts which would be adequate for our purposes. However, completion of this task would depend on the availability of reliable estimates of net fixed capital formation and net changes in inventories. The available data are still inadequate particularly in respect of certain basic statistics on construction, trade and transport margins, production of capital goods in the small enterprises sector, stocks held in the private non-corporate sector and valuation of machinery and building materials. It would be seen that the accounts of the households sector can be improved. Further data on cash factor incomes, cash consumption expenditures, cash transactions in land and buildings and statistics of inventories in trade etc. are also needed.

Banking

The coverage of the banking sector in the present accounts is not complete. For instance, cooperative banks (other than State cooperative banks) and cooperative credit societies are not covered. It is suggested that suitable surveys may be initiated, if necessary on a sample basis, to collect the required data relating to these institutions.

Corporate Enterprises

It would be necessary to extend the scope of the analysis of company finances conducted by the RBI so as to cover the entire corporate sector. For this purpose, special studies of the finances of cooperative non-credit societies may have to be taken up. Also the coverage of joint stock companies may have to be enlarged. The content and item coverage of the RBI analysis of company finances may also have to be modified suitably to accommodate the needs of flow-of-funds system of accounts. The RBI has initiated some preliminary steps in these directions.

Other Financial Institutions

As in the case of corporate enterprises, it would be necessary to improve the coverage of the RBI's analysis of private financial and investment companies. Moreover, the RBI's study of government financial corporations is confined only to IFC and State Financial Corporations and it may be necessary to extend the scope of analysis to other government financial corporations as well. Like-wise efforts may also be made to improve the scope and contents of the analysis of data relating to insurance and provident funds, etc.

Government

In the case of this sector, adequate material is being collected and published in the various government documents. The problem is to explore the possibility of adapting these statistics to the requirements of flow-of-funds analysis. In this connection, the CSO's analysis of data relating to government in the 'Estimates of of National Income' and "An Economic Classification of the Budget of the Central Government" done by the Ministry of Finance every year, help to provide that basic information which can be used for multiplicity of analytical, purposes. An extension of the scope of economic classification of the budgets of all public authorities and transactions of autonomous government enterprises would fill in a major gap in the construction of flow-of-funds accounts for the government sector. The present attempt to construct accounts for this sector has also revealed some other statistical deficiencies. This include the extreme inadequacy of data relating to the local authorities. The timely collection of these data by a suitable agency and their compilation in a form meaningful for economic analysis are also of primary importance for construction of comprehensive flow-of-funds accounts for the entire government sector.

The above review indicates that a considerable amount of data are available for construction of financial flows accounts on an annual basis. This work may be continued. In the non-official flows, there are gaps particularly in the households sector. Continued efforts have to be made to improve the data on non-financial flows specially in the households sector so that the work is put on a systematic basis thus making it possible to prepare consolidated accounts.

REVIEW COMMITTEE ON BOTANY IN INDIAN UNIVERSITIES, 1959—REPORT

New Delhi, University Grants Commission, 1963. 82p.

Chairman : Prof. P. Maheshwari.
Members : Dr. B.P. Pal; Rev. Fr. H. Santapau; Prof. T.S. Sadasivan; Dr. Shri Ranjan.
Secretary : Dr. B.D. Laroia.

APPOINTMENT

Early in 1959, the University Grants Commission felt it desirable to assess the present status and standards of teaching and research in various science subjects and the facilities available in the country for training in each subject and to estimate the impact of the grants made by the Commission during the First and Second Plan periods. The purposes for which these grants were made were rehabilitation, construction of laboratory buildings, purchase of seientific equipment, provision of workshop facilities, improvement of central and sectional libraries and revision of salary scales of university and college teachers. It was also felt that stock-taking of the results of the programmes followed by the Commission during the First and Second Plan periods would serve as a useful indicator and guide for formulation of the programmes for the Third Plan period. The Chairman of the University Grants Commission accordingly appointed Review Committees in all science subjects including Botany.

The Review Committee in Botany was appointed by the University Grants Commission in March 1959,

TERMS OF REFERENCE

The Botany Committee, like other Review Committees, was given wide terms of reference and was free to determine its own programme and procedure of work. Nevertheless, in order to carry out its assignment satisfactorily, the Committee was requested to specifically examine the following major problems :

(1) The stage of development achieved so far in the field of Botany in Indian Universities ;

(2) To make a qualitative and quantitative appraisal of the existing facilities for teaching and research at the under-graduate and post-graduate levels ;

(3) The trends of research, its potentialities and steps to be taken for expansion of training and research facilities in the various branches of the subject;

(4) To scrutinise the syllabi and examination systems at different levels of university education and to suggest steps for improvement and modernisation of the syllabi and the preparation of model syllabi;

(5) To suggest ways and means of coordination between university and non-university institutions and the improvement of amenities for both students and teaching personnel.

CONTENTS

Foreword; Preface; Introduction; Development of Botany in India; Universities; The Affiliated Colleges; An Appraisal of the Botanical Research in the Country; Improvements in Teaching; Syllabi and Curricula; Research Degrees; Examination System; Future Development of Botany (Botanical Manpower; Centres of Intensive Research; Hill Laboratories; Botanical Gardens, Museums and Herbaria; Training of Teachers; Coordination between Universities and other Institutions; Scientific Publications); Summary of Recommendations.

RECOMMENDATIONS

With the monetary support given by the University Grants Commission during the last few years the condition of the botany departments is much better than what it was a decade ago. However, a great deal still remains to be done. The more important of our recommendations are summarised below:

The teaher-pupil ratio should be improved and the ratio between the senior and the junior staff should be brought as close to a 50 : 50 basis as possible. For any large department there should be a senior teacher (Professor or Reader) for each of the following six subjects:

(i) Physiology;
(ii) Mycology and Plant Pathology;
(iii) Systematic Botany;
(iv) Morphology of Phanerogams;
(v) Morphology of Cryptogams; and
(vi) Genetics.

Those departments, which are working on certain borderline subjects will also need a Lecturer or Reader in biochemistry, biophysics, or biometry, as the case may be.

We also feel that the teaching load (an average of 18 hours per week) of a university or college teacher in botany is excessive and ought to be reduced to 15 hours or less.

The time of the head of a large department is taken up largely in extra-curricular and administrative work. Since this is highly uneconomical, if not wasteful, it is commended that such departments should have an Administrative Secretary to help the head of the department.

There should be a general overall increase in the emoluments of university teachers so that their salaries are comparable with those of the scientific services in the Government. There seems no reason why top men in the universities should be paid less than in the National laboratories. A certain number of National Professorships and Research Professorships ought to be created on an All-India basis to meet this difficulty.

Many departments are handicapped in their work because of lack of such special facilities as an insect-proof glasshouse for research on viruses, and small biotrons with temperature and humidity control for experimental work on plants, plant parts and tissue culture. These should no longer be considered as luxuries but as essential requirements of modern research.

The college departments are, as a rule, very poorly equipped to teach M.Sc. classes and more stringent conditions should be laid down before a college is permitted to open M. Sc. classes. On the whole it seems best that post-graduate instruction be left with the University departments, while the colleges should look after undergraduate teaching.

The chief points we wish to suggest regarding the syllabi are that more time should be available for field work and experimental botany involving such fields as physiology, microbiology and genetics. To make this possible a certain amount of reduction can be made in the morphological and descriptive aspects of the subject. We also think that there should be other combinations at the B. Sc. level besides the usual one of chemistry, botany and zoology. There are many aspects of botany for which physics/mathematics, chemistry and botany will form a more suitable combination and a better basis for admission to the M. Sc.

The present comprehensive examinations held at the end of three years for the Bachelor's degree and annually for the Master's degree are unsatisfactory. We favour the introduction of several tests during the year conducted by the teachers themselves. In our opinion 40 per cent of the marks should be assigned to such tests, and 60 per cent to the more comprehensive university examination. The latter may continue to be conducted by both external and internal examiners as at present.

The Committee favours the idea of two research degrees—the Ph. D. and D. Sc. For the Ph. D. the supervisor should be a member of the board of examiners, there should be a compulsory viva-voce examination, and the degree should be awarded only if the reports are unanimous. Apart from intensive work on a problem the candidate must acquire a good knowledge of the wider aspects of the subject. We note that the Madras university requires the candidate to appear in a written test as well. We consider this practice to be satisfactory and further suggest that a department should hold frequent seminars and discussions in which the Ph. D. students must be required to present their work from time to time before the teaching staff and other scholars. The D. Sc. degree should be awarded mainly on the basis of published work evaluated by a board of external examiners.

There are certain special requirements of botany departments such as botanical garden, museum and herbarium. These need to be developed adequately in order to give more life to the teaching of botany. For this it is necessary not only to provide block grants and recurring grants but also create additional posts of curators of the herbarium, museum and garden. Annual grants of Rs. 5,000 or so should also be available for field trips and excursions, and those departments which are situated in big towns should be provided with a jeep or other transport to facilitate field work so that teachers and students can have a better opportunity to see plants in their natural habitats.

Another important and universally felt need in the improvement of botanical teaching is the creation of at least four hill laboratories, at Mussoorie, Kodaikanal (or Ootacamund), Darjeeling and Mahabaleshwar. Two marine biology stations with phycological laboratories and motor-launches attached to them should be set up at Okha and Mandapam for algal research. All the six centres should provide hostel accommodation, together with some laboratory and library facilities for 15-20 students. For administrative purposes each laboratory could be put in charge of a particular university closest to the former but its facilities would be open to the students of any university who may like to visit it. We urge that this proposal, which does not involve much foreign exchange, ought to be given top priority in the Third Five-Year Plan. A national culture collection centre of living fungi and algae in an Indian University has been suggested for implementation at a very early date.

One of the major difficulties experienced by botanical laboratories is the lack of workshop facilities. The workshops in universities are generally attached to the physics department and work for the botany department is usually handled in a step-motherly fashion. Furthermore, the workshop mechanics are not very familiar with the equipment used in the botany departments. We, therefore, recommend that such facilities should be greatly augmented. In view of the foreign exchange restrictions it becomes more and more necessary to improvise our own apparatus. The central workshop in the university ought to be under the control of a Committee of all Heads of Departments with a rotating Chairmanship.

Besides, a botany department should have its own small workshop (one or two mechanics, a glass blower and one carpenter) for day-to-day work. In our opinion this is a matter of great urgency which should receive very careful attention.

It has been observed that generally only those students take up botany who fail to get admission in physics, chemistry or medicine. This is perhaps due to the impression that opportunities do not exist for suitable employment in this subject. For an agricultural country like India, biological research is sure to gain ground in the near future. We earnestly request the UGC to take cognisance of this and treat botany on a more generous footing with regard to staff, equipment and other facilities. At present no botany department has more than one Professor although there are several departments of physics and chemistry with three or four Professors. Steps should be taken to remedy this discrepancy.

For its grants to the various botanical laboratories the Commission has so far followed a more or less uniform policy. This was perhaps all right since all laboratories were very poorly equipped in the past. However, it now seems reasonable that the more active an institution is in pursuing research and in its output of Ph. D.'s and D.Sc.'s, the more adequately it should be financed by increasing its block grant, recurring grant and senior staff. The botany departments of the universities should be classified into A,B and C categories and increased support given to them on the basis of their productivity.

Many scholars experience a serious difficulty in the publication of their papers because of the high cost of the preparation of blocks for their illustrations. Grants for this purpose are sometimes made by the UGC but only on a matching basis. Since the Universities or the individuals are usually unable to provide their share, the whole scheme is rendered infructuous. In our opinion suitable grants should be made to universities for this specific purpose so that they can provide their share, or else the entire expenditure should be borne by the UGC without insisting on a matching grant.

In order to keep our scholars in touch with the work being done in other universities and to avoid duplication of research it is suggested that the UGC should publish a monthly bulletin giving the name of the author, title of work, place of publication, a short summary of the M.Sc. and Ph.D. theses, and a list of the problems of research undertaken by the staff and students.

AD-HOC COMMITTEE ON AUTOMOBILE INDUSTRY, 1959—REPORT

Delhi, Manager of Publications, 1960. 223p.+iip.

Chairmnn : Shri L.K. Jha.

Members : Rr. Adm. Daya Shanker ; Dr. S.K. Muranjan ; Dr. B. D. Kalelkar ; Prof. B.N. Das Gupta ; Shri D.D. Suri : Shri M.M. Gupta ; Shri V.K.R. Menon.

Secretary : Shri V.P.S. Menon.

APPOINTMENT

The *Ad-hoc* Committee on Automobile Industry was constituted under the Ministry of Commerce and Industry *vide* their Resolution No. A. E, Ind. 1 (11)/59 dated 8-4-1959.

TERMS OF REFERENCE

(a) To review the progress of the automobile industry and automobile ancillary industries and recommend measures to increase the indigenous content of the different vehicles in the shortest possible time, keeping in view the targets and schedules envisaged in 1956, when the manufacturing programmes of the different producers were approved ;

(b) To recommend measures to be taken to reduce the cost to the consumer of different vehicles (car, jeep and truck) under manufacture by the automobile industry and suggest the most appropriate pattern of organisation of the future expansion of the industry to ensure low cost production ;

(c) To examine the feasibility of producing a low-cost passenger car within the price range of Rs. 5,000 to Rs. 7,000 including within the scope of such examination not only schrmes previously presented to Government, but also other models of cars that have been developed in different countries and suggest ways and means of manufacturing such a car in the country ;

(d) To recommend targets of production of different types of vehicles for the Third Five-Year Plan ; and

(e) To indicate the financial implications including foreign exchange of development programmes that might be suggested under (a), (b) and (c) above.

By their letter No. A.E. Ind. 1 (11)/59, dated April 24. 1959, the Government of India desired that "in their studies relating to the manufacture of trucks, the Committee should bear in mind the growing surplus of motor spirit that is likely to arise over the next seven years and the need for diminishing rather than increasing this surplus.

CONTENTS

Introduction ; Some General Observations ; Progress in Indigenous Manufacture ; Economy and Efficiency in Production ; Ancillary ; Industy ; Foreign Exchange for the Industry ; Future Demand and Development ; The Production of a Cheap Car ; Investment and Taxation ; Price Policy ; Concluding Remarks ; Conclusions and Recommendations ; Annexures I to V ; Apppendices I to XV.

RECOMMENDATIONS

The recommendations made in the Report have not been discussed with the industry and it would be desirable to ascertain the reactions and comments of the industry before taking final decisions on them.

The decision to grant protection to the industry was sound. The achievement of self-sufficiency regarding transport vehicles is of great importance to the economy. Even in regard to passenger cars the consumer would have been far worse off in the present difficulties regarding foreign exchange there, had been no domestic industry.

The demand for vehicles today has gone up considerably. There is need for greater competition though the shortage of foreign exchange operates as a limiting factor.

Among the various possible alternatives to measure the progress of indigenous manufacture the best would be to take the ex-factory price of the complete vehicle in the country of origin and to deduct from it the percentage of value represented by components, either finished or semi-finished, which are still imported.

The indigenous content in different vehicles and engines worked on the basis of import licensing figures for the period October 1959 to March 1960 is given below :

S. No.	*Type of Vehicle*	*Indigenous Contents (Oct.' 59—March,' 60)*
1.	Hindustan Ambassador	70.5%
2.	Fiat 1100	47.0%
3.	Dodge diesel with Perkins engine	68.0%
4.	Standard Ten	32.5%
5.	Tata Mercedes Benz Truck	64.0%
6.	Tata Mercedes Benz Bus	71.0
7.	Leyland Comet	38.5%
8.	Jeep	65.0%
9.	Meadows Engines	50.0%
10.	Perkins P. 6 V Bare Exh. Diesel Engine	64.0%
11.	Bedford Diesel with Perkins Engine	46.0%

To encourage the development of ancillary industries and to give inducement to the automobile manufacturers to buy components from outside, in measuring the progress of different automobile units, no distinction should be made between units, who make more of the components required by them and units who buy more of such components from the ancillary industry.

While it has not been possible to compare the progress of each firm with its promise, a study of each programme and its fulfilment has been attempted.

Among cars, the Ambassador continues to be leader from the point of view of indigenous manufacture. In 1950-51 the important components of the engine, transmission and axle were made by Hindustan Motors. At the time of the first Tariff Commission Enquiry in 1953, the indigenous content was about 45 per cent which has gone up to 50 percent by the time of the Second Tariff Commission Enquiry in 1956. Today it is a little above 70 per cent.

Premier Automobiles are very much behind schedule in thelr Fiat 1100 programme. When their scheme was approved in November 1953, the aim was completion of the manufacture of engine, axles and transmission by the end of 1956. At the time of Second Tariff Commission Enquiry in 1956, apart from tyre, tube, batteries, etc., which were bought out from other industries, the items which Premier Automobiles were making were the fuel tank, silencer assembly, and the radiator for a limited number of vehicles. The indigenous content today is about 47 per cent.

The progress of Standard Motors has been the lowest among the car manufacturers. Standard Vanguard was approved in September 1953 and Standard 10 in October 1954. In both cases the programme aimed at the completion of the manufacture of engine, transmission and axles by the end of 1956. At the time of the second Tariff Commission Enquiry in 1956, they had made a few components for Vanguard but had made little progress with Standard 10. The indigenous content of Standard 10 today is about 32.5 per cent while their production of Vanguard has been discontinued.

Mahindra and Mahindra had got their programme for Jeep approved in June 1954 with the aim of completing the manufacture of engine, axles, and transmission by the end of 1958. At the time of the Second Tariff Commission Enquiry in 1956, they had made little progress. Today the vehicle is 65 per cent indigenous.

The Dodge truck of Premier Automobiles had a few indigenous items even in 1950-51. Their approved programme in 1953 aimed at the completion of manufacture of engine, transmission, and axles by the end of 1956, At the time of the Second Tariff Commission Enquiry in 1956, the important components of the engine and gear box were completed, but the alxe had yet to be developed. Meanwhile the consumer demand had gone over to diesel. Today their indigenous content is 68 per cent, taking into account the diesel engines supplied to them by other manufacturers.

The performance of Telcos on Tata-Benz trucks has been equal to their promise. The scheme was approved in 1953 with a manufacturing programme which aimed at the engine, transmission, gear box and axles being made indigenously by the end of 1959. They had made little progress at the time of the Second Tariff Commission Enquiry, but today the indigenous content is 64 per cent and 71 per cent on the truck and bus chassis respectively.

The Leyland Comet of Ashok-Leyland was approved in 1954 with a programme to make the important components by the end of 1959. Today their indigenous content is 38.5 per cent. Part of the delay was to complete reorganisation of the company's capital structure causing a major dislocation of their programme.

Bedford trucks were taken by Hindustan Motors only in 1958 in place of their abondoned Studebaker programme and they have lost no time in going ahead to place orders for the equipment needed for their programme.

There are certain items going into the vehicle, the production of which in India will entail heavy expenditure of foreign exchange for a nominal reduction in imports and whose cost of production will also be too high and impose a wholly unjustifiable burden on the consumer. Such uneconomic investment could be justified in an industry of strategic value but not in the case of passanger cars.

To consider the extent to which the price of vehicles in India is higher than in overseas countries, the comparison should be between the basic price of the same vehicle in India and abroad and not of different vehicles, and the incidence of taxation should be eliminated. A comparison on this basis of Ambassador Car and Tata-Benz truck prices in India and in their respective countries of orgin is made, from which it appears that the consumer price of these two vehicles is 38 per cent and 6 per cent respectively higher in India.

The net value of the production within the Automobiles factory itself, which indicates the extent to which the cost of the automobile is directly the responsibility of the automobile manufacturer. The percentage of the total cost of a vehicle in the hands of the automobile manufacturer himself is small and generally less than one third of the total cost of the vehicle. For the Hindustan Ambassador Car, the total cost of raw materials and components purchased from outside is a little more than the price of the built up car in the U.K.

The disparity between the Indian Costs and overseas purchase price is capable of considerable reduction by proper supervision and control.

The recommendations of Tariff Commission regarding the introduction of proper training schemes have been disregarded by all the manufacturers except Telco.

Enough attention is not being paid to technical supervision by some units.

The recommendations of Tariff Commission regarding the introduction of proper cost accounting have been disregarded by the manufacturers with the exception of Simpsons, who make Perkins Engines. The cost data available for examination were open to serious criticism and objection. The Government should instruct the industry to introduce an adequate system of cost accounting.

Though there had been since 1956 considerable improvement in the quality of automobiles made in India, sufficient care is not being taken to avoid minor but irritating defects creeping in at the assembly stage.

It would be desirable to set up an institution for the testing of the vechicles.

The progress made by the ancillary industry is substantial and the part played by it in increasing the indigenous content of vechicles is significant.

A study of the prices at which components are being supplied by the ancillary industry reveals :

(a) That in general the increase in domestic price over the price of the imported components is very much higher in respect of items supplied by ancillary industry than for items produced by the main automobile manufacturers.

(b) But some producers are able to buy their components from the ancillary industry at prices which are competitive and even cheaper than the price of the imported components, while others have a different tale to tell.

When any kind of special relationship exists between ancillary industry and the main producer, the prices changed by the former to the latter should be subject to close scrutiny.

In Indian conditions, it would be desirable, if even some of the major items, not generally considered to be the responsibility of the ancillary industry, were developed by the automobile manufacturers themselves on a cooperative basis. If such a venture does not materialise, it would be advisable for the Government to take the initiative in the matter.

Commercial transport vehicles should be looked upon as capital goods of the road transport industry. With similar expenditure of foreign exchange few other industries can stimulate such widespread employment with benefit both to the consumer and producer.

Since in the long run, the maintenance cost of the vechicle assumes greater importance than the initial price, increased availabilty of spates and servicing tools should be ensured even if it is at some sacrifice of increased production of vechicles.

To ensure that the consumer gets the spare parts at a reasonable price, import applications from

(a) Small fleet owners, who have organised themselves on a cooperative basis, and

(b) Automobile Associations, who are prepared to bulk the requirements of the spare parts required by their members, particularly for vehicles not in popular use,

may be considered sympathetically.

After the serious difficulties in regard to foreign exchange, which devleoped in 1957, the higher priority given by Government for importing components of commercial vechicles in preference to the components of cars was legitimate. However, the priority between capital goods and components needs consideration.

To prevent avoidable duplication of capacity and to rationalise and reduce to the minimum the expenditure of foreign exchange, the Government should ask the automobile manufacturers and ancillary industry to apply for all capital goods they wish to import in order to complete their manufacturing programme by the end of 1961.

Taxation on diesel oil will not be the answer to the growing inbalance between diesel and petrol. If taxation is to be used as an instrument, the imposition of an excise duty on diesel engines for road transport coupled with a reduction in the level of taxation on petrol and greater availability of transport vehicles filled with petrol engines would be the best approach to the problem.

One way in which the consumption of diesel in heavier road transport vehicles can be reduced and the consumption of petrol can be increased would be by marketing a mixture of diesel and petrol. A suitable programme for the introduction of mixed fuel should be taken in hand so that facilties for handling the mixed fuel could develop as a substitute for and not as an addition to the facilities for handling pure diesel.

Since a sudden change in the economics of diesel operation will impose a loss on the community and render some of the investment already made both in rupees and in foreign exchange infructuous, Government should take a clear-cut decision of policy on this subject at the earliest possible date.

The foreign exchange requirements of any new production programme of automobiles must rank in priority below the requirements for the maintenance of existing vehicles and completion of the existing production programmes. For new capacity expenditure on foreign exchange should be limited to capital goods for the project and import of components as a recurring feature should be virtually eliminated.

The conditions which necessitated the limitation of the area of internal competition to give each manufacturing unit a certain assured share of the market when demand was low no longer exist. The demand for three to five ton diesel vehicles is in excess of the total production capacity of the three units concerned, namely, Telco, Hindustan Motors and Premiers. These units should, therefore, be permitted to produce and sell as many vehicles as they can.

The demand for heavier vehicles of the Leyland Comet class is too small to introduce competition in this range at present but makers of medium vehicles should be allowed to market them with such variation as would enable them to carry heavier loads so long as the basic features of the vchicles are not altered and extra imports are not asked for,

For future development, the manufacturing units should order such plant and machinery as they may need to complete their programme at the very beginning. Once all orders have been placed the import of components for part assembly and part manufacture can be regulated according to availability of foreign exchange and the demand.

The target of capacity for commercial vehicles should be fixed at 60,000 Nos. for the Third Five Year Plan period. The consumers interests will be better served if the expansion to achieve the target of capacity is allowed on thc basis of each firm's ability to compete with the others in terms of cost, quality and servicing, rather than on any abstract considerations of equity as between the different firms concerned.

Demand for Leyland Tiger/Titan is limited. Increase in indigenous content is therefore likely to be accompanied by a marked increase in cost. For the present, Ashok Leyland should concentrate on the engine which has many uses for industrial purposes and for such components as can be developed with the equipment installed for the Comet. State Governments who need such vehicles may be allowed to import such components as cannot be supplied by Ashok Leyland or ancillary industries.

Light commercial vehicles have an important role to play. However, their demand would not justify setting up independent production. Where any firms have developed petrol engines for other purposes they should be permitted to market delivery vans and commercial vehicles using the same engines.

The target of capacity for cars fort he existing units

should be fixed at 30,000 Nos. for the Third Five year Plan period. If a cheap car is introduced the demand of the existing cars is likely to go down to some extent but there will also be an overall increase in demand to 40,000 Nos. through the creation of a new class of consumers.

The target of capacity for jeaps should be fixed at 10,000 Nos. for the Third Five-year Plan period. This demand is not adequate to be shared by another unit. The price of the jeep should however, come down with an increase in production. If this is not assured consideration may be given to licensing another unit.

In a planned and controlled economy such as exists in India capacity should not be created either in the public or private sector unless that capacity is needed by economy as a whole. This should be the criterion to decide as to whether it would or would not be desirable for the public sector to take on the production of automobiles for the people as distinct from production in Ordnance Factories to meet Defence needs.

Two alternatives are possible to meet the consumers, need for a car at more economic price, *viz*. by improving the quality, quantity and cheapness of the cars already on the manufacturing programme or by introducing a new vehicle altogether.

The type of vehicle known commonly as the 'Miniature' or 'Bubble Car' would not be suitable for Indian road conditions. size of family and climatic conditions, etc. Their development should be considered in the context of expansion of capacity sanctioned for making scooters, motor cycles and other two wheeled and three wheeled vehicles. Among the proposals relating to miniature cars, that of Bachraj Trading Corporation, can be developed with a relatively lower expenditure of foreign exchange because of the large commonality of components between the proposed vehicle and the three wheeler for which the firm has already been license d to manufacture.

Among the 24 applications for the manufacture of baby car only five applications merit consideration.

The car proposed to be manufactured by Hindustan Aircraft Ltd. is still in the development stage and has yet to be perfected and brought into regular production. It would, therefore, be premature to consider this proposal as an answer to the question put to the Committee.

For long distance journeys and for special purposes there is demand for bigger cars of the American type which is not large enough to sustain their manufacture in India. Premier Automobiles who assemble Dodge cars and supply some components including the engine of their own manufacture may be permitted to import components for assembly as and when considered desirable to meet the demand for this type of cars.

There is no room for a cheap car in addition to the Baby Hindustan; it is for Government to consider whether there is any commitment to permit Hindustan Motors to manufacture Baby Hindustan by virtue of the fact that initially a programme of manufacture had been approved many years ago.

There is widespread need for a medium car of the Standarrd Vanguard type. At the time of suspension of its manufacturing programme, Standard Motors had made better progress with this car than with Standard 10. Standard Motors are not equipped to produce Standard 10 in large numbers; moreover, this car undergoes frequent changes of design in the U. K. Therefore, Standard Motors should gradually give up Standard 10 in favour of Vanguard. They should also be permitted to market a light petrol delivery van using the same engine, axle and transmission as their Vanguard car. The 10 H.P. engine which they have already developed should also be put to similar use if they so desire.

The best production pattern for passenger cars would be the new economy car, the Fiat 1100, the Hindustan Ambassador and the Standard Vanguard. The Dodge may continue on an *ad hoc* basis.

It is not necessary to earmark or allocate particular figures of production to those vehicles which should be decided by consumers' choice and the size of the market.

The existing production capacity of the automobile industry as assessed by the Technical Committee is :

Cars	20,000
Commercial vehicles	28,000
Jeep and Jeep Station Wagons	5,500
Petrol engines	3,000

The total investment required for the Commercial vehicles on the target for the Third Five-year Plan is Rs. 67 crores on plant and machinery and Rs. 19.5 crores in buildings and land.

The likely investment to be made by the end of the Second Five-year Plan in commercial vehicles and Jeep would be Rs. 21 crores in plant and machinery Rs. six crores in land and buildings. The additional investment for the Third Plan Period would be Rs. 46 crores in land and buildings.

The total investment required for cars on the target of the Third Five year Plan would be Rs. 20 crores in plant and machinery and Rs. four crores in land and buildings. The likely investment at the end of the Second Five-year Plan would be Rs. 13.5 crores in plant and machinery and Rs. two and a half crores in land and buildings. The additional investment required for the Third Five Year Plan period would be Rs. six-and-a-half crores in plant and machinery and Rs. one and a half crores in land and buildings.

Any measure of taxation which would raise the cost

of the indigenous vehicles further at a time when there is general anxiety to see lower prices would not be advisable.

Government might consider fixing a uniform rate of duty on all automobile components.

Government might consider fixing flat rates of import duty on built-up commercial vehicles and built-up automotive engines at a level higher than the average import duty on components imported as components.

There is much to be gained by making the duty which applies to most components applicable to all components. To offset the increase in the cost of vehicles arising out of the arrangement, the excise duties on tyre, tube and batteries used as original equipment should be waived.

It might be advantageous to keep on increasing the import duty on components from year to year since it would help these firms which move ahead with their manufacturing programme to retain a competitive advantage.

The taxation policy applicable to the automobile industry should be influenced by long term rather than short term considerations. It would be as much in the interests of revenue as of the development of the automobile industry if the taxation policy was such as to keep the level of taxation per vehicle, as it leaves the factory somewhat low so as to stimulate the demand for vehicles to as high a level as the industry can cope with.

The automobile industry needs large investment to be economic and successful. Therefore, the price fixation policy should be such as to ensure a reasonable return to the investor in the automobile industry provided the unit works efficiently and economically.

The cost-plus system should not be used as a basis for long term price determination.

Prices can be more eflectively controlled by increasing the production of diflerent factories and giving the consumer the freedom to buy the vehtcle on a competitive basis ; until such conditions are created, some measure of price control may be necessary.

Since Government have taken certain steps through a Control Order in regard to passenger cars to ensure that the benefit of the lower prices go to the consumer the price control over cars should continue.

Since the ultimate consumer of the commercial vehicle is often not the person who buys the vehicle, but the person who pays for the use of its services which payment by and large is not subject to any control, price control over commercial vehicles should be abolished. The price at which commercial vehicles are purchased by State Transport Undertakings and other similar agencies should be settled by mutual negotiations.

The decontrol on commercial vehicles should enable both Hindustan Motors and Premier Automobiles to make internal adjustments to absorb a reduction in the prices of Ambassador and Fiat 1100 respeceively provided production is permitted to be maintained at the maximum level. After giving the necessary import licences for raw materials and components and providing four months to enable adjustments to be made and to ensure steady flow of raw materials, the current prices of Fiat 1100 and Hindustan Ambassador should be reduced as below :

	Current Rs.	Proposed Rs.	Reduction Rs.
Fiat 1100	9,783	9,283	500
Hindustan Ambassador	11,554	11,054	500

Standard 10 programme is never likely to be economic or successful particularly with the introduction of a new economy car and should therefore be given up by Standard Motors in favour of Standard Vanguard only.

The new Vanguard should be allowed to sell without price control for the first three months. Thereafter the new price for the Vanguard exclusive of Customs duty for actual imports other than raw material and of excise duties on tyres, tube and battery should not be more than 40 per cent higher than the basic price exclusive of purchase tax of the built-up Vanguard in U. K.

Four months from the date of issue of import licences for the Vanguard, the price of Standard 10 should be reduced by Rs. 400.

The price fixation in all cases should be inclusive of dealer's commission, the actual amount being not subject to determination by Government.

Since Jeep has no other competitor, it would be justifiable to retain control over prices. The current selling price of Jeep and Station Wagon should be reduced by Rs. 200 each straightaway. The new price of Jeep and Station Wagon would then become Rs. 12,421 and Rs. 18,422 respectively.

The prices of engines sold to vehicle manufacturers as original fitment should be reduced by Rs. 150. Sales in the replacement market need not be controlled.

Attention is also drawn to the following important recommendations:

(a) The industry should be enabled to place orders for its requirements of steel more than 12 months ahead to ensure timely supplies at the best possible prices.

(b) The rate of progress has been slowed down by difficulties of foreign exchange though most manufacturers should have ordered all their plants and machinery in accordance with their approved programmes of manufacture even before the restrictions on import of capital goods were imposed. The inadequacy of rupee finance and technical competence has been a greater obstacle to progress than shortage of foreign exchange.

(e) The road transport industry has an important bearing on the automobile industry. The pursuit of well coordinated policies by the different States, particularly uniformity on an all-India basis in fixing the Registered Laden Weights of vehicles will be of great value.

COMMITTEE ON SPECIAL MULTIPURPOSE TRIBAL BLOCKS 1959—REPORT

Delhi, Manager of Publications, 1960. 453p.+ivp.

Chairman : Dr. Verrier Elwin.
Members : Shri R. C.V.P. Noronha; Shri N. M. Wadiwa; Shri R.L. Bahl; Shri M.C. Nanavatty.
Secretary : Shri O.K. Moorthy.

APPOINTMENTS

Article 46 of the Constitution of India lays down that State shall promote with special care the educational and economic interests of the weaker sections of the people, and, in particular, of the Scheduled Castes and the Scheduled Tribes, and shall protect them from social injustice and all forms of 'exploitation'. In accordance with this policy, large sums of money have been spent and a number of schemes have been prepared, one of which is a programme, jointly undertaken by the Ministry of Home Affairs and the Ministry of Community Development and Cooperation, to set up 43 Special Multipurpose Tribal Blocks in the most undeveloped parts of tribal India. There has been considerable criticism of the works of these Blocks which were slow in getting started and tended to introduce unmodified, programmes devised for other parts of India with no special reference to tribal Needs.

In its resolution No. 20/170/58-SCT-III of the May, 1, 1959, the Ministry of Home Affairs of the Government of India accordingly appointed this Committee to examine the work and programme of these Blocks.

TERMS OF REFERENCE

(i) To study the working of the Special Multipurpose Tribal Blocks ; and

(ii) To advise the Government of India on how to implement the intensive development programme of the Blocks more effectively and give the programme a proper tribal bias.

CONTENTS

Introduction ; Evolution of the Scheme ; The Fundamentals of an Approach to the Tribes ; Staffing Problems ; Training ; Problems of Land and Agriculture ; Shifting; Cultivation ; the Problem of the Forests ; Animal Husbandry ; Communications ; Health Services; Education ; Social Education in the Tribal Areas ; Women's Programmes ; Rural Arts and Crafts ; Rural Housing and Colonies ; Indebtedness and Cooperation ; Tribal Culture ; Research ; The Block Surveys ; Methods of Reporting ; the Tribal Councils ; the Place of Non-Official Agencies ; Assessment of the Present Situation; the Future of the Special Tribal Blocks ; Epilogue; Appendices I to V ; Index.

RECOMMENDATIONS

The Fundamentals Of An Approach To The Tribes

The plans for tribal welfare need to be very simple. It is important, atleast in the initial stages, to concentrate on a few selected programmes, that have a vital bearing on the felt needs of the people, so as to secure ready understanding and willing participation the part of the tribals.

Mr. Albert Mayer believes that we are exceeding a realistic rate of expanding the C.D. programme, chiefly because, apart from the shortage of finance and supplies, it involves too many and too varied items both for the present quantity and the quality of our personnel and for the absorptive capacity of the village. The result is a greatly diluted reproduction of the substance and worth of the early prototype C.D. projects which only leads to cynicism among villagers and observers alike.

A wide distribution of free gifts of money or materials may have an undesirable effect. In the agricultural field, it is important that we should avoid the danger of giving too many free gifts for the tribal. In the field of housing, we should not put up buildings for him, which he may actually do better for himself. He should be helped to utilise his own resources and this aid should of course be on a non-loan basis. But we should not do those things which he is perfectly able to do himself. In particular, we would not recommend too much mechanised aid in the tribal areas. The tribal tends to become accustomed to governmental assistance, with the result that he cannot readjust himself easily when particular schemes come to the end.

The Staff And Its Approach

Both the Renuka Ray Committee and the Inaccessible Areas Committee have criticised the quality of the officials employed in the Multipurpose Blocks and other underdeveloped areas. The first finds that the Block Officials are not on sufficiently friendly terms with their people and seem to regard themselves as superior to them. 'A sense of awe, more than a feeling of friendly cooperation seems to prevail among the local tribals.' The second refers to the fact that service personnel of low calibre is all too often posted to these Blocks. 'Often enough official postings to such remote areas and deemed to be a form of punishment. Upon receiving posting orders, a common practice is to utilise all accumulated leave, and in the meantime, make every effort to have the posting orders cancelled. If such attempts are not successful, official eventually takes up duties as a last resort, and carries out his performance in a disprinted and uninterested way.'

Our own experience has been that the above observations are true to some extent but at the same time we would like to stress the fact that we have met a number of officials at all levels who were keen. enthusiastic and auxious to learn. Some of the V.L.W.'s appeared to us extremely good and nearly all the present P.E.O.'s were carrying on their work with sincerity, and often with intelligence, in face of almost overwhelming difficulties, not the least of which was the fact that their status was not sufficiently high for them always to exercise the gift of leadership over their own team or to deal effectively with representatives of the State Departments.

This suggests that a wrong attitude has been created among officials. One way whereby this has been done is through the way we talk, which tends to increase subconsciously the sense of superiority. The word 'backward' is a very dangerous one. It is being used *ad nauseam* all the time—backward tribes, backward areas, backward classes. How then can we avoid thinking of ourselves as advanced, elevated, progressive and thus superior ? And how can the educated tribals, so constantly described in these disparaging terms, fail to develop an acute inferiority complex with all its unhappy consequences? In any case, words like 'backward' and 'uplift' imply subjective judgments which are often based on a wrong sense of values. Who is backward—the simple honest tribesman or the merchant who exploits him ? Who is backward—the creative artist at her tribal loom, the gentle mother with her child among the hills, or the inventor of the atom bomb which may destroy her and all the world? Are these self-reliant, cooperative tribes the really backward as against the self-seeking, individualistic, crafty products of our industrial civilisation ?

The use of 'primitive' as equivalent to 'backward' is equally objectionable, and we comment elsewhere on the extraordinary suggestion that a list of tribes 'according to their primitiveness' should be prepared. The tribes were referred to recently in Parliament as 'these unfortunate people' and a recent publication by the Ministry of *CDSC* classifies them in a single sentence not only with the Scheduled Castes but also with the blind, and deaf and mute !

Another unfortunate term is "Scheduled Tribes" which makes them sound as if they really were museum specimens and which is resented by the educated. It is even unfortunate that it is usually used in the expression "Scheduled Tribes and Scheduled Castes" and that both groups, with their totally different problems, should be associated together and dealt with by one administrative organisation. This has undoubtedly lowered the social status of the tribes in public opinion.

Adaptation

Now let us admit frankly that it is very easy to talk about being dedicated to the tribes or loving them or being one with them. It sounds wonderful on paper, but it is by no means easy to carry out in practice. When a Block official is first appointed, in the first flush of his enthusiasm everything seems simple, but as the months go by, it becomes more difficult, for the tribal people are like people all over the world, Most of them are friendly, honest, hospitable, good, but just as anywhere else in the world, some of them are dishonest, mean, untruthful, treacherous. It is easy to love the friendly ; it is not easy to put up with those who cheat or betray you and, in some cases, an official or social worker in the tribal areas, who has begun well loses his enthusiasm and grows impatient with the people he is trying to serve. He becomes mentally hostile to them and feels that somehow he has been cheated. The hardships and loneliness of his life then begin to oppress him and what at first was a great adventure now becomes a rather dreary chore, and he applies for transfer or resigns. This is why it is essential that we should not be inspired merely by romantic sentiment, but build up within ourselves a store of inner strength, with an attitude based on knowledge and reason, so that when the testing days come we will not fail.

In fact, patience and even temper are qualities admired even by the most warlike tribes. They very strongly resent being shouted at or roughly treated. No one should ever, on any account whatever, strike or beat them. It is sometimes said that this is the best way of handling them, that they respect a 'man' who is not afraid of them, and that once they have been 'put in their place' they became devoted friends. Our experience is that such friendship is generally based on fear and that a blow is brooded over and resented for years.

Very important to tribal psychology is the love of truth and a belief in justice. This is why sincerity in an official is more important than academic or technical qualifications. The people expect him to tell them the truth even if it is unpalatable and nothing causes greater trouble than for him to make promises which he cannot fulfil. The frank, truth-speaking type is thus more likely to succeed than the glib, the smooth or the slick. The tribal people are becoming aware of the large sums of money now allocated for their benefit and are demanding a high standard of integrity in their officers. They may be profoundly disturbed by a discrepancy of only a few annas, which we may hardly notice.

In the P,E.O.'s report, he points out that, however liberal and generous the policy at the higher level may be, the tribals are often governed at the village level by the worst kind of petty official. We have already mentioned the tendency to send development workers to tribal areas as a punishment. This is even more marked in the Police and Revenue Departments. It has apperently been assumed that, because there is so much poverty and little incidence of crime in the tribal areas, bad officials will have less opportunity for taking bribes and exploiting the people.

This. however, is unfortunately not the case. Supervision by higher officials is inevitably weak in the remoter areas ; the tribal people are ignorant of the law ; and in any case they are unwilling to go to a District Headquarters to make complaints and are terrified of being summoned to a court which may be thirty or forty miles away from their homes and to which, if a case is raised against them, they may have to go a dozen times. In one such case a tribal had to walk an aggregate of over 3,000 miles before it was settled.

The tribal people suffer from the exactions of minor officials in the three main administrative Departments—Forest, Revenue and Police.

Forest

In the Multipurpose Block about which we have received this report, it is estimated that every Forest Guard is paid an annual tithe of seven-and-a half seers of grain by every tribal family in his beat as a sort of protection fee. This entitles the donors to free collection of fuel, fruit, gum, bamboos and thatching-grass from the forest without any interference. Should they need timber for building their houses, they obtain it by making additional payment in kind—a cow, chickens, ghee or wheat.

Some of the more enterprising tribals arrange with the local Forest Guard on a personal cash payment to be permitted to remove timber even from the Reserved Forests. If a tribal wishes to clear the forest for shifting cultivation he pays a fee of two rupees an axe. In some areas this fee, which is normally regarded as a kind of tax, is much higher. This, of course, is done on the understanding that if the tribal concerned is caught by the Ranger or the *D.F.O.* he will have to face the consequences and will not refer to the Forest Guard who has assisted him. The Forest Guards also make it their joint responsibility to provide the Forester of their beat with free food-provisions throughout the year.

Police

The incidence of crime is low, yet the unfortunate police constables have to live. Therefore, since crime is the most profitable source of income for a constable, crimes have to be committed. Non-official non-tribals of the locality help to 'frame' the tribals by putting up false complaints against them, placing, for example, bottles of illicit liquor in tribal house or the equipment for distillation in tribal fields, and then aranging to have them 'discovered' by the police.

Revenue

The Patwari is the Revenue official who in many areas collects land revenue and recovers arrears. He is supposed to give regular receipts but very often he conveniently forgets to issue them and the amount is put down as arrears. These gradually accumulate and are then demanded in a lump sum later on.

The Patwari also prepares an annual report in which he records the boundaries of the land cultivated by various tribal farmers. It often happens that when a new Patwari takes over charge, he finds that some of the people have encroached on Government lands and have been cultivating them for a number of years. In such cases he has an excellent opportunity to collect suitable gratification in cash. Those tribals who do not pay are reported in the Tahsil courts.

The Patwari is paid his protection money both in cash and kind according to the ability of the cuitivator and not on a flat rate for each house or family as in other cases.

The strongest weapon in the hands of village level officials is the threat of summons to a court and there are very few tribals indeed who can stand up against it. Quite apart from the waste of time and the economic loss on fines imposed, a tribal who is arrested and taken to court loses face and his social position is impaired.

Non-Official Non-Tribals :

We do not suggest, of course, that all subordinate officials or non-tribals outsiders in the tribal areas are corrupt and oppressive. Some are kind, helpful and friendly : some are themselves disturbed by what goes on. But there are still far too many of the wrong kind.

The heavy burden laid on the tribal people by Forest Laws, Prohibition Laws and the gradual advance of the rule of law in the realm of land possession. With the loss of their former freedom and their own simple and informal way of doing things, they have become bewildered in a world of red tape. It is said that every villager in a tribal area, if he is to survive, has to break some kind of law everyday of his life. This results in lowering the respect for law in general and imposed a sub-conscious sense of guilt.

We cannot blame the tribal for doing this, for if he does succeed in placing a complaint against an official, the latter may be transferred but his successor makes it his business to take it out of the complainant in order to ensure that he will not complain again.

If the Tribal Councils can he revived they will be a powerful instrument to check this kind of corruption and harassment. As education spreads in the tribal areas we may hope that the people will learn to stand up for themselves more vigorously. Already officers in the Multipurpose Blocks are, we are glad to say, generally strongly on the side of the tribals and their presence will help to ease the situation. The modification of the Forest and Land Laws, the establishment of rights to land, a general improvement in human relations between tribals and officials will all help. We suggest that not only development workers but officials of the Revenue, Forest, Police and Excise Departments should be given very careful briefing to create a new attitude; that there should be much stricter supervision; that Rasad books, as we suggest under the heading 'The Problem of the Forests', should be introduced everywhere; and that superior officers should not resent complaints made by the tribals (who are almost always very honest in what they say and will never make a complaint unless they are driven to despair) and should take immediate and drastic action where necessary.

Adaptation To Tribal Needs

A tribal bias means that we recognise and honour their way of doing things, not because it is old or picturesque but because it is theirs, and they have as much right to their own culture and religion as anyone else in India. It means that we must talk their language, and not only the language that is expressed in words but the deeper language of the heart. It means that we will not make the tribes ashamed of their past or force a sudden break with it, but that we will help them to build upon it and grow by a natural process of evolution. It does not mean a policy of mere preservation; it implies a constant development and change, a change that in time will bring unbelievable enrichment, as there is ever closer integration in the mainstream of Indian life and culture.

Museum Specimens

We might as well say that by preserving the sari we are keeping Indian women as museum specimens. We do not know of a single responsible person in India today who has the desire to hold back the development of the tribals in order to preserve them for study or as a picturesque enclave in our rather drab modern world. Even if anyone wished to do so, it would obviously be impossible under present conditions.

We feel, however, that in view of the fact that we are advocating the development of the people on the lines of their own tradition and genius, we should make it absolutely clear that we have no interest in any kind of artificial preservation of tribal customs or ways of living. Where they are good we should encourage them. Where they are less good we should try carefully to help the people to develop from within into something better. We fully recognise that as a result of our own recommendations great changes will come, not only in the comparatively small area which is at present subject to intensive development, but later throughout the whole of tribal India. We are suggesting for this purpose 30 crores of rupees for new Special Tribal Blocks. You do not keep people as museum specimens by spending very large sums of money on policies that are bound to cause far-reaching changes.

We would also stress the fact, again in order to avoid misunderstanding by those who may not take the trouble to read out Report, that there is no question whatever of isolating the tribal people. We have, in fact, placed the development of communications very high in the order of priorities and have strongly emphasised the need of opening up the entire tribal area. The unity of the hills and of the plains is as essential to the general national interest as it is to that of the hill and forest people themselves. At the same time we have stressed the need of caution, for too rapid a contact is not desirable and in the past, as a result of exposure to the outside world, some of the tribes have become psychologically maladjusted, culturally impoverished and grossly exploited by the outside world. We feel, however, that the 'middle path,' suggested by the Prime Minister, of bringing the good things of modern life to these people and of proceeding with caution and by a system of planned contact and adjusted exposure, should ensure that the evils that have affected them in the past will not affect them in the future. We may indeed look forward to an enriching process of mutual fertilisation : we have much to give the tribes and they have much to give us.

Staffing Problems

In view of the very special conditions of the tribal areas, the unusual problems that arise there and the urgency of developing them as rapidly as possible along the right lines, we feel that the post of P.E.O. in the future Special Tribal Blocks should be upgraded to that of a Class I officer. The remarkable success both in the development of the country and the emotional integration of the people with India as a whole in NEFA, in spite of quite extraordinary difficulties, has been at least partly due to the fact that men of sufficiently high calibre have been put in charge even of remote administrative centres covering comparatively small populations. If we are serious in demanding the best men to solve this vital problem throughout India, we are more likely to obtain them for class I posts.

Not all men are natural leaders and a Class II officer who has to control other officers of the same status sometimes feels it difficult to do so. Another difficulty is that a Class II officer, who has to deal with senior officers of other Departments, is often, not in a sufficiently strong position to make himself felt or to ensure the cooperation which is sometimes regrettably lacking. Thus in order to obtain men of higher calibre, to ensure that they will be able to lead and direct their team of workers, and to help in obtaining proper co-ordination, it will be of considerable benefit if the P.E.O.'s have the rank of Class I officials. Although this will cost more money and may create certain difficulties, we feel that the problem is so difficult, urgent and important that its solution should be put in the hands of really good Class I officials, which may include members of the I.A.S. and State Civil Service.

That the formal aspects of social education, such as conducting adult literacy classes and the establishment of libraries, should be handed over to the Education Departments of the States and should form part of their general programme. We have further suggested that the post of Social Education Organiser (to whom we would like to give many new duties) should be upgraded to a Class II post and its designation changed to that of Cultural Officer. We feel that this delicate and important task should be entrusted to someone who has higher educational and other qualifications than a Class III official.

The majority of us feel that it would be useful to add to the Multipurpose Blocks staff a Forest Extension Officer (he might be a Ranger on the strength of the Forest Department) who would act as liaison officer between his parent department and the Block officers, look into the grievances of the people, help to organise. Forest Cooperatives and generally promote the needs of the forest economy which is so important to many tribal groups. This post would not, of course, be necessary in areas where forest problems do not generally arise.

One of our members, however, feels that this official is not likely to prove effective.

It has also been suggested that a special Horticultural Extension Officer should be appointed, but we feel that in view of the need to keep the staff to a minimum, this is not really necessary.

On the question of staff, however, there are two points of view represented on the Committee. On the one hand it is felt that it will simplify matters if the additional officials, over and above those provided in a normal C.D. Block, are borne on the strength of their parent departments. Thus the Assistant Engineer and the Engineering Overseer should work under the direct supervision of the State P.W.D.; of course in collaboration both for planning and execution with the P.E.O. and the officials of the Community Development Department. Similarly, the Medical Officer, the Compounder and the two Midwives should be on the strength of the Public Health Department and the Extension Officer for Soil Conservation should be directly under the Agricultural Department. If this is done it will relieve the P.E.O. of some of the many problems that distract him and will give him better opportunity to concentrate on his fundamental task of improving agriculture and allied subjects. Other members of the Committee, however, feel that there is a danger that if these officials are not definitely part of the Block team, some of the work at present done by them may go by default.

It has also been suggested that the post of a Mobile Medical Officer is unnecessary since, in practice, his work is ineffective. The majority of us feel, however, that medical coverage in the tribal areas is so inadequate that we should not, on any account, reduce it and some of us have been Mobile Units doing very useful work in, for example, Andhra, Orissa and Assam.

The Employment Of Tribals On The Block Staff

With regard to the appointment of tribals on the staff, the position is very unsatisfactory.

We feel that insufficient attention is being paid to this problem. It can only be solved on a long-term basis, but if it is ever to be solved we should make a start now. In the Bastar District of Madhya Pradesh and in NEFA attempts are already being made to have a sort of aptitude survey of boys in the schools. Wherever a boy, exceptional in character and intelligence, is discovered, he is given special attention and is helped from the Primary to the Middle School period and is then given every opportunity to develop according to his capacity, either as V.L.W. or school-teacher or as a future administrator or technician. Local officials, in other words, help a boy to plan his future at an early stage and then help him to achieve it. This should be the special responsibility of the P.E.O. and of the Collector or Deputy Commissioner.

It is essential, of course, that this should be done very carefully and that boys should not be told that they will be fit to become district officers or leading politicians. It is necessary to look far ahead and estimate the number of posts in the tribal areas that will need to be filled over a period of years and then try to arrange that there will be coming up sufficient doctors, engineers, agriculturists and administrators for the future.

It is equally important to ensure that there will be a steady influx of boys and girls who will be able and willing to work as nurses, compounders, V.L.W.'s and teachers.

Methods of recruitment should be as simple as possible and candidates should not be asked to make long journeys for interviews. Where such journeys are necessary, T.A. should be paid to tribal candidates immediately and, after interview, information should be sent to them as soon as possible to inform them whether they have succeeded or failed. There have been cases where tribal candidates have waited for months hoping against hope that they have obtained a job and have never had any notification about it.

The method of recruitment through advertisement is not likely to succeed in the tribal areas for very few, even of the educated boys, see newspapers regularly and there should be some other means of informing them when there is a possible vacancy.

Transfers

Another problem concerns the length of time an official spends in his Block. In the tribal areas, success does not come in a hurry and one reason for the comparative failure of the staff to make contact with their people is the present system of frequent transfers. It is almost impossible to find an official at any level who has been in a multipurpose Block since its inception. Some Blocks have had three or even four successive P.E.O.'s in charge of them, and doctors, engineers, agriculturists and V.L.W.'s are continually changed. It is difficult to see how, under these circumstances, when he expects, or hopes, to have to leave in a few months, an official can come to know much about the people, get on really friendly terms with them, learn the language or indeed carry on his work with any hope of success.

The Situation In Badlipet

The P.E.O. of Badlipet gave us a valuable note on the staff situation in the course of which he pointed out that, even if 'some willingness is shown by a few in the beginning or at the time of posting, such persons after a short stay openly indicate their eagerness to escape at the earliest opportunity and start actively trying to achieve their object. Deliberate indifference towards duties, illness of self and family, difficulties about local languages, unhealthy climate, very difficult living conditions, the extreme backwardness of the area and great difficulties in achieving tangible results of work are some of the means and grounds used by the staff to get themselves transferred from this area. It is found that the special pay (25 per cent of basic pay) sanctioned by Government in June 1958 for the staff of this Block is not serving as a sufficient inducement and no keenness is shown by them to stay on in the Block on that amount.

The constant changes of the officers have a bad effect on the tribal people. While they may be relieved at the transfer of a bad officer, they are often greatly disturbed at the removal of a good one and, not being able to realise the whole situation, they tend to feel disappointed in the officer concerned and think he did not want to remain and work for them.

This is a very serious matter and one which has greatly slowed down progress in the multipurpose Blocks. If it continues, real progress may exist only on paper. Money may be spent, glowing reports may be put up, yet the essential change in the people's outlook, a sense of integration with India as a whole, will be lacking. We recommend that Block officials should much more carefully be chosen and appointed six months before the Block is to be opened, no matter what the financial or administrative difficulties may be, so that they can begin their surveys and make a start on the language. They should be asked to give an undertaking on their part that they will remain at least three years after the Block has started and the State on its side should guarantee that there will be no interference with the posting (except where this may be demanded by inferior work or for disciplinary reasons) and it should be understood that an official who remains in a Tribal Block for the full term will be eligible for accelerated promotion and special commendation in his confidential records. He may be given a special increment in recognition of exceptionally good work for which there are unusually good opportunities in the tribal areas.

Special Pay

In view of the difficulty of maintaining two establishments, for only a few of the Block officials are able to take their families with them (though every possible encouragement should be given to those who take their wives) we feel that special pay should be given to all officials working not only in the Multipurpose Tribal

Blocks but in all tribal Blocks.

We feel that it would be advisable to regularise the situation throughout India and we suggest that special allowances should be given not only to officials working in the Multipurpose Blocks but to officials working in all tribal areas, some of which are much more difficult and isolated than the Multipurpose Blocks themselves. It is important to ensure that these allowances should not only be given to members of the Block staff but to their colleagues in other Departments who are working within the Block area. Failure to do this naturally causes recentment and hampers coordination.

We suggest that if such officers were to be appointed they should belong to the senior grade and be positioned as District Development Officers or Tribal Welfare Officers of parallel status to, but working under, the local Deputy Commissioner or Collector, their duties being confined to the development of the tribal areas in the District. Some of the more senior might hold similar positions in relation to the Development Departments or Tribal Welfare Departments of the states.

The Renuka Ray Committee, the Inaccessible Area Committee as well as our own Committee have noticed that there is a tendency to send an official who has done badly elsewhere as a sort of punishment to a tribal area. The result is that the good men feel that some discredit attaches to them on their appointment and the bad men are respectful and in any case may be presumed to be unsuitable. It is essential that this attitude should change. In actual fact, it is surely an honour and privilege to be sent to the frontiers of civilization and a recognition that a man has special qualities if his superiors suppose that he will be able to stand the conditions of work there and succeed in spite of them. As we cease to think of or talk about the tribal people as 'backward' or unimportant and recognise that they are exactly the same as we ourselves; as we lay greater stress on their good qualities and discover more and more of the artistic and human contributions they can make to India, the general attitude may change and an officer going to a remote tribal village will do so in a spirit of adventure and a desire to meet the great challenge that such a place offers to his originality and creativeness.

Training

One of the major reasons why the development programme in the Multipurpose Blocks has failed to adapt itself to local conditions is the lack of adequate training of the staff in an appreciation of tribal life and culture.

We observed the curious fact that in some cases the trained S.E.O.'s were not deputed to the Multipurpose Blocks, but were posted in non-tribal Blocks in the same State. Except in Bihar there are hardly any trained workers working at the village level or in the V.L.W. circles with any orientation training. In view of the fact that very few tribals are as yet employed as V.L.W.'s and Extension workers, this means that on the whole the officials of the Multipurpose Blocks have a very limited, if any, orientation to tribal life. It is, as we have already said, due to this gap in the preparation of the minds and attitudes of the workers that the development programme has not succeeded in fulfilling its objective in the Multipurpose Blocks. We would, therefore, underline the need for such orientation before sending any worker to a Multipurpose Block. If such workers are not available or if the training facilities cannot be expanded with the required speed, it would actually be better to stagger the further programme of opening new Blocks in tribal areas rather than to develop it on a non-effective basis and then try to remedy it at a later stage.

The nature of this special training can be of three types :

(i) Orientation training of Extension workers in tribal affairs for a period of not less than three months. Our experience suggests that a short course of one month is inadequate. Training at this stage should not be too academic or be confined to anthropology and sociology. Its aim should be to make the workers conscious of the different stages in the development of the tribal people and the need to adapt the programme to their degree of receptivity. It should also create a proper understanding of the principles of tribal welfare, and should be related to the practical problems of life, explaining how tribal institutions and customs work in practice. It should, in fact, emphasise the main problems discussed in this Report, parts of which might be included in its syllabus.

(ii) Orientation training for V.L.W.'s and other workers in the villages. The same type of training, although at a different level, should be given to the V.L.W.'s as well as to Patwaris, Forest Guards and even police working in the villages. The period should be for three months at least and the training should be geared to the practical problems of the tribals with whom the trainees will be dealing.

(iii) Intensive training of one year for P.E.O.'s and Cultural Officers. As the P.E.O. is the head of the administration of a Multipurpose Block, he should play the major role in giving a tribal base to the development programme, but he will only be able to do this or guide his staff in the right direction if he is adequately trained himself. His training should include the theory and practice of social anthropology, sociology and tribal welfare.

The Cultural Officer will have a vital part to play by

understanding the social and cultural practices of the tribal people and helping them to relate them effectively to the changing conditions of life without any feeling of unhappiness, and for this he himself will require intensive training. This training can be given to him during a period of one year in addition to the training of the P.E.O. This officer should also have understanding of the various manifestations of tribal culture such as folk-songs, folk-dances and folk-lore.

We suggest that a Committee of experts in tribal welfare and administration should be constituted to examine this important matter. In addition, the services of the existing Research Departments and the Training Centres should be utilised effectively in promoting it. The Social Education Organisers' Training Centre, Ranchi, which is at present confined to the training of Social Education Organisers should be extended to all Extension workers and the courses suitably adjusted. What is required is a proper coordination of the Research Institutes and the Training Institutes, so that the findings of research can inspire and enrich the training programmes.

Although we have recommended the organisation of orientation courses in tribal life and culture for all Extension workers, we would emphasise that this suggestion is only meant to meet what we hope will be a temporary difficulty—that the general training is not geared to tribal problems. In the final analysis, the 'tribal' training should be an integral part of the regular job training. In fact, all job training should be related to the life of the people, no matter who they are. It is, therefore, necessary to emphasise that the training programme for all workers in the Multiprpose Blocks should be instituted in the tribal areas themselves—where the necessary atmosphere of tribal life prevails and the content of job training can be geared to tribal requirements. It would be altogether wrong to think of orientation training and job training as two different things. The very training for a given job should be rooted in tribal life, tradition and culture. For example, a V. L. W. will prove ineffective if he does not know how to gear his agricultural knowledge to the local traditions and practices. It is true that a knowledge of agriculture and how to improve it may be the same both for tribal and non-tribal areas, but its application will have to be in terms of the stage of development of the people, the existing methods of cultivation and the social or religious ideas about it. It is because of the lack of understanding of such ideas and practices that the programme of agriculture has not always been received by the people willingly and adopted enthusiastically. This also applies to other Extension workers. This matter needs serious attention if the programme is to fulfil the objectives of the Community Development movement. The P. E. O., as an administrator and coordinator of the programme, requires greater insight in tribal life and culture, if he is to succeed in helping and guiding his staff.

To meet this requirement, we suggest that the existing training centres should attend specially to the training of specific functionaries to work in the tribal areas. In other words, these centres should be reserved for workers coming from the tribal areas and who will return to them. With the expansion of the programme of Community Development to cover the whole of rural India, including tribal India, by 1963, there will be an enormous demand for workers, and some of the training centres could be profitably converted for the training of workers in tribal life and culture exclusively. For example, the Orientation Training Centre at Ranchi which is giving training to Block Development Officers for their own job should enlist all the B. D. O.'s and P. E. O.'s who are to work in the tribal areas and adjust the training to the requirements of tribal life and culture. Similarly, the training centres in cooperation, industries, panchayat, animal husbandry, agriculture and so on, situated in and around Ranchi may be specially reserved for training these functionaries to work in the tribal areas. In some cases, the States which have large tribal populations may help to work jointly in providing such training. If they are to undertake this new responsibility, the present Training Centre may require : (a) an orientation of the present teaching staff itself in tribal life and culture ; (b) some additional staff with advanced knowledge in social anthropology; (c) a research and study wing to develop the training programmes and relate them to tribal requirements. In addition, the existing Tribal Research Institutes will have to help these centres in the initial stage to adjust their programmes to their new responsibilities. This is a comprehensive approach and can only be developed gradually and on a long-term basis, but we must realise that if we mean business and really intend to fufil the constitutional responsibilities of guiding the tribal population through the difficult period of transition and change that now awaits them, we must take the subject of training more seriously, for it has had insufficient attention in the past.

But who will pay for this ? It is obviously necessary to make some special provision, if the training programme is to be established on a sound and permanent footing. The budget of the Multipurpose Blocks cannot spare much for it. Moreover, each Block budget has to be approved by the Block Development Committee or the Block Samiti and it would be difficult to get sanction for a training programme for each Block, and this would create a sense of insecurity and uncertainty among the officials to be trained. The necessary additional provision for training should be made in the Third Five-Year Plan under the heads of different Ministries responsible for specific subjects, such as Agriculture, Animal Husbandry, Health, Education, Industries, and so on. The Ministry of Community Development and Cooperation should provide funds for the job training of P.E.O.'s S.E.O.'s and Mukhya Sevikas and orientation training for all community development workers. The Ministry of Food and Agriculture should provide the necessary funds for the training of V.L.W.'s and Gram Sevikas. The Ministry of Home Affairs should help in establishing Tribal Research Wings at the different training centres.

Problems Of Land And Agriculture

The economic stability of the tribals can be ensured only through agriculture and it is obvious that there can be no progress in agriculture without suitable land to cultivate. In some of the tribal areas such as Bastar, there seems to be no shortage of land at present but in many other areas there is real land hunger. The Renuka Ray Committee has studied the entire situation and, though we ourselves are concerned only with the Multipurpose Tribal Blocks, we cannot emphasise too strongly that their circumstances cannot be considered in isolation and indeed, our conclusions should have a bearing on the entire tribal area, in view of the fact that we hope that it will be completely covered with Blocks during the Third Five-Year Plan period.

The Renuka Ray Committee has pointed out that 'the extension of the rule of law in the field of land rights has resulted in the progressive extinction of the original rights of the tribals which were their's, at least by virtue of the first occupation', and in an important sentence, with which we are in the strongest agreement it declares that 'even if it is not possible to reverse the process there should be no doubt or difficulty about arresting it and in restating the rights of tribal communities in land in unabiguous terms'.

We recommend that :

(a) The States should take up as a measure of priority a survey of the tribal areas in order to discover the amount of cultivable land availabie and the extent to which the tribal people have no established rights in the areas they cultivate;

(b) This should be followed by a vigorous and sincere attempt to establish the tribal people in their rights to the land which they have cultivated traditionally;

(c) Land Alienation Acts and similar protective measures should be carefully re-examined in the light of the present situation;

(d) The aim should be to ensure that every tribal has at least two-and-a-half acres of wet or five acres of dry land which he can cultivate, and in the establishment of colonies or in any scheme of settlement this should be regarded as the absolute minimum.

We regret that the P.E.Os' have not adopted a bolder and more imaginative attitude. The scope for flexibility in the schematic budget to suit local needs has not been fully explored. We hope that in the new Special Tribal Blocks to be opened in the Third Five-Year Plan, much greater attention will be paid to these subjects, so vital to the happiness, health and progress of the tribal people.

Shifting Cultivation

The Renuka Ray Committee has given emphatic support to three main problems of tribal agriculture; the restoration and preservation of the land rights of the tribal communities; the introduction of scientific shifting cultivation; and the improvement of agricultural practices for more and better production of food. The problem of shifting cultivation is indeed intimately related to the problem of tribal land. Although in some places there is plenty of land available on which to settle cultivators who hitherto have been living in the hills, there are many other areas where the pressure on land is causing intense economic and psychological distress to the tribal people. They are also very anxious about and resentful of proposals to bring them down from the hills they love and the land to which they are bound by many intimate ties of memory and religion. They fear that if they have to come down to the plains they will be involved in disputes with stronger and more progressive communities. At present many of them suffer from a sense of guiet and anxiety because they are continuing to practise their traditional methods of agriculture against the law and they are often subject to blackmail by minor officials.

The Renuka Ray Committee obeserves in its report that even if the full programme of rehabilitation is fulfilled. only 10 per cent of shifting cultivators can be settled in the next 15 years. In the Second Five-year Plain, a sum of two crores and 87.33 lakhs of rupees was set apart for the purpose. It goes on to say that : "It should thus appear to be a costly and long-drawn-out process and the results do not promise to be commensurate with the effort or the outlay. Recently, however, experiments are being made to introduce scientific jhuming in order to preserve the fertility of the soil and prevent erosion. If the experiments currently in hand in NEFA prove successful, as they promise to be, we might strike at a golden mean which wiil result in greater food production without unduly interfering with the tribal way of life. In the absence of any such approach, we are likely to be continuously beset with the present dilemma in which we can neither allow jhuming to go on unchecked nor do we have sufficient land, water and other material resources to offer an inexpensive and quick substitute. There are regions in or around tribal areas where land is available but has remained unallotted and in most cases even unsurveyed.

We feel on the whole that the dangers of shifting cultivation have been a little exaggerated in the past and we are supported in this view by a number of experts, even foresty experts. It is, therefore, advisable that we should proceed continously in weaning the people away from this practice. We may remember that even the weaning of children is not done in a single day.

To sum up, while it is most desirable that there should be a change over from shifting to more permanent type of cultivation, we should recognise that this cannot be done in a hurry and certainly not in the course of a brief five years. The change will have to be preceded by cautions and tactful propaganda and there areas where no alternative land is available and where, therefore, this practice will have to continue for a long time to come.

We feel that it is most important that this should be taken up immediately along the line suggested by Shri M. S. Sivaraman. This plan has recently been supported by both the Renuka Ray and Inaccessible Areas Committees.

We are unanimous in our opinion that shifting cultivation is an arduous and wasteful method and in fact, even if all our plans for scientific improvement succeed, it will be better that the people should take to settled cultivation. We look forward, therefore, to the day when ultimately all the tribal people will be living on prosperous farms of their own with undisputed right to their land. But until this is possible; until good land can be found w thin a reasonable distance of their original homes; until this land is properly surveyed and rights are given to the tribal people; until, infact, they themselves are psychologically adjusted to this great change and themse lves demand opportunities for a better type of cultivation, it would be wise to proceed with caution.

We should be very careful that in our enthusiasm for bringing shifting cultivation to an end we do not injure the people psychologically or socially. We do not consider that to uproot them from their homes and move them to distant places will be a good thing. We should not think in terms of bringing hill people down from their hills. We are to recognise and respect the tribal people's rights in land and forest and also their right to settle their own destinies by evolution from within and not by force imposed from outside.

The Problem Of The Forests

We recognise, of course, the importance of preserving India's forest wealth and would pay our tribute to the scientific knowledge and the devotion of hundreds of forest officers, who live under conditions of great difficulty in the most in accessible places and who have done so much to protect the trees which are among the great treasures of India. But no one can visit the tribal areas without feeling that there is a very serious conflict between the people of the soil and the officials who in the course of their duty, have to administer laws and regulations which press very heavily upon the tribal.

Pattas should be issued immediately to all tribals, who do not have them, in predominently forest areas in order to confirm their actual possession. This should be taken up as a matter of top priority if the tribal areas are really to make the progress we desire for them.

Where there is insufficient land available, tracts should be excised from the less valuable areas of the Protected Forests and be given exclusively to the landless tribals. A minimum holding of five acres of dry or two-and-a-half acres of wet land should be ensured. This is little enough but it may be unrealistic to ask for more.

Wherever there is a tank or other irrigation schemes, the land which can be irrigated should be allotted promptly and exclusively to the tribals.

A Forest Extension Officer should be appointed on the development team to act as a liaison officer with the Forest Department and promote the establishment of Forest Cooperatives.

The extraction of timber for housing schemes should be permitted on the authority of the P.E.O., who would of course maintain close cooperation with the Forest authorities,

Wood and bamboo should similarly be allowed for the encouragement of cottage industries even if the final product is for sale. If this is not done, cottage industries (which can help to relieve pressure on the land and thus on the forest) will just not prosper.

The present permit system should be abolished, or modified to allow the Extension Officers to act on behalf of the Forest Department.

Minor irrigations such as the ban on exracting grass or stone from the forest area, the collection of Mahua (bassia latifolia) flowers for food or seeds for oil should be removed. This brings little profit to Government and causes an altogether disproportionate resentment against the Forest officials.

Hunting rules should be modified to promote greater freedom to the tribals, even if they are only permitted to use spears, bows and arrows and traps. Ceremonial hunts should in no case be interfered with. At the same time vigorous educational propaganda should be carried on to persuade the people of the value of preserving the game and of hunting only during the open season.

Permission should be gtven to tribals to protect their

crops against all wild animals who damage them, and not merely against those which are classified as vermin.

Forest protection will only be really dffective when there is a mutual sense of trust and even affection between the Forest staff and the tribal people. For this a kind of public relations campaign is needed, and small exactions, irritations and unnecessary restrictions should be removed.

It is desirable that forest officials at all levels should have some orientation training to help them to understand the tribal point of view and thus adopt a more sympathetic attitude. Perhaps even more than the actual forest laws the attitude of some forest officials, and especially of the forest guards, who often adopt a dictatorial attitude towards the people, should be changed. We recommend that there should be some lectures at the Forest Research Institute to inspire trainees with a new approach.

Forests should be managed essentially in the interests of the tribals who inhabit the areas, subject to minimum safety precautions in regard to erosion and the national interest which must, of course, take priority.

Daily wages in the forest areas, whether paid by the Forest Department or by contractors, should be fixed on the basis of what they would be, if free and fair competition existed and should be related to the most favourable wages in the area. We feel that it is as essential to have a Forest Minimum Wages Act as it is to have an Agricultural Minimum Wages Act. The very fact that there is no such Act at present suggests the comparative indifference throughout the country towards the interests of tribal labourers.

Taking into consideration the tribal psychology, some share of the profits derived in a particular area by the Forest Department should be ploughed back in the form of increased wages if there is departmental working. This direct share in the profits would convince the tribal that his interests were linked with those of the forest; whereas contributions in the form of indirect benfit such as roads or schools will not convince him of the fidentity of interest.

Precautions should be taken to avoid hardship to forest villagers arising from demands for their labour at a time when they are themselves busy with agricultural operations.

Under existing circumstances and conditions, it will soon become impossible for Forest Villages to fulfil the labour supply function. In due course, the exploitation of forests may have to be entrusted to a semi-autonomous organisation like a State Trading Corporation. This organisation would undertake exploitation only and the function of the Forest Department would be limited to the technical aspects of the working of the forest and indicating the timber to be cut, If and when such a Corporation was set up it would become essential to have a standing labour force such as is even now maintained by private commercial concerns. The setting up of a standing labour force, based on the average labour requirement of all the forests within a particular zone (which might be conveniently made to coincide with the Forest Division) would ultimately solve the labour problem.

A Rasad (receipt) and services note-book should be maintained in each village (whether a Forest Village or an ordinary revenue village). The requirement of making an entry in this note-book should extend to employees of all Departments including the Police. Minimum rates for daily essentials, such as one generally required by Government servants on tour, should be laid down by the Collector, separately for each tract, keeping in mind the prevailing standard of prices.

The principles indicated above regarding Cooperatives may be accepted and details regarding selection of co-ops should be worked out well in time, so that Government's orders may be obtained promptly. Similar Cooperatives should be organised for the exploitation of minor forest produce.

In regard to *ad hoc* felling series, either (i) they should be departmentally worked, or (ii) if they are to be auctioned, all materials needed locally by villagers should be departmentally felled and extracted and then only the remaining material auctioned.

Where forest produce in a particular area is in excess of local requirements, this fact should be intimated to the revenue authorities who should then make available such surplus in the first place to the people of adjoining areas outside the zone. These materials would, however, not be available free, but would have to be paid for at half the market rates applicable to the area. After such demands were met, then only would the remaining produce be auctioned or disposed of commercially.

As we also suggest in another chapter, that when Forest Officers go on tour they should, whenever they have opportunity, give talks to the children in the schools about the value of trees, both to India as a whole and to themselves in particular, and on the need of cherishing the wild life of the country. The establishment of little zoos or aviaries, the keeping of animals as pets in the schools, might also help to create a greater sensitivity towards the wild life. A Forest Officer should also meet the Block officials from time to time and there should, in general, be a greater cooperation between the workers in the two fields of development and the Extension Officers themselves should have sufficient knowledge of forest problems; they should talk to the people about them and help them to understand the situation. If there can be sufficient modification of those forest laws which interfere with the people's progress, if the irritations caused by the malpractices of forest guards can be removed and if ebucation of this kind can be extended, there is no reason why in future there should not be a much happier psychological climate with the result that the people will work more vigorously.

The religion of the tribes leads them to believe that there are many spirits living in the trees and forests. There are special sacrifices to the forest gods; in many places offerings are made to a tree before it is cut and there are usually ceremonies before and after hunting. Tribal folktales often speak about the relations of human beings and the spirits of the trees and it is striking to see how in many of the myths and legends the deep sense of identity with the forest is emphasised. Here is a possible line for education of the people and we recommend a careful study of tribal folk literature to officials who have to deal with the subject. It will help them to understand the tribes better (for such literature should never be regarded as merely a collection of stories—it is very serious business) and may give them many points for educating them and gaining better relations.

Animal Husbandry

In order to better the conditions and to develop milch and draught cattle, cattle-consciousness should be produced among the tribals by means of audio-visual units, exhibitions and propaganda.

The incentive to improve the condition of their domestic animals should come from the tribals themselves and this can only be achieved if Government takes effective interest by speading facilities in the Block areas by providing the outlying dispensaries with medicines, instruments, medical staff and creating a congenial and enthusiastic atmosphere.

Facilities for educating men and boys in animal husbandry and veterinary training should be enlarged by including this subject in schools and colleges, or even by opening special schools. Local tribal boys should be given training as stockmen, veteninary compounders, and vaccinators-*cum*-compounders. This need not cost very much, yet it will surely go a long way in enriching the cattle population and developing poultry farming, pigeons, pisciculture and so on with a beneficial effect on the general economic condition of the tribal areas.

Officials employed in the Special Blocks should be mainly selected or recruited from the tribal areas themselves, for this will create a rural and tribal setting and there will be less need to draw trained veterinary personnel from the towns.

The present practice of dealing with the diseases, castration of bulls and other so-called crude methods in treating the animals can only be changed by a proper atmosphere and the introduction of educational facilities by Government.

It is important to develop Cooperatives to handle and market dairy products, fish, eggs and so on and to provide them with working capital.

Communications

We recommend that first priority should be given to the construction of Class I roads, even though these will be bound to be comparatively few in number in view of their much higher cost. We are confident that such roads will pay for themselves in a relatively short time, through the indirect benefits which they will bring to the area. Here will be something of obvious and tangible benefit, about which there can be no dispute and where expenditure can usually be carefully controlled. The cost of the main roads, and certainly those linking the Block with the District Headquarters should be a charge on the general State budget.

Road-planning for the entire Block area should be taken up at a very early stage and should ensure, in the first place, that the headquarters (which should itself be in the heart of the Block) will be connected by an all-weather motorable road to some main highway and secondly, that one or two main Class I roads should run through the entire area of the Block.

Culverts, bridges and causeways should in the first place be made to cover all the obstacles in the roads that are planned and while many of these will have to be fair-weather roads in the first instance, there should be a carefully considered plan for progressively transforming them as soon as possible.

It is more important to make roads linking the interior of the hills with the plains than to join remote villages in the interior with one another.

It is essential that some provisions for the maintenance and progressive improvement of roads should be made, for otherwise they may fall into disuse and much effort and money will be wasted. We cannot rely on the tribals to maintain the roads themselves for, in the first place, they have not the resources to do so and, secondly, they may not be particularly interested unless a road is of really vital importance to themselves.

The Cooperative Extension Officers should make it their special care to organise the tribal people into labour cooperatives to whom construction works will normally be given. Contractors should be eliminated as far as is humanly possible. This policy has been successful in the Araku Block and in parts of Assam.

The resources of the C.P.W.D., the State P.W.D., the Local Board and the Forest Department should be pooled for the planning, construction and maintenance of roads, and schemes should be drawn up on a 10-year rather than a five-year programme.

Roads, of course, can be a curse as well as a blessing to the tribal people. In some places they have been the means of corruption and exploitation. They have brought new diseases, moral decline and cultural decadence. They have made it easy for the money-lender, the rapacious merchant, the liquor-vendor, the lawyer's tout to penetrate deep into the hills and forest. They can bring money in, but they can also take money out. They have helped to destroy the hand-loom industry by the import of cheap bazaar cloth; they have brought vulgar and inferior goods to the very doors of the people. Difficult though it will be, we must try to ensure that this does not happen any longer and that every road is a pilgrim's way to a better and richer life, bringing health, food and enlightenment to the villages it serves.

Health Services

The Primary Health Centre is a unit whence integrated health care has to radiate into the homes of the tribal people. Its location should be decided by the Block Development Committee after taking into consideration the following criteria:—

(1) Service to the maximum number of people;

(2) Health problems of the area as revealed by a survey;

(3) People's participation; and

(4) Easy accessibility for referral services.

The buildings of the Primary Health Centre should be simple and inexpensive. They should be constructed as far as possible with locally available material (but there must be a really *pucca* Operating Theatre) and the design should conform to the local environment. The main criterion should be its utility and capacity to offer service. The establishment of sub-centres should also be of a similar pattern.

Medical coverage in almost all the Tribal Blocks is extremely inadequate and even when there is money and sometimes even when buildings for hospitals and dispensaries have been erected, doctors, nurses, compounders and midwives are unwilling to come and serve in such remote places.

In order to meet the very serious shortage of medical staff we suggest that as in Andhra Pradesh, there should be a certain period of service in a tribal area for all doctors as a condition of promotion, crossing the efficiency bar or for being sent for higher studies in India or abroad. Those doctors who serve well should receive special commendation in their Character Rolls and be considered for accelerated promotion.

Mobile Units should be placed as a matter of routine in centres at some distance, where practicable, from the main Health Centre and the Block headquarters. The value of these Mobile Units has been questioned, but we feel that in many Blocks they have done useful work and that provided the doctor or compounder attends regularly at specified places, specially if this is done on bazaar days, a lot of good can be done.

We feel, however, that it is unrealistic to provide these Mobile Centres in the tribal areas with ambulances or large vans which often cannot get along the rough roads or tracks even in the fine weather. An ordinary jeep is quite sufficient to take a doctor with his staff and medicines to a number of outlying villages. Serious cases can easily, by a little ingenuity, be accommodated in a jeep and brought back to hospital. It might even be considered whether an improved type of bullock-cart could not be sometimes used by the Mobile Units; in NEFA these Units have to move about in the most difficult country on foot, and doctors there have performed successful operations under the most impossible circumstances in village camps without any assistance from motor transport. Special financial provision will, of course, have to be made for this type of touring, as we have suggested elsewhere.

Medicine chests should be provided at the rate of atleast one for each V.L.W. circle. These chests can be kept under the charge of the V.LW. or school-teacher. The most important thing is that arrangements should be made to refill these chests and maintain them properly.

Maternal and Child Health Care are the essential services and deserve highest priority. In view of the difficulty in getting women to go to these areas, short training courses should be started for tribal women who are carrying out domicilary midwifery at present. This training should preferably be carried out on the spot and will require a mobile team of a health visitor and a trained midwife. It is essential for the staff to be fully conversant with the existing practices and beliefs in relation to maternal and child-health care, so that service training can be integrated with them. This scheme must always include health education for the improvement of nutrition, environmental sanitation, control of communicable diseases and improvement of other personal health services. For its effective development it may be necessary to enlist the active help and participation of the local Mahila Samithis and Health Committees.

Children of school-going age form a large section of the population and it is necessary to inculcate healthy habits and hygienic practices among them. A comprehensive programme for the medical examination of school children with adequate arrangements for the correction of defects, immunisation, improvement of environmental sanitation, supply of drinking water and provision of mid-day meals, should be developed. Kitchen gardens and orchards (as in Orissa) should be developed in every school.

The National Malaria Eradication Programme is already in operation in those areas where it is a problem.

In addition, steps should be taken for the eradication of certain other diseases like leprosy. yaws. goitre, small pox, V.D. and so on wherever they have a high incidence.

The provision of drinking-water wells is a subject which is beyond controversy, one which can do nothing but good, and which is of incalculable benefit to the tribal people. While it would be an exaggeration to say that most of the people have to walk three or four miles to get their water. there is no doubt that they do have difficulty in getting a supply of really clean drinking-water and we urge that this programme should be given very high priority. In some places the people do not used wells and prefer to draw water from running streams. Here cisterns, such as have been built in Orissa, can be a valuable substitute.

Health Education is one of the most important items of every basic health service.

To accomplish his goal the health educator should be familiar with the nature of the culture and the way of life of the people, their values, beliefs, traditions, customs and taboos about health and illness. He should understand the objectives for which the people are willing to strive, and conversely, the aspects of life that mean very little to them or they are as yet unable to understand. He should know what the people can understand and what they will reject. Having once learned these facts he can work with the people in planning and using educational measures which will harmonise with their life and character.

The Health staff should have accurate statistical data based on surveys conducted by the Department of Health or by other departments at its disposal which will give a fairly accurate picture of the local health problems. On the basis of this, the Medical Officers can plan their programme.

A great deal of good work has undoubtedly been done wherever it has been possible to position an adequate medical staff. The tribal people are beginning to realise the value of modern medicine and although at first they were unwilling to come to hospitals or dispensaries they are now doing so in ever greater numbers.

In view of the special nature of the work in the Multipurpose Blocks, it is essential that all the members of the health staff, and specially the doctors, should undergo orientation training in the basic philosophy of the general programme as well as in the special health problems of the locality. They must learn the latest developments in extension method and how to work with the tribal people.

Education

We feel that there should be great caution in starting compulsory education in the tribal areas. It was recently introduced in the Tamia Multipurpose Block and 45 matriculate teachers with no knowledge of the local language and no orientation to tribal life suddenly arrived and began their work. How can education forced upon at least partly unwilling people be successful under these circumstances ?

Compulsory education must, of course, come in the end. But so far as the tribal areas are concerned, we urge that it should be delayed until it can be done properly. For this we must first have a sufficient number of either teachers who are recruited locally or experienced and well-qualified teachers who are completely familiar with the local language. It is equally necessary to have Inspectors oriented to the tribal outlook and way of doing things. We should then ensure that there are text-books in the tribal languages for the lower classes and books for the more advanced classes specially prepared with reference to tribal needs. Perhaps more important than anything else is that, before compulsory education is brought to these areas, an educational policy suitable for them, which will be implemented at every stage and by every organisation which is dealing with the subject, should be properly worked out.

We feel that an attempt should be made to introduce a carefully-adapted form of basic education, with a special syllabus, such as has been done in Bastar and NEFA.

Clothes are often given free to the children in schools and these are not always of the most appropriate kind. It is better not to give white clothes, for they soon begin to look shabby and dirty, In some of the Orissa schools uniforms of an attractive green colour have been given. Similarly, girls should not be dressed up in frocks in the western style, but there should be some attempt to dress them at least in Indian fashion if there is no suitable tribal dress available.

It is important to maintain the spirit of self-reliance in the schools. There is a danger that we may make education too cheap; in the desire to attract boys and girls to school everything is given free. This has not been a tradition in the past.

It has been urged that all primary schools in tribal areas should be based on agriculture and forestry. At least two days in the week should be set apart for practical training in these subjects. Every school should have at least half-an-acre of land for practical work, and this land should not be used for gardening but for the growing of the common crops of the area. No hired labour should be engaged. There should also be an attempt to relate the programme to basic forestry.

It has been suggested at a high level that we should not at this stage at least open too many secondary schools in the tribal areas, for they tend to produce large numbers of boys and girls whose only desire is to get away from their villages and obtain clerical jobs in towns. We do, however, need a few really first-class secondary schools, as we have already said, to train up the brightest boys and girls to be the leaders of the future. Other secondary schools should aim at agriculture and vocational training; they should aim at turning out proficient technicians and not merely boys who have some smattering of agriculture or of a trade. These boys and girls, when they leave the secondary school, should be capable of earning a fairly good living by working at the trade they have been taught. It has been pointed out that for the next 15 or 20 years at least the welfare of the tribal will depend entirely on agriculture and it would be wise to concentrate on this subject rather than on general education. Under agriculture, of course, would be included such veterinary knowledge as is necessary for the cultivator—the proper protection of cattle, selective breeding, timely inoculation and so on.

The Orissa Government is making orchards of fruit-trees in the compounds of all their schools, the idea being to have about 50 trees attached to every school. This is a most admirable idea and we recommend that it should be followed with enthusiasm throughout the country.

Though we should not waste money on libraries in villages where everyone is illiterate, more attention should be paid to secondary school libraries, which should not consist only of publications supplied free by the Ministry of Community Development. Indeed, it will be hard to imagine a more unfortunate method of creating the habit of reading than to provide boys with literature of this kind. There should be books of adventure, children's stories, books about animals and birds, books about other countries—simple well-illustrated books that will catch the eye and attract the attention of the child. This will be expensive, but if we are to have education at all in the tribal areas, it ought to be expensive.

Literature should not only be for the young, but also for neo-literates, where possible in their own language.

The machinery for the award of scholarships has frequently been criticised. We suggest that:

(a) Scholarships should be sufficient to cover all expenses while at school and college, and not merely part of those expenses. Most tribal boys have no private resources.

(b) Such scholarships should be available to a boy at least a fortnight before he actually joins the school or college, so that he may have the funds to join.

(c) At present the quantum of the scholarship, in college particularly, is very inadequate, and payment is usually made after eight or nine months' delay. The result is that usually only those tribals who have private resources and who do not, therefore, really need scholarships, can afford to go to college.

(d) For the next five years at least all tribal boys and girls who wish to go forward with their education should be given opportunities to do so provided they pass the necessary examinations, irrespective of the marks they may obtain. Every attempt, however, should be made to persuade boys and girls to take up technical rather than arts subjects, for otherwise we may well produce a large number of unemployable Matriculates or Graduates who will suffer distress and frustration later on.

In the schools also there is considerable delay in receipt of the scholarships but here it is possible for the local authorities to make arrangements for loans, etc., to tide over the lean period before governmental assistance becomes available. Unfortunately all local authorities do not render such assistance. We do not blame them because a fairly heavy financial expenditure is involved. In one case, a person had practically to stand surety for a loan of several thousand rupees so that a Vanwasi Sewa Mandal school could continue to function until its grant was received.

The teaching of art is greatly neglected. In some ways this is perhaps fortunate, for the low level art teachers, who would normally be available, can do much more harm than good, and it has been found in India itself as well as in other countries that the stiff and formal drawing and painting instruction commonly given has deplorable results. On the other hand, provided plenty of raw materials are provided, such as drawing paper and paints or crayons, the development of free drawing and painting among tribal children has immense possibilities.

An experiment, which has been tried in Tripura, is to encourage the children to keep pets in their schools. There may be only two or three birds or animals, but the task of looking after them does create some sense of the need for the preservation and love of animals. Since wild life in the tribal areas of India is in danger of being exterminated, this is a matter of importance.

Some of the tribes have a remarkable facility for producing completely informal little dramas or one-act plays, as we may call them. They always represent something familiar to them—sometimes they show an oppressive official demanding free food and being rebuffed; sometimes they represent a quarrel over land; there may be a hunting scene or a parody of a wedding ceremony; the essential thing about such dramas is that they are not and never should be written down. The dialogue is always spontaneous and, because of this, is fresh and exciting.

More attention should be given by touring officers of all departments to visiting schools and giving talks on their own subjects. This is already being done in some places, but it is generally too haphazard, and insufficient atttention is paid to it. It should be recognised that the entire administration in a tribal area is engaged in one great task of education. Education, in fact, is far too important to be left to the educationists; a school should be the concern of everyone.

In areas where villages are small and widely separated from one another, there is scope for transforming some of the schools into inter-village schools or Ashram schools. Ashram schools, however, should not be of a puritanic type and the children should not be overstrained by being asked to get up very early in the morning for prayers and so on. Tribal children, indeed all children, must be thoroughly happy in their schools if they are to do them good. Sometimes, the hours are too long, even in day-schools, for tribal children, most of whom have to work very hard when they are at home.

It is of great importance that the crafts introduced in the Ashram schools should be those which the boys and girls are likely to carry on in later life and which will be of real economic value to them. In many of the schools spinning and weaving is adopted as an important craft. Unhappily, there are many tribal areas where weaving is taboo and though this may gradually be broken down, it is unlikely that it will succeed to any great extent.

Another important point which arises in some areas is the question of caste. As the tribal people come more and more into contact with the outside world they tend to take from our society its bad rather than its good points and to adopt the very things which India as a whole is eliminating from its life.

Another policy which may well be questioned is that of having residential Ashram schools in the actual villages from which the boys are enrolled. It is a question whether it is a good thing to take boys away from their homes and keep them 24-hours in a school which is actually in their own village, for it is very expensive and creates a drastic distinction between school and home.

We feel that it is not even desirable that the tribals should be deprived of a very important aspect of their diet. The Community Development Programme gives a fairly high place to the improvement of poultry, goats, pigs and other livestock and it seems rather inconsistent that on one side the tribals should be encouraged to breed these animals, either for personal use or for sale, and on the other should be taught that to eat them is wrong.

A carefully worked-out programme of tribal education, adjusted in some such way as we have suggested in this Chapter, would be a great adventure, original if not unique, and might do much to save the younger tribals from the frustration and disappointments that have been experienced by the preceding generation. While on the one hand we will ultimately have well trained tribal officers to develop their own areas, a process which is bound to continue for many years to come, we will have on the other a contented and enlightened peasantry who will not be ashamed to work with their hands and who will see in the farmer's life one of the ideal professions.

Social Education In The Tribal Areas

We feel that the whole programme of Social Education should be given a new orientation. It should not follow the uniform pattern adopted in non-tribal areas. To begin with, it should relate the programme with the prevailing folk-culture. It is necessary to realise that this is a more difficult thing than to introduce songs and dances of a non-tribal type, which in any case is not desirable.

As we have already said, if tribe has a youth dormitory, it needs to be recognised and promoted. If it is in a decaying condition, it needs to be revived with care. Wherever the system of Natya gharh is prevalent, it may be used to promote group life. The institution of the village god gives an excellent opportunity to relate the interest and energy of the villagers to the welfare of their village. If new social changes are to be introduced, and this is bound to happen with increasing outside contact, the social changes should be slow, at the pace of tribal receptivity and in harmony with the prevailing outlook and practice. Gradual exposure and conditioning through participation should be the two main tools to be used for bringing about social change rather than the imposition of an autside way of life. This is a difficult task and needs to be handled with care.

The Programme of Adult Education, specially literacy activity, needs only a little comment. Most of the tribes have their own languages or dialects. Therefore, if any activity of language is to be introduced, it should be related to the prevailing dialect.

While considering the nature of the services of the Social Education Organiser, we have come to the conclusion that its present grade is unlikely to attract people with the necessary imagination, sensitivity or knowledge. It requires a man of good academic qualifications, wide reading and with a fresh and original mind to handle this delicate and responsible task of relating a programme of cultural development and social change to the existing tribal situation. We recommend, therefore, that this post should be upgraded from Class III to Class II, to avoid any kind of rivalry with the P.E.O. (who is also Class II unless, as we have suggested, he is upgraded to Class I) the incumbents should normally be junior men, which is in any case desirable.

We suggest that the designation of the officer in-charge of the cultural and social programme, whose upgrading we have recommended above, should be 'Cultural Officer'. This is not meant to imply any change in the department to which he will belong. The change of designation is only suggested to emphasise the need of understanding the cultural life of the tribals and the degree to which it has developed. It will not mean that the officer will be removed from the parent department to which he belongs at present as a Social Education Organiser.

There is also need for artists and photographers, who could be supervised by the Cultural Officers. All States employ them, but there are many demands on them, and we suggest that special posts should be created expressly for the tribal areas. They could prepare illustrations for text-books in the tribal languages, illustrations which would be of things familiar to the childern. Thev could prepare calendars, and pictures for schools, charts and posters with the local background, as has been done very efficiently elsewhere. Photographers could produce pictures of the local people and scenes, which could be enlarged and used to decorate schools, hospitals, and Government institutions which at present are so drab and lifeless.

Social Education, as an education for social change, should be to some extent the responsibility of all development workers. Therefore, it is necessary for every Block Official to realise that a wrong attitude on his part may result in a wrong development of the tribals in terms of their social practices and attitudes to life.

Women's Programmes

We suggest that the whole approach to the women's programme requires reorientation. It may be advantageous to ask well-qualified and sensitive Mukhya Sevikas and Gram Sevikas, after their orientation to tribal life and culture, to experiment with different types of programme and thus determine the kind of activity that will be most suitable. The most important thing is to cut out the frills and concentrate on the less spectacular but far more vital problems of maternity, child-care and clean and happy homes.

Rural Arts And Crafts

The real progress of Arts and Crafts cannot be estimated in terms of finance, for a Block may put up a very good report on money spent which has actually been used on expensive and unsuitable buildings, non-tribal trainees or unproductive crafts. But, speaking financially, many of the Blocks have done reasonably well in this subject, having used a-quarter to a-third of their funds in the first three years. In the Araku Block of Andhra Pradesh and the Akrani Mahal of Bombay 57:47 per cent and 37:96 per cent respectively of the allocation has been spent, but the financial record of some of the other Blocks is hardly satisfactory.

In the Rongkhang Block, nothing has been spent on this subject in three years, though there are now ambitious plans to release a lot of money for it—we hope it will be done wisely. In Kushalgarh in Rajasthan, the home of the arts, only 8.75 per cent has been utilised and plans for the future seem singularly uninspired.

At the same time, in some Blocks far too much is being spent on the erection of elaborate buildings. For example, in one Block Rs. 44,000 is proposed for an industrial school and in another no less than Rs. 82,000 is to be used for an elaborate cottage industries centre which will be situated in a non-tribal village.

It is often difficult for the tribal people to obtain the raw material for their crafts: forest laws have done a great deal to discourage them, for even of wood.

Painting (except on walls with natural materials) has never developed because the people cannot afford or obtain paints and paper.

Lack of patronage and encouragement has also had its effect, and in the inaccessible areas there is little possibility of marketing tribal produce on a commercial basis.

Another restricting influence comes from the people themselves. There are taboos on the practice of various crafts. In most areas outside Assam, weaving is forbidden to the tribal communities; sometimes bamboo work is regarded as the monopoly of a Hindu Caste; iron-work can only be done by certain small groups which are regarded as taboo and dangerous. Among some Nagas, the human figure may only be carved by some-one who has taken a head, the image of a tiger only by someone who has actually killed a tiger.

It is most important that two types of survey should be made in regard to cottage industries. One is to discover what arts or crafts already exist, the other is to assess how these can be developed and what crafts can be introduced on an economically sound basis. This might be the responsibility of the State Directorate of Industries in cooperation with the Tribal Research Institute.

Research in economics has been badly neglected in all the Multipurpose Block areas and schemes are put up and started which no intelligent businessman would even consider. It is vital, before large sums of money are spent on erecting buildings for institutions or enlisting large number of trainees at considerable public expense, that everything to do with cottage industries should be carefully examined: to discover what kind and what quantity of articles can be consumed locally, and what can be exported. It will not always be possible to secure sales for tribal products on largely sentimental grounds and we cannot continue subsidising craftsmen for the rest of their lives.

We found a great deal of ignorance on the part of the Extension Officers regarding the actual arts that existed in their Blocks.

We should not think only in terms of trying to sell things. If we do that it will mean the final extinction of the tribal arts. For it is true that in many cases the tribal people cannot compete and are not likely to compete with their more expert neighbours. It has been reported from Madhya Pradesh that in that State cottage industries, except for purely local consumption, are of doubtful utility to the tribals. They are not sufficiently skilled, there are taboos on the undertakings of some handicrafts, which in any case would have to compete with the products of the very highly skilled craftsmen in the settled areas.

We should not at present introduce too many expensive machines. A report from Bastar has also recommended that we should not give 'too much mechanised aid' in the tribal areas. For the tribesman 'tends to become accustomed to governmental assistance, with the result that he cannot readjust himself easily when particular schemes come to an end.'

There are a number of arts which do not warrant full-scale training institutes and foı these we suggest some such scheme as has proved successful in north-eastern India.

The revival of wood-carving, at present almost entirely neglected, has great possibilities both for the development of the creative artistic spirit and for sale. There is a constant demand from tourists and others for something unusual and the ornaments and carvings on sale in most emporia are too often stereotyped and conventional. If the strength and originality of tribal carving can be preserved and revived, it will be possible to get a very ready sale in what we may call the luxury market.

Wood carving is in the blood of many tribes, though it has began to decline partly because of the general lack of enthusiasm and partly due to the difficulty of getting wood from the forest in modern times. A number of tribes make striking masks for use in dances. Careful survey will discover many other places where wood-carving has been known in the past and lingers on, even though it may now only be practised by a few individuals.

If it can be revived by the people themselves—it is doubtful if instructors from outside will succeed—this craft has great potentialities.

For the encouragement of the village arts a system of competitions might well be useful.

Another very important matter is that the Forest Departments of the States should encourage, and not frustrate, the tribal desire to follow their own arts.

We suggest that special enquiries should be made in all the Multi-purpose Blocks as to how far the existing forest rules militate against the development of cottage industries and that, if they do, the State Governments should immediately institute a simple and more liberal procedure.

The manufacture of bricks and tiles has received far too little attention and yet as part of the housing as well as of the cottage industries schemes, it is of the first importance. There is nothing more necessary than to provide tribal houses with fire-proof roofs. These houses are sometimes built close together and fire can rapidly spread through an entire village. The present tendency to import corrugated iron or aluminium sheets is not altogether satisfactory.

In north-eastern India the supreme craft, both for utility and art, is weaving but unfortunately, in most other parts of tribal India this valuable industry has disappeared, partly because of the competition of mill-cloth in the bazaars and partly because the people themselves have built up taboos on its practice, possibly as a result of propaganda by the established Hindu and Muslim hand-weavers who wanted to obtain a monopoly for their products. It should, however, be possible to revive hand-weaving in some of the tribal areas and attempts are being made to do this in all the States.

If, however, this is really to succeed, exclusive attention should not be given to the introduction of the fly-shuttle loom. At present, attempts to revive or 'improve' weaving in the tribal areas are almost everywhere made through the introduction of this type of loom.

We feel that those responsible for Women's Welfare Centres require orientation to the tribal background even more than the ordinary Block Officials, and that it is essential that steps should be taken to ensure this. We also suggest that designers with some artistic gift should go into the matter of discovering things that are natural to the tribal people for use in embroidery.

We agree with the suggestion of Renuka Ray Committee that the present system of paying stipends to trainees should be replaced by a new system of paying wages, even from the very beginning. A new trainee need not be expected to earn a full wage on the basis of his output, even less on the basis of the quality of his goods.

To create correct psychological atmosphere, the same kind of method might be adopted as in schools. The actual institutions, where boys and girls are trained, should resemble, as far as possible, their own homes. A cottage industries centre, in fact, might very appropriately be built up as a model tribal village in which the buildings will be made entirely of local materials but more carefully constructed, with better ventilation, a better type of floor and roof (of wood, tiles or bamboo shinghing) and improved technique in the making of the walls, whether they be of mud or of woven bamboo. The workshops should be made in the same simple style, except that a blacksmithy should be made fire-proof. The hostels should be of the traditional dormitory pattern in areas where such institutions exist or be built like a large local house where they do not. If the boys and girls grow up in these simple surroundings, they are less likely to look on themselves as sahibs or memsahibs when they have finished their training. Their institution which presumably will be visited by their parents and freinds, will also set an example to the villagers (as to how a village) and its homes can be improved.

Another most important matter, which is often neglected, is to issue immediately the tools and equipment with which the trainees will carry on their craft at the completion of their training. It often happens that there is a long gap between the end of the training and the receipt of equipment and this tends to discourage the trainees. Sufficient raw materials, such as yarn, iron, wood and so on, should be ensured for a period of at least six months in order that they may make a good start. It would be a good thing too, whenever a batch of trainees finishes its course, if a sort of passing out parade could be held at which some senior officer of the area should be present and should distibute the tools and give a talk about carrying on the work.

We gather that it is far from easy on the present rates of pay to obtain craft instructors who will be willing to travel from village to village and to live with the people.

There are many ways by which unncessary extravagance on cottage industries can be prevented.

We need not emphasise the importance of production and indeed, it has already been suggested that instead of speaking of training-*cum*-production centres we should call them production-*cum*-training centres. All the training should be organised with a view to the manufacture of beautiful, useful or saleable goods. There should be a few regular employees who would organise production to meet demands and all overhead charges should be taken into account in settling the price. These production units should be self-sufficient and profitable within a few years and it should be regarded as a serious failure if this does not happen. In this way the training programme may become more realistic. We recommend that 50 per cent of the amount allotted for Rural Arts and Crafts should be reserved for the production side. We should not, however, speak of production centres, for this implies that everybody must come to work in some sort of building. We should rather speak of production units, through which men and women living in their own homes will be encouraged to produce more through the supply of raw materials and marketing organisations.

Rural Housing And Colonies

The large sum of two-and-a-half lakhs has been allotted for rural housing. In some States a substantial proportion of this has been used for the erection of buildings for the staff. The remainder is spent or will be spent on the erection or improvement of so-called model houses for the tribal people.

This construction programme precedes the economic prosperity, uproots the old rural architecture, and divides the community socially and psychologically.

It will be generally agreed that these points are sound and realistic. The Rural Housing programme does indeed depend far too much on the import of materials from outside.

It is desirable to improve accommdation for animals, but it is surely a little expensive to put up pigsties at Rs. 750 a time!

Aesthetically these houses generally do not fit into the picture and where there are only one or two of them in a village they stand out, ugly and privileged, among the rest.

There seems to have been little research into the kind of houses that the tribal people like the lay-out of their villages or the economics of the business. Houses in the Multipurpose Blocks vary enormously from the leaf-huts of the Birhors or the tumble-down sheds of the poorer section of the population everywhere, to the very good houses of the more enterprising.

It is, therefore, important to help the poorer people to build better houses but it is equally important to ensure that these are of a type with which they are familiar.

A serious weakness in a normal tribal house is the lack of windows. The people generally claim that this keeps the houses cool in summer and warm in winter; that it keeps out mosquitoes and other stinging insects; that it prevents evil spirits getting in; and that since the walls rarely go right up to the roof they do in fact get sufficient ventilation. Furthermore, we must not think of a tribal house as if it was a kind of building where a great deal of light is required.

We feel that it is important that wherever the local style of building is to raise the houses on poles this should be followed and that in other places the plinth of the house should always be fairly high to protect from damp.

The first thing is to recognise that the improvement of rural housing is an educational, and not a constructional, programme.

For improving the existing houses, the first thing to do is to provide a fire-proof roof. A system of double roofing will ensure ventilation and carry off the smoke.

Priority, in short, should be given to the improvement of existing houses. New houses need only be provided under special circumstances.

The Renuka Ray Committee considers that housing for tribals 'need not receive a high priority in the schemes for tribal development, and envisages only three situations in which it will be required.' These are as follows:

(a) When tribals carrying on jhuming cultivation are allotted land for permanent settlement;

(b) When nomadic tribes have to be settled permanently at a particular place; and

(c) When tribals have been deprived of their house-sites, houses and land on account of the construction of dams, industrial plants or other development projects.

If the above suggestions are accepted, the housing programme will apply only to the very poorest and weakest section of the population. In view of this, it will be necessary to revise considerably the existing rules, which require either some sort of security or some kind of contribution from the beneficiaries. The poorest people will not be able to provide either. We suggest, therefore, that in such cases both security and contribution should be waived, that the amount of assistance in each case should be greatly reduced in order to spread the benefits over a wider field, that timber and bamboo should be made available without any restrictions, that the people should do the work themselves and be permitted to build where they like and not according to any type-plan whatever either for the architecture of the house or the lay-out of the village, and that there should be a careful system of education and propaganda to help them to build better houses on their own lines which would, at first at least, only introduce a few elementary improvements and gradually grow, by an organic evolution, into ideal tribal homes.

One great difficulty in the improvement of housing along traditional or indeed on any lines arises from the rules imposed by the Forest Departments with regard to cutting timber. This is normally permitted for building one's own house but, as in the case of materials needed for cottage industries, there is often a rule that the villager must obtain a permit or pass to do so (even though he may not have to pay for it) and generally a forest official goes to decide which tree or trees may be cut. This involves considerable delay and constant irritation to the tribal people who not only have to make long journeys to and from the forest offices but are even today, not always treated with much consideration when they arrive. They are kept waiting for long periods; perhaps the officer entitled to give passes is out on tour; and they have to go and come two or three times before they can get their passes. Sometimes they have to bribe the local forest guard or chowkidar before they can see the officer at all. This involves the people in a waste of time (and today if the development programmes are to succeed there is no time to waste for anybody) and expense and a psychological irritation which divides them from Government.

In any case, a great many trees are cut illegally and this is a bad thing, for it creates a sense of indifference to the law and antagonism to the Forest Department.

We suggest that these rules should be abrogated and that, if necessary, where this permission is abused, more stringent punishment should be awarded to defaulters. We feel, however, that provided the Forest Department and the people can achieve more friendly relations and can understand each other, this trouble may not arise at all.

The architecture and positioning of latrines is another matter of some importance. It is in a way rather ridiculous, when we consider the insanitary habits of people in the cities, to put up latrines at all in the hill and forest areas. Such latrines are rarely used and when they are used they soon become so insanitary and malodorous that the people do not go near them.

And further, in the layout of official quarters, schools and other institutions in the tribal villages, we have been constantly distressed by the geographical prominence given to the latrine. If latrines must be built far away from the buildings to ensure that the user gets thoroughly met when it rains, could they not somehow be concealed with bushes or placed at least where they will not be the most obvious feature in the landscape?

In a few Blocks, cement bathrooms are being erected. It is hard to see the necessity for these. For centuries the people have been bathing in the open without self-consciousness and to erect bathrooms, which are presumably intended to further a sense of modesty, is likely to have the opposite effect. It will make the people self-conscious about their bodies, which is undesirable, and may easily lead to the creation of class of Peeping Toms.

This is one of the many totally unnecessary schemes which confuse and overload our programmes and are due to local officials taking an urban approach to tribal problems.

We do not suggest that officials should live in tribal houses. It is necessary, in order to persuade officials to come to the Multipurpose Block areas, to make them comfortable but their general appearance should fit in with the surroundings. This is particularly true of houses for V. L. W.'s or others posted in interior villages away from a Block Headquarters. The style of house that is normally put up for them (and it is often the only building of the kind in a village) is inartistic and incongruous. Both from the aesthetic and social points of view it is important that this matter should be carefully considered.

We recommend that in future Blocks the allocation for buildings in headquarters should be reduced and that efforts should be made, wherever practicable, not only to adopt the general architectural pattern to harmonise with the rural scene but as far as possible to use local materials in construction. Tiles, where these are made, could be used for the roofs, and the walls and floors could be made of locally obtained wood. If this is done with imagination and skill, just and pleasant accommodation will be provided at lesser cost.

It is obviously important that officials should have good homes, but let them be homely where their tribal friends can feel at home.

A special aspect of the housing problem is the establishment of colonies; both by the Tribal Welfare and Development Departments and under the Block budgets.

Although there have been a few successsful colonies, these schemes do not, as the Renuka Ray Committee has pointed out, seem to have been successful in their object of settling the tribals.

There are instances of colonies habitable but lying unoccupied, for example, in Bigan Pandar in Keonjhar District, Orissa. There are also colonies which have been deserted wholly or partly, after the initial occupation. Again, there are colonies in which the houses have begun to fall either because they were very poorly constructed or because of neglience, for example, in the Adarshnagar and Sundarnagar colonies in the Banswara District, Rajasthan.

With a few exceptions, the colonies that have been established suffer from serious defects which account at least in part for their failure.

In the first place, the lay-out of the colonies is often unsuitable to the tribal areas. Most of the tribals are hill people and they like to have their houses on the side of hills and do not usually arrange them in their villages in geometrical patterns.

The architecture of the houses and the materials used are often not only far too expensive but inappropriate.

Then again, even when the land allotted to the people is scattered over a wide area the houses are all built close together in a colony. This is contrary to tribal custom, for the farmers naturally like to build their houses as near their land as possible.

We feel that, in view of the very considerable expense involved in setting up of a colony whether by the Tribal Welfare or the Development Departments, in view of the fact that it uproots the people and tears them away from surroundings to which they are tied by bonds of sentiment and religion, in view of the moral dangers implicit in artificially concentrating people together in this way, no more colonies should be opened for the time being, either by the Multipurpose Block Officials or by the Tribal Areas Departments in the various States.

Indebtedness And Cooperation

Indebtedness

We suggest:

Enactment of social legislation, and effective enforcement of it, to prevent money-lenders practising their profession among the tribals, at least in the Scheduled Areas. Various State Governments have taken legislative and executive measures to regulate money-lending and to provide relief to the indebted but they have not met with any measure of success and the money-lender continues to remain as powerful as ever. It now seems necessary that the Centre should examine the various types of legislation already in existence and prepare a model Act for enforcement by the States.

Effective legislation for the liquidation of tribal debts of more than three years' standing.

Effective machinery for conciliation and settlement even under the existing legislation.

Before these measures can be enforced, it is necessary to make a survey of the nature and extent of tribal indebtedness. The law should provide for an effective implementing agency. In case the effort for conciliation does not bear fruit, it will be necessary to provide legal aid to the tribals to face litigation, so that their poverty may not stand in the way of getting justice and their claims may not go by default.

An effective system of giving credit to the tribals, both for productive as well as non productive purposes.

Effective promotion of Social Education among the tribals to encourage thrift, to preserve their earnings through Small-scale Savings Societies, to look ahead. Women can be a powerful force to prevent their menfolk from extravagance.

We endorse the following recommendations of the Pachmarhi and Ranchi Seminars:—

'Before money-lenders can be removed from the scene, it will be necessary to provide an alternative source of credit. Government-sponsored credit institutions should be encouraged to give loans in suitable cases for unproductive purposes, such as marriage and funeral ceremonies. In particular, loans should specifically be made available for the purpose of redeeming old debts. Existing debts should be scaled down by the process of conciliation to a reasonable level (within the paying capacity of tribals); debts outstanding for three years or more may be made irredeemable.'

'The Reserve Bank of India may be requested to give loans to the Cooperative Societies of the tribal people who cannot by themselves alienate their lands.'

The problem of indebtedness will not be overcome unless an all-sided attack is made through legislative measures, administrative enforcement and the development of public opinion. This should be the responsibility of the development agencies and the Tribal Welfare Departments. It is imperative that the present vicious circle should be broken as soon as possible. It is also necessary to make further studies of the problem to determine other suitable measures for solving it. This should not mean any postponement of the implementation of the measures we have suggested, but should re-inforce them while simultaneous action is taken.

Cooperation

We endorse the following recommendations made by the Pachmarhi Seminar:—

A great deal of primary extension education work should precede the formation of Cooperative Societies.

Care should be taken to see that the rich or the influential sections of the people do not dominate the Cooperatives and monopolise their benefits.

'Service' Cooperatives should be formed as quickly

as possible so as to serve the largest number of tribal people. The Multipurpose Cooperatives already formed can serve the same purpose with slight modifications wherever needed.

The procedure for the advance of loans from these Cooperative Societies and the objects for which they are given should be suitably simplified and amended so that the tribal members can depend upon them and not have to look to the money-lenders.

The sale and marketing of the produce and supply of the tribal people's requirements at reasonable prices should receive special attention through Cooperative organisations.

Special concessions in the form of State participation in share capital, construction of godowns and provision of managerial staff is necessary.

Tribal Culture

For many of the tribal people have become so assimilated in the surrounding population and have lost so much of their own culture, language and art in the process that there is little to distinguish them from their neighbours. Yet a more careful enquiry will show, as it has shown in the Tamia Multipurpose Block, that even those tribes, which at first sight appear to have nothing of their own, have their own fine culture and way of looking at things. In particular, their psychology and the nature of their approach to people and problems is distinctive and nearly all of them retain a pride in their history, a desire to revive their own language, and a determination to preserve their own social customs.

It is, of course, difficult, if not impossible, to generalise about the tribes and this is, in fact, one of the difficulties of the Multipurpose Block Schemes.

It must be admitted, of course, that in many places tribal culture is in a state of decay. Contact with the outside world has tended to shake the people's faith in themselves. New religions have competed for their allegiance, new taboos have been introduced. There are many things in the development programmes which cannot easily be adjusted to the old way of life. Some bad things have disappeared, but many good and vitalising things are disappearing as well.

Tribal culture can be encouraged and developed firstly on the negative side by not doing anything that will discourage or destroy it. We are not to interfere, not to impose customs and ways of living that will make the people a second-rate copy of ourselves.

All Block Officials, including the V.L.W's should have careful briefing on the importance of tribal art and culture. They must learn to look for it and not to assume that it does not exist because it is not immediately evident.

Research

The Cultural Research Institutes

We recommend that the work of the Tribal or Cultural Research Institutes should be greatly intensified in a practical direction; that the publication of material should be accelerated; that the Development Departments should keep the research officers fully in the picture, consult them more frequently and at least consider what they say; and that they should be given their proper status as scientific bodies with freedom to express their views freely and dispassionately.

We suggest that every State with a large tribal population should have a Tribal Research Institute which should deal both with cultural and linguistic matters. These institutes might later be used, as in Ranchi, for giving orientation courses to development workers which should be very practical and to the point. Long-drawn schemes of academic research should not be taken up at the moment.

There is also need for some coordinating body, perhaps a cell in the Home Ministry, to give these institutes advice, generally supervise their work, and ensure proper coordination. This would also serve as a clearing house for information at the national level.

Publications

The recent seminars of field workers in the Multipurpose Blocks held at Ranchi and Pachmarhi, suggested the production of short booklets (of not more than 150 pages) on the different tribes. There are already a good number of monographs on the tribes of India and a large number of articles and papers in learned journals. Most of these are heavy and complicated, are out of print or were written very long ago and, even where they can be obtained, the ordinary field-worker may find them difficult to understand. There is a good deal of useful material in Census Reports and District Gazetteers but these are virtually inaccessible to officials in the interior. There is a need of well printed and well-illustrated, but simply written and very on-the-spot booklets about the tribes which can be of really practical use to officials.

Such booklets and other research material might be prepared by the following agencies :—

(1) The Indian Universities which have interested themselves in research of this kind, as for example, Saugar, Lucknow, Patna, Baroda, Gauhati and Delhi.

(2) The Tribal Research Institutes, the Bharatiya Lok Kala Mandal, the Rural Higher Education Institutes of Sriniketan, Udaipur, the Rajasthan Department of Research and the Tata Institute of Social Sciences in Bombay.

(3) Individual research scholars, whether from India or abroad, who are interested in cultural change.

There should be no lack of funds for this purpose, which might be obtained from the Research Programmes

Committee of the Planning Commission, the Ministry of Home Affairs, the Ministry of Information and Broadcasting (Publications Division), the Ministry of Community Development, which has its own budget for booklets of this kind, the States budgets or, in certain cases, the budgets of the Multipurpose Blocks.

The booklets might be prepared originally in English and then (if they are good enough) should be translated into Hindi, the regional language and, in some cases, into the tribal languages.

It has been suggested that these booklets should be divided into two parts. Part I might contain factual information dealing with the historical background, the environment (physical and economic), social relations, social customs and institutions, religious beliefs and practices, tribal law, systems of land tenure and so on, and Part II might deal with social, cultural and economic practices which could be related to the Community Development Programme with suggestions for suitable priorities, and a description of the results of contact with the outside world.

It is not only important to prepare new books; it is equally important to obtain existing books and to ensure that they are read. There is a very large body of literature about the Indian tribes but since, as we said, it is nearly all out of print, we suggest that it would be quicker and more practical to reprint some of the existing books and make them available to all officials dealing with the tribal areas which they describe then to depend on the production of new books which, to be quite realistic, may take several years to publish. Although some of these books are now not only out of print but out of date, the best of them could still prove of value even today. For example, the pioneer works of S. C. Roy on the Uraons, Birhors, Mundas and other tribes in Bihar would still be of considerable help in giving officials a background for their work and inspiring them to make their own enquiries. Even where customs and ideas have changed it will be an exciting and interesting task to compare the situation as outlined in the older books with what is happening now. There has been for some time past a proposal to reprint some of the older books on the tribes of Assam. There is a work by Playfair on the Garos which could surely be financed from the Damluk-Aga Block budget. The same thing could be done for Stack's book on the Mikirs from the Rongkhong budget and Gurdon's book on the Khasis out of the Mairang and Saipung-Darrang funds allotted for the purpose of research which so far have not been touched. There are similar books, parts of which at least might be reprinted, for most of the tribal people.

That this is necessary may be seen from the fact that not a single Extension Officer in the Mokhada-Talasari Block had read the useful book on the Warlis by Shri K. J. Save and no one in the Aheri Block was even aware of the existence of the late Sir W. V. Grigson's accounts of the Chanda tribals in the second edition of his Maria Gonds of Bastar and his Report on the Aboriginal Tribes of the Central Provinces.

Many of these older books fall into three sections, one dealing with the anthropological and social aspeets of the tribe, one with linguistics and the third containing a collection of folktales, It might simplify matters if, in reprinting, the section on folktales was omitted and printed as a separate book which could be used as supplementary reading material for schools. In addition, there are a very large number of tribal folktales already published in separate volumes. Most of these were recorded some time ago and many of them are probably now forgotten. They could be translated back into the local languages and would be greatly appreciated by the people. Selections from them could also be republished as books in English for the use of more advanced students.

Philology

Another very important subject of research is philology. Every State with a large tribal population, and especially where Multipurpose Blocks have been started, should have a trained linguist attached to it to study and encourage the local languages. Scholars in the Universities might be asked to 'adopt' a Block for this purpose and be paid an honorarium for doing so.

It will, of course, be impossible to preserve every little dialect and a beginning should be made with the most important tribal languages.

The work of the philologists, would be mainly of two kinds—first, the building up of a people's literature and secondly, the encouragement of officials in learning the tribal languages.

Learning The Tribal Languages

The Estimates Committee for 1958-59 of the Ministry of Home Affairs has recommended as follows :

'In order to understand the tribal problems in their proper perspective, the Committee consider it desirable that non-tribal officers and staff working in the Scheduled and Tribal Areas should learn the tribal languages. They suggest that Government may evolve a suitable scheme to encourage non-tribal officers and staff to learn the tribal languages.'

Yet although this matter has been emphasised over and over again at Conferences and in reports and directives, both from the Centre and the State Governments, it cannot be said that progress has been very encouraging. A great deal of fuss has been made about the difficulty of learning the tribal languages, but we should remember that the missionaries seem to have overcome the difficulty satisfactorily and it is indeed owing to their enthusiasm that many of these languages were first put down in writing through translations of the Bible, prayer-books and hymn-books. Even merchants have gone ahead of officials in learning these languages, for they know that by doing so they have a much better chance of extending their trade.

It is no excuse to say that the tribal languages have no script. They can be written down in Devanagri or in the regional or even roman script, if necessary.

In places, where Hindi or some regional language has become widely known, there is a particular danger in neglecting the tribal languages. There is an impression in such areas that there is no need for officials to learn them because they are able to carry on some sort of conversation with the people in the local lingua franca.

And very often, even where the men understand the regional language, the women do not, and women's programmes, of such vital importance, will not make real progress unless they are conducted in the tribal dialects.

But officials need a good deal of encouragement. They need guide-books of the same general kind as Victor Hugo's 'French Self-Taught' or other 'Easy Ways' of learning the European languages, which have been of help to generations of tourists. Such phrase-books, which could contain a skeleton grammar, a list of useful words and a number of phrases in common use arranged under suitable headings, would be of immense value to officials and social workers. At a later stage regular Grammars and Dictionaries should be prepared.

There are, in fact, a large number of books published during the last few decades on the various tribal languages. Many of these have been produced by missionaries and are practical hand-books to help their workers to learn the local language quickly. One such book is Canon G.S. Patwardhan's Manual of the Gondi Language as spoken in the Chanda district. There is another valuable book on Gondi as spoken in the Betul area by C.G.C. Trench and yet another on the Gondi of Bastar by A.N. Mitchell. Thus for one tribal language we have practical manuals available for three of its most important dialects, and the task of reprinting them might be taken up immediately. Problems of copyright would, of course, have to be solved but if the matter is pressed forward urgently, this should not take too long. We should not grudge the expense if we have to pay a certain amount of money for the purchase of copyright. But this does need to be done soon.

Money should also be made available for the starting of classes or to pay instructors who will watch officials both in Block Headquarters and in isolated villages.

The System Of Rewards

The giving of rewards to officials who can pass an examination in languages other than their own goes back to British times, the rewards being usually adjusted to the pay of the officer concerned. Proposals for the extending of such rewards in modern days have been made again and again but either nothing has been done or, where the rewards are given, they are, when applicable to the lower staff, so small as to give little encouragement.

At present there is great variety in the attitude of the different States to this subject.

The North-East Frontier Agency has laid down that there will be two exams., one a preliminary and the second of a higher standard which requires proficiency equal to that of an interpreter. The rewards for passing these examinations are as follows :

	For passing a Preliminary Examination	For attaining Interpreter's Standard
	Rs.	Rs.
Class I Officers	500	1,000
Class II Officers	350	650
Class III Officers	200	300

This system of rewards should be Standardised throughout the country and should be particularly generous to Grade III Officials. For it is the V.L.W., the Social Educational Organiser, as well as the doctors or the P.E.O. himself, none of whom are very highly paid and who thus can claim only a modest reward (in relation to their pay) when they pass an examination, who really matter from this point of view. They are the officials who are in real touch with the people and if they cannot express themselves freely it is impossible for them to get their message across. We suggest that, in the first place, wherever rewards are not given for passing an examination in the tribal languages, these should be instituted with any further delay. We further suggest that these rewards should not be linked to pay as hitherto but that they should be sufficiently substantial to encourage officials, even at the V.L.W. level, to take the matter up with enthusiasm. After all a Development Commissioner, who under the old scheme would earn a substantial reward, does not really need a tribal language nearly as much as a V.L.W. or S.E.O.

One of the greatest barriers to the learning of the tribal languages is not laziness or lack of interest, but is the sense of uncertainty that exists among all officers due to the constant transfers that are made. It is obviously unlikely that an officer will go to the trouble of learning a difficult language if he expects to be transferred elsewhere within six months or a year, and this seems to be perhaps the fundamental reason why so little progress has been made in this direction. That the present habit of constant transfers should come to an end, for once an officer knows that he has three or even five years to look forward to in any one lauguage area, he then has a real inducement, which is far more powerful than any monetary consideration, to study the local language.

Text-Books For Schools

Another very important matter is to prepare text-books in the local languages for schools. It has been laid down by Government of India that the mother tongue should be the medium of instruction in the primary stage. This will be impossible unless text-books are available. The text-books should also be illustrated by pictures which will be familiar to the tribal children. At present text-books prepared for urban children are being imported into the remotest tribal areas. Local folktales should be used instead of stories from the European or classical Indian tradition and these books should be brought into harmony with the rural and tribal scene. Within a few years over a hundred text-books in 13 different tribal languages have been produced by the NEFA Administration with a small staff, and if this is possible in NEFA, it should be possible anywhere.

The Block Surveys

We have observed that very little, if any, importance has been given to the study and survey of the social and economic conditions in the tribal villages. Wherever surveys have been conducted, they have been mainly confined to an examination of physical conditions. In most Blocks, some sort of survey was conducted in the pre-extension phase but no further systematic study was made when they were converted into Multipurpose Tribal Blocks.

The survey programme provides a mechanism which will enable the development workers to become sensitive to the special social and economic conditions of the tribal people, which are often so different to those elsewhere. It is important, therefore, that they should undergo this exercise of conducting the survey, first at the very beginning of the scheme, and thereafter by keeping the survey records uptodate from year to year. It is necessary for the Project Executive Officer to become aware of this important aspect of the programme and to get the survey conducted by all development workers, including the Extension Officers and the V.L.W.'s. Unless the P.E.O. becomes convinced of the importance of this, the programme is not likely to be built up on a suitably adjusted foundation.

The surveys can be of three types:

(a) A preliminary survey;
(b) A basic survey; and
(c) A specific survey.

The Preliminary Survey

The preliminary survey should, of course, be carried out by the P.E.O. and his staff at the very inception or even before the inception of a Block. It should be of an elementary character, rapidly conducted, to discover and to acquaint the Block Officials with the main features of the area in which they are to work. It should include: (a) figures of population and its distribution by age and sex; (b) the main characteristics of the physical environment with special attention to any obstacles to the development with of communications; (c) elementary data regarding the basic and supported economy of the villages; (d) existing living standards, (e) some information about the tribes and sub-tribes as well as the non-tribals living in the Block; and (f) the existing facilities for medical relief, education and welfare services. Even at this stage there should be an attempt to discover which is the most undeveloped part of the Block and where the poorest people are living.

The Basic Survey

As soon as possible after this preliminary survey there should be a basic survey which should also be carried out by the P.E.O. and his officials. The point of this is not to submit reports to Government but to serve as a kind of education or training which will enable the Block Officers to understand the difficulties of their area, the needs of their people and to allot priorities in their work. It should include some general information regarding the economy, social organisation, religion and daily life of the tribes. It should also study the general condition of the non-tribal population. It should obtain statistics for each family and its individual members in the village community. It should also take up such definite problems as the nature of the tribal arts and crafts and the possibility of developing them and finding a market for them. No cottage industries training centre should be started until this has been done. It should discover the possibilities of developing irrigation schemes; examine what kind of improved breeds of animals could be introduced, having regard to the elevation and climate; the possibilities of introducing cash crops, with reference to the nature of the soil, the rainfall and possible markets. Above all, it should make the staff sufficiently acquainted with the problems of communications so that their plans will be on a thoroughly realistic basis. This will involve a great deal more than mere paper-work, for the P.E.O. and his staff will have to tour throughout their entire area.

The Specific Survey

What we have called the specific survey should be the task of the Tribal Research Institutes, the Research Sections of the Universities or any other recognised research societies. It should go in detail into the question of indebtedness. It should study the people's food habits in relation to their food resources in order to discover ways of improving the standard of diet; the living conditions and problems of tribal children; the role of the younger generation in the development schemes; social problems that may affect the health and the morale of the community or which may interfere with its economic development. It should examine the land situation; how far forest rules can be adapted to tribal needs: the possibilities of improving tribal houses.

It is most important that the State Governments should try to make available to the Block workers any literature on the area and its tribal people which has already been published. It might be possible to get important sections of rare books cyclostyled and distributed to officials. Other books will, we hope, be reprinted.

In suggesting a series of surveys, it is not our intention to imply that the development programme should be delayed till they are completed. What is necessary is to recognise that the programme of survey is a continuous programme of understanding, both the tribals themselves and the work done among them and should, therefore, be integrally woven into the development programme. The nature of the survey conducted and the study made in the Multipurpose Tribal Blocks should be taken as a proof of the conviction, purposefulness and sincerity of the development workers in giving a tribal foundation to the development programme.

Methods Of Reporting

We suggest that there should be a section of every Annual Report in which the P.E.O.'s should attempt answers to the following questions:

(1) How many: (a) local, and (b) other tribal people are employed at different levels in your Block at present? What is their percentage in relation to the total number of staff at each level? Has there been any increase in the number employed during the past year? If the percentage is low, is there any special reason for it?

(2) How many members of your staff have passed a Language Examination in the past year? How many others have, at least, a working knowledge of the language which enables them to carry on a conversation on their own subject with the local people? How many have received rewards for proficiency in the language? How many are still unable to make themselves understood by the tribal people and unable to understand what they say? How many members of the Block staff have had orientation courses during the past year and what kind of courses did they attend? Has the result of this training made any appreciable difference to their work?

(3) What social education activities have been carried on and what sort of success have they really had? If a library, for example, has been opened, how many: (a) officials, and (b) local people use it? What kind of books and magazines do they prefer? Do audio-visual activities have any real effect? Which aspects of this programme have the greatest appeal? What kind of films have been selected? Has any attempt been made to ensure that these will appeal to the tribal people or have any relevance to their needs? Do the officers supervising film-shows explain the films properly before-hand and discuss their message with the people afterwards? How far is the propaganda carried on by the Block Officials having any real impact on the outlook of the people?

(4) What use is being made of tribal institutions, such as boys' dormitories or tribal councils, for development purposes? Are the indigenous tribal institutions decaying or has there been any progress in reviving them?

(5) Are money-lenders as active as they were last year? How are the Block Officers attempting to solve the problem of indebtedness? Is local economy developing in a way that is lessening the burden of indebtedness?

(6) Do the people show signs of becoming more and more dependent on Government help? Are they losing their self-reliance or are they beginning to show an independent spirit and really taking up the task of self-development even if they are not paid to do so? How far are you finding real cooperation from other Departments of Government?

(7) How far have the people themselves contributed actual ideas and suggestions in the past year that you have been able to include in the Block programme? Do you feel that they are satisfied with what is being done? Have they made any criticisms and if so, what are they? What signs are there that a genuine people's movement is coming into being in the Block area? Do the tribal members of the Block Advisory Committees play any significant role in their deliberations?

(8) Have you discovered in the past year any urgent needs of a new kind that might be dealt with for the benefit of the people?

(9) Has there been any real progress in reviving the arts and crafts of the people? Has the quality, as apart from the quantity, of their products improved during the last year? Are the people dancing and singing more, or less, than formerly? Have there been any obvious changes in the customs and conduct of the people? Are they observing their religious festivals in relation to agricultural and other practices or are these beginning to die out? Have any new food taboos been introduced?

(10) Where new agricultural methods have been introduced, are the people happy about them? Or, do they still desire to continue their traditional shifting cultivation where this exists? Have forest cooperatives been started and if so, how are they progressing? Are there any non-tribal members and if so, what positions do they hold?

(11) Where there are Statutory Panchayats, are the tribal people adequately represented and in general, how

are they working ? How many of the Sir Panchas are: (a) tribal, (b) non-tribal ?

(12) What is the morale of the officials in the Block ? Do they want to be transferred elsewhere or have they now begun to settle down and feel enthusiastic about their work ? What are their relations today with the local people and has there been any improvement during the past year ?

(12) What evidence is there that today the people are better fed, enjoy a richer cultural life and are happier than when the Block started ?

We may, of course, be accused of inconsistency, for we have stressed the importance of regular surveys and the submission of self-evaluation reports outlined in this chapter. What we have suggested, however, is not ordinary paper-work. What we are anxious to ensure is that there should be a continuous process of self-education which will sensitise members of the Block staff to the tribal situation and will progressively acquaint them with the people's ideals and aspirations.

The Tribal Councils

We recommend :

That in all homogeneous tribal areas, where the new Panchayat Acts have not been introduced, taking advantage of the provisions in these Acts (excepting Bombay) whereby the Governor can exempt a specified area or areas from the operation of the Panchayat Acts, they should not be introduced, but a serious attempt should be made to use the existing machinery instead.

If, however, the Panchayat Acts have been introduced in the tribal areas of any State, it is a matter for consideration whether the Scheduled Areas should not be exempted from their operation by virtue of the provision in the Act concerned. In the State of Bombay, recourse could be taken to para 5 of the Fifth Schedule of the Constitution for this purpose.

The above action may be taken in consultation with the Tribal Advisory Council constituted in each State.

In each tribal village, which is inhabited by people of one tribe, the existing machinery for settling disputes and administering the affairs of the village should be organised, in the first instance, into a simple Village Council, care being taken that at least one member of every clan in the village is represented. The Chairman should be the traditional headman of the village and if custom so directs the village priests or other traditional elders should also be represented.

Where there are members of more than one tribe in a village the same policy may be followed but it should be ensured that at least one member of each tribe should be represented.

Tribal group councils should be formed for groups of 10 to 15 villages and one representative should be chosen by each village as a member of the larger body. These simple councils should not be by formal election but should consist of the elders who have traditionally managed village affairs. The Chairman should be the leading Chief or Headman.

In the event of any dispute, the Chairman of the Council should be nominated by the Deputy Commissioner Collector.

In view of the fact that in many places the machinery for judicial and administrative work in tribal villages has fallen into disrepair, powers should be given to these Councils on a progressive basis. They may first be given various aspects of development work and the managing of ordinary or forest cooperatives. and they should be encouraged to settle village and inter-village disputes without having recourse to the ordinary courts.

We further suggest that as these Councils show their capacity for managing their own affairs they should be given more and more of the powers enumerated in the various Panchayat Acts until finally they can take over all their functions.

Wherever a Tribal Council exists at present in an organised form it should be recognised immediately; where, however, it still has to be revived and developed, the Deputy Commissioner on the advice of the P.E.O. should recommend its recognition when he is satisfied that it is ready to take over statutory powers.

In areas where the tribal population is in a minority and the population is a mixed one, it is evident that any Tribal Council that may exist cannot be vested with the powers of the Statutory Panchayats so far as they affect the non-tribal population. In such areas, if a village Panchayat is to be instituted, provision should be made to ensure that a fair proportion of the members is from the tribal groups. In areas where, although the tribals are in a majority, there is a substantial proportion of non-tribals, or in areas where the State Government feels that it would be difficult to abrogate the provisions of the State Acts that may have already been enforced, steps should be taken to ensure that the Panchayats recognise in there membership the constitution of the villages, and the Sir Panch in such cases should be a tribal to be nominated by the Deputy Commissioner.

The Place Of Non-Official Agencies

It has been widely recognised that specialised welfare services are among the most important characteristics of a Welfare State. In a democratic set-up the contribution of voluntary effort has been responsible in no small measure towards achieving this objective. A democracy working for social ends has to be broad-based on the willing assent of the people and not merely on the sanctions behind the administrative set up of the State. The willing corporation of the whole population backed by strong public opinion has, therefore, constituted the principal force and sanction behind all plan programmes,

Implementation of welfare schemes by non-official agencies which enlist public cooperation will lead to all citizens acquiring a significant awareness and sense of partnership in the fulfilment of plan objectives. As a Report of the Congress Planning Committee has said: 'It is necessary in a democratic framework that a large measure of the constructive activity of the nation is done under non-official auspices. These activities can satisfy the urge of the normal human being to be of some use to the community in his spare time and give some benefit of his special ability to those who are in need of it. These activities can also become the training ground of social service workers on a mass scale.'

'We feel that such organisations should receive all encouragement. The Social Welfare Board is doing its best in this direction. Care should be taken that their character as voluntary organisations is not impaired in the process. It is possible to meet the deficiencies of training facilities for the voluntary and salaried personnel of these agencies and also to make some arrangement for coordination of their administration and accounting functions. It is important, however, to give them a turn in the direction of the fulfilment of social objectives and especially in the case of those where they come in contact with those who have no work or capacity for work to give them a bias in the direction of producing goods and services'.

On the question of official contributions to non-official organisations, our Committee is generally in agreement that a measure of Government help by way of subsidy is essential for their growth and development but, however anxious we may be to promote non-official effort, the initiative and enthusiasm of these agencies should not be retarded by making over-generous grants and reducing too far their own duty to help themselves. When an institution is not able to find even a very small percentage, say five per cent or 10 per cent of the amount that it spends, it can hardly be supposed to have any hold on the sympathy of the public to satisfy them that they are necessary. If they are only spending authorities, the need for this will disappear and demoralisation may set in. An institution is entitled to live so long as the people want it to do so. We feel, therefore, that too great dependence on Government will tend to weaken the initiative of the voluntary organisations.

We recognise, however, that public contributions to non-official effort are dwindling for various reasons. We feel that non-official organisations which are implementing certain programmes such as Ashram Schools or Forest Labour Cooperative Societies as agencies of Government should receive the total cost of the schemes for non-recurring items, their own contribution taking the form of supervision and providing trained workers who have knowledge and enthusiasm.

Government should also ensure that the various non-official organisations should avoid duplication of activities not only as amongst themselves but also with those undertaken by Government in the same area. To achieve this, the scope of work of each non-official organisation and its field of activity should be clearly defined in an integrated and phased programme carefully planned in advance. Government should also ensure that an adequate accounting staff is provided to each of these organisations for the proper maintenance of accounts, which should be perodically audited by Government auditors. Without disturbing the continuity of the programmes, non-official organisations should be assured well in advance of the funds that will be made available so that they can assess the scope of the work that they can undertake.

Assessment Of The Present Situation

It is difficult to assess a fluid situation. We have figures of expenditure under the different heads of the Schematic Budget up to the end of September 1959, but it will not be fair to the Block officials to judge them by these, for there is little doubt that the picture is changing rapidly.

In their 48th Report for 1958-59, the Estimates Committee of Parliament commented adversely on this and pointed out that there was no justification for financing a Block, in which only a small percentage was tribal, from the funds earmarked for the Special Multipurpose Tribal Blocks, for this was bound to mean that the scheme would primarily benefit the non-tribals rather than the tribals. Moreover, there are still large underdeveloped areas with strong concentrations of tribals that have not been covered, and the Multipurpose Blocks should have been opened in them instead of in places with mixed populations or in areas with a low percentage of tribal people. Moreover, these Blocks are financed out of the grants made available to the State Governments by the Government of India under Article 275 of the Constitution, wherein it is specified that the money shall be earmarked specifically for the development of the Scheduled or Tribal Areas or for the welfare of the Scheduled Tribes.

We recommend that while opening future Blocks the location of their headquarters should invariably be in the heart and not on the outskirts of the area to enable the tribal people to get the maximum benefit of the programme.

The Schematic Budget has, in practice, proved an obstacle to the adaptation of the programme to urgent tribal needs. Although the State Governments have been empowered to transfer funds from one head to another within the same Block in any manner they consider necessary to meet local requirements, this power has not been used with sufficient imagination and knowledge. There are also rules which prevent, for example, any transfer of funds from certain subjects such as Rural Arts and Crafts, though this has now been rather grudgingly allowed. As the Renuka Ray Committee says, these powers have not been used freely or appropriately by the State Governments, the Schematic Budget tends to set a rigid pattern, which results in lopsided expenditure. Even though the PEO's have been told again and again that they should be flexible in their approach, what we may call a psychological paralysis has been created by the very existence of a 'Schematic' budget.

Among the villagers themselves, in the experience of both the Renuka Ray Committee and our own, Agriculture, Education and Public Health have rated very high in the scale of preference and it has been found that educational services have been utilised by 59.2 per cent, public health by 57.6 per cent and agriculture by 50 per cent. Rural Housing and Rural Arts and Crafts take the lowest place, being only 2.9 per cent and 0.36 per cent in the order of utilisation.

The Future Of The Special Tribal Blocks

We recommed that those Blocks which have spent their 27 lakhs in time should receive five lakhs of rupees for Phase II from the Home Ministry in addition to the five lakhs they will receive from the C. D. Ministry for this period. Otherwise, the sudden drying up of financial support may create serious problems, for the simple tribal people will not understand the situation. This money should, of course, be used to extend and complete the existing schemes and not be used to start new ones. Those Blocks which cannot spend their alloocation in time may receive for Phase II the extra five lakhs when they have used up the money given to them for Phase I and the period for spending this additional money may be similarly extended.

With regard to the opening of Special Tribal Blocks in the Third Five Year Plan period, we feel that the present experiment, although it suffers from the defects of all pilot projects, has been sufficiently successful to justify its extension. There may, however, be various modifications.

We feel that, in the first place, there has been a little too much money to be used wisely and profitably within five years, at least in the more inaccessible and undeveloped Blocks, which are of course the very areas we most want to help.

We suggest, therefore, that the Home Ministry's contribution to each of the new Special Tribal Blocks to be opened in the Third Five-Year Plan period should be reduced from 15 lakhs to 10 lakhs, in addition, of course, to the 12 lakhs which will be contributed by the Ministry of Community Development. We further recommend that in Phase II of these Blocks the Home Ministry should contribute five lakhs in addition to the five lakhs which we hope will be provided by the Ministry of Community Development. We expect that the Block authorities will be able to spend usefully the reduced sum of 22 lakhs of rupees within the five-year period and that it will not be necessary to extend it as is being done at present. We must recognise, however, that development in the tribal areas is going to take a long time and we earnestly hope that some special assistance will continue to be given for the Special Tribal Block areas for a period of 15 to 20 years.

We further suggest that development should be equal throughout the whole of tribal India. The entire area will be covered by C. D. Blocks by 1963 and this scheme will apply not only to the Scheduled and Tribal Areas but to all areas. In the Scheduled and Tribal Areas alone there are still 72.5 lakhs of tribal people who have not been covered by the Multipurpose Tribal Blocks scheme, but we do not see any reason why it should in future be confined only to the Scheduled and Tribal Areas. Even at present nine of the Multipurpose Tribal Blocks are outside these special areas. This will mean that there will be a large number of Blocks with predominantly tribal populations covered in Third Five-Year Plan.

Let us, for the sake of argument estimate that about 300 Special Tribal Blocks will be required to cover all the predominantly tribal areas. We suggest that if each of these Blocks receives from the Home Ministry 10 lakhs of rupees instead of 15 lakhs, it will be possible to spread the benefits of intensive development over all of them. Instead of giving 15 lakhs to each of, say, 100 Special Tribal Blocks, the Home Ministry might give 10 lakhs to each of 300 new Blocks. This will mean an expenditure (above the C. D. Ministry's contribution) during the Third Five-Year Plan of Rs. 30 crores, which is surely not too much to meet a problem of such magnitude.

We recommend that these new Blocks should not be confined to the Scheduled and Tribal Areas but should cover areas, wherever there is a tribal population of 55 per cent of the total, anywhere in India, provided the overall coverage for each Block is not more than 25,000 individuals in an area of 200 square miles.

We suggest elsewhere that funds available under the Education programme should be administered by the Education Departments of the States and we hope that sufficient funds will be available from other channels to further schemes for Education in the Block areas. At present the amount allocated under the schematic budget for Education is more a token grant than anything else and we feel that it would be better if a special provision is made outside the Block budget for this subject. It will also be more effective if Education is handled by a single agency.

We consider, however, that if this is to be done and

this large sum of money allotted, certain conditions must be fulfilled.

First and foremost, the State Governments should take the whole matter of developing their tribal areas much more seriously. They should ensure that planning is done well in advance and sanctions issued expeditiously. They should insist that all Departments should cooperate generously and enthusiastically with the P.E.O.'s in implementing the Special Block plans. They must realise that money is of little use unless it is made usable.

Block officials should be chosen and appointed at least six months before the formal opening of a Block and they should spend their time in surveying the area, learning the language and assessing priorities for development.

State Governments should not transfer any official who has been so appointed and trained, unless he proves a failure, for at least three years. No official, at any level, should be posted to a tribal area as a punishment; in fact, the best officials (including members of the I.A.S. and P.C.S.) should as a matter of routine, be appointed as part of their general training, for at least a year.

The State Governments should follow the suggestions made with regard to both the area and the population of the Blocks to be opened.

There should be a really serious attempt to relate the programmes and the way of doing things to the tribal background.

We suggest that in future the designation of the Special Multipurpose Tribal Blocks might be changed. It is too elaborate and after all every Block in the country is a multipurpose one. These Special Blocks only differ in having more money to spend and a small additional staff. They are, in fact, no more multipurpose than any others. We suggest that they should be called in future Special Tribal Blocks, which should be sufficient, for this is exactly what they are.

We feel that a Project Officer ought to spend at least 20 days a month outside his headquarters and that he should not confine himself to visiting villages which can be reached by road. There is a tendency for the officials at headquarters to dash out into the villages in the early morning and to return the same night. They will not really come to know their people or have any real impact upon them unless they live with them, sit with them in the evenings and share their life to some extent. It is specially necessary for officials to meet the people in the evenings for they are often so busy during the day that they either do not come to meet officials at all or, if they do, they have a sense of grievance that their work has been interrupted.

We suggest, therefore, that arrangements should be made to equip every Block with a number of good bullock-carts with tyre-wheels, ball bearings and so on and provide also a number of small tents. Such bullock-carts will be able to reach many places inaccessible to ordinary motor transport. Where this is impracticable we suggest that ponies should be provided and for shorter visits there should be a number of bicycles available. Payment for these things should be suitably provided.

We are not in favour of establishing any kind of means test to determine which of the people most deserve economic benefit. In the first place, any kind of survey of this kind will take a long time and it is unlikely that the investigators will discover the truth. In the second place, such enquiries may discourage the people from developing their fields or from building better houses. In some areas we have found that through fear of increased taxation the tribals are unwilling to improve their fields, for there is a deep and almost ineradicable objection among them to paying out money. They prefer to have a poor crop on which they will not have to pay anything to getting a better one which may involve payment of some sort of additional tax. Even a well-to-do person feels a certain nervous tremor when he is presented with a Wealth Tax form, and the simple tribal people are deeply suspicious of any attempt to assess their economic condition.

Epilogue

We agree that we should 'hasten slowly', advance with caution, give the tribes a breathing-space to adapt themselves to the new world. Whatever we do, that world will come upon them and they must be ready for it. Hunger, disease, exploitation, ignorance, isolation are evils whose cure cannot be delayed; they must be treated rapidly and efficiently.

We believe that in the programme of the Special Tribal Blocks, if it is planned wisely and implemented sincerely, India has an effective instrument to save her tribal people from poverty and fear, and develop them along the lines of their own genious.

COMMITTEE ON CALCUTTA DOCK WORKERS (REGULATION OF EMPLOYMENT) SCHEME, 1956, 1959—REPORT

Delhi, Manager of Publications, 1959. 64p.

Single Member Committee : Shri R.L. Mehta.

APPOINTMENT

Committee on Calcutta Dock Workers (Regulation of Employment) Scheme, 1956, was constituted under the Ministry of Labour and Employment vide Government of India's letter No. Fac. 175 (59)/59, dated May 9, 1959.

TERMS OF REFERENCE

(i) To review the working of the Calcutta Dock Workers (Regulation of Employment) Scheme, 1956;

(ii) To examine in particular the complaints received from different quarters about the administration of the Scheme; and

(iii) To make such recommendations to Government as the Committee may deem fit.

CONTENTS

Introductory; the Origin and Nature of Scheme; the Functioning of the Dock Labour Board; the Administrative Body; Miscellaneous Complaints; Conclusions; A Summary of Conclusions and Recommendations; Appendices I to III.

RECOMMENDATIONS

In order to encourage the development of an atmosphere of consultation rather than of bargaining the present practice of deciding all matters that come up before the Dock Labour Board by vote should be given up. Instead solutions should be hammered out by discussion. If this means restricting the activities of the Board to matters which can be made common ground the price is worth paying if the Board is to mature into a positive force for curing the ills of the docks industry in Calcutta. Proceedings should record only decisions and not discussions.

Its many Committees and Sub-Committees, of which there are more than a dozen should be replaced by one general purposes Committee on the Bombay model. All controversial and contentions matters should be referred to this Committee.

In the move away from the present antagonism between the stevedores and the dock labour towards a better understanding and consequently better working of the Board the employers should give the lead. If they do so, they will find labour meeting them half way.

The decision of the Board to reimburse the stevedores the expenditure incurred by them on leave, provident fund contributions and other benefits in respect of monthly workers goes against the grain of the Scheme and is one of the causes of financial difficulties in which the Board finds itself today. This reimbursement should stop forthwith. All financial responsibility in respect of monthly workers is that of the employers and they should discharge it.

The rate of levy has fluctuated far too suddenly and sharply in the past. The Board should make long-term plans regarding its income and with the experience it has so far gained arrive at a figure which, with minor adjustments, should hold the field over a fairly long period, balance the annual budget and leave a safe margin for the rainy day. For this purpose, a Stabilisation Fund should also be built up.

The practice of making provisional payments to workers should stop at once. These payments always start as a temporary measure to tide over a crisis and then continue indefinitely and the state of crisis is perpetuated. This puts a premium on delays and inefficiency, in the end making for more work, more delays and therefore more crisis and more provisional payments. The Calcutta Dock Labour Board at the moment is in the grip of such a vicious circle which must be broken at once.

The wrong decision of the Board to take over the statutory responsibility of employers for payment of compensation to workers for injuries sustained in the course of employment has cost it over four-and-a-half lakhs during the last three years. The Board must evolve a machinery to recover this amount as soon as possible and for the future insist on this responsibility being discharged by employers.

Interim dearness allowance of Rs. five p.m. paid to workers in pursuance of the interim recommendation of the Second Pay Commission is part of wages. Under the scheme wages are payable by empolyers. It was wrong of the Board to agree to pay this amount to workers even temporarily. The Board is still paying it at a cost of Rs. 50,000 per month. The Board must forthwith transfer this responsibility to employers to whom it belongs.

The Boards has not yet created the Dock Workers Welfare Fund as required by the Scheme. This Fund has to be built up with contributions from employers. Instead, in deference to the wishes of the employers that the contributions should come from the levy which they can recover from the shipping companies, the Board has agreed to set apart about Rs. Seven-and-a-half lakhs from the levy for welfare work. This is against the provisions of the Scheme; it inflates the levy and favours employers at the cost of the shipping companies and is not in the interest of traffic in the port of Calcutta. The Board should take early steps to build up a Welfare Fund with contributions from employers outside the levy.

Most workers carry much heavier loans and advances than what the rules permit and what their repaying capacity warrants. The total amount outstanding on August 1, 1959, was nearly Rs. seven lakhs Steps should be taken to recover this amount as soon as possible and future loans and advances should be regulated stringently. One way of doing this is to restrict them to loans permissible under the provident Fund Rules as in Bombay. For this the Provident Fund Rules will have to be finalised as soon as possible. The average monthly expenditure for operating the Loan Fund and advances is about Rs. 3,000. The average monthly disbursement of loans and advances is Rs. 30,000 and Rs. 1,10,000 respectively.

The Dock Labour Board has been balancing its budget by raising overdrafts since 1957. The amount overdrawn stood at Rs. 4,49,106 on July 11, 1959. This is mainly because of the "extra-curricular activities" undertaken by the Board do not leave it enough money to discharge its statutory responsibilities like payment of wages to workers. While borrowing for revenue expenditure is wrong, borrowing against securities some of them purchased with provident fund accumulations of workers and office staff is a crime. So is mortgaging of securities bought with money earmarked for capital expenditure. The Culcutta Board has indulged in all these irregularities. Bombay has no overdraft account and Bombay does not oblige employers by taking over their responsibilities. The Board should close the overdraft account as soon as possible and learn to live within its means. If they were not adequate the levy may be increased.

The Power-Samas machine was hired without taking such precautions as a person of ordinary prudence would normally take. By the time the two-years agreement for its hire is over which will be next month, this experiment will have cost the Board nearly Rs. one lakh. The machine has so far served no useful purpose and Rs. one lakh may be regarded as one of the many instances of infructious expenditure incurred by the Board.

Other instances involving avoidable waste are the hospital building completed at a cost of Rs. six-and a-half lakhs in February 1959, and still lying unused, the appointment of Messrs Beacons Limited, efficiency experts in 1957 to improve the efficiency of the Board at a cost of Rs. 15,000 and not giving effect to their recommendations to this day. Forethought, planning and coordination would have given better results in both these instances.

Contrary to clause 7(4) of the Scheme, which requires the Board to submit an annual report to Government together with an audited balance sheet, no report has yet been submitted for 1957-58 or 1956-57 or even 1955-56. This calls for serious attention.

The Board's accounts for the last three years have not yet been written up. The arrangement, it has made with its auditors—M/s. Basu & Co.—to prepare them on a remuneration of about Rs. 40,000, is most extraordinary, to say the least. This expenditure cannot be justified.

The scheme should be amended to specify dates for the submission of annual budget, the yearly report and the final accounts by the Board to Government.

The staff under the Board is in excess of requirements. No proposals for further increase should be entertained. Periodic or localised rush of work can be met by adjustments within the existing staff.

The Administrative Body is very tardy in implementing the Board's decisions and it does not seem to have ever been taken to task for this neglect.

The Board's record in welfare work is extremely poor. No houses for workers have yet been put up. The dockers have no canteen. The call stands are small and untidy. The booking counters are too few for the requirements of all the workers. Other creature comforts are either missing or unsatisfactory—drinking water does not always run in the taps, nor does flushing water in the latrines and the urinals.

Accumulations in respect of provident fund of workers and staff are still merged with the General Fund of the Board which is irregular. A sum of 5,17,000 in respect of workers' contribution alone was still in the General Fund on July 1, 1959. Immediate steps should be taken to transfer this amount to the workers' Provident Fund account. To manage this fund and the Staff Provident Fund, Boards of Trustees should be appointed as soon as possible.

There is no control on the register of workers. In the beginning, far too many persons were on it. Since then no systematic assessment of anticipated labour requirements has been made. This should be done periodically.

The number of registered tally clerks is so much in excess of requirements as to deny them a proper livelihood without the aid of minimum guarantee and attendance allowance which accounts for so high a levy as 190 per cent on tally clerks. This untenable position might be set right. The strength of tally clerks should not be more than one-twentieth of the total register of workers. Some tally clerks are not qualified for the job. They bring a bad name to all. Many ships therefore refuse their services.

The Employers on the Administrative Body are averse to undertaking any expenditure which they cannot pass on to the shipping companies. If employer-employee relations are to improve in the docks in Calcutta the stevedores should be prepared to do for their employees what a private employer does voluntarily as well as in accordance with the requirements of law.

The Administrative Body in Calcutta does not seem to have accepted the Scheme in the proper spirit. It still regards it as an imposition and takes an extremely narrow view of its functions. There are yet no signs that it will in the near future create the necessary goodwill for itself which is essential for the success of the Scheme.

Among its statutory functions it has not discharged any successfully, not even such elementary and routine responsibilities as to ensure :

(i) That casual vacancies are filled by leave reserve workers by rotational bookings;

(ii) That a worker does not wait at the call stand for more than an hour;

(iii) That normally no "pool" worker is employed in consecutive shifts;

(iv) That the "pool" workers receive payments promptly and correctly; and

(v) That the accounts regarding the cost of running the Scheme are maintained properly and submitted regularly to the Dock Labour Board together with an annual report and an auditor's balance sheet.

Individual system of booking should be introduced as in Bombay, instead of the present system of booking by gangs. This will not only prevent "ghosts" from drawing attendance allowance and/or taking bookings but also help the Administrative Body in filling up casual vacancies from amongst workers who are on attendance allowance and ensure equal opportunities for all and enable the Administrative Body to save on attendance allowance and minimum guarantee.

The provisions of Clause 37(4)(b) regarding the objections of pool workers to accept any employment in connection with dock work should be enforced.

Casual vacancies should be filled by the Administrative Body and not by Sirdars and Clause 30(2) of the Scheme be amended on the lines of the corresponding provision in the Bombay Scheme.

At present there are six rates of wages for nine workmen in a gang. This results in multiplicity of accounts which can be avoided by standardising their wages as in Bombay where there are only two rates of wages, one for all senior workers and the other for all junior workers.

Timings for bookings should be changed. Bookings for the morning shift which begins at 6.30 A.M. should start at 5.30 A.M. Booking for the afternoon and night shifts should be done in the afternoon. This will solve many difficulties. At present booking for the morning shift is done the previous evening. During the intervening period there is often re-shuffling of the vessels programme. This results in a large number of workmen being sent back on disappointment money. Sometimes, quite a few workmen who accept booking the previous evening, for various reasons, do not turn up the next morning, thus creating problems on the work-spot. It is therefore essential that there is as little as possible time lag between the booking and the commencement of work.

A separate lot of workmen should be earmarked for the day-shift booking and for the after noon and night shifts booking. There should be change-shift every fortnight.

Timings for placing indents for labour by employers should be so fixed that there is enough time for the booking staff to make allocation of labour. These times should be strictly adhered to.

The Administrative Body should send bills for wages to employers on the basis of allocations made by the booking section and not on the basis of the returns sent by employers. These wage bills should be made periodically, either weekly or after every 10 days. Then there should be one consolidated bill for all categories of workmen allocated, and should include levy and all other charges due to the Dock Labour Board. These bills must be paid within three to four days without any deductions. There should be no relaxation in this rule. If employers fail to pay their dues inspite of notice, the supply of labour to them should be immediately cut off as envisaged in Clause 52(6).

To ensure that in cases of default in payment by employers the Administrative Body has enough funds to fall back upon. The Administrative Body should insist on employers making adequate deposits as securities. These deposits should be reviewed every quarter to see that they cover the bills for the labour drawn.

The wage books should be revised along the Bombay model. They should be written up from day-to-day in accordance with allocations made and reconciled shift-wise and period-wise. The amounts due to workmen should agree with the amount billed to employers.

At present the Administrative Body makes *ad hoc* cash payments to workers from time to time on account of leave, wages, arrears of wages etc. This system is liable to abuse. All payments to workmen should be made along with the monthly wage payments.

The great variety of loans and advances to workers should cease. As in Bombay there should be no loans except mid-month advances or advances from the provident fund under the Provident Fund Rules.

Complaints regarding delays in payment of wages, incorrect payment, etc., are on the increase. The main reason for this is mismanagement in the Wages Section.

The Administrative Body should take effective steps to improve the efficiency of this section in particular.

Workmen should be issued with a confirmation slip every month. These slips should contain details of his earnings under various heads. In case of a discrepancy workmen can lodge complaints within three days of payment. No complaint received thereafter should be entertained.

The system of sanctioning leave to workers should be simplified. Proper records showing leave due and leave sanctioned should be maintained. The duplication of work between the Leave Section and the Leave Registration Section should cease.

Injury leave is being misused. There are cases where workmen have availed of injury leave with full pay for three months or so for slight bruises on fingers.

Though there is a system of staggered weekly off for workmen, in practice all workmen report for all the days of the week with the result that the workmen who attend continuously for seven days get an extra wage on account of weekly off payment. The weekly off was not intended for this purpose. If there is to be a weekly off it should be on a staggered basis and one-seventh of the total strength should be laid off every week automatically and no worker should be called upon to work on his off day except in an emergency.

Payment of overtime which is rampant encourages inefficiency. Even in such sections as Provident Fund, where there is no sudden rush of work, the staff earns overtime. To impose efficiency proper supervisory staff not entitled to overtime should be appointed and the practice of paying overtime discouraged. No overtime should be allowed for clearing arrears without the prior permission of the head of the department.

The service conditions of office staff, particularly their confirmation and promotion are not yet properly regulated. The decision of the Dock Labour Board taken in December 1958 to confirm 150 persons has not yet been implemented by the Administrative Body. It has also failed to nominate its representative on the Departmental Promotion Committee, Important administrative matters like these cannot be allowed to mark time indefinitely because of the non-cooperation of the Administrative Body. The Chairman should take the matter in his own hands and pass orders.

The office order of September 26, 1957, detailing the functions of the Administrative Body and the Secretary of the Dock Labour was wrong and unnecessary.

Since a large number of chipping and painting and coal workers has already been listed, the Calcutta Unregistered Dock Workers (Regulation of Employment) Scheme should be enforced in respect of them immediately.

The Listing Committee should be wound up and the Deputy Chairman entrusted with the work of listing and the work be finished in about four months. He may be assisted by the Secretary, Dock Labour Board.

The Listing Scheme may be amended to amalgamate into one category "stitchers and baggers" and "salt workers".

Early steps should be taken to register riggers.

The members of the Master Stevedores Association and the Calcutta Stevedores Association are the only registered stevedores in Calcutta. Thus they enjoy a monopoly of stevedoring in the docks. As required by the Scheme the Dock Labour Board should see that arrangements to register more stevedores are made as soon as possible.

The accounts of the Dock Labour Board should be audited by the Comptroller and Auditor General.

The Scheme may be amended to provide for the suspension of the Dock Labour Board. In the meantime the Dock Labour Board may continue. If its working does not improve the amendment should be made use of.

The Administrative Body should be suspended immediately and the Deputy Chairman should constitute the Administrative Body under clause 5(1) of the Scheme.

The Chairman of the Port Authority, ex-officio should continue to be the Chairman of the Dock Labour Board. The various aspects of working in a port are so inter-linked that a disturbance in one cannot but have repercussion in another. The Deputy Chairman who is a whole-time officer of the Board should have had field experience preferably of both labour and the docks, and, in any case, of at least, one of them.

The Secretary of the Dock Labour Board should be placed under the Deputy Chairman.

The present haphazed recruitment of staff for the offices of the Dock Labour Board and the Administrative Body should stop and one of the recognised methods be adopted.

COMMITTEE FOR COORDINATION AND INTEGRATION OF SCHEMES OPERATING IN THE FIELD OF PHYSICAL EDUCATION, RECREATION AND YOUTH WELFARE, 1959—REPORT

New Delhi, Ministry of Education, 1964. 88p.

Chairman : Dr. Hriday Nath Kunzru.

Members : Shri Mahavir Tyagi, Shri Asoka Mehta, Smt. Ammu Swaminadhan; Shri P.N. Kirpal; Shri H.C. Sarin; Shri A.A.A. Fyzee (Shri A.A.A. Fyzee resigned on September 26, 1960 and shri R.R. Singh was appointed in his place on January 5, 1961, he did not attend the meeting so Shri R.K. Kapur was appointed as member in his place on Aprll 10, 1961), Shri G.D. Sondi; Shri P.M. Joseph.

Secretary : Shri C.S. Nayar (on his transfer Shri P.M. Joseph was appinted as Member-Secretary).

APPOINTMENT

The Committee for Coordination and Integration of Schemes operating in the field of Physical Eduation, Recreation and Youth Wefare was constituted on May 26, 1959/Jaistha 6, 1881 (Saka) by the Ministry of Education, Government of India, under Resolution No. F.24-1/59-PE-2, dated May 26, 1959. The text of the letter intimating the appointment of the Committee is reproduced below :

"Wheareas, in pursuance of the recommendations of the Estimates Commttiee of the Lok Sabha, the Central Advisory Board of Physical Education and Recreation and other bodies, it has been considered necessay to examine the question of co-ordination and integration of different schemes and programmes in the field of Physical Education, Recreation and Youth Welfare, it is hearby resolved that a Coordination Committee (herein after referred to as the Committee) shall be established forthwith."

TERMS OF REFERENCE

(a) To evaluate the respective merits and to define the role of various schemes for Physical Education, Recreation, Character-building and Discipline, operating in educational institutions;

(b) To recommand measures for the proper coordination of approved schemes in order to avoid duplication and wastage of resources;

(c) To examine ways and means of developing the most useful schemes and activities for the promotion of Physical Education, Recreation, Character-building and Discipline among students.

CONTENTS

Introduction; Objectives, Organisation and Working of the Various Schemes: Evaluation of Achievements of Various Schemes; Suggested Policy for the Future; Miscellaneous; Summary of Recommendations; Annexures from I to VI.

RECOMMENDATIONS

1. Integrated Programme

(a) At the school stage, there should be an integrated programme, woven into the fabric of the educational system and consisting broadly of a basic curriculum compulsory for all and an optional curriculum. The basic curriculum should include a minimum programme of physical and cultural activities. The optional part should consist of activities like scouting, mountaineering, sports dance, drama, music, hobbies, social service, workshop activities, etc. One of the optional subjects must be compulsory, the choice being left to students. The content of such an Integrated programme should be worked out by a body of experts in the field of education, in consultation with the State Governments.

(b) No expenditure should be spared to develop the essential characteristics of the programme which should cover all schools.

(c) Once such an integrated programme is introduced (every effort should be made to expedite its early introduction) existing programmes under Physical Education, the A. C. C. and the National Discipline Scheme should no longer be continued as separate schemes. The scheme already prepared by the Ministry of Education for an integrated programme should be vetted by a body of experts on which the A. C. C. should be represented.

(d) The services of the Instructors working under old schemes should be availed of in implementing the new programme, after giving them such reorientation as might become necessary.

(e) Pending the introduction of the new integrated programme the National Discipline Scheme and the A. C. C. may continue but should not be allowed to expand.

(f) The continuation of the National Discipline

Scheme even in the interregnum should be made conditional on the satisfaction of the following conditions:

(i) Participation in the scheme for students should be voluntary and not compulsory.

(ii) The syllabus on 'mental training' should be suitably modified as the present syllabus does not appear to have been carefully worked out educationally or with reference to the capacity of the N. D. S. instructors to impart such training.

State Governments should also be invited to share a part of the expenditure on the N. D. S. so that they may take keener interest in its development.

(g) After the introduction of the integrated programme, extraneous character-building schemes should be allowed to flourish in schools only on a voluntary basis, and that too to the extent that they cover fresh ground not covered by the integrated programme.

2. Natioual Cadet Corps

(a) At the collegiate level, training in N. C. C. should be encouraged, as such training gives the country a potential corps of military officers. The training in N. C. C. at any stage should be imparted only on a voluntary basis. In implementing this scheme, every precaution should be taken to maintain the authority of the heads of educational institutions.

(b) The concessions granted to N. C. C. cadets by various Universities in the matter of qualifying marks or exemptions from papers are not justified academically and should be withdrawn as far as possible wherever they exist.

(c) While the N. C. C. existing pattern should continue undisturbed, the high cost of training under this programme should be reduced as far as possible without affecting its efficiency.

(d) Besides the facilities given to them for training in the N. C. C., college students should also be given the maximum facilities for participation in games and sports.

3. Scouting And Guiding

(a) Even after implementing the suggested integrated programme there should be full opportunities for students at all levels to take scouting/guiding as an extra-curricular activity on a voluntary basis.

(b) Adequate grants should be given to the Bharat Scouts and Guides to enable them to employ more staff to overcome organisational deficiencies and to implement their training programme. Every State should have at least one fully equipped centre for training scout masters.

(c) In order to provide for a regular flow of adequate leadership, scouting should be a subject of study in the normal and basic schools.

(d) There must be provision for supplying free uniforms and for meeting the camp expenditure from the school funds in respect of the poor and needy scouts.

(e) In order to stop the depletion of well trained and experienced leaders from the scout movement, remuneration to the scout leaders may be paid on the same basis as that on which it is paid to the leaders in other Youth Movements.

(f) To make scouting attractive in colleges steps should be taken to encourage mountaineering and hiking. The organisation should depute each year some scouts and guides from colleges for training in mountaineering at the Himalayan Mountaineering Institute, Darjeeling. Financial assistance should be extended to the organisation for this purpose.

4. Labour And Social Service Camps

(a) The organisation and control of the Labour and Social Service Camps should be vested in educational organisations. Outside agencies should be excluded from managing these camps. Strict control should be kept on the financial aspect and proper accounts should be rendered to the Ministry of Education by the appointed time.

(b) In matters of organisation, the main emphasis should be placed on the educational values of camping. Considering the age of the campers, the social service component of these camps is not of very greate value. Social service is undoubtedly useful, but need not be unduly stressed in these camps.

(c) For boys and girls in the age group 13—16 manual work in the camps should not be of more than two hours' duration per day. Boys and girls above 16 years of age may be asked if physically strong to do about three hours' manual work each day.

(d) Wherever possible, schools should adopt nearby villages for social service. This will create an abiding interest in social work among the students, establish collaboration between the students and the villagers and make follow-up action feasible.

5. Campus Works Project Scheme

More funds should be provided for increasing the number of projects under the Campus Works Project Scheme. The scheme temporarily suspended during National Emeregency should be revived as early as possible. Allocations for Labour and Social Service Camps should be pruned and the amounts so saved should be allocated to the Campus Works Projects Scheme.

6. Miscellaneous

(a) All school children should have smart uniforms. If, for any reason, it is not possible to arrange for uniforms for all, the students may at least have common belt or a common badge as a sign of belonging to a particular institution.

(b) Small labour and social service undertaking within the school campus should be encouraged. Full opportunities should be provided for educational institutions for organising creative programmes for recreational activities and for this purpose small scale workshops should be set up in a few big urban and rural schools.

(c) Hobbies should be encouraged, students should also be led to work for their institutions in small ways first and later on in bigger enterprises.

(d) Students should be encouraged to hold periodic camp fires, songs and dance shows and even simple dramatic plays in neighbouring mohallas or in nearby villages. Older students can hold magic lantern and documentary cinema shows, on health, better agriculture and balanced diet to these peoples.

(e) Students should be led to take interest in the preservation and development of nearby 'beauty spots'. Batches of students can be assigned to look after these spots.

(f) Morning assemblies should he held in every school and the school's work should begin with singing of the National Anthem, followed by other community songs.

(g) Each student must be taught how to salute, hoist and lower the National Flag. He should also have an understanding of what the Flag stands for.

(h) Three kinds of Honour Rolls should be set up in every educational institution—for academic work, for sports and for general good work and conduct. Cases of special behaviour or courageous action should be specially mentioned at periodic student and staff meetings.

(i) To inculcate a sense of descipline and a sense of responsibility in students they may be given a chance, by rotation, to act as monitors, prefects and supervisors etc. For disciplinary corrections of a minor nature, special committees of senior students should be nominated by the head of institution to look into such matters.

(j) The 'Tutorial System' should be introduced in all colleges under which the tutor acts as a moral guide to students when they are confronted with difficult problems. For the success of this system a tutor should not be entrusted with the care of more than six to eight students at a time.

(k) To encourage the spirit of comradeship and healthy competition, each school should introduce the 'House System' and organise art exhibitions, inter-house debates, discussions, literary competitions, team games, etc.

(l) Training colleges should not merely give training for the teaching of class room subjects but also include training in either sports, or music, or drama or crafts so that each teacher has dual qualifications.

(m) Educational tours should be encouraged but teachers should take care to ensure that the tours are made purposeful and not converted into more sight-seeing jaunts. The students should be asked to keep diaries of the places visited and those with well maintained diaries should be complimented.

(n) A net-work of youth hostels should be set up to encourage students to go on hikes, These hostels should be at places which attract tourists.

(o) Projects like Inter-University Youth Festivals and the Inter-University and Inter-State Sports Meets should be encouraged. Inter-village festivals, in which students should take a larger part are also commended.

WASTELANDS SURVEY AND RECLAMATION COMMITTEE ON LOCATION AND UTILISATION OF WASTELANDS IN INDIA (ANDHRA PRADESH), 1959—REPORT

New Delhi, Ministry of Food and Agriculture, 1961.
52p. viip.+ip.+Maps.

Chairman : Shri B. N. Uppal.

Members : Shri J.P. Mital; Shri F.C. Gera; Dr. J.K. Basu (retired; replaced by Shri M.S.V. Rama Rao).

Coopted Members : Shri M.P. Pai; Shri S.A. Quader; Shri C. Seshagiri Rao; Shri S.A. Abbas; Shri C.V.K. Reddy; Shri D.V.N. Raju; Shri M.K. Adeni.

Secretary : Shri A.S. Venu Gopalan.

APPOINTMENT

The uncultivated lands in the country may be broadly classified into the following two categories:

(a) Lands which are really adjuncts of village *abadis* and are meant to serve as pastures and fuel forests or sites for the extension of *abadis*, and

(b) Lands in large-sized blocks which have either

gone out of cultivation or have never been brought under cultivation.

With a view to utilising the latter category of lands which afford the greatest promise for increased agricultural production, the Government of India constituted this Committee, vide their letter No. F/1024/Spl./59, dated June 11, 1959.

TERMS OF REFERENCE

(i) To make a survey of land classified as "other uncultivated land excluding fallow lands" and "fallow lands other than current fallows" and locate areas where large blocks of land are available for reclamation and resettlement;

(ii) To suggest suitable measures for reclamation according to conditions in different areas and estimate the cost of reclamation and colonisation and the financial assistance and agricultural extension and training necessary for the settlers (the settlements being made on a cooperative basis);

(iii) To suggest the terms and conditions upon which settlement should be made, the areas to be allotted and the payments to be made by settlers' cooperative; and

(iv) To estimate the economic aspects of such reclamation in terms of the expenditure involved, the likely addition to food production and the employment and income that would become available to settlers and their families and to lay down the priorities *inter se* between different categories of reclaimable lands.

CONTENTS

Introduction; Preface; General Aspects; Description of Blocks and Measures for Reclamation; Disposal of Reclaimed Lands for Cultivation; Summary of Conclusions and Recommendations; Appendices A to H; Maps I and II.

RECOMMENDATIONS

Of the total area of 10.50 million acres under the heads "other uncultivated lands excluding fallows" and "fallows other than current fallows", an area of 1.89 lakh acres has been offered for reclamation in blocks of 250 acres or more. It appears that the bulk of the wastelands are found in small pieces scattered all over the State. Moreover, the allotment of wastelands to the members of the Scheduled Castes and the Scheduled Tribes, etc., has been going on for some time past, and it is possible that large areas of culturable waste have been disposed of in this manner.

The wastelands offered for reclamation in the State can be divided into the following three categories:

I. Areas infested with thick growth of jungle, shrubs and bushes;
II. Saline lands, and
III. Dry lands.

The distribution of wastelands in the three categories is as under :

Category			Area (Acres)
I	...	...	14,988
II	...	...	37,605
III	...	...	1,36,341
		Total	1,88,934

The wastelands included in category I are infested with thick jungle, shrubs and bushes, and are located in tracts with an average rainfall of 40-45 inches. The cost of reclamation varies from Rs. 100 to Rs. 500 per acre.

The saline lands included in category II, lying waste in the districts of Guntur and Krishna, can be rendered productive if adequate irrigation is provided and, whereever necessary, the drainage of these lands is improved by widening the existing drains or constructing new ones. The lands should also be protected by the construction of bunds with sluice gates so as to prevent the ingress of salt water during high tides and to control the outflow of the rain water. The cost of reclamation is estimated at about Rs. 190 per acre. These lands should be taken up for reclamation on a priority basis during the Third Plan period.

Most of the wastelands in category III are located in the districts of Nellore, Kurnool and Karimnagar, where the annual rainfall is 25 to 30 inches. In the Kurnool and Karimnagar districts where about 66,000 acres of wastelands have been offered for reclamation, crop growing is a gamble in the rains as this area suffers from low and variable rainfall. Suitable measures for soil and water conservation are necessary for sucessful cultivation in these scarcity areas. Contour bunding of eroded lands followed by a suitable system of dry farming should be adopted on a wide scale. These measures should, however, be undertaken on a complete watershed basis. As regards the Nellore district, the wastelands offered for reclamation in this district are likely to come under the command of the Nagarjunasaagar Project, and it is necessary that a rapid survey is made of these lands before irrigation is available from the project.

The entire area located for reclamation in the State belongs to the Government.

In order to bring under cultivation the wastelands belonging to Government, they should be allotted to the members of the Scheduled Castes and the Scheduled Tribes, etc., in accordance with the existing rules for the disposal of wastelands in the different areas of the erstwhile Hyderabad State, namely, the Telangana area, and the former Andhra State. These rules are fairly comprehensive and deal with the manner of disposal of wastelands. Some of the areas can be utilised for setting up cooperative colonies of landless labourers, the members of the Scheduled Castes and the Scheduled Tribes, etc.

A detailed soil survey for land-use should be carried out in each area proposed for reclamation, particularly in the areas included in category III.

After the reclamation measures have been carried out the responsibility for the follow-on cultivation operations in the reclaimed lands should be that of the normal staff of the Agricultre Department, which, if necessary, may be strengthened. For the proper utilization of reclaimed wastelands, the cultivators should be educated in the adoption of suitable soil management practices, including the dry farming system of cultivation in the wastelands included in category III. This can be done by organising trials and demonstrations of improved agricultural practices on cultivators' holdings, and by arranging for the supply of agricultural requisites such as improved dry farming implements, seeds, fertilisers, etc. We attach great importance to these trials and demonstrations as the success of the reclamation projects primarily depends upon the adoption of suitable soil management practices in the reclaimed lands. The responsibility for extension work in the reclaimed lands may be transferred to the Community Development Organisation after the initial period of demonstrations.

Wherever irrigation facilities can be provided by the construction of wells, loans for this purpose may be given on a liberal scale to the cultivators.

Most of the wastelands found in the Nellore district are likely to receive irrigation from the Nagarjunasagar Project. Since the cultivators in this area are not accustomed to wet cultivation, suitable systems of cropping under irrigated conditions should be demonstrated to the cultivators with a view to making the best use of irrigation when it becomes available.

Before the wastelands are allotted to the members of the Scheduled Castes and the Scheduled Tribes, etc., these should be reclaimed.

In any settlement project, the selection of suitable settlers is a vital factor contributing to its success. Accordingly, special attention should be given to this important aspect of the settlement work, so that the right type of settlers who have an aptitude for agricultural work and who are willing to do hard work, are selected.

In order that the settlement work is successful, it is necessary that the revenue/block agency should be associated with it, so that the problems of the settlers are attended to as expeditiously as possible. Experience has shown that, where the District Collectors and the Block Development Officers take personal interest in the settlement work, the projects are often successful.

At present, no reliable figures of additional yields of food crops expected to be obtained from the reclaimed lands are available. Crop-cutting experiments may, therefore, be conducted in the reclaimed lands during the Third Plan, particularly in the districts of Krishna, Guntur, Nellore, Kurnool and Karimnagar.

The total cost of reclaiming 1,37,710 acres of wastelands in categories I, II, and III, out of 1.89 lakhs acres offered for reclamation comes to about 1.74 crores, *i.e.*, Rs. 126 per acre. The estimated additional production from the reclaimed lands is 43,329 tons of foodgrains, valued at Rs. 1.18 crores. Thus the value of production will cover the cost of reclamation in two crop seasons.

The areas included in category II (saline lands) seem to be the most profitable in terms of additional food production which is about 20 maunds for an expenditure of about Rs. 190 per acre on land improvement. On the other hand, category III offers the greatest promise for increasing agricultural production since large areas of dry lands are available for cultivation. The wastelands in the Nellore district, most of which are expected to receive irrigation from the Nagarjunasagar Project, belong to this category. The extent of the area offered for reclamation in category I is small and the cost of its reclamation is relatively high.

The following order of priority may be assigned to the wastelands located in the State:—

Category		Priority
I	... ...	III
II	... ...	I
III	... ...	II

WASTELANDS SURNEY AND RECLAMATION COMMITTEE ON LOCATION AND UTILISATION OF WASTELANDS IN INDIA (BIHAR), 1959—REPORT

New Delhi, Ministry of Food and Agriculture, 1961.
50p+viiip.+Maps.

Chairman : Dr. B.N. Uppal.
Members : Shri F.C. Gera; Shri J.P. Mital; Dr. J.K. Basu (retired; replaced by Shri M.S.V. Rama Rao.)
Coopted Members : Shri T.P. Singh; Shri S.C. Mukherjee; Shri S.N. Chakravarti; Shri H. Prasad.
Secretary : Shri A.S. Venu Gopalan.

APPOINTMENT :

The uncultivated lands in the country may be broadly classified into the following two categories:

(a) Lands which are really adjuncts of village *abadis* and are meant to serve as pastures and fuel forests or sites for the extension of *abadis;* and

(b) Lands in large-sized blocks which have either gone out of cultivation or have never been brought under cultivation.

With a view to utilising the latter category of lands which afford the greatest promise for increased agricultural production, the Government of India constituted this Committee, vide their letter No. F/1024/Spl./59, dated June, 11, 1959.

TERMS OF REFERENCE

(i) To make a survey of land classified as "other uncultivated land excluding fallow lands" and "fallow lands other than current fallows" and locate areas where large blocks of land are available for reclamation and resettlement ;

(ii) To suggest suitable measures for reclamation according to conditions in different areas and estimate the cost of reclamation and colonisation and the financial assistance and agricultural extension and training necessary for the settlers (the settlements being made on a cooperative basis) ;

(iii) To suggest the terms and conditions upon which settlement should be made, the areas to be allotted and the payments to be made by settlers' cooperative; and

(iv) To estimate the economic aspects of such reclamation in terms of the expenditure involved, the likely addition to food production and the employment and income that would become available to settlers and their families and to lay down the priorities *inter se* between different categories of reclaimable lands.

CONTENTS :

Introduction; Preface; General Aspects; Description of Blocks and Measures for Reclamation; Disposal of Reclaimed Lands for Cultivation; Summary of General Conclusions and Recommendations; Appendices A to I; Maps I & II.

RECOMMENDATIONS

Of the total area of 4.84 million acres under the head "other uncultivated lands excluding fallows" and "fallows other than current fallows" about 89,000 acres only have been located in the State for reclamation in blocks of the sizes of 250 acres or more. This area is relatively small as only the blocks of wastelands which could be surveyed by the district authorities with the help of the local staff were reported to the Committee, although (according to the estimate of the State Government) over two million acres of wastelands in sizeable blocks are available in the lateritic belt of the State.

The wastelands found in the State may be broadly divided into the following two categories :

I. Eroded lands located in the lateritic belt of South Bihar and the Chotanagpur plateau, and

II. *Terai* lands (lands infested with pernicious grasses such as *kans*, *pater* etc.).

The distribution of wastelands in the two categories is as under :

Category	Area (Acres)
I	57,396
II	31,259
Total	88,655

The wastelands found in the lateritic belt of South Bihar and the Chotanagpur plateau are most undulating, with uplands and valleys. The soils are generally red and lateritic, varying in texture from sandy loam to loam, but the predominant type is sandy loam with *murum* on the surface. They are poor in organic matter. Land reclamation in these areas is primarily soil and water conservation work. The total cost of reclaiming

57,396 acres would amount to Rs. 91.83 lakhs. The average cost of reclamation would be Rs. 160 per acre.

Although there has been little opposition from the private owners of wastelands for undertaking soil conservation measures on their holdings forming part of a catchment, it is necessary to introduce legislation on the lines of the model Act prepared by the Government of India, empowering the State Government to undertake soil conservation measures in the State.

The expenditure on reclamation of eroded lands located in the tribal areas may be shared by the Centre and the State Government in the ratio of 3:1. In the non-tribal areas, where contour-bunding and other soil conservation measures are undertaken in private holdings, the expenditure should be shared as under :

(a) 75 per cent of the expenditure should be advanced as loan to the cultivator to be recovered in equal annual instalments spread over a period of 10-15 years, and

(b) 25 per cent should be treated as subsidy to be shared equally between the Centre and the State.

Land revenue should be collected from the cultivators of the reclaimed lands after a period of three years after reclamation, since these lands do not give any economic return in the initial period.

The wastelands near *bastis* should be assigned higher priority for reclamation over other lands, but large tracts of wastelands lying outside the *bastis* should also receive equal consideration if the owners construct dwelling houses on their holdings and pay a token sum for the reclamation of their lands to indicate their earnestness to cultivate them.

Manual labour should, as far as possible, be employed for such operations as contour-bunding while undertaking reclamation of uplands.

The selected projects on soil conservation should be on a complete watershed basis.

Field experiments should be laid out to study the different methods of bunding in the lateritic belt of the State, with a view to determining as to which method should be adopted with special reference to its cost and effectiveness.

The wastelands included in category II comprise areas located in the districts of Darbhanga, Saharsa and Purnea. The land in the Darbhanga district is flat and fertile, and can produce good crops of paddy, chillies, etc. Irrigation can be provided from the Kosi canals or by the installation of tube-wells. The area is, however, subject to floods during the rainy season and only one crop can be grown during the year. The cost of clearing and ploughing up the land with tractors is estimated at Rs. 100 per acre.

The area offered for reclamation in the Purnea and Saharsa districts is 16,459 acres only, although there are extensive belts of barren lands in these two districts. It is estimated that there are 200 sq. miles of such lands in the Purnea district alone. The lands are covered with coarse sand on account of the shifting of its course by the Kosi, and have a thin layer of six inches to nine inches of sandy loam or loamy sand on the surface with coarse or fine sand underneath. Crop growing is a hazard in these areas as the cultivation of the land disturbs the thin layer of the top-soil which is blown off by strong winds which prevail in these belts. When irrigation becomes available from the Kosi canals system, it may be possible to evolve a crop pattern in which forage legumes and erosion, resistant crops like groundnut are included in the rotation. The establishment of bamboo plantations as shelter belts will, however, be necessary as a protection to the cultivated lands from wind erosion.

Before irrigation becomes available in the wastelands located in the Saharsa and Purnea districts, a detailed soil survey should be conducted with a view to delineating these lands on the basis of proper land-use.

The wastelands for which information has been furnished by the State Government are owned either by private individuals or the Government. The wastelands belonging to private indlviduals can be handed over, after reclamation, to their respective owners for following-on cultivation. In order to bring the lands belonging to the Government under cultivation, allotments may be made to the members of the Scheduled Castes and Scheduled Tribes in accordance with the existing orders of the Governmrnt regarding land settlement. Cooperative colonies of the members of the Scheduled Castes and the Scheduled Tribes and landless labourers, may also be established in favourable areas to serve as pilot projects.

A detailed soil survey for land-use should be carried out in the areas proposed for reclamation, particularly in the lateritic belt of South Bihar and the Chotanagpur plateau, so that the requisite information on the proper utilisation of wastelands is available.

Every effort should be made to complete procedural formalities for the allotment of wastelands before the work of reclamation is taken up.

The execution of soil conservation projects in agricultural lands should be entrusted to one Government Department, say, the Agriculture Department, since this Department has also the necessary organisation and the specialist staff for advising the cultivators in regard to agricultural practices to be adopted in the reclaimed lands.

Reclamation of wastelands donated to the Bhoodan Samiti should be carried out under the technical guidance of the State Agriculture Department, or in accordance with the plans approved by that department.

Trials and demonstrations of improved agricultural practices should be organised on cultivators holdings so that they may adopt suitable soil management practices after reclamation. If necessary, the Agriculture Department may be strengthened to prove for special staff for carrying out intensive demonstrations and propaganda in the reclaimed areas for a period of two-three years. The responsibility for extension work may be transferred to the Community Development Organisation after the initial period of demonstration.

Green manuring should be extensively practised in the reclaimed lands in order to build up their organic matter content and to improve soil structure. The State Government should arrange for the supply of seed of green manuring crops free of cost for the first year after reclamation.

In the lateritic belt where irrigation is not available, percolation tanks or earthen embankments may be constructed across gullies to hold water. The construction of such tanks helps in the storage of rain-water for agricultural and other purposes, and also checks erosion on the down-stream side of the gullies

In the uplands which are not suitable for growing crops, cultivators should be encouraged to plant cashewnut, sisal, sabai grass, etc.

In order to carry out the large programme of soil conservation work in the State, the soil conservation wing of the Agriculture Department should be strengthened by the appointment of a full-time Joint Director of Agriculture (Soil Conservation), who may be assisted by Divisional Soil Conservation Officers and the necessary field staff.

The total cost of reclaiming 72,196 acres in categories I and II (exclusive of the areas of wastelands in the districts of Saharsa and Purnea comes to about Rs. 1.07 crores, *i.e.*, about Rs. 148 per acre. The estimated additional production from the reclaimed lands is 20,746 tons valued at Rs. 45.31 lakhs. The average cost of reclamation is, therefore, economic in terms of additional production.

A study of the cost of reclamation of lands in the two categories reveals that the areas located in the Darbhanga district (category II) are the most profitable in terms of additional food production which is about 15 maunds for an expenditure of about Rs. 100 per acre on land improvement. On the other hand, category I offers the greatest promise for increasing agricultural production since large tracts of eroded lands (estimated at two million acres) are reported to be available in the lateritic belt of the State. On an average, the cost of reclamation of land in the lateritic belt is Rs. 160 per acre, and the additional production, on a conservative estimate, is six maunds per acre.

The wastelands located in the Darbhanga district (category II) may be assigned the highest priority in view of the productive nature of these lands. The eroded wastelands in South Bihar and the Chotanagpur plateau (Category I) should be assigned on equally high priority because of the availability of large tracts of such lands in the State.

WASTELANDS SURVEY AND RECLAMATION COMMITTEE ON LOCATION AND UTILISATION OF WASTELANDS IN INDIA (GUJARAT), 1959—REPORT

New Delhi, Ministry of Food and Agriculture, 1963. 34p.+xp.—Maps.

Chairman : Dr. B.N. Uppal.
Members : Dr. J. K. Basu (retired; replaced by Shri M. S. V. Rama Rao); Shri F. C. Gera; Shri J. P. Mital.
Coopted Members : The Development Commissioners; The Revenue Secretary; The Secretary of the Agriculture Forest Department, or his nominee; A Representative of the Irrigation Department.

APPOINTMENT

The uncultivated lands in the country may be broadly classified into the following two categories :

(a) Lands which are really adjuncts of village *abadis* and are meant to serve as pastures and fuel forests or sites for the extension of *abadis* ; and

(b) Lands in large-sized blocks which have either gone out of cultivation or have never been brought under cultivation.

With a view to utilising the latter category of lands which afford the greatest promise for increased agricultural production, the Government of India constituted this Committee, vide their letter No. F/1024/Spl./59, dated June 11, 1959.

TERMS OF REFERENCE

(i) To make a survey of land classified as "other uncultivated land excluding fallow lands" and "fallow lands other than current fallows" and locate areas where large blocks of land are available for reclamation and resettlement;

(ii) To suggest suitable measures for reclamation according to conditions in different areas and estimate the cost of reclamation and colonisation and the financial assistance and agricultural extension and training necessary for the settlers (the settlements being made on a cooperative basis);

(iii) To suggest the terms and conditions upon which settlement should be made, the areas to be allotted and the payments to be made by settlers' cooperative; and

(iv) To estimate the economic aspects of such reclamation in terms of the expenditure involved, the likely addition to food production and the employment and income that would become available to settlers and their families and to lay down the priorities *inter se* between different categories of reclaimable lands.

CONTENTS

Introduction ; Preface ; General Aspects ; Description of Blocks and Measures for Reclamation ; Disposal of Reclaimed Lands for Cultivation ; Summary of General Conclusions and Recommendations ; Appendices A to H ; Maps I & II.

RECOMMENDATIONS

Of the total area of 5.29 million acres under the heads 'other uncultivated land excluding fallows' and 'fallows other than current fallows', 71,000 acres of wastelands in blocks of 250 acres or more have been located for reclamation. This area is relatively small as a large proportion of wastelands is found scattered in small blocks, and the figures of wastelands reported under the above two heads are not very reliable.

The wastelands offered for reclamation in the State may be broadly divided into the following two categories :

I. Dry lands, and

II. Saline lands.

The distribution of wastelands in the two categories is as under :

Category		Area (acres)
I ...	...	12,957
II ...	...	58,115
	Total	71,072

The wastelands included in category I are situated in a belt where low and variable rainfall is received, and hence crop growing is a hazard unless suitable measures are taken for conservation of soil moisture, and for preventing the loss of soil by erosion. Contour-bunding of eroded lands followed by the adoption of a suitable system of dry farming will rehabilitate these degraded lands.

The wastelands included in category II can be subdivided into two groups, namely, (a) *khar* lands and (b) *bhal* lands. For the reclamation of *khar* lands, a scheme is already in operation in the State under which the expenditure on reclamation is initially met by the Government, and when the reclaimed lands are disposed of to the owners or tenants, 60 per cent of the reclamation cost, together with a nominal occupancy price (when the lands belong to Government) is recovered from the grantees and the the balance is treated as subsidy. The cost of reclamation is estimated at about Rs. 120 per acre. The total area offered for reclamation in blocks of 250 acres or more is 53,361 acres, but it is reported that about five lakh acres of such lands are available in the State. In taking up *khar* lands for reclamation, high priority should be assigned to areas receiving a rainfall of more than 35-40 inches and/or having irrigation facilities.

The *Bhal* tract is situated in the south-east corner of Saurashtra, with an area of 200 sq. miles. The soil is mostly loamy, but patches of black soil are also found. The average precipitation is 18 to 20 inches. The total reclaimable area in the tract is estimated at 60,000 acres. The work on reclamation of *bhal* lands is still in an experimental stage and it is not certain to what extent this project will be a success. It is, therefore, necessary that the results of the experiments in progress should be carefully studied before undertaking any large scale projects of reclamation, since the cost of reclamation comes to about Rs. 350 per acre.

In the Little Banni tract of the Kutch district, an area comprising 10,000 acres each in villages Dhori Samrasar and Nirona, in the Bhuj taluk, is proposed for reclamation. The soil survey carried out in the area has indicated that the entire area of village Samrasar and about half of the area in village Dhori are suitable for cultivation, whilst the remaining area in villages Dhori and Nirona are unfit for this purpose due to high salinity. The annual precipitation in this tract is 10-1[illegible] inches. Three storage schemes are being executed in the tract with a view to providing irrigation to the land. These schemes, when completed, are expected to supply annually only 15 acre-inches of water per acre, for the area under command. With this meagre supply of irrigation, the cultivation of crops will be greatly restricted as the supplies of sub-soil water are also not only limited but its quality is not uniformly satisfactory

However. if the supply of irrigation water could be augmented, there is a possibility of establishing a small mechanised farm in the Samrasar area.

The vast grazing lands of the Banni tract should not be taken up for cultivation, since they are most suited for the development of pastures. Large numbers of professional cattle breeders have settled in the tract for generations, and entirely depend upon their livestock for their livelihood. However, before an all-round development of the tract can be undertaken, it is necessary to improve the communications in the tract so that it is easily accessible, and to make adequate arrangements for the supply of drinking water.

The entire area located for reclamation belongs to the Government, but the land included in category I vests in village panchayats.

In order to bring the wastelands belonging to the village panchayats under cultivation, the lands, after reclamation, may be allotted to the members of the Scheduled Castes, the Scheduled Tribes, etc. The expenditure on reclamation involving soil and water conservation measures may be shared as under :

(a) 75 per cent of the expenditure may be advanced as loans to the allottees to be recovered over a period of 10—15 years;

(b) 25 per cent of it should be treated as subsidy to be shared equally between the Centre and the State.

The expenditure on reclamation of *Khar* lands may be initially met by the Government. When the reclaimed lands are disposed of to the tenants, 60 per cent of the reclamation cost, together with a nominal occupancy price, may be recovered from the grantees and the balance may be treated as subisdy to be shared equally between the Centre and the State.

The work on reclamation of *Bhal* lands is still in an experimental stage, and it is not certain to what extent the project will be a success. If it is finally determined that the reclamation of these lands is economically feasible, the lands may be allotted to the landless labourers, members of the Scheduled Castes and the Schedules tribes, etc. Since the allottees will not have the means to undertake reclamation on their own, assistance from Government, both the financial and technical, should be forthcoming in ample measure. Accordingly, the Government should set up an organisation at the appropriate time for the reclamation of these lands, and allot them to landless labourers, etc., after reclamation.

The cost of reclamation of *Bhal* lands is estimated at Rs. 350 per acre. As this expenditure cannot be met from the profits of cultivation in early years, 75 per cent of the cost should be recovered in convenient instalments spread over a period of 15 years, the first instalment commencing from the sixth year after allotment. The balance of expenditure should be treated as subsidy to be shared equally between the Centre and the State.

A detailed soil survey for land-use should be carried out in each area proposed for reclamation, so that the lands are put to proper use.

After the reclamation measures have been carried out, the responsibility for the follow-on cultivation operations should be that of the normal staff of the Agriculture Department. The agricultural staff should suggest suitable cropping patterns and also introduce improved agricultural practices in the reclaimed areas. The extension staff of the Community Development Organisation can assist particularly in the demonstration of improved methods of cultivation and in arranging for the supply of agricultural requisites.

The cost of reclaiming 44,638 acres of wastelands in categories I and II (exclusive of the areas which cannot be brought under cultivation) comes to Rs. 48.55 lakhs, *i.e.*, Rs. 109 per acre. The estimated additional production from the reclaimed land is 9,231 tons, valued at Rs. 28.98 lakhs. Thus. the value of production will cover the cost of reclamation in two crop seasons.

A study of the economics of reclamation between the two categories of wastelands reveals that the areas included in category II are more profitable in terms of additional food production. On the other hand, the additional food production from the reclaimed lands included in category I is four maunds per acre for a small expenditure of Rs. 57 on reclamation. In these circumstances, the following order of priority may be assigned to the two categories of wastelands :

Category			Priority
I	...	...	1
II	...	...	2

WASTELANDS SURVEY AND RECLAMATION COMMITTEE ON LOCATION AND UTILISATION OF WASTELANDS IN INDIA (JAMMU AND KASHMIR), 1959—REPORT

New Delhi, Ministry of Food and Agriculture, 1962.
29p.+ivp

Chairman : Dr. B.N. Uppal.
Members : Dr. J.K. Basu (retired, replaced by Shri M.S.V. Rama Rao); Shri F.C. Gera; Shri J.P. Mital.
Coopted Members : Shri S.M. Agha; Shri Ghulam Nabi; Shri P.N, Kaul; Shri Dwarka Nath; Shri B.N, Nengi.
Secretary : Shri A.S. Venu Gopalan.

APPOINTMENT

The uncultivated lands in the country may be broadly classified into the following two categories :

(a) Lands which are really adjuncts of village *abadis* and are meant to serve as pastures and fuel forests or sites for the extension of *abadis*; and

(b) Lands in large-sized blocks which have either gone out of cultivation or have never been brought under cultivation.

With a view to utilising the latter category of lands which afford the greatest promise for increased agricultural production, the Government of India constituted this Committee vide their letter No. F/1024/Spl./59, dated June 11, 1959.

TERMS OF REFERENCE

(i) To make a survey of land classified as "other uncultivated land excluding fallow lands" and "fallow lands other than current fallows" and locate areas where large blocks of land are available for reclamation and resettlement;

(ii) To suggest suitable measures for reclamation according to conditions in different areas and estimate the cost of reclamation and colonisation and the financial assistance and agricultural extension and training necessary for the settlers (the settlement being made on a cooperative basis);

(iii) To suggest the terms and conditions upon which settlement should be made, the areas to be allotted and the payments to be made by settlers' cooperatives ; and

(iv) To estimate the economic aspects of such reclamation in terms of the expenditure involved, the likely addition to food production and the employment and income that would become available to settlers and their families and to lay down the priorities *inter se* between different categories of reclaimable lands.

CONTENTS

Introduction; Preface; General Aspects; Description of Blocks and Measures for Reclamation; Disposal of Reclaimed Lands for Cultivation; Summary of General Conclusions and Recommendations; Appendices A to H.

RECOMMENDATIONS

Of the total area of 0.91 million acres under the heads "other uncultivated land excluding fallows" and "fallows other than current fallows," only seventeen blocks comprising an area of 12,932 acres have been offered for reclamation in blocks of 250 acres or more in the districts of Kathua and Jammu. No blocks of wastelands of the requisite size have been reported from the remaining seven districts. The area offered for reclamation is relatively small as compared with the figures reported in the revenue records. It was explained that the revenue figures could not be relied upon and that most of the available wastelands were in scattered patches.

The distritution of wastelands in the two districts is given below :

District		Area
Kathua	...	1,946
Jammu	...	10,986
	Total	12,932

The wastelands located for reclamation in the districts of Kathua and Jammu except blocks 1 and 2 are mostly located along the creeks of the Chenab, Ujh, Tawi, Basantar and Devak, with the result that the areas remain flooded during the rainy season and any large scale habitation becomes somewhat precarious. These lands are generally covered with thick growth of pernicious weeds and grasses such as *Sarkanda, Kharkana,* etc., and can be reclaimed with tractors. The cost of clearance of weeds and bushes is estimated at about Rs. 75 per acre.

Some of the areas offered for reclamation are not

easily accessible. Further, it is difficult to eradicate the pernicious weeds and grasses unless facilities for mechanical cultivation are made available. The areas are mostly located along the cease-fire line with Pakistan, and will attract settlers only if the Government sets up military pickets for the protection of settlers and makes liberal grants for their housing and for agricultural requisites, such as bullocks, implements, etc. There are at present hardly any irrigation facilities in the blocks, but shallow, open wells can be dug at moderate costs as the water-table is quite high.

The wastelands in the State are owned either by private individuals, the Government, or the Custodian of Evacuee Property. Of the total area of wastelands located for reclamation, about 42 per cent belongs to Government and 46 per cent to private individuals. Only a very small percentage of wastelands belongs to the Custodian of Evacuee Property.

In order to make the wastelands included in blocks 3—17 fit for cultivation, the following measures need to be adopted :

(a) flood protection,
(b) clearance of weeds,
(c) arrangements for adequate security, and
(d) provision of irrigation.

Heavy cost is involved in undertaking the various reclamation measures and it would be beyond the capacity of individual cultivators to bring the areas under successful cultivation. The Government may also not find it convenient to spare large funds for this purpose.

The area of 1,340 acres included in blocks 1 and 2 may be taken up for reclamation. As regards the remaining blocks, their reclamation will not be profitable unless steps are taken to eliminate the hazards from annual floods and the situation along the Indo-Pakistan border has sufficiently eased to attract cultivators to settle in these lands. In the meantime, the State Forest Department may take steps to establish small woodlots in the wastelands under the Farm Foresty Schemes sanctioned in the Third Plan. These woodlots will serve to protect the wastelands from further erosion, and will augment the supplies of firewood in the State.

To bring the wastelands included in blocks 1 and 2 under cultivation, the following steps should be taken :

(i) Land reclamation charges should be borne by the State Government; and

(ii) Suitable subsidy should be given for sinking wells, for the purchase of bullocks, implements, seed, etc., and for building houses for residential purpose.

In addition, security arrangements should be made by the military authorities along the border with Pakistan.

The average yield, after reclamation, from wastelands included in blocks 1 and 2 will be about eight maunds per acre valued at Rs. 96. As the cost of reclamation will be about Rs. 80 per acre, the value of production will cover the expenditure on reclamation in one crop season.

WASTELANDS SURVEY AND RECLAMATION COMMITTEE ON LOCATION AND UTILISATION OF WASTELANDS IN INDIA (KERALA), 1959—REPORT

New Delhi, Ministry of Food and Agriculture, 1961.
29p.+ivp.+Maps.

Chairman : Dr. B.N. Uppal.
Members : Dr. J.K. Basu (retired, replaced by Shri M.S.V. Rama Rao); Shri F.C. Gera; Shri J.P. Mital.
Coopted Members : Shri C. K. Keralavarma ; Shri P. M. Mathew; Shri T.P. Kuttiamu.
Secretary : Shri A.S. Venu Gopalan.

APPOINTMENT

The uncultivated lands in the country may be broadly classified into the following two categories:

(a) Lands which are really adjuncts of village *abadis* and are meant to serve as pastures and fuel forests or sites for the extension of *abadis*; and

(b) Lands in large-sized blocks which have either gone out of cultivation, or have never been brought under cultivation.

With a view to utilising the latter category of lands which afford the greatest promise for increased agricultural production, the Government of India constituted this Committee, vide their letter No. F/1024/Spl./59, dated. June 11, 1959.

TERMS OF REFERENCE

(i) To make a survey of land classified as "other uncultivated land excluding fallow lands" and "fallow lands other than current fallows" and locate areas where large blocks of land are available for reclamation and resettlement;

(ii) To suggest suitable measures for reclamation according to conditions in different areas and estimate the cost of reclamation and colonisation and the financial assistance and agricultural extension and training necessary for the settlers (the settlements being made on a cooperative basis);

(iii) To suggest the terms and conditions upon which settlement should de made, the areas to be allotted and the payments to be made by settlers' cooperatives; and

(iv) To estimate the economic aspects of such reclamation in terms of the expenditure involved, the likely addition to food production and the employment and income that would become available to settlers and their families and to lay down the priorities *inter se* between different categories of reclaimable lands.

CONTENTS

Introduction; Preface; General Aspects; Description of Blocks and Measures for Reclamation; Disposal of Reclaimed Lands for Cultivation; Summary of Conclusions and Recommendations; Appendices A to F; Maps I and II.

RECOMMENDATIONS

Of the total area of 1.26 million acres under the heads "other uncultivated land excluding fallows" and "fallows other than current fallows" only seven blocks comprising 56,000 acres have been located in the State in blocks of 250 acres or more.

The distribution of wastelands in the different districts is given below:

District	Block No.	Area(Acres)
Kozhikode	1	3,323
Trichur	2	500
Falghat	384	1,000
Ernakulam	5	500
Kottayam	6	42,604
Tirvandrum	7	8,000
	Total	55,927

In the Kuttanad, over 1,20,000 acres are at present growing one crop of paddy since this area is subject to inundation by sea-water. If suitable measures are adopted, such as the construction of lands to prevent the ingress of salt water and the provision of irrigation facilities, much of this area can be double cropped. The construction of the Thottapilly spillway and the Thanirmukham barrier will bring a large proportion of this area under their command. It is estimated that at least 50,000 acres in the Upper Kuttanad can be easily converted into double-cropped lands at a cost of Rs. 500-600 per acre. These areas are capable of being developed into lands suitable for the cocoanut cultivation by growing paddy crops in them successively, for four or five years.

The lands in the Kozhikode district are infested with weeds, and shrubs. The soil is fertile. No irrigation is available. The cost of reclamation is estimated at Rs. 250 per acre.

Most of the lands located in the Trichur, district are already being cultivated unauthorisedly. The soil is fertile. Perennial irrigation will be available after the completion of the second stage of the Sholayur Project.

The wastelands in the Palghat district are located in the Attapaddy Valley which is a vast hilly area of about 280 sq. miles covered with forests. The soil is very fertile. There is possibility of providing perennial irrigation from natural channels. The cost of reclamation is estimated at Rs. 250 per acre.

A comprehensive scheme for the development of wastelands in the Attapaddy Valley should be formulated which would include a rapid reconnaissance survey for locating blocks of wastelands, construction of bunds across the Kookampalayam and Golikkadavu streams for augmenting irrigation water supply, improvement of A nakketty-Sholayur road, and settling tribal families on the land.

The block of wastelands located in the Ernakulam district is a marshy area, and is infested with bushes and shrubs. The soil is alluvium. The cost of reclamation involving the clearance of bushes and shrubs and filling the area with earth is estimated at Rs. 2,000 per acre.

The wastelands in the Kottayam district are located in the Munnar area. The areas mostly consist of lofty hills and steep valleys and hence are not suitabie for cultivation.

The wastelands in the Trivandrum district are located in a narrow strip of littaral sand of an average width of one mile running from south to north, from Velikayal to Kadinamkulam. The area is suitable for establishing cocoanut plantations. The cost of irrigation is estimated at Rs. 800 per acre, in addition to an expenditure of Rs. 1,000 per acre on the digging of pits for planting, transport of manure and silt for incorporation into the sandy soils, the price of seedlings, etc.

The wastelands belonging to private individuals will have to be acquired before they can be disposed of to landless labourers, the members of Scheduled Castes and the Scheduled Tribes, etc. The cost of acquisition is estimated at Rs. 100—200 per acre.

The lands belonging to the Government, after reclamation, may be allotted to landless labourers, members of the Schedule Castes and the Scheduled Tribes, etc., or to actual cultivators who have no lands of their own and who may be willing to do cooperative farming under the Cooperative Colonisation Scheme proposed by the State Government to be undertaken during the Third Plan period.

The cost of reclaiming 5,323 acres of wastelands located in the districts of Kozhikode, Trichur, Palghat and Ernakulam comes to about Rs. 20.80 lakhs. *i.e.,* about Rs. 400 per acre. The estimated additional production from the reclaimed lands is 37,500 maunds of paddy and 1,82,765 maunds of tapioca valued at Rs. 7.43 lakhs. Thus the value of production will cover the cost of reclamation in two or three crop seasons.

The wastelands found in the district of Trichur and Palghat would appear to be the most profitable in terms of the additional food production per acre, followed by the block in the Kozhikode district. The cost of reclamation of the marshy area in the Ernakulam district is not commensurate with the expenditure involved. The wastelands in the Munnar area (block 6) are not suitable for cultivation.

The following is the order of priority assigned to the areas included in blocks 1—5 and 7.

		Priority
Blocks 2-4 & 7	...	I
Block 1	...	II
Block 5	...	III

WASTELANDS SURVEY AND RECLAMATION COMMITTEE ON LOCATION AND UTILISATION OF WASTELANDS IN INDIA (MADHYA PRADESH), 1959—REPORT

New Delhi, Ministry of Food and Agriculture, 1961.
83p.+ivp.+Maps.

Chairman : Dr. B.N. Uppal.

Members : Shri J.P. Mital; Shri F.C. Gera; Dr. J.K. Basu (retired; replaced by Shri M.S.V. Rama Rao).

Coopted Members : Shri P.S. Bapna; Shri R.C. Murab; Shri N.D. Gupta; Shri M.L. Sood; Shri J.K. Verma.

Secretary : Shri A.S. Venu Gopalan.

APPOINTMENT

The uncultivated lands in the country may be broadly classified into the following two categories:

(a) Lands which are really adjuncts of village *abadis* and are meant to serve as pastures and fuel forests or sites for the extension of *abadis*; and

(b) Lands in large-sized blocks which have either gone out of cultivation or have never been brought under cultivation.

With a view to utilising the latter category of lands which afford the greatest promise for increased agricultural production, the Government of India constituted this Committee, vide their letter No. F/1024/Spl./59, dated June 11, 1959.

TERMS OF REFERENCE

(i) To make a survey of land classified as "other uncultivated land excluding fallow lands" and "fallow lands other than current fallows" and locate areas where large blocks of land are available for reclamation and resettlement;

(ii) To suggest suitable measures for reclamation according to conditions in different areas and estimate the cost of reclamation and colonisation and the financial assistance and agricultural extension and training necessary for the settlers (the settlements being made on a cooperative basis);

(iii) To suggest the terms and conditions upon which settlement should be made, the areas to be allotted and the payments to be made by settlers' cooperatives; and

(iv) To estimate the economic aspects of such reclamation in terms of the expenditure involved, the likely addition to food production and the employment and income that would become available to settlers and their families and to lay down the priorities *inter se* between different categories of reclaimable lands.

CONTENTS

Introduction; Perface; General Aspects; Descriptiou

of Blocks and Measures for Reclamation; Disposal of Reclaimed Lands for Cultivation; Summary of Conclusions and Recommendations; Appendices A to K, Maps I & II.

RECOMMENDATIONS

Of the total area of 22.75 million acres under the heads "other uncultivated lands excluding fallows" and "fallows other than current fallows", only 2.55 lakh acres have been located in the State for reclamation in blocks of 250 acres or more. This area is relatively small in view of the fact that the extent of arable wastelands available in the State is much less than that reported in the revenue records, and the bulk of wastelands is found in blocks smaller than 250 acres spread all over the State.

The wastelands in blocks of 250 acres or more have been located in 21 districts of the State. Large areas of wastelands have been reported in the districts of Morena, Shivpuri, Panna, Satna, Reva and Guna.

The blocks offered for reclamation are mostly infested with thick jungle growth, shrubs and bushes. No irrigation is available in most of the areas.

The wastelands in the State are owned by the private individuals, the Government, or the Bhoodan Organisation. More than 93 per cent of the wastelands belong to the Government, and only a small proportion of these lands is the property of private individuals, or is donated to the Bhoodan Organisation.

In order to bring the wastelands belonging to the Government under cultivation, cooperative colonies of landless labourers, members of the Scheduled Castes and the Scheduled Tribes, etc., may be set up, or these lands may be allotted to the members of the Scheduled Castes and the Scheduled Tribes, etc., in accordance with the existing regulations under the Land Revenne Code. As most of the wastelands are found in the districts where the density of population is low, the establishment of cooperative colonies of settlers seems to be the only feasible method of disposal of wastelands in these districts. The expenditure on the setting up of cooperative colonies is much more than that involved in reclaiming lands and allotting these to private individuals for cultivation. Larger allocations should, therefore, be made for settlement work and the State Government should make every effort to dispose of as large areas of wastelands as possible by organising cooperative colonies of settlers.

The lands donated to the Bhoodan Organisation are proposed to be allotted in accordance with the provisions of the State Bhoodan Yagna Act.

A rapid reconnaissance suvery of wastelands should be conducted quickly so that marginal lands are not allotted for arable cultivation.

In order to carry out the programme of reclamation, it will be necessary for the State Directorate of Agriculture to add to the existing strength of its tractors fleet.

After reclamation measures have been carried out, the responsibility for the follow-up cultivation should be that of the normal staff of the Agriculture Department, which, if necessary, may be strengthened. The agricultural staff should suggest suitable cropping patterns and also introduce improved agricultural practices in the reclaimed areas. The extension staff of the Community Development Organisation can assist, particularly in the demonstration of improved methods of cultivation and in arranging for the supply of agricultural requisites.

Wherever irrigation facilities can be provided by the construction of wells or tube-wells, loans may be given on a liberal scale to the cultivators.

Whenever allotments of Government lands are made to individuals, other than the members of the Schcduled Castes and the Scheduled Tribes, etc., it is necessary to ensure that the persons to whom the lands are allotted are able to cultivate them without any special financial assistance from the Government.

An enquiry to find out as to what percentage of lands allotted to the landless labourers, members of the Scheduled Castes and the Scheduled Tribes, etc. is brought under cultivation, seems necessary, with a view to ascertaining whether there are any lands which have not been cultivated, and the reasons for keeping them fallow. This will help the State Government in adopting such measures as will discourage the allottees from leaving the lands uncultivated.

There should be close coordination between the work of the Tribal Welfare Department and the Land Records Department in relation to the settlement projects, so that the funds at the disposal of these two departments are utilised in the best manner possible.

In view of the satisfactory progress made in the settlement projects during the Second Plan Period, the tempo of settlement work should be increased during the Third Five-Year Plan.

Special attention should be given to the selection of settlers as it is the most important factor contributing to the success of a settlement project.

Settlement projects should be undertaken to those districts where the prospects of settlement are more enconraging, *i.e.*, where irrigation and good fertile lands are available and the right type of settlers are forthcoming to take up cultivation, and the cost of settlement is not high, as compared to other districts.

For any settlement work to be successful, it is necessary that the Revenue/Block agency should be associated with it, so that the problems of the settlers are attended to as expeditiously as possible.

In the districts where the bulk of wastelands is found, the utilisation of wastelands involves not only reclamation but also the establishment of settlement colonies for arranging their cultivation as the size of holdings in these districts is large and there is, therefore, no desire on the part of the local settlers to move away from their existing holdings. The settlement of landless labourers and the members of the Scheduled Castes and the Scheduled Tribes is however, a social problem and the expenditure on this account should accordingly be treated separately from the cost of reclamation, which alone should be considered in determining the economic aspects of a reclamation project.

Of the total area of 2,55,137 acres of wastelands offered for reclamation in the different districts, the cost of reclaiming 53,512 acres located in the districts of Chhindwara, Raisen, Betul, Panna and Satna will exceed Rs. 250 per acre. These lands are badly eroded and are covered with thick jungle growth. In these circumstances, no expenditure should be incurred on the reclamation of these wastelends.

Crop-cutting surveys may be conducted in the reclaimed lands during the Third Five Year Plan, particularly in the districts of Guna, Shivpuri and Morena, where large blocks of wastelands are likely to be taken up for reclamation.

The cost of reclaiming 2,01,625 acres (excluding 53,512 acres which cannot be reclaimed at economic cost) comes to about Rs. 2.51 crores, *i.e.*, about Rs. 125 per acre. The estimated additional production from the reclaimed lands is about 46,600 tons valued at about Rs. 1.51 crores. Thus, the value of production will cover the cost of reclamation in two to three crop seasons.

The wastelands offered in the districts of Shivpuri, Guna, Damoh and Rewa seem to be very promising in increasing agricultural production, since the cost of reclaiming the lands is about Rs. 100 per acre, and there are also large areas of these wastelands, which have fertile alluvial or black soils. In the Guna district, however, there is scarcity of drinking water, and a rapid survey of the ground water resources would be necessary before undertaking any large-scale operations for reclaiming wastelands.

In the district of Morena, the cost of reclamation is rather high, *i.e.*, Rs. 225 per acre, but the estimated additional production of about eight maunds per acre will pay off the cost of reclamation in two or three crop seasons. Further, there are some blocks in this district which will be commanded by the Chambal River Project during the Third Plan period, and they should, therefore, receive high priority in the reclamation programme of the State. The wastelands in the Raigarh, Raipur, Bhind and Chhatarpur districts which are capable of yielding about eight to 10 maunds of foodgrains per acre, should be taken up for reclamation early. The cost of reclaiming wastelands in the districts of Vidisha, Dewas, Gwalior, Sehore, Seoni and Betul ranges from Rs. 50 to Rs. 100 per acre, but the additional production will hardly be three to four maunds per acre. Reclamation of wastelands in Tikamgarh may be taken up only when irrigation becomes available. The wastelands in the Jhabua district should not be taken up for reclamation for the present as the estimated production is low due to the gravelly nature of the soil.

Based upon the average cost of reclamation per maund of additional production and the rainfall and soil conditions obtaining in the different districts, we suggest the following order of priorities :

District	Priority	Area (Acres)
Chhatarpur, Raigarh, Bhind, Vidisha, Raipur, Shivpuri, Seoni, Rewa, Gwalior, Morena, Guna and Surguja	I	1,89,037
Dewas, Raisen, Damoh and Sehore	II	9,066
Tikamgarh and Jhabua	III	3,522

WASTELANDS SURVEY AND RECLAMATION COMMITTEE ON LOCATION AND UTILISATION OF WASTELANDS IN INDIA (MADRAS), 1959—REPORT

New Delhi, Ministry of Food and Agriculture, 1962.
40p.+ixp.+Maps.

Chairman : Dr. B. N. Uppal.
Members : Dr. J, K. Basu (retired; replaced by Shri M. S. V. Rama Rao); Shri F. C. Gera; Shri J. P. Mital.
Coopted Members : Shri D. A. Karthikeyan; Shri D. Ambrose; Shri K. R. Venkatesan; Smt. S Satyabhama; Shri T. R. Ramakrishnan.
Secretary ; Shri A. S. Venu Gopalan.

APPOINTMENT

The uncultivatd lands in the country may be broadly classified into the following two categories:

(a) Lands which are really adjuncts of village *abadis* and are meant to serve as pastures and fuel forests or sites for the extension of *abadis*; and

(b) Lands in large-sized blocks which have either gone out of cultivation or have never been brought under cultivation.

With a view to utilizing the latter category of lands which afford the greatest promise for increased agricultural production, the Government of India constituted this Committee vide their letter No. F/1024/Spl./59, dated June 11, 1959.

TERMS OF REFERENCE

(i) To make a survey of land classified as "other uncultivated land excluding fallow lands" and "fallow lands other than current fallows" and locate areas where large blocks of land are available for reclamation and resettlement;

(ii) To suggest suitable measures for reclamation according to conditions in different areas and estimate the cost of reclamation and colonisation and the financial assistance and agricultural extension and training necessary for the settlers (the settlements being made on a cooperative basis);

(iii) To suggest the terms and conditions upon which settlement should be made, the areas to be allotted and the payments to be made by settlers' cooperatives; and

(iv) To estimate the economic aspects of such reclamation in terms of the expenditure inovlved, the likely addition to food production and the employment and income that would become available to settlers and their families and to lay down the priorities *inter se* between different categories of reclaimable lands.

CONTENTS

Introduction; Preface,, General Aspects; Description of Blocks and Measures for Reclamation; Disposal of Reclaimed Lands for Cultivation; Summary of General Conclusions and Recommendations; Appendices A to H; Maps I and II.

RECOMMENDATIONS

Of the total area of 5.22 acres under the heads "other uncultivated land excluding fallows" and "fallows other than current fallows", about 38,000 acres have been located in the State for reclamation. This area is relatively very small as compared with the figures reported in the revenue records. It was explained, however, that the revenue figures could not be relied upon and that large areas of wastelands had already been allotted for cultivation to the members of the Scheduled Castes and the Scheduled Tribes, etc.

The wastelands offered for reclamation in the State may be broadly divided into the following three categories:

I. Dry lands.
II. Saline lands, and
III. Lands infested with thick growth of bushes and jungle.

The distribution of wastelands in categories I to III is given below:—

Category		Area (Acres)
I	... ...	28,266
II	... ...	8,000
III	... ...	2,200
	Total	38,466

Most of the wastelands in category I are found in the districts of North Arcot, South Arcot, Ramanathapuram; Salem and Tiruchirapalli. The entire area located in the Tirunelveli district and a part of the area in the Ramanathapuram district are not suitable for cultivation. The wastelands in the North Arcot, South Arcot and Ramanathapuram districts are low in fertility and can grow only seasonal crops. The lands in the Salem district are, however, fertile and, with provision of irrigation facilities, double cropping can be practised on these lands. In the Tiruchirapalli district the uplands may be put under crops like cashewnut on a plantation scale. The other wastelands may be utilised for growing millets.

It appears that of the 30,000 aeres allotted for individual culivation in the Attur taluk of the Salem district, a large part of this area has not been brought under cultivation due mainly to lack of irrigation facilities and the selection of settlers who did not have sufficient resources for reclaiming the lands and for follow-on cultivation operations. In the circumstances, large areas of wastelands are still available in the Attur taluk. A rapid survey should be conducted to locate these areas so that they could be taken up for cultivation.

The saline lands in category II are located in the Tanjore district. These are swampy lands, and are not suitable for cultivation due to their high salt content.

The lands in category III are situated in an area of heavy rainfall, and are suitable for growing rubber, tea pepper, etc. Some of the lands along the coast where rainfall is not heavy, seem to the suitable for gruwing crops like cashewnut, cocoanut, etc.

Most of the wastelands located for reclamation belong to the Government, and only a small area is privately-owned, The lands belonging to private individuals may, after reclamation, be handed over to their respective owners for their follow-on cultivation. The cost of reclamation of these dry lands in not likely to be high. The expenditure on contour-bunding of the dry lands may be shared between the Government and the cultivator on the basis of the existing pattern of financial assistance whereby 25 per cent ot the expenditure is treated as subsidy to the cultivator and 75 per cent is advanced as loan to be recovered over a period of 10—15 years.

A detailed soil survey for land-use should be carried out in each area proposed for reclamation, so that the lands are put to proper use. The State Government may apply for financial assistant to the Central Soil Conservation Board for conducting these surveys.

After reclamation measures have been carried out, the responsibility for follow-on cultivation should be that of the normal staff of the Agriculture Department. The agricultural staff should suggest suitable cropping patterns and also introduce improved agricultural practices in the reclaimed areas. The extension staff of the Community Development Organisation can assist, particularly in the demonstration of improved methods of cultivation and in arranging for the supply of agricultural requisites.

In the Attur taluk of the Salem district where about 5,500 acres have been located in blocks of 250 acres or more, and where more areas of wastelands are reported to be available, the rainfall is about 40 inches, but it is not well-distributed. However, the water-table in all the blocks is fairly high, and open wells can be sunk at a depth of 20—30 feet. Also, in the lands adjoining the hills, there are a number of streams which flow up to the end of February. There are thus adequate facilities for providing irrigation which seems to be necessary to ensure good crops. Similarly, in the district of Tiruchirapalli, facilities for irrigation will have to be provided for successful cultivation of the reclaimed lands. Accordingly, it is suggested that loans may be given on a liberal scale to the cultivators for sinking wells.

Some of the areas in the Salem and Tiruchirapalli districts are rocky, and it will be difficult to dig wells without the help of equipments like drills, blasting units, etc. It was reported that these equipments were not available in sufficient quantities in the State. As the lands in these two districts have great potentialities for agricultural production, suitable assistance may be given for the import of the necessary equipments for boring wells.

Before the wastelands are allotted to landless labourers, the members of the Scheduled Castes and the Scheduled Tribes, etc., these lands should be reclaimed.

In any settlement project, the selection of suitable settlers is a vital factor contributing to its success. Special attention should be given to this important aspect of settlement work so that the right type of settlers who have an aptitude for agricultural work and who are willing to do hard work are selected.

In order that the settlement work is successful, it is necessary that the revenue/block agency should be associated with it so that the problem of the settlers are attended to as expeditiously as possible. Experience has shown that where the District Collectors and the Block Development Officers take personal interest in the settlement work, the projects are often successful.

In view of the availability of large areas of wastelands in the Salem and Tiruchirapalli districts, and the satisfactory progress made in settling landless labourers on these lands, suitable provision should be made under the Third Five-Year Plan for executing settlement projects in these districts.

The cost of reclaiming 24,446 acres in category I (excluding 3,820 acres which are not suitable for cultivation) comes to Rs. 27.30 lakhs, *i.e.*, about Rs. 112 per acre. The estimated additional production from the reclaimed lands is 195,186 maunds of foodgrains, valued at Rs. 19.51 lakhs. Thus, the value of production will cover the cost of reclamation in about two seasons.

The cost of reclaiming 1,200 acres in category III (excluding 1,000 acres, the cost of reclamation of which is high) is estimated at Rs. 30.00 lakhs, *i.e.*, Rs. 250 per acre. Considering that these lands are suitable for growing crops like pepper, tea, rubber, etc., which are remunerative, their reclamation will be economical.

A study of the economics of reclamation of the

different blocks of wastelands in category I reveals that the lands in the Salem district are the most profitable in terms of additional food production, followed by blocks located in the Tiruchirapalli district. In other blocks, the cost of reclamation is not high; and by the adoption of suitable system of dry farming, the risk of crop failures can be reduced and normal crop yields obtained.

The following order of priority is assigned to the different areas :

District	Block No.	Priority
Salem and Kanyakumari	20—24 & 41	I
Tiruchirapalli	25—39	II
Chingleput, North Arcot, South Arcot, Ramanathapuram and Coimbatore	1, 2—6, 7—13, 16 and 17	III

WASTELANDS SURVEY AND RECLAMATION COMMITTEE ON LOCATION AND UTILISATION OF WASTELANDS IN INDIA (MAHARASHTRA), 1959—REPORT

New Delhi, Ministry of Food and Agriculture, 1963.
33p.+ixp.+Maps.

Chairman : Dr. B. N. Uppal.
Members : Dr. J. K. Basu (retired; replaced by Shri M. S. Y. Rama Rao); Shri F. C. Gera; Shri J. P. Mital; Shri R. V. Tamhane,
Coopted Members : Shri D. R. Pradhan; Shri D. D. Sathe; Shri S. P. Mohite; Shri D. A. Gadkary; Shri J. V. Karamchandani.
Secretary : Shri A. S. Venu Gopalan.

APPOINTMENT

The uncultivated lands in the country may be broadly classified into the following two categories :

(a) Lands which are really adjuncts of village *abadis* and are meant to serve as pastures and fuel forests or sites for the extension of *abadis*, and

(b) Lands in large-sized blocks which have either gone out of cultivation or have never been brought under cultivation.

With a view to utilising the latter category of lands which afford the greatest promise for increased agricultural production, the Government of India constituted this Committee, vide their letter No. F/1024/Spl./59, dated June, 11 1959.

TERMS OF REFERENCE

(i) To make a survey of land classified as"other uncultivated land excluding fallow lands' and "fallow lands other than current fallows" and locate areas where large blocks of land are available for reclamation and resettlement;

(ii) To suggest suitable measures for reclamation according to conditions in different areas and estimate the cost of reclamation and colonisation and the finanacial assistance and agricultural extension and training necessary for the settlers (the settlements being made on a cooperative basis);

(iii) To suggest the terms and conditions upon which settlement should be made, the areas to be allotted and the payments to be made by settlers' cooperatives; and

(iv) To estimate the economic aspects of such reclamation in terms of the expenditure involved, the likely addition to food production and the employment and income that would become available to settlers and their families and to lay down the priorities *inter se* between different categories of reclaimable lands.

CONTENTS

Introduction; Preface; General Aspects; Description of Blocks and Measures for Reclamation; Disposal of Reclaimed Lands for Cultivation; Summary of Conclusions and Recommendations; Appendices A to H; Maps I to III.

RECOMMENDATIONS

Of the total area of 10.09 million acres under the heads 'other uncultivated land excluding fallows' and 'fallows other than current fallows', an area of 48,020 acres only has been located in the State for reclamation in compact blocks of 250 acres or more. This area is relatively small in view of the fact that the bulk of wastelands has already been disposed of by the State Government, for cultivation on *eksali* lease by the members of the Backward Classes including the *Adivasis*.

The State Governments are doing their best to bring

the wastelands under cultivation as speedily as possible, but it is necessary that rapid surveys should be conducted to delineate the wastelands broadly on the basis of proper land-use so that the diversion of lands which are more suited for pasture, for arable cultivation may not in the end result in greater impoverishment of these lands due to soil erosion,

The wastelands found in the State can he brodly divided into the following two categories :

I. Dry lands, and

II. Lands infested with thick growth of bushes and jungle.

The distribution of wastelands in the two categories is as under:—

Category			Area (Acres)
I	...	...	36,710
II	...	...	6,310
			43,020

The wastelands included in category I are situated in tracts of low and variable rainfall ranging from 20 to 30 inches. These lands are generally poor and have barely a soil depth of six to 12 inches. The lands are suitable for the development of pastures and should not be opened up for arable cultivation, except in areas where there is moderate rainfall of 25 inches and above, and where the soil has sufficient depth to support the growth of crops. Even then, suitable water and soil conservation measures should be adopted for successful cultivation under conditions of low and variable rainfall, since the absence of such measures will result in the failure of crops during long periods of drought and also aggravate the problem of soil erosion. The average cost of reclamation of dry lands is estimated at Rs. 100 per acre.

The wastelands in category II are found in the districts of Chanda and Kolaba where there is sufficient rainfall. The cost of reclamation is estimated at Rs. 150—200 per acre.

The State Government have approved the Dina Irrigation Project in the Chanda district at an estimated cost of Rs. 2.44 crores. This project can command an area of about 30,000 acres, but only 18,000 acres of cultivated land are available for irrigation at the tail end of the canal. On the other hand, 30,500 acres comprising 12,500 acres of wastelands and 18,000 acres of class 'B' forest lands are available in the upper reaches of the canal, and if this area is taken up for reclamation, an additional area of about 12,000 acres will become available for irrigation and there will be a substantial reduction in the estimated cost of the project. In this connection, the following suggestions have been made :

(i) The forest lands may be released for cultivation.

(ii) The cost of reclaiming 12,500 acres of wastelands and 18,000 acres of class 'B' forest lands may be borne by the Agriculture Department, but not charged to the Dina Project.

(iii) The question of setting up lift irrigation projects along the Wainganga river should be investigated, so that the cultivated lands at the tail end which were to be irrigated from the projected canal from the Dina Irrigation Project, may receive their irrigation supply from the lift irrigation projects. There seem to be good prospects of setting up lift irrigation projects along the Wainganga.

(iv) The possibility of establishing a mechanised farm in the area to be irrigated from the Dina Project should be investigated.

Most of the wastelands in categories I and II belonged to the Government, and only a small area belongs to private individuals and village panchayats. It is likely that the bulk of the wastelands belonging to the Government have already been distributed, since the work of land distribution in the entire State was to be completed by March, 31, 1961.

The wastelands belonging to private individuals in category I may be reclaimed by undertaking suitable soil and water conservation measures, and the expenditure on these measures should be shared as under :

(a) 75 per cent of the expenditure may be advanced as loans to the cultivators to be recovered over a period of 10—15 years; and

(b) 25 per cent of it should be treated as subsidy to be shared between the Centre and the State.

The cost of reclamation of the land in category II is rather high, and it will not be within the reach of the cultivators to undertake reclamation measures on their own. The work should, therefore, be undertaken by the State Government on behalf of private individuals and the expenditure shared in the manner indicated for category I.

The lands belonging to village panchayats may, after reclamation, be given back to them for arranging follow-on cultivation.

The total cost of reclaiming 35,584 acres of wastelands in categories I and II (exclusive of the lands of which the cost of reclamation is reported to be very high, and of areas which cannot be brought under cultivation) comes to Rs. 38.20 lakhs, *i. e.*, Rs. 107 per acre. The estimated additional production from the reclaimed land is 6,532 tons, valued at Rs. 14.27 lakhs. Thus the value of production will cover the cost of reclamation in three crop seasons.

The following order of priority may be assigned to the two categories of wastelands :

Cetegory			Priority
II	...	...	1
I	...	...	2

WASTELANDS SURVEY AND RECLAMATION COMMITTEE ON LOCATION AND UTILISATION OF WASTELANDS IN INDIA (MYSORE), 1959—REPORT

New Delhi, Ministry of Food and Agriculture, 1961.
48p.+ivp.+Maps.

Chairman : Dr. B. N. Uppal.
Members : Dr. J. K. Basu (retired; replaced by Shri M. S. V. Rama Rao); Shri F. C. Gera; Shri J. P. Mital.
Coopted Members : Shri R. J. Rabello; Shri M. S. Swaminathan; Shri M. H. Minchigiah; Shri M. L. Subanna.
Secretary : Shri A. S. Venu Gopalan.

APPOINTMENT :

The uncultivated lands in the country may be broadly classified into the following two categories :—

(a) Lands which are really adjuncts of village *abadis* and are meant to serve as pastures and fuel forests or sites for the extension of *abadis*, and

(b) Lands in large-sized blocks which have either gone out of cultivation or have never been brought under cultivation.

With a view to utilising the latter category of lands which afford the greatest promise for increased agricultural production, the Government of India constituted this Committee, vide their letter No. F./1024/Spl./59, dated June 11, 1959.

TERMS OF REFERENCE

(i) To make a survey of land classified as "other uncultivated land excluding fallow lands" and "fallow lands other than current fallows" and locate areas where large blocks of land are available for reclamation and resettlement;

(ii) To suggest suitable measures for reclamation according to conditions in different areas and estimate the cost of reclamation and colonisation and the financial assistance and agricultural extension and training necesary for the settlers (the settlements being made on a cooperative basis);

(iii) To suggest the terms and conditions upon which settlement should be made, the area to be allotted and the payments to be made by settlers' cooperatives; and

(iv) To estimate the economic aspects of such reclamation in terms of the expenditure involved, the likely addition to food production and the employment and income that would become available to settlers and their families and to lay down the priorities *inter se* between different categories of reclaimable lands.

CONTENTS

Introduction; Preface; General Aspects; Description of Blocks and Measures for Reclamation; Disposal of Reclaimed Lands for Cultivation; Summary of Conclusions and Recommendations; Appendices A to H.

RECOMMENDATIONS

Of the total area of 8.25 million acres under the heads "other uncultivated lands excluding fallows" and "fallows other than current fallows", about 1,18,000 acres of wastelands in blocks of 250 acres or more have been located for reclamation. This area is relatively small as a large proportion of wastelands is found scattered in small pieces, and the figures of wastelands reported under the above two heads are not very reliable.

The wastelands offered for reclamation in the State may be broadly divided into the following four categories

I. Eroded lands;

II. *Kaval* (pasture) lands;

III. Lands infested with thick growth of jungle bushes and shrubs; and

IV. *Khar* (saline) lands.

The distribution of wastelands in the four categories is as under :

Category			Area (Acres)
I	...	...	7,031
II	...	...	22,031
III	...	...	81,433
IV	...	...	7,832
		Total	1,18,327

The wastelands included in category I are situated in a belt where low and variable rainfall is received, and hence crop growing is a hazard unless suitable measures are taken for conservation of soil moisture, and for preventing the loss of soil by erosion. Contour-bunding of eroded lands followed by the adoption of a suitable system of dry farming will rehabilitate these degraded lands.

The wastelands included in category II are located in tracts of low rainfall ranging from 20 to 30 inches

These lands are generally poor and have barely a small depth of six to 12 inches. The soil is gravelly red or mixed red and black as found in the districts of Chitradurga, Tumkur and Hassan, and it is lateritic in the Mysore district. These lands are suitable for the development of pastures, and should not be opened up for arable cultivation, axcept in areas where there is a moderate rainfall of 25 inches and above and the soil has sufficient depth to support the growth of crops. Even then, suitable soil and water conservation measures should be adopted for successful crop production.

The wastelands in category III are infested with thick growth of shrubs and bushes and can be developed for growing food and plantation crops. These lands are situated in tracts receiving a rainfall of 30--50 inches, or in areas of high rainfall ranging from 100 to 175 inches. The soil is either black or mixed read and black.

In category III is included a large-sized block comprising about 12,000 acres. It is situated near village Koppa, which is about 54 miles from Mysore and 12 miles from Periyapatna on the Mysore-Mercara road. The area is covered with thick jungle growth which is composed of fuel and timber trees The soil is black and rich in organic matter. In some places, red loamy soil is found, which is fertile and well-drained. The area has an assured and well distributed rainfall of about 50 inches and receives both the south-west and the north-east monsoons. At present no irrigation is available, but there are good, prospects of providing irrigation by undertaking repairs to the tanks which have gone out of use, or by providing lift irrigation from the river Cauvery. The area is ideally suited for setting up cooperative colonies of landless labourers.

The wastelands included in category IV comprising 7,832 acres of saline lands are in the Chitradurga and North Kanara districts. These lands, after reclamation, can grow good crops of paddy.

A systematic survey of saline-affected lands in the State should be organised by the State Government, and adequate provisions for reclaiming these lands should also be made under the Third Plan.

Most of the wastelands in categories I to III belong to the Government, and only a small area belongs to private individuals and village panchayats. In category IV (*Khar* lands), however, most of the lands are privately-owned. In order to bring the lands belonging to the Government under cultivation, allotments may be made to the members of the Scheduled Castes and the Scheduled Tribes, etc., in accordance with the existing rules for the disposal of wastelands in the different regions of the State.

The wastelands belonging to private individuals in categories I to II may be reclaimed by undertaking suitable soil and water conservation measures, and the expenditure on these measures shall be shared as under :

(a) 75 per cent of the expenditure may be advanced as loans to the cultivators to be recovered over a period of 10—15 years;

(b) 25 per cent of it should be treated as subsidy to be shared between the Centre and the State.

The *Khar* lands belonging to private individuals should be handed over, after reclamation, to their owners for follow-on cultivation.

The lands belonging to village panchayats may be given back to them for arranging follows-on cultivation.

A detailed soil survey for land-use should be carried out in each area proposed for reclamation, particularly in the eroded lands found in North Mysore, and in the districts of Chitradurga, Tumkur, Hassan and Mysore where *kaval* (pasture) lands have been offered for reclamation.

In order to carry out the programme of reclamation of wastelands in category III, it will be necessary for the State Directorate of Agriculture to add to the existing strength of its tractor fleet.

After the reclamation measures have been carried out, the responsibility for follow-on cultivation should be that of the normal staff of the Agriculture Department which, if necessary, may be strengthened. Trials and demonstrations of improved agricultural practices should be organised on cultivators' holdings, so that they may adopt suitable soil management practices in reclaimed lands. The responsibility for extension work may be transferred to the Community Development Organisation after the initial period of demonstration.

Wherever irrigation facilities can be provided by the construction of wells, loans for this purpose may be given on a liberal scale to the cultivators.

Before the Government wastelands are allotted to the members of the Scheduled Castes and the Scheduled Tribes, etc., these lands should be reclaimed, and the expenditure on reclamation borne by the Government.

Specal attention should be given to the selection of settlers so that the right type of settlers who have an aptitude for agricultural work and who are willing to do hard work, are selected.

In order that the settlement work may be successful, it is necessary that the revenue/block agency should be associated with it so that the problems of the settlers are attended to as expeditiously as possible.

The total cost of reclaiming 68,820 acres of wastelands in categories I, III and IV (exclusive of the lands of which the cost of reclamation has been reported to be very high, and of the forest areas which may not be available for cultivation) comes to about Rs. 1.65 crores, *i.e.*, about Rs. 236 per acre. The estimated additional production from the reclaimed lands is 20,530 tons valued at Rs. 67.29 lakhs. The average cost of reclamation, therefore, is economic in terms of additional production.

A study of the economics of reclamation between the three categories of wastelands reveals that the areas included in category IV (*khar* lands) are the most profitable in terms of additional production. On the other hand, category III offers the greatest promise for increasing agricultural production since large areas of lands infested with thick growth of jungle shrubs and bushes are available in the State. The extent of wastelands offered for reclamation in category I is small, but the adoption of a suitable system of dry farming in these lands not only reduces the risk of crop failures but appreciably increases the crop yields.

The wastelands included in category IV (*khar* lands) may be assigned the highest priority. The wastelands in category III should, also be assigned on equally high priority, since large tracts of these lands are available, which, when reclaimed, will assist in increasing agricultural production in the State. The wastelands included in category I may be assigned the next order of priority.

WASTELANDS SURVEY AND RECLAMATION COMMITTEE ON LOCATION AND UTILISATION OF WASTELANDS IN INDIA (PUNJAB), 1959—REPORT

New Delhi, Ministry of Food and Agriculture, 1961.
54p,+ixp.+Waps

Chairman : Dr. B. N. Uppal.
Members : Dr. J. K. Basu (retired; replaced by Shri M. S. V. Rama Rao); Shri F. C. Gera; Shri J. P. Mital.
Coopted Members : Shri Lal Singh; Shri S. C. Jain; Shri S. K. Misra; Shri H. L. Uppal; Shri P. S. Saggoo.
Secretary : Shri A. S. Venu Gopalan.

APPOINTMENT

The uncultivated lands in the country may be broadly classified into the following two categories :

(a) Lands which are really adjuncts of village *abadis* and are meant to serve as pastures and fuel forests or sites for the extension of *abadis*, and

(b) Lands in large-sized blocks which have either gone out of cultivation or have never been brought under cultivation.

With a view to utilising the latter category of lands which afford the greatest promise for increased agricultural production, the Government of India constituted this Committee, vide their letter No. F/1024/Spl./59, dated June 11, 1959.

TERMS OF REFERENCE

(i) To make a survey of land classified as "other uncultivated land excluding fallow lands" and "fallow lands other than current fallows" and locate areas where large blocks of land are available for reclamation and resettlement;

(ii) To suggest suitable measures for reclamation according to conditions in different areas and estimate the cost of reclamation and colonisation and the financial assistance and agricultural extension and training necessary for the settlers (the settlements being made on a cooperative basis);

(iii) To suggest the terms and conditions upon which settlement should be made, the areas to be allotted and the payments to be made by the settlers' cooperatives; and

(iv) To estimate the economic aspects of such reclamation in terms of the expenditure involved, the likely addition to food production and the employment and income that would become available to settlers and their families and to lay down the priorities *inter se* between different categories of reclaimable lands.

CONTENTS

Introduction; Preface; General Aspects; Description of Blocks and Measures for Reclamation; Disposal of Reclaimed Lands for Cultivation; Summary of General Conclusions and Recommendations; Appendices A to I; Maps I, IA & II.

RECOMMENDATIONS

The total extent of wastelands in the Punjab, according to the land utilisation statistics of 1957-58, is 2.06 million acres classified as "other uncultivated lands excluding fallows" (2.05 million acres) and "fallows other than current fallows" (0.01 million acres). Of this area of 2.06 million acres, 3.04 lakh acres have been located in the State for reclamation in blocks of the sizes of 250 acres or more.

The wastelands found in the State may be classified into the following five categories :

I. Lands infested with thick growth of jungle, bushes and shrubs;

II. Lands lying along the banks of the rivers, and infested with pernicious weeds and grasses;

III. Saline and alkaline lands;

IV. Eroded lands; and

V. Sand dunes or arid tracts.

The distribution of wastelands in categories I to III is as under :

Category			Area (Acres)
I	...	...	41,850
II	...	...	99,800
III	...	...	1,63,000

In addition, two million acres in category IV and four lakh acres in category V are reported to be available for reclamation, but their distribution in large-sized blocks is not known.

The blocks offered for reclamation in category I have great potentiality for food production as the lands in these blocks are fertile and irrigation is available in most of the areas. The cost of reclamation is estimated at Rs. 140 per acre. The total cost of reclaiming 41,850 acres would be Rs. 58.59 lakhs.

The system of getting the jungle clearance work done through contractors has proved quite satisfactory and should be continued. However, the practice of awarding contracts on an annual basis has resulted delays in the execution of work. It is suggested that contracts should be given for longer periods than one year, so as to enable the contracting companies to plan their work more efficiently. This procedure will result in greater output at lower costs.

The areas in category II are mostly situated along the river banks. The main problem of these areas is that the nallahs are silted up and do not function satisfactorily as natural drains, with the result that most of the areas are waterlogged and have consequently been rendered saline and alkaline. The areas are covered with thick grass growth and can be cleared only with tractors. Practically no irrigation facilities exist in most of the blocks.

The total expenditure on the reclamation of 99,800 acres in category II works out as under:

	Rs. lakhs
(a) Clearance of weeds	49.90
(b) Provision of drainage	30.00
(c) Removal of salinity and alkalinity	89.82
Total	169.72

The average cost of reclamation would be Rs. 170 per acre.

The total area of saline and alkaline lands available in large-sized blocks is 1,63,000 acres. The cost of reclamation of these lands is Rs. 250 per acre when the water-table is low, and Rs. 500 when the water table is high. It is suggested that at least 50,000 acres of affected land may be taken up for reclamation during the Third Five Year Plan period. The total cost reclamation will be Rs. 2.4 crores.

The methods of reclamation of the lands affected by salinity and alkalinity have been investigated by the Punjab Agriculture and Irrigation Departments, and suitable recomendations have been made. Pilot projects should be set up in the districts where the problem of salinity and alkalinity is acute, with a view to demonstrating to the cultivators the practical methods of reclaiming the affected lands. Provision should also be made for the supply of *dhaincha* seeds to the cultivators at subsidised rates.

In the reclamation of lands affected by salinity and alkalinity, it is essential that the physical and chemical properties of the affected lands should be studied with a view to devising suitable methods of reclamation. It is, therefore, necessary that a competent soil scientist should be associated with the irrigation engineer. We were glad to note that the State Government was fully aware of the importance of soil investigation in connection with the reclamation of waterlogged lands.

Eroded wastelands are mostly found in the hilly tracts of the districts of Gurdaspur, Hoshiarpur, Ambala, Kangra and Gurgaon. For their improvement measures such as contour-bunding and terracing are essential. There is need to evolve a suitable dry farming system of cultivation in order to check further deterioration of these lands. It is recommended that soil and water conservation measures may be undertaken on at least 1,25,000 acres over a period of five years. The cost of these measures will be Rs. 75 lakhs. Of the expenditure on contour-bunding, 25 per cent may be given as subsidy to the cultivators, and the balance treated as loan to be recovered in equal annual instalments spread over a period of 10 to 15 years.

The wastelands in the State are owned either by private individuals, the Government, the Custodian of Evacuee Property, or village panchayats. The lands owned by private individuals are brought under cultivation immediately after reclamation. There appears to be some delay in the allotment of Government lands after reclamation on account of the complicated procedures involved. It is suggested that such delays should be avoided as far as possible.

As regards the evacuee lands, these are returned, after reclamation, to the Custodian of Evacuee Property, who arranges for their follow-on cultivation either by permanent allotment or by temporary lease. The present rules do not provide for lease of more than one year and no cultivator comes forward to cultivate these lands for such a short period. It is suggested that the Punjab Government should allot the evacuee lands on a permanent basis for the resettlement of the landless peasants, ex-servicemen, Rai Sikhs, etc., in accordance with the scheme drawn up by the State Governments.

Lands belonging to the village panchayats are not allotted for follow-on cultivation immediately after reclamation. The State Government has set up a Directorate for the effective management of common lands, and it is hoped that this Directorate will quickly draw up plans for the resettlement and follow-on cultivation of these lands.

Detailed soil surveys for land use should be carried out in each area proposed for reclamation, so that the requisite information on the proper utilisation of land is available.

The staff of the Agriculture Department should suggest suitable cropping patterns and also introduce improved agricultural practices in the reclaimed areas so that the lands are put to the best use. The extension staff of the Community Development Department can play a useful role in the demonstration of improved methods of cultivation and in arranging for the supply of agricultural requisites.

In view of the large-scale reclamation work to be undertaken in the State, the work of land reclamation may be entrusted to a full-time senior officer who should be responsible for ensuring proper follow-on cultivation in the areas reclaimed, and for helping in the allotment of the wastelands to individuals and cooperative societies.

Since practically no irrigation facilities exist in the *bet* areas, construction of shallow, open wells may be encouraged by the grant of subsidy and loans on a liberal scale to the cultivators.

The *bet* lands in category II are infested with pernicious weeds and grasses which are difficult to eradicate unless facilities for mechanical cultivation are made available to the cultivators. The State Government should set up tractor stations to be managed by private tractor companies, so that the cultivators may be able to hire out tractors and tractor-implements for ploughing harrowing and other farm operations. The cultivators should also be encouraged to purchase tractors by the grant of loans recoverable in easy instalments.

As *bet* lands are subject to annual floods from the rivers, we recommend that a belt of thick growth of trees and grasses, at least 1,000 ft. in width, may be established along the river banks in order to provide protection to the lands from the floods and prevent erosion and under-cutting of the banks.

Crop-cutting surveys should be conducted in the reclaimed areas during the Third Five Year Plan period, in order to have an accurate idea of the additional food production due to the land improvement measures.

The total cost of reclaiming 3,16,650 acres of land in categories I to IV comes to Rs. 5.43 crores, *i.e.*, about Rs. 171 per acre. The estimated additional production from the reclaimed areas is 1,17,500 tons valued at Rs. 3.85 crores. In terms of additional production, the average cost of reclamation per acre is economic.

A study of the cost of the reclamation of lands in the different categories reveals that category IV offers the greatest promise for increasing agricultural production since the cost of land improvement per acre is the lowest, and there are also large areas of eroded lands where the adoption of soil and water conservation measures will produce quick and beneficial results for the needy sections of the farming community. In terms of additional production per acre, however, the lands in category I seem to be the most promising followed by the lands in categories III and II. The lands in category V are situated in tracts of low and variable rainfall and the returns are not expected to be commensurate with the investments on their improvement.

The following is the order of priority assigned to the different categories of lands on the basis of the additional production per acre and the cost of reclamation :

	Priority
Category I	1
Category IV	2
Category III	3
Category II	4

Although high priority has not been assigned to the reclamation of wastelands affected by salinity and alkalinity, it is hoped that, in view of the widespread damage to the cultivated lands caused by waterlogging, the State Government will give particular attention to the reclamation of saline and alkaline lands.

The reclamation of sand dunes in the arid tracts should be taken up only when irrigation is available in these areas. The cost of reclamation is quite heavy, and the returns are not commensurate with the expenditure on land improvement.

WASTELANDS SURVEY AND RECLAMATION COMMITTEE ON LOCATION AND UTILISATION OF WASTELANDS IN INDIA (UTTAR PRADESH), 1959—REPORT

New Delhi, Ministry of Food and Agriculture, 1963.
49p.+vip.+Maps.

Chairman : Dr. B. N. Uppal.

Members : Dr. J. K. Basu (retired ; replaced by Shri M. S. V. Rama Rao) ; Shri F. C. Gera; Shri J. P. Mital; Shri R. V. Tamhane.

Co-opted Members : Shri Satish Chandra; Shri Dashrath Singh; Shri S. K. Bhatnagar ; Shri Sumer Singh.

Secretary : Shri A. S. Venn Gopalan.

APPOINTMENT

The uncultivated lands in the country may be broadly classified into the following two categories :

(a) Lands which are really adjuncts of village *abadis* and are meant to serve as pastures and fuel forests or sites for the extension of *abadis*, and

(b) Lands in large-sized blocks which have either gone out of cultivation or have never been brought under cultivation.

With a view to utilising the latter category of lands which afford the greatest promise for increased agricultural production, the Government of India constituted this Committee, vide their letter No. F/1024/Spl./59, dated June 11, 1959.

TERMS OF REFERENCE

(i) To make a survey of land classified as "other uncultivated land excluding fallow lands" and "fallow lands other than current fallows" and locate areas where large blocks of land are available for reclamation and resettlement ;

(ii) To suggest suitable measures for reclamation according to conditions in different areas and estimate the cost of reclamation and colonisation and the financial assistance and agricultural extension and training necessary for the settlers (the settlements being made on a cooperative basis);

(iii) To suggest the terms and conditions upon which settlement should be made, the areas to be allotted and the payments to be made by settlers' cooperative; and

(iv) To estimate the economic aspects of such reclamation in terms of the expenditure involved, the likely addition to food production and the employment and income that would become available to settlers and their families and to lay down the priorities *inter se* between different categories of reclamable lands.

CONTENTS

Introduction; Preface; General Aspects; Description of Blocks and Measures for Reclamation ; Disposal of Reclaimed Lands for Cultivation ; Summary of Conclusions and Recommendations ; Appendices A to H; Maps I to II-C.

RECOMMENDATIONS

Of the total area of 10.20 million acres under the heads "other uncultivated land excluding fallows" and "fallows other than current fallows", only 30,460 acres have been located for reclamation in the State in compact blocks of 250 acres or more. (This is the figure as reported by the Revenue authorities, but the soil surveys carried out by the State Agricultural Department in a few districts have revealed the existence of over 2.8 lakh acres of *usar* lands in blocks of 200 acres or more, thus indicating the possibility of larger areas being available for reclamation.) This area is relatively small, considering that the actual extent of aralable wastelands in the State is much larger than the figures reported in the revenue records, although the bulk of these wastelands is found in blocks smaller than 250 acres in size.

The wastelands found in the State may be classified into the following two categories :

I. *Usar* lands, and

II. Lands infested with thick growth of jungle, bushes and shrubs.

The distribution of wastelands in categories I and II is as under :

Category			Area (Acres)
I	...	...	13,618
II	...	...	16,842

The area of *usar* lands offered for reclamation is small, but the surveys carried out by the State Agriculture Department have revealed the existence of extensive belts of degraded lands in the districts of Kanpur, Fatehpur, Aligarh, Mainpuri and Unnao. Although no surveys have yet been carried out in other districts, salinity and alkalinity are reported to be widely prevalent in the soils of Hardoi, Etawah, Rae Bareilly Pratapgarh, Mathura, Agra and Azamgarh districts.

There are certain types of *usar* lands which can be reclaimed more economically than others, and it is necessary to classify *usar* lands so as to suggest appropriate remedies for their reclamation. Broadly speaking, *usar* lands may be divided into the following four classes for reclamation:

(a) Land of which the permanent water-table is within six feet from the surface, or which is impermeable due to the formation of *kankar* or the existence of an indurated clay pan, or where both these conditions exist;

(b) Land where the permanent water-table lies between six and 10 feet from the surface, or which is semi-permeable due to the nascent formation of a pan or where both these conditions exist;

(c) Land in which the permanent water-table is beyond 10 ft. from the surface with no hard clay pan, but the clay fraction is in a deflocculated condition so that infiltration is impeded partially or completely; and

(d) Land of which the permanent water-table is beyond 10 ft. from the surface, with no hard pan and good permeability.

Much of the intractable *usar* land in Uttar Pradesh belongs to class (a) above. Under suitable management over a period of years, this type of land can at best be made to grow grass or such salt-resistant trees as *babul* (Acacia arabica) or *ber* (Zizyphus jijuba). Lands in class (b) can be rendered fit for cultivation but the expenditure of time and effort is disproportinately high. The use of soil amendments such as gypsum, press-mud etc., combined with the application of irrigation water to leach out harmful salts can be useful in reclaiming lands in class (c), but these amendments are generally too expensive. The soils in class (d) can, however, be readily reclaimed for agricultural purposes by the application of undecomposed bulky organic matter, together with the use of liberal quantities of irrigation water to leach out salts. The class of *usar* land offers the greatest scope for increasing agricultural production, since, on a rough estimate, over 50 per cent of *usar* land in the State belongs to this class.

The methods of reclamation of *usar* lands have been investigated by the State Agriculture Department, the National Botanic Gardens, Lucknow, and by individual farmers A good deal of useful knowledge about the practical methods of reclamation of *usar* has been accumulated over the past years, ond there is great need for the full use of the existing knowledge. The details about the practical methods of reclaiming *usar* are given.

Practically no information is available on the cost of reclamation of *usar* land of different types. The cost of reclamation of lands which have a low water-table and which are not impervious to water is, however, estimated at Rs. 325 per acre. If the soil has a hard clay pan, a mechanical ripper will be needed to break the pan and an additional expenditure of Rs. 80 per acre will be necessary in such areas.

The blocks included in category II are situated in the districts of Allahabad, Banda, Bijnore, Jalaun and Pilibhit. Most of the wastelands in the Jalaun district consist of ravines, and their reclamation will involve large financial outlay. The areas offered in the districts of Allahabad, Banda and Bijnore are dry lands and accodingly are not very productive. The lands in the Pilibhit district are quite productive, as they have ample underground water supply and are also suited for the cultivation of commercial crops like sugarcane.

For the utilisation of *usar* lands which are easier to reclaim, the State Government should set up a seperate organisation, and allot these lands to landless labourers, etc., after reclamation, since the work of reclamation involves a large outlay of money and the return on investment in early years is not sufficient to sustain a cultivating family without financial assistance from the Government. During the first two years each allottee should be paid on the basis of a means test which would take into account the wages for the work done by him against the amount required for his subsistence.

Of the total cost of reclamation of *usar* lands, 75 per cent of it should be recovered in convenient instalments commencing from the fourth year after allotment. The balance of the expenditure should be treated as subsidy and shared equally by the Centre and the State Government. It will also be necessary to give suitable financial assistance to the allottees in the form of loans for the purchase of implements, bullocks, etc., which may be recovered from the third year of the grant of the loans in five annual instalments at a concessional rate of interest.

Out of six lakh acres of *usar* lands availabe in large-sized blocks which are easy to reclaim, at least 50,000 acres of the easily reclaimable type of *usar* should be taken up for improvement during the Third Five Year Plan period. A sum of Rs. 1.625 crores will be required for this purpose.

Since most of the *usar* lands belong to Government, they may be disposed of at a nominal price to individuals or cooperative societies with the specific object of reclaiming them and bringing them under cultivation. Alternatively, these lands may be leased out on a long-term basis: Government may give to cultivators financial assistance in the form of loans at a low rate of interest, for the purchase of farm machinery such as tractors, rippers etc., and for the installation of tubewells.

The extent of wastelands in the districts of Allahabad, Banda and Bijnore is small, and these lands may be allotted, after reclamation, to landless labourers and the members of the Scheduled Castes and the Scheduled Tribes, in accordance with the existing instructions of the Revenue Department. Twenty-five per cent of the expenditure on reclamation should be treated as subsidy to the cultivators, and the balance as loan to be recovered in easy instalments spread over a period of 10—15 years. In the Pilibhit district, however, the utilisation of wastelands will involve the establishment of settlement colonies for arranging their cultivation.

A detailed soil survey for land-use should be carried out in each area proposed for reclamation so that the lands are put to proper use. Soil surveys of *usar* land have been conducted by the State Department of Agriculture in five districts of the State. It is suggested that these surveys should be extended to other areas where *usar* lands in large-sized blocks are likely to be available for reclamation. The State Government may apply for financial assistance to the Central Soil Conservation Board for carrying out these surveys.

After reclamation measures have been carried out, the responsibility for the follow-on cultivation operations should be that of the normal staff of the Agriculture Department. The agricultural staff should suggest suitable cropping patterns and also introduce improved agricultural practices in the reclaimed areas. The extension staff of the Community Development Organisation can assist, particularly in the demonstration of improved methods of cultivation and in arranging for the supply of agricultural requisites.

In view of the large-scale *usar* reclamation work to be undertaken in the State, the work of land reclamation may be entrusted to a Committee or Board which should be responsible for preparing *usar* reclamation projects, should have the power to sanction funds for their execution, should advise cultivators or cooperative societies regarding suitable methods to be adopted for reclamation, and finally should ensure proper follow-on cultivation operations in the reclaimed lands,

Pilot projects should be set up in the districts where mild *usar* is widely prevalent, so as to demonstrate to the cultivators practical methods of reclaiming *usar* lands. Some pilot projects have been started in the districts of Aligarh, Mainpuri, Etawah, Kanpur, Unnao, Hardoi, Sultanpur, Pratapgarh, Azamgarh and Ghazipur. We suggest that such projects may be extended to other districts.

There are partically no irrigation facilities in the *Tarai* tract of the State. The construction of shallow wells may be encouraged in this tract by the grant of subsidy and loans to the cultivators on a liberal scale.

The lands in the *Tarai* tract are fertile but they are infested with pernicious weeds and grasses which are difficult to eradicate unless facilities for mechanical cultivation are made available to the cultivators. Ordinarily, it would not be within the reach of the cultivators to own a tractor, and we would, therefore, recommend that Government should encourage the setting up of tractor stations to be mangaged by cooperative societies or by private tractor companies.

In view of the satisfactory progress made so far in the settlement projects undertaken by the State Government, larger allocations should be made for settlement work so that the entire area that may be available for reclamation in the Pilibhit district, is brought under cultivation.

In any settlement project the selection of settlers is the most important factor contributing to its success. Accordingly, special attention should be given to this aspect of settlement work so that the right type of settlers who have an aptitude for training and who are willing to do hard work are selected.

For any settlement work to be successful, it is necessary that the Revenue/Block agency should be associated with it so that the problem of settlers are attended to as expeditiously as possible.

Field experiments on the reclamation of *usar* lands have shown that in the fourth year after reclamation, the yield of paddy is abovt 12 maunds per acre. When the salinity is brought down to a low level, irrigated wheat can be grown with an average yield of 15 maunds per acre.

The wastlands in the districts of Allahabad, Banda and Bijnore can grow seasonal crops only as no irrigation is available. The average additional production from these lands is estimated at five maunds per acre. The wastelands in the Pilibhit district are fertile and, with the provision of adequate irrigation, double cropping can be practised. An average additional production of 10 maunds per acre can be estimated from these lands.

The cost of reclaiming 61,018 acres of land in categories I and II comes to about Rs. 1.73 crores, *i.e.*, about Rs. 284 per acre. The estimated additional production from the reclaimed lands is 24,901 tons, valued at Rs. 83.70 lakhs. Thus the value of production will cover the cost of reclamation in about two crop seasons.

The wastelands in category I may be assigned the highest priority. Amongst the various types of *usar*, the work of improvement and reclamation* should be confined to those areas where less intractable type of *usar* is found in large-sized, compact blocks, and there are adequate underground water resources.

The wastelands in the *Tarai* tract of the Pilibhit district included in category II should be assigned on equally high priority. The last in the order of priority are the dry lands in the districts of Allahabad, Banda and Bijnore.

WASTELANDS SURVEY AND RECLAMATION COMMITTEE ON LOCATION AND UTILISATION OF WASTELANDS IN INDIA (WEST BENGAL), 1959—REPORT

New Delhi, Ministry of Food and Agriculture, 1961.
51p.+ivp.+Maps.

Chairman : Dr. B.N. Uppal.
Members : Shri F.C. Gera; Shri J.P. Mittal; Dr. J.K. Basu (retired ; replaced by Shri M.S.V. Rama Rao).
Co-opted Members : Shri H. Banerjee ; Shri B. N. Banerjee ; Shri A. Chatterjee ; Shri A. Das Gupta ; Shri H. M. Brahma.
Secretary : Shri A. S. Venu Gopalan.

APPOINTMENT

The uncultivated lands in the country may be broadly classified into the following two categories :

(a) Lands which are really adjuncts of village *abadis* and are meant to serve as pastures and fuel forests or sites for the extension of *abadis* ; and

(b) Lands in Large-sized blocks which have either gone out of cultivation or have never been brought under cultivation.

With a view to utilising the latter category of lands which afford the greatest promise for increased agricultural production, the Government of India constituted this Committee, vide their letter No. F/1024/Spl./59, dated June 11, 1959.

TERMS OF REFERENCE

(i) To make a survey of land classified as "other uncultivated land excluding fallow lands" and "fallow lands other than current fallows" and locate areas where large blocks of land are available for reclamation and resettlement;

(ii) To suggest suitable measures for reclamation according to conditions in different areas and estimate the cost of reclamation and colonisation and the financial assistance and agricultural extension and training necessary for the settlers (the settlements being made on a cooperative basis);

(iii) To suggest the terms and conditions upon which settlement should be made, the areas to be allotted and the payments to be made by settlers' cooperative; and

(iv) To estimate the economic aspects of such reclamation in terms of the expenditure involved, the likely addition to food production and the employment and income that would become available to settlers and their families and to lay down the priorities *inter se* between different categories of reclaimable lands.

CONTENTS

Introduction ; Preface ; General Aspects ; Description of Blocks and Measures for Reclamation ; Disposal of Reclaimed Lands for Cultivation ; Summary of General Conclusions and Recommendations; Appendices A to G; Maps I and II.

RECOMMENDATIONS

Of the total area of 2.54 million acres under the head "other uncultivated lands excluding fallows" and "current fallows", about 1.13 lakh acres have been located in the State for reclamation in blocks of the sizes of 250 acres or more.

The wastelands found in the State may be broadly divided into following four categories :

I. Eroded Lands,
II. *Char* Lands,
III. *Terai* Lands (flat lands at the foot of the hills), and
IV. Saline Lands.

The distribution of wastelands in categories I to IV is as under :

Category		Area (Acres)
I	...	85,379
II	...	12,594
III	...	13,869
IV	...	1,798
	Total	1,13,640

The wastelands found in the districts of Midnapore, Purulia and Bankura falling in category I are mostly undulating, with large upland tracts made up of ridges alternating with valleys. The soils are generally red and lateritic, varying in texture from sandy loam to loam, but the predominant type is sandy loam with *murum* on the surface. Land reclamation in these areas is primarily soil and water conservation work. The average cost of reclamation would be Rs. 120 per acre.

It is necessary to introduce legislation on the lines of the model Act prepared by the Government of India and circulated to the State Governments, empowering the State Government to undertake soil conservation measures in the State.

The selected projects on soil conservation should be on a complete watershed basis.

Field experiments should be laid out to study the different methods of bunding in the lateritic and red soil tracts, with a view to determining as to which method should be adopted with special reference to its cost and effectiveness.

The *char* lands included in category II are very fertile and can produce good crops of paddy, sugarcane, jute, etc. The flood and erosion hazards make large-scale habitation in this area somewhat precarious, although settlements are possible at sites which are not subject to these hazards. The cost of removing the shrubs and bushes and ploughing up the land to make it fit for cultivation, is estimated at between Rs. 75 and Rs. 100 per acre.

The flat *terai* lands are very poor in nitrogen, phosphate, potassium and organic matter, and do not retain moisture for long, although they are located in an area with a rainfall of 120 to 180 inches. They are covered with shrubs and grasses. The cost of reclamation is estimated at Rs. 100 per acre.

The saline lands located in the Midnapore district are rich in organic matter and plant nutrients. Salinity in the lands is not high, but they are slightly eroded. To reclaim these lands, suitable ameliorative measures for the removal of salinity should be undertaken. The cost of reclamation is estimated about at Rs. 160 per acre.

The wastelands in the State are owned either by private individuals, the Government, or village panchayats. The wastelands belonging to private individuals can be handed over, after reclamation, to their respective owners for follow-on cultivation. In order to bring the lands belonging to the Government under cultivation, it is proposed to establish cooperative colonies of settlers from East Pakistan, or to allot these lands to the landless labourers, members of the Scheduled Castes and the Scheduled Tribes, etc. The common lands may be given to the village panchayats for arranging follow-on cultivation.

Detailed soil surveys for land-use should be carried out in each area proposed for reclamation, so that the requisite information on the proper utilisation of land is available.

In order to carry out the programme of soil conservation indicated in the report, we recommend the establishment of the Directorate of Agriculture of a separate wing of soil conservation under the Superintending Engineer and Joint Director of Agriculture (Engineering), who may be assisted by three Divisional Soil Conservation Officers and the necessary field staff.

After soil conservation measures have been carried out, the responsibility for the follow-on cultivation should be that of the normal staff of the Agriculture Department. The agricultural staff should suggest suitable cropping patterns and also introduce improved agricultural practices in the reclaimed areas.

Wherever irrigation facilities can be provided by the construction of shallow wells or tube-wells, loans and/or subsidy may be given to the cultivators on a liberal scale.

Green manuring should be extensively practised in the reclaimed lands in order to build up their organic matter content and to improve soil structure.

In the areas of the lateritic or red soil belt where irrigation facilities are not available, percolation tanks or earthen embankments across big gullies may be constructed to hold water. The construction of such tanks helps in the storage of rain-water for agricultural and other purposes, and also checks erosion on the down-stream side of the gullies.

In the Teesta *char* lands, advantage should be taken of the nearness of the sub-soil water from the ground level to grow winter crops by adopting suitable cultivation practices.

Although the *char* lands are fertile, sound agronomic practices should be developed so that the fertility of these lands is maintained at a high level.

The total cost of reclaiming 1,13.640 acres of land in categories I to IV comes to Rs. 1.32 crores, *i.e.*, about Rs. 116 per acre. The estimated additional production from the reclaimed lands is 42,895 tons valued at about 1.40 crores. The average cost of reclamation is, therefore, economic in terms of additional production, since the total expenditure involved can be recovered in one or two crop seasons.

A study of the cost of reclamation of lands in the different categories reveals that category II is the most profitable in terms of additional food production. On the other hand, category I offers the greatest promise for increasing agricultural production since large tracts of such lands are available and the average cost of their reclamation is also not high. The cost of reclamation of saline lands is also economic, but the area available is small. The wastelands in category III do not at present hold much promise for increased production, but the position will materially change when irrigation becomes available, for which there seem to be good prospects.

The following is the order of priority assigned to the different categories of wastelands on the basis of all relevant factors :

Category		Priority
Category I	...	1
Category II	...	2
Category III	...	3
Category IV	...	4

WORKING GROUP ON COOPERATIVE FARMING, 1959—REPORT

New Delhi, Department of Cooperation, Ministry of Community Development and Cooperation, 1959. 2 Vols.

Chairman : Shri N. Nijalingappa.

Members : Dr. Ram Subhag Singh; Sardar Gurbaksh Singh; Shri V. K. Rao; Shri B. D. Pande; Shri Ameer Raza; Dr. A. U. Sheikh; J. S. Patel; Shri V. M. Jakhade;

Secretary : Shri M. P. Bhargava.

APPOINTMENT

The Second Five Year Plan envisages that the main task during the Plan Period should be to take such essential steps as would provide sound foundations for the development of cooperative farming so that a substantial proportion of agricultural lands are cultivated on cooperative lines. More recently, the Government of India has accepted joint cooperative farming on a voluntary basis as the future agrarian pattern in India. Conditions have to be created in the country so that joint farming may have a fair chance of success. For this purpose, it is necessary to ensure that financial and other facilities, technical knowledge and guidance are available to those who voluntarily decide to establish joint farming societies.

The Government of India have, therefore, decided to set up this Working Group on Cooperative Farming vide their Notification No. E. 5-32/59-Coop. II, dated June 11, 1959, to help the formulation of a programme for this purpose based on available experience.

TERMS OF REFERENCE

(I) To examine the types and methods of organisation and management of joint farming societies with special refrence to:

(a) Preparatory work,

(b) Model bye-laws and registration,

(c) Management:

(i) Formulation of production plan;

(ii) Payment of ownership dividend;

(iii) Work distribution—formation of teams and groups;

(iv) Assenment of performance;

(v) Payment of remuneration to workers;

(vi) Maintenance of accounts;

(d) Mobilisation and fuller utilisation of manpower, cattle and other local resources;

(e) Measures necessary for setting up cottage and other subsidiary industries for increasing employment;

(f) Measures necessary for preservation and maintenance of individual initiative and at the same time fostering close contact, social cohesion and mutual obligation;

(II) To assess financial requirments and suggest how these should be met:

(III) To assess the requirements of administrative, supervisory and technical personnel at various levels;

(IV) To suggest arrangements for training of:

(i) Members;

(ii) Office-bearers;

(iii) Managers; and

(iv) Administrative, suprervisory and technical staff and formulate a phased programme of training.

(V) To recommend such other measures as may be considered necessary for promoting this programme of joint cooperative farming.

CONTENTS

Introductory; **Part I** : The Background; **Part II** : The Recommendations; **Part III**. Summary, Note and Annexures; Annexures; I to XIII.

RECOMMENDATIONS

Organisation Of Cooperative Farming Societies

Variations in soil, climatic and rainfall conditions and man-land ratio have to be taken into account in the organisation of a cooperative farming society.

It is not desirable to lay down a uniform pattern for cooperative farming society. Approach should be flexible. Suitable changes in the suggestions may be made in accordance with the local conditions and requirements without losing the essential ingredients.

Before registration, the members should have a clear appreciation of the need for joint efforts in increasing production, employment and income, working of the society, their rights and obligations and the source from which the necessary assistance would be available. A society should not be organised by raising exaggerated hopes. The members should have real desire to form such a society.

While it is necessary to allow and to give sufficient time for education and experience, this process should not become unduly long.

The progress of a society should be judged by its ability to implement its immediate as well as long-term programme of improvement, production and employment. Excessive enthusiasm for ambitious schemes which are beyond the resources should be restrained.

In case a society is promoted by an outsider, efforts

should be made to train one of its members to assume leadership in due course.

At present neither the public servants—officials and non-officials—nor the financial agencies are sufficiently enthusiastic about the development of cooperative farming possibly because of insufficient experience in the field. They should be properly educated, trained and re-oriented.

Traditional forms of cooperation in farming such as "Phad", "Gonchi", etc., in the country should be studied.

These forms should also be improved and popularised. Programmes relating to joint efforts should be encouraged to develop cooperative farming. These may be considered for registration as cooperative societies and assistance.

The minimum membership often or as laid down in the Act should be adhered to.

The chances of success would be greater if the membership is broad-based, homogeneity of interest is maintained, overwhelming majority of members participate in farm work and the economic status of members is more or less equal.

No compulsion should be imposed to bring the cultivators into a society.

Legislative measures compelling agriculturists to set up a society should not be undertaken. States which have already enacted such legislation should not enforce them. They should take early action to repeal such laws. Efforts should be directed to promote a spontaneous growth of cooperatives.

Optimum size of a cooperative farm would depend upon a number of factors such as average holding, location, rainfall, irrigation facilities, types of crops raised etc.

A cooperative farm need not necessarily cover the entire village. More than one farming society can be organised with advantage in a village of average size. Viability and mutual knowledge should be the prime considerations in this regard.

The denial of the right to vote or participate in management to a landless member is detrimental to the growth of cooperative farming. Such a practice should be modified.

In U.P. the land pooled by a person cannot be withdrawn unless the registration of the society is cancelled. This is against the voluntariness and should be amended.

Period of pooling should be five years. Even during this period, if a member wants to transfer the land to another member or the society itself, he should be allowed to withdraw. If a member has to leave the village, he should be allowed to resign; his land may be taken on lease.

Every retiring member who contributed land to the pool should get land in return.

Land of equal productivity end not necessarily the same piece or area of land should be given at the periphery without dislocating the schemes.

The lands should be classified according to the productive capacity and the fertility determined properly at the time of pooling to facilitate return for land.

Standards of productivity fixed should have general acceptance.

The return for land should be paid out of the farm business income and not out of the gross produce. The societies, however, should be free to settle the issue.

The value of the cattle, implements and other assets pooled, should be treated as deposits or share capital.

Management Of Cooperative Farming Societies

The decision-making power in a cooperative farming society should not rest in an individual or a small group but in the general body. If the decisions are imposed from outside, the democratic content is reduced and its autonomy curtailed.

The general meeting should also approve of : (i) production and Development Plans, (ii) Plan for employment, (iii) Cropping Scheme, (iv) Plan for Subsidiary Industries, and (v) Social Welfare Scheme.

Basic principles governing remuneration for work done and return for land contributed together with the priority *inter se* of the various improvement and irrigation programmes and their location should also be determined by the general body.

The practice of nominating the entire board of directors is against the principles of democracy and cooperation. This should be discontiued.

Some State Governments appoint nominees in the managing committee even without share capital participation. Government should not nominate any one on the managing committee which should consist of elected members only.

Appointment of Government officers as presidents diminishes considerably the initiative and sense of responsibility of members. This should not be done.

With a view to develop initiative and leadership and ensure participation of members, sub-committees each in charge of a specific subject may be appointed in societies having large membership. Where the membership is small, each member of the managing committee should have this responsibility. The sub-committee or member incharge should report the progress to the managing committee and general body meetings.

An assessment committee independent of the managing committee for performing the duties of an internal auditor should also be appointed.

The committee should consist of three members elected by the general body.

In order to minimise the chances of misapplication of funds, the President should be entrusted with sanctioning the expenditure, Treasurer with disbursements and Accountant-*cum*-Secretary with the accounts.

A secretary capable of maintaining accounts and registers should be appointed preferably from among the members. An outsider may be appointed when a suitable person is not available locally. In that case a member should also be trained to assume the responsibility. Secretary should also help in management and agricultural operations.

A secretary should have considerable acquaintance with the local people and conditions and have sufficient knowledge and experience of improved local practices.

He should also participate in farm-work for a minimum period along with other members.

Approval of the Registrar for appointment of the Secretary or Manager should not be necessary. The society should have full discretion to appoint a suitable person.

Income and distribution of profits should be determined according to the provisions of the bye-laws.

10 per cent of the net profits should be credited to reserve fund and invested according to the instructions of the Department. 15 per cent of the profits should constitute the Development Fund which should be utilised with the approval of the general body.

To finance educational, social and recreational activities, Common Good Fund should be created.

10 per cent of the net profits may be earmarked for Mutual Aid Fund to meet ceremonial expenses and unforeseen expenditures.

Share Redemption Fund should be created out of the Profits for retiring the share capital contributed by the Government.

Substantial part of net profits should go to members as bonus for the work done. Bonus on the basis of return received by them for the land pooled should also be paid. Non-members who have leased out their lands to the society should not be eligible for the bonus.

There should be no rigid and fixed pattern of distribution of profits. The society should be allowed discretion in evolving a suitable system from time to time.

Operation Of Cooperative Farming Societies

Timely and efficient performance of agricultural operations are essential for getting the maximum yield. The allotment of work, assessment of performance and determination of remuneration are of utmost importance.

Taking into account the available skill, number of working members and the size of the society, the manpower should be organised. On a not too small farm, formation of groups of members either on *ad hoc* or seasonal basis would facilitate better supervision and provide greater incentive. Same group should not continue on the same block for more than a season or two. This would check any tendency of disintegration and promote a sense of attachment to the society as a whole. The produce of the groups should be harvested and pooled jointly. The group producing more should be given requisite incentive.

For the success of a cooperative farming society it is necessary that the members have no separate common interest and they identify themselves with the area of its operation.

The system of providing substitute labour can be a source of weakness in the society.

Participation of overwhelming majority of members in the farm operation is an essential ingredient for the success of a society and also an indicator of its genuineness. Absentees should not normally be admitted as members. Instead, their land may be taken on lease and rent paid at the rates regulated under the law.

Office bearers and members of Managing Committee should also engage themselves in farm work during a year.

As farm experience is vital for deciding major issues and for fostering the spirit of equal partnerhip, members of the Managing Committee should not be elected from among the non-working members.

Every society should formulate a programme of production and employment including works of permanent improvement.

The differences in skill and ability of the workers should be properly evaluated and rewarded otherwise they may not put in their best which would ultimately affect production.

A large number of detailed norms need not be attempted in the existing conditions. Simple objective tests which would enable the workers to know what is expected of them should be laid down only in regard to important agricultural operations. The local knowledge and experience in this regard should be utilised.

An attempt to introduce 'norms' on the lines of the traditional standard and prevalent practices should be made. After the society has gained some experience it should improve upon or evolve new norms.

Suitable monetary rewards and recognition should be given to member or group for best performance and developing specialised skills and aptitude.

Although payment of remuneration at rates higher than prevailing local rates attracts members to work on the farm itself, its disadvantages in the form of increased cost of production, adverse effect on capital formation and financial stability should not be lost sight of.

Members should be supplied with farm produce such as foodgrains, vegetables, fruits, milk, etc. to meet their genuine needs. The value may be computed at rates prevailing at the time of harvest.

The scale of remuneration should be at par with the

local rates Profits should be distributed among members in proportion to the work done and land contributed. Total income and not the daily rates even if it is lower should be the real index of the success.

Where the available manpower cannot be absorbed in agricultural operations, industries allied to agriculture should be developed as an integral part of the scheme. Cottage, Small Scale and Village Industries should be set up on the basis of the available resources and skill and receive special attention.

The improvement schemes which a farming society is likely to undertake such as desilting of tanks, cleaning and deepening of old wells for irrigation, contour bunding and other soil conservation methods, collection and conservation of locally available organic manure, etc. provide opportunity of larger employment and do not call for the use of machinery. Usually labour intensive methods should be adopted for carrying out improvements.

Use of machinery can prove advantageous for purposes like reclamation of land, cooperative farming, however, need not necessarily lead to mechanisation.

Before going in for a tractor or other machinery, a society should carefully consider the need for and economics of such equipment. The extension staff should help the society in arriving at a right decision. The society owning such heavy machinery should get one of its members trained in their operation and maintenance.

In the use of machinery, distinction should be made between that which causes immediate displacement of labour and that which increases efficiency and employment. The use of the latter type of machinery such as pumps and engines for water lifting should not be ruled out on *a priori* consideration.

Consolidation of holdings of members of Cooperative Farming Societies would enable them to obtain economies of scale. It would, therefore. be advantageous to coordinate the programme of consolidation of lands and organisation of cooperative farming societies.

By pooling the scattered holdings, even without consolidation, the number of plots would be reduced and units of cultivation increased. Economies of scale would thus be available.

Although the total gain may not be so much as, when land and manpower are fully pooled, the advantages would be significant and positive as the pooled manpower could be utilised on making improvements of lasting nature on holdings not contiguously located.

While consolidation would facilitate progress, it should not be a condition precedent to formation of cooperative farming societies and promotional work should continue in all areas.

Where cooperative farming societies are liable for the agricultural income-tax, the tax should not be imposed on the society as such but on the individuals constituting the society after taking into account the income obtained and area held by them.

Accounts

The existing system of accounts in cooperative farming societies needs to be simplified. To begin with four books of original entry such as Cash Book, Stock Book, Work Register and Advance Register should be maintained and four other registers namely the Ledger, Members' Share Register, Land and *Haisiyat* Register and proceedings book should be maintained.

While marking attendance the names of persons absent on previous day should be read out and discrepancies, if any, corrected instantly.

Advances in cash or kind may be given to members as and when required.

Along with a reasonably accurate and simple system of accounting, a society should build up other internal safeguards including appointment of Assessment Committee, issue of pass books, etc.

A part-time worker who can spare a couple of hours every day should be able to maintain the accounts.

Forms of registers are given at Annexures.

The temptation to calculate the cost of each crop from each plot and to prescribe too many statements and returns should be resisted.

The society should be allowed to maintain forms and registers in manuscript. Such registers should, however, be properly bound and their pages serially numbered.

If a society is required to maintain detailed accounts for purposes of experimentation and research, a trained statistician should be provided and additional expenditure, if any, reimbursed.

Registration And Bye-Laws

Members should be allowed to make the necessary amendments in the model bye-laws provided these are not contrary to the basic principles of cooperation. If the proposed amendments are not admitted the reasons for their non-acceptability should be explained to the members.

Numbers of forms and statements prescribed for registration should be considerably reduced.

State Government should issue instructions to village officials and other concerned staff to supply the information required for registration by cooperative farming societies within a prescribed period of say two weeks. The Cooperative Department should also help the promoters in obtaining these.

A set of model bye-laws is suggested in Chapter II of Volume II.

Finance

In some States, cooperative farming societies cannot become members of land mortgage banks and thus cannot obtain long-term finance. The Act, Rule or Bye-laws should be suitably amended.

According to Land Reforms Acts, all lands belonging to the members of the cooperative farming socities except homestead lands vest in the society in U.P. and West Bengal. As such, Land Mortgage Banks should have no hesitation in furnishing long-term loans to such socities on land security. In a joint farming cooperative, ownership right should, however, be retained by individual members and should not vest in the society.

In some States, the members individually enter into an agreement with the society authorising it to pledge their lands as security or loans to be raised for agricultural or other needs. Land Mortgage Banks should make it possible to advance loans in such cases.

In order to facilitate transfer and sale of lands mortgaged as security, it may be necessary to modify the Land Reforms or other laws in some States.

Government guaranteee in regard to loans advanced by Land Mortgage Banks to cooperative farming societies is not necessary.

Where Land Mortgage Banks are not in a position or do not come forward to meet the long-term credit requirments of cooperative farming societies, the State Governments should provide timely and adequate long-term finance on the basis of agricultural development programme and without insisting upon hypothecation of land.

Central Cooperative Banks should supply the required medium-term credit whenever the societies can furnish landed security. In others, Government should provide the necessary finance.

Repaying capacity and not the tangible security should be the guiding principle in advancing short-term loans.

The farming society will have to get itself affiliated to the Central Bank operating in the area which should provide the necessary short-term finance.

As a result of the effective implementation of carefully drawn up production plans, better utilisation of resources including the credit obtained and other improvements, production on a cooperative farm will increase and the surplus produce will be sold through marketing societies which will help recovery of the loans. This is not always so in the case of individual cultivators. Central financing agencies, therefore, should not hesitate in providing short-term finance to these societies. There is no need for a Government guarantee for the same.

A farming society may need credit at about Rs. 130 per acre for irrigated land and Rs. 60 per acre for dry crops. In the initial stages, its borrowing capacity may not be adequate under the existing rules.

Relaxation of the multiple in favour of cooperative farming societies pending the recommendations of the Mehta Committee on Cooperative Credit is not favoured.

For strengthening the society's share capital, members should be persuaded to invest a portion of their extra income in the shares. It may take sometime before sufficient share capital is built up. In similar circumstances, Government have advanced loans to members of weavers' cooperative societies. In case of cooperative farming society, individual members should not be required to apply for loans from the Government and to invest the amounts received in the shares of the society.

In some States members of cooperative farming societies were given subsidy to enable them to purchase shares. Such a grant is not desirable.

For augmenting the resources of cooperative farming societies, Government should purchase shares subject to a suitable ceiling. This may be equal to or even larger than the members' contribution.

Share capital contributed by the Government may be returned over a period of 10 years through the creation of share redemption fund or members' contribution.

Government should not have its nominees on the Managing Committee of a society to which such a contribution has been made.

A sum not exceeding Rs. 2,000 per society for subscribing to the share capital by the State Government would be suitable. Contribution to each society should be made in the light of the shares collected from the members and its production programme. A total sum of Rs. 4.6 crores should be provided for a period of six years.

Maximum credit limit of a society should be fixed at the time of the registration. The limit once fixed should be in operation until some modification becomes necessary, The societies should be allowed to draw the amount of credit in instalments.

Cooperative farming societies should pay the same rate of interest as is charged from primary credit societies. No special concession in this regard need be given.

Seed Stores and Cooperative Banks should review their structure of interest rates and rationalise the same. But, the timely and adequate supply of finance and production requisites is of the highest importance.

A cooperative farming society will need assistance for financing its cottage and village industries schemes. They should receive perference in the allotment of assistance available under different schemes, of the various Boards and the Government. The Block Extension staff should help these societies in drawing up plans and in securing Government aids.

In some States, cooperative farming societies received assistance on a liberal scale. In majority of cases, however, the societies failed to receive timely and sufficient help from Government.

Adequate provision should be made in the budgets for providing loans to such societies. The Extension staff should help the societies in working out a suitable programme for land improvement. The tendency to draw aid merely because it is admissible under a schematic pattern of scme programme should be guarded against.

Assistance admissible under Grow More Food, Soil Conservation Schemes, etc., should be readily available to cooperative farming societies, changes in rules, if necessary, should be made. The block staff should help them in securing the aid for which they are eligble.

In order to expedite the implementation of the programme of development requiring long and medium-terms finance, a sum not exceeding Rs. 4,000 may be assured to each cooperative farming society. Rs, 9.28 crores may be required on this account during the next six years.

Wherever necessary, a cooperative farming society should be given financial assistance for construction of a godown-*cum*-cattle shed subject to the maximum of Rs. 5,000, 25 per cent of this as subsidy and the balance as loan. A provision of Rs. 11.6 crores should be made for societies to be set up upto the Third Plan.

In order to ensure that the managerial cost does not eat into the income of a farming society, subsidy on the following scale should be given for a period of three years :

	Rs.
First year	900
Second year	600
Third year	300

(On this basis Rs. 3.12 crores will be required upto the end of the Third Plan period.)

The Society should not take upon itself the liability of prior debts of a member. There should be no bar on admission of such persons as members. If the lands of such a person are covered by a usufructuary mortgage, he cannot be admitted as a member. He can be admitted as a member, if his hands are covered by a simple mortgage.

In the event of foreclosure, if the society wishes to retain the mortgaged land of one of its members, it should be allowed to do so and suitable legislation be enacted. The society should also be given a right of pre-emption to acquire the land if it so wishes.

The society should advance loans for ceremonial and other purposes and recover the same out of the members' income by way of remuneration for work and land, bonus and the like.

The society should also educate its members to avoid lavish expenditure and should borrow from the society only the bare minimum necessary for the occasion.

The society may also give advances to its members for meeting their consumption needs. In doing so, it should not be put to any loss. It should not also depend indefinitely on outside agencies for funds for this purpose.

A Mutual Aid Fund should be created out of the profits earned. Members should also be persuaded to put in a Chit Fund which should be utilised for helping them in meeting these expenses.

Inculcation of thrift and savings is one of the essentials of cooperative farming, as it would reduce its dependence on outside agencies for obtaining bulk of financial resources and make it more and more self-reliant. A portion of gains of members as well as the society should, therefore, be set aside for capital formation.

Administrative Machinery

The process of evolution from small scale subsistence farming to cooperative joint farming calls for a change in attitudes and voluntary restraints and development of skills in reducing social tensions and resolving personal conflicts as they arise.

Adequate preparation should be made to solve initial difficulties by carefully planned education and training of the members. Technical guidance and assistance should be continuously and readily available.

In order to educate the people in general, a programme of general social education in the advantages of the cooperative way of life should be undertaken. The pilot projects for the formation of cooperative farming societies should be taken up in cooperatively developed areas.

Complaints of departmental delays, inefficiency, unhelpful attitude or corruption continue to be a source of anxiety and dissatisfaction to cooperative farming societies. State Governments should review the existing policy and procedures so that the necessary facilities and concessions can be given to such societies promptly.

A Secretary should be appointed preferably from amongst the members. A non-member of the village or even an outsider may be appointed, if necessary. He should be in-charge of accounts and assist in the management and farm operations of the society.

The officials of the department concerned should be required to visit the society as frequently as possible and spend adequate time to help in drawing its plan for improvement and investments.

A Special Officer incharge of cooperative farming should be added to the block team in Blocks selected for intensive development. He should be an experienced agricultural graduate. A specially trained auditor should also be attached to the Block when needed.

In every block, where a sufficient number of cooperative farming societies have been established, a union may be set up. The main core of this union should be the elected representatives of its affiliated societies. Its membership should be small so that it can meet frequently. It need not in the beginning, have an office of its own or a separate clerical staff. Its meeting should be held at each cooperative farm by rotation. Its Chairman should be elected from among its non-official members.

Similar unions should be established at the district, State and National levels only when the movement has acquired sufficient strength at the village level to justify the creation of a higher federated structure.

Advisory Boards should be set up at the State and National levels immediately. These bodies would give their undivided attention to the promotion of cooperative farming movement.

State Boards should generally consist of Ministers, non-officials, representatives or organisations and officials connected with cooperation, agriculture and industry in the State at various levels. Minister for Cooperation in the State might be the Chairman.

In the development of cooperative farming, apart from technical and administrative problems, the human aspect is of the highest importance.

Promotional and educational work for creating a favourable atmosphere, interest and awakening among the masses can be performed more effectively by those devoted public workers who have worked among the rural people, have sympathy for the cause and have been engaged in cooperative farming and allied fields. State Government should obtain the services of one or two such eminent public workers for the Cooperative Department and assign to them specific functions and responsibilities.

Great care should be exercised in selecting these workers from among the people who have by their whole life demonstrated beyond doubt their intense conviction in the development of cooperative farming and devotion for constructive activity.

In order to ensure that non-official workers are in a position to give their entire attention to the work a suitable remuneration and sufficiently high status be given.

In addition to one or two public workers, a Joint Registrar (from the Services) should also be placed in special charge of cooperative farming.

The officers so appointed should also be *ex-officio* members of the State Board.

The National Cooperative Development and Warehousing Board which is responsible for planning and promoting various programmes of cooperative development including cooperative farming may not be able to devote the time and attention necessary for the new experiments as it has to deal with other equally vital and pressing problems regarding cooperative marketing and processing societies.

Government of India should constitute on the lines suggested a Cooperative Farming Advisory Board for planning and promoting cooperative farming with Minister for Community Development and Cooperation as Chairman.

The Government would be responsible for executing the programme recommended by the Board. For implementing the programme two eminent devoted public workers be carefully selected and given the rank of Additional or Joint Secretary in the Cooperative Department. An official of the rank of Joint Secretary should also be added. These three should form a team. They should be *ex-officio* members of the Board. Necessary subordinate staff may also be provided.

Staff should be carefully selected. Scales prevailing within the Government should not prove a limitation in getting most suitable persons.

Education And Training

The essentials for the sound development of Cooperative Farming are meeting of minds of the members, pooling of their intelligence, skill, manpower, land and other resources and that the members have the necessary knowledge and access to available information. The role of education, training and orientation programme is of the highest importance in this context.

The existing scheme of the training of members, office-bearers etc. would not be adequate as the problems in a Cooperative Farming Society are difficult from that of the credit or other types of societies.

By and large the training of Manager has not received due appreciation. This is one of the reasons of slow growth of Cooperative Farming. Education and training of Manager should be attended so promptly and courses organised.

Persons belonging to the same village can be more effective in placing the facts and the available experience in cooperative farming before the people and provide the leadership. Therefore, young promising farmers and village leaders should be imparted a two-week training course in cooperative farming.

These persons should be trained in batches at a residential cooperative farming training centre, each batch consisting of 40 participants. By the end of Third Plan, about two lakh farmers from one lakh villages should be trained.

Seminars for members of cooperative farming societies, members of Committees, Gram Sahayaks and agriculturists should be conducted in the villages at a central place. Each seminar should be of the duration of three days and the participants should be invited from a group of eight or 10 villages at the rate of five per village. 15 lakh members, Gram Sahayaks and agriculturists should receive education under this programme by the end of the Third Plan.

Three months' training courses for 26,000 Secretaries needed for societies in the Pilot Projects as well as in other areas should be arranged. Training should be given in farm management and planning, organisation, accounting and improved techniques of agricultural production. One week orientation courses for village level workers and other officials and the staff of cooperative institutions should also be arranged.

160 training centres should be established during the next four years. These may be located preferably at the existing training institutions wherever attached farm and accommodation facilities are available and which are located near successful co-operative farming societies. A large scale programme of building construction and land acquisition should be avoided. The centres should be run on austerity basis.

The training centres should be estimated at the rate of 20 in 1960-61, 30 in 1961-62, 45 in 1962-63 and 65 in 1963-64. Cost of the programme for 1960-61 to 1965-66 would be Rs. 361.44 lakhs out of which Rs. 241.44 lakhs would account for recurring expenditure at the rate of Rs. 37,430 per centre and Rs. 120 lakhs non-recurring at the rate of Rs. 75,000 per institute.

It is expected that these centres would train 18.12 lakh workers of different categories.

Every training centre should have a Principal and an Instructor. They should have sufficient knowledge and experience of Coperative Farming.

The trainers should be properly re-orintented before taking up the teaching work. Special officers and auditors should also be trained.

The National Institute of Cooperative Farming as recommended should conduct training and reorientation courses and carry out research. Univesities, Cooperative institutions and other appropriate agencies should also be associated with research projects.

Cooperative training institutions functioning under the guidance of the Central Committee for Cooperative Training should give more attention to cooperative farming either by way of some extra lectures or a special paper on the subject.

National Academy of Administration should provide for minimum of two lecturers on cooperative farming. Similar arrangements should be made in the training colleges and schools for officers of Provincial Civil Service and others.

The subject should receive greater attention in the training courses organised for the Community Development Staff.

Students Cooperative Farms should be organised at the educational and training centres to which a farm is attached.

Essay competition and debates on the subject should be arranged in universities and colleges and prizes awarded,

Popular literature on cooperative farming should be made available.

Government should give encouragement to writers and artists of Dramas, Skits. Ballads, Kirtan, Bhajan, etc. Audio-visual aid should also be utilised for promoting the movement.

The Programme

The development of cooperative farming cannot be regarded as a series of isolated experiments or projects. Besides educational activity, as the Village Panchayats gain in power and effectiveness and the coverage and scope of service cooperatives are progressively increased, a suitable atmosphere will be created for transition to cooperative joint farming on a large scale.

Intensive efforts should be made to organise cooperative farming societies composed of the willing agriculturists. Necessary guidance and facilities should be provided to these societies so that they may constitute a living example of the advantages of cooperative farming.

A cooperative farming society is a voluntary association of cultivators for better utilisation of resources including manpower and lands pooled, and in which the overwhelming majority of members participate in farm operations with a view to increasing agricultural production, employment and income.

A cooperative farming society, in our view, is a voluntary association of cultivators for better utilization of resources including man-power and lands pooled; and in which the majority of members participate ln farm operations with a view to increasing agricutural production, employment and income. Four types of cooperative farming societies are working at present; of these better farming and tenent farming societies are developed form of service cooperatives and should be distinguish from Cooperative Farming because there is no pooling of manpower and land in these societies and the members take the responsibility and risk of farm operations individualy. As such these societies need not be classified as co-operative farming societies.

Cooperative Farming Societies which do not really conform to the principles of cooperative farming and are not well-managed should not receive encouragement and assistance and action should be taken to weed them out. Existing promising societies should be helped.

A special officer in-charge of cooperative farming should be added to the Block staff in each project. An auditor should also be added when necessary. Adequate and timely financial assistances, technical guidance and other facilities should be assured.

By the end of the Third Plan it is expected that 20,000 new societies would come into existence in addition to 3,200 societies in the pilot project areas.

Financial assistance to cooperative farming societies should be related to production programme. A society in the pilot project should ordinarily be given assistance at the following scal:

(i) Rs. 4,000 as long and medium-terms loans;

(ii) Rs. 5,000 as loans and subsidies for godown-*cum*-cattle shed;

(iii) Rs. 2,000 as share capital contribution; and

(iv) Rs. 1,800 as managerial subsidy.

Short-term finance should be provided by the Central Cooperative Banks.

Similar assistance should be available to cooperative farming societies in other areas as well.

Procedural and other delays in obtaining assistance from Government and other institutions should be resolved.

In the allotment of Government and surplus lands preference should be given to cooperative farming societies. Besides developing cooperative farming on such lands, special efforts should be made to organise this on the existing holdings.

Financial requirements upto the end of the Third Plan of 3,200 societies in the pilot projects would be Rs. 409.60 lakhs and of the 20,000 other new societies would be Rs. 2,455 lakhs. Total requirements would be of the order of Rs. 2,864.60 Lakhs.

Cost of Education and Training Programme including that of 160 Training Centres, National Institute, etc., would be of the order of Rs. 424.4 lakhs up to the end of the Third Plan.

In addition to the staff required in the pilot projects, a special officer per district should be appointed for the work in other areas. An auditor may also be provided in each of these districts, if necessary.

Advisory Boards in the States and at the Centre should be constituted and men of ability, drive and devotion should be placed in position to render guidance at appropriate levels.

Total cost of the technical, advisory and organisational staff would be of the order of Rs. 237.44 lakhs.

Total outlay of the whole programme would be Rs. 3,526.44 lakhs.

As a result of the programme outlined, conditions would be created so that cooperative farming will emerge as a pattern of agriculture in the country.

HEALTH SURVEY AND PLANNING COMMITTEE, 1959—REPORT

New Delhi, Ministry of Health, 1961. 2 Vols.

Chairman : Dr. A. Lakshmanaswami Mudaliar.

Members : Shri Tirumal Rao; Dr. G. S. Melkote; Shri V. K .B. Pillai (resigned); Dr. C. O. Karunakaran; Lt. Gen. B, Chaudhuri; Lt. Col. Jaswant Singh (retired; replaced by Lt. Col. V. Srinivasan); Lt. Gen. D. N. Chakaravarti; Dr. Dukhan Ram; Dr. C. G. Pandit; Dr. V.S. Mangalik (resigned); Major K,N. Rao; Dr. (Miss) H. M. Lazarus; Dr. P. M. Mehta; Dr. K. C. K. E. Raja; Lt. Gen. B. M. Rao; Dr. R. V. Sathe.

Secretaries : Dr. K. C. K. E. Raja (resigned); Dr. T. R. Tewari.

APPOINTMENT

The Government of India in the Ministry of Health set up this Committee on June 12, 1959, to undertake the review of the developments that have taken place since the publication of the Report of the Health Survey and Development Committee (Bhore Committee) in 1946 with a view to formulate further health programmes for the country in the Third and subsequent Five Year Plan periods.

TERMS OF REFERENCE

(i) The assessment (or evaluation) in the field of medical relief and public health since the submission of the Health Survey and Development Committee's Report (The Bhore Committee);

(ii) Review of the First and Second Five-Year Plans Health Projects; and

(iii) Formulation of recommendations for the future plan of health development in the country.

CONTENTS

Volume I: Appointment of the Committee, Terms of Reference, etc. ; Introduction: Important Developments since the Health Survey and Development Committee's Report (1946); Role of International Organisations; Present State of the Nation's Health; Medical Care; Public Health; Communicable Diseases; Professional Education; Research; The Population Problem; Drugs and Medical Supplies; Legislation; Indigenous Systems of Medicine; Health Administration; Financial Aspect and Conclusions; **Volume II**: Appendices.

RECOMMENDATIONS

Constitutional Provisions

Although under the provisions of the Constitution of India 'Health' is primarily a State subject, and although more effective Central action and a larger measure of Centre-State and inter-State coordination is necessary, any amendment of the Constitutional provisions, to secure this, does not appear to be called for.

On the other hand, in keeping with the democratic traditions being built up in this country, the objective can be better achieved by the growth of healthy conventions, greater goodwill and better education; by a system of grants-in-aid by the Central Government in support of public health programmes of a national character like those of water supply and sanitation, eradication/control of communicable diseases, family planning and schemes of training of health personnel, by the setting up of an All-India Health Service, by the creation of regional organisations of the Central Health Directorate, by the Central Council of Health being made a more effective organ for policy-making and implementation in the matter of national health programmes, by the promotion of zonal Councils, on the lines of the Southern Regional Health Ministers' Council, and by the utilisation of the University Grants Commission, or a comparable agency that may be set up for the purpose of advancement of medical education and research.

International Collaboration

The assistace and support received from international bilateral and other agencies has been most valuable and it is to be hoped that it will continue to be forthcoming to supplement the national effort towards the attainment of a higher standard of health.

General

Having given due credit for the implementation by States of many health measures, it must be confessed that the general picture presented by health statistics of different States does not enable us to take too optimistic a view of the present state of health and of the future health protection of the citizens.

Unless the conscience of the citizens as a whole is stimulated to demand and accept better standards of health, unless the principles of sound hygiene are inculcated into the masses through health education and other efforts, and unless Governments feel strengthened in taking positive measures to promote health, it will be difficult for health authorities alone to ensure that the measures contemplated are actually implemented. There are at present wide variations as between States, not only in providing necessary facilities for health care but in the measure of control exercised by authorities in preventing the spread of epidemic diseases. This aspect should be attended to carefully.

While appreciating the efforts made by Governments to give relief and provide satisfactory methods of rehabilitation to displaced persons, the absence of a measure of willingness, on the part of the displaced persons themselves has created difficulties not only for the displaced persons but also for the populations of the States concerned and those of adjacent areas.

The increase in the number of hospitals, dispensaries and beds has not created the impression that might have otherwise been made because of large increase in the population.

The arrangements for medical care for the people have to be examined carefully. Overcrowding in hospitals, inadequate staff, non-availability of essential drugs and medicines, mixing of serious with minor cases, lack of coordination of hospital services and the close proximity of the out-patient department with the hospital proper, are some of the orgainsational defects which have to be remedied at an early date.

There is a maladjustment in the distribution of trained personnel who congregate in urban areas owing to lack of amenities and gainful employment in rural areas. Moreover, highly trained doctors of the medical profession are being utilised to carry out routine duties which can as well be done by lesser qualified people. The need is to conserve such highly trained personnel to jobs that they ought to be doing and to make greater use of auxiliary health personnel.

The attempt to start mass campaigns against certain diseases like tuberculosis, smallpox, cholera, leprosy and filariasis is commendable, but the method of dealing with these diseases individually will not be conducive to the organisation of unified efforts needed for the promotion of total health care. The health personnel engaged in such mass campaigns must be trained to tackle all health problems in any area. While the overall supervision for particular diseases may require special attention through specialists, in rural areas it is neither possible nor desirable to have separate agencies to deal with separate diseases.

The intensive steps taken at the time of the out-break of epidemics or at the time of sudden catastrophies have led to waste of effort and finance. Instead of sporadic efforts at the time of epidemics, large amounts can be conserved and more lasting results achieved if permanent measures for eradication of diseases are undertaken.

While it is noted with satisfaction that the position regarding plague is now more satisfactory than before and that there has been no epidemic of plague for several years, there are certain factors which do not tend to give us the confidence that recrudescence of plague may not occur.

In attempting to provide school hygiene it should be ensured that apart from providing minimum standards of sanitation in schools and colleges, conditions are made available to inculate in children proper health habits from the earliest stage.

Medical Care

It does not appear feasible for the State to provide

free medical service on the scale visualised by the Bhore Committee in the near future. It shold be considered fairly satisfactory if the ratio of one bed per 1,000 population, is achieved during the Fourth or Fifth Plan periods.

The question of financing of medical care, needs a careful study. The introduction of a system of graded changes for all hospital services, except in the case of the genuinely indigent patients, is called for. The possibility of the levy of a health cess is also worth exploring.

Steps need also be taken for the extension of medical care through the promotion of health insurance schemes. The initial steps taken in this direction in the form of the Employees State Insurance and Contributory Health Service Schemes, should be followed up by extending their scope by giving coverage to other sectors of the population in the case of the former and by bringing all Government servants within the purview of the latter, as early as possible.

The Governments should also encourage the development of medical care facilities on cooperative lines, on an experimental measure, through suitable subsidies.

The district hospital should occupy the key position in regard to medical care and should be expanded and strengthened with specialist facilities. Besides, there should be mobile teams of specialists to cover all areas of the district and to provide necessary supervisory and consultant facilities at the periphery. On the other hand, the Taluk hospitals should be developed to take over the routine medical, surgical, obstetrical and gynaecological needs of the area.

The primary health centre programme as it has developed bears no resemblance to that visualised by the Bhore Committee. It is felt that while the idea of the primary health centre is an excellent one, it will not serve any useful purpose if centres are established without adequate facilities, resources and personnel. The programme needs to be radically revised and it is suggested that the further opening of primary health centres on the existing pattern should be discontinued and any primary health centres that are opened hereafter should be on the pattern suggested to serve a population of upto 40,000 and should have full complement of staff recommended by that Committee. Further, the primary health centres already in existence should be upgraded by stages to reach the full-fledged pattern of the Bhore Committee.

It will be preferable to provide medical coverage to the rest of the rural population through mobile health units in mobile vans visiting them from district and Taluk headquarters than through poorly equipped and staffed primary health centres. Those requiring hospitalisation or intensive medical care can be brought in ambulances to the Taluk or district hospitals, for necessary treatment. When facilities in regard to personnel, finance and other requirements are sufficiently enlarged the Bhore Committee formula of the Primary Health Centres can be adopted.

The Primary Health Centre should provide residential accommodation to all the personnel of the centre and should have a bed strength of 10 including two beds for emergency cases.

There should be suitable conveyance including an ambulance and a jeep at every centre. Wherever possible the centre should be at a place where other activities such as education, agriculture, animal husbandry, etc. are concentrated.

It is suggested that before this new programme of Primary Health Centres is implemented on a large scale, each State should establish some model centres so that necessary adjustments can be carried out in the light of experience at a later stage. The model centres will be supported by hospital services at Taluk and district levels, by telephonic, ambulance and mobile service facilities. Facilities of the police wireless communication now available in the greater part of the country should be fully utilised

Apart from improving the conditions of service of the medical and auxiliary personnel serving in primary health centres, it is imperative that training should be given to prepare the large bulk of students, going through the medical colleges, for public health duties in rural areas and for improving the equipment and staffing of the primary health centres so as to allow a better standard of work to be undertaken.

The Primary Health Centre medical officers should not be allowed private practice, but should be given non-practising plus public health allowances together with residential accommodation. There should be one unified cadre of Assistant Surgeons in the State to man rural health centres as also hospitals at higher levels. All medical officers in that cadre should be given rural assignments by rotation and posting to a primary health centre should normally be after one or two years of service in a hospital under the supervision of a senior medical officer. Service in rural areas should be an essential condition for confirmation in Government service and for crossing the efficiency bar. Preference for post-graduate training should be given to those who have served in rural areas.

Taluk hospitals should have a minimum bed strength of 50 and should have three medical officers dealing with medicine, surgery, obstetrics and gynaecology. Such a hospital should serve as a referral centre for routine type of cases from two or three Primary Health Centres in that area. Of the three medical officers one should preferably be a woman medical officer for maternity and child health and family planning work. Good clinical side-room facilities should be available. One of the three medical officers should have had training in laboratory work.

Each District Headquarters Hospital should be expanded to 300 to 500 beds, of which 75 may be set apart for maternity and 50 for paediatrics. Specialist services medicine; surgery, obstetrics and gynaecology, eye, ear, nose and venereal diseases should be provided.

The specialists in medicine, surgery and obstetrics and gynaecology should have the status of a Civil Surgeon.

There should be an isolation unit of 50 beds attached to the District Hospital. The Tuberculosis Clinic and Public Health Laboratory at the District Headquarters should work in close association with the district hospital. There should also be a chronic and convalescent hospital, in order to relieve the congestion in the hospital and the consequent strain on the staff.

A number of district hospitals should be linked with the teaching hospital on a regional basis in order to get expert advice and assistance in the matter of investigation, diagnosis and treatment.

Every district and teaching institution should have a blood bank service. The headquarters of each State should develop a special department for blood transfusion service.

In planning hospital facilities the basis of one bed for every 1,000 population should be taken for each district. Hospitals at the Taluk level will provide 600 to 800 beds and the Primary Health Centres will provide 10 beds each. In addition, the beds available in private or voluntary hospitals should also be taken into consideration. The important thing is to ensure that from the smallest to the biggest hospital they function as an integral whole.

The planning and organisation of the Out-Patient Department deserves special care. It should be outside the compound of the In-Patient Department with a separate entrance. The casualty department for emergency cases, and the Orthopaedic department for accident cases should be attached to the Out-Patient Department. Certain other departments, such as eye and E.N.T. could also safely be situated in the Out-Patient Department building. There should be full facilities in the Out-Patient Department for X-Ray and laboratory services, immunisation and anti-rabic treatment. Special clinics like diabetic clinic, border-line mental clinic, chest clinic, could also be located in the Out-Patient Department.

There is a great need for special hospitals for children.

Apart from the provision made in district and Taluk hospitals and primary health centres for maternity beds, wherever possible, independent maternity hospitals should be brought into existence so as to increase within the shortest possible time hospital facilities for maternity cases. Maternity wards or maternity hospitals should be available in all large towns and cities and should be so spread over that facilities are afforded for women in different localities to get admission easily. It is desirable to encourage the habit of pregnant women attending the ante-natal clinic. As far as possible only booked cases should be ultimately admitted into maternity hospitals. Domiciliary visits should be paid by trained health visitors or midwives. Maternity hospitals should also have facilities for post-natal care.

The larger maternity hospitals should serve as training centres for nurses, mid-wives, nurse-midwives, medical students and other para-medical personnel who serve in the field of maternal and child care. A planned method of development of maternity homes and maternity hospitals with attached ante-natal clinics and facilities for the system of promoting booked cases, is recommended.

Each Taluk hospital should have 10 to 15 beds for isolation of T. B. cases. Similarly, at the district level where there is no separate T.B. hospital, 30 to 40 beds should be reserved for T.B. cases.

Each district hospital should have a Psychiatric Clinic and five to 10 beds may be earmarked for psychiatric cases.

Mental hospitals should be developed on a regional basis, the optimum bed strength being about 750.

Each teaching hospital should have a separate cancer clinic and each State should have a full-fledged hospital equipped with modern facilities for the surgery and radio-therapy of cancer.

It is also necessary to have leprosy hospitals for treatment of cases requiring isolation, surgery and rehabilitation.

In regard to blindness those concerned with preventive and social medicine should be properly instructed about the aetiology and incidence of eye diseases and the measures necessary for preventing them. Special surveys and provision of adequate number of beds are necessary. At the under-graduate level the students should be adequately trained in Ophthalmology. This will encourage them to take up Ophthalmology as a career.

Mass campaign against diseases like trachoma and other diseases, causing blindness like smallpox, etc., should be conducted.

There should be one Ophthalmic Hospital for each State with 300 to 350 beds, besides the provision made in the district hospitals.

Centres for the rehabilitation of the adult blind should be established.

Eighty to ninety per cent of deafness is preventible. This requires education of mothers and children on the simple causes of deafness.

Incidence of deafness is likely to increase with the rapid industrialisation of the country and with the frequent exposure of the human ear to loud noises.

Steps should be taken to remedy the situation.

Training of ear surgeons is necessary. Mechanical hearing aids should be manufactured in India.

The deaf schools in the country should be supervised and uniform standards of teaching prescribed by a National Committee.

Every State should have an Orthopaedic Hospital with wings for accident cases. Hospitals for handicapped children with physio-therapy, occupational therapy and other facilities should be organised in each State.

The existing institution for training workers in Physiotherapy at Bombay should be fully developed so as to enable it to take on limb fitting activities which are at present being done entirely by the Army Limb-Fitting Centre at Poona.

It is felt that in the present state of development of Dental Health Services, it may not be necessary to have full time Deputy or Assistant Directors in the State Health Directorates for Dentistry. It is suggested that Principals of Dental Colleges in the States where such exist, or the senior-most Dental Surgeon in the State should act as Consultant to Health Directorates to draw programmes for dental services.

At the district level a fully-equipped and staffed dental clinic should form part of the headquarters hospital. Besides the Dental Surgeon there should be a dental hygienist and a dental mechanic.

In each district there should in addition be a dental mobile van, which should visit the Taluks and other centres on a carefully drawn schedule. Cases referred from primary health centres for dental examination of school children can be examined in this manner.

It is suggested that some orientation in dental care may be given to the auxiliary health worker in each primary health centre, so that he may assist the dental hygienist.

The Armed Forces Medical Services can cooperate with their civilian counterparts in order to improve the health of the country and to train medical auxiliary personnel of which there is an extreme shortage in the civil side. A short period of service in the Armed Forces may usefully be rendered by every civilian medical officer. Interchange of specialists for limited periods, between the Armed Forces and Civilian Institutes is also highly desirable.

Medical Care in Railways

In an organised service like the railways it should be feasible to subject all employees to periodical physical examination.

It is necessary to provide checks against patients suffering from infectious diseases freely using the railway trains and platforms.

Stringent control is required in the matter of cleaning of railway carriages, the inspection of food and the manner of its vending or platforms and refreshment rooms.

The public health staff of railways requires to be trained at all levels. There appears to be no reason why the Railway Health Service should continue to remain in a water-tight compartment. A common cadre with the Central Health Service is suggested. While retaining the administrative structure of the Railway Health Service in general, it is time that railways drew upon the pool of the General Health Services for their medical personnel.

It should be possible to make suitable arrangements for advice and assistance from specialists in Government hospitals in bigger cities being made available to the railway hospitals as and when required and *vice versa*.

Factories

Special provisions should be made available for hospital, domiciliary and clinical care of workers. There should be separate hospitals for the insured patients except when specialist treatment is required.

There should be no discrimination whatsoever in the existing Government institutions between the Government servant, the insured patient or the civilian patient.

Plantations

By and large the health care facilities provided in plantations are poor and inadequate. Emphasis has largely been placed on providing expensive medical care facilities without adequate regard to the need of preventive health services. In a majority of plantations, sanitary facilities, facilities for health education, immunisation programmes, etc., have not been carried out on the required scale.

The provisions of the existing law in regard to health in plantations should be enforced by the State Health Departments.

Tribal And Backward Areas

The major public health problems are those of water supply and sanitation, malaria, tuberculosis, V.D., leprosy and nutritional disorders. The problem is made difficult because of the sparseness of the population, lack of communications and primitive voodooistic outlook of the majority of the tribes to disease. Over-zealousness in providing scientific medicine should not lose sight of the attitudes of the tribes and the village doctor should be treated as an ally by the health worker rather than a rival. The so-called civilising influences should be extended to the tribal people with judgement and discrimination so as not to do violence to certain cultural patterns peculiar to the tribes.

One of the most urgent needs of tribal areas is expansion of training facilities so that health assistants, health visitors, sanitary inspectors and other technicians are trained out of loca ltribal candidates. The standards of basic education applicable to the rest of the country should not be insisted upon for some time to come in such cases. The training centre at Passighat in NEFA should serve as a model and similar centres should be set up in all tribal areas to meet the needs of the tribal population.

To meet the shortage of doctors in tribal areas, suitable tribal students should be selected even while at school for training as doctors and should be given training in State Medical Colleges on condition that they will serve the tribal areas after qualifying.

Besides this, duty in the tribal areas for limited periods at least should be made compulsory for members of the Central Health Services and State Health Services.

Private Medical Practitioners

Closer liaison should be established between the private practitioners and the hospital authorities.

Government hospitals and dispensaries should profitably utilise the services of private practitioners on part-time or honorary basis.

Such practitioners should also be utilised in State Schemes of medical care like the Employees' State Insurance Scheme.

Private practitioners can cooperative with Government in problems of mass immunisation, school health, family planning and health education.

To secure the cooperation of private practitioners and to enable them to play a vital role in the matter of medical care to the public, they must be given refresher courses from time to time. Laboratory services at nominal cost and other facilities should be made available to them in the public institutions.

Public Health

Water Supply And Sanitation

Most States are not completely equipped with men and materials to carry out water supply and sanitation programmes. The organisational set up for handling the rural phase of the water supply and sanitation programme is lacking and there is a multiplicity of agencies entrusted with this programme, with the result that progress has been halting and results achieved doubtful. A re-orientation of the existing policy and procedures is necessary.

Full-fledged State Public Health Engineering Organisations should be brought into existence and all public health engineering works carried out in consultation with such departments in regard to designs, estimates, etc. where the execution is through recognised agencies.

The magnitude of the urban and rural water supply and sanitation programme will involve a large outlay the lowest estimate of which is of the order of Rs. 1,500 crores. The aim should be to accomplish this entire work within about 25 years, if any tangible improvements are to be expected. A much needed change in outlook in the management of water supply projects is called for.

The practice of Corporations and other local authorities undertaking water supply projects independently has proved unsatisfactory and the reeommendation of the Public Health Engineers' Conference for the formation of Water and Sewage Boards to serve a number of municipalities and other local authorities in an area is commended.

Another direction in which reorientation is necessary is legislation for conserving water sources and for regulating the exploitation of ground water.

It is suggested that the possibility of tapping perennial rivers throwing large quantities of unutilised water into the sea should be explored before their entry into the sea without affecting the reparian rights of any other States. Such water may be collected in reservoirs and carried through conduites to many vallages through storage tanks.

In areas where there are a large number of rainfed tanks they may be interlinked with one another wherever possible.

Another possibility of providing water in coastal areas may be by disalination of sea water.

A scheme for the provision of water supply to every village with a population of 5,000 before the end of the Fourth Plan is not too ambitious to put through.

It is of the utmost importance that drainage and sewerage schemes should run parallel to water supply schemes in urban areas.

Part of the money advanced by Government to local authorities for water supply schemes should be treated as grants. A condition should be made that the schemes undertaken with the help of loans from Government are integrated with drainage and sewerage schemes.

Another line of action will be research in the treatment of effluents in such a manner as to bring as high a return as possible with the least investment.

Methods of disposal of human excreta most suited to each area will have to be evolved. It is suggested that in every State a pilot project should be set up to study various methods of disposal of sewage and human excreta in rural areas.

The Committee is strongly of the opinion that suitable receptacles, hand-carts and other mechanical devices should be provided; and dignified and hygienic methods of collection and disposal of night-soil should be brought into practice.

It is felt that not only health education but also punitive measures should be instituted in order to prevent the use of open spaces for defecation

A satisfactory solution of the rural latrine programme will depend more upon an appeal to the civic consciousness of the community rather than on motivation of the individual villager. The Block Development Organisation in each area should take the responsibility to fabricate appropriate rural latrines and to supervise periodically the servicing of such latrines.

Competitions at the Block and Zila Parishad levels may be organised where some token of recognition of creditable effort on the part of individuals and communities for the improvement of rural hygiene, may be awarded. Efforts in this direction should be coordinated by the various agencies like the Community Development Blccks, Local Bodies, State Departments of Health, etc.

The sources of air pollution are many and the effects of such pollution on human health are multifarious. It is suggested that the programme for control of air pollution in the bigger cities of India should be given due attention by research, establishment of a monitoring machinery and legislation.

Meternal And Child Health

Greatest attention should rationally be given to the care of the health of the childern. There is no agency to ensure that a systematic follow-up of ante-natal, midwifery, post-natal, infant and child welfare services takes place. This work must be organised properiy.

Every effort should be made to develop and expand the net-work of maternity health centres so that with in a period of 10 years one midwife is in position for 5,000 to 6,000 population in rural areas, supported by a public health worker for twice that number.

The Departments of Social and Preventive Medicine should give due importance to maternity and child health. Under-graduates should have more experience and partical training in ante-natal and post-natal care and in mid-wifery.

Enough maternity beds must be provided in teaching hospitals to allow each under-graduate to do the normal quota of 20 cases. Training in mid-wifery should also be domiciliary.

Mid-wifery, paediatrics and health education should receive emphasis in the orientation and refresher courses for medical officers, public health nurses and auxiliary health workers.

The output of public health nurses, lady health visitors and auxiliary nurse-midwives should be increased considerably.

The maternity and child health services in hospitals should be coordinated properly with those of the M. C. H. Centres. The centres should register all expectant mothers and induce them to avail of all the services. The services rendered by maternity centres should include immunisation and nutrition education, apart from routine mother and child care. Maternity and child health centres' staff should give talks, demonstrations, film shows, family planning education, home visits and health education in the homes of the people. These centres should establish close liaison with agencies like Balvadis for the care of pre-school children.

Creches should be set up in commercial and industrial establishments.

For children, playgrounds should be provided.

Until there is an adequate number of trained midwives, the village *dai* should be trained for use in certain areas.

The Lady Health Visitor and Mid-wife posted to health centres should be responsible for health education, personal hygiene and nutrition.

Health centres and referral and district hospitals should form part of an integrated whole with telephone connections and ambulance services in order to attend to abnormal deliveries, surgical cases and blood transfusions.

The primary health centres and maternity and child health centres in rural areas should take a greater part in the programmes of immunisation of children and in the notification and checking of births and deaths. They should also attend of the distribution to food supplements like skimmed milk.

School Health

The Advisory Boards to be set up at the headquarters and district levels in States on which the Departments of Education, Health, Housing, Agriculture and Social Welfare, are represented, should play an important part in developing policies and programmes connected with the health services for school children.

Each Directorate of Health Services should have a Bureau of School Health Services to plan and initiate School Health Service programmes, to coordinate the activities of the Government, the local bodies and voluntary organisations and to establish close liaison with the Education Departments in the States.

General hygiene and sanitation in school premises and their surroundings should be improved. Every school must have a source of wholesome water supply, sanitary facilities and regular and proper cleaning up of the class rooms and the school campus.

Officers of the Primary Health Centres should consider it their duty to see that sanitary facilities in schools are adequately maintained.

The production of birth and vaccination certificates should be made compulsory for admission to schools.

Teachers should see to it that lists of students are prepared for re-vaccination after three years and such lists are made available to the medical officers of the Primary Health Centres for necessary action.

The school staff should actively assist in inoculation of pupils at the time of any epidemic.

The school feeding programmes being carried out in certain States should be watched carefully and steps taken in the light of experience to improve and extend them.

Kitchen gardens should be cultivated in a large majority of village schools for supplementing the menu for school meals.

The Primary Health Centre staff may not be able to cater to the medical coverage of the school population except in 20 to 25 villages. Therefore, for the remaining portion of the Block area the services of private medical practitioners in the nearest towns may be made use of either through a system of per capita fee or by payment of an honorarium. These private practitioners may do periodical examinations and inoculation, while minor ailments may be attended to by the Primary Health Centre staff and the more detailed investigations may be done by the district hospitals, the mobile specialists and the ambulance services, being recommended elsewhere.

Nutrition

In spite of the priority given to agriculture in the two Five-Year Plans, major emphasis was laid on the increase of food production only, and adequate attention was not paid to increasing the output of protective foods, for the vulnerable groups of the population.

A sound nutrition policy involves collaborative effort on the part of the Ministries of Food and Agriculture, Community Development, Education and Heath.

The sixty million acres of cultivable land still to be developed and the 70 million acres of fallow land in the country should be fully utilised for production of more food.

To cover deficiency in protective foods, milk production should be considerably increased. Production of more fodder, improving the breed of cattle, poultry farming and fish production are other ways for increasing protective foods. Special attention should be paid to the development of vegetables and fruits, exploitation of neglected sources of vegetable protein foods, development of kitchen and community gardens, fish culture and production of processed and synthetic foods.

More nutrition sections in the State Health Departments should be opened, and the existing ones should be considerably strengthened.

Qualified Nutritionists and Dieticians should be employed in public institutions.

Iron supplements, protein rich foods, vitamins, etc., should be supplied to the vulnerable groups in rural areas through Rural Health Centres, M.C.H. Centres, Schools, etc. Similar action should be taken in urban areas.

Clinical Research Units should be established in teaching hospitals for investigation of diseases associated with faulty diets, for analysis of food stuffs, for study of the effects of storage, processing and cooking and for the study of normal physical and physiological standards.

The training facilities for nutrition workers at the Nutrition Research Laboratory at Hyderabad and the All India Institute of Hygiene and Public Health, Calcutta, should be considerably enlarged and a Diploma should be given to those who undergo such training.

A large number of institutions for the training of dieticians and nutritionists and nutrition workers should be set up.

The recommendation of the Bhore Committee for the establishment of Chairs for Nutrition is reiterated.

Considerable precaution should be taken while storing and transporting foodgrains to see that such goods are not contaminated with other poisonous substances like follidol.

Mental Health

There is a general sense of complacence in regard to mental diseases. There is an urgent need for the setting up of preventive mental health services, for the expansion and improvement of curative services, for the institution of training facilities and for research and survey programmes.

Housing

Early steps should be taken to see that as far as possible, housing accommodation is made available to all employees of State and Central Governments, all industrial workers employed in large factories and all those who are associated with public utility concerns.

Any new industrial area should be sufficiently large and well planned to meet the requirements of industrial labour for housing and other amenities.

The creation of large towns will, no doubt, involve construction of multi-storied buildings but safeguards regarding perflation of air, easy transport facilities, ancillary necessaries like schools, hospitals playgrounds and parks should all be provided.

The removal of slums and provision of alternative accommodation to slum dwellers is another important point to remember.

Cooperative housing schemes should be encouraged.

The proposal of the Life Insurance Corporation to subsidise housing schemes should go a long way to solve the housing problem.

The type of houses in urban and rural areas should be considered carefully from the point of view of public health and sanitation.

The policies for Town and Country Planning laid by the Central Government should be taken full advantage of by the States. There should be a proper town and country planning before housing schemes are sanctioned. All schemes of housing should be regulated by special Boards on which the Health Engineering and Administrative authorities should be represented along with experienced non-officials.

Vital Statistics

Health statistics should not be confined to disease alone but must include, in future, information on the socio-economic and cultural pattern of the community.

More and more longitudinal studies should be made in future for purposes of problem measurement and concurrent evaluation.

State Bureaux of Health Intelligence should be established.

There must be coordination between the Vital and Health Statistical Units in States and the Registrar-General and international agencies.

Centres should be established for the training of officers and other persons engaged in Health Statistics work.

A Central Health Statistics Act should be enacted to bring about uniformity in the collection and reporting of health statistics throughout the country.

Health Education

In view of the great importance of the subject, all States should establish Health Education Bureaux which must work in cooperation with the Central Health Education Bureau to promote health education of the people and make them health-conscious.

Model Public Health Act

In the interest of public health all over the country, the time is to come when every State should have a Public Health Act of its own. Such an Act should induce all the subjects mentioned in the Model Public Health Act framed by the Ministry of Health.

Physical Education

Physical education has yet to receive its due emphasis in this country. The general public should be made aware of the contribution that physical education and sports can make to the balanced development of personality. There is need for a more widespread realisation on the part of all concerned that physical education including games and sports is an essential part of education and that no educational system can be called complete if physical education is not allowed to play its full role.

Communicable Diseases

General

Control of communicable diseases cannot be dealt with exclusively as a State subject. It should be simultaneously a Central responsibility. It will be too late and not very effective for the Centre to intervene only in the event of an inter-State spread of infection.

Taere should be an organisational set-up representing the Central Government and the States in each zone to deal with communicable diseases on the lines of the Regional Organisations set up for the Malaria Eradication Programme. Two or three experts concerned with Communicable Diseases should be associated with this organisation. This will tend to promote greater collaboration and more prompt action wherever necessary.

Some compensation (either under the Workmen's Compensation Act or under any other Legislation to be passed) should be given to the health personnel, medical and non-medical, who are exposed to unusual risks through contact with patients suffering from Communicable Diseases.

The development of a national outlook through the processes of cooperation and discussion is preferable to the enforcement of action for the control of Communicable Diseases by statutory sanctions.

Necessary measures to enforce the legal obligations in regard to the notification of Communicable Diseases should be promoted.

The network of Police Wireless Stations may be used for the transmission of intelligence about Communicable Diseases from rural areas to the nearest District Health Organisation.

Infectious Diseases Hospital

There is a prime need to improve the conditions of Infectious Diseases Hospitals so as to make them fit for the treatment of the sick. A modern isolation hospital with facilities for treatment of Smallpox, Cholera, Diphtheria, Plague and other epidemic diseases should be established by every municipality with a population of 50,000. In municipalities of smaller size, isolation wards should be attached to general hospitals for the purpose. In bigger cities like Bombay, Calcutta, Madras, Delhi and Kanpur, there should be as many as three to six separate isolation hospitals distributed in the different parts of the Corporation areas.

Apart from Infectious Diseases Hospitals, every General Hospital (including maternity hospitals) should have a small isolation block for the purpose of observation and treatment of cases suspected of Communicable Diseases.

Public Health Laboratories

Public Health Laboratories equipped to undertake Laboratory and field investigations must be considered as the Essential pre-requisites in any Communicable Diseases Programme. There should be a chain of such Laboratories in each State. Besides other facilities, they should have a mobile unit for field investigations. There should be a Blood Bank in such laboratories. These laboratories should cater also to the needs of private medical practitioners for the examination of clinical material in connection with the diagnosis of infectious diseases.

Epidemiological Units

Each State should have a fully equipped mobile epidemiological unit capable of proceeding at short notice to any part of the State for field and laboratory investigation on the outbreak of an epidemic.

In addition to the small epidemiological units in States, there should be a nucleus organisation at the Centre, the services of which can be called upon by any State in an emergency. The cooperation of the Armed Forces Medical Services may also be taken in this regard.

Malaria

While it is hoped that the Malaria Eradication Programme of the Government of India will achieve the targets in the course of the Fourth Plan period, if not in the Third, attention may be drawn to the following problems which are likely to crop up as a result of the mass campaign of this size :

(a) The question of the possible developments of resistance in the mosquito to the insecticides and the need for the completion of the programme before this becomes manifest on a wide scale ;

(b) The possibilities of insects other than malaria vectors becoming resistant to the insecticide in use, *e.g.*, the rat flea and sand-flies which transmit plague and kala-azar respectively ; and

(c) Careful consideration of the routine use of insecticide to insect-borne diseases of man and animals and also against agricultural pests, in present circumstances.

Filariasis

In view of the evidence of spread of filariasis it is essential to concentrate control measures in the urban centres.

The structure and functions of the existing control units should be so modified as to permit them to undertake effective anti-larval measures continuously.

Filariasis clinics should be established in suitable hospitals in areas where the disease is endemic.

There should be a separate section for filariasis in the epidemiological bureaux to be created in each State. This section should work in close cooperation with the Public Health Engineering Section of the State.

Health education on the problem of filariasis should be an integral part of the activity of the Health Education Bureau in the State.

One research-*cum*-training unit should be established in each State where filariasis is a major problem.

Control of filariasis is not amenable to a crash eradication programme as in the case of malaria. The effort will have to be continued for an appreciable time with adequate financial support before any tangible results can be obtained.

While anti-larval measures may be expected to stem the tide temporarily, only adequate drainage facilities can provide the long-term solution of the problem.

Tuberculosis

The emphasis on anti-tuberculosis work must continue to be on the public health aspects including protection of the vulnerable population, early detection of cases, control of the spread of infection and attempts at converting an infective case into a non-infective one within the shortest possible time.

Emphasis is also required on early detection of the disease in persons who come into contact with children as well as contacts of active cases.

While mass B.C.G. vaccination should continue during the Third Plan, active steps should be taken to integrate B.C.G. vaccination programme and other tuberculosis schemes.

Highest priority should be given to the establishment of T.B. clinics so that fully equipped and staffed clinics come into existence in each district with the least possible delay.

Since modern chemo-therapy has proved to be very effective and is likely to be the basis of any mass anti-tuberculosis programme, it is essential to ensure that adequate stocks of such drugs are made available at a reasonable cost.

The provision of a mobile van equipped with X-ray is essential at each of the T.B. clinics. The mobile vans should visit the Taluk hospitals and Primary Health Centres at stated intervals. The district clinic would become the basis from which the B.C.G. vaccination teams operate.

The setting up of demonstration and training centres in T.B., one for each State, must be considered as a *sine qua non* for the development of an efficient anti-tuberculosis service.

Owing to limited hospital beds and extremely poor housing conditions in the country, facilities for isolation of advanced or infective cases should be provided on a much larger scale than is contemplated at present, and at a much greater speed. At least 50,000 beds should be available in the country for purposes of isolation.

In order that atleast a part of the total need for hospitalisation can be met, it is suggested that the immediate aim should be for a bed strength of not less than 1,00,000.

Rehabilitation and after-care facilities need also to be provided simultaneously.

There should be an official in the Directorate of Health Services of each State exclusively in charge of the T.B. programme, both preventive and curative. The State T.B. Officers should have adequate training and experience and the entire T.B. Service, curative and preventive, should function as one unitary service in the State Health Directorate.

T.B. workers, as also others working for control of communicable diseases, should be given attractive remuneration and treated as part of the State Health Cadres, so that normal avenues of promotions are open to them. Private practice should not be permitted to doctors doing such work.

Government should give all possible encouragement to non-official and voluntary organisations working in the field of tuberculosis.

Leprosy

In the light of present circumstances, segregation cannot be considered as a practical approach for the eradication of leprosy. Emphasis has got to be laid on the early detection and treatment of cases.

A determined attempt should be made to train leprosy personnel both medical and para-medical at as many centres as possible. The para-medical workers should be used in as large a measure as possible, thus relieving medical officers from these duties which can adequately be performed by the former.

For some time to come, steps will have to be taken to provide facilities for rehabilitation of leprosy patients. Wherever possible simple physiotherapentic measures should be introduced at treatment centres and attempts should be made to educate patients to take care of their hands and feet. Centres for reconstructive surgery should be established at suitable places.

The work of the treatment and study centres in the Third Five Year Plan should be so organised as to permit an assessment of the leprosy problem in the near future.

The attempts so far made for the prevention of infection in children by segregating them from their infected parents have not produced any appreciable results.

Recent observations indicate the possible use of chemoprophylaxis in contacts as well as the use of B. C. G. vaccination but no positive data are yet available regarding the adequacy of these methods. This is a matter for research.

Small Pox

On the termination of the Small Pox Eradication Programme planned by Government, there should be a follow-up by a sustained programme of re-vaccination and primary vaccination of new born babies.

An improvement in the method of reporting of vital statistics and adequate supervision of the vaccination work is called for.

The present tendency towards multiplication of agencies for the conduct of immunisation and other preventive programmes, is wasteful and should be avoided.

Normal health agencies should take up the work now being done by independent units for tuberculosis, leprosy etc., by making a larger use of para-medical personnel under a qualified medical officer's supervision.

In addition to official health services the, services of private practitioners should be utilised on an increasingly large scale.

In order to develop immunisation programmes properly, States should carry out pilot studies in selected areas.

Up to now, no concerted and properly controlled vaccination drive has been organised. Haphazard measures can never achieve eradication of this disease. The experience gained recently in the pilot projects should be fully utilised when the Small Pox Eradication Programme is launched.

Inspite of our knowledge of the efficacy of vaccine lymph as a prophylactic against Small Pox and the continuing vaccination effort over a century, expected results have not been achieved in India, although limited local experience and experience in other countries show that an organised effort does yield results. Therefore, steps should be taken to deal with it more effectively making full preliminary arrangements such as recruitment and training of personnel, procurement of equipment, manufacture of adequate quantities of lymph etc., before the actual mass vaccination programme starts. The programme must be carried out within a short period of years taking care to see that new-borns are vaccinated within six months after birth. Thereafter surveillance services should be established to take care of children who have not had primary vaccination.

The urgency of the eradication programme is strongly emphasised. The programme should be pushed through on a coordination basis under the direction of a Central Authority.

Attention is particularly drawn to the need for developing the manufacture of freeze dried vaccine on a large scale.

Cholera

The recommendations made by the Expert Committee appointed by the Government of India in 1958, to review the question of Cholera and to recommend ways and means to deal with it, are fully endorsed. Extensive measures are needed in West Bengal area for the control of the disease because that area is the most important focus of infection in the country.

Trachoma

Taking into account the results of the country-wide studies conducted during the last five years and the efforts already initiated for the control of this disease, it is considered that instead of tackling the problem piece-meal, a comprehensive approach to extend the control activities, especially in those States where Trachoma is known to be a serious public health problem, should be made.

Venereal Diseases

Compulsory notification of Venereal Diseases cannot be an effective step so far as India is concerned. Indirect methods will have to be adopted. For this, proper monthly returns may be obtained from all the States on the different types of venereal diseases treated in all institutions. Serological surveys in selected groups of population, random sampling in highly endemic areas, serological testing of all pregnant women are some of the other sources of getting such information.

The measures to discourage prostitution and promisenity should be taken up by social welfare agencies and health education sections of the health services.

The National Venereal Diseases Control Programme should be instituted with the long-term objective of reducing the incidence of these diseases to a negligible proportion and eventually eradicating them. Sustained efforts would therefore have to be made for at least the next 20 or 25 years. Greater use will have to be made of epidemiological methods.

It is extremely important to have family contacts brought in for testing and treatment at clinics.

It is essential to continue and expand systemic programmes on all the therapeutic, educational, epidemiological fronts with periodical assessment of the results achieved. The programme should therefore be integrated with the existing public health services.

Free supply of penicillin (PAM) and antigen, to all units, strengthening of Maternity and Child Welfare units for testing of pregnant women and treatment of positive cases, continuation of mass campaigns in areas like Himachal Pradesh and Tehri Garhwal, expansion and strengthening of existing Training and Demonstration Centres, health education, financial assistance to voluntary agencies, establishment of a Central V.D. Reference Laboratory at Madras and regional reference laboratories at Bombay, Culcutta and Delhi, research, improvement of facilities at major sea ports for V.D. treatment, incorporation of training in V.D. in the training programmes of medical officers for Primary Health Centres and adequate remuneration to people working in the V.D. programmes, are steps that should be taken to achieve the objectives of V. D. programme.

Yaws is a controllable communicable disease. Resurvey and constant vigilance should be maintained by existing health units. Raising the social level of the population concerned will be another necessary measure. The control of yaws should be vested in State V.D. Control Officers.

Plague

Sporadic cases of plague are reported in certain areas of the country. Fleas concerned in the transmission of plague, are gradually developing resistance to D.D.T. There is evidence of changes in the rat population. B. Bengalenois, which is highly sensitive to plague infection, is replacing R. Norvegiens. This shift in rat population may create favourable conditions for triggering off the epidemic in human beings. The Public Health Departments of States should, therefore, be alert to the possibility of outbreaks of plague. In the potentially dangerous areas rat elimination measures should be undertaken on a priority basis. The epidemiological units proposed for the State Health Directorates should take over these functions at an early date.

Virus Diseases

In view of the practical difficulties in instituting quarantine measures against influenza, these need not be adopted in future. Facilities may be created at different centres for the production of influenza vaccines at short notice on the lines of the techniques developed by the Pasteur Institute, Coonoor. In the first instance vaccine should be made available for the protection of the special groups of the population such as the medical personnel, transport workers, etc.

Entero-virus infections should be studied in more detail.

There is a vide prevalence of poliomyelitis in the country in the younger age groups. Steps should be taken in time to prevent development of such infection in the later age groups. Salk Vaccine has been used extensively in many countries with encouraging results, although there is evidence to show that the immunity produced by this is comparatively of a short duration. A mass immunisation programme with Salk Vaccine is therefore not practical. It would appear that Sabin's oral vaccine is the vaccine of choice in organising mass immunisation programmes in this country against Poliomyelitis.

It is necessary to take steps for the production of oral polio vaccine in centres where facilities are available.

There is no specific treatment for infectious hepatitis, but special steps must be taken to investigate outbreaks of this disease in greater detail in future. It is possible to prevent its occurrence or spread by use of gamma globulin. Steps should therefore be taken to produce gamma globulin in the country.

Facilities should be created for a thorough epidemiological investigation of epidemic encephalitis in children.

Studies on the arthropod-borne virus diseases now being carried on in the Virus Research Centre, Poona, should be extended, because they will help in the elucidation of the etiology of many of these infections, the precise nature of which is yet unknown.

Unless there is overall improvement in environmental sanitation, no meterial impact will be made on the prevalence of such infections in the community. A serious attempt should be made to train as many scientists as possible to undertake work in the diverse aspects of the problem at as many centres as possible. As and when such trained personnel become available, attempts should be made to develop diagnostic service units for viral infections at suitable regional centres.

Knowledge concerning the purification of water supplies is necessary to study the entero-virus infections. Special facilities should, therefore, be created to develop measures of water purification.

Professional Education

Under-Graduate

Whether colleges are run by the State Government or private agencies the responsbility for rcognition of colleges rests with the universities concerned and no medical college should be started unless the conditions laid down by the universities have been fully statisfied.

While appreciating the urgency of stepping up training facilities and opening new medical colleges. it is necessary to see that full information is in possession of the State Government or the authority concerned before the universities are approached for recognition.

Before a new medical college is started by a State Government or other agency it should conform to a standard plan laid down for this purpose. The University should appoint a Commission consisting of experienced teachers and experts to decide whether all the conditions are satisfied or not.

State Governments should not start new colleges without the concurrence of the Planning Commission and of the Ministry of Health if grants are to be given.

It would perhaps be a safe target to aim to have one doctor for every 3,000 or 3,500 population at the end of the Fourth Plan period.

There should be one medical college for at least five million population, which would mean, taking into consideration the rapid increase in population, that there should be 90 medical colleges for the existing population and for the anticipated population in 1971, the number of medical colleges will have to be nearer 100. Similar targets must be fixed for dental, nursing, pharmaceutical and other para-medical training institutions.

In order to give as much personal attention to individual students as possible, the number of admissions to medical colleges should not ordinarily exceed 100.

More than one teaching hospital, properly equipped and staffed, may be utilised for under-graduate training; and it is not necessary to concentrate all students at one teaching hospital during the period of their clinical training.

In view of the shortage of medical and public health personnel, the age of retirement should be increased from 55 to 60, subject to physical and mental fitness.

Tho Central Government should give grants for under-graduate and post-graduate medical education, on the analogy of the grants being made by the U.G.C. for post-graduate technological education.

In deciding the location of medical colleges and while planning and constructing them the following considerations may be kept in view :

(a) Closer contact with Arts and Science Colleges;

(b) The site chosen should be sufficient for further expansion for construction of quarters etc.;

(c) It is not necessary to construct a medical college within city limits—in fact it may be desirable to build it in rural surroundings, provided facilities like electricity, water and roads are available;

(d) The campus for a medical college and hospital should be between 60 to 100 acres;

(e) For easy communication between department and department, and between departments and the hosipital, it will be necessary to have three to four storied buildings with lifts;

(f) Clinical theatres and demonstration rooms should be made available in the hosipital or in the out-patient poly-clinics; and

(g) The buildings for medical colleges may either be permanent using standard materials or they may be prefabricated structures which will cost much less, according to the discretion of State Governments;

(h) Provision should be made for libraries in the college buildings on the ground floor ;

(i) Hostel accommodation should be provided to at least 75 per cent of the students ; and

(j) A High-powered Committee with full authority to meet all plans should be set up to prepare a master plan.

English should continue to be the medium of instructions in medical colleges.

Graduates in mathematics and physical sciences and natural sciences should be encouraged to get admission to medical colleges, provided they possess First or Second Class Degrees and their pre-professional record is of the minimum standard prescribed for admission to medical colleges and provided also that in the pre-clinical course they take up study of the subjects which may not have been covered in the pre-university course.

Graduates may be selected in addition to those who have passed pre-professional examination. First and Second class graduates can be admitted to the first year of the medical course, if they have the basic pre-professional requirements for admission. At least 10 per cent of the total admissions should be reserved for such graduates.

A separate entrance examination for candidates seeking admission to medical colleges is not recommended.

The best course would be to select candidates on the basis of the result of the pre-university or equivalent examination.

Where interviews are considered desirable for selecting candidates, not more than 10 per cent of the total marks of the university examination in the subjects concerned should be assigned for the interview and the following factors should be taken into consideration at the interview, among others:

(i) Extra-curricular activities ;

(ii) Membership of N.C.C., Boy-Scouts, and Girl Guides ;

(iii) Sports ; and

(iv) Personality.

The assessment for sports should be on the basis of the candidate having reached university, inter-university or national ranking.

The Selection Committee for admission of candidates to medical colleges should consist of Principals of medical colleges along with a senior educationist of standing nominated by the Vice-Chancellor of the University concerned. There should be a common Selection Committee for all the medical colleges in a State.

Merit should be the only consideration in the selection of students.

In regard to reservation of seats for Scheduled Castes, Scheduled Tribes and Backward Communities, it is felt that in selecting from these groups only the best among the candidates are selected for medical colleges.

A minimum of five per cent of the total number of seats should be reserved for special cases like sons and daughters of parents migrating from one State to another, either for official duties or in connection with trade and business. This reservation will not include cases of students coming from outside India and nominated by the Government of India.

20 per cent of the seats may be reserved for women in certain States where there is a dearth of women students. The reserved quota of seats will include those admitted on merit. In the event of more than 20 per cent of girl candidates qualifying on merit, there would of course, be no occasion for any special reservation of seats for them. This special reservation should be only for a transitional period of 10 years.

The minimum age of admission to a medical college should be 17 *plus* on October 1, for candidates joining the integrated course of six years and 18 *plus* for candidates joining the regular medical course of five years.

The pre-clinical course of instructions should extend to 18 months and the main subjects of study and examination will be Physiology including Biophysics, Organic Chemistry, Bio-chemistry and Anatomy including Histology. Stress should be laid on the practical applications of the above subjects that will follow during the candidates clinical years.

The period of clinical training should extend to three-and-a-half years, the first six months being devoted to subjects like Elementary Statistics, Introduction to Psychology and Sociology and Introduction to Medicine.

Emphasis during clinical training should be on an integrated method of teaching, the professor of pre-clinical subjects also taking a part and responsibility in the matter.

Didactic lectures should be reduced to the minimum and there should be more of clinical lecture-demonstrations with audio-visual aids wherever possible.

A proper method of instruction will be to limit it to small groups not exceeding 30 students. Besides clinico-pathological conferences should be held regularly every week both on medicine and surgery and such conferences should be attended by senior students of the fourth and fifth year classes.

Too much emphasis on specialities should not be given in the under-graduate course, this being reserved for the post-graduate stage and the housemanship stage.

Students should not spend too much time in witnessing complicated operations in theatres. Such operations need be witnessed only by post-graduate students and house surgeons.

The last year of the medical course should be completely devoted to the study of Medicine, Surgery, Obstetrics and Gynaecology and applied aspects of preventive medicine.

The existing department of preventive and social medicines should be strengthened and facilities for the training of teachers in this subject should be developed.

The teaching of medical jurisprudence should in future be restricted to the broader aspects of jurisprudence including professional behaviour. But so long as a separate cadre of medical jurists is not established in each State and properly trained medical jurists are not made available, the teaching of medical jurisprudence should be continued on the present basis.

Examinations in all subjects, other than Medicine, Surgery, Obstetrics and Gynaecology together with applied aspects of preventive medicine and pathology should be completed by the end of the fourth year of the study.

The teaching of paediatrics and mental diseases should form part of the under-graduate training. At least a period of three months should be devoted to the medical and surgical aspects of paediatrics and a question or two on paediatrics should form part of the medicine and surgery papers.

So far as ophthalmology and otorhinolaryngology are concerned, a separate examination paper may continue to be prescribed where this practice has been in vogue.

Examinations by themselves will not serve the purpose of producing a well-qualified basic doctor. Greater importance should, therefore, be given to the training methods adopted to make the medical students more and more self-reliant. The interest which a student takes in a subject depends upon the particular Professor.

While the day-to-day evaluation of the student's work during the training period may be a commendable idea, in actual practice it is doubtful whether such an assessment, to the exclusion of an examination, will be possible, realistic or fair in colleges where a large number of students are admitted and where personal contacts between students and head of the department is not likely to be as intimate as they ought to be. This method of evaluation can be adopted only to this extent, *viz.*, that along with the standard attained by the student in his University examination, he may be given a certificate by the college coneerned giving his general attainment during the college career.

In regard to orientation in rural health, the system of having certain days of the week when students are taken to villages along with the teachers will be of some benefit. Visits to slums in urban areas should also be included. The Professor of Preventive and Social Medicines and his associates, as also clinical teachers, should take a prominent part in such study tours.

Teachers in medical colleges have generally too many students to teach and too little assistance. Teaching facilities are unsatisfactory. Well-qualified and experienced persons are not always available for teaching posts because of unattractive terms of service. Considerable difficulty is felt in getting qualified teachers for pre-clinical subjects. It is suggested that trained personnel in these subjects from the ranks of non-medical men may be utilised as auxiliaries in teaching, research and other institutions, so that the medical men may be freed from some of their present duties for devoting their time to certain important aspects of teaching and research.

In addition to the regular professional staff, teaching work should also be undertaken by other members of the staff who have post-graduate qualifications. A small number of students should be allotted to these people, so that intensive coaching is done when lectures and demonstration classes are not held.

Attention should be given to the number of teachers employed in medical colleges in relation to the number of students admitted, the qualifications of these teachers at different levels and their teaching experience. The time has come when some uniform nomenclature should be given to the different types of teachers. A simple classification will be :

(i) Professor, including Associate or Additional Professor;

(ii) Reader or Assistant Professor; and

(iii) Lecturer and Registrar.

Lower down in the Category will be Demonstrators and Tutors.

There should be some full-time paid units in all branches of study in medical colleges particularly in the pre-clinical, laboratory sciences and certain of the clinical subjects.

Full-time units should be available in medicine, surgery, obstetrics and gynaecology. All these full-time units should devote their time entirely to teaching and should not engage either in active or consulting practice. In view of difficulties in meeting the entire requirements of teaching and medical relief by full-time staff, part-time teaching units are necessary. Fully qualified persons should be appointed to work as honorary medical officers and assistant medical officers for teaching and for care of patients. The honorarium paid to them should be commensurate with their responsibilities and they should be given the same designation as Professors, Readers or Lecturers, provided they have the required qualifications and experience.

There should be a cadre of full-time teachers in the categories of Professors, Readers, and Assistant Professors, liable to transfer to other teaching institutions.

Lecturers should have an occasional experience of working in non-teaching hospitals as well as in the districts. Such people may be selected later for the posts of Ptofessors and Readers.

No tutor, demonstrator or registrar should be attached to a teaching hospital for more than five years.

Teachers of clinical subjects should have a minimum basic qualification of M. D., M. S. or an equivalent qualification. Teachers of non-clinical and pre-clinical subjects should have a minimum qualification of M. Sc. or Ph. D. Along with these qualifications they should have the requisite number of years of teaching experience.

The duties of Registrars should be specified where they function as lecturers besides collecting records. They should then be equated to the grade of lecturers. Where they work only as Tutors and Demonstrators, they should be equated to such posts.

Lecturers should all have post-graduate qualifications in the particular subjects or specialities. (A post-graduate diploma or degree in the clinical subjects or a M.Sc. or Ph. D. or equivalent in non-clinical subjects.)

Taking the basic number of admissions to the medical college to be 100, the teacher-student ratio inclusive of tutors and demonstrators in each department should be 1:5.

Considerable improvements of out-patient departments of teaching hospitals are necessary if the student is to have the full benefit of the variety of cases available in such departments.

The following minimum scales of pay are suggested for teaching staff:

Professors	...	Rs. 1,500—2,500
Associate Professors	...	Rs. 1,250—2,000
Readers (Asstt. Professors)	...	Rs. 1,000—1,500

Lecturers & Registrars	...	Rs. 600—1,000
Tutors & Demonstrators	...	Rs. 350—600

Class I scales of pay for those recruited to the Medical and Public Health Posts should be the same as the I. A. S. scales of pay, where it is a running scale depending on the length of service and not on the position held by an individual. The scale of pay of Class II posts should be the same as for other Class II posts in Central Government.

Internship has been found to be unsatisfactory and it should be replaced by one year's compulsory housemanship, with provisional registration as a part of the training course prior to final registration in the medical register. Three months of this housemanship period should be spent in Public Health Work and one of these three months should necessarily be spent in a Primary Health Centre as an Assistant to the Medical Officer-in-charge of the Centre. Such housemen should work under the supervision of the Medical Officer-in-charge and should undertake complete responsibility for all types of work pertaining to the Primary Health Centre. They should be provided with free accommodation and a subsistence allowance of not less than Rs. 150 per month. In general all housemen should be provided with free furnished accommodation within the hospital or as near the hospital as possible, together with a subsistence allowance of ot less than Rs. 150 per mensem.

Licentiate Course

It will be unfortunate if at the present stage, the proposal for the revival of a short-term medical course is accepted by Government. The licentiates and students trained in short-term courses are not at all likely to settle down in rural areas as is popularly believed. Moreover, rural areas cannot be treated on a differential basis from urban areas. On the other hand, the training of several categories of para-medical personnel suggested elsewhere would meet the problem of filling up the gap in medical manpower requirements.

Post-Graduate Education

The training of post-graduates and specialists is very important and urgent because they have to take a promiment place in all teaching institutions, in district and Takul hospitals and in industries.

The great paucity of candidates for post-graduate training in pre-clinical subjects should be remedied by grant of stipends.

It is felt that every medical college is not immediately fit to be a post-graduate centre for training in the several branches of medicine. The recognition given at present to some of these institutions should depend upon their satisfying the conditions in regard to equipment and personnel.

It is felt that the upgraded departments which were started as a temporary measure and which have already served their purpose, should be merged with post-graduate centres wherever established and no more upgraded departments should be created.

There should be at least one well-developed post-graduate centre of training in each State where all the specialities will gradually develop.

The maintenance of such post-graduate centres should be the entire responsibility of the Central Government for atleast the next 10 years if uniformity of standards is to be maintained. Attention is drawn in this connection to the position of the higher technological institutions in the field of engineering set up by the Government of India.

It is suggested that the Ministry of Health may follow the practice of the Ministries of Education and Scientific Research & Cultural Affairs, by giving through the U. G. C. lump-sum grants to post-graduate medical education centres.

During the Third Plan a beginning should be made to develop at least six such Regional Post-Graduate Centres with the assistance of the Government of India, besides the All India Institute of Medical Sciences, New Delhi. The Post-Graduate Centre at Calcutta should be taken over by the Government of India as a Regional Centre and strengthened for all disciplines. The remaining five Regional Centres should be located at Bombay, Madras, Hyderabad, Lucknow and Chandigarh.

The regional post-graduate centres referred to above should serve the surrounding States till such time as post-graduate centres are establish in each State.

Admission to the post-graduate centres should be on a regional basis.

Under-graduate teaching may also be imparted at the proposed post-graduate training centres till such time as it is possible to have separate under-graduate colleges at these places, the number of under-graduates to be trained being limited to 50 in each case.

The methods of selection of candidates for post-graduate study need careful examination. The numbers to be trained in a particular speciality must be strictly limited if proper training is to be given.

A National Council for Post-Graduate Education should take charge of the functions of inspection, recognition and approval of institutions giving post-graduate instruction. The manner in which post-graduate institutions have developed round outstanding individuals in many countries, is far more conducive to effective growth of centres of post-graduate education than a recognition given and continued on the strength of an assessment of the facilities available at the start. It is, therefore, necessary to lay down that recognition once given should not automatically continue. The teaching personnel should be of a high grade and should command the confidence of the medical profession. It would be essential to see that the candidates admitted to post-graduate studies come up to the standards required.

It would be a mistake to consider post-graduate medical education without considering also the necessity to provide post-graduate instruction in allied fields, such as, nursing, social medicine, anatomy, physiology, pharmacology, bacteriology, pathology, bio-chemistry and dentistry. The training given in post-graduate centres should be of a comprehensive nature including not only the basic medical sciences but some of the fundamental physical and biological sciences.

It is suggested that 80 per cent of the seats in these post-graduate centres should be filled by candidates from the States in the region and 20 per cent should be made available to candidates from other parts of India, until such time as each State has got its own post-graduate centre. Even then there should be available some seats for graduates from other regions.

In selecting the subjects for post-graduate training at any centre, emphasis should be on the qualifications of the teaching staff available there, besides equipment and other facilities.

Candidates for post-graduate training should have as a basic qualification either a Master of Surgery or a Doctor of Medicine or some basic post-graduate qualification before specialising in any subject. In selecting candidates for post-graduate studies, preference should be given to those who have passed the M.B.B.S. examination in the minimum period of time, those who have shown special aptitude in any branch of medicine and those others found suitable on their academic records.

There should be a Selection Committee for each post-graduate centre consisting of the Vice-Chancellor of the University where the centre is situated, three to five Principals of medical colleges of the region and the Director or the Deputy Director of Medical Education of the State concerned.

A large number of stipends should be available to candidates taking up post-graduate studies in these regional centres.

Opportunities should be given to post-graduate students and research workers to participate in teaching, so that they get practice in the method of teaching, such teaching being recognised for appointments to higher teaching posts.

For the posts of professors, additional and associate professors in the post-graduate training centre the scales of pay should be higher than those obtaining for similar posts in under-graduate institutions.

Granting of post-graduate diplomas is recommended, so that such diploma holders will be available for service in different positions other than those for teaching. Persons who are unable to obtain the requisite standard for a post-graduate degree at a regional centre, but who have otherwise attained a reasonable standard of proficiency may be given certificates on the analogy of certificates of Graded Specialists in the Armed Forces Medical Services and utilised in district and Taluk headquarters hospitals where specialists are badly needed.

It will be advantageous to have liaison between Indian Universities and some of the foreign universities so that teams of experts from other countries may be exchanged, seminars held and various problems concerning medical education discussed to mutual advantage. For this purpose State and Central Governments should provide adequate financial assistance.

Refresher courses for service doctors and private practitioners should be provided in greater degree. The courses should not merely consist of theoretical lectures but should be accompanied by practical demonstrations and seminars.

The training of the general practitioner should be the special responsibility of the profession, of post-graduate teachers and of specialists, and every training institution in the Faculty of Medicine should, therefore, make a special effort to see that refresher courses are given as frequently as possible and in a practical manner to the general practitioners.

Suitable units should be developed in districts and tehsils for giving opportunities for training of practitioners and for research in community organisation.

A Committee on Public Health Practice should be set up under the Indian Council of Medical Research and an Institute for Research in Public Health Practice should also be established in due course.

It is considered essential that a large number of technicians should be trained for multi-purpose duties in the field of medicine. All district headquarters hospitals and the larger hospitals with 200 beds can train such multi-purpose technicians.

Lay administrators for hospitals are not satisfactory. Hospital administrators should be specially trained so that they can work in close cooperation with medical personnel without unduly trenching on their professional duties or responsibilities.

The health and welfare of the student population in medical colleges and other training institutions should be paid greater attention. For this purpose, apart from proper hostel accommodation, facilities should be provided for periodical check-up, free treatment and accommodation in the hospitals, for keeping of all records of illness of each student and for running of canteens on a cooperative basis under the charge of qualified dieticians in all medical and other institutions.

Public Health Training

For community welfare higher standards of training

in the field of public health are necessary, and a large number of medical officers with a minimum period of one year's training in public health, after the basic qualification, should be employed to carry out public health and sanitation measures.

Schools of public health should therefore be established in every State in order to provide facilities for the training of medical officers in the field of public health as also various other categories of public health personnel, like public health engineers, sanitarians, public health nurses, maternity and child welfare workers, dieticians, epidemiologists, nutrition workers, malariologists and field workers. They should work in close cooperation with under-graduate and post-graduate institutions in the locality.

The Professor of Public Health in the School of Public Health should have a post-graduate degree in public health with five to eight years' experience in public health work. Similarly, teachers in maternity and child welfare should have a Diploma with sufficient training and experience in the subject. One of the senior professors may be appointed as the Director of the School of Public Health, while the administrative duties can be carried on by an Assistant Director.

Higher training in the School of Public Health should be in the nature of M.D. or Ph.D.

It is felt that there is a scope for a Degree in Public Health being instituted in a University for non-medical personnel, the course of studies covering general public health, communicable diseases and their prevention including immunisation, broad aspects of environmental sanitation, public health statistics and school health. Such pensions can be of assistance to the trained public health worker of the Faculty of Medicine and can relieve the Health Officers of Municipalities of routine duties in the public health field.

Public health priniciples and hygiene should be inculcated in the minds of pupils even at the primary school stage, along with practical demonstrations.

Dental Education

The out-turn of existing dental colleges should be doubled.

There should be a minimum of one dental college in each State.

Facilities should be provided for the training of dentists registered in part B of the Dental Register.

There should be increased facilities for post-graduate training of dentists, so that the requisite number of teachers for dental colleges may become available.

The training of dental hygienists and mechanics should be undertaken at all dental colleges. Dental hygientists may be used for elementary dental services in rural areas until fully qualified dentists become available.

Nursing

There should be three grades of nurses *viz.*, the basic nurse with four years of training, the auxiliary nurse midwife with two years of training and the nurse with a Degree qualification.

Candidates admitted to the general nursing course should have the minimum qualification of matriculation or equivalent ; and the candidates for the Degree course should have passed the higher secondary or pre-university examination.

In view of the need for securing a larger number of recruits for the nursing profession the age of admission can be relaxed to 16 in suitable cases as a transitional measure particularly in States where there are difficulties in recruiting candidates at the age of 17.

The medium of instruction should preferably be English for the general nursing course, while the Degree course should be taught only in English.

Nurse pupils should not be over-burdened with the routine duties in hospitals, but more attention should be given to training and practical experience. They should not be subjected to too many spells of night duty in hospitals.

A large number of hospitals in the country can be utilised for Nursing Schools. District headquarters hospitals with a bed strength of 75 to 100 should also be utilised for this purpose.

The minimum number of admissions to the course should be 12.

Student nurses should be provided free furnished accommodation in hostels, free board, free supply of uniforms, laundry arrangements, free books, free medical services, medical check-up twice a year and suitable recreational facilities. The stipend during training should be a minimum of Rs. 35 increasing by Rs. 10 every year.

The recommendations of the Committee set up by the Central Council of Health (Shetty Committee) in regard to scales of pay and ratio of nurses to hospital beds etc. are endorsed.

There should be a Nursing Advisory Committee in each school for advising on admissions and welfare of the trainees.

Each nursing school should have its own separate budget.

The training of auxiliary nurse-midwives should be continued and extended, because it will be necessary for a long time to come to have a second line of trained personnel to meet the needs of the country.

The number of auxiliary nurse-midwives to be trained should be phased in such a way that there will be one auxiliary nurse-midwife for 5,000 population by the end of 15 years.

The training of midwives should also be continued and they should replace the *dais* who are now being utilised at certain places.

The time has come when fresh thinking on the type of training at present given to health visitors should be done. There should, instead, be a Public Health Nurse with a basic nursing qualification and one year's further training particularly in domiciliary care and other public health aspects of community work.

The contiunance of the training of *dais* in certain States as temporary measure is recommended, till such time as a sufficient number of midwives are trained to replace them.

Any person trained in one category of nursing should get an opportunity of being trained in the next higher grade, under conditions to be specified by the Indian Nursing Council.

There should also be higher training for the general sick nurse, public health nurse, pediatric nurse, mental nurse, theatre sister, sister tutor and nursing administrator.

Promotion of Degree course nurses or basic nurses to posts of higher responsibility should be considered only after a minimum of three to five years of practical experience after qualification, has been put in.

Male nurses should be trained only for certain types of work *e.g.*, mental hospitals, V. D. clinics and rehabilitation centres.

In general, sufficiently attractive terms should be given to young girls in order to enable them to take to the nursing profession rather than the clerical profession.

Other Para-Medical Personnel

There is an urgent need for different types of medical and public health auxiliaries to help doctors and public health workers in various fields. A separate class of persons, called 'Auxiliary Health Workers' should be trained mainly in the field of health to assist public health officers. Such auxiliary health personnel may also be used at Primary Health Centres.

Para-medical personnel recruited at present for individual diseases such as B.C.G., leprosy, malaria and filariasis should be given further necessary training in other diseases in order to make them multi-purpose personnel and to attach them to the urban or rural centres. Otherwise there is likely to be an immense loss of man-power.

Hospital architects should be specially trained. There should be a cell for hospital architects in each Public Health Engineering Department.

Medical and public health technicians, pharmacists, sanitary inspectors, etc., discharged from the Armed Forces every year should be employed in State Health Services either by relaxing where necessary the standards normally required or by giving them an additional short course of training to make up for any deficiencies.

Medical Research

If the medical profession of this country is to occupy the place, it should in the international world, contributions in the field of medical research are as important as contributions in other fields. India cannot for all times be a debtor country in this respect. Research should form a prominent part in the nation's activities in the field of medicine, greater importance should be given to it and necessary facilities made available.

Manufacture of sera and vaccine in the existing research institutes in India may have to continue for some time, but it should not be a permanent feature. The main function of these institutes must be research. The manufacturing side may be separate wings of the institutes manned suitably by trained staff but under the overall supervision of the Director.

Apart from operational aspects of research, the institutes should be the source for two types of research activity, *viz.* : (a) fundamental research and research in regard to certain aspects of diseases which may be referred to the institutes, and (b) field research to make available to the State concerned valuable data on certain epidemiological conditions or on certain rare diseases which may spring up from time to time or on problems which arise in the very process of giving effect to remedial measures suggested for certain diseases.

The research sections of such institutes should have responsibility only in regard to quality testing, standardisation and further research.

It is hoped that ultimately the production side will be taken over by the private or public sector, subject to quality testing being done by an independent organisation responsible to the State.

Research centres must keep in close touch with the international organisations and it should be their endeavour not merely to cooperate with schemes of research as may be undertaken by international centres but also to serve the very necessary purpose of disseminating the latest information in regard to causation of diseases, methods of treatment and measures for the eradication of diseases.

The Indian Council of Medical Research should be a Central Organisation to collect information from international centres and make it available to the profession through the research centres referred to above.

For this purpose the trained personnel at the various research centres will have to be strengthened.

Educational institutions cannot divest themselves of the responsibility for research and the best teaching is imparted in those colleges where there is an academic atmosphere of research. Every encouragement should, therefore, be given to research in medical colleges in the country.

Any teacher in a medical college who is genuinely interested in research can always find it possible to devote a portion of his time for this purpose.

The assistance of various disciplines, both in the faculty of medicine and in allied faculties, is essential for research and the cooperation of the Department of Bacteriology Pathology, Bio-chemistry Public Health, Radiology, etc., should be obtained by considerably reducing the routine work that is being done in these departments and by augmenting the staff.

A research unit should be set up in every medical college with a Pathological, Bacteriological and Bio-chemical section besides such other sections as may be necessary for the investigations that have to be carried out.

There should be an animal house in each medical college which should not merely be a shed for animals but should approximate to conditions where hospital treatment can be given to such animals. The animal house may suitably be situated in the top floor of the college building, with separate provision for an operation theatre and post-operative ward for animals.

Every post-graduate medical centre must have research facilities and there should be a separate ward of 10 to 15 beds available for the purpose with special nurses for looking after the patients and for periodical observations and maintenance of relevant records.

Research on indigenous drugs which is now being done in some of the medical institutions should be extended.

As in the case of medical college research units the budget of the various research centres in the country should be separate and specific sums for research must be earmarked.

In institutions where a large amount of research work is being done there should be an attached statistical section.

Wherever possible, there should be close coordination between the university departments of science and the departments of medicine in the matter of research.

While teachers in medical colleges are expected to interest themselves in research, it is necessary to give them the help of trained research workers or persons with aptitude for research, so that a good deal of routine experimentation and maintenance of records can be done by them.

The proposal of the Indian Council of Medical Research to award a number of fellowships to help medical colleges to extend their research activities is commended.

While the responsibility for medical research has been mainly that of the I.C.M.R. so far, it is suggested that Governments at the Centre and State levels should realise their responsibility to a larger extent and should contribute financially and otherwise to foster research. The responsibility for stimulating research work in the country will, however, largely rest with the I.C.M.R.

The reconstitution of the I.C.M.R. is also called for in the light of past experience.

In each State a Committee should be constituted to consider research programmes and recommend adequate grants for the same. A permanent allotment should be made for this purpose to different institutions, teaching or otherwise, which are expected to carry on research. The expenditure on equipment, drugs, or appliances should be met by Government.

The time is come when in the larger interests of the country there should be established an All-India cadre of research workers, with persons chosen from amongst trained research workers or workers with an aptitude for research who should devote their whole time to research problems. It is noted that a proposal for an All-India cadre of research workers has recently been approved by the I.C.M.R.

Whatever may be the method for eradication or control of diseases, it is necessary to have from the start an evaluation unit which will at the commencement draw up the manner in which the results of these operations can be recorded and interpreted. Otherwise, at the end of a long period of research work no definite conclusions can be arrived at regarding the success or otherwise of the scheme. This Evaluation Organisation should have an All-India pattern.

The working of these evaluation teams and the expense therefor should be part and parcel of the partcuilar programme for which the Evaluation unit is appointed, although advice and guidance in regard to methods to be adopted by the teams may be forthcoming from the I.C.M.R.

Such evaluation teams will be useful not only in the field of medicine but also in the case of many other projects.

So far as industries are concerned, two types of research work are urgently needed, *viz.,* one for the industry itself in order to improve methods of production and the other and more important being connected with the health, welfare and safety of industrial workers.

In all big industries there must be one or more units for carrying on research in regard to industrial health and the expenditure for research must come largely from the industry itself. Technical advice and assistance for such research should be forthcoming from the Council of Scientific and Industrial Research and the Indian Council of Medical Research. The industrial research units should work in close cooperation with the Employees' State Insurance Corporation.

The health and welfare of the people and of the employees of various departments are at present being looked after by different Ministries of Government, namely, Railways, Labour, Health, Industry, etc. It is recommended that the resources of all these Ministries should be pooled together and coordinated at a high level to ensure the best utilisation of funds for schemes relating to industrial health and research.

Population Problem

Voluntary and social organisations have a large part to play in impressing on the public the necessity of family planning and urgency of the problem by propaganda, education and mass contacts. Financial aid should be given by the Government in an adequate measure to such organisations for this purpose. All possible steps should, therefore, be taken for the increasing association and participation by voluntary and social organisations, particularly in regard to measures of mass contact and education of the public in family planning. The creation of autonomous family planning boards is not, however, considered to be in the best interests of the movement.

The dimensions and the urgency of the problem are such that the appointment of a State Minister in the Health Ministry who could give all his time and attention to this work, would be justified.

Much more intensive demographic, sociological and anthropological study is necessary for deciding the methods of family planning best suited to each area.

The National Council on Population which has already been set up under the Chairmanship of the Home Minister has a Demographic Advisory Committee. It is felt that this Demographic Advisory Committee should continue to function under the Ministry of Health.

The educative part of the family planning programme should be adjusted to the availability of services. Indigenous production of contraceptives should have been taken in hand simultaneously with the launching of the family planning programme on a national scale. Therefore, a priority no less higher than that of any other major project should now be given to the project of setting up of plants for the production of contraceptive appliances in the country. Priority should also be given in the meantime for foreign exchange for the import of certain contraceptives.

The All India Radio should be increasingly utilised for propaganda on family planning. In addition, educative material in all regional languages through films, posters, pamphlets, charts, graphs, plays, shows and other means should be utilised for family planning educational purposes.

Family planning activity should be included within the scope of primary health centres, community development blocks, the Central Social Welfare Board and other similar organisations. The workers in the community development and Panchayat Raj organisations should be oriented in family planning and utilised to bring home to the people in rural areas the necessity for control of population.

The help of political parties should also be enlisted for propaganda purposes.

With the existing social patterns and cultural background of the teachers and the taught in the large majority of schools and colleges, the inclusion of sex education may not be desirable. Education on the biological lines of life may, however, be imparted in colleges.

The demand for sterilisation operations is gaining momentum and it is noted that some States, have undertaken large scale sterilisation according to certain established procedures. This is one of the many-sided attacks on the family planning problem. The after-effects of sterilisation should, however, be studied carefully.

Laboratory and field research in regard to oral contraceptives should be identified.

Drugs And Medical Supplies

There is a case for going into the cost structure of manufactured drugs and bringing the cost down. This can be done under the provision of the Industries (Development and Regulations) Act.

It is recognised that while in recent years the final stages of manufacture of drugs have developed fairly fast and a large number of sizeable factories have come up, the extent of dependence on imported raw materials and intermediaries has only been slightly reduced. The indigenous pharmaceutical industry has therefore to contend with competent know-how, big capital, world-wide sales, unfair competition from mushroom units, and a long and a tortuous licensing procedure under the Industries (Development and Regulations) Act.

The industry as a whole has not promoted any significant research activity, either on a collective or on an individual basis. The situation needs to be remedied.

The universal complaint with regard to excise restrictions on the use of alcohol appears to call for finding ways and means of the regulations not coming in the way of legitimate manufacture.

There should be close-coordination between the Drugs Control Organisation and the Development Wing of the Ministry of Commerce and Industry and the policy in respect of setting up of pharmaceutical industry should be based on the need of the ultimate consumer rather than on the industrial policy of Government in other respects. It is felt therefore, that the present dual control should be done away with and the licensing for drugs manufacture should be the function of the Ministry of Health. There should be an appropriate organisation in the Ministry of Health in-charge of an officer of standing, capable of dealing with his counterpart in the Ministry of Commerce and Industry at the highest secretariat level.

If the pharmaceutical industry is to prosper and if the health of the nation is to be safeguarded, no quarter should be given to any manufacturer merely on the ground of his being a small scale manufacturer.

The Drugs Control Organisation by and large may be said to be extremely inadequate in comparison with the growing needs. It is recommended that in States where any substantial drug manufacture is going on, a fully equipped analytical laboratory should be established with the financial support from manufacturers. Research Wings should be attached to selected laboratories. Strict measures should be taken to enforce the conditions of licensing.

In the training of drug control inspectors it would be useful to have at least one or two inspectors adequately trained in "Law", so that the number of acquittals new resulting from technical flaws may be avoided.

An Expert Committee consisting of the top men in various specialities should be set up to examine the question of reducing the list of medicinal items permitted to be stocked and sold in the country and to work out a list of the essential drugs and formulations. Normally the import, manufactures, distribution and sale of drugs and formulations should be confined to the list prepared by the Expert Committee. The list will of course, have to be reviewed and revised periodically. In the meantime, Central and State Governments should give a lead by restricting the use, preparation and supply to State hospitals of those drugs and formulations included in the National Formulary. The use of proprietary preparations in Government institutions should be discouraged.

The responsibility for the manufacture and sale of sera and vaccines should be that of Government. Such sale should be on a no-profit-no-loss basis.

The manufacture of drugs coming under the indigenous systems of medicine should be controlled to ensure standard quality and satisfactory conditions of manufacture. For this purpose, drugs used in indigenous medicine should be brought under the provision of the Drugs Act.

Regarding Patent Law, as applied to the pharmaceutical industry, it is recommended that a patent should be for the process and not for the product, the specifications of the process clearly described to leave no room for doubt or for blocking the efforts of others in revising the process. The period covered by the patent should be reduced to between five and 10 years, extensions not being granted as a matter of course. There should be automatic revocation of patents in the event of manufacture not being undertaken within four years of the grant of such patent. There should be compulsory provisions for the grant of manufacturing licenses under the patent within the period of one year after the date of such an application.

The efforts made so far for the manufacture of instruments, hospital appliances, laboratory equipment, etc., have been sporadic and unorganised. There are no standards, little technical know-how and imported raw materials are not readily available. The country should become self-sufficient as early as possible in the manufacture of these instruments and equipment. A panel should be set up to study the position with regard to the estimated requirements of such instruments and appliances, particularly optical and electronic, and to work out detailed specifications. After the recommendations of the panel are received one of the corporations in the public sector may be entrusted with the manufacture; or a new factory in the public sector may be established; or private sector may be allowed to undertake the manufacture. The Technical Organisation in the Ministry of Defence for laying down standards for inspection and testing of instruments and appliances, should be taken advantage of and made to include civilian needs within their scope and functions.

Based on the existing Defence Services Institutions, similar organisations should gradually be built up in collaboration with the Ministries of Defence and Commerce and Industry.

In order to encourage private entrepreneurs in this field a strong technical advisory organisation should be set up in the Ministry of Commerce and Industry to provide guidance and help.

Medical stores depots should be modernised, expanded and made to work as public corporations for the manufacture and supply of drugs to meet the needs not only of civil departments, but also of the Defence Services. The Civil and Defence Medical Stores Organisations should be merged. They should cover the needs of railways too. For a more effective and expeditious programme of procurement and distribution, the number of depots will have to be increased progressively, so as to provide a closer regional coverage, the ultimate target being one medical stores depot for each State.

It would be in the interests of research in general, and of the industry in particular, if ways and means could be found for inducing the pharmaceutical industry to pool their resources with the object of promoting research on medicinal plants. One of the practical ways of giving effect to this suggestion will be to insist on the setting apart by the industry of a certain proportion of their profits for research. This may be in the form of a cess, as is being done in the case of cotton and textile industries.

The drug research programme outlined by the Council of Scientific and Industrial Research is endorsed.

There is a large scope for the expansion of the activities of the CIMPO under the Ministry of Scientific Research and Cultural Áffairs, in regard to cultivation of medicinal plants.

Legislation

While it is realised that a great deal has been done to coordinate the standards of training in the different medical colleges under the provisions of the Indian Medical Council Act, a number of difficulties have been felt in this matter by the Universities and the medical colleges. It would not be in the interest of medical education to divest Universities of their responsibilities or to make them feel that they are merely to carry out the recommendations of the Indian Medical Council.

The Universities should no doubt accept the standards laid down by the Indian Medical Council and also their advice in regard to major matters relating to professional education, while they should be free to implement details at their discretion.

The main responsibility for recognition of medical qualifications should no doubt be that of the Indian Medical Council, subject to the provisions of the Act and also subject to the final approval of the Government of India which acts in this case like the Privy Council of Great Britain.

There is no necessity for the Indian Medical Council to seek the approval of the Medical Councils of other countries in regard to recognition of degrees awarded in India. This requires serious consideration.

Recognition of degrees should be with reference to a University and not with reference to individual colleges. The suggestion that individual colleges should be recognised by the Council is not one which is consistent with the position of the Universities nor will it improve the standard. A certain amount of time should be allowed for improvement and it is here that the Council's advice would be most valuable. However, some temporary measures may have to be taken to bring the new medical colleges coming rapidly into existence to the required standard. In such cases as a temporary expedient, individual colleges may be inspected and reported upon for purposes of recognition.

While the Universities should get all the advice of the Indian Medical Council they should also see that such advice is implemented with the cooperation of the State Government or other management,

The agency which carries out inspection of medical colleges should be much more broadbased and should inspire confidence. Such an inspecting body should consist of an educationist, a representative of the University concerned and three experts nominated by the Council, who should be serving or have served as professors of medical colleges for not less than 10 years. There should be two or three permanent inspectors of the Council, one of whom will be a member of this inspecting body. A representative of the State Government in the case of Government colleges and a representative of the management in the case of other institutions may be co-opted as an observer.

The Indian Medical Council as at present constituted may not be in a position to review the recommendations of the Post-graduate Committee. In order, therefore, to safeguard and promote the interests of Post-Graduate Medical Education, it is, suggested that the Post-Graduate Committee of the Indian Medical Council should be reconstituted and designated as the Post-Graduate Medical Council with 20 members, 10 of whom will be elected by the Indian Medical Council, five elected on a zonal basis by the Universities and five nominated by the Central Government. All the 20 members should possess the prescribed qualification, *viz.*, 10 years of post-graduate teaching experience. The recommendations of the Post-graduate Council should be forwarded directly to the Government of India, the Indian Medical Council being simultaneously apprised of those recommendations.

The qualifications granted by the Dental, Nursing and other Councils in the form of University degrees should be regulated on the same lines as is now being done in the case of the Indian Medical Council.

With regard to the Diploma and other qualifications in Nursing, Dentistry, Pharmacy, etc., standards must be laid down with the approval of the Government of India.

It is not desirable to allow disparities between the provisions of the different Acts to continue and it is suggested that the Dental, Nursing and Pharmacy Acts should be amended so as to bring them in line with the Indian Medical Council Act.

Although certain standards of training have been laid down for Pharmacists by the Pharmacy Council, it is felt that as a transitional measure it may be necessary to have somewhat lower qualifications prescribed. This matter may be considered by the Pharmacy Council in consultation with Government of India in the interests of uniformity. The State Medical Council should be the agency to see that the general code of ethics is observed by medical practitioners, a reference being made to the Indian Medical Council before the removal of a name from the State Register. Unqualified persons now in practice should be placed in a separate section of the medical register. Persons possessing qualifications included in the Medical Council Schedule shall alone be placed in the main section of the State Register, and have the right to elect a representative to the Medical Council.

It is imperative that steps should be taken to ensure that registration is made an essential pre-requisite before anyone sets up practice. After initial registration subsequent registration should be open only to those who possess recognised qualifications in one or another system of medicine through recognised institutions. The practice of medical profession by persons other than those mentioned above should be made a penal offence.

Legislative action is called for in regard to radiological clinics, use of isotopes and other practices involving radiation hazards.

In the interests of public health all over the country, the time is come when every State should have a Public

Health Act of its own on the basis of the Model Public Health Act framed by the Ministry of Health.

In regard to the Drugs Act, an adequate and honest inforcement machinery should be provided. The inspecting and prosecuting agency should be independent of local authorities and should be directly under the State Governments. Facilities for analysis should be provided at Public Health Laboratories on a larger scale than at present. The punitive provisions of the Drugs Act should be made more stringent.

Legislative sanction for autopsy examination of dead bodies to enable donation of eyes for corneal grafting, etc. is not likely to have any effect. Methods of persuasion and education are likely to lead to better results.

The Indian Lunacy Act is outdated and completely out of content in the present day outlook on mental diseases. No further time should be lost in amending the Act to bring it in line with the present day requirements.

Indigenous Systems Of Medicine

Training in Ayurveda and other indigenous systems should be in the Shudha in place of the integrated system.

The Central Government should establish in collaboration with State Governments a Central Institute of Medicine for finding authentic and original manuscripts and books in Ayurveda scattered in different parts of the country and for publishing them for the benefit of students and teachers.

Chairs of Indian system of medicine should be established in all Medical Colleges.

The student of Ayurveda should have a good knowledge of Sanskrit : similarly, the students of Siddha system should be well-versed in Tamil and the student of the Unani System of Medicine in Arabic.

They should have the minimum basic qualification of school leaving certificate or matriculation.

The preparation of syllabus and courses of study should be left to experts in Ayurveda, Siddha and Unani.

The period of study should be about three to four years, fo that students will be able to concentrate their attention solely on Ayurveda, Siddha or Unani.

The need for giving a Degree qualification in modern medicine is recognised provided the students are trained upto the standard. The students who qualify in Ayurveda should be given opportunities to be trained in the modern system of medicine after completing the Ayurveda course and after they pass the prescribed examination. The duration of training for the modern system should be three to four years in such cases.

For the majority of those qualifying in Ayurveda, subsequent training in modern medicine should be for a period of two to three years and should cover preventive medicine, obstetries and gynaecology and principles of surgery, so that after such training their services can be utilised in the health services. Such training will not, however, entitle them to a Degree in modern medicine.

The development of post-graduate centres in Ayurveda, eventually one for each region, is desirable and such a development should be guided by the experience gained at Jamnagar. To encourage graduates in the modern medicine to join such post-graduate centres, the establishment of Chairs of Indian Medicine already recommended will prove helpful.

Research in indigenous systems should be done in the Central Institute of Medicine and in modern medical colleges. Research in respect of medicinal plants, drugs and diseases will be an important function of the various post-graduate and research centres.

Post-graduate training should also be available to both medical men trained in modern medicine who have had an intensive training in Ayurveda after their M.B.B.S. and to Shuddha Ayurvedic men who have taken a degree in modern medicine.

The growth of a body of trained personnel on the lines indicated above is essential in the interests of Ayurveda and modern medicine and the integration of two systems of medicine will eventually come about as a result of the labours of such scientific workers.

The Central and State Governments should provide sufficient financial support to trainees in indigenous systems of medicine.

Selection for post-graduate education in indigenous systems of medicine should be on merit and candidates so selected should be given stipends.

The establishment of a separate council of Ayurveda on the lines of the Medical Council of India is advocated, to set the required standards of training and to ensure uniformity throughout the country. Similar councils for Siddha and Unani will also be of advantage and there should be a coordinating committee for the three systems.

The newly constituted Council of Ayurveda Research should work in close collaboration with the I.C.M.R.

The task of developing appropriate standards for medicinal preparations in Ayurveda throughout the country would appear to be very necessary although it may present formidable difficulties. In this task a Central Institute of Indian Medicine, the Post-Graduate Regional Institutes, the Research Wings attached to Modern Medical Colleges should all collaborate. State pharmacies should be established and should become the source of all drugs utilised in Ayurvedic hospitals and in dispensaries, maintained by Government and local bodies.

Administrative Organisation

The abolition of the post of Public Health

Commissioner and the merger of the organisation with the Directorate-General of Health Services, while good in itself, has indirectly resulted in the weakening of the epidemiological, statistical and other aspects of public health activity, due to inadequacy of staff and the drying up of the sources from which the Directorate recruited experienced health administrators. On the other hand, due to increased activities in the health field as a result of the Five-Year Plans the need of leadership and coordination at the Central level has become more pronounced.

It is felt that the Director-General of Health Services should for all purposes, enjoy the status of an Additional Secretary to the Government.

While in matters of administration and financial nature the normal channel of communication should be through the Secretary to the Ministry of Health, in purely technical matters the Director-General's views and recommendations should be dealt with at the highest level without the intervention of the Secretariat.

Technical advice given by the Heads of Health Services should be directly available to the Minister for Health at the Centre or in the States, subject of course, to comments on financial and administrative angles by the Secretary of the Ministry/Department.

A well-staffed and well-equipped Health Intelligence Bureau in the Directorate-General of Health Services is called for. This bureau's task will be to keep itself up-to-date in health intelligence, serve as a model for States and be capable of organising programmes for the training of health statisticians and epidemiologists.

If the Central Government is to play the role which it should in the matter of fostering and developing all aspects of medical education, it is essential that a separate division on Medical Education should be formed in the Directorate-General of Health Services. This will be more imperative if the regional organisations which are being recommended elsewhere come into existence.

Similar divisions for Medical Education should be set up in the States, with a Deputy Director of Health Services being in independent charge, as Director of Medical Education.

A division of Planning should also be a distinct unit of the Directorate-General of Health Services under a Senior Deputy Director-General.

Yet another aspect of administrative organsiation which deserves serious consideration is that of a permanent machinery in the Directorate for evaluation which would become a normal feature of all major health plans. This machinery for evaluation will be independent of the administrative agency concerned with particular schemes.

Strong Health Education Bureaux should be set up in the Central and State Health Directorates. There should be close liaison between the State and the Central Health Education Bureaux so as to evolve common methods of approach in matters connected with the health education of the public. Audio-visual aids and other methods now adopted in Western countries should be studied and suitably modified to meet the requirements of India.

The State Governments should also, as in the Central Government, establish separate public health engineering divisions as an integral part of the Directorate of Health Services. The Chief Public Health Engineer in the State should have the status of an Additional Director of Health Services.

There should be a separate section dealings with international health matters in the Directorate-General of Health Services. It is essential that a destinct and well-defined cell should come into existence to deal with policy decisions on administrative and financial matters of all United Nations agencies, so that it will be able to brief the Indian delegation to the World Health Assembly fully. The Head of this cell in the Directorate should invariably be the Secretary to the Delegation to the World Health Assembly.

The association of non-official experts and leaders in the various professional fields with the health administrations in the country in an advisory capacity should result in not only placing experts at the disposal of the Health Services but also in giving a broader base and a more popular stance to the health policies of Government. Consultative bodies representing the Medical, Dental, Nursing, Pharmaceautical and Public Health Engineering professions should therefore be set up at the Central and State levels to advise the Health Ministers on programmes and policies. The tenure of members of such advisory committees should be three years with provision for gradual replacement of sitting members by fresh ones.

In the interests of better coordination and more effective Centre-State participation in the large number of schemes in which the State is the executive agency but in which the Centre has a financial and functional stake, an administrative tier at a regional level covering three or four States should be brought into existence on the analogy of such organisations in the Ministry of Scientific Research and Cultural Affairs. Such regional offices should be under the charge of officers of the status of a D.D.G. and would serve as a two-way channel for intelligence purposes and also as a liaisoing agency for schemes of professional education, communicable diseases control, eradication programmes and other matters of common interest. A regional committee, consisting of the Directors of Health Services of the States, Secretaries to Governments of States, some non-official members and representatives of professional organisations, *i.e.*, Medical, Nursing, Dental and Pharmacist bodies concerned, may be set up which may meet twice a year or oftener to discuss matters of common interest.

The technical set-up in States should be headed by the Director of Health Services assisted by a suitable number of Deputy Directors including one for Public Health, one for Medical Relief, a Deputy Director for Professional Education, a Drugs Controller an officer-in-charge of Maternity and Child Health, School Health and Family Planning, a Deputy or Assistant Director of Nursing Services and a Deputy Director or Assistant Director for Planning. There should be, in addition, a Public Health Engineer with the status of an Additional Director of Health Services.

The Public Health Engineering Organisation in every State should be attached to the Health Departments and not to the Public Works Departments.

The Public Health Engineers of Municipalities and local bodies should be members of the Public Health Engineering Service under the over-all control of the Public Health Engineer of the State.

Statistical and epidemiological units should be developed as part of the public health section of each State Directorate.

There should be State Health Advisory Boards consisting of Ministers dealing with Health, Housing, Education, Industry, Labour and Local Self-Government. The Chairman of some of the Zila Parishads and a few members of Legislatures should also be on this body, along with the President of the State Branch of the Indian Medical Association. The State Health Advisory Board should survey the health programmes initiated in the State so that these programmes are fully coordinated and implemented and should advise Government in regard to measures necessary for improvement of health conditions of all sections of the population.

For placing emphasis on preventive aspects of medical care at the peripheral level it is necessary to bring into existence in each State regional organisations between the headquarters and the districts. These regional organisations should be in-charge of a Deputy or Assistant Director of Health Services with two or three District Health and Medical Officers, Superintendents for M.C.H., Family Planning and Communicable Diseases and Assistant Public Health Engineers. All hospitals with 300 beds and more should be under the direct control of the Regional Director, all other rural institutions being left to the District Medical and Health Officer.

The designation of the officer in charge of health at the district level should be District Medical and Health Officer. He will be responsible for medical care, public health and environmental sanitation and will co-ordinate the work of all hospitals with a bed strength of less than 300.

In order to coordinate the activities of the District Medical and Health Officer and the Regional Director, there should be a coordination Committee under the Chairmanship of the Regional Director, the Superintendents of Hospitals and the District Medical and Health Officer being members.

The Medical Officers, Health Visitors, Auxiliary Nurse Midwives and Sanitary Inspectors attached to Primary Health Centres should belong to the State cadre and should be under the Director of Health Services through the District Medical and Health Officer in regard to technical and disciplinary control. The remaining staff, other than Class IV, should be from a district cadre. Disciplinary action against this staff should only be taken in consultation with the medical officer in charge of primary health centres, with a right of appeal to the Zila Parishad.

The problem of integration of medical and public health services should not be postponed, because of certain initial difficulties. In a long-term programme, periodical shifting of personnel from medical to public health and vice versa will be desirable if the problems of medical relief and public health are to be dealt with properly.

An All-India Health Cadre should be brought into existence. This service will man posts in Central Ministries other than Defence and provide a quota for State posts, to which officers may be seconded, thus enabling qualified and experienced persons being made available in various fields of work in different regions of the country. The structure of the All-India Health Services should be on the lines of the I.A.S. The Central Health Service now under the consideration of the Health Ministry should be enlarged to provide a deputation quota, so that the requirements of States may be met from time to time. The posts of medical officers under the Employees State Insurance Schemes in the various States should be made a part of the All-India Cadre. The time has come when consideration should be given to the pooling of medical officers for all Central Institutions through the Health Ministry.

A separate cadre of medical jurists should be established, to whom all important and complicated cases will be referred. These medical jurists should be specially trained.

The question of seconding officers of the Armed Forces Medical Services to the Civil Department, which proved a great success before Independence, should be revived. Similarly, it will be desirable that people recruited for the Civil Medical Service should have experience of work in the Defence Forces.

There should be a permanent organisation for morlidity survey in the country. This organisation should function in cooperation with special surveys for other communicable diseases and with epidemiological units.

SPECIAL SUB-COMMITTEE FOR DEVELOPMENT OF MINOR AND NON-EDIBLE OILS, 1959—REPORT

Hyderabad, Indian Central Oilseeds Committee. 120p.

Chairman : Dr. S.M. Sikka.

Members : Chief Conservator of Forests, Bombay (Maharashtra State); Chief Conservator of Forests, Uttar Pradesh; Chief Conservator of Forests, Mysore State; Chief Conservator of Forests, Kerala State; Chief Conservator of Forests, Assam State; Chief Research Officer, Minor Forest Products, Forest Research Institute, Dehra Dun; Dr. J.G. Kane; A Representative of the Non-Edible Oil Section, Khadi and Village Industries Commission, Bombay; Mr Mathias/Shri R.K. Lal, Raw Material Purchasing Department, M/s Hindustan Lever Ltd., Bombay; Shri G.V. Swaika.

Convenor : Secretary, Indian Central Oilseeds Committee, Hyderabad.

APPOINTMENT

In view of the importance of the development of minor and non-edible oilseeds in the country, the President, Indian Central Oilseeds Committee vide Government of India, Ministry of Food and Agriculture, letter No. 11-37/58-Com. II, dated June 17, 1959, constituted a "Special Committee for Development of Minor and Non-Edible Oils".

TERMS OF REFERENCE

(a) To review the work, so far done with regard to the development of minor and non-edible oilseeds with particular reference to :

(i) Collection of data regarding the existing and potential resources of these oilseeds ;

(ii) Their economic collection ;

(iii) Technological research done with regard to their processing and utilisation, etc ; and

(iv) Actual utilisation of the oils in the industry.

(b) To indicate the future lines of development in all its aspects, taking into view the important role which these oilseeds are destined to play in the economic development of the country ; and

(c) Suggest a coordinated development plan, both for short-term and long-term periods, indicating priorities.

CONTENTS

Introduction ; Non-Edible Oilseeds and Oils ; Resources Survey of Non-Edible Oilseeds ; Collection of Non-Edible Oilseeds; Planting of Non-Edible Oilseeds-bearing. Trees in Compact Blocks ; Processing and Utilisation of Non-Edible Oilseeds and Oils ; Trade in Non-Edible Oilseeds ; Technological Research on Non-Edible Oilseeds and Oils ; Development of Tung Cultivation in India ; Red Oil Palm ; Recommendations of the Special Committee ; Appendices I to VIII.

RECOMMENDATIONS

(a) Resources Survey Of Non-Edible Oilseeds

(i) Work on the development of non-edible oilseeds might be undertaken in order of following priorities :

First Priority : Mahua, Neem, Karanj and Undi.

Second Priority : Kusum, Khakan, Dhupa, Kokum.

Third Priority : Nahor

Fourth Priority : Pisa and Sal.

(2) Pilot projects for collection and utilisation of non-edible minor oilseeds be started both in the forest and non-forest areas. The State Governments might be requested to submit schemes for establishing pilot projects for survey and sample collection of non-edible oilseeds in forest areas.

A model scheme for sample survey of non-edible oilseeds in forest areas with the specific objective to make a survey of the eleven approved species, which offer scope for commercial utilisation may be drawn up and forwarded to State Governments for drawing up schemes on these lines.

(b) Collection Of Non-Edible Oilseeds

(3) The question of constituting an Autonomous Board for the development of non-edible and minor oils, might be considered at a later stage. In the meanwhile, the work should be started as a wing of the Indian Central Oilseeds Committee and a Special Officer with the required staff might be appointed for the purpose. The present Special Committee with such additions as may be required, be continued to guide and direct the work connected with the development of non-edible oilseeds.

(4) Separate leaflets on each of the important non-edible oilseeds covering all aspects like availability, collection, storage, extraction, utilisation, etc., may be published by the Indian Central Oilseeds Committee.

(5) The possibility of forming Forest Labour Co-operative Societies, on lines similar to those in Maharashtra State may be examined by other States.

(6) Pilot projects for collection and utilisation of

non-edible minor oilseeds should be started both in the forest and non-forest areas. For non-forest areas, not already tapped, 20 centres for seed collection might be established under the Khadi and Village Industries Commission in the first instance and these may be extended subsequently to new areas.

(7) A small note on Kusum seed and its oil covering all aspects, viz., organisation of collection, drying, storage, processing of seed, extraction of oil, characteristics of oil, utilisation, etc., might be prepared which may be forwarded to the Chief Conservators of Forests of the States. The State Governments might be requested to submit schemes for the collection of Kusum seed.

(8) The Forest Departments might undertake the plantation of non-edible oilseed-bearing trees like neem, Khakan, mahua, etc. in their afforstation and wasteland reclamation programmes. The importance of raising plantations of non-edible oilseeds, particularly in wastelands, might be brought to the notice of the Central Board of Forestry so that they could take up the matter effectively with the State Forest Departments. Some portion of land from the soil conservation areas and new irrigation projects could also be set apart for this purpose. The Public Works Departments of the States might take up the plantation of neem, mahua and karanj trees on Highways. The Agriculture Department of the Central State Governments might be approached to examine the possibility of planting neem, mahua and karanj trees along boundary lines and roadsides of big agricultural farms. Seeds might be supplied by the Indian Central Oilseeds Committee free of cost.

(9) The State Governments might consider the question of enacting legislation prohibiting the felling of mahua trees. They might also examine the question of regeneration of mahua trees in areas where they have been removed. Schemes for distribution of mahua seeds and seedlings similar to the one sanctioned in Madras State might be invited from other States. The trees should be planted in compact blocks in order to facilitate the collection of seeds.

(c) Utilisation Of Non-Edible Oilseeds And Oils

(10) Information regarding availability of large quantities of sal seed and utility of its oil in soap making might be brought to the notice of the solvent extraction factories and soap manufacturing concerns.

(11) Data regarding the number of solvent extraction plants installed, their capacity, utilised capacity, etc., might be collected. In cases where solvent extraction factories evinced some interest, the question of formulating schemes for organising collection of sal seed might be considered by the Forest Departments.

(12) Indian Standards Institution might be requested to draw up standard specifications for neem and other non-edible oils which had been commercially exploited.

(d) Research Work On Non-Edible Oilseeds And Oils

(13) A note on 10 to 12 non-edible oilseeds which were available in plenty and on which research work was necessary, indicating the areas where the seeds are available, their quantities and uses, research work so far done further work required may be prepared by Dr. J.G. Kane and Shri R.L. Badhwar.

(14) The machinery for depulping, drying and decortication evolved by Prof. Sharp, Harcourt Butler Technological Institute, Kanpur, and the Village Industries Research Institute, Wardha should be supplied to the 20 centres set up under the Khadi and Village Industries Commission for field trials.

(15) Suitable prizes might be awarded for the fabrication of improved designs of machinery for depulping and decortication of non-edible oilseeds.

(16) A small scheme for research work on storage and extraction of oil from sal seed and its utilisation may be sponsored.

(17) Results of the "Scheme on Extraction of Kamala Oil" sanctioned at the Department of Chemical Technology, Bombay might be awaited before further action is taken on the collection of Kamala seeds.

(e) Development Of Tung Cultivation In India

(18) The West Bengal Government might prepare a scheme for the development of tung cultivation and submit it for consideration of the Indian Central Oilseeds of Committee. The possibility of extending cultivation of tung oil in Punjab hills and Wynad area of Mysore and Kerala may be explored.

(19) The information regarding the prevailing high prices and the demand of tung oil might be brought to the notice of tea estates and in case they were interested in tung plantations, the seed might be supplied to them free of cost by the Indian Central Oilseeds Committee.

(f) Development Of Red Oil Palm Cultivation In India

(20) Strenuous efforts should be made to take up the cultivation of the Red Oil Palm on a planned and scientific basis.

KONKAN COASTAL SHIPPING SERVICES COMMITTEE, 1959—REPORT

New Delhi, Ministry of Transport and Communications, 1960. 150p.+iip.+Map & Charts.

Chairman : Shri P. S. Rau.
Members : Shri A. Ramaswami Mudaliar; Shri Asoka Mehta; Shri Babubhai M. Chinai; Shri S. G. Barve; Shri C. P. Srivastava; Thri V. P. Varde; Shri Wamanrao Rane of Ratnagiri.
Secretary : Shri A. V. Subramania Iyer.

APPOINTMENT

The Bombay Steam Navigation Company, a subsidiary company of Scindias, who are operating passenger services on the West Coast from Bombay to Dabhol, Vengurla and Purnagad had represented in 1955 that they were incurring heavy losses in maintaining the services. At the same time representations were also received by Government from various passenger associations for a reduction in the existing level of fares. This matter was examined by a one-man Commission consisting of Shri N. S. Lokur, Chairman, Railway Rates Tribunal, and on its recommendations the Government of India allowed the Shipping Company to increase fares by 10 per cent with effect from September 1, 1956.

The Bombay Steam Navigation Company have again represented to Government that the quantum of increase in the fares allowed in 1956 is not adequate to cover their losses in maintaining the service and unless fares are further increased or other substantial financial help is given to them, they would be forced to discontinue the services. Government have also received several representations from the travelling public urging a reduction in the existing fares.

Having regard to the fact that a large number of industrial labour in the Konkan Coast is dependent upon the passenger services, Government consider it essential to find a solution, which will be equitable both to the Company and to the travelling public, so that the services could be maintained without any interruption. They have accordingly set up this Committee under the Ministry of Transport and Communications. Notification No-35-MS (17) 57, dated June 29, 1959, to go into the entire question of maintenance of steamer services on the Konkan Coast.

TERMS OF REFERENCE

(i) To examine and report on all problems both immediate and long term, connected with the continuance of the passenger services on the Konkan Coast by the Bombay Steam Navigation Company (1953) Ltd., in order to meet adequately the requirements of the travelling public at reasonable fares.

(ii) To examine if it thinks necessary the connected problems of the Bombay Harbour Service and such other matters as may be brought to its notice during the course of its enquiry, which have a hearing on the question of maintenance of the steamer service on the Konkan. Coast.

CONTENTS

Appointment of the Committee-Terms of Reference; Meetings of the Committee — Memorandum from the B. S. N. Co. — Issue of Questionnaire—Tour of Ports—Taking Oral Evidence; the Konkan Region—General Description and Physical Features—Rivers and Creeks—Population and Towns; Historical Survey of the Konkan Coastal Passenger Services; Previous Enquiries into Konkan Passenger Fares; Scindia-Bombay Steam Amalgamation Scheme-To what Extent this has a Bearing on the Present Enquiry; Communications—Road and Railway Development in Konkan; Steamer Services—needs of Travelling Public—Frequency—Ports of call—Also Future Traffic Trends in so far as can be Foreseen at Present; Present Cost of Steamer Services — To what Extent Susceptible of Reduction; Losses at Present Fares —How these should be met; Long-term Pattern of Konkan Steamer Services — Type of Ships to be Ordered in Replacement of the Existing Ones — Additional Cost of the Services and How it Should be met; Harbour Services and their Future Regulation; Ports and Port Facilities; Miscellaneous; Summary of Recommendations; Acknowledgments and Conclusion; Appendices I to XII.

RECOMMENDATIONS

The Scindia Company should treat the loan granted by them to the B. S. N. Co., as without interest in future.

The construction or improvement of the following feeder roads should be undertaken without delay.

(1) **Shriwardhan** : A *Pucca* road from Bag Mandla to Shriwardhan — distance 12 miles.

A road from Hareshwar to Shriwardhan (distance 25 miles). This will connect Bankot and Hareshwar Shriwardhan.

(2) **Palshet, Boria**: The road between Hedvi and Veldur *via* Guhagar should be improved. It is also advisable to connect Boria with Chiplun a distance of 38 miles.

(3) **Karbone** : A road should be constructed between Chiplun and Korbone, a distance of nine miles.

(4) **Tivri** : The road from Ganpatipule should be extended upto Tivri *via* Malgund — a distance of about four miles — and the road from Ratnag ri to Ganpatipule should be improved. This will connect Tivri with Ratnagiri Port, a distance of 32 miles.

(5) **Jaygad** : The road between Tivri and Jaygad (distance nine miles) should be improved.

(6) **Purnagad** : The road between Purnagad and Ranpar (six miles) should be raised in class.

The road between Ratnagiri and Purnagad should be improved and raised in class.

(7) **Musakazi** : The road between Rajapur and Musakazi should be improved.

(8) **Achra** : The road between Achra and Malwan should be made a first class metalled road.

(9) **Vijaydurg** : Roads should be constructed (i) between Karul Ghat and Tarala *via* Vaibhawadi; and (ii) between Khare-Patan and Kusur.

(10) **Deogad** : A road from Deogad to Achra is necessary.

Of the three ports of Revdanda, Hareshwar and Purnagad, which were formerly being served by coastal steamers but have since been closed for passenger traffic, there is no need to consider the reopening of Revdanda and Hareshwar for such traffic. As regards Purnagad the question whether this port presents any difficulty for steamers calling after mid-day or at night needs invetigation by the Port Officer of the Maharashtra Government without any loss of time. In the meantime the Schedules of the steamer services to be adopted for the immediate future should be so framed as to include a call at Purnagad at least twice a week.

The pattern of steamer services on the Konkan Coast that we would recommend for the immediate future is as follows:

Dabhol Line : This service to continue as at present.

Purnagad Line : To operate from October 1, till January 31, once a week. From February 1, this service to operate thrice a week till the end of the season.

Vengurla Line : This service to operate on the same lines as prior to "rationalisation" of the services, from September 1, to September 30, and from February 1, to the end of the season. From October 1, this service to cater for the minor ports of the Purnagad line twice a week till January 31.

With the improvement of the services as suggested by us, viz. the re-introduction of the Purnagad Line, it would appear reasonable to assume that annual passenger traffic would be about 6.75 lakhs in future.

The operating expenses incurred by the B. S. N. Co. (1953) Pvt. Ltd., are not unreasonable under any of the heads under which such expenses fall but the item of interest charges to Scindias should in future be excluded from such expenses.

We estimate that, at the existing rates of fares, there will be a shortfall in the Company's revenue as compared with the expenses for the coming two years as follows:

	(Rs. lakhs)
1960-61	4.29
1961-62	4.93

In order to make good this short-fall, we recommend an increase in fares of eight per cent with immediate effect.

The company's claims to be reimbursed past losses cannot be accepted.

It would not be feasible to start a monsoon service on the Konkan Coast at present. Nor is there any compelling need for this at the moment.

The Maharashtra Government should arrange for a hydrographic survey of the ports of Ratnagiri, Dabhol, Jaigad, Vijaydurg and Devgad as soon as possible. These ports should be visited by the Port Adviser to the Government of India and a nautical expert (e.g. the Principal Port Officer of Maharashtra Government during the monsoon and arrangements made for taking observations over a suitable period of time of the wind, tide and other conditions at each port. The question whether or not all weather facilities could and should be provided at any of these ports would depend on the data collected on these lines. In the meantime the construction of alongside berthing facilities at Jaigad, Vijaydurg and Devgad for the fair weather season should be designed for all weather conditions and wherever possible for a draft of 15ft.

For the long term future, while the Dabhol and Vengurla line services may continue as at present with a daily service for six days in the weak, the Purnagad line should have a tri-weekly service throughout the fair season from the beginning of September to the end of May.

The total number of ships required for the Konkan service for the long term future is six,

The new ships to be ordered for the Konkan Coastal services should be powered by diesel engines and should have a service speed of 14 to 15 knots. They should provide benches to seat 25 per cent of the passengers, and should be so constructed as to enable a greater proportion or the whole number of passengers being provided with seats on benches if that should prove more popular than the existing mode of travel on the bare deck. They should also incorporate certain other improvements on the lines suggested by us.

The SS *Hiravati* may be allowed to be scraped.

Orders for two new ships to replace the existing ships, *Chandravati* and *Ratnagiri*, should be placed immediately.

Orders for a third new ship to bring up the strength of the Company's fleet to a total of six ships should also be placed immediately.

With the introduction of the three new ships the operating costs of the Konkan steamer services are expected to go up by Rs. 9.71 lakhs per annum. This additional costs should be borne by the Central Government the Maharashtra Government and the travelling public as follows:

(i) The Central Government should provide a loan to the Company for the purchase of the new ships repayable in twenty annual instalments, free of interest. This would mean a contribution by the Central Government by way of waiver of interest of Rs. 3.6 lakhs in the first year diminishing at the rate of Rs. 18,000 per annum over a period of twenty years. This would work out to an average annual contribution to Rs 1.89 lakhs;

(ii) The Maharashtra Government should make a like contribution in the shape of a direct subsidy to the Company of Rs. 1.89 lakhs p a.;

(iii) The travelling public should bear the balance in the shape of a further increase in fares of seven per cent.

These arrangements will be subject to review at the end of five years, or even earlier, should any material change occur in the meantime in the circumstances under which the Konkan shipping services operate.

As regards the loans to be paid by the Central Government for the purchase of ships, we consider that the terms on which they should be granted should be similar to those governing the grant of loans to shipping companies generally for the purchase of ships for coastal trade, except that the loans in this case should be (i) paid on adequate security to be furnished by the Scindia S. N. Co. Ltd., (ii) made repayable in twenty equated annual instalments, and (iii) free of interest.

We feel that the subsidy scheme suggested by us should be preferred to nationalisation and should be implemented with immediate effect. We would, however, like to qualify this recommendation to the extent that if, from experience over a reasonable period, our scheme is found not sufficiently conducive to the public interest, Government should be free to re-examine the whole question in all its aspects, not excluding the desirability of nationalisation. In the terms and conditions subject to which loans are granted to the Company for the purchase of the new ships, it should be made clear that in the event of nationalisation of the service, Government would have the right to acquire these ships at their book value, less depreciation.

The Maharashtra Government should promulgate rules under Section 6 (1) (a) of the Indian Ports Act, 1908, applicable to the minor ports of Rewas and Dharamtar and the Government of India should promulgate similar rules applicable to the major port of Bombay, for regulating the Harbour Services.

The B. S. N. Company should continue to run the Harbour Services all the year round as an integral part of their Konkan coastal services. Their Monsoon services should, however, in future cover not only Rewas and Dharamtar but also Uran (Mora).

We do not recommend any futher increase in fares so far as the harbour services are concerned.

The administration of the harbour services should be taken over by the Mahrashtra Government from the Collector of Central Excise, Bombay.

Siltation has become particularly acute at Rewas, Dharamtar, Dabhol, Jaigad, Ratnagiri and Malwan. It requires to be tackled urgently first by making the necessary hydrographic surveys for ascertaining the extent of siltation that has occurred at the various places and then by dredging the entrance bars and inner harbours of the ports to restore them to their original depths.

The Survey Sub-Division of the Marine Division of the Maharashtra Government should complete the hydrographic surveys of all the Konkan ports within as short a time as possible.

We lend our full support to the State Government's proposal for the purchase of a second dredger for the Konkan ports. We would also recommend that when the Central Dredger Pool is set up it should treat the dredging of the approach channels to the Konkan ports as deserving of high priority.

Dredging is necessary particularly at the following ports and provision should be made for it in the Third Five Year Plan.

Mora, Rewas, Deogad, Vijaydurg, Vengurla, Jaigad and Malwan.

As the Konkan ports handle a large volume of passenger traffic, the hydrographic surveys of these ports and the publication of up-to-date navigational charts in respect of them should be undertaken and completed by the Chief Hydrographer to the Indian Navy as a top priority programme. The ports requiring immediate survey are Janjira, Dabhol, Jaygad, Vijaydurg and Malwan.

Larger plan charts should be provided in respect of small ports on the Konkan Coast such as—Shriwardhan, Harnai, Palshet, Boria, Tivri, Ranpur, Purnagad and Achra. Tide tables for the ports of Dabhol, Jaygad and Malwan should also be prepared.

Construction of passenger coastal berths with dolphins and gangways should be taken up at the ports of Devgad, Vijaydurg and Jaigad in the Third Five Year Plan.

Whatever doubts there may be regarding the constitutional position relating to light houses should be cleared with the least possible delay and the lighthouse projects envisaged for the Konkan ports taken up and completed without further loss of time. In particular,

(i) The lights now being maintained by the B.S.N. Co.,

should be taken over by Government immediately;

(ii) The Perch Rock at Malwan should be permanently marked by a buoy and it should be so founded as to ensure that the buoy will not shift its position under any conditions of tide, weather, etc;

(iii) A light should be provided at the Korlai Fort to enable the B.S.N. Co.'s ships to pass through fishing stakes safely.

The improvement schemes included in the First and Second Five-Year Plans for the various Konkan ports should be completed as quickly as possible and the following further schemes taken up in the Third Five-Year Plan :

Dabhol : Provision of water supply.

Deogad : Provision of water supply.

Vijaydurg : (i) Provision of water supply. (ii) Construction of passenger shed with canteen, W.C.'s etc.

Vengurla : Provision of water supply.

Janjira : (i) Electrification of Khora Wharf. (ii) Provision of water supply at Khora Wharf. (iii) Construction of a passenger shed at Khora.

Jaigad : Provision of water supply.

Malwan : Provision of water supply.

Achra : Construction of passenger shed with W. C.'s etc.

The B.S.N. Co., and the State Transport Corporation should jointly draw up an integrated scheme for the provision of adequate communication facilities at the various Konkan ports, with a view to its being sponsored by the Bombay Government to the Central Government and the D.G., Posts & Telegraphs.

The Government of Maharashtra should take over direct administration of all the Konkan ports within as short a time as possible.

The B.S.N. Co., should as far as possible give timely warning to passengers of likely cancellations and delays to ships.

Mechanisation of "Padaos" (passenger lighters) is not practicable. At ports where alongside facilities for passengers are not provided the question of providing suitable tugs or launches for the towage of the "Padaos" may be considered. We would particularly recommend this for the port of Ratnagiri.

Continuous vigilance should be exercised by the authorities concerned as well as the Deck Passenger Welfare Committee at Bombay to ensure that so far as the Konkan services are concerned the recommendations of the Deck Passenger Committee are strictly enforced and implemented.

In order to facilitate the revival of creek services the State Government should get the creeks surveyed and desilted by dredging.

As soon as suitable road connections to Janjira, Shri-Wardhan, Palshet, Boria, Ranpar and Achra are provided, State Transport omnibus services should be extended to these ports.

The steamer services and the State Transport bus services should be so timed that the steamer passengers as soon as they lend at a port have a State Transport bus ready to take them to their interior destinations and vice versa.

The State Road Transport Corporation and the B.S.N.Co. should in consultation with each other explore the feasibility of introducing through booking arrangements at all Konkan ports where the volume of passenger traffic is comparatively large.

There should be a small Standing Committee consisting of the General Managers of the State Transport Corporation and the B.S.N. Co., a senior representative of the Maharashtra Government (preferably the Secretary of the Department concerned with Communications and Transport) and an M.L.A. or two representing the Konkan public, to maintain close coordination between State Transport and steamer services. This Committee should specially be consulted by the State Transport Corporation and the B.S.N. Co., before either of them effect any changes in the routing, time schedules, etc., of their respective services.

The B.S.N. Co., in recruiting home-trade masters and mates should take into account not merely their technical competence and experience as navigating officers, but also the fact that their officers have to handle a large volume of passenger traffic and should therefore conform to some reasonable standard of general education and have some personality and qualities of leadership.

INDIAN PRODUCTIVITY TEAM ON INDUSTRIAL MANAGEMENT ORGANISATION AND TRAINING IN WEST GERMANY, U.K. AND U.S.A., 1959—REPORT

New Delhi, National Productivity Council, 1961 87p.+viiip.

Leader : Shri I.P. Anand.

Dy. Leader : Shri R.M. Aggarwal.

Members : Shri M. V. Arunachalam ; Shri G. R. Damodaran ; Shri S. D. Joshi ; Shri J. K.

Jhunjhunwala ; Shri Robin Kakti ; Shri B. D. Somani ; Shri Sudhir Ghosh ; Shri K. A. Varugis.

Secretary Shri R. N. Warriar

APPOINTMENT

In July 1959, the National Productivity Council of India decided to sponsor, with the aid of the International Cooperation Administration of the U.S. Government, the visit of a Productivity Study Team to West Germany, the United Kingdom and the United States of America to make a survey of productivity techniques and practices in the field of industrial management organisation and training and to make suitable recommendations for the adoption of those techniques and practices by Indian industry.

TERMS OF REFERENCE

To visit industrial organisations and other institutions in West Germany, the united Kingdom and the United States of America ; to carry out an intensive survey of productivity techniques and practices in the field of management organisation and training particularly covering the topics given below ; and to make suitable recommendations to the National Productivity Council, bearing in mind the present progress of Indian industry and the overall pattern of industrial development in the country.

1. (a) Management organisation structure of various types of organisations.

(b) Methods and extent of delegation of responsibility and authority.

(c) Techniques and systems of management controls.

2. (a) Machinery and procedure (i) for policy making and implementation; (ii) for "progress planning" and development.

(b) Place of and techniques for (i) recruitment ; (ii) promotion (iii) training; (iv) incentives of top and middle management personnel.

3. Methods of, and programmes for, executive development and management succession.

4. Role of professional management consultants, educational institutions and Government in improving management methods and arranging management training programmes.

CONTENTS

The Team : Preface ; Acknowledgements ; Introduction ; Industrial Management—India; Review of Visits in India ; Industrial Management—West Germany, U.K. and U.S.A., Personnel for Management ; Education and Training for Management; Role of Research in Industry; Role of Management Consultants ; Role of Industrial and Professional Associations ; Recommendations ; Appendices I to V.

RECOMMENDATIONS

In the light of the experiences gained from the study tour, the team makes the following recommendations for the advancement of industrial management organisation, education and training in our country.

I. Industrial Management

It is recommended :

(1) That the top management of each organisation should clearly lay down the goal of the enterprise, taking into account the organisation's responsibility to its employees, shareholders, consumers, the State and the community;

(2) That the senior management should formulate a philosophy of management, in the light of which junior managers will be able to take decisions ;

(3) That an overall plan of action should be drawn up for the organisation, in conformity with its philosophy; that such plans should cover the long-term prospects of the organisation, for a period of at least five to 10 years, and that such plans should admit of flexibility;

(4) That each management should be encouraged to develop a sound organisation structure of its own and that this should be made clear, logical, flexible, taking into account the specific requirements of the organisation ;

(5) That Indian Industry should be encouraged to consider the feasibility of introducing a two-tier structure at the top level, one representing the trusteeship interest and the other responsible for administration or operation, on the analogy of the practice obtaining in West Germany;

(6) That scope should be afforded for suitable senior management personnel to be associated at Board level in order that their competence, experience and loyalty may be made available for making a valuable contribution to the Industry at this level ;

(7) That the total participation of all personnel should be gained for the promotion of efficient management, through the constitution of Committees for joint consultation, communication and coordination ;

(8) That industries should be encouraged to make proper delegation of functions to lower levels and match authority with delegated responsibility ;

(9) That wherever industries have not yet developed organisation charts and mannuals, they should be encouraged to do so ;

(10) That industries should be encouraged to devise ways and means of improving the communication system ; and

(11) That industries should be encouraged to use extensively such control techniques as standard costing, budgetary control, inventory control, etc.

II Personnel For Management

It is recommended :

(1) That a well-defined and integrated personnel policy for obtaining and retaining key Managerial Personnel should be developed in each industry, and that a personnel budget be prepared periodically, suited to its present and prospective requirements;

(2) That each industry should be encouraged to adopt scientific selection procedures and to improve such procedures wherever they are in practice;

(3) That industries should be encouraged either to institute regular development programmes of their own or, where these are not possible, to avail themselves of facilities offered by such organisations as the National Productivity Council, the Management Associations, the Administrative Staff College, etc.

(4) That all industries should be required to define their promotion policy, which should be on the basis of merit assessed through proper procedures of evaluation of executive performance;

(5) That the executive remuneration policy should ensure satisfactory status and salary for all executives through a judicious combination of direct and indirect incentives; and

(6) That where proprietory succession prevails, prospective top executives should be suitably trained to become professionally competent also.

III Education and Training For Management

It is recommended:

(1) That Universities which do not at present offer courses in Management, but are located in and near industrial areas, should be encouraged by the Government of India, through adequate aids, to consider the feasibility of instituting courses in Management at the Under-Graduate, Graduate and Doctoral levels;

(2) That the National Productivity Council should explore ways and means for creating the right climate through conferences, seminars and the like for acceptance, by industry, of the functional values of education for Management offered by the Universities;

(3) That the National Productivity Council should likewise create scope for Universities to recognise the value of the body of knowledge and skills available within industries in India and elsewhere, for inclusion in their curricula;

(4) That a National Institute of Management should be established with responsibility for offering advanced education in Management and also for conducting basic and applied research, and that this institution should be a joint undertaking of industry and the State;

(5) That full-time as well as part-time programmes of education for Management and sandwich courses should be sponsored by Technological Institutions, Chambers, of Commerce and other allied Associations for the benefit of personnel in Industry;

(6) That full-time residential Executive Development Programmes, on the model of the Summer Schools of American Universities, should be sponsored in India by the proposed Central Institute of Management; and

(7) That Industries, either by themselves or jointly with Universities, should be persuaded to institute Fellowship like the Sloan Fellowship Programme, designed to develop senior executives with high promise to become industrial statesman of our country.

IV Research In Industry

It is recommended:

(1) That the Ministry of Scientific Research and National Resources should be requested to take such steps as are necessary to coordinate all fundamental and basic research and to disseminate the results;

(2) That basic research should be undertaken by research organisations sponsored by the Government, Universities and also Research Institutions supported by Industrial Associations; and

(3) That applied research dealing mainly with process and product development, should be undertaken by individual industries and that, where the industries by themselves cannot independently establish and operate such research projects, an organisation of related industries should be undertake this task with or without the assistance of the Government.

V Management Consultants

To bring to surface the nature of the need for the Management Consultant, his importance and the value of his services to industries, it is recommended:

(1) That surveys and researches should be sponsored and undertaken by the National Productivity Council in selected segments of industry in the public and private sectors respectively, to demonstrate to industries the enhancement in production accruing from the services of professional management consultants;

(2) That the findings of these efforts should be duly disseminated to the field;

(3) That, to suggest ways and means thus surfaced, the National Productivity Council should take the lead in stimulating interest among leaders of industry:

(a) To recognise the value of associations like NUMAS in the UK, and NAM and BAHIL in America, through study circles organised for the purpose;

(b) To encourage them to sponsor, and build up similar organisations in our country; and

(4) That National Productivity Council should undertake an evaluation of the existing resources available to the industry for professional consultancy.

VI Associations

It is recommended:

(1) That the All-India Management Association should, on the model of the British Institute of

Management in the United Kingdom, undertake all activities that are of common interest to their constituents, such as research, collection and dissemination of statistical data, guidance in industrial relation matters, etc.;

(2) That all-India organisations like the Federation of Indian Chambers of Commerce, Associated Chambers of Commerce, etc., should be requested to consider the desirability of organising Service Sections like the one organised by the National Union of Manufacturers of England (NUMAS) to undertake advisory service for small and medium industries and to make market surveys and studies;

(3) That all-India organisations should be requested to evolve a code of conduct on the analogy of the one prescribed by the National Association of Manufacturers of the United States to promote fair trade practices and also to enhance the prestige of Indian industry abroad;

(4) That all-India organisations should be persuaded to take a leading role, in collection with the National Productivity Council, in sponsoring various development programmes, seminars, conferences, symposia, group discussions, etc., thus not only providing a meeting ground for exchange of ideas, but also ensuring wider acceptance of modern methods of management; and

(5) That Directors of training in Indian Industries should be encouraged to come together in conferences and seminars and be stimulated to organise themselves into a society like ASTD in America which will help them refresh their skills and knowledge and keep them alreast of progress in these days of rapid technological advancement.

STUDY TEAM ON COMMUNITY DEVELOPMENT INDUSTRIAL PILOT PROJECTS, 1959—REPORT

Delhi, Ministry of Community Development and Cooperation, 1960. 124p.

Leader : Shri S.D. Misra.
Members : Shri R. Srinivasan; Shri L.C. Jain; Dr. P.C. Alexander; Shri Anil De; Shri Mahmood Butt; Shri Abid Hussain; Shri V.R. Rao.
Secretary : Shri P.M. Mathai.

APPOINTMENT

The Study Team on Community Development Industrial Pilot Projects was constituted under the Ministry of Community Development and Cooperation (Department of Community Development) vide The Government of India's Memorandum No. 1 (10) (xxii)/59-Prg-II, dated July 21, 1959, to survey the work of the Pilot Projects, to assess their contribution to the programme of Community Development and to examine their structure and functions with a view to suggesting correctives.

TERMS OF REFERENCE

(a) To study the working, achievements and failures of the pilot projects bearing in mind the objectives with which they were initiated, and to assess and recommend experiences suitable for application or multiplication in the development of village and small scale industries in blocks.

(b) While making recommendations, the following points should be specially taken into consideration:

(i) Methodology of industrial potential survey for a block and also a group of blocks if required and how to plan an industrial programme for a block;

(ii) Development of marketing, local as well as outside, supply of raw material, credit, technical know-how, etc.;

(iii) Industrial extension agency required for a block taking into consideration the set up at district and divisional levels, etc.;

(iv) Training required for rural artisans both for improving the skill and also creating new skill;

(v) Development of suitable agencies like industrial cooperative societies in the development of village and small scale industries;

(vi) Coordination of various departments and non-official bodies who are engaged in the field and their role;

(vii) Minimum industries programme for a block and providing the necessary financial and other resources;

(viii) Role of panchayats and block samities and other local official bodies in the development of industries in the block;

(ix) Indicators recommended for calling reports on industries programmes in the blocks in order to assess the achievements and impact of the programme.

(c) The team will also analyse the causes of any failure or bottlenecks holding up the programme and recommend the measures required to be taken by the

State Governments as well as the Central Governments in order to accelerate the development of village and small scale industries in the blocks.

CONTENTS

Introductory; Aims and Objectives; Programme Implementation and Case Studies; The Pilot Projects; Assessments and Lessons; The Future Programme; Industrial Potential Surveys and Progress Reports; Summary of Report; Appendices I to V.

RECOMMENDATIONS

During the Third Plan, financial, organisational and technical assistance should be provided to 300 traditional artisans in each block. This assistance should be based on certain criteria for aid.

At least five new industrial cooperative societies should be developed in each block, i.e. about 25,000 for the 5,000 blocks. Besides Industries Extention Officer for a block, some crafts specialists and other technical hands should be provided depending on local needs to assist Industries Extention Officers. The Block Development Committee may approve the grant of financial and other aids for individual artisans or cooperatives. A sum of Rupees one lakh may be provided for each block for this programme under the Third Plan. For 5,000 blocks, a sum of Rs. 50 crores (loans 25 crores and grants 25 crores) is necessary for organisational, financial and technical aid to rural artisans.

It is necessary to give the traditional industries strong technical support. This could be done by providing common facilities centres, where required, employing equipment and techniques which individual artisans or small units cannot afford or by providing improved tools and equipment, electric power and technical know-how and marketing assistance. Such a programme may be taken up in 2,500 blocks. There already exist certain villages in which commercial and industrial activities have tended to develop and take roots. In most of the blocks, one or two such centres can be found. One of these should be selected for establishing a common facility unit. Such a centre may be called a "Rural Industries Centre". The funds provided in the plan for Rural Industries Centre should be placed at the disposal of the Block Development Committee, or Panchayat Samiti. Each Rural Industries Centre should bs expected to create opportunities for additional employment for about 100 persons, besides providing technical, marketing and other facilities to traditional industries. 2,500 Rural Industries Centres may be started under Third Plan at the rate of about 300 in the first year, 500 in the second year, and about 600 each in the third, fourth and fifth years of the Plan. Each such centre should be provided with about 2.5 lakhs for five years. It is estimated that an outlay of about Rs. 35 crores will be required during the Third Plan.

There are certain areas in the country where village industries have already reached, more or less, the stage of development which we expect them to obtain in the areas around the Rural Industries Centres. To provide increased employment, it is necessary that industries in such areas should be further developed by the establishment of rural or small Industrial Estates. The direction of the Estate should be entrusted to a Committee or Corporation whose functions should include surveys and prospecting of industrial potential in the area, development of sites, providing built-up space, power, help in drawing plans, construction of factory buildings, procuring finance, raw materials, technical know-how, etc. At the rate of two blocks per district, 600 rural estates may be established in the country during the Third Plan; say 50m. in the first year, 100 in the second year 150 in the third year, fourth year and fifth year of the plan. An outlay of Rs. 15.5 crores is proposed for this purpose.

The underlying idea behind the measures, we have recommended is to create conditions of balanced growth of economy where additional employment opportunities are created and dispersed as widely as possible. It is necessary to tone down the further expansion of metropolitan cities and big towns and to provide employment opportunities for the population in a group of villages (say in a block) as close to their present abode as feasible. It is not only employment opportunities which cause the influx of the population to the cities, but also the numerous social amenities which are available in big towns and which are almost completely absent in the remote areas. Even if provision was made for one centre in a block (a group of 100 villages) which could act as a frontier check-post of migration and provide opportunities for local industrial growth, it would be necessary to have at least 5,000 such check-posts in the country. To be effective, these check-posts must offer both the opportunities of industrial employment as well as social amenities. Establishment of such a network of small townships is obviously a matter of long-term pursuit. It is accordingly suggested that a pilot project may be established in one district in each State during the Third Plan. With the object of building up one small township in every block in the selected districts. In the long run, each Rural Industries Centre would develop sufficient industrial opportunities as well as social amenities to become a small township. In short the suggestion is that one district, in each State, intensive efforts should be made to achieve in a period of five years (it may even extend to seven years) a picture of a decentralised structure of society which should develop all over the country over a long period of time.

A total provision of about Rs. two crores may be made for each pilot project district, or a total of Rs. 28 crores during the Third Plan. To ensure integrated and effective development these districts should be identical with those already selected for intensive and comprehensive development of agriculture under the 10-point programme recommended by the Ford Foundation Team.

Training Programme

At least 50 artisans in each block should be given training during the Third Plan. A provision of Rs. 30 crores may be provided for this programme.

Marketing Facilities

A well organised network of emporia and sales depots for distribution of goods extending upto block and Taluk level is envisaged. Sales Depots will also supply raw materials to industries. As far as possible, composite sales depots are to be set up at each block, or Taluk level to avoid duplication and wastage. As the cooperatives grow, the depots can be handed over to them. A provision of Rs. seven crores is suggested.

Rural Electrification

Special attention should be given to extension of electricity to at least the proposed Centres, industrial estates and block-level townships. Small industrialists and farmers are not in a position to pay for the entire cost of electrification. There is no doubt an element of subsidy by the State is called for in view of the high cost of extending elecrticity to the villages. On account of the importance of rural electrification, a high-power committee may be appointed by the Ministry of Irrigation & Power to go into the entire question of rural electrification in all its various aspects.

Popular Participation

The Government will act in this field as a promotor, initiator and will for most part enable the individual corporations and cooperatives to do the job.

Organisation of Artisans

The programme should give full encouragement, assistance and counsel in the organisation of associations, trade unions and cooperatives.

Educational Tours

Educational tours for artisans should be organised on the lines conducted for farmers. A provision of Rs. 20 lakhs is proposed.

Craft Museums

Regional craft museums may be set up for rural arts and crafts, preferably at the block level.

Policy and Research

It is important that the Third Plan should clearly extend the field of reservation or demarcate the sphere of production in regard to industries which are located in the rural areas and/or considered essential for development for socio-economic reasons. It should be the policy of the Government of India that during the Third Plan, any State Government which expects assistance for hand-pounding of paddy and village oil industry should clearly indicate that. Areas where these industries are promoted should be banned from starting rice hullers and oil expellers respectively. Such a step would avoid waste of money and efforts and also would enable planned development of village industries where they would be really needed. For taking proper policy decisions in such matters, research should also be encouraged. An Action or Research Institute may be established for this purpose.

Rural Cell

At the Government level, both at the Centre and in the States, special Rural Cells should be located in the Industries, Ministry and State Departments. These Cells should be practically charged with the responsibility of a watch-dog for implementation of this programme.

COMMITTEE ON TRANSPORT POLICY AND COORDINATION, 1959—REPORT (PRELIMINARY)

New Delhi, Planning Commission, 1961. 212p.+vip.

Chairman : Shri K. C. Neogy.

Members : Shri Vishnu Sahay (replaced by Shri B. N. Jha); Shri R. L. Gupta; Shri K. B. Mathur (replaced by Shri Kripal Singh); Shri A. K. Roy (replaced by Shri L. K. Jha); Shri S. Ranganathan; Shri G. V. Ayyar.

Secretary : Shri K. L. Luthra.

APPOINTMENT

The Planning Commission and the Ministries of Railways and Transport & Communications have had under consideration for some time past suggestions relating to the coordination of different means of transportation, especially rail and road transport, and their future development having regard to the needs of the growing economy of the country. It has been felt that a comprehensive examination of these problems at this stage will be of material assistance in the formulation of plans of future development in the field of transportation It has accordingly been agreed in consultation with the Ministries of Railways and Transport and Communications to constitute a Committee to study the problems involved, and to make recommendations on the measures required to secure the necessary coordination between different means of transport and on long-term policies and considerations which should guide their future development. Accordingly this Committee was constituted vide Government of India Resolution dated July 22, 1959.

TERMS OF REFERENCE

Taking into account the existing stage of development of the various means of transport and the economic political, social and strategic purposes which the transport machinery is designed to serve, the committee should recommend;

(a) What broadly should be the long-term transport policy of the country, so that the development of the transport machinery may be effected in consonance with our growing needs, with economy and efficiency, avoiding duplication to the maximum extent practicable;

(b) In keeping with the policy defined under item (a) what should be the role of the various means of transport in the country during the next five to 10 years; and

(c) What is the best mechanism for the regulation and coordination of the various means of transport, so that the transport needs of the country are met in an efficient and economic manner consistent with the larger interests of the country?

CONTENTS

Introduction; Development and Regulation of the Indian Railways — A Historical Retrospect; the Role of Railways as a Public Enterprise; Administrative Organisation of the Indian Railways; Development and Regulation of Road Transport; Licensing Policies Pertaining to Commercial Road Transport; Existing State of Organisation of Road Transport Industry and its Capacity to Undertake Public Service Obligations; Recent Trends in the Distribution of traffic between Road Transport and Railways ——A Factual Assessment; Recent Trends in Railway Finances; Inherent Advantages of Road and Railway Transport and their Comparative Costs; More Important Methods of Coordination and their Applicability in India; Road-Rail Coordination in Respect of Passenger Traffic; Requirements in Regard to the Future Development of Railways and Road Transport; Main Questions at Issue; Appendices 1 to 24.

RECOMMENDATIONS

Adjustment Of Rates On The Basis Of Costs

A good deal of thought has been given in some foreign countries in recent years to the possibility of revising railway freight structure in a manner so as to make the railway rates correspond to the costs of haulage. The main consideration guiding such thinking has been the growing competition between railways and road transport. On services in respect of which the railway charges have been high in relation to costs, the railways almost everywhere in the world have laid themselves open to the competition of road transport which has affected adversely their financial position.

Uneconomic Branch Lines

The Committee has requested the Railway Board to make an attempt to estimate the financial results of working selected lines in the various zones and let the Committee have an idea of the losses involved in operating these lines.

It was urged that Light Railways could not afford any further diversion of traffic to road transport resulting in losses of revenue and that a separate code of principles should be evolved for regulating motor transport in the areas served by the Light Railways. The Committee has gone into the problem of Light Railways at some length and has had prolonged discussions with the representatives of the State Governments concerned. It is admitted by all concerned that some of these railways at least could not be discontinued and replaced by road transport services in the near future. It will be a matter for consideration how these railways could be made to pay their way during the period that they are required to continue in sevice.

Non-Paying Suburban Passenger Services

The Committee has asked the Railway Board to let it have an indication of the losses incurred by the Indian Railways on such services. It is doubtful, however, whether on the basis of the statistics compiled by the Indian Railways, it is possible to have a very exact estimate of these losses.

Amenities For Passenger Travel

It is difficult to make an estimate of the financial losses involved in the provision of such amenities over the entire railway system.

Obligation In Respect Of Staff

In several regions of the country, the railways as a Central Government undertaking, have to pay scales of wages which are substantially higher than the scales admissible to the employees of the State Governments within whose territories the railways function. This obligation, therefore, involves a social burden on the railways which the comparatively smaller units in the other means of transport are not called upon to bear. It should be possible to work out an estimate of the financial burden imposed on the railways on this account although this will require detailed calculations.

Preference For Certain Types Of Traffic Under Government Directions

Under Section 27-A of the Indian Railways Act, the Central Government may direct any Railway Administration in the public interest, to give preference to the transport of such goods or class of goods, as may be specified by it. It is impossible to make any estimate of the financial implications involved in the Indian Railways carrying out such orders of Government from time to time.

Administrative Organisation Of The Indian Railways Central Administrative Organisation

Under the existing set-up, the Minister is in touch with the day-to-day administration of the railways and in his discretion can deal with any matter concerning the administration. Parliament exercises control over the railway administration as over any other department of the Government.

Detailed administration of the Railways is at present the direct responsibility of a Central Ministry. And policy matters relating to the other forms of transport, in so far as they are subject to Central control or supervision, are the concern of another Ministry. Such a division of respensibility in the field of transport policy, adds to the difficulty of coordination. According to one view, so long as the Ministry of Railways remains responsible for detailed administration of the railways as at present, it would be open to serious objection to entrust to it, at the policy making level, the fortunes of other forms of transport also.

The Committee has observed certain tendencies which, if continued, might have serious implications from the point of view of the larger interests of the country. The Committee has not been able to give any detailed thought to this matter.

It seems to our Committee that the best initial test of what the public need is given by what they will pay for. If, thereafter, there are other considerations which make it desirable for members of the public to travel or freight to be carried on some routes at prices below the cost, it should be for the Government and not the Commission to decide.

Licensing Policies Pertaining To Commercial Road Transport

Grant of Temporary Permits

The Committee has also noticed that in several States temporary permits are being issued under clause (c) of Section 62. These permits are issued ostensibly 'to meet a particular temporary need' and do not require countersignature for inter-regional or inter-State operations (vide Sub-Section 4 of Section 63). At the instance of the Committee, the Ministry of Transport and Communications have collected figures from some of the States in regard to the number of temporary permits issued for distances of 300 miles and above and the available information for a period of six months, i. e. from January to June, 1960, is presented in a statement at Appendix 6. It will be observed that a large number of temporary permits are being issued by various Regional/State Transport Authorities for distances of 300 miles and above. These permits can broadly be placed in the following four categories :

(a) First, in some of the States, temporary permits are issued for the newly acquired vehicles pending the issue of regular permits which must necessarily take time.

(b) Second, in the case of the States which have not yet arrived at reciprocal agreements between themselves, the inter-State operations are allowed under temporary permits or temporary countersignatures.

(c) Third, some State Governments in the reciprocal agreements in respect of inter-State traffic have made a provision for the issue of a certain number of temporary permits in addition to the regular permits provided for under the agreements.

(d) Fourth, temporary permits are issued by a few States for long distance haulage between important towns ; as far instance, between Delhi and Calcutta, Delhi and Bombay, Delhi and Bangalore and Bombay and Calcutta, etc.

The Committee is not aware of the procedure that is followed by the Regional/State Transport Authorities to assess the genuineness or otherwise of the need for temporary permits.

The Committee has no detailed information as regards the possible effects of the liberal policy with regard to the grant of permits on the coordination within the road transport industry itself.

It is possible that the liberal policy followed by the State Governments in regard to the countersignatures of permits or the issue of long distance permits may, in certain cases, be due to the impression that the railway facilities available in the regions or the routes concerned are not adequate to meet the demands of traffic. Moreover, there may be genuine demands for long distance haulage by road in particular cases because of the special needs of traffic in question. On the other hand, in numerous cases, the demand for long distance haulage by road transport may arise largely because of the fact that the freight charged by road transport in respect particularly of high-priced goods is substantially lower than that charged by the railways.

Existing State Of Organisation Of Road Transport Industry And Its Capacity To Undertake Public Service Obligations

Possibility of Extension Of Social Obligations To Road Transport

There are many regions in the country where road transport is the only means of transport available or has to carry by for the largest part of traffic. The Committee has no evidence to show that the road transport industry in these regions has had a tendency to get better organised so as to be able to undertake such obligations as are necessary to be undertaken under conditions of virtual monopoly. The basic question to consider is whether the road transport industry could be so organised that it can be depended upon to undertake the public service obligations similar to those which are placed on the railways. The Committee has not been able to get any definite answer to this question even from the experience of the foreign countries in which road transport has come to occupy an important place in the economy. The Committee does not have enough factual material in regard to the experience of West Germany. However, the observation of the Commission on German Federal Railways quoted will give an indication of the difficulties which might be expected in enforcing any fixed freight structure on the road transport industry even when the industry may be reasonably well organised, as in West Germany.

Recent Trends In The Distribution Of Traffic Between Road Transport and Railway—A Factual Assessment

Estimates Of Traffic Carried By Road Transport

There has been a phenomenal growth in the volume of traffic moved by the railways under the five-year plans. However, to judge from the growth of the number and capacity of motor vehicles, there has been a proportionately larger expansion of the traffic moved by commercial road transport over this period. The share of road transport in high-priced goods i. e., the commodities other than coal and mineral ores, has increased in still higher proportions over the period.

The share of road transport in passenger traffic has shown a gradual increase during the period.

It is not easy to determine to what extent, if any, the expansion of traffic on road transport has been at the expense of the railways; or in other words, to what extent the traffic has been diverted from the railways to road transport.

Recent Trends In Railway Finances

Long-Term Trends In Railway Finances—Need For Careful Examination

In the first place, the contributions which the railways expect to make to the Depreciation Reserve Fund during the coming five years will be just a little more than the amount required to meet the actual cost of replacement requirements during the period and the balance available in the Fund will increase only by about Rs. 20 crores over the present small figure of about Rs. 21 crores. This is a very meagre balance considering that at the end of the Third Plan the total capital-at-charge of the railways will be Rs. 2,313 crores. The balances in the Fund have been almost denuded as a result of the large withdrawals during the second plan period which were inevitable on account of the back-log of replacements from the past. The contributions to the Depreciation Reserve Fund are at present estimated on the basis of the actual requirements of replacements and the railways' capacity to finance them during the period of each Convention. It is possible to take a view that the contributions to the Depreciation Reserve Fund should be calculated after carefully revaluing the capital-at-charge on the basis of the present replacement costs. The Committee has not gone into detailed calculation on this basis. It can, however, hardly be questioned that the railways' contribution to the Depreciation Reserve Fund during the Third Plan period might well have been at a somewhat higher figure if only the railways could afford it. This would enable the railways to start with a reasonable balance in the Fund in the Fourth Plan for replacements.

Secondly, the expenditure met out of the Railway Development Fund has exceeded the net surplus since 1957-58 and the railways have had to take temporary loans from the General Revenues to meet the expenditure. For the period of the Third Plan, the actual expenditure chargeable to the Fund is much more than the amount available with the Railways. The Comptroller and Auditor General is understood to have questioned the desirability of financing the Development Fund by temporary loans from the General Revenues and to have suggested that the Fund should rely only on railway surpluses and the expenditure therefrom should be restricted to the amounts available and for purposes for which the Fund was originally created. The Convention Committee (1960) while appreciating the view of the Auditor General expressed doubt about the practicability of implementing this suggestion 'during a period of developing economy'. Nevertheless, if it is not in the public interest to curtail the unremunerative expenditure chargeable to the Railway Development Fund, it will be a matter for consideration whether the railway should be burdened with the interest load on such expenditure.

We have, however, to consider the long-term prospects of railway finances against the background of the position as revealed for the Third Plan period. Several factors have to be taken into account which will influence the railways' financial position in the long run. The increases in rates on low-rated commodities, such as foodgrains, coal and raw materials of industries, will react generally upon the economy as a whole, and particularly on the costing pattern of important industries in the various regions of the country. On the other hand, the future pattern of rates on what may be described as high-rated commodities at present on the railways, will have to be considered carefully having regard to the possibilities of development of road transport and other means of transport.

Inherent Advantages Of Road And Railway Transport And Their Comparative Costs

Inherent Advantages Of Rail Transport

The railways are also considered more suitable than road transport for long haul passenger service. It is considered to offer the advantages of greater safety, better reliability, and more comfort and convenience.

The railways are considered especially suitable for suburban passenger services in the larger cities.

The respect of goods services, the railways are obviously at a disadvantage in regard to speed of delivery, particularly for short and medium distance traffic, or door to door delivery services, or personal attention being paid to the consignments of individual customers. There are also complaints from the users about the loss or damage to goods in transit and pilferage of goods and delays in settling claims on the part of railways. Many of these disadvantages are such as will be inherent in any big organisation like the railways. It is necessary for the railways as a commercial undertaking, however, to organise its working in a manner so as to mitigate, to the extent possible, these inherent weaknesses in their operations. The Indian Railways recently have taken several steps which may be mentioned in this connection. These include (i) introduction of quick transit services and express goods services, (ii) supply of container services, (iii) collection and street delivery services, and (iv) opening of out-agencies and city booking agencies, etc.

Comparative Costs Of Railway And Road Transport

The inherent advantages of railway and road transport must reflect themselves in the comparative costs of these two modes of transport, provided that the 'costs' are interpreted in wide terms so as to include not merely economic but also social costs to the community at large.

It is not an easy matter to determine 'the economic and social cost to the community' of any particular service performed by the railways and road transport.

There are thus numerous difficulties involved in any elaborate cost analysis of rail and road operations, if such an analysis is to be attempted for determining the relative role of the two means of transport.

The present system of expenditure accounts on the Indian Railways is determined by the needs wholly of budgetary and general administrative control. The expenditure is booked under heads like maintenance, replacements, additions, staff, fuels, stores, etc., and this system of accounting does not lend itself to any scientific analysis of costs of haulage of any particular type of traffic hauled by the railways. Most of the expenses incurred in the traffic operations are treated as a whole and are not allocated between the various types of traffic. What we have on the railways are the figures of overall average cost of hauling a ton of goods per mile. These average figures have not much meaning for purposes of comparison of costs of specific types of traffic handled by the railways with corresponding costs of haulage by road transport.

All that we wish to say is that this study like other studies done on the subject in the past, does not provide an answer to the main question which needs to be considered in any comparison of the costs of haulage by railway and road transport; namely, whether and to what extent the cost of wear and tear caused to the roads by the operation of commercial vehicles and also their share of interest on the capital investment in the construction of roads are, in practice, met from the taxes which these vehicles pay to the Exchequer. This question does not easily lend itself to any scientific examination. In the first place, not all the taxes paid by road transport can be taken to represent the contribution of road transport to the cost of maintenance and construction of roads.

Secondly, an important basic question that needs to be studied is the extent of damage to roads caused by the use of various types of vehicles.

The Committee wished to pursue further the studies of average costs by these two means of transport in the considerations obtaining in India but the existing system of accounting of the railways or, for that matter, of the road transport undertakings sets serious limitations to these studies being made very scientific.

More Important Methods Of Coordination And Their Applicability In India

Adjustment Of Freight Rates On The Basis Of Costs

We may, for the present, overlook the fact that adjustment of rates on the basis of the average costs will itself lead to reduction in the volume of traffic in these commodities and, therefore, will result in increase in the average cost of haulage of these commodities.

Reimbursement To Transport Undertakings Of The Cost of Unremunerative Services And Other Public

Service Obligations

It will be a matter for careful consideration whether it is possible to make an assessment of the financial burden placed on the railways on account of these obligations and whether Government can undertake to reimburse the cost of these obligations to the railways in the near future. Moreover, if the railways are to be treated as a purely commercial undertaking, an important question to consider will be whether they can adopt strictly economic and commercial criteria while opening up new lines and whether and to what extent Government should directly subsidise the railway lines which are unremunerative and have to be opened or maintained by the railways on considerations other than commercial.

Integration Of Transport Services

It has been suggested that the railways should have a substantial share in this corporation say, about 35 per cent or more, and that the corporation should be required to have a reasonable rate structure so that it could not under-out the railways. It is claimed that, under this arrangement, unhealthy competition will be prevented and at the same time the railways would be assured a share in the profits of the corporation which would compensate them for loss of traffic in any region of the country. There are several aspects of the proposal which need to be carefully studied. It will, for instance, have to be considered whether there should be one such corporation to operate road transport services all over the country or there may be several such corporations. Then again, what should be the extent of participation of the State Governments and the private operators in the corporation and how the share allocated to the State Governments should be distributed among different States. Another important question to consider is how the proposed corporation would function vis-a-vis private operators who will still be operating the comparatively short distance routes or, say, intra-State routes in case the operations of the corporation are confined to inter-State routes only.

Coordination Through Suitable Organisation And Regulation Of Road Transport

The regulation of motor transport industry which is the third alternative solution to the problem of coordination, can take various forms, of which the most important are the following:

(a) Regulation of rates and fares,

(b) Regulation of entry into the industry through appropriate authorisation or licensing by the State, and

(c) Restrictions on the operation of goods vehicles beyond certain distances or restrictions on the types of services to be provided, etc., etc.

The Committee has been trying to collect material so as to be able to study in detail the experience of some of the industrially advanced countries in securing coordination between different means of transport, particularly railways and road transport, by suitable regulatory measures.

Special Problems In Regard To Regulation Of Transport Agencies In India

Two specific issues will require to be considered in detail in this connection:

(a) the division of responsibility between the Centre and the States as regards regulation of road transport and (b) the need for and the form of any Central Organisation to be entrusted with the responsibility of coordinated development of all means of transport in the country.

As far as we have been able to find out. the division of responsibility in respect of road transport and railways as it obtains in India, is not to be found in any other country.

Under the present set-up, therefore, there is no agency at the Centre which has adequate responsibilities in regard to coordination of all means of transport in the country.

Road-Rail Coordination In Respect Of Passenger Traffic

We have not considered it necessary to examine in detail the problem of coordination between the passenger services provided by the private operators and the railways.

A notable feature of the expansion programmes of some of the nationalised transport undertakings is the introduction of long distance bus services. Several State Government undertakings have introduced long distance services in recent years. The Committee has not been able to get data about these services, but are given to understand by the Railway Board that, in several cases, the long distance services provided by these undertakings have had a tendency to affect the railways adversely.

The Committee considered it desirable to ascertain from the Railway Board their experience of the results of association with such corporations as have been in operation for some time.

The Committee considered whether the objective of road-rail coordination could not be achieved through some alternative means, i.e., by setting up Advisory Boards in the States with the railways represented on them. In this connection, the Railway Board have expressed the view, which is shared by the Committee, that there is a great deal of difference between the railways being represented on an Advisory Board and their being on the Board of Directors of a corporation. In the latter case, they would have a formal *locus standi* and their representative could deal with the other Directors on an equal footing.

In the Committee's opinion, the most important

consideration in favour of the corporation form of management is the need to achieve, by mutual agreement, coordination between two public undertakings namely, State road transport on the one hand and the railways on the other. The utility of the Corporation lies mainly in the fact that this form of management provides a forum for the two public authorities to arrive at a mutual understanding and enables the railways to put forward their views effectively in an informal atmosphere.

The Committee supports the policy of corporations being constituted with the railways' participation for the management of nationalised road transport undertakings in the States. The Committee, in fact, after through examination of the issues involved, is merely confirming the policy adopted by Government quite some years back.

The Committee would like to make is clear that it supports this policy simply from the point of view of securing coordination between the railways and the nationalised road transport undertakings of the State Governments and that it has not been influenced by considerations relating to the comparative efficiency of corporations vis-a-vis departmental undertakings. This may be a relevant consideration, but does not fall within the purview of the Committee.

The Committee is aware of the difficulty which the Government have had in the past in getting this policy implemented by some of the State Governments. It is understood that the main reason for some of the State Governments being disinclined to accept this policy is that corporations would be subject to income-tax. It will, however, be appreciated that if some of the State Governments do not set up corporations and thus avoid payment of their share of income-tax leviable on the road transport undertakings, they may be said to benefit themselves at the expense of the other State Governments who have set up corporations and pay income-tax on their earnings, while sharing in the divisible pool of income-tax. This point may well deserve to be examined by the Finance Commission so that any differentiation in the practical operation of the formula relating to sharing of the income-tax proceeds by individual State Governments may be removed by necessary adjustments of their share of the pool.

Requirements In Regard To The Future Develpment Of Railways And Road Transport

Elements Of Uncertainty In The Estimates Of Traffic For The Third Plan

We have to take into account the likely changes in the pattern of movement of commodities like foodgrains, and iron and steel in respect of which the objective in the Third Five-Year Plan is to attain a measure of self-sufficiency.

Third, it is difficult at this stage to make an assessment of the impact of expansion programme of the road transport industry on the railways and vice versa.

Projections Of Traffic Requirements In Future

It will be appreciated that the element of uncertainty in the long-term projections will be much greater than that pertaining to the projections of traffic for a relatively short period of the Third Plan.

The Difficulties Involved In The Allocation Of Future Traffic Between Railways And Road Transport

We have also to take into account the possibilities of technological advances both in railways and road transport in future which may materially influence the economics of the two means of transport and their capacity to carry traffic in the country.

Considerations Relating To Opening Up Of New Lines

While the developmental and strategic roles of the railways must no doubt be important considerations in considering future expansion of the railway system in any country, it will be relevant in this connection to study the recent development in some of the industrially advanced countries of the world.

Considerations Relating To Road Development Programme

There is the problem of missing bridges on arterial routes. On the National Highways alone, 80 major bridges will remain to be provided at the end of the Second Five-Year Plan of which 47 will be in various stages of progress.

Having regard to the limitation of resources, it will be a matter for consideration what priority should be given to the programmes relating to the up-grading of surfaces of the arterial and other important roads in the country and the provision of missing bridges on them and whether these roads will have the necessary capacity to carry all the traffic that is likely to be generated in the next five to 10 years as also in the long run. This question has an important relevance in any consideration of the allocation of traffic in future between railways and road transport.

Main Questions At Issue

We have also pointed out that there is a tendency on the part of the interests concerned to ask for extensions of the railway system which are not always justified an economic or commercial considerations. Likewise, road transport facilities are also being sought to be extended without proper thought being given to needs of coordination. Although the overall resources available both for railway and road development are limited, because of local pressure demands for unnecessary duplication of facilities in certain regions are not easy to resist.

Furthermore, we are very conscious of the fact that, as has been the experience of other countries, there will come a time when serious problems may arise. It would be a pity if we did not, with the experience of other countries to guide us, and particularly when we have adopted a policy of planned development, take steps from now on to prevent such a situation developing. The road transport system in the country is still in an early stage of development, and as the output of vehicles from indigenous sources goes up, there will be much greater opportunities for the transport of goods by road. At the sametime, the movement of goods which seem basically more suitable for rail transport either because of their bulk or the length of haulage, e.g., ores for export as well as for our metallurgical plants and other similar industries, will also go up steadily. It is necessary to consider the factors which determine the appropriateness of railways and road transport for different types of goods and passenger traffic. It is much better to direct investment in right channels with a clear-cut conception of our objectives and policies than to seek remedial measures after infructuous investment has been made. Such an approach to the problem necessitates a consideration of some fundamental issues.

The Committee, according to its terms of reference in fact, has been asked to define the role of the various means of transport in the country during the next five to 10 years in keeping with the long-term transport policy which the Committee might recommend for the country. Before considering a suitable scheme of coordination for the next five to 10 years, therefore, it is necessary that we should give careful thought to all the various questions which are relevant in formulating a long-term policy for the country.

Referred to three alternative approaches to the problem of coordination. First, there is the possibility of allowing free unrestricted competition between different forms of transport. Second, the necessary coordination may be achieved through appropriate Government regulation. In this approach, thought has to be given not only to the objectives of the policy to be followed but also to the machinery to be used to implement it. The third alternative is of the rail and road services being integrated into one single unit, when the problem is of coordination not from outside but within the authority responsible for the joint management of all forms of transport.

We are emphatically of the view that it would be wrong to dismiss summarily the first and third alternatives, particularly because it cannot be claimed that the second has met with complete success in the other countries. Our transport system has to develop a great deal during the next 10 years if it is to keep pace with the programmes of industrial development on which we have embarked. It is essential that we should take a long-term view of the question and, in doing so, we should not hesitate to consider any changes in respect of our existing policies regarding the railways and roadways, however radical they may seem, if they are likely to secure a more efficient and economic development of our transport system as a whole. To rely on regularly measures, to be devised *ad hoc* as and when any signs of unhealthy competition appear will not, in our view, be the right answer to the questions confronting us. Having regard to our wide terms of reference, which cover long-term policies, we consider it desirable to elecit public opinion on each of the three alternatives discussed above and to draw the attention of the Planning Commission and the Government to some of the fundamental issues which have to be considered and on which a long-range view has to be taken before a national transport policy can be formulated.

We have felt, however, that in most instances, such judgements and opinions are formed without a full appreciation of the implications of the view taken.

We hope that by placing before the public a fairly detailed analysis of the present situation, we shall get the kind of informed criticism and advice which is most valuable in the formulation of a long-term policy.

We have, in the questions set out at the end of this chapter, tried to pose squarely the question of allowing railways the freedom to operate as a purely commercial undertaking and competing an equal terms with other forms of transport. This is followed by a second set of questions relating to policy of regulation. These questions arise out of the experience gained in working the existing system of coordination of which reference has been made earlier. The third set of questions refers to the possibility of eventually achieving coordination through integration of rail and road services. Nationalisation of the entire road transport system will itself raise many problems, though it may be achieved by suitable stages. We feel that this question also should be considered along with the other two possibilities referred to above.

Our final questions relate to what, after all, is the most important issue, viz., the criteria which should govern future investment in the development of different forms of transport in the country. The more carefully this policy is thought out and implemented, the less serious is the problem of coordination likely to be.

The questions that we have listed in this chapter are of basic importance and will require to be given detailed thought in any consideration of long-term policy for coordinated development of railways and road transport. While discussing several matters of policy in the earlier chapters we have raised other relevant questions as well. To avoid repetition, we are not recapitulating them in this chapter, although some of them are extremely important. In giving further thought to all these issues we shall be greatly helped if we have before us the reaction of all sections of the community.

Questions

1. Could railways and road transport, and for that matter, all other means of transport be treated as commercial undertakings and be enabled to complete with each other on equal terms ? If so,

(a) It is possible for the railways to be relieved of their obligation to provide services which do not pay, or alternatively, is it possible to assess the cost to the railways of providing uneconomic services and to reimburse them this cost from public revenues ? If a distinctive section of a railway such as a branch line is proved to be a source of continuous loss will it be possible to permit the railways to discontinue the sections ?

What reforms, if any, will be needed in the present accounting practice of the railways so as to enable the railways to ascertain the profitability or otherwise of their operations in respect of different sections of a zone or individual lines, etc ?

(b) Is it possible to relieve the railways of their statutory obligations to accept all traffic offering without discrimination and their obligation not to discriminate between customers in regard to charges payable, leaving them free to quote competitive rates which may differ in different areas and for different customers ?

(c) As an alternative to (a) and (b) above, is it possible to impose similar obligations on other forms of transport ?

2. What should be the financial obligation, if any, of the railways towards Central Revenues under such a system ?

3. If the railways are to function as a purely commercial undertaking with complete freedom to quote competitive rates, would this policy involve any significant change in the organisational set-up of the railways and their relationship with Government ; and if so, what would be the nature of such changes ? Will there be a special case for the railways being managed through a corporate body in such a set-up ?

4. If the road transport system is not restricted to certain areas by permits, how would it be possible to ensure the availability of adequate transport facilities at a reasonable cost in the less-developed and rural areas and hilly tracts where short-distance transport is involved and where rail communication may not be available ?

5. What increase will be required in railway rates on the low-rated commodities like coal and other raw materials for industries and foodgrains, such as may be necessary to enable the railways to make a reasonable margin of profit on their overall operations after taking into account effect of possible reduction in the rates on the high-rated categories of traffic? How might such adjustments in the railway rating structure, react upon the economy in general and the costing pattern of important industries in the various regions of the country ?

6. To what extent could the Inter-State Transport Commission be made an effective body to ensure coordination between railways and road transport in respect of (a) Inter-State operations and (b) intra-State operations ?

7. Would it be possible under the existing Constitution to set up a central organisation entrusted with adequate responsibility for coordination of all forms of transport ? If so, what form should this organisation take ?

If not, what change in the Constitution may be necessary to secure effective coordination through regulation and to set up an appropriate coordinating body ?

8. If any such organisational reforms be adopted, would it be advisable to entrust the overall control, at policy level, of all forms of transport (including railways) to a single Ministry so as particularly to facilitate effective coordination ? Could the Ministry directly responsible for the detailed administration of the railways be entrusted with the responsibility of controlling, at policy level, other forms of transport also ?

9. If coordination is to be achieved through regulation, then in what manner could it be ensured that regulation would result in a rational distribution of traffic between road transport and railways having regard to their respective suitability for particular types of traffic?

(a) To what extent may any type and bulk of freight traffic and the distance to be traversed broadly constitute elements of suitability for road and rail transport respectively? and

(b) In the case of passenger traffic, are there any district elements of respective suitability for road and rail transport ?

10. Which of the following forms of regulation would suit the conditions in India ?

(a) Should the licensing policy to be adopted be modelled on a system prevailing in the United States of America in respect of inter-State operations under which the service to be provided and the route or area to be covered and the charges to be levied by the carriers are regulated, but there is no restriction on the number of vehicles to be acquired on each licence for the service prescribed ? Or

(b) Should the licensing policy be designed on the model obtaining in West Germany under which the total number of long distance licences valid for distances over a given radius (50 kilometres in West Germany) is fixed by the Federal Government and the long distance road transport industry is subject to fixed tariff rates which are almost the same as the railway rates ? Or

(c) Should the system be more in line with the one obtaining in Great Britain which aims at regulation of the number of public haulage vehicles, but has very little control over the type of work on which they are subsequently engaged or over the rates which are charged but which permits the railways to quote competitive rates without any restrictions in regard to non-discrimination of rates or the publication of rates etc. ? Or

(d) Should the licensing system, as in some of the States in Australia, aim at restriction on distance or areas over which road transport services should be provided ? Or,

(e) Should the licensing policies in India broadly represent a combination or modification of some of the features mentioned above ?

11. To what extent can the taxation of road transport vehicles be used as an alternative to, or to supplement the system of regulation through permits ? To what extent could the present system of taxation on the road transport industry be modified so as to increase the taxes on vehicles carrying particular types of goods or those operating over long distance and correspondingly to reduce the taxes for the other types of traffic or for short distance operations ?

12. Should a broad-based scheme be contemplated for the integration, rather than mere coordination, of road and rail services under a nationalised system, in which the Central and State Governments may participate on suitable terms ?

13. Should nationalisation of long distance road transport services be undertaken on selected routes with a view to securing coordination between rail and road services on these routes ?

14. If nationalisation of goods transport services is contemplated as a method of coordination, what should be the form of organisation to operate these services ? More particularly, will it be appropriate to manage these services through a corporation or corporations in which the railways, State Governments and private operators participate ?

Could the railways, in any circumstances, be entrusted with the operation of road transport services as an integrated part of the railway operations ?

15. As regards the future extension or development of roads and railways in the country, what should be the guiding criteria in deciding on such extensions ? Should the effort be to develop either road transport or rail transport only, having regard to the suitability for rail or road transport of the bulk of the traffic offering in any particular area ?

16. Before any road or rail project is undertaken in any area, should technical and economic surveys be made for the purpose of ascertaining whether road or rail transport, exclusively would meet the needs of the situation at lesser cost than the other, and should decision be taken on the result of such surveys so as to avoid the provision of the costlier service ?

17. What should be the guiding principles that should be followed in choosing the alignments of new roads and railways ?

18. Should the railways be expected to provide new lines even if they are unremunerative from a commercial point of view ? If such services have to be provided, should the financial burden be debited to the sponsoring authorities rather than to the railways ?

REVIEW COMMITTEE FOR MATHEMATICS IN INDIAN UNIVERSITIES, 1959—REPORT

New Delhi, University Grants Commission, n.d. 98p.+vip.

Chairman : Dr. B. R. Seth.
Members : Dr. Ram Behari; Dr. B. N. Prasad; Dr. P. L. Bhatnagar; Dr. R. P. Bambah; Dr. C. R. Rao; Dr. Alladi Ramakrishnan.
Secretary : Dr. B. D. Laroia.

APPOINTMENT

In 1959, the University Grants Commission appointed 'Reviewing Committees' in a number of important subjects to broadly survey and assess the standard of teaching and research and the facilities available for the purpose, and to recommend steps to be taken (including modifications of syllabuses) in order to raise the general level of academic attainment and research in the universities. Knowledge these days is expending at such a rapid pace that a serious and sustained effort is required if teaching is to be kept even reasonably up-to-date. The value and necessity of "Reviewing Committees" is apparent, and, if anything, these are all the more important in the context of our development plans for expansion of higher education and research, specially in the fields of science and technology.

The Review Committee for Mathematics and Statistics was constituted in August, 1959.

TERMS OF REFERENCE

The Committee had wide terms of reference and was free to datermine its own programme and procedure of work. The Committee could also visit some of the Indian Universities and other institutions. At its first meeting the Committee laid down the following items for study and investigation:

1. The present state of development in Mathematics and Statistics;

2. A qualitative and quantitative appraisal of the existing facilities for teaching and research;

3. Trends of research, its potentialities and steps to be taken for expansion of training and research facilities invarious disciplines of the subject;

4. Syllabi and examination system at different levels of university education, improvement and modernisation of syllabi, preparation of model syllabi;

5. Ways and means of co-ordination between institutions including university and non-university centres of teaching and research;

6. Improvement of facilities for students and teaching personnel.

CONTENTS

Foreword; Introduction; A Brief Historical Sketch of Mathematical Research in India; Syllabus; Examination System; Future Developments; Summary of Recommendations; Appendices I to IV.

RECOMMENDATIONS

'Model syllabi' for under-graduate and post-graduate courses are recommended in order to indicate the standard of training desired in Mathematics and to prepare a student for service and research. The syllabi need to be reviewed and revised once in every five years.

The extent of formal lectures should be reduced and reduction compensated by introduction of tutorials and seminars to develop the reasoning capacity and the habit of independent reading in the student.

Due recognition should be given to the sessional work in order to reduce the entire dependence on the annual examination only at the end of the course. In order to do this, a beginning may be made by alloting 25 per cent of the marks for sessional work and gradually increase it to 40 per cent or even 50 per cent.

There should be no Third Division awarded at the Master's Degree level.

The University Grants Commission should recognise a selected number of centres in prescribed fields. These centres should form an integral part of a university or an institute of higher learning.

Each centre should be formed around a group of distinguished workers in the field. The nucleus should consist of eight or 10 active workers.

The University Grants Commission should give grants on a 100 per cent basis to these centres for any additional expenditure on account of staff, library, equipment, buildings, publications, symposia, visiting professorships, casual visiting lecturerships, visits of members of other centres or universities, conferences, etc.

The division of the posts at the centres into various cadres should not be too rigid. If a member of the staff is deemed at any time by an expert committee to be fit for promotion to a higher rank, his post should be upgraded. Thus the number of professorships, readerships, fellowships may vary within reasonable limits at each centre. The recruitment of all staff connected with the centre should be done by selection committees with which the University Grants Commission is actively associated.

Admission to the centres should be on an All-India basis and on merit alone. An adequate number of fellowships should be available at each centre. Each centre should have an intensive programme of study and research. It should also arrange symposia, summer schools, refresher courses for both college and school teachers.

The centres may submit plans to invite visiting professors from other universities and countries. If approved, the University Grants Commission should provide all expenses thus incurred. Integreted plans extending over a number of years should be drawn up for visiting mathematicians. The visitors during the period of one plan should be so chosen that their individual contributions supplement those of other visitors and members of the centre. The programme of every visiting professor should be up in consultation with all other centres interested in the subject of specialisation so that maximum benefit may be taken from his visit.

Centres must cooperate with each other and have inter-centre plans.

Creative workers should be encouraged and facilities should be given to them to get away from their routine work of teaching to do some research. For this purpose it is desirable to set up on the basis of inter-university collaboration an institute where the workers can come at their will to spend six months to a year without any formal duties.

Steps should be taken to recognise academic attainments and research abilities of persons. Steps may be evolved to get continuous supply of efficient teachers by proper methods of selection and give them necessary amenities. Stress may be laid on research potential and achievements particularly for the senior posts. While fixing the initial salary of the teachers, the period spent by him in research should be given due recognition.

Such of the teachers who have for some reason or other detached themselves from research and modern developments should be required to undergo advanced training.

Younger teachers should be able to take study leave early in their career and all senior teachers should be eligible to get one year's leave once in five or six years for academical purposes.

A university teacher engaged in research should not have a teaching load in excess of nine hours per week. The head of the department, who also has to do the administrative work and guide research students, should not have more than six hours of teaching load per week. No teacher should be called upon to do more than 15 hours of teaching work including tutorials. Out of these 15 hours not more than nine hours should be for post-graduate teaching.

Suitable working rooms and library facilities should be provided to all workers.

Exchange of professors among the Indian Universities and visits by distinguished foreign scholars should be encouraged.

The University Grants Commission should give special importance to the organisation and holding of summer institutes, summer schools. symposia, etc., for university and college teachers and should make special provisions for this purpose in their budget.

Somposia : Topics selected for the symposia must be highly specialised and the invitees are to be chosen on the basis of their current status in the subject. The duration of symposia can be three to six days and the proceedings may be published.

Summer School : The purpose of summer schools could be to organise extensive lectures on few selected topics by invited lecturers and admission would be by application. Regarding the summer schools it may not be possible to organise a single summer school for the whole country. It is, therefore, saggested that regional summer schools be held and the venues for each region can be selected by rotation. The summer school should preferably be organised during long vacation to extend from a period to four to six weeks.

Summer Institutes : The Primary aim of summer institutes will be to bring together research workers for extensive discussions both formal and informal. The duration should be for four to six weeks. The participation should be by invitation.

Suitable publicatlon grants may be given by the University Grants Commission to encourage publication of research material in recognised journals by individual research workers. An *ad hoc* grant may be given to each university to encourage original publication as well as for purchase of reprints of each of such publication for purposes of general distribution.

COMMITTEE ON LARGE-SIZED MECHANISED FARMS, 1959—FIRST REPORT

New Delhi, Ministry of Food and Agriculture, Department of Agriculture, n.d. 36p.+Map.

Chairman : Shri K. R. Damle.
Members : Shri Joginder Singh; Shri Kanwar Sain; Dr. B. N. Uppal; Maj. Genl. T. Mahadeo Singh; Dr. P. S. Lokanathan; Shri Nawab Singh.

APPOINTMENT

The variety of measures have been and are being taken from time to time to help solve the food problem of our country. The establishment of Central Mechanised Farm, Suratgarh in August 1956, covering a gross area of roughly 30,000 acres in Rajasthan under the direct control of the Central Government is yet another project launched with the same objective in view. This Farm set up with the aid of a composite unit of agricultural machinery and equipment received as gift from the Government of U.S.S.R. has kept on making steady progress right from its inception to-date and has nearly achieved its principal objective, namely, production and multiplication of improved seeds.

Encouraged by the success achieved at the Central Mechanised Farm, Suratgarh and in the context of the important role played by State Farms in U.S.S.R. in the building up of large stocks of foodgrains, the Cabinet took a decision in February, 1959 to appoint a small committee of experts to examine in detail the economics of large State-owned farms in the light of the experience gained at the C.M.F., Suratgarh with a view to setting up more such farms elsewhere in the country on the pattern of the central Mechanised Farm, Suratgarh. Such an examination in consonance with the objective aimed at, has necessarily to take into account, among other things, initial capital outlay on buildings, machinery and equipment, availability of large compact blocks of land with adequate irrigation facilities or potentiality for immediate development of such facilities.

Pursuant to the Cabinet's decision referred to above, the Ministry of Food and Agriculture (Department of Agriculture) appointed this Committee vide their Memorandum dated August 5, 1959, to examine the possibility of setting up of more mechanised Farms on the lines of the Suratgarh Farm.

TERMS OF REFERENCE

(i) To consider in detail the economics of operation of State-owned mechanised farms in the light of the experience obtained in the case of Suratgarh Farm, taking into account all the relevant factors such as the cost of machinery, development of land, construction of essential buildings, running expenses, etc.;

(ii) To submit proposals for the setting up of new State farms, taking into account the avilability of land and irrigation facilities, giving separate financial forecast for seasonal and perennial irrigation;

(iii) To consider any other relevant matter that might be placed by the Government of India before the Committee.

CONTENTS

Introduction; Examination of States Proposals; Suggestions for New Farm; Appendices I to VIII.

RECOMMENDATIONS

Introduction

In order to make the task of the Committee easy, enquiries had already been made from all States with the exception of Union Territorries and the two States of Assam and Jammu and Kashmir in regard to the availability of suitable compact blocks of land answering the following essental requirements :

(a) Adequate irrigation facilities;

(b) Compactness of the area;

(c) Ready availability of land for cultivation;

(d) Soil and terrain with a view to ensuring effective utilisation of machinery throughout the year;

(e) Adequate means of communications; and

(f) Proximity to established markets for disposal of Farm produce.

The reasons for excluding the Union Territories and the States of Assam and Jammu and Kashmir seem to be the improbability of locating large compact blocks of the required size in the mountainous or sub-mountainous region where Assam and Jammu and Kashmir happen to be located and the comparatively small size of the Union Territories.

As per our terms of reference, we now proceed to examine the economics of large State-owned farms in the light of the experience gained hitherto at the Central Mechanised Farm, Suratgarh. Before we commence this examination, we would like to draw attention to the fact that the final result derived from our analysis of the economics of the Suratgarh Farm should not be made the sole criterion to determine the remunerative aspect of such farms as may be located at sites having ideal conditions. This Farm, it may be pointed out, has hitherto been run largely on non-perennial irrigation, perennial irrigation having been made available through a system of lift irrigation for a small area of only about 3,000 acres and that too from the year 1958 onwards.

The gross area of the Central Mechanised Farm, Suratgarh is roughly 30,000 acres of which 22,000 acres are earmarked for cultivation. 2,000 acres for orchards, 1,500 acres for animal husbandry schemes and the balance of 4,500 acres is accounted for by sand dunes, roads, buildings, and channels, etc. The total capital investment on the Farm, including the cost of the gift machinery would be of the order of Rs. 227.64 lakhs of which a large component of Rs. 118.00 lakhs is accounted for by buildings both residential and non-residential. The balance of Rs. 109.64 lakhs is made up of Rs. 95.00 lakhs for machinery plus Rs. two lakhs being the likely cost of foundation stock for projected schemes of animal husbandry Rs. 10.00 lakhs for land development including reclamation and Rs. 2.64 lakhs towards compensation paid to the owners lessees displaced from the occupied area. The last mentioned figure of Rs. 2.64 lakhs includes a sum of Rs. 1.55 lakhs paid as compensation for kutcha houses, wells, tanks etc. owned by the persons displaced from the occupied area. Spreading the total capital investment on the area of 25,000 acres utilised for production activities the investment per acre works out to Rs. 900/-. The share of capital investment accountable towards, Land Development, in this particular case is considerably low, because of the fact that very little of what is termed as heavy reclamation work was required to be undertaken in the Farm area. The land under the Farm was fairly even and flat and some growth of scrubs, thorny bushes existed only in a small section of the farm area. In areas where reclamation involves clearance of thick jungle growth, the cost of reclamation, judging from the experience of Central Tractor Organisation will vary from Rs. 250 to 300 per acre.

Examining the normal running expenses incurred at the C.M.F. Suratgarh, we find that they have increased with the expansion of farming operations over larger areas from year to year. The increase in the running expense is not directly proportional to the increase in the cultivated area for the obvious reason that overheads like expenditure on administrative and supervisory staff do not go up in the same proportion; rather, these remain more or less constant. During 1959-60, when roughly 90 per cent of total cultivable area had been brought under crops, the running expenses amounted to Rs. 21.60 lakhs. We estimate that the running expenses, when the farm is fully developed, will work to Rs. 36.00 lakhs. Thereafter there will be only nominal increases resulting from grant of annual increments to staff drawing pay in time scales of pay. Our estimate is that the operational expenses will revolve round a figure of Rs. 175/- per acre.

The details of the running expenses given in Appendix II can be regarded as fairly realistic, allowing a margin of five per cent for fluctuations. It will be seen that the expenditure on staff represents 33-1/3 per cent of the total running expenses which we consider a little on the high side but nonetheless justifiable on a venture of this magnitude. We are, however, inclined to believe that it should be possible to bring about some saving in the expenses on labour if more labour-saving devices could be devised after carrying out experiments keeping in view the local requirements. We strongly emphasise this, as it will also reduce our dependence on manual labour which it is difficult to get in that sparsely populated area and consequently the wages demanded are high.

Coming to the income aspect of the scheme, we find that despite natural calamities and inadequacy of irrigation supplies, the farm has been able to register profits in the years 1956-57, 1958-59 and 1959-60. We are given to understand that the figures of profits mentioned in the relevant Profit and Loss Accounts are yet to be certified by the Accountant General, Rajasthan. Normally, such encouraging results would not have been achieved in the initial stages when only a portion of total Farm area was put under cultivation. We are led to infer that this may be due to the virginity of the soil contributing to better yields and in no small measure to better cultivation under mechanised mode of farming. We have good reasons to believe that the present level of yields can be maintained by application of manures and fertilizers in a greater degree to help soil recoup its fertility. We feel that in this farm or any other farm, given the necessary facilities particularly perennial irrigation, it should be possible to get a return of six per cent over the initial capital investment after recovering in full the running expenditure including invisible charges like interest on capital, depreciation on capital assets, etc. From this it follows that the entire investment can be recovered in a period of 16 years or say 20 years, making allowance for one year in every slab of four years when normal production may not be achieved due to natural calamities and other unforeseen factors peculiar to agriculture.

Examination Of States Proposals

The Committee regret to point out that the response from States to the enquiries regarding availability of land was poor. Data about compact blocks of 30,000 acres or more answering the essential requirements laid down, had been called for. Most of the States took unduly long time to send their replies. Considering the feeble response, the Committee decided to obtain data about small blocks of 10,000 acres or more. Even after the reduction made in the size of the block, the response from States was no better. We now proceed to discuss in the following paragraphs such proposals as were received from States.

The States who sent in positive proposals are Rajasthan, Bombay, Andhra Pradesh, Punjab, Mysore, Orissa, and Bihar. Madhya Pradesh had at one stage suggested some sites, but on actual surveys carried out by them they intimated that the sites suggested earlier were no longer available. While the Committee desired to locate farms in all parts of the country it was mainly concerned in locating such places where land was readily available and irrigation facilities were assured, so that immediate food production could be undertaken. The proposals from each State are discussed below :

(1) **Bombay** : Two sites were suggested. One is suggested in Banni area in Kutch district and the other in Karad Taluka of North Satara District. (The former is now a part of Gujarat State and the latter is in Maharashtra). The land offered in Banni area is all Government land and it answers practically all the essential requirment laid down. The Committee consider it quite suitable but for one major defect. This area is seasonally in undated by sea and any scheme to prevent its flooding would be in the nature of a major project involving a big outlay and requiring several years to complete. The land offered in Karad Taluk measures 28,984 acres and is mainly within the jurisdiction of a local Sugar Factory. All this is private land and is under cultivation. The State Government suggested that it could be considered for introduction of mechanised farming on cooperative basis. For setting up of a State Farm in this area, the entire land would have to be acquired which will involve payment of heavy compensation. Besides, acquisition of land on such a large scale will take a long time to complete. For these reasons we do not recommend any of the two sites suggested in the composite State of Bombay as suitable for the purpose in view.

(2) **Bihar** : Five blocks were suggested of which the largest one measuring 30,000 acres was withdrawn by the State Government themselves on close examination it was not found to be suitable. Three blocks of 10,000 acres each are suggested in the districts of Monghyr, Gaya and Bhagalpur respectively. None of these answers fully the essential requirements laid down. Irrigation facilities are practically non-existent in the Monghyr Block. In the other two blocks only partial irrigation can be given from two local irrigation projects, namely Lilazam Scheme in Gaya and Badna Dam in Bhagalpur. The State proposed to enlarge the small order of irrigation on the two local schemes by undertaking construction of percolation tanks. These would have only assured lift irrigation sources. The fourth block is of 25,000 acres and is located in the district of Purnea. The entire block lies in the command of the Araria Branch Canal of the Eastern Kosi Main Canal System and will receive irrigation after completion of the major Kosi Project. This and the other three blocks are presently occupied by private cultivators. For setting

up a State Farm land, acquisition on a large scale will have to be resorted to. For this and other reasons stated above we do not recommend any of the four blocks in Bihar for the purpose in view.

(3) **Orissa :** One block of 10,000 acres in Nawapura Sub-division of Orissa was suggested. The land is all State owned, but it does not answer the essential requirements laid down. Apart from lack of irrigation facilities and satisfactory means of communication, there is thick growth of jungle and here and there stony patches are found in the area. This very site was offered by the State Government when similar enquiries had been made from the States early in 1956. The Site Selection Committee then constituted to examine the various sites did not approve of it for these very reasons. We endorse the finding of the earlier Committee and do not recommend it.

(4) **Punjab :** A block of 30,000 acres forming part of the land under the State Government Livestock Farm, Hissar was offered. The offer made was subject to the condition that if a Farm were to be set up there, it would be run by the State Government and that the present character of the Farm as a Livestock Breading Farm, would be maintained. This implied that emphasis would continue to be laid on fodder crops in preference to cereals. While we do recognise that the area is quite suitable from all points of view, we do not support the idea of setting up a State Farm there in view of the conditions imposed by the State Government. The State Farms, we have in view are primarily intended for raising cereals.

(5) **Mysore** : Four blocks of 10,000 acres each in Raichur District where irrigation from Tungbhadra is planned were offered with the suggestion that they be considered for establishment of mechanised farms on co-operative lines. All this land is owned by private cultivators. Large-scale acquisition of land will be necessary and heavy sums may have to be paid towards payment of compensation to owners. This process of land acquisition would be time consuming and land will not be available for immediate increase in food production. We do not, therefore, recommend any of these four blocks for the purpose in view. The possibility of locating a suitable block in Periyapatna-Hunsur Talukas of Mysore District was also explored. On examination of the data placed before us, we found that a major portion of this area is under forest. The clearance of forest will be costly and take a long time to complete. As it did not serve our objective, the proposal was dropped.

(6) **Madhya Pradesh** : Two tentative sites, one in Morena district and the other in Guna district had been suggested. Both were subsequently withdrawn. Lately, the State Government have located a block in Betul which has been suggested for consideration. Even before this offer came, the Committee had examined it with the help of data received from the State Government by the Wastelands Reclamation and Surveys Committee. This area does not have any irrigation arrangement. Construction of new works would be time consuming and may not serve the entire area. Also, the topography of the areas is uneven and is cut up at various places by numerous nalas. Reclamation and levelling of land is likely to be costly. We do not, therefore, recommend this area for setting up of large mechanised farm.

(7) **Andhra Pradesh :** Two blocks, one in Godavari North Canal Project (Kadam) area and the other in Emmiganur Block under the Tungabhadra Canal were proposed. The block in Kadam area is of 29,000 acres while the other are in the command of Tungbhadra Canal is of 28,000 acres. The particulars furnished originally by the State Government did not give complete information. It had to be called for and as the State Government took long to furnish the desired information, Shri Mahavir Prasad, Irrigation Adviser had to go to Hyderabad towards the close of June, 1960. He had detailed discussions with the concerned Irrigation Engineers and other officers of the State Government. Both the blocks suggested are in the command of Irrigation Projects that were undertaken recently. Local people have been anxiously looking forward to receiving benefits from new irrigation works that are in hand and it is doubtful if the people of the area would willingly hand over their lands for setting up of large State Farms. (The bulk of the land in both the sites is under private ownership at present). Land acquisition is thus likely to be unpopular in both the areas. Even if special procedures are laid down for land acquisition, the process of land acquisition will at least take one year to complete. The cost of dry land in both the blocks ranges from Rs. 400 to Rs. 600 per acre and that of wet land is about Rs. 1,000 per acre. Besides, about 10 per cent of the area is stated to be under scrub jungle, the reclamation of which may cost about Rs. 150 per acre. In view of the rolling topography of the blocks some land levelling work will also be necessary adding to the cost of land development. Irrigation arrangements contemplated for these two areas are mainly for single crop cultivation. For double cropping under mechanised mode of cultivation additional water supplies will have to be arranged. The present intensity of the irrigation system is low round about 30 per cent and to fully meet the irrigation requirements of mechanised farming complete overhaul of the irrigation system would be necessary and it may not be possible to attain the required percentage of intensity at the farm unless irrigation commitments in other parts of the projects command are withdrawn or drastically curtailed. Predominance of black-cotton soil in the two areas is yet another handicap to intensive mechanised cultivation. Much as the Committee wished to locate at least one

large State Mechanised Farm in the South, we cannot recommend any of the two areas for the purpose.

(8) **Rajasthan**: Initially the State Government recommended two blocks of land in the command of the Rajasthan Canal. Later they increased the number of blocks to four—all these are in the command of the Rajasthan Canal. These four blocks occupy different places in the commanded area of the Rajasthan Canal and their distance from the main Branch of the Canal varies. One of these blocks measuring 30,854 areas in contiguous to the Suratgarh Farm. Possibilities of reaching Rajasthan Canal water to the different sites depend upon the progress of construction on Rajasthan Canal. Looking to the progress of work hitherto made on the project, the State Government have informed us that non-perennial irrigation supplies can be made available to the first site contiguous to the Suratgarh Farm from 1962 onwards. The non-perennial supplies will be start from middle of June and continue till middle of September each year. The supplies will be plentiful during July and August and any quantity of water can be made available during these two months. There is little hope of continuing the non-perennial supplies during the month of October. In fact, water supplies even in the latter half of September would be satisfactory only once in two years. The Rajasthan Canal is not likely to get perennial supplies from its source earlier than 1970. Till then farming under non-perennial irrigation is possible. The State Government who were approached to arrange for perennial supplies of about 20 cusecs from Gang Canal, regretted their inability to do so. A supply of 20 cusecs was thought to be sufficient for 5,000 acres which could be sown with wheat. The only possibility to provide some perennial irrigation to the new Farm is to divert the existing supply of 15 cusecs made available to the Suratgarh Farm from Gang Canal. This was given to the Suratgarh Farm in 1958 on the expenses understanding that it would be withdrawn after the Bhakra Canal becomes fully perennial towards the close of 1962. This, in our opinion, would be desirable, especially as Rajasthan Government representatives have agreed to give an additional 15 cusecs supply for Suratgarh Farm from Bhakra System. It would involve construction of a five to six mile long channel at a cost of about Rs. 1.50 lakhs which will have to be borne by the Government of India. The maintenance will be taken care of by the State Government.

The land is more or less even excluding the areas under sand dunes which account for a total area of about 8,000 acres and these are spread all over the Farm area. The soil is mostly light-loam. Out of 30,854 acres an area of about 17,000 acres is already under cultivation. A major portion of these 17,000 acres is let out an annual temporary leases. The cultivated area will have to be acquired on payment of compensation to the owners/lessees to the tune of Rs. 1.70 lakhs (Rs. 1.03 lakhs towards cost of *abadi*, tanks, wells, etc. and Rs. 0.67 lakhs towards cost of displacement). The tenants/lessees displaced from the occupied area will be allotted undeveloped land elsewhere in the same area. The compensation payable to them will have to be met by the Government of India, as was done in the case of land, etc., acquired for Suratgarh Farm. Regarding rental charges the rafes settled for Suratgarh Farm may be adoped with the only difference that these be assessed on 17,000 acres initially. For the balance area the charges may be paid according as it is developed from year to year.

Considering the relative merits of the site contiguous to the Suratgarh Farm, the Committee recommend it for establishment of another Central Mechanised Farm which will need to be developed according to a phased programme spread over a number of years depending upon the availability of perennial and non-perennial water. In the initial stages, the new Farm can be run as an extension of the existing Suratgarh Farm and it should not be necessary to employ any large additional managerial staff for it. Ony operational and ministerial staff to the extent necessary will have to be recruited. Nor will it be necessary to have any separate Base Workshop there, because the one at Suratgarh Farm can meet the requirements of the new Farm. The existing communicational facilities serving the farm area will need to be developed and expanded. An approach road of about three miles in length will be required to connect the Farm with the *pucca* Anoopgarh—Sarupsar road passing through Jetsar. This will involve an expenditure of Rs. 1.8 lakhs which will be met by the Government of Rajasthan. Besides, the existing Railway Station at Jetsar, one new Railway Station at a suitable point between Jetsar and Mohangarh should be got built through the Railway Board in due course. The existing Jetsar Railway Station will need to be expanded to permit of extra goods booking facilities. This too should be arranged for by the Railway Board. It will also be necessary to have a net-work of *pucca* roads within the Farm area to facilitate movement of machinery and produce. *Pucca* roads in the new farm as against the *Kutcha* ones in the Suratgarh Farm will in the long run prove to be economical, as wear and tear of motor vehicles, etc. will be less. Also, maintenance of *pucca* roads will be less expensive. The total length of internal roads within the Farm area will be about 22 miles and will cost roughly Rs, 12.00 lakhs. Two main *pucca* roads in Suratgarh Farm are made by Rajasthan Government under their normal programme of constructing works in the area. Till perennial supplies become available it will be necessary to put up two to three tubewells to supply drinking water to the employees of the farm and labour force.

(9) **Madras, Uttar Pradesh, West Bengal and Kerala:** The replies received from the States of Madras, Uttar Pradesh, West Bengal and Kerala were all in the negative, They have no suitable blocks of the required size to recommend. The Committee guided by its desire to locate big farms in different parts of county made a fresh approach to the Government of Uttar Pradeth to specially comb their districts of Pilibhit and Bahraich to locate one or two suitable blocks of the required size. The Government of Uttar Pradesh did undertake a survey of the possible areas in the two districts mentioned above, but the result was not fruitful. The possibility of utilising a large block of land in Pannagarh in West Bengal which was declared surplus to the requirements of the Ministry of Defence some years back was considered. Enquiries made from the Ministry of Defence revealed that the said block of land was no longer available.

Having made a recommendation for establishment of one new farm on the site contiguous to Suratgarh, we now proceed in the next Chapter to submit specific proposals for the proposed farm.

Suggestions For The New Farm

The tract which we have recommended for the establishment of another Central Mechanised Farm extends over two tehsils, namely, Anoopgarh and Raisinghnagar of Sri Ganganagar District. The area is very sparsely populated and the new *Abadis* that have sprung up in the area have hardly any title to be called villages. No civic amenities are available there. It will not be incorrect to treat the entire area as undeveloped. For proper layout and development of the farm area consistent with the requirements of large-scale mechanised farming, a proper plan has to be thought of and implemented in stages. Even the few facilities that are available in Suratgarh do not exist in this area and communications are particularly non-existent.

The Government of Rajasthan are willing to give land for the new Farm on the some terms and conditions as have been proposed in the case of land taken over for the Suratgarh Farm. The land taken over for the Suratgarh Farm will be on lease for a period of 15 years with a provision for renewal of the lease for another 15 years at the option of the lessee. No separate lease money is to be paid, but only land revenue, Malkhana, etc., are to be recovered at the approved rates. The total amount payable on this account will be about Rs. 1,10,000, so long as the Bhakra Canal continues to be non-perennial and will be increased to about Rs. 1,80,000, when the canal becomes perennial. In other words the maximum rent payable will be about Rs. six per acre per annum. Compared to the rent charges from temporary lessees, the rent settled in the case of Suratgarh Farm land is markedly less. As in the case of Suratgarh Farm we do not recommend outright purchase of land for the new Farm. If the lands were to be purchased outright the initial investment on the scheme will increase manifold and it will not be worthwhile to do so. The price of land in the area is stated to vary from Rs. 100 to Rs. 300 per acre. The purchase of land alone will, therefore, involve an expenditure of Rs. 100 lakhs. With a view to encouraging the State Government to take over such farms at some stage or the other say after 30 years, it would be preferable if the Central Government take over the land on lease basis rather than go in for outright purchase. We, therefore, recommend that the land for the new Farm should be taken on lease for a period of 30 years in the first instance. The period of lease may be extended in the light of conditions then obtaining.

The land development and cultivation programme at the new Farm has necessarily to be phased over a number of years. On the basis of perennial supplies for 2,500 acres to be diverted from the Suratgarh Farm and non-perennial supplies to be made available from Rajasthan Canal it should be possible to tackle an area of 10,000 acres in the first year of operation of the Farm and in the second year area can be increased to 12,500 acres. A tentative cropping programme for the first two years is indicated in Appendix IV. It may be modified after results of detailed soil analysis, which we strongly recommend, are made known. This may also have to be adjusted to suit the quantum of non-perennial irrigation, especially during the Rabi season. A tentative cropping pattern for the entire cultivable area under perennial irrigation is also outlined in Appendix IV. The proposed cropping pattern will make for maximum use of the machinery and irrigation supplies. In order to make full use of the perennial supply during the months of March, April and May, a small percentage of the area has been suggested for cash crops like Cotton and Sugarcane right from the second year onwards. On the basis of the assurances given by the State Government, it should be possible to start cultivation operations in June, 1962.

Good deal of initial planning work will have to be done before actual farming operations could start in kharif, 1962, apart from construction of essential buildings. Keeping this in view, we recommend that a Project Officer in Class I Senior Scale of pay with nucleus staff should be appointed as early as possible and in any case not later than March, 1961. It would be of great advantage if the Project Officer could be one having practical experience of working in large mechanised farms with knowledge of local conditions.

The requirements of machinery and equipment for the new farm have to be related to the proposed cropping patterns and the nature of land development work required to be done in the area. Keeping in view these considerations and the generally accepted formula of one H.P. for five acres cultivation, the requirement of machinery and equipment for the new farm has been drawn and details are given in Appendix V. The items of machinery which can be transferred from the existing stock of machinery from the Suratgarh Farm are also given. The cost of the equipment has been estimated on the basis of the prices quoted for similar machinery obtained or received as gift for the Central Mechanised Farm, Suratgarh. At the new farm it would be a good idea to obtain similar machinery because it would mean an over all economy in spares and flexibility in exchange of equipment available at the existing farm and that proposed to be purchased for the new farm. Also the Base Workshop being completed at Suratgarh will be able to undertake major overhaul and repairs of this type of equipment. The total cost of the machinery and equipment required to be purchased for the new farm will be Rs. 66 lakhs in round figures. In course of time it will be necessary to replace items of machinery going out of use due to normal wear and tear for which necessary provision has to be made at the appropriate time.

The building programme for the new farm will require to be phased in keeping with its over-all development programme. The building programme suggested for the new farm along with its phasing is outlined in Appendix VI. Buildings shown in first year should be ready by April, 1962. In according priorities to various works for actual execution the non-residential buildings have been assigned a higher place as compared to the residential ones. The total outlay on the building programme for the new farm will be of the order of Rs. 130.50 lakhs inclusive of the departmental charges which have been worked out at 16 per cent of the total outlay on works. Excluding the departmental charges the total outlay on residential component of the building programme works out to Rs. 51.39 lakhs and that on the non-residential component to Rs. 60.90 lakhs. The plinth areas proposed for various types of residential quarters are those based on the latest austerity standard fixed by the Government of India for provision of houses in various projects in the public sector. These differ slightly from those adopted for similar or comparable types of quarters built at Suratgarh. Looking to the extreme climatic conditions in this sandy region of Rajasthan we feel that the plinth area viz. 400 sq. ft. as against 475 sq. ft. adopted earlier for the pay group of Rs. 60-150 is considered to be rather low. We suggest that it may be raised a little so that the living accommodation may be enough for a family of an average size. Quite a sizeable number of operational and ministerial staff will be entitled to this type of quarters, because the type-wise distribution of quarters has been done on the basis of minimum of the pay scale. The same procedure was adopted while determining the types of quarters for various pay scales obtaining at Central Mechanised Farm, Suratgarh.

The building programme recommended by us provides for a net-work of *pucca* roads covering a length of 22 miles which would cost Rs. 12 lakhs. We consider it might be possible to bring about some appreciable saving in the outlay on internal communications by substituting *pucca* roads by rail-track of 1½ ft. width. In that case it will be necessary to purchase some six or seven trolleys with two Diesel-driven Locomotives which would in turn replace some transport vehicles. We recommend that the economics of laying a rail-track *vis-a-vis pucca* roads may be examined in detail in consultation with the experts of the Railway Board.

The C.P.W.D., in our opinion, has taken a long time in execution of the various works at the Central Mechanised Farm, Suratgarh. This is because C.P.W.D. did not have any organisation in the area. On the other hand Rajasthan Canal Administration are now setting up an organisation. We therefore, recommend that the construction of buildings, roads, etc., in the new farm be entrusted to the Rajasthan Canal Project Administration who have agreed to undertake it on the basis of the State P.W.D. (B.&R.) Rules. The Project Administration may be paid the usual departmental charges which should not exceed departmental charges of the C.P.W.D.

The requirements of staff for the new farm as shown in Appendix VII are based on the phased cultivation programme outlined in Appendix IV. Further, they generally conform to the organisational set-up obtaining in the Central Mechanised Farm, Suratgarh. In consideration of the paramount need for economy without impairing general efficiency, slight changes have been made at the Officers' level. In regard to the operational staff we would strongly recommend a training programme being undertaken at Suratgarh in agricultural operations of Rabi 1961 so that trained personnel are available for the new farm when operations are started in June 1962. This would mean appointment of a nucleus operational staff some months in advances of June, 1962.

A rough idea of the financial results expected at the new farm under (i) with partial perennial irrigation and (ii) with perennial irrigation could be had from the statistics furnished in Appendix VIII. It is expected that the farm will start yielding profits right from the close of the first year of its working. The margin of profit is not likely to increase so long as the non-perennial supplies continue. It will go up appreciably when perennial supplies become available.

To sum up, from among the proposals received from the States not many blocks have the necessary facilities. For this reason the Committee has not been able to suggest many sites. It sees immediate prospects of starting farms in the State of Rajasthan. This does not, however, mean that all efforts to locate such blocks in other parts of the country, especially in the South, should not be encouraged. It is also our impression that States have not yet fully appreciated the advantages of having large-sized State mechanised farms and due attention and thought has not been devoted to this important matter by them. A further effort should be made after new areas of wastelands are opened up on completion of major irrigation projects that may be launched in the Third Five-Year Plan.

We recommended that a new farm may be set up in the area proposed in the Anupgarh and Raisinghnagar Tehsils of Sri Ganganagar district in Rajasthan. This recommendation of ours is based on such important considerations as (i) ready availability of land involving little of heavy reclamation work, (ii) immediate prospects of supply of irrigation and (iii) proximity of the site to the Central Mechanised Farm, Suratgarh. The sites suggested in other States do not compare favourably with the one recommended by us, if the three important considerations mentioned above are taken into account.

Appendix II

Details Of Running Expenses Of The Central Mechanised Farm Suratgarh On Full Development

		Rs. (in lakhs)
1.	Pay and Allowance of Officers and Staff	12.00
2.	Labour	6.00
3.	Petrol, Oil and Lubricant	6.00
4.	Spare parts	3.00
5.	General Stores	1.60
6.	Seeds	2.00
7.	Manure and Insecticides	1.00
8.	Land Revenue	1.80
9.	Gunny Bags	0.50
10.	Customs Duty	0.70
11.	Miscellaneous Office Contingency	1.00
	Total	35.60

Appendix IV

Cropping Programme For The Proposed Mechanised Farm At Jetsar And Its Estimated Income

Conditions

1. Seasonal supplies of irrigation will be available from middle of June to middle of September.
2. 15 cusecs of perennial supply of irrigation will be available from the very first year.

First Period--10,000 Acres

Crops under Seasonal			Crops under Perennial			
Kharif		Rabi	Kharif		Rabi	
	ac			ac		ac
Bajra	2500	—	Bajra	500	Mustard	1500
E. Maixe	1000	—	E. Paddy	500	Gram	500
E. Paddy	500	—			Wheat	2000
Til, Ground-nut and Guar for seed	1000	—				
	5000			1000		4000

Income

		Area	Yield per acre	Total Yield in mds.	Rate per mound	Amount Rs.
1	2	3	4	5	6	7
(i) Kharif Crops						
1.	Bajra	3,000	10	30,000	14/-	4,20,000
2.	E. Maize	1,000	15	15,000	12/-	1,80,000
3.	E. Paddy	1,000	15	15,000	12/-	1,80,000
4.	Til, Ground-nut and Guar for seed	1,000	5—10	5,000(—) 10,000(—)	30/-(—) 15/-(—)	1,50,000
		6,000				9,30,000

1	2	3	4	5	6	7
(ii)	**Kharif Fodder**					
1.	Bajra Karbi	3,000	30	90,000	1/-	90,000
2.	Maize Karbi	1,000	20	20,000	1/-	20,000
3.	Paddy Straw	1,000	15	15,000	0.50	7,500
						1,17,500
(iii)	**Rabi Crops**					
1.	Mustard	1,500	8	12,000	25/-	3,00,000
2.	Gram	500	10	5,000	12/-	60,000
3.	Wheat	2,000	15	30,000	15/-	4,50,000
						8,10,000
					Total Income Rs.	18,57,500

Second And Subsequent Years—12,500 Acres

Seasonal				Perennial			
Kharif		Rabi	Kharif			Rabi	
	ac.				ac.		ac.
1. Bajra	3000	—	1.	Sugarcane	200	Mustard	1500
2. E. Maize	1000	—	2.	Cotton	300	Gram	500
3. E. Paddy	1000	—	3.	Bajra	500	Wheat	2000
4. Til, Ground-nut and Guar for Seed	1000	—	4.	Green manuring	1000		
			5.	E. Paddy	500		
	6000				2500		4000

Income

		Area	Yield per ac. Mds.	Total Yield in Mds.	Rate per Mds.	Amount	
1	2	3	4	5	6	7	8
(i)	**Kharif Crops**						
1.	Bajra	3500	10	35,000	14/-	4,90,000	
2.	E. Maize	1000	15	15,000	12/-	1,80,000	
3.	E. Paddy	1500	15	22,500	12/-	2,70,000	
4.	Til, Ground-nut and Guar for Seed	1000	5/10	5000/ 10000	30/- 15/-	1.50,000	
5.	Sugarcane	200	800	1,60,000	1/50	2,40,000	
6.	Cotton	300	8	2,400	35/-	84,000	
							14,14,000
(ii)	**Kharif Fodder**						
1.	Bajra Karbi	3500	30	1,05,000	1/-	1,05,000	
2.	Maize Karbi	1000	20	20,000	1/-	20,000	
3.	Paddy Straw	1500	15	22,500	0.50	11,250	
							1,36,250

1	2	3	4	5	6	7	8
(iii)	**Rabi Crops**						
1.	Mustard	1500	8	12,000	25/-	3,00,000	
2.	Gram	500	10	5,000	12/-	60,000	
3,	Wheat	2000	15	30,000	15/-	4,50,000	
							8,10,000
						Total Income	23,60,250

Eleventh Year—21,000 Acres

Condition

Perennial supplies of irrigation will be available for the whole Farm area.

Karif		Rabi		Total
	Acres		Acres	Acres
1. Bajra	1000	1. Wheat	10,000	
2. Maize	1000	2. Gram	500	
3. Paddy	1000	3. Mustard & Toria	3,500	
4. Cotton	500			
5. Sugarcane	500			
6. Green Manuring	3000			
	7000		14,000	21,000

Income

		Area Ac.	Yield Mds.	Total yield Mds.	Rate per Mds.	Amount Rs.	Total Rs.
(i)	**Kharif Crops**						
1.	Bajra	1000	15	15,000	14/-	2,10,000	
2.	Maize	1000	20	20,000	12/-	2,40.000	
3.	Paddy	1000	20	20,000	15/-	3,00,000	
4.	Cotton	500	8	4,000	35/-	1,40,000	
5.	Sugarcane	500	650	3,25,000	1/50	4,87,500	
	(newly planted—800 mds. per acre)						
	Ratoon —500 mds. per acre)						13,77,500
(ii)	**Kharif Fodder**						
1.	Bajra Karbi	1000	40	40,000	1/-	40,000	
2.	Maize Karbi	1000	25	25,000	1/-	25,000	
3.	Paddy Straw	1000	20	20,000	0.50	10,000	
							75,000
(iii)	**Rabi Crops**						
1.	Wheat	10,000	20	2,00,000	15/-	30.00,000	
2.	Gram	500	15	7,500	12/-	90,000	
3.	Mustard & Toria	3,500	12	42,000	25/-	10,50,000	
							41,40,000
						Grand Total	55,92,500

Appendix V

Phased Requirement Of Machinery

Sl. No.	Description of Machinery	Unit Price	First year		Second year		Third to 10th year		11th year		Total by the end of 10th year	Remarks
			No.	Amount	No.	Amount	No.	Amount	No.	Amount		
1	2	3	4	5	6	7	8	9	10	11	12	13
		Rs.		Rs.		Rs.		Rs.		Rs.		
1.	Tractor chain Type S-80 80 H.P.	50,000	6	3,00,000	—	—	—	—	—	—	6	6 Nos. S-80 tractors will be transferred from CMF, Suratgarh in first year.
2.	Tractor Chain Type DT-54 54 H.P.	30,000	5	1,50,000	—	—	—	—	—	—	5	5 Nos. —Do—
3.	Tractor Wheel Type (4-wheel drive) 35 drawbar H.P.	14,000	27	3,78,000	11	1,54,000	—	—	39	5,46,000	77	
4.	Motor Grader	38,000	1	38,000	—	—	—	—	—	—	1	
5.	Bowzer for transporting diesel	60,675	3	1,82,025	—	—	—	—	2	1,21,350	5	
6.	Water tankers app. 800 Glns. capacity	6,500	3	19,500	—	—	—	—	2	13,000	5	
7.	Mobile Crane 15-ton capacity	1,20,000	1	1,20,000	—	—	—	—	—	—	1	
8.	Trucks (a) 2½-three ton capacity	24,000	5	1,20,000	2	48,000	—	—	3	72,000	10	
	(b) five ton capacity	35,000	4	1,40,000	1	35,000	—	—	5	1,75,000	10	
9.	Light Vehicles (a) Jeep	14,000	3	42,000	2	28,000	—	—	2	28,000	7	
	(b) Station Wagon	18,000	1	18,000	—	—	—	—	1	18,000	2	
10.	Low bed diesel tractor trailor 25-ton capacity	1,50,000	1	1,50,000	—	—	—	—	1	1,50,000	2	
11.	Trolly Five ton capacity	4,000	6	24,000	—	—	—	—	9	36,000	15	
12.	Workshop Equipment :											
	(i) Lathe	10,000	3	30,000	—	—	—	—	3	30,000	6	
	(ii) Drill	3,000	3	9,000	—	—	—	—	3	9,000	6	
	(iii) Generator diesel operated	20,000	3	60,000	—	—	—	—	—	—	3	
	(iv) Compressor diesel	8,000	1	8,000	—	—	—	—	5	40,000	6	Electrically fitted after 10 years

1	2	3	4	5	6	7	8	9	10	11	12	13
	(v) Electric welding set	7,000	3	21,000	—	—	—	—	3	21,000	6	
	(vi) Gas welding set	2,000	3	6,000	—	—	—	—	3	6,000	6	
	(vii) Blacksmith-cum-carpenter equipment set	3,500	4	14,000	—	—	—	—	4	14,000	8	
	(viii) Battery charger	2,000	1	2,000	—	—	—	—	5	10,000	6	
	(ix) Tools grinding machine	1,000	3	3,000	—	—	—	—	3	3,000	6	
	(x) Valve lapping machine	3,250	1	3,250	—	—	—	—	—	—	1	
	(xi) Electric equipment testing stand	3,700	1	3,700	—	—	—	—	—	—	1	
	(xii) Harvester combine repair and tools	2,100	1	2,100	—	—	—	—	1	2,100	2	
	(xiii) Oil pump testing stand	6,700	1	6,700	—	—	—	—	—	—	1	
	(xiv) Stand for equalising fans	2,300	1	2,300	—	—	—	—	—	—	1	
	(xv) Complete set of tools for assembling and dismantling of tractors	2,500	4	10,000	—	—	—	—	4	10,000	8	
	(xvi) Set of tools for machanics	200	14	2,800	—	—	—	—	16	3,200	30	
	(xvii) Set of tools for valve seat cutting and grinding	4,000	1	4,000	—	—	—	—	—	—	1	
	(xviii) Spring testing machine	400	1	400	—	—	—	—	—	—	1	
	(xix) Injector testing machine	150	1	150	—	—	—	—	—	—	1	
	(xx) High pressure pump for washing machinery	1,100	3	3,300	—	—	—	—	3	3,300	6	
	(xxi) Hand Crane	4,000	3	12,000	—	—	—	—	2	8,000	5	(will be manufactured in CMF, Suratgarh workshop).
	(xxii) Radiator testing stand	4,300	1	4,300	—	—	—	—	—	—	1	
	(xxiii) 100-ton hydraulic press	15,800	1	15,800	—	—	—	—	—	—	1	
	(xxiv) 20-ton hydraulic press	5,000	1	5,000	—	—	—	—	—	—	1	
	(xxv) Vehicle Servicing Station :											
	(a) Hydraulic lift	10,000	1	10,000	—	—	—	—	—	—	1	
	(b) Compressor	2,000	1	2,000	—	—	—	—	—	—	1	
	(c) High pressure pump	1,100	1	1,100	—	—	—	—	—	—	1	
	(d) Lubricating unit	600	1	600	—	—	—	—	—	—	1	
	Agriculture Machinery :											
	(i) Dozer attachment	7,000	3	21,000	—	—	—	—	2	14,000	5	
	(ii) Ditcher attachment	23,514	2	47,028	—	—	—	—	1	23,514	3	
	(iii) Scraper tractor driven 10 cyds. cap.	10,000	1	10,000	—	—	—	—	—	—	1	

1	2	3	4	5	6	7	8	9	10	11	12	13
(iv)	Plow M.B. 4 bottom hydraulically operated	4,000	5	20,000	—	—	—	—	—	—	5	
(v)	Plow M.B. 3 bottom hydraulically operated	3,000	18	54,000	—	—	—	—	7	21,000	25	
(vi)	Disc. plow 3 Disc.	4,000	10	40,000	—	—	—	—	15	60,000	25	
(vii)	Offset harrow	3,500	24	84,000	8	28,000	—	—	28	98,000	60	
(viii)	Cultivator for inter-cultivation	2,200	3	6,600	—	—	—	—	2	4,400	5	
(ix)	Maize planter	1,850	3	5,550	—	—	—	—	—	—	3	
(x)	Cotton planter	2,900	—	—	1	2,900	—	—	2	5,800	3	
(xi)	Seed drills knife type single row planting	3,500	6	21,000	—	—	—	—	9	31,500	15	(In first year 6 can be spared from Suratgarh.)
(xii)	Seed drill disc type single row planting	3,500	15	52,500	—	—	—	—	10	35,000	25	15 Nos. do.
(xiii)	Zigzag harrow	500	15	7,500	—	—	—	—	15	7,500	30	Can be spared from Suratgarh.
(xiv)	Roller or clod crusher	1,500	6	9,000	—	—	—	—	9	13,500	15	In first year 6 sets can be spared from Suratgarh.
(xv)	Ridgers	2,500	—	—	2	5,000	—	—	3	7,500	5	
(xvi)	Land levellors	2,500	6	15,000	—	—	—	—	4	10,000	10	
(xvii)	Hole angers	1,500	1	1,500	—	—	—	—	1	1,500	2	
(xviii)	Harvester combine self propelled diesel drives											
	(a) Big	50,000	4	2,00,000	—	—	—	—	26	13,00,000	30	
	(b) Small	35,000	2	70,000	—	—	—	—	8	2,80,000	10	
(xix)	Cultivator model KP-4-M	3,000	9	27,000	—	—	—	—	11	33,000	20	Can be spared from Suratgarh.
(xx)	Root cutter	4,000	1	4,000	—	—	—	—	1	4,000	2	
(xxi)	Maize cob sheller & cob crusher set	6,000	2	12,000	—	—	—	—	—	—	2	
(xxii)	Winnowing machine	7,000	6	42,000	—	—	—	—	9	63,000	15	
(xxiii)	Wooden sohagas	100	24	2,400	8	800	—	—	28	2,800	60	
	Total	26,76,103		3,01,700						33,40,964		

1	2	3	4	5	6	7	8	9	10	11	12	13
	Railway freight custom duty and other clearing charges	1,23,897		8,300						1,49,036		
	Grand Total	28,00,000		3,10,000						34,90,000		

Total cost of machinery Rs. 66,00,000.

Appendix VI

Phased Requirement Of Non-Residential Buildings For Proposed Central Mechanised Farm At Jetsar (Rajasthan)

Sl. No.	Description of Building	Plinth area in sq. ft.	Unit cost of const-ruction	first year of construction *i.e.* 1961-62		Second year of construction *i.e.* 1962-63		11th year when the whole perennial supply is available		Remarks
				No. of Bldgs.	Amount	No. of Bldgs.	Amount	No. of Bldgs.	Amount	
1	2	3	4	5	6	7	8	9	10	11
					Rs.		Rs.		Rs.	
1.	Central running repair shop	6,500	1,65,000	1	1,65,000	—	—	—	—	
2.	Block repair shop	1,200	25,000	2	50,000	—	—	2	50,000	
3.	Service stations	964	27,000	1	27,000	—	—	4	1,08,000	
4.	Petrol oil and lubricant ramp	3,400	11,000	1	11,000	—	—	4	44,000	
5.	Combine and implement shed	2,500	50,000	3	1,50,000	—	—	2	1,00,000	
6.	Shed for seed drills and winnowing machine	2,000	40,000	3	1,20,000	—	—	2	80,000	
7.	Tractor and vehicle sheds	4,000	80,000	3	2,40,000	—	—	2	1,60,000	
8.	Central stores (mechanical)	4,048	80,000	1	80,000	—	—	—	—	
9.	Central stores (agriculture and plant protection)	3,000	60,000	1	60,000	—	—	—	—	
10.	Block stores	2,000	40,000	3	1,20,000	—	—	2	80,000	
11.	Grain godown and thrashing floor	9,000	1,80,000	3	5,40,000	—	—	3	5,40,000	
12.	Central office	5,000	85,000	1	85,000	—	—	—	—	
13.	Block office	500	8,500	3	25,500	—	—	2	17,000	
14.	Hospital for six beds	2,000	40,000	--	—	1	40,000	L.S.	40,000	(Addition to be made in existing hospital.)
15.	Post and telegraph office	500	10,000	—	—	1	10,000	L.S.	5,000	(Addition to be made in existing P.&T. office.)

1	2	3	4	5	6	7	8	9	10	11
16.	Primary school for centre	1,000	15,000	—	—	1	15,000	—	—	
17.	Primary school for block	500	7,500	—	—	1	7,500	2	15,000	
18.	Secondary school for centre	4,000	60,000	—	—	1	60,000	—	—	
19.	(a) Rest house	5,000	75,000	1	75,000	—	—	—	—	
	(b) Kitchen block and outhouses for above	1,500	25,000	1	25,000	—	—	—	—	
	(c) Furniture for rest house	L.S.	10,000	L.S.	10,000	—	—	—	—	
20.	(a) Field hostel	2,000	40,000	—	—	1	40,000	—	—	
	(b) Furniture for above	L.S.	5,000	—	—	L.S.	5,000	—	—	
21.	Community centre	500	10,000	2	20,000	—	—	2	20,000	
22.	Labour sheds	600	7,200	10	72,000	5	36,000	10	72,000	
23.	Shops sheds with residential accommodation	400	6,000	8	48,000	8	48,000	4	24,000	
24.	Pucca roads in centre and blocks	per mile	60,000	3 miles	1,80,000	—	—	2 miles	1,20,000	
25.	External services for lights	per block	50,000	2	1,00,000*	—	—	2	1,50,000	*50,000 for central block 25,000/- for each block.
26.	Sanitary disposal central block	L.S.	50,000	—	—	L.S.	50,000	—	—	
27.	Sanitary disposal other blocks	L.S.	30,000	—	—	2	60,000	2	60,000	
28.	Drainage system	L.S.	10,000	—	—	1	10,000	L.S. 2	20,000	
29.	Water supply	L.S.	1,50,000	—	1,50,000	—	—	L.S.	50,000**	**In 2 blocks.
30.	Tubewells	L.S.	30,000	2	60,000*	3	60,000	—	—	*3 trial boring @ 10,000 each of which one will be successful and cost of pump and engine 30,000 each year.
31.	Farm minor for 15 Cs. supply	L.S.	1,50,000	L.S.	1,50,000	—	—	—	—	
32.	External roads	per mile	60,000	3 miles	1,80,000	—	—	20 miles	12,00,000	
	Total				27,43,500		4,41,500		29,05,000	Total—60,90,000.

N.B. : Jetsar Farm will take advantage of the Base Workshop at Suratgarh.

Phased Cost Of Residential Buildings For The Proposed Central Mechanised Farm at Jetsar (Rajasthan)

Sl. No.	Description of buildings	Plinth area in sq. ft.	Unit cost of construction	First year of construction		Second year of construction		11th year when the whole perennial area is available		Remarks
				No. of Bldgs.	Amount	No. of Bldgs.	Amount	No. of Bldgs.	Amount	
1	2	3	4	5	6	7	8	9	10	11
		sq. ft.								
1.	Type VI Qrs. above Rs. 1,500 p.m.	2100 +240 +225 for servant and garrage =2665	38,500	—	—	—	—	—	38,500	
2.	Type V Qrs. Rs. 751-1500 p.m.	1500	22,500	2	45,000	2	45,000	—	—	
3.	Type IV Qrs. 301-750 p.m.	900	13,500	10	1,35,000	—	—	5	67,500	
4.	Type III Qrs. Rs. 151-300 p.m.	600	9,000	40	3,60,000	4	36,000	37	3,33,000	
5.	Type II Qrs. Rs. 150 p.m	400	6,000	128	7,68,000	29	1,74,000	136	10,56,000	
6.	Type I Qrs.	365	5,600	77	4,31,200	12	67,200	99	5,54,400	
7.	Internal Servicing (Electricity)	17,21,200	@12½%	—	2,17,400	@12½%	40,300	@12½%	2,56,200	
8.	Internal servicing (Sanitation)	17,21,200	@12½%	—	2,17,400	@12½%	40,300	@12½%	2,56,200	
	Total—Non-Commercial buildings				21,74,000		4,02,800		25,61,800	= 51,38,600
	Total Commercial buildings				27,43,500		4,41,500		29,05,000	= 60,90,000
	Grand Total				49,17,500		8,44,300		54,66,800	= 112,28,600
	Say				49,25,000		8,50,000		54,75,000	= 112.50,000
	Add departmental charges @16% of the total outlay									18,00,000
										1,30,50,000

Appendix VII

Phased Requirements Of Staff For Propose Central Mechanised Farm At Jetsar (Rajasthan)

Sl. No.	Particulars		First year	Second year	11th year	Total	Remarks
1	2		3	4	5	6	7
		Rs.					
1.	General Manager	1800	—	—	1	1	
2.	Agronomist	1100--1400	—	1	—	1	
3.	Agri. Officer	700—1250	1	—	—	1	
4.	Div. Engineer	700—1250	—	1	—	1	
5.	Asstt. Mech. Engineer	350—900	1	—	—	1	
6.	Asstt. Engr. (Irri.)	350—900	—	—	1	1	
7.	Farm Supdt.	400—950	—	—	1	1	
8.	Administrative Officer	620—900	1	—	—	1	
9.	Accounts Officer	590—900	1	—	—	1	(Rs. 590—900) if taken on deputation).
10.	Stores Officer	400—950	1	—	—	1	
Operational Staff							
11.	Senior Agri. Asstt.	325—575	4	—	2	6	1 for Plant Protection.
12.	Junior Agri. Asstt.	210—425	7	—	2	9	
13.	Chargeman	250—425	3	—	2	5	
14.	Asstt. Chargeman	168—256	- -	—	5	5	
15.	Mechanics	150—240	9	—	11	20	
16.	Tractor Drivers	140—175	27	9	30	66	
17.	Mate Grade I	110—131	10	2	10	22	
18.	Mate Grade II	70— 85	24	—	21	45	1 with each mechanic, 5 in each block, 4 for servicing and 1 for pump in each block.
19.	Grader Operator	150—240	1	—	—	1	
20.	Fieldman	110—180	26	6	52	84	In non-perennial one Fieldman for 400 acres and in perennial 1 for 250 acres.
21.	Agri. Mate	70— 85	26	6	52	84	
22.	Surveyor	150—240	1	—	—	1	
23.	Overseer	180—380	1	—	—	1	
Workshop Staff							
1.	Foreman	350—475	1	—	—	1	
2.	Asstt. Chargeman	168—256	1	—	1	2	
3.	Mechanics	150—240	4	—	4	8	
4.	Jr. Mechanics	140—175	1	—	1	2	
5.	Crane Operator	125—155	1	—	1	1	
6.	Mate II trainee	70 — 85	4	—	4	8	
7.	Electrician	125—155	2	1	3	6	
8.	Machineman	110—131	3	—	3	6	
9.	Welder	125—155	3	—	3	6	

1	2		3	4	5	6	7
10.	Generator attendent	110—131	3	—	3	6	
11.	Truck Driver	110—139	12	3	10	25	
12.	Jeep Driver	110—139	4	2	3	9	
13.	Painter	110—131	1	—	—	1	
14.	Upholsterer	140—175	1	—	—	1	
15.	Carpenter-cum-Blacksmith	110—131	3	—	3	6	
Office Staff							
1.	Office Supdt.	350—475	1	—	—	1	
2.	Head Clerk	210—320	—	1	1	2	
3.	Commercial Acctt.	270—575	1	—	—	1	
4.	Divisional Acctt.	270—575	—	—	—	1	For internal checking of Blocks accounts.
5.	Stenographer	130—330	1	1	2	4	
6.	Asstt. Statistician	210—320	1	—	—	1	
7.	Upper Div. Clerk	130—300	8	2	6	16	
8.	Lower Div. Clerk	110—180	26	5	15	46	
9.	Asstt. Storekeeper	205—280	1	—	1	2	
10.	Asstt. Storekeeper (Agri.)	205—280	1	—	—	1	
11.	Binkeeper	110—180	2	—	2	4	
12.	Fieldman store	110—180	3	—	2	5	
13.	Security Supervisor	250—380	1	—	—	1	
14.	Head Guard	75— 95	3	—	3	6	
15.	Guards	70— 85	18	6	18	42	
16.	Daftri	75— 85	1	—	1	2	
17.	Farrash	70— 85	1	—	—	1	

Appendix VIII
Financial Forecast For The New Farm At Jetsar

Sl. No.	Particulars	1st year Rs. in lakhs	2nd year Rs. in lakhs	11th year Rs. in lakhs	Remarks
		With partial perennial irrigation		With perennial irrigation	
1.	Pay of Officers and Staff	4.31	5.30	11.04	
2.	Other charges (labour, petrol, oil and lubricant and stores misc. etc.)	8.81	9.15	20.72	
3.	Depreciation on machinery equipment including custom duty freight @ 10 per cent	2.80	3.11	6.60	
4.	Depreciation on tents and tarpauline ponies @ 10 per cent	0.05	0.07	1.16	
5.	Depreciation on buildings @ 2—1/2 per cent	1.42	1.67	3.26	
6.	Interest on capital	3.19	3.65	7.04	
7.	Audit charges	0.04	0.05	0.08	
8.	Proportionate share of reclamation for 10,000 acres in first year, 12,500 acres in second year and 21,000 acres in 11th year	0.27	0.33	0.56	
		20.89	23.33	50.46	

1	2	3	4	5
	Less reclamation charges capitalised charged off in 15 years @ 40 per acre for 10,000 acres in first year, 2,500 acres in second year and 8,500 acres in 11th year.	4.00	1.00	3.40
		16.89	22.33	47.06
	Income from produce	18.57	23,60	55.92
	Net Project	1.68	1.27	8.86

N.B.: Net profit during the second year is less because non-perennial area has increased by 50 per cent while the perennial area has remained constant.

COMMITTEE ON RELIGIOUS AND MORAL INSTRUCTION, 1959—REPORT

New Delhi, Ministry of Education, 1960. 23p.

Chairman : Shri Sri Prakasa.
Members : Shri G.C. Chatterji; Shri A. A. A. Fyzee.
Secretary : Shri P. N. Kirpal.

APPOINTMENT

The Committee on Religious and Moral Instruction was appointed by the Ministry of Education, Government of India vide their letter No. F. 1-1-/59-SE1 dated, August 17, 1959 to make a detailed study of the entire question of religious and moral instruction in educational institutions.

TERMS OF REFERENCE

(i) To examine the desirability and feasibility of making specific provision for the teaching of moral and spiritual values in educational institutions.

(ii) If it is found desirable and feasible to make such provision.

(a) To define broadly the content of instruction at various stages of education; and

(b) To consider its place in the normal curriculum.

CONTENTS

Foreword; Report

RECOMMENDATIONS

The teaching of moral and spiritual values in educational institutions is desirable, and specific provision for doing so is feasible within certain limitations.

The content of such education in moral and spiritual value should include a comparative and sympathetic study of the lives and teachings of great religious leaders and at later stages, their ethical systems and philosophies. The inculcation of good manners, social service and true patriotism should be continuously stressed at all stages.

We regard it most important that in any educational scheme, the home should not be left out; and we suggest that through mass media such as leaflets, talks, radio and the cinema, and through voluntary organisations, the faults and drawbacks of our homes both in the matter of their physical orderliness and their psychological atmosphere, should be pointed out and instruction given as to how these can be removed. If this is done in an impersonal manner, it would not hurt anyone, but would draw the attention of the persons concerned to their own shortcomings, thus inducing and encouraging them to eradicate these.

It would be very desirable, as suggested by the University Education Commission, to start work everyday in all educational institutions with a few minutes of silent meditation either in the class room or in a common hall. There could be some sort of prayer also which need not be addressed to any deity or ask for any favour, but which may be in the nature of an exhortation for self-discipline and devotion to some ideal. Occasionally, in these Assembly Meetings inspiring passages from great literature, religious as well as secular, and pertaining to all important religions and cultures of the world, could be read with profit. Community singing of inspiring songs and hymns can be most effective at the school stage.

Suitable books should be prepared for all stages — from primary to university — which should describe briefly in a comparative and sympathetic manner the basic ideas of all religions as well as the essence of the lives and teachings of the great religious leaders, saints, mystics and philosophers. These books should be suitable to the various age groups in different classes of schools and colleges, and should be a common subject of study for all. Collections of poems and selected passages from Sanskrit, Persian, English and the regional languages should be made for the use of young people. These publications will give sound instruction and perhaps teach true wisdom; they will also tell young people what duties they owe to themselves and to others. Suitable books should be prepared for different stages of education which would help in the inculcation of patriotism and social service. These should particularly concentrate on deeds of heroism and self-sacrifice in the cause of the country and in the service of others. We attach very great importance to the preparation and production of such books. Authors should be selected with the greatest care and their manuscripts should be revised in consultation with eminent authorities. The entire programme of preparing and distributing such publications should be operated by a central agency set up under the auspices of the Union Ministry of Education.

In the course of extra-curricular activities, learned and experienced persons may be invited to deliver lectures on inter-religious understanding. Educational broadcasts and group discussions may be organised to stimulate interest in the study of moral and spiritual values.

Special stress should be laid on teaching good manners and promoting the virtues of reverence and courtesy which are badly needed in our society. Traditional ways of learning proper conduct from such teachers as the Muslim Maulvis in the north may be encouraged. An all out effort, in the nature of a crusade by all concerned is called for and nothing should be spared for the successful propagation of good manners and courtesy.

Some form of physical training should be compulsory at every stage. This can be graded from Clubs and Boy Scouts to Auxiliary and National Cadet Corps. Games and sports should be encouraged and the dignity of manual work and social service to the community should be taught. At present, very few students take to these activities. Our suggestion is that everyone should take up some activity of this kind and thus learn habits of cooperating with others, and imbibe the spirit of sportsmanship.

The following suggestions merely indicate a broad framework of instruction in moral and spiritual values at different stages of education :

Elementary Stage

(a) The school assembly should be held for a few minutes in the morning for group singing.

(b) Simple and interesting stories about the lives and teachings of prophets, saints and religious leaders should be included in the syllabus for language teaching.

(c) Wherever possible the interest of the child may also be aroused by the use of audio-visual material, especially good quality photographs, filmstrips and coloured reprints showing great works of art and architecture closely connected with the main living religions of the world; such material could be used in the teaching of Geography.

(d) In the school programme, two periods a week should be set aside for moral instruction. In these classes the teacher should relate interesting stories drawn from the great religions of the world and explain broadly their ethical teachings. Dogmas and rituals of religion should be excluded from moral instruction.

(e) Through school programme, the attitude of 'service' and the realisation that 'work is worship' should be developed in the child.

(f) All schemes of physical education and all forms of play in the school should contribute to the building of character and the inculcation of the spirit of true sportsmanship.

Secondary Stage

(a) The Morning Assembly should observe two minutes' silence followed by readings from the scriptures or great literature of the world or an appropriate address. Community singing should also be encouraged.

(b) The essential teachings of the great world religions should be studied as part of the curriculum pertaining to social studies and history. Simple texts and stories concerning different religions may be included in the teaching of languages and general reading.

(c) One hour a week should be assigned to moral instruction. The teacher should encourage the habit of discussion in his class. Apart from this regular class instruction, suitable speakers may be invited to address the students on moral and spiritual values. Joint celebrations may be organised on the occasion of important festivals of all religions. Knowledge and appreciation of religions other than one's own and respect for their Founders, should be encouraged in various ways including essay competitions and declamations.

(d) Organised social service during holidays and outside class hours should be an essential part of extra-curricular activities. Such service should teach the dignity or manual labour, love of humanity, patriotism and self-discipline. Participation in games and sports should be compulsory and physical education, including sex hygiene should be a normal part of school programme.

(e) Qualities of character and behaviour of students should form an essential part of the overall assessment of a student's performance at school.

University Stage

(a) Students should be encouraged to meet in groups

for silent meditation in the morning. These meetings should be supervised by the senior staff on a voluntary basis.

(b) A general study of different religions should be an essential part of the general education course in degree classes. In this connection, the following recommendations of the University Education Commission (Radhakrishnan Commission) are commended :

(i) That in the first year of the degree course, lives of the great religious and spiritual leaders like Gautama the Buddha, Confucious, Zoroaster, Socrates, Jesus, Samkara, Ramanuja, Madhava, Mohammad, Kabir, Nanak and Gandhi be taught.

(ii) That in the second year, some selections of a universalist character from the scriptures of the world be studied.

(iii) That in the third year, the central problems of philosophy of religion be considered. Standard works for such studies should be prepared carefully by specialists who have deep knowledge of and sympathy for the religious systems about which they write.

(c) A post-graduate course in Comparative Religion may be instituted. Due importance should be given to the study of the following subjects in the appropriate Honours and M. A. courses in the fields of Humanities and Social Science.

(i) Comparative Religion.

(ii) History of Religions.

(d) A fairly long period of social service should be introduced by all Universities. In the organisation and conduct of such service, considerable attention should be given to the learning and practice of moral and spiritual values.

From the broad suggestions outlined above, it is evident that we are in favour of a comparative and sympathetic study of religions and the teaching of their underlying philosophies and ethical codes. The Constitution provides that religious instruction given in institutions under any endowment or trust, should not be interfered with even when such institutions are helped by the State. We suggest that the sort of instruction that we have recommended should be imparted in all institutions, and if any special religion is particularly taught in some institutions, this should be in addition to what we have proposed. There is no question of conscience involved in this; the instruction proposed by us is essential for the building of character and the making of proper citizens, and by its very nature it cannot possible injure the susceptibilities of any religious group. We confidently hope that the effective implementation of the suggestions made above will create a proper atmosphere in our educational institutions, so that they may train not only technicians or professional experts but also humane and balanced citizens who can contribute to the hoppiness and well-being of their countrymen and of humanity as a whole.

COMMITTEE ON ARCHIVAL LEGISLATION, 1959—REPORT

New Delhi, National Archives of India, 1960. 143p.+ivp.

Chairman : Dr. Tara Chand.

Members : Dr. Raghubir Sinh; Dr. Bisheshwar Prasad; Shri Mohibbul Hasan; Dr. P.M. Joshi; Shri Fateh Singh; Shri R.S. Sarkar; Shri Nizamuddin Ahmed (replaced by Shri K.R. Ramachandran); Dr. S. Gopal.

Secretary : Shri K.D. Bhargava (replaced by Shri S. Roy).

Appointment

The Committee on Archival Legislation was constituted under the Government of India vide the Ministry of Education's Resolutions No. F. 6-13/59-A-10, dated August 19, 1959, to advise the Government regarding the desirability or otherwise of making a law applicable to the archives in India, to enquire into the working of National and State archives and to suggest means for improving their Administration.

Terms of Reference

(i) To examine (a) the condition of public records and the rules and instructions relating to the preservation, administration and maintenance thereof and public access thereto; (b) Dr. Raghubir Sinh's "The Historical Records (of national importance) Bill, 1957" and the opinions received thereon; and (c) the Destruction of Records Act of 1917 and the Antiquities (Export Control) Act, 1947, and other Acts bearing on archival problems; and

(2) To submit our recommendations on the following :

(i) How far in the interest of the proper preservation and administration of public records, it is desirable for the Government of India to exercise supervision over the State records or any part thereof, including the records of the former Princely States which are with various State Governments as a result of merger;

(ii) In order to exercise such supervision to consider what steps should be taken to declare the State records or parts thereof to be of national importance;

(iii) Whether the executive authority in respect of the records which may be declared to be of national importance should be exercised directly by the Government of India or left with the State Governments;

(iv) The feasibility of transferring "ancient and historical records other than those declared by Parliament to be of national importance" from the State List to the Concurrent List of the Seventh Schedule of the Constitution of India;

(v) Whether it is desirable to have a statutory enactment for the management and disposal of the records of the Central Government and such other public bodies which have an all-India character;

(vi) To consider the desirability of a plan for establishing zonal repositories for such records as may be declared of national importance and/or the records of the Government of India's agencies in each zone;

(vii) What further measure, if any, can be taken for effectively preventing the destruction or disposal of manuscripts and records in private custody which are considered to be of national importance.

CONTENTS

Introduction; The State of Public Records and Problems Relating to Them; The problems Relating to Coordination of Archival Work on an All-India Basis; The Need and Scope of Law Relating to Archives; The National Archives of India; The Problem of Private Archives; Summary of Recommendations; Appendices I to VI.

RECOMMENDATIONS

In making the recommendations embodied in the preceding sections whether they relate to the Union or the States our main object has been to ensure that—

(i) No public records which are of value remain uncared for;

(2) All public records which are fit for permanent preservation are regularly sorted out from those which are ephemeral and are retired regularly to the appropriate archival repositories, and then made available to the public for use in due course;

(3) Proper accommodation is provided for all records worthy of preservation by the Governments concerned;

(4) That only such steps are taken as are administratively and financially practicable.

While we believe that the responsibility for management, selection and transfer of records to the appropriate repositories must be shouldered by the creating Departments concerned, we are at the same time of the opinion that the archival departments whether of the Union or of the States should be made responsible for coordinating these activities, and should supervise on behalf of the Government as a whole the manner in which they are conducted by the department concerned.

We also consider that within the framework of the present law it is not possible to ensure the desiderata mentioned above and have pointed out that the need for supplying a statutory frame-work to what in our view are the fundamental principles underlying these desiderata. We have at the same time made it clear that the details are to be left to be worked out in the shape of statutory rules which may have the force of law. We have in this connection explained the reasons why it is not possible for the Union to take over the control or the administration of the State Archives either by law or by any other means, and to provide, consequently, for their adequate up-keep and to effect coordination in archival work all over the country. Although we believe it is not possible to enact a single Central Law that would provide both for the Union and the State Archives, we consider it at the same time very necessary that there should be a single Central body exercising coordinating functions in respect to public archives of all categories whether of the States or of the Union. Such a body in our view should be as fully representative as possible of both the Union and State Governments, and should act in an advisory capacity. As to private archives we do not consider that it is possible either for the Union Parliament or State Legislatures to enact laws affecting them. The grounds on which we have based our conclusion will be found fully explained in the body of the Report. We summarise below our main recommendations.

A. Legislation

(1) Procedure to be Followed : (a) As an interim and urgent measure there should be enacted separate Central and State laws governing respectively archives in the Union and in each of the States, the Central law being enacted by the Parliament and the State laws by the appropriate State Legislatures.

(b) An advisory body to be called the Indian Archival Council should likewise be constituted by Presidential Order (under Article 263 of the Constitution) to advise both the Union and the State Governments on all matters connected with the management, administration, preservation, disposal and public use of records and to coordinate the archival activities of the public offices in the country.

(c) Steps should also be taken to amend the Constitution by making a suitable entry in the Concurrent List to enable the framing of a single law that would take care of both the Union and the State Archives and make possible the setting up of a statutory advisory Council.

(2) **Scope and Contents of Laws:** The scope and the contents of the Central Law should be on the lines

indicated in paras 109-119. The law should specify the different classes of public records which it intends to cover and define clearly the responsibilities of the Central Government in respect of them. It should make Government responsible not only for their care, management disposal and preservation, but for facilitating their use by the public. It should ensure that all record-owning bodies make suitable arrangement for regular selection of those records which are to be permanently preserved and for the disposal of all papers which may on review be found to be ephemeral, and for retirement to the National Archives of all records which may be 25 years old, subject only to the restrictions mentioned in para 111. The law should also ensure that no records earlier than 1860 are destroyed on any account whatever. It should provide records being thrown open to the public in general after they become 40 years old.

The law should define the powers and responsibilities of the Director of Archives in respect of public records and should invest him with the legal custody of all records in his charge. It should authorise him to do whatever may be necessary or expedient for maintaining or improving the utility of the National Archives, and particularly to undertake, the tasks outlined in para 114, to coordinate, supervise and guide all operations in public bodies connected with the management, administration, preservation, selection, disposal and retirement of their records; and to eliminate ephemeral records in his custody subject to the restrictions mentioned in para 110, or any other restriction which the Government may think necessary.

The law should provide for special arrangement being made for the records of the Supreme Court, Parliament and the Statutory Bodies of all-India character mentioned in para 109 on the lines indicated in paras 117 and 118.

(3) **Rules to be Framed Under the Law :** There should be a provision for rules of business and other rules being framed within the frame-work of the Statute to enable the implementation of the purposes of the Statute. What these rules should include have been generally indicated in paras 120-122 and explained in greater details in paras 34-53, 59-61. More important among them will be specified below.

The State laws should be framed as far as possible on the model of the Central Law keeping in view the varying circumstances of the individual States concerned.

(4) **Indian Archival Council** : It should have 15 members representing each of the 15 States and 10 additional members to be nominated by the Central Government of which no less than four are to represent the Central Government including the Director of Archives, Government of India. The Education Minister (or any other Minister who may be in-charge of the Archives) should be the Chairman. Members should be appointed by the President for a term of five years. The Director of Archives is to act as the Secretary. The Council should have in addition the services of a whole-time Administrative Secretary. The Council should also have a Standing Committee of seven members selected from among the members of the Council. Its functions should be defined on the lines indicated in paras 132-136. Besides performing advisory, inspection and coordinating duties, it should also take charge of the work of the National Register of Private Archives. It should have a staff of its own and its expenses should be a charge on the Central Revenues. After the body has been constituted it will be necessary to terminate the Indian Historical Records Commission and all its adjuncts.

B. Special Points Relating to Union Archives

I. Management, Disposal, Preservation And Retirement Of Records

Special thought should be given to the problems in management, accommodation and preservation created by the present rapid growth in the volume of records and an all-out effort be made to ensure that public records of value are not swamped by ever-growing mass of trivial material.

A careful study should be made of the relation between the over-growth and the existing documentation and disposal practices, and these practices should be so improved as to make possible regular and easy separation of important papers from trivial and the periodical elimination of the latter.

Ways and means should be found for adopting the existing filming practices to the requirements outlined in para 39 (b and d) and para 46.

Special attention should be devoted in this connection to the implications of Sections 85-86, 90 and 106 of the **Manual of Office Procedure.**

It should be made obligatory on public offices (a) to keep their records arranged in the original order of their creation, (b) to refrain from disturbing that order on any account whatever, and (c) from dividing records on the ground of any organisational or jurisdictional change, any redistribution of functions or on any other ground.

No changes which may be introduced in the filming practice should be forced on files already in existence or closed.

Public Offices should subject their records to a *First Review* not later than five years after they have passed out of active use and destroy those which need not be retained further for their own Departmental purposes. The question to be answered when reviewing a file should be : whether the file is likely to be needed by the Department should a circumstance similar to that which led to its origin happens to arise again. No use should be made of any historical criterion at this stage. The review should be conducted exclusively by Departmental officers appointed for the purpose.

All files surviving the First Review should be subjected to a Second Review when they reach their 25th year. In this review a representative of National Archives of India should be associated with the Departmental Officers entrusted with the task and the historical criterion should be applied wherever possible. Any paper deemed unworthy of further retention at this review should be disposed of either by destruction or any other method found suitable.

No original of any file which may have been printed should be destroyed on any account whatever. No more than one printed copy should be retained for permanent preservation where originals have survived in complete form and only two printed copies should be retained where originals are non-existent.

No records of a date earlier than 1860 should be destroyed on any account whatever.

No records relating to the period 1860-1923 which have already been appraised for disposal should be subjected to another review. Where such a review is necessary it should be carried out in collaboration with the National Archives of India. No documents of the period are to be destroyed except in consultation with the latter.

Steps should be taken to collect precise information on the various types of records which do not fall into the category of files with a view to deciding how they should be disposed of.

Records surviving the First Review should be regarded as semi-current (or intermediate) records till they reach their 25th year. They should be housed in intermediate repositories to be set up for the purpose.

All files surviving the Second Review (which is to be conducted when they reach their 25th year) should be regarded as mature for retirement and should be transferred immediately to the National Archives of India. Three reforms would be necessary to make this retirement possible :

(a) The National Archives should be stripped of all non-archival materials except books or documents bearing on Archives Science, modern Indian History and related subjects, and the acquisition of non-archival manuscripts should be discontinued.

(b) Appraisal should be made of such archival collections as have been transferred to National Archives without any prior review.

(c) Extension should be made to the present building to make possible housing of additional records.

All Central records ripe for retirement should be housed in the National Archives premises irrespective of their present location and no zonal repositories should be built up outside New Delhi to house non-current records of such Central agencies as may be located in other places.

II. Procedures For Control And Coordination

The management of matters relating to public records should be entrusted to a single Ministry or a single organ of government and the relations between that organ and the Director of Archives, who is to discharge his functions under the latter's guidance, should be precisely defined in the Rules of Business to be framed under the proposed Statute.

A consolidated body of general administrative orders and rules are to be framed within the framework of the Statute which should spell out the basic principles and procedures relating to archive-making and archive administration.

Each Ministry and Central Department should have a Departmental Record Officer, who should be made responsible for the care of its records from the time when they are created until they are either destroyed or retired to the National Archives.

The powers and responsibilities of the Director of Archives, Government of India, should as already recommended, be statutorily defined. He should be in full charge of the National Archives and of all records therein, and it should be his duty to take all practicable steps for their preservation and for increasing their utility. He should be authorised to ensure regular transfer to his custody all records from the different public bodies which may be ripe for retirement. He should be entrusted with the responsibility of coordinating, guiding and supervising all operations in the public bodies connected with the management, administration, preservation, selection, disposal and retirement of their records. It should be incumbent on the public bodies to conduct all these operations under his guidance and advice.

All public bodies mentioned in para 62 should be included in the system of control outlined above subject to such exceptions as mentioned in the same para, as also in para 117.

C. Public Access To Records

Public access to records should be controlled in accordance with the recommendations made in paras 83, 112, 122.

D. The National Archives Of India

The following recommendations are made with a view to enabling the National Archives of India to play an active role in the system of coordination and control outlined above.

The acquisition policy of the National Archives should be redefined in the light of recommendations made in paras 53 (i). The present practice of retiring to the Department any material other than non-current records (records of permanent value older than 25 years) should cease. Apart from Central Government's records the Department should acquire only such private archives as throw light an important phases of modern Indian history or which may help to fill in gaps in the existing holdings of the Department. These acquisitions should exclude private archives of mere regional or local importance. The acquisition programme should also include transcripts of records and documents bearing on modern Indian history that may be available in foreign repositories, public as well as private.

Preservation, repair and photo-duplication programmes of the Department should be limited to the Central Government's records. So far as the records or documents of bodies other than Central Government are concerned the activities of the National Archives should not extend beyond advisory work.

Top-most priority should be given by the Department to the task of arrangement, analysis and listing of records, which should be limited to important collections and series.

The existing practice of publishing full texts or calendars of entire record series or selections from them should be discontinued as soon as the programmes in hand have been completed, and the privilege of full publication should be extended only to special collections enumerated in para 157. The editing and publication of Educational Records should be taken out of the hands of the National Archives and should either be undertaken by an appropriate branch of the Ministry of Education or entrusted to a suitable institution. The pubilcation of **The Indian Archives** should continue.

Programme of microfilm publication as described in para 159 should be taken up with a view to supply scholars with cheap copies of documents of their interest.

The training in Diploma Course should be modified on the lines indicated in para 160.

The Research Fellowship Scheme should be taken out of the hands of the National Archives and entrusted to Universities or historical research institutes.

The Status of the Director of Archives should be raised in order to enable him to discharge the additional duties devolving on him. The National Archives should be raised to the position of an Attached Office.

The following organisational changes should be effected in the Department as early as possible :

(a) The Records and Reference Division should be split up into three separate Divisions : (i) **Records Administration**—to look after acquisition, arrangement, listing and other ancillary duties ; (ii) **Research and Reference**—to take care of all research, reference and other public relations duties and have also the management of the Library; (iii) **Liaison and Record Management**—to be entrusted among others with periodical examination of records outside the National Archives premises, their systematic review, their regular retirement to the National Archives. They will also have to advise the record creating Departments on methods of arrangement, preservation and disposal.

(b) The three independent publication divisions should be consolidated into a single division. There should not be a separate Persian or Oriental Records Division.

(c) All divisions should be placed in charge of an Assistant Director except that of Liaison and Record Management which should be under a Deputy Director. The present cleavage between Administration and other Divisions should be removed, and the former should be placed under an Assistant Director with the same experience, training and qualifications as his colleagues of other Divisions. All Assistant Directors should undergo a training in Office administration to enable them to take charge of administration whenever required. There should be a system of regular transfer of officers from one Division to another.

(d) All supervisory staff, except those in Preservation Division, should be merged into one common cadre subject to the proviso that those who by reason of their qualifications do not fit in the cadre can be absorbed elsewhere.

(e) The existing multiplicity in levels of supervision should be removed as early as possible, and the existing three grade of Archivists, Assistant Archivists (Grade I) and (Grade II) should be merged in one suitable running scale. Reforms on the same lines should be effected in the Preservation Division as well.

(f) Recruitment should be started at the level of Archivist (or the lowest supervisory post in the Department), all higher posts being filled by promotion when suitable candidates are available, in the Department. All appointees should be selected by the Union Public Service Commission on the basis of a written test, after which they should undergo a traininig in the National Archives.

(g) Steps should be taken to do away with existing multiplicity of scales among the manual (skilled or semi-skilled) workers in the Department and to give them a better scale of pay.

Top-most priority should be given to the construction of the proposed annexe to the present National Archives premises and arrangement should be made for air-conditioning the stacks as well as work-rooms where records are handled.

E. Special Points Relating To State Archives

It should be urged on the States to reorganise their archives on the same lines as indicated in respect of Archives of the Union, with such modifications as the varying local conditions may justify. Very high priority should be given to the task of developing State Archives and of setting up properly equipped repositories for housing them conformably to scientific standards.

The primary responsibility of administering State Archives should rest with the State Governments themselves. Neither the ownership nor the administrative control of these records should be rested in the Centre. It is not possible to sort out any portion of the State Archives on the basis of their being of national importance nor to declare them by law as such. There is consequently no need to set up zonal repositories for administering State records of 'national importance'.

Coordination of archival activities in the States should be secured (a) through a system of uniform laws providing for all State Archives; (b) through a Central Advisory Body (Indian Archival Council) fully representative both of the Union and the State Governments discharging advisory functions in respect of public archives of all categories; and (c) if possible, through a system of grants in-aid to be given to States needing help for the development of their own archives. The proposed arrangement for grants should, if it materialises, be processed through the Indian Archival Council.

Archival laws affecting States should be enacted by the State Legislatures. These laws should provide for all public bodies under the control of the States, and should also cover State Legislatures, High Courts and other Courts in the States and the Local Governments (District Boards, Municipalities, etc.) subject to special arrangement being made in each case with regard to their management, appraisal, retirement and accessibility.

No special treatment requires to be made for the records of the defunct princely States. They are to be treated as integral part of the archives of the States in which they have merged. The records of the defunct Bhopal State which were taken over by the Central Government should be restored to the Madhya Pradesh Government.

The State laws should make provision for public access to the State Archives, which in our view, should be governed by the same conditions as specified by us in respect of Union Archives.

F. Private Archives

It is not practicable to bring private archives of any category within a system of effective public control either by declaring them by law to be of national importance or by any other means. The task of their preservation and maintenance are best left to private initiative which, may where necessary, be reinforced by State-aid flowing either from the Centre or from the States in which they are located. Universities, learned institutions, libraries and historical societies should be encouraged to acquire and arrange for preservation of collections which may be worthy of permanent preservation, and financial assistance may be extended to such institutions where called for, by the Central as well as the State Governments. Public repositories and archival institutions should, where necessary, supplement private efforts in this behalf by acquiring by gift, loan or purchases, collections which may be of unique importance. The activities of the National Archives and of the State Archives in the field should be restricted in the manner indicated respectively in paras 148, 150, 184.

A survey and registration of private records should be under-taken on the basis of cooperation between the Union and the State Governments and the processing of the work should be entrusted to the Indian Archival Council, which is to take charge of the National Register of Records.

The Antiquities (Exports Control) Act of 1947 should be suitably amended to prevent migration and unauthorised export of private archives. Dr. Raghubir Sinh's bill (1957) for amending this Act will meet the purpose if the definition of the term 'antiquity' as suggested in that Bill is appropriately revised.

Paras Mentioned In The Recommendations

Desirability Of Two Stage Review

34. We are, therefore, forced to the conclusion that the narrower the range of the retention periods that may be fixed for a record group, the small is likely to be the number of papers that may mature for review in a particular year and the lighter and simpler is likely to become the task of annual reviewing. If, for instance, a Department would arrange to have only two retention periods for all files created by it, namely five and 25 years, it will considerably simplify and reduce the task of annual reviewing. It will in that case have to examine in any year only papers relating to two years, viz., those which are five years and 25 years old. Under such a procedure, moreover, all files in a Department which may be required to be kept beyond five years will need only two reviews, one when it reaches its fifth year and the other when it becomes 25 years old. English public offices have simplified the problem of record disposal beyond expectation by adopting an analogous procedure of two-stage review. It needs to be carefully examined whether, in view of the enormous labour which the prevailing processes involve and the complexities they often give rise to, it will not be advisable to try to assimilate these processes to the two-stage review outlined above with such modifications as the particular circumstances of our public offices may justify. How such a procedure will actually work we propose to explain in a subsequent paragraph.

Historical Criterion In Appraisal Work

35. We have so far been looking at the problem strictly from the point of view of the administrator, but since most records acquire with passage of time values other than purely administrative — values, for instance, to the historian, the genealogist or researchers in other

fields, it is necessary to examine how far the present reviewing practices adequately safeguard the interests of research. It is no doubt true that an administrative department is primarily concerned only with such records as may serve its own administrative purposes. But in-view of the growing public interest in records as historical material, governments in almost all civilised countries have been devoting greater and greater attention to the potential research value of all public records under their control. In India, the importance of records as materials for history was first officially recognised in 1862 when following a recommendation from the Record Committee, Government of India agreed to preserve administratively inactive records in the interest of research. But it was only in 1913 that the need was for the first time felt for framing a set of record disposal rules emphasising the importance of the use of a historical criterion in selecting records for retention. The need for the application of that criterion received further emphasis in the rules proposed by the Indian Historical Records Commission in 1944, which led to a revision of the 1913 rules. The Section (108) in the present manual dealing with the question is based more or less on the above revised rules. That section very rightly stresses that :

"Care should be taken to see that the files containing papers which are important, however, indirectly, as sources of information on any aspect of history, whether political, military, social, economical, etc., or which are, or may in future prove to be of biographical or antiquarian interest are not to be destroyed.

36. There cannot be two opinions on the appropriateness of the instructions. But the question to which we have to find an answer is how and by whom the instructions are to be carried out. One possible way is to assess the potential historical value of the files at the time of their initial classification as 'A', 'B', or 'C', i. e., at the time of their closing. But this is not without its difficulties. In the first place, the initial classification being a gigantic task has inevitably to be entrusted to junior officers (Section Officers) in the Department, who having no actual experience of research, have no conceivable means to forecast with certainty what papers the future historian, economist or sociological researcher, as the case may be, is likely to consider important. Historical research, moreover, is in no may related to the normal work of a record-creating Department, and it is possibly not fair that the departmental officers concerned should be required to take decisions on a matter which, on any view, is clearlyoutside their normal experience. Further-more, the time of closing a file is not the stage at which it is possible for any person, however knowledgeable or qualified, to determine authoritatively which among the papers house and therein are going to acquire historical importance at a future date. The perspective needed for arriving at such a judgment can be obtained only after sufficient time has elapsed.

37. What is possible to assess at the time of the initial review, therfore, is the administrative value of the files undergoing appraisal, and the right persons to conduct this review are those who may have the requisite administrative experience. If at the time of the review the question to be answered by the reviewing officer is put in the form : "Is this paper likely to be of historical importance, or to be useful for economic, sociological or genealogical research?"; it may not be possible for him to see the basis on which he should provide the answer. If on the other hand, the question is put, indirectly in the form : "is the Department likely to require this paper any longer for its own Departmental purposes ?"; it becomes immediately intelligible to him in terms of the experience gained by him in the course of his normal work. The two forms of the question will, in our view practically become synonymous of the meaning of the word 'Departmental purposes' is not kept confined simply, to the question specifically dealt with in the file, but is so extended as to include the possibility of the file being needed as a precedent or as a guide to possible action, should a similar set of circumstances arise in future. A correct answer provided to the question, in that case, will ensure that a paper is not destroyed merely because the activities with which it dealt have ceased. We also believe that the initial review if conducted on this basis will, in practice, guarantee the survival of almost all Departmental papers which an historian, may wish to see preserved. The task of initial reviewing, however, cannot in our view be entrusted either to an historian or an archivist as neither of them has the Departmental experience needed for the assessment of paper from the purely administrative point of view.

38. It is, therefore, difficult to resist the conclusion that if the use of the historical criterion is to produce any satisfactory results it should be applied not at the time of the initial reviewing of the Departmental files, but after they have become sufficiently mature to bring about the perspecitve necessary for assessing their historical significance. At what stage of its life span a file should be regarded as so mature is a question on which there is likely to be divergent opinions. We are, however, inclined to the view that the purpose we have in mind will be roughly met if the stage is fixed at a point when a file is at least 25 years old. 25 years is usually reckoned as the normal length of an entire generation, and in our view a transaction or an event must be at least a generation old to become capable of being studied in its correct perspective. The same considerations ought to be valid also for transactions recorded in public files. The period needed by a file to attain the requisite maturity should thus on no account be reckoned as less than 25 years.

Desiderata For Reviewing Procedure

39. This brings us back to the two stage review, already outlined by us, of all files other than those which can be initially detected as ephemeral and can, in consequence, be eliminated fourthwith. It will be necessary to bear in mind several points if we have to operate successfully the two-stage review mentioned above :

(a) The First (or initial) Review of a file should not be normally deferred to a date far removed from its actual closing. This should, in fact, be conducted before the meaning of the transactions of which the files in question are the tangible evidence has completely faded from memory. In our view, five years should normally be regarded as the maximum interval which may be allowed between the recording of a file and its appraisal from the administrative point of view.

(b) For the same reason, efforts should be made to close all files after a specified period (say, a year). In case the transaction dealt with in a file has not been completed with the specified period all succeeding papers relating to the transaction should be placed and dealt with in a new file opened on the same subject and bearing the same reference number. Only by this means can it be ensured that the First Review of a file is not unduly delayed, and taken up at a stage when the significance of the transaction embodied in it has been completely forgotten.

(c) The files which can be identified at their very start as policy records, meant for permanent perservation should not normally figure in the First Review. The review should, as far as possible, be restricted only to those records which, although they cannot be identified as of permanent value either at the time of their creation or at the time of their closing, may yet be needed even after they have passed out of current use.

(d) The filing practice of each Department should be so adopted as to ensure that (i) a file's contents are adequately described by its title, (ii) that no file is used to house papers on a subject other than it was originally intended to deal with, (iii) that files dealing with policy decisions are not cluttered with papers relating to the particular application of those decisions, and (iv) that on no account matters of mere routine are allowed entry into a regular file of any category whatever. The desiderata outlined above are already stressed in one form or another in the **Manual of Office Procedure** (*vide* Sections 85-86, 90, 106). Since, however, they form the foundation on which a practicable reviewing procedure can be built up, we have found it necessary to lay particular stress on them. If strictly followed, they will make possible the defining of the narrowest possible range within which a file or a group of files can be opened, and will thereby prevent the growth of unwieldy files attracting papers on a wide multiplicity of topics. More over, by enabling automatic isolation of important papers from mere routine it will considerably lighten the task of the reviewer, the greater part of whose time is unnecessarily taken up with mere sorting out of papers requiring examination.

(e) While conducting the review, steps should be taken, if possible, for the use of a schedule showing in detail the specific categories of files which are capable of examination by classes and need not be reviewed individually. To be of real use such a schedule should strictly correspond to the system of classification to which the files to be reviewed owe their origin, and should on no account include artificial or imaginary classes into which it will be difficult to place a file. The files which elude such a classification will have, of course, to be assessed individually. But the number of such files will be greatly reduced if careful thought is given both to the classification of files while they are in making, and on the preparation of schedules for the purpose of review.

(f) The prevailing practice of destroying the originals of files that have been printed should cease. It is usual to edit out of printed copies any document or writing which although it may have formed integral part of an important transaction, is believed to have outlived its usefulness, in consequence of the transaction having been completed. Such printed files fail to present complete documentation of the transactions they are required to embody. A printed file, moreover, is no substitute for its original and it is the original which should, in our view, be maintained as permanent record of Government.

(g) All files surving the first Review should be retained till they reach their 25th year, and the practice of according to them varying retention periods should discontinue. This would necessitate their being subjected to a Second Review of their attaining maturity. The necessity for such a re-appraisal follows from the fact that while the First Review makes possible early elimination of all ephemeral papers, which constitute the greater bulk cf the annual accumulation of operational files, and the retention of all papers likely to be of historical value, it cannot ensure that all surviving papers are necessarily of historical importance. The latter requirement can be met only if the surviving files are appraised a new after they have reached a certain stage of maturity. We have already explained why we think that no file can be regarded as having attained this stage before reaching its 25th year. It is only at this stage that the historical criterion, the importance of which has been very rightly emphasised in the manual, can be applied to a paper with reasonable chance of success. But while the First Review, which, as we have seen, can be conducted purely from the administrative point of view, is to be entrusted to the creating Department concerned, the Second Review will require a collaboration between the latter and the National Archives of India. The archivists are the persons most in contract with research workers, and their knowledge of what the latter wish to consult can be of great use in exercising the historical criterion. Because of the greatly reduced bulk of the surviving papers and the perspective brought about by the passage of time, we have every hope that a collaboration between Archivists and Departmental Officers will make it comparatively easy to apply the historical criterion to the papers at the Second Review. Any paper which is deemed unworthy of retention at this review may be marked as fit for permanent retention in the National Archives of India.

(h) If the purpose of the proposed two-stage appraisal is to be fulfilled it will further be necessary to allot the task of deciding what papers are to be retained at both the stages to more senior and experienced staff than is perhaps possible under the existing arrangement. We note that the Weeding Sub-Committee of the Local Records Sub-Committee, which very recently examined the entire disposal question, has recommended the assigning of the task to specially qualified Departmental Record Officers to be appointed for the purpose by each record-creating Department; and we heartily endorse the proposal. We would furter recommend that the Officer should be responsible, under the Departmental head concerned, for the general care of all Departmental papers from the time when they are created or received in office till they are disposed of either by destruction or by retirement to the National Archives. It is he who should also be made responsible for deciding, in consultation with the appropriate administrative staff, which papers it was necessary for the Department to retain further for its own Departmental purposes' at the time of the First Review. On him would equally rest the responsibility of collaborating with the National Archives in finally selecting papers for retirement when they become mature for the proposed Second Review. The need for the proposed concentration in the same hands of the onerous tasks of both handling a Department's current and semi-current papers and conducting their review necessarily follows from the fact that arrangements made by a Department for handling its active papers are as much a part of the process of public administration as the selection of documents for preservation. We refrain from making any specific recommendations as to what place he should occupy in the Departmental office structures, but his status would need to be higher than at present given to Section Officers, and we would urge on all Departments the importance of appointing a capable and trained official to the post.

Economy Involved In The Procedure

40. The proposed arrangement should not necessitate a big increase in expenditure. The extra cost which it may entail will be much less than the amount which the Departments will be obliged to spend in future years, on staff, accommodation, and preservative materials, if the present rate of archival accumulation is not effectively controlled. That the arrangements we are proposing will effect substantial economy in many ways will be clear from the following facts. It will, in the first place, obviate the necessity felt at present for fixing separate retention periods for each individual file at the time it is closed and will release the staff engaged on this task for more important Departmental work. It will equally obviate the necessity of perpetually reviewing 'A' and 'B' files which are now required to be appraised ever 10 years. The reason of this is that the initial classification of files which we are advocating, and which forms the basis of the arrangement proposed, provides for the automatic separation, at their very start, of policy (important) files from those relating to mere cases, virtually making redundant their reclassification for the same purpose at the time of recording. Since, moreover, all files, barring those which can easily be identified as policy files, are due for review on the expiry of five years, the greater bulk of the ephemeral papers occurring among them are normally expected to be weeded out at the time of the First Review. The reduced bulk of the surviving papers is bound to lighten considerably the task of appraisal at the time of the Second Reviewing. This will not only simplify reviewing procedures but will effect real economy in the time now being spent on the task of the reviewer. We note that the two stage review we have in view has also been strongly recommended by the Weeding Sub-Committee already referred to. We are definitely of the opinion that it will be worth while to try the procedure suggested in the interest not only of administration and the research scholars but of economy in money, space and time.

Appraisal Of Ricords Already In Existence

41. The reforms suggested will be readily applicable to all Departmental files still in currency or to be opened in future and, with slight adjustment, also to all closed files which owe their existence to a system of subject-classification (i.e., practically all files dating from 1923). The adjustment proposed will consist in the careful revision of all existing destruction and retention schedules, on the basis of the file-classification systems in use, and the use of these revised schedules at the time of the First Review proposed. Care should be taken in the course of the review to see that not more than one printed copy of a file is retained of which the original has survived in complete form and that only two printed copies are retained where originals are non-existent. The same procedure should apply to the records relating to the period 1901-1922 subject to the proviso that no collection included in this class need to be re-appraised which has already been subjected to the weeding operation.

42. The records before 1900 stand on an altogether

different footing. They relate to a time when the administrative agencies were much less active in record-production than in the present century, and the proportion of ephemeral papers in them is likely to be comparatively small. Moreover, within this group, the records ante-dating 1859 deserve special treatment in as much as the greater bulk of them constitute the proceedings of the Supreme Council and contain little that may now be regarded as useless. Even a routine paper like a voucher or a bill coming down from this period may, by virtue of its uniqueness, have greater inportance than a paper of the same type belonging, for instance, to the twentieth century, of which it is easy to find almost boundless examples. It would, therefore, be safe to accept it as a rule that no record which is of an earlier date than 1860 should on any account be destroyed. With regard to the records beyond 1860 and prior to 1900 the review proposed should be restricted only to those collections which have never been appraised so far, and should always be conducted in collaboration with the National Archives of India. The procedure suggested is not likely to create any complication as the bulk of the records of this discription still with the creating bodies cannot be very great. As in the case of post-1900 records only one printed file should by preserved of which the original is available. No document, moreover, is to be destroyed except in consultation with the National Archives of India.

Records Other Than Files

43. The review procedures outlined above take note only of Departmental files or proceedings. It is necessary for our purpose to take into account also those papers which fall outside the category of files. Some outstanding categories of these are given below:

(a) Unregistered papers such as forms, registers, diaries, ledgers, etc., of which a seemingly unending variety is in use in almost every Department and continue to occupy a considerable portion of the space reserved for official papers. The Secretariat Manual (Sec. 115) lists some six varieties, but there seem to be many more in use in offices outside the Secreteriat. The Accountant General, Central Revenues, alone has not less than 286 varieties of documents of this type.

(b) Personal papers like service records and other kinds of information about persons or families kept in forms, *e.g.*, census and income-tax returns.

(c) Standard types of papers giving information about business concerns, firms and the like (*e.g.*, those with the Ministry of Commerce and Industry, Ministry of Finance, etc.) or merely statistical information.

Information is lacking on the precise nature or extent of any of these categories, and while it is conceivable that the greater bulk of these can safely be weeded out, the possibility cannot be totally ruled out of their containing some material (however small in volume) which may be of use to the future researcher. We, therefore, consider it desirable that a survey should be undertaken with a view to determining the criteria in accordance with which these records should be periodically disposed of.

The Problem Of Management : Records In Currency.

44. The necessary complement of the disposal procedure, we have advocated above, is a sound record-management programme that will take care of all preservable records from the time of their birth till their final retirement. The first pre-requisite of such a programme is that, the papers in a Department should be brought on record in such a way that they accurately reflect not only the organisation and functions of that Department but the complete history of its activities, and also render possible their prompt identification. This requirement can hardly be met under the existing practice of filng which, as we have seen, is based on a list of subject-headings, numbered serially without any predetermined order of classification. While the broad subject-heads, which are pre-determined, have usually some fixed numerical symbols tied to them, the symbols attached to the sub-divisions within the subject-heads, which are flexible, tend to vary. The result is that the same numerical symbols have different meanings not only for different Ministries or different sections within the same Ministry, but for the same section for different years. The file-numbers are of little help in ensuring the expected physical grouping of the files dealing with related subjects or even aspects of the same subject. They tend to drift apart and after travel so far away from each other as to render almost impossible any study of the complete history of the transactions they reflect. Moreover, as we have seen, the practice leads to mingling up of important papers with routine and enclosing in the same file papers dealing with a wide variety of topics. No file-register can under this arrangement be of much use either in identifying or tracing a document.

45. The lacunae are often sought to the remedied by annual indexes. But indexes in very few Departments are quite up-to-date. Since, more-over, the files created according to the prevailing methed do not admit of proper indexing, the indexes complied in the circumstances often fail to serve as satisfactory keys to the information needed by a user. A recent official enquiry has revealed that transactions have often to the conducted without reference to their past history because papers embodying that history are not easy to trace. This shows the inadequacy of the existing arrangement.

46. We have already stressed the need for adopting the present practice in such a manner that the subject headings as well as the different sub-divisions within

them are grouped together strictly on the basis of their logical relation to each other. It needs to be explained that closely corresponding to the arrangement of subjects in the scheme there should also be a scheme of numerical symbols under which each symbol is to be permanently tied to the subject it represents. This would not only enable a file to get automatically numbered as soon as the theme on which it is to be opened has been decided on, but will ensure exclusion from the file matters alien to its theme. Moreover, as the files in a Department are to be arranged according to their number, and the numbers are to correspond strictly to the arrangement in the proposed scheme of the subjects then symbolise, the files will, if the scheme is strictly followed, get automatically arranged in an order which will be the exact reflection of the origanic relation in which the topics they deal with stand. Given a subject it will normally be possible to know the appropriate numerical symbol and given a number it will be equally possible to know the exact scope of the file it symbolises and its precise location in the series. The file registers, under the reform proposed, would serve as an efficient key to the records figuring in them and the logical arrangement of subjects which the reform presupposes will make indexing a much simpler proposition. The measures described above, we may add, do not involve any departure from what is laid down in the **Manual of Office Procedure**. What we have endeavoured to do here is to spell out some of the procedures outlined therein as also to place special emphasis on other. Similar suggestions, we note, have been made by the Weeding Sub-Committee in its Report dated January 15 and February 10, 1958.

47. A further pre-requisite of a sound record management policy is that the arrangement of the files in a Department should strictly follow the order dictated by the classification scheme to which they owe their origin. On no account should an attempt be made at any reclassification, renumbering or retitling of any file in violation of this original order. There can be noticed a general tendency to divide, disperse, reclassify or even renumber records, following every reorganisation or redistribution of the functions of a record-creating body. This tendency has in the past inevitably led to the dismemberment of many record-series and often to the total disappearance of valuable records or record-groups. It is important to stress here that any alteration in original order of files whether dictated by administrative changes or by a simple desire to be logical can end only by rendering totally useless the existing index registers and other reference aids and making almost impossible the location of the documents wanted or any study that may be attempted of complete history of the transactions they reflect. The only advisable course would be to ensure that whenever any inter-Departmental or inter-Sectional redistribution of functions takes place, only the incomplete files relating to the functions transferred to a unit should move to that unit to be integrated with the new files to be opened on the subject by the latter. Files already closed should not be affected by the change, and should continue to remain as part of the records of the parent unit. If any of them are needed by the unit concerned they can be transferred as on loan, subject to the condition they return to the parent collection as soon as they have served their purpose. By the same count any change introduced in the file classification system of a Department should affect only the records post-dating that change. The reform should in no circumstances be forced on any file already closed.

Records Semi-Current And Non-Current

48. An essential feature of an efficient record-management programme is a well-planned system of administering the records which have passed out of currency. Under the existing arrangement, all closed files are required to be retained by the creating units (Sections) for three years and thereafter they are to be keep in the Departmental Record Rooms for five more years, at the end of which they are to be retired to National Archives repository. As however, very few Departments have properly planned record rooms of their own the Sections are obliged to retain with them a mass of records exceeding the three years limit. A recent official enquiry showed that the present accumulations in the Secretariat office rooms constitute about 50 per cent of the records actually housed in the temporary resting places allotted for them mostly in the Secretariat basements. The eight year limit fixed for the retirement of records to the National Archives is scarcely adhered to in actual practice. As we have noticed, the papers accumulated in the Secretariat Offices alone already cover about 40. linear miles of space. The gap between the rule and the practice is wide enough to justify radical rethinking, and if the disposal procedure outlined by us is to be tried the present system will require a thorough revision

49. We have suggested in para 39 (a) above that five years should be regarded as the maximum length of time upto which files can be kept in Department unreviewed and that all files should be subjected to the proposed First Review on or before the fifth year of their existence. The date on which the files in a Section become mature for the review is in our opinion the date most convenient for their transfer to the appropriate Departmental Record Room. The changed procedure will ensure the regular transfer of records from the appropriate Sections only after they had been stripped of the greater bulk of their ephemeral components, and will help to relieve substantially the prevailing congestion in storage space.

50. The records surviving the First Review should

be regarded as having passed from the stage of currency to that of semi-currency. It is a stage in which records are less frequently required in administration. The stage continues till they become mature for their retirement to their permanent home in the appropriate repository. We have shown in para 39(g) why we feel that no record should be deemed fit for retirement till it has reached its twenty-fifth year and has survived the final review to which it is to be subjected at that stage. An exception should in our view be made in respect of the records of such agencies, organisations or bodies which may becme defunct without their functions being inherited by a successor body. These records should be regarded as fit for retirement as soon as the bodies originating them have ceased to function, since there is not likely to be any successor body to take care of them.

Intermediate Repositories

51. The eight year limit prescribed in the **Manual** is in our view too short for the purpose, as it can never bring about the perspective necessary for the correct selection of a document for permanent retention. The records still to reach this age of maturity (intermediate records) are, as we have seen, being indifferently kept mostly in office-rooms and rarely in rooms exclusively allotted to them. It seems essential that all records in the intermediate stage should remain under the control of the creating Departments themselves and placed in properly maintained repositories conforming to scientific requirements. One possible alternative is to organise such repositories as in the United States of America on the basis of sole occupancy by the Federal Records Service. The other and more economical way would be to follow the model in the United Kingdom and set up repositories on the basis of joint occupancy by the Departments.

Retirement Problems

52. Strictly speaking, all non-current records deserving permanent retention, and nothing but such records, should be retired to the National Archives repository. In actual practice the greater bulk of the records of this description is lying with their originating Departments and those retired include not only non-current records but records, still in semi-currency, both embodying a large quantity of ephemeral contents. The transfers are usually effected sporadically and haphazardly, priority generally being given to the accumulations for which the owning Department has no space. Care is hardly ever taken for keeping intact the original order of the retired records or to provide them with properly drawn up lists. It is also a common experience to see the records of different provenance having been hopelessly mixed up at the time they are finally retired. The chronological limit for retirement varies from Department to Department, and even so there is no certainty that all preservable records prior to this limit have actually been transferred to the National Archives. The limit of 25 years we have recommended for the purpose of retirement should, we suggest, be made obligatory on all Departments, an exception being made only of such collections as may be frequently needed by the owning Departments even after they have passed this limit. It should be made equally obligatory on the Departments to retire records in an orderly manner without violating the principle of provenance.

53. The retirement procedure outlined above is, however, incapable of immediate implementation owing to shortage of space in the National Archives premises and till that shortage is removed the creating Departments themselves will have to retain with them their existing accumulations. Three measures are necessary to relieve the prevailing pressure on space :

(1) Expurgating the National Archives repository of all non-archival accretions for which it has no use. This would include (a) a huge mass of books, pamphlets and reports accumulated in the Departmental Library which have no bearing either on archives keeping or on Modern Indian history : (b) the fairly big collection of Oriental manuscripts which deal mostly with religions, literary, astrological, etc., topics and very rarely with history, and which are never needed either by the staff working in the Department or the research workers visiting it. The manuscript collection is likely to grow in bulk with coming years in consequence of a recent decision of Government to build up in the National Archives a repository of non-archival manuscripts. It is not our intention to suggest that such manuscripts do not require to be cared for. But what we do wish to emphasize is that they should on no account be allowed precedence over the Central Government's own records, which, being unique, are irreplaceable, and which would most certainly be lost for good unless immediate arrangement is made for their proper housing.

(2) Appraisal of such record collections as have been transferred to the National Archives without any prior review. A review is particularly necessary for the records of the defunct Residencies which are believed to contain a fairly large quantity of ephemeral papers.

(3) **Additions To The Present Buildings**

However much the bulk of the existing contents of the National Archives may be reduced, it is clear that even to house the records of permanent value lying outside that repository it would need extra space that cannot at present be provided in the present building. A proposal for the contruction of an annexe to the building has been, we understand, under consideration since 1945, but it has not been so far implemented owing to financial reasons. Further postponement of this work will in our view be a measure of doubtful economy. The longer delay the more difficult and more expensive is sure to become the task of keeping the records at present uncared for even in a reasonably good state of repair.

Problem Of Zonal Repositories

54. It is incumbent on us to examine in this context the possibility of setting up zonal repositories for housing the records of such central agencies as may be located outside Delhi. The main argument in favour of such a step is that it would remove the prevailing congestion in the National Archives premises. The argument, however, is not one which will carry conviction. Dottinh the country with a number of miniature National Archives respositories is not likely to prove less expensive than effecting legitimate extensions in the present building in New Delhi. Even the construction of an additional repository in the Capital is sure to be more economical than the proposed dispersal of records among various centres, as in the first case the records housed in the additional building can have easy access to the repair facilities provided in tee present premises. Any dispersal of Central records that may be taken up will impose on the public the additional burden of having to maintain an enormous additional staff and to acquire additional technical equipment. Besides, such a step would greatly add to the difficulty of research scholars, whose studies usually embrance the records of a number of Departments. Difficulties will also arise when work is transferred from one Department to another, for every time such a change takes place records wiil have to be moved from one zonal office to another. The other alternative would be to keep the records of the same provenance dispersed among several repositories. Neither of these alternative would be desirable.

55. There is one other point requiring to be examined in this connection. The Central Agencies located outside the Capital fall into three broad categories: (1) those whose activities embrace the whole of India (like Geological Survey, Anthropological Survey, Indian Forest Research Institute, etc.): (2) those whose activities affect an entire state or a bigger region embracing several states: (3) small units or field offices serving a very small area like a Division, District, a town or even a village (Post Offices, Customs Offices, Income-tax Offices). While the records created by the first two categories are sure to contain a substantial quantity of preservable material, there is little likelihood of anything of permanent value being found among the records of the last. The greater bulk of the last mentioned class of records consists of what may be regarded as particular transaction papers kept in forms, registers, ledgers, etc., and may be eliminated without much harm as soon as they have served their administrative purpose. There is thus no particular need for setting up zonal repositories to cater to the need only of this class of records. As regards the records mentioned under (1) and (2) above it will be possible to accommodate the preservable part among them in the repository at New Delhi, if the procedure suggested for the periodical appraisal and substantial reduction is scrupulously followed. The advantages of concentration of all records of permanent value in a Central repository are so obvious and the disadvantages of their dispersal among several zone offices are so many that the latter step in our view does not merit any serious consideration. The question whether zonal repositories may be developed for housing State records which may be declared of national importance is a separate issue and will be discussed in its proper place,

Need For Unified Control And Coordination

56. It is essential to the successful implementation of the various programmes outlined in paras 34-53 above that there should be a system of effective and unified control over the entire field of archival activities of all public offices under the Union. Such a system at present is conspicuous by its absence. As already pointed out, barring a few, no public office has any obligation statutory or of any other kind either to administer or to dispose of its records. So far as the task of disposal is concerned the Destruction of Records Act (1917) empowers the Central Government to frame rules in respect of their own records and any other public records "which do not relate to the purposes of the States", but it does not require them to do so. In actual practice this power has never been exercised and no rules have consequently been framed under the Act. Such rules as exist whether they relate to the management of records or their disposal are advisory rather than mendatory in character, and they are more often violated than observed".

57. There is, moreover, under the existing system to single authority having the exclusive control over all matters pertaining to the Central Government's records. Till 1910 the late Home Department used to exercise something roughly approaching such a control. But this was limited to the issue of general instructions affecting record making and record disposal, both the manner and the extent of their application being left entirely to the discretion of the individual Departments. Till 1891 there was no Central repository to house inactive records, and it was only in 1898 that necessity was felt for the first time for the regular retirement of such records from all Central Departments. Even so the use of any compulsion in this respect was never thought of. When in 1892 rules were first formulated for systematic selection of inactive records with a view to their retirement to the central repository their application was limited to the Home Department only. Precisely the

same was the case with a set of more comprehensive rules framed seven years later (Order No. 197, 30 September 1899) with the same object in view. The position did not improve any way when, following the creation in 1910 of the Department of Education, the portfolio of Archives was transferred to that body. This in practice meant nothing more than the Education Department was henceforth to look after the records retired to the Central Repository, while Home was to shoulder, as before, all responsibilities in respect of records in currency and semi-currency. In 1913 as Inter-Departmental Conference entrusted the former Department with the duty of framing a set of rules to govern the disposal of non-current records. But the same body also decided that the individual Departments should have the power to add or subtract from these rules so far as their own records were concerned. In the end, the majority of the Departments, viz., Foreign, Army, Public Works, Commerce and Industry, Revenue and Agriculture compiled special rules of their own. The Education Department's competence to frame such rules, though admitted in theory, was thus denied in practice. The Department, moreover, had little voice either in planning record management programmes or in determining the manner or the method of record retirement.

58. Since 1954 the responsibility of the Ministry (formerly Department of Home Affairs affecting archival matters has partly devolved on the Organisation and Methods Division of the Cabinet Secretariat, which now formulates rules embodying, among others, record-making and record-disposal procedures. Since, however, archives still continue to be within the portfolio of the Ministry (formerly Department) of Education, the latter is often consulted by the bodies concerned on matters chiefly affecting disposal, retirement and accessibility of records. But the advice tendered has no binding force, and the Ministry hardly has any decisive voice in determining the archival policy of the Central Government. It is only over the records retired to the Central repository that the Ministry exercises anything approaching effective control. But even here its role is that of a mere custodian and its powers are extremely limited. It cannot, for instance, control the way in which the records are to be retired nor the manner in which they should be borrowed or returned by the owning Departments. The upshot of all this is that in most matters affecting archives the Departments enjoy the fullest conceivable autonomy, and such over-all control as the present system permits is divided among several authorities and that too not in a very logical manner.

Machinery For Overall Control

59. The only way to remove the existing anarchy in the archival field is to demarcate precisely the respective spheres of the various authorities concerned and to vest in a single Minister or a single Organ of the Executive the sole responsibility in respect of overall supervision and coordination of the archival activities of all public offices under the Union. The Minister charged with this responsibility should have the power not only to instruct the owning Departments on all matters affecting their archives, but also to maintain continual check on the archival work done by each and to see that the procedure outlined in paras 34-53 above was strictly followed. This inevitable corollary of this would be to defive the powers and responsibilities of the Minister in this respect by a statutory enactment, without which in our considered view it will not be possible for him to function properly. It will be equally necessary to have a consolidated body of general administrative orders issued within the framework of the enactment, that would spell out the basic principles and procedures relating to archive-making and archive-administration. It will further be the duty of the Minister to report to Parliament on the working of the law proposed. The change suggested is not likely to impinge on the general responsibilities of either the Ministry of Home Affairs or the Organisation and Methods Division in respect particularly of records in the making and in current and semi-current stage except to the extent, that, after the change has taken place, none of the authorities will be within their competence to issue any rule or instruction which may be inconsistent with either the act or the executive orders promulgated under it.

Role of the National Archives In Records Management

60. Under the reform suggested the National Archives will be necessity, be required to play a more active role in the record management operations of the Central Government than it is competent to do at present. The efficient administration on non-current records by the National Archives is largely dependent on the owning Departments making, keeping and reviewing their records properly and transferring regularly to the former's custody those selected for preservation. While these are matters for which the Departments themselves should continue to be responsible, the National Archives should be entrusted with the duty of coordinating the arrangements to be made for the selection and the retirement of the Departmental records for permanent preservation. To enable the National Archives to meet this obligation we suggest that an Officer in the Department, not below the rank of a Deputy Director, should be exclusively charged with the task of the supervision of the coordination programme. He should have the assistance of liaison officers to help him in his work.

The primary duty of the staff would be to ensure that the review and selection work was being done by the Department concerned in the proper manner, and while they are not actually to participate in the operations themselves they might assist the Departmental Record Officers by suggesting ways and means by which they can be carried out most efficiently. At the time of final review, however, the liaison staff would be required to collaborate actively with the Departmental Officers concerned in the selection of records fit for permanent preservation. It will be equally the duy of the National Archives to advise the Departments on the methods of preservation and to assit them in maintaining proper standards in the various archival programmes undertaken by them.

61. The collaboration of the sort we have in view will not only lead to a positive improvement in the quality of the archive-work done in the various Departments but will eventually succeed in standardising their archival policies and procedures. Several changes in the organisation of the National Archives and also in the scope of its present activities will be necessary in order to enable it to concentrate on this collaboration. We propose to deal with this subject in a separate section below. But it will be appropriate to point out here that a necessary corollary of the reforms we are suggesting is that the head of the National Archives should be given a better status than he enjoys under the existing arrangement. If the new system is to work, as we want it to, the Director of Archives will have to bear the lion's share of the statutory responsibilities devolving on the Minister responsible for Archives. It seems only logical that his status and powers should be commensurate with and accurately reflect, the magnitude, of these responsibilities and we strongly recommend that the proposed statute should precisely define not only the scope of his duties but that of his powers as well.

Public Offices To Be Included In The Proposed System

62. It remains to decide which of the record creating bodies apart from the Ministries should be included in the proposed system of control. The principal categories of such bodies are enumerated below :

(1) **Departments Subordinate to the Secretariate or the Attached Offices.** These roughly fall into five categories : (a) those having all-India jurisdiction ; (b) those whose jurisdiction effects an entire state or a bigger region embracing several States ; (c) those whose activities are limited to a small area like a Division or a District ; (d) Small units and field offices serving or very small area like a sub-division, town or even a village ; (e) Educational and Research Institutions run by a Government Department.

In para 55, we have explained the reasons why we consider it necessary that the records emanating only from (a) and (b) above should be included in the proposed record management programme, and we have nothing further to add. As regards class (c) our suggestion is that for the purpose of inclusion in the programme a rigid criterion should be used in distinguishing important institutions from those which are of minor importance. While the papers of the former may certain valuable material, those of the latter are likely to be for the most part ephemeral in character, and may in the majority of cases be eliminated as soon as they have served their purpose, without jeopardising the cause of research.

(2) **Bodies Outside the Secretariat, but forming Integral Part of the Central Government set-up** (e.g. Union Public Service Commission, the Comptroller and Auditor General, Planning Commission, Prime Minister's Secretariat, President's Secretariat, Cabinet Secretariat). These should obviously be included in the system proposed. A word need to be said in respect of the Comptroller and Auditor General, some of whose records have a quasi-judicial character. But the problem relating to their retirement to the National Archives may be solved by enacting that the legal validity of any record will not be affected by its removal to a repository in accordance with the provisions of the Statute. The 25-year limit prescribed for retirement of records may not be found applicable either to the Cabinet Secretariat records or those of the President's or the Prime Minister's Secretariats. While we agree that this limit may be altered by arrangement with the authorities concerned, we should like to stress that no relaxation in other measures of reforms suggested by us would be justified.

(3) **Boards, Committees, Commissions etc., Set up under the authority of the Government of India** : The records of the temporary bodies of the above description should be treated as part of the Archives of the Ministries processing their work. When these have been set up on a permanent basis they should be treated as though they were independent Government Departments. In either case they should come under the purview of the system proposed.

(4) **Statutory bodies of All-India Character** : Many of these we believe are already covered by categories (2) and (3) above. Some deviate from the types composing those categories. They do so by virtue of their being entrusted with functions widely different from those normally discharged by the Secretariat Departments. We have little precise information on the nature of their records, but in view of the voluminous nature of their periodical accruals, of which only a small fraction may be found to be of permanent interest, and also in view of the wide divergence between their documentation practices and those of the Secretariat, we do not think it will be practicable to force on them the reforms which are primarily applicable to the latter. While these bodies should be placed under a statutory obligation to

arrange for methodical selection of records with a view to preservation of those having permanent interest no attempt should be made to bring them within the system of executive control we wish to see established in respect of other Departments. It would follow logically that their records should be retired to the National Archives for permanent preservation by special arrangement. They should be allowed to frame rules in respect to all archival matters within the frame-work of the proposed enactment.

(5) **Nationalised Enterprises and Undertakings.** The same consideration should in our view apply as for the bodies mentioned in sub-para (4) above.

(6) **Parliament.** The records of Parliament would include not only those of the Lok Sabha and Rajya Sabha Secretariats but those of all Legislative bodies of pre-Independence days as also those emanating from the Constituent Assembly. While we do not think it will be quite consistent with the established constitutional practice to vest in the executive control over these records, we wish particularly to emphasise the need for having a statutory provision for their systematic arrangement and preservation; under the control of the authorities concerned while they are in the current or semi-current stage, and their regular retirement to the National Archives as soon as they become inactive. The procedure for retirement should be settled by arrangement between the National Archives and the Parliamentary Secretariats.

(7) **The Supreme Court** has its own arrangements for keeping and disposing of records. While we consider that the Court should have a statutory obligation to select and preserve records of permanent value in accordance with the accepted standards, we do not think it will be appropriate to interfere with the power the Court possesses for dealing with its own records.

It remains to add that even where a category of public records is excluded from the system of executive control we are proposing, the technical advice of the National Archives should be made available to their owners, whenever there is a call on such service.

83. We have examined very carefully the various aspects involved in the question and feel convinced that a uniform procedure with regard to public access to records should be arrived at without further delay. Our recommendations in this respect are as follows :

(1) All records, including those marked confidential, which are 40 years old, should generally be thrown open to the public.

(2) Open records should be treated as open to every citizen of the Indian Union. After the open period there should be limited access period (extending say upto 10 years) records relating to which should be accessible to qualified users. Records beyond this limit should be open to researchers only with the permission of the appropriate Ministry.

(3) Records made accessible to the public should not be subjected to any kind of censorship or any other restrictions as regards their use.

Scope of the Law

109. The scope of the proposed law should in our view embrace the records of (1) all Ministries, Departments and other offices of the Government of India wherever located and whether existing or defunct, (2) all statutory and non-statutory bodies of all-India character, temporary or permanent, set up, controlled, administered and financed by the Government of India, (3) all nationalised undertakings and enterprises whether industrial, commercial or of any other sort, (4) the Union Parliament, and (5) the Supreme Court. So that there may not be any scope for misunderstanding as to what may or may not constitute 'records' for the purposes of the law, we would recommend that the term should be defined as precisely and lucidly as possible. It should in our view include records in any form or on whatever material prepared (e.g., rolls, codices, sheets, files, dossiers, films, photographs, charts, plans, diagrams, sound recordings, etc.)

Central Government's Responsibilities

110. The law should clearly define the responsibilities of the Central Government in respect of the different classes of records indicated in the preceding paragraphs. Government is responsible not only for the care, management, disposal and preservation of all these records, but for ensuring that reasonable facilities are given to the public for their consultation after they reach the stage of non-currency. The law should ensure that all Ministries and other Central bodies which may be responsible for the records housed outside the National Archives of India, make suitable arrangements for regular selection of those records which are to be permanently preserved and for their safe-keeping, and for the disposal either by destruction or any other way of all papers which may on review be found to be of ephemeral character. The law, in our opinion, should make it quite clear that no records of a date earlier than 1860 are to be destroyed on any account whatever.

111. The law should further make it obligatory on the public bodies concerned to retire to the National Archives repository all their records which have been selected for permanent preservation not later than 25 years after their creation. It is necessary for us to indicate here two possible cases in respect of which the 25 years limit proposed may not work, (1) the case in which the records to be retired pertain to a body which has become defunct and whose functions have not been taken up by any other body, and (2) the case in which a public body may want to retain for purposes of administration

or for any other special reason, certain records or certain categories of records although they may have exceeded the 25 years limit. In the first case our view is that the law should provide for the retirement of the records as soon as the creating or the owning body becomes defunct. In the second case, the law should permit the public bodies concerned to withhold their retirement with the consent and approval of the Central Government.

The public bodies concerned should have the statutory authority to recall any records which may have been retired to the National Archives.

Accessibility

112. As we have recommended earlier, all public records which may be more than 40 years old should be made available for public inspection in the National Archives of India. It is at the same time our view that the Director of Archives, Government of India, should be made responsible for ensuring that reasonable facilities are available to the public for inspecting and obtaining copies in whatever form (manuscript, typescript, facsimile, photographic) of any public records in his custody that may have been thrown open to research. He should further be empowered to permit any person to inspect records beyond the limit fixed if the latter has obtained special authority in that behalf given by a competent officer of the public body concerned.

Role Of The Director Of Archives

113. For reasons already explained it is considered necessary by us that the powers and responsibilities of the Director of Archives in respect of public records should be statutorily defined. He should, in the first place, have the full charge of the National Archives and of all records therein, and it should be his duty to undertake all practicable steps for the preservation of records under his charge. In the second place, he should have the legal custody of all records in his charge, and to enable him to discharge his functions in this respect, it should be provided in the law that the transfer of any public records to his custody by their owners will not affect their legal validity and that a copy of or extract from any public records in his custody certified as true and authentic by the Director of Archives or any other officer authorised by the latter and sealed with the seal of the National Archives should be admissible as evidence in any legal proceedings in the same way as their originals.

114. The Director, moreover, should, under the proposed law, have the power to do whatever may appear to him necessary or expedient for maintaining or improving the utility of the National Archives. Powers should in particular be vested in him for compiling and making available guides to and lists, calendars and edited texts of the records in his custody; bringing out publications concerning the activities of and facilities available in the National Archives; regulating the conditions under which members of the public may inspect records in his charge or use this facility in the National Archives; accepting responsibilities for safe-keeping of any records other than public records which may be received as gift or loan; lending records for display at exhibitions or for other special purposes with the concurrence of the appropriate public body; and ensuring regular transfer to his custody of all records from the different public bodies which may be ripe for retirement.

115. We also consider it necessary that the Director of Archives should be entrusted with the responsibility of coordinating, guiding and supervising all operations in the public bodies connected with the management, administration, preservation, selection, disposal and retirement of their records, while the latter should be pleaced under an obligation to conduct all these operations under the guidance and advice of the Director of Archives. It should be open to the Director of Archives to postpone retirement of any class of records until arrangement has been completed for their reception in the National Archives whenever he is convinced that such a course would be justified in the interest of their proper administration.

116. With a view to eliminating any ephemeral materials that may still be found among the records in the custody of the Director of Archives the latter should in our view be required to subject all these records to a continued review, and be authorised to destroy or dispose of in any other way, with the concurrence of the public body concerned, and papers which are duplicated in the public records selected for permanent preservation or any other papers which on any other ground may be thought unfit for permanent retention. This power he is to exercise subject to the restrictions referred to in para 110 or any other restrictions that the Government may think necessary. He should, moreover, maintain a list of all records which may be destroyed in this way.

Categories Of Records Needing Special Tratment.

117. Among public records mention may be made of those of the Supreme Court which has its own arrangements for keeping and disposing of records. The proposed law in our view should authorise the Supreme Court to continue to make, as before, its own rules regarding management, administration and selection of records for permanent preservation. The Court should be equally empowered to make arrangement for the preservation in its own custody of all its records as may be of permanent value and frame its own rules for public access to them.

118. The other records needing special treatment include those of Parliament and the statutory bodies of all-India character mentioned in para 109 above. These bodies should, in our view, be empowered to make their

own arrangements for systematic management, review and disposal of their records and determine the time-limit or procedure of their retirement to the National Archives of India for their permanent preservation.

Report On The Working Of The Law

119. To keep the Parliament informed of the actual working of the proposed law we consider it essential that a report in that behalf should be annually placed before both houses of the Parliament.

Rules To Be Framed Under The Law

120. We have explained earlier that the statute we have in view can deal only with the general principles relating to archival matters and that so far as the actual application of these principles is concerned it will be necessary to provide for them in rules framed on the basis of the statute itself. The field which should be covered by these rules has been indicated earlier. But here we propose to draw particular attention to some important points which, in our view, ought to be given special emphasis in these rules. In the first place, we consider it desirable that the management of matters relating to public records should be entrusted to a single Ministry or a single organ of the Government and that the relations between the Minister and the Director of Archives, who is to discharge his functions under his guidance and direction should be precisely defined in these rules. Secondly, we believe that for the proper implementation of the reforms we are advocating it is desirable that all public bodies brought within the purview of the proposed law should adapt their documentation, arrangement, preservation and disposal procedures to the requirements indicated by us, and that it should be made particularly obligatory on them to keep their records arranged in the original order of their creation and to refrain from disturbing that order on any account whatever. It should be made equally incumbent on them not to divide their records on the ground of any change that may occur in their respective jurisdictions whether by way of contraction or expansion or any redistribution that may take place in their prescribed functions, or on any other ground whatever. Any division of archival assets that may be necessitated by any administrative, jurisdictional or organisational change should, as already pointed out by us, be strictly limited to records on which action yet remains to be completed.

121. With regard to the disposal of records we think it necessary to stress that special care should be taken by all public bodies concerned while reviewing the records relating to the period 1860-1900, and that none of them should be actually destroyed, even though found to be administratively unimportant, except with the concurrence of the Director of Archives, Government of India. A list should be maintained by the Ministries of all records destroyed in accordance with the procedure. As to the records in the Director of Archives' own custody it should be made incumbent on him to send annually for examination to the proposed Central Advisory Council the lists of all papers selected for destruction. He should be authorised to destroy them if no advice is received from the Council to the contrary within a period of six months fromt their submission.

122. There is one other point which in our view should figure in the statutory rules proposed. We have already recommended that the law should provide that all records which may be 40 years old should be made accessible to the public. We have also suggested that the records of later years and less then 40 years old should be accessible to qualified research workers, including University sponsored students upto a limit of 10 years. It will, of course, be open to Government to prohibit the availability of records less than 40 years old. It is desirable that the proposed statutory rules should make provision for this limited access period and vest in the Director of Archives descretionary power to permit scholars t consult records falling within the prescribed limits.

Functions Of The Council

132. The functions of the Advisory Council as we have already stressed should primarily be advisory and the scope of its activities should relate to all problems vitally affecting the up-keep as well as the use of public records of all categories whether of the Union or of the States. Its additional duty should be to explore ways and means by which the archive work of the entire country can be conducted on a scientific basis and in conformity with uniform standards and bring about such coordination between the activities of the Central and State Archives as would promote gradual development of uniform archival procedures and practices all over the country.

Compilation And Dissemination Of Technical Information

133. To promote all these objects it would be necessary for it to pool information on the state of archives and in regard to the administrative arrangements at the Centre and in the States, to study carefully the problems connected with these archives, to endeavour to find solutions for them, and to offer these solutions to the authorities concerned. This will entail an extensive study not only of the archival methods in use in India but also those in progressive countries in Europe and America, and it will be incumbent in our view on the Advisory Council to try to take full advantage of the experience acquired and advances made in the field in the leading archives of the world. As a logical corollary, it will be

one of the duties of this body to build up under its aegies a body of useful technical information on different aspects of archive-keeping and to make arrangements for its dissenination among those needing them. The last task, we think, can he best accomplished by systematic issue of reports or circulars embodying the requisite technical information.

Inspection Of Archives Repositories

134. To enable the body to discharge efficiently its advisory or coordinating functions it will be necessary to authorise it to arrange for periodical inspection of the archive repositories whether belonging to the different States or to the Centre. The. body should have the authority to entrust the duty of inspection to any of its members or any other person whom by reason of his special experience in the field, it may consider competent, to discharge this duty. Reports on the inspection carried out and all recommendations made on its basis should as a matter of routine be placed before the Governments responsible for the archives. It will be equally the duty of the Advisory Council to examine any lists of records worked out for destruction that may be submitted to it annually either by the National Archives of India or any State Archives, and the Council will be within its right to tender to the parties concerned whatever advice it may feel necessary on the desirability or otherwise of any papers included in the lists. While we consider that it should be open to the Government concerned to accept or reject the advice tendered, we think it desirable that it should be made incumbent on the latter to keep the Advisory Council informed of its reactions to the latter's proposals and of the progress made in implementing them where they are found acceptable. This will provide the Council with an opportunity to explain to the Government concerned the implications of its recommendations and to try to resolve any difference of opinion that may arise.

Grants-in-Aid To States

135. There is yet another field in which the Advisory Council may play an active and useful role. Earlier we have called attention to the fact that archive work has not been placed on a sound footing in many States for lack of sufficient funds, and in the course of our talks with official representatives of almost every State we visited, we gathered that each State was only too eager to re-organise their records, conformably to scientific standards if requisite financial assistance could be found. We feel that this is a matter for active consideraiion by the Central and the State Governments, and while we are not in a position to make any positive recommendation, we do recommend that the Central Government should consider the desirability of giving financial assistance to the States so that they may without undue delay and consquent apprehension of damage to the records provide suitable accommodation and proper equipment for preservation of their archives. If this view is found acceptable to the Government, the proposed arrangement of grants may be processed through the Advisory Council which may be required to examine each case on its merits and make the requisite recommendation to the Government. This body, if constituted on the lines we have indicated, will be in the best position to assess the needs of each State requiring help and to draw up a realistic proposal on the basis of actual facts studied and examined by it.

National Register Of Private Archives

136. Finally, the Council will also be of substantial help in promoting the project which, we understand, the Central Government have undertaken, of conducting, in collaboration with the State Governments a survey of important archives in private custody, and of preparing a National Register of such records. The Central Government have set up a small Central Committee for drawing up the survey programmes and for coordinating and guiding the activities of the different State Governments in this behalf. The Central Government also make an annual grant to the State Governments participating in the scheme. We learn from the proceedings of the second meeting of the National Register Committee (September 3, 1960) that in their opinion the task undertaken is not making sufficient progress owing, among other reasons, to the absence both at the Centre and in the States of appropriate organisations that would give full-time attention to the task. The Committee has, therefore, recommended that the National Register Committee should be reconstituted so as to include representatives from such State Governments as may cooperate in the programme and that the body should help in effectively coordinating the work done in the States. While agreeing with the main recommendations of the Committee, we wish to point out that the central advisory body if constituted on the lines indicated by us would provide the exact machinery which in the Committee's view will be able to undertake better planning and better coordination of the survey activities. As the Advisory Council is to be fully representative of the State Governments and will in addition consist of eminent University Professors and archival experts its voice is sure to carry as great a weight in all matters relating to archives in private custody as in those connected with State Archives. We therefore, find no hesitation in recommending that the functions of the National Register Committee as outlined in the Committee's proceedings should be entrusted to the Advisory Council, which through its Standing Committee, will be in a better position to supervise and guide all operations necessary to be carried out in this behalf.

Private Papers

148. In recent years, the Department has also acquired a number of private papers (including story, historical documents, and fragments of family or personal archives) by gift or by purchase. There does not seem, however, any well-defined policy in this respect, and we recommend that the acquisition programme of the Department should be limited as far as possible to private archives which may throw light on important phases of modern Indian history or which may help to fill in the gaps in the existing holdings of the Department. Among these should be classed private papers of statesmen, high government officials, writers, scientists, and all eminent Indians who have played or may play a significant role in the country's history. Private papers of mere local or regional importance should, in our view, be excluded from the programme. The right place to house them are State Archives or local museums or institutions.

Microfilm Copies

150. Before we conclude this topic it is necessary for us to emphasise that the primary duty of the National Archives is to house only such non-current records of the Central Government as may be deemed fit for permanent preservaton and that all other acquisition programmes which we have recommended should be regarded as forming its secondary duty only. A microfilm collection, a collection, of private archives and a library of printed books and documents bearing on modern Indian history are no doubt necessary adjuncts to the Department's archival holdings, but the scope of these collections should be strictly limited to the object which they are required to fulfil, namely, that of supplementing the information furnished by the available records. They should on no account be allowed to grow as independent units pursuing independent acquisition policies.

Changes Suggested

157. We are, therefore, of the view that the present practice of publishing the full text or abridged summaries of a record series in its entirety or selections from them should cease as soon as the programmes in hand have been completed, and that the privilege of full publication should be extended only to such special collections as may relate to a phase of history of which there is at present little or no knowledge, or may reflect a period for which few authorities exist, or to documents which once printed would continue to be read for their intrinsic worth by a wide public and not merely by a limited class of readers. So far as the Educational Records are concerned, we would recommend that the entire task of their editing and publication should be taken out of the hands of the National Archives and should either be undertaken by an appropriate Branch of the Ministry of Education itself or entrusted to any suitable institution.

Research And Reference Work

159. One of the most important functions of the National Archives is to make its archival holdings and the information contained in them easily available to all persons wanting to consult them whether for research or for other academic purposes. Besides supplying records for reference to official agencies and researchers who work in the Departmental Research Room, the Department undertakes to furnish information available in records or in published documents to all types of investigators whose number is steadily on the increase. Prolonged researches are often undertaken on behalf of both Government agencies and members of the public for collecting information bearing on their subjects of enquiry. There are arrangements for supply to scholars and other interested parties of copies of documents wanted by them in type scripts as well as microfilm and photostatic transcripts. One obstacle which impedes the consultation by the public of the archival holdings of the Department is as we have already seen in Section II(D) above the absence of a well-defined policy in respect of public access to records, but the reforms, we have suggested in that section, if carried out, will help in removing this obstacle. Another impediment to research to which we need to call attention is the absence of proper lists for several important series in the Department, but we have already recommended that the listing work should be given the top-most place in the Department's list of priorities. Another way by which the cause of research may be served will be to take up a project of what in United States Archives is known as microfilm publication. The object of such a project is to keep ready for distribution at cost microfilm copies of selections from important record collections or series.

Training In Archives-Keeping

160. Since 1943, the Department has been conducting courses of training in archives-keeping with the object of providing suitably trained personnel for performing archival duties particularly in the official record repositories in the country. The course at peresent includes a year's training in different aspects of archive-science, on the successful completion of which the trainees are awarded diplomas. There are arrangements for the award of five stipends of Rs. 150 each per month to the most deserving among the trainees while the trainees deputed by State Governments and other official agencies outside Delhi are each given a special allowance of Rs. 75 per month. The scheme, however, suffers from the defect that under it there is no obligation

on the part either of the Central Government or of the States to fill all vacancies in arrhival posts necessarily with the holders of the National Archives diploma. The scheme has so far failed to attract really talented students because at present it offers no hope whatever of suitable employment even on the successful completion of the training course. As a modification in the present scheme, we would suggest that the trainees be selected in future against actual vacancies either in the National Archives or any other record office whether of the Central Government or of the States outside the National Archives of India. The selection of the candidates for the posts may be left to the Union or the State Public Service Commission as the case may be, who, if necessary, may subject them to a written test. Training facilities, in our view, should normally be made available only to the candidates who have passed the Public Service Commission's tests and they should be posted only after they have successfully completed the training in the National Archives.

Deposits In Repositories

184. What we have recommended above in regard to collection of private archives by Universities applies equally to principal public libraries as well as the National Library. The latter has embarked on a project for the collection of papers of our national leaders and this deserves the fullest support of all concerned. The public libraries in the States should as far as possible concentrate their efforts on bringing together papers relating to their respective regions. In this connection it may also be useful to promote. State Historical Societies with the object of collecting original materials on regional history. The efforts of these bodies in the field of private archives should further be supplemented by the State Archives. Earlier, we have recommended that State Archives should be divested of all non-archival functions, but that does not preclude the possibility of their receiving for deposit some collections of private papers. The scope of these collections should, however, be confined to such papers as may help to supplement the official archives in the custody of the State repositories concerned or to fill gaps in their holdings. The rest of the private papers and manuscripts should best be deposited in libraries and institutions mentioned earlier.

MINER'S BOOTS COMMITTEE, 1959—REPORT

New Delhi, Ministry of Labour and Employment,
1960. 61, II p.

Chairman : Shri K. N. Subramanian.
Members : Shri N. S. Mankiker; Shri P. C. Ahluwalia; Shri D. N. Sen (coopted).
Secretary : Shri A. P. Veera Raghavan.

APPOINTMENT

The Miners' Boots Committee was constituted under the Ministry of Labour and Employment on September 2, 1959 for the purpose of evolving specifications for a suitable type of footwear for miners.

TERMS OF REFERENCE

(i) To draw up suitable specifications, conforming to certain basic minimum standards, for the footwear to be supplied to coal mine workers, considering the essential requirements of health and safety, the habits of the Indian Miner, and the reasonableness of the cost in the light of existing economic conditions; and

(ii) To examine whether the types of footwear already approved by the Department of Mines are suitable for the purpose and whether the prices charged are reasonable.

CONTENTS

Introductory; Historical Background; Considerations Involved; Specifications Recommended; Cost and Related Matters; Patterns approved by the Mines Department, Summary of Conclusions and Recommendations; Acknowledgement; Appendices A to C.

RECOMMENDATIONS

A survey conducted in the Jharia coalfield in 1947-48 showed that about 55 per cent of underground workers, 49 per cent of surface workers and 11 per cent of clerical and technical staff were infected by hookworm and that use of footwear had a significant effect in reducing the incidence of hookworm.

About one-third of the serious accidents in coal mines cause injuries to the leg. About 60 per cent of leg injuries are injuries to the toes and the ankle. If, therefore, the toes, and the ankle, together with the heel and the sole, are protected, one would have gone a long way towards reducing the number of injuries to miners.

A knee boot, which would protect the shin, is out of

the question in present conditions and slippers are not an adequate protective footwear.

Leather boots are the proper footwear for use in mines, but as workers are not accustomed to wearing heavy footwear and are themselves anxious to have shoes in the beginning, they should be given the option to choose between boots and shoes for a preparatory period of two years. At the end of the two year period only boots should be issued. In order that workers may find it comparatively easy to change over from shoes to boots, both should be of the same materials and constructed in the same manner, the shoes being in all respects a replica of the lower portion of boots.

Shoes will invariably be used not only during the period of work but during off-time. This will happen much less when shoes are replaced by boots. This should be borne in mind while eventually evaluating the life of the footwear that is being recommended by the Committee. Enquiries into actual experience should take into account the extent to which the footwear has been used outsite working hours.

As workers will not be able to buy socks in the existing economic conditions, a soft leather lining should be provided as a partial substitute for socks.

There should be steel toe caps fitted inside, capable of resisting an impact from a blow of 100 ft. lb.

Carbon steel of special quality for the manufacture of toe caps will be available from indigenous sources. But till indigenous manufacturers take up manufacture in sufficient numbers, toe caps may have to be imported. As toe caps are of good quality steel, it would be possible to use them again after being salvaged from discarded footwear.

Leather sole and heel (with hobnails) are better than rubber sole and heel for the majority of workers, in non-gassy mines. Option may, however, be given to workers, in non-gassy mines to choose between leather sole and heel (with or without hob-nails) and rubber sole and heel, after being informed of the difficulties in repairing rubber sole and heel, because for some occupations requiring walking or pushing up gradients, rubber may give a better grip than leather on the ground.

Rubber sole and heel may be the standard for gassy mines, as naked steel in the form of hobnails cannot be allowed in them.

Leather is the best for uppers in preference to canvas or rubber.

The footwear should be waterproof as the wearer has often to walk or work on wet ground.

Both boots and shoes should have laces and not buckles.

The bigger employers should try to provide mechanical arrangements for brushing and cleaning like revolving brushes. Others must provide hand brushes, dubbin and cleaning rags in central places under the charge of a responsible person or persons.

Employers should make arrangements to set up repair shops in suitable centres in cooperation with workers on a no-profit-no-loss basis. These shops can also sell hobnails, laces, etc., which will be required by workers from time to time. The more important workshops must have arrangements for repairing rubber soles also.

The question of giving training in footwear repair to disabled miners in rehabilitation centres may be explored by the Coal Miners Labour Welfare Fund.

Each employers' organisation or each employer as the case may be, should pool all requirements and place bulk orders on competitive terms. In placing orders a condition may be imposed that a certain percentage of the bulk orders will be subject to test at the expense of the manufacturer. In each case a joint purchase committee should be set up to take charge of all arrangements for the procurement and supply of footwear including the issue of tenders, selection of samples, timely securing of supplies, testing of quality, recovery of workers' contribution and proper fitting of workers. The purchase committee should consist of representatives of the employer or employers' organisation and of the workers in equal proportion together with the Regional Labour Commissioner concerned or an officer designated by him.

The Government Test House, Alipore, which is easily accessible to employers in the major coal producing areas, may be the best place for getting samples tested. If it be found that special tests on toe caps cannot easily be carried out, it would be sufficient if the steel used conformed to the composition and hardness indicated in Annexure 2 to Appendix B.

The specifications recommended by the Committee are in Appendix B. Any scope for effecting improvements in these specifications in future can be considered by the Indian Standards Institution.

The life of boots and shoes conforming to these specifications will be 12 months as compared to life of about four months or so of the canvas boots introduced in 1958.

The approximate price of shoes and boots conforming to these specifications is estimated at about Rs. 19 and Rs. 22. When tenders are invited, a more favourable rate may be obtained as a result of competition.

It would not be unreasonable to expect employers and workers to pay about Rs. 10 or Rs. 11 each for a pair of sturdy footwear costing about Rs 19 to Rs. 22.

Bonus, where it is due, might be a suitable source for meeting the workers' share of the cost. Where bonus is not due, recoveries may, if possible, be made in quarterly or half-yearly instalments. This must, however, be left for adjustment between employers and workers.

The question whether the use of the approved pattern

of footwear should be made compulsory may be examined at a future time after a substantial number of workers have got accustomed to the use of footwear.

None of the six patterns of boots approved by the Mines Inspectorate in the past was suitable for use in mines. There was, however, some justification for selecting such types, as hard and heavy boots might have proved unacceptable to workers.

The prices of the boots approved by the Mines Inspectorate were not unreasonable.

Appendix B

Specifications Recommended

I

Specifications For Protective Boots For Miners to

Scope

This specification prescribes the requirements of protective boots for use by miners.

Description

The boot described in this specification is ankle high and is made from printed grain chrome upper leather and waterproof sole (either treated leather or rubber). The toe is reinforced by steel toe cap and the tongue is padded up. The leather sole and heel are fitted with rustless metal toe and heel tips (also called plates). Each boot having leather sole is also further reinforced with 13 rustless hobnails, if required by the purchaser.

Materials

Upper Leather: Chrome tanned printed grain upper leather, cow, calf or young buffalo, conforming to I.S.I. specification No. IS : 578-1954.

The shade of the upper leather shall be as previously agreed to between the purchaser and vendor and approved by the former.

Lining Material

Leather vegetable tanned, cow, calf, sheep or goat skin of good quality for the vamp.

Bottom Material

Vegetable tanned leather for bottom components shall be well tanned and compressed buffalo leather, conforming to I.S.I. specification No. IS : 579-1954. The outer sole leather shall be further treated by wax-oil mixture to impart waterproofness. (A typical oil wax composition is indicated at Annexure 1.)

Moulded rubber sole and heel of good quality, which shall be durable in wear and give satisfactory grip on the rocky surface with steep gradient. (For guidance, a typical design of rubber sole and heel is illustrated in diagram),

The type, quality and shade of the sole shall be as agreed to between the purchaser and vendor and previously approved by the former.

Threads

Upper Closing : Thread linen 3-cord No. 18, 5-cord No. 18 and 3-cord No. 50.

Bottom Stitching : Thread linen 10 cord No. 18 and 12 cord No. 18.

Steel Toe Cap : Moulded toe cap made from high tempered carbon steel sheet conforming in respect of impact test to the British Standards Institution specification No. 953 of 1952 Grade II and in respect of composition and hardness to Annexure 2. In the absence of facilities for the impact test in accordance with the British Standards Specification, steel toe cap conforming to the requirements of Annexure 2 shall be considered acceptable. The shape and design of the steel toe cap shall be according to diagram 5.

Tape : Cotton tape $\frac{3}{4}$ in. (19 mm) or drill strips 3/4 in. turned in at the edges.

Bottom filling Material : Tarred felt or cork sheet or any other suitable material such as gummed or tarred newar or durry which do not crumble or shift during use.

Eyelets : Brass or brass coated steel eyelets for boots, jappaned, or otherwise coated to a shade, matching the colour of the upper leather.

Toe Compound : Cement and gum compound.

Rivets : Brass $\frac{1}{2}$ in. (12.5 mm), $\frac{9}{16}$ in. (14.3 mm) and $\frac{3}{4}$ in. (19 mm) spear pointed.)

Screw Wire : Brass No. 2 in accordance with the details given at Annexure 3.

Heel Pin : Iron rust proofed $1\frac{1}{8}$ in. (29 mm).

Laces Leather : 34 in. (86 cm) in length, $\frac{1}{6}$ in. (4.2 mm) in width and 1.75 mm. to 2.0 mm. in thickness, made from well fat liquored and well dubbined chrome tanned leather, matching the colour of the boot upper. The average breaking strength of the laces (between 24 in. grip) shall be not less than 45 lbs. and the colour of laces shall be post to wet rubbing.

Shank : Iron shank properly moulded, free from rust and sharp edges.

Heel Tip and Toe Tip : Steel, rustproofed in accordance with Annexure 4 and diagram 6.

Heel tip rail 7/8 in. (21 mm) and toe tip nail 3/4 in. (19 mm) : Steel rustproofed and in accordance with diagram 6.

Lasting Tacks : Iron (8 mm) and $\frac{1}{2}$ in. (12.5 mm) rustproofed.

Components

Each component of the boot shall comply with the following requirements :

S. No.	Component	Material	Thickness	
			Min.	Max.
(i)	Vamp	Prime part of side cow or young buffalo	1.50 mm.	1.75 mm.
(ii)	Quarters	Remaining best portion of side, cow or young buffalo	1.75 mm.	2.50 mm.
(iii)	Toe cap and outside counter with Jug loop and strengthening pieces	Do	1.25 mm.	1.75 mm.
(iv)	Full helows tongue and seat sock	Remaining portion of leather, soft and pliable	0.75 mm. 1.00 mm.	1.00 mm. 1.25 mm.
(v)	Vamp lining	Cow, calf, sheep or goat leather	1.00 mm.	1.25 mm.
(vi)	Tongue lining	Raised woollen cloth	Weight 12 ozs/sq. yd.	
(vii)	Insole	Well struck and rolled shoulders	6 Irons	7 Irons
(viii)	Through middle sole	Do (For boots having leather outer soles)	7 Irons	8 Irons
(ix)	Through middle sole	Do (For boots having rubber outer soles)	4 Irons 8 Irons	5 Irons 9 Irons
(x)	Outer soles	Prime part of bend treated for waterproofness.		
(xi)	Moulded rubber sole and heel	As per quality and design previously approved.		
(xii)	Lifts and split lifts	Compressed bellies	5 Irons	8 Irons
(xiii)	Stiffeners	Well struck shoulders and bellies	4 Irons	5 Irons
(xiv)	Top fillings	Prime part of bend treated for waterproofness.	7 Irons	8 Irons
(xv)	Shanks	Steel Shank	Previously approved.	
(xvi)	Steel toe cap	Steel	Previously approved.	

Construction

The protective boots for miners shall be made to the pattern, shape and design shown in diagram 1 or 2. The construction shall be by composite method i.e., riveted stitched and screwed. The boots shall be made on well fitting broad toe lasts previously approved by the purchaser. Lasts taken from model No. 10883, as used for army boots which cater for various foot widths in the same size are recommended.

Prior to commencing supplies the vendor shall tender to the purchaser a pair of boots for approval.

Manufacture

The various components of the boots shall be cut to the thickness, shape and design as required.

The upper components, specially the vamps and tongues shall be properly skived.

The upper shall be closed on lock stitch machines, the counter, back and tongues with linen thread 3-cord No. 18, sides and toe caps with 5-cord No. 18 taping with 3-cord No. 50. The number of stitches shall be 7 to 8 per inch. There shall be two rows $\frac{1}{8}$ inch (3 mm) apart on the toe caps and counters and two rows $\frac{1}{4}$ inch (6 mm) apart on the sides. All loose ends of stitching threads shall be properly secured.

The tongue shall be full bellows and so fitted that wrinkles do not appear where it is joined with the vamp. A layer of raised woollen cloth shall be stitched to the flesh side of the tongue to act as a cushioning padding.

Six eyelets shall be fitted in each facing. Each eyelet shall be peoperly clenched without distortion.

The counter shall be turned over to within $\frac{1}{2}$ in. (12 mm) of the top of the leg so as to form a jug loop, as shown in diagram 1 and 2. The top of the quarters shall be reinforced by stitching a one inch (25 mm) wide leather strip at the back.

The back seams shall be reinforced by stitching a $\frac{3}{4}$ in. (19 mm) wide cotton tape or drill strip over the back seams.

The heel stiffener shall be reinforced with cement toe compound to make it hard and strong. The steel toe cap shall be pre-moulded to the exact shape and contour of the last. The edges of the steel cap shall be free from sharp points or burrs.

All bottom components shall be properly prepared and moulded before use. The insoles shall be properly feathered and shall be lightly buffed on the grain side. The outer leather soles shall be open channelled.

The outer sole may be pieced under the heel provided the joint shall not less than one inch (25 mm) behind the breast of the heel. The piece sole shall be of the same quality as the sole and of corresponding thickness.

In the case of a leather soled boot the heel shall consist of whole cut or two pieced lifts, one split lift and tip filling complete with metal heel tip. The tip filling shall be attached by $\frac{3}{4}$ in. (19 mm) spear pointed brass rivets and the tip heel by rustless heel tip nails.

The uppers shall be tightly laced up to the fourth eyelet before lasting so that the quarters meet on the instep. Prior to the insertion of the steel toe cap the upper shall be pulled over and the vamp lining lasted to the insole. The protective steel toe cap shall then be positioned and firmly secured to the insole. The boots shall be properly lasted so that the uppers are properly embedded to the last. In order to ensure a firm attachment of the uppers to the insole, a clear half inch lasting allowance all round the upper shall be provided. The stiffener shall not be cut short in any way but shall come adequatey under the lasting. The lining shall be properly cleared during lasting. The boots shall remain on the lasts for a minimum period of twenty-four hours.

A metal shank shall be fitted to the waist of the insole. The bottom shall be filled with tarred felt or sheet cork or other suitable material previously approved.

The full leather middle soles shall be attached by means of $\frac{1}{2}$ in (12 mm) long rivets at the rate of four rivets per inch. All rivets shall be properly clenched to the insoles.

All stitching threads for sole sewing shall be properly waxed before use.

The attachment of the soles and heels of rubber and leather soled boots shall be as follows:

Boots With Leather Soles and Heels. The leather sole shall be securely stitched with the middle sole in an open channel by the lock stitch method using 10 and 12 cord linen thread for machine made boots and 10 cord thread for hand made boots. The number of stitches shall be 5-6 per inch (2-3 per cm.). The loose ends of all stitching threads shall be secured.

The outer sole shall be screwed all round by means of brass screw wire No. 2 spaced one inch apart. The screw wire shall penetrate all the bottoming layers and shall be clenched properly to the insole.

The built up moulded and compressed heel shall be securely attached by means of 12 heel pins $1\frac{1}{8}$ in. long (29 mm) from the inside by machine or hand.

Boots With Rubber Soles and Heels: The rubber sole shall be positioned on top of the middle sole and securely stitched with the middle sole in an open channel by the lock stitch method using 10 and 12 cord linen thread for machine made boots and 10 cord linen thread for hand made boots. The number of stitches shall be 5-6 per inch (2-3 per cm.). The loose ends of the stitching threads shall be secured.

The rubber heel shall be securely fixed by a suitable number of $1\frac{1}{8}$ in. (29 mm) heel pins from the outside, a leather lift being positioned in between the rubber sole and the rubber heel prior to attachmant if and when required.

Finishing Applicable to both Leather and Rubber Soled Boots: The height of the heel when finished shall be $1\frac{1}{8}$ in. to $1\frac{1}{4}$ in. (29 mm to 32 mm) and the heel shall be in proper alignment with the tread of the sole.

The sole and heel edges of leather soled boots shall be carefully trimmed, scoured and set black or brown as required to give a smooth finish.

The sole and heel edges of the rubber soled boots shall be scoured and finished smooth.

The upper shall be finished bright by polishing to give an attractive appearance.

A seat sock shall be provided with every boot and shall be firmly pasted.

All boots with leather soles shall be fitted with a rust proof metal toe plate and by toe tip nails. 13 hobnails shall be fitted in each boot if required.

A pair of leather laces previously approved shall be provided with each pair of boots.

Each boot shall be legibly and indelibly marked with the manufacturer's name or recognised trade mark at the waist of the insole. The size and fitting number shall be marked on the waist of outer sole.

In appearnce, general workmanship and finish and in all other respects not defined in this specification the boots shall be equal to the approved sample.

II

Specifications For Protective Shoes For Miners

Scope

This specification prescribes the requirements of protective shoes for use by miners.

Description

The shoe described in this specification is in Derby design with four eyelets and is made from printed grain chrome upper leather and water proof sole (either treated leather or rubber). The toe is reinforced with steel toe cap and the tongue is padded. The shoe is lined throughout. The leather sole and heel are fitted with rustless metal toe and heel tips (also called plates). Eeah shoe having leather sole is also further reinforced with 13 rustless hobnails if required by the purchaser.

Materials

Upper Leather: Chrome tanned printed grain leather cow, calf or young buffalo conforming to ISI specification No. IS: 578-1954.

The shade of the upper leather shall be as previously agreed to between the purchaser and the vendor and approved by the former.

Lining Material: Leather vegetable tanned cow, calf, sheep or goat skin of good quality.

Cotton drill for the vamp (with a minimum B.S. of 450 lbs. in the warp direction and 250 lbs. in the weft direction in six width between 4 in grip).

Bottom Material

Vegetable tanned leather for bottom components shall be well tanned and compressed buffalo leather, conforming to ISI specification No. IS: 579-1954. The outer sole leather shall be further treated by wax oil mixture to impart water proofness. A typical oil-wax composition is indicated at Annexure 1.

Moulded rubber sole and heel of good quality, which shall be durable in wear and give satisfactory grip on steep, rocky surface. For guidance, a typical design of rubber sole and heel is illustrated in diagram 7.

The type, quality and shade of the sole shall be as agreed to between the purchaser and the vendor and previously approved by the former.

Threads

Upper Closing: Thread linen 3-cord No. 50 and 3-cord No. 18.

Bottom Stitching: Thread linen 8 cord No. 18 and 10 cord No. 18.

Steel Toe Cap

Moulded toe cap made from high tempered carbon steel sheet conforming in respect of impact test to the British Standards Specification No. 953 of 1952 Grade II test and in respect of composition and harness to Annexure 2. In the absence of facilities for testing the impact test in accordance with the British Standards Specification, steel toe cap conforming to the requirements of Annexure 2 shall be considered acceptable. The shape and design of the steel toe cap shall be according to diagram 5.

Tape: Cotton tape $\frac{3}{4}$ in. (19 mm) or drill strips $\frac{3}{4}$ in. (19 mm) turned in at the edges.

Bottom Filling Material: Tarred felt cork sheet or any other suitable material such as gummed or tarred newar or durrie which does not crumble or shift during use.

Toe Compound: Cement and gum compound.

Rivets: $\frac{1}{2}$ in. (12 mm) and $\frac{3}{4}$ in. (19 mm) spear pointed.

Heel Pins: Iron, rust proofed 1in. (25 mm).

Eyelets: Brass or brass coated steel eyelets jappaned or otherwise coated to a shade matching the colour of the upper leather.

Screw Wire: Brass No. 2 in accordance with the details given at Annexure 3.

Shank: Iron shank properly moulded free from rust and sharp edges.

Toe Tip, Heel Tip, Nail Toe Tip $\frac{3}{4}$ in. (19 mm) And Nail Heel Tip $\frac{7}{8}$ in. (21 mm): Steel, rustproofed and in accordance with Annexure 4 and diagram 6.

Hobnails: Steel rustproofed in accordance with diagram 5.

Laces Fabric: Cotton, black or brown matching the colour of the upper having a length of 23 in.$\pm$1 in. The laces shall have a minimum breaking strength of 80 lbs. between 7in. grip.

Components

Each component of the shoe (see diagrams 3 and 4) shall comply with the following requirements:

S. No.	Component	Material	Thickness Min.	Thickness Max.
(i)	Vamp	Prime part of side cow or young buffalo		
(ii)	Quarters	Remaining best portion of side cow or young buffalo	1.5	1.75 mm.
(iii)	Back strap	Remaining portion of the leather	1.5 mm	1.75 mm.
(iv)	Tongue	Remaining portion of the leather	1.00 mm	1.5 mm.
(v)	Vamp & quarter lining	Cow, Calf, sheep or goat leather	0.75 mm	1.00 mm.
(vi)	Seat sock	Do	0.75 mm	1.00 mm.
(vii)	Tongue lining	Raised woollen cloth	0.75 mm	1.00 mm.
(viii)	Insole	Well struck & rolled shoulder	Weight 12 ozs/sq. yd. 6 Irons	7 Irons

(ix)	(a) Full middle sole	Well struck and rolled shoulder (For shoes having leather outer sole)	5 Irons	6 Irons
	(b) Full middle sole	Well struck and rolled shoulder (For shoes having rubber soles and heels).	3 Irons	4 Irons
(x)	Outer sole	Prime part of bend treated for water proofness	8 Irons	9 Irons
(xi)	Tip filling	Do	7 Irons	8 Irons
(xii)	Moulded rubber sole and heel	As per quality and design previously approved		
(xiii)	Lifts and split lifts	Compressed bellies	5 Irons	8 Irons
(xiv)	Stiffener	Well struck shoulder or belly	4 Irons	5 Irons
(xv)	Steel toe cap	As previously approved	......	......
(xvi)	Shank	Steel shank previously approved.	......	......
(xvii)	Hobnails	Steel previously approved	......	......

Construction

The protective shoes for miners shall be made to the pattern, shape and design as illustrated in diagrams 3 and 4. The shoes shall be made on well fitting broad toe lasts previously approved by the purchaser. Lasts taken from model No. 10883 as used for army boots which cater for various foot widths in the same size, are recommended.

Prior to commencing supplies the vendor shall tender to the purchaser a pair of shoes for approval.

Manufacture: The method of construction shall be by the composite method.

The various components of the shoes shall be cut to the thickness, shape and design as required. The vamp and tongue shall also be in one piece. All upper components shall be properly prepared, including skiving and beading as necessary.

The upper shall be machine closed with lock stitches using linen thread 3-cord No. 18 and 3-cord No. 50. The number of stitches shall be 10-12 per inch (4.5 per cm). There shall be one row of stitches on the quarters, back strap and tongue and two rows on facings all with 3-cord No. 50 and three side rows with 3-cord No. 18. All loose ends of the stitching threads shall be properly secured. All threads for welt and sole stitching shall be properly waxed before use. The quarters shall be lined with leather, the vamp with drill, and the tongue with raised woollen cloth. Four eyelets shall be fitted in each facing, each eyelet being properly clenched without distortion.

The prepared heel stiffener shall be reinforced with cement toe compound to make it hard and strong. The steel toe cap shall be premoulded to the exact shape and contour of the last. The edges of the steel toe cap shall be free from sharp points or burrs.

The bottom components shall be properly prepared and moulded before use. The insoles shall be feathered and the outersoles channelled. The insoles may be lightly buffed on the grain side if required.

Prior to inserting the steel toe cap the upper shall be pulled over and the vamp lining lasted to the insole. The protective steel toe cap shall then be positioned and firmly secured to the insole. The upper shall then be properly lasted to ensure a sung embedding of the uppers to the last and at least a half inch lasting allowance shall be provided all round the upper. The upper linings shall be properly cleared all round. The shoes shall remain on the last till they are perfectly dry and the toe and stiffeners are set hard and strong. A steel shank shall be fitted to support the waist, and the bottom properly filled with the bottom filling material previously approved.

The making operations for different types of construction shall be as follows.

Composite Construction With Leather Outersole And Heel

The full leather middle sole shall be riveted by means of $\frac{1}{2}$ in. (12 mm) spear pointed brass rivets, at the rate of four rivets to the inch.

The outer sole shall then be stitched in an open channel with the middle sole using thread linen 8-cord and 10-cord for machine stitching and 10-cord for hand stitching, and further reinforced by means of brass screw wire No. 2, spaced one inch apart all round. The stitches shall not be less than five nor more than six per inch.

A piece sole may be used provided the joint is positioned at least one inch (25 mm) behind the breast of the heel. The soles shall be properly levelled.

It shall be ensured that all rivets and screws penetrate all bottoming the layers and are properly clenched to the insole.

The leather heel shall consist of two to three whole cut lifts, one split lift, one tip filling complete with metal heel tips and shall be properly pre-moulded and compressed. The tip filling shall be attached by means of $\frac{3}{4}$ in. (19 mm) brass rivets and the heel tip by means of heel tip nails. The heel shall then be attached by means of 12 heel pins, one inch long (25 mm) from the inside in case of machine made shoes and for hand made shoes the heel shall be fixed from outside by a minimum of 14 heel pins which shall be further reinforced from the inside by four to six heel pins

Composite Construction With Rubber Sole And Heel

The through middle shall be riveted all round, at the rate of 4 rivets to the inch (25 mm).

The rubber outersole shall be positioned on top of the leather middle and stitched using 8 and 10-cord linen thread for machine sewing and 10-cord linen for hand stitching. The number of stitches shall be five or six per inch.

The rubber heel shall be securely attached using a suitable number of one inch (25 mm) long heel pins from the outside, using a whole cut leather lift placed in between the rubber heel and the rubber sole, if and when required.

Finishing (Applicable To All Constructions)

The height of the heel when finished shall be one inch (25 mm). The heel shall be in proper alignment with the tread of the sole.

The sole and heel edges of leather soled shoes shall be carefully trimmed, scoured and set black or brown as required to give a smooth finish. The sole and heel edges of rubber soled shoes shall be scoured and finished smooth.

The upper shall be finished bright by polishing to give an attractive appearance.

A seat sock shall be provided for all shoes. Each shoe shall be supplied with a fabric lace equal in quality to that used in the approved sample.

All shoes having leather sole shall be fitted with a rustproof metal toe plate by toe tip nails. Each shoe shall also be fitted with 13 hobnails, if required by the purchaser.

Each shoe shall be legibly and indelibly marked with the manufacturer's name or recognised trade mark at the seat sock. The size and fitting number shall be marked on the waist of the outersole.

In appearance, general workmanship and finish and in all other respects not defined in this specification, the shoes shall be equal to the approved sample.

Annexure 1

Composition Of Oil Wax Mixture For Imparting Waterproofness To Vegetable Tanned Sole Leather

Mineral oil, BOC 103	4 parts
Bees wax	1 parts
Paraffin wax	1 parts
Rosin	$\frac{1}{2}$ parts

Melt the above wax-oil composition and bring it to a temperature of 140°F. Into the molten mixture at 140°F dip the dry cut soles and keep them immersed for 15 to 20 minutes. Take out the soles, allow them to strain and cool overnight, keeping them in a vertical position. Slicker away the excess grease from the surface.

Annexure 2

Composition And Hardness Of Steel For The Steel Toe Cap

The medium carbon steel for the steel toe cap shall conform to the following requirements:

Composition

The medium carbon steel shall consist of the following ingredients in the proportion by weight:

Carbon	0.55 to 0.65%
Manganese	0.52 to 0.80%
Sulphur	0.05% maximum
Phosphorus	0.05% maximum
Silicon	0.1 to 0.35%

Hardness

450 to 500 VPN at a load of 10 kilograms.

Thickness

The thickness of the steel sheet shall be 0.0625 in. to 0.0670 in. (16 B G to 17 B G).

Annexure 3

Requirements Of Brass Screw Wire

Metal	Diameter	Depth of thread	Angle of threads	No. of threads per inch	Hardness at 10 kilso
	'A'	'B'	'C'		
Brass	0.9-1.00 in.	0.015-0.118 in.	95°-98°	20	185-200 V.P.N.

The details 'A', 'B' and 'C' are shown in diagram 8.

Practical Test

The screw wire shall not break when bent at an angle of 90° repeatedly four times.

Annexure 4

Size Of Heel And Toe Tips

Boot/shoe sizes	Tips toe sizes	Tips heel sizes
3 to 5	$2\frac{7}{8}$ in.	$2\frac{7}{8}$ in.
6 to 7	$2\frac{7}{8}$ in.	3 in.
8 to 9	3 in.	$3\frac{1}{8}$ in.
10 to 11	$3\frac{1}{8}$ in.	$3\frac{1}{4}$ in.

COMMITTEE ON COOPERATIVE CREDIT, 1959—REPORT

New Delhi, Ministry of Community Development And Cooperation, Department of Cooperation, 1960. 256 p.

Chairman : Shri Vaikunth L. Mehta.
Vice-Chairman : Shri T.M. Narayanaswami Pillai.
Members : Shri Tarapado Chaudhary; Shri K. Achuta Reddy; Shri B. Venkatappiah; Shri V.K. Rao; Shri B.P. Patel; Shri M.R. Bhide; Shri Siddique Hasan; Shri T.V. Reddi; Shri C. Narasimham; Shri K. Ramamurthy.
Secretary : Shri A. Palaniappa Mudaliar.

APPOINTMENT

The cooperative movement in India originated in the desire to organise and develop a special institutional agency for the provision of credit for agriculture. Through nearly six decades the emphasis on credit has never ceased. Meeting in November 1958, the National Development Council suggested that suitable arrangements for more adequate agricultural credit through cooperative agency should be worked out in consultation with the Reserve Bank of India. The Working Group on Cooperative Policy appointed by the Government of India in November, 1958 for considering the administrative and organisational arrangements for implementing the resolution of the National Development Council on cooperative policy, stated in its report that the problem of providing adequate credit was important and required careful and immediate consideration and suggested that it should be speedily examined by the Government of India, the State Governments, the Reserve Bank of India, and others concerned. It proposed that definite decisions should be taken so that adequate credit, so essential for any programme of increased agricultural production was made available through the cooperative agency. Later, the entire question of agricultural cooperative credit came up for consideration at a conference of the State Ministers in charge of cooperation held at Mysore in July 1959. The conference recommended that an Expert Committee consisting of representatives of the Planning Commission, the Department of Cooperation, Agriculture and Community Development of the Government of India, the Reserve Bank of India, the State Bank of India, two or three representatives of the State Governments and two or three representatives of non-official cooperative opinion should go into the whole question and make concrete suggestions as to how to expand credit for agricultural production on a considerable scale.

In pursuance of this recommendation, the Government of India, Ministry of Community Development and Cooperation, in their Notification No. F-11-25/59-Coop. I dated September 5, 1959, appointed this Committee.

TERMS OF REFERENCE

To examine and make definite recommendations on :

(i) (a) The existing standards for credit limits prescribed under the Cooperative Societies Act, rules or the bye-laws of the societies in the different States and (b) their justification from the point of view of the principles of sound cooperative banking;

(ii) The loan policies and practices of cooperative credit institutions from the apex to the primary level;

(iii) The working in community development blocks and in other areas of (1) a few representative societies which have (a) suffered losses in successive years, (b) got heavy overdues outstanding for more than two years, (c) repeatedly defaulted to the central banks, or (d) gone into liquidation, as also (2) of a few good societies in different States from the point of view of the following criteria, among others, viz. (a) adequacy of credit, (b) coverage of families, (c) inclusion of the smaller farmers and tenants, (d) utilisation of loans for productive purposes, (e) recovery of loans, (f) repayment to the central financing agency, and (g) deposits and encouragement of thrift generally;

(iv) The measures necessary for increasing the borrowing power of primary credit societies to the extent necessary in this connection; and in the same context, the question of revising the existing standards for fixing credit limits and the conditions under which it should be effected with a view to providing more effective credit for agricultural production plans; and

(v) The desirability of share capital participation by the State in village societies and if the Committee is in favour of it, the terms and conditions subject to which such State participation should take place.

CONTENTS

Introduction; Agricultural Production Programmes; Progress of Cooperative Credit Primaries; Progress of Cooperative Credit Financing Banks; Trends in Cooperative Policy; Reorganisation and Revitalisation of Primary Credit Societies; Credit for Cultivating Members; Credit Limits—Primary Credit Societies; Credit Limits—Central and State Cooperative Banks;

Augmenting Internal Resources—Share Capital; Augmenting Internal Resources—Deposits; External Resources—The Role of the Reserve Bank; Other External Resources; Cooperative Marketing; Legislative, Administrative and Organisational Arrangements; Special Funds and Guarantees; Conclusion; Summary of Conclusions and Recommendations; Appendices I to VI.

RECOMMENDATIONS

Agricultural Production Programmes

There is generally no agricultural production plan for each village much less for each family. Even the plans that are now being drawn up in a few cases cannot be said to be on the lines contemplated by the Government of India. What really exists in each State is a plan of State aid for agricultural production drawn up by the State under various heads such as minor irrigation, land development, manuers, improved seeds, etc., and these are prepared by the departments concerned and targets set out for each year.

Any production plan to be drawn up in a systematic manner and to be implemented and supervised successfully, would require the employment of a large technical staff which is not available today. For drawing up such programmes the ground has to be prepared by a detailed survey of various aspects of agricultural production. Measures have to be taken for popularising improved production techniques to be followed by an adequate credit programme. In the absence of adequate staff and supplies, the preparation of production programmes for all cultivating families does not at present seem feasible.

There is no production plan for a village or family with which proposals for expansion of credit could be correlated. Every farmer has a plan of his own and, therefore, arrangements should be made for providing necessary facilities including credit, so that farmers are enabled to raise good crops on their lands.

In areas served by new irrigation projects, the question of finance will require special attention. With the extension of irrigation facilities, when farmers switch over from dry to irrigated farming, there is likely to be an appreciable increase in the demand for medium-term and long-term agricultural credit. In the case of crops like rubber, cocoanut, etc., where the yield will begin only a few years after planting, the problem of providing credit will require special treatment.

A dynamic programme of agricultural credit and distribution will be required to enable the farmer to take full advantage of the agricultural plans and the facilities that would be available for increased agricultural production. Cooperatives will have, therefore, to strengthen themselves financially and otherwise and extend their range of credit and distribution operations, so that all farmers are enabled to take full advantage of the facilities provided under the schemes of agricultura improvement in the Third Five-Year Plan.

Progress Of Cooperative Credit-Primaries

The average working capital of primary agricultural credit societies on June 30, 1958, for the country was Rs. 8,031. It exceeded Rs. 10,000 in Andhra Pradesh, Bombay, Kerala Madras, Mysore, Tripura and Delhi. It was only in Bombay that the average was above Rs. 20,000. The percentage of overdues to loans outstanding exceeded 25 in Bihar, Mysore, West Bengal Delhi and Himachal Pradesh. Nearly one-third of the societies in the country worked in loss or did not make any profit during 1956-57 and 1957-58. Of the 1.35 lakh agricultural credit and multi-purpose societies audited during 1956-57, about 22,000 were in A and B categories, about 81,000 in C and about 22,000 in D and E, while about 10,000 societies were unclassified. A large number of C class societies require considerable reorganisation and revitalisation. Some of these may even have to be liquidated, if attempts to revive their working fail.

The working of primary credit societies cannot be viewed with complacency, as it indicates lack of sufficient vitality and strength on their part. The existence of a fairly large number of dormant and weak socilties is an impediment in the way of new schemes designed to widen the scope and utility of cooperative organisations in the rural areas. For any scheme of expansion of agricultural credit, efforts have to be on parallel lines, one for the organisation of new societies and the other for the reorganisation and revitalisation of a large number of existing societies.

Progress Of Cooperative Credit Financing Banks

Out of 418 central cooperative banks and banking unions functioning in the country at the end of June 1958, 185 or about 44 per cent did not come up to the minimum standards regarding owned funds and working capital recommended by the Reserve Bank's Standing Advisory Committee on Agricultural Credit. It is imperative that in the context of the increased responsibilities they will be called upon to bear in an expanded programme of agricultural credit, the banks should build up quickly their resources and expand their loan business.

While introducing land reforms, State Governments should ensure that the interests of land mortgage banks are not adversely affected. All land owners, occupancy tenants and tenants in the process of becoming owners, should have an unfettered right to mortgage their rights in favour of a cooperative society. State Governments should give a definite assurance to make good the loss sustained by land mortgage banks as a result of land or tenancy reforms. If steps to safeguard the interests of land mortgage banks are taken simultaneously with the introduction of land reforms, the banks can be expected to finance the new class of land owners as well. For this purpose central land mortgage banks may have to take the initiative in developing their business for which Government may give subsidies in the initial period for appointment of managerial and valuation staff.

Reorganization And Revitalisation Of Primary-Credit Societies

A systematic programme of rectification, consolidation and revitalisation of the large number of dormant primary credit societies should be chalked out before they can be relied upon to play their part in the expansion of rural credit.

Since the number of inactive societies requiring careful attention is admittedly large, it will be necessary to appoint special staff for the purpose. Where the number of dormant societies is large, one or more inspectors may be posted in each district to attend to rectification. In States where the total number of societies to be rectified and revitalised runs into 500 or more, one or more Assistant Registrars may be appointed for expediting the work.

All societies, old and new, should be strong enough not only to function efficiently at the start, but to weather the strains and difficulties which will be inevitable as they assume additional and heavier responsibilities as time progresses. One of the main aims of future endeavour should be the promotion of viable units of cooperative service and business. A viable unit is that which may be expected within a reasonable time to render the more important of the services expected of credit societies both adequately and to as large a number of producers as possible, without depending upon financial assistance from Government except for a limited period. The society should have the ability not only to command the services of competent personnel, but at the end of the stipulated period be able to meet fully the expenditure incurred on such personnel as well as the expenditure on rent, audit and supervision and provide for education fund, reserves and a reasonable return on share capital.

A society requires services of two kinds, those consisting in direction, guidance and participation generally. These have been available so far on a voluntary basis; but there are others involving managerial duties, clerical work, keeping of accounts and so on. Even these services may in some areas or in individual instances be available on an honorary or near-honorary basis. In terms of the country as a whole, the services of competent and trained managers, accountants, clerks, etc, are not available except on the basis of remuneration.

The cooperative aspect is as important as that of viability, the coorperative society cannot afford to enlarge itself into an impersonal institution. The membership should not be too large and the area too extensive. No village included in a society should be at a distance of more than three or four miles from the headquarters village. The majority are of the view that the population covered should not exceed 3000 (i.e. 600 families or 500 cultivating families).

The need for flexibility in the approach to the pattern of organisations should not be overlooked. There has to be flexibility not only in respect of the details of the pattern itself, but of the process of choice and decision whereby patterns suitable to different areas are adopted by those who are most affected. Such patterns must fall within a broad framework of policy. But, subject to this consideration, it is necessary that State Governments which are primarily responsible for cooperation should be left free to choose, in consultation with local cooperators and cooperative financing banks, the type most fitted for different areas of their States.

The pattern of Government assistance should in its turn be a flexible one, the main test being that it will help promote viable societies of the type required in the different areas, in relation to the condition of those areas. The proposals in this regard are as follows:—

(a) **Share Capital:** The State Government should be satisfied that the society is viable in the light of the broad criteria mentioned above. The contribution of share capital from the State should range from Rs. 1,000 to Rs. 10,000 on a matching basis. Further, the society should undertake to collect additional share capital of not less than Rs. 3,000 from its members over a period of three to five years.

(b) **Subsidy:** A subsidy of Rs. 1,200 to be given for a period not exceeding five years should be available to all viable societies brought under the State programme. Where a society is already receiving or has been promised assistance on the basis of existing schemes such as the revitalisation programmes, the present position should not be disturbed.

(c) **Grants:** Outright grants for contribution to 'special bad debt reserves' should be available to all societies, whether or not viable (provided, of course, their audit classification is not D or E).

Credit For Cultivating Members

By and large, the grant of loans to individuals follows landed property rather than the productive purpose for which the loans are taken. This practice has an adverse effect on agricultural production. The various land reform measures in the different States seek to confer on tenants protection against arbitary eviction and ensures to them a good share of the crops raised by them. Their status and economic position are bound to improve in future. It is, therefore, necessary that cooperatives provide funds even to this class of cultivating members, provided they are honest and possess the necessary repaying capacity and produce sureties who, however, need not necessarily be owners of land.

A primary credit society should not deny a loan to a person merely on the ground that he does not own land or cannot produce owners of land as sureties. The primary test for judging the credit worthiness of an individual is his repaying capacity and to that extent he can be advanced a loan by the society on the basis of his requirements for agricultural production.

In judging the production needs, account should be taken of the nature of the crops grown, of the fertilisers, manures, better seeds, etc., which the cultivator is going to use and also of the likely effect of these improved methods of cultivation on the borrower's income and his repaying capacity. The judgment in that behalf should be left to the managing committee or the general body of the society itself.

The scope for misapplication of the loans obtained by a member can be minimised by supplying in kind as large a part of the loans as possible. It will be necessary to channel the distribution of the available quantities of seeds, fertilisers agricultural implements, etc., through primary credit societies.

The share capital held by a member in the society occupies an important place in the system of cooperative credit. It is a measure of his interest in the financial stability and soundness of the society. It also creates a sense of responsibility and ensures his loyalty to the society. Further, it is a good way of promoting thrift among members. Individual members, therefore, should be required to contribute to the society's share capital in certain proportion of their borrowings. This principle should be adopted in limited as well as unlimited liability societies.

The borrowings of an individual may not exceed eight to 10 times his paid-up capital in the society. By-laws of societies should contain specific provisions to secure this linking. However, a member whose loan requirements do not exceed Rs. 200 may be allowed to subscribe to two shares of Rs. 10 each, but pay up only Rs. 5 per share in the first instance and the balance in the next two years in two instalments of Rs. 2.50 each.

In view of the need for making adequate credit available to all cultivators in relation to the acreage under cultivation and the kind of crops raised, absolute limits for loans to individuals prescribed in the by-laws or otherwise may be reviewed in the light of the increased costs of cultivation. There should, however, be a ceiling for individual loans so as to ensure that the needs of small and medium cultivators are not sacrificed in favour of the big cultivators. There may be instances where the grant of loans above the general ceiling may be necessary. Exceptions may be made on the merits of each case where the borrower gives satisfactory evidence that the additional credit limit will be utilised by him for increasing agricultural production.

Borrowings of an individual against pledge of jewels (gold and silver in bars or ornaments) or goods or fixed deposit receipts may, if necessary, be in excess of the general ceiling prescribed by the by-laws of the society. It will be necessary, however, to fix ceilings for each such class of loans so as to ensure that the benefit of credit facilities from the primary credit society is restricted to cultivators and not passed on to others, e.g., traders, merchants, etc.

Discretion to prescribe the nature of security for a loan to an individual should necessarily be left to the managing committee of a society. Insistence on mortgage security for short-term loans denies the benefit of cooperative credit to a large section of agricultural community. Members should be allowed short-term loans on the production of two sureties from fellow members, whether or not they own land, provided the amount for which they stand surety is within prescribed limits.

All borrowings—short-term or medium-term—by an individual should be within the credit limit fixed for him by his society. It does not seem necessaey to prescribe a ratio between short-term and medium-term loans taken by an individual.

Insistence on mortgage security for all medium-term loans, irrespective of the amounts, results denying such loans even to tenants who have a heritable tenancy right but no right to mortgage it. As a general rule, mortgage security need not be insisted upon for loans below Rs. 500. Loans between Rs. 500 and Rs. 1,000 may be given on the borrower creating a charge on his land. For loans above Rs. 1,000 it would be desirable to obtain mortgage security.

When the benefits of improvement take time to accrue repayment of a medium-term loan in annual instalments beginning at the end of the first year may cause hardship to a borrower. Central banks and societies may examine the question of making the first instalment payable, in such cases, at the end of the second or third year when the investment on the land will begin to yield additional income. Similar facility will be desirable in respect of long-term loans, particularly when such loans are required for plantation crops like rubber which begin giving income from the seventh year or so.

In order to facilitate the issue of long-term loans for land improvement, land mortgage banks may, for the purpose of valuation of land, take into consideration not the existing but the anticipated value. To cover the risk involved, the State Governmeut might provide guarantee to land mortgage banks to cover the difference between the value before and after land improvement.

Credit Limits : Primary Credit Societies

For the type of viable unit visualised and the services village societies are expected to undertake, organisation of societies on the basis of limited liability would be more suitable.

The owned funds of a cooperative society serve as a margin of security for creditors and also help it to absorb the shock of overdues. What the owned funds are to a limited, liability society, the net assets are to an unlimited liability society. The credit limits for limited liability societies are fixed, generally, at eight times the owned funds and for unlimited liability societies at one-eighth of the net assets of members. By and large these limits have not so far stood in the way of the societies raising adequate funds. It is urged that these limits will prove inadequate to implement the expansion of credit now envisaged. After a careful examination of the suggestion, in the context of the factors determining the credit worthiness of the societies in the eyes of the creditors, of the actual position in regard to reserve borrowing power of the societies on the basis of the existing standards and also the improvement that is likely to result in it from the additions to their owned funds in the case of limited liability societies and from a proper valuation of the assets of the members of unlimited liability societies, it seems that it may not be necessary to commence, as a rule, the present limits in respect of all limited and unlimited liability societies.

In special circumstances there may be need for increased credit limits for the societies. Where the Registrar is satisfied about the need, he may fix the maximum limit of a limited liability society between ten to twelve times its owned funds and that of an unlimited liability society upto one-sixth of the value of the net assets of members, after taking into account various factors such as the efforts made by the society to build up its share capital, the existence of special schemes of credit and of effective linking of credit with marketing, the attempts made to extend credit facilities to the weaker sections of the agricultural community, the adequacy or otherwise of the existing arrangements for recovery, the record in the matter of advances and recoveries, the efficiency of management etc, and after consulting the central cooperative bank to which it is affiliated. The fixation of credit limits beyond eight times the owned funds for limited liability societies and one-eighth of net assets for unlimited liability societies may be reviewed periodically so as to assess the performance of the society.

The practice of some central banks to insist on cent per cent repayment of the loans due to them from a society as a condition of making fresh advances in unduly rigid and denies credit to members who have repaid their dues punctually. At the same time, a central bank should not continue to finance a society irrespective of the degree of default, firstly of members to the society and secondly of the society to the central bank. Some standards in that regard should be prescribed by each central cooperetive bank after taking local circumstances into account.

Credit Limits : Central And State Cooperative Banks

Owned funds for the purpose of determining, the borrowing power of a Cooperative bank, may apart from the paid-up capital and statutory reserve fund, include other funds of a permanent nature creatred out of profits, such as building fund, stabilisation fund, sinking fund for defentures, other than in central land mortgae banks. This definition may be accepted by the Reserve Bank when fixing credit limits with reference to owned funds of State and central cooperative banks.

By and large, State and central cooperative banks have adequate borrowing power on the basis of the existing standards. Account has to be taken of the fact that owned funds of the banks will grow automatically with the expension of business by the linking of the borrowings of the various units with their share capital. Further, State Governments will continue to contribute to the share capital of the banks. Finally, the revised definition of owned funds will mean an increase in such funds for some banks, thus giving them larger borrowing power. It may not therefore, be necessary, as a rule, to revise the existing standards which are generally 10 to 12 times the owned funds for central cooperative banks and 15 times the owned funds for State cooperative banks. In individual cases, in the context of special schemes of agricultural credit or of the extension of credit facilities to medium and small cultivators by a substantial proportion of primary credit societies affiliated to the bank, or of procurement and distritution of controlled commodities through cooperatives or of the financing on a large scale of marketing and processing societies against pledge of goods the credit limits fixed on the above standards may prove inadequate. In such an event the Registrar may fix limits at higher levels after examining each case on merits. Liberalisation may be done in each case in consulation with the state cooperative bank (so far as central banks are concerned) within the range of 12 to 15 times for central banks and 15 to 20 times the owned funds for state cooperative banks. The revision so made may be reviewed periodically. Liberalisation in the circumstances described above should not result in slowing down the process of collecting more share copital from constituents and should not also lead to the Government contributing less to the share capital of the bank than they would otherwise have done.

Augmenting Internal Resources: Share Capital

Judged by past performance, it appears that mobilization of reasources through deposits will be a slow process in primary credit societies. Share capital as a means of promoting thrift in the cooperative movement at the base has a more satisfactory record and holds out better promise for the future.

Apart from inspiring greater confidence among creditors, to strengthening of the share capital base services to increase the internal resources of primary credit societies and thereby reduces their reliance for funds on outside agencies. It would, therefore, be desirable for the societies to make systematic efforts to augment the share capital even beyond the level of 10 per cent of the borrowings recommended. The additional contributions should be realised at the time of harvest when a member sells his produce or on any other occasion when he can conveniently part with some portion of his savings.

There should also be a link between shareholding and borrowings in central banks so that their owned capital will increase automatically and proportionately with the increase in their loan operations. Primary credit societies should be required to contritute to the share capital of the central cooperative bank at the rate of 1/20 of their borrowings. Societies that do not borrow from the central cooperative bank should also be required to contritute to its share capital in recognition of its role as a balancing centre for all cooperative societies in a district.

As there does not appear to be any large scope for central cooperative banks building up their share capital by enrolling more individual members, no special attempts may be made in that direction.

Several members would contribute to the share capital of primary credit societies in instalments. The societies could also require some cash resources for the non-credit activities undertaken by them. Thus the resources needed for credit and non-credit business will be large and can be raised only when the capital base of the societies is strong. Further, a broad capital base is required at the primary level so that the shock of overdues is aborbed to as large an extent as possible at that level and the liquidity and financial stability of the institutions above it are not seriously affected. For all these reasons the share capital of primary credit societies will need strengthening by contributions from Government.

Partnership of the State should ordinarily correspond to the efforts made by individual members of societies. The extent of Government contribution may be governed by the following :

(i) The share capital contributed by the State should not be more than the contribution made by individual members of societies;

(ii) The contribution of share capital from the State may range from Rs. 1,000 to Rs. 10,000. The minimum contribution of Rs. 1,000 should, however, be available only if the society undertakes to collect additional share capital of not less than Rs. 3,000 from its members over a period of three to five years; and

(iii) The contributions may be continued from the initial level for a period of five to eight years, during which the society may be expected to reach the optimum level and may not, therefore, require any further additions.

There may be no rigidity in the matter of duration of State partnership and in the manner in which share capital held by the Government is retired. During the period when an additional contributions from the State are made, there may be no retirement. After the optimum level is reached, the process of retirement should start and might be completed during the next five to eight years. Such retirement should be so regulated as not to affect the interest of creditors. In particular, the central cooperative bank should be consulted in the matter of the programme of retirement.

Government should be a partner in the real sense and participate in the risk of business in the same manner as any other share holder. In other words, the Government's capital will also serve as margin of security to creditors. Further, the State should not enjoy any privileged position in the matter of dividends vis-a-vis the other share holders.

Government may stop making further contributions to the share capital of a society and may even withdraw the share capital already contributed after giving due notice of its desire to do so both to the society and to its creditors, if they find that the society does not show a progressive attitude towards the admission of small and medium cultivators and towards financing them on the basis of their production needs and repaying capacity.

It would be advantageous for the partnership of the State to be indirect at the primary level, i.e. through the apex and central cooperative banks. This will help strengthen the federal character of the cooperative credit structure.

In indirect partnership, the right to make nominations should vest in the central cooperative bank. The neminees of the Government or of the central bank should not have the right to veto. Government nomination should not lead to interference in the day-to-day working of the societies.

State partnership may ordinarily be in societies which, in the course of a few years, are likely to become self-sufficient. In unlimited liability societies, State partnership may be resorted to where it will increase their borrower power. The question may, however, be decided after examining the legal position. The State should take shares in society only if 60 percent of its members decide in its favour and the central bank to which it is affiliated endorses the resolution of the general body of the society.

Augmenting Internal Resources : Deposits

The success of the cooperative credit movement in the country will in the ultimate analysis, depend upon the extent to which self-reliance is fostered at the primary livel. At the same time, conditions will have to be created at this level so that primary credit societies may be in a position to mobilise savings in the rural areas. No agency, cooperative or other, can hope for success unless it inspires confidence and invokes local interest.

One of the grounds for recommending a viable unit at the primary level is that it will be in a position to inspire confidence in, and provide the necessary services to, the depositors. In addition to the financial and administrative strengthening of primary credit societies, it will be necessary for them to offer sufficiently attractive rates of interest. These may provide the required incentives for persons in rural areas to deposit their savings with primary societies.

The cooperative structure being federal, the higher financing institutions have a responsibility towards meeting the credit requirements of members of primary societies which constitute the base. The need, therefore, for State and central cooperative banks making special efforts for tapping deposits from urban areas cannot be over-emphasised.

The following measures are suggeted for this purpose.

(i) Substantial contributions may be made by Government to the share capital of cooperative banks to impart to them the financial strength necessary to inspire confidence among the dipositors.

(ii) In the face of competition for available funds from commercial banks Central and State Governments etc. the banks should offer competitive rates of interest on deposits.

(iii) State Governments should remove the restrictions which stand in the way of local bodies, educational institutions, etc., depositing their funds with cooperative banks.

(iv) The banks should provide reasonable banking facilities to individuals such as opening current accounts, collecting cheques and bills, issuing demand drafts, etc.

(v) The banks should take up the question of opening branches in suitable centres.

(vi) Influential non-official chairmen and directors can play a useful role in inducing urban population to keep their funds with cooperative banks and hence the practice in some States of having officials as chairmen of the banks should be discontinued.

The suggestion that Government may guarantee deposits in cooperative banks as a measure of augmenting their resources is not practicable.

Cooperative credit societies and banks and the staff employed by them should not be asked to do propaganda in favour of National Savings Certificats or be appointed as agents for collecting contributions to these Certificates. No pressure should be exercised on depositors in cooperatives to withdraw their diposits for investment in the Certificates or on the cooperative themselves to invest funds in them.

What counts with the cultivator is not the rate at which he obtains credit from his society, but its adequacy and timeliness. This should not be taken to indicate that credit may be provided without regard to its cost to the ultimate borrower. The rate of interest charged to him should be a realistic one in the context of the prevailing money rates and the existing need of the co-operatives to attract larger funds by way of diposits. It is not possible to suggest a rate which would be appropriate or the margins that may be retained at the different levels. The factors that are relevant in this context vary widely from bank to bank and from society to society that no uniform rates or margins can be suggested. As far as possible the highest margin may be allowed at the primary level as compared with the other two levels of the structure, to enable the primary credit societies to acquire greater financial strength.

Financing banks should not charge differnt rates of interest on loans for the same purpose according to the source of funds. The resources obtaind from all sources should be pooled and an average borrowing rate worked out. The rates charged to the lower institutions should be based upon this average rate.

The State Bank of India has agreed to provide interim finance to central land mortgage banks against the guarantee of State Governments. Where the State Governments are unable to provide the necessary finance, the banks may approach the State Bank of India for the purpose.

With the existing competition for funds in the money market, it is possible that land mortgage banks may not always succeed in getting subscriptions to their debentures. The cooperative movement itself can provide some assistance to land mortgage banks in this regard. State and central cooperative banks have to maintain fluid resources according to certain prescribed standards against their deposits and certain other liabilities. Debentures of land mortgage banks can serve as a suitable medium for the maintenance of fluid resources.

External Resources: The Role Of The Reserve Bank

The part played by the Reserve Bank of India in the progress achieved by the cooperative credit structure in the provision of agricultural finance has been very significant. The increasing reliance of same State cooperative banks on the Reserve Bank is in itself not an indication of the weakness of the banks, but may on the contrary, be a sign of a rapidly developing agricultural economy in the area. But where the borrowings from the Reserve Bank constitute a very large part of the agricultural lendings of a bank, the question does arise whether maximum efforts are being made to mobilise resources such as deposits as also to divert a reasonable proportion of such resources to agricultural finance. The proportion of financial accommodation from the Reserve Bank has, therefore, to be considered in the light of many factors, such as the pace of agricultural development in an area and the strength and efficiency of the cooperative credit structure.

When a rapid agricultural development is envisaged and the cooperatives have been chosen as the best agency for the provision of credit, it will be unrealistic to expect them in the near future to raise the necessary resources, wholly or in the bulk, from owned funds and deposits. Self-help and self-reliance are undoubtedly the guiding principles of cooperation. But to achieve self-sufficiency will be relatively a slow process. The Reserve Bank, therefore, is likely to have to play a prominent part in this context for many years to come.

The need for greater assistance from the Reserve Bank should be viewed in the context of the policy pursued by the Bank over the past decade. This policy is part of the larger objective of building up a strong, sound and country-wide structure of cooperative credit for agriculature and other purposes. The Bank will, in the context of providing short and medium term credit to coopertives on a more liberal scale than at present, therefore, be entitled to take into account the efforts made by the cooperative movement in (i) increasing its financial strength and operational efficiency (ii) developing its resources through share capital and deposits with a view to promoting greater self-sufficiency and (iii) extending the provision of agricultural credit.

The following criteria may be adopted by the Reserve Bank of granting short-term accommodation for agricultural purposes to State cooperative banks on behalf of central banks.

(i) The distinction made at present between 'normal' and 'exceptional' limits may be removed so that the normal credit limit to which A and B class central banks will be eligible will be four times and three times their owned funds respectively.

(ii) In adition to the above, an A class central bank may be sanctioned a limit not exceeding twice its owned funds and a B class bank equal to its owned funds on the following conditions.

(a) For the amount outstanding against a bank out of the limit sanctioned by the Reserve Bank in excess of the 'normal' limit as indicated in (i) above, the bank should show outstanding loans against societies for agricultural purposes for twice the amount borrowed. In other words, of the excess of loans outstanding against societies for agricultural purposes over and above the 'normal' limit, only 50 per cent can be from funds provided by the Reserve Bank, the other half being provided by the bank out of its own resources.

(b) The outstanding loans for the above purpose, i.e. for normal or additional limits, will not include any overdue loans. It will also be necessary to ensure that the real position of overdues is not concealed by extensions granted without proper examination of the merits in each case.

(c) In computing a bank's own resources for the purposs mentioned in (a), borrowing from the State cooperative bank, the State Bank of India and Government will be excluded. Account will be taken of the funds derived from the bank's share capital, reserves and deposits.

(iii) A C class central bank may be sanctioned a limit upto three times its owned funds against the guarantee provided by Government. The limit may be raised to four times in special circumstances. Simultaneously, there should be a systematic programme of rectifying the defects in these banks. The facility for loans against Government guarantee may be for a period of three years during which the programme of rectification and consolidation of the bank should be completed. The State Government may review the position in this behalf at the end of each year.

Any liberalisation in the present standards for sanctioning medium-term loans by the Reserve Bank, i.e. equal to the owned funds of a central bank, will be possible only if the resources in the long-term operations Fund out of which such loans have to be sanctioned are appreciably augmented. The Reserve Bank may be authorised by the Government of India to credit Rs. 15 crores annually to the Fund as against Rs. five crores which are being contributed now.

The provision of more medium-term credit from the Reserve Bank should be co-related to the efforts made by a central bank in raising more medium-term funds in the form of share capital and fixed deposits. The Reserve Bank may sanction an additional limit to a central cooperative bank up to twice the increase in fixed deposits and share capital registered during the year prior to that for which the limit applies provided, however that the 'normal' and the 'additional' limits do not together exceed twice the owned funds of the bank. For the purpose of the additional limit, the increase in share capital taken into account should exclude that received from Government during the year. The above formula may be applicable to all central banks, irrespective of their audit classification. The limits proposed are with reference to the medium-term loan outstandings and not to the amounts borrowed every year.

Other External Resources

With a view to enabling marketing societies to avail themselves of larger facilities than hitherto from the State Bank of India, the bank may examine whether instead of having physical custody of the produce, it can protect its interests effectively by arranging, if necessary, periodical inspection and by requiring the societies to furnish, at frequent intervals, statements of the stock held by them.

At the village level there should be only one institutional agency for the supply of credit, *viz.*, the cooperative and the policy of the Government should be such as will eventually lead to that result. Funds intended for disbursement as taccavi, short-term or medium-term, should be placed at the disposal of the cooperative credit structure.

Provision has been made under the Community Development Programme for issue of loans in block areas for purposes such as sinking of wells, land improvement, etc. Wherever a cooperative society exists, medium-term loans should be channelled through it alone and that for this purpose, appropriate funds should be placed at its disposal.

In routing *taccavi* through the cooperatives, if the State Government consider that the rate of interest on loans for a particular purpose or for a class of persons or for a particular area should be fixed at a particular level, the cooperatives may be required to issue such loans at that rate and the difference between an institution's actual lending rate and its economic lending rate may be made good by the State Government by providing the necessary subsidy.

The Government of India may take up with the authorities in the United States, the question of allocating a part of the "P.L. 480 Funds" to the cooperative credit structure for the provision of medium-term and long-term finance for promoting agricultural development. The necessary details of the organization, etc., that may have to be set up for utilising the funds, in case they are made available, may be worked out by the Government in consultation with the Reserve Bank.

The Life Insurance Corporation of India should make substantial contributions, to the debentures floated by land mortgage banks, particularly in areas which are less favourably situated in the matter of raising funds. Where the Corporation has agreed to a definite subscription, land mortgage banks should reserve that part of their debenture issue for allotment to the Corporation

Where legislation in regard to investment of the Trust Funds does not provide for investment in debentures of land mortgage banks, such a provision should be made as expeditiously as possible. Large sums that are available under the Provident Funds might also be allowed to be invested in these debentures.

Cooperative Marketing

The linking of credit with marketing, besides enabling members of credit societies to reap the benefit of organised marketing, helps in the recovery of loans out of sale proceeds of the produce. The arrangments for linking credit with marketing should be strengthened throughout the country.

If the linking of credit with marketing has not been established to the extent desired or even necessary, it is largely because of the fact that marketing societies have not till now acquired any hold over agriculturists, except in certain areas in a few States and in respect of some cash crops. The reasons for this state of affairs are many and varied.

It will be necessary to provide more godowns for primary credit societies, which can serve as auxiliary to those set up by marketing societies. The programme for construction of godowns by primary credit societies should be proceeded with as part of the Third Five-Year Plan.

For cooperative marketing to succeed, marketing societies should be permitted and enabled to make outright purchases from the producers. To protect these societies from the risk of loss in making outright purchases on a large scale, State Governments should fix a certain minimum price at which they would be prepared to purchase from the cooperative societies.

The suggestion for establishing a link between credit and marketing by requiring a member of a credit society by law to bring to the marketing society agricultural produce at least equal in value to the amount of crop loan raised by him from the credit society, is not favoured. The introduction of a compulsory levy might cause hardship either because the grower may like to retain the crop raised by him for consumption and pay the loan from other sources of income, or because he may be able to get a better price elsewhere than the one at which the cooperative marketing society offers to purchase.

When a decision is taken by the State to take up trading in foodgrains, Government should ensure that the interests of the members who bring their poduce to marketing societies are not placed at a disadvantage as compared to those dealing with private traders.

Legislative, Administrative And Organisational Arrangements

State Governments may, in the light of the recommendations made in the report, consider what further changes will be necessary in their laws and take action to get them suitably amended.

Where necessary, the Cooperative Societies Act may be amended to provide for a member creating a charge on his property by signing a declaration in writing so that he can be saved from the trouble and expense involved in registration of mortgage deeds.

State Governments may provide in the Cooperative Societies Act for charge being created in favour of a society on the crops raised by a member and also frame appropriate rules for enforcement of the charge.

Steps may be taken to amend the Cooperative Societies Act, where necessary, so as to vest in the Registrar the power to execute awards passed for the recovery of cooperative dues. He should be given sufficient and special staff for this purpose. It is necessary to ensure that the procedure for recovery prescribed under the Civil Procedure Code is strictly observed by the staff appointed by the Registrar and, therefore, it will be desirable to train the staff in this respect and to place it under a senior and experienced judicial officer who may himself be attached to the office of the Registrar.

The majority are of opinion that in the context of the expansion of credit envisaged in the future through the cooperatives, Central cooperative banks will have to assume responsibility for supervision of primary credit societies affiliated to and financed by them.

A supervisor has to perform a variety of functions. He should, therefore, be incharge of such number of societies as he can reasonably be expected to supervise efficiently. It will be necessary to reduce the change of a supervisor which at present varies from State to State. The question of further strengthening the machinery for supervision may be examined by the central cooperative banks and the cooperative departments.

In States where it is not the practice to nominate the Registrar or the Deputy or Assistant Registrars on the boards of the apex and central cooperative banks, the Cooperative Societies Act should be amended to vest in the Registrar the power to inspect, on his own motion, apex and central cooperative banks and primary societies. This power may be delegated by the Registrar to officers working under him. It may be necessary, however, to prescribe that the power to inspect a State cooperative bank may not be delegated by the Registrar to an officer below the rank of a Joint or Additional Registrar. Similarly, the power to inspect a Central cooperative bank may not be delegated to an officer below the rank of a Deputy or Assistant Registrar. For primary societies, a person not below the rank of an inspector may be appointed.

The Registrar cannot fulfil his responsibility unless he keeps in close touch with the working of societies by getting their accounts audited under his direction and control. In Punjab and Uttar Pradesh where the Registrar is not responsible for audit of cooperative societies, steps may be taken to transfer the control of audit to the Registrar.

Audit of cooperative societies is in arrears in many States. This is not a happy position. The need for auditing all cooperative societies efficiently and promptly will be much greater in the context of the programmes for expansion of agricultural credit. Wherever the staff for audit is not adequate, steps may be taken by the State Government concerned to appoint the necessary additional staff so that all the societies and banks are audited every year. The number of societies under an auditor may be reviewed in the light of the increase in the volume of transactions that may take place in primary credit societies and the change of an auditor may be fixed by the States with due reference to these transactions.

The existing position of staff in the cooperative departments and cooperative institutions may be reviewed by the State Governments and federal agencies concerned and additional staff provided for where necessary, so that the increased responsibilities of the various authorities can be discharged satisfactorily.

Special Funds and Guarantees

Production in agriculture is affected by cycles of short-falls. Some dependable provision is essential to enable cooperative banks to tide over financial difficulties arising from widespread adverse seasonal conditions and the consequent failure on the part of members of cooperative societies to repay their loans when even the banks' resources are inadequate to meet such situations.

The constitution and strengthening of the Agricultural Credit Stabilisation Fund at various levels of the cooperative credit structure is essential. It should be obligatory on financing banks and primary credit societies to build up this Fund to the extent possible. It is necessary for banks and societies to provide in their by-laws not only for the manner in which the Fund shall be constituted, but also for the purposes for and the manner in which it will be utilised.

The Reserve Bank may frame rules governing its National Agricultural Credit (Stabilisation) Fund so that cooperative financing agencies may know the circumstances under which assistance from the Fund may become available to them.

The need for the Governments setting up Relief and Guarantee Fund will be greater when the cooperatives undertake to finance agriculturists on a much bigger scale than hitherto. State Governments should make suitable provision in that behalf in the Third Five Year Plan. It will also be necessary to frame rules for the purpose. The model rules circulated by the Government of India may be adopted by State Governments with such modifications as may be considered necessary to suit local conditions.

Agricultural finance, as such, involves greater risk than finance for commerce which is largely based upon tangible security. The extension of credit facilities to a class of persons to whom they were so far denied and also to the class of persons who were getting credit inadequately, may amount to the cooperative credit agencies being called upon to shoulder heavier responsibilities and greater risks than they have been undertaking so far. These institutions have shown some hesitation in providing credit for production on the basis of repaying capacity to landless tenants and others who are sometimes described as marginal or sub-marginal cultivators. If a system can be devised by which primary societies are enabled by suitable assistance to withstand accumulation of overdues and ultimate losses arising out of such overdues, it would help them and the financing banks to go ahead with programmes for expansion of agricultural credit.

A guarantee given by Government to make good the loss suffered by a society could be invoked only when the processes of recovery of the dues from the primary borrower and his sureties have been exhausted. Most societies and banks may not be inclined to take up the financing of all classes of cultivators on the expanded scale now envisaged, on the mere assurance that their ultimate losses will be met partially after they are finally determined.

In order that cooperative credit institutions may undertake the financing of all classes of cultivators in earnest and without mental reservations, some incentive in a more concrete form than a Government guarantee is necessary. The incentives may be as under.

(a) Government may give an outright contribution to the funds of each society at three per cent of the additional loans made by it during a year over and above the loans advanced by it in the preceeding year. The assistance proposed may be shared equally between the Central and Slate Governments.

(b) Government may also make an outright contribution at one per cent, similarly, to Central cooperative banks in respect of the additional finance provided by them.

(c) The advances to be taken into account for the purpose of the assistance will be, in either case, those made for financing agricultural production. Since, by and large, loans given against pledge of produce or jewels are not for production, such loans should be excluded for this purpose.

(d) The contribution recommended above may be made by the Governmet in the year 1961-62 in respect of the increase, in the loans registered by societies and banks in 1960-61, over the figure of loans advanced in 1959-60.

(e) Contributions from the Government may be given for the first two years without examining how far the increase in the loan business is reflected in the expansion of credit facilities to the weaker sections of the community. Before contributions are made in the third year, Government may withhold assistance from a society which has not made any satisfactory progress in that direction.

(f) The contributions received by societies and central banks should be credited by them to a special bad debt reserve which will be distinct from the bad debt reserve created out of their profits.

(g) The special bad debt reserve of the societies should be kept as a deposit with the Central Bank to which they are affiliated. It should be permissible for the bank to invest its special bad debt reserve in its business.

(h) The special bad debt reserves may be drawn upon with the permission of the Registrar. Rules may be framed for the purpose. While withdrawal by a primary credit society from the reserve may be made to cover the entire amount of loss, the withdrawal by a Central Bank may be only to the extent of two-thirds of the loss, the balance being borne by the bank.

The assistance from the State, on the lines recommended above, will serve as the needed catalytic agent and provide the moral, more than the material, assurance that may be necessary before the benefit of cooperative credit is extended to all sections of the agricultural community.

Conclusion

Credit from the cooperatives should no doubt be adequate for the production requirments of a cultivator, but should not be so facile or so inadequately supervised as to render possible its use for consumption rather than for increasing production. Any misuse of the extended facilities may give a set back to the attempts made to build up strong cooperative credit system.

Within the framework of the broad principles which may be applied to the country as a whole, the greatest possible freedom should be allowed to State Governments who are responsible under the constitution for Cooperation and no less to the people associated with the movement. Provision of various aids from Government should not be intended or used for compelling societies to adopt a particular pattern of organisation.

Once a policy is adopted after the fullest consideration, adherence to that policy for a fairly long period is essential so that it may have scope for operation over a reasonable length of time. It is only then that the effects of such a policy can be assessed. The importance of periodical evaluation of the results connot be underrated. Such an evaluation may be undertaken, through a small committee, by the Ministry of Community Development and Cooperation in collaboration with the Reserve Bank of India. With this committee, an economist and a non-official co-operator should be associated. The evaluation reports should provide the basis for adjustments or changes in policy, in case they are deemed necessary after consultation with the various interests concerned.

To the extent it is possible to secure the services of suitable persons to associate themselves actively in the direction and management of cooperative organisations at various levels, the cooperative movement can be expected to establish itself firmly in the country. It is, therefore, of vital importance that such leadership should be encouraged for the promotion of the movement.

The role of the State will consist in providing the assistance required by the institutions during the period of their initial growth, but should not extent to the internal management of societies and banks, which should be left to the representatives of the members themselves. This will involve discontinuance of the practice, obtaining in some States of officials occupying responsible positions in boards of directors—such as those of chairman and vice-chairman. The posts of managing directors and secretaries should be normally filled by the board of management or the general meeting, appointment to these posts being made by Government only for special reasons and for specified periods.

It will be necessary to draw in, for the management of cooperative institutions, public-spirited workers who will subordinate their personal interests and party and political considerations to the common good of the people.

To meet the requirements of scheduled tribes and scheduled areas, special steps may become necessary. Some of the conditions attached to the grant of financial aids of various descriptions may have to be modified or relaxed. The duration of such aids also may have to be extended.

ASSESSMENT COMMITTEE ON VIJNAN MANDIRS, 1959—REPORT

New Delhi, Ministry of Scientific Research and Cultural Affairs, 1960. 84p.+vp.

Chairman : Shri Balwantray G. Mehta.
Members : Shri M.P. Bhargava; Shri Muhammed Khuda Bukhsh; Shrimati Yashoda Reddy; Shri C. Ramachandran (coopted); Thakur Phool Singhji (coopted).
Secretary : Shri N.K. Sreenivasan.

APPOINTMENT

The Assessment Committee on Vijnan Mandirs was constituted under the Ministry of Scientific Research and Cultural Affairs, vide their Order No. 1/19/59-VM-I, dated September 14, 1959 to review the working of the Vijnan Mandirs and consider the desirability of enlarging their scope by the addition of cultural activities.

TERMS OF REFERENCE

(a) How far have the Vijnan Mandirs fulfilled their objectives?

(b) What are the difficulties they have faced and how can these be overcome?

(c) Is there any need to change the nature and extent of the assistance given by the States?

(d) The desirability of widening the scope of Vijnan Mandirs and of adding a Cultural Wing to them.

(e) Any other suggestions for improving the work of the Vijnan Mandirs.

CONTENTS

Part I:—Introduction; Historical Survey (Vijnan Mandir—Concept and Approach); Factual Picture Today; A Review of the Scheme; Need for Vijnan Mandir; Programme of Work; Extension Through Service; Administrative Set-up; Organisational Arrangements; Recruitment and Training; Cultural Wing; Conclusion;

Part II:—Summary of Recommendations; A note on Financial Implications.

RECOMMENDATIONS

Factual Picture Today

In a few Vijnan Mandirs both the Vijnan Mandir Officer and the Assistant Vijnan Mandir Officer were drawn from the same group of Science and not from complimentary groups. There is need to post the staff on a rational basis for proper balancing of work.

A Review Of The Scheme

Inspections which provide first-hand knowledge of local difficulties, to be effective, should be conducted as frequently as possible.

Proper shape and content must be given to the programme of work, bearing in view the objectives of the scheme and the capacity and limitations of Vijnan Mandirs.

Need For Vijnan Mandirs

If an adventitious programme like Vijnan Mandirs is to really help the educational process, they should be properly located, equipped and staffed.

An institution like the Vijnan Mandir close to the village and related to its immediate needs should primarily strike the horizon of the villager and improve his mental state.

A scheme like this which has been developed to a certain stage should be carried on to obtain results. If these "little islands of science" are to help in developing a scientific temper among the people, they should be properly worked.

Programme Of Work

Vijnan Mandirs have to concentrate on adults of

significant age-groups who are not yet too old to learn and who have not had any formal education.

Vijnan Mandirs should educate villagers on sanitation, health and hygiene, balanced diet and nutrition, pest and plant diseases, taking into account available resources in the rural areas.

In places where no Science Clubs have been set up, the Vijnan Mandir Officers should persuade teachers to organise them. They should also assist in starting such Clubs for interested groups.

Vijnan Mandirs should mobilise the agency of progressive farmers to reach the people.

Vijnan Mandir Officers should participate in the meetings of agencies like Youth Clubs, Community Centres and Mahila Samaj inside the Blocks where they are located.

The agency of trained teachers should be mobilised by Vijnan Mandirs and utilised as 'intermediaries' to create science-consciousness among rural people.

There is need for providing a museum which will be realistic and functional. The exhibits should carry suitable explanatory notes in regional language.

Exhibits might be stocked at convenient centres in the States and sent to the various Vijnan Mandirs according to pre-arranged programme.

A pattern for eqipping the museum for the guidance of State Governments and other agencies who might be invited to work the scheme, should be laid down.

The Committee of experts in the Planning Commission, which we have recommended separately to go into the entire question of equipment and training concerning Vijnan Mandirs, might also consider the manner in which the Vijnan Mandir museum should be equipped and organised.

Vijnan Mandirs should be equipped with audio-visual aids like projectors, films, film-strips and slides to enable them to arrange educational shows.

Every Vijnan Mandir should draw up a programme of talks, lectures, demonstrations, etc., sufficiently in advance and this programme should be implemented systematically and continuously.

Lectures and talks should be prepared with due regard to the psychology of the village adult and this aspect should also be taken care of in the training programme of Vijnan Mandir Officers. Records should be kept of such lectures and talks.

The favourable atmosphere provided by fairs and festivals should be exploited to the best advantage by Vijnan Mandirs for dissemination of scientific knowledge. Better facilities should be afforded to them to arrange exhibitions, etc. on a wider and more efficient basis.

With the assistance of Social Education Organisers and Gram Sevikas and voluntary agencies. Vijnan Mandir Officers should reach the womenfolk and educate them no subjects like environmental hygiene, nutrition child-care, house-keeping and family planning.

Vijnan Mandir library should make available scientific and technical knowledge of a higher type. The library should also be equipped with popular scientific literature in regional languages.

The Ministry should draw up a scheme to encourage production of popular scientific literature by scholars and other experts by giving them necessary financial and other assistance.

Easy literature dealing with rural problems such as rural housing, road making, minor irrigation, utilisation of waste products, etc., should be made available to Vijnan Mandirs.

Brochures and other literature as also leaflets produced by state agencies, together with information on the results of investigations on fields trials conducted by them on various rural problems should be supplied to Vijnan Mandirs.

With the assistance of the National Library, Sahitya Parishads and other competent agencies, a suitable bibliography of scientific books may be prepared.

Vijnan Mandirs may collect useful information from different sources, process it and make it intelligible to the common man. They may also serve as a liaison with the National, the Regional and the State laboratories and other research institutes and refer to them for investigation and advice such problems as cannot be solved at their level. In other words the Vijnan Mandir may function as a 'clearing house' for local scientific knowledge.

Educational programmes launched by Vijnan Mandirs should have a practical bias and be closely related to the daily problems of the villager.

Vijnan Mandirs should educate villagers about the causes of common diseases and how they could be prevented by adopting some simple and prompt measures.

Vijnan Mandirs should play an important part in educating villagers on 'First Aid' measures to be adopted in certain emergencies.

Vijnan Mandirs should take note of the work done in the field of balanced diet and nutrition by other agencies and pass it on through all available media of communication to the villager.

Vijnan Mandirs should investigate the diet habits of the people and suggest suitable remedies to correct imbalances in consultation, if necessary, with other expert agencies.

Elementary ideas of genetics, moral and sex hygiene and child-care may be spread by Vijnan Mandirs.

Vijnan Mandirs may educate villagers on the need for family planning.

Scientific information with regard to soil improvements, conservation of soil and moisture, water application methods; improved agricultural practices, plant protection, food preservation, etc., should be spread by Vijnan Mandirs.

Vijnan Mandirs should enlighten farmers on methods of raising high-yielding and nutritious grasses and on methods of preservation of the nutritional value of available fodder.

Vijnan Mandirs should disseminate knowledge on the need for castration of over-aged and other scrub bulls and for prophylactic treatment like inoculation and other precautionary measures against diseases like rinderpest and advise on care and sanitary upkeep of livestock.

Vijnan Mandirs should suggest ways for the utilisation of available local resources to the best advantage.

Cottage industries provide Vijnan Mandirs with a first-rate opportunity to apply their minds to the problem of more efficient production at the village level and to suggest ways and means for better production through the introduction of improved tools and methods.

Efforts should be made to garner village 'wisdom' born of practical experience before it is irrevocably lost. Vijnan Mandirs should study the local practices and habits and, where necessary, refer them to higher institutions for proper appraisal.

The programme of work in Vijnan Mandirs should be elastic and adjusted to accommodate local needs. Modifications in the programme may be considered by local committees.

Vijnan Mandirs should act as catalytic agents to *supplement*, and not to *supplant* the work of other agencies.

Some order of priority has to be observed in the execution of programme. The different items included in the programme might be taken up generally in the order in which they have been dealt with in this chapter.

Vijnan Mandirs should maintain records in respect of every village. An illustrative pro-forma may be prescribed.

All observations made and advices given should be entered carefully in the register maintained for the purpose.

Definite lines may be prescribed for Vijnan Mandirs for evaluation of achievements without introducing rigidity into the process.

Vijnan Mandirs should be asked at the beginning of each year to send up a plan for the year in consultation with local committees. The plan, as finally approved, may be the basis for evaluating the work done by Vijnan Mandirs.

An elastic job chart may be prescribed in regard to different items. These could be supported by quarterly reports from Vijnan Mandirs.

Even in regard to intangible benefits, some action may be taken to evaluate the work. There may be an initial survey at the time a project is launched, followed by a second survey after a period of time. The change in the picture as presented by two survey reports would give some indication of the impact made by the project in question.

Extension Through Service

Service is essential to give a richer content to education. Kept within reasonable limits, service programmes will not only not detract from the importance of utility of Vijnan Mandirs, but positively help in the educational process.

Vijnan Mandirs may undertake simple analysis of soil and advise people in rural areas on matters like soil deficiencies, manurial recommendations and suitability of water for irrigation.

Facilities may be provided in Vijnan Mandirs for simple pathological examination. Apart from helping diagnostic work, such examination in the presence of the villager has a real educational value. Some arrangement may be made with the nearest hospital or the Primary Health Centre for supervision of the work and for interpretation of the results of pathological investigations.

Vijnan Mandirs may undertake simple examination of water to assess suitability for irrigation and consumption.

Facilities for detection of food adulteration may also be provided in Vijnan Mandirs. The Sub-Committee to be set up in the Planning Commission may consider what additional equipment is required for this purpose.

Administrative Set-up

Vijnan Mandirs should be built up from below and not wholly from above. The Centre, apart from having sponsored the scheme, should provide the necessary financial assistance and technical guidance. But the needs of the people and their demands should shape and strengthen the structure from below.

Before a final pattern is evolved for the administration of Vijnan Mandirs, the scheme should be given a further and fuller trial through different methods listed.

There is need for recognition of the vital role of voluntary agencies and other institutions of the people in the implementation of a National scheme such as Vijnan Mandirs. If Vijnan Mandirs are to be brought closer to the life of the people, full advantage will have to be taken of the work of all such voluntary agencies and institutions which have established places of their own in the life of rural community.

Rural Institutes which have already inspired confidence in the minds of the people may he invited to work Vijnan Mandirs, according to the general pattern laid down by the Government.

A survey should be made of voluntary agencies which by dint of devoted service, have created the necessary atmosphere for development work and those among them which are willing to implement the Vijnan Mandir Scheme should be given necessary facilities. These agencies should have the freedom to develop the scheme along their own lines consistent with the objectives laid down for it. They should be ready to accept inspection and audit by the states in which they are located, while responsibility for higher training and technical guidance of the personnel and over-all evaluation might remain with the Centre.

In the initial stages, both recurring and non-recurring expenditure on the administration of Vijnan Mandirs may be met by the Centre. After a period of time, the Rural Institutes and other voluntary agencies administering the scheme should be asked to bear a portion of the expenditure. The balance should be shared between the Centre and the States in the same ratio as may be decided upon in respect of Vijnan Mandirs which will be integrated with selected Blocks

Even after integration with selected Blocks, Vijnan Mandirs may work in close association with educational institutions.

Vijnan Mandirs may fall in line with the new pattern envisaged under democratic decentralisation and accept some control by Panchayat Samitis.

Vijnan Mandir officers may be made ex-officio members of the functional sub-committees at the Block and the District levels.

The relations between Block Development Officers and Vijnan Mandir Officers should be similar to those that subsist between the Block Development Officers and the Doctors in the Primary Health Centres.

For purposes of administrative control, Vijnan Mandir Officers should be placed under the State Education Department.

Vijnan Mandirs may function as part of a comprehensive programme of educational and training institutions and agencies like selected Blocks. There might be an internal evaluation of the scheme which will be administered by different authorities followed by an assessment by an external agency after a suitable period.

Establishment of Vijnan Mandirs should be suitably phased.

75 per cent of the non-recurring expenditure on buildings (including staff quarters) transport, furniture, equipment, etc., should be met by the Centre and the remaining 25 per cent by the States, subject to suitable monetary ceilings.

For the first three years recurring expenditure on pay and allowances, etc., should be met by the Centre. Thereafter, a formula may be negotiated for apportionment of costs between the Centre and the States.

Organisational Arrangements

Suitability of site and accommodation for Vijnan Mandir work and other factors should be kept in the selection of sites for locating Vijnan Mandirs. The needs of backward areas should also be considerd.

A type design for the Vijnan Mandir building should be prepared.

Provision of suitable residential accommodation for the staff is necessary.

The jurisdiction of a Vijnan Mandir should be coterminous with the Block.

No restrictions need be placed on participation by Vijnan Mandirs in fairs, festivals and other occasions of importance in other Blocks of the District.

Vijnan Mandirs should have the freedom to establish contacts with educational institutions, Panchayat Samitis and other village groups interested in Vijnan Mandir Work, etc., if they are located outside the Block.

Each Vijnan Mandir should have a minimum of two officers drawn from complementary subjects to supplement each other's work.

In selecting officers suitable women candidates may be considered for appointment to one of the posts.

Each Vijnan Mandir may have a laboratory assistant, trained in pathological work. Laboratory assistant should also function as museum-keeper.

To enable the village people to keep their equipment in good repair and also help in running the projectors, there is need for a mechanic close at hand. The mechanic should also function as driver.

Vijnan Mandir Officers may be provided, where necessary, with some clerical assistance. However, the facilities available in institutions with which Vijnan Mandirs may be integrated should be kept in view before separate clerical assistance is provided.

Vijnan Mandir Officers should be declared Drawing and Disbursing Officers and invested with powers of 'Head of Office'.

Vijnan Mandir Officers may also be invested with powers to incur expenditure on individual items up to certain limits. Provision should also be made for relaxation of these limits up to certain ceilings in respect of proposals which have the concurrence of the local committees or other specified local authorities.

The present imprest of Rs. 50 is inadequate and may be increased to Rs. 100.

Vijnan Mandir Officers may be declared as the appointing authority for Class IV staff.

Vijnan Mandir Officers may be vested with powers to impose minor penalties on Class III staff working under their control.

Vijnan Mandirs should be provided with a mobile van fitted with a generator and fixtures for transporting laboratory equipment and audio-visual aids. However, the facilities available in those institutions with which Vijnan Mandirs may be integrated should be taken into account.

A separate Advisory Committee for Vijnan Mandirs may not be necessary. But the functional sub-committees envisaged for the Panchayat Samitis and the Zila

Parishads for education and allied activities should include the Vijnan Mandir Officers.

Vijnan Mandir sub-committee should be set up for the Rural Institutes and other bodies which might run the Vijnan Mandirs in future.

There should be a Standing Committee with representatives of the Centre, the States and concerned institutions to ensure uniformity in the administration of Vijnan Mandirs in accordance with the policy evolved by the Centre and also to review the progress made from time to time.

While internal assessment of the working of Vijnan Mandirs may the conducted by the agencies which will be responsible for the actual administration of Vijnan Mandirs, some external assessment may be entrusted to the Programme Evaluation Organisation of the Planning Commission.

If Vijnan Mandirs are attached to institutions like Rural Institutes, a budget with ceilings for different items may be drawn up for each Vijnan Mandir.

Recruitment And Training

A good master's degree in Science should be the minimum qualification as at present for the Vijnan Mandir Officers and the Assistant Vijnan Mandir Officers.

The senior officer in a Vijnan Mandir should be an M.Sc., in Agriculture with research or teaching experience. The junior officer may be drawn from the physical sciences, preferably, Chemistry. Persons with some field experience and ability for writing and lecturing on popular scientific topics in the regional language may be preferred.

The Vijnan Mandir Officers may form part of suitable cadres in the States and their scales of pay should be such as to attract young men of talent with an aptitude for a work of this type and who can do justice to their work.

Non-official organisations like Rural Institutes which may be willing to work the scheme according to the pattern laid down by the Centre should be left free to adopt their own scales of pay, subject to suitable ceilings to be fixed for purposes of grants by the Centre.

Vijnan Mandir Officers with sufficient promise may be given preference for appointment in the extension wings of research laboratories, agricultural colleges and teachers' training colleges.

As far as possible, Vijnan Mandir Officiers may be recruited from the teaching staff of science or agricultural colleges.

60 per cent of the posts of Assistant Vijnan Mandir Officers should be filled by departmental candidates and the remaining 40 per cent by direct recruitment.

25 per cent of the posts of Vijnan Mandir Officers may be filled by promotion of Assistant Vijnan Mandir Officers. The remaining vacancies may be apportioned between departmental candidates and direct recruits on the basis of 60 per cent and 40 per cent respectively.

For making appointments in Vijnan Mandirs, persons with a rural background may be preferred, other conditions being equal.

In view of the qualifications prescribed for the Vijnan Mandir Officers and their responsibilities, conferment of gazetted status on them is essential.

The programme for the training of Vijnan Mandir Officers and Assistant Vijnan Mandir Officers may cover the following aspects:

(i) Training in extension methods, processes of communication, etc.;

(ii) Training at an Orientation Training Centre,

(iii) Training in museum techniques;

(iv) Visits to selected Vijnan Mandirs and conducted tours;

(v) Some specialised training at institutions like the Indian Agricultural Research Institute; and

(vi) Training in nutrition.

A Sub-Committee may be set up in the Planning Commission to consider (i) the adequacy and suitability of equipment supplied to Vijnan Mandirs; (ii) the facilities available at the existing trianing centres for the training of Vijnan Mandir Officers and (iii) the arrangements to be made to fill the gap.

The question whether the existing training institutions controlled by the Ministry of Community Development and Cooperation could be utilised for imparting training to Vijnan Mandir Officers should be examined in Consultation with that Ministry.

Vijnan Mandir Officers should receive training in the science of human relations and human values in the institutions imparting training to Social Education Organisers.

Refresher courses for the staff already in position should be held at regular intervals to bring them into touch with the latest developments.

Even after the reorganised set-up suggested by the Committee gets stabilised, the practice of holding Annual Conference of Vijnan Mandir Officers should continue.

At suitable intervals, the Vijnan Mandir Officers should be deputed to attend special refresher courses for about a month or two in an appropriate institution in the State where they are working.

Those who have completed three years of service may be made quasi-permanent.

Cultural Wing

Vijnan Mandirs should concentrate on dissemination of scientific knowledge. To add a cultural wing now to Vijnan Mandirs may involve a fundamental change in the basic concept of the scheme, not justified by the circumstances.

COMMITTEE ON IMPROVEMENT IN QUALITY AND ECONOMY IN PRODUCTION IN THE GOVERNMENT OF INDIA PRESSES, 1959—REPORT

New Delhi, Ministry of Works, Housing and Supply, 1960. 38p.

Chairman : Shri K.G.S. Pisharody.
Members : Shri U.S. Mohan Rao; Shri G.S. Bhasin.
Secretary : Shri B.C. Sen Gupta.

APPOINTMENT

The Government feels that there is considerable room for improving the quality and reducing the cost of printting at the Government of India Presses. It has, therefore, been decided that a Committee should be appointed to make an investigation into Government Printing and submit a report on the steps that may be necessary to:

(i) Bring about an improvement in the quality of printing at the Government of India Presses; and

(ii) To effect economy in Government Printing consistent with the requirements for quality printing.

Accordingly, the Government of India under the Ministry of Works, Housing and Supply constituted this Committee vide their letter No. S. & P. II-43(23)/59, dated September 29, 1959.

TERMS OF REFERENCE

(i) To bring about an improvement in the quality of printing at the Government of India Presses; and

(ii) To effect economy in Government printing consistent with the requirements for quality printing.

CONTENTS

Introduction; General Survey; The Essential Problem; Aspect; Structural; Aspect; Functional; Supervision; Control and Management; Personnel; Conclusion (Summary of Main Recommendations); Appendices A to C.

RECOMMENDATIONS

Replacement of the Asst. Manager (Adm.) in the Presses by an Administrative Officer of a higher status who can take independent decisions.

Better utilisation of the services of the Labour Officers in a manner not incompatible with their neutral roles.

Optimum strength in a Government of India Press should not be more than 1000 in two shifts, the press being organised over a period of time in self-contained and balanced production units.

Wastage due to idling of machines should be avoided by:

(a) Synchronisation of construction of building with installations of machinery and supply of power.

(b) Preventive maintenance by setting up self-contained electrical-cum-mechanical branches in all the Government of India Presses.

(c) Stocking of spare motors in each press.

Purchase of machines should be confined to a minimum number of standard makes.

Steel furniture should be provided in all branches of the press and stacking and storage of paper should be systematic.

Fixation of a definite time-limit for return of proof and issue of final print order.

As an economy measure, debit should be raised by the Chief Controller of Printing and Stationary against indenting departments in respect of all infructuous exdenditure which, in his judgement, is clearly attributable to them for reasons other than public interest, to be paid from their contingencies.

Manager of the Presses should be given full discretion with regard to choice of type, paper, style of printing and general presentation according to suitability and availability of materials. In the case of publicity, scientific and technical materials, details of typography and specifications should be finalised by the indenting department.

A planning section should be set up in each of the Government of India Presses for proper planning, programming and progressing of all jobs on the basis of availability of equipment, materials, etc.

The pattern of supervision should be reorganised.

A well-formulated Incentive Bonus Scheme should be introduced simultaneously in all the Government of India Presses.

The revised edition of the Handbook for the Government of India Presses should be brought out as quickly as possible.

A drill for operatives should be enforced based on instructions contained in the Handbook for the Government of India Presses and the production methods detailed in para 7 of Chapter V.

Introduction of a Job Costing System on the lines indicated in paras 9—15 of Chapter V in all the Government of India Presses linked up with the Incentive Bonus Scheme.

Review of individual performances of operative and group performances of branches through statistical returns.

Holding of well-defined trade tests for recruitment and where necessary for promotion.

All promotion posts from lower to higher operational levels should be converted into selection posts.

Introduction of Merit Rating Cards to replace existing Character Rolls.

Imparting of systematic training to the operatives through a specially trained practical printer whose services might be obtained through one of the Foreign Aid Programmes.

Institution of annual awards of merit certificates and prizes to the best workers and shields and trophies for the best production.

Regular periodical inspection of the Government of India Presses by the Controller of Printing.

Annual Conference of the Managers of the Government of India Presses and participation by the Department in all-India and Regional Conferences.

Chapter V Paras 7, 9 to 15

Drill for Operatives

7. It was observed by the Committee that dispite the fact that detailed instructions regarding the various operations in the Case Room, Machine Section and Bindery are given in the Handlook for the Government of India Presses, there is no evidence that these instructions are being followed in the various branches of the Government of India Presses. Indeed, it was brought to the notice of the Committee that copies of the Handbook are not avilable in all the Government of India Presses. It would appear that, some years ago, an attempt was made to revise the handbook to bring it up-to-date but the revision of the Handbook has not yet been completed although the General Manager of the Government of India Press, New Delhi, was engaged on the work for the last few years. It is understood that some chapters have been revised but the work is still incomplete. As this is the Bible for all the Government of India Presses, it is imperative that the revision of the Handbook should be completed as early as possible and the copies of the revised edition made available to all the Government of India Presses. Meanwhile, it is recommended that the relevant chapters relating to the instructions to operatives of the various branches of the Press may be reprinted and copies supplied to all the Presses so that the Managers could enforce a drill based on these instructions. The Committee would like to draw special attention to the instructions for Machine-men regarding packing cylinders, adjustment of rollers, care of roller bearings, care of rollers, quality of printing and washing formes, care of machines, condition of machines, adjusting machines, electric motors and their maintenance, contained in pages 333-334 of the Handbook reproduced in Appendix "B". These instructions, although elementary, are fundamental for improving quality of printing and maintenance of machines and should, in any case, be implemented in all the Government of India Presses with suitable modifications without any further delay. In addition, the Committee would recommend the following production methods :

Composing Section

(a) Regular checking of the height of mechanically-set matter and of the composition and quality of metal used.

(b) The imposition of pages of type without removing the page-card.

(c) The use of one-piece chases (particularly those with two cross-bars which assist the registering of formes), mechanical quoins for the imposition of colour work, and high-speed precision galley and forme proof presses.

(d) Checking to ensure that formes are free from imperfections before they are sent for printing.

(e) Pre-make reády before formes are put on the machines for printing.

Machine Room

(a) Periodical and regular checking of the impression of machines by the use of test blocks (Test blocks should be available from manufacturers).

(b) The use of precision metal mounting bases for blocks and stereos.

(c) The fixing of standard thickness of cylinder dressing for each machine, and the adoption of cylinder packing charts.

(d) The use of hard cylinder packing.

Cost Control

9. One of the basic tasks to which the Committee addressed itself during its deliberations regarding productive efficiency in Government of India Presses was to find out whether an independent evaluation of the output of the Presses is possible. In this connection, the existing Costing System in the Government of India Presses was examined in some detail. A costing system in order to be an instrument of control should provide for the computation of the expenditure involved in running a particular unit and for determining the value of the work done in that unit. As the Government of India Presses are run on a no-loss-no-profit basis, if a press is run efficiently, the cost of running the press and the value of work turned out by the press should balance over a period. The costing system that has been obtaining in the Government of India Presses envisages the value of the output to be arrived at by adding the actual value of paper, binding and other materials used and the total expenditure incurred by the press direct and indirect during the year. In this process it will be observed there is no real comparison between the cost of running

the press and the value of work turned out in the press during the year. Wastage in capacity is also not immediately brought to light. Costing system, we feel, should be such as to provide the means to judge the efficiency of a unit by comparing costs of production with values of production and not merely aim at allocating the expenditure *inter se* the using Department whether it is paying or non-paying. A proper costing system should, in other words, enable the cold eye of the outsider being applied to the cost of production vis-a-vis the value of the work turned out in order to assess the degree of efficiency. Only a system which enables an independent evaluation of the work done can reveal how far capacity available in a press has been used to the optimum extent. It was realised that such an evaluation is not possible in the system that has been obtaining in the Government of India Presses.

10. An attempt has, however, been made recently in the new Job Costing System formulated by the officer on Special Duty and at present in operation, on an experimental basis, in the Government of India Press, New Delhi, to evolve a method of determining the value of work on the basis of fixed hourly rates, although hourly rates have so far been worked out only in the Machine Section. In the Machine Section, the various machines are grouped according to the size etc. into two or three broad categories and hourly rates have been worked out, taking into account the expenditure incurred on this section and the number of hours the various machines could he worked after allowing for the normal overhauling and other unavoidable stoppages. The value of the output of each machine is arrived at by multiplying the actual number of productive hours the machine has run and the hourly rate fixed for it. The total value of the output of the various machines in the Machine Section can then he compared with the total expenditure incurred in respect of that Section over a given period. It after making due allowances for factors other than shorter number of working hours, there is still a gap, such a gap can be deemed to represent unutilised capacity. The hourly rates already fixed for machines in the Government of India Press, New Delhi, may require rechecking in the other major Government of India Presses so that suitable hourly rates could be worked out in respect of broad categoeries of machines in all the Government of India Presses.

11. This concept, namely the data necessary for translating the time into cost furnished in the form of hourly rate for each operation can be extended further to the Case Room and the Bindery as well and a costing system could be evolved to enable the Management to review the efficiency in each branch of the Press. A simple formula that can be adopted for calculating hourly rates in a branch, such as composing, is to divide the cost of running the department by the total number of chargeable hours, the chargeable hours being equivalent to the total number of attendance hours by the productive operatives less the number of hours lost on account of absenteeism and non-productive hours. For instance, out of 365 days of a year, we lose on an average 52 Sundays, 16 gazetted holidays, 12 holidays (Saturdays), 12 days casual leave and 30 days earned leave. The total loss of absence can thus be equated to 122 days in all. This gives a balance of 243 days. The total number of attendance hours per operative is 1,944 for the day shift. This multiplied by the number of operatives will give us the total number of hours for which we can expect the production from the operatives. The value of work produced in any period of the year (weekly, monthly, quarterly or half-yearly) will, therefore, be equivalent to the chargeable productive hours multiplied by the hourly rate. In certain departments like the Bindery where we have both machine and man-power, it should be possible to work out an hourly rate for the machine and for the productive personnel. The hourly rates for the Case Room and the Bindery for the first year may be worked out in the manner indicated above on the basis of the data available in the press for the last three years. Thus, hourly rates can be fixed in respect of all the operations in the productive branches of a press on the basis of the data available in the press for the last three years. Thus, hourly rates can be fixed in respect of all the operations in the productive branches of a press on the basis of the data available to the management regarding the productive chargeable hours of each branch of the press for the preceding years and the total expenditure incurred on each branch during the corresponding years. It would be advantageous then to compare the hourly rates obtaining in the various Government of India Presses in respect of the same category of operations and to enquire into the factors responsible for the variation. Such a comparative assessment of efficiency of the various branches of individual Government of India Presses should enable the Centroller of Printing to make a judicious distribution of printing jobs among various Government of India Presses with a view to getting the jobs executed at as reasonable a cost as possible.

12. If the difference between the expenditure incurred on running the department, i.e., the cost involved in the production of the work turned out in that department and the value of production calculated on the basis of the hourly rate fixed as indicated in the preceding paragraph, is very wide over a given period, say six months or a year, there is a definite case for review to determine whether the efficiency of the department has been increasing or decreasing during the period having regard to all the variable factors responsible for the difference in the actual utilisation of productive hours (or hours charged to a job). In so far as the job evaluation itself

is concerned, it is necessary to go by the actual time spent, as the Government Presses are not working for profit, but in so far as the control of personnel is concerned, the individual's output can be computed and compared with the norms fixed. The Incentive Bonus Scheme now in operation in the Government of India Press, New Delhi, has given a basis for assessment of individual output in hours. It is the considered view of the Committee that by linking up the Incentive Bonus Scheme with the new Job Costing System also in operation in the same press which can be further developed on the lines indicated above, an effective control on efficiency and expenditure could be ensured and corrective measure, wherever necessary, taken expeditiously.

The actual productivity of each branch in terms of hours should be computed. For determining the rated output per hour, it is necessary to determine the standards of performance of each category. In the case of purely manual workers, this should follow the time-study based on elements of operation in any work. In the case of machines, however, the rated output as given by the manufacturers cannot be accepted as basis for determining the norms. On the other hand, the actual cruising speed on the basis of experience over a number of years correlated with the length of run and the quality of jobs should be accepted as the basis for determining the norms. For the present, the output of individuals should be computed in terms of hours on the basis of norms already fixed in the Incentive Bonus Scheme in operation in the Government of India Press, New Delhi.

The difference between the possible hours of production and the actual productivity of each branch in terms of hours over a given period, say a year, should be carefully studied with a view to judge the degree of efficiency, to determine whether the norms require revision or whether there is deliberate under-production on the part of the operatives. Along-side collection of this information, it would be necessary to study under ideal conditions, the output of individuals for the purpose of finding out whether the norms are reasonable or low.

The Committee also studied the costing system proposed to be followed in the Bombay Government Press which is based on an average unit costing system evolved by the Technical Sub-Committee of the Conference of Heads of Printing and Stationery Departments of the Southern States. This system consists in a break-up of the total productive work in well-defined physical units (on standard time basis) and dividing the total departmental cost over the number of units produced in order to fix the unit rate. The cost of a job or work done is worked out by multiplying the units of output in each branch of the press by the unit cost. On a detailed examination of the system, the Committee felt that in arriving at a uniform unit of output for each branch of a press, the Bombay system oversimplifies a number of complicated and variable factors. The resulting analysis, therefore, in the view of the Committee, will not bear a close relation to the actual cost involved. The system may be satisfactory so far as the Bombay Government Presses are concerned where the variety of work is limited and conditions of working are, more or less, uniform. In the Government of India Presses, on the other hand, which are dealing with multifarious types of work, this system would not be appropriate. Even the existing Costing System in most of the Government of India Presses provides one statement which exhibits the direct expenditure incurred in the press as also the indirect charges, such as rent rate, taxes, pensionery charges etc., and another statement containing the actual share of expenditure that should be attributable to the department using the press indicating separately the cost of printing, author's correction, binding charges, materials as also the work done for the department through the press from outside sources. Although these statements may not mirrior the cost of each job separately, then give clearly progressive cost incurred during the course of a year for printing jobs for the various departments of the Government of India. This system is, in fact, accurate and takes into consideration work in progress and expenditure incurred on a particular job up to the end of the financial year, although the job itself may not be completed during the course of the year. As has been mentioned earlier, this system is capable of further improvements on the lines formulated in the new Job Costing System in operation, on an experimental basis, in the Government of India Press, New Delhi, and in the manner indicated in para 11 above. Such a modified system would be an effective instrument for judging productive efficiency and controlling cost in all the Government of India Presses providing the management of the individual presses as well as the controlling organisation in the Headquarters the necessary means for an effective control on efficiency and expenditure.

Appendix B

Special Instructions for Machinemen

Packing cylinders. When fitting new packing on cylinders machinemen are particularly cantioned against putting too great a thickness. The correct amount of packing can easily be ascertained by placing the edge of a straight rule or neglect on it, and see that the neglect or rule is only just clear of the planed ends of the cylinder which run over bearings at the sides of the bed. The test should be made after all overlay sheets are on the cylinder. It too much packing is placed on the cylinder it will cause slurring, and the type will also be seriously worn through friction, the diameter of the printing surface of the cylinder being greater than the length of the bed.

Adjustment of Rollers. The adjustment of the rollers

require close attention to see that they only run over the forme lightly and do not press too hard against each other. If they run on the forme too hard they will be cut, and will also clog up the type, thus causing dirty printing. If they press too hard against each other they become overheated.

Care of Roller Bearings. When placing rollers in position on machine the machineman must see that the ends of the stocks are carefully wiped to remove all grit and avoid unnecessary wear to the roller bearings: the roller bearings and gear wheels should then be oiled.

Care of Rollers: Machinemen will pay particular attention to their roller to keep them in good condition. Before leaving work each day the machinemen must have all rollers washed up with kerosene oil and thoroughly wiped with clean waste to remove all traces of grease. If this is not done the rollers will not take the ink properly and will deteriorate rapidly. Machinemen are supplied with all the necessary kerosene and waste for keeping their rollers in good order and will be liable to fines and/or disciplinary action if their rollers are spoiled through failure in complying with this rule. In the same way pressmen will be held responsible for the condition of their rollers.

Quality of Printing: While printing is in progress the machineman, or pressman will watch the sheets carefully to see that the ink is kept uniform through all the copies, and that no type draws out of the forme or quads or spaces work up. He will also see that the sheets are being fed correctly, so that sheets which have to be printed both sides, as in book-work, will register accurately. Only first class work will be accepted, and if any work is defective or badly printed, the workman at fault will be liable to a fine of six pies for every defective sheet which has to be reprinted.

Washing Formes: After a forme has been printed off the machineman, or pressman, will send it to the forme-washers, who will thoroughly brush the forme with the potash provided and swill it with a liberal quantity of water. The forme-washers will be responsible that all-ink is removed from the type and furniture and the potash entirely washed away. Type kept standing or distributed in dirty condition will not print clearly next time it is used. Those responsible for a breach of the rule will make themselves liable to punishment.

Care And Conditions Of Machines And Motors

Care of Machines: Before starting work in the morning operatives will carefully examine their machines to see that all parts are properly adjusted. Machines are to be thoroughly cleaned so that no dirt or foreign substance is allowed to get into the working parts. All working parts and bearings are to be carefully oiled, and the process is to be repeated at intervals during the day to such parts as are subject to excessive friction.

Condition of Machines: Operatives are held personally responsible for the condition of the machines under their charge. Carelessness or wrongful use on their part resulting in damage to the machines will be punishable by fines and/or by disciplinary action. Allowance will be made for fair wear and tear.

Adjusting Machines: Any defect in the machine is to be immediately reported by the operative to the foreman who will report to the overseer. The latter will, if necessary, instruct the mechanical branch to do the necessary repairs or adjustments. Should an operative fail to report defects and the machine sustain damage through being worked while in a defective state, he will be liable to fines and/or disciplinary action.

Electric Motors and their Maintenance: These motors are under the direct charge of the mechanic, who will see that they are very carefully cleaned, supplied with oil and maintained in perfectly efficient working order. Minor faults will be immediately attended to by the mechanic; but any serious fault will be reported to the Manager to be communicated to the Executive Engineer, Electrical Division, who undertake all repairs which cannot be carried out by the mechanic. The motor must not be allowed to run when there is no forme on a machine, and the Machineman must stop the motor directly he has completed printing a forme.

MINE SAFETY EQUIPMENT COMMITTEE, 1959—REPORT

Delhi, Manager of Publications, 1961. 81p.+vip.

Chairman : Shri G. S. Jabbi.
Members : Shri K. S. R. Chari; Shri K. J. Welsh; Shri V. M. Sundara Rajan; Shri B. H. Engineer; Shri R. N. Sharma.
Secretary : Shri G. S. Marwaha.

APPOINTMENT

While considering the question of availability of safety equipment in mines the, Conference on Safety in Mines (1958-59) convened by the Government of India recorded that certain equipment and material were vital to the safe working of mines. Some of these, such as fire-resistant brattice, incombustible dust, etc., are of simple nature and easy manufacture, whilst others have to be imported in large quantities because either they are not manufactured within the country or the capacity of indigenous poducers is small. Noting that nine operators cannot be expected to observe vital provisions of safety ligislation unless the necessary material and equipment are available within the country, the Conference recommended that a Committee may be constituted to consider the whole problem and to recommend measures to meet the same.

Vide their letter No. MI-27 (5)/59, dated October 26, 1959, addressed to the Chief Inspector of Mines in India, the Government of India in the Ministry of Labour and Employment set up this Committee to assess the mining industry's requirements for sefety equipment and to recommend measures to meet the same.

TERMS OF REFERENCE

(i) To determine the requirnents of mines of safety material and equipment in the immediate as well as foreseeable future;

(ii) To evaluate the production capacity of existing indigenous manufactures;

(iii) To make suggestions for the manufacture of safety material and equipment not produced in the country at present; and

(iv) To assess the requirement of raw material for indigenous production of sefety material and equipment.

CONTENTS

Summary of Observations and Recommendations: Introductory; General Conditions; Requirements of Coal Mines; Requirements of Metalliferous Mines; Indigenous Manufacture; The Problem of Spares; Import of Mine Sefety Equipment; Mine Safety Equipment Advisory Board; Miscellaneous; Appendices A to R.

RECOMMENDATIONS

Assessment Of Requirements

It is extremely difficult to assess the requirements of mines still to be opened, for mine safety equipment, to any degree of accuracy. All that is possible is to make 'an inspired guess'.

The Committee has confined itself only to such equipment and material as are required for ensuring safety in mines. For purpose of assessment, the various items have been broadly classified into items which are consumed from day-to-day (i.e. Consumable Material) and those which are provided at only infrequent intervals (i.e. Capital Equipment).

After making certain assumptions with regard to projected outputs of mineral ores and to the requirements of standard units of mines, the total reqirements for safety equipment and material are worked out at Appendix I (Coal Mines), Appendix L (Metalliferous Mines) and Appendix M (All Mines).

Indigenous Manufacture

The existing programmes for indigenous manufacture should be scrutinised, and suitably revised and expanded, so as to ensure that the country becomes self-sufficient as regards its requirements of safety machinery and equipment of a a basic industry like mining. The only exceptions are those items whose manufacture is highly specialised or whose demand is not sufficient for economic production within the country.

The Problem Of Spares

Easy availability of spares of the right specifications forms an important aspect of the whole problem. 'Spares' are vital not only to increased production but also to the maintenance of existing production levels. This is particularly so, in respect of safety material and equipment which has often to be of approved design and standard.

As most of the machinery already in use in Indian mines is of foreign manufacture and most of the spares and parts are of proprietory design, these parts would have necessarily to be imported.

Indigenous manufacture of spares can only be undertaken under licence of the original makers and only in case of standardise equipment and in case of parts whose requirements are fairly high. In any programme of indigenous manufacture of safety equipment, however, adequate capacity for manufacturing spare parts should be provided right from the beginning.

Probelms Of Import

In order to ensure that safety of persons employed in the most hazardous of peace-time industries is not jeopardised due to non-availability of safety equipment and material, it is vital that the mining industry's requirements for import of safety equipment and of spare parts are met in full and in time.

Imports of safety equipment and material should be allowed without undue delay, even in case of material manufactured indigenously, if

(a) The standard of indigenous manufacture has not been established to the satisfaction of safety authorities; or

(b) The delivery date is too long or has been unduly postponed; or

(c) The range of indigenous manufacture does not cover the actual requirements.

The Certifying Authority (for recommending Import applications) for Mine Safety Equipment should be the office of the Chief Inspector of Mines.

Most of the requirements for spares should be permitted to be imported through Established Importers, so that spare parts are readily available on open sale.

A Standing Mine Safety Equipment Advisory Board should be set up to costantly review, and to advise on, the availability of mine safety equipment.

Appendix I

Estimated Annual Requirements Of Coal Mines For Safety Equipment And Material (1961 And 1965)

	1961			1965			Remarks
	For new mines opened during the year	For old mines	Total	For new mines opened during the year	For old mines	Total	
1	2	3	4	5	6	7	8
1. **Permitted Explosives etc. (in respect of Gassy Mines only) :**							
Permitted explosives (tons)	—	—	900	—	—	1,700*	
Sq. S. explosives (tons)	—	—	1,080	—	—	2,040*	
Elec. Detonators (millions)	—	—	90	—	—	170	
Shotfiring Cable (million metres)	—	—	9	—	—	17	
Approved Exploders :							
Single-shot	—	—	80	—	—	80	
Multi-shot	—	—	80	—	—	80	
Multi-shot Exploder batteries	—	—	1,080			2,040@	
2. **FLP Equipment (for gassy mines only except where otherwise stated) :**							
FLP Motors	—	—	600	—	—	600	
Gate end boxes	—	—	160	—	—	160	
Switchgear							
H.T. Oil immersed	—	—	132	—	—	132	
L.T. Oil immersed	—	—	180	—	—	180	
Air break type	—	—	240	—	—	240	
Transformers :							
Mining type	—	—	32	—	—	32	
Drill type	—	—	160	—	—	160	
Lighting	—	—	80	—	—	180	
FLP Light fittings	—	—	1,600	—	—	1,600	
Telephones (Intrinsically safe; as well as ordinary mining type for use in non-gassy mines)	360	240	600	360	1,440	1,800	

* In addition, about 3,500 tons (in 1961, rising to 4,300 tons in 1966) of non-permitted high explosives would be required for non-gassy mines (excluding the requirements of open-cast mines) plus detonators and short firing cable for the same.

@ The actual demand may be smaller, due to the expected use of continental type (battery-less) multi-shot exploders.

1	2	3	4	5	6	7	8
Shaft signalling equipment (Sets)	48	20	68	48	68	116	Assuming 5 yr. life.
Signalling bells (Intrinsically safe; as well as ordinary mining type for use in non-gassy mines)	300	120	420	300	420	720	Assuming 5 yr. life.
Cable in 1000 ft. : (for all Underground Mines) :							
Armoured	270	260	530	270	390	660	
Trailing (C.C. Machines)	60	200	260	60	580	640	
Trailing (Drills)	180	600	780	180	1,740	1,920	
Telephone	24	24	48	24	36	60	
Cable vulcanisers			24			24	
3. **Winding equipment :**							
Winding Rope Cappels	120	90*	210	120	120	240*	
Safety Hooks	120	90	210	120	120	240	
Distribution Plates	120	90	210	120	120	240	
Chains (1,000 ft.)	6	45	10.5	6	6	12	
Keeps (Sets)	60	45	105	60	60	120	
Automatic Contrivances	60	45**	105	60	60	120	
Depth Recorders	60	45	105	60	60	120	
Continuous Speed Recorders (including for fans)	90	70	160	90	90	180	
4. **Haulage equipment :**							
Haulage rope cappels	170	180	350	170	270	440	Made locally
Haualge clips	216	216	532	216	532	748	
Intercoupled Run-away Switches and stop blocks	—	—	90	—	—	90	
Fire-resistant Conveyor belting (1000 ft.)	200	75@	325	200	300	500	Assuming that only 2/3 of the additional underground output would be conveyed.

* At present there are about 560 shafts deeper than 45 metres in coal mines.

** At present there are 100 shafts deeper than 150 metres. Many of these are still to be fitted with automatic contrivances.

@ About 60,000 ft. of belt conveyors are in use at present.

1	2	3	4	5	6	7	8
5. Wire Ropes :							
Guide Rope (1000 ft.)	210	210	420	210	420	630	
Winding Rope (1000 ft.)	84	126	210	84	252	336	
Haulage Rope (million ft.)	0.97	6.88	7.85	0.97	11.20	12.17	
Flexble Rope (million ft.)	1.2	2.2	3.4	1.2	7.00	8.2	
5A. Manila Rope (1000 ft.)	15	25	40	15	100	115	
6. Mine Supports :							
Prop Withdrawers	240	—	240	240	—	240	
Timber (1000 tons)	—	—	345	—	—	500	
Steel Supports (tons)	—	—	50	—	—	500	
7. Pumps etc.							
Main Pumps	72	28	100	72	42	116	
Dip pumps	96	48	144	96	96	192	
Face Pumps	192	96	288	192	192	384	
Pipes 5″—8″ (1000 ft.)	120	60	180	120	120	240	
2″—4″ (1000 ft.)	420	210	630	420	420	840	
½″—1″ (1000 ft.)	120	400	520	120	600	720	
8. Lighting :							
Elec. Cap Lamps (1000's)	30	50*	80	30	80	110	
Cap Lamp batteries (1000's)	—	—	70	—	—	250	
Cap Lamp bulbs (1000's)	—	—	480	—	—	1,700	
Lamp Gauzes (1000's)	—	—	30	—	—	50	
Lamp Glasses (1000's)	—	—	15	—	—	25	
Oil Safety Lamp (1000's)	4.8	—	4.8	4.8	—	4.8	
9. Ventilation :							
Main Fans	—	—	30	—	—	30	
Booster Fans	—	—	30	—	—	30	
Face Fans	—	—	150	—	—	150	
Flexible air ducting (1000 yds)	30	60	90	30	180	210	
Fire-Resistant Brattice cloth (1000 yds)	60	260	320	60	480	540	
Continuous Recording :							
Water gauges	—	—	72	—	—	72	
Methanometers	72	28	100	72	100	172	
Gas Analysis Apparatus	—	—	30	—	—	30	
Anemometers	—	—	72	—	—	72	

* Including 30,000 every year for supply to existing non-gassy mines.

1	2	3	4	5	6	7	8
Hygrometers	—	—	72	—	—	72	
Gas-indicator tubes (Emergency equipment requirements cannot be estimated)							
10. **Dust Control, Fire-Fighting and Rescue Epuipment :**							
Fire Eutinginshers	—	—	750	—	—	750	
Fire Pumps	—	—	35	—	—	35	
Hose Pipes (1000 ft.)	36	36	72	36	72	108	Assuming 5 yr. life.
Sel-contained breathing Apparatus	—	—	72	—	—	72	
Resuscitating Apparatus	—	—	30	—	—	30	
High Pressure Pumps	—	—	6	—	—	6	
Incombustible dust (1000 tons)	—	—	36	—	—	84	
11. **Protective Equipment :**							
Safety Belts etc.	240	360	600	240	1,160	1,400	
Hard Hats (1000's)	32	48**	80	32	80	112	
Miners' Boots (1000's)	32	200	232	32	350	382	
12. **Medical**							
Ambulance Vans	10	5	15	10	8	18	Assuming 10 yr. life.
Station FA Kits	700	990	1,690	700	1,700	2,400	Assuming 4 yr. life.
Officials' FA Kits (1000's)	3.6	9.9	13.5	3.6	17.0	20.6	Assuming 2 yr. life.
13. **Surveying :**							
Theodolites	33	17	50	33	17	50	
Miners' Dials	66	34	100	66	34	100	
Dumpy Levels	33	17	50	33	17	50	

** Inclunding 30,000 every year for supply to existing mines.

Appendix L

Estimated Annual Requirements Of Metalliferous Mines For Safety Equipment And Material (1961 And 1965)

(Items 1, 2, 5, 6, 7 and 8 are mainly for underground mines)

	1961			1965			Remarks
	For new mines opened during the year	For old mines	Total	For new mines opened during the year	For old mines	Total	
1	2	3	4	5	6	7	8
1. **Communications :**							
Telephones (Mining type)	30	30	60	30	70	100	
Shaft signalling equipment (sets)	4	4	8	4	6	10	
Telephone Cables (1000 ft.)	2	2	4	2	2	4	
2. **Winding Equipment :**							
Winding Rope Cappels	5	30*	35	5	40	45	
Safety Hooks	5	30	35	5	40	45	
Distribution Plates	5	30	35	5	40	45	
Chains (1000 ft.)	0.5	3.0	3.5	0.5	4.0	4.5	
Keeps (sets)	3	12	15	3	17	30	
Automatic Contrivances	3	3**	6	3	5	8	
Depth recorders	3	3	6	3	5	8	
Continuous Speed Recorders	3	3	6	3	5	8	
3. **Haulage Equipment :**							
Haulage rope Chappels	75	50	125	75	75	150	
Haulage Clips	80	60	140	80	80	160	
Intercoupled Run-away Switches and Stop blocks	50	—	50	50	—	50	
Wire Ropes etc. :							
@ Guide Ropes (1000 ft.)	17	23	50	17	33	60	
Winding Ropes (1000 ft.)	7	43	50	7	53	60	
Haulage Ropes (1000 ft.)	240	480	720	240	960	1,200	
Flexible Rope (1000 ft.)	200	400	600	200	800	1,000	
4A. Manila Rope (1000 ft.)	40	40	80	40	80	120	
5. **Mine Support :**							
Prop. Withdrawers	20	—	20	20	—	20	
Timber (1000 tons)	—	—	50	—	—	60	
Steel Supports (tons)	25	75	100	25	125	150	

* At present there are 180 vertical shafts (deeper than 45 metres); fitted with winding engines in the metalliferous mines.

** At present there are 35 shafts deeper than 150 metres.

@ Mostly rigid guides are used.

1	2	3	4	5	6	7	8
6. **Pumps etc. :**							
Main pumps	6	6	12	6	9	15	
Dip pumps	8	8	16	8	12	20	
Face pumps	12	12	24	12	18	30	
Pipes 5"—8" (1000 ft.)	10	5	15	10	15	25	
2"—4" (1000 ft.)	35	15	50	35	20	55	
½"—1" (1000 ft.)	30	15	45	30	20	50	
Alkathene Pipes (1000 ft.)	5	2	7	5	3	8	
7. **Lighting :**							
Carbide Cap Lamps (1000's)	2	3*	5	2	8*	10	
8. **Ventilation :**							
Main Fans	3	7*	10	3	7	10*	
Face Fans	12	18	30	12	18	30	
Flexible Air Duct (1000 yd.)	3	17	20	3	27	30	
Water gauges	6	14	20	6	14	20	
Gas analysing apparatus	2	2	4	2	2	4	
Anemometer	6	6	12	6	6	12	
Hygrometer	6	6	12	6	6	12	
9. **Fire fighting and Rescue etc. :**							
Fire extinguishers	—	—	250	—	—	250	
Fire Pumps	—	—	20	—	—	20	
Hose Pipes (1000 ft.)	10	10	20	10	15	25	
10. **Protective Equipment :**							
Safety Belts etc.	400	1,600	2,000	400	2,400	2,800	
Hard Hats (1000's)	6	9**	15	6	14**	20	
Miners' Boots (1000's)	6	9**	15	6	14**	20	
11. **Medical :**							
Ambulance Vans	—	—	9	—	—	9	
Station FA Kits	200	800	1,000	200	1,000	1,200	
Officials' FA Kits (1000's)	1.5	4.5	6.00	1.5	7.5	9.0	
12. **Surveying :**							
Theodolites	10	5	15	10	5	15	
Dials	40	20	60	40	20	60	
Dumpy Levels	20	10	30	20	10	30	

* Includes provision for fitting more fans in existing mines.
** Includes provision for supply to miners in existing mines.

Appendix M

Total Estimated Annual Requirements For Mine Safety Equipment And Material (1961 To 1965)

(All figures have been rounded off)

	In 1961	rising to	In 1965	Remarks
1. **Permitted Explosives**				
etc. (for gassy mines only)				
Permitted Explosives (tons)	900	—	@ 1,700	
EqS Explosives (tons)	1,100	—	@ 2,050	
Electric (copper)	90	—	170	
Detonators (Millions) Shot-firing Cable (m. metres)	9	—	17	
Approved Exploders				
Single Shot	80	—	80	
Multi Shot	80	—	80	
Exploder batteries	1,100	—	2,050	
2. **FLP Equipment** (for gassy mines only, except where otherwise indicated)				
FLP Motors	600	—	600	
Gate-end boxes	160	—	160	
Switchgear: H.T. Oil immersed	140	—	140	
L.T. Oil immersed	180	—	180	
Air Bred type	240	—	240	
Transformers: Mining type	50	—	50	Suitably adjusted for non-gassy mines.
Drill type	250	—	250	Do.
Lighting	125	—	125	Do.
FLP light fittings	2,500	—	2,500	Do.
Telephones	650	—	1,900	Do.
Shaft signalling equipment	75	—	115	Do.
Signalling bells	425	—	725	Do.
Cables (1000 ft.) Armoured	530	—	660	Do.
Trailing (c.c. machines)	260	—	640	
Trailing (drills)	800	—	1900	
Telephone	50	—	65	Suitably adjusted for non-gassy mines.
Cable vulcanisers	25	—	25	Do.
3. **Winding Equipment**				
Wing Rope cappels	250	—	300	
Safety Hooks	250	—	300	
Distribution Plates	250	—	300	
Chains (1000 ft.)	14	—	16.5	
Keeps (sets)	120	—	150	
Automatic Contrivances	110	—	130	
Depth Recorders	110	—	130	
Continuous Speed Recorders (including for fans)	166	—	190	
4. **Haulage Equipment**				
Haulage Rope Cappels	475	—	600	

@ An estimate of additional requirements of other mines is given below:

	tons	tons
High explosives for opencast mines	3,600	9,600
High explosives for underground mines	4,000	5,000

Plus necessary detonators and cables etc.

	In 1961	rising to	In 1965	Remarks
Haulage Clips	675	—	900	
Intercoupled Run away switches and Stop blocks	140	—	140	
Fire resistant Conveyor belting (1000 ft.)	400	—	600	Suitably adjusted for opencast mines.
5. Wire Ropes etc.				
Guide Rope (1000 ft.)	470	—	700	
Winding Rope (1000 ft.)	260	—	400	
Haulage Rope (mill. ft.)	8.5	—	13.25	
Flexible Rope (mill. ft.)	4.0	—	9.25	
5A. Manila Rope (1000 ft.)	80	—	235	
6. Mine Support				
Prop withdrawers	260	—	260	
Timber (1000 tons)	400	—	560	
Steel for support (tons)	150	—	650	
7. Pumps etc.				
Main Pumps	110	—	115	
Dip Pumps	150	—	200	
Fire pumps	300	—	400	
Pipes 5 in.—8 in. (1000 ft.)	200	—	265	
2 in.—4 in. (1000 ft.)	680	—	900	
½ in.—1 in. (1000 ft.)	500	—	800	
Alkathene pipes (1000 ft.)	525	—	725	
8. Lighting				
Elec. Cap Lamps (1000's)	85	—	120	
Cap Lamp batteries (1000's)	70	—	275	
Cap Lamp Bulbs (millions)	0.5	—	1.8	
Oil Safety Lamps (1000's)	5	—	5	
Safety Lamp Gauzes (1000's)	30	—	50	
Safety Lamp Glasses (1000's)	15	—	25	
9. Ventilation				
Main Fans	40	—	40	
Booster Fans	30	—	30	
Face Fans	180	—	240	
Flexible air-ducting (1000 ft.)	110	—	180	
Fire retarding brattice cloth (1000 yds.)	320	—	540	
Continuous recording water gauges	95	—	95	
Methanometers	100	—	172	
Gas analysing apparatus	35	—	35	
Anemometers	75	—	75	
Hygrometers	75	—	75	
Gas-indicator tubes Emergency Equipment—requirement cannot be estimated.				
10. Dust Control, Fire Fighting and Rescue Equipment				
Fire Extinguishers	950	—	950	
Fire Pumps	50	—	50	
Hose Pipe (1000 ft.)	95	—	120	
Self contained breathing app.	75	—	75	
Resuscitating apparatus	30	—	30	
High Pressure Pumps	6	—	6	

	In 1961	rising to	In 1965	Remarks
Incombustible Dust (1000 tons)	36	—	84	
11. Protective Equipment				
Safety Belts	2,600	—	4,200	
Hard Hats (1000's)	95	—	125	
Miners' Boots (1000's)	250	—	400	
12. Medical				
Ambulance Vans	25	—	25	
Station FA kits (1000's)	2.6	—	3.5	
Official's FA kits (1000's)	20	—	30	
13. Surveying				
Theodoliter	65	—	65	
Miner's Dials	160	—	160	
Dumpy Levels	80	—	80	

FERTILISER DISTRIBUTION ENQUIRY COMMITTEE, 1959—REPORT

New Delhi, Ministry of Food and Agriculture, Department of Agriculture, 1960. 117, vp.

Chairman : Dr. J. S. Patel.
Member : Shri K.C. Chetty; Shri Veda P. Sethi; Shri C.R. Ranganathan.
Coopted Members : Shri R.H. Engle.
Secretary : Shri O.P. Sharma.

APPOINTMENT

The existing distribution system has been developed in an *ad hoc* manner largely during a period of fertiliser shortages. Complaints of imperfect working of the system have been received from time to time and attempts have been made to patch it up. A comprehensive review of the distribution system has become necessary. Further, to achieve the high targets of agricultural production, greatly increased quantities of fertilisers will have to be used. It is essential that the fertilisers are made available to the farmer in time over the whole country. This calls for an overhaul of the existing distribution system to cope with the greatly increased tonnage of fertilisers. With these objects in view the Fertiliser Distribution Enquiry Committee was constituted under the Ministry of Food and Agriculture (Department of Agriculture) vide their letter No. 20-55-59-M, dated November 19, 1959.

TERMS OF REFERENCE

(i) To study the system followed for assessing the demand of nitrogenous fertilisers, the mode of distribution in vogue and to recommend steps for improvements, wherever necessary;

(ii) To study the role of the distribution agencies employed and their share in the distribution margin allowed and to recommend such adjustments as may be necessary in the distribution margin;

(iii) To recommend steps that should be taken to ensure that the cultivators get the fertilisers of the required quality and at the notified price; and

(iv) To study the system in vogue for the distribution of super-phosphate and the cost of distribution and to suggest improvements as may be considered necessary.

CONTENTS

RECOMMENDATIONS

General

The consumption of nitrogenous fertilisers in the country has gone up very rapidly from 2.82 lakh tons in 1951-52 to 11 lakh tons in 1959-60 in terms of sulphate of ammonia. It has been planned to increase this consumption to 50 lakh tons in 1965-66. Similarly the consumption of phosphatic fertilisers has gone up from 6,880 tons in 1951 to 38,887 tons in 1959 and is expected to rise to four lakh tons in 1965-66 in terms of O.

In the many pronged attack to increase rapidly the agricultural production, the fertilisers occupy a pivotal position. The large increase in consumption programmed for the Third Five-Year Plan cannot be attained unless (a) the prices of fertilisers and agricultural produce are so related that it is profitable for the farmer to use the fertiliser, (b) the arrangements for distribution, including stocking and sales are orderly and adequate (c) sales promotion is vigorously pursued by the fertiliser distributors and is actively supported by the extension work for teaching the farmers, and (d) the required quantities of fertilisers are made available both from indigenous productions as well as from imports so that the consumption is steadily stepped up year after year as it would not be possible to create a very large demand all of a sudden. It has also to be recognised that so long as the shortage of fertilisers is acute, the extension and sales promotion agencies may not feel called upon to put forth their best efforts.

There is at present an acute shortage of nitrogenous fertilisers but the supply of phosphates exceeds the demand. The country has, however, to prepare for a situation of more plentiful supplies.

The problems of distribution differ according to the consumption level attained and the organisational stage reached by the cooperative movement in the State.

Mixtures And Complex Fertilisers

The use of fertilisers in mixed form should be encouraged to promote balanced fertilisation and assist in stretching the limited supplies of nitrogen over larger areas.

The use of balanced fertilisers should be promoted by assisting the farmer to buy mixtures suited to his soils and crops and also ensuring reasonable prices for mixtures.

The use of mixtures should be extended through suitable assurances to mixing firms and mixture manufacturers.

The mixtures may be marked in granulated form to safeguard the farmer against fraud and adulteration.

To protect the farmers, all states should fix the composition of mixtures in conformity with the established fertiliser recommendations. These recommendations should be reviewed annually.

Crop requirements in any State can be supplied adequately with a maximum of six grades of mixtures including the complex fertilisers.

Since farmers generally do not know how to make the best use of mixed or complex fertilisers, it will require careful education to acquaint them with this type of fertilisers.

The first priority for liquid fertiliser should be for use in the manufacture of mixed fertilisers.

The use of liquid fertiliser on small farms is a problem which must be studied.

As a general practice it is not advisable to mix micronutrients with fertilisers. It is advisable that micronutrient elements be applied only on the recommendation of a qualified scientist.

Since in the trade of mixtures, opportunities for malpractices are great and may not be easily detected by the farmers, it is essential to institute a good system of sampling and check at the various stages. For this purpose it is necessary to appoint a sufficient number of inspectors and to see that they regularly draw a large number of samples and to ensure that analyses keep pace with the progress of checking. It is also desirable to entrust the compounding of mixtures to reliable and reputable firms and parties, who in order to maintain their reputation would not permit malpractices to prevail either at their own end or of their agents. The grades of mixtures should be expressed in whole numbers.

To increase the consumption of mixtures the following methods are recommended:

(a) The prices of mixtures should be reasonable.

(b) Nitrogenous fertilisers should be made available to the mixing firms at the pool price and in increasingly larger quantities.

(c) Loan facilities should be extended to the farmers for purchase of approved mixtures.

(d) Under specified conditions a rebate should be given to mixture manufacturers so as to reduce the cost of mixtures. A small profit may be made by Central Fertiliser Pool from the sale of nitrogenous fertilisers so as to finance the scheme of rebates on mixtures.

The price of mixtures should be fixed on a uniform basis taking into consideration the unit costs of the various fertiliser elements in the mixtures. So far as nitrogen is concerned the unit cost of organic and inorganic nitrogen should be based on the average cost of all nitrogenous fertilisers in current supply. The prices fixed should be periodically reviewed.

Control Of Quality, Licencing And Registration

Regular drawal of samples for test analysis from straight fertilisers as well as mixtures at various stages in their marketing is the only effective instrument for enforcing the control over their quality. The number of samples so far taken and examined by the States is very low.

The dealers' licensing fees should not be deterrent. The fees fixed for the issue of dealers' licences should be regarded as a means of regulation of trade and not as a measure of revenue collection. The Committee suggests a fee of Rs. five for the issue of a retail dealer's licence and a fee of Rs. 50 for the issue of a wholesale dealer's licence, on an annual basis. As the Fertiliser (Control) Order is a Central Order and as the fees are approved by the Controller of Fertilisers there ought to be a measure of uniformity in their fixation throughout the country.

The registration fee for mixtures should also be reasonable and uniform for the reasons stated above.

As the fertiliser year now corresponds to the financial year, the licensing year should be the same as the financial year and the licences may be issued for three years at a time if the licencee so desires.

The definition adopted for wholesalers and retailers should be uniform throughout the country and in accordance with the sense usually connoted.

Training Of Sales Personnel

As the farmers learn how to use fertilisers more effectively, distributors will need better trained men to sell these materials. To develop men with adequate qualifications, training courses should be planned and put into operation at an early date.

New developments in the fertiliser industry demand well trained men and new procedures of distribution. In addition to the knowledge of salesmanship, a thorough and complete understanding of the fertilisers in the market and how they should be used by the farmer are necessary for the salesman.

Fertiliser sales personnel should be given short training on fertilisers so that they may be able to advise farmers as to how, when and where to use the fertilisers. These courses may be organised by the Cooperative Departments with the help icultural Extension staff.

The research, extension and educational groups in the agricultural field must work diligently to develop in formation as to the value of various fertiliser materials and educate the farmer to use them economically through demonstrations carried out in their fields.

An understanding between the sales organisation and extension and research groups can be best obtained by yearly joint meetings to discuss fertiliser problems which have arisen during the year.

Distribution

Coordination Of Distribution

Only a single agency should coordinate distribution and allocate supplies of fertilisers to districts. In several States, besides the State Department of Agriculture, the Apex Cooperative Society also functions as a coordinating agency. If this work is done by one agency at the State level it will avoid duplication of work and staff and lead to an economy in expenditure.

Estimates Of Demand

Wherever the work relating to distribution of fertilisers in entrusted to a Cooperative Department, the State Agriculture Department and the District Agricultural Officers should be closely associated with the estimation of demand of fertilisers.

Influential farmers and dealers in fertilisers at Taluk headquarters should also be consulted while framing the estimates. The states should be encouraged to prepare a realistic estimate of demand. The Central Fertiliser Pool, while allocating the fertilisers to the State should take into consideration the past consumption as also the achievements in respect of increased production.

Despatch Instructions

The States should be given, in the beginning of the year an indication of the likely allocation of fertilisers, quarter by quarter, so that they may be ready with despatch instructions sufficiently in advance of the commencement of the supplies. To enable this being done, release of foreign exchange should be secured sufficiently in advance and the orders should also be placed in time.

Stock Returns And Checking

Information about the stocks of fertilisers in the retail depots is at present not being regularly received and analysed. The stacking of bag in the depots is often unsatisfactory which makes physical verification difficult. It is essential that arrangements should be made for regular checking of the accounts as well as the stocks at the depots.

Administrative Charges

In most of the States, administration charges are included in the cost of distribution of fertilisers. In Madras and Bombay, administrative charges vary according to the cost of the fertiliser, the costlier, the fertiliser, the higher, the charge. Since the cost of administration and transport by road are independent of the price of fertilisers, the committee feels that there is little justification for linking administrative charges with the price of the fertilisers.

The State Governments have been involved in the distribution of fertilisers because of the Central Fertiliser Pool and do not look upon fertiliser business as an opportunity to make profit. The cost of establishment at the State level should be frequently reviewed and kept at the minimum. The Committee considers that the cost of administrative charges should not ordinarily exceed rupee one per ton.

Cost Of Road Transport

The cost of transport by road should be pooled at the states' level so that the fertiliser can be sold at a uniform price throughout the state irrespective of the distance of the fertiliser depot, and so that the tendency to sell fertiliser only at the rail head is discouraged. To simplify the operation of this freight-pool, it is suggested that from out of the controlled price a rebate may be allowed to retailers according to notified rates of transport for scheduled distances from the wholesale depot to the retail depots. Notified rates may be revised from time to time, but as a working basis the following rebates which operated in Maharashtra State may be considered:

1. For six to 10 miles... Rs. 0.50 per ton/mile.
2. For 11 to 20 miles... Re. 0.37 per ton/mile.
3. For 21 and over miles... Re. 0.25 per ton/mile.

It will facilitate the working of rebates if distances of retail depots from the rail head depots are tabulated and communicated in advance to both the parties. Where the cost of ferrying fertilisers across rivers is high, a special rebate may be allowed for this purpose from the pooled transport cost.

To reduce the incidence of road transport cost, arrangements should be developed for taking delivery of fertilisers in wagon loads at the largest possible number of railway stations and particularly in Taluk (Tehsil) and Mandi rail heads.

Transport Costs On Hills

In hill areas where the fertiliser has to be transported by mules or even on head loads the cost of transport is very high. Such high transport cost is at present being subsidised in certain areas like Himachal Pradesh, Manipur and Tripura. These *ad hoc* arrangements need to be recognised as a regular feature to be financed by the Central Fertiliser Pool and extended to all states with similar tracts which are difficult of access.

To promote economy in the cost of transport in hilly areas, a progressive switch over to concentrated fertilisers may be planned. In areas where road transport is at present subsidised and in areas where it is contemplated to introduce this subsidy it may be restricted to concentrated high analysis fertilisers so as to transport a larger quantity of plant food at the same cost.

Shortage

Only a few States have furnished figures of shortage and spillage of fertilisers. In the committee's view these are generally due either to pilferage or leakage in transit and handling, the former not being a significant factor. Leakage is largely due to use of hooks during loading and unloading. This damaging practice, it is hoped, will vanish when packaging is done in small bags of 50 kilograms. Since, however, certain shortages occur at present the Committee recommends a provision of Rs. 1.50 per ton.

Sales Tax On Fertilisers

While it is recognised that sales tax in an important source of revenue' to the states, its incidence in some states is as high as Rs. 20 per ton of sulphate of ammonia. As both the central and the State Governments are endeavouring to keep the cost of fertilisers down, it is recommended that the exemption of fertilisers from the sales tax may be considered by the States.

Certain commodities have been recognised as of special importance in inter-State trade or commerce under the Central Sales Tax Act, 1956. Since fertilisers, which are manufactured in a limited number of factories, are to be used throughout the country, the Committee considers that fertilisers should also be classed as goods of 'special importance' in inter-State trade and commerce.

Interest Charges

In certain States, interest on capital invested is added to the cost of distribution. The incidence of interest differs from State to State. The Committee considers that in the most unfavourable circumstances, fertilisers may have to be stored by the wholesalers for five to six months and by the retailers for two months. As the lifting of the stock from the wholesale godowns will be spread over, the period of incidence if interest should not be more than three months. Taking into account the period of two months, which at present lapsed before the debit is raised against the State Governments, the Committee considers that of the Central Pool raises the debit after three months from the date of consignment, no interest charges need be provided for the period for which the stock remains with the wholesalers. Presumably it would be possible to meet this additonal interest for one month from the present pool price structure of the Central Pool and if not, a suitable provision for one month may be made. As retail sales will be spread over, interest charges for not more than one month need be provided for the retailers. The Committee, therefore, recommends that:

> The Central Pool may raise the debits for the value of the stocks supplied after three months from the date of consignment. The sale of fertilisers to the retailers should be made by the wholesalers on payment of value and a provision of Rs. two may be made in the distribution charges on account of interest on capital employed at the retailers' end.

Commissions For Distributors

The apex distributing agents and the wholesale agents at present utilise most of the commission with the result that very little is left for the retail distributors who sufer from lack of incentive to sell fertilisers. The wholesalers should be discouraged from undertaking retail sales. The Committee recommends that in order to provide adequate incentive to the retailers to enter into this business the rate of commission should be increased from the apex level to the village level and these should be fixed by the State Governments taking the above factors into consideration.

It is necessary to keep down the expenses of internal distribution by eliminating unnecessary intermediary functionaries. Only the Marketing Cooperative Society at the Taluk level and the Primary Society at the village level have a real service to render in fertiliser distribution. If there is an Apex Coordinating agency at the State level, the State Government should only act as a channel of communication between the apex agency and the Central Pool and undertake financial responsibility for the supply of fertilisers from the Central Pool to the State.

Cost Of Distribution

On the whole, the Committee considers that it is possible to cover the cost of distribution within a margin of Rs. 30 per ton for sulphate of ammonia.

Supply On Consignment Basis

The system of supplying fertilisers on consignment basis to the Primary Cooperative Societies does not work well as the societies often fail to remit in time the sale proceeds to the State Governments and utilise them for their other business. Since the required supervision and check over the Primary Societies is not likely to be provided for some more time, the fertiliser may be supplied on a consignment basis only to the wholesalers and the retailers should be asked to lift the stocks after payment.

Fertiliser Loans

The farmers should be afforded sufficient credit facilities for the purchase of fertilisers. The loans should be given in kind (not in cash) and the rate of interest should be reasonable.

Working Hours Of Depot

The cooperative depots should remain open for the sale of fertilisers at hours convenient to farmers so that they are enabled to purchase fertilisers when they are free from farm work.

Storage And Warehousing

As the demand for fertilisers is seasonal it would be cheaper if different commodities required by the cultivators are stored in the same godown. The Committee, therefore, recommends that the setting up of separate depots exclusively for dealing in fertilisers should be discouraged with a view to lowering the cost of their distribution.

The present difficulty about the storage of fertilisers especially in the off-season is likely to diminish when the new factories are set up during the Third Plan. In the meantime the congestion in the depots can be minimised by instituting a system of 'off-season sales rebates' so that farmers are induced to take delivery of the fertilisers during the lean months. In this manner, the farmers will also be certain of having the fertilisers in time for their needs.

The warehouses and godowns should be so constructed as to suit the local climatic conditions and also with a view to doing away with avoidable handling. It should be possible to store in the same godowns, besides fertilisers, other agricultural requirements and commodities so that storage expenses will be reduced and the cultivator will be able to secure most of his requirements at one and the same place.

Phosphates Promotion

The sales of superphosphate are poor in those States where there is a monopoly of distribution by the Government or Cooperative Societies. To increase its consumption, it is suggested that the State Governments may encourage the superphosphate manufacturers to build up their sales organisations and to develop sales by providing incentives. These organisations can also assist in selling fertiliser mixtures. The manufacturers would also utilise the cooperative societies for this purpose, as they are already doing in some cases.

The progress of consumption of phosphatic fertilisers is much behind the schedule envisaged in the second Plan. In view of the urgent need to promote balanced fertilisation as well as to reduce the prevalent high costs of Indian-made superphosphates, the committee recommends that a subsidy of 25 per cent be granted on all purchases of superphosphate and that this be operated in the form of rebate granted to manufacturers on the lines indicated for the mixtures and that the cost of this subsidy be borne by the Central Fertiliser Pool.

Cheaper Fertilisers

Fertilisers should be supplied to farmers at as low a price as possible. When the cost of fertilisers is low, the net profit to the farmers is higher which gives him our inducement to use more fertiliser and raise agricultural production.

The present prices of nitrogenous fertilisers in India are very high as compared with the prices ruling in other countries. The prices of food grains also do not justify a high level of prices for fertilisers. The Committee considers that the prices of nitrogenuos fertilisers now ruling are susceptible to substantial reduction without in any way impairing the financial position of the Pool and its ability to take the tasks of subsidy recommended for mixtures and super phosphate.

The present prices of muriate of potash and sulphate of potash are also very high and require a substantial reduction on grounds of equity and promoting their free use.

Marketing Of New Brands

To promote the use of new or comparatively less popular fertilisers it is considered expedient to allow a larger commission than admissible on the basis of equivalent nutrient value of the popular brand.

Many of these societies are reluctant to undertake the sale of new and comparatively less popular fertilisers. It should be made clear to the cooperaitve societies that they cannot pick and choose the fertiliser which they wish to sell and that they must market the entire range of fertilisers.

To push up the sales of fertilisers the salesmen may be paid bonus(say at 20 nP. per bag of two cwt.) in addition to their pay or honorarium provided they show improvement over past performance. The Central Fertiliser Pool may also consider a prize scheme for encouraging sales of unpopular or new fertilisers and mixtures. These prizes may be awarded through the State Government to the primary societies which have shown good progress.

Marketing Corporation

The present organisation of the Central Fertiliser Pool is considered inadequate. In the next few years greatly increased quantities of fertilisers are to be procured and distributed. If the Committee's recommendations regarding subsidy on mixtures and phosphatic fertilisers are to be implemented, increased responsibility will rest upon the Pool. The Pool will also have to undertake propaganda work for promoting the use of new fertilisers. The Committee recommends that the duties now performed by the Central Fertiliser Pool and the anticipated additional responsibilities may be entrusted to an organisation which may be called the Central Fertiliser Marketing Corporation. This Corporation should enjoy a liberal measure of autonomy while working under the direction and superintendence of the Department of Agriculture.

A Committee of experts may be consitituted to draft a constitution of the proposed Corporation after studying the methods adopted fore ensuring effective marketing and distribution of fertilisers in advanced countries, such as U.S.A., Western Europe and Japan.

COMMITTEE FOR DRAFTING A GRANT-IN-AID CODE AND PREPARING A SCHEME FOR A FIELD COUNSELLING SERVICE, 1959—REPORT

New Delhi, Central Social Welfare Board, 1961. 114p.+viip.

Chairman : Dr. J.F. Bulsara.

Dy. Chairman : Smt. Achamma J. Matthai.

Members : Smt. Ashoka Gupta; Smt. Indumati Chimanlal; Smt. Tara Ali Baig; Shri Prem Narain; Shri Lal Advani; Shri P.D. Kulkarni; Shri M.S. Gore (resigned); Shri V.V. Sastri.

Assistant Secretary : Shri D. Paul Chowdhary.

Secretary : Shri R.S. Krishnan.

APPOINTMENT

The Committee for Drafting a Grant-in-Aid Code and Preparing a Scheme for a Field Counselling Service was constituted under the Central Social Welfare Board at its 27th meeting held in New Delhi on December 10, 1959.

TERMS OF REFERENCE

(1) To determine whether the existing categories of institutions and associations for grants should remain as at present (vide C.S.W.B. Programmes of Assistance-Policy and Procedure—July 1959—pp. 10.11);

(2) Within these categories:

(a) Whether all grants under the first three categories should be for a period of five years at a time, even if such period extends beyond the plan period; and

(b) Whether the ceiling for individual grants requires variation and, if so, to what extent;

(3) To review the present conditions for matching the Board's grant and to suggest modifications as considered necessary or advisable;

(4) To consider the need for enlarging the scope of the purposes for which grants will be given by the Central Social Welfare Board, and, within this enlarged scope:

(a) To determine the quantum of grant for a particular purpose for a particular unit; and

(b) To suggest ways and means to ensure that every institution, given a grant for a specific purpose, adheres to that purpose;

(5) To suggest means of coordination,

(a) Between grant-giving bodies; and

(b) Between grant-receiving institutions themselves in a local area, so as to ensure that a number of small grants are not given to several institutions in the same area for the same purpose, and that, with suitable grants particular programmes are adequately implemented;

(6) To specify clearly various conditions of utilising the grants, to devise measures which will help the institutions to fulfil the conditions, and which will further ensure their fulfilment;

(7) To suggest methods of minimising delays in the processing of applications for grants and giving adequate guidance to institutions,

(a) Before an application for a grant is considered: and

(b) After a grant has been sanctioned:

(8) To advise whether it is desirable to permit a part of the grant to be utilised for administrative expenditure including the maintenance of accounts; and also whether an institution, which undertakes to help several others in an area to maintain their accounts, should be allowed to use a part of the grant to that institution in order to meet some of the expenditure involved in rendering such assistance. To suggest whether and to what extent auditing of accounts by a Chartered Accountant need not be insisted upon, and in that case to suggest what other alternative safeguards could be adopted;

(9) To specify, with a view to decentralisation,

(a) The extent to which the power of sanction of grants could be delegated to State Social Welfare Advisory Boards, and

(b) Whether certain categories of applications could be considered as and when received, instead of at periodic meetings of the State Boards and the Central Board;

(10) To advice to what extent the principles and procedures suggested by the Committee could with advantage be adopted by other Governmental grant-giving bodies;

(11) To suggest such other ways and means as would tend to make the use of grants-in-aid more effective in promoting fruitful welfare services to the community;

(12) To advise on the establishment of an appropriate Field Counselling Service, inclusive of all details connected with its efficient functioning.

CONTENTS

General; Report of the Committee; Explanation: Answering the Terms of Reference; Annexures 1 and 2.

RECOMMENDATIONS

Composition Of The Report

According to the Committee's terms of reference in paragraph 2 above, the two main tasks which the Committee was charged with were:

(A) Framing a code to govern the grants given by the Central Social Welfare Board to encourage and promote voluntary welfare services on the widest possible scale in the country, and

(B) Formulating a Scheme for a Field Counselling Service, which may be helpful to voluntary welfare organisations in improving the standards of their welfare services.

The Committee accordingly submits herewith

(i) Rules for the administration of the Grant-in-aid Programme of the Central Social Welfare Board, together with 8 Appendices, which form a substantive part of the Rules,

(ii) Outline Scheme for a Field Counselling Service and,

(iii) A Brochure elaborating the general standards briefly enunciated in Appendix IV to the Rules, for the guidance of voluntary welfare institutions and organisations providing welfare services to the community or to the needy and handicapped sections thereof (Annexure I).

The Rules Of The Central Social Welfare Board For The Administration Of The Grant-in-Aid Programme

In these rules:

'Aided' organisations refer to those which have received a grant from the Board earlier.

'Unaided' organisations refer to those which apply for grant to the Board for the first time.

'Approved' means approved by the Central Social Welfare Board.

The 'Board' unless otherwise specified or indicated by the context, means the Central Social Welfare Board.

'Inspector' means one of the Central Social Welfare Board's Inspector or any other person employed by the Board for the purpose of inspection.

'Normal' activity or programme refers to the nature and extent of the activity or programme of welfare service carried out by the organisation during the financial year previous to that during which the application is made.

'Normal' expenditure refers to the recurring expenditure during the financial year previous to that in which the application is made.

'Organisation' includes institution, association, society or a like corporate body.

'Registered' means registered under the societies Registration Act 21 of 1860 or other appropriate Act.

The funds of the Central Social Welfare Board are utilized to carry out the functions adumbrated in the Resolution No. F. 2-6/53-D.2, dated August 12, 1953, to the Government of India, Ministry of Education, New Delhi. According to this resolution the functions of the Central Social Welfare Board are:

(i) Generally to assist in the improvement and

development of social welfare activities, and

(ii) In particular

(a) To cause a survey to be made of the needs and requirements of social welfare organisations;

(b) To evaluate the programmes and projects of the aided agencies;

(c) To coordinate the assistance extended to social welfare activities by various Ministries in the Central and State Governments;

(d) To promote the setting up of social welfare organisations on a voluntary basis in places where no such organisations exist; and

(e) To render financial aid, when necessary, to deserving organisations or institutions on terms to be prescribed by the Board.

Accordingly the Central Social Welfare Board shall provide from time to time a suitable amount for its grant-in-aid programme.

The Central Social Welfare Board prescribes the following rules and lays down the following terms and conditions on which financial aid will be rendered to voluntary welfare organisations and prescribes the procedure which will be followed in the administration of its grant-in-aid programme.

The Central Social Welfare Board may make grants for the following purposes to an organisation or institution:

(a) Welfare Services of Children,

(b) Welfare Services for Women,

(c) Welfare Services for the Handicapped,

(d) Welfare Services for the Aged and Infirm,

(e) Rehabilitative services for persons released from correctional institutions or for persons who have left non-correctional institutions,

(f) Rehabilitative services for cured leprosy or tuberculosis patients,

(g) Training of welfare personnel as specified from time to time,

(h) Promoting coordination among welfare organisations or institutions in an area or region,

(i) Any other welfare scheme or service for the community or a section thereof, handicapped or otherwise as approved or sponsored by the Central Social Welfare Board from time to time according to felt need and within the means at the Board's disposal.

The Board shall exclude from the purview of its grants the following organisations, institutions, activities or services:

(a) Activities, services and institutions which are the direct responsibility of gevernment departments or statutory bodies, except for a part of the activities or services of a welfare nature to be initiated or aided for a limited period as agreed upon between the Central Social Welfare Board and the department or body concerned.

(b) Welfare institutions and activities substantially financed by Government, Central, State or local.

(c) Such other activities, services and institutions as the Board may decide from time to time for specific reasons.

Grants may be given to meet wholly or in part, as the case may be, the approved expenditure of the;

(a) Consolidation and improvement, of an existing welfare service,

(b) Development and expansion of an existing welfare service,

(c) Extension of an existing welfare service to another area,

(d) Provision of a new welfare service not hitherto undertaken. 'Consolidation and Improvement' refers to the continuance of the already existing welfare service on a more systematic basis and includes the improvement of its qualitative aspects according to the standards laid down and requirements specified by the Board. 'Development and expansion' refers to the quantitative aspects of the existing welfare service and includes the simultaneous improvement of its qualitative aspects according to the standards laid down and requirements specified by the Board.

If the context so indicates 'development and expansion' may also include the extention of an existing welfare service to a new area, or the provision of a new service not undertaken hitherto by the grant-seeking organisation.

The grants may cover the recurring expenditure on such items as salaries of personnel, food and clothing for the inmates, rent of premises and organisational or administrative expenditure, and they may cover non-recurring expenditure on such items as equipment and/or furniture essential for the conduct of the welfare activity or institution, a mobile van, a building and/or addition and alteration to premises.

The non-recurring expenditure of a welfare service and the grant given therefor should be shown and accounted for separately from the recurring expenditure and the grant given therefor.

The amount of the grant to be sanctioned to an organisation will be determined by the Board after taking into consideration its constitution, character, status, standing, efficiency, the volume and quality of its activities or services and the cost thereof. In addition, in assessing the grant the Board will take into consideration the income and grants received by the organisation or institution from various sources including the grants or payments from other Government Departments, Central, State or Local, and the aggregate sum made available to the Board for grants by the Government of India.

In order to avoid duplication and overlapping, while considering applications for grant, care should be taken to see that ordinarily grants are not repeated to several organisations for the same welfare service in a particular area or locality.

A scale prescribing the maximum amounts of grants for activities, services and programmes will be laid down by the Board from time to time for purposes of guidance and observance by the person concerned.

The amounts of grants to be given for various purposes and programmes shall not exceed the maximum limits determined by the Board.

The grants may be sanctioned for one year, for the full or part plan-period, or in a lump sum on a non-recurring basis. They may be paid in such instalments and by such dates as the Board may determine from time to time.

One of the objects of the grant-in-aid programme being to elicit, encourage and foster the maximum possible effort within their competence and capacity by voluntary welfare organisations and local communities, their will be a qualifying contribution in cash, kind and/or personal service made by the organisations conducting or undertaking a welfare activity or service and seeking financial aid for the purpose from the Board.

Where the Board considers the necessity of initiating or fostering a new programme of welfare service to satisfy a local or national need, the Board may provide full or a major part of the approved expenditure of the service for a limited period as laid down by it from time to time.

While calcutating the qualifying contribution of the organisation, among its other assets and resources, reasonable allowance may be made for the probable cost of personal service rendered by voluntary workers, which otherwise may have to be paid for, and for the rental value of premises owned by the organisation keeping in mind the Board's grant towards its acquisition or construction, if any.

An application for two grants simultaneously, one being for the consolidation and improvement of an existing welfare service and the other for the development and expansion of the same service or its extension to another area, may not be entertained.

Where an application is considered for a grant for the development and expansion of an existing welfare service, the volume of expansion should be within reasonable limits and such as the organisation will be able to sustain on its own in the case of the future stoppage of the grant. The cost of development and expansion should therefore be a reasonable proportion or percentage of the average annual expenditure of the existing service.

Where an application is considered for the consolidation and improvement or for the development and expansion of an existing welfare service, the annual expenditure of that service for the financial year previous to its application should be ascertained. Further, the quantitative aspects of expansion and the qualitative aspects of improvement should be laid down item by item and the expenditure thereon-clearly ascertained so that the subsequent checking of the accomplishment or otherwise of the consolidation and improvement or the development and expansion programme may be possible and could be enforced. Similar procedure should be adopted also with regard to applications for grant for an extension of the existing welfare service to another area or the provision of a new service not undertaken so far.

In any five-year plan period no organisation or institution shall be paid a total amount of grants exceeding rupees one lakh for several programmes of welfare undertaken by it in any one village, town or city.

Another object of the grant-in-aid programme being to improve the general level and quality of welfare services in the country, the Board will lay down standards of services and administration to be observed and attained by the organisations receiving grants from the Board.

In order to assist the grant-receiving and other voluntary welfare organisations in the conduct, maintenance, improvement, development and expansion of their welfare services or for starting a new activity or service, the Board may provide a Counselling Service of expert or experienced social workers at the Central and State levels, which will function as per the instructions of the Board and which may be availed of by such organisations on the terms and conditions prescribed by the Board.

The grants will be sanctioned entirely at the discretion of the Board and the Board may withhold or make a deduction from the sanctioned grants, if the requirements of these Rules and the conditions subject to which grants are made are not fulfilled or if the applying agency has since come into resources for the purpose for which the grant had been sanctioned.

The Board makes no commitment for the continuance of a grant on the expiry of the grant period and in no case beyond the plan period.

When making a grant for the provision of welfare activities or services as aforesaid, the Board may in addition to any requirements of these rules attach to the grant such conditions for securing the continuity of the activities or services as it may think proper.

All activities, services, projects and programmes for which grants are sought under these Rules and the premises in which they are carried on, must be open to inspection by one or more of the Board's Inspectors or any other person or persons employed or deputed by the Board for the purpose of inquiry, inspection or report. Such Inspector or person shall be afforded all the facilities he requires for informing himself as to those activities, services, projects, programmes, or premises and he shall be given access to all the records and accounts of the organisation.

All organisations and institutions seeking a grant from the Board should get themselves registered, preferably before applying for a grant, or within the period stipulated by the Board in case a grant has been already sanctioned.

Ordinarily applications for aid should reach the Board by the dates fixed for the purpose and in the forms prescribed for various types of aid.

Such registers, records and accounts must be maintained and such information and returns must be furnished by the organisations and institutions receiving grants as the Board may require.

The benefits of the activities or service for which a grant is sought from the Board should be available to needy and deserving persons irrespective of caste, creed, race or religion.

If any question arises as to the interpretation of these Rules, or as to whether any of the requirements thereof have been fulfilled, of as to the amount of any grant payable thereunder, the decision of the Board shall be final. In order to expedite the disposal of such references to the Board, it may authorise its Standing Committee to deal with the same in the manner prescribed by it.

Whenever a doubt arises as to the interpretation of the provisions of the Rules and discretion has to be used by a member of the Board or the Office Staff in assessing the application for a grant, determining the quantum of grant, considering the fulfilment or otherwise of the conditions of utilising the grant, the discretion may be used in such a manner as to lead to simplicity in the operation of the grant-in-aid system and fairness to the grant-receiving organisation. Decision or action taken in a bonafide manner by a Board or staff member will receive due protection.

For facilitating the work of the Central Social Welfare Board throughout the country, it may delegate its powers and functions to the Social Welfare Advisory Boards of the States and Union Territories subject to the conditions and restrictions laid down by the Board in this behalf from time to time.

The Social Welfare Advisory Boards of States and Union Territories shall exercise such powers and functions as are delegated to them by the Board from time to time strictly under these Rules and further subject to the conditions and restrictions laid down by the Board.

Within the broad frame-work of the Rules, the Central Social Welfare Board may from time to time frame sub-rules or issue directives and instructions to regulate the detailed administration of its grant-in-aid programme.

These Rules may be cited as the grant-in-aid Rules of the Central Social Welfare Board, 1961.

Appendix I (Rule 5)

Illustrative But Not Exhaustive List Of Activities, Services And Schemes

(a) **Welfare Services For Children**

(i) Institutions for the care, protection, education and rehabilitation of the socially handicapped (e.g. orphans, destitutes, foundlings, children of unmarried mothers, waifs & strays).

(ii) Temporory Homes for the children (e.g. uninfected children of leprosy and T.B. patients, children from broken homes, children of unattached women workers employed or under training).

(iii) Day-care centres including creche, Balwadi, nursery school or Pre-primary school.

(iv) Recreational and Cultural Centres and Holiday Homes for children of low income families.

(v) Infant Health Centres.

(vi) Child Guidance Clinics.

(b) **Welfare Services For Women**

(i) Institutions and Reception Centres for the care, protection, training and rehabilitation of (a) destitute women and those in distress, (b) rescued women.

(ii) Women's welfare organisations (Mahila Mandal, Bhagini Samaj and such others) conducting Social Education (including domestic science and hygiene and extra-curricular activities for adolescent girls), Literacy classes, Arts and Crafts, Recreational activities, etc.

(iii) Maternity Centres in places where such service is not easily available.

(iv) Condensed Course of Training for Women.

(v) Hostels for Working Women (for low income groups).

(vi) Family Counselling Agencies.

(c) **Welfare Services For The Handicapped**

(i) Institutions and Services for the care and rehabilitation of the physically and mentally handicapped and for the supply of aids to them. (Grants for the education and training of the handicapped may be given temporarily so long as the Ministry of Education is unable to provide for the same).

(ii) Hostels for the working handicapped.

(iii) Small production units for the handicapped.

(iv) Special schools and residential institutions for children in need of special instruction (e.g. mentally retarded or those who have been under long hospitalised treatment or orthopaedically handicapped).

(d) **Welfare Services For The Aged And The Infirm**

(i) Homes, day care centres or clubs for the aged.

(ii) Infirmaries for the chronic ill.

(e) **Services For Persons Released From Correctional Institutions**

(i) Rehabilitation services e.g. Aftercare hostels, workshops, job placement and small financial assistance wherever necessary.

(f) **Services For Cured Leprosy And T.B. Patients**

(i) Rehabilitation services e.g. Aftercare hostels, workshops, job placement and small financial assistance.

(g) **Training Of Welfare Personnel**

(i) Training or Orientation of salaried workers of voluntary welfare agencies.

(ii) Refresher courses for the trained welfare workers.

(iii) Short-term or orientation courses for voluntary social workers.

(h) **Coordination**

Meeting expenditure of agencies carrying out coordination in a specific geographical area and in a field of social service.

(i) **Other Welfare Services For The Community**

(i) Urban Community Centres including welfare aspects of slum improvement, clearance and prevention.

(ii) Short-term specialised courses of training for adult women seeking employment.

(iii) Other specialised courses of training for women as approved by the Board.

(iv) Dormitories and Night Shelters.

(v) Small production units set up by voluntary welfare institutions.

(vi) Holiday Homes for children.

(vii) Community Welfare Services in rural areas.

(viii) Welfare Services for the children of women, who have formed themselves into a cooperative in a socio-economic programme.

(j) **Medical Social Work Offering Welfare Services To Patients In Medical Institutions**

Appendix II (Rule 6)

Services Excluded By The Board From Its Purview

(a) Programmes exclusively for the welfare of Scheduled Castes, Scheduled Tribes and other Backward Classes including denotified tribes.

(b) Labour Welfare Schemes meant exclusively for the benefit of labour employed in factories, mines, plantations, industrial establishments, and similar other concerns.

(c) Youth and Students' Welfare Programmes provided for under the Central or State Governments.

(d) 'Family Planning' Services.

(e) Libraries except when they form part of a composite welfare programme.

(f) General medical aid except when it forms part of a composite welfare programme.

(g) Grants for supplementing per capita grants given by the State Governments in discharge of a statutory responsibility.

(h) Welfare activities undertaken by the Gram Panchayats.

Appendix III (Rules 12-16)

Scale Of Grants And Qualifying Contributions

The amount of grant should not exceed the amount requested by the organisation or the actual need whichever is less.

Ordinarily an unaided organisation, applying to the Board for a grant for the first time, may be considered for a grant for the consolidation and improvement of its existing welfare service.

An unaided organisation of less than five years standing asking for a grant for the first time may be considered for a grant for one year for the purpose of consolidation and improvement of its welfare service upto an amount not exceeding Rs. 5,000 subject to the provisions of the Rules and the following conditions:

(a) that the amount of the Board's grant does not exceed the organisations own qualifying contribution calculated on the basis of its normal recurring expenditure on the service.

(b) that the amount of grant does not exceed 75 per cent of the cost of improvement worked out item by item, and

(c) that the organisation undertakes to meet 25 per cent of the expenditure of improvement and to maintain its normal activity of service.

Such grant as above or a lesser grant as applied for or considered necessary may be repeated on an annual basis and the standard of performance of the organisation may be watched. The minimum period for watching the performance of the organisation should be two years and the maximum five years, whereafter if the standard of its service is found to be satisfactory, its application may be considered for a plan period grant.

If an organisation, newly started but otherwise found dependable, applies for a grant for welfare service in an area which is poor, remote, backward or difficult, where welfare services are scarce or non-existent, and which the Board approves as an area where welfare services need to be specially encouraged, the application may be considered for a one year grant up to a maximum amount of 75 percent of the total approved expenditure of the project or service, provided the organisation has collected or gives satisfactory assurance to meet at least 25 per cent of the required expenditure as its qualifying contribution. The amount of grant in such cases shall not exceed Rs. 5,000 per annum.

Such grant as above may be continued on an annual basis upto the Plan period or a maximum period of five years, provided the service rendered by the organisation is found to be satisfactory. Only after the organisation has proved its capacity to provide the welfare service as per the standards laid down by the Board should its application be considered for a plan period grant.

Organisations, receiving annual grants which come to satisfy the standards of welfare service, laid down by the Board, may be put on a Plan period basis if they apply for the continuance of the grant.

If an unaided organisation established over a period of five years or longer, asks for a grant for the improvement of its welfare services, the Board may consider the application for a Plan period grant not exceeding an amount calculated at the rate of Rs. 5,000 per annum, subject to the provisions of the Rules and the following conditions:

(a) That the amount of the Board's grant per annum does not exceed the organisation's qualifying contribution by way of its normal expenditure;

(b) That the amount of grant does not exceed 75 per cent of the approved expenditure of improvement worked out item by item;

(c) That the organization undertakes to meet 25 per cent of the expenditure of improvement and to maintain its normal activity or service; and

(d) That such grant for improvement is not repeated beyond five years.

If an organisation, qualifying by its standing, status and standard of services asks for a grant for the development and expansion of its existing welfare service, for the extension of its service to another area or for providing a new service not undertaken hitherto and the Board considers the organization eligible for such grant, the Board may consider the application for a plan period grant not exceeding an amount calculated at the rate of Rs. 10,000 per annum, subject to the provisions of the Rules and the following conditions:

(a) That the amount of the Board's grant per annum does not exceed the organisation's own normal recurring expenditure on its existing welfare service;

(b) That the amount of grant does not exceed 75 per cent of the approved expenditure of the development and expension or extension to another area of the existing service, or the expenditure for the provision of a new service, worked out item by item; and

(c) That the organisation undertakes to meet 25 per cent of the expenditure of development and expansion and to maintain its normal activity or service.

When an organization, which has been given a grant in one Plan period for less than five years, is considered for a full five-year grant in the succeeding Plan period, necessary adjustments may be made for calculating the amount of grant to be given.

Grants for the next Plan period to organizations aided in an earlier Plan period will be given on a tapering or diminishing basis, the idea being that the beneficiaries, the group, neighbourhood or community should progressively share as far as possible in the expenses of the service, the benefits of which they have been enjoying.

The amount of the Board's grant to be given to aided organizations for continuing their approved programme of service during the succeeding Plan period should not exceed 50 per cent of the approved total recurring expenditure of the programme, or the amount requested by the organisation, whichever is less, all other provisions of the Rules being observed as usual while considering the applications for the continuance of such grants during the succeeding Plan period.

Ordinarily the principle of tapering the amount of grant (as from 75 to 50 per cent) be applied to each aided organisation after a lapse of five years.

In no case should the grant in a succeeding Plan period exceed the grant given for the same programme in the preceding Plan period.

If for any reason the grant given for a programme of service to an aided organisation on a yearly basis in an earlier Plan period is to be continued on an annual basis in a succeeding Plan period, the same criterion of tapering may be applied as for full Plan period grants.

As regards the proportion of grants to be given for the continuance of the programmes of service during the next further and succeeding Plan periods, the Board may review the position in the fourth year of the Third Five Year Plan, i.e. in 1964-65 and in the fourth year of the succeeding Plans as considered advisable in order to reach necessary decisions regarding the proportion of grants to be given in each succeeding Plan period.

If an aided organization asks for a grant for the consolidation and improvement or the development and expansion of a programme of service not aided before, and the Board considers it eligible for such grant, the application may be considered on the same basis as if it were made for the first time.

Building

The maximum amount of grant for the purchase or construction of a building and for additions and/or alterations thereto shall not exceed a sum of Rs. 25,000 subject to the following conditions:

(a) That the grant-receiving organization will match the Board's grant with an equal amount of its own, the land if any to be calculated at its actual value not exceeding 25 per cent of the Board's grant for the purpose of the qualifying contribution.

(b) That the standing, nature and quality of service, the volume of annual expenditure thereon, the need for the proposed building and the financial stability of the organization will be taken into consideration while assessing its eligibility for a grant, and special conditions may be attached to the grant as considered advisable by the Board.

Mobile Van

The maximum amount of grant for a mobile van with necessary equipment for the proper conduct of a specific welfare service shall not exceed a sum of Rs. 18,000 subject to the following:

(a) That the grant-receiving organisation will meet the remaining cost of the van and equipment, if any, and its running expenses;

(b) That the same considerations for assessing the eligibility of the organisation applying for a grant will apply as in the case of one applying for a grant for a building.

The above two non-recurring grants may be given to deserving organisations over and above the maximum plan-period grants for the consolidation and imrpovement or development and expansion of their welfare service programmes, subject to the proviso that the maximum amount of grant of Rupees one lakh to an organisation under Rule 21 shall be inclusive of the grants for building and mobile van and any of the specific schemes mentioned below.

Equipment

The amount of grant for non-recurring expenditure on apparatus equipment, furniture, utensils, etc. included in the total grant for a welfare service should not ordinarily exceed a sum of Rs. 5,000 in any one service or programme subject further to the following:

(a) The non-recurring expenditure of a welfare service should be separated from the recurring expenditure;

(b) The non-recurring grant for equipment and furniture should be in proportion to the expenditure of the welfare service;

(c) A grant for equipment for a particular service shall not be repeated except on a recognised basis as to the durability of various items of the equipment as laid down by the Board.

(d) Ordinarily such grant for equipment shall not be repeated within a period of less than three years.

Grants For Specific Schemes Sponsored By The Board

The Central Social Welfare Board may sponsor the provision of a specific needed welfare service on its own initiative. In such cases the Board may invite applications from recognized voluntary welfare organisations or entrust the carrying out of its programme to selected organisations. The details of the cost should be carefully worked out in such cases and the working of the programme reviewed from time to time to ensure efficiency of service. In such cases the Board may provide the major portion of the expenditure of an approved programme without insisting on a cent per cent matching basis. In such cases a part of the qualifying contribution may come in the form of personnel service, which may have otherwise to be paid for, the use of premises where the programme is conducted, and the general management and supervision of the organisation undertaking the execution of the programme or provision of the service.

Specific schemes sponsored so far by the Board from time to time are as follows:

		Rs.
(i)	Condensed Course of Training for Adult Women to be completed in two years	30,000
	Additions to building for the above	5,000
(ii)	Hostels for working women (one year)	15,000
(iii)	Urban Community Welfare Project to be conducted over a period of three years	25,000
(iv)	Dormitories or Night Shelters for the homeless	(To be determined by the Board from time to time)
(v)	Hostels for the working blind (one year)	-do-
(vi)	Holiday Camps for children	-do-

Appendix IV (Rule 22)

Standards

Standards will apply to the following:

(i) Welfare Service

(ii) Premises where the service is conducted.

(iii) Personnel employed or working to render the service.

(iv) General Administration.

The welfare service provided by the institutions should be prompt, efficient and adequate to meet the need.

It should be carried out economically so as not to be wasteful of the resources in men, money and material, which are limited in comparison to the vast need of the country.

The premises where the service is provided should be kept scrupulously clean and tidy, both within and without and so also the surroundings.

The equipment, furniture and other belongings of the institution and the workers and inmates should be kept in proper places and/or receptacles in an orderly manner.

The rooms where the inmates sleep and work should

not be over-crowded and should be properly lighted and ventilated.

The essential facilities and amenities for the comfort and convenience of the inmates such as clean water supply, washing and bathing facilities, latrines and storage space should be adequate and in proportion to the number of inmates living or working in the institution.

The beds, bedding and clothing of the inmates should be kept scrupulously clean. The clothing should be tidy and adequate.

Care should be taken to see that the inmates receive adequate balanced food and nutrition.

Provision should be made for the adequate medical care of the inmates by way of preventive inoculations, regular periodical check-up, isolation and treatment whenever necessary.

A genuine effort should be made to eproduce in institutions an atmosphere of a home, family and community and not one of impersonal indifference. Contact should be maintained with the local community. Discipline among the staff and inmates should arise spontaneously out of the general conduct, courteous and considerate behaviour and the tone of management of the institution, and should not necessarily have to be forced through rigorous measures of fines and penalties.

Where children under twelve are lodged, particular effort should be made to create the atmosphere, intimacy and warmth of a home and family and not of an impersonal institution.

The staff of the institution should be specifically oriented to observe the above attitude and spirit of helpfulness to the inmates. They should also be given the necessary awareness of uptodate techniques and methods of teaching and treatment available in their particular field of service. They should be given facilities to acquire the knowledge of the technical side of their work if they have not been specifically trained for the purpose.

Particular attention should be paid to orient the staff to observe the tenets of good human relations in dealing both with the subordinate staff and the inmates of the institution.

The general supervision and administration of the institution and the management's relationship with staff and voluntary workers should be such as to evoke response and cooperation and make for an efficient discharge of their functions, duties and responsibilities by the staff and the inmates.

All attempts of the service should be directed towards the ereation of a spirit of self-reliance and for the rehabilitation of the inmates to the normal life of a citizen within a minimum possible period.

The affairs of the institution or the service should be supervised by a proper Committee appointed or elected according to the constitution, and there should be periodic meetings of the committee to look after or check the work being done.

Proper accounts of the income and expenditure of the institution, service or activity should be kept and arrangements made to see that this is done regularly by the staff or voluntary workers entrusted with the task.

The Board would like to see the principle of self-help fostered by the grant-receiving institutions or organisations, rendering a welfare service, charging a reasonable fee from the beneficiaries taking advantage of the service. However, in such cases where otherwise deserving beneficiaries are unable to pay the fee, the service should not be refused to them.

Organisations providing palliative, curative and/or rehabilitative welfare services would do well to pay attention to the preventive aspects of the social ill or problem they are dealing with, and take such measures as lie in their power to prevent the spread of the ill or mitigate its incidence, and also move the authorities concerned to take such preventive measures as are considered desirable or as the authorities deem fit.

Appendix V (Rule 26)

General Conditions

An organisation or institution aided by the Central Board should

1. Have a regularly constituted and representative Managing Committee.
2. Exercise reasonable economy in utilising the Board's grant.
3. Maintain its normal level of activities and efficiency and raise sufficient funds to meet its qualifying contribution.
4. Utilise the grant for purposes approved by the Board and within the period for which it was sanctioned.
5. Maintain proper accounts in order to reveal how the Board's grant and their own contribution have been utilised.
6. Conform to such further special conditions as are attached to the grant.
7. Get its accounts audited by a Chartered Accountant or by the Audit Department of the State Government and send to the Board, soon after the period of utilisation of the Board's grant, a statement of accounts clearly showing the expenditure from the grant an approved items, and the normal and/or matching expenditure.

Where a grant to an institution does not exceed Rs. 2,000 in one year the Central Board may accept the accounts if certified by a local gazetted officer.

In case auditing is expected to take time an unaudited statement prepared from the organisation or institution's books, should be sent immediately to be fellowed by an audited statement as soon as it is available.

8. The second or subsequent instalment will be released on the basis of a progress report and a statement of (unaudited) accounts.

The audited statement of accounts should follow.

Appendix—VI (Rule 29)

Time Schedule *

Advertisement :	Between June 10-15
Receipt of applications;	By August 15
Preliminary scrutiny of applications by the office and calling for required information, etc. :	By August 31
Forwarding applications and the copy of the inquiry made by the office to the visiting members :	By September 15
Visit and scrutiny of applications by members :	By October 31
Preparation of the summarised application in a prescribed form and forwarding the same to the members of the State Boards :	By November 15
Meeting of the State Boards to dispose of the applications :	Between Decembre 1 and 7
Forwarding the recommendations of the State Boards in the prescribed form to the Central Social Welfare Board :	By December 15
Communication of the approval and/or decision of the Central Social Welfare Board to the State Boards and applying organisations and institutions :	By February 15
Release of first instalment of grant :	April 30 to May 30

* This time-schedule will not apply to applications for grants for building mobile van, or for special schemes sponsored by the Board. Such applications for grants may be considered as and when received or by such dates as Board may determine from time to time.

Appendix VII (Rule 30)

Proforma of Budget Estimate/Accounts in respect of.........For the year (s)

(a) Normal (average) strength of beneficiaries......
(b) Additional number to be taken during the year.......
(c) Total ....

Receipts	Average of the last 3 years	For the last year: Budgeted	For the last year: Actual as per statement of accounts	Proposed for the year (s)	Payments	Average of the last 3 years	For the last year: Budgeted	For the last year: Actual as per statement of accounts	Proposed for the year (s)

Receipts

I. Grants :
(a) Central Government (Ministry)
(b) State Government (Department)
(c) Local Bodies (Town)
(d) Other grant
II. Donations
III. Subscriptions
IV. Sale-proceeds
V. Interest
VI. Rent of Buildings
VII. Fees
VIII. Other receipts (to be specified)
IX. Grant from Central Social Welfare Board
Total

Payments

I. Recurring
1. Salaries of staff
2. Food and clothing
3. Raw materials for crafts
4. Medicines.
5. Rent.
6. Light, water, etc.
7. Contingencies
8. Other items (to be specified).
Total ____________
II. Non-recurring:
1. Building, etc.
2. Van
3. Equipment, etc.
4. Other items.
Total ____________

Grand Total (I & II)

(i) The list of heads of accounts is not exhaustive. An agency could adopt the above form as far as possible leaving out items not applicable/or adding other items of receipts and payments if necessary.

(ii) The value of donations in kind and voluntary services which may have to be otherwise paid for to be shown separately against the relevant item with entry on both the sides.

(iii) A separately sheet relating the figures with the work of consolidation and improvement or development (expansion) and giving explanation for each of the major items provided in the budget may be attached with the estimates.

(iv) If the institution has more than one activity, the figures for the Receipts and payments of different activities should be shown separately in the Budget/Accounts.

(v) Against items 1,7 and 8 under 'Recurring Payments the estimated administrative expenditure on items like rent, salaries of clerical and accounts staff audit fee, stationery, etc. may be clearly shown.

Appendix VIII (Rule 35)

Delegation Of Powers to The Social Welfare Advisory Boards Of States And Union Territories

All applications for one year grants and all applications asking for five year plan period grants not exceeding a maximum amount of Rs. 5,000 provided the same organisation has not simultaneously applied for a plan period grant for another activity or service, may be disposed of by the Social Welfare Advisory Boards subject to the confirmation of their decisions or by the Central Social Welfare Board as per Regulation X of the Board and subject further to any specific instructions issued by the Board from time to time. All subsequent actions relating to the sanctioned grants, their release and utilisation may be taken by the Social Welfare Advisory Boards.

The Social Welfare Advisory Boards shall consider, dispose of and deal with the applications for one year grants in accordance with the rules of the Central Social welfare board for the administration of the grant-in-aid programme and any specific directives which the Central Social Welfare Board may give in that behalf from time to time.

If there is any doubt about the interpretation of the Rules, instructions or directives of the Board, the same may be got clarified as far as possible before the grants are sanctioned or instalments thereof released.

All applications other than for one year grants may be also routed through the Social Welfare Advisory Boards, who shall process them as per the rules, instructions and directives of the Central Social Welfare Board and forward their recommendation on each application in the manner and by the date required by the Board.

All decisions of the Board may generally be communicated to the applying agencies through the Social Welfare Advisory Boards or copies of the letters communicating the decisions may be sent simultaneously to them for their information and necessary action as in the case may be.

One copy of every application for aid with all relevant information shall be forwarded to the Central Social Welfare Board for purposes of record, analysis, collection of relevant statistics and any other action which the board may take thereon.

CHAIRMAN INDEX

INDEX